www.wadsworth.com

wadsworth.com is the World Wide Web site for Wadsworth and is your direct source to dozens of online resources.

At *wadsworth.com* you can find out about supplements, demonstration software, and student resources. You can also send email to many of our authors and preview new publications and exciting new technologies.

wadsworth.com
Changing the way the world learns®

NINTH EDITION

WORLD POLITICS

Trend and Transformation

CHARLES W. KEGLEY, JR.
University of South Carolina

EUGENE R. WITTKOPF
Louisiana State University

THOMSON
—————✶————— ™
WADSWORTH

Australia • Canada • Mexico • Singapore • Spain
United Kingdom • United States

DEDICATION

To our wives, Debra and Barbara, for their loving support for our endeavors, in and through this book, to make the world, through education, a better place for future generations.

THOMSON

™

WADSWORTH

Publisher: Clark Baxter
Executive Editor: David Tatom
Development Editor: Stacey Sims
Assistant Editor: Heather Hogan
Editorial Assistant: Dianna Long
Technology Project Manager: Melinda Newfarmer
Marketing Manager: Janise Fry
Marketing Assistant: Mary Ho
Advertising Project Manager: Nathaniel Bergson-Michelson
Project Manager, Editorial Production: Ray A.K. Crawford
Print/Media Buyer: Rebecca Cross

Permissions Editor: Sarah Harkrader
Production Service: Shepherd, Inc.
Photo Researcher: Mary Reeg
Copy Editor: Michelle Livingston
Cover Designer: Brian Salisbury
Cover Image: top left-Corbis Images; top right-AP/Wide World Photos; bottom left-Sally Weiner Grotta, The Stock Market; bottom right-AP/Wide World Photos
Cover Printer: Coral Graphics
Compositor: Shepherd, Inc.
Printer: RRD-Williard

For more information about our products, contact us at:
Thomson Learning Academic Resource Center
1-800-423-0563

For permission to use material from this text, contact us by:
Phone: 1-800-730-2214   **Fax:** 1-800-730-2215
Web: http://www.thomsonrights.com

Library of Congress
Control Number: 2002113977
Student Edition ISBN: 0-534-57442-4
Instructor's Edition ISBN: 0-534-57444-0

Wadsworth/Thomson Learning
10 Davis Drive
Belmont, CA 94002-3098
USA

Asia
Thomson Learning
5 Shenton Way #01-01
UIC Building
Singapore 068808

Australia
Nelson Thomson Learning
102 Dodds Street
South Melbourne, Victoria 3205
Australia

Canada
Nelson Thomson Learning
1120 Birchmount Road
Toronto, Ontario M1K 5G4
Canada

Europe/Middle East/Africa
Thomson Learning
High Holborn House
50/51 Bedford Row
London WC1R 4LR
United Kingdom

Latin America
Thomson Learning
Seneca, 53
Colonia Polanco
11560 Mexico D.F.
Mexico

Spain
Paraninfo Thomson Learning
Calle/Magallanes, 25
28015 Madrid, Spain

BRIEF TABLE OF CONTENTS

Controversy Boxes and Maps   xvii

Preface   xx

About the Authors   xxviii

PART I: TREND AND TRANSFORMATION IN WORLD POLITICS   3

1   Exploring Twenty-First-Century World Politics   5

2   Theories of World Politics   29

PART II: THE GLOBE'S ACTORS AND THEIR RELATIONS   59

3   Foreign Policy Decision Making   61

4   Great-Power Rivalries and Relations   97

5   Nonstate Actors in the Interstate System   135

6   The Global South in a World of Powers   187

PART III: THE POLITICS OF GLOBAL WELFARE   225

7   Humans and Global Challenges to the Protection of Human Rights   227

8   Does Globalization Spell the End of Borders as Boundries?   265

9   Markets and Money in the New Global Political Economy   303

10   Population Pressure, Resource Depletion, and the Preservation of the Global Environment   351

PART IV: MILITARY CONFLICT AND ITS CONTROL   401

11   The New Face of Twenty-First-Century Armed Conflict   403

12   Military Power and National Security in the Age of Globalized Terrorism   449

13   Coercive Diplomacy and Intervention in the Age of Global Terrorism   495

14   The Realist Road to Security through Alliances, the Balance of Power, and Arms Control   531

15   The Liberal Institutional Paths to Peace   569

PART V: THE PROBLEMATIC TWENTY-FIRST CENTURY   611

16   Ten Questions about Twenty-First-Century Global Prospects   613

References   R-1

Index   I-1

Photo Credits   C-1

CONTENTS

Controversy Boxes and Maps   xvii

Preface   xx

About the Authors   xxviii

PART I: TREND AND TRANSFORMATION IN WORLD POLITICS   3

CHAPTER 1
EXPLORING TWENTY-FIRST-CENTURY WORLD POLITICS   5

The Investigative Challenge   8

How Perceptions Influence Images of Reality   12
   The Nature and Sources of Images   12
   The Role of Images in World Politics   12

Different Levels of Analysis   17

The Book's Approach: Actors, Issues, and Their Interactions   18

Facing the Future: Key Questions to Confront at the Dawn
of the New Millennium   20
   Are States Obsolete?   20
   Is Globalization a Cure or a Curse?   21
   Is Technological Innovation a Blessing or a Burden?   22
   Will Geo-Economics Supersede Geopolitics?   22
   What Constitutes Human Well-Being on an Ecologically Fragile Planet?   23

Key Terms   24

Suggested Reading   25

Where on the World Wide Web?   25

InfoTrac® College Edition   27

CHAPTER 2
THEORIES OF WORLD POLITICS   29

Understanding World Politics   31
   The Elusive Quest for Theory   31
   The Evolution of Theoretical Inquiry   32

Liberalism   32
   The Liberal Worldview   33
   The Liberal Reform Program   34

Realism   35
   The Realist Worldview   36
   Realism in the Nuclear Age   38
   The Limitations of Realism   38

The Neorealist or "Structural" Extension of Realism 41

The Neoclassical Extension of Realism 42

Neoliberalism 43

Transnational Interdependence as a Neoliberal Counter Worldview
to Realism 45

International Regimes 48

Alternative Theories 49

Theorizing about Theory: The Constructivist Conception 49

Key Terms 55

Suggested Reading 55

Where on the World Wide Web? 56

InfoTrac® College Edition 57

PART II: THE GLOBE'S ACTORS AND THEIR RELATIONS 59

CHAPTER 3
FOREIGN POLICY DECISION MAKING 61

The Emergence of the Modern State System 63

The Global and Domestic Determinants of States' Foreign
Policy Behavior 63

Geopolitics 65

Military Capabilities 67

Economic Conditions 68

Type of Government 69

The Unitary Actor and Rational Decision Making 73

States as Unitary Actors 73

Policy Making as Rational Choice 74

Impediments to Rational Choice 76

The Bureaucratic Politics of Foreign Policy Decision Making 80

Bureaucratic Efficiency and Rationality 81

The Limits of Bureaucratic Organization 81

Attributes of Bureaucratic Behavior 85

The Consequences of Bureaucratic Policy Making 87

The Role of Leaders in Foreign Policy Decision Making 88

Leaders as Makers and Movers of World History 88

Factors Affecting the Capacity to Lead 89

Refinements to the History-Making Individuals Model 91

Constraints on Foreign Policy Making: Problems and Prospects 91

Key Terms 93

Suggested Reading 93

Where on the World Wide Web? 94

InfoTrac® College Edition 95

CHAPTER 4
GREAT-POWER RIVALRIES AND RELATIONS 97

The Quest for Great-Power Hegemony 99

The First World War 101
  The Causes of World War I 101
  The Consequences of World War I 104

The Second World War 106
  The Causes of World War II 107
  The Consequences of World War II 112

The Cold War 113
  The Causes and Evolutionary Course of the Cold War 113
  The Consequences of the Cold War 121

The Future of Great-Power Politics: A Cold Peace? 122
  A Twenty-First-Century Multipolar World 122

Key Terms 131

Suggested Reading 131

Where on the World Wide Web? 132

InfoTrac® College Edition 133

CHAPTER 5
NONSTATE ACTORS IN THE INTERSTATE SYSTEM 135

Nonstate Actors, Intergovernmental Organizations (IGOs), and
Nongovernmental Organizations (NGOs): An Introduction 137

Global IGOs 140
  The United Nations 140
  The Organization of the United Nations: System and Structure 143
  Other Prominent Global IGOs: The World Trade Organization,
  the World Bank, and the International Monetary Fund 147
  The European Union as a Model Regional IGO: A Rite of Passage
  for "Euroland"? 155

Other Regional IGOs 158

Nongovernmental Organizations (NGOs) 161
  Nonstate Nations: The Indigenous Ethnic Groups of the Fourth World 163
  Religious Movements 167
  Multinational Corporations and Transnational Banks 173
  Reevaluating NGOs' Capacity to Transform World Politics 177
  Nonstate Actors: Saviors or Stranglers of the State? 180

Key Terms 182

Suggested Reading 183

Where on the World Wide Web? 183

InfoTrac® College Edition 185

CHAPTER 6
THE GLOBAL SOUTH IN A WORLD OF POWERS 187

The Colonial Origins of the Global South's Plight 191
    The First Wave of European Imperialism 194
    The Second Wave of European Imperialism 196
    Colonialism, Self-Determination and Decolonization
    in the Twentieth Century 198

North and South Today: Worlds Apart 200

Theoretical Explanations of Underdevelopment 202
    Classical Economic Development Theory 203
    Two Structural Theories: Dependency Theory and World Systems 203
    Closing the Gap? The Global South's Prospects 205

The Global South's Foreign Policy Response to a World Ruled
by the Great Powers 207
    In Search of Power 208
    The Search for Wealth in a Globalized World 210
    Trade, Aid, Investment, Debt Relief—or Nothing? 213

The Future Role of the Global South 219

Key Terms 220

Suggested Reading 221

Where on the World Wide Web? 221

InfoTrac® College Edition 222

PART III: THE POLITICS OF GLOBAL WELFARE   225

CHAPTER 7
**HUMANS AND GLOBAL CHALLENGES TO THE PROTECTION
OF HUMAN RIGHTS** 227

Putting People into the Picture 229

How Does Humanity Fare? Assessing the Human Condition 231
    Measuring Human Development and Human Security 234
    Political and Economic Preconditions for Human Development 235
    Human Development in the Age of Globalization 239

The Global Refugee Crisis 241

Indigenous Peoples: Precarious Life in the Fourth World 245
    The Threat of National Disintegration to Human Security 248

Gender Politics: The Subordinate Status of Women and
Its Consequences 249

Human Rights and the Protection of People 253

Responding to the Agony of Human Rights Abuse 256

Key Terms 261

Suggested Reading 262

Where on the World Wide Web? 262

InfoTrac® College Edition 263

CHAPTER 8
DOES GLOBALIZATION SPELL THE END OF BORDERS AS BOUNDARIES? 265

What is Globalization? 269

    The Global Information Age 270

    The Media: Markets or Monopoly? 276

    Global Health or Global Infection? 280

    Global Migration 282

The Globalization of Finance 283

The Globalization of Trade 286

Globalization and the State: What Future? 297

Key Terms 300

Suggested Reading 300

Where on the World Wide Web? 301

InfoTrac® College Edition 302

CHAPTER 9
MARKETS AND MONEY IN THE NEW GLOBAL POLITICAL ECONOMY 303

The Global Context for Interpreting Contemporary World Economic Change 305

    The Shadow of Past Commercial Policy Philosophy 306

    The Clash between Liberal and Mercantile Values 307

    Hegemony: A Precondition for Economic Order and Free Trade? 313

The Changing Free-Trade Regime 319

Monetary Matters: Can Financial Regimes Promote Growth? 321

    The Nuts and Bolts of Monetary Policy 321

    The Bretton Woods Monetary System 325

    The End of Bretton Woods 328

    Floating Exchange Rates 330

    Plans for Reforming the International Financial Architecture 332

From Currency Concerns to Trade Troubles in the Twenty-First Century 335

    Emerging Unilateral Trade Policies 335

The Fate of Free Trade: Triumph or Trouble in a Global Age? 341

    Premises for a Future Global Economy 344

    Global Economic Destiny? 345

    Playing Games with Prosperity on a Global Scale: Tricks-of-the-Trade Debate 345

Key Terms 348

Suggested Reading 349

Where on the World Wide Web? 349

InfoTrac® College Edition 350

CHAPTER 10
POPULATION PRESSURE, RESOURCE DEPLETION, AND THE PRESERVATION OF THE GLOBAL ENVIRONMENT 351

Population Change as a Global Political Challenge 353

Understanding Growth Rates: The Persian Chessboard 353

The Demographic Divide Between Global North and Global South 357

Population Momentum 358

From Population Explosion to Population Implosion—A Demographic Transition? 359

New Plagues? The Global Impact of Tuberculosis and HIV/AIDS 361

The International Response to Population Issues 363

Food Fights: The Clash of Optimists and Pessimists 365

A Prescription for Optimism or Pessimism? 368

Environmental Security and Sustainable Development: An Overview 369

The Ecopolitics of Energy 372

Global Patterns of Oil Consumption 372

Running on Empty: Is Energy Security an Elusive Goal? 373

The Ecopolitics of the Atmosphere 378

Climate Change 378

Climate-Change Culprits 381

Ozone Protection 383

The Ecopolitics of Forests and Biodiversity 384

Shrinking Forests and Dust Bowls 385

Biodiversity 388

Toward Preservation: The International Response 389

Trade, the Environment, and Sustainable Development 392

Toward Sustainability? 395

Key Terms 396

Suggested Reading 396

Where on the World Wide Web? 397

InfoTrac® College Edition 398

PART IV: MILITARY CONFLICT AND ITS CONTROL 401

CHAPTER 11
THE NEW FACE OF TWENTY-FIRST-CENTURY ARMED CONFLICT 403

Continuities and Change in Armed Conflict 405

Rival Theories of the Causes of Aggression 408

The First Level of Analysis: Individuals' Human Nature 409

The Second Level of Analysis: States' Internal Characteristics 411

The Third Level of Analysis: Cycles of War and Peace in the Global System   418

Armed Conflict within States   424

     The Characteristics of Civil War   425

     The Causes of Civil War   427

     The International Dimensions of Internal War   431

Terrorism   433

Key Terms   446

Suggested Reading   446

Where on the World Wide Web?   447

InfoTrac® College Edition   448

CHAPTER 12
MILITARY POWER AND NATIONAL SECURITY IN THE AGE OF GLOBALIZED TERRORISM

449

Power in International Politics   450

The Elements of State Power   451

     Inferring Power from Capabilities   453

     The Changing Nature of World Power   455

The Quest for Military Capabilities   457

     Trends in Military Spending   458

     Changes in Military Capabilities   460

     Trends in Weapons Technology   468

The Great Powers' National Security Strategies   477

     The U.S.'s New Security Policies   477

     Russia Adjusts to its New Geostrategic Circumstances   482

     China's Global Clout and Security Posture   483

     Japan's Search for a Strategy   486

     Germany and the European Union Search for a Strategic Vision   488

The Search for Security in an Insecure World   490

Key Terms   492

Suggested Reading   493

Where on the World Wide Web?   493

InfoTrac® College Edition   494

CHAPTER 13
COERCIVE DIPLOMACY AND INTERVENTION IN THE AGE OF GLOBAL TERRORISM

495

The Place of Coercive Diplomacy in World Politics   496

The Security Dilemma   499

Nuclear Deterrence and Defense   501

     Superpower Deterrence and Defense Policies   502

Deterring Terrorism   509

     Military Intervention   511

     International Crises   514

     The Future of Conventional Military Coercion   516

Boycotts, Not Bullets, as Weapons: Sanctions as Instruments of Coercion 519

Key Terms 527

Suggested Reading 528

Where on the World Wide Web? 528

InfoTrac® College Edition 529

CHAPTER 14
THE REALIST ROAD TO SECURITY THROUGH ALLIANCES, THE BALANCE OF POWER, AND ARMS CONTROL 531

Alliances and Their Impact on National and Global Security 534

The Balance of Power 536

Assumptions of Balance-of-Power Theory 536

The Rise, Fall, and Revival of Collective Security as a Substitute for Power Balances 540

Models of the Balance of Power in the Twenty-First Century 541

Multipolarity 544

Unipolarity Redux 549

Controlling Military Power through Arms Agreements 553

Arms Control versus Disarmament 553

The Superpowers Negotiate Arms Control 554

Multilateral Diplomacy: The Checkered Disarmament and Arms Control Record 556

The Problematic Future of Arms Control 557

Military Power and the Search for a Twenty-First-Century Peace 564

Key Terms 565

Suggested Reading 565

Where on the World Wide Web? 566

InfoTrac® College Edition 567

CHAPTER 15
THE LIBERAL INSTITUTIONAL PATHS TO PEACE 569

International Law and World Order 570

Law at the International Level: Core Principles 572

The Limitations of the International Legal System 575

The Legal Control of Warfare 578

International Organizations and World Order 586

The United Nations and the Preservation of Peace 587

Regional Security Organizations and Conflict Management 595

Political Integration: The Functional and Neofunctional Paths to Peace 596

World Federalism: A Single Global Government 596

Functionalism 598

Neofunctionalism 600

Political Disintegration 602

A Democratic Peace: Can Votes Stop Violence? 603

Liberal Institutions and World Order: From Security to Stability? 605

Key Terms 607

Suggested Reading 608

Where on the World Wide Web? 608

InfoTrac® College Edition 609

PART V: THE PROBLEMATIC TWENTY-FIRST CENTURY 611

CHAPTER 16
TEN QUESTIONS ABOUT TWENTY-FIRST-CENTURY GLOBAL PROSPECTS 613

Toward the Future: Critical Questions at the Start of the New Millennium 615

1. Should Global Interests Be Placed Ahead of National Interests? 615

2. If War between States Is Obsolete, What Is the Purpose of Military Power? 616

3. Can the New Global Terrorism Be Contained? 619

4. Will Separatist Conflict within States Lead to Hundreds of New States? 622

5. Will the Great Powers Intervene to Protect Human Rights? 622

6. Will Globalization Tie the World Together or Tear It Apart? 623

7. Is Realism Still Realistic and Is Liberalism Still Too Idealistic? 626

8. Is the World Preparing for the Wrong War? 627

9. Is This the "End Of History"? 628

10. Is There a Reordered Global Agenda? 629

A New World Order or New World Disorder? 630

Key Terms 632

Suggested Reading 632

Where on the World Wide Web? 633

InfoTrac® College Edition 633

References R-1

Index I-1

Photo Credits C-1

CONTROVERSY BOXES AND MAPS

CONTROVERSY BOXES

Chapter 1   Should We Believe What We See?   14

Chapter 2   Can Behavioral Science Advance the Study of International Relations?   40

Neoliberalism versus Neorealism: Which theory Makes the Most Reasonable Assumptions?   44

What's Missing in Realist Theories of Interstate Relations? The Feminist Critique   46

Chapter 3   Are Democracies Deficient in Foreign Affairs?   71

Policy and Personality: Do Leaders Make a Difference?   92

Chapter 4   Was Ideology the Primary Source of East-West Conflict?   115

Why Did the Cold War End Peacefully?   121

Chapter 5   Are Religious Movements Causes of War or Sources of Transnational Harmony?   171

Chapter 6   Multinational Corporations in the Global South: Do They Help or Hurt?   216

Chapter 7   Are National Security, Environmental Security, and Human Security Competing Goals?   246

Chapter 8   Does Globalization Mean the End of the Age of States?   270

Is Globalization Producing Prosperity or Poverty?   292

Chapter 9   Globalization's Growing Pains: Is the World Trade Organization a Friend or Foe?   322

Chapter 10   How Many People Can Earth Support?   366

Chapter 11   Does Nationalistic Love of Country Cause War with Foreign Nations?   419

Can the War Against Global Terrorism Be Won?   444

Chapter 12   Does High Military Spending Lower Human Security?   458

A Revolution in Warfare? The Next Generation of Lethal and Nonlethal Weapons   474

Chapter 13   Is It Ethical to Wage Preemptive War to Preserve Peace?   504

Chapter 14   Are Allies Friends or Foes? Reconsidering the Advantages and Disadvantages of Allies to a State's Security   535

Is a Unipolar, Bipolar, or Multipolar System the Most Stable? Three Schools of Thought on the Relationship of Polarity and International Peace   552

Chapter 15   Legal Limits on Sex for Sale? International Law versus States' Rights on Prostitution   573

MAPS

World Map   Inside Cover

Map 1.1   Mercator Projection   15

Map 1.2   Peter's Projection   15

Map 1.3   Orthographic Projection   15

Map 3.1   Geographic Influences on Foreign Policy   65

Map 3.2   The Map of Freedom: The Location of Democratically Governed Countries at the Start of 2003   72

Map 4.1   Territorial Changes in Europe Following World War I   105

Map 4.2   World War II Redraws the Map of Europe   108

Map 4.3   The Emerging Centers of Power in the Twenty-First Century Global Hierarchy   123

Map 5.1   The UN's Headquarters and Global Network   145

Map 5.2   Africa's IGOs   160

Map 5.3   The Indigenous Cultures of the Fourth World   166

Map 5.4   The World's Major Civilizations: Will Their Clash Create Global Disorder?   168

Map 5.5   Major Religions of the World   169

Map 6.1   The Global North and Global South   189

Map 6.2   The Great North-South Divide in Wealth and Population   192

Map 6.3   Global Imperialism, 1914   194

Map 7.1   The Percentage of People Living Below the Poverty Line, 1984–2000   233

Map 7.2   The Map of Human Development   238

Map 8.1   The International Flow of Finance Capital   285

Map 8.2   The World Trade Organization Goes Global   287

Map 9.1   Ranking Countries by Their Economic Freedom and Political Risk   338

Map 9.2   Putting Politics into the Management of Free Trade: The Global Network of International Trade Organizations   340

Map 10.1   The Spread of the Deadly HIV/AIDS Plague   362

Map 10.2   Global Warning about Global Warming: Who's to Blame?   381

Map 10.3   Loss of Forest and Ground to Deserts   386

Map 10.4   Measuring Environmental Sustainability and Locating Biodiversity Bastions and Endangered Biodiversity Hot Spots   390

Map 11.1   A World at War: States Threatening to Collapse in Civil Wars, 2002   431

Map 11.2   The Dance of Death in the Middle East's Cauldron of Terror—the West Bank Flash Point   439

Maps 12.1 and 12.2   Two Measures of Military Power Potential: National Wealth and the Size of National Armies   454–455

Map 12.3   Military Expenditures   458

Map 13.1   Nuclear-Weapon Armed Countries, Today and Tomorrow   508

Maps 13.2 and 13.3   Vulnerable to Sanctions—Countries Dependent on Trade and Energy Imports   522–523

Map 14.1   The Enlarged NATO and the New Geostrategic Balance of Power   546

Map 14.2   Trick or Treaty? Can Arms Control Treaties Arrest the Proliferation of Weapons?   561

Map 15.1   UN Peace Missions since 1948   592

Map 15.2   The European Union Expands   601

Maps on CD

Map 1.1 Mercator Projection 15

Map 1.2 Peter's Projection 15

Map 1.3 Orthographic Projection 15

Map 3.1 Geographic Influences on Foreign Policy 65

Map 4.1 Territorial Changes in Europe Following World War I 105

Map 4.2 World War II Redraws the Map of Europe 108

Map 4.3 The Emerging Centers of Power in the Twenty-First Century Global Hierarchy 123

Map 5.3 The Indigenous Cultures of the Fourth World 166

Map 5.5 Major Religions of the World 169

Map 6.1 The Global North and Global South 189

Map 6.2 The Great North-South Divide in Wealth and Population 192

Map 8.1 The International Flow of Finance Capital 285

Map 8.2 The World Trade Organization Goes Global 287

Map 10.2 Global Warning about Global Warming: Who's to Blame? 381

Map 10.3 Loss of Forest and Ground to Deserts 386

Map 11.1 A World at War: States Threatening to Collapse in Civil Wars, 2002 431

Maps 12.1 and 12.2 Two Measures of Military Power Potential: National Wealth and the Size of National Armies 454–455

Map 13.1 Nuclear-Weapon Armed Countries, Today and Tomorrow 508

Map 14.2 Trick or Treaty? Can Arms Control Treaties Arrest the Proliferation of Weapons? 561

Map 15.1 UN Peace Missions since 1948 592

PREFACE

At the start of the twenty-first century, much was said about the prospects of the new millennium in which there would arise a "new world order." Talk about possible global transformations reached frenzied proportions, buoyed by the rising hope that the peace between states and rising prosperity within them during the 1990s would persist. Many people set their sights on the promise of a stable global future. Those expectations were abruptly shattered on September 11, 2001, when a shocked world witnessed the terrorist destruction of the World Trade Center in New York. Almost immediately, visions of world politics shifted as a new mood of doom and gloom set in about the probability that, rather than peace, the twenty-first century would be colored by the resumption of past patterns of violence on the world stage.

Our age does not have, as yet, a name. True, we are in a post–Cold War, post–twentieth-century, post–September 11 phase. But those labels do not adequately describe the period of transition through which world history is moving. We have left something behind but do not yet possess sufficient confidence about the future to predict how later generations will classify the defining characteristics of world affairs in our present period of history. Rapid changes sweeping world politics pose an enormous challenge to policymakers, scholars, and especially students. Without a single overriding issue like the Cold War, or the continuing threat of global terrorism, to structure thinking about global affairs, little agreement exists about which dimensions of world politics will come to the fore as the twenty-first century unfolds to define our age.

It is the purpose of the ninth edition of *World Politics: Trend and Transformation* to provide the framework students need to put changes and continuities into perspective. The book combines the latest available data with contemporary debates in international relations to prepare students to assess the possibilities for the global future and its potential impact on their lives. *World Politics* aims to provoke such critical thinking by presenting a picture of the evolving relations among global actors, the historical developments that affect those actors' relationships, and the salient contemporary global trends that those interactions produce. The major theories scholars use to explain the dynamics underlying international relations—realism, liberalism, and their variants—frame our study. At the same time, this book incorporates the reconstructed theories newly advanced to interpret contemporary developments (such as constructivism) and resists the temptation to over simplify world politics with a superficial treatment that would mask complexities and distort realities.

OVERVIEW OF THE BOOK

To help students make sense of political complexities, *World Politics* is organized into five parts. Part I introduces the central issues and major theories in the study of international relations. Part II identifies the major actors in the global arena and discusses the processes by which those actors make decisions. Part III looks at issues of global welfare, beginning with a new chapter focusing on humans as important agents in international relations and the various threats of prevailing global conditions to human rights. It then discusses the impact of globalization on international trade and economic relations and on the linkage between population demographics and the ecological environment, whose preservation is necessary for the saga of the human story to continue. Global conflict is the subject of Part IV, including warfare, terrorism, national security, arms races, and rival approaches to peace. The text concludes with Part V, in which ten questions provoked by presently unfolding trends in world politics are posed to stimulate thinking about the global future.

CHANGES IN THE NINTH EDITION

Content and Organization

Many global changes have taken place in the thirty-six months since the publication of the eighth edition. They required revisiting every passage of the manuscript and integrating the latest developments with the most current information available as the book went to press. This edition incorporates the most recent available indicators of global trends and addresses the most important issues on the global agenda, ranging from human development and the empowerment of women to the number of terrorist acts and military interventions in progress, and from fluctuations in foreign direct investments by multinational corporations to changes in the globalized political economy. In addition, coverage has been expanded to take account of new departures in theory that attempt to interpret recent global developments.

Without identifying every modification in the new edition, attention is drawn to the most important changes in each chapter. Those familiar with previous editions will immediately note that some modifications reduced the number of chapters to sixteen (to more closely match the number of weeks in a typical semester. The new organization reflects the following major revisions:

- Chapter 1, "Exploring Twenty-First-Century World Politics," has been revised to further highlight the impact of perception on the social construction of images and theories of international relations. The five questions that conclude the chapter anticipate future trends in global politics and have been updated to account for recent changes in a global system rife with controversy. Some of these questions are revisited in greater length in the final chapter.

- Chapter 2, "Theories of World Politics," builds on the two major theoretical interpretations of world politics, the realist and liberal traditions, by introducing coverage of theoretical inquiry constructivism and by relating more explicitly to concrete global issues, thereby encouraging students to appreciate the contribution of political theory to an understanding of international relations.

- Chapter 3, "Foreign Policy Decision Making," more instructively illuminates the obstacles to rational choice facing both state and nonstate actors, such as international organizations and multinational corporations when they make policy choices to cope with changing international circumstances. New case material is introduced about the impediments to rational decision making presented by "bureaucratic politics" and interagency competition, featuring the failures in the U.S. intelligence community to identify the planning by the Al Qaeda terrorist network to destroy the World Trade Center on September 11, 2001.

- Chapter 5, retitled "Nonstate Actors in the Interstate System," merges Chapters 6 and 7 from the eighth edition. It now places the streamlined and updated material ahead of the discussion of the Global South countries to better emphasize the profound and sometimes harmful impact that IGOs and NGOs, such as powerful multinational corporations, have on the impoverished conditions in many less-developed countries. New analyses of both the World Trade Organization and the International Monetary Fund are provided to better cover the activities and impact of these global actors, which increasingly find themselves under attack as symbols of the problems attributed to globalization and the rules created by global institutions. Moreover, a new discussion is provided on how the push and pull among IGO and NGO nonstate actors exerts pressure for globalization while countervailing coalitions among them lessen their influence over sovereign states. This new chapter allows the discussions of the United Nations and the expanding European Union to be consolidated in Chapter 15.

- Chapter 6, formerly Chapter 5 in the eighth edition, is retitled "The Global South in a World of Powers" and takes a fresh, critical look at the widening gap between an impoverished and youthful Southern Hemisphere and a wealthy and aging Northern Hemisphere. It emphasizes how the less-developed countries are often marginalized by the great powers and the institutions of global governance that they create. Expanded coverage is provided of the impact of globalization on the Global South and their foreign policy responses to it. The focus is confined to the conditions facing Global South *countries* as a level of analysis, with material in a new Chapter 7 dealing with conditions experienced by people at the individual level of analysis.

- Chapter 7, "Humans and Global Challenges to the Protection of Human Rights," is an entirely new chapter that pulls together materials formerly scattered throughout the previous edition dealing with the individual in relation to the global forces that shape his or her experiences. In looking at world politics through a lens that gives each individual primacy, the new chapter isolates the so-called individual level-of-analysis in order to punctuate the supreme importance of individual experience in the overall scheme of world history, while capturing the ways in which each person's encounter is mediated by social, political, religious, and linguistic institutions and traditions. The new chapter gives the issues of human security and human rights, such as gender equality, the special separate treatment they deserve, as these issues assume increasing significance in comparison to traditional concerns about entire countries' national security without regard for the security of welfare of the people living in them. Included in this new chapter are new discussions of ethics—the moral principles that speak to the challenge of protecting the human rights and civil liberties of people such as refugees and displaced persons—people who are victimized by the proverbial "man's inhumanity to man" that is a tragic component of contemporary international politics.

- Chapter 8, retitled "Does Globalization Spell the End of Borders as Boundaries?" has been repositioned to introduce the problems and politics of global welfare issues examined in the next two chapters. The potential decline in states' sovereign power is considered as a global trend, not only in the liberal democracies of the Global North but also in the "failed states" of the Global South. The chapter has been revised to highlight the growing controversies between winners and losers in the process of globalization by addressing the intensifying popular backlash against globalization. The new chapter reviews divided opinions about whether globalization is a process that states have the power to control.

- Chapter 9, retitled "Markets and Money in the New Global Political Economy," takes into account newly evolving perspectives in commercial liberalism, mercantilism, and hegemonic stability theory to evaluate whether sustained prosperity, free trade, and the management of hypercurrency volatility, banking crises, and rising debt will continue and, if so, if the liberal international economic order will erode. The chapter pays attention to the influence of a globalized marketplace on international and national economic conditions, while taking into account the hegemonic supremacy of the United States as the dominant player in the international political economy, whose position and recent new protectionist policies raise questions about the preservation of the liberal trade regime.

- Chapter 10, now titled "Population Pressure, Resource Depletion, and the Preservation of the Global Environment," repackages in a revised and abridged merged version Chapters 10 and 11 from the eighth edition. The consolidation permits a direct linkage to be drawn between population growth pressure and the question of how the global ecology might be preserved through sustainable growth. Also explored are the opportunities and problems associated with the "birth dearth" in the aging Global North compared to the continuing population explosion in many Global South countries as they relate to the problematic status of recently negotiated new legal regimes to control global warming and common environmental problems associated with biotechnology and genetic engineering.

- Chapter 11, now titled "The New Face of Twenty-First-Century Armed Conflict," has been updated to examine the so-called new age of global terrorism in the aftermath of September 11, with a fresh interpretation provided of the causes, characteristics, and control of terrorism today. The chapter also covers recent changes in the incidence of other types of warfare, specifically expanding discussion of the wave of internal rebellions in failing states.

- Chapter 12, now titled "Military Power and National Security in the Age of Globalized Terrorism," punctuates the new military doctrines that have been promulgated by the United States and the other great powers to wage a worldwide war against global terrorism and to prevent the use of weapons of mass destruction, and the shifting distribution of military expenditures toward those goals. The so-called revolution in military technologies that makes new methods of warfare available are also discussed, and the chapter introduces the latest declassified estimates of the global distribution of arms sales.

- Chapter 13, "Coercive Diplomacy and Intervention in the Age of Global Terrorism," brings up-to-date the discussion of how states increasingly exercise military influence by methods short of war. The use of military intervention for humanitarian and peacekeeping purposes and the controversies surrounding such interventionism are given prominence; so, too, is the radical U.S. strategic shift from deterrence to the preemptive prevention of violence by attacking potential aggressors before they can undertake anticipated military actions. In addition, changes of the uses of economic sanctions as a method of coercive diplomacy are built into the revised discussion.

- Chapter 14, "The Realist Road to Security through Alliances, the Balance of Power, and Arms Control," has been refocused to sharpen awareness of the similarities and differences in the realist and liberal approaches to world order. Incorporated is coverage of NATO's expansion by seven new members in November 2002 and the U.S.-Russian SORT nuclear weapons reduction agreement in 2002, as well as the changing laws giving increased license to humanitarian military interventions.

- Chapter 15, "The Liberal Institutional Paths to Peace," reexamines, in light of the post–9/11 wave of terrorism, the controversies surrounding the possibility of preserving peace by promoting the enlargement of the coalition of liberal democratic states, which have seldom if ever waged war against one another. Also added is a new assessment of the European Union's decision to expand to twenty-five members.

- Chapter 16, "Ten Questions about Twenty-First-Century Global Prospects," concludes with a series of questions designed to generate critical thoughts about the trends and issues identified in the preceding chapters and the dilemmas they pose for the global future. A new section on the controversies surrounding the means for containing global terrorism has been added, and two overlapping questions from the previous edition have been condensed into a refashioned and refocused issue. These ten questions have been revised thoroughly, and the discussion presents the most recent assessments of the global prospect, while relating them to enduring issues in international relations.

Design and Pedagogy

This ninth edition of *World Politics* features an attractive new interior design and the following pedagogic improvements to make the intellectual journey through world politics easier than ever for students.

- **The reorganization of the table of contents to reduce the number of chapters to 16.** The merger of several chapters, the addition of an entirely new chapter, and the repositioning of some topics makes a more orderly and organized presentation of topics. The instructor is not required to follow the book's presentation in sequence from start to end, as each chapter and part is self-contained.

- **Chapter *Topics and Themes* revised to parallel chapter headings.** Each chapter begins with a new outline of major topics that correspond to the chapter headings and titles of featured sections. By breaking each topic into separate components, students can more easily navigate each chapter.

- *Controversy* **boxes presenting essential debates.** As a sense of change grips much of the world, discourse about international relations gives rise to questions that inspire intense new debate, such as rival hypotheses about the causes of global terrorism and contending prescriptions for combating it. Each *Controversy* identifies a major issue on which there are opposing positions. The essays, several newly written to deal with new issues, encourage students to consider rival viewpoints and develop their own opinions. Addressing both classic dilemmas in international affairs and the most-heated current debates, Controversy boxes offer excellent starting points for class debates or research papers.

- **Comprehensive marginal glosses for all key terms.** Responding to the popularity of the marginal glosses introduced in the seventh edition, marginal glosses for *all* key terms in the text are provided, and the number of key concepts introduced has been increased to expand the students' understanding of concepts that will be used to interpret world politics for the rest of their lives. For complex terms with multiple meanings, the marginal glosses provide the explanation that is most relevant to the topic being discussed, along with a cross-reference to alternate definitions and meanings, enabling students to compare different uses of the term as it applies to different topics and to broaden their understanding of its meaning.

- **Expanded up-to-date map and illustration program.** Over three dozen new maps, tables, photographs, or figures broaden the book's coverage, provoke interest, and enable students to visualize the ideas that now command attention. These new photographs and illustrations have been selected with an eye toward introducing the timeliest topics, including a detailed caption that identifies the picture and explains its relevance to the larger issues discussed in the text.

- **Updated "Where on the World Wide Web?" listings.** Responding to the new and rapidly changing information available on the Internet, the "Where on the World Wide Web?" section at the end of each chapter has been updated and expanded to list major Web sites that students can explore for further information on the topics discussed in the chapter. Each Web listing is accompanied by a lively annotation describing the site's contents and suggesting activities and research that students can pursue on the site.

- **InfoTrac® College Edition.** Four months of FREE anywhere, anytime access to InfoTrac® College Edition, the online library, is automatically packaged with this book. The new and improved InfoTrac® College Edition puts cutting edge research and the latest headlines at readers' fingertips, giving access to an entire online library for the cost of one book. This fully searchable database offers more than 20 years' worth of full-text articles (more than 10 million) from almost 4000 diverse sources, such as academic journals, newsletters, and up-to-the-minute periodicals including *Foreign Affairs, International Security, Foreign Policy, World Politics, Time, Newsweek, Science,* and *USA Today.* A listing of the most current articles from the database relevant to the subject matter appears at the end of each chapter.

- **Revised list of suggested reading.** To bring the most recent scholarship and commentary to the attention of students for further study, a thoroughly revised list of authoritative books and articles appears at the end of each chapter, incorporating groundbreaking published research within the past two years into this inventory of essential books and journals for further reading.

SUPPLEMENTS

International Relations Interactive CD-ROM

For the first time, *World Politics* includes a CD-ROM packaged free with every new copy of the text. The CD-ROM gives you; access to Online MicroCase exercises that allow you to work with actual data, map exercises exploring the current demographic information of selected countries, historical maps and related exercises that supply context for the events of today, Internet and Info-Trac ® College Edition research activities, and more.

Instructor's Resource Manual with Test Bank

An *Instructor's Resource Manual with Test Bank* supports the ninth edition of *World Politics*. The manual includes chapter outlines to guide lectures; thematic guides suggesting a variety of approaches to covering each chapter's material; learning objectives; suggested readings for instructors; creative teaching aids for each chapter, including simulations, teaching cases, and multimedia offerings; and a test bank containing over five hundred new or revised essay and multiple-choice questions. A computerized version of the test bank and manual is also available on CD-ROM.

The Wadsworth Political Science Resource Center at http://politicalscience.wadsworth.com

Here you will find information on how to better surf the Web, links to general political Web sites, a career center, issues in the news, a monthly current events quiz, and more—including the following materials:

- A *Citizen's Survival Guide*
- *Spanish Equivalents for Important Terms in American Government.*
- *Terrorism: An Interdisciplinary Perspective*

Book Companion Web Site at http://politicalscience.wadsworth.com/kegley9/

Offering a rich array of teaching and learning resources, this site includes tutorial quizzing, InfoTrac ® College Edition activities, Internet exercises, Web links, and instructor resources.

ACKNOWLEDGMENTS

Many people have contributed to making the ninth edition the most timely and useful version of *World Politics* since the book was first published in 1981. In addition to those whose assistance helped establish *World Politics* as the field's leading text in its previous editions, we wish to acknowledge the special assistance and advice of those who have contributed specifically to this edition.

We greatly appreciate the constructive comments and suggestions offered by reviewers. In particular, we express our gratitude to the professional scholars who provided blind reviews of the revised manuscript, including Kevin D. Archer, Point Loma Nazarene College; Steve Chan, University of Colorado, Boulder; Paul Christensen; David A. Dickson, University of Memphis; Deborah Gerner, University of Kansas; Deborah Moore Haddad, Ohio University; Virginia Haufler, University of Maryland; Clinton G. Hewan, Northern Kentucky University; Richard D. Hughes, California State University, Sacramento; Matthias Kaelberer, University of Northern Iowa; William W. Newman, Virginia Commonwealth University; Thomas Oatley, University of North Carolina at Chapel Hill; Iraj Paydar, Shoreline Community College; Richard Price, University of Minnesota; Neil Richardson, University of Wisconsin—Madison; Lt. Col. Skip Shackelford, United States Air Force Academy; Scott Tollefson, Kansas State University; and Stephen Wrage, United States Naval Academy. We also wish to thank Roger Coate and Donald Puchala of the Walker Institute of International Studies at the University of South Carolina, Richard Grimmett at the Congressional Research Office, Ted Robert Gurr at the University of Maryland, Margaret G. Hermann at Syracuse University, Jeffrey Pickering at Kansas State University, Gregory A. Raymond at Boise State University, Joseph Reap at the U.S. Department of State, Jonathan Wilkenfeld at the University of Maryland, and Rodney Tomlinson at the U.S. Naval Academy for providing and sharing data which made the update of statistical information possible. We are also grateful to John Soares, who diligently collected sites for the "Where on the World Wide Web?" boxes and to Professor Lynn Kuzma at the University of Southern Maine for revising the *Instructor's Resource Manual with Test Bank*.

Deserving of special gratitude are our highly skilled, dedicated, and helpful editors at Wadsworth: Senior Developmental Editor Stacey Sims and Executive Editor David Tatom who exercised extraordinary professionalism in guiding the process that brought this edition into print, assisted by the Project Management of Ray Crawford and the support of Dianna Long, Joohee Lee and Sarah Harkader. Assistant Editor Heather Hogan and Technology Project Manager Melinda Newfarmer worked diligently together in developing the CD-ROM that accompanies the new edition. In addition, Peggy Francomb and the staff at Shepherd, Inc. as well as Michelle Livingston, our copyeditor, contributed immeasurably to the preparation, polish, and production of the book; both were extraordinary.

Beyond the Wadsworth staff and their associates, we are pleased to acknowledge the enormous contribution of Linda Logan to the preparation of a complete manuscript, and to the research and proofreading assistance provided by Mary Schwartz, Wendy Halbert, Min Ye, and Long Wang, Daniel Sabia, Robert Palmer, Holli Buice, and Amanda Cunningham.

Charles W. Kegley, Jr.
Eugene R. Wittkopf

ABOUT THE AUTHORS

CHARLES W. KEGLEY, JR. is the Pearce Professor of International Relations at the University of South Carolina. A graduate of the American University and Syracuse University, and a Pew Faculty Fellow at Harvard University, Kegley serves on the Board of Trustees of the Carnegie Council on Ethics and International Affairs and is a past president of the International Studies Association (1993–1994). Kegley has held faculty appointments at Georgetown University, the University of Texas, Rutgers University, and the People's University of China. Recently published among his four dozen books are *The New Global Terrorism* (2003); *Controversies in International Relations Theory* (1995) and, with Gregory A. Raymond, *From War to Peace* (2002); *Exorcising the Ghost of Westphalia* (2002); *How Nations Make Peace* (1999); *A Multipolar Peace? Great-Power Politics in the Twenty-First Century* (1994); and *When Trust Breaks Down: Alliance Norms and World Politics* (1990). He has also published his primary research in many scholarly journals.

EUGENE R. WITTKOPF is the R. Downs Poindexter Distinguished Professor of Political Science at Louisiana State University. A graduate of Valparaiso and Syracuse Universities, Wittkopf has held appointments at the University of Florida and the University of North Carolina at Chapel Hill. Wittkopf is author of *Faces of Internationalism: Public Opinion and American Foreign Policy* (1990); coeditor of *The Future of American Foreign Policy* (4th edition, 2004); and *The Domestic Sources of American Foreign Policy: Insights and Evidence* (2004). He has also published extensively in many scholarly journals. In 1997, he received the highest award given by Louisiana State University in recognition of faculty contributions to research and scholarship when he was named the LSU Distinguished Research Master of Arts, Humanities, and Social Sciences.

Kegley and Wittkopf have both been recipients of the Distinguished Scholar Award in Foreign Policy of the International Studies Association. Together, Kegley and Wittkopf have coauthored and edited a number of leading texts, including *American Foreign Policy: Pattern and Process* (6th edition, 2003); *The Global Agenda* (6th edition, 2001); *The Future of American Foreign Policy* (1992); *The Nuclear Reader* (2nd edition, 1989); and *The Domestic Sources of American Foreign Policy* (1988).

TREND AND TRANSFORMATION IN WORLD POLITICS

The world has moved into a new century and new millennium. How are we to think about the global future? Part I introduces you to the study of world politics in a period of rapid change. It opens a window on the many trends that are unfolding, some of them in contrary directions, whose combined force may transform many aspects of international relations that, only recently, we expected to persist.

There are obstacles to understanding world politics accurately. Chapter 1 explains how our perceptions of global realities can lead to distortions and provides a framework for getting beyond these barriers. Within this framework, major influences on ever changing international conditions are divided into three categories—the individual, the state, and the global "levels of analysis." Chapter 2 introduces the major theories that scholars have developed over the years to help policymakers and citizens better describe, explain, and predict the evolving nature of international relations. Such theories are important, because they are the tools that can help us construct more accurate images of the complexity of world politics and better interpret emerging trends and transformations.

EXPLORING TWENTY-FIRST-CENTURY WORLD POLITICS

T O P I C S   A N D   T H E M E S

- The challenge of investigating international affairs
- How perceptions influence images of reality
- Different levels of analysis: Individuals, states, and the global system
- The book's approach: Actors, issues, and their interactions
- Facing the future: Key questions to confront

- CONTROVERSY SHOULD WE BELIEVE WHAT WE SEE? THE ORGANIZATION OF OBSERVATIONS AND RIVAL PROJECTIONS OF GLOBAL REALITIES

Global warming is blamed for the blazing heat waves and droughts that have swept the globe, like that pictured here in Allahabud, India, in August 2002. Arresting global warming is a global issue.

Great things are achieved by guessing the direction of one's century.

—GIUSEPPE MAZZINI, Italian political leader, 1848

Now the world faces new circumstances whose implications it is just beginning to discover, and the problem of order has become even more complex than before.

—STANLEY HOFFMANN, political scientist, 1998

Picture yourself preparing to return home from a three-week vacation on an island where you had no access to the news. When you departed—the first week of September 2002—you understandably were haunted by memories of the horrifying day of September 11, 2001. A year earlier terrorists instilled fear worldwide when they destroyed the Twin Towers of the World Trade Center in New York City and hit the Pentagon. On your departure nearing the first anniversary of that awful day, a sense of vulnerability remained as you went through tight airport security under the anxious eyes of "homeland security" forces placed at airports to prevent future terrorist attempts.

The sense of fear—of terror—was experienced on your return, as you wondered once anew how and why, in today's world, such an astonishingly terrible assault happened to create a transforming "date with history," arguably as momentous as the historical turning point when the surprise bombing of Pearl Harbor by the Japanese on December 7, 1941, drew the United States into World War II.

However, your vacation allowed you to take a break from the doom and gloom that has prevailed since 9/11. It permitted you to experience peace and quiet. Your "break" was a true break from the realities of today's often frightening world. Now, however, upon your return, you cannot help but to become curious about what happened while you were away. As you pick up the newspapers piled outside your door, headlines catch your eye. They tell you that many events occurred in the short time you were gone. For starters, headlines inform you that the UN's World Summit on Sustainable Development convened in Johannesburg, South Africa, seeking to construct a plan to reduce poverty and preserve earth's natural resources, and that at that global conference, the United States was heckled and booed by delegates upset with the perceived U.S. failure to address these problems. Next, you read confirmation of the perils of poverty and environmental despoliation in a report headlined "Save the Planet? It's the Rich vs. the Rich as the United States and Europe Engage in a Hot Fight over Strategies for Survival." Citing evidence about the growing gap in incomes between rich and poor people, the report also summarized the findings of the Intergovernmental Panel on Climate Change which documented that the increase in global warming in the past thirty years "is attributable to human activities" and that it is likely that an intense struggle for scarce water (Earth's most indispensable resource) could easily breed a wave of future wars. You then read that UN Secretary General Kofi Annan warned that "In some respects [environmental] conditions are worse [in 2002] that they were ten years ago."

Deflated by this pessimistic forecast for the long-term future, you turn to CNN next and hear that while you were away global investors lost another $1 trillion in stocks in addition to the $6 trillion their savings had eroded since January 2001, and that fears of another huge global recession escalated as confidence in the future of the global political economy plummeted. At the same time you are told that the threat of a global trade war is rising, you are informed that the World Trade Organization backed the European Union in a ruling that authorized $4 billion in retaliatory tariffs against the United States (as compensation for the U.S. illegal system of tax breaks for corporations). Perplexed, you turn off the television set and connect to the Internet looking for some reassuring news. However, you find little. Instead, you learn that the Bush administration announced its plans to militarily attack Iraq, when the president from his month-long vacation at his Texas ranch argued that a pre-emptive strike to oust Saddam Hussein was necessary. President Bush claimed the Iraqi dictator was on the verge of acquiring nuclear capabilities and was intent on using weapons of mass destruction against his American enemy and its allies. However, reading on, you discover that the pledge to remove Saddam Hussein by force has met with strong opposition within President Bush's own administration and among congressional leaders in the president's Republican Party. In addition you learn that harsh critiques of the invasion plan were now being voiced by former President Bush's most trusted national security advisers (Brent Scowcroft, James A. Baker III, and Lawrence Eagleburger), and that the criticism was mounting further, with leaders in Europe, the Middle East, and elsewhere condemning the plan as dangerous and counterproductive. Meanwhile, you learn that a new wave of terrorist suicide-bombings has swept Jerusalem, and that Israel has countered with retributive attacks in Palestine.

The scenario just described is not hypothetical. These events actually occurred between August 20 and September 7, 2002. Undoubtedly, many individuals experienced dismay, fear, and confusion during this turbulent period and the equally volatile periods preceding and following that three-week span. Putting this information about unfolding events together, you cannot help but be reminded that the world matters and that those changes in it affect your circumstances and future powerfully. The "news" you received is not really new, because it echoes many old stories from the past about the growing sea of turmoil sweeping contemporary world circumstances. Nevertheless, the temptation to wish that this depressing kind of chaotic world would just go away is overwhelming. If only the unstable world would stand still long enough for a sense of predictability and order to prevail. Alas, that does not appear likely. You cannot escape the world or control its turbulence, and you cannot single-handedly alter its character.

We are all a part of the world, and the world is an integral part of each of us. Hence, if we are to live adaptively amidst the fierce winds of global change, we must face the challenge of discovering the dynamic properties of world politics. Because every person is influenced increasingly by world events, all must confront the challenge of investigating how the global system works and how the process of globalization is remaking our political and economic world. Only through learning how our own decisions and behavior contribute to the global condition, as well as those of powerful state governments and nonstate transnational actors, and how all people and groups in turn are heavily conditioned by changes in world politics, can we address what U.S. President Bill Clinton in 1993 defined as "the question of our time—whether we can make change our friend and not our enemy."

THE INVESTIGATIVE CHALLENGE

How can we best understand the political convulsions that confront the globe's more than six billion people almost daily? How can we anticipate their future significance? And how can we understand which factors and forces most influence the world's future? At the beginning of the twenty-first century, we have been engulfed in futurist talk. We have been forced to use unfamiliar language—"new century," "new millennium," "new world"—and to speculate, What will the new world be like? Will it be different? As global conditions change, will the human victims and beneficiaries change in the process? Or will the patterns of the past endure?

How can we visualize our probable human destiny and see beyond the confines of our immediate time? To start, it is important to appreciate the interaction of previous ideas and events with current realities. As philosopher George Santayana cautioned, "Those who cannot remember the past are condemned to repeat it." Similarly, British Prime Minister Winston Churchill advised, "The farther backward you look, the farther forward you are likely to see." Thus, to understand the dramatic changes in world politics today and to predict how they will shape the future, we will view them in the context of a long-term perspective that examines how the **international political system**—the patterns of interaction among world political actors—has changed and how some of its fundamental characteristics have resisted change. What do evolving diplomatic practices suggest about the current state of world politics? Are the episodic shock waves throughout the world clearing the way for a truly new twenty-first-century world order? Or will many of today's dramatic disruptions ultimately prove temporary, mere spikes on the seismograph of history?

■ **international political system**
the patterns of political interaction among actors in the global arena.

We invite you to explore these questions with us. To begin our search, let us explore how the differences between continuities, changes, and cycles in world history can help us orient our effort.

Every historical period is marked to some extent by change. Now, however, the pace of change seems more rapid and its consequences more profound than ever. To many observers, the cascade of events at the start of the twenty-first century implies a revolutionary restructuring of world politics. Numerous integrative trends point to that possibility. The countries of the world are drawing closer together in communications, ideas, and trade, as the integration of national economies has produced a globalized market, forming interdependent bonds among countries and cultures. Globalization is changing the way the world works. Likewise, disintegrative trends are shaking the globe and restructuring the way it operates. The proliferation of conventional and unconventional weapons, global environmental deterioration, and the resurgence of nationalism and ethnic conflict all portend a restructuring marked by disorder. The opposing forces of integration and disintegration point toward a **transformation** in world politics as extensive and important as the system-disrupting convulsions following World Wars I and II and the **Cold War** between the United States and the former Soviet Union and their allies.

Distinguishing meaningful transformations (true historical watersheds) from temporary changes (sudden changes that at first shock and scare everyone, but then, with the passage of time, fade in importance) is difficult. The moment of transformation from one system to another is not immediately obvious. Still, certain times are especially likely candidates. Major turning points in world politics usually have occurred at the ends of major wars, which typically disrupt or destroy preexisting international arrangements. In the twentieth century, World Wars I and II and the end of the Cold War stimulated fundamental breaks with the past and set in motion major transformations, providing countries with incentives to rethink seriously the premises underlying their interests, purposes, and priorities. Similarly, many concluded that the terrorist attacks on September 11, 2001 (9/11) produced a fundamental transformation in world affairs. Indeed, many felt that 9/11 changed everything, perhaps forever: In U.S. President George W. Bush's words, "Night fell on a different world," adding later "This is our life now. . . . The battle's just begun."

Despite all that appears radically different since the 9/11 terrorist attacks, much also remains the same in world politics. In fact, as political journalist Robert J. Samuelson noted on the first anniversary of 9/11, "What is most striking about the past year is how little has changed. . . . What no one can know is whether September 11 marked the beginning of the end for global terrorism or whether these theoretical threats will someday materialize. . . . We are swamped with hypotheticals. Whether September 11 becomes a defining moment in history, or just an isolated tragedy depends on how all the hypotheticals turn out." Thus, entrenched continuities after 9/11 persist, to our amazement. We often expect the future to automatically bring changes and later are surprised to discover that certain patterns from the past have reappeared. Given the rapid changes that are occurring alongside enduring continuities, these are uncertain times, and it is dangerous to make firm predictions about the shape of the global future. Because some aspects of the future are likely to be characteristic of the past, even assuming or asserting that a major transformation in world politics is under way is risky.

■ **transformation**
a change in the characteristic pattern of interaction among the most active participants in world politics of such magnitude that it appears that one "global system" has replaced another.

■ **Cold War**
the forty-two-year rivalry between the United States and the Soviet Union, as well as their competing coalitions, between 1949 and 1991, which sought to contain each other's expansion through an arms race and win worldwide predominance for capitalism (U.S.) or communism (USSR) (see p. 113).

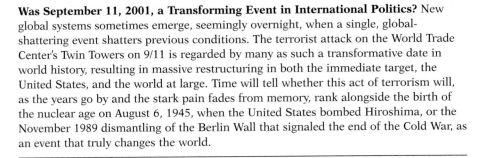

Was September 11, 2001, a Transforming Event in International Politics? New global systems sometimes emerge, seemingly overnight, when a single, global-shattering event shatters previous conditions. The terrorist attack on the World Trade Center's Twin Towers on 9/11 is regarded by many as such a transformative date in world history, resulting in massive restructuring in both the immediate target, the United States, and the world at large. Time will tell whether this act of terrorism will, as the years go by and the stark pain fades from memory, rank alongside the birth of the nuclear age on August 6, 1945, when the United States bombed Hiroshima, or the November 1989 dismantling of the Berlin Wall that signaled the end of the Cold War, as an event that truly changes the world.

How can we determine when an existing pattern of relationships gives way to a completely new international system? Following Stanley Hoffmann (1961), we will proceed by assuming that we have a new international system when we have a new answer to one of three questions: (1) *What are the system's basic units?* (e.g., states or supranational institutions for global governance); (2) *What are the predominant foreign policy goals that these units seek with respect to one another?* (e.g., territorial conquest or material gain through trade); and (3) *What can these units do to one another with their military and economic capabilities?*

These criteria might lead us to conclude that a new system has now emerged. First, new trade partnerships have been forged in Europe, the cone of South America, North America, and the Pacific Rim, and these trading blocs may behave as unitary, or independent, nonstate actors as they compete with one another. Moreover, international organizations, such as the World Trade Organization and the European Union, now sometimes flex their political muscles in contests with individual states, and transnational religious movements, such as Islamic fundamentalism, challenge the **global system** itself—a system that international law still defines as composed primarily of **states** consisting of various nationality groups who perceive themselves as unified by a common language, culture, or ethnic identity. At the same time, some states have disintegrated into smaller units. In 1991, the former Soviet Union fragmented into fractious political entities searching for national identity and autonomy. Other national units could disintegrate as well—peacefully, like the former Czechoslovakia, or violently, like the former Yugoslavia.

Second, territorial conquest is no longer the predominant goal of most states' foreign policies. Instead, their emphasis has shifted from traditional military methods of exercising influence to economic means. Meanwhile, the ideological contest between democratic capitalism and the Marxist-Leninist communism of the Cold War era no longer comprises the primary cleavage in international politics, and a major new axis has yet to become clear, even though many conclude that 9/11 marked the beginning of a new age dominated by a global war between terrorists and those who resist them.

Third, the proliferation of weapons technology has profoundly altered the damage that states can inflict on one another. Great powers alone no longer control the world's most lethal weapons. Increasingly, however, the great powers' prosperity depends on economic circumstances throughout the globe, reducing their ability to control their growth rates at precisely the time when their capabilities to militarily dominate others have eroded.

The profound changes in the types of actors (units), goals, and capabilities of recent years have dramatically altered the power ranking of states that defines the structure of international politics. Still, the hierarchies themselves endure. The *economic hierarchy* that divides the rich from the poor, the *political hierarchy* that separates the rulers from the ruled, the *resource hierarchy* that makes some suppliers and others dependents, and the *military asymmetries* that pit the strong against the weak all still shape the relations among states, as they have in the past. Similarly, the perpetuation of international **anarchy,** in the absence of institutions to govern the globe and chronic national insecurity continue to encourage preparations for war and the use of force without international mandate. Thus change and continuity coexist, with both forces simultaneously shaping contemporary world politics.

The interaction of constancy and change makes it difficult to predict whether the twenty-first century will bring a wholly new and different international system. What is clear is that this interaction will determine future relations among global actors. This, perhaps, explains why **cycles** so often appear to characterize world politics: Periodic sequences of events occur that resemble patterns in earlier periods. Because the emergent international system shares many characteristics with earlier periods, historically minded observers may experience déjà vu—the illusion of having already experienced something actually being experienced for the first time.

The challenge, then, is to observe unfolding global realities objectively in order to describe and explain them accurately, and hence to understand their future impact. This requires that we understand how our images of reality shape our expectations. It also requires a set of tools for analyzing the forces of

■ **global system**
a worldwide system primarily of states comprising nationality groups who perceive themselves as unified by language, culture, or ethnic identity.

■ **state**
an independent, territorially defined community in the global system administered by a sovereign government (see p. 11).

■ **anarchy**
a condition in which the units in the global system are subjected to few if any overarching institutions to regulate their conduct (see p. 142).

■ **cycles**
the periodic reemergence of conditions similar to those that existed previously.

constancy and change that affect our world. Thus, the remainder of this chapter will briefly examine the role that images of reality play in our understanding of world politics, and then will describe the theoretical orientation of the book. Chapter 2 will examine the theoretical perspectives we will use in this book to interpret trends and transformations in world politics.

HOW PERCEPTIONS INFLUENCE IMAGES OF REALITY

We all carry mental images of world politics—explicit or implicit, conscious or subconscious. But whatever our level of awareness, our images simplify "reality" by exaggerating some features of the real world while ignoring others. Thus we live in a world defined by our expectations and images.

These mental pictures, or perceptions, are inevitably distortions, as they cannot fully capture the complexity and configurations of even physical objects, such as the globe itself (see Controversy: Should We Believe What We See?). Thus many of our images of the world's political realities may be built on illusions and misconceptions. Even images that are now accurate can easily become outdated if we fail to recognize changes in the world. Indeed, the world's future will be determined not only by changes in the "objective" facts of world politics but also by the meaning that people ascribe to those facts, the assumptions on which they base their interpretations, and the actions that flow from these assumptions and interpretations—however accurate or inaccurate they might be.

The Nature and Sources of Images

The effort to simplify one's view of the world is inevitable and even necessary. Just as cartographers' projections simplify complex geophysical space so we can better understand the world, each of us inevitably creates a "mental map"— a habitual way of organizing information—to make sense of a confusing abundance of information. Although mental maps are neither inherently right nor wrong, they are important because we tend to react according to the way the world appears to us rather than the way it is. How we *view* the world (not what it is really like) determines our attitudes, our beliefs, and our behavior. Political leaders, too, are captives of this tendency. As Richard Ned Lebow (1981) warns, "Policymakers are prone to distort reality in accord with their needs even in situations that appear . . . relatively unambiguous."

Most of us—policymakers included—look for information that reinforces our preexisting beliefs about the world, assimilate new data into familiar images, mistakenly equate what we believe with what we know, and deny information that contradicts our expectations. We process information using **schematic reasoning;** that is, we rely on learned ways of psychologically perceiving new information and we interpret it in light of our memories (Rosenberg 1988). We use information shortcuts both to make political judgments and to help orient our attitudes and beliefs toward specific events and policy issues. A schema thus aids in the organization of information and shapes our perceptions of the world.

■ **schematic reasoning** the process of reasoning by which new information is interpreted according to a memory structure that contains a network of genetic scripts, metaphors, and stereotypical characters.

We assemble and organize information about the world to help us simplify it. This is necessary "to cope with an extraordinarily confusing world by structuring views about specific foreign policies according to [our] more general and abstract beliefs" (Hurwitz and Peffley 1987). Our preexisting values and beliefs encourage us to accept some images as accurate while rejecting from consciousness others that are incongruent with our prior beliefs, a psychological conflict known as **cognitive dissonance** (see Festinger 1957). The mind selects, screens, and filters what it perceives. Thus our view of world politics depends not only on what happens in the world but also on how we interpret and internalize those events; **social constructivism** informs us that our mental maps inevitably help to shape our attitudes about, and images of, global issues. Several factors influence our perceptions of international relations:

- Our psychological needs, drives, and dispositions (e.g., trust or mistrust), which are ingrained in our personalities as a result of early childhood experiences.

- Our views of international affairs (e.g., tolerance or fear of cultural diversity) as filtered through the socialization or learning we receive as children.

- The images of international realities advanced by the most popular and powerful groups, comprised of leaders and scholars throughout the world, which present core ideas for discussion that offer a compelling, socially constructed shared worldview about the meaning and nature of international life.

- Our images of world history as shaped by the teachers and books to which we are exposed.

- Opinions about world affairs articulated by our frequent associates, such as close friends.

- Attitudes expressed by policymakers, political pundits, and others whose expertise we respect.

- The positions we occupy and the various roles we perform (student, parent, bureaucrat, policymaker, diplomat, etc.).

Tolerance of ambiguity and receptivity to new ways of organizing thinking vary among individuals and personality types. Some people are receptive to diversity and therefore better able than others to revise perceptual habits to accommodate new realities. Nevertheless, to some extent, we are all prisoners of the perceptual predispositions that have shaped us and that in turn shape our attitudes, beliefs, and images of world politics. This is why political **ideologies** tend to develop and to attract adherents, who join groups to express their common beliefs.

The Role of Images in World Politics

We must be careful not to assume automatically that what applies to individuals applies to entire countries. Still, leaders' images of historical circumstances often predispose them to behave in particular ways toward others, regardless of "objective" facts. For instance, the loss of twenty-six million Soviet lives in the "Great Patriotic War" (as the Russians refer to World War II) created an exaggerated fear of foreign invasion, which caused a generation of Soviet policymakers to perceive U.S. defensive moves with considerable suspicion and often

■ **cognitive dissonance**
the general psychological tendency to deny discrepancies between one's preexisting beliefs (cognitions) and new information.

■ **social constructivism**
a liberal-realist theoretical approach advocated by Alexander Wendt that sees self-interested states as the key actors in world politics, whose actions are determined not by anarchy but by the ways states socially "construct" and then respond to the meanings they give to power politics so that as their definitions change, cooperative practices can evolve.

■ **ideology**
a set of core philosophical principles that a group of leaders and citizens collectively holds about politics, the interests of political actors, and the ways people ought to ethically behave.

SHOULD WE BELIEVE WHAT WE SEE?
The Organization of Observations and Projections of Global Realities

Many people assume that "seeing is believing" without questioning whether the ways they have organized their perceptions are accurate. But is there more to seeing than meets the eye? To view and interpret reality, do we perceive in ways that may produce a biased distortion? Students of perceptual psychology think so. They maintain that seeing is not a strictly passive act: what we observe is partially influenced by our preexisting values and expectations (and by the visual habits reinforced by the constructions society has inculcated in us about how to view objects). Students of perception argue that "what you see is what you get" and that two observers looking at the same object might easily see different realities. To illustrate this, perceptual psychologists are fond of displaying the drawing below, which, depending on how the viewer looks at it, can be seen as either a goblet or two faces opposing each other. Both images are possible.

This principle has great importance for investigation of international relations, where, depending on one's perspective, people can vary greatly on how they will view international events, actors, and issues. From competing images often arise intense disagreements.

To appreciate the kind of controversies that can result from the fact that different people can easily see different realities when they look at the same thing from different perspectives, consider something as basic as viewing objectively the location and size of the continents in the world. There exists a long-standing controversy among cartographers about the "right" way to map the globe, that is, how to make an accurate projection, and the accuracy of their rival maps matter politically because they shape how people view what is important. All maps of the globe are distorted, because it is impossible to perfectly represent the three-dimensional globe on a two-dimensional piece of paper. The difficulty cartographers face can be appreciated by trying to flatten an orange peel. You can only flatten it by separating pieces of the peel that were joined when it was spherical. Cartographers who try to flatten the globe on paper, without "ripping it" into separate pieces, face the same problem. Although there are a variety of ways to represent the three-dimensional object on paper, all of them involve some kind of distortion. Thus cartographers must choose among the imperfect ways of representing the globe by selecting those aspects of the world's geography they consider most important to describe accurately, while making adjustments to other parts.

Cartographers' ideas of what is most important in world geography have varied according to their own global perspectives. These three maps (Maps 1.1, 1.2, and 1.3) depict the distribution of the Earth's land surfaces and territory, but each portrays a different image. Each is a model of reality, an abstraction that highlights some features of the globe while ignoring others. In examining these three ways of viewing and interpreting the globe, evaluate which projection you think is best. Which features of global reality are most worthy of emphasizing to capture an accurate picture? What does your answer reveal about your values and view of the world?

MAP 1.1
Mercator Projection

This Mercator projection, popular in sixteenth-century Europe, is a classic Eurocentric view of the world. It retained direction accurately, making it useful for navigators, but placed Europe at the center of the world and exaggerated the continent's importance relative to other landmasses. Europe appears larger than South America, which is twice Europe's size, and two-thirds of the map is used to represent the northern half of the world and only one-third the southern half. Because lines of longitude were represented as parallel rather than convergent, it also greatly exaggerates the size of Greenland and Antarctica.

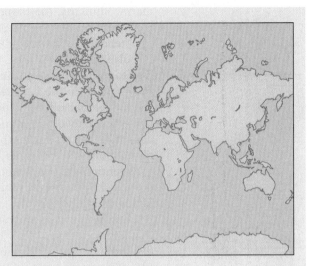

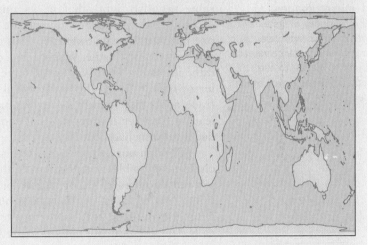

MAP 1.2
Peter's Projection

In the Peter's projection, each landmass appears in correct proportion in relation to all others, but it distorts the shape and position of landmasses. In contrast with most geographic representations, it draws attention to the less-developed countries of the Global South where more than three-quarters of the world's population lives today.

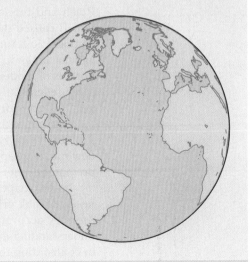

MAP 1.3
Orthographic Projection

The orthographic projection, centering on the mid-Atlantic, conveys some sense of the curvature of the Earth by using rounded edges. The sizes and shapes of continents toward the outer edges of the circle are distorted to give a sense of spherical perspective.

alarm. Similarly, the founders of the United States viewed eighteenth-century European power politics as corrupt, contributing to two seemingly contradictory tendencies later evident in U.S. foreign policy: (1) America's isolationist impulse (its disposition to withdraw from world affairs), and (2) its determination to reform the world in its own image. The former led the country to reject membership in the League of Nations after World War I; the latter gave rise to the U.S. globalist foreign policy after World War II, which committed the country to active involvement nearly everywhere on nearly every issue. Most Americans failed to recognize that others might regard such a far-reaching international policy position as arrogant or threatening; they saw in active U.S. interventionism only good intentions. As President Jimmy Carter once lamented, "The hardest thing for Americans to understand is that they are not better than other people."

Because leaders and citizens are prone to ignore or reinterpret information that runs counter to their beliefs and values, mutual misperceptions often fuel discord in world politics, especially when relations between countries are hostile. Distrust and suspicion arise as conflicting parties view each other in the same negative light—that is, as **mirror images** develop. This occurred in Moscow and Washington during the Cold War. Self-righteousness often leads one party to view its own actions as constructive but its adversary's responses as negative and hostile. When this occurs, conflict resolution is extraordinarily difficult, as the Cold War and the recurrent ethnic conflicts and acts of global terrorism illustrate. Thus fostering peace is not simply a matter of expanding trade and other forms of transnational contact, or even of bringing political leaders together in international summits. Rather, it is a matter of changing deeply entrenched beliefs.

■ **mirror images**
the tendency of states and people in competitive interaction to perceive each other similarly—to see others the same way others see them.

Although our constructed images of world politics are resistant to change, change is possible. Overcoming old thinking habits sometimes occurs when we experience punishment or discomfort as a result of clinging to false assumptions. As Benjamin Franklin once observed, "The things that hurt, instruct." Dramatic events in particular can alter international images, sometimes drastically. The Vietnam War caused many Americans to adjust their previous images about the use of force in contemporary world politics. The defeat of the Third Reich and revelations of Nazi atrocities committed before and during World War II caused the German people to confront their past as they prepared for a democratic future imposed by the victorious allies. The use of atomic bombs against Japan in the waning days of World War II caused many to confront the horrors of modern warfare and the immorality of weapons of mass destruction. More recently, the unexpected collapse of communist rule in the Soviet Union and Eastern Europe prompted policymakers and political commentators alike to reexamine their assumptions about foreign policy priorities in a new, post–Cold War system. Often such jolting experiences encourage us to construct new mental maps, perceptual filters, and criteria through which we may interpret later events and define situations.

As we shape and reshape our images of world politics and its future, we need to think critically about the foundations on which our perceptions rest. Are they accurate? Are they informed? Might they be adjusted to gain greater understanding and empathy? This rethinking is one of the challenges we face in confronting the world politics of the twenty-first century.

DIFFERENT LEVELS OF ANALYSIS

To predict which forces will dominate the future, we must recognize that many forces are operating at the same time. No trend or trouble stands alone; all interact simultaneously. The future is influenced by many determinants, each connected to the rest in a complex web of linkages. Collectively, these may produce stability by limiting the impact of any single disruptive force. If interacting forces converge, however, their combined effects can accelerate the pace of change in world politics, moving it in directions not possible otherwise.

Many international relations scholars agree that world politics can best be understood by focusing on one (or more) of three levels. Known as **levels of analysis,** this classification distinguishes: (1) individuals, (2) states or other nonstate global actors, and (3) the entire global system.

The **individual level of analysis** refers to the personal characteristics of humans, including those responsible for making important decisions on behalf of state and nonstate actors, as well as ordinary citizens whose behavior has important political consequences. Here, for example, we may properly locate the impact of individuals' perceptions on their political attitudes, beliefs, and behavior, and explore the question of why each human being is a crucial part of the global drama and why the study of world politics is relevant to our lives and future.

The **state level of analysis** consists of the authoritative decision-making units that govern states' foreign policy processes and the internal attributes of those states (e.g., their type of government, level of economic and military power, and number of nationality groups), which both shape and constrain leaders' foreign policy choices. The processes by which states make decisions regarding war and peace and their capabilities for carrying out those decisions, for instance, fall within the state level of analysis.

The **global level of analysis** refers to the interactions of states and nonstate actors on the global stage whose behaviors ultimately shape the international political system and the levels of conflict and cooperation that characterize world politics. The capacity of rich states in the **Global North** to dictate the choices of poor states in the **Global South** falls properly within the global level of analysis. So does the capacity (or incapacity) of the UN to maintain peace.

Examples abound of the diverse ways in which global trends and issues are the product of influences at each level of analysis. Protectionist trade policies by an importing country increase the costs to consumers of clothing and cars and reduce the standard of living of citizens in the manufacturing states. Such policies are initiated by a *state* government (national level), but diminish the quality of life of *people* living both within the protectionist country and those living abroad (individual level) and reduce the level of *global* trade while threatening to precipitate retaliatory trade wars. Of course, for some developments and issues, factors and forces emanating primarily from one or two particular levels provide more analytical leverage than do those from the other level(s). Accordingly, as we confront specific global issues in subsequent chapters, we will emphasize those levels of analysis that provide the most informative lens for viewing them. In the next section, we outline the path to discovery that *World Politics* will pursue.

■ **levels of analysis**
the different aspects of and agents in international affairs that may be stressed in interpreting world politics and explaining global phenomena, depending on whether the analyst chooses to focus on "wholes" (the complete global system and large collectivities) or on "parts" (individual states or people) (see p. 231).

■ **individual level of analysis**
an analytical approach that emphasizes the psychological and perceptual variables motivating people such as those who make foreign policy decisions on behalf of states and other global actors.

■ **state level of analysis**
an analytical approach that emphasizes how the internal attributes of states influence their foreign policy behaviors (see p. 104).

■ **global level of analysis**
an analytical approach that emphasizes the impact of worldwide conditions on foreign policy behavior.

■ **Global North**
a term used to refer to the world's wealthy, industrialized countries located primarily in the Northern Hemisphere.

■ **Global South**
a term now often used instead of "Third World" to designate the less-developed countries located primarily in the Southern Hemisphere.

Greg Baker/AP/Wide World

Globalization's Seeds of Change? At a time in world history rife with collapsing failed states, a worldwide war to combat terrorism, and ethnic wars within states and by state governments against minorities living within their national borders, many have pinned their hopes for future peace and prosperity on the effects of "globalization"— the expansion of international trade and the integration of the global economy. That aspiration and expectation is captured by this photo showing happy Chinese celebrating in June 2002 China's new membership in the World Trade Organization (WTO), a symbol of and catalyst for globalization. Critics, of course, see the WTO as a sinister force breeding inequality and the loss of national identity.

THE BOOK'S APPROACH: ACTORS, ISSUES, AND THEIR INTERACTIONS

Because world politics is complex and our images of it are often discordant, scholars differ in their approaches to understanding the contemporary world. In this book, we adopt a multilevel, multi-issue perspective that frames the investigation by looking at: (1) the characteristics, capabilities, and interests of the principal "actors" in world politics (states and various nonstate participants in international affairs); (2) the principal welfare and security issues—the key issues—on the **global agenda;** and (3) the patterns of cooperation and contention that influence the interactions between and among actors and issues. As we probe these interactions, we will discover why **politics**—the exercise of influence to affect the distribution of particular values, such as power, prestige, or wealth—is the most pervasive and controversial aspect of international affairs.

A multilevel, multi-issue perspective is useful, not only because it takes into account the interaction of constancy and change in the new millennium but also because it avoids dwelling on any particular events, countries, individuals, or transitory phenomena whose long-term significance is likely to diminish. Instead, the perspective seeks to identify behaviors that cohere into general

■ **global agenda**
the primary issues, problems, and controversies on which states and humanity concentrate their attention and to which they allocate resources.

■ **politics**
to Harold Lasswell, the study of "who gets what, when, how and why?" (see p. 33).

global patterns—trends and transformations that measurably affect global living conditions. Thus we explore the nature of world politics from a perspective that places general patterns into a larger, lasting theoretical context, providing the conceptual tools and theories that will enable us to interpret subsequent developments.

Our journey into the dynamics of world politics begins in Chapter 2 with an overview of the major realist and liberal theoretical traditions that scholars and leaders use most to interpret world politics, as well as the **constructivist** interpretations they develop as a theoretical account of how both realism and liberalism are socially constructed sets of assumptions about how best to view world politics. This provides the intellectual background for the description, explanation, and prediction of the issues and developments that are treated in the remaining chapters.

Chapter 3 begins the analysis of actors, issues, and their interactions with a close examination of foreign policy decision-making processes *within* states, which remain the principal actors in world politics. Chapter 3 also covers the individual level of analysis, as we consider the role of leaders in making foreign policy, but the bulk of the chapter addresses how other forces at the state or domestic level can constrain the impact of individuals.

We will then turn our attention to each of the types of actors in world politics and examine how their characteristics and capabilities affect their interests and influence in the world. **Great powers** (those wealthy countries with the biggest militaries) are the focus of attention in Chapter 4. In Chapter 5, we extend the account to cover two groups of **nonstate actors** (intergovernmental organizations—IGOs—on the one hand and nongovernmental organizations—NGOs—such as transnational ethnopolitical movements, religions, and multinational corporations on the other) and demonstrate how these actors interact with states and increasingly challenge the supremacy of all states, including even the great powers, by either transcending or subverting states' sovereign control over their destinies. Then, in Chapter 6, we incorporate into the picture the place of the weaker states, that is, the less-developed countries of the Global South, explaining how the fate of this group of states is shaped by their relations with great powers and with nonstate actors and international institutions active in world politics.

The next group of chapters properly falls within the global level of analysis. Here we shift attention to global issues and inquire into how the characteristics, capabilities, and interests of the principal actors in world politics affect interactions and outcomes of the principal welfare and security issues on the global agenda. Welfare issues—the so-called **low politics** of problems relating to economics, population, and the environment—are the subjects of Chapters 7 through 10, topics that have assumed center stage in discussions of world politics in the age of globalization. Also discussed in Chapter 7, "Humans and Global Challenges to the Protection of Human Rights," is the role of individuals in the advancement of human welfare and human development. Next, in Chapters 11 through 15, we examine the so-called **high politics** of security issues—the threat of armed conflicts and war that traditionally have commanded primary attention on the global agenda, as well as the major approaches to the prevention of war and the preservation of peace. In the final chapter, Chapter 16, we offer contending perspectives about the probable shape of the global future.

■ **constructivism**
a scholarly approach to inquiry emphasizing the importance of agents (people and groups) and the shared meanings they construct to define their identities, interests, and institutions—understandings that influence their international behavior.

■ **great powers**
the most powerful countries, militarily and economically, in the global system.

■ **nonstate actors**
all transnationally active groups other than states, such as organizations whose members are states, and nongovernmental organizations whose members are individuals and private groups from more than one state.

■ **low politics**
a category of global issues related to the economic, social, demographic, and environmental relations between governments and people.

■ **high politics**
issues related to the military, security, and political relations of states (see p. 179).

FACING THE FUTURE: KEY QUESTIONS TO CONFRONT AT THE DAWN OF THE NEW MILLENNIUM

Chapter 16 concludes our inquiry into the trends and transformations comprising contemporary world politics. It draws on the ideas and information presented in earlier chapters in order to address ten questions on the global issues that will dominate political discourse during the next decade. We anticipate those questions here by posing several that will also inform our inquiry in the chapters that follow.

Are States Obsolete?

The territorial state has been the primary actor in world politics for more than four centuries. Resurgent nationalism and civil warfare throughout the world attests to the continuing quest by national independence movements for self-governance and statehood, since the principal motive of each nationalistic separatist movement is to become a sovereign independent state. The disintegration of failed states and the creation of new members of the international community in recent years accounts for the expansion of the number of UN member states from 166 in 1991 to 190 in September 2002 when Switzerland joined the world organization. If today's fragile failed states break into even smaller separate states, with various nationalities within them gaining independence and becoming sovereign states, the UN could have 400 to 500 members in the twenty-first century. Some estimate that the number of independent states in the global system could grow from 207 in 2000 to more than 800 by the year 2025. Others wonder if states will fade in the twenty-first century, with globally engaged "citistates" assuming their place by the year 2100 as the organizing principle for world affairs (Peirce 2000).

In some respects, the territorial state is flourishing because it is still needed to give people identity, raise taxes, provide safety nets for the needy, protect the environment, and provide military security. At the same time some states are failing to adequately meet such traditional goals as providing for the poor, generating economic growth, preventing pollution, maintaining domestic stability, or countering terrorism. In fact, many have proclaimed "the end" of **state sovereignty** (Opello and Rosow 1999) and its supreme authority in the face of growing challenges from home and abroad. To them, "The one trend that is sure to dominate the coming . . . quarter-century is the decline of the power of the state" (Zakaria 1999) because "a wide variety of forces has made it increasingly difficult for any state to wield power over its people and address issues it once considered its sole prerogative" (Stanley Foundation 1993).

"While states may not be about to exit from the political stage, and while they may even continue to occupy center stage, they do seem likely to become vulnerable and impotent" (Rosenau 1995). The question to be confronted is if

> even where sovereignty still appears intact, states [can any] longer . . . retain sole command of what transpires within their own territorial boundaries. . . . The notion of the nation-state as a self-governing, autonomous unit appears to be more a normative claim than a descriptive statement. (Held et al. 1999, 8–9)

■ **state sovereignty**
under international law, the status of states as equals in that, within their territory, a state's government is subject to no higher external authority.

As global trends transform twenty-first-century world politics, the question is whether the state can cope with the challenges it now faces. Auguste Comte, a nineteenth-century French political philosopher, argued that societies create institutions to address problems and meet human needs. When institutions are no longer able to perform these functions, they disappear. Today, as the managerial capabilities of states fail to inspire confidence, we must ask if states have a future.

Is Globalization a Cure or a Curse?

Globalization has become a popular shorthand term to describe a number of basic dimensions of world politics; it is used as an adjective, a noun, and a verb to refer alternatively to a process, a product, a policy, or a predicament. Globalization in general describes the internationalization and integration of the global community into a single society without barriers and national boundaries. Most observers would agree with one among many possible definitions of globalization—as "the increasing scale and importance of exchanges of people, products, services, capital, and ideas across international borders" (Auguste 1999). However, globalization is perhaps also interpreted not only as a condition but in addition is best seen as the culmination of what a quarter of a century ago was commonly called **interdependence**—the increasing degree since the mid-1970s to which the quality of life within states was rapidly and visibly becoming dependent on conditions in other states.

Interdependent globalization lies at the heart of the external challenges states now face. As the range of global issues has expanded and the integration of national economies has created a worldwide market and global culture, globalization in a borderless world has reduced states' ability to govern their affairs. Mutual vulnerabilities have reduced states' autonomy by curtailing their control of their own national fates, and globalization has erased the traditional distinctions between what is national and what is international, what is private and what is public, and what is domestic and what is foreign.

From one perspective, an awareness of the common destiny of all, alongside the declining ability of many sovereign states to cope with global problems through national means, will energize efforts to put aside interstate competition. According to this reasoning, conflict will recede as humanity begins to better recognize how little protection national borders and oceans provide it against the multiple challenges arising from the global revolution in travel, communications, and trade—shared problems that can only be managed through collective, multilateral cooperation. As Thomas Friedman (1999b) argues, globalization, "with its economic integration, digital integration, its ever-widening connectivity of individuals and nations, its spreading of capitalist values and networks to the remotest corners of the world [is creating] a much stronger web of constraints on the foreign policy behavior of those nations which are plugged into the system." Consequently, because globalization makes it imperative that states cooperate, we should welcome the continued tightening of interstate linkages.

From another, more pessimistic perspective, the irreversible process of globalization will not lead to transnational collaboration, but to competition. Regardless of how compelling the need or how rewarding the benefits, increased contact and the trend toward an integrated single society of states

■ **globalization**
the integration of states through increasing contact, communication, and trade, creating a holistic, single global system in which the process of change increasingly binds people together in a common fate (see p. 45).

■ **interdependence**
when the behavior of international actors greatly affects others with whom they have contact, and the parties to the exchange become mutually sensitive and vulnerable to the others' actions (see p. 307).

will breed enmity, not amity. According to this view, globalization empowers advantaged states but constrains the prospects of weak states, producing new inequalities in a highly stratified global hierarchy in which the gap between the wealthy and the poor continues to widen. Because its benefits will not be distributed equally, globalization will likely generate conflict between winners and losers. Intertwined economies will sour relations more often than sweeten them. Under conditions of fierce competition, scarcity, and resurgent nationalism, the temptation may be irresistible to seek isolation from the assault of globalization on national identity and autonomy by creating barriers to trade and other transactions. The temptation to achieve political benefits by military force will also continue: "Interdependence promotes war as well as peace" (Waltz 2000). Thus the tightening web of globalization foretells danger as well as opportunity.

Is Technological Innovation a Blessing or a Burden?

"The dynamics of globalization unleashed by technology," James N. Rosenau (1995) concludes, "are the dominant catalyst in world affairs." The consequences, however, are not certain. Like globalization, which technology engenders, technological innovation solves some problems but causes others. Not only can technological innovations create new ways of preventing or treating disease, but they can also enhance the sophistication and destructiveness of weapons of war. As Meg Greenfield (1997) correctly reminds us, "Illness, ignorance, and want have obviously not been eliminated. But millions upon millions of people living today, who not all that long ago would have been direly afflicted by all three, will never know them in anything like their once common form if they know them at all." Nevertheless, no generation but ours has faced the kind of random violence made possible and accessible by modern weapons technology.

Discoveries in microelectronics, information processing, transportation, energy, agriculture, communications, medicine, and biotechnology profoundly affect our lives and shape our future (Dyson 1997). They have united the globe into a single international market and common culture, while paradoxically breaking down people's sense of citizenship and community (Barber 1995). "There appears to be a fundamental lag between the current rate of technological change and the rate of adjustment to these changes among decision makers" (Blumenthal 1988). Technological change requires enlightened management. But is this possible in a greedy, disintegrative world in which science and technology are often selfishly exploited without serious consideration of their impact on and ethical consequences for humanity at large?

Will Geo-Economics Supersede Geopolitics?

Throughout modern history, states have competed with one another militarily for position and prominence in the hierarchy of international power. For more than three centuries, world politics has been largely a record of preparing for, waging, and recovering from interstate war. Military might was equated with prestige and influence, and military conquest became the means to economic as well as political preeminence.

In the view of some, the battlefield in world politics has shifted to economic issues. National destinies will be determined by commercial competition, not military conquest. If issues of **geo-economics** (the distribution of wealth) become more important than conventional issues of **geopolitics** (the distribution of political and military power), will states' foreign policies also change? If wealth is converted into political muscle, nationalistic pride can give rise to competition and self-assertiveness. But economic interdependence and tight commercial relationships can also collapse into trade disputes and political rivalry. Nevertheless, the apparent shift of priorities to the economics of world politics is certain to alter the distribution of twenty-first-century global power. This shift is also likely to decrease the barriers of long-standing state borders.

What Constitutes Human Well-Being on an Ecologically Fragile Planet?

The worldwide quest for **human rights** requires people and governments to define and distinguish the fundamental values to which they are entitled. Throughout history, many have placed money and prosperity as their first priority. However, that value preference has been challenged, and the once popular **limits-to-growth proposition**—the belief that the world cannot forever increase its productive capacity—has been replaced by the maxim of sustainability. Sustainability emphasizes "the growth of limits" in the global ecology (the total pattern of relations between organisms and their environment on Earth). Thus **sustainable development** means learning to live off earth's interest without encroaching on its capital, in order that the planet can continue to provide the means to life that makes the pursuit of other values such as political freedom and religious principles possible.

    Gross national product (GNP)—the total monetary value of goods and services produced in a state during a specified period, usually a year—is the common measure of states' relative economic well-being. It is an index of relative standards of living "closely bound up with human welfare. . . . Human welfare has dimensions other than the economic one. But it is widely held that the economic element is *very* important, and that the stronger the economy the greater the contribution to human welfare" (Daly and Cobb 1989). Indeed, many states' values are highly materialistic; money is perceived as a means to a secure and happy national existence—almost a human rights entitlement. To the inhabitants of most Global South less-developed countries, growth in GNP may mean more food, better housing, improved education, and an increased standard of living. However, affluent people in the Global North already enjoy these basic amenities; therefore, additional income usually allows them to satisfy comparatively trivial needs. When basic needs are fulfilled, conspicuous consumption and greed pose a danger to other values.

    The global impact of population growth, as well as the continued quest for economic growth, are great. People consume, and the more people there are, the greater will be levels of consumption, depletion of the world's resources, and pollution and the higher will be the toll on earth's ecological system. Unbridled exploitation and consumption, in the ever enduring quest for a higher standard of living that neglects the needs of future generations, will ultimately prove self-destructive. As Mikhail Gorbachev, the last president of the Soviet Union, warned in 1988, we must halt "humanity's aggression against nature."

■ **geo-economics**
the relationship between geography and the economic conditions and behavior of states that define their levels of production, trade, and consumption of goods and services.

■ **geopolitics**
the relationship between geography and politics and their consequences for states' national interests and relative power.

■ **human rights**
political rights and civil liberties recognized internationally as inalienable for individuals in all countries (see p. 512).

■ **limits-to-growth proposition**
the theory that earth's capacity to support life has natural limits and that if important resources such as fresh water are depleted, many will perish.

■ **sustainable development**
economic growth that does not deplete the resources needed to maintain growth (see p. 371).

■ **gross national product (GNP)**
the total monetary value of goods and services produced in a state during a specified period (see p. 68).

Looking beyond Earth's Problems As we consider the future, we must ask ourselves whether technological innovation is inevitably the anwer to our concerns. Although we are now able to send satellites into space and receive photos from planets we will never visit, we remain unable to eliminate hatred or aggression, or to achieve peace on earth.

These ideas challenge the core values of Western civilization. Although sustainable development is an attractive goal, even it will be hard to realize. Sustainable economic welfare requires economic growth managed to limit natural resource depletion and environmental damage, while protecting people's rights of leisure and liberty. But can this kind of growth in a finite world proceed infinitely? How long can finite energy sources sustain uncontrolled consumption before automobiles sputter to a stop, industries grind to a halt, and lights go out? How many pollutants can the atmosphere absorb before irreparable environmental damage results? And how many people can a delicately balanced ecosystem support?

Understanding today's world requires a willingness to confront complexity. A true but complicated idea always has less chance of success than a simple but false one, the French political sociologist Alexis de Tocqueville (1969) cautioned in 1835. The challenge is difficult but the rewards warrant the effort. Humankind's ability to chart a more rewarding future is contingent on its ability to entertain complex ideas, to free itself from the sometimes paralyzing grip of the past, and to develop a questioning attitude about rival perspectives on international realities. On that hopeful yet introspective note, we begin our exploration of world politics in a new millennium.

KEY TERMS

international political system	cycles	levels of analysis
transformation	schematic reasoning	individual level of analysis
Cold War	cognitive dissonance	state level of analysis
global system	social constructivism	global level of analysis
state	ideology	Global North
anarchy	mirror images	Global South

global agenda   high politics   geopolitics
politics   state sovereignty   human rights
constructivism   globalization   limits-to-growth proposition
great powers   interdependence   sustainable development
nonstate actors   geo-economics   gross national product (GNP)
low politics

SUGGESTED READING

Baylis, John, and Steve Smith, eds. *The Globalization of World Politics,* 2nd ed. New York: Oxford University Press, 2001.

Dark, K. R. *The Waves of Time: Long-Term Change and International Relations.* New York: Continuum, 2000.

Dawson, Christopher. *Dynamics of World History.* Wilmington, Del.: ISI Books, 2002.

Friedman, Thomas L. *Longitudes and Attitudes: Exploring the World after September 11.* New York: Farrar Straus and Giroux, 2002.

Head, David, Anthony McGraw, David Goldblatt, and Jonathan Perraton. *Global Transformations.* Stanford, Calif. Stanford University Press, 1999.

Holsti, Ole R., Randolph M. Siverson, and Alexander L. George, eds. *Change in the International System.* Boulder, Colo.: Westview Press, 1980.

Hughes, Barry B. *International Futures: Choices in the Face of Uncertainty,* 4th ed. Boulder, Colo.: Westview Press, 2002.

Kegley, Charles W., Jr., and Eugene R. Wittkopf, eds. *The Global Agenda: Issues and Perspectives,* 6th ed. New York: McGraw-Hill, 2001.

Kliot, Nurit, and David Newman, eds. *Geopolitics at the End of the Twentieth Century: The Changing World Political Map.* Portland, Ore.: Frank Cass, 2000.

Mazarr, Michael J. *Global Trends 2005: An Owner's Manual for the Next Decade.* London: Palgrave, 2001.

Rochester, J. Martin. *Between Two Epochs: What's Ahead for America, the World and Global Politics in the 21st Century.* Upper Saddle River, N.J.: Prentice Hall, 2002.

Worldwatch Institute. *State of the World 2003.* New York: W. W. Norton, 2003.

WHERE ON THE WORLD WIDE WEB?

The World Wide Web's (WWW or Web) features make it a powerful tool for providing access to global information sources. Using the Web, you have instant access to documentation of important international events and agreements. Online information is current and often more complex than traditional sources. It quickly reflects the changing nature of international events. The Web's international reach also permits users to locate opinions and perspectives from individuals across the United States and around the world. Many from the international community post their work on the Web. Every day more sources become available online as individuals and institutions discover the wonders of the Web.

The "Where on the World Wide Web?" sections that accompany each chapter provide you with interesting Web links to explore. Through this investiga-

tion, you will become an active participant in the globalization of world information (see Chapter 8 for a discussion of the Internet's role in the globalization process). You will also gain a greater understanding of the concepts and terms discussed in *World Politics*.

As you begin to examine the trends and transformation of world politics, it is important that you understand the evolution of international events and keep abreast of the ever changing world of international politics. The Web links listed here will help you analyze current events.

American Journalism Review **News Link**
http://www.newslink.org/news.html

If you are interested in "going to the source" for your news, check out the *American Journalism Review*'s Web site. This site provides links to electronic newspapers from the United States or anywhere in the world. Even campus papers are accessible through this site. You can read the news in a foreign language or try to find an English version. You may want to compare the same news story found in different newspapers around the world to see how different countries interpret the same event.

CNN Interactive World News
http://www.cnn.com/WORLD/

Surf the Web site of the news organization that changed the way world news is reported by providing constant, minute-by-minute coverage of breaking news stories from around the world. CNN's World News main page is divided according to world region and reports the top stories in each area. Over the course of a week, compare and contrast the content of the top stories from each region. Do you see a pattern concerning the type of news stories reported for each area?

Foreign Affairs Online
http://www.people.virginia.edu/~rjb3v/rjb.html

This comprehensive Web site has been specifically designed to assist students and other individuals interested in international law, international relations, and U.S. foreign policy. It has links to general references, map resources, foreign states, the United Nations system, international organizations, international legal entities, think tanks, and media resources. This is an important gateway to numerous international affairs resources on the Web, so you may want to bookmark it.

The National Geographic Society
http://www.nationalgeographic.com/maps/index. html

Publisher of the popular *National Geographic* magazine, the society has created an impressive Web tool called the MapMachine Online Atlas, one of the best interactive map sets on the Web. Viewers can choose many different types of interactive maps. For instance, the Dynamic Maps, which use geographic information systems (GIS), display population densities, ecoregions, weather patterns, earthquake fault lines, mineral deposits, and other features anywhere in the world. The Atlas Maps identify 191 independent states and provide a brief overview of each state.

A quick click anywhere on the map gives key geographic, demographic, and economic data. As Chapter 1 explains, all maps focus on specific features while ignoring other features, which leads to distortions. Compare the Map Machine maps with those found in the box, Controversy: Should We Believe What We See? The Organization of Observations and Projections of Global Realities, in this chapter. Are the "dynamic" maps more accurate representations of reality? What distortions do they depict?

National Public Radio Online
http://www.npr.org/

As an alternative to reading the news, access National Public Radio Online. This site lets you listen to the top news stories and is updated every hour. You can also search the entire site for stories of particular interest from a variety of NPR radio shows. You may also want to take a minute to cruise the discussion area and give your thoughts on the headline stories. You will need to download the RealAudio player to listen to the news stories at this site.

New York Times on the Web
http://www.nytimes.com

"All the news that's fit to print" is available online following a free registration. International news stories are easily accessed by clicking on the "International" news category. Keep in mind that the *Times* is a news source produced in the United States and may have American biases. While you read the news stories, think of ways in which they may have an "American slant."

University of Texas Library On-line Map Collection
http://www.lib.utexas.edu/maps/index.html

If you've ever wondered exactly where Rwanda, Kosovo, Taiwan, or Pakistan is, this site can help. The Perry-Castañeda Library Map Collection of the University of Texas at Austin is an extensive collection of electronic maps. It features regional as well as state maps according to political and shaded relief criteria. When reading about a specific country in *World Politics*, make sure you can locate the country and identify its neighbors. This will give you a better understanding of international events.

INFOTRAC® COLLEGE EDITION

George, Alexander L. "Knowledge for Statecraft," *International Security* Summer 1997.

Rothkopf, David J. "Cyberpolitik: The Changing Nature of Power in the Information Age," *Journal of International Affairs* Spring 1998.

Selle, Robert R. "Yen for Adventure—Geopolitics," *World and I* April 2002.

Hoffmann, Stanley. "Clash of Globalizations," *Foreign Affairs* July–August 2002.

For more articles, enter:

"political science" in the Subject Guide, and then go to subdivision "analysis."

"international relations" in the Subject Guide, and then go to subdivision "analysis."

THEORIES OF WORLD POLITICS

T O P I C S   A N D   T H E M E S

- Thinking theoretically to interpret global issues
- The liberal orientation
- The realist orientation
  The neorealist extension of realism
  The neoclassical extension of realism
- The neoliberal revision of liberalism
  International regimes
  Feminist theory
  Complex interdependence
- Alternative theories
  Behavioralism
  Postmodern deconstructivism

- **THEORIZING ABOUT THEORY** THE CONSTRUCTIVIST CONCEPTION
- **CONTROVERSY** CAN BEHAVIORAL SCIENCE ADVANCE THE STUDY OF INTERNATIONAL RELATIONS?
- **CONTROVERSY** NEOLIBERALISM VERSUS NEOREALISM: WHICH THEORY MAKES THE MOST REASONABLE ASSUMPTIONS?
- **CONTROVERSY** WHAT'S MISSING IN REALIST THEORIES OF INTERSTATE RELATIONS? THE FEMINIST CRITIQUE

One of the authors of your text, Charles Kegley, lectured in Poland in 2001, on the future of the theoretical study of world politics. His challenge was the same as yours—interpreting theoretically the meaning of a changing world for the global citizens facing the turbulent, interconnectness of the twenty-first century.

It's important that we take a hard, clear look . . . not at some simple world, either of universal goodwill or of universal hostility, but the complex, changing, and sometimes dangerous world that really exists.

—JIMMY CARTER, U.S. president, 1980

The present generation, and even more its successors, encounter a special challenge. For we are living through not only an exceptional period of fluidity in international relations but through an even more profound upheaval in how publics and leaders view the world around them.

—HENRY A. KISSINGER, former U.S. secretary of state, 1999

Imagine yourself the newly elected president of the United States. You are scheduled to deliver the State of the Union address on your views of the current world situation and your foreign policy to deal with it. You face the task of both defining those aspects of international affairs most worthy of attention and explaining the reasons for their priority. To convince citizens these issues are important, you must present them as part of a larger picture of the world. Therefore, based on your perceptions of world politics, you must identify a general framework from which to consider global issues. You must, in short, think *theoretically*. At the same time, you must be careful, because your interpretations will necessarily depend on your assumptions about international realities that your citizens might find questionable. The effort to explain the world, predict new global problems, and sell others on a policy to deal with them is bound to result in controversy because even reasonable people often see realities differently.

When leaders face these kinds of intellectual challenges, they fortunately benefit from the existence of a body of theoretically informed ideas from which they can draw guidance. In this chapter we distinguish among the major theoretical perspectives policymakers and scholars use to interpret international relations. Since perceived "realities" of international affairs that these theories seek to explain influence the content of the theories, we will examine how perceived changes in underlying international conditions have shaped various theories. In addition, our review of contending political theories will identify the intellectual heritage that informs this book.

UNDERSTANDING WORLD POLITICS

Social scientists construct different theories to make international events understandable. Over time, a **paradigm,** or dominant way of looking at a particular subject, such as international relations, arises and influences judgments regarding which characteristics of the subject are most important, what puzzles need to be solved, and what analytic criteria should govern investigations. These paradigms or "fundamental assumptions scholars make about the world they are studying" (Vasquez 1997) tend eventually to be revised in order to explain new developments in world affairs. Thus, the theories that guide the thinking of policymakers and scholars in different historical circumstances tell us much about world politics itself.

■ **paradigm**
derived from the Greek *paradeigma* meaning an example, a model, or an essential pattern; a paradigm structures thoughts about an area of inquiry.

The Elusive Quest for Theory

Throughout history, paradigms have been revised or abandoned when their assertions have failed to mirror the prevailing patterns of international behavior. Major wars have been especially potent in bringing about significant changes in the theoretical interpretation of world affairs. "Every war . . . has been followed in due course by skeptical reassessments of supposedly sacred assumptions" (Schlesinger 1986) and has influenced "what ideas and values will predominate, thereby determining the ethos of succeeding ages" (Gilpin 1981). Three such system-transforming wars dominated the twentieth century: World War I, World War II, and the Cold War. Each has shaped policymakers' perceptions of world politics, and each has provided lessons critical to developing policy programs that can best preserve world order in the twenty-first century.

This chapter will concentrate on the two core perspectives that throughout history have most influenced thinking about international affairs and that continue to guide theorizing: liberalism and realism and their neoliberal and neorealist variants that have commanded a large following in the last two decades. In addition, we shall ground these two major theoretical traditions in the **constructivism** approach. The constructivism approach is used to explain how *all* paradigms depend for their acceptance on the extent to which theoreticians and other groups reach general agreement, or an *intersubjective consensus,* on the most meaningful ways to define in detail the core concepts of international affairs and communicate these shared images and understandings. Constructivism provides a lens for examining the fads of intellectual fashions—that is, the formulations that make particular theoretical interpretations socially accepted and popular.

■ **constructivism**
a scholarly approach to inquiry emphasizing the importance of agents (people and goups) and the shared meanings they construct to define their identities, interests, and institutions— understandings that influence their international behavior.

The Evolution of Theoretical Inquiry

When the formal study of international relations began at the dawn of the twentieth century, the world abounded with optimism. Many people believed that peace and prosperity had taken root and would persist. The Hague peace conferences in 1899 and 1907 had inspired hope of controlling arms and sparing Europe another series of wars like those between 1848 and 1870. Moreover, numerous individuals—including the Scottish American industrialist Andrew Carnegie, who gave much of his fortune to the cause of world peace—assumed that as industrialization progressed and the costs and risks of war increased, the chance of protracted war among the great powers would decline dramatically (see also Angell 1910).

In those tranquil times, students of international relations studied history to glean insight on the events of the day. The study of international relations consisted mainly of commentary about personalities and events, past and present. Rarely did scholars seek to generalize theoretically about the lessons of history or about the principles or "laws" that might account for states' characteristic responses to similar stimuli or influences. Sir Halford Mackinder (1919) and Alfred Thayer Mahan (1890) were exceptions. Both sought to generate theoretical propositions pertaining to the influence of geographic factors on national power and international politics—efforts that laid the foundations for the study of political geography, which survives today as an important **geopolitical** approach to world politics (see Demko and Wood 1994).

The large-scale death and destruction that World War I exacted from 1914 to 1918 destroyed the sense of security that had made the **current history approach** popular. This catastrophic war was a painful lesson that stimulated the search for knowledge to address contemporary policy problems in a theoretical context. However interesting descriptions of recent or past wars might be, they were of doubtful use to a world in search of ways to prevent wars of mass destruction. For those purposes, policymakers and scholars needed a **theory**—a statement attempting to account for general phenomena or patterns rather than explaining unique or individual circumstances—that could reliably predict war and instruct leaders on the best policies to prevent it.

LIBERALISM

World War I initiated a paradigmatic revolution in the study of international relations, in which several perspectives competed for attention. While the current history approach continued to claim some disciples in the waning days of World War I, after Russia's Bolshevik Revolution Marxist-Leninist thought became increasingly influential, with its critique of capitalism's creation of inequality, class conflict, and imperialistic war. In the 1930s, with the rise of Adolf Hitler in Germany, national socialism (or fascism) also challenged conventional European thinking about world politics. Nazism, the German variant of national socialism, was particularly provocative. Not only did Nazism glorify the role of the state (as opposed to that of the individual) in political life, it also championed war as an instrument of national policy.

■ geopolitics
the relationship between geography and politics and their consequences for states' national interests and relative power.

■ current history approach
a focus on the description of contemporary and particular historical events rather than theoretical explanations to explain broader patterns of international relations.

■ theory
a set of hypotheses postulating the relationship between variables or conditions, advanced to describe, explain, or predict phenomena and make prescriptions about how positive changes ought to be engineered to realize particular ethical principles (see p. 308).

Pioneers in the Liberal Quest for World Order Influenced by David Hume and Jean-Jacques Rousseau, Immanuel Kant (left) in *Perpetual Peace* (1795) helped to redefine modern liberal theory by advocating global (not state) citizenship, free trade, and a federation of democracies as a means to peace. Richard Cobden (right) primarily foresaw the possibility of peace across borders; in his view, if contact and communication among people could expand through free trade, so too would international friendship and peace, secured by prosperity that would create interdependence and eliminate the need for military forces to pursue rivalries.

The Liberal Worldview

Emerging as dominant, however, was a perspective known as **liberalism.** At the core of liberalism is an emphasis on the impact ideas have on behavior, the equality, dignity and liberty of the individual, and the need to protect people from excessive state regulation. Liberalism views the individual as the seat of moral value and virtue and asserts that human beings should be treated as ends rather than means. It emphasizes ethical principle over the pursuit of power and institutions over capabilities as forces shaping interstate relations, and defines **politics** at the international level more as a struggle for consensus than a struggle for power and prestige.

Because advocates of liberalism were inspired by their interest in ideals, after World War I they are sometimes referred to as **idealists,** even though they were a diverse group within the larger liberal tradition. Post–World War I idealism, as advocated by such scholars and policymakers as Alfred Zimmerman, Norman Angell, James T. Shotwell, and Woodrow Wilson, derived from ancient liberal philosophy and has been interpreted variously in different periods. These idealists drew their philosophy from such liberal thinkers as Immanuel Kant, Thomas Jefferson, James Madison, John Stuart Mill, John Locke, David Hume, Jean-Jacques Rousseau, and Adam Smith (see Doyle 1997, Howard 1978, and Zacher and Matthew 1995).

■ **liberalism**
a paradigm predicated on the hope that the application of reason and universal ethics to international relations can lead to a more orderly, just, and cooperative world, and that international anarchy and war can be policed by institutional reforms that empower international organizations and laws.

■ **politics**
to liberal idealists, the search for agreement about shared values to foster cooperation within a global community (see p. 18).

■ **idealists**
people inspired by the liberal theoretical tradition who believe that the pursuit of ideals like world peace can change the world by reducing the disorder often exhibited in world politics.

Collectively, the post–World War I liberal idealists embraced a worldview that emphasized the power of ideas in controlling global destiny, based on the following beliefs:

1. Human nature is essentially "good" or altruistic, and people are therefore capable of mutual aid and collaboration through reason and ethically inspired education.

2. The fundamental human concern for others' welfare makes progress possible.

3. Sinful or wicked human behavior, such as violence, is the product not of flawed people but of evil institutions that encourage people to act selfishly and to harm others.

4. War and international anarchy are not inevitable and war's frequency can be reduced by strengthening the institutional arrangements that encourage its disappearance.

5. War is a global problem requiring collective or multilateral, rather than national, efforts to control it.

6. Reforms must be inspired by a compassionate ethical concern for the welfare and security of all people, and this humanitarian motive requires the inclusion of morality in statecraft.

7. International society must reorganize itself in order to eliminate the institutions that make war likely, and states must reform their political systems so that democratic governance and civil liberties within states can protect human rights and help pacify relations among states.

While not all liberal idealists subscribed to each of these tenets with equal conviction, they shared a moralistic, optimistic, and universalistic image of international affairs as taking place within a global community.

The Liberal Reform Program

Although liberal idealists after World War I differed significantly in their prescriptions for reforming the international political system (see Herz 1951), they generally fell into one of three groups. The first group advocated creating international institutions to replace the anarchical and war-prone balance-of-power system, characterized by coalitions of independent states formed to wage war or to defend a weaker coalition partner from attack. In place of this unregulated competitive system, idealists sought to create a new one based on **collective security.** This approach dealt with the problem of war by declaring any state's aggression an aggression against all who would act in concert to thwart the aggressor. The League of Nations was the institutional embodiment of collective security through international organization, reflecting simultaneously the liberal idealists' emphasis on international institutions and the possibility of international cooperation for global problem solving.

A second group emphasized the use of legal processes such as mediation and arbitration to settle disputes and avoid armed conflict. This facet of the idealists' policy prescriptions was illustrated by the creation in 1921 of the Permanent Court of International Justice to litigate interstate conflicts and by the ratification of the **Kellogg-Briand Pact** of 1928, which "outlawed" war as an instrument of national policy.

■ **collective security**
a security regime agreed to by the great powers that set rules for keeping peace guided by the principle that an act of aggression by any state will be met by a collective response from the rest (see p. 540).

■ **Kellogg-Briand Pact**
a multilateral treaty negotiated in 1928 that outlawed war as a method for settling interstate conflicts.

A third group followed the biblical injunction that states should beat their swords into plowshares and sought disarmament as a means to ending war. This orientation was exemplified by efforts during the 1920s, such as those negotiated at the Washington and London naval conferences, to secure arms control and disarmament agreements.

Several corollary ideas gave definition to the liberals' emphasis on encouraging global cooperation through international institutions, law, and disarmament. These included:

- The need to substitute attitudes that stressed the unity of humankind for those that stressed parochial national loyalties to independent sovereign states.
- The importance of individuals—their essential dignity and fundamental equality throughout the course of history, and the corollary need to protect and promote human rights and civil liberties.
- The use of the power of ideas through education to arouse world public opinion against warfare.
- The promotion of free international trade in place of states' economic competition.
- The replacement of secret diplomacy by a system of "open covenants, openly arrived at."
- The termination of interlocking bilateral alliances and the power balances they sought to achieve.

In seeking a more peaceful world, some liberal reformers promoted the ideal of **self-determination**—giving nationalities the right through voting to become independent **states**—as a means to redraw the globe's political geography to make **nations'** borders conform to ethnic groupings. Related to this was U.S. President Woodrow Wilson's call for democratic domestic institutions. "Making the world safe for democracy," liberals believed, would also make it secure and free from war, because democracies historically have almost–never urged war against one another. Wilson's celebrated Fourteen Points speech to Congress in 1918 proposed the creation of the League of Nations and, with it, the pursuit of other liberal idealists' aims such as free trade to create wealth and a global harmony of states' interests. This speech, perhaps better than any other statement, expressed the idealistic sentiments of the liberal worldview and program.

Although a tone of idealism dominated policy rhetoric and academic discussions during the interwar period, with the exception of the League of Nations and the precedent-setting Washington Naval Disarmament Treaties, little of the liberal reform program was ever seriously attempted, and even less of it was achieved. When the winds of international change again shifted and the Axis Powers pursued world conquest, enthusiasm for liberal idealism as a worldview receded.

■ **self-determination**
the principle that the global community is obligated to give nationalities their own governments (see p. 198).

■ **state**
a legal entity with a permanent population, a well-defined territory, and a government capable of managing sovereign authority over the nations or nationality groups living within its legal borders (see p. 35).

■ **nation**
a collection of people who, on the basis of ethnic, linguistic, or cultural affinity, perceive themselves to be members of the same group (see p. 63).

REALISM

The drive for global conquest that led to World War II provoked strong criticism of the liberal idealist paradigm. Critics blamed the outbreak of war on what they believed to be the so-called idealists' naive legalistic and moralistic

Realist Pioneers of Power Politics In *The Prince* (1532) and *The Leviathan* (1651) Niccoló Machiavelli and Thomas Hobbes, respectively, emphasized a political calculus based on interest, prudence, power, and expediency above all other considerations. This formed the foundation of what became a growing body of modern realist thinking that accepts the drive for power over others as necessary and wise statecraft.

assumptions about the possibility of peace and progress through human aspiration, and alleged that idealists were utopians who neglected the harsh realities of power politics and humans' innate compulsion to put their personal welfare ahead of the welfare of others (Carr 1939). The lessons the critics drew from the period between World War I and II led many to construct a revised set of perceptions and beliefs.

Advocates of the new, ascendant paradigm known as **realism,** or **realpolitik** as a specific philosophy, emerged to frame an intellectual movement whose message reads like the antithesis of idealism. Among the principal prophets of this new worldview were E. H. Carr (1939), George F. Kennan (1951, 1954), Hans J. Morgenthau (1948), Reinhold Niebuhr (1947), and Kenneth W. Thompson (1960). Realism deserves careful scrutiny because its socially constructed worldview continues to guide much thought about world politics.

The Realist Worldview

As a political theory, realism can trace its intellectual roots to the ancient Greek historian Thucydides and his account of the Peloponnesian Wars between Athens and Sparta (431–404 B.C.E.), the writings of Kautilya (minister to the Maurya emperor of India more than two thousand years ago), and especially the sixteenth-century political thought of the Italian theorist Niccoló Machiavelli and the seventeenth-century English philosopher Thomas Hobbes.

■ **realism**
a paradigm based on the premise that world politics is essentially and unchangeably a struggle among self-interested states for power and position under anarchy, with each competing state pursuing its own national interests (see p. 106).

■ **realpolitik**
the theoretical outlook prescribing that countries should prepare for war in order to preserve peace.

Realism, as applied to contemporary world politics, views the state as the most important actor on the world stage since it answers to no higher political authority. Moreover, conflicts of interests among states are assumed to be inevitable. Realism also emphasizes the ways in which the anarchical nature of international politics dictates the choices that foreign policymakers, as rational problem solvers who must calculate their interest in terms of power, must make. (See Chapter 3 for discussion of the "rational" actor.)

Within the realist paradigm, the purpose of statecraft is national survival in a hostile environment. To this end, no means is more important than the acquisition of **power,** and no principle is more important than **self-help.** In this conception, **state sovereignty,** a cornerstone of international law, gives heads of state the freedom—and responsibility—to do whatever is necessary to advance the state's interests and survival.

To the hard-core realist, respect for moral principles is a wasteful and dangerous interference in the rational pursuit of national self-advantage. To these proponents of power politics, questions about the relative virtues of the values within this or that ideological system cannot be allowed to interfere with sound policy making. A state's philosophical or ethical preferences are neither good nor bad—what matters is whether they serve its self-interest. Thus, the game of international politics revolves around the pursuit of power: acquiring it, increasing it, projecting it, and using it to bend others to one's will. At the extreme, realism appears to accept war as normal and rejects morality as it pertains to relations between individuals.

At the risk of oversimplification, realism's message can be summarized in the form of ten assumptions and related propositions:

1. People are by nature narrowly selfish and ethically flawed and cannot free themselves from the sinful fact that they are driven to watch out for themselves and compete with others for self-advantage.

2. Of all people's evil ways, none are more prevalent, inexorable, or dangerous than their instinctive lust for power and their desire to dominate others.

3. The possibility of eradicating the instinct for power is a utopian aspiration.

4. International politics is—as Thomas Hobbes put it—a struggle for power, "a war of all against all."

5. The primary obligation of every state—the goal to which all other national objectives should be subordinated—is to promote its **national interest** and to acquire power for this purpose.

6. The anarchical nature of the international system dictates that states acquire sufficient military capabilities to deter attack by potential enemies and to exercise influence over others.

7. Economics is less relevant to national security than is military might; economic growth is important primarily as a means of acquiring and expanding state power and prestige.

8. Allies might increase a state's ability to defend itself, but their loyalty and reliability should not be assumed.

9. States should never entrust the task of self-protection to international security organizations or international law and should resist efforts to regulate international behavior through global governance.

■ **power**
the factors that enable one actor to manipulate another actor's behavior against its preferences.

■ **self-help**
the principle that in anarchy actors must rely on themselves (see p. 450).

■ **state sovereignty**
under international law, the principle that the governments of states are subject to no higher external authority (see p. 63).

■ **national interest**
the goals that states pursue to maximize what is selfishly best for their country.

10. If all states seek to maximize power, stability will result by maintaining a balance of power, lubricated by shifts in the formation and decay of opposing alliances.

Realism in the Nuclear Age

The dour and pessimistic realist thinking that dominated policy making and academic discourse in the 1940s and 1950s fit the needs of a pessimistic age. World War II, the onset of rivalry between the United States and the Soviet Union, the expansion of the Cold War into a global struggle between East and West, the stockpiling of nuclear weapons, and the periodic crises that threatened to erupt into global violence all confirmed the realists' emphasis on the inevitability of conflict, the poor prospects for cooperation, and the divergence of national interests among incorrigibly selfish, power-seeking states.

The realists' constructed picture of international life appeared particularly persuasive after World War II, given the prevailing patterns of conflictual interstate relations. States and their incessant competition were accordingly seen as the defining elements of global reality; all other aspects of world politics became secondary. At the same time, the view that a threatening international environment demanded that foreign policy take precedence over domestic problems also appeared cogent; the global level of analysis was emphasized as a determinant of the behavior and policies of states and individual decision makers (Vasquez and Elman 2003).

As the historical imperatives of "power politics" required unceasing attention to the threat of war, the logic of realpolitik asserted that military security was the essence of world politics.

The Limitations of Realism

However persuasive the realists' constructed image of the essential properties of international politics, their contentions and conclusions were frequently at odds and even contradictory.

> Critics . . . noted a lack of precision and even contradictions in the way classical realists use such concepts as "power," "national interest," and "balance of power." They also see possible contradictions between the central descriptive and prescriptive elements of classical realism. On the one hand, as Hans Morgenthau put it, nations and their leaders "think and act in terms of interests defined as power," but on the other, diplomats are urged to exercise prudence and self-restraint, as well as to recognize the legitimate national interests of other nations. Obviously, then, power plays a central role in classical realism. But the correlation between the relative power balance and political outcomes is often less than compelling, suggesting the need to enrich analyses with other variables. (O. Holsti 2001, 125)

Thus, once analysis moved beyond the belief that people are wicked and the rhetoric requiring that foreign policy serve the national interest, important questions remained: What policies best serve the national interest? Do alliances encourage peace or instability? Do arms promote national security or provoke costly arms races and war? Are states more prone to act aggressively when they are strong or weak? Are the interests of states better served through competition or through cooperation? If humankind is unchanging, then how do we explain the observable evolution and transformation of the international system? Indeed, how do we explain the growth of collaborative multilateral institutions, economic expansion, and states' observable willingness to abide by ethical principles and agreements rather than to exploit others ruthlessly when the opportunity arises?

Because many of the assumptions of the realist paradigm were not testable, realism began to be questioned (Waltz 2000; Vasquez and Elman 2002). Realism offered no criteria for determining what data were significant and what epistemological rules to follow to interpret relevant information. Even the policy recommendations that purportedly flowed from its logic were often divergent. Realists themselves, for example, were sharply divided as to whether U.S. intervention in Vietnam served American national interests and whether nuclear weapons contributed to international security.

A growing number of critics also pointed out that realism did not account for significant new developments in world politics. For instance, it could not explain the creation of new liberal trade and political institutions in Western Europe in the 1950s and 1960s, where the cooperative pursuit of mutual advantage rather than narrow self-interest appeared to dominate (at least in economic, if not always in military, affairs). Other critics began to worry about realism's tendency to disregard ethical principles and about the material and social costs that some of its policy prescriptions seemed to impose, such as retarded economic growth resulting from unrestrained military expenditures. Consequently, by the end of the 1960s, realism found itself bombarded by criticism, especially by **behavioral scientists** who sought to replace realist thought and polemics with theories tested against evidence (see Controversy: Can Behavioral Science Advance the Study of International Relations?).

Despite realism's shortcomings, much of the world continues to think about world politics in the language constructed by realists, especially in times of global tension. This happened, for example, in the early 1980s when the Cold War competition between the United States and the Soviet Union entered an embittered new phase, and their arms race accelerated. Because realism provides great insight into the drive for national security through military means, it tends to be used to explain such phenomena as the outbreak of bloody wars in the 1990s in the former Yugoslavia.

Two schools of thought within the realist theoretical tradition have recently arisen to overcome realism's recognized limitations and to reconstruct it as a general theory: "neorealism" and "neoclassical realism." In its explanation for why interstate conflict persists, **neorealism** emphasizes the anarchic nature of global society without governance rather than the traditional realist emphasis on the unceasing lust for power inherent in human nature. For this reason, neorealism is sometimes referred to as **structural realism** because it emphasizes the potent influence of the global power structure on states' behavior within it. The second reconstructed version of realism, known as **neotraditional realism,** reacted against the limitations of structural realism by returning to the original roots of realism, which placed considerable emphasis on the ways leaders of states made foreign policy decisions.

■ **behavioral scientists** scholars who apply scientific methods to the study of world politics.

■ **neorealism** a theoretical account of states' behavior that explains it as determined by differences in their relative power instead of by other factors, such as their values, types of government, or domestic circumstances (see p. 92).

■ **structural realism** a theory that emphasizes the influence of the world power structure on the behavior of the states within the global hierarchy, defined primarily by the distribution of power (see p. 190).

■ **neotraditional realism** a body of recent realist theorizing that departs from neorealism by emphasizing the motives behind states' foreign policies more than global structure and that focuses on the internal influences on states' external behavior instead of the global determinants of states' foreign behavior.

CAN BEHAVIORAL SCIENCE ADVANCE THE STUDY OF INTERNATIONAL RELATIONS?

How should scholars construct theories to interpret international behavior? The answer to that question has never been satisfactorily resolved, and the long-standing debate about how best to construct theories of international relations continues today. Some scholars, known as advocates of "postmodern **deconstructivism,**" challenge the ability of intellectuals to provide a satisfactory theoretical account of why states and people act as they do in international relations. These scholars devote their efforts to criticizing and "deconstructing" the theories of world politics to expose their inherent limitations. Most scholars remain motivated by the theoretical quest to interpret and comprehend the complexities of international relations, and challenge the pessimistic view that world politics defies meaningful understanding, despite the obstacles and limits to knowledge. What do you think? Is the scientific analysis of patterns of international relations a realistic undertaking? Or are explanations of international relations impossible, as deconstructionists argue? In formulating your opinion, take into consideration the progression of this intellectual debate over the past five decades.

This evolving epistemological controversy took an important step in the 1960s and early 1970s when dissatisfaction with realism's shortcomings intensified and a movement known as **behavioralism** arose to challenge realism, which the behavioralists called "traditionalism," as well as other modes of studying international relations. Behavioralism was not a new theory of international relations so much as a new method of studying it, based largely on the application of scientific methods to the study of global affairs (see Knorr and Rosenau 1969; Knorr and Verba 1961).

Behavioralism advances principles and procedures for investigating international phenomena to reach generalizations or statements about international regularities that hold across time and place. Science, the behavioralists claim, is primarily a generalizing activity. From this perspective—a view consistent with that of many "traditional" realists and liberals—a theory of international relations should state the relationship between two or more variables that specifies the conditions under which the relationship(s) hold and explain

why the relationship(s) should hold. To uncover such theories, behavioralists lean toward using comparative cross-national analyses rather than case studies of particular countries at particular times. Behavioralists also stress the need for data about the characteristics of countries and how they behave toward one another. Hence, the behavioral movement encourages the comparative and quantitative study of international relations (see, for example, Rosenau 1980; Singer 1968).

What makes behavioralism innovative is its attitude toward the purposes of inquiry: replacing subjective beliefs with verifiable knowledge, supplanting impressions and intuition with testable evidence, and substituting data and reproducible information for mere opinion. In this sense, behavioralists embrace liberalism's "high regard for modern science" and its "attacks against superstition and authority" (Hall 1993). In place of appeals to the "expert" opinion of authorities, behavioral scientists seek to acquire knowledge cumulatively by suspending judgments about truths or values until they have sufficient evidence to support them. They attempt to overcome the tendency of traditional inquiry to select facts and cases to fit preexisting hunches. Instead, all available data, those which contradict as well as those which support existing theoretical hypotheses, are to be examined. Knowledge, they argue, would advance best by theorists assuming a cautious, skeptical attitude toward any empirical statement. The slogans "Let the data, not the armchair theorist, speak," and "Seek evidence, but distrust it" represent the behavioral posture toward the acquisition of knowledge.

Although some behavioral research speaks directly to the moral issues that differentiate realism and liberalism, it is sometimes criticized for neglecting the ethical aspects of poverty, hunger, violence, and other global problems. This accusation led to a **postbehavioral movement** which called for a new research agenda that would focus on new issues (see Easton 1969). Nonetheless, postbehavioralists rarely have recommended discarding scientific methods, despite the harsh criticism of behavioral science by "postmodern deconstructionists."

The Neorealist or "Structural" Extension of Realism

In his influential book *Theory of International Politics* (1979), the pioneer of neorealism, Kenneth N. Waltz, set out to convert the loose and disjointed body of realist thought into a formal theory (Waltz 1995). "To systematize political realism into a rigorous, deductive systemic theory of international politics" (Keohane 1986b), neorealism dismisses explanations developed at the individual and state levels of analysis and argues that explanations at the global system level are sufficient to account for the main trends in world politics. As Waltz (1995) expressed his neorealist conceptualization of the determinants of international behavior, "international structure emerges from the interaction of states and then constrains them from taking certain actions while propelling them toward others."

In neorealism, as in realism, anarchy or the absence of central institutions above states is the most important and enduring property of the structure of the system. States remain the primary actors, acting according to the principle of self-help and seeking to ensure their own survival. Thus, it is the neorealists' view that states do not differ in the tasks they face, only in their capabilities. Capabilities define the position of states in the system, and the distribution of capabilities defines the structure of the system and shapes the ways the units interact with one another.

Power also remains a central concept in neorealism. However, the quest for power is not considered an end in itself, as in realism; nor does it derive from human nature. Instead, states always pursue power as a means of survival. As Waltz (1979) explains, the "means fall into two categories: internal efforts (moves to increase economic capability, to increase military strength, to develop clever strategies) and external efforts (moves to strengthen and enlarge one's own alliance or to weaken and shrink an opposing one)." Furthermore, because the instinct for survival drives states, neorealism asserts that balances of power form automatically, regardless of whether "some or all states consciously aim to establish and maintain a balance, or whether some or all states aim for universal domination" (Waltz 1979). Once the global system is formed, its structure "becomes a force that the units may not be able to control; it constrains their behavior and interposes itself between their intentions and the outcomes of their actions" (Ruggie 1983).

Although neorealists recognize that states' goals sometimes "fluctuate with the changing currents of domestic politics, are prey to the vagaries of a shifting cast of political leaders, and are influenced by the outcomes of bureaucratic struggles," they contend that such factors as whether governments are democracies or dictatorships tell little about the process whereby states come to pursue the goal of balancing power with power. Instead, framed at the **global level of analysis,** "structural constraints explain why the [same] methods are repeatedly used despite differences in the persons and states who use them" (Waltz 1979).

> In its stress on the structure of the international system, that is, the state of anarchy among sovereign states, [neo]realism attaches little or no importance to what is going on inside states—what kind of regimes are in power, what kind of ideologies prevail, what kind of leadership is provided. According to [neo]realists, the foreign policies of all states are basically driven by the same systemic factors—they are like so many billiard balls, obeying the same laws of political geometry and physics. (Harries 1995, 13)

■ **deconstructivism**
postmodern theory that the complexity of the world system renders precise description impossible, and that the purpose of scholarship is to understand actors' hidden motives by deconstructing their textual statements.

■ **behavioralism**
an approach to the study of international relations that emphasizes the application of scientific methods (see p. 406).

■ **postbehavioral movement**
an approach to the study of international relations that calls for increased attention to the policy relevance of scientific research.

■ **global level of analysis**
an analytical approach to world politics that emphasizes the impact of worldwide conditions on the behavior of states, nonstate and other international actors.

Neorealist theory also helps to explain why the prospects for international cooperation and change often appear so dim and why states are naturally wary of others and strive to compete. The anarchical structure of the system compels states to be sensitive to their *relative position* in the distribution of power.

> When faced with the possibility of cooperating for mutual gain, states that feel insecure must ask how the gain will be divided. They are compelled to ask not "Will both of us gain?" but "Who will gain more?" If an expected gain is to be divided, say, in the ratio of two to one, one state may use its disproportionate gain to implement a policy intended to damage or destroy the other. Even the prospect of large absolute gains for both parties does not elicit their cooperation so long as each fears how the other will use its increased capabilities. (Waltz 1979, 105; see also Snidal 1993)

Impediments to global cooperation thus result not from the parties' attitudes toward potential collaborative efforts, but rather from the insecurity that the anarchical system breeds. "The condition of insecurity—at the least, the uncertainty of each about the other's future intentions and actions—works against their cooperation" (Waltz 1979), as does states' fear of dependence on others.

The Neoclassical Extension of Realism

Alongside neorealism, another group of realists who share a dim view of cooperation in world politics has arisen, advocating what is called "neotraditional realism." This theoretical movement seeks to transcend Waltzian neorealism's exclusive focus on the global level of analysis, which they argue incorrectly neglects classical realism's attention to the determinants of foreign policy at the individual and state levels of analysis (see Vasquez 1998). To neoclassical theorists the sources of states' foreign policy choices are best explained not by changes in the global structure, but by leaders' perception of national interests and capabilities: "Statesmen, not states, are the primary actors in international affairs, and their perceptions of shifts in power, rather than objective measures, are critical" (Zakaria 1998b). Hence, "a new breed of realist scholars have embraced the richer formulation of traditional, pre-Waltzian realists, who focus more on foreign policy than systemic phenomena. While not abandoning Waltz's insights about international structure and its consequences, neoclassical realists have added [factors at the state and individual levels of analysis] such as domestic politics . . . , state power and intentions, and statesmen's perceptions of the relative distribution of capabilities . . . to better explain historical puzzles and foreign policy decision making" (Schweller 1999).

Many scholars and policymakers disagree with the view of the neorealists and the neoclassical realists about the prospects for international cooperation. They point out that the record suggests that patterns can change and that increased interdependence can lead to even higher levels of cooperation. This expectation lies behind the so-called neoliberal challenge to realism and neorealism (Doyle and Ikenberry 1997; Kegley 1995).

NEOLIBERALISM

In the last decade of the twentieth century, dissatisfaction with realism and neo-realism began to rise. Arguing that it was time for a new, more rigorous liberal alternative to realism, critics pointed to several shortcomings: (1) power-politics perspectives failed to predict the peaceful end of the Cold War and international social change in general; (2) research suggested that the "under-lying theory of war and peace [of realism and neorealism was] flawed" (Vasquez 1993) because realists "oversimplified the concept of power and misunderstood the lessons of history" (Kober 1990); and (3) it appeared that realism's approach would "not be an adequate guide for the future of international politics" (Jervis 1992), because the broadened global agenda included many questions and problems that realist theory could not cover. The problems of AIDS, ecological deterioration, global warming, economic underdevelopment, and the globaliza-tion of trade and markets were among those for which the realistic approach was seen as deficient.

"Some students of international politics," Kenneth Waltz (2000) complains, "believe that realism is obsolete. They argue that although realism's concepts of anarchy, self-help, and power balancing may have been appropriate to a bygone era, they have been changed by changed conditions and eclipsed by better ideas. New times call for new thinking, changed conditions require revised theories or entirely new ones." Among these students, Fareed Zakaria (1992–1993) asked, "is realism finished?" Jeffrey Legro and Andrew Moravsik (1999) questioned "is anybody still a realist?" and Patrick James (1993) proclaimed that neorealism was "a research enterprise in crisis." In addition, as Waltz notes, many critics went beyond calling for a revision and replacement of realist theorizing by advo-cating that "the recovery of liberalism" (Little 1993) be treated as a theoretical goal in international relations. This view gained a following among policymak-ers. For example, in accord with Francis Fukuyama's conclusion (1992b) that there were "good reasons for examining aspects of the liberal international legacy once again," U.S. President Bill Clinton in 1995 maintained that "In a world where freedom, not tyranny, is on the march, the cynical calculus of pure power politics simply does not compute. It is ill-suited to the new era."

In light of this growing sentiment, in the early 1990s **neoliberalism** emerged, a new approach to world politics that concentrates on the ways inter-national organizations and other nonstate actors promote international cooper-ation. This analytic departure goes by several labels including "neoliberal insti-tutionalism" (Grieco 1995), "neoidealism" (Kegley 1993), and "neo-Wilsonian idealism" (Fukuyama 1992a).

Neoliberalism seeks to build theories of international relations by giving the basic tenets of classical liberalism and post–World War I liberal idealism a fresh examination. Taking heart in the international prohibition, through com-munity consensus, of such previously entrenched practices as slavery, piracy, dueling, colonialism, the slaughter of certain animals, and unrestrained exploitation of the planet's ecology, neoliberalism emphasizes the prospects for progress, peace, and prosperity. Studies of regional integration—processes whereby sovereign states might be politically unified—began to flourish in the 1950s and 1960s, paving the way for the new liberal theories that emerged in the 1990s. The expansion of trade, communication, information, technology,

■ **neoliberalism**
a perspective that accounts for the way international institutions promote global change, cooperation, peace, and prosperity through collective programs for reforms (see p. 500).

NEOLIBERALISM VERSUS NEOREALISM
Which Theory Makes the Most Reasonable Assumptions?

The issues dividing neoliberal and neorealist theorizing center on the different assumptions they make about the following six topics (David Baldwin, 1993, 4–8). Looking at the world, which set of assumptions do you think is the most accurate for interpreting twenty-first-century world politics?

- *The Nature and Consequences of Anarchy.* Whereas everyone recognizes that the global system is anarchical because effective institutions for global governance are lacking, neorealists argue that anarchy does not matter much and in fact may be preferable to the restraints of world government. Neoliberals see anarchy as a big problem that can be reformed through creation of strong global institutions.
- *International Cooperation.* Although neorealists and neoliberals agree that international cooperation is possible, neorealists think cooperation is difficult to sustain whereas neoliberals believe cooperation can be expected because collaboration produces rewards that reduce the temptation to selfishly compete.
- *Relative versus Absolute Gains.* Both neorealists and neoliberals are concerned with relative gain as well as absolute gain. Neorealists believe that the desire to get ahead of their competitor by obtaining relative gains is the primary motive, while neoliberals believe that states are motivated by the search for opportunities to cooperate that will produce absolute gains for all parties to the cooperative exchange.
- *Priority of State Goals.* Both national security and national economic prosperity are seen as important state goals by neorealists and neoliberals, but neorealists stress security as the most important, while neoliberals believe states place a greater priority on economic welfare.
- *Intentions versus Capabilities.* Contemporary neorealists maintain that the distribution of states' capabilities is the primary determinant of their behavior and international outcomes. Neoliberals maintain that states' intentions, interests, information, and ideals are more influential than is the distribution of capabilities.
- *Institutions and Regimes.* Both neorealists and neoliberals recognize that states have created a variety of new international regimes and institutions to regulate their relations since World War II. Neoliberals believe that institutions such as the World Trade Organization create norms that are binding on their members and that change patterns of international politics. On the other hand, neorealists emphasize that organizations like the UN are arenas where states carry out their traditional competition and political rivalry for influence.

and immigrant labor propelled Europeans to sacrifice portions of their sovereign independence to create a new political community out of previously separate units. These developments were outside of realism's worldview, creating conditions that made the call for a theory grounded in the liberal tradition convincing to many who had previously been skeptical of realism.

Neoliberalism departs from neorealism on many assumptions (see Controversy: Neoliberalism versus Neorealism). In particular, neoliberalism focuses on the ways in which influences such as democratic governance, public opinion, mass education, free trade, liberal commercial enterprise, international law and organization, arms control and disarmament, collective security and multilateral diplomacy, and ethically inspired statecraft can improve life on our planet. Because they perceive change in global conditions as progressing through cooperative efforts, neoliberal theorists maintain that the ideas and ideals of the liberal legacy today can describe, explain, predict, and prescribe international conduct in ways that they could not during the conflict-ridden Cold War.

Like realism and neorealism, neoliberalism does not represent a cohesive intellectual movement or school of thought. Neoliberals operate from different assumptions, examining different aspects of the processes through which international change and cooperation might be promoted. Some, like neorealists, embrace a structural theory that examines the characteristics of the global system. Others concentrate on the characteristics of the units and subunits that comprise it, such as types of governments (democracies or dictatorships) and the leaders who govern states. Still other neoliberals give primary attention to the influence of international institutions such as the UN and nonstate actors such as multinational corporations. All neoliberals, however, share an interest in probing the conditions under which the convergent and overlapping interests among otherwise sovereign political actors may result in cooperation.

To illuminate these similarities and differences among neoliberals, consider two theoretical perspectives that paved the way for neoliberalism's acceptance and are a part of its orientation: "transnational interdependence" and "international regimes." For the sake of brevity, we have selected only these two examples from among the many other divergent strands within neoliberal theorizing (see Zacher and Matthew 1995) such as **feminist theory** and its critique of previous theorizing in general and realism in particular (see Tickner 2002, Chapter 7, and, in particular, Controversy: What's Missing in Realist Theories of Interstate Relations?).

Transnational Interdependence as a Neoliberal Counter Worldview to Realism

In the 1970s, a new analytical perspective known as "transnational relations" arose to question realism's key assumption that states are the only important actors on the global stage. With **complex interdependence** as its central concept, this theoretical departure advanced a "synthesis of liberal and realist perspectives [by] constructing a way of looking at world politics that helps us understand the relationship between economics and politics, and patterns of institutionalized international cooperation." It asked how under conditions of complex interdependence world "politics would be different than under realist conditions" (Keohane and Nye 2001a) and answered by arguing that differences were substantial because sweeping changes in international relations fostered by technological innovations and the information revolution were increasingly challenging realism's oversimplified view of world politics. Emphasizing the growing importance of **nonstate actors,** such as multinational corporations and international organizations, the transnational interdependence perspective anticipated what is now called **globalization.** States were becoming increasingly dependent on, sensitive to, and mutually vulnerable to one another in ways that were eroding their sovereign control and independence. This modified theory needed to be accounted for to supplement realism's account for only state-to-state relations. In this sense, by highlighting the multiple channels through which both state and nonstate actors were visibly engaging in active transnational contact and communication worldwide, transnational interdependence represented a holistic conception of world politics as the sum of its many interacting parts in a global society (see O. Holsti 2001).

The transnational interdependence school also questioned realism's assumption that national security issues were truly dominant in states' decision-making

■ **feminist theory**
a body of scholarship that emphasizes gender in the study of world politics (see p. 231).

■ **complex interdependence**
a theory stressing the complex ways in which the growing ties among transnational actors make them vulnerable to each other's actions and sensitive to each other's needs.

■ **nonstate actors**
all transnationally active groups other than states, such as organizations whose members are states (IGOs) and nongovernmental organizations (NGOs) whose members are individuals and private groups from more than one state.

■ **globalization**
the integration and growing interdependence of states through their increasing contact and trade. This creates a single united global society within a single culture in order to tie people together in a common fate, thereby reducing the capacity of states to control their national destinies.

WHAT'S MISSING IN REALIST THEORIES OF INTERSTATE RELATIONS?
The Feminist Critique

Many scholars are dissatisfied with existing theories of world politics because nearly all fail, in their opinion, to give sufficient attention to certain important factors and forces. No theory can possibly cover everything comprehensively; however, if a theory ignores a key variable or issue in the effort to simplify the essential features of world politics, that theory will fail to capture the true complexity of international relations. Yet people disagree about what is essential. Determining which features should be emphasized is controversial, because certain questions are more interesting to some students than others (as the debate between realists and liberals illustrates).

Do you think mainstream realism and liberalism ignore any crucial factors in world politics? To stimulate your thinking about what is essential and what has potentially been ignored, consider the issue of gender. Until recently, most theories paid little attention to this variable, and thus failed to account for such crucial trends as the chronic and widening inequalities in income and freedom between men and women.

Feminist theory, a body of scholarship that emphasizes the importance of gender as a factor in world politics, arose in the 1960s in response to the pronounced realist depersonalization of state-centered accounts of foreign policy. In particular, feminist theory attacked the exclusion of women in discussions about public and international affairs as well as the injustice and unequal treatment of women this prejudice caused. The mainstream realist literature on world politics underestimated or ignored the plight and contributions of women, treating differences in men's and women's status, beliefs, and behaviors as unimportant. Gender roles were also ignored, along with the evidence that sexism is a pillar of the war system (Reardon 1985). In the realists' masculine image of sovereign rulers, "Fame, wealth, and women were prizes to be won in

battle. For the typical prince, war was a means to reputation and glory" (Tickner 1999). In the feminist critique, a remedy for this problem might be to give women the prominence and power in policy making that traditional practices denied them (see Beckman and D'Amico 1994; Peterson and Runyan 1993).

As feminist theory crystallized, it moved away from focusing on a history of discrimination against women and began to direct much of its criticism at realism. In particular, many gender studies alleged that realism, formulated and dominated by males, ignored the human roots of global conditions and promoted an essentially masculine interpretation of international relations that was inattentive to human rights and rife with rationales for aggression.

Derived in part from liberal principles supportive of fair play, justice, and the philosophical acceptance of love over power, feminist theory moved beyond this initial critique of realism's bias to chart an independent theoretical course (Enloe 2001). This perspective has focused on the performance of women as leaders of government and as members of infantry combat units (Grant and Newland 1991), as well as on theoretical explorations of the plight of women in business and in the less-developed countries of the Global South.

Perhaps of greatest influence in the field of international relations, however, has been feminist theory's rejection of the realist preoccupation with states' military strategies in favor of developing strategies for world security (see Tickner 2002). In this sense, feminist theory, like neoliberalism generally, is motivated by the quest for discovering paths to greater international cooperation. In liberating conventional theory from its narrow focus, can feminist theory open a window on the full range of international activity and point the way toward a fuller appreciation of the ways in which human beings influence the global condition?

agendas. Under conditions of mutual vulnerability, it seemed that states' foreign policy agendas had become "larger and more diverse" and that alongside the continuing potential threat of war, trade, monetary, and environmental issues had begun to crowd the global agenda to such an extent that these nonmilitary issues were beginning to make a broader range of "governments' policies, even those previously considered merely domestic, impinge on one

Pedro Ugarte/AFP

Free At Last? For most of recorded history, women were deprived of the basic human right of voting in elections, as is explained by feminist theory, an extension of neoliberal theorizing in international relations. With recent reforms, that situation has begun to change, as shown in this photo of Somaliland women singing as they line up to cast their ballots for the first time on May 31, 2001, at a polling station in Hargeisa, Somalia, during a referendum on the 1997 constitution.

another" (Keohane and Nye 1988). In addition, this neoliberal challenge to realist theorizing disputed the popular realist conception of military capabilities as the only effective means of exercising influence in international politics, particularly among the industrialized democracies. It was argued that "Intense relationships of mutual influence exist between these countries, but in most of them force is irrelevant or unimportant as an instrument of policy" (Keohane and Nye 1988, 2001b).

Advocates of the transnational interdependence perspective extended many of these insights in order to account for the growing role of transnational institutions in global affairs, such as the United Nations and the emerging nongovernmental organizations (NGOs) such as human rights groups. Thus, Robert O. Keohane and Joseph S. Nye's (1977, 1989, 2001a) *Power and Interdependence*, the definitive treatise on the new extensions of liberalism, paved the way for attempts "to combine the great theoretical traditions of realism and liberalism" to capture the changes in international relations that were unfolding (Keohane and Nye 2001a). Note that the pioneering transnational interdependence perspective did not altogether reject realism. Rather, the primary concern of its proponents was to identify "the conditions under which the assumptions of realism were sufficient or needed to be supplemented by a more complex model of change" (Nye 1987; see also Keohane and Nye 2001a). Keohane and Nye drew on realism, in part, to account for the willingness of states to see their interests served by the creation of international regimes, or the norms for behavior that are created when cooperation becomes institutionalized and actors expect them to be followed, even though this necessitates a sacrifice of sovereignty.

Transnational interdependence has become a central component of the neoliberal perspective and continues to be widely used to interpret cooperative agreements between states under the continuing twenty-first-century conditions of anarchy and fear of dependence and exploitation.

International Regimes

Although the international system is still characterized by anarchy, its nature is more properly conceptualized as an ordered anarchy and the world as a whole as an "anarchical society" (Bull 1977), because cooperation, not conflict, is often the observable outcome of relations among states.

■ **international regimes**
a perspective that explains the benefits of actors supporting particular rules to regulate a specific international activity, such as disposal of toxic wastes.

Given this reality, the question arises: How can **international regimes** based on coordinated cooperation be established and preserved? Interest in this question derives from two goals: first, "a desire to understand the extent to which mutually accepted constraints affect states' behaviors" (Zacher 1987), and second, a desire to devise strategies for creating a less disorderly "world order."

Regimes are institutionalized or regularized patterns of cooperation in a given issue area, as reflected by established rules. Because the international regime perspective necessarily looks primarily at global institutions and the ways in which norms influence states to behave according to more global than national interests, it is perhaps best viewed as an attempt to reconcile the liberal and realist perspectives on world politics (Haggard and Simmons 1987).

The global trade and monetary rules created during and after World War II are vivid examples of international regulatory regimes. These rules, as well as particular sectors within the trade system, have been the focus of considerable inquiry from the regime perspective. Together, the trade and monetary regimes comprised a Liberal International Economic Order (LIEO) that limited government intervention in the world political economy and otherwise facilitated the free flow of goods and capital across national boundaries. The General Agreement on Tariffs and Trade (GATT) that preceded the World Trade Organization (WTO) and the International Monetary Fund (IMF) played important institutional roles in the LIEO and reconfirmed the importance of international institutions in fostering transnational cooperation (see Chapter 9 for elaboration).

■ **low politics**
the category of global issues related to the economic, social, demographic, and environmental aspects of relations between governments and people.

Most illustrations of the regime perspective appear in the **low politics** arena of economic and humanitarian relationships; until recently, relatively few "security regimes" (Jervis 1982) had emerged in the high politics defense issue area. Early exceptions were the nuclear nonproliferation regime and the regime that the United States and the Soviet Union used to manage their crises (see George 1986). But after the Cold War, the pressures of globalization can be expected to foster creation of regimes in widening areas of international conduct. This is likely to accelerate efforts to grapple theoretically with the causes and consequences of multilateral approaches to collective problem solving.

Alternative Theories

Having studied the liberal and realist traditions, keep in mind that this coverage is very selective. At least six additional major schools of thought regarding particular aspects of world politics also deserve attention, and each will be introduced—along with still other theoretical subspecialties linked to them—in later chapters where they best help to interpret the topic covered. First, as explained in Chapter 3, decision-making theory accounts for the ways leaders and other actors seek to make policy choices rationally and the limits to this aspiration. Second, as introduced in Chapter 4, long-cycle theory seeks to explain the historical ebb and flow of world politics, global leadership, and systemwide war (Modelski and Thompson 1996). The rise and fall of the great powers and empires is its central concern. Third, dependency theory, first treated in Chapter 6, examines the pattern of dominance and dependence that characterizes the unequal relationship between the world's rich and poor states (Packenham 1992). Fourth, to understand how cooperation among states is encouraged to deal with problems primarily in the realm of low politics (Chapters 8–10), hegemonic stability theory—a hybrid of liberal/neorealist theory (Gill 1993b)—examines what happens when a clearly predominant state, a "hegemon," exercises leadership and control of the global system by setting and enforcing the rules governing international trade, finance, investment, and other issues, such as environmental regulation (see Gilpin 2000). Fifth, to expand this coverage and move to other topics dealing with global security, world-system theory looks at system dynamics from a long-term, structural perspective, emphasizing its economic underpinnings to explain the Western capitalist societies' rise to dominance and the lack of economic development in many other geographic areas (Chapters 6–10) and their military repercussions (Chapter 11) (see Wallerstein 1980). Sixth, to systematically organize inquiry about how states fit into international phenomena from diverse levels of analysis, advocates of the comparative study of foreign policy seek to probe the similarities and differences in states' international circumstances, national attributes and capabilities, foreign policy decision-making processes, and individual policymakers (see Hermann and Sundelius 2004). Still other streams of theorizing within both the liberal and realist traditions will be introduced in those chapters that address directly the problems investigated.

THEORIZING ABOUT THEORY: THE CONSTRUCTIVIST CONCEPTION

To understand our changing world and to make reasonable prognoses about the future, we must begin by arming ourselves with an array of information and conceptual tools, entertaining rival interpretations of world politics, and questioning the assumptions on which these contending worldviews rest. Because there are a great (and growing) number of alternative, and sometimes incompatible, ways of organizing theoretical inquiry about world politics, the challenge of capturing the world's political problems cannot be reduced to any one simple yet compelling account, such as the five major theoretical traditions stressed here (see Table 2.1). Each paradigmatic effort to do so in the past,

TABLE 2.1

The Quest for Theory: Four Major Perspectives

Feature	Realism	Neorealism	Liberalism	Neoliberalism	Constructivism
Key Units	Independent states	The international system's structure	Institutions transcending states	Individuals; "penetrated" states and nonstate transnational actors	Social groups, their socially constructed images of international conditions
Core Concern	War and security	Struggle for position and power under anarchy	Institutionalizing peace	Fostering interstate cooperation on the globe's shared economic, social, and ecological problems	Social collectivities' shared meanings and images of contemporary international life; the theoretical implication of these visions
Major Approach	Balance of power	Balance of terror; military preparedness and deterrence	International law; international organization; democratization	Complex interdependence and regimes	Advocacy of normative innovation through construction of new images; tracing assumptions within various theoretical traditions; discovering how and why they color mental maps of world affairs
Outlook on Global Prospects	Pessimistic/stability	Pessimistic	Optimistic/progress	Expectation of cooperation and creation of a global community	Neither optimist nor pessimistic, depending on the most popular or socially accepted visions about the potential for humanity to engineer changes that either improve or harm future global conditions

Motives of Actors	National interests; zero-sum competition; security; power	Power, prestige, and advantage (relative gains) over other states	Collaboration; mutual aid; meeting human needs	Global interests (absolute gains); justice; peace and prosperity; liberty; morality	Contingent upon the socially constructed explanations about the basic drives of international actors, in various epochs
Central Concepts	Structural anarchy; power; national interests; balance of power; polarity	Structural anarchy; rational choice; arms races	Collective security; world order; law; integration; international organization	Transnational relations; law; free markets; interdependence; liberal integration; liberal republican rule; human rights; gender	Ideas; identities; ideals; images—all as socially constructed by various groups
Prescriptions	Increase national power; resist reduction of national autonomy	Preserve nuclear deterrence; avoid disarmament and supranational organizations	Institutional reform	Develop regimes and promote democracy and international institutions to coordinate collective responses to global problems	Broaden understanding of the ways international actors construct their images of international relations to clarify the limitations of rival theoretical interpretations and the policies on which they are based

■ **deconstruction**
postmodern theory
postulating that the
complexity of the world
system renders precise
description impossible, and
that the purpose of
scholarship is to understand
actors' motives by
deconstructing their textual
statements.

■ **chaos theory**
the application of
mathematical methods to
identify underlying,
episodically recurring
patterns in rapidly changing
and seemingly
unconnected relationships
(as many global
phenomena appear) in
order to better interpret
complex reality.

■ **epistemology**
the philosophical
examination of how
knowledge is acquired and
the analytic principles
governing the study of
phenomena.

■ **social constructivism**
a liberal-realist theoretical
approach advocated by
Alexander Wendt that sees
self-interested states as the
key actors in world politics;
their actions are
determined not by anarchy
but by the ways states
socially "construct" and
then respond to the
meanings they give to
power politics, so that as
their definitions change,
cooperative practices can
evolve.

whether derived from liberalism or from realism, has ultimately been abandoned as developments in world affairs eroded its continuing relevance. Although grand theories fade with the passage of time, they often regain their attractiveness when global transformations make them useful once again. In fact, world politics is so resistant to clear, comprehensive, and convincing analysis that some so-called **deconstructionists** contend that international complexity defies description, explanation, and prediction (see Controversy: Can Behavioral Science Advance the Study of International Relations?). Deconstructionists share the philosophical view that all peoples' conceptions of global realities are relative to their understandings and that, because there is no objective principle, the validity of which is independent of one's own personal point of view, any interpretation is as valid as any other, and there is no point in attempting to develop a shared conception of the world.

Most other scholars continue to struggle in the pursuit of theory and knowledge about international affairs. For example, scholars adhering to **chaos theory** attempt to find new methods for modeling the kind of turbulent global change that is occurring in the world. However, because there exists no single general-purpose theory able to account for all questions regarding international relations, a number of scholars have returned to reconsider the basic questions of **epistemology** that are fundamental to evaluating the relative value and validity of rival theoretical frameworks. How do we know what to believe? What principles of analysis can lead us to recognize the strengths and weaknesses of various theories? How do we separate fact from fiction and sense from nonsense? What is the relative descriptive accuracy and explanatory power of different theories, and how much confidence should be placed in their explanations of world politics? To what extent, in short, should we accept the perspective of *any* theory, such as realism or liberalism, and the claims all such theories make about what should count as knowledge of international affairs?

Increasingly, many students of international relations have turned to **social constructivism** to interpret both international life and the various substantive theories others have built to help understand international affairs. Strictly speaking, "constructivism is not a theory of international politics;" rather, it helps to "clarify the differences and relative virtues" of alternative theories (Wendt 2000). Beyond that, constructivism provides a lens for thinking critically about how theories of international relations can be constructed, and the kinds of premises and assumptions that are reasonable for any theorist to make as a starting point for explaining world politics. Constructivism follows Alexander Wendt's argument, therefore, that

> students of international politics must answer these questions, at least implicitly, since they cannot do their business without making powerful assumptions about what kinds of things are to be found in international life, and how they are related, and how they can be known. These assumptions are particularly important because no one can "see" the state or international system. International politics does not present itself directly to the senses, and theories of international politics often are contested on the basis of ontology [ideas about the nature of existence] and epistemology, i.e., what the theorist "sees." (Wendt 2000:5)

Constructivism thus provides a pathway to theoretical interpretation by reminding students that perceptions about world politics must be organized for inquiry to be conducted, that is, first put together in a manner that identifies what is believed important, matters most, and is worthy of observation and analysis (recall Controversy: Should We Believe What We See?, Chapter 1, pp. 14–15).

Constructivism is best seen as a conceptualization of international affairs—a way of organizing perceptions about the subject—as a first step to investigating international phenomena theoretically and to evaluating more formal existing streams of theorizing. It attempts to bridge the gap between neoliberal and neorealist theories by accepting many key assumptions shared by both approaches while critically rejecting realism's failure to pay attention to the powerful role of ideas and norms in world politics. Constructivists emphasize the importance of shared ideas and understandings that are developed between actors on the world stage through their interactions. These shared experiences define their interests, identities, and images of the world in which they interact (Wendt 2000; see also Hopf 1998; Onuf 1989 and 2001; and S. Smith 1997). Constructivism is helpful because it reminds us that how we think about the world matters. All theories are necessarily socially constructed based on communication among the agents in international relations, and these constructions of shared meanings through social learning provide states and other actors with the mental models of international politics on which they act. This method of viewing international politics represents a welcome theoretical departure, because it reminds us that shared images influence the ways actors in the global arena see themselves and behave (Checkel 1998). Further, this emphasis on subjective beliefs helps us appreciate that the practices in statecraft and the identities of global actors or agents are products of shared ideas rather than, as the realists would have it, simply products of the objective or material structure of the international system. As we move into the twenty-first century, it is likely to become increasingly popular to interpret world politics from a constructivist theory that focuses on the collective norms and culture of people and state actors. Those shared norms will define their reality and influence their relations within that constructed vision (see Desch 1998).

Note the underlying premises that have made social constructivism so popular. It is hard to argue against the principle that international reality is defined by the ways people construct their images of it (Onuf 1989). Our visions are derived from our point of view, because all people are intellectual prisoners of the collective conceptions of the world. All conceptions and theories are shaped by the social pressures within groups for those groups' members to construct similar images or worldviews, ones that define global reality for them and provide a springboard for theoretical interpretation. Moreover, awareness of the influence of these socially constructed sets of collective images of world affairs, their inherent subjectivity, and their inability to fully capture global realities contributes to appreciation of the limits of valid theoretical interpretation and accurate representation of our subject matter. Constructivism cautions us to be skeptical of all claims of truth.

In addition, constructivism opens a window to insightful analysis. It brings to inquiry the possibility of learning through analysis, from which policymakers can construct more accurate pictures of international realities and use them to engineer change. Beginning with a stress on the power of ideas, constructivists counter, for example, structural realism's failure to overlook "what is often a more determinant factor, namely, the intersubjectively sharpened ideas

Defending Reason against Deconstructionist Criticism Pope John Paul II is shown here signing the "Fides et Ratio" encyclical in October 1998 that defends using reason to discover bedrock truths. Arguing that faith and reason are not incompatible, the statement describes deconstructionism as a nihilistic philosophy that breeds skepticism because it questions our ability to know anything for certain and rejects "the pursuit of truth through reason." Yet in a bewildering, complex world, it is easy to appreciate why some theoreticians give up the effort to discover the underlying principles of world politics, claiming that the challenge is hopeless.

Arturo Mari/AP/Wide World

that shaped behavior by constituting the identities and interests of actors" (Copeland 2000). The socially accepted ideas, norms, and values held by powerful state and nonstate actors are seen as making a difference in constructing an international consensus about the rules that should govern international society. Not only do "ideational structures shape the very way actors define themselves—who they are, their goals, and the roles they believe they should play" (Copeland 2000)—but also they shape the prevailing ideas in each age about the global condition and the prospects for humanity to escape the problems posed by states in an anarchic arena. When a new consensus materializes about norms—what is legal and illegal—the modified shared global culture prepares the way for **transformation** in world politics. Because "reality is in the eye of the beholder," agreement on the redefinition of reality enables the pattern of international relations to change from one epoch to another. Thus, "Changing attitudes toward slavery and racial and other forms of discrimination are illustrative of [constructivist] phenomena to which proponents of this approach point" (Dougherty and Pfaltzgraff 2001).

■ **transformation**
a change in the characteristic pattern of interaction among the most active participants in world politics of such magnitude that it appears that one "international system" has replaced another.

As we seek to understand the changing global conditions, we must be humble in recognizing the limitations of our understandings of world politics and at the same time inquisitive about its character. The task of interpretation is complicated because the world is itself complex. As one scholar frames the challenge:

> Conceptually speaking, world affairs today can be likened to a disassembled jigsaw puzzle scattered on a table before us. Each piece shows a fragment of a broad picture that as yet remains indiscernible. Some pieces depict resurgent nationalism; others show spreading democracy; some picture genocide; others portray prosperity through trade and investment; some picture nuclear disarmament; others picture nuclear proliferation; some indicate a reinvigorated United Nations; others show the UN still

enfeebled and ineffective; some describe cultural globalization; others predict clashing civilizations.

How do these pieces fit together, and what picture do they exhibit when they are appropriately fitted? (Puchala 1994, 17)

All theories are maps of possible futures. Theories can guide us in fitting the pieces together to form an accurate picture. However, in evaluating the usefulness of any theory to interpret global conditions, the historical overview in this chapter suggests that it would be wrong to oversimplify or to assume that a particular theory will remain useful in the future. Nonetheless, as the American poet Robert Frost observed in 1911, any belief we cling to long enough is likely to be true again someday, because "most of the change we think we see in life is due to truths being in and out of favor." So in our theoretical exploration of world politics, we must critically assess the accuracy of our impressions, avoiding the temptation to embrace one worldview and abandon another without any assurance that their relative worth is permanently fixed.

KEY TERMS

paradigm
constructionism
geopolitics
current history approach
theory
liberalism
politics
idealists
collective security
Kellogg-Briand Pact
self-determination
state
nation

realism
realpolitik
power
self-help
state sovereignty
national interest
behavioral scientists
neorealism
structural realism
neotraditional realism
behavioralism
deconstructivism
postbehavioral movement

global level of analysis
neoliberalism
feminist theory
complex interdependence
nonstate actors
globalization
international regimes
low politics
deconstruction
chaos theory
epistemology
social constructivism
transformation

SUGGESTED READING

Carlsnaes, Walter, Thomas Risse, and Beth A. Simmons, eds. *Handbook of International Relations.* London: Sage, 2002.

Dougherty, James E., and Robert L. Pfaltzgraff, Jr. *Contending Theories of International Relations,* 5th ed. New York: Addison Wesley-Longman, 2001.

Doyle, Michael W. *Ways of War and Peace.* New York: Norton, 1997.

Elman, Colin, and Miriam Fendius Elman, eds. *Progress in International Relations Theory: Appraising the Field.* Cambridge, Mass.: MIT Press, 2003.

Ferguson, Yale H., and Richard W. Mansbach. *The Elusive Quest Continues: Theory and International Politics.* Upper Saddle River, N.J.: Prentice Hall, 2003.

Fierke, Karin M., and Knud Erik Jørgensen, eds. *Constructing International Relations: The Next Generation.* London: M. E. Sharpe, 2002.

Katzenstein, Peter J., Robert O. Keohane, and Stephen D. Krasner, eds. *Exploration and Contestation in the Study of World Politics.* Cambridge, Mass.: MIT Press, 2000.

Kegley, Charles W., Jr., ed. *Controversies in International Relations Theory: Realism and the Neoliberal Challenge.* New York: St. Martin's Press, 1995.

Keohane, Robert O., and Joseph S. Nye, Jr. *Power and Interdependence: World Politics in Transition,* 2nd ed. Glenview, Il.: Scott, Foresman/Little, Brown, 1989.

Puchala, Donald J., ed. *Visions of International Relations: Assessing an Academic Field.* Columbia: University of South Carolina Press, 2002.

Viotte, Paul R., and Mark V. Kauppi. *International Relations Theory,* 4th ed. Boston: Allyn & Bacon, 2002.

Wendt, Alexander. *Social Theory of International Politics.* Cambridge, Eng.: Cambridge University Press, 2000.

WHERE ON THE WORLD WIDE WEB?

Contemporary Philosophy, Critical Theory, and Postmodern Thought
http://www.cudenver.edu/~mryder/itc_data/postmodern.html

The University of Colorado at Denver's School of Education has created a Web site that helps students understand the ideas behind critical theory and postmodern thought. Read about the main authors of postmodern thought and then access their works.

Data on the Net
http://odwin.ucsd.edu/idata/

Try your hand at being a behavioral social scientist. The University of California at San Diego has created a gateway Web site from which you can browse the collection of several hundred Internet sites of numerous social science statistical data. On the home page, type in a topic that interests you, and receive data that is relevant to your topic.

Feminist Theory and Gender Studies
http://csf.colorado.edu/isa/ftgs/

This is the home page of the Feminist Theory and Gender Studies Section (FTGSS) of the International Studies Association. Through this site you can access the archives of FEMISA, a moderated discussion list where individuals discuss issues related to gender and international studies. You can also subscribe to the FEMISA list and join the lively debate.

Feminist Theory Web Site
http://www.cddc.vt.edu/feminism/

The Center for Digital Discourse and Culture at Virginia Tech University hosts the award-winning Feminist Theory Web Site. This site provides one of the most extensive lists of research materials and information for students, activists, and scholars interested in women's conditions and struggles around the world, with a staggering 5,425 bibliographical entries and 593 links to other Internet sites. Its stated goals are to encourage research and dialogue between individuals in different countries around the world. True to its international focus, the site can be accessed in English, Spanish, or French. Those interested can read complete bibliographies from various fields as well as obtain information on women's movements and activities anywhere in the world. As noted in this chapter, much literature on world politics has ignored the plight and contributions of women. This Web site will undoubtedly contribute to remedying this situation.

Niccoló Machiavelli
http://www.philosophypages.com/ph/macv.htm

The writings of Nicolo Machiavelli (1469–1527) are often cited as the base of realist thinking in international relations. As this chapter explains, the realist worldview is primarily concerned with a state's drive for power. Visit this site for a complete informational resource on Machiavelli's life and times. There is also a link to his famous book on how to rule, *The Prince,* which you can read online.

President Woodrow Wilson
http://gi.grolier.com/presidents/aae/bios/28pwils.html

As Chapter 2 notes, Woodrow Wilson's celebrated Fourteen Points speech before a joint session of Congress on January 8, 1918, "expressed the sentiments of the liberal world view and program." The *Academic American Encyclopedia,* produced by Grolier Online, features this speech along with information on Wilson's life and times. Take a moment to read the Fourteen Points. In retrospect, did Wilson's speech aim to prevent another war or establish American international dominance in a new world order? Which philosophy do you think underlies current U.S. foreign policy, liberalism or realism?

INFOTRAC® COLLEGE EDITION

Legro, Jeffrey W., and Andrew Moravcsik. "Is Anybody Still a Realist?" *International Security* Fall 1999.

Jervis, Robert. "Realism, Neoliberalism, and Cooperation," *International Security* Summer 1999.

Kurth, James. "Inside the Cave: The Banality of I.R. Studies," *The National Interest* Fall 1998.

Hoffmann, Stanley. "The Crisis of Liberal Internationalism," *Foreign Policy* Spring 1995.

For more articles, enter:

"realism theory" in Keywords.

"neorealism" in Keywords.

"liberalism" in the Subject Guide, and then go to subdivision "international aspects."

THE GLOBE'S ACTORS AND THEIR RELATIONS

Shakespeare said that "all the world's a stage and all the men and women merely players." When it comes to international politics, not just people, but also organizations, groups, and countries have a variety of roles to play on the global stage. Part II identifies the major actors in world politics today and describes the roles they perform and the policies they are pursuing.

Each chapter in Part II focuses on a prominent type of global actor. We begin with states (Chapter 3), using them as an example to show the processes all transnational actors use to make foreign policy decisions. We also identify the factors that sometimes interfere with the actors' ability to make rational choices about their interests and policies. In Chapter 4 special attention is given to the actors with the greatest military and economic capabilities—the great powers. Next in Chapter 5, we examine the growing role of non-state actors—intergovernmental organizations such as the United Nations and European Union and nongovernmental organizations of private actors such as Greenpeace and Amnesty International—whose members actively work for global changes. This broad category also includes multinational corporations, ethnopolitical groups, and religious movements. Finally, Chapter 6 deals with the weaker, economically less-developed countries whose fates are shaped so much by the great powers and by multilateral institutions and actors, known collectively as the Global South because the majority of them are located on the earth's southern hemisphere.

FOREIGN POLICY DECISION MAKING

T O P I C S   A N D   T H E M E S

- The emergence of the modern state system
- The global and domestic determinants of states' foreign policy behavior
- The unitary actor and rational decision making
- The bureaucratic politics of foreign policy decision making
- The role of leaders in foreign policy decision making
- Constraints on foreign policy making: Problems and prospects

- **CONTROVERSY** ARE DEMOCRACIES DEFICIENT IN FOREIGN AFFAIRS?
- **CONTROVERSY** POLICY AND PERSONALITY: DO LEADERS MAKE A DIFFERENCE?

U.S. President George W. Bush addressing the United Nations on September 10, 2002, giving the multilateral world body an ultimatum by warning the Security Council to authorize U.N. military action against Saddam Hussein.

Foreign policy is the system of activities evolved by communities for changing the behavior of other states and for adjusting their own activities to the international environment.

—GEORGE MODELSKI, political scientist, 1962

Much of the anguish of foreign policy results from the need to establish priorities among competing, sometimes conflicting, necessities.

—HENRY A. KISSINGER, former U.S. secretary of state, 1999

■ **actor**
an individual, group, state, or organization that plays a major role in world politics.

In studying world politics we typically use the term **actor** to refer to the agents who are the globe's primary performers. These transnational players include countries (for example, the United States and Japan), international organizations (the United Nations, or UN, and the Nordic Council), multinational corporations (General Motors and Sony), as well as nonstate actors such as nongovernmental international organizations (the World Wildlife Federation), indigenous nationalities (the Kurds in Iran, Iraq, and Turkey), and terrorist groups (the Al Qaeda global network). The conventional image is that of a stage on which players in the global drama act out their assigned roles. The leading actors dominate center stage, and the supporting players move along the periphery.

We will discuss each type of actor in later chapters, but here we will focus on countries, usually called "states." We particularly emphasize the ways states make foreign policy decisions designed to cope with challenges from abroad. The processes by which states decide on foreign policy will illuminate the factors that influence how other types of transnational actors make foreign policy choices as well. States demand primary attention, however, because international law gives them special status as the principal holders of economic and military capabilities in world affairs, and assigns to states alone the legal right to use armed force.

THE EMERGENCE OF THE MODERN STATE SYSTEM

As a network of relationships among independent territorial units, the modern state system was born with the Peace of Westphalia in 1648, which ended the Thirty Years' War in Europe. Thereafter, European rulers refused to recognize the secular authority of the Roman Catholic Church, replacing the system of papal governance in the Middle Ages with geographically and politically separate states that recognized no superior authority. The newly independent states were all given the same legal rights: territory under their sole control, unrestricted control of their domestic affairs, and the freedom to conduct foreign relations and negotiate treaties with other states. The concept of **state sovereignty**—that no one is above the state—captures these legal rights.

The Westphalian system still colors every dimension of world politics and provides the terminology used to describe the primary units in international affairs. Although the term "nation-state" is often used interchangeably with "state" and "nation," technically the three are different. A **state** is a legal entity that enjoys a permanent population, a well-defined territory, and a government capable of exercising sovereignty. A **nation** is a collection of people who, on the basis of ethnic, linguistic, or cultural affinity, perceive themselves to be members of the same group. Thus the term "nation-state" implies a convergence between territorial states and the psychological identification of people within them. However, in employing this familiar terminology, we should exercise caution because this condition is relatively rare; there are few independent states comprising a single nationality. As we shall explain in Chapter 5, most states are populated by many nations, and some nations are not states. These "nonstate nations" are ethnic groups, such as Native American tribes in the United States, Sikhs in India, or Basques in Spain, composed of people without sovereign power over the territory in which they live.

When we speak generically about **foreign policy** and the decision-making processes that produce it, we mean the goals that officials heading states (and other transnational actors) seek abroad, the values that underlie those goals, and the means or instruments used to pursue them. To begin our inquiry into how foreign policy choices are made, we first consider the setting for states' choices and the circumstances outside national borders that make such choices necessary. Next we look at decision making as a rational process before considering two ways of viewing national decision making: the bureaucratic politics and the history-making individual models. We conclude by examining how states' national attributes influence their foreign policy behavior.

■ **state sovereignty**
a state's supreme authority to manage internal affairs and foreign relations (see p. 20).

■ **state**
a legal entity with a permanent population, a well-defined territory, and a government capable of exercising sovereignty.

■ **nation**
a collection of people who, on the basis of ethnic, linguistic, or cultural affinity, perceive themselves to be members of the same group.

■ **foreign policy**
the decisions governing authorities make to realize international goals.

THE GLOBAL AND DOMESTIC DETERMINANTS OF STATES' FOREIGN POLICY BEHAVIOR

Geostrategic location, military might, economic prowess, and system of government are all variables that affect foreign policy choices. Still, due to the diversity of states, as well as their different locations and positions within the contemporary global system, it is difficult to generalize about the influence of any one factor or combination of factors.

FIGURE 3.1
**The Major Sources of States' Foreign Policy Decisions:
Influences at Three Levels**

The factors that shape states' foreign policies can be
categorized at three basic levels. At the global level are
those structural features of the international system such
as the prevalence of civil wars and the extent of trade
interdependence. At the state level are internal or domestic
influences such as the state's type of government or the
opinions of its citizens. At the individual level are the
characteristics of the leader—his or her personal beliefs,
values, and personality. All three levels simultaneously
affect decisions, but their relative weight usually depends
on the issues and circumstances at the time of decision.

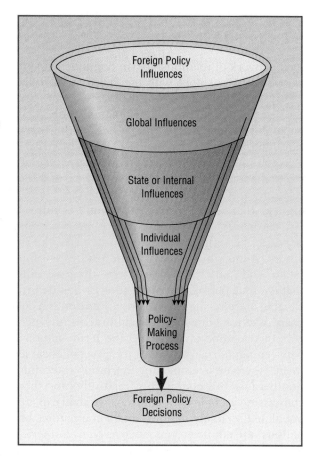

■ **levels of analysis**
the different aspects of and
agents in international
affairs that may be stressed
in interpreting world politics
and explaining global
phenomena, depending on
whether the analyst
chooses to focus on
"wholes" (the complete
global system and large
collectivities) or on "parts"
(individual states or
people).

■ **intermestic**
those issues confronting a
state that are
simultaneously international
and domestic.

To determine the relative impact of specific factors under different circumstances, we must first distinguish between the international and internal influences on policy choices. Note the **levels of analysis** pictured in Figure 3.1. In
classifying the determinants not only of states' foreign policies but also of
trends in world politics generally, the levels-of-analysis concept introduced in
Chapter 1 helps to describe the multiple influences on states' decision-making
processes. Recall that states and the global system make up two distinct levels:
the state level encompasses domestic characteristics, and the global or international system level encompasses interstate relations and changes in these relations over time. Although these two traditionally discrete realms have become
increasingly fused in what is called **intermestic** politics, as the need for leaders
to coordinate their domestic and foreign policies has increased with the **globalization** of twenty-first-century international relations, this categorical distinction is still useful for purposes of analysis.

Global or "external" influences on foreign policy include all activities occurring beyond a state's borders that structure the choices its officials make. Such
factors as the content of international law, the number of military alliances,
destruction of forests and animal species, and the changing levels of international trade sometimes profoundly affect the choices of decision makers.
Internal or "domestic" influences, on the other hand, are those that exist at
the level of the state, not the system. Here attention focuses on variations in

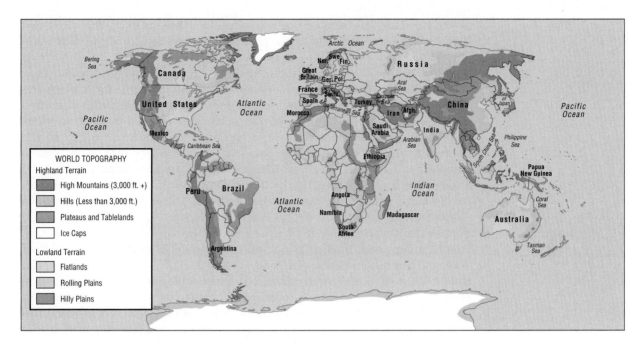

MAP 3.1

Geographic Influences on Foreign Policy

How countries act toward others is shaped by the number of neighboring states on their borders and whether they are protected from invasion by natural barriers such as mountains and oceans. This map suggests how the separation of the United States from Eurasia has encouraged an isolationist policy during many periods in U.S. history, until recently. Note also how topography, location, and other geopolitical factors may have influenced the foreign policy priorities of Great Britain, Germany, China, Finland, and states in South America—hypotheses advanced by the geopolitics approach to international politics.

states' attributes, such as military capabilities, level of economic development, and types of government, that may influence different states' foreign policy behavior. Examples of both types of influences follow.

Geopolitics

One of the most important influences on a state's foreign policy behavior is its location and physical terrain. The presence of natural frontiers, for example, may profoundly guide policymakers' choices (see Map 3.1). Consider the United States, which has prospered because vast oceans separate it from Europe and Asia. The advantage of having oceans as barriers to foreign intervention, combined with the absence of militarily powerful neighbors, permitted the United States to develop into an industrial giant and to practice safely an isolationist foreign policy for over 150 years. Consider also mountainous Switzerland, whose topography has made neutrality an attractive foreign policy option.

Similarly, maintaining autonomy from continental politics has been an enduring theme in the foreign policy of Great Britain, an island country whose physical separation from Europe served historically as a buffer separating it from entanglement in major-power disputes on the Continent. Preserving this

■ **globalization**
the accelerating process by which increasing interstate interconnectedness has eroded the traditional distinction between states' domestic and international affairs (see p. 45)

■ **states' attributes**
state characteristics that shape foreign policy behavior, such as their size, wealth, and the extent to which their leaders are accountable to their citizens in comparison with other states.

protective shield has been a priority for Britain and helps to explain why Great Britain has been so hesitant in the past twenty years to accepting full integration in the European Union (EU) (see Chapter 15).

Most countries are not insular, however; they have many states on their borders, denying them the option of noninvolvement in world affairs. Germany, which sits in the geographic center of Europe, historically has found its domestic political system and foreign policy preferences profoundly affected by its geostrategic position. Located in the center of Europe, Germany in the twentieth century has struggled through no less than six major radical changes in governing institutions, each of which pursued very different foreign policies: (1) Kaiser Wilhelm II's empire, (2) the Weimar Republic, (3) Adolf Hitler's authoritarian dictatorship and imperialistic wars to establish a 1,000-year Reich to rule the world, its two post–World War II successors, (4) the capitalist Federal Republic in West Germany, (5) the communist German Democratic Republic in East Germany, and, finally, (6) a reunited Germany after the end of the Cold War, now committed to liberal democracy and full integration in the European Union. Each of these governments was preoccupied with its relations with neighbors, but responded to the opportunities and challenges presented by Germany's position in the middle of the European continent with very different foreign policy goals. For each government, however, isolationistic withdrawal from involvement in continental affairs was not a viable geostrategic option.

In much the same way, extended frontiers with the former Soviet Union shaped the foreign policies of China and Finland. Finland's neutrality in the Cold War helped ensure its survival in the face of a powerful and threatening neighbor. China, on the other hand, has long regarded its relationship with the now defunct Soviet Union as unequal, and in the late 1960s the two communist giants clashed militarily as the Chinese sought to rectify past injustices. The "unequal treaties" between China and outside powers, which encapsulate other perceived injustices, resulted in part from China's vast size and indefensible borders, which made it an easy target for the great powers that had carved it into spheres of influence in previous centuries.

Like China, the Latin American countries reside geographically near a much stronger power, the United States, whose capabilities are in part a function of geophysical resources. Latin America has long been the object of studied interest and frequent intervention by the giant to the north. The U.S. presence provoked a bitter response among Latin American countries for many decades, because they felt they could not compete on an equal footing with the U.S. economic and military powerhouse. Their foreign policy of resistance to so-called Yankee **imperialism** was driven by their vulnerable circumstances. Understandably, many other poor Global South countries without many resources also see that, given their weak geo-economic condition, their foreign policy goals should be geared to opposing imperialism—what former Egyptian President Gamal Abdel Nasser defined as "the subjugation of small nations to the interests of the big ones."

History is replete with other examples of geography's influence on states' foreign policy goals, which is why geopolitical theories are useful. The **geopolitics** school of realist thought and political geography generally stresses the influence of geographic factors on state power and international conduct. Illustrative of early geopolitical thinking is Alfred Thayer Mahan's (1890) *The Influence of Sea Power in History*, which maintained that control of the seas shaped

■ **imperialism**
intentional imposition of one state's power over another, traditionally through territorial conquest, but more recently through economic domination, denying the victim population freedom to have a voice in the conquering regime's decisions.

■ **geopolitics**
the theoretical postulate that states' foreign policies are determined by their location, natural resources, and physical environment.

national power. Thus states with extensive coastlines and ports enjoyed a competitive advantage. Later geopoliticians, such as Sir Halford Mackinder (1919) and Nicholas Spykman (1944), stressed that not only location but also topography, size (territory and population), climate, and distance between states are powerful determinants of the foreign policies of individual countries. The underlying principle behind the geopolitical perspective is self-evident: Leaders' perceptions of available foreign policy options are influenced by the geopolitical circumstances that define their states' place on the world stage.

Geopolitics is only one aspect of the global environment that may influence foreign policy. In other chapters we will discuss additional global factors. Here, we comment briefly on three internal attributes of states that influence their foreign policies: military capabilities, level of economic development, and type of government.

Military Capabilities

The proposition that states' internal capabilities shape their foreign policy priorities is supported by the fact that states' preparations for war strongly influence their later use of force (see Levy 2001; Vasquez 1993). Thus while all states may seek similar goals, their ability to realize them will vary according to their military capabilities.

Because military capabilities limit a state's range of prudent policy choices, they act as a mediating factor on leaders' national security decisions. For instance, in the 1980s Libyan leader Muammar Qaddafi repeatedly provoked the United States through anti-American and anti-Israeli rhetoric and by supporting various terrorist activities. Qaddafi was able to act as he did largely because neither bureaucratic organizations nor a mobilized public existed in Libya to constrain his personal whims and militaristic foreign policy preferences. However, Qaddafi was doubtlessly more highly constrained by the outside world than were the leaders in the more militarily capable countries toward whom his anger was directed. Limited military muscle compared with the United States precluded the kinds of belligerent behaviors he threatened to practice.

Conversely, Saddam Hussein, the Iraqi dictator, made strenuous efforts to build Iraq's military might (partly with the help of U.S. arms sales) and by 1990 had built the fourth-largest army in the world. Thus the invasion of Kuwait became a feasible foreign policy option. In the end, however, even Iraq's impressive military power proved ineffective against a vastly superior coalition of military forces, headed by the United States. The 1991 Persian Gulf War forced Saddam Hussein to capitulate and withdraw from the conquered territory. Eleven years thereafter, in 2002 when the anti-Iraqi coalition crumbled after its attempted enforcement of UN sanctions to prevent Iraqi armament failed, Iraq was now defiant.

The new U.S. president, George W. Bush, claimed that Iraq was poised to militarily confront its primary enemy, the United States. Iraq's potential military muscle was said to give Saddam Hussein the capabilities to threaten its more powerful foe. Thus, military might as a determinant of national security policy was underscored once again when President Bush chose to face the challenge that still existed after his father left the White House in 1992—how to deter Iraq's Saddam Hussein from arming himself with nuclear warheads and other weapons of mass destruction and possibly sharing them with terrorists to attack the United States and its allies. The potency of military capabilities as a driving influence on foreign policy decisions was made apparent in September 2002 when Bush announced a "new Bush doctrine" pledging to use military force to remove Mr. Hussein from office, that is, to undertake an unprovoked attack on an enemy state to coerce disarmament and regime change.

It was not surprising that Bush's Iraqi policy at once met with staunch criticism at home and abroad, even from members of his own administration and political party, because a preemptive attack without prior aggressive provocation would violate the established norm in international law prohibiting a premeditated attack to prevent an anticipated action. As former U.S. Secretary of State Henry Kissinger warned at the time, the danger is that every country could conclude that preemption is an acceptable practice; he counseled, "we cannot have a doctrine of pre-emption for all eternity" which would encourage any state to attack any adversary that it felt was threatening it. Nevertheless, this episode of a showdown with Iraq illustrates well the power of perceived shifts in the balance of military capabilities between enemies as a determinant of foreign policy decisions.

Economic Conditions

The level of economic and industrial development a state enjoys affects the foreign policy goals it can pursue. Generally, the more economically developed a state is, the more likely it is to play an activist role in the global political economy. Rich states have interests that extend far beyond their borders and typically possess the means to pursue and protect them. Not coincidentally, states that enjoy industrial capabilities and extensive involvement in international trade also tend to be militarily powerful—in part because military might is a function of economic capabilities.

The United States today stands out as a superpower precisely because it benefits from a combination of vast economic and military capabilities, including extensive nuclear weapons capabilities. This enables the United States to practice unrestrained globalism; its "imperial reach" and interventionist behavior are seemingly unconstrained by limited wealth or resources. For this reason, **gross national product (GNP)** is often used in combination with other factors to identify great powers and by itself is an important element in predicting the extensiveness of states' global interests and involvements.

■ **gross national product (GNP)** measure of a state's production of goods and services within a given period of time (see p. 23).

Although economically advanced states are more active globally, this does not mean that their privileged circumstances dictate adventuresome policies. Rich states are often "satisfied" ones that have much to lose from the onset of revolutionary change or global instability and that usually perceive the status quo as best serving their interests (Wolfers 1962). As a result, they often forge international economic policies to protect and expand their envied position at the pinnacle of the global hierarchy.

Levels of productivity and prosperity also affect the foreign policies of the poor states at the bottom of the hierarchy. Some dependent states respond to their economic weakness by complying subserviently with the wishes of the rich on whom they depend. Others rebel defiantly, sometimes succeeding (despite their disadvantaged bargaining position) in resisting the efforts by great powers and powerful international organizations to control their international behavior.

Koji Sasahara/POOL/AP/Wide World

The Burden of Foreign Policy Choice for Global Leadership George W. Bush was inaugurated on January 20, 2001, facing the awesome challenge of constructing a new U.S. foreign policy for the turbulent twenty-first century. In 2002, in the wake of the 9/11 terrorist attacks, he confronted his most severe foreign policy crisis—how to reconcile competing values to rationally decide how to deal with Iraqi dictator Saddam Hussein while pursuing his "war on global terrorism" to fulfill his pledge that war "will not end until every terrorist group of global reach has been found, stopped, and defeated."

Thus generalizations about the economic foundations of states' international political behavior often prove inaccurate. Although levels of economic development vary widely among states in the global system, they alone do not determine foreign policies. Instead, leaders' perceptions of the opportunities and constraints that their states' economic resources provide may more powerfully influence their foreign policy choices.

Type of Government

A third important attribute affecting states' international behavior is their political system. Although neorealism predicts that all states will act similarly to protect their interests, a state's type of government demonstrably constrains important choices, including whether threats to use military force are carried out. Here the important distinction is between **constitutional democracy** (representative government) on one end of the spectrum and **autocratic rule** (authoritarian or totalitarian) on the other.

In neither democratic (sometimes called "open") nor autocratic ("closed") political systems can political leaders survive long without the support of organized domestic political interests, and sometimes the mass citizenry. But in democratic systems those interests are likely to be politically potent, spread beyond the government itself, and active in their pressure on the government to make policy choices that benefit them. Public opinion, interest groups, and the mass media are a more visible part of the policy-making process in democratic systems. Similarly, the electoral process in democratic societies more meaningfully frames choices and produces results about who will lead than typically occurs in authoritarian regimes, where the real choices are made by a few elites behind closed doors. In short, in a democracy, public opinions and preferences may matter and, therefore, differences in who is allowed to participate and how much they exercise their right to participate are critical determinants of foreign policy choices.

■ **constitutional democracy**
government processes that allow people through their elected representatives to exercise power and influence the state's policies.

■ **autocratic rule**
a system of authoritarian or totalitarian government where unlimited power is concentrated in a single person.

Compare, for example, the foreign policy of Saudi Arabia, controlled by a king and royal family, with that of Switzerland, governed by a multiparty democratic process. In the former, foreign policy decisions have sometimes been bold and unexpected, as exemplified by the Saudi royal family's revolutionary policies in summoning U.S. military forces to its territory during the 1991 Persian Gulf War, in contravention of long-standing Arab policies designed to prevent Western encroachments against Muslim lands. In Switzerland, where voting and mass political participation heavily influence decisions about Switzerland's international activities, the government has pursued the policy of neutrality without deviation since 1815, and, as an indicator of its traditional foreign-policy independence, did not join the UN until September 2002.

The proposition that domestic stimuli, and not simply international events, are a source of foreign policy is not novel. In ancient Greece, for instance, the realist historian Thucydides observed that what happened within the Greek city-states often did more to shape their external behavior than what each did to the others. He added that Greek leaders frequently concentrated their efforts on influencing the political climate within their own polities rather than on managing relations with other Greek city-states. Similarly, leaders today sometimes make foreign policy decisions for domestic political purposes—as, for example, when bold or aggressive acts abroad are intended to influence election outcomes at home or to divert public attention from economic woes. This is sometimes called the "scapegoat" phenomenon or the **diversionary theory of war** (Levy 1989b).

■ **diversionary theory of war**
the contention that leaders initiate conflict abroad as a way of increasing national cohesion at home by diverting national public opinion away from controversial domestic issues.

Some see the intrusion of domestic politics into foreign policy making as a disadvantage of democratic political systems that undermines their ability to deal decisively with crises or to bargain effectively with less democratic adversaries and allies (see Controversy: Are Democracies Deficient in Foreign Affairs?). Democracies are subject to inertia. They move slowly on issues, because so many disparate elements are involved in decision making and because officials in democracies are accountable to public opinion and must respond to pressure from a variety of domestic interest groups (groups mobilized to exercise influence over the future direction of their country's foreign policies, especially on issues highly important to them). A crisis sufficient enough to arouse the attention and activity of a large proportion of the population may need to erupt in order for large changes in policy to come about. As the French political sociologist Alexis de Tocqueville argued in 1835, democracies may be inclined to "impulse rather than prudence" because they overreact to perceived external dangers once they recognize them. "There are two things that a democratic people will always find difficult," de Tocqueville mused, "to start a war and to end it." In contrast, authoritarian governments can "make decisions more rapidly, ensure domestic compliance with their decisions, and perhaps be more consistent in their foreign policy" (Jensen 1982). But there is a cost: Nondemocracies "often are less effective in developing an innovative foreign policy because of subordinates' pervasive fear of raising questions." In short, the concentration of power and the suppression of public opposition can be dangerous as well as advantageous.

The impact of government type on foreign policy choice has taken on great significance following the rapid conversion of many dictatorships to democratic rule. These liberal government conversions have occurred in three successive "waves" since the 1800s (Huntington 1991b). The first wave occurred between 1878 and 1926 and the second between 1943 and 1962. The third wave began in the 1970s when a large number of nondemocratic countries began to

ARE DEMOCRACIES DEFICIENT IN FOREIGN AFFAIRS?

History suggests that democracies enjoy faithful allies and lose fewer wars than do nondemocracies but, despite these achievements, democracies may make foreign policy choices in ways that are less rational and efficient than autocracies (see Siverson and Emmons 1991). For this reason, one realist thesis argues that democracies are decidedly inferior to nondemocratic regimes. Does the nature of democratic rule help or hinder those governments' capacities to realize their goals under anarchy? In evaluating this controversy, consider the views of a leading American policymaker and realist political scientist, George F. Kennan, who advanced the following thesis:

> I sometimes wonder whether a democracy is not uncomfortably similar to one of those prehistoric monsters with a body as long as this room and a brain the size of a pin. He lies there in his comfortable primeval mud and pays little attention to his environment; he is slow to wrath—in fact, you practically have to whack his tail off to make him aware that his interests are being disturbed; but, once he grasps this, he lies about him with such blind determination that he not only destroys his adversary but largely wrecks his native habitat. You wonder whether it would not have been wiser for him to have taken a little more interest in what was going on at an earlier date and to have

seen whether he could not have prevented some of these situations from arising instead of proceeding from an undiscriminating indifference to a holy wrath equally undiscriminating. (Kennan 1951, 59)

Against this criticism of democratic governments' tendency to react without foresight or moderation in foreign policy, defenders of liberal democratic governance such as Immanuel Kant, Thomas Jefferson, and Woodrow Wilson have argued just the opposite: that giving people power through the ballot and a voice in the making of foreign policy decisions restrains leaders in those countries from extreme or excessive choices, such as initiating a war on a whim. Thus, to liberals, democratization makes a positive contribution, enabling the leader of a democracy to bargain successfully with nondemocracies, since other states know that democratic governments are likely to have the support of the people and to honor their agreements.

What do you think? Are democratic procedures for making foreign policy decisions an aid or a handicap? What arguments and evidence can you provide to support your general conclusion about this timeless controversy?

convert their governments to democratic rule. In a remarkable global transformation from past world history, the once radical idea that democracy is the ideal form of decision making has triumphed. Today, as the year 2003 began, according to Freedom House three-fourths of the world's countries were fully or partially democratic (see Map 3.2).

This sea change has prompted widespread speculation that we many be witnessing the **end of history**—meaning "the end of mankind's ideological evolution and the universalization of Western liberal democracy as the final form of government" (Fukuyama 1989; Mandelbaum 2002). If this trend continues, the contagious expansion of democratic states could transform the war-prone pattern of past international relations.

The recent growth of democracy has emboldened neoliberals to predict that a **democratic peace** will develop—that a twenty-first century increasingly dominated by liberal democracies will be a safer century. Their reasons for this prophecy vary (see also Chapters 11 and 15) but rely on the logic that Immanuel Kant outlined in his 1795 treatise *Perpetual Peace*. Kant believed democracies would act very differently than nondemocracies in their foreign relations: they would form a separate peace with each other. The basis for this

■ **end of history**
the thesis advanced by Francis Fukuyama that because liberal democracy and a market economy are the only workable options for modern societies, the contest with centrally planned governance has ended (see p. 628).

■ **democratic peace**
the theory that although democratic states sometimes wage wars against other states, they do not fight each other (see p. 416).

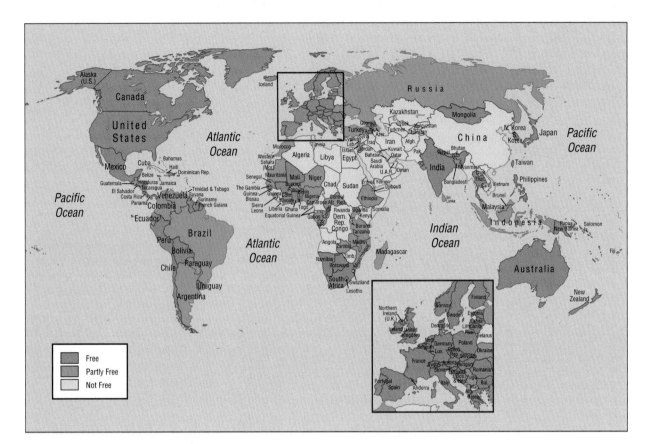

MAP 3.2

The Map of Freedom: The Location of Democratically Governed Countries at the Start of 2003

Throughout most of modern history, the majority of states were ruled autocratically and the people living in them were not free. However, since the mid-1970s, an increasing number of states have undertaken political reforms leading to democratic governance and civil liberties. This map shows the location in the year 2002 of (1) the eighty-five "free" countries whose governments provide their citizens with a high degree of political and economic freedom and safeguard basic civil liberties, (2) the fifty-nine "partly free" electoral democracies, and (3) the forty-eight "not free" states, where citizens' human rights and liberties are systematically abused or denied. Liberal democratic peace theory predicts that if the trend toward the spread of liberty worldwide continues so that democracy really, as some assert, has "established itself as a universal norm" (Muravchik 2002), then peaceful relations among the growing community of the liberal democracies is to be expected.

SOURCE: Adapted from "Liberty's Ebb and Flow" by Michael Kilborn in *The Christian Science Monitor*, May 9, 1997, pp. 18–19. Reproduced with permission. Copyright © 1997 The Christian Science Monitor (www.csmonitor.com). All rights reserved. Data originally reported on Freedom House website at www.freedomhouse.com. Used with permission.

prediction rested on Kant's recognition that in democracies leaders are accountable to the public, and that because ordinary citizens have to supply the soldiers and bear the human and financial cost of imperialistic policies, they would constrain leaders from initiating foreign wars (especially against other liberal democracies similarly constrained by norms and institutions that respect compromise and civil liberties). From this reasoning derived the neoliberal democratic peace argument that liberal democracies are natural forces for international peace.

Much empirical evidence supports this **neoliberal** proposition that, as stated in 1994 by President Bill Clinton, "Democracies don't attack each other." Whereas liberal democracies fight wars often with nondemocracies, in the last two centuries there have been no major wars waged by one democracy against another (Ray 1995; Russett 2001). This fact poses a serious challenge that when it comes to war, liberal democracies are no different from illiberal states (since both, realism avers, act on their perceptions of their national interests, not their ideologies, and will respond to similar external threats with the same kind of military responses). The overall record shows that, contrary to realism's premise, the type of government and, more specifically, whether leaders are accountable to opposition groups through multiparty elections, strongly influence foreign policy goals (see Kegley and Hermann 2002). Many developments in world politics examined in Chapters 11 and 15 will draw further attention to the internal roots of external behavior.

Having described the international settings to which policymakers respond and the internal factors that influence their decisions, we now turn to how foreign policy decisions are reached. We begin with the rational model of decision making.

THE UNITARY ACTOR AND RATIONAL DECISION MAKING

According to realist theorizing, the primary goal of foreign policy is to ensure state survival. From this viewpoint, strategic calculations about national security are the primary determinants of policymakers' choices. Domestic politics and the process of policy making itself are of secondary concern.

States as Unitary Actors?

Realism, in both its classical and neorealist forms, emphasizes that changes at the **global level of analysis** determines state action. It assumes that foreign policy making consists primarily of adjusting the state to the pressures of an anarchical world system whose essential properties will not vary. Accordingly, it presumes that all states and the individuals responsible for their foreign policies confront the problem of national survival in similar ways. Thus all decision makers are essentially alike in their approach to foreign policy making:

> If they follow the [decision] rules, we need know nothing more about them. In essence, if the decision maker behaves rationally, the observer, knowing the rules of rationality, can rehearse the decisional process in his own mind, and, if he knows the decision maker's goals, can both predict the decision and understand why that particular decision was made. (Verba 1969, 225)

Because realists believe that leaders' goals and their corresponding approach to foreign policy choices are the same, the decision-making processes of each state can be studied as though each were a **unitary actor**—a homogenous or

■ **neoliberalism**
a perspective that accounts for the way international institutions promote global change, cooperation, peace, and prosperity through collective reform approaches (see p. 500).

■ **global level of analysis**
an analytical approach to world politics that emphasizes the impact of worldwide conditions on the behavior of states, IGOs, NGOs, and other international actors.

■ **unitary actor**
a transnational actor (usually a sovereign state) assumed to be internally united, so that changes in its internal circumstances do not influence its foreign policy as much as do the decisions that actor's leaders make to cope with changes in its global environment.

monolithic unit with few or no important internal differences that affect its choices. One way to picture this assumption is to think of states as billiard balls and the table on which they interact as the state system. The balls (states) continuously clash and collide with one another, and the actions of each are determined by its interactions with the others, not by what occurs inside it. According to this realist view, the leaders who make foreign policy, the types of governments they head, the characteristics of their societies, and the internal economic and political conditions of the states they lead are unimportant.

Policy Making as Rational Choice?

■ **rational choice**
decision-making procedures guided by careful definition of situations, weighing of goals, consideration of all alternatives, and selection of the options most likely to achieve the highest goals.

The decision-making processes of unitary actors that determine national interests are typically described as rational. We define rationality or **rational choice** here as purposeful, goal-directed behavior exhibited when "the individual responding to an international event . . . uses the best information available and chooses from the universe of possible responses that alternative most likely to maximize his [or her] goals" (Verba 1969). Scholars describe rationality as a sequence of decision-making activities involving the following intellectual steps:

1. *Problem Recognition and Definition.* The need to decide begins when policymakers perceive an external problem and attempt to define objectively its distinguishing characteristics. Objectivity requires full information about the actions, motivations, and capabilities of other actors as well as the character of the international environment and trends within it. The search for the information must be exhaustive, and all the facts relevant to the problem must be gathered.

2. *Goal Selection.* Next, those responsible for making foreign policy choices must determine what they want to accomplish. This disarmingly simple requirement is often difficult. It requires the identification and ranking of *all* values (such as security, democracy, and economic well-being) in a hierarchy from most to least preferred.

3. *Identification of Alternatives.* Rationality also requires the compilation of an exhaustive list of *all* available policy options and an estimate of the costs associated with each alternative.

4. *Choice.* Finally, rationality requires selecting the single alternative with the best chance of achieving the desired goal(s). For this purpose, policymakers must conduct a rigorous means-ends, cost-benefit analysis guided by an accurate prediction of the probable success of each option.

Policymakers often describe their own behavior as resulting from a rational decision-making process designed to reach the "best" decision possible. Indeed, some past foreign policy decisions do reveal elements of this idealized process, described well by former U.S. Secretary of State Henry Kissinger when he observed that

> an effective decision-making process must . . . reflect well-thought-out policy choices—that is, they must answer these questions: What are we trying to achieve, or what are we trying to prevent? What consequences do we expect from this decision, and what steps do we have in mind for dealing

with them? What is the cost of the proposed action? Are we willing to pay that price, and for what length of time? (Kissinger 1999, 1067)

The 1962 Cuban Missile Crisis, for example, illustrates several ways in which the deliberations of key U.S. policymakers conformed to a rational process (Allison and Zelikow 1999). Once Washington discovered the presence of Soviet missiles in Cuba, President John F. Kennedy formed a crisis decision-making group and charged it to "set aside all other tasks to make a prompt and intensive survey of the dangers and all possible courses of action." Six options were ultimately identified: do nothing; exert diplomatic pressure; make a secret approach to the Cuban leader Fidel Castro; invade Cuba; launch a surgical air strike against the missiles; or blockade Cuba. Before the group could choose among these six, it had to prioritize goals. Was removal of the Soviet missiles, retaliation against Castro, or maintaining the balance of power the objective? Or did the missiles pose little threat to vital U.S. interests? Until it was determined that the missiles posed a serious threat to national security, "do nothing" remained an option.

Once the advisers agreed that their goal was removing the missiles, their discussion turned to evaluating a surgical air strike versus a blockade. They eventually chose the latter because of its presumed advantages, including the demonstration of firmness it permitted the United States and the flexibility about further choices it allowed both parties.

President Bill Clinton's decision to commit the United States to participate in and lead NATO's military intervention in Kosovo following acts of genocide by Yugoslavia dictator Slobodan Milosevic's Serbian troops against the Albanian Kosovar minority in 1999 is often cited as another example of crisis decision making that conforms in part to the model of rational choice. After carefully weighing various options, a single choice from among the identified alternatives was selected: air strikes and massive bombardment to force Yugoslavia to stop the human slaughter, to surrender, and to accept NATO's military occupation of Kosovo. Whether the decision proved wise was highly debated, but few observers doubted that the Clinton administration had attempted, in collective consultation with its NATO allies, to reach what they thought was the "best" decision through a rational policy-making process.

The elusive quest for rational decision making was also illuminated in the crises that the second Bush administration faced. Most members of the closed circle of George W. Bush's U.S. advisers in September 2001 claimed that they were faithfully following the rules for rational choice in their declared war against "global terrorism" following 9/11 and, later in September 2002, in their decision to attack Iraqi dictator Saddam Hussein. For example, the administration in the latter case launched a campaign in public diplomacy to persuade all states that it was in their best interests to recognize the imminent danger posed by the possibility that Iraq was illegally obtaining weapons of mass destruction, and took its argument to the UN. The message was clothed in the language of deliberate logical choice to convince skeptics that the costs and benefits of all options had been carefully weighed.

However, like beauty, rationality often lies in the eye of the beholder and reasonable, clear-thinking people can disagree and often do disagree about the facts and about the wisdom of foreign policy goals. Note that counterarguments of Bush's war planning were also couched in terms of rationality—criticisms which attacked the premises on which Bush's big plans for a major war were based. For example, one Australian observer complained that "Unless Bush can mount a more persuasive case that Saddam is uniquely dangerous, Iraq's overthrow by force would send a powerful message that might is right and that the United States alone determines the rules of the game. This would be a repudiation of norms that have governed the conduct of international relations for the past half-century" (Dupont 2002). At home, critics also questioned the rationality of the decision process. Republican Senator Chuck Hagel, for instance, praised the president's September 10, 2001, ultimatum as an important first step in the decision process which cast the confrontation with Iraq as a multilateral global issue and not a bilateral fight. However, Hagel worried that Bush failed to address the important questions required of a national choice: "If we invade Iraq, what allies will we have? Who governs after Saddam? What is the objective? Have we calculated the consequences, particularly the unintended consequences? What does [a war with Iraq] mean for the unfinished work with Afghanistan? For the Israeli-Palestinian conflict? For the tenuous truce between nuclear-armed India and Pakistan? . . . I support the Bush administration policy of regime change in Iraq [but] we must recognize, however, there are no easy, risk-free options. . . . Sending young men and women into war should never be taken lightly. Elected leaders should ask tough questions before sending them into a situation that may result in the ultimate sacrifice" (Broder 2002).

What this debate in the fall of 2002 demonstrated was (as constructivism warns) that rationality is a decision-making goal to which all international actors aspire, but that it is difficult to determine when the criteria for rational choice have been met. This raises the question: what are the barriers to rationality?

Impediments to Rational Choice

Despite the apparent application of rationality in these crises, rational choice is often more an idealized standard than an accurate description of real-world behavior. Theodore Sorenson—one of President Kennedy's closest advisers and a participant in the Cuban missile deliberations—has written not only about the steps policymakers in the Kennedy administration followed as they sought to emulate the process of rational choice but also about how actual decision making often departed from it. He described an eight-step process for policy making that is consistent with the model we have described: (1) agreeing on the facts; (2) agreeing on the overall policy objective; (3) precisely defining the problems; (4) canvassing all possible solutions; (5) listing the possible consequences that flow from each solution; (6) recommending one option; (7) communicating the option selected; and (8) providing for its execution. But he explained how difficult it is to follow these steps, because:

> [e]ach step cannot be taken in order. The facts may be in doubt or dispute. Several policies, all good, may conflict. Several means, all bad, may be all that are open. Value judgments may differ. Stated goals may be imprecise. There may be many interpretations of what is right, what is possible, and what is in the national interest. (Sorensen 1963, 19–20)

Despite the virtues rational choice promises, the impediments to its realization in foreign policy making are substantial, which is why an eminent his-

Photo by Barbara Kinney/White House/NEWSMAKERS/Getty Images

Diplomatic Ties—Rituals in a Global Diplomatic Culture Israeli Prime Minister Yitzhak Rabin, Egyptian President Hosni Mubarak, Jordan's King Hussein, U.S. President Bill Clinton, and the Palestine Liberation Organization's Yasser Arafat made history by signing an accord in September 1995 to expand Palestinian self-rule on the West Bank. The agreement was reached through step-by-step bargaining to realize common objectives presumably carefully decided on by rational choice. Fateful diplomatic ties, like neckties, can sometimes go askew, despite the best intentions. Five months later, the celebratory mood of the moment vanished when Rabin was assassinated by a terrorist as punishment for his act of courage.

torian concluded a "phenomenon noticeable throughout history regardless of place or period is the pursuit by governments of policies contrary to their own interests" (Tuchman 1984). In fact, **bounded rationality** is typical (Simon 1997). Some of the barriers that make errors in foreign policy so common are human, deriving from deficiencies in the intelligence, capability, and psychological needs and aspirations of foreign policy decision makers. Others are organizational, since most decisions require group agreement about the national interest and the wisest course of action. Reaching agreement is not easy, however, as reasonable people with different values often disagree about goals, preferences, and the probable results of alternative options. Thus the impediments to rational policy making are not to be underestimated.

Scrutiny of the actual process of decision making reveals other hindrances. Available information is often insufficient to recognize emergent problems accurately, resulting in decisions made on the basis of incomplete information. Moreover, the available information is often inaccurate, because the bureaucratic organizations political leaders depend on for advice screen, sort, and rearrange it. Compounding the problem is decision makers' susceptibility to **cognitive dissonance**—they are psychologically prone to block out negative, or dissonant, information and perceptions about their preferred choice and to

■ **bounded rationality** the concept that decision makers' capacity to choose the best option is often constrained by many human and organizational obstacles.

■ **cognitive dissonance** the general psychological tendency to deny discrepancies between one's preexisting beliefs (cognitions) and new information (see p. 13).

look instead for information that justifies that choice. This explains why policymakers sometimes pay little heed to warnings and overlook information about dangers, so that they repeat their past intellectual mistakes.

In addition, determining what goals best serve national interests is difficult: "Decision making often takes place within an atmosphere marked by value-complexity and uncertainty. The existence of competing values about a single issue forces value trade-offs; uncertainty refers to the absence of complete and well-organized information on which to base a confident policy choice" (Walker 1991).

Furthermore, decision makers' inability to rapidly gather and digest large quantities of information constrains their capacity to make informed choices. Because policymakers work with overloaded **policy agendas** and short deadlines, the search for policy options is seldom exhaustive. "There is little time for leaders to reflect," observes former U.S. Secretary of State Henry Kissinger (1979). "They are locked in an endless battle in which the urgent constantly gains on the important. The public life of every political figure is a continual struggle to rescue an element of choice from the pressure of circumstance." In the choice phase, then, decision makers rarely make value-maximizing choices. Instead of selecting the option with the best chance of success, they typically end their evaluation as soon as an alternative appears that seems superior to those already considered. Herbert Simon (1957) describes this as **satisficing** behavior. Rather than "optimizing" by seeking the best alternative, decision makers are routinely content to choose the first option that meets minimally acceptable standards. Because they frequently face "unresolvable" choices that preclude satisfaction across competing preferences, often only "admissible" ones appear available (see Levi 1990). In short, decisionmakers are prone to rush to judgments—rapidly estimating whether rival options are good or bad and reacting according to these constructed expectations about likely gains and losses.

The ability to make decisions is hindered by individuals' difficulties in abandoning formed opinions and their tendency to overreact in crises. **Prospect theory** informs us that when making choices, decision makers proceed by "framing" their choices from a perceived "reference point" based on past experiences about potential gains and losses and react differently about what they expect to gain or lose from particular choices by overvaluing losses relative to comparable gains. Because "people tend to value what they have more than comparable things they do not have, [there results an] observed tendency toward status quo choices" (Levy 1997). Prospect theory suggests that leaders do not make decisions according to the rational-choice model; they let their needs and expectations affect when they will be receptive to taking risks and when they will be psychologically reluctant to take the risk of making policy changes to achieve gains. One implication of this theory and evidence is that when leaders strike out by taking risks to initiate bold new foreign policy directions, they will have great difficulty admitting and correcting those choices if they later prove to be mistaken. Like investors who take big risks in the hope of making big profits but hold losing investments too long, policymakers view the prospects of new policies hopefully but cling to failed policies long after their deficiencies have become apparent. This—along with the "sunk-cost fallacy" that having paid for something, people are unwilling to waste it no matter what the consequences, as well as people's tendency to select the option that looks preferable judging by some past reference point rather than one with better

■ **policy agenda**
the changing list of problems or issues to which governments pay special attention at any given moment.

■ **satisficing**
the tendency for decision makers to choose the first available alternative that meets minimally acceptable standards.

■ **prospect theory**
the social psychological theory that international decision making is constrained by formed opinions and tendencies to overreact in crises, that decisions tend to be made based on the perceived prospects of choices to fulfill objectives, and that policymakers engage in risk-averse behavior in making choices about probable gains but are risk-acceptant when making choices about anticipated losses.

prospects for future gains—may account for leaders' reluctance to make and implement corrective policy decisions for fear of public criticism (Bostdorff 1993).

The assumption that states are unitary actors partially explains the discrepancy between the theory and practice of rational decision making. Most leaders must meet the often incompatible demands of domestic politics and external diplomacy, and it is seldom possible to make policy decisions that respond rationally to both sets of goals. Domestic policy traditionally referred to governmental decisions affecting people's behavior within the state's borders and foreign policy to external relations. However, in an age of globalization and state interdependence, it is often difficult to know where domestic policy ends and foreign policy begins. Policies at home often have many consequences abroad. Similarly, foreign activities usually heavily influence a state's internal condition. This is why many leaders are likely to fuse the two sectors in contemplating policy decisions.

To better capture the way most leaders proceed as they make policy decisions, Robert Putnam coined the phrase **two-level games.** Challenging the assumptions of realism, he asserted that leaders should formulate policies simultaneously in both the diplomatic and domestic arenas and should make those choices in accordance with the rules dictated by the "game."

> At the national level, domestic groups pursue their interests by pressuring the government to adopt favorable policies, and politicians seek power by constructing coalitions among these groups. At the international level, national governments seek to maximize their own ability to satisfy domestic pressures, while minimizing the adverse consequences of foreign developments. Neither of the two games can be ignored by central decision makers so long as their countries remain interdependent, yet sovereign. (Putnam 1988, 434)

In addition to the complications undermining the separation of foreign and domestic decision making, states are administered by individuals with varying beliefs, values, preferences, and psychological needs, and such differences generate disagreements about goals and alternatives that are seldom resolved through tidy, orderly, rational processes. These procedures may be better described as **muddling through,** or making incremental policy changes through small steps (Lindblom 1979). As one former U.S. policymaker put it, "Rather than through grand decisions or grand alternatives, policy changes seem to come through a series of slight modifications of existing policy, with new policy emerging slowly and haltingly by small and usually tentative steps, a process of trial and error in which policy zigs and zags, reverses itself, and then moves forward" (Hilsman 1967).

Despite the image that policymakers seek to project, the actual practice of foreign policy decision making is an exercise that lends itself to miscalculations, errors, and fiascoes. Policymakers tend "to avoid new interpretations of the environment, to select and act upon traditional goals, to limit the search for alternatives to a small number of moderate ones, and finally to take risks which involve low costs" (Coplin 1971). Thus, although policymakers can sometimes absorb new information quickly under great pressure and take calculated risks through deliberate planning, more often the degree of rationality "bears little relationship to the world in which officials conduct their deliberations" (Rosenau 1980).

■ **two-level games**
a concept referring to the growing need for national policymakers to make decisions that will meet both domestic and foreign goals.

■ **muddling through**
the tendency for leaders to make foreign policy decisions by trial-and-error adjustments in an attempt to cope with challenges.

TABLE 3.1

Foreign Policy Decision Making in Theory and Practice

Ideal Rational Process	*Actual Common Practice*
Accurate, comprehensive information	Distorted, incomplete information
Clear definition of national interests and goals	Personal motivations and organizational interests bias national goals
Exhaustive analysis of all options	Limited number of options considered; none thoroughly analyzed
Selection of optimal course of action for producing desired results	Course of action selected by political bargaining and compromise
Effective statement of decision and its rationale to mobilize domestic support	Confusing and contradictory statements of decision, often framed for media consumption
Careful monitoring of the decision's implementation by foreign affairs bureaucracies	Neglect of the tedious task of managing the decision's implementation by foreign affairs bureaucracies
Instantaneous evaluation of consequences followed by correction of errors	Superficial policy evaluation, uncertain responsibility, poor follow-through, and delayed correction

■ **constructivism**
a scholarly approach to inquiry emphasizing the importance of agents (people and goups) and the shared meanings they construct to define their identities, interests, and institutions— understandings that influence their behavior.

Indeed, **constructivism** advances a conception of decision makers as those individuals greatly shaped by the socially accepted shared understandings of national interests and foreign policy within their own policy-making community and culture and that these dominating ideas inevitably reduce their capacity to make fully rational choices.

Although rational foreign policy making is more an ideal than a reality, we can still assume that policymakers aspire to rational decision-making behavior, which they may occasionally approximate. Indeed, as a working proposition, it is useful to accept rationality as a picture of how the decision process *should* work as well as a description of key elements of how it *does* work (see Table 3.1).

THE BUREAUCRATIC POLITICS OF FOREIGN POLICY DECISION MAKING

Picture yourself as a head of state charged with managing your nation's relations with the rest of the world. To make the right choices, you must seek information and advice, and you must see that the actions your decisions generate are carried out properly. Who can aid you in these tasks? Out of necessity, you must turn to those with the expertise you lack.

In today's world, states' extensive political, military, and economic relations require dependence on large-scale organizations. Leaders turn to these organizations for information and advice as they face critical foreign policy choices. Although this is more true of major powers than of small states, even those without large budgets and complex foreign policy bureaucracies seldom make decisions without the advice and assistance of many individuals and administrative agencies (Korany 1986). Organizations perform vital services, enhancing the state's capacity to cope with changing global circumstances.

In the United States, for instance, the State Department, Defense Department, and Central Intelligence Agency are all key participants in the foreign policy machinery. Other agencies also bear responsibility for specialized aspects of U.S. foreign relations, such as the Treasury, Commerce, and Agriculture Departments. Similar agencies characterize the foreign affairs machinery of most other major powers, whose governments face many of the same foreign policy management challenges as the United States.

Bureaucratic Efficiency and Rationality

Bureaucratic management of foreign relations is not new. However, with the internationalization of domestic politics during the twentieth century, the growth of large-scale organizations to manage foreign relations has spread. Bureaucratic procedures based on the theoretical work of the German social scientist Max Weber are commonplace, primarily because they are perceived to enhance rational decision making and efficient administration.

Bureaucracies increase efficiency and rationality by assigning responsibility for different tasks to different people. They define rules and standard operating procedures that specify how tasks are to be performed; they rely on record systems to gather and store information; they divide authority among different organizations to avoid duplication of effort; and they often lead to meritocracies by hiring and promoting the most capable individuals. Bureaucracies also permit the luxury of engaging in forward planning designed to determine long-term needs and the means to attain them. Unlike heads of state, whose roles require attention to the crisis of the moment, bureaucrats are able to consider the future as well as the present. The presence of several organizations can also result in **multiple advocacy** of rival choices (George 1972), thus improving the chance that all possible policy options will be considered.

■ **bureaucracies**
the agencies, regulatory commissions, and departments that conduct the functions of a central government.

■ **multiple advocacy**
the concept that better and more rational choices are made when decisions are reached in a group context, which allows advocates of differing alternatives to be heard so that the feasibility of rival options receives critical evaluation.

The Limits of Bureaucratic Organization

What emerges from our description of bureaucracy is another idealized picture of the policy-making process. Before jumping to the conclusion that bureaucratic decision making is a modern blessing, however, we should emphasize that the foregoing propositions tell us how bureaucratic decision making should occur; they do not tell us how it does occur. The actual practice and the foreign policy choices that result reveal burdens to bureaucracy as well as benefits.

Consider again the 1962 Cuban Missile Crisis, probably the single most threatening crisis in the post–World War II era. The method that U.S. policymakers used in orchestrating a response is often viewed as having nearly approximated the ideal of rational choice. From another decision-making perspective, however, the missile crisis reveals how decision making by and within organizational contexts sometimes compromises rather than facilitates rational choice.

In his well-known book on the missile crisis, *Essence of Decision* (1971), Harvard political scientist Graham Allison identifies two elements in the **bureaucratic politics model** (see also Allison and Zelikow 1999; Caldwell

■ **bureaucratic politics model**
a description of decision making that sees foreign policy choices as based on bargaining and compromises among government agencies.

■ **policy networks**
leaders and organized interests (such as lobbies) that form temporary alliances to influence a particular foreign policy decision.

■ **caucuses**
informal groups that individuals in government join to promote their common interests.

■ **standard operating procedures (SOPs)**
rules for reaching decisions about particular types of situations.

1977; C. Hermann 1988). One, which he calls "organizational process," reflects the constraints that organizations and coalitions of organizations in **policy networks** place on decision makers' choices. The other, "governmental politics," draws attention to the "pulling and hauling" that occurs among the key participants and **caucuses** of aligned bureaucracies in the decision process.

One way in which large-scale bureaucratic organizations contribute to the policy-making process is by devising **standard operating procedures (SOPs)**—established methods to be followed in the performance of designated tasks. For example, once the Kennedy administration opted for a naval quarantine of Cuba, the Navy could carry out the president's decision according to previously devised procedures. These routines, however, effectively limit the range of viable policy choices. Rather than expanding the number of policy alternatives in a manner consistent with the logic of rational decision making, what organizations are prepared to do shapes what is and is not considered possible. In the Cuban crisis, a surgical air strike was seen as preferable to the blockade, but when the Air Force confessed that it could not guarantee complete success in taking out the missiles, the alternative was dropped.

Governmental politics, the second element in the bureaucratic politics model, is related to the organizational character of foreign policy making in complex societies. Not surprisingly, participants in the deliberations that lead to policy choices often define issues and favor policy alternatives that reflect their organizational affiliations. "Where you stand depends on where you sit" is a favorite aphorism reflecting these bureaucratic imperatives. Consequently, many students of governmental politics observe that professional diplomats typically favor diplomatic approaches to policy problems, while military officers routinely favor military solutions.

Because the players in the game of governmental politics are responsible for protecting the nation's security, they are "obliged to fight for what they are convinced is right." The consequence is that "different groups pulling in different directions produce a result, or better a resultant—a mixture of conflicting preferences and unequal power of various individuals—distinct from what any person or group intended" (Allison 1971). Rather than being a value-maximizing process, then, policy making is itself intensely political. Thus one explanation of why states make the choices they do lies not in their behavior vis-à-vis one another but within their own governments. And rather than presupposing the existence of a unitary actor, "it is necessary to identify the games and players, to display the coalitions, bargains, and compromises, and to convey some feel for the confusion" (Allison 1971). From this perspective, the decision to blockade Cuba was as much a product of who favored the choice as of any inherent logic that may have commended it. Once Robert Kennedy (the president's brother and the attorney general), Theodore Sorensen (the president's special counsel and "alter ego"), and Secretary of Defense Robert McNamara united behind the blockade, how could the president have chosen otherwise?

Governmental politics—fighting among insiders within an administration and the formation of factions to carry on battles over the direction of foreign policy decisions—are chronic in nearly every country (but especially in democracies accepting of participation by many people in the policy-making process). Consider again the United States. Splits among key advisors over important foreign policy choices have been frequent. For example, under presidents Nixon and Ford, Secretary of State Henry Kissinger fought often with James

Photo courtesy of White House/Getty Images

Collective Decision Making During crises that threaten a country's national security, decisions usually are made by the head of state and a small group of advisers rather than by large-scale bureaucracies. George W. Bush and advisers in the White House "Situation Room" make plans for war against Iraq in October 2002.

Schlesinger and Donald Rumsfeld, who headed the Department of Defense, over strategy regarding the Vietnam war; Jimmy Carter's national security advisor, Zbigniew Brzezinski, repeatedly engaged in conflicts with Secretary of State Cyrus Vance over the Iran hostage crisis; and under Ronald Reagan, Caspar Weinberger at Defense and George Shultz at State were famous for butting heads on most policy issues. Such conflicts are not necessarily bad because they force each side to better explain its viewpoint, and this allows heads of state the opportunity to weigh their competing advice before making decisions. However, battles among advisors can lead to paralysis and to rash decisions that produce poor results.

That possibility became evident more recently, in the fall of 2002, when serious divisions within George W. Bush's own administration developed over how and why the president's goal was to wage war against Saddam Hussein in Iraq. Fissures became transparent as key officials opened a debate in public over how best to invade another country, or even the wisdom of an invasion as opposed to the continuation of containment through diplomacy. On one side emerged an influential cabal of superhawks, the so-called get Saddam hardliners eager to use America's overwhelming military power and unconcerned about the reactions of long-time U.S. allies to such an unilateral military undertaking. Beating the war drums were Defense Secretary Donald Rumsfeld and his Deputy Paul Wolfowitz, supported by Vice President Dick Cheney and Chair of the Pentagon Defense Policy Board Richard Perle, as well as House Majority Whip Tom Delay, a conservative Republican Congressman.

Opposing a military invasion to solve a political problem were Secretary of State Colin Powell, who rejected a preemptive strike without provocation to overthrow a foreign leader whose acquisition of weapons of mass destruction and support for the 9/11 terrorist attacks had not been established. Backing Powell were a coalition of unlikely critics of the president's war goals. They included Dick Armey, the top Republican house majority leader, who warned that "If we try to act against Saddam Hussein, as obnoxious as he is, without proper provocation, we will not have the support of other nation states [and] an unprovoked attack on another nation would not be consistent with what we have been as a nation or what we should be as a nation."

Weighing in on the critique was former Secretary of State Larry Eagleburger in the first Bush administration, who counseled that no action should be taken until proof is presented that Saddam has his finger on the trigger of nuclear or other weapons of mass destruction. Former President Bush's most trusted national security advisors, Brent Scowcroft and James A. Baker III, also sided with the doves in the battle for the president's ear, with Mr. Scowcroft arguing that "Saddam's goals have little in common with the terrorists who threaten us" and that the Iraqi leader would not risk nuclear blackmail because he is a "power-hungry survivor" who knows America's response would be devastating.

In one way or another, those questioning President George W. Bush's war plans all reflected Colin Powell's qualms, based on his experience as a general in the U. S. Army about the unacceptable costs of an ill-considered war. As Powell (the only combat veteran among Bush's senior aides) wrote in *My American Journey*, "Many of my generation, the career captains, majors, and lieutenant colonels seasoned in that war, vowed that when our turn came to call the shots, we would not acquiesce in half-hearted warfare for half-baked reasons that the American people could not understand or support."

As rumors of war spread and the intergovernmental debate between these two opposed groups of policymakers and advisors intensified, the national security policy-making decision process fell into disarray. The battle in Washington dominated the headlines, and the president had difficulty fulfilling the promise he made in his January 2002 State of the Union Address: "We'll be deliberate." Looking askance at what he termed "the Babel over Babylon," Fareed Zakaria (2002b), the former editor of *Foreign Affairs*, summarized the disturbing way in which a major foreign policy decision about war was unfolding, and the bureaucratic bases for its clumsy processes, when he concluded that "The reason for this seeming irrationality is that the real target of Cheney's and Rumsfeld's efforts is not Saddam Hussein but Colin Powell. Their strategy is a bureaucratic one, designed to box in a colleague rather than Iraq's dictator. Parlor politics have trumped power politics in the Bush administration." "There's no question that the world would be a better place without Saddam's regime," observed Samuel R. Berger, President Bill Clinton's national security advisor," but "if we don't do this operation right, we could end up with something worse. We need to be clear and open about the stakes, the risks and the costs that genuine success—meaning a more secure America and a more secure world—will require." The obstacles to that kind of calculated rational decisionmaking are illuminated further by examining more closely the characteristics of bureaucratic behavior.

Attributes of Bureaucratic Behavior

In addition to their influence on the policy choices of political leaders, bureaucratic organizations possess several other characteristics that affect decision making. One view proposes that bureaucratic agencies are parochial and that every administrative unit within a state's foreign policy-making bureaucracy seeks to promote its own purposes and power. Organizational needs, such as large staffs and budgets, come before the state's needs, sometimes encouraging the sacrifice of national interests to bureaucratic interests, as bureaucrats come to see their own interests as the state's. Bureaucracies fight for survival, even when their usefulness has vanished.

> Programs that don't concoct some new argument or other for their continuing indispensability also tend to survive. This is because of [an] immutable law of government: even the most anachronistic, abysmal, extravagant and counterproductive government program will do at least one thing that is hard to assault. (Greenfield 1995)

Bureaucratic parochialism breeds competition among the agencies charged with foreign policy responsibilities. Far from being neutral or impartial managers, desiring only to carry out orders from the head of state, bureaucratic organizations frequently take policy positions designed to increase their own influence relative to that of other agencies. Characteristically, they are driven to enlarge their prerogatives and expand the conception of their mission, seeking to take on other units' responsibilities and powers.

The tragic surprise terrorist attack on September 11, 2001 (9/11) provides a telling example of these ascribed characteristics of bureaucratic politics. 9/11 was regarded by many as the worst intelligence failure since Pearl Harbor. U.S. intelligence agencies, it was later discovered, received numerous reports before 9/11 that terrorists were planning to attack the United States, and that the use of hijacked airliners as weapons was a strategy; two months before September 11, a CIA briefing warned President Bush, "We believe that bin Laden will launch a significant terrorist attack against U.S. or Israeli interests in the coming weeks. The attack will be spectacular and designed to inflict mass casualties." Alarmed U.S. citizens asked, why, with an enormous army of agencies gathering intelligence, weren't the multitude of messages and warnings about the attack on September 11 on the World Trade Center and the Pentagon translated in time to prevent the disaster? Why weren't those dots connected? Why were the warnings ignored? The answer accepted by most analysts was that America's chaotic system of intelligence was paralyzed by the morass of cross-cutting bureaucracies responsible, who engaged in turf battles with one another and did not share the vital information with each other that arguably could have identified the Al Qaeda plot and prevented it. The problem was miscommunication and noncommunication; the signals about the attack were not forwarded to the executive branch in time. Why? Morton Abramowitz, a former assistant secretary of state in the Reagan administration, offered in August 2002 this explanation:

> Three features pervade the making of foreign policy in Washington today: massive overload, internal warfare and the short term driving out the long

term. These problems exist in every administration. They are worse in this one. . . . In the war on terrorism [George W. Bush] has embarked on a huge overhaul of the government and bureaucracy that promises uncertain benefits, at least in the short run while demanding significant attention to detail, turf battles and congressional consultations. Running foreign policy is a challenge in any era. Running it with the additional problems generated by September 11 is a feat. Moreover, while the clash of views is healthy and often produces better policy, this foreign policy team is beset by internal wars. . . . War is fought daily in the high-level bureaucratic trenches; ideology is very much in play. And that infighting has accentuated stasis or inconsistencies in both policies and rhetoric.

What this episode revealed is the extent of the crippling effects of struggles within and between bureaucracies. In the case of the United States, more than fifty units of government are involved with national security policy, and agencies like the CIA, the FBI, and the INS in the State Department are habitually loath to share information with each other for fear of compromising "sources and methods." Each agency competes with its rivals and engages in finger pointing and scapegoating as a blood sport. Moreover, as FBI Special Agent Coleen Rowley testified in June 2002, "There's a mutual-protection pact in bureaucracies. Mid-level managers avoid decisions out of fear a mistake will sidetrack their careers while a rigid hierarchy discourages agents from challenging superiors. There is a saying: 'Big cases, big problems; little cases, little problems; no cases, no problems.' The idea that inaction is the key to success manifests itself repeatedly" (Toner 2002). These types of problems are difficult to control, and few students of public administration believe that they can automatically be overcome through massive reorganization and restructuring. That is why critics of President George W. Bush's plan to create a new Department of Homeland Security were doubtful about its prospects for infusing greater rationality into national security policy in general and counterterrorism in particular. Sympathizing with the fact that "Mr. Bush is somewhat in the position of trying to steer an 80,000-ton supertanker with nothing more substantial that a sail boat rudder," George Melloan (2002a) noted that through creation of a Homeland Security Department President Bush was "no doubt hoping that in the process he could rationalize some of those [decision making] efforts [but that] given the national tendency of bureaucrats to expand their remits, he will be lucky if he doesn't end up with more duplication and dead-weight than he has now. As Ronald Reagan once commented, 'a government bureau is the nearest thing to eternal life we'll ever see on this earth.'"

When put into perspective, we discern some key properties of bureaucratic politics. Among them, we see especially that bureaucratic organizations seek to protect their own interests. They attempt to reduce interference from and penetration by the political leaders to whom they report as well as from other government agencies. Because knowledge is power, a common device for promoting organizational exclusivity is to hide inner workings and policy activities from others. The "invisible government" operating within the U.S. National Security Council during the Reagan administration illustrates this syndrome. Lieutenant Colonel Oliver North used his authority as a staff member of the council to orchestrate a secret arms-for-hostages deal with the Iranian government, part of what became popularly known as the Iran-Contra Affair.

The natural inclination of professionals who work in large organizations is to adapt their outlook and beliefs to those prevailing where they work. Every bureaucracy develops a shared "mind-set" or dominant way of looking at reality akin to the **groupthink** characteristic that small groups often develop (Janis 1982). An institutional mind-set or socially constructed consensus discourages creativity, dissent, and independent thinking; it encourages reliance on standard operating procedures and deference to precedent rather than the exploration of new options to meet new challenges. This results in policy decisions that rarely deviate from conventional preferences.

■ **groupthink**
the propensity for members of a group to accept and agree with the group's prevailing attitudes, rather than speaking out for what they believe (see p. 411).

The Consequences of Bureaucratic Policy Making

A corollary of the notion that bureaucracies are often self-serving and guardians of the status quo is the idea that they defy directives by the political authorities they are supposed to serve. To thwart unpopular demands by authorities, bureaucracies often slow down and act inefficiently. At other times, bureaucratic sabotage is direct and immediate, again as vividly illustrated by the Cuban Missile Crisis. While President Kennedy sought to orchestrate U.S. action and bargaining, his bureaucracy in general, and the navy in particular, were in fact controlling events by doing as they wished.

> [The bureaucracy chose] to obey the orders it liked and ignore or stretch others. Thus, after a tense argument with the navy, Kennedy ordered the blockade line moved closer to Cuba so that the Russians might have more time to draw back. Having lost the argument with the president, the navy simply ignored his order. Unbeknownst to Kennedy, the navy was also at work forcing Soviet submarines to surface long before Kennedy authorized any contact with Soviet ships. And despite the president's order to halt all provocative intelligence, an American U–2 plane entered Soviet airspace at the height of the crisis. When Kennedy began to realize that he was not in full control, he asked his secretary of defense to see if he could find out just what the navy was doing. McNamara then made his first visit to the navy command post in the Pentagon. In a heated exchange, the chief of naval operations suggested that McNamara return to his office and let the navy run the blockade. (Gelb and Halperin 1973, 256)

Bureaucratic resistance is not the only inertial force promoting status quo foreign policies. The dynamics of governmental politics, which reduce policy choices to the outcome of a political tug of war, also retard the prospects for change. From the perspective of the participants, decision making is a high-stakes political game in which differences are often settled at the least common denominator instead of by rational cost-benefit calculations. As former U.S. Secretary of State Henry Kissinger described the process:

> Each of the contending factions within the bureaucracy has a maximum incentive to state its case in its most extreme form because the ultimate outcome depends, to a considerable extent, on a bargaining process. The premium placed on advocacy turns decision making into a series of adjustments among special interests—a process more suited to domestic than to foreign policy. . . . The outcome usually depends more on the pressure or the persuasiveness of the contending advocates than on a concept of overall purpose. (Kissinger 1969, 268)

Thus it is not surprising that bureaucracies throughout the world are frequently the object of criticism by both the political leaders they ostensibly serve and the citizens whose lives they so often affect.

THE ROLE OF LEADERS IN FOREIGN POLICY DECISION MAKING

The course of history is determined by the decisions of political elites. Leaders and the kind of leadership they exert shape the way in which foreign policies are made and the consequent behavior of states in world politics. "There is properly no history, only biography" is the way Ralph Waldo Emerson encapsulated the view that individual leaders move history.

Leaders as Makers and Movers of World History

■ **history-making individuals model**
an interpretation of foreign policy behavior that equates states' actions with the preferences and initiatives of the highest government officials.

This **history-making individuals model** of policy decision making equates states' actions with the preferences and initiatives of the highest government officials. We expect leaders to lead, and we assume new leaders will make a difference. We reinforce this image when we routinely attach the names of leaders to policies—as though the leaders were synonymous with the state itself—as well as when we ascribe most successes and failures in foreign affairs to the leaders in charge at the time they occur. The equation of U.S. foreign policy with the **Nixon Doctrine** in the 1970s, the **Reagan Doctrine** in the 1980s, the **Clinton Doctrine** in the 1990s, and the **Bush Doctrine** in 2001 are recent examples.

■ **Nixon Doctrine**
President Richard Nixon's position that U.S. allies should bear a greater share of the burden for their defense.

Citizens are not alone in thinking that leaders are the decisive determinants of states' foreign policies and, by extension, world history. Leaders themselves seek to create impressions of their own self-importance while attributing extraordinary powers to other leaders. The assumptions they make about the personalities of their counterparts, consciously or unconsciously, in turn influence their own behavior (Wendzel 1980), as political psychologists who study the impact of leaders' perceptions and personalities on their foreign policy preferences demonstrate (see Kelman 1965).

■ **Reagan Doctrine**
the Reagan administration's pledge of U.S. support for anticommunist insurgents who sought to overthrow Soviet-supported governments.

One of the dilemmas that leader-driven explanations of foreign policy behavior pose is that history's movers and shakers often pursue decidedly irrational policies. The classic example is Adolf Hitler, whose ruthless determination to seek military conquest of the entire European continent proved disastrous for Germany. How do we square this kind of behavior with the logic of realism, which says that survival is the paramount goal of all states and that all leaders engage in rational decision making? If the realists are correct, even defects in states' foreign policy processes cannot easily explain such wide divergences between the decisions leaders sometimes make and what cold cost-benefit calculations would predict.

■ **Clinton Doctrine**
the Clinton administration's policy of active engagement in world affairs to support enlargement of the peaceful liberal democratic community.

■ **Bush Doctrine**
the unilateral policies of the George W. Bush administration proclaiming that the United States will make decisions only to meet America's perceived national interests, not to concede to other countries' complaints or gain their acceptance.

We can explain this divergence in part by distinguishing between procedural rationality and instrumental rationality (Zagare 1990). **Procedural rationality** is the foundation of the realists' billiard ball image of world politics. It views all states as acting similarly because all decision makers engage in the same "cool and clearheaded ends-means calculation" (Verba 1969) based on a careful weighing of all possible alternative courses of action. **Instrumental**

■ **procedural rationality**
a method of decision making based on having perfect information and carefully weighing all possible courses of action.

rationality is a more limited view, which says simply that individuals have preferences and, when faced with two or more alternatives, they will choose the one they believe will yield the preferred outcome.

The implications of these seemingly semantic differences are important. The idea of instrumental rationality demonstrates that rationality does not "connote superhuman calculating ability, omniscience, or an Olympian view of the world," as is often assumed when the rational-actor model we have described is applied to real-world situations (Zagare 1990). They also suggest that an individual's actions may be rational even though the process of decision making and its product may appear decidedly irrational. Why did Libya's leader, the mercurial Muammar Qaddafi, repeatedly challenge the United States, almost goading President Ronald Reagan into a military strike in 1986? Because, we can postulate, Qaddafi's actions were consistent with his preferences, regardless of how "irrational" it was for a fourth-rate military power to take on the world's preeminent superpower. This and many other examples serve as a reminder of the importance of the human factor in understanding how decisions are made. Temptation, lack of self-control, anger, fear of getting hurt, religious conviction, bad habits, and overconfidence all play a part in determining why people make the kinds of decisions they do.

■ **instrumental rationality**
a conceptualization of rationality that emphasizes the tendency of decision makers to compare options with one another and select the one that has the best chance of success.

Factors Affecting the Capacity to Lead

Despite the popularity of the history-making individuals model, we must be wary of ascribing too much importance to individual leaders. Their influence is likely to be subtler, a probability summarized by U.S. President Bill Clinton in 1998 when he observed, "Great presidents don't do great things. Great presidents get a lot of other people to do great things." Henry Kissinger, once described as "the most powerful individual in the world in the 1970s" (Isaak 1975), in a commencement address at the University of South Carolina in May 1985 urged against placing too much reliance on personalities:

> [There is] a profound American temptation to believe that foreign policy is a subdivision of psychiatry and that relations among nations are like relations among people. But the problem [of easing protracted conflicts between states] is not so simple. Tensions . . . must have some objective causes, and unless we can remove these causes, no personal relationship can possibly deal with them. We are [not] doing . . . ourselves a favor by reducing the issues to a contest of personalities.

Most leaders operate under a variety of political, psychological, and circumstantial constraints that limit what they can accomplish and reduce their control over events. In this context, Emmet John Hughes (1972), an adviser to President Dwight D. Eisenhower, concluded that "all of [America's past presidents] from the most venturesome to the most reticent have shared one disconcerting experience: the discovery of the limits and restraints—decreed by law, by history, and by circumstances—that sometimes can blur their clearest designs or dull their sharpest purposes." Abraham Lincoln in 1864 summarized his presidential experience with the conclusion, "I have not controlled events, events have controlled me."

The question at issue is not whether political elites lead or whether they can make a difference. They clearly do both. But leaders are not in complete control, and their influence is severely constrained. Thus personality and personal political preferences do not determine foreign policy directly. The relevant question, then, is not whether leaders' personal characteristics make a difference, but rather under what conditions their characteristics are influential. As Margaret G. Hermann has observed, the impact of leaders is modified by at least six factors:

> (1) what their world view is, (2) what their political style is like, (3) what motivates them to have the position they do, (4) whether they are interested in and have any training in foreign affairs, (5) what the foreign policy climate was like when the leader was starting out his or her political career, and (6) how the leader was socialized into his or her present position. World view, political style, and motivation tell us something about the leader's personality; the other characteristics give information about the leader's previous experiences and background. (Hermann 1988, 268)

The impact of leaders' personal characteristics on their state's foreign policy generally increases when their authority and legitimacy are widely accepted by citizens or, in authoritarian or totalitarian regimes, when leaders are protected from broad public criticism. Moreover, certain circumstances enhance individuals' potential influence. Among them are new situations that free leaders from conventional approaches to defining the situation; complex situations involving many different factors; and situations without social sanctions, which permit freedom of choice because norms defining the range of permissible options are unclear (DiRenzo 1974).

■ **political efficacy**
the extent to which policymakers' self-confidence instills in them the belief that they can effectively make rational choices.

A leader's **political efficacy** or self-image—that person's belief in his or her own ability to control events politically—combined with the citizenry's relative desire for leadership, will also influence the degree to which personal values and psychological needs govern decision making (DeRivera 1968). For example, when public opinion strongly favors a powerful leader, and when the head of state has an exceptional need for admiration, foreign policy will more likely reflect that leader's inner needs. Thus Kaiser Wilhelm II's narcissistic personality allegedly met the German people's desire for a symbolically powerful leader, and German public preferences in turn influenced the foreign policy that Germany pursued during Wilhelm's reign, ending in World War I (Baron and Pletsch 1985).

Other factors undoubtedly influence how much leaders can shape their states' choices. For instance, when leaders believe that their own interests and welfare are at stake, they tend to respond in terms of their private needs and psychological drives. When circumstances are stable, however, and when leaders' egos are not entangled with policy outcomes, the influence of their personal characteristics is less apparent.

The amount of information available about a particular situation is also important. Without pertinent information, policy is likely to be based on leaders' personal likes or dislikes. Conversely, the more information leaders have about international affairs, the more likely they are to engage in rational decision making (Verba 1969).

Similarly, the timing of a leader's assumption of power is significant. When an individual first assumes a leadership position, the formal requirements of that role are least likely to restrict what he or she can do. That is especially true during the "honeymoon" period routinely given to new heads of state, during which time they are relatively free of criticism and excessive pressure. Moreover, when a leader assumes office following a dramatic event (a landslide election, for example, or the assassination of a predecessor), he or she can institute policies almost with a free hand, as "constituency criticism is held in abeyance during this time" (Hermann 1976).

A national crisis is a potent circumstance that increases a leader's control over foreign policy making. Decision making during crises is typically centralized and handled exclusively by the top leadership. Crucial information is often unavailable, and leaders see themselves as responsible for outcomes. Not surprisingly, great leaders (e.g., Napoleon Bonaparte, Winston Churchill, and Franklin D. Roosevelt) customarily emerge during periods of extreme tumult. A crisis can liberate a leader from the constraints that normally would inhibit his or her capacity to control events or engineer foreign policy change.

History abounds with examples of the seminal importance of political leaders who emerge in different times and places and under different circumstances to play critical roles in shaping world history. Mikhail Gorbachev dramatically illustrates an individual's capacity to change the course of history. Many experts believe that the Cold War could not have been brought to an end, nor Communist Party rule in Moscow terminated and the Soviet state set on a path toward democracy and free enterprise, had it not been for Gorbachev's vision, courage, and commitment to engineering these revolutionary, system-transforming changes. Ironically, those reforms led to his loss of power when the Soviet Union imploded in 1991.

Refinements to the History-Making Individuals Model

Having said that the history-making individuals model may be compelling, we must be cautious and remember that leaders are not all-powerful determinants of states' foreign policy behavior. Rather, their personal influence varies with the context, and often the context is more influential than the leader (see Controversy: Policy and Personality: Do Leaders Make a Difference?). The "great person" versus **zeitgeist** (spirit of the times) debate is pertinent here. At the core of this enduring controversy is the question of whether certain times are conducive to the emergence of leaders or whether famous leaders would have an impact whenever and wherever they lived (see Greenstein 1987). That question may be unanswerable but it reminds us at least that multiple factors affect states' foreign policy decisions. The history-making individuals model alone appears too simple an explanation of how states react to challenges from abroad.

■ **zeitgeist**
the "spirit of the times," or the dominant cultural norms assumed to influence the behavior of people living in particular periods.

CONSTRAINTS ON FOREIGN POLICY MAKING: PROBLEMS AND PROSPECTS

Can states respond to the demands that external challenges and internal politics simultaneously place on their leaders? For many reasons, that capability is increasingly strained.

Foreign policy choice occurs in an environment of uncertainty and multiple, competing interests. On occasion, it is also made in situations when policymakers

POLICY AND PERSONALITY: DO LEADERS MAKE A DIFFERENCE?

Some theorists, such as **neorealists,** embrace the assumption of rationality and assume that any leader will respond to a choice in the same way: the situation structures the reaction to the existing costs and benefits of any choice. But does this assumption square with the facts? What do we know about the impact of people's perceptions and values on the way they view choices? Political psychology tells us that the same option is likely to have different value to different leaders. Does this mean that different leaders would respond differently to similar situations?

Consider the example of Richard Nixon. In 1971, Americans took to the streets outside the White House to protest the immorality of Nixon's massive bombing of Vietnam. His reaction to this perceived threat was to shield himself from the voice of the people, without success, as it happened. Nixon complained that "nobody can know what it means for a president to be sitting in that White House working late at night and to have hundreds of thousands of demonstrators charging through the streets. Not even earplugs could block the noise."

Earlier, on a rainy afternoon in 1962, John F. Kennedy faced a similar citizen protest. Americans had gathered in front of the White House for a Ban the Bomb demonstration. His response was to send out urns of coffee and doughnuts and invite the leaders of the protest to come inside to state their case, believing that a democracy should encourage dissent and debate.

Nixon saw protesters as a threat; Kennedy saw them as an opportunity. This comparison suggests that the type of leader can make a difference in determining the kinds of choices likely to be made in response to similar situations. More important than each president's treatment of the protesters, however, was whether he actually changed his policy decisions based on the protests. Although Kennedy was hospitable to protest-ers, he did not ban nuclear weapons; in fact, military spending under Kennedy grew to consume half of the federal budget. Many would protest that Kennedy alone could not be expected to eliminate nuclear weapons—that the zeitgeist was dominated by fear of the Soviet Union and intense concern for national security. The protesters in 1971, however, were more in keeping with the spirit of the times. Although they alone may not have persuaded Nixon to alter his policies in Vietnam, widespread protest and discontentment with the war, as well as America's inability to win, eventually prompted Nixon to order the gradual withdrawal of U.S. troops, ending American participation in the Vietnam War. These outcomes suggest that leaders are captive to zeitgeist, or larger forces that drive international relations in their times.

What do you think? Did Kennedy and Nixon choose courses of action that reflected who they were as individuals? Or would any president in their respective eras have made similar choices?

AP/Wide World

■ **neorelism**
theoritical account of states' behavior as determined by differences in their relative power (see p. 39).

are caught by surprise and a quick decision is needed. Preoccupied with sunk costs, short-run results, and postdecisional rationalization, the stress these conditions produce impairs leaders' cognitive abilities and may cause them to react emotionally rather than analytically.

The trends and transformations currently unfolding in world politics are the products of countless decisions made daily throughout the world. Some decisions are more consequential than others, and some actors are more important than others. Throughout history, great powers such as the United States have at times stood at the center of the world political stage, possessing the combination of natural resources, military might, and the means to project power worldwide that earned them great-power status. How such major powers have responded to one another has had profound consequences for the entire drama of world politics. To better understand this, we turn our attention next to the dynamics of great-power rivalry on the world stage.

KEY TERMS

actor	end of history	bureaucratic politics model
state sovereignty	democratic peace	policy networks
state	neoliberalism	caucuses
nation	global level of analysis	standard operating procedures
foreign policy	unitary actor	(SOPs)
levels of analysis	rational choice	groupthink
intermestic	bounded rationality	history-making individuals model
globalization	cognitive dissonance	Nixon Doctrine
states' attributes	policy agenda	Reagan Doctrine
imperialism	satisficing	Clinton Doctrine
geopolitics	prospect theory	Bush Doctrine
gross national product (GNP)	two-level games	procedural rationality
constitutional democracy	muddling through	instrumental rationality
autocratic rule	contructivism	political efficacy
elitism	bureaucracies	zeitgeist
pluralism	multiple advocacy	neorealism
diversionary theory of war		

SUGGESTED READING

Allison, Graham, and Philip Zelikow. *Essence of Decision: Explaining the Cuban Missile Crisis,* 2nd ed. New York: Longman, 1999.

Hagan, Joe D., and Margaret G. Hermann. *Leaders, Groups, Coalitions: Understanding the People and Processes in Foreign Policymaking.* Boston: Blackwell, 2001.

Hermann, Charles F., Charles W. Kegley, Jr., and James N. Rosenau, eds. *New Directions in the Study of Foreign Policy.* Boston: Allen & Unwin, 1987.

Hermann, Margaret G., and Bengt Sundelius, eds. *Comparative Foreign Policy Analysis: Theories and Methods.* Upper Saddle River, N.J.: Prentice Hall, 2004.

Kegley, Charles W., Jr., and Gregory A. Raymond. *From War to Peace: Fateful Decisions in International Politics.* Boston: Bedford/St. Martin's, 2002.

Korany, Bahgat. *How Foreign Policy Decisions Are Made in the Third World.* Boulder, Colo.: Westview Press, 1986.

Kubalkova, Vendulka, ed. *Foreign Policy in a Constructed World.* London: M. E. Sharpe, 2001.

Levy, Jack S. "Prospect Theory, Rational Choice, and International Relations," *International Studies Quarterly* (March 1997): 87–112.

Marqaudt, Michael J., and Nancy O. Berger. *Global Leaders for the Twenty-First Century.* Albany: State University of New York Press, 2001.

Ray, James Lee. *Democracies and International Conflict*. Columbia: University of South Carolina Press, 1995.

Snyder, Richard C., H. W. Bruck and Burton Sapin. *Foreign Policy Decision Making (Revisited)*. London: Palgrave, 2003.

t'Hart, Paul, Eric K. Stern, and Bengt Sundelius, eds. *Beyond Groupthink: Political Group Dynamics and Foreign Policy-Making*. Ann Arbor: University of Michigan Press, 1997.

Wittkopf, Eugene R., Charles W. Kegley, Jr., and James M. Scott. *American Foreign Policy: Pattern and Process*, 6th ed. Belmont, Calif.: Wadsworth/ Thomson Learning, 2003.

WHERE ON THE WORLD WIDE WEB?

Cuban Missile Crisis
http://hyperion.advanced.org/11046/

The Cuban Missile Crisis is often cited as an event that brought the superpowers to the brink of nuclear war. This site provides an in-depth account and analysis of the crisis and the actors and issues involved. Read dossiers of the primary players, hear segments of the ExComm meeting, and see U-2 spy plane photos. At the end, take an online quiz to see how well you understand the crisis.

Freedom, Democracy, Peace; Power, Democide, and War
http://www2.hawaii.edu/~rummel/

The democratic peace theory presented in Chapter 3 contends that "although democratic states sometimes wage wars against other states, they do not fight each other." (see pp. 69–73). Political scientist Rudolph J. Rummel has devoted his career to research on the causes and conditions of collective violence and war with a view toward helping bring about their resolution or elimination; he supports the democratic peace proposition. Visit his Web site to analyze his work. What evidence do you think supports the democratic peace proposition? How persuasive are his arguments? *Caution:* Some of the pictures on the site contain graphic violence.

Freedom House
http://www.freedomhouse.org/

Founded by Eleanor Roosevelt and Wendell Willkie, this nonprofit organization focuses on threats to peace and democracy. Each year since 1972, Freedom House has published comparative ratings for countries and territories around the world, evaluating levels of political rights and civil liberties. Map 3.2 (p. 72) in your text uses data on the spread of democratic liberty throughout the world provided by Freedom House. Examine specific countries' "freedom records." Which have radically improved? Why do you think this is so?

The Presidents: PBS's *The American Experience*
http://www.pbs.org/wgbh/amex/presidents/indexjs.html

This inclusive Web site features some of the most prominent U.S. presidents of the twentieth century, including Theodore Roosevelt, Franklin Roosevelt, Dwight Eisenhower, Harry Truman, John Kennedy, Lyndon Johnson, Richard Nixon, and Ronald Reagan. Sections focus on the U.S. foreign policy achievements of each president. Chapter 3 introduces the history-making individuals model of government that equates a state's foreign policy with the preferences and initiatives of the highest government officials. Familiarize yourself with the foreign policy achievements of some U.S. presidents. Do you believe the history-making individuals model is a legitimate explanation of foreign policy? What are the limits to the model?

INFOTRAC® COLLEGE EDITION

Meagher, Michael R. "In an Atmosphere of National Peril: The Development of John F. Kennedy's World View," *Presidential Studies Quarterly* Summer 1997.

Pious, Richard M. "The Cuban Missile Crisis and the Limits of Crisis Management," *Political Science Quarterly* Spring 2001.

Hoekstra, Douglas J. "Presidential Beliefs and the Reagan Paradox," *Presidential Studies Quarterly* Summer 1997.

Rhodes, Edward. "Do Bureaucratic Politics Matter? Some Discomfiting Findings from the Case of the U.S. Navy," *World Politics* October 1994.

For more articles, enter:

"John F. Kennedy" in the Subject Guide, and then go to subdivision "military policy."

"Ronald Reagan" in the Subject Guide, and then go to subdivision "military policy."

"bureaucratic politics" in Keywords.

GREAT-POWER RIVALRIES AND RELATIONS

T O P I C S   A N D   T H E M E S

- The quest for great-power hegemony
  Long-cycle theory
  Hegemonic stability theory
- The causes and consequences of World War I
  Structuralism
  Rational choice and great-power relations
- The causes and consequences of World War II
- The causes and consequences of the Cold War
- The future of great-power politics: A cold peace?

- **CONTROVERSY** WAS IDEOLOGY THE PRIMARY SOURCE OF EAST-WEST CONFLICT?
- **CONTROVERSY** WAS MILITARY CONTAINMENT NECESSARY?
- **CONTROVERSY** WHY DID THE COLD WAR END PEACEFULLY?

The Big Three (Winston Churchill, Franklin Roosevelt, and Joseph Stalin) discuss peace at Yalta, 1945.

America's most enduring contribution to world affairs is that it is not like the other great powers of history, which routinely used force to impose their will. This is an extraordinarily important legacy. If it is abandoned in favor of hegemony—obsessed power politics, America will lose its exceptionalism and become just today's biggest boy on the block.

—JONATHAN CLARKE, British diplomat, 2001

The United States has been described as bestriding the world like a colossus. Looking more closely, we see that U.S. dominance varies across realms and that many relationships of interdependence go both ways. . . . Over the longer term, we can expect globalization itself to spread technological and economic capabilities and thus reduce the extent of U.S. dominance.

—JOSEPH S. NYE, JR., former U.S. Undersecretary of state, 2002

W ho's number one? Who's gaining on the leader? What does it mean for the future if the strongest is seriously challenged for predominant position?

These are the kinds of questions sports fans often ask when the rankings of the top teams are adjusted after the preceding week's competition. World leaders also adopt what former U.S. Secretary of State Dean Rusk once called a "football stadium approach to diplomacy." And many people throughout the world habitually make comparisons of countries, asking which states are the biggest, strongest, wealthiest, and most militarily powerful and evaluating which states are rising and which are falling relative to one another. When making such rankings, both groups are looking at world politics through the lens of realism. They see a globe of competitors, with winners and losers in an ancient contest for supremacy. And they look most closely at the shifting rankings at the very top of the international hierarchy of power—at the rivalry and struggle among the "great powers." Moreover, they picture this conflict as continual. As Arnold J. Toynbee's (1954) famous cyclical theory of history explains: "The most emphatic punctuation in a uniform series of events recurring in one repetitive cycle after another is the outbreak of a great war in which one power that has forged ahead of all its rivals makes so formidable a bid for world domination that it evokes an opposing coalition of all the other powers."

Toynbee's conclusion lies at the center of realism. The starting point for understanding world politics, maintains Hans J. Morgenthau (1985), the leading post–World War II classical realist theorist, is to recognize that "all history shows that nations active in international politics are continuously preparing for, actively involved in, or recovering from organized violence in the form of war." Cycles of war and peace colored twentieth-century world politics, with three global wars breaking out. World Wars I and II were fought with fire and blood; the Cold War was fought by less-destructive means but with equal intensity. Each of these three global wars set in motion major transformations in world politics, and have set the stage for the unfolding twenty-first century. In this chapter we explore the causes and consequences of these past great-power rivalries and their implications for the future. By examining their origins and impact, we can better anticipate whether in the twenty-first century the great powers will again fail to control their rivalries, and the world will once again experience the dangerous possibility of another global war.

THE QUEST FOR GREAT-POWER HEGEMONY

Great-power war was not unique to the twentieth century. Changes in the balance of power over the past five hundred years have regularly preceded war's outbreak (see Chapter 11). For this reason, the relationship between the great powers' rise and fall and global instability is a core concern in theories of world politics.

One viewpoint, **long-cycle theory,** seeks to explain why over the past five centuries periods of war have been followed by periods of peace, with shifts in the cycle usually occurring in concert with changes in the major states' relative power (see Modelski and Thompson 1999). During this long cycle, each global war led to the emergence of a victorious **hegemon,** a dominant global leader capable of dictating the rules governing the conduct of international political and economic relations (see Nye 2001). With its acquisition of unrivaled power, the hegemon reshapes the existing system by creating and enforcing rules to preserve its own dominant position, exercising power to maintain, for its own benefit, order in the global system.

Hegemony characteristically imposes an extraordinary tax on the world leader, which must bear the costs of maintaining economic and political order while protecting its position and preserving its empire. In time, as the weight of global responsibilities takes its toll, new rivals rise to challenge the increasingly vulnerable world leader. Historically, this struggle for power has set the stage for another global war, the demise of one hegemon and the ascent of another.

■ **long-cycle theory**
a theory that focuses on the rise and fall of the leading global power as the central political process of the modern world system

■ **hegemon**
a single, overwhelmingly powerful state that exercises predominate influence over the global system (see p. 422)

TABLE 4.1

The Evolution of Great-Power Rivalry for World Leadership, 1495–2025

Dates	Preponderant State(s) Seeking Hegemony	Other Powers Resisting Domination	Global War	New Order after Global War
1495–1540	Portugal	Spain, Valois, France, Burgundy, England, Venice	Wars of Italy and the Indian Ocean, 1494–1517	Treaty of Tordesillas, 1517
1560–1609	Spain	The Netherlands, France, England	Spanish-Dutch Wars, 1580–1608	Truce of 1609; Evangelical Union and the Catholic League formed
1610–1648	Holy Roman Empire (Hapsburg dynasty in Spain and Austria-Hungary)	Shifting ad hoc coalitions of mostly Protestant states (Sweden, Holland) and German principalities as well as Catholic France against remnants of papal rule	Thirty Years' War, 1618–1648	Peace of Westphalia, 1648
1650–1713	France (Louis XIV)	The United Provinces, England, the Hapsburg Empire, Spain, major German states, Russia	Wars of the Grand Alliance, 1688–1713	Treaty of Utrecht, 1713
1792–1815	France (Napoleon)	Great Britain, Prussia, Austria, Russia	Napoleonic Wars, 1792–1815	Congress of Vienna and Concert of Europe, 1815
1871–1914	Germany, Austria-Hungary, Turkey	Great Britain, France, Russia, United States	World War I, 1914–1918	Treaty of Versailles creating League of Nations, 1919
1933–1945	Germany, Japan, Italy	Great Britain, France, Soviet Union, United States	World War II, 1939–1945	Bretton Woods, 1944; United Nations, 1945; Potsdam, 1945
1945–2010	United States, Soviet Union	Great Britain, France, China, Japan	Cold War, 1945–1991	NATO/Partnerships for Peace, 1995; World Trade Organization, 1995
2010–2025	United States	China, European Union, Japan, Russia	A cold peace or hegemonic war, 2010–2025?	A new security regime to preserve world order?

Long-cycle theory also draws attention to the fact that world politics has usually been transformed by a outbreak of a major, general war. "Only after such a total breakdown has the international situation been sufficiently fluid to induce leaders and supporting publics of dominant nations to join seriously in the task of reorganizing international society to avoid a repetition of the terrible events just experienced" (Falk 1970). Table 4.1 summarizes 500 years of the cyclical rise and fall of great powers, their global wars, and their subsequent efforts to restore order.

The central premise of long-cycle theory is disarmingly simple, and for this reason it is not without critics. Must great powers rise and fall as if by the law of gravity—what goes up must come down? There is something disturbingly deterministic in a proposition that implies that global destiny is beyond policymakers' control. Fundamental hypotheses are difficult to confirm. Long-cycle theorists disagree on whether economic, military, or domestic factors produce these cycles, as well as about their comparative influence in different historical epochs. Still, long-cycle theory provokes questions about whether this entrenched cycle can be broken. It also invites critical consideration of **hegemonic stability theory.** That theory assumes that a stable world order requires a dominant global leader to punish aggressors who challenge the status quo and prevent the explosive competition of **enduring rivalries** between competing great powers from escalating into a major systemwide war. Many great powers have become entangled in long-term struggles "to occupy the same territory, control the same markets, or monopolize overlapping positions of influence [and] in the process they [have] become competitors for these objectives" (Thompson 1999b). The persisting clashes between Britain and France (1066–1904), France and Germany (1815–1955), and the United States and Japan (1905–1945) are examples of enduring rivalries that historically have produced significant interstate conflict. Long-cycle theory and hegemonic stability theory enable us to see the dynamics of great-power rivalries "from the standpoint of the present, future, and the past . . . to better understand all the other things that happen in international relations" (Thompson 1999b). For this purpose, this chapter inspects the three great-power wars of the twentieth century and the lessons these uncontained rivalries suggest for the twenty-first century.

■ **hegemonic stability theory**
a body of theory that maintains that the establishment of hegemony for global dominance by a single great power is a necessary condition for global order in commercial transactions and international military security (see p. 313).

■ **enduring rivalries**
prolonged competition between great powers or other pairs of countries whose perpetual conflicting interests often lead to war.

THE FIRST WORLD WAR

World War I rumbled onto the global stage when a Serbian nationalist seeking to free his ethnic group from Austrian rule assassinated Archduke Ferdinand, heir to the Hapsburg throne of the Austrian-Hungarian Empire, at Sarajevo in June 1914 (the same location where NATO's 1999 intervention in Yugoslavia was centered). This assassination sparked a series of moves and countermoves by states and empires distrustful of each other's intentions in the two months that followed, shattering world peace.

Before the assassination, two hostile alliances had already formed, pitting Germany, Austria-Hungary, and the Ottoman Empire against France, Britain, and Russia. The strategic choices of the two alliances culminated in World War I. By the time the first major European war in the previous century had ended, nearly ten million people had died, three empires had crumbled, new states had been born, seven decades of communist rule in Russia had begun, and the world geopolitical map had been redrawn in ways that paved the way for the rise of Adolf Hitler in Nazi Germany.

The Causes of World War I

How can such a catastrophic war be explained? The multiple answers converge around structural explanations, which hold that World War I was inadvertent, not the result of anyone's master plan. It was a war bred by uncertainty and

The Price of Superpower Predominance? Throughout history, reigning hegemonic great-power leaders have been feared, envied, and hated by both great-power rivals and subordinate states and cultures. Shown here in 2002 is one example: Arabs displaying their intense dislike of the United States and its post–9/11 foreign policies.

■ **counterfactual reasoning**
speculations about historical events and developments that ask how the world might have changed had certain momentous foreign policy choices not been taken or had other conditions prevailed (see p. 475).

■ **structuralism**
the proposition that states' behavior is shaped primarily by the changes in the properties of the global system, instead of by individual heads of states or by changes in states' internal characteristics.

circumstances beyond the control of those involved, one that people neither wanted nor expected. Some revisionist historians, using **counterfactual reasoning** (Ferguson 1999), regard World War I (and other great-power wars) as far from inevitable. One called World War I "a tragic and unnecessary conflict . . . because the train of events that led to its outbreak might have been broken at any point during the five weeks of crisis that preceded the first clash of arms, had prudence or common goodwill found a voice" (Keegan 1999).

Structuralism. **Structuralism,** a neorealist theory, sees the changing distribution of power within the global system as the primary factor determining states' behavior. The power distribution determines whether coalitions will form and peace will prevail. Many historians find a structural interpretation framed at the **global level of analysis** convincing because on the eve of World War I the great powers' prior rearmament efforts as well as their alliances and counteralliances (the Triple Alliance of Germany, Austria-Hungary, and Italy, initiated in 1882 and renewed in 1902, and the Entente Cordiale between Britain and France, forged in 1904) created a momentum that, along with the pressures created by the mobilization of armies and arms races, dragged European statesmen toward war (Tuchman 1962).

A related element in the structuralist explanation focuses on the nineteenth century, when Britain dominated world politics. An island country isolated by temperament, tradition, and geography from continental affairs, Britain's sea power gave it command of the world's shipping lanes and control of a vast empire stretching from the Mediterranean to Southeast Asia. This dominance helped to deter aggression. However, Germany would mount a challenge to British power.

After becoming a unified country in 1871, Germany prospered and used its growing wealth to create a formidable army and navy. With strength came ambition and resentment of British preeminence. As the predominant military and industrial power on the European continent, Germany sought to compete for international position and status. As Kaiser Wilhelm II proclaimed in 1898, Germany had "great tasks outside the narrow boundaries of old Europe." With Germany ascendant, the **balance of power** shifted as its rising power and global aspirations altered the European geopolitical landscape.

Germany was not the only newly emergent power at the turn of the century, however. Russia was also expanding and becoming a threat to Germany. The decline in power of the Austrian-Hungarian Empire, Germany's only ally, heightened Germany's fear of Russia, as seen by its extreme reaction to Archduke Ferdinand's assassination. Germany, fearing an unfavorable shift in the balance of power in the event of a long war, became convinced that a short, localized, and victorious war was possible. Accordingly, while the advantages seemed clear-cut, Germany gave Austria-Hungary a "blank check" to crush Serbia, which proved to be a serious miscalculation.

To Germany's imperial rulers, the risk involved in the blank check made sense from the viewpoint of preserving the Austrian-Hungarian Empire. The disintegration of the empire would have left Germany isolated, without an ally. Unfortunately for Germany, its guarantee provoked an unexpected reaction from France and Russia. The two powers joined forces to defend the Slavs. Britain then abandoned its traditional "splendid isolation" and joined France and Russia in the Triple Entente in opposing Germany and its allied Central Powers. The immediate objective was to defend Belgian neutrality. The war later expanded across the ocean when in April 1917 the United States, reacting to German submarine warfare, entered the conflict. For the first time ever, war became truly global in scope.

This chain reaction and the rapidity of escalation that led to World War I fit the interpretation that it was an "inadvertent war." Simply put, European leaders were not in full control of their own fate. Still, historians ask why they miscalculated so badly. Did they simply fail to recognize their primary interest in successfully managing the crisis? If so, was this because their alliances gave them a false sense of assurance, blinding them to danger and dragging them into a conflict that was not a part of anyone's design?

Rational Choice. Rational choice theory provides an alternative interpretation of World War I. From this perspective, framed at the **individual level of analysis,** the war's outbreak was a result of German elites' preference for a war with France and Russia in order to consolidate Germany's position on the continent, confirm its status as a world power, and divert domestic attention from its internal troubles (Kaiser 1990). The people gathered at the Imperial Palace in Berlin are believed to have pressured Europe over the brink.

If the **rational choice** model of decision making (see Chapter 3) offers an accurate interpretation, then World War I is best seen as a consequence of the purposive goal of rival great powers to compete against one another for global power, a drive that realists believe is an "iron law of history." It resulted from "an attempt by Germany to secure its position before an increasingly powerful Russia had achieved a position of equality with Germany (which the latter expected to happen by 1917)" (Levy 1998b).

■ **global level of analysis**
an analytical approach to world politics that emphasizes the impact of worldwide conditions on the behavior of states, IGOs, NGOs, and other international actors.

■ **balance of power**
the theory that peace and stability are most likely to be maintained when military power is distributed so that no single power or bloc can dominate the others.

■ **individual level of analysis**
an analytical approach to the study of world politics that emphasizes the psychological and perceptual origins of the foreign policy behaviors of international actors, with special attention to leaders.

■ **rational choice**
the theory that decision makers choose on the basis of what they perceive to be the best interests for themselves and their states, based on their expectations about the relative usefulness of alternative options for realizing goals. Sometimes called "expected-utility theory," this model derives from realist theories (see p. 410).

As these rival interpretations suggest, the causes of World War I remain in dispute. Structural explanations, which emphasize the global distribution of power, and rational choice explanations, which direct attention to the calculations and goals of particular leaders, partially help us to understand the sequences that produced the world's first truly global war. We must, however, consider additional factors that, in association with these underlying causes, led to the outbreak of the globe's first world war.

■ **state level of analysis**
an analytical approach to the study of world politics that emphasizes how the internal attributes of states explain their foreign policy behaviors.

■ **nationalism**
a mindset glorifying a particular state and the nationality group living in it, which sees the state's interests as a supreme value (see p. 418).

Other Explanations. At the **state level of analysis,** some historians argue that domestic factors within countries were influential causes. In particular, many view the growth of **nationalism,** especially in southeastern Europe, as having created a climate of opinion that made war likely. Different groups began to champion their own state above all others. As nationalistic feelings intensified, they aroused long-suppressed ethnic and national hatreds, which strained European statesmen's ability to avoid war.

Domestic unrest inflamed these nationalistic passions, as did the pressure for war applied by munitions makers who played on nationalistic sentiments. The Austrian-Hungarian Empire's reaction to the assassination crisis suggests that the potency of national passions fed Austria-Hungary's diabolic image of the enemy, its hypersensitivity about the preservation of the empire, and its overconfidence in its military capabilities.

The Germans and Russians were also driven by intense nationalism, an uncritically passionate, patriotic love of country that caused them to make serious miscalculations. Germany's insensitivity to others' feelings prevented it from understanding "the strength of the Russians' pride, their fear of humiliation if they allowed the Germans and Austrians to destroy their little protégé, Serbia, and the intensity of Russian anger at the tricky, deceptive way the Germans and Austrians went about their aggression" (White 1990).

Despite these national passions, World War I would not likely have unfolded without Anglo-German commercial rivalry, the Franco-Russian alliance, Germany's blank check to Austria-Hungary, and—perhaps most importantly—the formation of two entangling alliances. "One cannot conceive of the onset of World War I without the presence of the Triple Entente, which existed as an alliance of ideologically dissimilar governments" uniting Britain, France, and Russia (Midlarsky 1988). Consequently, the division of the multipolar balance-of-power system that drew the growing number of great-power contenders into **bipolar** coalitions—and the absence of a hegemon to maintain order—may have made war inevitable, even though "political leaders in each of the great powers . . . preferred a peaceful settlement" of their differences (Levy 1990–91).

■ **bipolar**
an international system with two dominant power centers.

The Consequences of World War I

World War I destroyed both life and property and changed the face of Europe (see Map 4.1). In its wake, three empires—the Austrian-Hungarian, Russian, and Ottoman (Turkish)—collapsed, and in their place the independent states of Poland, Czechoslovakia, and Yugoslavia emerged. In addition, the countries of Finland, Estonia, Latvia, and Lithuania were born. The war also contributed to the overthrow of the Russian czar in 1917 by the Bolsheviks. The emergence of communism under the leadership of Vladimir Lenin produced a change in government and ideology that would have consequences for another seventy years.

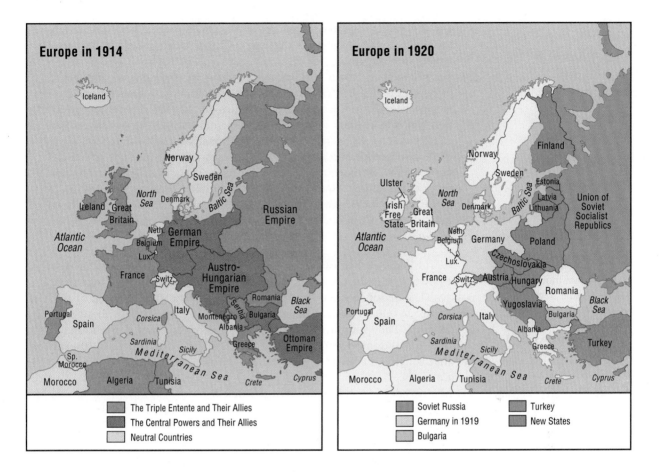

MAP 4.1

Territorial Changes in Europe following World War I

World War I redrew the boundaries of Europe. The map on the left shows state boundaries on the eve of the war in 1914, as well as the members of the two major opposing coalitions that formed. When the guns fell silent after the war, the victors met at Versailles in Paris and drafted a punitive peace settlement that stripped vast territories from the defeated German and Austrian-Hungarian Empires as well as from the western front of the Russian Empire, which disintegrated in the Bolshevik revolution that deposed the czar and brought the communists into power in the new Union of Soviet Socialist Republics (USSR). The map on the right shows the new borders in 1920, with the nine new states that emerged from the war.

SOURCE: From *Strategic Atlas, Comparative Geopolitics of the World's Powers*, revised edition, by Gerard Chaliand and Jean-Pierre Ragau. Copyright © 1990 by Gerard Chaliand and Jean-Pierre Rageau. Reprinted by permission of HarperCollins Publishers, Inc.

Despite its costs, the coalition consisting of Britain, France, Russia, and (later) the United States and Italy defeated the threat of domination posed by the Central Powers (Germany, Austria-Hungary, Turkey, and their allies). Moreover, the war set the stage for a determined effort to build a new global system that could prevent another war.

For most Europeans, the Great War had been a source of disillusionment. . . . When it was all over, few remained to be convinced that such a war must never happen again. Among vast populations there was a strong conviction that this time the parties had to plan a peace that could not just terminate a war, but a peace that could change attitudes and build a new type of international order. . . .

For the first time in history, broad publics and the peacemakers shared a conviction that war was a central problem in international relations. Previously, hegemony, the aggressive activities of a particular state, or revolution had been the problem. In 1648, 1713, and 1815, the peacemakers had tried to resolve issues of the past and to construct orders that would preclude their reappearance. But in 1919 expectations ran higher. The sources of war were less important than the war itself. There was a necessity to look more to the future than to the past. The problem was not just to build a peace, but to construct a peaceful international order that would successfully manage all international conflicts of the future. (Holsti 1991, 175–176; 208–209)

■ **realism**
the school of thought which maintains that because interstate competition is natural, states should prepare for war in order to avoid it.

■ **liberal theory**
the school of thought which argues that progress at peace is possible through institutional reforms that control international anarchy.

■ **Kellogg-Briand Pact**
a multilateral treaty negotiated in 1928 that outlawed war as a method for settling interstate conflicts.

World War I evoked revulsion for war and theories of **realism** that justified great-power competition, arms races, secret alliances, and balance-of-power politics. The deadly cost of this war led the peacemakers gathered at the Versailles Palace outside Paris to question realpolitik assumptions about the rules of statecraft. They sought instead to guard against the threat of another world war and global domination through a reformed program rooted in **liberal theory** that sought to construct political and commercial cooperation among the great powers.

The two decades following World War I were the high point of liberal idealism. That liberal philosophy was given expression in Woodrow Wilson's "Fourteen Points" address, the creation of the League of Nations, the Five Power Treaty (signed by Japan, Britain, France, Italy, and the United States at the Washington Navel Conference in February 1922 that put a ceiling on the building and modernization of large warships), the **Kellogg-Briand Pact** (which in 1928 legally prohibited war as an instrument of foreign policy), the Four Power Treaty (pledging Japan, France, Britain, and the United States not to attack one another's colonies), and the Nine Power Treaty (that placed China off limits to further great-power imperialism). Nevertheless, the liberal idealists' proposals failed to deter the resumption of great-power rivalry. Another system-transforming global war was on the horizon.

THE SECOND WORLD WAR

Although it lost World War I, Germany did not lose its desire for global status and influence. On the contrary, Germany's aspirations intensified. Thus conditions were ripe for the second great-power war of the twentieth century, as Germany again pursued an aggressive course.

Global in scope, World War II was a struggle for power cast in the image of realism. It pitted a fascist coalition striving for world supremacy—the Axis trio of Germany, Japan, and Italy—against an unlikely "grand alliance" of four great powers who united despite their incompatible ideologies—communism in the case of the Soviet Union and democratic capitalism in the case of Britain, France, and the United States.

The world's fate hinged on the outcome of this massive effort to meet the Axis threat of world conquest and restore the balance of power. The Allied powers achieved success in a six-year ordeal, but at a terrible cost: each day 23,000 lives were lost, as the war resulted in the death of 53 million people worldwide (for an account of the campaigns that "called so many to pay the ultimate price for victory," to prevent the German and Japanese regimes "founded on racial superiority, slavery, and genocide" from imposing their values on the rest of humanity, see Murray and Millett 2000).

The Causes of World War II

Several factors revived Germany's hegemonic ambitions. Domestically, German nationalism inflamed latent **irredentism** and rationalized the expansion of German borders both to regain provinces previously lost in wars to others and to absorb Germans living in Austria, Czechoslovakia, and Poland. The rise of **fascism**—the Nazi regime's ideology championing racism, flag, fatherland, nationalism, and imperialism—animated this renewed imperialistic push and preached the most extreme version of realism, **machtpolitik** (power politics), to justify the forceful expansion of the German state and the other Axis powers aligned with Germany. "Everything for the state, nothing outside the state, nothing above the state" was the way Italy's dictator, Benito Mussolini, constructed his understanding of the fascist political philosophy, in a definition that embraced the extreme realist proposition that the state was supreme— entitled to rule by force every dimension of human life.

Germany also resented the punitive terms imposed by the victors of World War I (France, Great Britain, Italy, Japan, and the United States). Reflecting French demands, the harsh Peace of Paris (the Versailles treaty) insisted on the destruction of Germany's armed forces, the loss of territory (such as Alsace-Lorraine, which Germany had absorbed following the Franco-Prussian war of 1870–1871), and the imposition of heavy reparations to compensate the Allies for the damage that German militarism had exacted. In addition, the Austrian-Hungarian Empire was splintered into divided political units.

Not only was the Peace of Paris punitive, more significantly and painfully it prevented Germany's reentry into the international system as a coequal member; Germany was denied membership in the League of Nations until 1926. As a result of its exclusion, Germany sought to recover by force its perceived rightful status as a great power.

Proximate Causes. Why did the victorious great powers permit German rearmament? A key reason was that Britain's hope for Anglo-American collaboration to maintain world order vanished when the United States repudiated the Versailles peace treaty and retreated to a policy of **isolationism,** withdrawing from active international involvements. As a result, Britain and France each fought for its own advantage in the treatment of Germany. While France wanted to deter Germany's readmission as an accepted member of the international community and prevent its recovery, Britain, in contrast, preferred to preserve the new balance of power by encouraging German rearmament and revival as a counterweight against the chance that France or the Soviet Union might dominate continental Europe.

■ **irredentism**
movement by an ethnonational group to regain control of territory by force so that existing state boundaries will no longer divide the group.

■ **fascism**
a far-right ideology that promotes extreme nationalism and the establishment of an authoritarian society built around a single party with dictatorial leadership.

■ **machtpolitik**
the German realist philosophy in statecraft that sees the expansion of state power and territory by use of armed force as a legitimate goal.

■ **isolationism**
a policy of withdrawing from active participation with other actors in world affairs and instead concentrating state efforts on managing internal affairs.

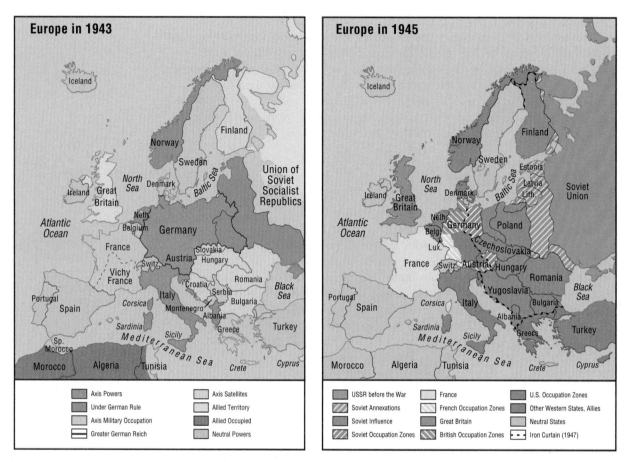

MAP 4.2
World War II Redraws the Map of Europe

The Axis coalition of great powers, composed of Germany, Italy and Japan, sought to conquer and divide the world in World War II and almost succeeded. The map on the left shows the extent of German expansion in Europe at the height of its aggression in 1943, when Nazi Germany occupied Europe from the Atlantic Ocean and Baltic Sea to the Soviet Union's borders. The map on the right shows the new configuration of Europe after the "Grand Coalition" of Allied forces—Great Britain, the United States, and the Soviet Union—defeated the Axis's bid for supremacy. The Allies partitioned Germany into four sections occupied by British, French, Russian, and American troops and carved out other territorial changes that returned to the Soviet Union most of the land that it had lost at the end of World War I. Later, Germany was divided into two independent countries, the Federal Republic of Germany (West Germany) and the German Democratic Republic (East Germany).

SOURCE: Europe in 1945 from *Strategic Atlas, Comparative Geopolitics of the World's Powers,* revised edition, by Gerard Chaliand and Jean-Pierre Rageau. Copyright © 1990 by Gerard Chaliand and Jean-Pierre Rageau. Reprinted by permission of HarperCollins Publishers, Inc.

■ **appeasement**
a strategy of making concessions to an aggressor state without retaliation in the hope that, satisfied, it will not make additional claims on the territory of its neighbors.

Acquiescence to German rearmament and other militaristic maneuvers led to the policy of **appeasement,** or pacifying potential aggressors with concessions. Adolf Hitler, the German dictator who by the mid-1930s controlled Germany's fate, pledged not to expand German territory by force. He betrayed that promise in March 1938 when he forced Austria into union with Germany (the *Anschluss*). Shortly thereafter he demanded the annexation of the German-populated area of Sudetenland in Czechoslovakia (see Map 4.2). Fear of further

German expansion led to the September 1938 Munich Conference attended by Hitler, British Prime Minister Neville Chamberlain, and leaders from France and Italy (Czechoslovakia was not invited). Based on the erroneous conviction that appeasement would halt further German expansionism and lead to "peace in our time," Chamberlain and the others agreed to Hitler's demands.

Rather than satisfying Germany, appeasement whetted its appetite and that of the newly formed fascist coalition of Germany, Italy, and Japan, which aimed to overthrow the international status quo. Japan, disillusioned with Western liberalism and the Paris settlements, and suffering economically from the effects of the Great Depression of the 1930s, embraced militarism. In the might-makes-right climate that Germany's imperialistic quest for national aggrandizement helped to create, Japanese nationalists led their country on the path to imperialism and **colonialism.** Japan's invasions of Manchuria in 1931 and China proper in 1937 were followed by Italy's absorption of Abyssinia in 1935 and Albania in 1939, and both Germany and Italy intervened in the 1936–1939 Spanish civil war on the side of the fascists, headed by General Francisco Franco, while the Soviet Union supported antifascist forces.

■ **colonialism**
the rule of a region by an external sovereign power.

After Germany occupied the rest of Czechoslovakia in March 1939, Britain and France formed an alliance to protect the next likely victim, Poland. They also opened negotiations with Moscow in hopes of enticing the Soviet Union to join the alliance, but failed. Then, on August 23, 1939, Hitler, a fascist, and the Soviet dictator Joseph Stalin, a communist, stunned the world with the news that they had signed a nonaggression pact, promising not to attack one another. Now confident that Britain and France would not intervene, Hitler invaded Poland. Britain and France, honoring their pledge to defend the Poles, declared war on Germany two days later. World War II began.

The war expanded rapidly. Hitler next turned his forces to the Balkans, North Africa, and westward, as the mechanized German troops invaded Norway and marched through Denmark, Belgium, Luxembourg, and the Netherlands. The German army swept around the Maginot line, the defensive barrier on the eastern frontier that France boasted could not be breached; within six weeks France surrendered, even though Germany's forces were measurably inferior to those of France and its allies (only deficient French decision-making practices and overconfidence in technology enabled the German surprise attack to succeed—see May 2000). The alarming and nearly bloodless German victory forced the British to evacuate a nearly 340,000-strong expeditionary force from the French beaches at Dunkirk. Paris itself fell in June 1940. Meanwhile, to keep the United States from participating in the looming war, in September 1940 Japan forged the Tripartite Pact with Germany and Italy that pledged the three Axis powers to come to each other's aid if attacked by another nonbelligerent great power, such as the United States.

In the months that followed, the German air force, the Luftwaffe, pounded Britain in an attempt to force it into submission as well. Instead of invading Britain, however, the Nazi troops launched a surprise attack on the Soviet Union, Hitler's former ally, in June 1941. On December 7, 1941, Japan launched a surprise assault on the United States at Pearl Harbor. Almost immediately, Germany also declared war on the United States. The unprovoked Japanese assault and the German challenge ended U.S. aloofness and isolationism, enabling President Franklin Roosevelt to forge a coalition with Britain and the Soviet Union to oppose the fascists.

■ **multipolarity**
the distribution of global power into three or more great-power centers, with other states allied with one of the rivals.

■ **political economy**
a field of study that focuses on the intersection of politics and economics in international relations.

■ **protectionism**
barriers of foreign trade, such as tariffs and quotas, that protect local industries from competition for the purchase of the products local manufacturers produce.

■ **imperialism**
the policy of expanding state power through the conquest of foreign territory (see p. 549).

Underlying Causes. Many historians regard the reemergence of **multipolarity** in power distribution as a key factor in the onset and expansion of World War II. The post–World War I global system was placed "at risk when the sovereign states, which were its components, became too numerous and unequal in power and resources, particularly when (as happened after 1919) the great powers were reduced in number and new, lesser states proliferated" (Calvocoressi, Wint, and Pritchard 1989). In 1914, Europe had only twenty-two key states, but by 1921 the number nearly doubled. When combined with resentment over the Versailles treaty, the Russian Revolution, and the rise of fascism, the increased number of states and the resurgence of nationalistic revolts and crises made "the interwar years the most violent period in international relations since the Thirty Years' War and the wars of the French Revolution and Napoleon" (Holsti 1991).

The collapse of the international economic system during the 1930s also contributed to the war. Great Britain found itself unequal to the leadership and regulatory roles it had performed in the world **political economy** before World War I. Although the United States was the logical successor, its refusal to exercise leadership hastened the war. "The Depression of 1929–1931 was followed in 1933 by a world Monetary and Economic Conference whose failures—engineered by the United States—deepened the gloom, accelerated nationalist **protectionism,** and promoted revolution" (Calvocoressi, Wint, and Pritchard 1989). In this depressed global environment, heightened by deteriorating economic circumstances at home, Germany and Japan sought solutions through **imperialism** abroad.

The League of Nations' failure to mount a collective response to the acts of aggression symbolized the weak institutional barriers to war. When Germany withdrew from the League of Nations in 1933, followed by Italy in 1937, war clouds gathered and the League of Nation was powerless to dispel them.

The Soviet Union's invasion of neutral Finland in 1939 provoked public indignation. In a final act of retaliation, the League of Nations expelled the Soviet Union, but the burden of defense fell on the shoulders of the victim. Ninety thousand fiercely independent Finns gave their lives in the victorious "Winter War" over the Soviet invaders while the rest of the astonished world watched.

At the state level of analysis, psychological forces also led to World War II. These included "the domination of civilian discourse by military propaganda that primed the world for war," the "great wave of hypernationalism [that] swept over Europe [as] each state taught itself a mythical history while denigrating that of others," and the demise of democratic governance (Van Evera 1990–91).

In the final analysis, however, the importance of leaders stands out. The war would not have been possible without Adolf Hitler and his plans to conquer the world by force. World War II arose primarily from German aggression. Professing the superiority of Germans as a "master race" and virulent anti-Semitism and anticommunism, Hitler chose to wage war to create an empire that he believed could resolve once and for all the historic competition and precarious coexistence of the great powers in Europe by eliminating Germany's rivals.

The broad vision of the Thousand-Year Reich was . . . of a vastly expanded—and continually expanding—German core, extending deep into

Topham/Image Works

The Rise of Hitler and German Nationalism In the 1930s the nationalistic ideologies of national socialism and fascism—realist philosophies that regarded the state as supreme, accepted dictatorship, and called for expansion at the expense of neighboring countries—took root in Germany and Italy. Consistent with the realist view that states have an inherent right to expand, Adolf Hitler's propaganda experts staged dramatic political rallies to glorify the Führer (leader), persuade the German people of the need to persecute the Jews, and expand German borders by armament and aggression.

Russia, with a number of vassal states and regions, including France, the Low Countries, Scandinavia, central Europe, and the Balkans, that would provide resources and labor for the core. There was to be no civilizing mission in German imperialism. On the contrary, the lesser peoples were to be taught only to do menial labor or, as Hitler once joked, educated sufficiently to read the road signs so they wouldn't get run over by German automobile traffic. The lowest of the low, the Poles and Jews, were to be exterminated. . . .

To Hitler . . . the purpose of policy was to destroy the system and to reconstitute it on racial lines, with a vastly expanded Germany running a distinctly hierarchical and exploitative order. Vestiges of sovereignty might remain, but they would be fig leaves covering a monolithic order. German occupation policies during the war, whereby conquered nations were reduced to satellites, satrapies, and reservoirs of slave labor, were the practical application of Hitler's conception of the new world order. They were not improvised or planned for reasons of military necessity. (Holsti 1991, 224–225)

A brutal war fought at terrible human cost, World War II was much more than a hegemonic struggle. Why and how the war was fought, at great sacrifice, may be best seen as springing from an epic clash between divergent ideologies—

between one conception of civilization founded on moral values against another philosophy seeking to destroy it. In both the European and Pacific fronts, the Allies faced an enemy whose ideologies, "founded on racial superiority, slavery, and genocide" (Murray and Millett 2000), sustained a war longer than the mere pursuit of personal, national gain would, from a purely rational choice perspective, seem to justify. World War II was fought over ethical values for which people were willing to die.

The Consequences of World War II

Having faced ruinous losses in Russia and a massive Allied bombing campaign at home, Germany's Thousand-Year Reich lay in ruins by May 1945. By August, the U.S. atomic bombing of Hiroshima and Nagasaki forced Japan to end its war of conquest as well, and brace itself, after its shattering defeat and followed by six years of U.S. military occupation, to meet the challenge of "starting over" by socially constructing acceptance of new values.

The Allied victory over the Axis redistributed power and reordered borders, resulting in a new geopolitical terrain. The Soviet Union absorbed nearly six hundred thousand square meters of territory from the Baltic states of Estonia, Latvia, and Lithuania, and from Finland, Czechoslovakia, Poland, and Romania—recovering what Russia had lost in the 1918 Treaty of Brest-Litovsk after World War I. Poland, a victim of Soviet expansionism, was compensated with land taken from Germany. Germany itself was divided into occupation zones that eventually provided the basis for its partition into East and West Germany. Finally, pro-Soviet regimes assumed power throughout Eastern Europe (see Map 4.2, p. 108). In the Far East, the Soviet Union took the four Kurile Islands—or the "Northern Territories," as Japan calls them—from Japan, and Korea was divided into Soviet and U.S. occupation zones at the thirty-eight parallel.

What is more important than these dimensions of the peace settlement is the system-transforming impact of the Allied victory. "World War II brought an end to the great-power rivalries of Europe, to the extension of much of those rivalries to much of the world through imperialism, and to European dominance of the world's economic development and culture" (Murray and Millett 2000). In the immediate wake of World War II one global system ended, but the defining characteristics of the transformed new system had not yet become clear.

The prevailing sense of confusion amidst chaos after the war generated much uncertainty and mistrust. The agreements governing goals, strategy, and obligations that had guided the Allied effort began to erode even as victory neared. Victory only magnified the great powers' growing distrust of one another's intentions in an environment of ill-defined borders, altered allegiances, power vacuums, and economic ruin.

The "Big Three" leaders—Winston Churchill, Franklin Roosevelt, and Joseph Stalin—met at the **Yalta Conference** in February 1945 to design a new world order, but the vague compromises they reached concealed the differences percolating below the surface. Following Germany's unconditional surrender in May, the Big Three (with the United States now represented by Harry Truman) met again in July 1945 at Potsdam. The meeting ended without agreement, and the facade of Allied unity began to fade.

■ **Yalta Conference**
the 1945 summit meeting among Franklin D. Roosevelt, Joseph Stalin, and Winston Churchill to resolve postwar territorial issues and voting procedures in the United Nations to collectively manage world order.

World War II, like previous great-power wars, paved the way for a transformation in world politics. Allied collaboration after the war to create a new international organization to manage the postwar international order gave birth to the United Nations (UN). Consistent with the expectation that the great powers would cooperate to manage world affairs, China was promised a seat on the UN Security Council along with France and the Big Three. The purpose of the Security Council was to guarantee that all of the dominant states would share responsibility for preserving peace.

After the war, the United States and the Soviet Union remained the two great powers that were still strong, with the capacity to impose their will. The vanquished, Germany and Japan, fell from the ranks of the great powers. The other major-power victors, especially Great Britain, had exhausted themselves and also slid from the apex of the world-power hierarchy. Thus, as the French political sociologist Alexis de Tocqueville had foreseen in 1835, the Americans and Russians now held in their hands the destinies of half of mankind. In comparison, all other states were dwarfs. In this atmosphere, observers of various ideological persuasions began to debate whether the twentieth century would become "the American century" or "the Russian century." In what eventually became known as the Cold War, Washington and Moscow used the fledgling UN not to keep the peace, but to pursue their competition with each other. As the third and last great-power war of the twentieth century, the Cold War and its lessons still cast shadows over the twenty-first-century geostrategic landscape.

THE COLD WAR

The second great war of the twentieth century not only had brought about a system dominated by two superstates, the United States and the Soviet Union, it also had hastened the disintegration of the great colonial empires assembled by imperialist states in previous centuries, thereby emancipating many peoples from foreign rule. The emergent global system, unlike earlier ones, featured a bipolar distribution of power consisting of many sovereign states outside the European core area that were dominated by the two most powerful. In addition, the advent of nuclear weapons radically changed the role that threats of warfare would play in world politics. Out of these circumstances grew the competition between the United States and the Soviet Union for hegemonic leadership.

The Causes and Evolutionary Course of the Cold War

The origins of the twentieth century's third hegemonic battle for domination are debated because the historical evidence lends itself to different interpretations (see Gaddis 1997). Several postulated causes stand out. The first is advanced by realism: the **Cold War** resulted from the **power transition** that propelled the United States and the Soviet Union to the top of the international hierarchy, which made each naturally suspicious of the other and their rivalry inescapable. Circumstances gave each superpower reasons to fear and to struggle against the other's potential global leadership and encouraged each superpower competitor to carve out and establish dominant influence in its own **sphere of influence,** or specified area of the globe.

■ **Cold War**
the forty-two-year (1949–1991) rivalry between the United States and the Soviet Union, as well as their competing coalitions, which sought to contain each other's expansion and win worldwide predominance.

■ **power transition**
a narrowing of the ratio of military capabilities between great-power rivals that is thought to increase the probability of war between them (see p. 482).

■ **sphere of influence**
a region of the globe dominated by a great power.

A second interpretation holds that the Cold War was simply an extension of the superpowers' mutual disdain for each other's professed beliefs about politics and economics. U.S. animosity toward the Soviet Union was stimulated by the 1917 Bolshevik revolution, which brought to power a government that embraced the Marxist critique of capitalistic imperialism. U.S. fears of Marxism stimulated the emergence of anticommunism as an opposing ideology. Accordingly, the United States embarked on a missionary crusade of its own to contain and ultimately remove the atheistic communist menace from the face of the earth.

Similarly, Soviet policy was fueled by the belief that capitalism could not coexist with communism. The purpose of Soviet policy, therefore, was to push the pace of the historical process in which communism eventually would prevail. However, Soviet planners did not believe that this historical outcome was guaranteed. They felt that the capitalist states, led by the United States, sought to encircle the Soviet Union and smother communism in its cradle, and that it was the Soviet obligation to resist. As a result, ideological incompatibility may have ruled out compromise as an option (see Controversy: Was Ideology the Primary Source of East-West Conflict?). Although the adversaries may have viewed "ideology more as a justification for action than as a guide to action," once the interests that they shared disappeared, "ideology did become the chief means which differentiated friend from foe" (Gaddis 1983).

A third explanation describes the Cold War as rooted in psychological factors, particularly in the superpowers' misperceptions of each other's motives. In this view, conflicting interests and ideologies were secondary to misunderstandings. Mistrustful actors are prone to see only virtue in their own actions and only malice in those of their adversaries. When such **mirror images** exist, hostility is inevitable (Bronfenbrenner 1971). Moreover, when perceptions of an adversary's evil intentions are socially constructed and become accepted as truth, **self-fulfilling prophecies** can develop. Prophecies are sometimes self-fulfilling because the future can be affected by the way it is anticipated. This tendency is illustrated by arms races: mistakenly fearing that a rival is preparing for an offensive war, a potential victim then arms in defense, thereby provoking the fearful rival to fulfill the prophecy by defensively building more weapons. The result is a classic illustration of the **security dilemma**, as each enemy's efforts to increase its own security by arming actually leads to a decline in security on both sides.

Additional factors beyond those rooted in divergent interests, ideologies, and images undoubtedly combined to produce this explosive Soviet-American hegemonic rivalry. To sort out the relative causal influence at the start of the Cold War and to grasp more completely the primary causes driving the dynamics of this great-power rivalry (and others in general), scholars have found it useful to evaluate how the Cold War changed over a forty-two-year period in order to identify the causes that contributed to changes in the U.S.-Soviet rivalry. The character of the Cold War shifted over the course of its duration, and several conspicuous patterns persisted that illustrate the larger historical pattern of great-power rivalries (Thompson 1999b).

- Periods of intense conflict alternated with periods of relative cooperation; reciprocal, action-reaction exchanges were also evident (friendly U.S. initiatives toward the Soviet Union were reciprocated in kind).

■ **mirror images**
the tendency of states and people in competitive interaction to misperceive each other—to see others the opposite way they see themselves (see p. 203).

■ **self-fulfilling prophecy**
the tendency for one's expectations to evoke behavior that helps to make the expectations become true (see p. 16).

■ **security dilemma**
the central problem faced by all sovereign states in an anarchic global system in which a state's arming for ostensibly defensive purposes provokes other states to arm in response, with the result that the national security of all declines as their armaments increase.

CONTROVERSY   WAS IDEOLOGY THE PRIMARY SOURCE OF EAST-WEST CONFLICT?

Cold War America was gripped by a "Great Fear" not simply of the Soviet Union but of communism. Senator Joseph McCarthy led the most infamous hunt for communist sympathizers in government, Hollywood production companies blacklisted supposed communist sympathizers, and average American citizens were often required to take loyalty oaths at their offices. Everywhere communism became synonymous with treasonous, un-American activity. As the nuclear arms race escalated and the U.S. government took military action to contain the Soviet Union, its justification was almost always expressed in terms of ideology. The threat, as the population learned to perceive it, was that of an atheistic, communistic system that challenged the fundamental American principles of democratic capitalism, and that according to the **domino theory** which states that communism was driven to knock over one country after another, Soviet communism was inherently expansionistic. The other side also couched its Cold War rhetoric in terms of ideology, objecting to the imperialistic, capitalist system that the Soviets said America planned to impose on the whole world.

Some would argue that fear of the other side's world dominance may have been more important in the Cold War than pure ideology. Both the American and the Soviet governments may have entered the Cold War to secure their relative power in the world order as much as to protect pure principles. After all, the United States and the Soviet Union had managed to transcend differing ideologies when they served as allies in World War II. After World War II, however, a power vacuum drew them into conflict with each other, and as they competed, ideological justifications surfaced.

Everyone has a psychological need to clarify their values and define them through the lens of an **ideology** or a belief system that expresses their convictions and enables them to explain what is of interest to them. Realism, liberalism, and Marxism-Leninism are all examples of such ideologies of international politics. Ideologies help us to interpret life and its meaning and are for that reason indispensable for organizing thought and values. But commitment to an ideology may at times cause hatred and hostility. Institutional proponents of particular ideologies are prone to perceive other ideologies competitively—as challenges to the truth of their own ideology's core beliefs. However, ideology can also become an excuse for less noble ambitions or for general fears. Although scholars are still debating the causes of the Cold War, we need to ask whether it was, in fact, an ideological contest over ideas or a more general contest for power—in which the two governments proselytized about communism and capitalism to win peoples' hearts and minds.

What do you think? Was the Cold War really an ideological contest between international communism and the free-market capitalism espoused by the liberal democracies or were there other, more powerful forces involved? In considering your opinion, take into account the end of the Cold War, in which the Soviet communistic system crumbled. Communist theoretician Vladimir Lenin described the predicament that he perceived to underlie the Cold War—prophetically, it turned out— when he predicted: "As long as capitalism and socialism exist, we cannot live in peace; in the end, either one or the other will triumph—a funeral dirge will be sung either over the Soviet Republic or over world capitalism."

- For reasons of expediency, both rivals were willing to disregard their respective professed ideologies whenever their perceived national interests rationalized such inconsistencies; for example, each backed allies with political systems antithetical to its own when the necessities of power politics seemed to justify doing so.
- Both rivals consistently made avoidance of all-out war their highest priority. Through a gradual learning process involving push and shove, restraint and reward, tough bargaining and calm negotiation, the superpowers created a **security regime.**

■ **domino theory**
a metaphor popular during the Cold War which predicted that if one state fell to communism, its neighbors would also fall in a chain reaction, like a row of falling dominoes.

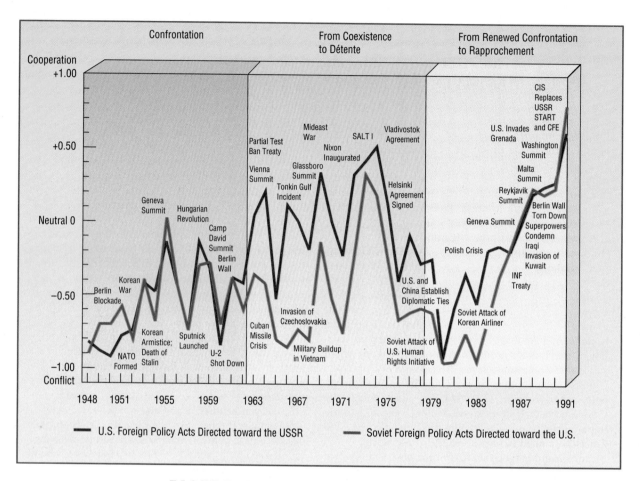

FIGURE 4.1

Key Events in the Evolution of the U.S.-Soviet Relationship during the Cold War, 1948–1991

The evolution of U.S.-Soviet relations during the Cold War displays a series of shifts between periods of conflict and cooperation. As this figure shows, each superpower's behavior toward the other tended to be reciprocal, and, for most periods prior to 1983, confrontation prevailed over cooperation.

■ **ideology**
a set of core philosophical principles that leaders and citizens collectively hold about politics, the interests of political actors, and the ways people ought to ethically behave.

These characteristics become visible when we inspect the evolution of the superpowers' relationship by dividing the Cold War into three chronological phases, shown in Figure 4.1.

Confrontation, 1945–1962. A brief period of wary Soviet-American friendship soon gave way to mutual antagonism when the Cold War began. In this short period of **unipolarity**—one characterized by a single dominant power center in the global system—the United States alone possessed the capacity to devastate its adversaries with the atomic bomb.

Despite this restraining factor, all pretense of collaboration rapidly vanished as the superpowers' vital security interests collided in countries outside their clearly defined respective spheres of influence. At this critical juncture,

George F. Kennan, then a diplomat in the American embassy in Moscow, sent to Washington his famous "long telegram" assessing the sources of Soviet conduct. Kennan's ideas were circulated widely in 1947, when the influential journal *Foreign Affairs* published his views in an article signed simply "X." In this article, Kennan argued that Soviet leaders forever would feel insecure about their political ability to maintain power against forces both within Soviet society and in the outside world. Their insecurity would lead to an activist—and perhaps aggressive—Soviet foreign policy. However, the United States had the power to increase the strains under which the Soviet leadership would have to operate, which could lead to a gradual mellowing or final end of Soviet power. Thus, Kennan concluded: "In these circumstances it is clear that the main element of any United States policy toward the Soviet Union must be that of a long-term, patient but firm and vigilant *containment* of Russian expansive tendencies" (Kennan 1947, emphasis added).

Soon thereafter, President Harry S Truman made Kennan's assessment the cornerstone of American postwar foreign policy. Provoked in part by violence in Turkey and Greece, which he and others believed to be communist inspired, Truman declared, "I believe that it must be the policy of the United States to support free peoples who are resisting attempted subjugation by armed minorities or by outside pressures." Eventually known as the **Truman Doctrine,** this statement defined the strategy that the United States would pursue for the next forty years, over Kennan's objections (1967, 361). This strategy, called **containment,** sought to prevent the expansion of Soviet influence by encircling the Soviet Union and intimidating it with the threat of a military attack.

A seemingly endless series of new Cold War crises soon followed. They included the communist coup d'état in Czechoslovakia in 1948; the Soviet blockade of West Berlin in June of that year; the communist acquisition of power on the Chinese mainland in 1949; the outbreak of the Korean War in 1950; the Chinese invasion of Tibet in 1950; and the on-again, off-again Taiwan Straits crises that followed. Nonetheless, superpower relations began to improve in the 1950s. After the Soviets broke the U.S. atomic monopoly in 1949, shifts in the balance of power prompted a movement away from confrontation. The risks of massive destruction necessitated restraint and changed the terms of the struggle. In particular, both superpowers began to expend considerable resources recruiting allies, promising to protect new client states from external attack through a strategy known as **extended deterrence.** Thus the Cold War expanded across the entire globe, producing a distribution of military power characterized by **bipolarity,** with the United States and its allies at one pole and the Soviet Union and its allies at the other.

Because the Soviet Union remained strategically inferior to the United States, Nikita Khrushchev (who succeeded Stalin upon his death in 1953) pursued a policy of **peaceful coexistence** with capitalism. Nonetheless, the Soviet Union at times cautiously sought to increase its power in places where opportunities appeared to exist. As a result, the period following Stalin's death saw many Cold War confrontations, with Hungary, Cuba, Egypt, and Berlin becoming the flash points.

A dark shadow loomed over hopes for superpower peace. As the arms race accelerated, the threats to peace multiplied. In 1962, the surreptitious placement of Soviet missiles in Cuba set the stage for the greatest test of the superpowers' capacity to manage their disputes—the Cuban Missile Crisis. The

■ **security regime**
norms and rules for interaction agreed to by a set of states to increase their security.

■ **unipolarity**
a condition in which an international system has a single dominant power hegemon capable of dominating all other states (see p. 550).

■ **Truman Doctrine**
the declaration by President Harry S Truman that U.S. foreign policy would use intervention to support peoples who allied with the United States against external subjugation.

■ **containment**
a strategy to prevent a great power rival from using force to alter the balance of power and increase its sphere of influence (see p. 486).

■ **extended deterrence**
a great power's commitment to its allies to use its military might to prevent them from being attacked by an enemy.

■ **bipolarity**
a condition in which power is concentrated in two competing centers so that the rest of the states define their allegiances in terms of their relationships with both (see p. 542).

■ **peaceful coexistence**
Soviet leader Nikita Khrushchev's 1956 doctrine that war between capitalist and communist states is not inevitable and that inter-bloc competition could be peaceful.

superpowers stood eyeball to eyeball. Fortunately, one (the Soviet Union) blinked, and the crisis ended. This "catalytic" learning experience both reduced enthusiasm for waging the Cold War by military means and expanded awareness of the suicidal consequences of a nuclear war.

From Coexistence to Détente, 1963–1978.   The growing threat of mutual destruction, in conjunction with the growing parity of American and Soviet military capabilities, made coexistence or nonexistence appear to be the only alternatives. Given this equation, finding ways to coexist became compelling. At the American University commencement exercises in 1963, U.S. President John F. Kennedy explained why tension reduction had become essential:

> Today, should total war ever break out again—no matter how—our two countries would become the primary targets. It is an ironical but accurate fact that the two strongest powers are the two in the most danger of devastation. . . . We are both caught up in a vicious and dangerous cycle in which suspicion on one side breeds suspicion on the other and new weapons beget counterweapons.
>
> In short, both the United States and its allies, and the Soviet Union and its allies, have a mutually deep interest in a just and genuine peace and in halting the arms race. . . .
>
> So let us not be blind to our differences, but let us also direct attention to our common interests and to the means by which those differences can be resolved. And if we cannot end now our differences, at least we can help make the world safe for diversity.

Kennedy signaled a shift in how the United States hoped thereafter to bargain with its adversary, and the Soviet Union reciprocally expressed its interest in more cooperative relations. That movement took another step forward following Richard Nixon's election in 1968. Coached by his national security adviser, Henry A. Kissinger, President Nixon initiated a new approach to Soviet relations that in 1969 he officially labeled **détente.** The Soviets also adopted this term to describe their policies toward the United States, and relations between the Soviets and Americans "normalized." Arms control stood at the center of the dialogue surrounding détente. The **Strategic Arms Limitation Talks (SALT),** initiated in 1969, sought to restrain the threatening, expensive, and spiraling arms race by limiting the deployment of antiballistic missiles. As Figure 4.1 shows, cooperative interaction became more commonplace than hostile relations. Visits, cultural exchanges, trade agreements, and joint technological ventures replaced threats, warnings, and confrontations.

From Renewed Confrontation to Rapprochement, 1979–1991.   Despite the careful nurturing of détente, its spirit did not endure. In many respects, the Soviet invasion of Afghanistan in 1979 catalyzed détente's demise. As President Jimmy Carter viewed it, "Soviet aggression in Afghanistan—unless checked—confronts all the world with the most serious strategic challenge since the Cold War began." In retaliation, he advanced the **Carter Doctrine** declaring America's willingness to use military force to protect its access to oil supplies from the Persian Gulf. In addition, he attempted to organize a worldwide boycott of the 1980 Moscow Olympics and suspended U.S. grain exports to the Soviet Union.

■ **détente**
in general, a strategy of seeking to relax tensions between adversaries to reduce the possibility of war.

■ **Strategic Arms Limitations Talks (SALT)**
two sets of agreements reached during the 1970s between the United States and the Soviet Union that established limits on strategic nuclear delivery systems.

■ **Carter Doctrine**
President Jimmy Carter's declaration of U.S. willingness to use military force to protect its interests in the Persian Gulf.

Biber/Sipa

Easing Tensions: U.S.-Soviet Détente As East-West tension waned, cooperation increased during the détente phase of U.S.-Soviet relations in the late 1960s. A considerable part of this departure from past confrontation was due to compromises at the bargaining table. Pictured here, President Richard Nixon, one of the architects of the U.S. **"linkage" strategy** along with Secretary of State Henry Kissinger, is toasting with Soviet Premier Leonid Brezhnev and fellow dignitaries at their meeting to discuss approaches to relaxing tensions between the superpowers.

■ **linkage strategy**
a set of assertions that claims leaders should take into account another country's overall behavior when deciding whether to reach agreement on any one specific issue.

Relations deteriorated dramatically thereafter. President Ronald Reagan and his Soviet counterparts (first Yuri Andropov and then Konstantin Chernenko) delivered a barrage of confrontational rhetoric. Reagan asserted that the Soviet Union "underlies all the unrest that is going on" and described the Soviet Union as "the focus of evil in the modern world." The atmosphere was punctuated by Reagan policy adviser Richard Pipes's bold challenge in 1981 that the Soviets would have to choose between "peacefully changing their communist system . . . or going to war." Soviet rhetoric was equally unrestrained and alarmist.

As talk of war increased, preparations for it escalated. The arms race resumed feverishly, at the expense of addressing domestic economic problems. The superpowers also extended the confrontation to new territory, such as Central America, and renewed their public diplomacy (propaganda) efforts to extol the virtues of their respective systems throughout the world. The **Reagan Doctrine** pledged U.S. support for anticommunist insurgents who sought to overthrow Soviet-supported governments in Afghanistan, Angola, and Nicaragua. In addition, American leaders spoke loosely about the "winability" of a nuclear war through a "prevailing" military strategy that included the threat of a "first use" of nuclear weapons in the event of conventional war. Relations deteriorated as these moves and countermoves took their toll. The new Soviet leader,

■ **Reagan Doctrine**
a pledge of U.S. support for anticommunist insurgents who sought to overthrow Soviet-supported governments (see p. 88).

Mikhail Gorbachev, in 1985 summarized the alarming state of superpower relations by fretting that "The situation is very complex, very tense. I would even go so far as to say it is explosive."

However, the situation did not explode. Instead, prospects for a more constructive phase improved greatly following Gorbachev's advocacy of "new thinking" in order to achieve a **rapprochement** or reconciliation of the rival states' interests. He sought to settle the Soviet Union's differences with the capitalist West in order to halt the deterioration of his country's economy and international position. Shortly thereafter, Gorbachev embarked on domestic reforms to promote democratization and the transition to a market economy, and proclaimed his desire to end the Cold War contest. "We realize that we are divided by profound historical, ideological, socioeconomic, and cultural differences," he noted in 1987 during his first visit to the United States. "But the wisdom of politics today lies in not using those differences as a pretext for confrontation, enmity, and the arms race." Soviet spokesperson Georgi Arbatov elaborated, informing the United States that "we are going to do a terrible thing to you—we are going to deprive you of an enemy."

Surprisingly, to many adherents to **realist theory** who see great-power contests for supremacy as inevitable and strategic surrender or acceptance of defeat an impossibility, the Soviets did what they promised: they began to act like an ally instead of an enemy. The Soviet Union agreed to end its aid to and support for Cuba, withdrew from Afghanistan and eastern Europe, and announced unilateral reductions in military spending. Gorbachev also agreed to two new disarmament agreements: the START Treaty (Strategic Arms Reduction Treaty) for deep cuts in strategic arsenals, and the Conventional Forces in Europe (CFE) Treaty to reduce the Soviet presence in Europe. In addition, the Soviet Union liberalized its emigration policies and permitted greater religious freedom.

The pace of steps to rapprochement then accelerated, and the "normalization" of Soviet-American relations moved rapidly. The Cold War—which began in Europe and centered on Europe for forty-two years—began to crumble in 1989 when the Berlin Wall came down and truly ended there in 1991 when the Soviet Union dissolved, accepted capitalist free-market principles and initiated democratic reforms. To nearly everyone's astonishment, the Soviet Union acquiesced in the defeat of communism, the reunification of Germany, and the disintegration of the Warsaw Pact (see Controversy: Why Did the Cold War End Peacefully?). The conclusion of the enduring rivalry between East and West, and with it the end of the seventy-year ideological dispute as well, was such a history-transforming event that, without serious opposition to liberal capitalism, the *end of history* was proclaimed by Francis Fukuyama (1992b). "Liberalism seemed to have triumphed—not merely capitalism but democracy and the rule of law, as represented in the West, and particularly in the United States" (Keohane and Nye 2001a).

The collapse of the Cold War suggested something quite different from the lesson of the twentieth century's two world wars which had implied that great-power rivalries are necessarily doomed to end in armed conflict. The Cold War was different; it came to an end peacefully, as a combination of factors contributed at various stages in the Cold War's evolution to transform a global rivalry into a stable, even cooperative, relationship. This suggests that it is sometimes possible for great-power rivals to reconcile their competitive differences without warfare.

■ **rapprochement**
in diplomacy, a policy seeking to reestablish normal relations between enemies.

■ **realist theory**
the view that states are unitary global actors in relentless competition with each other for position and power in the international hierarchy.

CONTROVERSY WHY DID THE COLD WAR END PEACEFULLY?

How history is remembered is important because those memories shape future decisions about the management of great-power rivalries. Why did the Cold War end without the use of armed force? That question remains a puzzle that still provokes much controversy, in part because the Cold War's abrupt end came as such a surprise to most observers and, in the unanticipated outcome, also undermined confidence in the adequacy of conventional realist theories that argued that no great power would ever accept without a fight the loss of position to another hegemonic rival.

What do you think? What was the cause of the Cold War's collapse? In considering your view on this issue, take into account some divergent opinions.

From one perspective, the policies George Kennan recommended in his famous "X" article now appear prophetic. In his version of nonmilitary containment, Kennan anticipated that this would "promote tendencies which must eventually find their outlet in either the breakup of or the gradual mellowing of Soviet power." Many believe that this was precisely what did happen, albeit more than forty years later!

Neorealists, in contrast, emphasize the contribution that nuclear weapons, and the West's superior military power and extended deterrence through alliances, made to forcing the Soviet Union's surrender. In 1991, for example, an adviser to U.S. President Reagan, Richard Perle, articulated the realist view in his contention that people "who argued for nuclear deterrence and serious military capabilities contributed mightily to the position of strength that eventually led the Soviet leadership to choose a less bellicose, less menacing approach to international politics."

Liberals and neoliberals voice another interpretation about causes, as Ted Galen Carpenter (1991) did when he observed that many Russian demonstrators "who sought to reject communist rule looked to the American system for inspiration. But the source of that inspiration was America's reputation as a haven for the values of limited government, not Washington's $300-billion-a-year military budget and its network of global military bases."

Although no consensus has materialized about the ways in which these factors individually or in combination put an end to the Cold War, a fundamental question resides at the center of this postmortem. Did military containment force the Soviet Union into submission? Or did Soviet leaders succumb to the inherent political weaknesses of communism, which caused an internal economic malaise that left them unable to conduct an imperial policy abroad or retain communist control at home? In other words, was the end of Communist Party rule accepted because of the intimidation of U.S. military strength? Or was the outcome produced by other political and economic influences within the Soviet Union, as suggested in 1991 by Georgi Arbatov, director of the USSR's Institute for the USA and Canada Studies, who countered the realist perspective by arguing "that President Reagan's 'tough' policy and intensified arms race . . . persuaded communists to 'give up' is sheer nonsense. Quite to the contrary, this policy made the life for reformers, for all who yearned for democratic changes in their life, much more difficult. . . . The conservatives and reactionaries were given predominant influence. . . . Reagan made it practically impossible to start reforms after Brezhnev's death (Andropov had such plans) and made things more difficult for Gorbachev to cut military expenditures."

Sorting out the contribution of different causes to ending the Cold War will doubtless intrigue historians for decades, just as determining the causes for its onset has done. The lessons drawn from this forty-two-year drama remain important because they affect how leaders are likely to manage new great-power rivalries in the twenty-first century.

The Consequences of the Cold War

In accepting the devolution of its external empire, Russia made the most dramatic peaceful retreat from power in history. The collapse of the East-West contest left the world facing unfamiliar circumstances. No longer was there "a clear and present danger to delineate the purpose of power, and this basic shift invalidated the framework for much of the thought and action about international affairs in the East and West since World War II" (Oberdorfer 1991).

The end of the Cold War has altered the face of world affairs in profound and diverse ways. The immediate consequence of the Cold War's end is a transformed global hierarchy in which Russia is no longer a challenger to U.S. hegemonic leadership. Communism's disappearance into the dustbin of history inspired hope for international peace but, at the same time, raised the specter of new kinds of global instability. As then President George Bush lamented in November 1991, "The collapse of communism has thrown open a Pandora's box of ancient ethnic hatreds, resentment, even revenge."

One consequence warrants particular attention: Following Russia's decline, can we expect another fifty years of great-power peace? Or will the transformed balance of power be a prelude in the twenty-first century to new great-power rivalries and possibly war?

THE FUTURE OF GREAT-POWER POLITICS: A COLD PEACE?

A peaceful future is not certain. The insights of long-cycle and realist theories predict pessimistically that prevailing trends in the diffusion of economic power will lead to renewed competition, conflict, and perhaps even warfare among the great powers, and that the range of new problems and potential threats will multiply.

To realists, great-power rivalry for power and position is likely to resume because the international anarchy that promotes it continues to shape the international conduct of states. Realists also foresee probable instability resulting from the changes unfolding in the global system's structure if U.S. hegemony begins to decay as rivals rise to challenge U.S. leadership.

A Twenty-First-Century Multipolar World

While the distribution of power in the Cold War system was bipolar, the post–Cold War world promises to be very different. Russia's demise produced a new unipolar structure. In early 1991, when it victoriously fought the Persian Gulf War, the United States basked in a "unipolar moment." It was the "one first-rate power [with] no prospect in the immediate future of any power to rival it. . . . [It was] the only country with the military, diplomatic, political and economic assets to be a decisive player in any conflict in whatever part of the world it [chose] to involve itself" (Krauthammer 1991).

This condition is not likely to last far into the new millennium, however. As Map 4.3 and Figure 4.2 show, the long-term trajectories of history unmistakably point to a world in which China, and perhaps other great powers, will rise to challenge U.S. financial prominence and even if U.S. military supremacy remains unchallenged (see Emmott 2002; Nye 2002a; Wallerstein 2002). China and others are growing in economic power (more rapidly) relative to the United States, and this suggests that the pecking order of the world's countries is likely to change in the early twenty-first century. One pro-

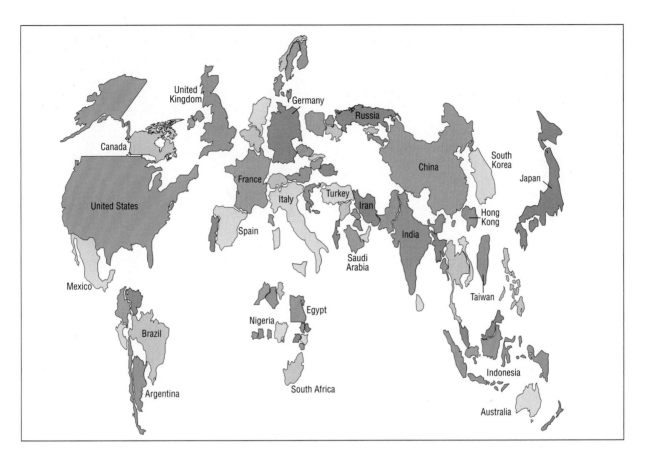

MAP 4.3
The Emerging Centers of Power in the Twenty-First Century Global Hierarchy

To estimate which countries are the most powerful and which are relatively weak, analysts frequently rely on the size of states' economies, because that measure predicts the power potential of each state (that is, their relative capacity to project power and exercise global influence). The map on the left pictures the proportionate economic clout of the leading great powers (measured by purchasing power parities), showing the United States, China, Japan, India, and Germany as today's leading economic powerhouses. Figure 4.2 on page 124 projects the probable rank order of the largest economic powerhouses by the year 2020, and postulates that in the short-term future the global hierarchy of power will look quite different from today, with China at the apex of economic power.

SOURCE: *Economist* (2002), 24.

jection provides clues on how to draw the probable geopolitical map of the future:

> Half a century from now, the world will not be unrecognizably different from the place it is now; it will be neither the more or less frontierless globe some optimists still hope for, nor the trampling-ground of monsters some pessimists used to fear. But nor will it be the same as the world of the

FIGURE 4.2

Projection of the Fifteen Largest Global Economies by 2020

Using purchasing power parities (PPPs) to account for differences in countries' price levels, the World Bank forecasts the probable size of the largest economies. The projections show that the rank order of the largest economic powerhouses by 2020 will be substantially different from today's. The political and military consequences are not predicted, but long-cycle theory postulates that the economic changes will breed political and even military conflict.

SOURCE: McGranahan (1995), 59; see also World Bank (2002b).

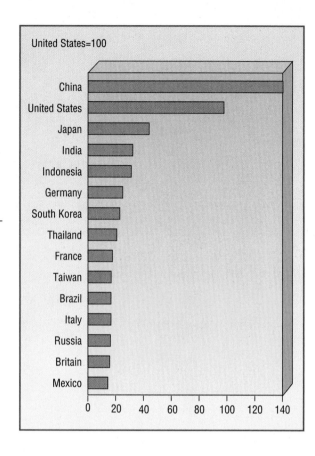

42 years of the Cold War, which was a two-sided confrontation between the communist and anti-communist alliances, or the world of the 150 years before that, which was a maneuvering for supremacy among four or five countries all of which sat in the part of the map called Europe, with America and Japan joining in only near the end.

The new pattern will consist of several powers, as in pre–Cold War days, but the competing powers will be spread more evenly over the map; one of these powers will start with a large lead over the others, but it is not sure how long it will keep that lead; and neither is it clear how many of the five or six possible competitors will actually decide to join in the struggle. These things will become known only when the two main questions of the next decade or so are answered. Those questions are whether the United States and Europe continue their present partnership, or go their separate ways; and which of the other potential members of the coming multi-power world raises its head first. (*Economist*, July 31, 1999, 4)

■ **multipolar**
an international system with more than two dominant power centers.

■ **balance of power**
the theory that peace and stability are most likely to be maintained when military power is distributed so that no single power or bloc can dominate the others.

Such a future **multipolar** world would be structured very differently from previous balance-of-power distributions in which either one (unipolarity) or two (bipolarity) countries possess overwhelming power. The multipolar global agenda requires continuing concern about military security and **balance-of-power** politics—the focus of realism—alongside mounting concerns about the great powers' economic relations—the focus of liberal international relations theory.

Stephen Shaver/AFP

A New Global Hegemon? China is a rising economic giant that many expect to become the globe's wealthiest country. In the West this has generated the fear that as China becomes a modern military power it will seek hegemony and use force to cause trouble abroad. Shown here are Chinese Peoples' Liberation Army soldiers marching with bayoneted rifles while performing official honor guard duties at a welcoming ceremony in Beijing—a show of strength at Tiananmen Square by the Chinese army, and a symbol of China's potential to project power.

The Challenge of Multipolarity. The character of a new multipolar structure may be very different from the stability that has characterized the unipolar and bipolar phases of international politics since World War II. In part this is because the emergence of a number of comparatively equal great powers will introduce more complexity and uncertainty about allegiances and alignments, and "in an international system characterized by perhaps five or six major powers . . . order will have to emerge much as it did in past centuries: from a reconciliation and balancing of competing national interests" (Kissinger 1994).

Many theorists point out the dangers inherent in multipolar distributions of power. Their warnings are inspired by the historical record, which suggests that if we look to the past to anticipate the future, we have many reasons to fear the reemergence of this kind of system. Today's hopes for great-power cooperation in the new millennium have many precedents. The end of every previous great-power war has been followed by an initial hopeful burst of collaborative institution building to forge a stable new order among the victorious powers. But each of these great-power designs for a new security regime, constructed at the conclusion of a multipolar period's war, ultimately proved temporary when the postwar sense of urgency faded. Precedents include the Peace of Westphalia (1648), the Treaty of Utrecht (1713), the Concert of Europe (1815), the League of Nations (1919), and the UN (1945). In each case, as the great powers' relative strength changed, collaboration gave way to competition. Sooner or later, *every* previous multipolar system collapsed, as one or more of the major powers expressed dissatisfaction with the existing hierarchy, rejected the rules by which they had agreed to manage their relations, and attempted to overturn the status quo by force. Rivalry has routinely resulted in a hegemonic struggle for supremacy ending in a new catastrophic general war, each more destructive than the last. This invites the sobering conclusion that

> in a world of sovereign states a contest among them over the distribution of power is the normal condition and . . . such contests often lead to war. . . . The reasons for seeking more power are often not merely the search for security or material advantage. Among them are demands for greater prestige, respect, deference, in short, honor. Since such demands involve judgments even more subjective than those about material advantage, they are still harder to satisfy. Other reasons emerge from fear, often unclear and intangible, not always of immediate threats but also of more distant ones, against which reassurance may not be possible. The persistence of such thinking in a wide variety of states and systems over the space of millennia suggests the unwelcome conclusion that war is probably part of the human condition and likely to be with us for some time yet. (Kagan 1995, 569)

Multipolar politics looks especially menacing when we take into account the interplay of military and economic factors in the perceived rankings of the great powers. In such a system, differentiating friend from foe will be more difficult because allies in military security are likely to be rivals in trade relationships. In Lester Thurow's (1992) apt phrase, the great powers are likely to go "head to head" on the economic battlefield. In this arena we can expect China and perhaps a reascendant Russia, India, and South Korea to join the fray. The U.S.-China and U.S.-Russia disputes in late 1999 about security issues and NATO enlargement at the very time they were also arguing about "fair trade" and the use of intervention to protect human rights within national borders illustrate the tensions that can easily escalate between powers at the pinnacle of the global hierarchy. So, too, have tensions escalated between the United States and the other great powers in 2002 over the conduct of America's war on global terrorism, the Middle East and Persian Gulf, and numerous trade agreements and environmental protection treaties (see Chapters 9, 10, and 15).

The diffusion of wealth predicts the likely intensification of great-power political competition. Throughout history, changes in comparative economic advantage have preceded political competition. When multipolarity has existed, economic rivals have struggled to protect their wealth and have competed politically for economic position, with military conflict usually following (Rusi 1997).

A "new cold war" could emerge between any pair of great powers, such as between the globe's two major contenders for supremacy, the United States and China, if their competition escalates and they practice containment to prevent their rival's quest for hegemony. However, this kind of armed rivalry need not develop; cooperation could increase instead. Quite different and inconsistent political types of great-power relations could emerge in the economic and military spheres. The probability of economic rivalry and conflict is generally high, whereas the likelihood of security cooperation for many of these same relationships is also high. For example, the United States, Japan, and China exhibit conflict in their commercial relations but nevertheless also display continuing efforts to manage their security relations collaboratively (as shown by their cooperation in fighting terrorism). Table 4.2 presents a projection of the kind of

TABLE 4.2

The New Great-Power Chessboard: Simultaneously Unfolding Military and Economic Rivalries

	Military Rivalry						*Economic Rivalry*				
	United States	Japan	Germany	Russia	China		United States	Japan	Germany	Russia	China
United States	—					United States	—				
Japan	L	—				Japan	H	—			
Germany	M	M	—			Germany	H	H	—		
Russia	M	H	H	—		Russia	L	L	M	—	
China	H	H	H	M	—	China	H	H	M	M	—

Note: The symbols H = high, M = medium, and L = low signify the likelihood of bilateral relationships that may develop in the twenty-first century.
How the great powers will align militarily and economically in the twenty-first century is difficult to predict. A wide variety of strategic and trade relationships are possible. To complicate the task of prediction, in the first decade of the twenty-first century the paradox exists that many of the pairs of great powers that are the most active trade partners are also the greatest military rivals. This table depicts the bilateral great-power relationships in their military and economic dimensions and illuminates the question of whether economic cooperation will help to reduce potential military competition.

cross-cutting bilateral relationships that could develop among the great powers in the twenty-first century. It estimates the probability of military cooperation and economic conflict between any pair of the five major powers.

Awareness of these different possibilities may have been behind U.S. Secretary of State Lawrence Eagleburger's warning in 1989:

> The issue . . . is how well the United States accomplishes the transition from overwhelming predominance to a position more akin to a "first among equals" status, and how well America's partners—Japan and Western Europe—adapt to their newfound importance. The change will not be easy for any of the players, as such shifts in power relationships have never been easy.

Few observers see advantages resulting from the emerging situation. As former U.S. Secretary of State Henry A. Kissinger surmised in 1993, this poses a serious challenge because "the United States has very little experience with a world that consists of many powers and which it can neither dominate nor from which it can simply withdraw in isolation."

Yet, we have no way of knowing whether the future will resemble the gloomy past history of multipolar systems. Patterns and practices can change, and it is possible for policymakers to learn from previous mistakes and avoid repeating them.

Responding to Multipolarity's Challenge. What, then, can the great powers do to prevent the resumption of their rivalry? What security policies should they pursue in order to avoid the dangers of shared power and rapid transitions in their position and strength in the great-power hierarchy?

The answers are highly uncertain. As we will discuss in Chapters 12–15, debate about the methods of guaranteeing international security in Washington, Beijing, Tokyo, Berlin, and Moscow today revolves around four basic options. Each is actively under consideration, and each will become more or less practical, prudent, or problematic for each great power depending on the circumstances that materialize in tomorrow's multipolar world.

A **unilateral** conception of a great power's role represents one possible option. Acting alone is especially attractive for a self-confident great power assured of its independent strength. With sufficient power, a potential hegemon can be self-reliant. Unilateralism can involve isolationism; an attempt to exert hegemonic leadership; a strategy of **selective engagement** that concentrates external involvements on vital national interests; or an effort to play the role of a "balancer" who skillfully backs one side or another in a great-power dispute, but only when necessary to maintain a military equilibrium between the other great-power disputants. At the extreme, unilateralism can lead the global leader to play the role of international bully, seeking to run the world. More commonly, unilateralism derives from the desire for control over the flexible conduct of a great power's foreign relations, independent of control by or pressure from other great powers. This, clearly, was the motive behind the landmark document signed by European leaders in June 1999 at the Cologne European Union (EU) Summit, which formally committed the EU to a common policy on security and defense. The purpose is to give the EU a "capacity for autonomous action," enabling it to act independently without U.S. approval or support. To implement the goal of acting unilaterally, the EU began to build its own independent "Eurocorps" military force following the 2000 Treaty of Nice. Likewise, the **Bush Doctrine** also captures the spirit and motives of unilateral approaches. That doctrine defiantly rejects "the liberal internationalist view of the world [that] the U.S. is merely one among many—a stronger country, yes, but one that has to adapt itself to the will and the needs of 'the international community.' " Instead, the U.S. administration under President George W. Bush is seen as having constructed the view that "America is no mere international citizen. It is the dominant power in the world, more dominant than any since Rome. Accordingly, America is [believed to be] in a position to reshape norms, alter expectations and create new realities. How? By unapologetic and implacable demonstrations of will" (Krauthammer 2001).

In the first decade of the twenty-first century, the predominance of the United States in the global hierarchy of power places it in a supreme position to practice a "go-it-alone" unilateralism. All the other great powers are relatively dependent on others and therefore, recognizing their need to address international problems cooperatively with others, emphasize multilateral approaches to foreign policy. The power of the United States in comparison with the other great power rivals permits it to embrace the unilateral posture of the Bush Doctrine. The United States, with 4.7 percent of global population, accounts for more than 31 percent of global gross domestic product, 36 percent of global defense spending, and 40 percent of global spending on research and development (Emmott 2002, 4; see also Chapter 12). With this kind of superpower status, the United States alone can afford to act independently on the world stage without the support of allies and global organizations. However, on many issues, such as counterterrorism, the U.S. colossus remains dependent on the cooperation of others (Nye 2002b), and accordingly at times is driven toward multilateral foreign policy approaches.

Moreover, with its superpower status the United States finds itself paying a price for its stature and unilateralism—it often faces vocal "anti-Americanism"

■ **unilateral**
an approach that relies on self-help, independent strategies in foreign policy.

■ **selective engagement**
a great-power grand strategy using economic and military power to influence only important particular situations, countries, or global issues by striking a balance between a highly interventionist "global policeman" and an uninvolved isolationist (see p. 514).

■ **Bush Doctrine**
the unilateral grand strategy of the George W. Bush administration to preserve a unipolar world under U.S. hegemony by keeping U.S. "military strength beyond challenge" by any other great power.

from abroad. With military and economic might comes criticism by many who hold "the view that the United States is basically a global bad guy, a nation that was founded on the impulses of materialism and expansionism [as the U.S. discovered after 9/11, and which] is hated by many good people around the world because it is an imperial bully [and] hated by many bad people around the world because it is a beacon of freedom and opportunity" (Menand 2002).

The above circumstance and unilateral response could change if and when the United States experiences a decline in its power position that reveals the limits of American supremacy and that decay is recognized. Some believe that such a hegemonic decline is already underway: for example, Immanuel Wallerstein (2002) argues that "Today, the United States is a superpower that lacks true power, a world leader nobody follows and few respect, and a nation drifting dangerously amidst a global chaos it cannot control. . . . The real question is not whether U.S. hegemony is waning but whether the United States can devise a way to descend gracefully, with minimum damage to the world, and to itself." This assessment will be tested by time, but what is certain is that the United States will, like the other great powers, also at times pursue other strategies when its perception of its interests appear to justify it.

Cultivation of a specialized relationship with another great power, similar to that between Great Britain and the United States in the twentieth century, illustrates a second approach that some pairs of great powers might pursue. The Joint Declaration on the Multipolar World and a New World Order signed by China and Russia in April 1997 suggested the kind of strategic bilateral partnerships that are likely to develop in a climate of fear in the future, as well as the most probable reasons why such alliances may be forged between powers that have suffered from frosty relations in the recent past. Convinced that a dominant United States aims to contain their influence, and asserting that "no country should claim hegemony for itself or pursue policy from positions of strength and monopolize international affairs," Moscow and Beijing announced their agreement to warm relations by joining together to counterbalance the United States as the world's lone superpower. That announcement led to a new agreement between the United States and Japan in 1999 to strengthen their specialized defense relationship by agreeing to new defense guidelines that would allow Japan to provide military support in "areas surrounding Japan" such as Taiwan. Beijing promptly responded in accordance with the realpolitik rules of balance-of-power politics. Claiming that the United States had "only one goal, the hegemonic domination of the world" propelled by military might, the enlargement and eastward expansion of NATO and strategic partnership with Japan, China strengthened its new alliance with Russia to counterbalance the perceived threat of a U.S.-EU-Japanese attempt to squeeze their countries from both east and west. Such dances among global giants, with the rapid formation and expansion of short-term specialized relationships among pairs of great powers in a climate of suspicion, is exactly the kind of national security maneuvering many expect to occur in the twenty-first century under conditions of multipolarity. Still other types of specialized relations between pairs of great powers could follow, at various levels of mutual support and commitment. There are several variants of this strategic option, including informal understandings, cooperation (sometimes termed **ententes**), and alliances formalized by treaties.

A third strategy under consideration is construction of a **concert,** or a cooperative agreement among the great powers to manage the international

■ **entente**
an agreement between states to consult if one is attacked by another party.

■ **concert**
a cooperative agreement among great powers to manage jointly the international system.

system jointly and to prevent international disputes from escalating to war. The Concert of Europe, at its apex between 1815 and 1822, is the epitome of previous great-power efforts to pursue this path to peace. The effort to build a great-power coalition to wage a war against global terrorism by the Bush administration following 9/11 is a more recent example of an attempt to contruct a concert.

Finally, some policymakers recommend that today's great powers unite with the lesser powers in constructing a true system of **collective security.** The principles rationalizing the formation of the League of Nations in 1919 exemplify this multilateral approach to peace under conditions of multipolarity, as did the 1999 pledge by Russia to cooperate with NATO following the intervention in Kosovo to build a twenty-first-century security partnership.

■ **collective security**
a security regime agreed to by the great powers setting rules for keeping peace, guided by the principle that an act of aggression by any state will be met by a collective response from the rest (see p. 540).

Whichever combination of approaches predominates in the strategies forged to prevent great-power rivalries from escalating to war in a multipolar future, it is clear that the choices the great powers make about war and peace will determine the fate of the world. To realists, there is every reason for concern. Even though to the liberal point of view the growth of interdependent globalization can act as a barrier to war, realists warn that "interdependence promotes war as well as peace. . . . Given the expectation of conflict, and necessity of taking care of one's interests, one may wonder how any state with the economic capability of a great power can refrain from arming itself with the weapons that have served so well as the great deterrent" (Waltz 2000). This prospect for a coming great-power arms race does not bode well for a twenty-first century peace, because major changes in a number of great powers and their relative power are probable, and throughout history rapid changes in the great powers' balance of power have been followed by war.

> Our generation, therefore, so far as political realism is concerned, is wandering in a zone of historical ambiguity, a political no-man's-land between, on the one hand, the state system with its balance-of-power politics now rendered globally lethal by nuclear weapons and, on the other, an evolving world order; between a fatally flawed nation-state traditionalism and a newer globalism that is powerless in its infancy. Under these circumstances political realism must detach itself from time-honored links to the balance-of-power state system and find a new mooring. (Gulick 1999, 17)

The future is largely in the hands of the great powers, because "powerful states make the rules" (Keohane and Nye 2001a). What kinds of rules and institutions will they create, and will their creations increase or decrease the prospects for global security? In Chapter 5, we examine the international institutions that have been parented by the great powers as well as the potential contribution that might be made by other nonstate actors such as nongovernmental organizations (NGOs), and consider the role that they perform in transforming world politics–from war to peace or from peace to another general war.

KEY TERMS

long-cycle theory
hegemon
hegemonic stability theory
enduring rivalries
counterfactual reasoning
structuralism
global level of analysis
balance of power
individual level of analysis
rational choice
state level of analysis
nationalism
bipolar
realism
liberal theory
Kellogg-Briand Pact
irredentism
fascism
machtpolitik
isolationism

appeasement
colonialism
multipolarity
political economy
protectionism
imperialism
rational choice
Yalta Conference
Cold War
power transition
sphere of influence
mirror images
self-fulfilling prophecy
security dilemma
domino theory
ideology
security regime
unipolarity
Truman Doctrine
containment

extended deterrence
bipolarity
peaceful coexistence
détente
Strategic Arms Limitation Talks
  (SALT)
Carter Doctrine
linkage theory
Reagan Doctrine
rapprochement
realist theory
multipolar
balance of power
security regime
unilateral
selective engagement
Bush Doctrine
entente
concert
collective security

SUGGESTED READING

Kadera, Kelly M. *The Power-Conflict Story: A Dynamic Model of Interstate Rivalry.* Ann Arbor: University of Michigan Press, 2001.

Kegley, Charles W. Jr., and Gregory A. Raymond. *A Multipolar Peace? Great-Power Politics in the Twenty-First Century.* New York: St. Martin's Press, 1994.

Kennedy, Paul. *The Rise and Fall of the Great Powers.* New York: Random House, 1987.

Kissinger, Henry. *Diplomacy.* New York: Simon & Schuster, 1994.

Leebaert, Derek. *The Fifty-Year Wound: The True Price of America's Cold War Victory.* Boston: Little, Brown, 2003.

Mearsheimer, John J. *The Tragedy of Great Power Politics.* New York: W. W. Norton, 2001.

Melko, Matthew. *General War among Great Powers in World History.* Lewiston, N.Y.: Edwin Mellen, 2001.

Murray, Williamson, and Allan R. Millett. *A War to Be Won: Fighting the Second World War.* Cambridge, Mass.: Harvard University Press, 2000.

Nye, Joseph S., Jr. *The Paradox of American Power: Why the World's Only Superpower Can't Go It Alone.* New York: Oxford University Press, 2002.

Pfaff, William. "The Question of Hegemony," *Foreign Affairs* 80 (January/February, 2001): 50–64.

Rusi, Alpo M. *Dangerous Peace: New Rivalry in World Politics.* Boulder, Colo.: Westview Press, 1997.

Thompson, William R., "Why Rivalries Matter and What Great Power Rivalries Can Tell Us about World Politics," pp. 3–28 in William R. Thompson, ed., *Great Power Rivalries.* Columbia: University of South Carolina Press, 1999.

WHERE ON THE WORLD WIDE WEB?

The Avalon Project—World War II
http://www.yale.edu/lawweb/avalon/wwii/wwii.htm

Yale Law School has ambitiously undertaken to collect and house digital documents relevant to the fields of law, history, economics, politics, diplomacy, and government. This site links you to documents relating to World War II. As Chapter 4 explains, the end of World War II generated much uncertainty and mistrust. While visiting the archive, read the text of the agreements reached at the Yalta Conference at which Roosevelt, Churchill, and Stalin tried to resolve territorial issues after World War II. Did the agreements reached at Yalta make the Cold War inevitable?

Cold War
http://www.cnn.com/SPECIALS/cold.war/

Chapter 4 discusses the causes, characteristics, and consequences of the Cold War. Learn more about the most recent great-power rivalry by exploring CNN's award-winning, comprehensive, Cold War Web site. Navigate interactive maps of the nuclear testing sites in the American Southwest. Learn more about the key players and then play an interactive game to see which Cold War players you recognize. Hear sound bites and match them to the statesman who made them. Tour Cold War capitals through 3-D images. See espionage weapons and hear real-life spy stories.

Race for the Superbomb
http://www.pbs.org/wgbh/amex/bomb/sfeature/index.html

On this highly enlightening site, PBS re-creates the competition between the United States and the Soviet Union in their race to stockpile nuclear weapons. This Web site brings home many aspects of the Cold War rivalry discussed in Chapter 4. Have you ever wondered if you could survive a nuclear blast if a bomb exploded fifty miles away? Nuclear Blast Mapper will analyze the "zones of destruction" for any location. If you survived the blast, find out if you would survive the fallout. Then, take a virtual tour of a secret government bunker maintained as shelter for lucky congressmen in case of a nuclear attack. Not scared enough? Take a Panic Quiz to determine your panic quotient.

Senator Joe McCarthy: A Multimedia Celebration
http://webcorp.com/mccarthy/

A multimedia site where students can see and hear the most famous speeches and hearings given by Joe McCarthy. This is an important site for contemporary students who have trouble understanding "what all the fuss was about."

Soviet Exhibit
http://sunsite.unc.edu/expo/soviet.exhibit/entrance.html

This Web site is a virtual tour of the Library of Congress's Soviet Archives exhibit. Go to the first floor to see the Internal Workings of the Soviet System or proceed directly to the second floor to see the Soviet Union and the United States. Shuttle buses take you to other pavilions or let you visit the Restaurant. You can even leave messages for a current or future friend at the Post Office.

The World War I Document Archive
http://www.lib.byu.edu/~rdh/wwi/

The World War I Military History List has assembled a group of primary documents from World War I. Read the treaties, scan personal reminiscences, see photos, and access links to other resources. Chapter 4 puts forth theories concerning the cause of World War I. Some state that the switching alliances in Europe brought on the war. Others claim that the rational choices of individual German leaders who wanted to consolidate power led to a declaration of war. And finally, many assert that state factors, such as the rise of nationalism in Germany, were responsible for the war. After reading the documents in the archive, which theories do you think best explain the advent of World War I?

INFOTRAC® COLLEGE EDITION

Howard, Michael. "The Great War," *The National Interest* Summer 2001.

Skidelsky, Robert. "Imbalance of Power (History of the Grand Alliance during World War II)," *Foreign Policy* March 2002.

Brooks, Stephen G., and William C. Wohlforth. "Power, Globalization, and the End of the Cold War: Reevaluating a Landmark Case for Ideas," *International Security* Winter 2000.

Waltz, Kenneth N. "Structural Realism after the Cold War," *International Security* Summer 2000.

For more articles, enter:

"World War, 1914–1918" in the Subject Guide.

"World War, 1939–1945" in the Subject Guide.

"cold war" in the Subject Guide.

NONSTATE ACTORS IN THE INTERSTATE SYSTEM

TOPICS AND THEMES

- Nonstate actors: What are IGOs and NGOs?

- Global IGO Actors
  The United Nations
  The World Trade Organization, the World Bank, the International Monetary Fund, and other global IGOs

- The European Union and other regional IGOs

- NGOs on the world stage
  Nonstate nations and the indigenous ethnic groups of the Fourth World
  Religious movements
  Multinational corporations and transnational banks
  Reevaluating NGOs' capacity to transform world politics

- Nonstate actors: Saviors or stranglers of the state?

- **CONTROVERSY** ARE RELIGIOUS MOVEMENTS CAUSES OF WAR OR SOURCES OF TRANSNATIONAL HARMONY?

At the United Nations, U.S. President George W. Bush insists on September 11, 2002 that Iraq must be disarmed, and warns "we have been more than patient."

For all its faults, the United Nations remains the only universally representative and comprehensively empowered body the world has to deal with threats to international peace and security.

—GARETH EVANS, former foreign minister of Australia, 2002

No reason exists why—in addition to states—nationalities, diasporas, religious communities and other groups should not be treated as legitimate actors. . . . In the emerging global politics, however, state sovereignty and authority are withering and no alternative, such as some system of world government, is about to fill the vacuum.

—SAMUEL P. HUNTINGTON, realist theoretician, 2001

The 1648 Peace of Westphalia, which ended the Thirty Years' War, also ended the secular authority of the Pope by creating sovereign and independent territorial states. The history of world politics for the past 350 years has largely been a chronicle of interactions among states that remain the dominant political organizations in the world. States' interests, capabilities, and goals significantly shape world politics. However, the supremacy of the state has been severely challenged in recent years. Increasingly, world affairs are being influenced by intergovernmental organizations that transcend national boundaries—global international organizations such as the United Nations (UN) and regional organizations such as the European Union (EU). In addition, there exist many ways that individual people band together as coalitions of private citizens in groups to play influential roles in international affairs. Religions, nationalities based on ethnic and linguistic heritages, and multinational corporations are examples of nongovernmental organizations. Diverse in scope and purpose, these nonstate actors push their own agendas and increasingly exert global influence.

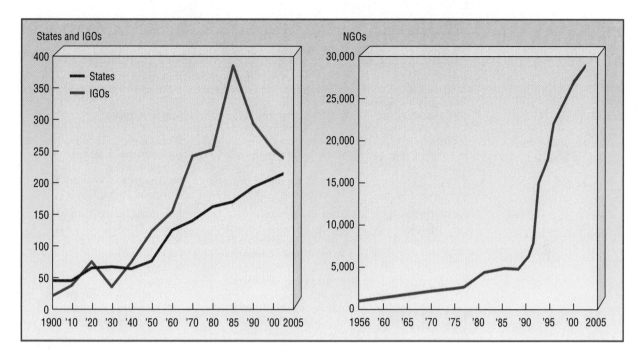

FIGURE 5.1

The Number of States, IGOs, and NGOs since 1900

The number of independent states increased greatly in the twentieth century—especially since the decolonization movement began after World War II—but the number of intergovernmental organizations (IGOs) and especially nongovernmental organizations (NGOs) has grown even more rapidly.

SOURCES: Figures for states are based on the Correlates of War (COW) project at the University of Michigan under the direction of J. David Singer: States, Polity III data (Jaggers and Gurr 1995); IGOs and NGOs from Yearbook of International Organizations 1993/1994 (1993: p. 1699), and moving averages from selected prior volumes. Reprinted with permission of the Union of International Associations, Belgium.

NONSTATE ACTORS, INTERGOVERNMENTAL ORGANIZATIONS (IGOS), AND NONGOVERNMENTAL ORGANIZATIONS (NGOS): AN INTRODUCTION

There are two principal types of nonstate actors: **intergovernmental organizations (IGOs),** whose members are states, and **nongovernmental organizations (NGOs),** whose members are private individuals and groups. Both types existed prior to the twentieth century and both are now very pervasive. The Union of International Organizations, which maintains comprehensive, up-to-date information on both types, records that their numbers increased sharply during the nineteenth century, as international commerce and communications grew alongside industrialization. In 1909, there were 37 IGOs and 176 NGOs. By 1960 there were 154 IGOs and 1,255 NGOs, and at the start of 2003 these numbers had risen to 243 and 28,775, respectively (see Figure 5.1).

IGOs are purposely created by states to solve shared problems. This gives the IGOs whatever authority they possess for the purposes states assign them. In this sense, IGOs are more important than NGOs because their members are states and, as such, are a product of the *interstate* system at the **global level of analysis** that decisions by states have produced.

■ **intergovernmental organizations (IGOs)** institutions created and joined by states' governments, which give them authority to make collective decisions to manage particular problem(s) on the global agenda.

TABLE 5.1

A Simple Classification of Intergovernmental Organizations (IGOs)

| Geographic Scope of Membership | *Range of Stated Purpose* | |
	Multiple Purposes	Single Purpose

Global	United Nations
	World Trade Organization
	UNESCO
	Organization of the Islamic
	   Conference
		World Health Organization
		International Labor
		   Organization
		International Monetary Fund
		Universal Postal Union

Interregional,
  regional,
  subregional
	European Union
	Organization for Security
	   and Cooperation in Europe
	Organization of American
	   States
	Organization of African
	   Unity
	League of Arab States
	Association of Southeast
	   Asian Nations
		European Space Agency
		Nordic Council
		North Atlantic Treaty
		   Organization
		International Olive Oil
		   Council
		International North Pacific
		   Coffee Organization
		African Groundnut Council

■ **nongovernmental organizations (NGOs)** transnational organizations of private citizens maintaining consultative status with the UN; they include professional associations, foundations, multinational corporations, or simply internationally active groups in different states joined together to work toward common interests.

■ **global level of analysis** an analytical approach to world politics that emphasizes the impact of worldwide conditions on the behavior of states, IGOs, NGOs, and other international actors.

In interpreting the spectacular growth of IGOs, keep in mind that identifying these nonstate actors is not easy. In principle, IGOs are defined not only by the fact that their members are the governments of states, but also by their permanence and institutional organization; IGOs meet at relatively regular intervals and have specified procedures for making decisions and a permanent secretariat or headquarters staff. If these definitional criteria were relaxed, an additional 4,907 international bodies ("special type") would qualify for inclusion as IGOs, as would more than 47,098 other nongovernmental associations that share characteristics with NGOs (*Yearbook of International Organizations, 2001/2002*, vol. 3, 1784). IGOs vary widely in size and purpose. Only thirty-four qualify as "intercontinental organizations" and only thirty-five are, like the UN, "universal membership" IGOs. The rest, accounting for more than 72 percent of the total, are limited in their scope and confined to particular regions. Table 5.1 illustrates these differences. The variation among the organizations in each subcategory is great, particularly with single purpose, limited-membership IGOs. The North Atlantic Treaty Organization (NATO), for example, is primarily a military alliance, while others, such as the Organization of American States (OAS), promote both economic development and democratic reforms. Still, most IGOs concentrate their activities on specific economic or social issues of special concern to them, such as the management of trade, or of transportation.

The expansion of IGOs has created a complex network of overlapping international organizations which cooperate with one another to deal with a wide range of global issues. They support one another to work, for example, on issues as varied as trade, defense, disarmament, economic development, agriculture, health, culture, human rights, the arts, illegal drugs, tourism, labor,

Grassroots Recruitment for Global Change NGOs are nonprofit, grassroots groups that advocate a wide variety of causes in order to set the global agenda in ways consistent with their ideology. In this advertisement, the Earthjustice Legal Defense Fund seeks to protect endangered species of plants and animals. Nearly twenty-nine thousand NGOs are active throughout the globe.

women's plight, education, debt, the environment, crime, humanitarian aid, civilian crisis relief, telecommunications, science, globalization, immigration, and refugees.

NGOs also differ widely. Due to their number and diversity, they are even more difficult than IGOs to classify. In 2002, the Union of International Associations categorized the major "conventional" NGOs as split, with 7.5 percent as "universal," 16.2 percent as "intercontinental," and the vast majority, 75 percent, as "regionally oriented." Functionally, NGOs span virtually every facet of political, social, and economic activity in an increasingly borderless globalized world, ranging from earth sciences to health care, language, history, culture, theology, law, ethics, security, and defense.

> Non-governmental organizations are not a homogeneous group. The long list of acronyms that has accumulated around NGOs can be used to illustrate this. People speak of NGOs, INGOs (International NGOs), BINGOs (Business International NGOs), RINGOs (Religious International NGOs), ENGOs (Environmental NGOs), QUANGOs (Quasi-Non-Governmental Organizations—i.e., those that are at least partially created or supported by states), and many others. Indeed, all these types of NGO and more are among those having consultative status at the UN. Among the NGOs . . . are the Academic Council on the UN System, the All India Women's Conference, the Canadian Chemical Producers Association, CARE International, the World Young Women's Christian Association, the World Wide Fund for Nature International, the World Wide Fund for Nature (Malaysia), the Union of Arab Banks, the Women's International League for Peace and Freedom, the World Energy Council, the World

Federation of Trade Unions, and the World Veterans Association. Thus it is difficult to generalize about NGOs at the UN. (Stephenson 2000, 270)

In general, the socially constructed image of NGOs widely accepted throughout the world is highly positive: humanitarian movements dedicated to improving the human condition rather than seeking to benefit themselves at the expense of others. However, some NGOs arguably unite people for collective action in ways that can harm others. Nonetheless, most commentary emphasizes the constructive international role that most NGOs perform. An example is the World Bank's definition of NGOs as "private organizations that pursue activities to relieve suffering, promote the interests of the poor, protect the environment, provide basic social services, or undertake community development."

In general, the term "NGO" can be applied to all nonprofit organizations that are independent of government. It thus is also customary to think of NGOs as intersocietal organizations that contribute to negotiations between and among states in the hope of reaching agreements for global governance on nearly every issue of international public policy. NGOs link the global society by forming networks to advocate for policy changes. For this purpose, many NGOs interact formally with IGOs. For instance, more than one thousand NGOs actively consult with various agencies of the extensive UN system, maintain offices in hundreds of cities, and hold parallel conferences with IGO meetings to which states send representatives. Such partnerships between NGOs and IGOs enable both types to work (and lobby) together in pursuit of common policies and programs.

Although widespread geographically, NGOs are most active in the advanced Global North industrial democracies. "This is so because open political systems, ones in which there is societal pluralism, are more likely to allow their citizens to participate in nongovernmental organizations, and such [democratic governments] are highly correlated with relatively high levels of economic development" (Jacobson 1984).

In this chapter, we will discuss some prominent and representative IGOs, including the UN, the EU, and various other regional organizations, and investigate the impact of NGOs, including ethnic nationalities and indigenous peoples, religious movements, and multinational corporations. The chapter's purpose is not simply to describe these nonstate actors, but to provoke you to question the extent to which their activities undermine states' continuing autonomy. Thus, the focus throughout will be on state governments' capacity to manage global change and the role of nonstate actors in that process.

GLOBAL IGOS

The United Nations

The United Nations (UN) is the best-known global organization. What distinguishes it from most other IGOs is its nearly universal membership, including today 190 independent states from every region (see Figure 5.2). The UN's nearly fourfold growth from the fifty-one states that joined it at the UN's birth in 1945 has been spectacular, but the admission process has from the start been governed by political conflicts that show the extent to which the organization

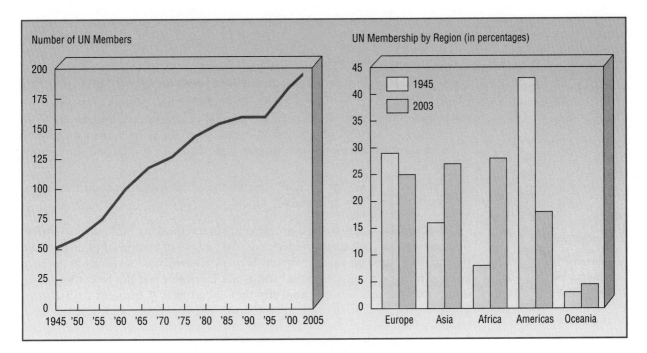

FIGURE 5.2
The Changing Membership of the United Nations, 1945–2005
As the figure on the left shows, the UN's membership has seen episodic bursts of growth from 51 states in 1945 to 190 in 2003 with the admission of Switzerland—and newly independent East Timor (the world's 208th sovereign state) is expected to join next. Over nearly six decades of expansion, the United Nations has increasingly included Global South countries (see figure on right). This shift has influenced the kinds of interests and issues the UN has confronted, expanding the global agenda from the priorities of the great powers in the Global North to include those important to the developing states in the Global South.
SOURCE: United Nations.

reflects the relationships of the five great powers that created it and govern it through veto authority in the Security Council.

In principle, any sovereign state accepting the UN's regulations and principles can join, but the great powers have often let **realpolitik** political considerations dictate what countries were admitted. During the Cold War, both the United States and the Soviet Union prevented countries aligned with their adversary from joining, and the controversy has continued about Taiwan ever since. In the 1970s the United States recognized the communist government in China and engineered the transfer of the "China seat" from the so-called Republic of China in Taiwan. Because China insists that Taiwan in not an independent state but instead a rebel province of the mainland, Taiwan cannot rejoin the world organization. Similar political barriers stand in the way of Palestine gaining UN admission by declaring its statehood.

The UN's Purposes and Expanding Agenda. In addition to its nearly universal membership, and its pervasive **politics** mirrowing world politics, the UN

■ **realpolitik**
the theoretical outlook prescribing that countries should put their own national interests above concern for the global community.

■ **politics**
the exercise of influence.

is also a multipurpose organization. As Article 1 of the UN Charter states, its objectives are to:

- Maintain international peace and security
- Develop friendly relations among nations based on respect for the principle of equal rights and self determination of peoples
- Achieve international cooperation in solving international problems of an economic, social, cultural, or humanitarian character and in promoting and encouraging respect for human rights and for fundamental freedoms for all
- Function as a center for harmonizing the actions of nations in the attainment of these common ends

Peace and security figured prominently in the thinking of those responsible for creating the UN and its predecessor, the League of Nations. Following each twentieth-century global war, world leaders created new institutions to keep peace. The liberal conviction that war is not inevitable but can be controlled by reforming the international **anarchy** that encourages it inspired both efforts. The first, the League of Nations, sought to prevent a recurrence of the catastrophic First World War by replacing the balance-of-power system with one based on **collective security.** When the league failed to restrain Germany, Japan, and Italy during the 1930s, it collapsed. At the start of World War II, the U.S., British, and Russian allies began planning for a new international organization—the UN—to maintain the postwar peace after victory. However, faith in the UN's ability quickly eroded. The world organization soon became paralyzed by the unforeseen **Cold War** conflict between the United States and the Soviet Union. When the chill of the Cold War began to thaw in 1989, the UN's mission underwent a transformation.

The UN has sought from its birth to combine the dual goals of preserving peace and improving the quality of life for humanity. These twin missions have carried the UN into nearly every corner of the complex network of interstate relations. The UN's conference machinery has become permanent: it has provided a mechanism for the management of international conflict, and increasingly the UN has become involved in a broad range of global welfare issues.

The history of the UN reflects the fact that both rich countries and developing countries have successfully used the organization to promote their own foreign policy goals, and this proud record has bred hopes throughout the world that the UN will be able to manage an ever changing and growing agenda. The UN Millennium Summit attended in September 2000 by 150 world leaders, which led to the ratification of nearly 300 treaties and conventions, made explicit the UN's **ideology** as expressed in its "six fundamental values" essential to international relations in the twenty-first century: freedom, equality, solidarity, tolerance, respect for nature, and a sense of shared responsibility. However, the UN's ambitions may exceed its meager resources. The UN has been asked to address an expanding set of pressing military and nonmilitary problems, and its plate is full. Consider the wide array of world conferences that the organization has been asked to sponsor since the 1970s: human environment (1972, 2002), law of the sea (1973), population (1974, 1984, 1994, 1999), food (1974, 1976), women (1975, 1980, 1985, 1995), human settlements (1976), basic human needs (1976), water (1977, 2002), desertification (1977), disarmament (1978,

■ **anarchy**
an absence of governmental authority, or an absence at the global level of a supranational authority to regulate relations between states.

■ **collective security**
a security regime created by the great powers that sets rules for keeping peace, guided by the principle that an act of aggression by any state will be met by a collective response from the rest.

■ **Cold War**
the forty-two-year rivalry between the United States and the Soviet Union, as well as their competing coalitions, which sought to contain each other's expansion through an arms race, and win worldwide predominance for capitalism (U.S.) or communism (USSR).

■ **ideology**
a set of core philosophical principles that a group of leaders and citizens collectively hold about politics, the interests of political actors, and the ways people ought to ethically behave.

1982, 1988), racism and racial discrimination (1978, 2002), technical cooperation among developing countries (1978), agrarian reform and rural development (1974, 1979), science and technology for development (1979), new and renewable sources of energy (1981), least-developed countries (1981), aging (1982), the peaceful uses of outer space (1982), Palestine (1947, 1982), the peaceful uses of nuclear energy (1983), the prevention of crime and the treatment of offenders (1985), drug abuse and illicit trafficking in drugs (1987, 1990, 1998), the protection of children (1990), the environment and economic development (1992, 2002), transnational corporations (1992), indigenous peoples (1992, 1994), internationally organized crime (1994), social development (1995), housing (1996), human rights (1993, 1997), global warming (1992, 1997, 2002), international trafficking of children for prostitution (2000), and principles for world order (2000). These conferences, in effect, comprise a list of "the most vital issues of present world conditions," and "represent a beginning in a long and evolving process of keeping within manageable proportions the major problems of humanity" (Bennett 1988).

The UN's agenda has grown over time, and it is certain that the number of issues and problems on the global agenda that the UN will be asked to manage will continue to grow in variety and complexity. In response to the demands that have been placed upon it, the United Nations has evolved over its more than fifty-year life into a vast administrative machinery, with offices and staff not only in the UN Headquarters in New York but also in centers spread throughout the globe (see Map 5.1, p. 145). To estimate the capacity of the United Nations to meet the huge burdens that the UN has been asked to carry across many issues, it is useful to expect how the United Nations has been organized.

The Organization of the United Nations: System and Structure

The UN's limitations are perhaps rooted in the ways it is organized for its ambitious and wide-ranging purposes. The Security Council is one of six principal organs established by the UN Charter; the others are the General Assembly, the Economic and Social Council, the Trusteeship Council, the Secretariat, and the International Court of Justice. In the General Assembly—the only organ that represents all member states—decision making follows the principle of majority rule, with no state given a veto.

Unlike the Security Council, which is empowered by the UN Charter to initiate actions including the use of force, the General Assembly can only make recommendations. The founders of the UN did not foresee that this limited mandate would later be expanded to allow the General Assembly to participate with the Security Council in managing security. The General Assembly, which has grown in numbers and importance, has assumed wider responsibilities and is now the primary body for addressing security as well as social and economic problems. The growth of the General Assembly's power may not be sufficient, however. As Secretary-General Kofi Annan noted in Tokyo in May 1997, the original UN design is outdated: it "reflects the world of 1945 and not the economic and political realities of today," and this failure to adapt to changing times lies at the core of complaints that the UN is unprepared to control the threats facing humanity in the twenty-first century.

That inadequacy is not necessarily permanent, however. Look at the UN's history. In response to the challenge of managing the world's many problems, the UN has adaptively evolved into an extraordinarily complex network of

Meeting Place for the World The United Nations headquarters in New York (pictured at right) is home to the Security Council, the General Assembly, the Secretariat, and a variety of departments and other agencies. The UN has evolved over its life into a huge bureaucracy with an equally huge global agenda.

UN/DPI photo

overlapping institutions, some of which (the UN Children's Fund or UNICEF or the United Nations University, for example) fulfill their mission in part through NGOs. The UN has also increasingly come to rely on the many NGOs that are not under its formal authority. This collaboration blurs the line between governmental and nongovernmental functions, but UN-NGO cooperation helps the UN's mission. In the process, the UN has become not one organization but a decentralized conglomerate of countless committees, bureaus, boards, commissions, centers, institutes, offices, and agencies scattered around the globe, with each of its many specialized activities managed from offices in various cities (see Map 5.1).

If any of these various units in the UN's widespread family occupies a central role in the UN's overall structure, it is the General Assembly. Countries in the Global South—seizing advantage of their growing numbers under the one-state, one-vote rules of the General Assembly—have guided UN involvement in directions of particular concern to them. This has reflected the enormous growth of diverse affiliated agencies created to address the full array of the world's problems and needs. Today, a coalition of the less-developed Global South countries comprising three-fourths of the UN and led by the **Group of 77** previously nonaligned states, along with the "Fifth Committee" (which deals with the UN budget), seeks to resist domination by the Global North and to protest that the UN ignores economic and social needs and fails to respect the Global South's special interests. The Global South's power in numbers gives it enormous clout.

North-South differences over perceived priorities are most clearly exhibited in the heated debate over the UN's budget. This controversy centers on how members should interpret the organization's charter, which states that "expenses of the Organization shall be borne by the members as apportioned by the General Assembly."

■ **Group of 77 (G-77)** a coalition of the world's poor countries formed in 1964 to press for concessions from wealthy Global North states (see p. 211).

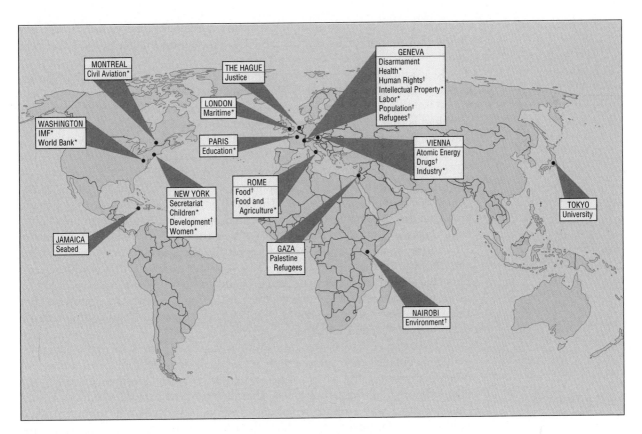

MAP 5.1
The UN's Headquarters and Global Network
The United Nations has sought since its creation to address the continuously expanding problems on the global agenda. To reduce the gap between aspiration and accomplishment, as shown on this map the United Nations has spread its administrative arm to every corner of the globe in order to fulfill its expanded mission of serving what Annan has called "a noble experiment in human cooperation."
*Specialized agencies.
†Funds and programs.
SOURCE: *The UN Handbook.*

The UN budget consists of three distinct elements: the core budget, the peacekeeping budget, and the budget for voluntary programs. States contribute to the voluntary programs and some of the peacekeeping activities as they see fit. The core budget and other peacekeeping activities are subject to assessments.

The precise mechanism by which assessments have been determined is complicated, but, historically, assessments were generally allocated according to states' capacity to pay. Although this formula is under attack in many wealthy states, it still governs. Thus the United States, which has the greatest resources, contributes 22 percent of the core UN budget (and is also the primary contributor to UN peacekeeping and voluntary programs), whereas the poorest 70 percent of the UN's members pay the minimum (0.01 percent) and contribute only $13,000 annually. By this agreement, the richest states pay more than three-fourths toward the UN's $1.2 billion budget in the fiscal year 2003.

Resistance to this budgetary formula for funding UN activities has always existed. It has grown progressively worse, in large part because when the General Assembly apportions expenses, it does so according to majority rule. The problem is that those with the most votes (the less-developed countries) do not have the money, and the most prosperous countries do not have the votes. Wide disparities have grown so that by 2002 the ten largest contributors to the UN commanded only ten votes, but were expected to pay 75 percent of its cost. At the other end of the spectrum, the poorest members paid only 25 percent of the cost but commanded 175 votes. This deep imbalance has led to many fierce financial disputes between the more numerous Global South developing countries that wield considerable influence over the kinds of issues on which the UN's attention and resources were focused and the great powers' concern about the UN's priorities, administrative efficiency, and expenses. The wealthy members charge that the existing budget procedures institutionalize a system of taxation without fair representation. The critics counter with the argument that the great-power members should bear financial responsibilities commensurate with their wealth and influence.

At issue, of course, is not simply money, which is paltry (averaging less than eighteen cents for each person in the world each year). Differences in images of what is important and which states should have political influence are the real issues. Poor states argue that needs should determine expenditure levels rather than the other way around. Major contributors, sensitive to the amounts asked of them and the purposes to which the funds are put, do not want to pay for programs they oppose. The United States in particular was historically the most vocal about its dissatisfaction and was still in arrears more than $1.2 billion in 2001 until the 9/11 terrorist attack, when the United States promptly paid its debt as it sought UN support to wage a global war against terrorism.

Even though the Global South countries have usually managed to set the agenda in the General Assembly, like the United States they also regularly failed to pay for it or to spend time lobbying for political support from other important UN groups. In fact, in early 2002 about 90 percent of the Global South members were also in arrears, and the unpaid assessments exceeded $3.1 billion.

In response to persisting cash flow problems and rising complaints about the UN's "bloated bureaucracy" and inefficient administration, Secretary-General Kofi Annan undertook what he called "bold reforms—the most extensive and far-reaching reforms in the history of the Organization." His initiative consolidated the programs under his control, reduced costs, corrected corruption and waste, and reassigned administrative responsibilities to different units in order to make the UN more efficient. These massive reforms cut the Secretariat's administrative costs by one-third, from 38 percent of the core budget to 25 percent and put the savings into a development fund for poor countries. The assessments of some Global North members were also adjusted: the United States pays 22 percent of the core budget, and Japan now pays 19.6 percent, Germany 9.8 percent, but France 6.5 percent, Russia only 2.9 percent and China only 0.9 percent. The reorganization plan merged the score of disparate programs into five categories and created the UN's first deputy secretary-general position. The new budget for the 190 members puts the UN financial house on a firmer if leaner foundation.

The future of the UN nonetheless remains uncertain. However, many supporters feel optimistic about the organization's long-term prospects, because past crises have been overcome and the UN's many important previous contributions to world peace and development have given most countries a large stake in its survival. The great gap between the mandates that the UN's members ordered, and the means they allowed for fulfilling them, may yet be closed. Failure would spell disaster.

In contemplating the UN's future agenda, it is sobering to reflect on Kofi Annan's warning that "The global agenda has never been so varied, so pressing or so complex. It demands of the international community new approaches, new resources and new commitments of political will." It is also sobering, given the UN's history, to recall that the agenda of issues that the UN is asked to address is likely to continue to be controversial and divisive. The UN is likely to remain an arena for heated exchanges among its diverse members, and the lack of consensus is likely to compromise the organization's capacity to forge new approaches and generate new resources to solve new global problems.

In the twenty-first century, the UN is likely to continue to play an active role in the areas both of social and economic enhancement and of peace and security. As we will examine in Chapter 15; however, the prospects for future UN peacekeeping are uncertain, and the capacity for the globe's most powerful IGO to engineer progress in the social and economic realm is also likely to be severely tested. The challenge will be great, because the UN is expected to serve the economic and social development needs of 190 states and 6 billion people with less money than the annual budget for New York City's police department. In the final analysis, the UN can be no more than the mandates and power that the member states give to it. As one high-level UN civil servant, Brian Urquhart, described the world's political dilemma, "Either the UN is vital to a more stable and equitable world and should be given the means to do the job, or peoples and governments should be encouraged to look elsewhere. But is there really an alternative?"

Other Prominent Global IGOs: The World Trade Organization, the World Bank, and the International Monetary Fund

Beyond the UN, literally hundreds of other IGOs are active internationally. Few are truly global, including as members every independent state. Unlike the UN, most IGOs include as members a large but incomplete list of today's sovereign states. In addition, the most influential, visible, and controversial IGOs usually have less-formal procedures in place to make policy decisions. To round out the sample, we look briefly at three of the most prominent of these other IGOs, all of which are specialized in their focus on the international political economy: the World Trade Organization, the World Bank, and the International Monetary Fund.

In each example, note that these nonstate global actors were created by the great powers for the purposes of their sponsors in response to the great powers' need for a stable international economic order, even at the voluntary sacrifice of sovereignty. IGOs such as the UN and these other IGOs "involve multilateral cooperation leading to the formation of international **regimes** on a global

■ **regimes**
norms, rules, and procedures for interaction agreed to by a set of states.

level . . . to achieve gains [states] want [which requires] they cooperate" (Keohane and Nye 2001a). To design governing institutions on a world — and human — scale, IGOs are representative of a partial step by states toward that goal. However, "states retain many of their present functions," and stand as obstacles to full-scale global governance, even if "effective governance of a partially—and increasingly—globalized world will require more extensive international institutions . . . to promote cooperation and help resolve conflict" (Keohane 2002).

The World Trade Organization.   After World War II, the United States prepared a preliminary blueprint for the International Trade Organization (ITO). The organization was to be one of three major institutions—along with the World Bank and the International Monetary Fund—to support the postwar world economy. Like the bank and the fund, as first conceived the ITO was to function as a specialized agency within the overall framework of the UN. While early negotiations for the anticipated ITO were going on, many states urged an immediate attack on trade barriers through an ad hoc conference that would function as a temporary arrangement until the ITO came into operation. Meeting in Geneva in 1947, twenty-three states negotiated a vast number of **bilateral** tariff concessions that were written into a final act called the General Agreement on Tariffs and Trade (GATT) which became a less-ambitious regime to guide trading practices.

The failure of the ITO nonetheless had given impetus to the GATT approach and led to the establishment of substitute international machinery. Unlike the ITO, GATT was based on executive agreements rather than a treaty, which meant that U.S. participation in GATT did not require U.S. Senate ratification.

GATT settlement procedures for dealing with tariff barriers to trade were sorely strained when world economic conditions took a turn for the worse, and these problems helped galvanize support for a stronger, more official IGO to address the rising economic threats to global trade and prosperity. This worldwide recession set the stage for the eventual passage of GATT and the birth of the World Trade Organization (WTO). The Uruguay Round of GATT deliberations that began in 1986 was significantly affected by the passing of the Cold War and the fall of communism in Russia and Eastern Europe. All these newly capitalist states undertook economic reforms and applied for GATT membership. Like all other major decisions creating today's key IGOs, the WTO's creation was supported by the United States and the world's other dominant economic actors in the **G-7** (Japan, Germany, Great Britain, France, Canada, and Italy). The Uruguay Round of the negotiations concluded in 1993 when the GATT members agreed to replace their temporary organization with a permanent World Trade Organization (WTO). The WTO began operations on January 1, 1995. The United States became a charter member of the new organization, and countries not yet members such as China, which later joined in 2002, were put on "fast track" for WTO membership.

The World Trade Organization was not exactly the ITO envisaged immediately following World War II, but it is nevertheless the most ambitious undertaking yet launched to regulate world trade. Unlike GATT, which functioned more as a coordinating secretariat, the World Trade Organization (WTO) is a full-fledged intergovernmental organization with a formal decision-making structure at the ministerial level. Organized as a fair-trade policeman, WTO is

■ **bilateral**
relationships or agreements between two states.

■ **G-7**
a group of the major most-advanced industrialized democracies, composed of the United States, Britain, France, Japan, Germany, Canada, and Italy, that meets in regular economic summit conferences; now known as the G-8 with the addition of Russia.

mandated to manage disputes arising from its trading partners. Functioning equally in overseeing trade in manufactures and agricultural commodities, the WTO was given authority for enforcing rules, which gives it the character of a court, and since 1995 the rules of the WTO authorize third parties to adjudicate conflicts among the WTO's more than 145 members.

"Ensuring trade flows as smoothly, predictably and as freely as possible" is the WTO's declared central purpose. However, the World Trade Organization has consistently sought to expand this agenda and the IGO's powers to lower trade barriers and thereby raise living standards through new initiatives. The WTO hopes to move well beyond the goals of reducing tariffs in agriculture, services, and traditional sectors to such areas as intellectual property rights. The present goal of the WTO is to transcend the existing matrix of free-trade agreements between pairs of countries and within particular regions or free-trade blocs and replace them with an integrated and comprehensive worldwide system of liberal or free trade.

Quite understandably, this liberal agenda poses a threat to some states, their sovereignty, and their perceived inability to successfully compete in the global capitalistic marketplace. At the heart of the complaint is the charge that the WTO undermines the traditional rule of law prohibiting interference in sovereign states' domestic affairs, including management of economic practices *within* the states' territorial jurisdiction. The WTO does, indeed, spark controversy because it undermines the **nonintervention norm** established at the 1648 Peace of Westphalia, for the WTO does in fact compromise and protract the conventional freedom given to sovereign states. However, the WTO, it should be kept in mind, developed as a result of agreements powerful states reached to voluntarily surrender some of their sovereign decision-making freedom, under the conviction that this pooling of sovereignty was a **rational choice** that would produce greater gains than losses. Nonetheless, the WTO seems destined to remain an IGO target for criticism precisely because the WTO's authority comes, particularly to some states, at what is perceived as a very high cost, namely, the reduction of a state's ability of regulate economic activities by businesses within their domestic economy.

The clout of the WTO is also somewhat uncertain and is widely perceived in the Global South as greater than probably actually exists. True, the WTO's purpose was to replace GATT with a permanent, highly administrated, and efficient IGO to pursue the same goals of liberalizing and expanding world trade. In fact "the Dispute Settlement process within the WTO gives it the strongest enforcement capacity of all international organizations" (Smith and Moran 2001). However, even though the WTO holds unprecedented responsibilities for administrating those multilateral trade agreements its members approve, the WTO cannot by itself manufacture its own agreements and does not possess the supranational authority to regulate any state's substantive economic policies. The WTO is only a formal institutional home available for member states to negotiate and implement the treaties which they voluntarily accept. The philosophy guiding the WTO is predicated and dependent on the vision its members have chosen to support—that open markets and free governments competing in global trade without discrimination contribute to the welfare of all countries. The continuation of that constructed vision depends, in the last analysis, on the willingness of the states which are members to abide by that

■ **nonintervention norm** a fundamental international legal principle, now being challenged, that traditionally has defined as illegal interference by one state in the domestic affairs of another sovereign state.

■ **rational choice** the theory that decisionmakers choose on the basis of what they perceive to be the best interests of themselves and their states, based on their expectations about the relative usefulness of alternative options for realizing goals. Sometimes called "expected utility theory," it was derived from realist theories.

philosophy. In addition, it would be inaccurate to characterize the WTO as a democratic IGO:

> In theory, the WTO was to promote greater democracy and transparency in global trade negotiations by allowing each member country a single vote in contrast to the financially weighted voting system used in the World Bank and the International Monetary Fund (IMF). In practice, however, there is little evidence of democracy within the WTO operations. The United States, the European Union (EU), Canada, and Japan (dubbed "the Quad") have routinely hammered out agreements in informal, "green room" meetings, named after the site of these secret conferences at the WTO's General headquarters. The Quad then uses its considerable economic and political influence to build "consensus" around these decisions made without participation from the full WTO membership. (Smith and Moran 2001, 69)

Like most IGOs, therefore, the WTO is an organization dominated by the great powers.

The World Bank. Created in July 1944 at the United Nations Monetary and Financial Conference held in Bretton Woods, New Hampshire, attended by forty-four countries, the World Bank was at first designed to support reconstruction efforts after the Second World War and to assist in "the development of productive facilities and resources in less developed countries." The International Bank for Reconstruction and Development (IBRD) and the International Development Association (IDA) were the twin IGO institutions created at the conference, but the term "World Bank" was coined as a shorthand way to informally refer to the IBRD alone.

From its inception, the International Bank for Reconstruction and Development was intended to be the central unit in UN lending operations. Within the UN system, the agencies of the World Bank group, along with the International Monetary Fund, are responsible for most of the capital aid transfers to the developing countries. Coordination between the World Bank agencies and the IMF is provided by the World Bank/IMF Development Committee. The committee functions both as an advisory body to the two boards of governors and as an action body to encourage "foreign capital flows of all kinds" to the developing states. Its membership includes twenty-two finance and development ministers from the boards of governors.

Administratively the World Bank is an IGO run according to its Articles of Agreement, which proclaim that "all the powers of the Bank shall be vested in the Board of Governors, consisting of a governor and an alternate appointed by each member in such manners as it may determine." A governor customarily is a member country's minister of finance, its central bank, or an equivalent official. The board cannot delegate decisions on many matters such as modifying the Bank's capital stock, suspending the Bank's operations and redistributing its assets, or allocating the Bank's net income. The Board of Governors delegate responsibility for the routine operations of the bank to its twenty-four directors of its executive board. The five countries with the largest number of shares in the World Bank's capital stock (the United States, Germany, Japan, France, and the United Kingdom) appoint their own executive directors, and the remaining executive directors are either appointed (Saudi Arabia), elected by their states (China, Russia, and Switzerland), or elected by groups of countries.

The Bank's president is also selected by the executive directors and is the chairman of the executive board, but cannot vote unless it is needed to break a tie vote. The president acts as a CEO in charge of the Bank's operating staff and is responsible, with the approval of the executive director, for the organization, appointment, and dismissal of the Bank's administrative staff. The Articles of Agreement state that the president and staff of the Bank "own their duty entirely to the Bank and to no other authority." During its first fifty years, the Bank has had nine presidents, the latest of which, since 1995, is James D. Wolfensohn.

The World Bank's organization consists not only of the president, but also three managing directors, a General Counsel and senior vice president for Management and Personnel Services, and fourteen vice presidents (six responsible for the Bank's regions: Africa, East Asia and Pacific, South Asia, Europe and Central Asia, Middle East and North Africa, and Latin America and Caribbean). The Articles of Agreement require the president to "pay due regard to the importance of recruiting personnel on as wide a geographical basis as possible" and require that the Bank's principal office be located in the territory of the member holding the largest number of Bank shares. Because the United States has more shares than any other member, the Bank's headquarters are in Washington, D.C. The Bank also has offices in New York (the World Bank Mission to the United Nations), Paris (the European Office), London, and Tokyo. Seven regional missions, fifty-nine resident missions, and a number of smaller offices exist to administratively support the central offices.

Unlike the United Nations, which has a one country/one vote system, the World Bank has a system of weighted voting. Each member is entitled to two hundred and fifty votes and receives one additional vote for each share held in the Bank's capital stock. The number of shares allocated is based on a quota so that the richer countries contribute to more shares than the developing countries. This system recognizes the differences among members' holdings and is intended to protect the interests of the great powers that make more substantial contributions to the World Bank's resources. If a country's economic situation changes over time, its quota is adjusted and its allocation of shares and votes changes accordingly. That said, the United States still has veto power and exercises, with the other economic powerhouses, preponderant influence over the Bank's decisions.

The World Bank is run by bankers to present the image that its board of governors seeks to project as a guardian of financial interests. The World Bank operates on the ideological principles governing contemporary international finance, and its loan criteria are aimed at protecting its creditors' interests. This constructed image of itself as a beacon of hope and help and a barrier against the collapse of global capitalism is prudent for its success, since most of the World Bank's loan funds are obtained, not from governments, but from borrowing in private capital markets. Loan applicants must use a "project" approach which requires the applicant to demonstrate that the loan will finance a rationally planned undertaking that will contribute to the productive and earning capacity of the recipient country. The World Bank, like all banks, must lend funds that promise to make a return for its creditor investor countries in order to ensure their continuing support. For many years, the World Bank therefore frowned on loans for social projects, like building hospitals and schools or for slum clearance. Historically it also was reluctant to provide general-purpose loans, or loans to meet rising debt or to resolve balance-of-payment problems; but this has declined in recent years. In fact, the World Bank's lending policies underwent substantial modification in the latter half of the 1980s and 1990s when it began to encourage economic growth in major debtor Global South countries. This was a departure from policy in the World Bank's traditional use of funds for "self-liquidating projects" generating revenues large enough to service the debtor's debt payments. Today, the World Bank bases its loaning policies on the capacity of the recipient country's entire economy to produce enough growth to repay the loans provided for that purpose. On average, World Bank loans have financed only twenty-five percent of the cost of projects; to provide the balance, other investors are now required to support the World Bank.

Over the years both the self-image and operations of the World Bank have changed—from a strictly financial IGO to that of a development agency dedicated to solving problems of economic and political development and, recently, environmental sustainability. Instead of remaining aloof and merely passing judgment on loan applications, the World Bank now assists states in their development planning, helps prepare project proposals, and provides training for senior development officials. Its economic survey missions actively monitor the resource and investment potential of member countries and determine priorities for country and regional projects. The World Bank has also participated increasingly in consortium arrangements for financing private lending institutions. It has demonstrated repeatedly that it is also dedicated to the promotion of political development, defined as liberal democratic governance, by its recent insistence on democratic reforms as a condition for economic assistance. Like the G-8, the World Bank has a clear and consistent commitment to liberalism; it is an active promoter of both free trade and free governments.

Despite its increased pace of activity, the World Bank has never been able to meet all the needs for financial assistance of the developing states. The repayment of loans in hard currencies has imposed serious obstacles on impoverished and indebted borrowing states of the Global South that do not benefit from revenues through active participation in global trade. Many developing states are currently overstraining their debt-servicing capacities, and new loans could easily exacerbate the world debt crisis (see Chapter 6). Moreover, since economic activity is habitually controlled predominantly by private companies in many developing Global South states, making loans to relatively small firms without government guarantees is risky, although it is widely regarded as essential to economic development. This has led some critics to conclude that whereas the World Bank has functioned effectively as an international bank, it has failed as an IGO (especially to critics who fondly recall the early post–World War II years when the developing countries fought vigorously to have the UN create a major capital grants institution, but lost the battle). The deficiencies of the World Bank, however, have been partly offset by the establishment of another lending IGOs, the International Monetary Fund.

The International Monetary Fund.   Prior to World War II, the globe had suffered from the absence of institutional mechanisms to manage orderly rules for the exchange of money across borders. As that world war neared its end, the United States led the Allies in creating the International Monetary Fund (IMF) (alongside the World Bank) at the 1944 Bretton Woods Conference for this goal.

The IMF sought a multilateral solution to a multilateral problem—guarding against the continuation of the selfishly competitive "beggar-thy-neighbor" practices of currency restrictions and devaluations at others' expense that had destroyed the world economy in the 1930s. Cast in the mold of commercial **liberalism,** the IMF sought to create a global institution to maintain currency-exchange stability, primarily for orderly currency relations among the wealthy powers but secondarily as a lender of last resort for poor as well as rich countries experiencing financial crises.

Those were the IMF's origins at its birth. Since then, the global marketplace has expanded and, with that growth, has come the increasingly economic interdependence of all states, or **globalization** through the integration of national economies. As a result, the conditions in which the IMF were created have vanished, and with global transformations the IMF has evolved to perform new roles.

The IMF is now one of the sixteen specialized agencies within the UN system. Each IMF member is represented on its governing board, which meets annually to fix general policy. Day-to-day business is conducted by a twenty-two-member executive board chaired by a managing director who is also administrative head of a staff of approximately two thousand employees. The primary purpose of the IMF is stabilizing international monetary exchange rates. This powerful financial IGO derives its operating funds from its member states. Contributions (and thus voting strength) are based on a country's national income, monetary reserves, and trade balance. The IMF's voting thus is weighted according to a state's monetary contribution to the IMF, giving a larger voice to the wealthier states.

In addition to stabilizing exchange rates in order to facilitate international trade, the chief aims of the IMF, as set forth in its Articles of Agreement, include:

- promoting international monetary cooperation
- facilitating the expansion of international trade
- promoting exchange stability
- establishing a multilateral system of payments
- fostering members' confidence in the IMF
- allocating the resources available
- shortening the duration of, and reducing the degree of disequilibrium in, members' balances of payments

The IMF's operations are administrated by a code of conduct governing exchange rate policies and restrictions on payments, primarily in the interest of promoting freer exchange of currencies. The IMF is, in this capacity, a multilateral forum for government consultation on major monetary questions. Beyond this, the IMF seeks to provide exchange stability through two instruments: influencing currency values and permitting members experiencing financial crises to recover by drawing foreign exchange from the IMF. The regime underlying the IMF assigns it the task of performing as a pooling arrangement, based on the requirement that all members will contribute to a common bank of monetary reserves from which they can draw to overcome short-term deficits in their balance of payments. In this regard, the IMF is designed to serve as a lender of last resort when one of its members is threatened by an economic downturn that

■ **liberalism**
a paradigm predicated on the hope that the application of reason and universal ethics to international relations can lead to a more orderly, just, and cooperative world, and that international anarchy and war can be policed by institutional reforms that empower organizations and international laws for global governance.

■ **globalization**
the integration of states, through increasing contact, communication, and trade, to create a holistic, single global system in which the process of change increasingly binds people together in a common fate.

could destroy its economy. Contributions are based on a quota system set according to a state's national income, gold reserves, and other factors affecting each member's ability to contribute. In this way, the IMF operates like a credit union that requires each participant to contribute to a common pool of funds from which it can borrow when the need arises. This is the cooperative spirit of liberalism in practice. Each member contributes twenty-five percent of its quota in hard currency (presently, the U.S. dollar, British pound, French franc, German mark, or Japanese yen)—the so-called credit tranche—with the remainder in its own currency. Each member then has a right to purchase foreign exchange from the IMF in amounts equal to the value of its credit tranche, but the maximum may run much higher. The currency pool is designed to maintain stable exchange values among all members' currencies. When a member suffers a short-term deficit in its balance of payments that cannot be financed through commercial banks, purchases of foreign exchange from the IMF are made available to carry it through the temporary crisis.

The IMF, as a standard practice, usually attaches conditions to large borrowings to ensure that the problems that produced the large deficit are remedied. The IMF has been subjected to considerable criticism for exercising the power given it to specify such often strict financial conditions for its loans. The IMF's expanded power to include terms of conditionality has also been used to demand environmental protection and democratization, including empowerment of women in the members' political system. Critics contend that in so expanding its original mandate, the IMF has deviated from its charter which called for making lending decisions strictly on economic bases.

As an IGO created to meet real shared global problems, the IMF has arguably served the goals for which it was created fairly well. However, the IMF has grown beyond its original mission, adapting policies to global transformations and responsibilities. Although still the preferred (and necessary?) IGO for coping with the chronic financial crises since the 1980s in a turbulent world economy under conditions of globalization (see Chapters 8 and 9), the IMF is widely perceived to have become overextended and overburdened. It is therefore in need of discarding its expanded role and returning "to its original mandate [by concentrating] on preventing and mitigating financial crises, especially liquidity and banking crises, leaving such tasks as reducing poverty to the World Bank." As Don Babai (2001a) elaborates, "The IMF has been subjected to a mounting barrage of criticism in recent decades [in part because] the IMF has remained the preserve of the powerful and affluent even as its membership, [184] strong by [2003], has expanded to include [almost] every country. . . . The IMF remains the preferred instrument for coping with financial crises. . . . The IMF will continue to occupy the position of *primus inter pares* [first among equals] in the hierarchy of international, financial institutions. But that position will not resolve the larger issues affecting the role of the IMF in a world in which the globalization of financed institutions has increased the vulnerability of countries. . . ."

Like the other major IGOs created by the great powers, the IMF is resented by the less powerful, who find that the IMF's beneficial intentions are betrayed by the domination and inequalities its programs, crafted by the great economic powers, have caused for the least-developed Global South countries most in need. As shall be seen in Chapter 6, the Global South often looks at the great powers, who manage IGOs like the IMF, as operating from a double standard.

The European Union as a Model Regional IGO:
A Rite of Passage for "Euroland"?

The tug of war between individual states and groups of states within the UN, the World Bank, and the IMF are reminders of an underlying principle that IGOs are run by the states that join them. This severely inhibits the IGOs' ability to rise above interstate competition and independently pursue their own purposes. Because they cannot act autonomously and lack the legitimacy and capability for independent global governance, universal IGOs are often viewed more as instruments of their state members' foreign policies and arenas for debate than as independent nonstate actors.

When states dominate universal international organizations like the UN, the prospects for international cooperation decline because, as **realist** theorists emphasize, states are fearful of any multilateral organizations that compromise their vital national interests. This limits IGOs' capabilities for multilateral decision making to engineer global change.

A rival hypothesis—that cooperation among powerful states is possible and that international organizations help produce it—emerges from **neoliberal theory.** This viewpoint is especially pertinent to the European Union (EU). The EU is a good example of the powerful (global) role played by some regional IGOs. In many respects the EU is unique, if for no other reason than that it stands as the globe's greatest example of peaceful international cooperation producing an integrated **security community** with a single economy and a common currency. The EU is also dedicated to liberal democratic governance and shares a preference for free-market capitalism tempered in Europe's search for **Third Way** values such as compassion for human suffering. Moreover, the EU, or what has become known as "Euroland," is not, strictly speaking, a freestanding supranational organization for the collective management of European domestic and foreign affairs. The EU coexists with a large number of other European IGOs, in which it is nested and with which it jointly makes decisions. Of these, the Organization for Security and Cooperation in Europe (OSCE) and the Council of Europe stand as regional institutions of equal European partners, free of dividing lines, designed to manage regional security and promote the human rights of minorities through democratization. In this overlapping network of European IGOs, the EU nonetheless is prominent as the primary example of a powerful regional institution and of a regional organization that has transformed itself from a single- to a multiple-purpose nonstate actor.

The process of European integration began with the creation of the European Coal and Steel Community (ECSC) in 1951, the European Atomic Energy Community (Euratom) in 1957, and the European Economic Community (EEC) in 1957. They centered initially on trade and development. Since the late 1960s, the three have shared common organizational structures, and, in successive steps, have enlarged their mission as they came to be called "the European Community." Its membership has grown and its geographical scope also has broadened as the EU has expanded in a series of waves to encompass fifteen countries as of 1997: Belgium, France, Germany, Italy, Luxembourg, and the Netherlands (the original "six"); Denmark, Ireland, and the United Kingdom (which joined in 1973); Greece (1981); Portugal and Spain (1986); and Austria, Finland, and Sweden (1995). At its April 1998 summit in Brussels, the EU reached a new milestone in its path toward enlargement, when it formally opened negotiations aimed at bringing as many as ten countries from Eastern

■ **realist**
a paradigm based on the premise that world politics is essentially and unchangeably a struggle among self-interested states for power and position under anarchy, with each competing state pursuing its own national interests.

■ **neoliberal theory**
a philosophy which maintains that peaceful change with prosperity can be encouraged through cooperation in institutions that knit the states and peoples of the world together into a true global community.

■ **security community**
a group of states whose high level of noninstitutionalized collaboration results in the settlement of disputes by compromise rather than by force.

■ **Third-Way**
an approach to governance advocated primarily by European leaders such as British Prime Minister Tony Blair and France's socialist Prime Minister Lionel Jostin who, while recognizing few alternatives to liberal capitalism, seek to soften the cruel social impact of free-market individualism by progressively allowing government intervention to preserve social justice and the rights of individuals to freedom from fear of the deprivations caused by disruptions in the global economy.

and Central Europe plus Cyprus into its membership, pending the applicants' ability to meet the EU's economic conditions for entry and to provide satisfactory indication of its commitment to democracy. At its November 2002 summit in Prague, the fifteen EU members confirmed that goal when they agreed to admit ten new members by 2004 (Cyprus, the Czech Republic, Slovakia, Estonia, Hungary, Latvia, Lithuania, Malta, Poland, and Slovenia). This bold enlargement creates the globe's biggest free trade bloc, and transforms the face of Europe by ending the continent's division. The idea of a single Europe remains compelling for many Europeans who are haunted by the specter of European nationalities and states that have been fighting each other ever since the Pax Romana collapsed eighteen hundred years ago. Consolidation is in Europe's future, providing that the resurrection of intra-European discord and perhaps even a surge of civil wars does not terminate this ambitious experiment in the integration of formerly separated countries.

Organizational Components and Decision-Making Procedures. The EU's institutional structure has changed over time, as the organization has grown and expanded its authority over its members, to transform the EU toward governance beyond the nation-state. The principal institutions for governance, as shown in Figure 5.3, include a Council of Ministers, the European Commission, a European Parliament, and a Court of Justice. The EU's central administrative unit, the Council of Ministers, consists of cabinet ministers drawn from the EU's member states, who participate when the most important decisions are made. In this respect, the EU is an association of states similar to the UN. But the EU is more than this, as evidenced by the "enlargement" of the EU's authority over its 25 members, which has grown so that the EU is truly much more than the sum of its parts.

The Council of Ministers represents the governments of the EU's member states and retains final authority over the policy-making decisions. The council sets general policy guidelines for the **European Commission,** which consists of twenty commissioners (two each from Britain, France, Germany, Italy, and Spain, and one each from the remaining member states). Commissioners are nominated by EU member governments and must be approved by the European Parliament. Headquartered in Brussels, the European Commission was created to construct common economic policies for the original six member states and to oversee their administration. Today the primary functions of the European Commission are to propose new laws for the EU, oversee EU treaties, and execute the decrees of the European Council. A professional staff of seventeen thousand civil-service "Eurocrats" assist the commission's administrative bureaucracy in proposing and directing decision making (by majority vote) for the EU and the Council of Ministers. The commission proposes legislation, implements EU policies, and represents the European Union in international trade negotiations. It also manages the EU's budget, which, in contrast with most international organizations, derives part of its revenues from sources not under the control of member states.

The European Parliament represents the political parties and public opinion within Europe. It has existed from the beginning of Europe's journey toward political unification, although at its creation this legislative body was appointed rather than elected and had very little power. That is no longer the case. The European Parliament is now chosen in a direct election by the citizens of the

■ **European Commission**
The executive organ administratively responsible for the European Union.

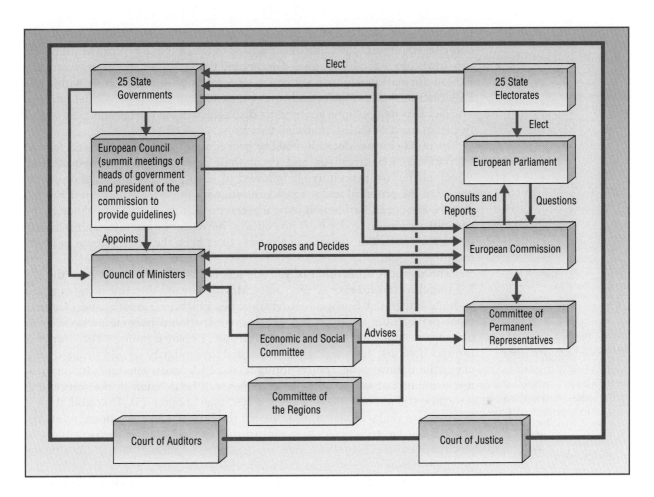

FIGURE 5.3
The European Union's Governmental Structure
The EU is a complex organization, with different responsibilities performed by various units. This figure charts the principal institutions and the relationships among them that collectively lead to EU decisions and policies.
SOURCE: *The Economist,* Oct. 23, 1999, p. 16. Copyright © 1999 by The Economist Newspaper Ltd. All rights reserved. Reprinted with permission. Further reproduction prohibited. www.economist.com

EU's member states. Its 626 deputies debate issues at the monumental glass headquarters in Brussels and at a lavish Strasbourg palace in the same way that democratic national legislative bodies do. The European Parliament shares authority with the Council of Ministers representing member governments, but the Parliament's influence has increased over time. The deputies elected through universal suffrage pass laws with the council, approve the EU's budget, oversee the European Commission, and can overturn its acts. This last element in the Parliament's authority gives it substantial clout, which it has not been hesitant to exercise. For example, in July 1999 the Parliament accused the previous group of commissioners of cronyism and corruption and forced their resignation.

The European Court of Justice in Luxembourg has also grown in prominence and power as European integration has gathered depth and breadth.

From the start, the court was given responsibility for adjudicating claims and conflicts among EU governments as well as between those governments and the new institutions the EU created. Comprising fifteen judges, the court interprets EU law for national courts and rules on legal questions that arise within the EU's institutions and hears and rules on cases concerning individual citizens. The fact that its decisions are binding distinguishes the European Court of Justice from most other international tribunals.

In practice, two decision-making procedures have been followed for the adoption of EU directives and regulations: consultation and cooperation. Which of the two procedures is followed to adopt regulations depends on the nature of the proposal under consideration, with the principal difference being that the European Parliament plays a greater role in the cooperative than in the consultive process. Under both procedures, however, the twenty commissioners of the European Commission in Brussels have been the driving force in European integration.

The political unification of Europe has been built step-by-step as the EU has marched toward ever greater unity. Moving beyond the nation-state toward a single integrated European federation has not been smooth, and disagreement persist over the extent to which the EU should become a single, truly united superstate, a "United States of Europe." Debate continues also over how far and how fast such a process of **pooled sovereignty** should proceed, and about the natural geographical limits to the EU's "enlargement"—its ultimate membership and boundaries. There issues will be debated in the future, and only time will tell how they will be resolved (see Chapter 15). That said, the EU represents a remarkable success story in the history of international relations. Who would have expected that competitive states which have spent most of their national experiences waging war against one another would consolidate, put their clashing ideological and territorial ambitions aside, and construct a "European-ness" identity built on unity and confederated decision making? The EU has moved above the nation-state as a *supranational* regional organization pledged to giving the EU dominion over its 25 members' internal affairs and control over common foreign and military policies, while at the same time developing a sense of solidarity and belonging among the regions' peoples.

■ **pooled sovereignty** legal authority granted to an IGO by its members to make collective decisions regarding specified aspects of public policy heretofore made exclusively by each sovereign government.

Other Regional IGOs

Since Europe's 1950s initiatives toward economic and political integration, more than a dozen regional IGOs have been created in various other parts of the world, notably among states in the Global South. Most seek to stimulate regional economic growth, but many have drifted from that original single purpose to pursue multiple political and military purposes as well. The major regional organizations in the Global South include:

- The Asia Pacific Economic Cooperation (APEC) forum, created in 1989 as a gathering of twelve states without a defined goal. APEC's membership has grown to eighteen countries (including the United States) that collectively account for forty percent of the globe's population and more than half of global GDP. At its November 1994 meeting in Jakarta, APEC set for itself the explicit goal of free trade.

- The North Atlantic Treaty organization (NATO), a military alliance created in 1949 primarily to deter the Soviet Union in Western Europe. The security IGO has expanded its membership and broadened its mission to promote democratization and to police civil wars and terrorism outside its traditional territory within Europe. The United States and Canada are also members.

- The Association of Southeast Asian Nations (ASEAN), established in 1967 by five founding members to promote regional economic, social, and cultural cooperation. In 1999 it created a free-trade zone among its ten Southeast Asian members as a counterweight outside the orbit of Japan, China, the United States, and other great powers so ASEAN could compete as a bloc in international trade. ASEAN's expansion has created an identity crisis, with fears of new divisions between the older and wealthy "haves" and the newer and less-wealthy "have-not" members, which include communist Vietnam, Laos, Cambodia, and the impoverished Myanmar (formerly Burma). ASEAN today struggles with political, economic, and environmental problems that beset the region and that cannot be managed without the combined efforts of this regional IGO.

- The Caribbean Community and Common Market (CARICOM), established in 1973 to promote economic development and integration among its fourteen members.

- The Council of Arab Economic Unity (CAEU), established in 1964 from a 1957 accord to promote economic integration among its twelve Arab members.

- The Economic Community of West African States (ECOWAS), established in 1975 to promote regional economic cooperation among its seventeen members.

- The Organization of the Islamic Conference (OIC) coordinates a large number of activities among fifty Islamic states (plus the Palestine Liberation Organization) for the purpose of promoting Islamic solidarity in economic, social, cultural, and political affairs. While not technically a regional IGO, the OIC orchestrates preventive diplomacy, does not condone the use of terrorism, and is not concerned with promoting fundamentalist Islamic religious principles.

- The Latin American Integration Association (LAIA), also known as Asociación Latinoamericana de Integración (ALADI), established in 1981 to promote freer regional trade among its eleven members.

- The Southern African Development Community (SADC), established in 1992 to promote regional economic development and integration among its twelve members.

- The South Asian Association for Regional Cooperation (SAARC), established in 1985 to promote economic, social, and cultural cooperation among its seven members.

As these examples illustrate, many IGOs are organized on a regional rather than global basis. The governments creating them usually concentrate on one or two major goals (such as liberalizing trade or promoting peace within the region) instead of attempting through collective action to address at once the complete range of issues that they face in common, such as environmental protection and democratization, in addition to economic and security cooperation. Africa illustrates the tendency at the regional level. (See Map 5.2). As one assessment explains:

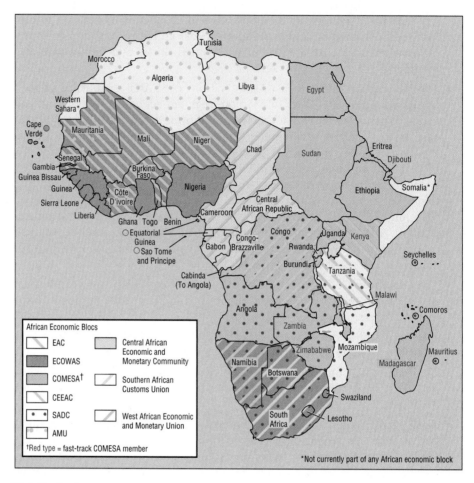

M A P 5 . 2
"Africa's IGOs"

Within strife-torn Africa, fragile states created a myriad network of regional IGOs, with multiple, crosscutting memberships. This map shows Africa's major economic IGOs. Created in the spirit of free trade, they enjoy continuous support from the multilateral World Trade Organization, even though trade blocs compromise the WTO's goal of trade liberalization at the global level. To the WTO's way of thinking, through regional IGOs, improved administrative capabilities are believed likely to eventually prepare Africa for fuller participation in and integration with the multilateral global regime advocating reduced barriers to international trade.

SOURCE: From *The Economist*, Feb. 10, 2001, p. 77. Copyright © 2001 by The Economist Newspaper, Ltd. All rights reserved. Reprinted with permission. Further reproduction prohibited. www.economist.com

Africa has been experimenting with economic integration for half a century. The fruits of those efforts have included big, multipurpose groups such as the Economic Community of Western African States (ECOWAS), the Common Market for Eastern and Southern Africa (COMESA), the Economic Community of Central African States (CEEAC), the Southern African Development Community (SADC) and the Arab Maghreb Union (AMU). They have also included smaller, less globally oriented blocs such as the Economic Community of the Great Lakes Countries, the Mano River Union and the EAC.

Global credibility has been hard to come by. Many alliances lack the authority and bureaucratic sophistication to deal with the big powers. Moreover, the blocs can lie dormant for years at a time while their members endure political turmoil. As a result, Africa's alliances have concentrated more on liberalizing trade within the region than with the rest of the world. What progress there is has been slow. Protectionism is easy to justify, since less-developed, less-diversified economies are also less able (it is argued) to weather the transition to free trade. For this reason, separate blocs of more liberalized countries exist within the larger ones. Most countries are members of more [than] one bloc. (*Economist,* February 10, 2001, 77)

It is hazardous to generalize about organizations as widely divergent in membership and purpose as the above list suggests, alongside many other, older IGOs whose function is to perform particular missions, such as the International Telecommunication Union founded in 1865, the World Meteorological Organization (1873), the Universal Postal Union (1874), the International Labour Organization (1919), and the International Civil Aviation Organization (1944). Regional IGOs seek to coordinate their programs, but none have managed to collaborate at a level that begins to match the institutionalized collective decision making achieved by the EU. The particular reasons why many regional IGOs sometimes fail and are often ineffective vary, but at bottom all IGOs are limited by national leaders' reluctance to make politically costly choices that would undermine their personal popularity at home and their governments' sovereignty. Nonetheless, these attempts at regional cooperation demonstrate many states' acceptance of the fact that they cannot individually resolve many of the problems that confront them collectively.

Because the state is clearly failing to manage many transnational policy problems, ironically it finds itself acting as the primary agent of the same cooperative management efforts that are eroding the state's power. Collective problem solving through the growth and expanding power of IGOs is likely to continue. Globalization and the force of a shrinking, borderless world are increasing the influence of international institutions; in turn, IGOs' expanding webs of interdependence are infringing on the power of states and changing the ways in which they network on the global stage. These IGOs and processes promise to transform world politics, which is why "almost any discussion of public policy nowadays seems to begin and end with the same idea: The state is in retreat [and] its power to rule is fading" (Crook 1997).

Another set of agents in the transnational transformation and globalization of world politics are nonstate actors such as NGOs, ethnonational movements, and multinational corporations, which are also highly active and increasingly influential. We now turn our attention to their behavior and impact.

NONGOVERNMENTAL ORGANIZATIONS (NGOS)

If you are like many other people in the world, there is at least one problem and possibly more that are of great concern to you. You would like to see the world change. How can you help make the world a better place? You are likely to realize that you cannot engineer global changes all by yourself. However, you probably recognize that other people share your concerns and that by joining together with them you can exercise power; you can join with other, like-minded people in the world and raise your collective voices.

In today's world, increasing numbers of people have found that through joining private interest groups they can participate in the global system and lobby to influence international decision making. They have joined as members of one or more nongovernmental organizations (NGOs), of which there are almost thirty thousand now in existence worldwide. NGOs are private international actors whose members are not states, but are instead volunteers drawn from the populations of two or more states who have formed organizations to promote their shared interests and ideals in order to influence the policies of state governments and intergovernmental organizations (IGOs).

These NGOs tackle many global problems, seeking changes in the world for causes such as disarmament, women's rights, environmental protection, and human rights. Most of them pursue objectives that are highly respected and constructive, and therefore do not provoke controversy or arouse much opposition. For example, NGOs such as Amnesty International, the International Chamber of Commerce, the Red Cross, Save the Children, the World Wildlife Federation, and Global Youth Connect (to support young people who are victims of human rights abuses) enjoy widespread popular support. Others, however, are more controversial because they push for changes which, were they to succeed, would threaten the interests of other groups who have a stake in preserving the status quo. For example, NGOs such as the Union of Concerned Scientists and Doctors Without Borders are interested in reducing military spending, and this threatens the budgets of members of the "military industrial complex" whose jobs and income depend on continued high government spending on defense. Hence, many NGOs work at cross-purposes in a competitive struggle to redefine the global agenda.

What makes NGOs increasingly prominent on the world stage is that their bargaining activities have led to the successful creation of **regimes,** or new sets of rules that help to regulate some important transnational problems. NGOs "are now influencing decisions and helping to set agendas that were once determined solely by governments and corporations, from policies on international trade and investment to initiatives on literacy, international aid, and human rights. . . . NGOs have used their flexibility, small scale, technical expertise, and connections to the grass roots to spark something of an 'organization revolution'—forging an effective middle ground between the state and the free market" (Runyan 1999). At the same time, the demands of NGOs have shaken the sovereign control by state governments over their foreign policies. The challenge to states by minority racial or religious NGOs has been especially severe in fragile or failing states where revolt by NGOs has led to the collapse of the state, and even in some strong states NGO pressure has led to the **devolution** of the central government's power. NGOs are making borders porous and states vulnerable both to external pressures and to challenges from within their boundaries. As NGOs rise in numbers and influence, a key question to contemplate is whether what may be termed a "nongovernmental global society" will materialize to corride the traditional global system centered on sovereign states, and, if so, whether this structural transformation will democratize, or disrupt, global governance.

Let us look at the major NGOs to better evaluate if they are contributing to the erosion of state sovereignty and whether their impact spells promise, or

■ **regimes**
norms, rules, and procedures for interaction agreed to by a set of states.

■ **devolution**
states' granting of political power to minority ethnopolitical national groups and indigenous people in particular national regions under the expectation that greater autonomy will curtail their quest for independence as a new state.

Getty

NGOs: New Gods Overseas Nearly thirty thousand NGOs exist and are influential activists pursuing their own agendas—and publicity—throughout the globe. Increasingly, they work together with IGOs such as the United Nations, and because they are often respected, rich state governments have increasingly turned to NGOs to perform services such as distributing foreign aid or providing humanitarian relief.

peril, for twenty-first-century world politics. Today a small subset of increasingly active and self-assertive major nonstate actors receive the most attention and provoke the most controversy. To simplify our task, we will focus on three of the most visible politically active types of NGO nonstate actors: ethnopolitical groups or **nonstate nations,** religious movements, and multinational corporations.

Nonstate Nations: The Indigenous Ethnic Groups of the Fourth World

The images of the all-powerful state and of governments as sovereign and autonomous rulers of unified nations are not very realistic. These images exaggerate the extent to which the state resembles a **unitary actor,** as realists often ask us to picture it. In truth, the unitary actor conception is misleading, because many states are divided internally and are highly penetrated from abroad, and few states are tightly unified and capable of acting as a single body with a common purpose.

Although the state unquestionably remains the most visible actor in world affairs, as **constructivism** emphasizes, **nationalism** and nationality should be seen as potent cultural factors defining the core loyalties and identities of many people that influence how states act. Many people pledge their primary allegiance not to the state and government that rules them, but rather to a politically active minority group with which they most associate themselves. One broad category of such national groups is **ethnopolitical groups** whose members share a common nationality, language, cultural tradition, and kinship ties. They view themselves as members of their nationality or ethnic group first and of their state only secondarily. **Ethnicity** is "a phenomenon associated with

▪ **nonstate nations**
national or ethnic groups struggling to obtain power and/or statehood.

▪ **unitary actor**
a transnational actor (usually a sovereign state) assumed to be internally united, so that changes in its internal circumstances do not influence its foreign policy as much as do the decisions that actor's leaders make to cope with changes in its global environment.

■ constructivism
a scholarly approach to inquiry emphasizing the importance of agents (people and groups) and the shared meanings they construct to define their identities, interests, and institutions-understandings that influence their international behavior.

■ nationalism
a mindset glorifying a particular state and the nationality group living in it that sees the state's national interests as a supreme value.

■ ethnopolitical groups
people whose identity is primarily defined by their sense of sharing a common ancestral nationality, language, cultural heritage, and kinship ties.

■ ethnicity
perceptions of likeness among members of a particular racial or linguistic grouping leading them to act prejudicially toward outsiders in other kinship or cultural groups.

■ ethnic nationalism
devotion to a cultural, ethnic, or linguistic community within an existing state.

■ ethnic groups
a group of people of the same nationality who share a common culture, set of ancestors, or language.

■ indigenous peoples
the native ethnic and cultural inhabitant populations within countries ruled by a government controlled by others, referred to as the "Fourth World."

contact between cultural linguistic communal groups . . . characterized by cultural prejudice and social discrimination. Underlying these characteristics are the feelings of pride in the ingroup, and the exclusiveness of its members. It is a phenomenon linked . . . to forms of affiliation and identification built around ties of real or putative kinship" (Nnoli 1993).

Ethnic nationalism (people's loyalty to and identification with a particular ethnic nationality group) in world affairs reduces the relevance of the unitary state. Many states are divided, multiethnic societies made up of a variety of politically active groups that seek, if not outright independence, a greater level of regional autonomy and a greater voice in the domestic and foreign policies of the state. "Nearly three quarters of the world's larger countries (116 of 161) have politically significant minorities," and 275 minority groups comprising one sixth of the world's population are at risk from persecution worldwide (Gurr 2001, 175). Relations between **ethnic groups** are a key element in the equation of relations between NGOs and the state, as contact is customarily widespread between groups who define their identity by their common ancestry. These ethnic divisions and the lack of unity within states make thinking of international relations as exclusively homogeneous interactions between unified states—the realist "billiard ball model"—dubious.

Ethnopolitical Challengers to the State in the Fourth World. **Indigenous peoples** are the ethnic and cultural groups that were native to a geographic location now controlled by another state or political group. The globe is populated by an estimated six thousand separate indigenous nations, each of which has a unique language and culture and strong, often spiritual, ties to an ancestral homeland. In most cases indigenous people were at one time politically sovereign and economically self-sufficient. Today there are an estimated 300 million indigenous people, more than 5 percent of the world's population, scattered in more than seventy countries; some have placed the number as high as 650 million (The State of Indigenous People 2002). This segment of global society is conventionally referred to as the **Fourth World** to heighten awareness of the poverty and deprivation that confront many native or tribal indigenous peoples.

It is extremely difficult to classify and count the abundant variety of politically active nonstate nations struggling for power and/or statehood. Perhaps the best way of making a rough estimate is by observing linguistic similarity. A huge number of ethnolinguistic divisions separate cultures. "Measured by spoken languages, the single best indicator of a distinct culture, all the world's people belong to 6,000 cultures; 4,000 to 5,000 of these are indigenous ones" (Durning 1993, 81).

Still, this indicator may be somewhat misleading, since the belief systems and backgrounds that incite ethnopolitical movements by indigenous peoples are varied and often overlapping. Beyond language, these movements are based on numerous combinations of cultural, racial, and religious orientations. This is why indigenous ethnopolitical movements pursue many different goals.

One characteristic of nonstate nations or ethnopolitical movements stands out as a defining attribute amidst these differences: most transcend the existing borders that separate the more than two hundred sovereign states currently recognized as independent under international law. Indigenous peoples (as mea-

Allen Tannenbaum

Indigenous Peoples Organize Many subnational groups of nations and indigenous peoples reside on the territory of existing states which govern them.

sured by the proportion of a country's total population in which minority ethnic, national, or racial groups) comprise a significant percentage of the majority of the population and are scattered widely within many of the globe's pluralistic states (see Map 5.3). Indigenous peoples such as the sizable Kurdish minorities of Turkey, Iraq, and Syria have members living in more than one of the globe's existing independent states. Linked together by common ancestry across national borders, these peoples form transnational **cultural domains** that share a common heritage and place higher value on ideals other than patriotic loyalty to particular states. Our world is composed of at least eight distinct transnational cultural communities, including European, Chinese, Russian, Hispanic, Islamic, Hindu, and both Black African and South African identities (Chaliand and Rageau 1993, 37). And, as a popular extension of this pessemistic thesis, Samuel P. Huntington (1996, 2001a) predicts that a **clash of civilizations** would occur between or among the seven or eight major "universalistic civilizations," such as a world war between the West and Islam (see Map 5.4). He stresses the constructivist interpretation that people identify with, and organize their activities around, the cultural values in their separate civilization, not their state, and forecasts that conflict between such NGO-centered transnational groupings is likely. That prediction proved rather prophetic on September 11, 2001, when the Al Qaeda terrorist network attacked the United States to vent the anger of its extremist Islamic members against the West (see Chapters 1, 3, and 11; Howell 2003). That proposition suggests the need to turn from ethnic groups as NGOs to consider how religious movements operate as transnationally active NGOs.

■ **Fourth World**
a term used to recognize the native natuional groups residing in many so-called united states who, although often minorities, occupied the state's territory first and refuse to accept domination, seeking instead to create a new state for themselves by splitting existing states or to gain greater political freedom to govern themselves.

■ **cultural domains**
groups that share a common intellectual heritage and values and do not recognize national borders when they define their identities and loyalties.

■ **clash of civilizations**
political scientiest Samuel Huntington's controversial thesis that in the twenty-first century the globe's major civilizations will conflict with one another, leading to anarchy and warfare similar to that resulting from conflicts between states over the past five hundred years.

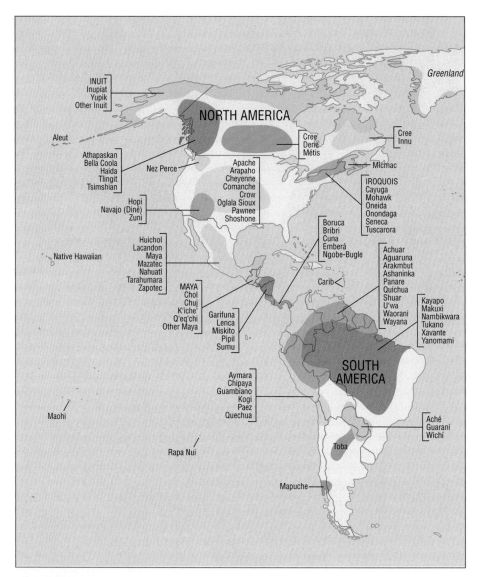

MAP 5.3
The Indigenous Cultures of the Fourth World

More than five thousand indigenous peoples live in many countries throughout the globe and are concentrated regionally. As Julian Burger of the UN's Office of the High Commissioner for Human Rights noted in 1999, "All over the world indigenous peoples are asserting their cultural identity, claiming their right to control their futures, and struggling to regain their ancestral lands." To protect their human rights and national identity, Fourth World groups have organized meetings, such as the World Conference of Indigenous Peoples in Rio de Janeiro, Brazil, in May 1992. As a result of their lobbying, the UN named 1993 the International Year of the World's Indigenous Peoples. Many minority groups and indigenous peoples long denied self-determination are seeking to govern themselves by pursuing independence through separatist movements. If every major "racial or ethnic group won independence," U.S. President Bill Clinton observed in October 1999, "we might have 800 countries in the world."

Note: Colors indicate regional concentrations of indigenous peoples.
SOURCE: Julian Burger, United Nations. Adapted from "Vanishing Cultures" by Wade Davis, *National Geographic*, August 1999, pp. 66–67. NG Maps/NGS Image Collection.

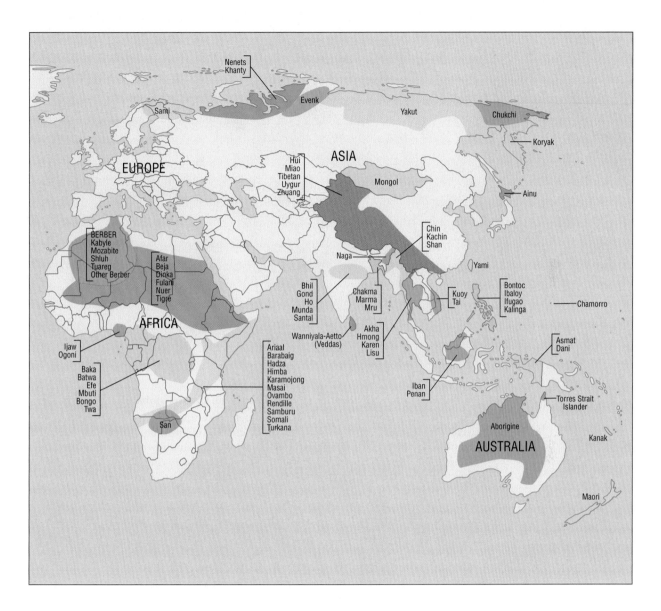

Religious Movements

In theory, religion would seem a natural worldwide force for global unity and harmony. Yet millions have died in the name of religion. The Crusades between the eleventh and fourteenth centuries were originally justified by Pope Urban II in 1095 to combat Muslim aggression, but the fighting left millions of Christians and Muslims dead and, "in terms of atrocities, the two sides were about even [as both religions embraced] an ideology in which fighting was an act of self sanctification" (*Economist,* January 5, 1996). Similarly, the "not so holy wars" in the religious conflicts during the Thirty Years' War (1618–1648) between Catholics and Protestants killed nearly one-fourth of all Europeans.

Many of the world's more than 6 billion people are affiliated in some form with a **religious movement**—a politically active organization based on strong

■ **religious movement**
a set of beliefs, practices, and ideas administered politically by a religious group to promote the worship of its conception of a transcendent diety or principles of conduct.

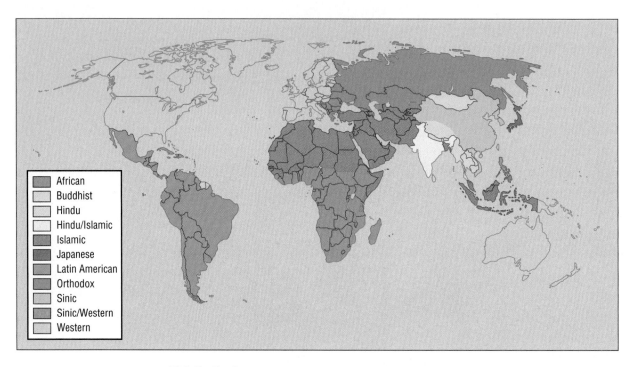

MAP 5.4
The World's Major Civilizations: Will Their Clash Create Global Disorder?
According to the controversial thesis of Samuel P. Huntington, a global war in the
twenty-first century is likely to result from a "clash of civilization." This map shows the
location of the world's major civilizations, according to Huntington—the Sinic or
Chinese, Japanese, Hindu, Islamic, Buddhist, Western, Latin America, the Orthodox
Christians in Eastern Europe and Russia, African, Sinic/Western in the Philippines, and
Hindu/Islamic in India.
SOURCE: Huntington (1999b), 17.

religious convictions. At the most abstract level, a religion is a system of
thought shared by a group that provides its members an object of devotion and
a code of behavior by which they can ethically judge their actions. This definition points to commonalities across the great diversity of organized religions in
the world, but it fails to capture that diversity. The world's principal religions
vary greatly in the theological doctrines or beliefs they embrace. They also differ widely in the size of their followings, in the geographical locations where
they are most prevalent (see Map 5.5), and in the extent to which they engage
in political efforts to direct international affairs.

These differences make it risky to generalize about the impact of religious
movements on world affairs. Those who study religious movements comparatively note that a system of belief provides religious followers with their main
source of identity, and that this identification with and devotion to their religion
springs from the natural human need to find a set of values with which to evaluate the meaning of life and the consequences of choices. Unfortunately this
need sometimes leads believers of a religious creed to perceive the values of
their own religion as superior to those of others, which often results in intoler-

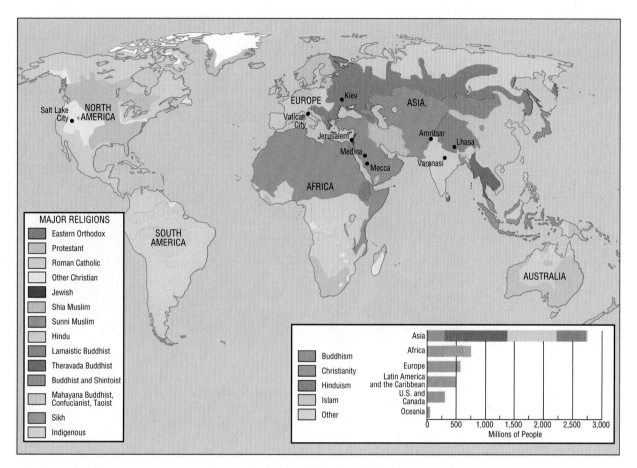

M A P   5 . 5
Major Religions of the World

People everywhere seek a power higher than themselves to give meaning and purpose to their lives, and many accept one or another of the world's major religions for this purpose. There are compelling reasons for the quest, in an otherwise rootless and chaotic world, because life for many people is shallow without a deity to respect and a religious code of conduct to follow. This map shows where the world's major religious affiliations have attracted a dominant following. The chart on the bottom right provides an estimate of the number of people who adhere to the four largest religions in the world today—Buddhism, Christianity, Hinduism, and Islam. High birthrates in Asia and Africa make Islam the world's fastest growing major religion.

SOURCE: Adapted from *National Geographic*, August 1999 supplement: NG Maps/NGS Image Collection.

ance. The proponents of most religious movements believe that their religion should be universal—that is, accepted by everyone throughout the world. To confirm their faith in their religious movement's natural superiority, many organized religions actively proselytize to convert nonbelievers to their faith, engaging in evangelical crusades to win over followers of other religions. Conversion is usually achieved by persuasion through missionary activities. But at times conversion has been achieved by the sword, tarnishing the reputations of

Peter Aventurier/Liasison Agency

The Fusion of Church and State Religion, politics, and violence are seldom seen as contributing to one another. But in many countries, religious bodies are supported by the armies of the state and the state supports the transnational activities of religious movements. Consider South America, for instance, where the powerful Roman Catholic Church has often worked hand in hand with the governments the church supports. At the same time, proponents of "liberation theology" have joined forces with revolutionary groups in the so-called Marxist-Catholic alliance to bring about reforms in the repressive governments they oppose.

some international religious movements (see Controversy: Are Religious Movements Causes of War or Sources of Transnational Harmony?).

In evaluating the impact of religious movements on international affairs, it is important to distinguish carefully the high ideals of doctrines from the activities of the people who head these religious bodies. The two realms are not the same, and each can be judged fairly only against the standards they set for themselves. To condemn what large-scale religious movements sometimes do administratively when they abuse the principles of the religions they manage does not mean that the principles themselves deserve condemnation. Moreover, although many students of international relations draw a causal linkage between the activities of religious movements and the outbreak of political conflict and terrorism (Juergensmeyer 2003; Schwartz 1997), this does not apply to all religions. Consider the Hindu ideology of tolerance of different religions, which teaches that there are many paths to truth and accepts pluralism among diverse populations. Similarly, Buddhism preaches pacifism, as did early Christianity, which prohibited Christians from serving in the armies of the Roman Empire (later, by the fourth century, only Christians were permitted to serve, as church and state became allies). But, notwithstanding the propensity for religious institutions to subordinate their beliefs to the state in order to survive and

ARE RELIGIOUS MOVEMENTS CAUSES OF WAR OR SOURCES OF TRANSNATIONAL HARMONY?

After 9/11, debate about the impact of religion on international conflict intensified, because many believed that the terrorist attacks were motivated by religious fanatics in the Islamic Al Qaeda global terrorist organization. As a result, the "religious roots of terrorism" (Juergensmeyer 2003) have received much attention, as have religions and religious bodies acting as NGO global actors more generally.

"To do harm, to promote violence and conflict in the name of religion," said Pope John Paul II in Egypt after fighting between Christians and Muslims left twenty-three people dead in February 2000, "is a terrible contradiction and a great offense against God. But past and present history give us many examples of such misuse of religion." Yet it is difficult to understand the religious origins of violence because most people equate religion with peace, compassion, and forgiveness, not hatred or intolerance. Indeed, because high ideals inspire the believers of nearly all the world's major religious movements, many of the principles religions espouse are very similar and conducive to peaceful relations between people. They all voice respect and reverence for the sanctity of life and acceptance of all people as equal creations of a deity, regardless of race or color. These are noble ideals. Religions speak to universal principles, across time and place—to enduring values in changing times. Moreover, they recognize no boundaries for their eternal validity—no north, south, east, or west—but only true virtue wherever found and the relevance of moral precepts (e.g., the prohibition of killing and the value of working for the betterment of humankind) throughout the world.

If all the world's great religious movements espouse universalistic ideals, why are those same religions increasingly criticized as sources of international conflict—of exclusivism, hatred, terror, and war? This, in the age of religious conflict and political violence, is a percolating controversy. What do you think?

In evaluating the role of religious NGOs in international affairs, consider first the view of sociologists of religion who contend that religious hostility results from the fact that universalistic religions are managed by organizations that often adopt a particularistic and dogmatic outlook (see Juergensmeyer 2003). The

virtues that religions uphold ironically can become weapons against those who do not hold such views. Followers of a religion may conceive the world and history through an ideological lens that views one deity protecting a single people against inferior others and, in an effort to believe in unshakable doctrines, rejects the attempt to separate what they wish to be true from what they or other religions think to be true. This constructed reality inspires an ethic that justifies violence, plunder, and conquest, in part because outsiders tend to be seen as threatening rivals whose loyalty and allegiance to other deities represents a challenge to their own religion's claim of universality. In a word, religious movements often practice intolerance— disrespect for diversity and the right of people to freely embrace another religion's beliefs. The next logical step is for fanatics to paint these imagined enemies as evil, unworthy of mercy, and to justify brutal violence against them.

However, using this violence as an argument against religion is controversial. It is dangerous to accept stereotypes of religious groups as responsible for relentless barrages of terrorism. Paganistic and atheistic societies recognizing no higher deity have equally long histories of waging violent wars against external enemies and their own people. Meanwhile, many religions perform ably the mission of peace making, and in fact most religious bodies have historically coexisted peacefully for centuries.

It is important for you to weigh objectively the evidence about the impact of religious NGOs on world affairs. In so doing, take into account the impact of this controversy on theories of world politics and world order. The inclination of extremist religious movements to evoke prejudice and aggression has led some realist theorists of international politics to conclude that such movements are more a menace than a pacific influence. Observing that most wars have been fought in the name of religion, these realist critics ask the world to acknowledge the viciousness and mean-spiritedness of followers who betray their religion's humanistic and global values by championing a style of religious thought which denies that morality is about nourishing life, not destroying it. What do you think?

to increase public popularity, many observers maintain that otherwise pacificist and humanitarian religions at times are inclined to oppose each other violently, despite their professed doctrines of tolerance. When they do, religious movements become sources of international tension, especially when they become radical, heavily involved in political action on a global scale, and fanatically dedicated to the promotion of their cause. The leaders of **extreme militant religious movements** are convinced that those who do not share their convictions must be punished, and that compromise is unacceptable.

■ **extreme militant religious movements** politically active organizations based on strong religious convictions, whose members are fanatically devoted to the global promotion of their religious beliefs.

While not all radical religious movements involved in politics are alike, they share certain similar characteristics:

1. Militant religious political movements tend to view existing government authority as corrupt and illegitimate because it is secular and not sufficiently rigorous in upholding religious authority or religiously sanctioned social and moral values.

2. They attack the inability of government to address the domestic ills of the society in which the movement exists. In many cases the religious movement substitutes itself for the government at the local level and is involved in education, health, and other social welfare programs.

3. They subscribe to a particular set of behavior and opinions that they believe political authority must reflect, promote, and protect in all governmental and social activities. This generally means that government and all of its domestic and foreign activities must be in the hands of believers or subject to their close oversight.

4. They are universalists: unlike ethnic movements, they tend to see their views as part of the inheritance of everyone who is a believer. This tends to give them a trans-state motivation, a factor that then translates their views on legitimacy of political authority into a larger context for action. In some cases, this means that international boundaries are not recognized as barriers to the propagation of the faith, even if this means they resort to violence.

5. They are exclusionists: they relegate all conflicting opinions on appropriate political and social order to the margins—if they do not exclude them altogether. This translates as second-class citizenship for any nonbeliever in any society where such a view predominates.

6. Finally, they are militant, willing to use coercion to achieve the only true end. (Shultz and Olson 1994, 9–10)

■ **irredentism** efforts by an ethnonational or religious group to regain control of territory by force so that existing state boundaries will no longer separate the group.

■ **secession, or separative revolts** the attempt by a religious or ethnic minority to break away from an internationally recognized state.

Although militant religious movements are not the only nonstate actors whose ideologies and activities may contribute to violence, many experts believe that they tend to stimulate five specific types of international activities. The first is **irredentism**—the attempt by a dominant religion or ethnic group to reclaim previously possessed territory in an adjacent region from a foreign state that now controls it. The group often rationalizes the use of force for this purpose. The second is **secession,** or **separative revolts**—the attempt by a religious (or ethnic) minority to break away from an internationally recognized state in a secessionist or separative revolt. Third, militant religions tend to incite migration, the departure of religious minorities from their countries of origin to escape persecution. Whether they move by force or by choice, the result, a fourth consequence of militant religion, is the same: the emigrants create diasporas, or communities that live abroad in host countries but maintain economic, political, and emotional ties with their homelands. Finally, a fifth effect of militant religions is **international terrorism** in the form of support for radical coreligionists abroad (see Chapter 11).

■ **international terrorism**
the use of terrorism against targets in other countries.

If we critically inspect the compound consequences of the activities of militant religious movements, we come away with the impression that religious movements not only bring people together but also divide them. Religious movements often challenge state authority, and religious-driven separatism can tear countries apart. The possible result, some predict, is that over time "the world may fracture into 500 states from the current 200" (UNDP 1994). Against this prophecy, we must contemplate another dimension of the sometimes close connection between religions and states: Many states actively support particular religions while repressing minority religions. States and religions are closely allied in many countries, with each reinforcing the other's power through many channels of contact, communication, and cooperation.

In the information age of disappearing boarders, money matters, and this makes multinational corporations also increasingly influential as nonstate actors connecting cash flow and people together globally in ways that may be eroding the sovereignty that states have previously taken as an unchanging given.

Multinational Corporations and Transnational Banks

Multinational corporations (MNCs)—business enterprises organized in one society with activities in another growing out of direct investment abroad—are a third major type of IGO. MNCs have grown dramatically in scope and potential influence with the **globalization** of the world political economy since World War II (see Chapters 8 and 9). As a result of these growing resources of power, they have provoked both animosity and enthusiastic acceptance. As advocates of liberal free trade and as active contributors to the globalization of world politics, MNCs generate both credit for the positive aspects of free trade and globalization and blame for their costs.

■ **multinational corporations (MNCs)**
business enterprises headquartered in one state that invest and operate extensively in other states.

■ **globalization**
the integration of states, through increasing contact, communication, and trade, to create a holistic, single global system in which the process of change increasingly binds people together in a common fate.

The numbers and immense size of MNCs add to the controversy surrounding their role and impact. At the start of the twenty-first century, the UN estimated that more than 53,000 MNCs and their 450,000 foreign affiliates had global assets in excess of $13 trillion and global sales of more than $9.5 trillion. This total financial clout is estimated to account for more than one-fifth of the world's economy, one-third of the world's exports, and one-third of the world's stock of all **foreign direct investment (FDI),** formally defined by the IMF as "ownership of assets in one country by residents of another for purposes of controlling the use of those assets."

■ **foreign direct investment (FDI)**
an investment in a country involving a long-term relationship and control of an enterprise by non-residents and including equity capital, reinvestment of earnings, other long-term capital, and short-term capital as shown in the balance of payments.

MNCs also employ more than 75 million people, although most of the existing MNCs are small and employ fewer than 250 people, and "it is commonplace to find service companies that maintain fewer employees working abroad in 15 countries" (Stopford 2001, 73). Today most multinational corporations are "'flag planters,' colonial outposts of basically domestic companies with some plant, or mines, or sales organizations in a few foreign lands" (Jain and Chelminski 1999). About twenty percent of all MNC employees work in the developed countries of the Global North, but MNCs penetrate the labor force throughout the world beyond their administrative staffs headquartered in the Global North. However, MNCs are very important NGOs in today's globalized world because each MNC typically generates one additional lower-wage job for each job through subcontracting in the corporate headquarters, bringing the number of jobs associated with MNCs to at least 150 million.

■ **transnational banks (TNBs)**
the globe's top banking firms, whose financial activities are concentrated in transactions that cross state borders.

MNC expansion has been facilitated by **transnational banks (TNBs),** another type of global NGO whose revenues and assets are primarily generated by financial transactions in the international economy. TNBs have become major forces in the world political economy. They have contributed to the globalization process that has led to financial integration worldwide at the same time that globalization has made international banks critical to global economic stability (as illustrated by the collapse of lending following occasional banking crises and the costs of recapitalizing, reorganizing, or liquidating insolvent banks by foreign countries). At the start of 2000, the combined assets of the world's twenty largest banks exceeded $425 trillion, a staggering figure attesting to the consolidation of the highly profitable control of financial resources in a highly globalized economy. The major banks in the world have formed strategic alliances and "big banks have been merging across borders to make themselves even bigger" (Stopford 2001) with an eye toward maximizing their already huge revenues. The mergers among some of the largest TNBs from the United States, the eurocurrency area, and Japan and Britain are a sign of global banking's slow but steady consolidations. The TNBs funnel trade and help to reduce the meaning of states' borders by making each state's economy dependent on other states' economies through the transfer of capital through international loans and investments. "The current environment of the MNC in the era of globalization is thus one of emergent alliances and coalitions across a broad array of actors" (Katzenstein and Leonway 2001). Together, TNBs and MNCs redistribute wealth and income in the world economy, contributing to the economic development of some states and the stagnation of others. One feared consequence in the Global South is that the TNBs advance the rich Global North at the South's expense, because about four-fifths of foreign direct investment is funneled into the richest countries with the poorest countries typically receiving very little. Like MNCs, therefore, TNBs spread the rewards of globalization unequally and inequitably, increasing wealth for a select group of countries and marginalizing the others.

Through their loans to the private sector, TNBs have made capital highly mobile and expanded the capacity of MNCs to lead the way in reducing differences across countries' tastes, lifestyles, and consumer products sold. As MNCs have grown in scope and power, concern has understandably been raised about whether their efforts to remove national barriers to foreign investments and trade is undermining the ability of seemingly sovereign states to control their own economies and therefore their own fates and cultures.

The benefits and costs attributed to MNCs as they have risen to a position of prominence since World War II have been many and complex, and this has made them highly controversial nonstate actors, especially in the Global South where people frequently see MNCs as the cause of exploitation and poverty (see Chapter 6).

MNCs are seen as increasingly influential IGOs because the world's giant producing, trading, and servicing corporations have become the primary agents of the globalization of production. Table 5.2 captures their importance in world

TABLE 5.2

Countries and Corporations: A Ranking by Size of Economy and Revenues

Rank	County/Corporation	GNP/Revenues (Billions of Dollars)	Rank	County/Corporation	GNP/Revenues (Billions of Dollars)
1	United States	9996.24	51	NIPPON TELEGRAPH & TELEPHONE	103.23
2	Japan	4619.81	52	ENRON	100.79
3	Germany	1921.97	53	Eygpt, Arab Rep.	96.17
4	United Kingdom	1434.87	54	Ireland	95.07
5	France	1317.11	55	Singapore	93.49
6	Italy	1080.87	56	AXA	92.78
7	China	1070.72	57	SUMITOMO	91.17
8	Canada	698.79	58	IBM	88.40
9	Brazil	641.95	59	Colombia	87.00
10	Spain	564.67	60	Malaysia	86.13
11	Mexico	563.83	61	MARUBENI	85.35
12	Korea	490.99	62	Iran	82.55
13	Inida	474.98	63	Philippines	78.87
14	Australia	385.30	64	VOLKSWAGEN	78.85
15	Netherlands	371.35	65	HITACHI	76.13
16	Taiwan, China	320.98	66	SIMENS	74.86
17	Argentina	289.32	67	Chile	74.66
18	Switzerland	242.02	68	ING GROUP	71.20
19	Russia	236.16	69	ALLIANZ	71.02
20	Sweden	235.17	70	MATSUSHITA ELECTRIC INDUSTRIAL	69.48
21	Belgium	229.21	71	E. ON	68.43
22	EXXON MOBIL	210.39	72	NIPPON LIFE INSURANCE	68.05
23	Turkey	197.68	73	DEUTSCHE BANK	67.13
24	WAL-MART STORES	193.30	74	SONY	66.16
25	Austria	192.30	75	AT&T	65.98
26	GENERAL MOTORS	184.63	76	VERIZON COMMUNICATIONS	64.71
27	FORD MOTOR	180.60	77	U.S. POSTAL SERVICE	64.54
28	Saudi Arabia	167.81	78	PHILIP MORRIS	63.28
29	Hong Kong, China	163.25	79	CGNU	61.50
30	Denmark	160.95	80	Pakistan	61.48
31	Indonesia	160.17	81	J. P. MORGAN CHASE	60.07
32	Norway	158.01	82	CARREFOUR	59.89
33	Poland	156.78	83	CREDIT SUISSE	59.32
34	DAIMLERCHRYSLER	150.07	84	NISSHO IWAI	58.56
35	Royal DUTCH/SHELL GROUP	149.15	85	HONDA MOTORS	58.46
36	BRITISH PETROLEUM	148.06	86	Peru	58.17
37	GENERAL ELECTRIC	129.85	87	BANK OF AMERICA	57.75
38	Thailand	129.70	88	BNP PARIBAS	57.61
39	South Africa	129.28	89	Algeria	57.02
40	MITSUBISHI	126.58	90	NISSAN MOTOR	55.08
41	Finland	121.76	91	TOSHIBA	53.83
42	TOYOTA MOTOR	121.42	92	PDVSA	53.68
43	MITSUI	118.01	93	ASSICURAZIONI GENERALI	53.33
44	Greece	114.79	94	FIAT	53.19
45	Venezuela	114.73	95	Hungary	52.48
46	CITIGROUP	111.83	96	MIZUHO HOLDINGS	52.07
47	ITOCHU	109.76	97	New Zealand	51.91
48	Portugal	105.91	98	SBC COMMUNICATION	51.48
49	TOTAL FINA ELF	105.87	99	BOEING	51.32
50	Israel	105.70	100	TEXACO	51.13

By integrating production and marketing their products worldwide, MNCs are dominating the global economy. As a result, MNCs rival many countries in wealth and are translating that income into influence as NGO actors. The value of MNC global mergers and acquisitions rose five-fold in the 1990s, to over $3.6 trillion in 2000 (Economist, January 27, 2001, 61). This trend suggests that "every day the line between companies and countries blurs a bit more . . . as the walls around the world disappear. . . . . The sheer size and power that some of these companies are amassing" (see Figure to right), which, leaves few ways to prevent "big monopolies from overwhelming consumers and preventing big business from overwhelming democratic government," observers Thomas Friedman (2000).

SOURCE: MNC revenues, Fortune August, 2001; <www.fortune.com/indexw.jhtml?channel=/editorial/site_map.html/>); countries' GDP, *The World Economic Outlook* (WEO) Database, IMF (May, 2001).

politics, ranking firms by annual sales and states by GNP. The profile shows that of the world's top one hundred economic entities, among the top fifty multinationals account for only fourteen, but in the next fifty, they account for thirty-seven. MNCs' financial clout thus rivals or exceeds that of most countries.

Although the growth of multinational firms is a global phenomenon, a telling feature of the distrubution of wealth is that the Global North is home to about 90 percent of MNC parent corporations. Historically, the United States has been the home country for most of the largest multinationals, and including the G-7 liberal democracies account for four-fifths of all parent corporations and also for a similar share of both the stock and flow of foreign direct investment. A major consequence is that FDI is now increasingly regional. The direction of MNCs' investments reinforces—perhaps causes—the growing regionalization of the world political economy across a range of dimensions, not only in investment but also in finance, and trade (see Chapters 8 and 9).

In addition to their global reach and economic power, MNCs' involvement in the domestic political affairs of local or host countries is also a controversial issue. In some instances this concern has extended to MNCs' involvement in the domestic politics of their home countries, where they actively lobby their governments for more liberal trade and investment policies that will enhance the profitability of their business activities abroad. In turn, both host and home governments have sometimes used MNCs as instruments in their foreign policy strategies. Perhaps the most notorious instance of an MNC's intervention in the politics of a host state occurred in Chile in the early 1970s when International Telephone and Telegraph (ITT) tried to protect its interests in the profitable Chiltelco telephone company by seeking to prevent the election of Marxist-oriented Salvador Allende as president and, once Allende was elected, pressured the U.S. government to disrupt the Chilean economy. Eventually Allende was overthrown by a military dictatorship.

Because MNCs assist in promoting free trade and are active participants in the process by which governments have reached agreements on rules liberalizing economic transactions in the global marketplace, it is tempting to conclude that MNCs are a threat to state power. However, this interpretation overlooks the fact that at the same time MNCs have grown in size, the regulatory power of states has grown.

> Only the state can defend corporate interests in international negotiations over trade, investment, and market access. Agreements over such things as airline routes, the opening of banking establishments, and the right to sell insurance are not decided by corporate actors who gather around a table; they are determined by diplomats and bureaucrats. Corporations must turn to governments when they have interests to protect or advance. (Kapstein 1991–1992, 56)

Still, the blurring of the boundaries between internal and external affairs adds potency to the political role that MNCs unavoidably play as nonstate actors at the intersection of foreign and domestic policy. The symbolic invasion of national borders by MNCs can be expected to arouse the anger of many local nationalists who fear the loss of income, jobs, and control to foreign corporate interests. Because multinationals often make decisions over which national political leaders have little control, their growing influence appears to be contributing to the erosion of the global system's major organizing principle—that the state alone should be sovereign. "The growth of trade within MNCs reduces states' control by making it more difficult to collect taxes" (Wolf 2001). Because "the reach and influence of multinationals, large and small, is far greater than the official statistics suggest [and] the relationship between governments and multinationals is characterized by a complex distribution of benefits," states have every reason to feel that MNCs are stripping away their sovereign control inasmuch as "multinational corporations increasingly demand the freedom they need to optimize their operations across borders" (Stopford 2001). And in fact, in some respects states *are* losing control of their national economies as MNCs merge with one another and, in the process, cease to remain tied to any one parent state, or region.

Controlling the resulting webs of corporate interrelationships, joint ventures, and shared ownership for any particular national purpose is nearly impossible. Part of the reason is that about one-third of world trade in goods and services occurs *within* multinationals, from one branch to another. Joint production and **strategic corporate alliances** to create temporary phantom "virtual corporations" undermine states' ability to identify the MNCs they seek to control. "There is widespread concern that MNCs are becoming truly 'stateless' [as] the explosion of strategic alliances is transforming the corporate landscape" with more than 10,000 strategic alliances estimated to be forged each year recently (Stopford 2001, 74–75). "You can't find targets any more, and if you aim at a target you often find it's yourself," observes Richard J. Barnet, coauthor of *Global Reach* (Barnet and Müller 1974).

The multinationals' potential long-run influence is depicted in *Global Dreams: Imperial Corporations and the New World Order:*

> By acquiring earth-spanning technologies, by developing products that can be produced anywhere and sold everywhere, by spreading credit around the world, and by connecting global channels of communication that can penetrate any village or neighborhood, these institutions we normally think of as economic rather than political, private rather than public, are becoming the world empires of the twenty-first century. The architects and managers of these space-age business enterprises understand that the balance of power in world politics has shifted in recent years from territorially bound governments to companies that can roam the world. As the hopes and pretensions of government shrink almost everywhere, these imperial corporations are occupying public space and exerting a more profound influence over the lives of ever larger numbers of people. (Barnet and Cavanagh 1994, 14)

As multinational corporations play increasingly larger roles in world politics, the community of sovereign states will be forced to confront the many issues raised by an economic and business sector that has turned global. How will they respond? Assessing the future requires a theoretical examination of contemporary thinking regarding the MNCs and the other types of NGOs.

■ **strategic corporate alliances**
cooperation between multinational corporations and foreign companies in the same industry, driven by the movement of MNC manufacturing overseas.

REEVALUATING NGOS' CAPACITY TO TRANSFORM WORLD POLITICS

"In global politics, interest group pluralism is growing" as citizens increasingly participate in NGOs in order to gain power "in the global institutions that shape people's daily lives" (Falk and Strauss 2001). Inspired by this trend, many people see NGOs as a democratic force in world politics that can empower individuals by giving them a voice in the decisions leading to transformations in international affairs. NGOs, many believe, can exert influence over the direction of global conditions. This viewpoint maintains that "alongside the necessary and imperfect interstate institutional framework, there is developing an informal political process that supplements the formal process of cooperative relations among states. . . . These organizations and the multiple channels of access across borders," Robert Keohane and Joseph Nye (2001a) explain, "are able to put increasing leverage on states. . . . The combination of private, transgovernmental, and transnational actors is creating an incipient, albeit imperfect, civil society at the global level."

constructivist
a scholarly approach to inquiry emphasizing the importance of agents (people and groups) and the shared meanings they construct to define their identities, interests, and institutions-understandings that influence their international behavior.

Is this **constructivist** image of the processes by which trends and transformations in world politics are determined realistic or exaggerated? Are NGOs influential? Or is a rival hypothesis—that NGOs remain relatively powerless in global governance—more accurate?

In support of the later viewpoint, "a counter-argument [can be] made that NGOs have tended to reinforce rather than counter existing power structures, having members and headquarters that are primarily in the rich Global North countries. Some also believe that NGO decision-making does not provide for responsible, democratic representation or accountability" (Stephenson 2000). According to this thesis, world politics is still controlled by states—especially the great powers; it is a world ruled by the powerful, in which nonstate actors have little real influence. Even the United Nations, so this assessment concludes, "still represents a predominately state-centric approach to global governing at a time when this approach is being questioned and undermined" (Knight 2000).

realism
a paradigm based on the premise that world politics is essentially and unchangeably a struggle among self-interested states for power and position under anarchy, with each competing state pursuing its own national interests.

Seen through the spectacles of **realism,** the critical choices that direct global destiny are made by the most powerful states. Global governance is not a product of the values and interests of the world's more than 6 billion people at large, organized into thousands of nongovernmental organizations; it is dominated by a privileged minority, namely, the great powers which possess the means to see that the most important global policy decisions are made to protect their national interests.

Juxtaposed to this conclusion is an alternative explanation—whereas individuals do influence international policy by organizing themselves into groups to petition powerful governments on behalf of their shared interests and values, their individual efforts are compromised by the opposition of other NGOs resisting the first group of NGOs' endeavors to push international relations in a particular direction. Skeptics also point out that many NGOs represent powerful vested interests that work secretly behind the scenes to lobby for global policies that protect both the powerful through private commercial interests and the great powers who are their primary clients at the expense of collective interests. Thus, the question is raised: precisely how influential and effective are grassroot NGOs in their efforts to lobby the powerful for new global rules and **regimes** that put human welfare and the collective interests of all humanity above particular, parochial national interests? Studies of the impact of NGO pressure on global policy making suggest some conclusions that reduce confidence in the expectation that NGO pressure can lead to far-reaching reforms, even transformations, in the conduct of international relations:

regimes
norms, rules, and procedures for interaction agreed to by a set of states.

- Interest group activity operates as an ever present, if limited, constraint on global policy making, but the impact *varies with the issue* and their influence is weakest on the most important problems on the global agenda.

- Similarly, the occasions when private NGOs are most influential are rare. The influences are greatest with respect to a particular issue—such as nuclear nonproliferation—when in the interests of the great powers.

- As a general rule, NGOs are relatively weak in the **high politics** of international security, because states remain in control of defense policy and are relatively unaffected by external NGO pressures. Conversely, the NGOs' clout is highest with respect to issues in **low politics,** such as protecting endangered species (e.g., whales) or combatting global warming, which are of concern to great and small powers alike.

- The influence between state governments and NGOs is reciprocal, but it is more probable that government officials manipulate transnational interest groups than that NGOs exercise influence over governments' foreign policies.

- Single-issue NGO interest groups have more influence than large general-purpose organizations.

- NGOs sometimes seek *inaction* from governments and maintenance of the *status quo;* such efforts are generally more successful than efforts to bring about major changes in international relations. For this reason NGOs are often generally seen as agents of policy continuities.

■ **high politics**
geostrategic issues of national and international security that pertain to matters of war and peace.

■ **low politics**
the category of global issues related to the economic, social, demographic, and environmental aspects of relations between governments and people.

The foregoing characteristics of NGO efforts to redirect global policy suggest that the mere presence of such groups, and the mere fact they are organized with the intent of persuasion, does not guarantee their penetration of the global policy-making process. On the whole, NGOs have participation without real power and involvement without real influence, given that the ability of any *one* to exert influence is offset by the tendency for *countervailing powers* to materialize over the disposition of any major issue. That is, as any particular coalition of NGOs works together on a common cause and begins to be powerful, other groups threatened by the changes advocated tend to spring up to balance it. When an interest group seeks vigorously to push policy in one direction, other nonstate actors—aroused that their established interests are being disturbed—are stimulated to push policy in the opposite direction. Global policy making consequently resembles a taffy pull: every nonstate actor attempts to pull policy in its own direction while resisting the pulls of others, with the result that often it appears that the quest for consensus proves elusive and the international community's posture toward many global problems fails to move in any single direction.

This balance process between opposing actors helps to account for the reason why so few global issues are resolved. Competition stands in the way of consensus, and contests of will over international issues are seldom settled. No side can ever claim permanent victory, for each decision that takes international policy in one direction merely sets the stage for the next round of the contest, with the possibility that the losers of the moment will be winners tomorrow. The result is usually a kind of continuous battleground over the primary issues on the global agenda, from which materializes no permanent resolution of the struggle. The debate and contests between those wishing to make protection of the environment a global priority and those placing economic growth ahead of environmental preservation provides one among many examples.

As the world grows more interdependent and transactions across state borders increase through the movement of people, information, and traded products, it is likely that world politics nonetheless will be increasingly affected by the activities of both IGO and NGO nonstate actors. Even though nonstate actors are unlikely to join together in a common cause to pressure the international community for radical reforms, their activities (however divided) are likely to challenge the ironlike grip that sovereign states have exercised for more than 350 years in determining the global system's architecture and rules. Ever since the Peace of Westphalia in 1648, states—and especially great powers—have ruled supreme. Nonstate actors were largely pawns at the states' mercy, to be moved at the states' will.

However, states' grip over trends in world politics *has* weakened, and nonstate actors are flexing their muscles in ways that directly challenge states' sovereign control over both their foreign and domestic policies. Despite their diversity and divisions, nearly all nonstate actors are animated by a desire to protest the existing organizational apparatus of international relations, in the hope that their voice will produce institutional and legal reforms. Are the pillars of the Westphalian system beginning to crumble, as some analysts of contemporary international relations claim (see Falk and Strauss 2001; Kegley and Raymond 2002a)? Let us conclude our introduction to nonstate actors with some observations about the rise of nonstate actors and the potential challenge they may make to the states in the global system.

NONSTATE ACTORS: SAVIORS OR STRANGLERS OF THE STATE?

As it becomes increasingly misleading "to view the world as consisting of territorial units each exerting supreme authority within its borders" (Falk 2001b), an accurate conceptualization of contemporary world politics must acknowledge the growing influence of NGOs and IGOs as partners and independent actors. Having observed their diversity and wide-ranging impact, one generalization certainly is apt: nonstate actors will continue to be widely seen as posing a threat to the overriding prominence of states in the management of world affairs. Czech President Václav Havel voiced this sentiment in July 1999 when he argued, "There is every indication that the glory of the nation-state as the culmination of every national community's history . . . has already passed its peak [and] that human beings are more important than the state. In this new world, people—regardless of borders—are connected in millions of different ways: through trade, finance, property, and information."

IGOs and NGOs are both seeking to change the face of international affairs and reshape the global agenda (as a coalition of 160 NGOs from all regions did in October 1998 when they met in Toronto to organize to control the shipment of small arms that they believed were causing misery and destruction worldwide). These global actors were collectively interested in turning the world of states upside down (Clegg 1999).

The question for the twenty-first century is whether the nation-state system will survive, given the challenges from IGOs, NGOs, and the gales of globalization to their continuing domination. Consider one among many assessments:

> Even if a few states can still defend their territory against an invading army,
> not even the most powerful can protect its people and cities against a dev-

Beth A. Keiser/AP/Wide World

Rage against Rising Institutional Symbols of Interdependence In the recent past, the meetings attended by finance ministers at such powerful IGOs as the World Bank or the International Monetary Fund drew little interest or publicity. Now, with increasing criticism of the globalization of national economies, these meetings are in the limelight. A backlash against the rising power of multilateral corporations—the primary force driving the interdependence of the international economy—is evident, and the major financial IGOs are the most convenient target for protests against IGOs and MNCs, which are increasingly perceived to act like governments. This image is expressed by those who typically portray MNCs as "inherently exploitative . . . globetrotting sweatshop operators, indifferent polluters, and systematic tax evaders" (Stopford 2001). Seen here is one recent outburst, when the meeting of the World Trade Organization mobilized a broad-based coalition of NGOs to challenge this global trend perceived to threaten nationalistic values.

astating surprise attack by guided missiles, and none can control the flow of images and ideas that shape human tastes and values. The globalized "presence" of Madonna, McDonald's, and Mickey Mouse make a mockery of sovereignty as exclusive territorial control. A few governments do their best to insulate their populations from such influences, but their efforts are growing less effective and run counter to democratizing demands that are growing more difficult to resist. . . . Interdependence and the interpenetration of domestic and international politics, the mobility and globalization of capital and information, and the rising influence of transnational social movements and organizations are among the factors that make it anachronistic to analyze politics as if territorial supremacy continues to be a generalized condition or a useful fiction. In particular, sovereignty, with its stress on the inside/outside distinction as between domestic and international society, seems more misleading than illuminating under current conditions. (Falk 2001b, 790–791).

This by no means indicates that the era of state dominance is over, however. States retain a (near) monopoly on the use of coercive force in the global system, and they continue to shape the transnational interactions of nonstate actors. The state still molds the activities of nonstate actors more than its behavior is molded by them. It "may be anachronistic, but we have yet to develop an alternative form of societal organization that is able to provide its members with both wealth and power" (Kapstein 1991–1992). It is also true that "a gain in power by nonstate actors does not necessarily translate into a loss of power for the state" (Slaughter 1997). We must conclude that whereas it would be premature to abandon the focus on the state in world politics, it would be equally mistaken to exaggerate the state's power as a determinant of the globe's fate and dismiss the expanding role that nonstate actors are playing within the tightening web of interdependent globalization that is eroding the power of states. We cannot ignore the shifts occurring "away from the state— up, down, and sideways—to supra-state, sub-state, and, above all nonstate actors— new players that have multiple allegiances and global reach" (Slaughter 1997). In the new globalized market, it is difficult to distinguish corporations, countries, and other actors in an era of collapsing states and reemergent nations. This is particularly true for the multiethnic, less-developed countries of the **Global South.** It is to their circumstances, in a world dominated by great powers and huge corporations, to which we turn in the next chapter.

■ **Global South**

a term now often used instead of "Third World" to designate the less-developed countries located primarily in the Southern Hemisphere.

KEY TERMS

intergovernmental organizations (IGOs)
nongovernmental organizations (NGOs)
global level of analysis
realpolitik
politics
anarchy
collective security
Cold War
ideology
Group of 77
regimes
bilateral
G-7
nonintervention
rational choice
liberalism
globalization
realist

neoliberal theory
security community
Third Way
European Commission
pooled sovereignty
regimes
devolution
realism
nonstate nations
unitary actor
constructivism
nationalism
ethnopolitical groups
ethnicity
ethnic nationalism
ethnic groups
indigenous peoples
Fourth World
cultural domains

clash of civilizations
religious movement
extreme militant religious movements
irredentism
secession, or separative revolts
international terrorism
multinational corporations (MNCs)
globalization
foreign direct investment (FDI)
transnational banks (TNBs)
product-cycle theory
strategic corporate alliances
constructivist
realism
regimes
high politics
low politics
Global South

SUGGESTED READING

Appleby, R. Scott. *The Ambivalence of the Sacred: Religion, Violence, and Reconciliation.* Boulder, Colo.: Rowman & Littlefield, 2000.

Barnet, Richard J., and John Cavanagh. *Global Dreams: Imperial Corporations and the New World Order.* New York: Simon & Schuster, 1994.

Broad, Robin, ed. *Global Backlash: Citizen Initiatives for a Just World Economy.* Lanham, Md.: Rowman and Littlefield, 2002.

Caporaso, James A. *Challenges and Dilemmas of European Union.* Boulder, Colo.: Westview Press, 2000.

Florini, Ann M., ed. *The Third Force: The Rise of Transnational Civil Society.* Washington, D.C.: Carnegie Endowment for International Peace, 2001.

Gruber, Lloyd, *Ruling the World: Power Politics and the Rise of Supranational Institutions.* Princeton, N.J.: Princeton University Press, 2000.

Harrison, Lawrence E., and Samuel P. Huntington. *Culture Matters: How Values Shape Human Progress.* New York: Basic Books, 2001.

Iriye, Akira. *Global Community: The Role of International Organizations in the Making of the Contemporary World.* Berkeley, Calif.: University of California Press, 2002.

Krasner, Stephen D., ed. *Problematic Sovereignty: Contested Rules and Political Possibilities.* New York: Columbia University Press, 1999.

Wallace, William, and Daphne Jostelin, eds. *Non-state Actors in World Politics.* London: Palgrave, 2002.

Weiss, Thomas G., David P. Forsythe, and Roger A. Coate. *The United Nations and Changing World Politics*, 3rd ed. Boulder, Colo.: Westview Press, 2000.

White, Nigel D. *The United Nations System.* Boulder, Colo.: Lynne Rienner, 2002.

Ziring, Lawrence, Robert E. Riggs, and Jack C. Plano. *The United Nations: International Organization and World Politics*, 3rd ed. New York: Harcourt, 2000.

WHERE ON THE WORLD WIDE WEB?

European Union
http://europa.eu.int/index.htm

The EU is an IGO with regional membership and multiple purposes. Chapter 5 characterizes the authority structure of the EU as one of pooled sovereignty, under which the member states grant the EU legal authority to make some collective decisions for them. After entering the Europa Web site, explore the main institutions of the EU. How does the Court of Justice differ from the UN's International Court of Justice? How many political groupings are represented in the European Parliament? How might these divisions affect the formation of a unified EU foreign policy?

International Monetary Fund
http://www.imf.org/

The International Monetary Fund (IMF) is an IGO with global membership that was created to promote international monetary cooperation and facilitate the expansion and balanced growth of international trade by promoting exchange stability. It does this by making monetary resources temporarily available to its members. Choose two or three countries of interest to you and see how they have interacted with the IMF. Examine the "current topics" section. What are the main issues discussed here? Which countries or groups of countries are affected?

North Atlantic Treaty Organization
http://www.nato.int

The North Atlantic Treaty Organization (NATO) is a military alliance that includes the European states, the United States, and Canada. It was originally formed to protect Europe from the Soviet threat after World War II. Since the end of the Cold War, it has been restructured; it now has an auxiliary membership, the Partnership for Peace (PfP). To see

PfP's membership, click on the "Partnerships" link from the NATO homepage and then click on the Partnership for Peace link. What characteristics do the PfP member countries share? Although once a regional collective defense organization, NATO has had to redefine its mission since the end of the Cold War. NATO's involvement in Bosnia was the first venture into new terrain. Many question whether it is appropriate for an organization designed for mutual self-protection from external attack to be involved in policing civil wars in Europe. What do you think?

Organization of American States
http://www.oas.org/

The Organization of American States (OAS) is a multipurpose IGO with regional members from North and South America. It is the "principal forum in the hemisphere for political, economic, and social dialogue." The OAS is concerned with issues such as democracy, human rights, trade, environment, and education. Explore one of these challenges by selecting "Key OAS Issues" from the "About the OAS" drop-down menu. How might the United States and other hemispheric countries differ in their views of the challenge and the best way to solve it?

United Nations
http://www.un.org/

The United Nations (UN) is an IGO with global membership that performs multiple purposes. The UN Web site is organized according to the organization's primary concerns: peace and security, international law, humanitarian affairs, economic and social development, and human rights. Chapter 5 has introduced you to the major UN organs—the General Assembly, the Security Council, Economic and Social Council, and Secretariat. Which organ focuses on which areas of concern?

World Health Organization
http://www.who.int/

The main goal of the World Health Organization (WHO) is the attainment by all peoples of the highest possible level of health. It defines health as the "state of complete physical, mental, and social well-being and not merely the absence of disease or infirmity." The WHO has been hailed as one of the best examples of how an international organization can benefit the world community. Review the WHO's major achievements and the challenges it faces. Do you think it is

possible for the WHO to achieve its goals? Do you agree with its expanded definition of health that includes social well-being?

The World Trade Organization
http://www.wto.org/

The World Trade Organization (WTO) is an IGO with a global membership and multiple purposes. Its mission is to ensure that trade flows between states as smoothly, predictably, and freely as possible. Decision making within the WTO is by consensus among all 145 member countries. Trade agreements are then ratified by members' parliaments. The WTO also uses a dispute settlement process that focuses on interpreting agreements and ensuring that member countries' trade policies follow them. Click on "WTO News" and "Trade Topics." What important issues is the WTO currently addressing?

Academic Info Religion
http://www.academicinfo.net/religindex.html

Many American students are unfamiliar with the belief systems of non-Western religions. Do you know the difference is between Lamaistic and Theravada Buddhists? Find out by visiting the Academic Info Religion Web site. This site links you with Internet resources for the study of the world's religions. Read passages from the Koran and the Old and New Testaments. Compare and contrast Taoist, Zen, Mormon, Hindu, Gnostic, and Nag Hammadi texts. If your tastes lean more toward mythology and alchemy, you will find them here, too.

Nathanson Center for the Study of Organized Crime and Corruption
http://www.yorku.ca/nathanson/

International organized crime is an increasingly influential nonstate actor for which the "creed is greed." The Nathanson Center at York University in Canada analyzes organized crime and corruption as part of its commitment to educate the public. Focusing primarily on North American organized crime, this site has an extensive bibliography of articles, books, and reports that is a good start for anyone researching this topic. It also offers links to Web sites on different international criminal organizations, including the Italian-Sicilian Mafia, the Japanese Yakuza, the Chinese Triads, and outlaw motorcycle gangs. Alternatively, it lists links by specific type of crime.

Patterns of Global Terrorism

http://www.usis.usemb.se/terror/

The U.S. Department of State has compiled a Web site that reviews region-specific information on terrorism from 1995 through 2000. Choose a year, then view appendices for a chronology of terrorist attacks, background information on specific terrorist groups, and attack and casualty statistics. Choose a terrorist group. What are its demands? Should the United States ever negotiate with terrorists? Why or why not?

Terrorism Research Center

http://www.terrorism.com/index.shtml

This site is a good source for research on terrorism and links to other Web sources on terrorism. Look at the Terrorist Profiles for discussion and analysis of groups.. Keep in mind that one NGO group's "freedom fighters" may be another group's "terrorists."

INFOTRAC® COLLEGE EDITION

Huebner, David, and Raja Haddad. "UN-Paid Dues: The Costs of Cooperation," *Harvard International Review* Summer 2002.

Thiessen, Marc A. "When Worlds Collide," *Foreign Policy* March 2001.

Calleo, David. "A Choice of Europes," *The National Interest* Spring 2001.

Peang-Meth, Abdulgaffar. "The Rights of Indigenous Peoples and Their Fight for Self-Determination," *World Affairs* Winter 2002.

For more articles, enter:

"United Nations" in the Subject Guide, and then go to subdivision "management."

"Europe" in the Subject Guide, and then go to subdivision "politics and government."

"indigenous peoples" in the Subject Guide.

THE GLOBAL SOUTH IN A WORLD OF POWERS

T O P I C S   A N D   T H E M E S

- The politics of marginalization: The Global South in the international hierarchy
- Global North and Global South today: Worlds apart
- The colonial origins of the Global South's plight
- Theoretical explanations of underdevelopment
- Closing the gap? The Global South's prospects
- The Global South's foreign policy response to a world ruled by the great powers
- The Global South's problematic future

- **CONTROVERSY** MULTINATIONAL CORPORATIONS IN THE GLOBAL SOUTH: DO THEY HELP OR HURT?

At the G-8 Summit in Alberta, Canada, in June 2002, Nigerian President Olusegun Obasanjo is invited to meet with the great power leaders, in a gesture to open up to Global South participation in international decision making controlled by the Global North.

A global human society based on poverty for many and prosperity for a few, characterized by islands of wealth surrounded by a sea of poverty, is unsustainable.

—THABO MBEKI, president of South Africa, 2002

In this unified world, poverty is our collective enemy. We must fight it because it is morally repugnant, and because its existence is like a cancer—weakening the whole of the body, not just the parts directly affected.

—JAMES D. WOLFENSOHN, president of the World Bank, 2002

Earth is divided into two hemispheres, north and south, at the equator. This artificial line of demarcation is, of course, meaningless except for use by cartographers to chart distance and location on maps. However, this divide captures a constructed view of international realities that has become a popular way of describing a basic fact: the countries of the world are unequal. There exists an international hierarchy that separates the rich and the poor states, the weak and the strong, the powerful and the powerless. And it is not by coincidence that today these two groups of state actors are located on either side of the equator (see Map 6.1)

Life for the countries in the Northern Hemisphere is very different from that in the Southern Hemisphere. The disparities between the "haves" and the "have nots" are profound, and for many Global South states the gap is growing. The division in status and power in this highly stratified society of states poses problems—a major issue on the global agenda for all humanity—for which solutions must be found if the world is to experience a peaceful and stable twenty-first century. As the ancient Greek political philosopher, Aristotle, warned, "wide differences in income are a source of war." The urgent moral need to reduce poverty and the war it breeds was argued in 2002 by British

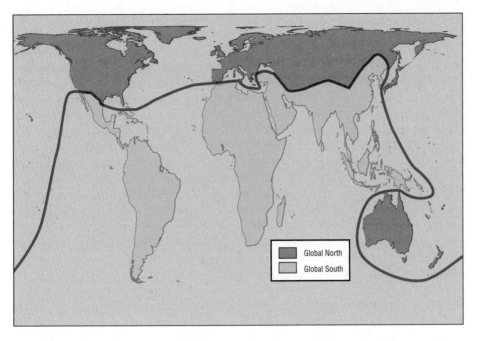

M A P 6 . 1
The Global North and Global South
The countries of the Global North are those that are wealthy, democratic, and technologically innovative, with declining birthrates and aging populations. In contrast, the countries in the Global South are home to 80 percent of the world's population, but the impoverished people living there possess only 15 percent of the globe's wealth.

Prime Minister Tony Blair: "One illusion has been shattered on September 11: that we can have the good life of the [Global North] irrespective of the state of the rest of the world . . . . The dragon's teeth are planted in the fertile soil of wrongs unrighted, of disputes left to fester for years, of failed states, of poverty and deprivation."

Poverty and inequality has existed throughout most periods of recorded history. But today the level of relative deprivation between rich and poor states has reached unprecedented proportions. The states in the less-developed Global South find themselves marginalized and left neglected by the wealthy states rapidly benefitting from rising prosperity in the age of globalization (see Chapter 8). Most of the countries in the Global South are frustrated by their inability to play catch-up and close the gap with rich-countries. Simply put, the global gap between rich and poor states of the Global South "has not closed. Instead, it has widened" (Hausmann 2002). Mired in abject poverty, these states have had their identities shaped by their subordinate position in the global hierarchy of power. They find themselves reduced in their self-image to thinking of themselves as distinct from the advantaged, without real hope of escaping the crushing conditions that have become an entrenched way of life.

It is the purpose of this chapter to examine the causes and consequences of this chronic inequality among the more than 200 states in the global system. Why is it that the great power experience abundance while the disadvantaged

■ **global level
of analysis**
an analytical approach to
world politics that
emphasizes the impact of
worldwide conditions on
the behavior of states,
IGOs, NGOs, and other
international actors.

■ **structural realism**
a theory associated with
neorealism that emphasizes
the influence of the
structure of world power on
the behavior of the states
within it.

■ **state level of analysis**
an analytical approach to
the study of world politics
that emphasizes how the
internal attributes of states
explain their foreign policy
behaviors.

■ **individual level
of analysis**
an analytical approach to
the study of world politics
that emphasizes the
psychological and
perceptual origins of the
foreign policy behaviors of
international actors, with
special attention to leaders.

poor countries desperately try simply to survive? What is it about global life that has bred such inequality?

Most analysts begin to address this question at the **global level of analysis.** The popularity of this approach derives from the fact that the relative power and position of each state in the global system is assumed to be potently determined by changes in the system's structure. How groups of states such as those in the less-developed Global South unfavorably fare in comparison with those in the advanced industrialized economies of the Global North is not believed to be accidental. Following the logic of **structural realism,** analysts believe that the global system has properties built into it which account for the inability of most Global South countries to engineer self-sustained growth and development at rates which would enable them to close the gap with the wealthy states. As a preface to our inquiry, let us briefly elaborate on the reasoning underlying this perspective. It needs to be underscored that this chapter investigates the above question about international inequalities by inspecting the Global South states as international actors in world politics—that is, at the global and **state level of analysis.** Later, in Chapter 7, we will look at the human dimensions of welfare issues by inspecting peoples' inequalities as they exist both across the entire globe as well as within particular states. There at the **individual level of analysis,** we will focus on humanitarian concerns and the barriers to human development and human rights.

Part of the basis for the resentment, envy, and sense of exploitation that the Global South countries feel stems from the fact that the modern state system, of which they are members, was created by the great powers in the 1648 Peace of Westphalia following the Thirty Years' War in Europe (recall Chapter 3). Today's less-developed countries had no voice in creating the rules and the global IGO institutions that govern both them and all sovereign states. The rules and laws that still cast their shadow over international affairs more than 350 years after Westphalia were constructed by the most powerful actors on the world stage, the so-called great powers. Those great powers constructed a system to serve their parochial self-interests by creating rules that would not only help them regulate their relationships with one another but also, and more importantly, enable them to conduct diplomacy in ways that would preserve their predominant positions at the top of the global pyramid of power, even at the expense of deterring the rise of less-powerful states seeking to join them (see Kegley and Raymond 2002a).

Indeed, the international organizations that have over time grown in number and influence (see Chapter 5) were created by the great powers to benefit themselves, but not necessarily all state members of the global community at large. Thus, to understand the origins and persistence of the inequalities of states in international society, we must make no mistake about the modern global system's most defining characteristic: it was initially, and remains, a socially constructed reality *by, of,* and *for* the powerful states, designed primarily to serve their interests and needs. The overarching motive was not the creation of a global civil society inspired by values of justice, but, in the realist construction, inspired by self-interest defined by power. The global system is understandably, given these assumptions, not designed as a system for equals; nor did the great powers design the global system with an eye to preventing the victimization of the weak and disadvantaged. In this sense, therefore, the inequalities that today divide into a class system the rich from the poor, and the mighty from the defenseless in terms of military capabilities, are part of a much longer historical pattern. It is important to look at the plight and predicament of the Global South countries by first recognizing the long-term global forces that have created the position of weakness from which they now struggle to escape.

To understand how the Global South countries today are attempting to survive in a world of the powerful, we need to begin by taking into consideration the legacy and impact of **colonialism** on the **indigenous peoples** whose territories were colonized by European imperial conquerors. These conquerors arbitrarily drew borders around their new territorial possessions without regard for the ethnic and linguistic divisions within the native populations they subjugated. Almost all the now independent sovereign states in the Southern Hemisphere were at one time colonies, including such contemporary powerhouses as the United States.

THE COLONIAL ORIGINS OF THE GLOBAL SOUTH'S PLIGHT

Despite their legal status as independent entities, sovereignty could not erase the colonial heritage and vulnerabilities that the former colonies faced. Indeed, the new poor states born after World War II were thrust to the international periphery, dominated by the wealthy great powers at the core of the transformed international system following the Second World War. The term **Third World** was first used to distinguish the growing number of newly independent but economically less-developed states that tended to share a colonial past from those states that identified with either the East or the West in the Cold War struggle, but it soon took on largely economic connotations. The Third World had failed to advance toward levels of economic development comparable to those of the **First World** industrialized great powers, like western Europe, North America, and Japan. The so-called **Second World** consisting of the Soviet Union and its allies in other communist countries was distinguished by a communist ideological commitment to planned economic policies rather than reliance on market forces to determine the supply and demand for goods and services. Today the states comprising the former Second World have almost totally vanished from the global scene, with liberalism triumphant and nearly all states committed to free-market capitalism. The Second World describes the handful of "countries in transition" that have yet to join the World Trade Organization and accept its rules of free markets and free governments.

The term *Third World* carries Cold War baggage that makes it no longer useful. Today the terms **Global North,** which refers to what was previously known as the First World, and **Global South,** which refers to the rest of the world, are popular. As always, the placement of particular states within these categories is sometimes problematic. Considerable diversity exists within the countries of the Global South, even though it is common to describe them as a single group quite distinct from the similarly diverse great powers. Generally, four major dimensions differentiate the Global North and South: politics, technology, wealth, and demography.

■ **colonialism**
the rule of a region by an external sovereign power.

■ **indigenous peoples**
the native ethnic and cultural inhabitant populations within countries ruled by a government controlled by others, referred to as the "Fourth World."

■ **Third World**
a Cold War term to describe the developing countries of Africa, Asia, the Caribbean, and Latin America.

■ **First World**
the relatively wealthy industrialized countries that share a commitment to varying forms of democratic political institutions and developed market economies, including the United States, Japan, the European Union, Canada, Australia, and New Zealand.

■ **Second World**
during the Cold War, the group of countries, including the Soviet Union and its then–Eastern European allies, that embraced central planning to propel economic growth.

■ **Global North**
a term used to refer to the world's wealthy, industrialized countries located primarily in the Northern Hemisphere.

■ **Global South**
a term now often used instead of "Third World" to designate the less-developed countries located primarily in the Southern Hemisphere.

GROSS NATIONAL INCOME

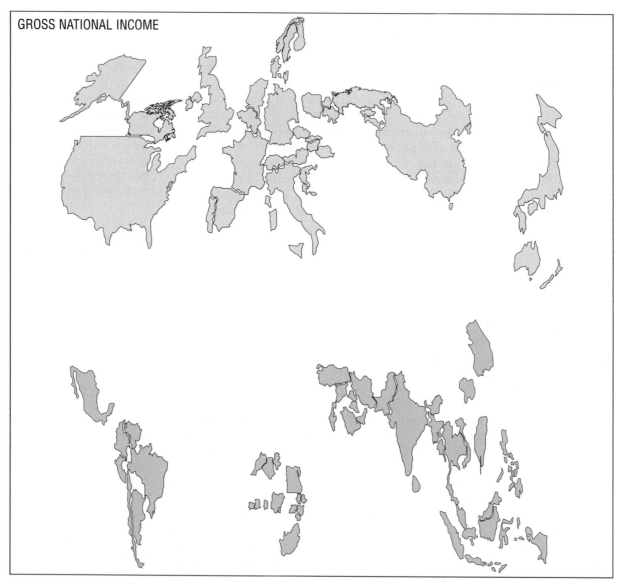

MAP 6.2
The Great North-South Divide in Wealth and Population

If the countries in the globe were redrawn to reflect the size of their economies and populations, as shown here, huge differences would be visible. Most of the wealth is in the Global North, and most of the people are in the Global South. If prevailing trends persist as expected, the disparities will continue to widen the existing division between rich and poor.

SOURCE: Adapted from WORLD DEVELOPMENT REPORT 1999/2000: by World Bank, Copyright © 2000 by the International Bank for Reconstruction and Development/The World Bank. Used by permission of Oxford University Press, Inc.

States comprising the Global North are democratic, technologically inventive, wealthy, and aging, since their societies tend toward zero population growth (see Map 6.2). Some states in the Global South share many of these characteristics, but none shares them all. Saudi Arabia is rich but not democratic; China is

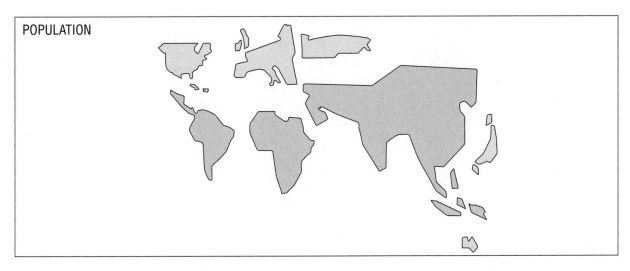

POPULATION

aging but only a fraction of its slow-growing population has recently become wealthy; India is democratic but burdened with an enormous and growing population; and Singapore is both wealthy and technologically innovative, with a comparatively modest population growth rate, but is not democratic. Beyond these are many states that are not democratic, technologically innovative, or wealthy, but who are experiencing rapid population growth that increasingly strains overtaxed social and ecological systems. These, the **least developed of the less-developed countries** (LLDCs) are sometimes described today as the "Third World's Third World." Many, but not all, are in Africa, south of the Sahara.

■ **least developed of the less-developed countries (LLDCs)** the most impoverished members of the Third World in the Global South.

The Global South is home to more than 85 percent of the world's people but commands less than 15 percent of its wealth. These disparities, illustrated in Map 6.3, underlie the long festering "North-South conflict" more than do political and technological differences. Relations between the wealthy north and the poor south have been governed by struggle because of the fears and resentments that differences in status and unequal opportunities to compete economically naturally arouse. These conflicts are likely to intensify if globalization continues to widen the rich-poor gap.

The emergence of the Global South as an identifiable international actor is a distinctly contemporary phenomenon. Although most Latin American countries were independent before World War II, not until then did the floodgates of decolonization first open. In 1974, Great Britain granted independence to India and Pakistan, after which **decolonization**—the freeing of colonial peoples from their dependent status—gathered speed. Since then, a profusion of new sovereign states have joined the global community, nearly all carved from the British, Spanish, Portuguese, Dutch, and French empires built under colonialism four hundred years ago.

■ **decolonization** the achievement of sovereign independence by countries that were once colonies of the great powers.

Today, few colonies exist, and the decolonization process is complete. However, the effects persist. Most of the ethnic national conflicts now so prevalent have colonial roots, as the imperial powers drew borders within and between their domains with little regard for the national identities of the indigenous peoples. (The divisions among these "nonstate nations" to this day undermine the sense of solidarity so important to the political stability of many multi–ethnic Global South countries.) Similarly, the staggering poverty facing Global South countries are partly a product of imperial pasts, when the European powers exploited their overseas territories. Although European powers have

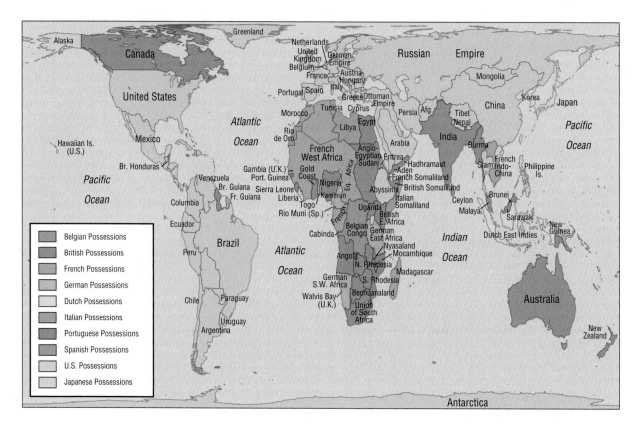

MAP 6.3
Global Imperialism, 1914

The ten major imperial powers competed for colonies throughout the globe in the present-day Global South, and on the eve of World War I their combined territories covered much of the world.

largely renounced political claims to their former colonies, the Global North maintains an active economic presence in many countries of the Global South. Thus, as viewed through the eyes of nationalist leaders in many of the emerging states, the disparity between the rich North and the poor South is the consequence of **neocolonialism** (or **neoimperialism**)—unequal trade exchanges through which the advantaged exploit the disadvantaged by penetrating the latter's markets and by institutionalizing economic processes for this purpose.

■ **neocolonialism (neoimperialism)**
the economic rather than military domination of foreign countries.

The First Wave of European Imperialism

The first wave of European empire building began in the late fifteenth century, as the Dutch, English, French, Portuguese, and Spanish used their military power to conquer territories for commercial gain. As scientific innovations made the European explorers' adventures possible, merchants followed in their wake, "quickly seizing upon opportunities to increase their business and profits. In turn, Europe's governments perceived the possibilities for increasing their own power and wealth. Commercial companies were chartered and

Rene Burri/Magnum

New States After the decolonization process runs its complete course, more new countries can be expected because many existing states are fragmenting. When World War I broke out, only sixty-two independent countries existed; at the beginning of the twenty-first century there were more than two hundred. Many new sovereign states are very small. Pictured here is the "micro" state of Nauru, which has a president, a Supreme Court, and the full apparatus of government to rule its tiny population. Half the globe's countries have populations smaller than the U.S. state of Massachusetts.

financed, with military and naval expeditions frequently sent out after them to ensure political control of overseas territories" (Cohen 1973).

The economic strategy underlying the relationship between colonies and colonizers during this era of "classical imperialism" is known as **mercantilism:** an economic philosophy advocating government regulation of economic life to increase state power and security. European rulers believed that power flowed from the possession of national wealth measured in terms of gold and silver, and that developing mining and industry to attain a favorable balance of trade (exporting more than they imported) was the best way to accumulate the desired bullion. "Colonies were desirable in this respect because they afforded an opportunity to shut out commercial competition; they guaranteed exclusive access to untapped markets and sources of cheap materials (as well as, in some instances, direct sources of the precious metals themselves). Each state was determined to monopolize as many of these overseas mercantile opportunities as possible" (Cohen 1973). To maximize national power and wealth, states saw the conquest of foreign territory as a natural by-product of active government management of the economy.

By the end of the eighteenth century the European powers had spread themselves, although thinly, throughout virtually the entire world, but the colonial empires they had built now began to crumble. Britain's thirteen North American colonies declared their independence in 1776, and most of Spain's possessions in South America won their freedom in the early nineteenth century. Nearly one hundred colonial relationships worldwide were terminated in the half-century ending in 1825 (Bergesen and Schoenberg 1980, 236).

■ **mercantilism**
a government regulatory trade strategy for accumulating state wealth and power by encouraging exports and discouraging imports (see p. 306).

As Europe's colonial empires dissolved, belief in the mercantilist philosophy also waned. As the Scottish political economist Adam Smith argued in his 1776 treatise, *The Wealth of Nations*, national wealth grew not through the accumulation of precious metals but rather from the capital and goods they could buy. Smith's ideas about the benefits of the "invisible hand" of the unregulated domestic and international marketplace laid much of the intellectual foundation for **classical liberal economic theory.** Following the thinking of Smith and other liberal free-trade theorists, faith in the precepts of **laissez-faire economics** (minimal government interference in the market) gained widespread acceptance (see also Chapter 9). European powers continued to hold numerous colonies, but the prevailing sentiment was now more anti-than proimperial.

■ **classical liberal economic theory**
a body of thought based on Adam Smith's ideas about the forces of supply and demand in the marketplace, emphasizing the benefits of minimal government regulation of the economy and trade.

■ **laissez-faire economics**
the philosophical principle of free markets with little governmental regulation (see p. 309).

■ **sphere of influence**
the area dominated by a great power (see p. 113).

■ **communism**
an ideology maintaining that if society is organized so that every person produces according to his or her ability and consumes according to his or her needs, a community without class distinctions will emerge and sovereign states will no longer be needed.

■ **Marxism-Leninism**
communist theory as derived from the writings of Karl Marx, Vladimir Lenin, and their successors, which criticizes capitalism as a cause of class struggle, the exploitation of workers, colonialism, and war.

The Second Wave of European Imperialism

Beginning in the 1870s and extending until the outbreak of World War I, a second wave of imperialism washed over the world as Europe, joined later by the United States and Japan, aggressively colonized new territories. The portion of the globe that Europeans controlled was one-third in 1800, two-thirds by 1878, and four-fifths by 1914 (Fieldhouse 1973, 3). As illustrated in Map 6.3, in the last twenty years of the nineteenth century Africa fell under the control of seven European powers (Belgium, Britain, France, Germany, Italy, Portugal, and Spain), and in all of the Far East and the Pacific, only China, Japan, and Siam (Thailand) were not conquered. But China was divided into **spheres of influence** by the foreign great powers which carved China into separate zones of commerce that the great powers individually controlled and exploited for profit, and Japan itself also imperialistically occupied Korea and Formosa (Taiwan). Elsewhere, the United States expanded across its continent, acquired Puerto Rico and the Philippines in the 1898 Spanish-American War, extended its colonial reach westward to Hawaii, leased the Panama Canal Zone "in perpetuity" from the new state of Panama (an American creation), and exercised considerable control over several Caribbean islands, notably Cuba. The preeminent imperial power, Great Britain, in a single generation expanded its empire to cover one-fifth of the earth's land area and comprised perhaps one-fourth of its population (Cohen 1973, 30). As British imperialists were proud to proclaim, it was an empire on which the sun never set.

Having abandoned their earlier acquired empires, why did most of the great powers—and those that aspired to great-power status—engage in this expensive and often vicious competition to control other peoples and territories? What explains the new imperialism? The answers are rooted in economics and politics.

Economic and Political Explanations for the New Imperialism. With the Industrial Revolution, capitalism grew, emphasizing the free market, private ownership of the means of production, and the accumulation of wealth. Theorists following Karl Marx, who called themselves adherents of **communism,** saw imperialism's aggressive competition as caused by capitalists' need for profitable overseas outlets for their surplus ("finance") capital. One of them was the Soviet leader Vladimir Lenin, who made distinctive contributions to the communist thinking later described as **Marxism-Leninism.**

Karl Marx Challenges Imperialism Pictured on the left is the German philosopher Karl Marx (1818–1883), whose revolutionary economic theory argued that "the history of all hitherto existing society is the history of class struggle." Imperial conquest of colonial peoples could only be prevented, Marx warned, by humanity's shift from a capitalist to a socialist economy and society. Pictured on the right is the kind of imperialistic activity that provoked his wrath: ruthless, aggressive, and bent on acquiring property for profit, Britain's nineteenth-century imperial forces marched into battle to seize foreign territory.

In his famous 1916 monograph *Imperialism, The Highest Stage of Capitalism*, Lenin argued that military expansion abroad was produced by the "monopoly stage of capitalism." Lenin concluded that the only way to end imperialism was to abolish capitalism. Classical or liberal economists, on the other hand, regarded the new imperialism not as a product of capitalism as such but rather as "a response to certain maladjustments within the contemporary capitalist system which, given the proper will, could be corrected" (Cohen 1973). What the two perspectives shared was the belief that economics explained the new imperialism: "The fundamental problem was the presumed material needs of advanced capitalist societies—the need for cheap raw materials to feed their growing industrial complexes, for additional markets to consume their rising levels of production, and for investment outlets to absorb their rapidly accumulating capital" (Cohen 1973). Thus, from both the Marxist and classical liberal perspectives, the material needs of capitalist societies explained their imperial drive.

World-system analyses, like Marxist theories, also embrace an economic explanation. **World-system theory** postulates that a single capitalist world economy emerged during the "long 16th century" from 1450 to 1640, which created a world division of labor separating "core" (industrial) areas from those in

■ **world-system theory**
a theory that claims the perpetual and widening inequity among states is explained by capitalism's international division of labor and production, which over time allows the wealthy core countries to become richer while the peripheral states supplying raw materials and cheap labor become poorer.

the globe's (nonindustrial) "periphery" (Wallerstein 1980). Northwest Europe first emerged as the core. As the Industrial Revolution proceeded, the core states exchanged manufactured goods for raw agricultural and mineral materials secured at bargain prices by taking advantage of willing sellers and cheap labor in the colonial territories at the periphery.

This perspective emphasizes colonization as the principal method for imperial control over foreign lands. After 1870 colonies effectively became occupation zones in which a small number of European sojourners coerced an indigenous population into production for the global economy (Boswell 1989).

Political factors also explain the new imperialism. In his influential 1902 book, *Imperialism*, J. A. Hobson argued that the jockeying for power and prestige between competitive empires had always characterized the great powers' behavior in the European balance-of-power system, and that imperialism through overseas expansion was simply a global extension of this inter-European competition for dominance.

By the 1800s Britain emerged from Europe's perpetual conflict as the world's leading power. By 1870, however, British hegemony was on the wane. Germany emerged as a powerful industrial state, as did the United States. Understandably, Britain tried to protect its privileged global position in the face of growing competition from the newly emerging core states, and its efforts to maintain the status quo help to explain the second wave of imperial expansion—especially in Africa, whose partition served the imperial powers at the expense of local populations.

The British-sponsored laissez-faire system of free trade promoted rapid economic growth in a number of colonial territories, but economic development elsewhere proceeded even more rapidly. Western Europe, North America, Australia, and New Zealand were able to complete their industrial revolutions during this period and to advance as industrial societies. Thus the gap between the world's rich and poor countries began to widen.

Colonialism, Self-Determination, and Decolonization in the Twentieth Century

The climate of opinion turned decidedly anti-imperial when the 1917 Versailles peace settlement that ended World War I embraced the principle of national **self-determination** advocated by U.S. President Woodrow Wilson. Self-determination meant that indigenous nationalities would have the right to decide which authority would represent and rule them. Wilson and others who shared his liberal convictions believed that freedom of choice would lead to the creation of states and governments content with their territorial boundaries and therefore less inclined to make war. In practice, however, the attempt to redraw states' borders to separate nationality groups was applied almost exclusively to war-torn Europe, where six new states were created from the territory of the former Austrian-Hungarian Empire (Austria, Czechoslovakia, Hungary, Poland, Romania, and the ethnically divided Yugoslavia). Other territorial adjustments were also made in Europe, but the proposition that self-determination should be extended to Europe's overseas empires did not receive serious support.

Still, the colonial territories of the powers defeated in World War I were not simply parceled out among the victorious allies, as had typically happened in the past. Instead, the territories controlled by Germany and the Ottoman

■ **self-determination** the liberal doctrine that people should be able to determine the government that will manage their affairs. (see p. 248).

Empire were transferred under League of Nations auspices to countries that would govern them as "mandates" pending their eventual self-rule. Many of these territorial decisions gave rise to subsequent conflicts such as in the Middle East and Africa after, for example, the League of Nations called for the eventual creation of a Jewish national homeland in Palestine and arranged for the transfer of control over South-West Africa (now called Namibia) to what would become the white minority regime of South Africa.

The principle implicit in the League of Nations mandate system gave birth to the idea that "colonies were a trust rather than simply a property to be exploited and treated as if its peoples had no rights of their own" (Easton 1964). This set an important precedent for the negotiations after World War II, when territories of the defeated powers placed under the United Nations (UN) trusteeship system were not absorbed by others but were promised eventual self-rule, and support for self-determination gained momentum. The decolonization process accelerated in 1947, when the British relinquished political control of India and Pakistan. War eventually erupted between these newly independent states as each sought to gain control over disputed territory in Kashmir, in 1965 and 1971, and again as the nuclear-armed states clashed in 2002. Violence also broke out in Indochina and Algeria in the 1950s and early 1960s as the French sought to regain control over colonial territories they had held before World War II. Similarly, bloodshed followed closely on the heels of independence in the Congo when the Belgians granted their African colony independence in 1960, and it dogged the unsuccessful efforts of Portugal to battle the winds of decolonization that swept over Africa as the 1960s wore on.

Despite these political convulsions, decolonization for the most part was not only extraordinarily rapid but also remarkably peaceful. This may be explained by World War II's having sapped the economic and military vitality of many of the colonial powers. World-system analysts contend that a growing appreciation of the costs of empire also eroded support for colonial empires (Strang 1990, 1991). Regardless of the underlying cause, colonialism became less acceptable in a world increasingly dominated by rivalry between East and West. The Cold War competition for political allies and the fear of large-scale warfare gave the superpowers incentives to lobby jointly for the liberation of overseas empires. Decolonization "triumphed," as Inis Claude (1967) explains, "largely because the West [gave] priority to the containment of communism over the perpetuation of colonialism."

The UN also contributed to the "collective delegitimization" of colonialism. With colonialism already in retreat, in 1960, Global South states took advantage of their growing numbers in the UN General Assembly to secure passage of the historic Declaration on the Granting of Independence to Colonial Countries and Peoples. "The General Assembly proclaimed that the subjection of any people to alien domination was a denial of fundamental human rights, contrary to the UN Charter, and an impediment to world peace and that all subject peoples had a right to immediate and complete independence. No country cast a vote against this anticolonial manifesto. . . . It was an ideological triumph" (Riggs and Plano 1994).

As the old order crumbled—and as the leaders in the newly emancipated territories discovered that freedom did not translate automatically into autonomy, economic independence, and domestic prosperity—the conflict between the rich Global North and the emerging states of the Global South began. And it continues today. While some see future international struggle as centered on a **clash of civilizations** (Huntington 1996), others argue that on account of cascading **globalization** a "civilizational clash" is "not so much over Jesus Christ, Confucius, or the Prophet Muhammad as it is over the unequal distribution of world power, wealth, and influence, and the perceived historical lack of respect accorded to small states and peoples by larger ones" (Fuller 1995). The widening gap between the developed and the developing world spells global turmoil in the future, as suggested by those (Crenshaw 2003) who trace the post-9/11 global terrorism to international inequalities.

NORTH AND SOUTH TODAY: WORLDS APART

The Global South is sometimes described today as a "zone of turmoil" in large measure because, in contrast with the Global North where "peace, wealth, and democracy" prevail, most of the world's people live amidst "poverty, war, tyranny, and anarchy" (Singer and Wildavsky 1993). A particularly noteworthy difference is that the states in the Global North are democratic and rarely fight one another, whereas in the Global South, violent conflict remains rife both within and among many states.

Democracy has spread rapidly and widely since the 1980s, becoming the preferred mode of governance throughout much of the Global South. However, some of the Global South's recent additions to the liberal democratic community have governments whose commitment to regular elections and human rights are fragile. Furthermore, many Global South countries lack well-developed domestic market economies based on entrepreneurship and private enterprise. Nonetheless, because the Global North's history suggests that free markets spawn the large middle class that is a precondition for free governments (Mazarr 1999), the continuing expansion of Global South market economies under capitalism appears likely to hasten democratization, although the continued enlargement of the liberal democratic community is not guaranteed.

Differences in technological capabilities also separate North and South. Typically, Global South countries have been unable to evolve an indigenous technology appropriate to their own resources and have been dependent on powerful Global North multinational corporations (MNCs) (see Chapter 5) to transfer technical know-how. This means that research and development expenditures are directed toward solutions of the Global North's problems, with technological advances seldom meeting the needs of the Global South. And in the information age, technology has not been distributed equally geographically: the highest density of computer connections to the Internet is in the Global North (see World Bank 2002a and Chapter 8).

The fact that 85 percent of the world's population is poor is both a reflection and cause of these unequally distributed resources. To measure the disparities, the World Bank differentiates the "low-income" and "middle-income" economies in **developing countries**—whose **gross national income (GNI)** in 2000 averaged $6,356 billion—from the "high-income" **developed countries**— above this level averaging $24,891 billion for each state (World Bank 2002b, 233). Among the developing countries, wide variations in economic performance (growth and inflation rates, debt burdens, and export prices, for exam-

■ **clash of civilizations**
Samuel Huntington's controversial thesis that in the twenty-first century the globe's major civilizations will conflict with one another, leading to anarchy and warfare similar to that resulting from conflicts between states over the past five hundred years.

■ **globalization**
the integration of states through increasing contact, communication, and trade to create a holistic, single global system in which the process of change increasingly binds people together in a common fate (see p. 45).

■ **developing countries**
a category used by the World Bank to designate those countries with an average GNI (in 2000) each year below $6,356 billion.

■ **gross national income**
a measure of the production of goods and services within a given time period, which is used to delimit the geographic scope of production. GNI measures production by a state's citizens or companies, regardless of where the production occurs. An alternative measure is gross domestic product (GDP), which measures production occurring within the territory of a state, regardless of the national identity of the producers.

■ **developed countries**
a category used by the World Bank to designate those countries with a GNP (in 2000) above $631 billion annually.

TABLE 6.1

Two Worlds of Development: An International Class Divide

Characteristic	Developing Global South	Developed Global North
Number of countries	158	50
Population (millions)	5,154	903
Population density (people for each sq. km)	52	29
Women in policy positions (%)	6%	16%
Land area (thousands of sq. km)	101,491	32,315
GNI ($ billions)	$6,356	$24,891
Average growth rate of the domestic economy, 1990–2000	3.5%	2.5%
Foreign direct investment ($ millions)	$185,390	$727,130
Exports ($ billions)	$1,748	$6,350
Exports as percent of GDP	51%	32%
Average years of citizens' schooling	6.5	10
Internet secure servers	5,573	115,650
Life expectancy at birth	64	78
Percent of population living in cities	41%	79%
Percent of roads paved	32%	93%
Number of motor vehicles for each 1,000 people	60	610
Personal computers for each 10,000 people	20	393
Television sets for each 1,000 people	185	641
Mobile phones for each 1,000 people	51	532

World GDP, $trn, 1995 $

■ Low and middle-income countries
□ High-income countries

1960 2000 2015 2050
Forecast

Where people live on the earth influences how they live. As this information shows, the situation is much more favorable—and the quality of life is relatively advantageous—in the developed countries of the Global North than it is in the Southern Hemisphere where nearly all the Global South countries are located. As the World Bank predictions in the attached figure show, global trends indicate that the discrepancy between the rich and the poor will grow considerably by the year 2050.

SOURCES: World Bank (2002a and 2002b); figure on the division of world economies by 2050, From *The Economist*, July 6, 2002, p. 4. Copyright © 2002 by The Economist Newspaper Ltd. All rights reserved. Reprinted with permission. Further reproduction prohibited. www.economist.com

ple) and international circumstances (such as the availability of oil and other fuels) are evident.

Numbers paint pictures and construct images, and the data on the division between Global North and Global South point to brutal disparities and inequalities. When we compare the differences on some key indicators differentiating low- and middle-income countries from high-income countries, at the peak of development, we discover huge gaps (see Table 6.1).

This picture darkens even more when focus is shifted to the plight of the poorest in the low-income developing countries. More than 2.4 billion people (two-fifths of humanity) live in one of the 63 countries at the bottom of the

■ **least developed of
the less-developed
countries (LLDCs)**
the most impoverished
states in the Global South.

■ **barter**
the exchange of one good
for another rather than the
use of currency to buy and
sell items.

global hierarchy, sometimes called by the International Monetary Fund the **least
developed of the less-developed countries (LLDCs),** where, typically, **barter**
of one agricultural good for another (rather than money) is used for economic
exchanges. These countries are not emerging or reemerging to break the chains
of their destitution; they are falling behind the other Global South countries.

The low-income LLDCs are not participants in the global market: they
account for less than 0.3 percent of world trade, and their meager exports are
largely confined to inexpensive primary products, including food stuffs (cocoa,
coffee, and tea), minerals (copper), hides, and timber. Because these low-
income countries consume most of what they produce, theirs is typically a subsistence economy, and the prospects for change are dim, because most of these
least-developed countries have been bypassed by direct foreign investment and
ignored by foreign aid donors (World Bank 2002b).

High rates of population growth since 1990 have contributed to the widespread poverty of LLDCs. Likewise, it will take only twenty-five years for the
LLDCs' total population to double, compared with two and a half centuries for
the Global North. LLDCs' economic growth rates in the recent past have averaged less than 0.1 percent each year. Growth rates elsewhere have almost uni-
formly been higher. This is a powerful reason why the rich minority gets richer
while the poorest of the poor will likely become even poorer.

Despite wide differences, a daunting scale of misery and marginalization
thus is evident across the Global South, from which only a fraction of its countries have begun to escape. For most Global South countries, the future is bleak,
and the opportunities and choices most basic to freedom from fear and poverty
are unavailable. The aggregate pattern underlying global trends in the last
twenty years shows that more than sixty countries today are worse off than they
were and are falling ever further behind the levels achieved by the countries in
the Global North. When we consider that nearly all the population growth in
the twenty-first century will occur in the Global South, the poorest countries
cut off from circulation in the globalized marketplace, it is hard to imagine how
the gap can close, and how the soil of poverty can be prevented from producing terrorism and civil war.

This tragic portrayal of unspeakable despair for so many Global South
states raises the basic theoretical question: Why does the Global South, at this
historical juncture, suffer from such dismal destitution?

THEORETICAL EXPLANATIONS
OF UNDERDEVELOPMENT

■ **development**
the processes through
which a country increases
its capacity to meet its
citizens' basic human needs
and raise their standard of
living.

Why has the Global South lagged so far behind the Global North in its comparative level of well-being and **development?** And why have the development
experiences even within the Global South differed so widely?

The diversity evident in the Global South invites the conclusion that underdevelopment is explained by a combination of factors within developing countries and in their relationships with the Global North. Some theorists explain
the underdevelopment of most developing economies alongside the escape of
others by looking primarily at differences between Global South states. Other
theorists focus on the position of developing countries in the global political

economy. We shall briefly discuss three variants on these interpretations: classical economic development theory, structuralist theories of dominance and dependence, and neoclassical theory.

Classical Economic Development Theory

Based on the definition of development—as constructed in the West—as increases in income, liberal economic development theories of **modernization** first emerged in the early post–World War II era. They argued that the major barriers to development were posed by the Global South countries' own internal characteristics. To overcome these barriers, most classical theorists recommended that the wealthy countries supply various "missing components" of development, such as investment capital through foreign aid or private foreign direct investment.

Once sufficient capital was accumulated to promote economic growth, these liberal theorists predicted that its benefits would eventually "trickle down" to broad segments of society. In this way, everyone, not just a privileged few, would enjoy the benefits of rising affluence. Walt W. Rostow, an economic historian and U.S. policymaker, formalized this theory in his influential book *The Stages of Economic Growth* (1960). He predicted that traditional societies beginning the path to development would inevitably pass through various stages by means of the free market and would eventually "take off" to become similar to the mass-consumption societies of the capitalist Global North. Even though the rich are likely to get richer, it was argued, as incomes in the world as a whole grow, the odds increase that a preindustrialized economy will grow faster and eventually reduce the gap between it and richer countries. That prognosis and the policies on which it was based were ultimately rejected by the impoverished Global South. Leaders there did not buy the classical liberal argument that the Global North became prosperous and assumed control of global economic power because their open societies concentrated on work, invention, skill, and investment in schools and tools to make them winners in the global marketplace (see Landes 1998; Thurow 1999). Economists in the Global South were persuaded by the rival structural theories that attribute the Global South's plight to the links between developing countries and the global political economy.

Two Structural Theories: Dependency Theory and World Systems

Two prongs of structuralism merit attention, as both locate the causes and potential cures of most developing countries' persistent underdevelopment in their positions of dependence on the dominant great powers. The first is dependency theory and its liberal variant, called "dualism." The second, which we have already introduced, is world-system theory.

Dependency theory builds on Lenin's theory of imperialism, but goes beyond it to account for changes that have occurred since Lenin first wrote his Marxist interpretation of capitalism as a cause of inequality and domination. Its central proposition is that the relationship between the advanced capitalist societies at the core of the world political economy and the developing countries at the periphery is exploitative, and that the underdevelopment of the Global South has been caused by world capitalism's impact: the division of the globe into two halves, one modern and the other backward.

■ **modernization**
a view of development popular in the Global North's liberal democracies that argues that wealth is created through efficient production, free enterprise, and free trade, and that countries' relative ability to create wealth depends on technological innovation and education more than on natural endowments such as climate and resources.

■ **dependency theory**
a theory that less-developed countries are exploited because global capitalism makes them dependent on the rich countries which create exploitative rules for trade and production.

Although the dependency theory literature is vast and arouses many controversies (see Caporaso and Levine 1992; Packenham 1992), dependency theorists all reject Rostow's stages-of-growth thesis, arguing that underdevelopment "is not a stalled stage of linear development, a question of precapitalism, retarded or backward development, but rather a [product of the less-developed countries'] structural position in a hierarchical world division of labor" (Shannon 1989). In short, the Global South's underdevelopment results from its subordinate position in a world political economy dominated by capitalistic industrialized great powers.

Andre Gunder Frank (1969) wrote a definitive structural interpretation of chronic underdevelopment in Latin America; he argued that "the now-developed countries were never underdeveloped, though they may have been undeveloped." The reason, he asserted, was colonialism—the historical expansion of the capitalist system that "effectively and entirely penetrated even the apparently most isolated sectors of the underdeveloped world."

Other theorists—frequently called *dependentistas*—share Frank's concern about the "enslavement" of the Global South by the capitalist Global North. "The relation of interdependence between two or more economies, and between these and world trade," Theotonio Dos Santos (1970) argues, "assumes the form of dependence when some countries (the dominant ones) can expand and can be self-sustaining, while others (the dependent ones) can do this only as a reflection of that expansion, which can have either a positive or a negative effect on their immediate development." Hence, **dependency** is seen as resulting from a situation "in which the economy of certain countries is conditioned by the development and expansion of another economy to which the former is subjected."

Dependent countries are vulnerable to penetration by outside forces. Dependency theorists argue that the overseas branches of giant MNCs headquartered in the Global North are the primary agents of neocolonial penetration because they transfer profits from the penetrated societies to the penetrators. Foreign investment—whether private or in the form of aid from other governments—is also an instrument of penetration. Technological dependence and "cultural imperialism," through which Global South societies become saturated with ideas and values alien to their indigenous cultures, are among the consequences. Once penetration by advanced capitalist states has occurred, continues the dependency theory argument, the inherently unequal exchanges that bind the exploiters and the exploited are sustained by elites within the penetrated societies, who sacrifice their country's welfare for personal gain.

The argument that a privileged few benefit from dependency at the expense of their societies is logically similar to **dualism.** Dualism refers to the existence of two separate economic and social sectors operating side by side. Dual societies typically have a rural, impoverished, and neglected sector operating alongside an urban, developing, or advanced sector—but with little interaction between the two. Thus whatever growth occurs in the industrial sector in dual societies "neither initiates a corresponding growth process in the rural sector nor generates sufficient employment to prevent a growing population in the stagnant sectors" (Singer and Ansari 1988). MNCs contribute to dualism by promoting "the interests of the small number of well-paid modern-sector workers against the interests of the rest by widening wage differentials . . . and worsen the imbalance between rural and urban economic opportunities by

■ **dependency**
a condition of retarded economic growth believed to result from the Global South's subordination and structural exploitation by the Global North's advanced capitalistic market economies, making the Global South especially vulnerable to cycles of expansion and contraction.

■ **dualism**
the existence of a rural, impoverished, and neglected sector of society alongside an urban, developing, or modernizing sector, with little interaction between the two.

locating primarily in urban areas and contributing to the flow of rural-urban migration" (Todaro 2000).

World-system theorists share dependency theorists' view that the world is divided into a core (the advanced capitalist states), a periphery (the developing states), and a semiperiphery composed of ascending countries climbing from the periphery and declining countries falling from the ranks of the wealthy core. However, they take a longer-term structural perspective on the emergence of disparities between the two (in terms of classes, much as Karl Marx did).

For world-system theory a critical issue is the core-periphery distinction. "Within the world division of labor, core states specialize in the production of the most 'advanced' goods, which involves the use of the most sophisticated technologies and highly mechanized methods of production ('capital-intensive' production). [This means] that core states specialize in the production of sophisticated manufactured goods." Within the periphery, on the other hand, economic activities "are relatively less technologically sophisticated and more 'labor intensive'. . . . For most of the modern era, production for export was concentrated on raw materials and agricultural commodities" (Shannon 1989). Historically, states on the periphery have also been militarily inferior to core states and less well-organized administratively, which limited their ability to compete with the capitalist states.

World-system theorists cannot easily explain the industrialization now taking place in the periphery's emerging markets. To account for this, they have coined the term "semiperiphery" to accommodate geographic areas or countries (such as the **Newly Industrialized Countries (NICs)** that are moving in an intermediate position between the core and the periphery. Dependency theorists also have difficulty explaining these countries' growth. To interpret this anomaly, they sometimes use the term **dependent development** to describe the industrial development of peripheral areas in a system otherwise dominated by the Global North. The term suggests the possibility of either growing or declining prosperity, but not outside the confines of a continuing dominance-dependence relationship between North and South.

Closing the Gap? The Global South's Prospects

Is it possible for the Global South to escape the vicious cycle of poverty? When we look at the situation from the perspective of the poorest of the poor countries, the prospects appear dismal. However, there is a basis for optimism that can be found if you broaden the picture and see the conspicuous exceptions to the general pattern of persistent poverty. Destitution is not necessarily permanent. Although many Global South countries appear to be mired in persistent poverty, some Global South countries have managed to break the chains of underdevelopment. By pursuing bold paths for growth, they have seen their fortunes rise and are poised to enter the ranks of the advanced Global North economies. The ability for some developing countries to escape the syndrome that still affects the rest of the Global South suggests that others can succeed as well.

Consider one category of Global South states whose relative wealth contrasts sharply with the LLDCs' poverty: those Global South states that have fossil fuels to consume and export. The sixteen developing-country exporters of oil and other fuels, and especially the twelve members of the Organization of

■ world-system theorists
a theory that claims there is an international division of labor in which core states specialize in the capital-intensive production of sophisticated manufactured goods and peripheral states concentrate on the labor-intensive production of raw materials and agricultural commodities.

■ newly industrialized countries (NICs) and newly industrialized economies (NIEs)
the most prosperous members of the Global South, which have become important exporters of manufactured goods as well as important markets for the major industrialized countries that export capital goods.

■ dependent development
the industrialization of peripheral areas within the confines of the dominance-dependence relationship between North and South, which enables the poor to become wealthier without ever catching up to the core Global North countries.

Petroleum Exporting Countries (OPEC), have escaped the LLDCs' grim fate. Notably, OPEC members Kuwait, Qatar, and the United Arab Emirates have risen to the high-income group's standards of living rivaling those of Global North countries.

Another category of Global South countries that inspires hope are the emerging or "middle-income" economies, or the so-called newly industrialized economies (NIEs) particularly in Asia, that have experienced even greater success than the oil-exporting countries. Their achievement lies in moving beyond the export of primary products to the export of manufactured goods. Today the NIEs are among the largest exporters of manufactured goods and the most prosperous members of the Global South, and have climbed from the periphery into the **semiperiphery.** The so-called **Asian Tigers** (South Korea, Singapore, Taiwan, and Hong Kong) have taken advantage of comparatively low wage rates to aggressively promote export-led economic growth. Pursuing strategies similar to the imperial powers of the past, the governments' neomercantilist practices include protecting infant industries from foreign competition and providing financial incentives for manufacturing industries. Spectacular economic growth has followed. With their population growth generally in check, the Asian Tigers have joined the ranks of the world's wealthiest states, and still other "new tigers" such as India have emerged as exports and foreign investment have stimulated a booming economy.

Neither geography nor current levels of economic performance identify well the emerging markets with the greatest potential. What most distinguishes these countries engineering an economic revolution is that their governments have stabilized the value of their currencies, brought inflation under control, and privatized the businesses once owned by the government. In addition, many opened themselves to foreign investment. This change in philosophy about the causes of and cures for underdevelopment formerly prevalent throughout the Global South was a concession in Global South thinking, stimulated in part by **neoliberal** pressure for reforms by such powerful global IGOs as the World Bank and the International Monetary Fund.

> [The NIES believed that for] competitive free markets to flourish, privatizing state-owned enterprises, promoting free trade and export expansion, welcoming investors from developed countries, and eliminating the plethora of government regulations and price distortions in . . . product and financial markets, both economic efficiency and economic growth will be stimulated. . . . [They concluded that] what is needed, therefore, [was] not a reform of the international economic system or a restructuring of dualistic developing economies or an increase in foreign aid or attempts to control population growth or a more effective central planning system. Rather, it [was] simply a matter of promoting free markets and laissez-faire economics within the context of permissive governments that allow the "magic of the marketplace" and the "invisible hand" of market prices to guide resource allocation and stimulate economic development. (Todaro 1994, 85–86)

The success of the free-market practices of the Asian NIEs in elevating themselves from the rest of the Global South inspired faith in the neoclassical theorists' NIEs' export-led strategies for economic growth and encouraged others to emulate their strategies. The neoclassical predictions that market

■ **semiperiphery**
to world-system theorists, countries midway between the rich "core" or center and the poor "periphery" in the global hierarchy, at which foreign investments are targeted when labor wages and production costs become too high in the prosperous core regions.

■ **Asian Tigers**
the four Asian NIEs that experienced far greater rates of economic growth during the 1980s than the more advanced industrial societies of the Global North.

■ **neoliberal**
a perspective that accounts for the way international institutions promote global and prosperity through reforms such as the creation of free markets and acceptance of free trade.

economies will thrive where government management of the market is minimal, and their argument that entrepreneurial success is more likely to occur where basic democratic political freedoms are protected, led to widespread acceptance of liberal theory, which appeared triumphant (Mandelbaum 2002). Because success is often its own reward, these reforms heightened cries for additional reforms in the Global South countries in order to remove still other obstacles standing in the way of economic growth. These include pressure by the UN, the IMF, and the World Bank for poor countries to pay more attention to attacking corruption and to protecting the environment and speeding up transitions toward fuller democratic governance—based on the liberal ethical premise that, properly understood, development is contingent upon the increase of freedom and civil liberties (Mandelbaum 2002).

The achievements of the NIEs and the emerging markets alongside the stagnant or plummeting financial fate of the poorest Global South countries provoke policy questions: Despite these differences and the inequalities between Global South states, is there a commonality, a consensus, that unites them as a group? Does the Global South share a socially constructed collective vision around which they have built a common posture? How have the weak responded to the situation they inherited—being vulnerable states among the strong? How have the relatively powerless sought to deal with the great powers, on whom they have been dependent? The Global South countries are situated in a global system at the bottom of the global pyramid of power, facing mighty great powers as well as the influential **nonstate actors** those great powers have created (IGOs, such as the United Nations, see Chapter 5). What strategies have the Global South countries forged to deal with their perceived exploitation resulting from having had to struggle from a position of weakness in a world of powers?

■ **nonstate actors**
all transnationally active groups other than states, such as organizations whose members are states (IGOs) and nongovernmental organizations (NGOs) whose members are individuals and private groups from more than one state.

THE GLOBAL SOUTH'S FOREIGN POLICY RESPONSE TO A WORLD RULED BY THE GREAT POWERS

The vast political, economic, and social differences separating North and South indicate that the Global South is "weak, vulnerable, and insecure—with these traits being the function of both domestic and external factors" (Ayoob 1995). Coping with this insecurity has long been a primary foreign policy goal of Global South states, and efforts to overcome these insecurities have often brought the Global South into contention with the Global North. Ironically, the end of the Cold War reduced the great powers' security interest in providing economic aid to Global South countries. Without foreign assistance, the Global South is now experiencing a burst of new armed conflicts (see Chapter 11). The globalization of finance and trade threatens to further expand the economic vulnerabilities of poor Global South states.

As realists insist, power and wealth are states' core motives and are realized through military and economic prowess. Strategies designed to maximize power and prosperity continue to preoccupy foreign policy thinking in the Global South, where different states take different approaches to increasing prosperity. Let us examine how the Global South countries are pursuing their objectives, particularly in their relationships with the Global North.

In Search of Power

The states emerging after World War II struggled on separate tracks to find a foreign policy approach that could provide them with the power and prosperity they lacked. The **nonaligned states** were determined to strike a neutral course in the Cold War contest, while a broader group (including, for example, many Latin American states allied with the United States that had secured independence in the nineteenth century) concentrated their efforts more directly on severing their economic dominance by and dependence on the Global North.

Nonalignment. The nonalignment movement began in 1955, when twenty-nine Asian and African countries met in Bandung, Indonesia, to devise a strategy to combat colonialism. In 1961 leaders from twenty-five countries, mostly former colonies, met in Belgrade, Yugoslavia, where they created a lasting political coalition, the **Nonaligned Movement (NAM),** whose membership would later grow to more than one hundred countries.

Because the new states sought to avoid entrapment in the Cold War, they tried through nonalignment to maximize their own gains while minimizing their costs. The strategy energized both the United States and the Soviet Union to renew their efforts to woo the uncommitted Global South "neutrals" to their own network of allies. The Cold War competitors became willing players in a bipolar **zero-sum** contest where one side's gains were the other's losses, often offering economic and military aid to win friends and influence allies.

The Cold War's end ended much of the competitive rationale for providing foreign aid and eroded the bargaining leverage nonalignment had provided the Global South. As a strategy, nonalignment "died" with the Cold War. The original justification for nonalignment no longer exists. But the passions for the improvement of the Global South behind it live on.

The challenge facing the nonaligned states today is how to promote their interests in a world where few listen to their voices. The nonaligned Global South can complain, but its bargaining power to engineer institutional reforms is limited. This weakness is displayed in the UN, where the most influence the Global South has mustered has symbolically been to delay serious proposals to make Germany and Japan permanent members of the Security Council by insisting that a nonaligned state or one of the larger developing countries (such as Brazil, Indonesia, Mexico, or South Africa) also be given a seat among the mighty. Weak states have some vocal power in numbers, but no clout or control. Thus, the Global South worries that the twenty-first century will witness "the reemergence of a more open and explicit form of imperialism, in which national sovereignty is more readily overridden by a hegemonic power pursuing its own self-defined national interest" (Bienefeld 1994).

Zones of Turmoil. These concerns are rooted in past experience: many developing countries felt betrayed and invaded when they became the battle-ground on which the superpowers conducted covert activities, paramilitary operations, and proxy wars. The Global South became the world's killing fields; more than 90 percent of the inter- and intrastate conflicts and 90 percent of the

---

■ **nonaligned states**
countries that do not participate in military alliances with rival blocs for fear that formal alliance will lead them to unnecessary involvement in war.

■ **Nonaligned Movement (NAM)**
a group of more than one hundred newly independent, mostly less-developed states that joined together as a group of neutrals to avoid entanglement with the superpowers' competing alliances in the Cold War and to advance the Global South's common interests in economic cooperation and growth.

■ **zero-sum**
the perception in a rivalry that if one side gains, the other side loses (see p. 316).

casualties in the past half-century occurred within it (see Chapter 11). The threat of civil war continues. More than 178 wars have erupted in the Global South since 1945, and most of these occurred after the Cold War ended in 1989 (Gleditsch et al. 2002). The danger of anarchy and violence *within* Global South countries has reached epidemic proportions. The Global South is a zone of danger, populated by many **failed states** which do not have governments strong enough to preserve domestic order.

Paradoxically, part of the insecurity facing Global South countries is due to the fact that most are multiethnic societies composed of a variety of **nonstate nations,** or nationality groups. Many of these suffer from a history of hatred and conflict with one another. Maintaining cooperation among competing eth-nonational groups poses a major challenge, especially because many of these nonstate actors, such as Palestine, are actively seeking independence in order to acquire statehood as new sovereign states. The potential for failed states in many Global South states is great, which is why many experts predict that by the middle of the twenty-first century there may exist as many as five hundred states.

The chief cause of concern about Global South political instability resides not from the potential for separatist activist groups within Global South countries to undermine central governments by challenging their sovereignty or, more dangerously still, by waging open rebellion. Although this is a serious problem, it is compounded exponentially by the scourge of poverty. "Poverty and conflict are not unrelated," warned in 2001 Nitin Desai and Jayantha Dhanapala, both undersecretaries at the United Nations; "They often reinforce each other. Poverty is a potent catalyst for conflict and violence within and among states, particularly at a time when poor countries and peoples are increasingly aware of the relative affluence of others." The situation is explosive in the information age under conditions of globalization, where knowledge of vast differentials in wealth is now news everyplace (see Chapter 8).

As with many other aspects of the Global South's conditions, those states' capacity to contain domestic violence, in a borderless globe of interdependence, rests largely in the hands of the great powers. The Global South countries must face the task of deciding the fateful question of whether they dare call upon the great powers and the international organizations those powers dominate for help when violence, terrorism, and anarchy prevail and collapsing Global South countries require external **military intervention** to restore order. The cry for assistance poses risks, because where there is outside involvement there tends to follow outside influence, some of which may be unwelcome. There is a fine line between external involvement and interference. On top of this concern, it was not clear (until the United States in 2002 asserted the right to unilaterally take preemptive military intervention in dangerous Global South trouble spots such as Iraq to eliminate the threat) that the great powers had sufficient interests in getting involved in Global South civil wars. They still have not agreed to a **doctrine** to guide great power decisions about when, where, why, and how the great powers should collectively become involved within Global South borders where violence, terrorism, and ethnic cleansing are occurring.

Arms Acquisitions. Faced with seemingly endless conflict at home or abroad, it is not surprising that the Global South has joined the rest of the world's quest to acquire modern weapons of war—including in some cases

■ **failed states**
countries whose governments have so mismanaged policy that their citizens, in rebellion, threaten to disintegrate the state (see p. 282).

■ **nonstate nations**
national or ethnic groups struggling to obtain power and/or statehood.

■ **military intervention**
overt or covert use of force by one or more countries that cross the borders of another country in order to affect the target country's government and policies.

■ **doctrine**
the guidelines a state or an alliance specifies to identify the conditions under which it will use military power and armed force for political purposes abroad.

(China, India, Iraq, North Korea, Pakistan) nuclear weapons. As a result, the burden of military spending (measured by the ratio of military expenditures to GNP) is highest among those least able to bear it. In the Global South military spending typically exceeds expenditures on health and education; impoverished states facing ethnic, religious, or tribal strife at home are quite prepared to sacrifice expenditures for economic development in order to acquire weapons.

Few Global South states produce their own weapons. Weak Global South governments, paralyzed by fears of separatist revolts, have invested increased proportions of their country's modest national budgets in arms rather than seek to reduce poverty by reallocating scarce revenues from the military to social and economic development. Most Global South countries have increased their military spending to purchase arms produced in the Global North at higher rates than their wealthy Global North counterparts do (Grimmett 2002).

What makes the Global South's militarization so counterproductive is that the Global South's national security has fallen while the Global North is a "zone of peace," with few threats from other rich and democratic states. The contrast is most paradoxical when considering the sale of weapons. The Global North sells most of its arms to the unstable Global South states, most of whom pose the greatest threat to world order. Since 1994, most arms transfers have been delivered to the Global South (Grimmett 2002). Therefore, in responding to a world of powers, the Global South appears to be increasing its dependence for arms purchases on the very same rich states whose military and economic domination they historically have most feared and resented.

The Search for Wealth in a Globalized World

The persistent underdevelopment of most developing states underlies their drive for greater wealth, a better life for their people, and a higher position in the hierarchy of global power. Breaking out of their dependent status and pursuing their own industrial development remains their greatest foreign policy priority.

To this end, some Global South states (particularly those in Latin America) have pursued development through an **import-substitution industrialization** strategy designed to encourage domestic entrepreneurs to manufacture products traditionally imported from abroad. Governments (often dictatorships) have been heavily involved in managing their economies and in some cases became the owners and operators of industry.

Import-substitution industrialization eventually fell from favor, in part because manufacturers often found that they still had to rely on Global North technology and even component parts to produce goods for their domestic markets. The recent preference is for **export-led industrialization,** based on the realization that "what had enriched the rich was not their insulation from imports (rich countries do, in fact, import massively all sorts of goods) but their success in manufactured exports, where higher prices could be commanded than for [Global South] raw materials" (Sklair 1991).

As exemplified by the NIEs, the shift toward export-led growth strategies has transformed many Global South countries from being suppliers of raw materials into manufacturers of products already available in the Global North. Thus a new international division of labor is emerging as production, capital, labor, and technology are increasingly integrated worldwide and decision mak-

■ **import-substitution industrialization**
a strategy for economic development that involves encouraging domestic entrepreneurs to manufacture products traditionally imported from abroad.

■ **export-led industrialization**
a growth strategy that concentrates on developing domestic export industries capable of competing in overseas markets.

ing has become transnational. "The old ideas of national autonomy, economic independence, self-reliance, and self-sufficiency have become obsolete as the national economies [have] become increasingly integrated" (Dorraj 1995).

Not all Global South economies are positioned to survive in this highly competitive globalized market. Many of the least-developed countries remain heavily dependent on raw materials and other primary products for their export earnings, and even some of the NIEs have not moved beyond the dependent development stage, as their export goods are in the old, declining industries of the Global North whose technology is easily transferred to the semiperiphery. While some benefit from such integration and prosper, others remain immune from the alleged benefits of globalization, and are especially vulnerable to recessions in the global economy.

How to cope with dominance and dependence thus remains a key Global South concern. As they search for status and economic security, let us next evaluate the Global South's key strategies in their relations with the Global North.

A New International Economic Order?   The emerging Global South countries were born into a political-economic order with rules they had no voice in creating. Beginning in the 1950s they began to seek the means to control their own economic futures, centering their efforts on the UN where their growing numbers gave them greater influence than they could otherwise command. In the 1960s they formed a coalition of the world's poor, the **Group of 77** (known in diplomatic circles simply as the **G-77**) and used their voting power to convene the UN Conference on Trade and Development (UNCTAD). UNCTAD later became a permanent UN organization through which the Global South expresses its interests concerning development issues.

A decade later the G-77 (then numbering more than 120 countries) again used its UN numerical majority to push for a **New International Economic Order (NIEO)** to counter the **Liberal International Economic Order (LIEO)** championed by the United States and the other capitalist powers since World War II. Motivated by the oil-exporting countries' rising bargaining "commodity power," the Global South sought to compel the Global North to abandon practices perceived as perpetuating their dominance and dependence. Later, the heated debate shifted as the Global South began to petition collectively for a redistribution of world health. Not surprisingly, the Global North rebuffed the South's reform efforts, and the North-South exchange gradually degenerated into a dialogue of the deaf.

The Global South's determination to revise the existing rules is now little more than a footnote to the history of a struggle between rich and poor states. Many of the NIEO issues remain on the global agenda, as do key philosophical controversies about the extent to which states should manage international economic transactions. Whereas the liberal philosophy underlying the LIEO recommends limited government intervention, "economic nationalists" advocate that their states act aggressively to promote national prosperity. "The nationalist considers relative gain to be more important than mutual gain [and seeks] to change the rules or regimes governing international economic relations in order to benefit themselves disproportionately with respect to other economic powers" (Gilpin 2001). Clearly that competitive viewpoint remains popular in many Global South countries (as well as some in the Global North), even as privatization and a return to market mechanisms rather than state-run

■ **Group of 77 (G-77)** the coalition of Third World countries that sponsored the 1963 Joint Declaration of Developing Countries calling for reforms to allow greater equity in North-South trade.

■ **New International Economic Order (NIEO)** the 1974 policy resolution in the UN that called for a North-South dialogue to open the way for the less-developed countries of the Global South to participate more fully in the making of international economic policy.

■ **Liberal International Economic Order (LIEO)** the set of regimes created after World War II, designed to promote monetary stability and reduce barriers to the free flow of trade and capital.

enterprises have become widely accepted for generating growth. As we will discover in Chapter 9, the tension between liberalism and mercantilism applies broadly to core contemporary issues in the global political economy.

Regional Trade Regimes. With the failure of reform envisioned by the NIEO, the integration of Global South countries into the globalization process will occur according to the rules dictated by the Global North. Are there alternatives? Can regional arrangements enable Global South states to take advantage of growing economic interdependence to achieve their development goals?

To promote growth through regional economic agreements, in the 1990s the global economy began to subdivide into three "trade blocs"—one in Europe, with the European Union (EU) as its hub; a second in the Americas, with the United States at the center; and a third in East Asia, with Japan and China dominant. Consider some recent developments:

- *In the Americas:* The North American Free Trade Agreement (NAFTA), formalized in 1993, brought Canada, Mexico, and the United States into a single free-trade area whose market size rivals that of the EU to create hemisphere-wide free-trade area, in which tariffs among member countries are eliminated.

- *Also in the Americas:* The Mercosur agreement, which links Argentina, Brazil, Paraguay, and Uruguay (Latin America's largest trade bloc), hopes to incorporate the Andean Group (Bolivia, Colombia, Ecuador, Peru, and Venezuela) in its free-trade union.

- *In Asia:* The association of Asia-Pacific Economic Cooperation (APEC), an informal forum created in 1989 that has committed itself to creating a free-trade zone during the next twenty-five years.

- *Also in Asia:* The members of the Association of Southeast Asian Nations (ASEAN), first established in 1967 by Brunei, Indonesia, Malaysia, the Philippines, Singapore, and Thailand and now including Vietnam, agreed to set up a free-trade area.

- *In Africa:* The Southern African Development Community (SADC) formed in 1980 has pledged to develop a free-trade area and common currency.

Will the lofty expectations of these regional politico-economic groups be realized? In the past political will and shared visions have proven to be indispensable elements in successful regional trade regimes. Economic complementarity is another essential component, as the goal is to stimulate greater trade among the members of the free-trade area, not simply between it and others. If one or more members export products that each of the others wants, the chances of the regime's success are greater; if, on the other hand, they all tend to export the same products or to have virtually no trade with one another (typically the case in Africa), failure is more likely.

Prospects for the success of regional trade regimes seem greatest when Global South countries cobble their futures to Global North states—but, complain Global South leaders, on terms that the North dictates. That conclusion hardly bodes well for regional economic agreements as an effective method for balancing the North-South relationship.

Trade, Aid, Investment, Debt Relief—or Nothing?

The developing countries have long pleaded for "trade, not aid" to improve their global position, turning to the NIEs' experience to support the view that access to the Global North's markets is critical to Global South economic growth. But many Global South countries have not improved their lot, often for two major reasons. First, market access has become increasingly difficult because domestic pressure groups in Global South countries have lobbied their governments to reduce the imports of other countries' products that compete with their own industries. Trade may be preferred to aid, but political barriers often interfere with free trade.

Second, the character and distribution of foreign aid have changed as criticism of its effectiveness and effects has risen. Consequently, levels of foreign aid have stagnated. **Foreign aid** comes in a variety of forms and is used for a variety of purposes. Some aid consists of outright grants of money, some of loans at concessional rates, and some of shared technical expertise. Although most foreign aid is bilateral and is termed **official development assistance (ODA)**—meaning the money flows directly from one country to another—an increasing portion is now channeled through global IGO institutions such as the World Bank, and hence is known as "multilateral aid." Moreover, the purposes of aid are as varied as its forms. Commonly stated foreign aid goals include not only the reduction of poverty through economic development, but also human development, environmental protection, reduced military spending, enhanced economic management, the development of private enterprise, increased power for women, the promotion of democratic governance and human rights, and humanitarian disaster relief and assistance to refugees. However, security objectives traditionally have figured prominently as motives of donors in the allocation of both economic aid and military assistance, and still do. For example, the United States continues to target Israel and Egypt as major recipients to symbolize friendship, maintain a balance of power, and tilt the scales towards peace in the Middle East.

The assumption that development will support other goals, such as fostering solidarity among allies and promoting commercial advantage, free markets, or democratization, still underpins most donors' assistance programs. Today, however, many of these traditional justifications are under widespread attack in numerous donor countries. This is especially true of the United States, which has now been overtaken by Japan as the world's most generous donor country of bilateral aid through multilateral institutions. Overall global official development assistance has in fact declined since peaking in 1991 (see Figure 6.1).

Many aid donors have become frustrated with the slow growth rates of many of the Global South recipients and impatiently have grown doubtful of the effectiveness of their aid programs, despite strong evidence that foreign aid has made a positive difference (Easterbrook 2002). Critics particularly resent what they perceive to be an entrenched state of mind in many Global South cultures that stands in the way of development, which—while bemoaning poverty—at the same time condemns the profit motive, competition, and consumerism at the heart of the spirit of capitalism. "The revolution of economic development occurs when people go on working, competing, inventing, and innovating when they no longer need to be rich," argues Mariano Grondona, an Argentinian political scientist, in a statement that expresses the Global North's faith in hard work, economic competition, and individual entrepreneurial creativity as necessary cultural values crucial to progress and prosperity (in Samuelson 2001b).

■ **foreign aid** economic assistance in the form of loans and grants provided by a donor country to a recipient country for a variety of purposes.

■ **official development assistance (ODA)** grants or loans to countries from other countries, usually channeled through multilateral aid organizations, for the primary purpose of promoting economic development and welfare.

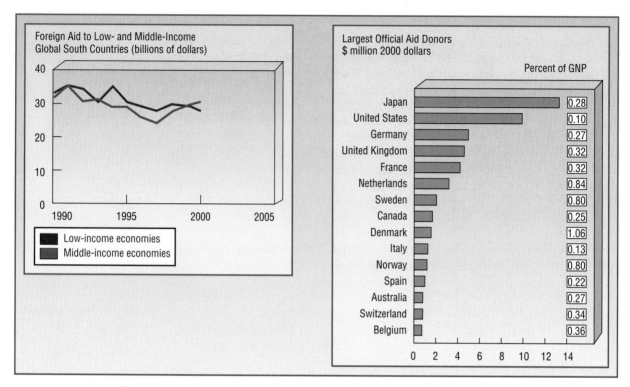

FIGURE 6.1

The Decline of Global North Foreign Aid to the Global South

Official development assistance (ODA) from Global North donors has not grown over the past decade at at pace commensurate with the rate of global economic growth. In 2001 it totaled only $53.7 billion, or less that 0.001 percent of the global economy (*Vital Signs 2002*, 119). As the figure on the left shows, since 1990, "the real value of aid to developing countries has fallen 8 percent," and only half goes to the poorest Global South countries (World Bank 2002a, 14). The bar on the right shows the top fifteen Global North foreign aid donors' official aid disbursements in 2000, as well as the percent of their income their donation represents. Only four countries (the Netherlands, Denmark, Sweden and Norway) meet the UN international target recommending donors to give 0.7 percent of their national income for assistance. In absolute terms, Japan was by far the globe's most generous donor, giving over $15.3 billion. But that represented 0.28 percent of its GDP, only half of what the UN would like. The second biggest donor, the United States, gave $9.6 billion—just 0.1 percent of its GDP in aid (*Vital Signs 2002*, 119).

SOURCES: World Bank Atlas, 2002. p. 14. Copyright © 2002 by the International Bank for Reconstruction and Development/The World Bank. Reprinted with permission. Vital Signs 2002, p. 40.

■ **two-level game**
a concept referring to the growing need for national policymakers to make decisions that will meet both domestic and foreign goals.

The shift to market-oriented models has led many donors to conclude that foreign aid is no longer as needed and may even be detrimental. The emergent climate of opinion, moreover, has spawned more "conditionality," or demands that recipient countries must meet to receive aid. Almost one-fourth of official development assistance is "tied, meaning that the procurement contracts were limited to the donor country or a group of countries. Driven by domestic political interests," donors are playing a **two-level game** that "goes against the very free-market principles that most donors are trying to encourage in developing countries and results in inefficient use of aid. It has been estimated that tying aid reduces its value by 15–30 percent" (World Bank 2001, 2000).

On top of this practice of tying aid, donors are highly selective in choosing the countries they target for assistance, especially when they treat foreign aid as a subsidy for their domestic corporations producing exports. Although most donors distribute aid to the poorer countries, "currently about a third of aid goes to middle-income countries, whose average GNP per capita is roughly six times that of low-income countries" and considerable sums are even contributed to high-income countries (World Bank 2001, 196). The result is that the poorest of the poor Global South countries (where the incidence of poverty is greatest) are receiving the least assistance and are suffering the most from the recent declines in foreign aid. Their resentment is reflected in the LLDCs' socially constructed image of foreign aid from rich countries, which sees it as a moral obligation, as repayment for years of unequal exchange perpetuated through colonialism and imperial rule.

Recently, however, many Global South leaders have joined Global North critics of foreign aid, interpreting it as an instrument of neocolonialism and neoimperialism and resenting the conditionality criteria for receiving aid imposed by the International Monetary Fund and other multilateral institutions, and they have joined the chorus of experts advocating trade and investment as substitutes for aid. Without lobbying, it appears unlikely that aid will expand above the current low level of only 0.6 percent of all Global South developing countries' GNPs (World Bank 2001, 315). The prevailing mood against alleviating the Global South's poverty through greater foreign assistance could, of course, change. As J. Brian Atwood, a former administrator of the U.S. Agency for International Development, noted in February 2001: "[At a time when many Global South leaders] are already tapping into disenchantment over the widening rich and poor, and some are challenging globalization itself as an imposition of the West," foreign assistance to support "sustainable development strategies to deal with global problems from drug trafficking to climate change are an essential policy . . . . It is still better to prevent conflict than to have to care for victims." Foreign aid to foster international cooperation and thereby stimulate the Global South's lasting development remains not only a noble humanitarian goal but an objective directly tied to the Global North's long-term parochial national interests.

"There is a widely held fiction that masses of money are poured into aid. In fact, industrialized countries spend roughly one quarter of one percent of their gross domestic product for assistance to the world's poor countries," argued James D. Wolfensohn, the World Bank's president, in 2001. His viewpoint gained greater acceptance following the Bush administration's announcement in 2002 that it would sharply increase U.S. foreign aid (provided it is delivered overseas through "faith-based" NGOs and other private relief organizations, and recipients would help the United States wage its war against global terrorism). Wolfensohn argued that "aid works, and we can do more to make it work for more people." That goal, if pursued, could restore to the global agenda a strategy in which many Global South leaders still believe is the most effective means to overcoming their subordinate international position.

In addition to foreign aid, another strategy sitting center stage in the Global South's strategies for escaping destitution and stagnant economic growth has been to encourage multinational corporations (MNCs) to funnel an increasing share of their **foreign direct investment (FDI)** into its countries, thereby increasing its export earnings to gain a greater share of global trade. This strategy for economic growth has always been the target of critics who question whether the investment of capital by multinational corporations (and, to a lesser extent, private investors) into local or domestic business ventures is really a financial remedy. The strategy has always been controversial, because there are

■ **foreign direct investment (FDI)** an investment in a country involving a long-term relationship and control of an enterprise by nonresidents and including equity capital, reinvestment of earnings, other long-term capital, and short-term capital as shown in balance of payments, accounts.

MULTINATIONAL CORPORATIONS IN THE GLOBAL SOUTH: DO THEY HELP OR HURT?

Within the Global South, there has existed widespread concern about the impact of MNCs' activities on the local economy and its growth rate. Part of the concern stems from the historic tendency for MNCs to look to Global South countries as production sites so they can take advantage of cheap labor for production and avoid labor-union pressure that for years was virtually nonexistent. MNCs are privileged nonstate actors, with such vast resources that their decisions about investments largely determine the direction of development. MNCs can either promote or inhibit development, depending on if they channel investments and, when they do, how they operate in the host country. Despite these concerns about MNCs as powerful, potentially neocolonial, nonstate actors that may compromise national sovereignty and undermine local prosperity, many Global South countries have overcome their fears and now welcome global companies to stimulate rapid growth despite the many risks and costs that MNCs' penetrations often incur.

MNCs continue to be alternately praised and condemned, depending on how their performance is viewed. The record is mixed and can be evaluated on different criteria. Following is a "balance sheet" summarizing the major arguments for and against MNCs. Using this summary of contending interpretations, you can easily see why the role and impact of MNCs as important NGOs is so controversial. What do you think? Do MNCs help or harm the Global South's ability to develop rapidly and to close the gap in wealth with the Global North? On the whole, is the impact of multinational corporations constructive or exploitative?

Positive
- Increase the volume of trade.
- Assist the aggregation of investment capital that can fund development.
- Finance loans and service international debt.
- Lobby for free trade and the removal of barriers to trade, such as tariffs.
- Underwrite research and development that allows technological innovation.
- Introduce and dispense advanced technology to less-developed countries.
- Reduce the costs of goods by encouraging their production according to the principle of comparative advantage.
- Generate employment.
- Encourage the training of workers.
- Produce new goods and expand opportunities for their purchase through the internationalization of production.
- Disseminate marketing expertise and mass advertising methods worldwide.
- Provide investment income to facilitate the modernization of less-developed countries.
- Generate income and wealth.
- Advocate peaceful relations between and among states in order to preserve an orderly environment conducive to trade and profits.
- Break down national barriers and accelerate the globalization of the international economy and culture and the rules that govern international commerce.

Negative
- Give rise to oligopolistic conglomerations that reduce competition and free enterprise.
- Raise capital in host countries (thereby depriving local industries of investment capital) but export profits to home countries.
- Breed debtors and make the poor dependent on those providing loans.
- Limit the availability of commodities by monopolizing their production and controlling their distribution in the world marketplace.
- Create "sanctuary markets" that restrict and channel other investments to give MNCs an unfair advantage.
- Export technology ill suited to underdeveloped economies.
- Inhibit the growth of infant industries and local technological expertise in less-developed countries while making Global South countries dependent on Global North technology.
- Conspire to create cartels that contribute to inflation.
- Curtail employment by driving labor competition from the market.
- Limit workers' wages.
- Limit the supply of raw materials available in international markets.
- Erode traditional cultures and national differences, leaving in their place a homogenized world culture dominated by consumer-oriented values.
- Widen the gap between rich and poor countries.
- Increase the wealth of local elites at the expense of the poor.
- Support and rationalize repressive regimes in the name of stability and order.
- Challenge national sovereignty and jeopardize the autonomy of the states.
- Create cartels with other MNCs that share markets in order to cut competition.

Robert Nickelsberg/Time Magazine

Not the choice of a New Generation Many nationalists blame multinational corporations for the problems of their countries' economies and social conditions. Foreign firms often face a backlash. In 1995, Hindu nationalists in India—the world's largest democracy—protested economic reforms that would open the country's borders to liberal trade and investment. These and other opponents pledged to drive some of the world's best-known brands out of the Indian market.

many hidden costs or "externalities" associated with permitting corporations controlled from abroad to set up business within the host state for the purpose of making a profit. Who is to be the ultimate beneficiary, the foreign investor or the states in which the investments are made? Considerable risks are entailed, as are a number of trade-offs among competing values (see Controversy: Multinational Corporations in the Global South: Do They Help or Hurt?).

The primary danger with this strategy is the potential for foreign investments to lead to foreign control, the erosion of sovereign governments' capacities to regulate the economy within their borders, and the probability that the multinational foreign investors will not invest their profits locally but channel them abroad for new investments or disburse them as dividends for their wealthy Global North shareholders (see Chapters 8 and 9). However, despite the risks, many developing countries have relaxed restrictions in order to attract foreign investors, with emphasis placed less on liberalizing investment restrictions and encouraging open domestic economic competition than on offering tax and cash enticements and opportunities for joint ventures. This has stimulated a recent surge in the flow of capital investments to the Global South (see Figure 6.2). However, keep in mind that four-fifths of all FDI is channeled to the Global North, and the poorest Global South countries (the LLCDs) benefit from only 3.4 percent of investments from abroad (World Bank 2002a, 286).

The impact of this new infusion of foreign investments in the developing countries has been substantial, given the relatively small economies of the Global South. It has paved the way for emerging markets in the Global South to

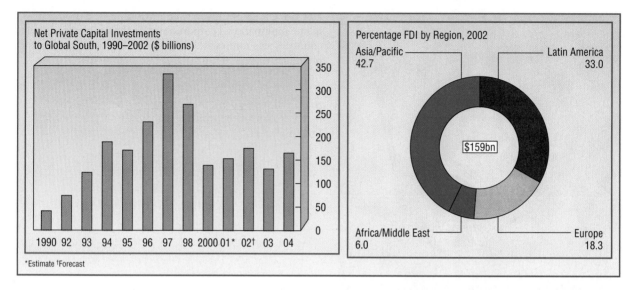

FIGURE 6.2

The Rise and Fall of Capital Investments in the Global South, 1990–2002

Since the early 1990s many Global South countries have competed for capital investments from abroad to stimulate economic growth. As the figure on the left shows, they largely succeeded until 1997, after which private capital inflows have declined to about $159 billion in 2002. As the chart on the right shows, about half the investments were going in 2002 to the emerging market European countries, but the poorer Global South were evenly split between Asia and Latin America as the leading contenders for the rest.

SOURCE: From *The Economist,* May 4, 2002, p. 102. Copyright © 2002 by The Economist Newspaper, Ltd. All rights reserved. Reprinted with permission. Further reproduction prohibited. www.economist.com

expand their rates of economic development despite the resistance of local industries in the Global South threatened by the competition and critics who have complained about the income inequalities that the investments are causing. Such fears and consequences notwithstanding, an intensified push among the Global South developing countries to compete for foreign investment capital in order to liberate themselves form dependence and destitution seems likely.

The prospects for either foreign aid of for foreign direct investments to contribute to the future development of, and relief of poverty in, the Global South will depend on a number of other factors. Foremost is the extent to which the staggering level of debt facing many Global South countries can be managed.

In 2001 the World Bank identified fifty-seven Global South countries, more than 80 percent of them in Africa, as burdened by "unsustainable debt" and in need of relief, noting that "many heavily indebted poor countries spend as much as a fifth of their annual budgets on debt service. . . . . . [B]ecause this is often more than the amount spent on social programs, debt servicing is viewed by many as a severe impediment to improving the lives of the world's poor" (World Bank 2001, 201). "Inspired by the biblical concept of Jubilee—to cancel external debt to the poorest," explained World Bank President James D. Wolfensohn in 2001, "religious leaders, rock stars and concerned men and women all over the world have galvanized public action and inspired official policy."

Debt relief—to slash the amount owned by these fifty-seven countries by more than two-thirds—is reflective of the changing attitudes toward the poorest Global South countries by the great powers and the IGO multilateral institutions that the great powers have created, such as the World Bank. They have distributed more than $56 billion in relief to the financially distressed Global South countries, $11 for each person in 2002 (World Bank 2002a, 362). The Jubilee 2000 movement for the cancellation of crushing debt targets the **heavily indebted poor countries (HIPCs),** which today owe a total of about $419 billion (about half is "bilateral" debt owed to governments, a third to international lending organizations, and the rest to private banks and other creditors [World Bank 2002a, 266]). It was predicated on the proposition that "the development of debt means the death of development" (Michael 2001, 78). Part of the motive was driven by compassion and part by the economic self-interests of the Global North, which see in debt relief a pragmatic method for arresting the collapse of the LLDCs' economies that pose a substantial threat to the continued growth of the entire world economy in the age of interdependent globalization.

It was enlightened awareness of the magnitude of this threat which prompted the Group of Eight (G-8) wealthy industrialized democracies to launch their program to assist the Heavily Indebted Poor Countries (HIPCs) with debt relief. The World Bank's "Enhanced HIPC initiative" with an allocated $128 billion for 2002, and the International Monetary Fund's "Enhanced Structural Adjustment Facility," are the primary products of this attempt to reduce the widening disparities between the Global North and Global South. Whether these programs will succeed will depend on the degree to which the Global South countries can undertake, with minimal corruption, the often painful liberalizing political reforms for democratic governance that are widely seen as a requirement for sustained economic growth (Kim and Wolfensohn 1999). Other parts of the equation include the prospects for still other reforms—such as implementation of the OECD's proposed Corporate Conduct Code for Third World Nations (Lewis 1999), or the capacity of Latin America's proposed **Fourth Way** alternative to neoliberalism, calling for increases in government funding for social services and education to foster economic growth, while accepting market economies, privatization of state-run corporations, global economic integration, and free trade (see Conger 1999).

■ **Heavily Indebted Poor Countries (HIPCs)** the subset of countries identified by the World Bank's Debtor Reporting System whose ratios of government debt to gross national product are so substantial that they cannot meet their payment obligations without experiencing political instability and economic collapse.

■ **Fourth Way** a strategy proposed for development in the Global South emphasizing government subsidies to help citizens contribute to growth within a free-trade market economy.

THE FUTURE ROLE OF THE GLOBAL SOUTH

It is useful to remember the historical trends underlying the emergence of the Global South as an actor on the global stage, rather than rely on analysts' socially constructed concepts that became popular and shaped its identity. Those states who came to regard themselves as its members share important characteristics. Most were colonized by people of another race, experienced varying degrees of poverty and hunger, and felt powerless in a world system dominated by the affluent countries that once controlled them and perhaps still do. Considerable change occurred among the newly emergent states as post–World War II decolonization proceeded, but much also remained the same. Thus, the concept "Third World" continues to describe a state of mind that will galvanize the Global South in the twenty-first century as it seeks to overcome the disorder and destitution that afflict so many people living there.

The relationships between the world's developed and developing countries will no doubt continue to change, but exactly how remains uncertain. A turn inward, toward isolationist foreign policies, in the Global North could lead to a posture of "benign neglect" of the Global South. Conversely, a new era of

North-South cooperation could commence, dedicated to finding solutions to common problems ranging from commercial to environmental and security concerns. Elements of both approaches are already evident. Although the fate of the Global North and the IGOs those great powers lead remains to be determined, it is clear that the Global South is, for the time being, in a world dominated by the most powerful state and nonstate actors, and the choices of the powerful will strongly influence the Global South's self-image and ultimate fate. "Development was—and continues to be for the most part—a top-down, ethnocentric, and technocratic approach that treats people and cultures as abstract concepts, statistical figures to be moved up and down in the charts of 'progress.' . . . It comes as no surprise that development became a force so destructive to cultures [throughout the Global South], ironically in the name of people's interests" (Estobar 2000).

In looking at a variety of actors in the global arena—from states such as the great powers, nonstate actors such as IGOs like the United Nations and NGOs like multinational corporations, and the countries of the Global South—it is important not to overlook an important fact: all of these global actors are composed of people. They are collectivities, or groups, made up of human beings. Humans' values are therefore at the center of any interpretation of global welfare, and it is to the existing international circumstances that affect all of humanity that we appropriately turn in Part III, where we inspect the factors and forces shaping how people live.

global level of analysis

KEY TERMS

structural realism
state level of analysis
individual level of analysis
colonialism
indigenous peoples
Third World
First World
Second World
Global North
Global South
least developed of the less-
    developed countries (LLDCs)
decolonization
neocolonialism (neoimperialism)
mercantilism
classical liberal economic theory
laissez-faire economics
sphere of influence
communism
Marxism-Leninism
world-system theory
self-determination

clash of civilizations
globalization
developing countries
gross national income (GNI)
developed countries
barter
development
modernization
dependency theory
dependency
dualism
world system theorists
newly industrialized countries
    (NICs)
dependent development
semiperiphery
Asian Tigers
neoliberal
nonstate actors
nonaligned states
Nonaligned Movement (NAM)
zero-sum

failed states
nonstate nations
military intervention
doctrine
import-substitution
    industrialization
export-led industrialization
Group of 77 (G-77)
New International Economic
    Order (NIEO)
Liberal International Economic
    Order (LIEO)
foreign aid
official development assistance
    (ODA)
two-level game
foreign direct investment
Heavily Indebted Poor Countries
    (HIPCs)
Fourth Way

SUGGESTED READING

Barthilow, Horace A. *The Foreign Policies of the Global South.* Boulder, Colo.: Lynne Rienner, 2003.

Cassidy, John. "Helping Hands: How Foreign Aid Could Benefit Everybody," *The New Yorker* (March 18, 2002), 60–66.

Fields, Gary S. *Distribution and Development: A New Look at the Developing World.* Cambridge, Mass.: MIT Press, 2001.

Griffiths, Robert G., ed. *Developing World 02/03.* Guilford, Conn.: McGraw-Hill/Dushkin, 2002.

Hey, Jeanne A. K., ed. *Small States in World Politics: Explaining Foreign Policy Behavior.* Boulder, Colo.: Lynne Rienner, 2003.

Landes, David S. *The Wealth and Poverty of Nations: Why Some Are So Rich and Some So Poor.* New York: Norton, 1998.

Packenham, Robert A. *The Dependency Movement: Scholarship and Politics in Dependency Studies.* Cambridge, Mass.: Harvard University Press, 1992.

Ryrie, William. *First World, Third World,* 2nd ed. London: Macmillian, 1999.

Thurow, Lester C. *Building Wealth: The New Rules for Individuals, Companies, and Nations in a Knowledge-Based Economy.* New York: Harper-Collins, 1999.

Todaro, Michael P. *Economic Development,* 7th ed. New York: Addison Wesley, 2000.

Weatherby, Joseph N., et al. *The Other World: Issues and Politics of the Developing World,* 4th ed. New York: Longman, 2000.

World Bank. *World Development Report 2003.* New York: Oxford University Press, 2003.

WHERE ON THE WORLD WIDE WEB?

The Age of Imperialism
http://www.smplanet.com/imperialism/toc.html

Chapter 6 begins with a discussion of European imperialism and its effects on the Global South. To extend your analysis of imperialism, review the Small Planet's Web site. Recommended by the History Channel, this site chronicles American expansion in the Pacific, the Spanish-American War, the Boxer Rebellion, and U.S. intervention in Latin America. See historic photos of the battleship *Maine,* maps of the regions, and portraits of the participants. Read letters, anti-imperialist essays from the past, and cartoons. You can even download movie clips.

Many U.S. citizens have trouble understanding the plight of the Global South. Use the following Web sites to familiarize yourself with these countries and the problems they face. Your might choose a country from each of the following regions: Latin America, Asia, Africa, and the Middle East. Using the Web sites listed here, compare and contrast each of the countries in terms of political and economic structures. Keep the following questions in mind: What type of government does each country have? Which industrial revolution has it experienced? What primary goods does each country import and export? Based on your findings, can you identify the biggest obstacles for each country in the development process?

African Studies WWW
http://www.sas.upenn.edu/African_Studies/AS.html

The University of Pennsylvania's African Studies Center has created a Web site that provides extensive links to country-specific information as well as a bulletin board that lists current events and important documents. A multimedia archive allows you to view African sculptures. Check out the Alligator Head from Nigeria. Why is the Standing Male Figure from Zaire impaled on so many blades?

Asian Studies WWW Virtual Library
http://coombs.anu.edu.au/WWWVL-AsianStudies.html

This global collaborative project provides bibliographic and hypertext access to scholarly documents, resources, and information systems concerned with or relevant to Asian Studies. The Asian Studies WWW Virtual Library Web site is divided according to global, regional, and country-specific areas. It provides a wealth of information on the region as well as specific countries. This site is well monitored, and each link is checked for its accuracy and content.

The Center for Middle Eastern Studies
http://menic.utexas.edu/menic/

The Middle East Network Information Center at the University of Texas at Austin is an inclusive source for general as well as country-specific information. Read about various countries' history, culture, business, energy resources, and government. View maps and scan the newspapers of the region. Learn more about Islam, Judaism, and Christianity and how these religions interact in the region. Click the News and Media link and hear Arabic spoken on numerous radio stations.

Political Database of the Americas
http://www.georgetown.edu/pdba/

A joint project of Georgetown University, the Organization of American States, and the Canadian Foundation for the Americas, this database provides documentary and statistical political information on Latin America, including constitutions, electoral laws, political parties, legislative and executive branch information, and election data. Look in the Links section to find Web sites of newspapers and embassies and consulates.

The following Web sites provide general information on international development.

United Nations Conference on Trade and Development (UNCTAD)
http://www.unctad.org/en/enhome.htm

From the UNCTAD homepage, go to the Least Developed Countries sub-site and investigate the backgrounds of the countries that the United Nations has deemed the poorest countries in the world. Examine the various policies UNCTAD has for helping the Least Developed Countries. Which do you think have the best chance of succeeding? Why?

United Nations Development Program (UNDP)
http://www.undp.org/

This United Nations branch helps countries in their efforts to achieve sustainable human development. As discussed in Chapter 6, the fulfillment of basic human needs (food, water, clothing, shelter, sanitation, health care, employment, and dignity) are important measures of a country's development level. The UNDP focuses its efforts on assisting countries in the Global South to design and carry out national development programs. Examine the various projects of the UNDP. Which have had the greatest impact on development?

U.S. Agency for International Development (USAID)
http://www.usaid.gov/

USAID is the federal government agency that implements foreign economic and humanitarian assistance programs to advance the political and economic interests of the United States. It assists countries recovering from disaster, trying to escape poverty, and engaging in democratic reforms. On the homepage you can choose regions from the Where section. Now you are able to explore U.S. aid efforts in each country of the world. What are the U.S. aid priorities in each region? Do you think aid should be tied to advancing U.S. interests or given to the needy without strings attached?

Virtual Library on International Development
http://w3.acdi-cida.gc.ca/Virtual.nsf/

This Canadian site outlines international development issues by topic, region, country, and organization. You can click on the outlines to discover links to organizations, news, and resources. The reference desk advises you of upcoming conferences and events related to international development and links you to libraries, periodicals, and reports of value in the study of international development.

INFOTRAC® COLLEGE EDITION

Streeten, Paul. "Beyond the Six Veils: Conceptualizing and Measuring Poverty," Journal of International Affairs Fall 1998.

Blinder, Alan S. "Eight Steps to a New Financial Order," Foreign Affairs September-October 1999.

Bhagwati, Jagdish. "The Poor's Best Hope—Trading for Development," The Economist (US) June 22, 2002.

Goldman, Michael. "Constructing an Environmental State: Eco-Governmentality and other Transnational Practices of a 'Green' World Bank," Social Problems November 2001.

For more articles, enter:

"International Monetary Fund" in the Subject Guide, and then go to subdivision "evaluation."

"World Bank" in the Subject Guide, and then go to subdivision "economic policy."

"developing countries" in the Subject Guide.

PART III

THE POLITICS OF GLOBAL WELFARE

What factors most affect the welfare of the world's people? World politics may be played out on a large stage, but with the expansion of international commerce and communication, a new era of globalization has arisen, knitting the world into a tight web of interdependence. Money, goods, and people travel across national borders at an accelerating pace. The effects of glob-alization are felt locally because to an increasing extent what happens in one place influences what happens every place, and how people live any one place affects how people live every-where else. The chapters in Part III draw attention to "human security"—the welfare of the peoples of the world—and the ways that state-to-state rela-tions and global institutions are transforming humanity's living standards and future prospects. This section explores the human condition at the start of the twenty-first century, looking at humanity as agents on the world stage and the degree to which human rights are pro-tected and violated (Chapter 7), the ways in which globalization is transforming international relations (Chapter 8), how changes in international trade and monetary affairs affect world politics (Chapter 9), and how the nexus between popula-tion demographics and the earth's ecological system (Chap-ter 10) influence human and global prosperity—the quality of life, the degree of liberty, and the expectation of personal security.

HUMANS AND GLOBAL CHALLENGES TO THE PROTECTION OF HUMAN RIGHTS

T O P I C S   A N D   T H E M E S

- Human agency: Putting people into the picture
- Profiling the human condition: Changing levels of human despair and development
  The global refugee crisis
  Indigenous people: Life in the fourth world
  Gender: The subordinate status of women
- Human rights and the protection of people
- International ethics: Reconciling national interests and human interests
- Humanitarian intervention: Should might be used for the protection of human rights?

- CONTROVERSY ARE NATIONAL SECURITY, ENVIRONMENTAL SECURITY AND HUMAN SECURITY COMPETING GOALS?

After years of being forbidden to learn, in 2002 in Mazar-i-Sharif, Afghan women are being taught to read and write.

Recognition of the inherent dignity and of the equal and inalienable rights of all members of the human family is the foundation of freedom, justice and peace in the world.

—UNIVERSAL DECLARATION OF HUMAN RIGHTS, 1948

[There is] a new, more profound awareness of the sanctity and dignity of every human life, regardless of race or religion. From this vision . . . flow three key priorities for the future: eradicating poverty, preventing conflict and promoting democracy. If today, after the horror of 11 September, we see better, and we see further, we will realize that humanity is indivisible. New threats make no distinction between races, nations or regions. A new insecurity has entered every mind, regardless of wealth or status.

—KOFI ANNAN, United Nations Secretary-General, accepting the Nobel Peace Prize for the UN, 2002

When we think about international relations, we think about the most influential actors and agents that engage in transnational activities—the sovereign states that are regarded as the great powers (Chapter 4), the global institutions or IGOs that states create (Chapter 5), and the general products of countries' decisions made by state agents that produce global trends, such as the accelerating pace of globalization which so profoundly shapes the way the world works. From this perspective, world politics revolves around relations between states and intergovernmental organizations, and most other agents or actors are taken into view only to the degree to which they influence the relationships among the mighty state and nonstate global actors.

The predominant state-centric constructed image of the forces and factors that drive world affairs is helpful in understanding some properties of international relations, such as dynamics of war and economic conditions that propel the rise and fall of the great powers in their rivalry to attain hegemony. However, such a simplifying construction fails to capture the role played by human agency—by the people comprising the human race. Peoples' individual choices are consequential because they combine to produce global trends and thereby contribute to transformations shaping the common fate of all people.

If you, as a student of international affairs, are to develop a more complete comprehension of the forces behind the prevailing trends in world politics, it is important to ask the question: how do humans—that is, ordinary individual people—act as agents of global change? What conception of human agency should be constructed? In short, to borrow the famous phrase in Karl Marx's *Capital,* the story of the world is *de te fibula narrator*—"this story is about you."

PUTTING PEOPLE INTO THE PICTURE

Until relatively recently, in the unfolding evolution of international history the theoretical study of world politics neglected the faceless billions of everyday people. It pictured the mass of humanity as marginalized victims, or left them invisible by painting peoples' fates as controlled by forces over which hapless people have little influence. "There is something in the nature of historical events," reflected Herbert Butterfield (1944) in expressing this view, "which twists the course of history in a direction that no man ever intended." Similarly, Fernand Braudel (1973) wrote that "when I think of the individual, I am always inclined to see him imprisoned within a destiny in which he himself has little hand, fixed in a landscape in which the infinite perspectives of the long-term stretch into the distance both behind and before."

When thinking about world affairs, people—the average person—long have been relegated to a mere "subject" whom rulers were traditionally permitted to manipulate to advance their states' national interests. "For millennia, human beings saw nothing odd about slavery, about selling and disposing of persons as if they were things" (Ignatieff 2001a). That vision has been rejected throughout the world. A consensus now supports the view that people are important, that they have worth, and that therefore **ethics** and **morality** belong in the study of international relations. As defined by Ronald Dworkin (2001), "Ethics includes convictions about what kinds of lives are good or bad for a person to lead, and morality includes principles about how a person should treat other people." These principles apply to interstate relations, and are at the heart of all analyses of human rights in world politics.

That consensus notwithstanding, many observers embrace traditional **realism's** assumptions that vast global forces make people powerless. They recognize that people participate politically, but claim they have no real power, because an invisible set of powerful forces described as the "system" gives most human beings only superficial involvement without real influence.

This denigration of the importance and influence of individual human agency today seems increasingly strange, because classic thinking about the world has long concentrated on people: on the essential character of human nature. As the anthropologist Robert Redfield (1962) argued, "Human nature is itself a part of the method [of all analysis]. One must use one's own humanity as a means to understanding. The physicist need not sympathize with his atoms, nor the biologist with his fruit flies, but the student of people and

■ **ethics**
criteria for evaluating right and wrong behavior and motives by individuals and groups.

■ **morality**
principles about the norms for behavior that should govern actors' interactions.

■ **realism**
the view that states are unitary global actors in relentless competition with each other for position and prosperity in the international hierarchy, dedicated to the promotion of their own interests at the expense of other states.

AFP Photo

Human Rights versus States' Rights How a state treats its own citizens was, until very recently, its own business under the nonintervention rule in international law protecting states from external interference in their domestic affairs. Now the global community has defined the humane treatment of people as a fundamental human right, and the UN Security Council has stretched the traditional definition of threats to international peace in order to authorize various kinds of intervention to protect the universal human rights of people within states. Shown here is an example of the kind of state behavior at the center of the debate: to defer crime, China's leaders have ordered the execution of hundreds of alleged criminals, and many other states have complained that this gross violation of civil liberties without fair trial warrants reprisals.

■ **civil society**
a community composed of citizens that create institutions that protect civil liberties (such as free speech and freedom from arbitrary governmental interference) and that use peaceful methods for conflict resolution.

institutions must employ [one's] natural sympathies in order to discover what people think or feel." A humanistic interpretation is needed that gives people status and value. Moreover, in the global community's fledging **civil society** there has recently emerged a normative consensus about the inherent moral worth and status of humans and the concomitant obligation of states to recognize and protect that status. Morality matters, because most states have publically proclaimed the ethical standard that states should respect "the universalist claim that all human beings have the same moral status; to accept universal human rights [is to make on states] the moral demand to respect the life, integrity, well-being and flourishing of . . . *all* human beings" (Vandersluis and Yeros 2000a), as punctuated in the ringing *Universal Declaration of Human Rights*. People, according to this perspective, are now empowered, even made by global agreement the ultimate concern, and therefore no longer are reduced as "simply hapless victims of fate, devoid of any historical agency" (Saurin 2000).

It is the purpose of this chapter to evaluate the unfolding debate about the human prospect and the ethics of **human rights.** Given "the increasing willingness to regard concern for human rights violations as acceptable justification for various kinds of international intervention, ranging from diplomatic and economic **sanctions** to military action, in the domestic affairs of states," we shall investigate the challenges posed by that lofty humanitarian ideal rooted in **liberalism** in order to explain why "the doctrine of human rights is a political construction intended for certain political purposes and to be understood against the background of a range of general assumptions about the character of the contemporary international environment" (Beitz 2001).

As described in Chapter 10, there are now more than 6 billion people on the face of the earth, and world population is growing. Between 2 and 4 billion more people will be added to the planet's population between now and the last quarter of the twenty-first century. With these numbers come concerns. Will humanity be valued, and human welfare and rights protected?

These are critical questions. Where does humanity fit into the prevailing and most popular **paradigms** or theoretical orientations which policymakers and scholars construct about what matters in world politics, such as neorealism and neoliberalism? For the most part, classical realism worships the state and its rulers' sovereign freedom and, except for building its image of international reality from a pessimistic conception of human nature, ignores the role of leaders and the NGOs people form (see Chapter 2). Liberals attach more importance to humans, following the ethical precept of the philosopher Immanuel Kant that people should be treated as ends and not means, and that therefore peoples' human rights should be safeguarded. **Feminist theory** goes further, countering realist logic by making humanity the primary **level of analysis** (see Chapter 2).

HOW DOES HUMANITY FARE? ASSESSING THE HUMAN CONDITION

"Man is born free, and everywhere he is in chains," the eighteenth-century French political philosopher Jean Jacques Rousseau bemoaned in his famous 1762 book, *Social Contract*. Times have since changed. But in many respects Rousseau's characterization of the human condition remains valid. How should we evaluate the depth of human deprivation and despair against this fact? Can the poorest proportion of humanity sever the chains of their disadvantages, so as to realize their human potential for development and obtain the high ideals of human security, freedom, and dignity.

There are many reasons for conceiving of individuals as objects for concern and compassion. Among them, the inequalities and disparities evident in people's standards of living cannot help but to evoke sympathy for the plight of most people, but especially for those in the less-developed Global South countries. One American college student painfully learned this during his first visit to South America, where he found a reality far different from his own experience growing up in the southern United States. He was moved to write:

> I spent the first 24 years of my life in South Carolina. When I left . . . for Colombia [South America], I fully expected Bogota to be like any large U.S.

■ human rights
the political rights and civil liberties recognized by the international community as inalienable and valid for individuals in all countries by virtue of their humanity.

■ sanctions
punitive actions by one state against another to retaliate for its previous objectionable behavior.

■ liberalism
a paradigm predicated on the hope that the application of reason and universal ethics to international relations can lead to a more orderly, just, and cooperative world, and that international anarchy and war can be policed by institutional reforms that empower organizations and international laws for global governance.

■ paradigm
derived from the Greek *paradeigma*, meaning an example, a model, or an essential pattern; a paradigm structures thoughts about an area of inquiry.

■ feminist theory
a body of scholarship emerging from the social feminist movement to promote the political equality of women with men, critiquing sexual biases and challenging gender roles that encourage female subordination and warfare.

■ level of analysis
the focus on which inquiring centers, depending on whether analysis concentrates of individuals, states, or the global system.

city, only with citizens who spoke Spanish. When I arrived there I found my expectations were wrong. I was not in the U.S., I was on Mars! I was a victim of culture shock. As a personal experience this shock was occasionally funny and sometimes sad. But after all the laughing and the crying were over, it forced me to reevaluate both my life and the society in which I live.

Colombia is a poor country by American standards. It has a per capita GNP of $550 and a very unequal distribution of income. These were the facts that I knew before I left.

But to "know" these things intellectually is much different from experiencing first-hand how they affect people's lives. It is one thing to lecture in air conditioned classrooms about the problems of world poverty. It is quite another to see four-year-old children begging or sleeping in the streets.

It tore me apart emotionally to see the reality of what I had studied for so long: "low per capita GNP and maldistribution of income." What this means in human terms is children with dirty faces who beg for bread money or turn into pickpockets because the principle of private property gets blurred by empty stomachs.

It means other children whose minds and bodies will never develop fully because they were malnourished as infants. It means street vendors who sell candy and cigarettes 14 hours a day in order to feed their families.

It also means well-dressed businessmen and petty bureaucrats who indifferently pass this poverty every day as they seek asylum in their fortified houses to the north of the city.

It means rich people who prefer not to see the poor, except for maids and security guards.

It means foreigners like me who come to Colombia and spend more in one month than the average Colombian earns in a year.

It means politicians across the ideological spectrum who are so full of abstract solutions or personal greed that they forget that it is real people they are dealing with.

Somewhere within the polemics of the politicians and the "objectivity" of the social scientists, the human being has been lost. (Wallace 1978, 15–16)

Despite wide differences that enable a proportion of humanity to enjoy unprecedented standards of living, a daunting scale of poverty and misery is evident throughout the world (see Map 7.1), from which only a small fraction of people in many countries have begun to escape. One indicator is money. As measured by the World Bank's common standard of $1 a day, vast numbers of people—1.3 billion—live in extreme poverty, and almost half of humankind—3 billion—seek to survive on $2 a day. Income inequality is a serious global problem, from which many difficulties and disputes result. What are we to expect about prospects from a situation in which, in 2002, over 150 countries had GNPs less than the amount spent worldwide at Wal-Mart (World Bank 2002a, 233–234; *Economist* 2002, 58). Simply put, like the gap between states (Chapter 6), the gap between rich and poor *people* is increasing: "In the past 15 years, per capita income has declined in more than 100 countries and individual consumption has dropped by about one percent annually in more than

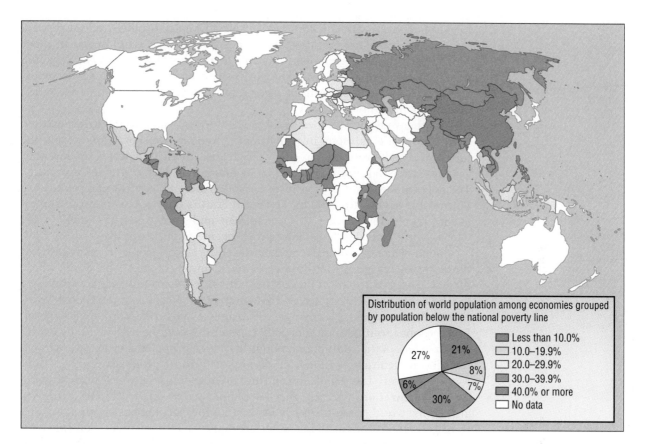

Distribution of world population among economies grouped by population below the national poverty line

- Less than 10.0%
- 10.0–19.9%
- 20.0–29.9%
- 30.0–39.9%
- 40.0% or more
- No data

27% 21% 8% 7% 30% 6%

MAP 7.1

The Percentage of People Living Below the Poverty Line, 1984–2000

As this map shows, if measured according to the World Bank's standard of $1.08 dollars or less a day, huge proportions of the world's population live in desperate conditions of extreme poverty. For them, basic human needs are unavailable, and without food or shelter abstract talk about human rights is practically meaningless, as the quest to merely survive another day is the overriding concern.

SOURCE: 2002 *World Bank Atlas*, p. 24. Copyright © 2002 by the International Bank for Reconstruction and Development/The World Bank. Reprinted with permission.

60. The number of poor people will increase sharply . . . to more than 100 million from 40 million, if current trends continue, according to World Bank estimates" (Speth 1999a, 6).

Consumption patterns show other discrepancies. The division between the rich and the poor is a growing source of resentment and conflict, for the facts show that only one-fifth of the globe's wealthiest people consume "anywhere from two- thirds to nine-tenths of its resources. The proportions reflect the figures given in the United Nations' regular *Human Development Report*, which show the richest fifth of humanity having, for example, 90 percent of all Internet accounts, 74 percent of all phone lines, 82 percent of all export markets" (McGurn 2002, 23). "The poorest 20 percent of the world's population receives only 0.2 percent of global commercial bank lending, 1.3 percent of global investment, 1 percent of global trade and 1.4 percent of global income" (Saurin 2000, 208). Nearly one of every four people in the world live in extreme poverty (UNDP 2002, 18). A select few are thriving, and the rest are barely surviving: "the world's three richest individuals are now worth more than the forty-eight poorest nations" (Easterbrook 2002, 17). Crushing poverty for one-half of humanity against rising abundance for a small minority is a recipe for hopelessness, desperation, and violence such as terrorism and even suicidal martyrdom.

Another indicator besides the absence of income and available resources is the deplorable conditions in which many humans live. For many people the future is bleak, resembling what the realist English political philosopher Thomas Hobbes described in 1651 as "solitary, poor, nasty, brutish, and short." The opportunities and choices most basic to freedom from fear and poverty are unavailable for most people in the Global South's developing countries experiencing much slower rates of development and human security than in the Global North, and the "have-nots" prospects are plummeting.

Much evidence captures the extreme suffering of people in many parts of the world, but especially in the low-income countries of the Global South where life has changed little from that of their ancestors. For example, life expectancy in the Global South averages less than sixty years, whereas in the Global North it exceeds eighty years. Human agony is also starkly evident in other respects. In the Global South, infant mortality rates are among the highest in the world; less than half of the adult population is literate (a proportion even lower among women); agriculture remains the dominant form of productive activity; and four out of every five people live in rural areas even as the world is undergoing rapid urbanization. "Among the 4.4 billion people in developing countries around the world, three-fifths live in communities lacking basic sanitation; one third go without safe drinking water; one quarter lack adequate housing; one-fifth are undernourished; and [nearly] one-third of the people in the poorest countries, mostly in Sub-Saharan Africa, can expect to die by age 40" (Speth 1999a, 6).

Given the serious deprivations in many aspects of life facing so many people, there are many reasons for humanitarian concerns. The denial to most humans of the inalienable rights to which all humans are presumably entitled— "the life, liberty, and the pursuit of happiness" of which the U.S. Declaration of Independence speaks—attests to the extent to which fundamental human rights are not being met. It is this problem which in 2002 prompted Mary Robinson, the UN High Commissioner for Human Rights, to "call on global actors— corporations, governments and the international financial organizations— to join with globalized civil society and share responsibility for humanizing **globalization.**"

To make the promotion of human rights the globe's major priority, a precise measure of human welfare is needed. How can human welfare—its level and the prospects for humanity's escape from poverty—best be gauged?

Measuring Human Development and Human Security

The human dimension of development first gained attention in the 1970s, partly in response to the growing popularity of **dependency theory** advanced by Global South leaders who attributed persistent poverty to exploitation caused by dependent relationships of the less-developed countries with the wealthy Global North. It also was a reflection of the realization that more is not

■ **globalization**
the integration of states, through increasing contact, communication, and trade, to create a holistic, single global system in which the process of change increasingly binds people together in a common fate (see p. 239).

■ **dependency theory**
a perspective that perceives the international economic system as responsible for the less developed Global South countries' dependence on, and exploitation by, the wealthy Global North countries.

necessarily better. Advocates of a basic **human needs** perspective sought new ways to measure development beyond those focusing exclusively on economic indicators such as the average income for each person in each country. In 1990 Mahbud ul Haq, a famous social scientist, constructed for the United Nations Development Program (UNDP) a **Human Development Index (HDI)** to measure states' comparative ability to provide for their citizens' well-being. Successive *Human Development Reports* have provoked fresh debate about the meaning of human development in international forums, including, for example, the 1995 World Summit for Social Development.

The HDI, as the UNDP most recently defines it, continues to seek to capture as many aspects of human development as possible in one simple, composite index and to rank human-development achievements. While no multiple-indicator index (a detailed set of statistical measures) can monitor progress in human development, the HDI comes close as an estimating procedure, by measuring "three dimensions of the development concept, living a long and healthy life, being educated and having a decent standard of living" (UNDP 2002).

The HDI is a more comprehensive measure than per capita income and has the advantage of directing attention from material possessions toward human needs. Income is only a means to human development, not an end. Nor is it the sum total of human lives. Thus, by focusing on aspects of human welfare beyond average income for each person—by treating income as a proxy for a decent standard of living—the HDI provides a more comprehensive picture of human life than income does. By this measure, the evidence provides a basic profile of the extent to which humanitarian aspirations are succeeding and failing.

The HDI ranges from 0 to 1. The HDI value for a country shows the distance that it has already traveled toward the maximum possible value of 1 and allows for comparison with other countries. The difference between the value achieved by a country and the maximum possible value shows how far it has to go; the challenge for every country is to find ways to reduce that discrepancy.

Look at the ability of countries to contribute to the human development of the people living within their borders, as measured by the HDI. We derive a revealing picture of the way personal welfare is provided (see Table 7.1 and Figure 7.1). These indicators raise important questions about the relationship of national economic growth to human development. "The index assumes that the need is not so much for more consumption or for less, but for a different pattern of consumption for human development. . . . Poor people and poor countries need to accelerate the growth of their consumption, but they need not follow the path trodden by the rich and high-growth economies. . . . And patterns of consumption that harm society and reinforce inequalities and poverty can be changed" (UNDP 1998, iii).

Humanitarian goals for human development vary greatly in the countries of the world. Why is this the case? Let us consider several explanations.

Political and Economic Preconditions for Human Development

Many factors affect the extent to which people's human rights to live a good life are provided. Among them, one correlate stands out: Political freedom—the degree to which countries rule themselves democratically and protect citizens' civil liberties—is a potent determinant of human development. That is, where democracy thrives, there also thrives human rights and human development.

■ **human needs**
those basic physical, social, and political requirements, such as food and freedom, required for survival and security

■ **Human Development Index (HDI)**
an index that uses life expectancy, literacy, average number of years of schooling, and income to assess a country's performance in providing for its people's welfare and security.

TABLE 7.1

Fastest and slowest progress in human development, 1975–2000
(For 174 countries with available data)

Country	1975 HDI	2000 HDI	Absolute change 1975–2000
Starting from high human development (.80–1.00)			
Fastest progress Ireland	0.82	0.92	0.10
Luxembourg	0.83	0.92	0.09
Australia	0.84	0.94	0.10
Slowest progress New Zealand	0.85	0.92	0.07
Denmark	0.87	0.94	0.07
Switzerland	0.87	0.93	0.06
Starting from medium human development (0.40–0.79)			
Fastest progress Tunisia	0.51	0.72	0.21
China	0.52	0.73	0.21
Algeria	0.51	0.70	0.19
Indonesia	0.47	0.68	0.21
Egypt	0.43	0.64	0.21
Slowest progress Zimbabwe	0.55	0.55	0.00
Guyana	0.68	0.71	0.03
Romania	0.75	0.78	0.03
Starting from low human development (0–0.49)			
Fastest progress Nepal	0.29	0.49	0.20
Pakistan	0.34	0.50	0.16
Bangladesh	0.33	0.48	0.15
Slowest progress Central African Republic	0.33	0.36	0.03
Congo, Dem. Rep. of the	0.42?	0.43	0.01
Zambia	0.45	0.43	0.20

SOURCE: UNDP (2002), 151–152.

When using the Human Development Index to measure the human welfare and development of people within various populations, countries stack up somewhat differently than when using a gross measure such as the Gross Domestic Product (GDP)—the total each year of each country's production of goods and services as measured by money. The correlation between national wealth and human welfare is not exact. As Table 7.1 shows, countries' levels of human development are changing at different rates.

Recall the states where democracy and political liberties exist (see Map 3.2, "The Map of Freedom," p. 72). Now compare their location with Map 7.2 showing the various levels of human development in countries across the globe. The two go hand in hand: where democracy flourishes, human development flourishes. But in autocratic governments not ruled by the will of the people, human rights are denied and human development fails to occur. That is why the UN has put so much emphasis on promoting democracy. *The Human Development Report 2002,* for example, made this linkage its theme:

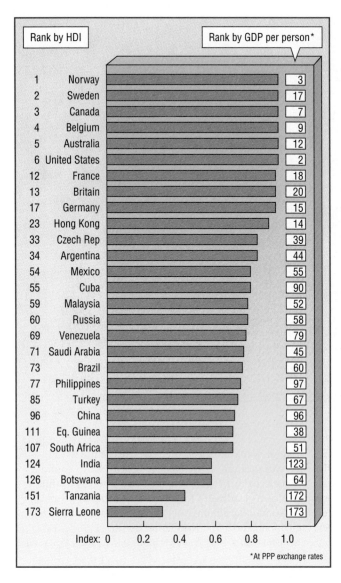

Rank by HDI		Rank by GDP per person*
1	Norway	3
2	Sweden	17
3	Canada	7
4	Belgium	9
5	Australia	12
6	United States	2
12	France	18
13	Britain	20
17	Germany	15
23	Hong Kong	14
33	Czech Rep	39
34	Argentina	44
54	Mexico	55
55	Cuba	90
59	Malaysia	52
60	Russia	58
69	Venezuela	79
71	Saudi Arabia	45
73	Brazil	60
77	Philippines	97
85	Turkey	67
96	China	96
111	Eq. Guinea	38
107	South Africa	51
124	India	123
126	Botswana	64
151	Tanzania	172
173	Sierra Leone	173

Index: 0   0.2   0.4   0.6   0.8   1.0

*At PPP exchange rates

FIGURE 7.1
The Human Development Index

In 2002, Norway overtook Sweden on the HDI measure of human development for first place, and Sierra Leone finished at the bottom for the 173 countries that were ranked that year on the HDI index; compare the HDI rankings with those recorded for the GDP per person to see how closely the HDI and the GDP indicators correspond. All measures of standards of living are controversial. Note, for example, another problem with the HDI is that "it does not include measures of other aspects of human development such as leisure, security, justice, freedom, human rights and self-respect. It would be possible to register a high HDI in a zoo or even a well-run prison. And, although at low incomes illness often leads to death, the HDI has no independent indicator of morbidity, absence of which is surely one of the most basic needs. Life can be nasty, brutish, and long" (Streeten, 2001).

SOURCE: *The Economist*, Aug. 3, 2002, p. 82. Copyright © 2002 by The Economist Newspaper Ltd. All rights reserved. Reprinted with permission. Further reproduction prohibited. www.economist.com

This Report is about politics and human development. It is about how political power and institutions—formal and informal, national and international—shape human progress. And it is about what it will take for countries to establish democratic governance systems that advance the human development of all people—in a world where so many are left behind.

Politics matter for human development because people everywhere want to be free to determine their destinies, express their views and participate in the decisions that shape their lives. These capabilities are just as important for human development—for expanding people's choices—as being able to read or enjoy good health. (UNDP 2002, 1)

Alongside democracy, national economic growth also contributes to human development. Democracy is not sufficient in itself, although democratization aids in helping countries develop economically (recall Chapter 6). For human development goals protecting basic human rights to be met, prosperity also

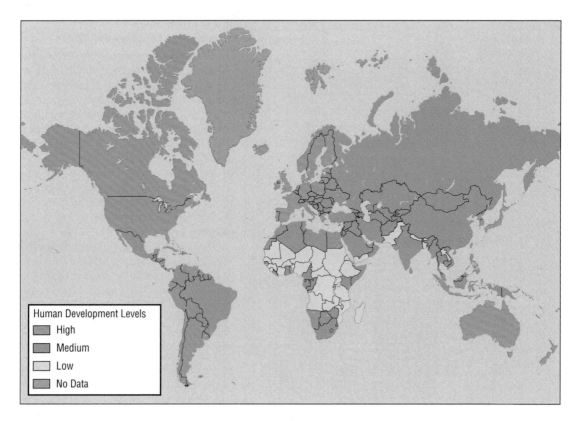

M A P 7 . 2
The Map of Human Development

This map measures the level of human development in the countries of the world, using the HDI scale. Note the wide variation. Although poorer Global South countries have made big gains in the past quarter century (following political reforms leading to greater democracy and economic reforms leading to free markets), a gap in peoples' quality of life and in their levels of human development is apparent that parallels to some degree the gap between the Global North and the Global South.

SOURCE: United Nations Human Development report, 2002; United Nations Development Programme 2002, pp. 38–41.

clearly helps. Strong evidence supports the liberal proposition that "the richer the country the freer," because "as peoples' basic security needs are met in richer countries, they turn their attention to important secondary concerns—such as liberty, a desire for which seems to be inherent in human nature but can only emerge reliably when more fundamental issues of personal safety, food, shelter, and other basic needs are met" (Mazarr 1999). Thus, when countries are grouped and ranked according to their human development performance, their rankings correspond, fairly strongly, to their per capita GDP levels. As we might expect, the level of human development is highest in the Global North, where economic prosperity is also highest on average; conversely, the quality of life is generally lower in the Global South where per capita economic output is substantially lower. National wealth contributes to human development. However, as a *Human Development Report* in 1999 noted, "the link between economic prosperity and human development is neither automatic nor obvious. Two countries with similar income per capita can have very different HDI values; countries with similar HDI values can have very different income levels. . . . Of the 174 countries, 92 [Ranked] higher on the HDI than on GDP per capita [at **purchasing power parity**] (**PPP** $), suggesting that these countries [had] been effective in converting income into human development. But for 77 countries the HDI rank [was] lower than the GDP per capita (PPP $) rank. These countries have been less successful in translating economic prosperity into better lives for people" (UNDP 1999, 129). In short, income alone is not a good predictor of human development. How countries politically organize themselves to promote the human welfare of their citizens makes a crucial difference.

Some question the trickle-down hypothesis (that if the rich first get richer eventually the benefits will trickle down to help the poor) while accepting the evidence that meeting basic human needs promotes long-term economic growth (Moon and Dixon 1992). Others maintain that redistributive policies to meet basic human needs or otherwise enhance human welfare and growth-oriented policies through trickle-down effects work at cross-purposes, because the latter can only be attained at the expense of the former. And many now recommend fostering human development through a **Third Way** strategy that combines the efficiency of a free enterprise capitalistic market with the compassion of governmental economic planning and regulation in an effort, through a fused administrative system, to produce the greatest good for the greatest number. Proponents agree that this mixed approach would enable a free market to generate rapid growth while providing a safety net for those most in need of assistance and that the formula is the best solution for engineering economic growth with a moral human purpose.

Human Development in the Age of Globalization

The rapid transfer of global capital and investment across borders that is integrating the world's economies has led to widespread speculation that **globalization**—the emergence "of a single global economy transcending and integrating the world's major economic regions" (Held and McGrew 2001)—will provide a cure for the chronic poverty facing the majority of humanity. There exists "a widely shared image of globalization—a worldwide process of converging incomes and lifestyles driven by ever larger international flows of goods, images, capital, and people as formidable equalizers [because] greater economic openness has made small parts of the changing world full-fledged members of the global village . . . so that globalized islands of prosperity are thriving in many developing nations" (Heredia 1999).

However, critics of globalization complain that it is the culprit: relative deprivation is caused by globalization, not cured by it. They see globalization as a part of the problem of human suffering, not the solution, because globalization clearly is not benefiting the people that need help most. Capital may flow more freely around the world, but it flows most slowly to the places and people where it is most scarce. A skeptical political economist from Mexico cautions: "Developing countries today are a much more heterogeneous group than at the beginning of the postwar period, [but] globalization is not helping them become more equal. The poorest are not catching up with the fastest. . . . More and more people across the planet have become increasingly exposed to the amenities of the global marketplace, although mostly as permanent window shoppers

■ **purchasing power parity (PPP)**
an index that calculates the true rate of exchange among currencies when parity—when what can be purchased is the same—is achieved; the index determines what can be bought with a unit of each currency.

■ **Third Way**
an approach to governance advocated primarily by European leaders such as British Prime Minister Tony Blair and France's socialist Prime Minister Lionel Jostin who, while recognizing few alternatives to liberal capitalism, seek to soften the cruel social impact of free-market individualism by progressively allowing government intervention to preserve social justice and the rights of individuals to freedom from fear of the deprivations caused by disruptions in the global economy.

■ **globalization**
the merger of states' economies and cultures through contact and communication to knit the globe into a tightening web of interdependence.

and silent spectators. The large majority of humankind, however, is rapidly being left outside and far behind" (Heredia 1999). Stated differently, some critics disturbed by the widening gap between the rich and poor see "the race to the bottom caused by globalization, [with] the plight of the poor [expanding because they] are paying the price for everyone else's prosperity. 'One aspect is for sure in the globalization process: labor is suffering most'" (Rembert Weakland, cited in McGurn 2002).

Like the controversy about whether globalization brings benefits or misery (see Chapter 8), human development is an ideological and policy issue that colors much of the debate about the roots of global inequality and rival approaches for its alleviation. The general record of HDI changes presents an arresting picture of both unprecedented human progress and unspeakable human misery, of humanity's advance on several fronts alongside its retreat on others. The gap between rich and poor people continues to widen. But that provides only a crude reflection of the simultaneously unfolding trends toward both progress and decline.

The past thirty years display a checked record, with some remarkable achievements in human development alongside daunting challenges that remain which warn how far progress must still travel in order for people to lead lives to their full potential. Consider both the positive improvements and the areas of human development still in urgent need of remedy. As the United Nations summarizes,

> Human development challenges remain large in the new millennium. Across the world we see unacceptable levels of deprivation in people's lives. Of the 4.6 billion people in developing countries, more than 850 million are illiterate, nearly a billion lack access to improved water sources, and 2.4 billion lack access to basic sanitation. Nearly 325 million boys and girls are out of school. And 11 million children under age five die each year from preventable causes—equivalent to more than 30,000 a day. Such deprivations are not limited to developing countries. In OECD countries more than 130 million people are income poor, 34 million are unemployed, and adult functional illiteracy rates average 15 percent.
>
> The magnitude of these challenges appears daunting. Yet too few people recognize that the impressive gains in the developing world in the past 30 years demonstrate the possibility of eradicating poverty. A child born today can expect to live eight years longer than one born 30 years ago. Many more people can read and write, with the adult literacy rate having increased from an estimated 47 percent in 1970 to 73 percent in 1999. The share of rural families with access to safe water has grown more than five-fold. Many more people can enjoy a decent standard of living, with average incomes in developing countries having almost doubled in real terms between 1975 and 1998. . . . The basic conditions for achieving human freedoms were transformed in the past ten years as more than 100 developing and transition countries ended military or one-party rule, opening up political choices. And formal commitment to international standards in human rights has spread dramatically since 1990. These are only some of the indicators of the impressive gains in many aspects of human development.
>
> Behind this record of overall progress lies a more complex picture of diverse experiences across countries, regions, groups of people and dimensions of human development. (UNDP 2001, 9–10)

Although progress in human development has occurred and will likely persist, so will trends toward declining human welfare, making the early twenty-first century appear to be both the best of times and the worst of times. Thus, the future of world politics will be not only a struggle between the Global North and Global South but also a contest between those who see global regress as inevitable and those who see global progress as possible. In the wake of the 9/11 advent of global terrorism and, with it, the virtual globalization of terrorism, globalization holds the key to humanity's future: Globalization is forging greater interdependence, yet the world seems more fragmented—between rich and poor, between the powerful and the powerless, and between those who welcome the new global economy and those who demand a different course. The September 11, 2001, terrorist attacks on the United States cast new light on these divisions, returning strategic military alliances to the center of national policymaking and inspiring heated debates on the danger of compromising human rights for national security." (UNDP 2002)

THE GLOBAL REFUGEE CRISIS

Another sign of concern about **human security** is expressed by the refugee crisis that now prevails. The vast majority of the world's population are either immigrants or the offspring of their immigrant parents or ancestors. Migration is pervasive, and it is politically controversial in many countries where existing, long-term residents are fearful of having foreigners as their neighbors. In Britain and France, for example, which continue to receive large numbers of immigrants from their former colonies, and also in Israel which has absorbed a flood of immigrants, state governments struggling with absorbing tens of thousands of new migrants are frequently targets of nationalistic criticism. The Middle Eastern oil producers also have received large numbers of migrants in recent years. But the United States, historically a place of escape from religious and political persecution and a land of economic opportunity, is an exception. The United States provides a home for fewer and fewer refugees; in 2002 the United States reduced the maximum number of refugees it would annually accept to 70,000, down from 200,000 in the mid-1980s. To balance this fact, it should be acknowledged that more than a million migrants are estimated to illegally enter the United States each year.

Refugees are individuals whose race, religion, nationality, membership in a particular social group, or political opinions make them targets of persecution in their own homelands and who migrate from their country of origin, unable to return to it. According to the UN High Commissioner for Refugees (UNHCR), the world's refugee population has grown each year since 1960, swelling rapidly to an all-time peak of more than 27 million in 1995, after which it declined at the start of 2003 to the still-staggering number of 20 million, or one out of each 300 persons throughout the world (see Figure 7.2). The total combined number of people "of concern" between 1960 and 2002 altogether exceeded 400 million refugees. This estimate does not count another 56 million returnees (former refugees who have returned home), 20 to 30 million internally **displaced people** living in situations similar to those of refugees but held hostage in their own countries and prevented from crossing borders to

■ **human security**
a concept that refers to the degree to which the welfare of individuals is protected and advanced, in contrast to national security which puts the interests of states first.

■ **refugees**
people who flee for safety to another country because of a well-founded fear of persecution.

■ **displaced people**
people involuntarily uprooted from their homes but still living in their own countries.

Refugees on the Run on Desperate Roads That Lead Nowhere Many refugees (and there are many—in excess of 20 million each year) are literally homeless people in search of sanctuary. Pictured here is the makeshift tent housing for 80,000 Afghan refugees at Jalozal in Pakistan, where in 2001, the "Pakistani government has refused to call it a refugee camp, fearing it would encourage Afghans to view it as a destination." The UN budgeted to help 800,000 Afghan refugees return to their homeland in January 2002 following the war against the terrorists supported by the Taliban, but since then 1,500,000 returned (Harper's, October 2002, 11).

■ **ethnic cleansing**
the extermination of an ethnic minority group by a state, in violation of international law since the mid-1990s, before which governments could treat the people within their territory as they wished.

■ **failed states**
countries whose governments have so mismanaged policy that they have lost the loyalty of their citizens who, in rebellion, seek independence to create their own state.

freedom, or the additional 4 million people who are illegally smuggled across borders by crime rings each year (*Foreign Policy,* March/April 2002, 31).

Refugees and displaced persons alike are often the victims of war. For example, the Persian Gulf War in 1991 created a refugee population of 5 million; genocide in Rwanda in 1994 drove more than 1.7 million refugees from their homelands; and 3.5 million Afghans sought asylum from the terror in 2001. The persecution, **ethnic cleansing,** and armed conflict that accompanied the breakup of the former Yugoslavia uprooted nearly 3 million victims, moving Europe to the list of continents with large numbers of refugees–over 6 million—for the first time since World War II. The U.S. war on terrorism in 2002 sought to root out the Taliban Al Qaeda terrorists in Afghanistan, but the conflict created what the UN termed a "major humanitarian catastrophe" for more than 3.6 million Afghan displaced people facing famine and freezing–in 2002 in excess of thirty percent of the global refugee population. As of November 2002, Asia had the greatest number of persons of concern, with nearly 8.5 million followed by Africa with 6.1 million and Europe with 5.6 million people (*www.unhcr*).

A large proportion of the world's refugees and displaced people flee their own homelands when ethnic and religious conflicts erupt in **failed states,** where governments have collapsed and no authority has gained acceptance to restore domestic law and order. In addition, human rights abuses provide a compelling explanation of why millions leave their homelands. "Refugees know

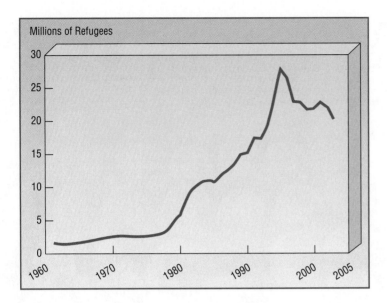

FIGURE   7.2
The Chronic World Refugee Crisis

The number of refugees receiving assistance from the UN has risen exponentially in the last four decades. More than 400 million people are estimated to have fled their home countries to avoid persecution or starvation, and at least 11.3 million are today refugees who have found asylum in another country (UNDP 2002, 219). This mass exodus is a symptom of human rights abuses worldwide and a symbol of the globalization process that is creating a borderless world. Meanwhile, others estimate that more than 50 million additional people have been internally displaced, living like refugees in their own countries.

SOURCE: Adapted from World Population Prospects. The United Nations is the author of the original material. Reprinted by permission of United Nations Publications.

---

that they cannot expect, at home, the protection of the police, access to a fair trial, redress of grievances through the courts, prosecution of those who violate their rights, or public assistance in the face of disaster. . . . Forcing people to flee is a violation of the human right to remain peacefully in one's home. The direct denial of other basic rights, including the rights of civilians not to be targeted in military actions, often provides the immediate impetus for flight" (Newland 1994).

People also leave home in search of economic opportunity. Legal migrants—particularly young people in the **Global South** without productive employment—are among those leaving at record rates—mostly to Global North countries. Migration also is increasingly occurring *between* developing Global South countries.

Some leaving their home states are the best educated and most talented, causing a serious **brain drain,** but most are not. The majority of migrants take low-wage jobs shunned by local inhabitants. Typically this means migrants earn less than the citizens of those states but more than they would earn in their homelands when performing the same tasks. Host countries increasingly welcome migrants (as Europe did during the 1970s guest worker era) not only because they accept low wages for undesirable jobs, but also because in many

■ **Global South**
a term now often used instead of "Third World" to designate the less-developed countries located primarily in the Southern Hemisphere.

■ **brain drain**
the exodus of the most educated people from their home country to a more prosperous foreign country where the opportunities for high incomes are better, which deprives their homeland of its ability to contribute to its economic development.

Seamus Conlan, F.S.P./Liaison Agency

Ethnic Cleansing Hate and hostility have traditionally led to terrorism and genocide. Racial and ethnic prejudice have commonly resulted in intercommunal warfare, such as the U.S. government's policy of expulsion and extermination of Native Americans, Nazi Germany's annihilation of 6 million Jews, and Japan's death marches and enslavement of those it conquered in the early victories of World War II. More recently, in 1994 ethnic conflict escalated to genocide in Rwanda as the Hutu militia attacked the Tutsi, and later as the Tutsi-dominated Rwandan Patriotic Front retaliated against the Hutus. This photo depicts the results of one such bloodbath, where as many as 1 million Tutsis died.

places the host pays little if anything for migrants' health, education, and welfare needs. On the other hand, the home (sending) countries sometimes encourage people to emigrate as a way of reducing unemployment or exporting unwanted elements of the population, such as criminals, or in the expectation that the emigrants will send much of their income back to their needy families in their homeland.

■ xenophobia
the suspicious dislike, disrespect, and disregard for members of a foreign nationality, ethnic, or linguistic group.

Xenophobia (fear of foreigners) is on the rise. Many refugees are finding the doors to safe havens closing. Although "countries such as Italy and Ireland, which once benefited by exporting their burgeoning populations, now urgently need immigrants" to reduce labor shortages, the barriers are rising, because legal migration in Europe is severely restricted. Only a fraction of the 450,000 applying for political asylum in 2001 in twenty-five European countries received sanctuary (*Economist*, March 31, 2001, 15). Security concerns stimulated by terrorist fears are sometimes at work, as in the United States, where many believe the catastrophic New York World Trade Center bombing on September 11, 2001, would not have occurred had immigration controls been tighter. A wave of illegal immigrants has contributed to the rising tide of anti-immigration sentiments. Ironically, in a country born of immigrants where in 2000 immigrants accounted for

12 percent of U.S. workers (*Parade,* February 25, 2001, 5), thousands of refugees who earlier would have found safe haven in the United States have been repatriated to their homelands or otherwise denied a chance to apply for political **asylum.**

A combination of push and pull factors has propelled migration to the forefront of the globalization of population dynamics. Human rights violations, environmental degradation, overpopulation, famine, war, and ethnonational clashes and **atrocities** within states—all *push* millions beyond their homelands. Migrants also are *pulled* abroad by the promise of political freedom elsewhere, particularly in the democratically ruled Global North countries. Indeed, the recent growth of immigration to the Global North from the Global South is related to the shrinking of the world (through revolutions in communication and transport), and the growing reach and absorptive power of global capitalism.

Shutting the door is increasingly viewed as a solution. This raises critical ethical issues. "Some states, especially leading industrial countries, have toughened their domestic refugee legislation and criteria for granting asylum" (www.unhcr). Where will the homeless, the desperate, the weak and the poor find **sanctuary**— a safe place to live where human rights are safeguarded? Will the rich countries act with compassion or respond with indifference? And more broadly, what is the best way to view human security and reconcile it with **national security?** This choice may involve irreconcilable values, and this makes human security and human rights a highly debatable issue (see Controversy: Are National Security, Environmental Security, and Human Security Competing Goals?)

The conclusion is invited: the welfare and survival of everyday people are endangered, and the need for their protection is increasing. But that is not the end of the story. Other people suffer even more.

■ **asylum**
the provision of sanctuary to safeguard refugees escaping from the threat of persecution in the country where they hold citizenship.

■ **atrocities**
brutal and savage acts against targeted citizen groups or prisoners of war, defined as illegal under international law.

■ **sanctuary**
a place of refuge and protection

■ **national security**
a country's psychological freedom from fears that the state will be unable to resist threats to its survival and national values emanating from abroad or at home.

INDIGENOUS PEOPLES: PRECARIOUS LIFE IN THE FOURTH WORLD

As noted in Chapter 5, where we first addressed the topic of nonstate actors (NGOs), **indigenous peoples** are representative of one type of ethnic and cultural groups that were once native to a geographic location now controlled by another state or political group. The globe is populated by an estimated six thousand separate indigenous nations, each of which has a unique language and culture and strong, often spiritual, ties to an ancestral homeland. In most cases indigenous peoples were at one time politically sovereign and economically self-sufficient. There are today at least 300 million indigenous peoples comprising more than 5 percent of the world's population scattered in more than seventy countries; some estimate the number as high as 600 million (*The State of Indigenous People* 2002; see also Map 5.3, pp. 166–167). Recall that this segment of global society is conventionally referred to as the **Fourth World** to heighten awareness of the poverty and deprivation that confront many native or tribal indigenous peoples without a homeland or self-rule (Wilmer 1993).

Many indigenous peoples feel persecuted because they feel that their livelihoods, lands, cultures, and lives are threatened. In part, these fears are inspired by the 130 million indigenous peoples who were slaughtered between 1900 and

■ **indigenous peoples**
the native ethnic and cultural inhabitant populations within countries ruled by a government controlled by others, referred to as the "Fourth World."

■ **Fourth World**
a term used to recognize the native natuional groups residing in many so-called united states who, although often minorities, occupied the state's territory first and refuse to accept domination, seeking instead to create a new state for themselves by splitting existing states or to gain greater political freedom to govern themselves.

CONTROVERSY

ARE NATIONAL SECURITY, ENVIRONMENTAL SECURITY, AND HUMAN SECURITY COMPETING GOALS?

How should "security" be defined? Policymakers disagree. Some see security primarily in terms of "national security"; others in terms of "environmental security" or "human security." The basis for the disagreement is competing conceptions of who and what is most important on the global agenda. One tradition gives states first priority and assumes that protecting national security must be put ahead of human security to manage shared problems such as environmental issues. Other groups challenge this conception and give primacy to the security of individual people, arguing that environmental protectionism must therefore be seen as a global priority, because all people depend on a clean, healthy environment for survival.

What do you think? In considering the issue, take into consideration the following interpretation, which frames the issue in the contemporary policy debate within national capitals and international organizations (IGOs and NGOs).

The traditional concept of national security that evolved during the Cold War viewed security as a function of the successful pursuit of interstate power competition. . . . Environmental security represents a significant departure from this approach to national security. It addresses two distinct issues: the environmental factors behind potentially violent conflicts, and the impact of global environmental degradation on the well-being of societies and economies. The idea that environmental degradation is a security issue when it is a cause of violent conflict appears to be consistent with the traditional definition of national security. However, . . . [the] focus on threats that do not involve an enemy state or political entity disturbs many theorists and practitioners of national security, for whom the only issues that should be viewed as "security" issues are those that revolve around conflict itself. . . .

The case for environmental security rests primarily on evidence that there has been serious degradation of natural resources (fresh water, soils, forests, fishery resources, and biological diversity) and vital life-support systems (the ozone layer, climate system, oceans, and atmosphere) as a result of the recent acceleration of global economic activities. These global physical changes could have far-reaching effects in the long run.

Each of these environmental threats to global well-being is subject to significant empirical and scientific uncertainty. . . . The uncertainties . . . are comparable, however, to those associated with most military threats that national security establishments prepare for. Military planning is based on "worst-case" contingencies that are

Graeme Ewens/Panos Pictures

Human Courage in the Face of Urbanization

considered relatively unlikely to occur, yet military preparations for such contingencies are justified as a necessary insurance policy or "hedge" against uncertainty. . . .

The relationship between scarce natural resources and international conflict is not a new issue. But unlike traditional national security thinking about such conflict, which focuses on nonrenewable resources like minerals and petroleum, the environmental security approach addresses renewable resources—those that need not be depleted if managed sustainably Porter (1995), 218–220.

SOURCE: Excerpt reprinted with permission from *Current History* magazine (May, 1995), p. 218–222. Copyright © 1995 Current History, Inc.

1987 by state-sponsored **genocide** in their own countries (Rummel 1994). The tragedy is of a magnitude of staggering proportions.

> During the twentieth century there were not only two world wars but at least six major cases of genocide—the mass killing of Armenians by Turks in 1915, of Jews (and other groups such as the Gypsies) by Hitler, of Cambodians by the Khmer Rouge, of the Kurds of northern Iraq by Saddam Hussein, of the Tutsi of Rwanda by the Hutu, and of Croats, Muslims, and the Albanians of Kosovo by the Serbs. In all cases except the Kosovo Albanians, the international community and its Western leaders failed to act in time.
>
> In 1948, halfway through this bloodiest of centuries, the United Nations General Assembly approved the text of the Genocide Convention, which outlaws the destruction by a government, in whole or in part, of a national, ethnic, racial, or religious group as such. Some forty years later the United States ratified the convention, and in the very last years of the century, the Hauge tribunal held hearings that led to the first conviction for genocide under the convention—of the Serb General Radislav Krstic for his part in the killings of Bosnians. Successive horrors have shamed governments into making some reluctant progress, but it is still far from certain that the nations of the world will act in time and with sufficient determination when genocide once again threatens some unfamiliar region. (Urquhart 2002, 12)

"The tragedy of the Nazi holocaust led a Polish jurist, Raphael Lemkin, to coin the word *genocide* from the Greek word *genos* (race, people) and the Latin *caedere* (to kill) and to begin action aimed at the international prohibition of genocide, which would in turn provide the necessary international legal basis for action against this crime. . . . Today . . . it is universally recognized that genocide is the gravest international crime and the most dangerous violation of human rights and that the international community is morally and politically responsible to take steps to prevent its occurrence and to punish persons responsible for crimes amounting to genocide" (Turk 2001).

Aroused nationalists are now fighting back across the globe in rebellion against the injustice, misery, and prejudice they perceive states to have perpetrated against them (see Gurr, et al. 2002). This is not to suggest that all indigenous minority groups are bent on tearing existing states apart, or on using violence to attain power. The members of many such **nonstate nations** are divided about objectives, and militants who are prepared to fight for independence are usually in a minority. In fact, most Fourth World indigenous movements only seek more representative clout in redirecting the policies and allocation of resources within existing states and are eliciting the support of NGOs and IGOs to pressure states to recognize their claims and protect their civil liberties and human rights. They strive to gain substate autonomy, not **sovereignty.**

A substantial number of indigenous movements in the last decade have successfully negotiated settlements resulting in **devolution**—the granting of political power to increase local self-governance to ethnopolitical national groups and indigenous peoples by the state, resulting in protagonists gaining concessions for greater local political power in exchange for accepting state sovereignty. Examples include the Miskitos in Nicaragua, the Gagauz in Moldova, and most regional separatists in Ethiopia and in India's Assam region. Yet, as

■ genocide
the deliberate extermination of an ethnic or minority group.

■ nonstate nations
national or ethnic groups struggling to obtain power and/or statehood.

■ sovereignty
the legal doctrine that states have supreme authority to govern their internal affairs and manage their foreign relations with other states and IGOs.

■ devolution
states' granting of political power to minority ethnopolitical national groups and indigenous people in particular national regions under the expectation that greater autonomy will curtail their quest for independence as a new state.

suggested by the U.S. war against international terrorism after September 11, 2001, and the "perpetual crisis" and action-reaction chain of militant hostility between Israel and the Palestinians, resolving clashes between established and aspiring states through terror and other forceful methods represents an entrenched trend.

The potential levels of discontent were made clear by the alarming threat of civil unrest painted by the official 2002 Communist Party's *China Investigation Report,* which warned that millions of Chinese are angered by rampant inequality, corruption, ethnic and religious conflicts, and the wrenching damage from China's end of its old state-run economy. It is difficult to foresee what will result from this and other cases of internal minority protests. One possibility is governmental devolution and the decentralization of state control to pacify nationalist separatist movements. Europe, today one of the world's most stable but ethnopolitically divided regions, could serve as a model for the twenty-first "devolution" century. However, from Kosovo to Kurdistan and from Palestine to Afghanistan, we observe an alternative scenario: freedom fighters impatient with the map they have inherited, struggling to become an independent state. Fighting by oppressed minority groups and between tribal ethnic factions has spread. The chaos that engulfed the impoverished and anarchic Afghanistan after 2001, which became the soil for the new wave of global terrorism, provides a striking example of the pregnant threat to human rights posed by failed states.

In another even more gloomy scenario presenting grave dangers for humanity, a **clash of civilizations** will unfold to terrorize humanity (see Chapter 5). In the wake of the 9/11 terrorist attack by Islamic extremists on the United States, Huntington's thesis (1999a) appears convincing that "almost everywhere in the contemporary world people are espousing cultural and civilizational identities" and that **ethnocentrism** within a particular group that perceives itself as a special civilization threatens to undermine the ideal of universal human rights, applicable to all of humanity.

The Threat of National Disintegration to Human Security

Indigenous peoples are now highly mobilized because "they were largely pushed to inaccessible and unproductive lands by earlier waves of colonization [and] now find that even these lands are coveted by outsiders" (Watson 1997). In response, many today pursue **self-determination** to protect themselves and control the resources on their territories. This quest for greater self-governance can sometimes be achieved through the peaceful separation of formerly unified states. This happened in Czechoslovakia on December 31, 1992, when that country split peacefully through the so-called velvet divorce into the independent Czech Republic and Slovakia.

However, aroused nationalist passions are prone to escalate to violence. An extreme example is the bloody warfare that has racked the former Yugoslavia since 1991, when the Bosnian Serbs and Croats both committed atrocities in the name of **ethnic cleansing**—a program of genocide to murder the rival nationality. The war in Kosovo was its culmination. What Italian President Oscar Luigi Scalfaro described in 1997 as a new "danger of racial, religious, and tribal hatred" follows the tragic pattern of twentieth-century genocides. Genocide caused the death of 500,000 to 1,100,000 ethnic minorities in the Soviet Union between 1943 and 1947, 80,000 to 1,000,000 ethnic Chinese and com-

■ **clash of civilizations**
political scientist Samuel Huntington's controversial thesis that in the twenty-first century the globe's major civilizations will conflict with one another, leading to anarchy and warfare similar to that resulting from conflicts between states over the past five hundred years.

■ **ethnocentrism**
a propensity to see one's nationality or state as the center of the world and therefore special, with the result that the values and perspectives of other groups are misunderstood and ridiculed.

■ **self-determination**
the doctrine that asserts nationalities have the right to determine what political authority will represent and rule them.

■ **ethnic cleansing**
the extermination of an ethnic minority group by a state government or rival majority ethnic group.

munists in Indonesia between 1965 and 1966, and 100,000 to 282,000 Kurds in Iraq between 1984 and 1991 (Barbara Harff, as cited in Sadowaski 1998, 18).

The goal expressed in the UN Charter of promoting "universal respect for, and observance of, human rights and fundamental freedoms" for everyone is a challenge for many nationally diverse countries, because protecting the human rights and civil liberties of minority populations is inherently difficult. The divisions of most states into segregated fragments along ethnic and cultural lines are different from the political partitions that divided Korea, Vietnam, Germany, and China into separate states. The majority of states can be described as inherently fragile because they are composed of multiple nationalities that can splinter. Consider the degree to which minority groups compose many states: for example, the share of indigenous populations in Bolivia is 70 percent; Peru, 40 percent; Mexico, 12 percent; the Philippines, 9 percent; and Canada, 4 percent. Cultural diversity is also captured by the number of distinct languages spoken in "megadiversity" countries, of which Indonesia's 670 languages, Nigeria's 410, India's 380, Australia's 250, and Brazil's 210 are exceptional examples (Durning 1993, 83, 86). Such states are not culturally, linguistically, or politically "united."

Racism and intolerance are hothouses for fanatical **irredentism,** fanaticism, and bloodshed. The inherent ethnocentrism underlying **ethnonationalism**—the belief that one's nationality is special and superior and that others are secondary and inferior—undermines the concept of human rights which "has attained increasingly broad support and is now firmly established under international law [and that stipulates] that human rights apply to everyone—by virtue of their humanity—everywhere, and at all times" (Clapham 2001). Nationalists are prone to marginalize and oppress "outside" nationalities, and to reject conciliation and compromise with them.

Although interethnic competition is a phenomenon that dates back to biblical times, it is a contemporary plague. According to *The Minorities at Risk Project* (see Gurr 1993, 2001), over 450 ethnopolitical minority groups have been involved in serious, often violent, struggles since 1945, and there exist many risks of new and escalating ethnic wars of tribal terrorism and warfare, challenging "the duty of all states," as proclaimed by Article 5 of the 1993 Vienna Declaration, "to promote and protect all human rights."

To the extent that conflict within and between ethnically disunited and divided states becomes a major axis on which twenty-first-century world politics revolves, the advent of a new era of tribal terrorism spreading worldwide could unfold. Such a breakdown would destroy "the duty of all states to promote and protect human rights" proclaimed in Article 5 of the 1993 Vienna Declaration.

■ **irredentism**
efforts by an ethnonational or religious group to regain control of territory by force so that existing state boundaries will no longer separate the group.

■ **ethnonationalism**
a belief system valuing an ethnic or national community above other possible objects of devotion, such as a state or the human community unit large.

GENDER POLITICS: THE SUBORDINATE STATUS OF WOMEN AND ITS CONSEQUENCES

In population conferences during the twentieth century's final decade, the critical role of women was recognized as a human rights concern, and a global consensus emerged about the need to improve the status of women if human

TABLE 7.2

Important Steps on the Path toward Human Rights and Women's Rights

Year	Conference	Key Passage or Issue of Treaty or Covenant
1968	United Nations International Conference on Human Rights (Teheran)	"Parents have a basic human rights to decide freely and responsibly on the number and spacing of their children."
1974	World Population Conference (Bucharest)	"The responsibility of couples and individuals [should take] into account the needs to their living and future children, and their responsibilities towards the community."
1975	International Women's Year Conference (Mexico City)	"The human body, whether that of woman or man, is inviolable, and respect for it is a fundamental element of human dignity and freedom."
1979	Convention on the Elimination of All Forms of Discrimination against Women (Women's Convention, New York)	Article 12 calls on countries to "take all appropriate measures to eliminate discrimination against women in the field of health care in order to ensure, on a basis of equality of men and women, access to health care services, including those related to family planning."
1984	World Population Conference (Mexico City)	"Governments can do more to assist people in making their reproductive decisions in a responsible way. [Family planning is] a matter of urgency."
1992	United Nations Conference on Environment and Development (Rio)	Agenda 21 calls for "women-centered, women-managed, safe and accessible, responsible planning of family size and service."
1993	United Nations World Conference on Human Rights (Vienna)	The Vienna Declaration includes nine paragraphs on "The Equal Status and Human Rights of Women," and, for the first time recognizes that "violence against women is a human-rights abuse."
1994	International Conference on Population and Development (Cairo)	ICPD Program of Action "reaffirms the basic human rights of all couples and individuals to decide freely and responsibly the number and spacing of children and to have the information, education, and means to do so."
1995	United Nations Fourth World Conference on Women (Beijing)	Sets a wide-ranging, ambitious agenda for promoting human development by addressing gender inequality and women's rights.
1999	United Nations Conference on World Population (The Hague)	Drafts recommendations on humane assistance for international family planning programs in light of the possibility that global population could start to decline late in the twenty-first century.
2002	World Summit on Sustainable Development (Johannesburg)	Drafts resolutions to combat abject and dehumanizing poverty, stressing the importance of reform to encourage gender equity and the rights of women in order to stimulate sustainable economic growth.

■ **gender empowerment index** the UN Development Program's attempt to measure the extent of gender equality across the globe's countries, based on estimates of women's relative economic income, high-paying positions, and access to professional and parliamentary positions.

development was to progress. These conferences are signposts that increasingly depict women's controlling their own bodies and reproductive fate as a basic human right, recognizable under international law (see Table 7.2). The conferences have educated the world to the incontrovertible evidence that women's status in society, and especially their education, has an important influence on human development, and that women's treatment is a human rights issue that affects everyone.

As measured by the UN's **gender empowerment index,** women throughout the world continue to be disadvantaged relative to men across a broad spectrum of educational statistics, such as literacy rates, school and college enrollments, and targeted educational resources. Women also enjoy less access to

AP/Wide World

The Gender Gap in Human Development
Women throughout the world have every reason to protest the unequal treatment and opportunities they receive in nearly all countries and have mobilized to lobby for human rights and changes in policy to close the serious "gender gap in employment." Here, in 1997, women demonstrators in Seoul, South Korea, give voice to their unfair treatment.

advanced study and training in professional fields, such as science, engineering, law, and business. In addition, within occupational groups, they are almost always in less-prestigious jobs, they face formidable barriers to political involvement, and everywhere they receive less pay than men. Although these and other gender differences have narrowed in recent years, in most countries **gender inequalities** remain firmly rooted.

Indeed, gender inequalities—differences in living standards between men and women—remain widespread both within and across states, despite the measurable improvement in the daily lot and future prospects of millions of women during the past several decades. Although many facets of human development are improving, the prevalent worldwide gender gap remains especially wide throughout and within the Global South. Women's share of earned income in developing countries is less than a third of men's. Worse still, women account for a much smaller proportion of the nonagricultural workforce than men, and their pay in that sector for the same work is routinely less. Females hold fewer

■ **gender inequalities** differences between men and women in opportunity and reward that are determined by the values that guide states' foreign and domestic policies.

teaching positions at all levels of education and fewer Ph.D.s, and their share of administrative and managerial jobs is minuscule. Much the same holds true in politics; "given the current institutional, legal, and socioeconomic constraints to [women's] access to opportunities" (UNDP 1995), women hold 14 percent of the seats in parliaments worldwide and only 6 percent of national government posts (*State of the World 2002*, 145; UNDP 2001, 210–229).

Furthermore, gender differences continue at the most basic levels of human development: more girls than boys die at a young age and females' access to adequate health care is more restricted. Despite the fact that "since the eighteenth century feminists, scholars and activists have taken up the task of revealing just how much political life has been built on presumptions about femininity and masculinity . . . there is abundant evidence now that regimes and the states beneath them in fact have taken deliberate steps to sustain a sort of hierarchical gendered division of labor that provides them with cheapened, often completely unpaid, women's productive labor" (Enloe 2001). Thus it is easy to conclude that women remain victims of human rights abuse and discrimination nearly everywhere, as reflected in the grim statistic that "women and their dependent children constitute at least 70 percent of all current refugees [while] it is usually male refugees within [UN administered refugee] camps who presume to have authority, often using it to strengthen men's militias, while preventing women from gaining access to UN literacy classes" (Enloe 2001, 313). It was not until 2001 that "sexual enslavement" was established at The Hague as a war crime, a fact feminists point out as an example of the traditional disregard for women's human rights.

So-called gender myopia, denying the existence of the many barriers that deny women equal freedoms and privileges enjoyed by men, is pervasive, although the need to extend women equal human rights for economic growth was recognized at the September 2002 Johannesburg World Summit on Sustainable Development. "The river of thought on human rights and development runs inexorably toward the emancipation of women everywhere and the equality of men and women," notes one report (*State of the World 2002*), which warns sadly, "but eddies and rivulets carry the water backwards every day—as when pregnant girls are expelled from school, or when the genitals of young women are cut in a ritual destruction of their capacity for sexual pleasure."

Addressing women's rights is difficult because the issues touch deeply entrenched as well as widely divergent religious and cultural beliefs. In many Islamic countries, for example, women must hide their faces with veils in public, and women and men are often completely separated in social and religious activities. For many in liberal Western countries, these traditions are difficult to understand. On the other hand, Western conceptions of feminism and women's rights, typically focused on social, political, and economic equality of the sexes, are foreign to women elsewhere, where the issues are personal and the goals pragmatic: "access to capital, the right of inheritance, basic education for girls, a voice in the political establishment and medical systems that let them make choices, especially in reproductive health" (Crossette 1995).

In 1995, in Beijing, the UN convened its fourth World Conference on Women, the largest-ever gathering of women. Many of the issues regarding women's rights, along with the arguments provoked by differing religious and cultural traditions, surfaced during the conference as attention focused on gender issues. The concept of "gender empowerment"—the conviction that "only when the potential of all human beings is fully realized can we talk of true human development" (UNDP 1995)—gained acceptance as an **ideology** or lens through which to view the core issues on the global agenda.

Feminist theory is a departure from classical realist theory that seeks to rectify the ways conventional but distorted images of world politics are socially constructed (see Chapter 2). The objective is to sensitize the world to the neglect of gender and the place of women in global society and to offer an alternative theoretical vision that empowers women and secures their basic human rights, while also challenging realist theories which honor the state and military power.

> ■ **ideology**
> a set of core philosophical principles that a group of leaders and citizens collectively hold about politics, the interests of political actors, and the ways people ought to ethically behave.

HUMAN RIGHTS AND THE PROTECTION OF PEOPLE

Laws regulating the practices that sovereign states may use have grown. These restraints include the principles of discrimination and **noncombatant immunity,** which in times of war attempt to protect innocent civilians by restricting military targets to soldiers and supplies. The message of the 1949 Geneva Convention that even wars have limits has been strengthened. The delegates at that historic conference, whose focus was to make new rules for warfare, understood that the causes of war and the problems of peace are best dealt with separately. "For war to be as merciful as possible sparing noncombatants and, in particular, civilian populations it is best if the law that governs the rules of war be distinct from all possible political consideration. This principle, the separation between causes of war and rules of war, became increasingly validated. . . . The world at large is so disgusted by acts of barbarity that governments and supranational bodies see it as their duty to intervene more and more to try to curb some of the more lurid atrocities that emerge here and there" (Sommaruga 1999).

> ■ **noncombatant immunity**
> the legal principle that military force should not be used against innocent civilians.

This change in the rules of war is representative of a larger sea change in the international consensus about human rights. That phase has advanced from a mere slogan to a program of action. New humanitarian norms have now been accepted globally, which have created a human rights **international regime** backed by enforcement institutions. The human rights revolution has advanced moral progress by breaking states' monopoly on international affairs and over citizens (Ignatieff 2001b). In this sense, liberalism triumphed and realism was repudiated, for the human rights movement has rejected the harsh realist vision expressed by Thomas Hobbes, who argued in the seventeenth century that because world politics is "a war of all against all, the notions of right and wrong, justice and injustice have there no place." Moreover, international law has fundamentally revised the traditional realist protection of the state by redefining the relationship of states to humans. As Kofi Annan in 1999 defined the new conception of human rights, "States are now widely understood to be instruments at the service of their people, and not *vice versa*. At the same time . . . the fundamental freedom of each individual, enshrined in the Charter of the UN and subsequent international treaties—[has] been enhanced by a renewed and spreading consciousness of individual [human] rights. When we read the Charter today, we are more than ever conscious that its aim is to protect individual human beings, not to protect those who abuse them."

> ■ **international regime**
> the set of rules, norms, and decision-making procedures that coordinates state behavior within a given issue area.

Piers Benatar/Panos Pictures

The Victimization of Children as the Ultimate Violation of Human Rights Women are not the only victims of the invisible forces that exploit the human rights of people. Another group of victims—to which every living human at one time belonged—are children. The UN Children's Fund estimates that some "200,000 children a year are trafficked in West and Central Africa. Girls are affected worst; most end up as domestic workers or prostitutes. Boys are forced to work on coffee or cocoa plantations or as fishermen" (*Time*, April 30, 2001, 39). Shown here is one tragic case: a starving farmer in Afghanistan, Akhtar Mohammed, watching his ten-year-old son, Sher, whom he traded to a wealthy farmer in exchange for a monthly supply of wheat. "What else could I do?" he asked "I will miss my son, but there was nothing to eat."

As a principle, human rights is a transnational ethical movement that supports the view that human beings should come first, ahead of other objects of identity such as the state. It recognizes humanity as members of the human community, in anticipation of the creation of a global civil society. Hence, a cosmopolitan vision is embraced:

- "Citizenship is not a condition that requires a state in the first instance; citizenship is a social status that requires mutual recognition of human moral worth" (Vandersluis and Yeros 2000a).

- People are valuable and equally entitled to certain "inalienable" rights, and therefore *everyone* deserves protection from the denial of those basic fundamental rights by virtue of their moral status as human beings and autonomous individuals, interconnected throughout the globe.

- Human rights is *universal.* Universality "means that human rights apply to everyone by virtue of their humanity—everywhere and at all times" (Clapham 2001).

- Human rights obligates all actors on the world stage to observe, respect, and protect these rights; this includes states, so that even they have clear duties that transcend borders and sovereign rights, because a moral demand is made "to respect the life, integrity, well-being and flourishing of others [and this ethical obligation] applies to all human beings" (Vandersluis and Yeros 2000a).

The persecution of individuals responsible for human rights violations in times of war attests to this accountability, which is now accepted in international law as a normative change that greatly reduces the traditional right of rulers to commit crimes against humanity in the name of defending the state: "states are no longer able to treat their citizens as they think fit" (Held and McGrew 2001).

When on December 10, 1948, the UN General Assembly proclaimed the *Universal Declaration of Human Rights,* it took a giant step in defining these rights and the liberal philosophy which inspired that declaration. "The declaration establishes a broad range of civil and political rights, including freedom of assembly, freedom of thought and expression, and the right to participate in government. The declaration also proclaims that social and economic rights are indispensable, including the right to education, the right to work, and the right to participate in the cultural life of the community. In addition, the preamble boldly asserts that 'it is essential, if man is not to be compelled to have recourse, as a last resort, to rebellion against tyranny and oppression, that human rights should be protected by the rule of law'" (Clapham 2001). These rights have since been codified and extended in a series of treaties, such as the 1981 *African Charter of Human and Peoples Rights* and the 1993 Second *Vienna World Conference on Human Rights.* As one authority, Charles R. Beitz, summarizes:

> Together these documents, which often are referred to collectively (and . . . misleadingly) as the International Bill of Rights, constitute an authoritative catalog of internationally recognized human rights.
>
> There are various ways to classify the rights enumerated in these documents. For our purposes it is useful to think of internationally recognized human rights as falling roughly into five categories, although it is less important to agree about categories than to appreciate the scope and detail of the enumerated rights.
>
> 1. Rights of the person refer to life, liberty, and security of the person; privacy and freedom of movement; ownership of property; freedom of thought, conscience, and religion, including freedom of religious teaching and practice "in public and private;" and prohibition of slavery, torture, and cruel or degrading punishment.
> 2. Rights associated with the rule of law include equal recognition before the law and equal protection of the law; effective legal

    remedy for violation of legal rights; impartial hearing and trial; presumption of innocence; and prohibition of arbitrary arrest.

3. Political rights encompass freedom of expression, assembly, and association; the right to take part in government; and periodic and genuine elections by universal and equal suffrage.

4. Economic and social rights refer to an adequate standard of living; free choice of employment; protection against unemployment; "just and favorable remuneration;" the right to join trade unions; "reasonable limitation of working hours;" free elementary education; social security; and the "highest attainable standard of physical and mental health."

5. Rights of communities include self-determination and protection of minority cultures. (Beitz 2001, 271)

RESPONDING TO THE AGONY OF HUMAN RIGHTS ABUSE

From any perspective, the scale of the chronic poverty, political victimization, and suffering that afflicts such a large proportion of humanity cannot but provoke compassion and outrage. Only the most heartless can feel indifferent about the extent of suffering documented in this chapter. True, some observers are not alarmed by the growing absolute and relative inequalities that exist across a variety of measures of the human condition; but few are so callous as to feel no empathy with the plight of millions of hapless victims throughout the world. When we look at the way ordinary people live in the real world, almost no one would conclude that the basic human rights defined above through consensus in the international community are being protected. There is great distance between the high ideal of human rights and its realization.

    The policy question facing the world is what steps can and should be taken to alleviate human suffering and to safeguard human rights. Agreement has yet to be reached on the extent to which the international community has a responsibility to react, to respond, and to intervene in order to protect human rights and rebuild broken humans. As the International Commission on Intervention and State Sovereignty noted in its December 2001 report, *The Responsibility to Protect*, the policy challenge is of great magnitude:

> Millions of human beings remain at the mercy of civil wars, insurgencies, state repression and state collapse. This is a stark and undeniable reality, and it is at the heart of all the issues with which this Commission has been wrestling. What is at stake here is not making the world safe for big powers, or trampling over the sovereign rights of small ones, but delivering practical protection for ordinary people, at risk of their lives, because their states are unwilling or unable to protect them.

> But all this is easier said than done. There have been as many failures as successes, perhaps more, in the international protective record in recent years. There are continuing fears about a "right to intervene" being formally acknowledged. If intervention for human protection purposes is to be accepted, including the possibility of military action, it remains imperative that the international community develop consistent, credible and enforceable standards to guide state and intergovernmental practice.

Photograph by Fred Peer, Camera Press London

Cruel and Unusual, or Simply Usual? The UN Human Rights Commission holds annual sessions that deal with accusations that some UN members are violating the human rights provisions enacted by international treaties. Shown here is the kind of human rights abuse that some countries practice: a photo of a person being punished according to Saudi Arabia's Islamic laws.

The search for agreement about the principles that should guide a **regime** "to establish clearer rules, procedures and criteria for determining whether, when and how to intervene" to protect human rights has proven elusive. The global community has not yet agreed upon a set of legal justifications for **humanitarian intervention** to protect civilians. The major paradox is this: "In major arenas of international politics concerns about human rights are more prominently expressed than ever before, and there is some reason to believe that these concerns increasingly motivate action. Yet, within contemporary political thought human rights are often regarded with suspicion" (Beitz 2001).

Advocating the protection and promotion of human rights is one thing high on the agenda of liberalism; yet taking the steps necessary for these goals is resisted by realists, who see the promotion and protection of state sovereignty as a priority. Hence, the promotion of human rights is primarily a *political* problem on the global agenda. The issue is not whether there exists a compelling human need and moral obligation to express concerns about populations at risk of slaughter, ethnic cleansing, starvation, or persecution; the issue is about how and if to forge a just response, when any response will comprise an interference in the internal or domestic affairs of a sovereign state. Humanitarian intervention is destined to remain inherently controversial.

■ **regime**
norms, rules, and procedures for interaction agreed to by a set of states.

■ **humanitarian intervention**
the use of peacekeeping troops by foreign states or international organizations to protect endangered people from gross violations of their human rights and from mass murder.

However, the mandate to permit intervention for humanitarian purposes appears to be growing in strength. The rationale for acceptance of humanitarian intervention to protect human rights has been advocated by the executive director of the NGO Amnesty International:

> Here is the grandpappy of "realism," diplomat George Kennan: "I would like to see [the U. S.] government gradually withdraw from its public advocacy of democracy and human rights. . . . I don't think any such questions should enter into our diplomatic relations with other countries. If others [private parties] want to advocate changes in their conditions, fine—no objection. But not the State Department or the White House. They have more important things to do."
>
> "Realists" regard the pursuit of rights as an unnecessary, sometimes even a dangerous extravagance, often at odds with our national interest. What they seem rarely to garner is that in far more cases than they will allow, defending human rights is a prerequisite to *protecting* that interest. What we require is not less realism but a more expansive, sophisticated, comprehensive form of it—a "new realism" for an interconnected age. . . .
>
> Fortunately the connection between human rights and national interest is becoming more clear to an ever-expanding circle of observers. As *The Economist*, that bastion of respect for capitalist values, editorialized not too long ago, "Morality is not the only reason for putting human rights on the West's foreign-policy agenda. Self-interest also plays a part. Political freedom tends to go hand in hand with economic freedom, which in turn tends to bring international trade and prosperity. And governments that treat their own people with tolerance and respect tend to treat their neighbors in the same way. Dictatorships unleashed the First and Second World Wars, and most wars before and since." (Schulz 2001, 13, 14)

Humanitarian intervention "refers to a range of unilateral or collective actions taken by the international community to provide assistance to the population of a target state experiencing unacceptable and persistent levels of human suffering caused by natural disaster, deliberate government policy, or state collapse" (Malaquias 2001). The decision to engage in humanitarian intervention will always be controversial, because it will raise very big questions about the legitimacy of intervention in a sovereign state: Was the cause just, and were the human rights violations committed sufficiently serious to make outside involvement necessary? The answers will always be uncertain. However, human rights has gained the stature of accepted international law. As a result, we can expect human rights to receive continuing attention, as long as people continue to be in need of help when they are caught in emergency situations such as the threat of famine or genocide:

> There is a determination to ensure that states and governments are held accountable for failing to live up to their international obligations. We care about rights because we care about each other. The language of human rights obligations is the simplest way to express that sense of sympathy and outrage. Concerned citizens will continue to demand change as long as the inherent dignity of any human being remains threatened, unprotected, and unrealized. (Clapham 2001, 370)

We most vividly see the rising importance assigned ethically to human rights protection in international legislation in one area where, traditionally, these rights were more blatantly ignored: the conduct of war. The change has been sparked in great measure by the fact that **noncombatants**—that is, innocent civilians and ordinary people not engaged in fighting—have become the primary victims in warfare. In recent years, the ratio of civilians to soldiers killed in wars has reversed the historic pattern: today ninety civilian casualties result for every ten military losses (Pfaff 1999, 8). To prevent the horror of civilian casualties and contain the mass slaughter that increasingly has taken place inside national frontiers, the global community in revulsion has made a radical revision in the rule of international law. For the first time, international law holds leaders of countries accountable for **war crimes** as war criminals. Traditionally, international law prohibited leaders from allowing their militaries to undertake actions in violation of certain principles accepted by the international community, including the protection of innocent noncombatants. However, when violations occurred, there was little that could be done except to condemn such actions. Another weakness was that traditional international law did not hold government leaders to the same standards to which it held soldiers and military officers who committed atrocities against enemy civilians and captured soldiers. Although international law set standards for both individuals and states, leaders were free from jurisdiction under the doctrine of "sovereign immunity," even when their commands flouted the laws of war. Though they might behave as criminals, leaders were treated with respect because they were the people with whom the global community had to negotiate to settle conflicts.

While many people and states still commit war crimes without facing punishment, the resumption of war crime tribunals in 1993 signaled to would-be perpetrators the global community's intolerance for these atrocities. In 1999, the prosecutor's office of the UN's International Criminal Court (ICC) indicted seventy-seven people and arrested seven for crimes in Bosnia. Building on this step, a permanent world criminal court was created in The Hague to try leaders for the most terrible of mass crimes, especially acts of genocide such as those occurring in ethnopolitical conflicts. Thus a goal the UN had pursued for half a century became a reality: the world community now has an international court with teeth, through a treaty approved by almost all states.

Moreover, heads of state are now held accountable for war crimes against humanity, removing the protection they had received under traditional international law. Ever since the Hague Tribunal's 1997 founding statute, a head of state can be charged with war crimes committed at any time the leader was in office; even a sitting head of state can now be indicted for war crimes. In fact, Slobodan Milosevic of Yugoslavia and President General Augusto Pinochet of Chile were indicted in 1999, and, in September 2002, Milosevic, the ex-Yugoslavian president, faced prosecutors at The Hague, who accussed him of war crimes as the mastermind behind the genocide planned to wipe out Bosnia's Muslims in the 1991–1995 wars. (Milosevic portrayed Serbs as victims of ethnic aggression and, claimed his policies had aimed at peace, not war.) The criminalization of rulers who have been alleged sponsors of state terrorism raises the legal restraints on the initiation and conduct of war to an all-time high, despite the refusal in 2002 of the United States to adhere to this treaty.

The global community has impressively expanded its legal protection of human rights. As Table 7.3 shows, a large number of conventions have been

■ **noncombatants**
those not engaged in fighting during wartime such as teachers and children, who, like soldiers, are often exposed to harm.

■ **war crimes**
acts performed during war that the international community defines as illegal crimes against humanity, such as atrocities committed on an enemy's prisoners of war and civilians or the state's own minority population.

TABLE 7.3

Legal Steps in the Development of International Human Rights Protection: Some Major Conventions

1948	Universal Declaration of Human Rights
1949	Convention on the Prevention and the Punishment of the Crime of Genocide
1950	Convention for the Suppression of the Traffic of Persons and the Exploitation of the Prostitution of Others
1951	Convention Relating to the Status of Refugees
1953	Convention on the Political Rights of Women
1959	Declaration of the Rights of the Child
1965	International Convention on the Elimination of All Forms of Racial Discrimination
1966	International Covenant on Civil and Political Rights
1966	Optional Protocol to the International Covenant on Civil and Political Rights
1967	Convention on the Elimination of All Forms of Discrimination against Women
1967	Declaration of Territorial Asylum
1969	Inter-American Convention on Human Rights
1973	Principles of International Co-Operation in the Punishment of War Crimes and Crimes against Humanity
1976	International Covenant on Economic, Social, and Cultural Rights
1977	Protocols on Humanitarian Law for International Armed Conflicts and Noninternational Armed Conflicts
1981	Covenant of Civil and Political Rights
1981	Declaration on the Elimination of All Forms of Intolerance and of Discrimination Based on Religion or Belief
1984	Convention against Torture and Other Cruel, Inhumane, or Degrading Treatment or Punishment
1989	Second Optional Protocol to the International Covenant on Civil and Political Rights, Aiming at the Abolition of the Death Penalty
1989	Convention on the Rights of the Child
1991	Convention on the Prevention and Suppression of Genocide
1992	Declaration of Principles of International Law on Compensation to Refugees
1993	Vienna Convention on Human Rights
1993	Declaration on the Rights of Persons Belonging to National or Ethnic, Religious or Linguistic Minorities
1993	Declaration on the Elimination of Violence against Women
1994	African Convention on Human and Peoples' Rights
2000	Convention Prohibiting Trafficking of Women and Children for Prostitution
2000	International Convention for the Suppression of the Financing of Terrorism

This inventory of some of the major conventions since the Universal Declaration of Human Rights was proclaimed in 1948 documents the extraordinary growth of human rights legislation.

enacted in the last fifty years that have steadily endowed individuals with power, rights, and respect—rights ensuring that people are treated as worthy of the freedom and dignity traditionally granted by international law to states and rulers. "The old assumption that national sovereignty trumps all other principles in international relations is under attack as never before; . . . the age of human rights is upon us. In these post-communist, postmodern times, human rights seem to have become the dominant moral narrative for thinking about world affairs. No longer does national sovereignty provide blanket protection for human rights abusers. In the eyes of many Western intellectuals, there is a New World Moral Order—one ruled by ideals like civil society, humanitarianism and, first and foremost, human rights" (Rieff 1999, 67).

That said, the persistence of horrendous atrocities and human suffering makes a mockery of the standards for a just global civil society called for by the *Universal Declaration of Human Rights*. "As with most declarations of faith, their adherents—first and foremost governments—have frequently failed to live up to them [even though] practically all governments say they accept the basic code of conduct these declarations expound. The continuing effort to achieve and maintain those standards is the frontier between civilization and barbarism" (Urquhart 2001).

"Moral universalism is a late and vulnerable addition to the vocabulary of mankind" (Ignatieff 2001a). The humanitarian vision to promote human rights and to provide a moral shield against man's proverbial "inhumanity to man" remains a huge challenge on the global agenda. To now put people first is to live up to high ideals, and the world has a long way to go to achieve that aspiration. Eleanor Roosevelt was an early champion of human rights, and it was her energetic leadership that was largely responsible for global acceptance in 1948 by nearly all governments of the *Universal Declaration of Human Rights*. Her noble pursuit shows that one person can make a difference in transforming world politics. In thinking about humans and humanity, we can profit by the inspiration of her nightly prayer: "Save us from ourselves and show us a vision of a world made new."

In the chapters that follow in Part III, we will examine the primary issues on the politics of global welfare, helping us better envision the world as it presently exists and contemplate the prospects for a transformed world—a world made new.

KEY TERMS

ethics	level of analysis	refugees
morality	globalization	displaced people
realism	dependency theory	ethnic cleansing
civil society	human needs	failed states
human rights	Human Development Index (HDI)	Global South
sanctions	purchasing power parity (PPP)	brain drain
liberalism	globalization	xenophobia
paradigm	Third Way	asylum
feminist theory	human security	atrocities

sanctuary	clash of civilizations	ideology
national security	ethnocentrism	noncombatant immunity
indigenous peoples	self-determination	international regime
Fourth World	ethnic cleansing	regime
genocide	irredentism	humanitarian intervention
nonstate-nations	ethnonationalism	noncombatants
sovereignty	gender empowerment index	war crimes
devolution	gender inequalities	

SUGGESTED READING

Beitz, Charles R. "Human Rights as a Common Concern," *American Political Science Review* 95 (June 2001): 269–282.

Franck, Thomas M. "Are Human Rights Universal?" *Foreign Affairs* 80 (January/February 2001): 191–204.

Goldstein, Joshua. *War and Gender.* Cambridge, Mass.: Cambridge University Press, 2002.

Hyndman, Jennifer. *Managing Displacement: Refugees and the Politics of Humanitarianism.* Minneapolis: University of Minnesota Press, 2000.

Jackson, Robert. *The Global Covenant: Human Conduct in a World of States.* New York: Oxford University Press, 2001.

Lauren, Paul Gordon. *The Evolution of International Human Rights: Visions Seen.* Philadelphia: University of Pennsylvania Press, 1999.

Power, Samantha, and Graham Allison. *Realizing Human Rights: Moving from Inspiration to Impact.* London: Palgrave, 2001.

Ratner, Steven R., and Jason S. Abrams. *Accountability for Human Rights Atrocities in International Law.* New York: Oxford University Press, 2001.

Schulz, William F. *In Our Own Best Interest: How Defending Human Rights Benefits Us All.* Boston: Beacon, 2001.

Shelton, Dinah. *Remedies in International Human Rights Law.* Oxford University Press, 2001.

Tickner, J. Ann. *Gendering World Politics: Issues and Approaches in the Post-Cold War Era.* New York: Columbia University Press, 2002.

United Nations Development Program (UNDP). *Human Development Report 2003.* New York: Oxford University Press, 2003.

WHERE ON THE WORLD WIDE WEB?

Amnesty International
http://www.amnesty.org/

Amnesty International (AI) is an international nongovernmental organization (NGO) with a global reach and a specific purpose. Its activities are concentrated on prisoners around the world who are detained solely for their beliefs, color, sex, ethnic origin, language, or religion. Amnesty International advocates the release of all prisoners of conscience, the availability of a fair and prompt trial for political prisoners, and the abolishment of the death penalty, torture, and other cruel and inhumane treatment of prisoners. What are some of the current issues of Amnesty International?

Fourth World Documentation Project
http://www.cwis.org/fwdp.html

The Center for World Indigenous Studies created this Web site to document and make available important materials related to the social, political, strategic, economic, and human rights problems that indigenous peoples face. The site is organized according to region and has links to international agreements and resolutions.

NativeWeb
http://www.nativeweb.org

The NativeWeb has both a resource center and a community center. Research the native peoples of the world by clicking on the "resource center" link, or click the "communities" link to discuss current issues on the message board. You can also participate in an on-line chat.

NetAid
http://www.netaid.org

NetAid is a new, long-term effort to use the unique networking capabilities of the Internet to promote development and alleviate extreme poverty across the world. NetAid issues periodic calls to action on items of urgency and focuses attention on what works. Read about efforts aimed at ending hunger, helping refugees, saving the environment, securing human rights, and relieving debt. This site also suggests actions you can take to address some of these issues.

Beijing '95: Women, Power, and Change
http://www.womensnet.org/beijing/

WomensNet brings you a Web site devoted to the implementation and follow-up of the 1995 UN Fourth World Conference on Women. Through this site, interested individuals can read the Final Report on the Fourth World Conference on Women. What influence did nongovernmental organizations have on the issues presented at the conference? What were some of the problems they experienced?

The United Nations and the Status of Women: Setting the Global Gender Agenda
http://www.un.org/Conferences/Women/PubInfo/Status/Home.htm

Table 7.2 chronicles a quarter-century of progress on women's rights. As you see, the UN and its programs have provided the most important international forums on women's rights. This Web site explains the major UN programs that advance women's rights, including the Committee on the Elimination of Discrimination against Women, UN Actions for Women, Commission on the Status of Women, Women in Development, and the Convention on the Elimination of All Forms of Discrimination against Women.

United Nations High Commissioner for Refugees
http://www.unhcr.ch/

Any study of human rights requires that one consider migration. The UN High Commissioner for Refugees leads and coordinates international action for the worldwide protection of refugees and the resolution of refugee problems. This Web site offers a wealth of information on refugees, and is a good place to start examining the issues involved. The "Protecting Refugees" link describes one of the fundamental aspects of the UNHCR. The "Statistics" link gives you current numbers on refugees, worldwide as well as by country. Explore the "News" link to examine important current topics.

INFOTRAC® COLLEGE EDITION

Patrinos, Harry Anthony. "The Cost of Discrimination in Latin America," *Studies In Comparative International Development* Summer 2000.

Chi-Ying Chung, Rita. "Psychosocial Adjustment of Cambodian Refugee Women: Implications for Mental Health Counseling," *Journal of Mental Health Counseling* April 2001.

Ballard-Reisch, Deborah S., Paaige K. Turner, and Marcia Sarratea. "The Paradox of Women in Zimbabwe: Emancipation, Liberation, and Traditional African Values," *Women and Language* Fall 2001.

Schulz, William, Robin Fox, and Francis Fukuyama. "The Ground and Nature of Human Rights: Another Round," *The National Interest* Summer 2002.

For more articles, enter:

"indigenous peoples" in the Subject Guide, and then go to subdivision "economic aspects."

"refugees" in the Subject Guide, and then go to subdivision "care and treatment."

"human rights" in the Subject Guide, and then go to subdivision "analysis."

CHAPTER 8

DOES GLOBALIZATION SPELL THE END OF BORDERS AS BOUNDARIES?

TOPICS AND THEMES

- What is globalization?
- The globalization of communications in the information age
- The globalization of contagious disease through transnational contact
- The globalization of finance
- The globalization of trade
- The globalization of production
- Globalization and widening inequalities?
- Globalization, the state, and global governance: What future?

- **CONTROVERSY** DOES GLOBALIZATION MEAN THE END OF THE AGE OF STATES?
- **CONTROVERSY** IS GLOBALIZATION PRODUCING PROSPERITY OR POVERTY?

The first McDonald's franchise opens in Lebanon.

What is globalization? The short answer is that globalization is the integration of everything with everything else. A more complete definition is that globalization is the integration of markets, finance, and technology in a way that shrinks the world from a size medium to a size small. Globalization enables each of us, wherever we live, to reach around the world farther, faster, deeper, and cheaper than ever before and at the same time allows the world to reach into each of us farther, faster, deeper, and cheaper than ever before.

—Thomas Friedman, political journalist, 2002

Today . . . everything affects everything else. . . . Good things are going to happen in a more global world but foreign policy crises are about what goes wrong. In the short run, I'm pessimistic. . . . There is still nothing like a global leviathan or a centralizing force. The world is coming together, but the international bureaucracy atop it is so infantile and underdeveloped that it cannot cope with growing instability.

—Robert Kaplan, political journalist, 2002

Stock prices tumble as foreign investors sell investments across borders with lightning speed, while your parents fret about their ability to meet their bills. Industrial and financial tycoons merge their multinational companies to form a global business colossus, and you discover that your local bank is now controlled overseas and your new employer is headquartered abroad and plans to restructure by cutting the workforce. As the Federal Reserve System lowers U.S. interest rates, skittish currency traders sell billions of dollars and buy euros. Another U.S. manufacturer shifts production overseas, substituting foreign workers without trade unions for local union workers. A bomb explodes in your hometown, and a friend's family member dies from the violence believed caused by foreign terrorists. Meanwhile, clad in Levi jeans and Calvin Klein shirts, university students in Istanbul chat with friends in America on cellular phones as they sip raki in a local bar, while the music of Bono from U–2 plays in the background.

What in the world is going on? The answer: globalization. Capital, commerce, advanced technology, and information are spreading worldwide at record speeds, producing the complexity and chaos associated with what is today widely known as **globalization.** "Globalization" is a shorthand for a cluster of interconnected phenomena that together are transforming world politics. It is used to describe, alternatively, a process, a policy, a predicament, and the product of vast, invisible international forces producing massive changes worldwide. Most would probably agree that globalization is a permanent trend leading to a global phenomenon.

Globalization is a hot topic. Money, goods, people, technology, and ideas are moving across national borders at an accelerating pace. As the world is rapidly becoming interconnected, linked tighter and tighter into a single, integrated global community and market, globalization is transforming world affairs profoundly.

This interdependence creates both possibilities and problems. On the one hand, globalization is uniting the world and generating unprecedented new levels of wealth. On the other hand, globalization is making national boundaries and state governments less important and, by creating some winners and many losers, it is also producing greater inequalities. Globalization is leading to the simultaneous integration and disintegration of states, to the growth of some states' power and the erosion of many other states' authority, and few global actors know how to adaptively respond to the force of globalization's changes.

It is understandable, therefore, that globalization is so controversial. It is a small world, after all; but is that good or bad? People cannot seem to agree. In fact, there is even disagreement about what globalization is, even if the word *globalization* "has become the most ubiquitous in the language of international relations [and] has spawned a new vocabulary: *globaloney* (why all the hype when the global economy was more integrated in the age of Queen Victoria?); *globaphobia* (the new, mainly mistaken, backlash); *globeratti* (the members of the international nongovernmental organizations [NGOs] who travel around the world from conference to conference, except when they are on the Internet mobilizing for the next conference), and so on" (Ostry 2001). In addition to trying to agree on what globalization encompasses is the larger issue about globalization's consequences. Consider one assessment:

> Days of speeches at the World Economic Forum [in Davos] and at the counter-gathering in Porto Alegre, Brazil, about the benefits and evils of globalization benumb the brain. Has globalization triumphed? Is it threatened by a backlash of which demonstrations and their suppression are the precursors? Or is everyone thinking at cross-purposes?
>
> Is the globalization divide just a replay of the North-South debate of two decades ago? Or perhaps yet another divide is emerging, with most of Asia opting out of what it sees as an acrimonious ideological debate that slows progress on pragmatic trade issues.
>
> In one corner are those who seem to believe that globalization is an ideology to be preached rather than the consequence of other, mostly

■ **globalization**
according to the International Monetary Fund, "the increasingly close international integration of markets both for goods and services and for capital" (see p. 45).

beneficial forces—technological change plus the efforts of major countries to reduce barriers to movement of goods, money and ideas. They are under the illusion that it is new, but globalization has been proceeding in fits and starts, with occasional major setbacks, for centuries. Nor is it measured by Internet penetration.

Many assume that globalization represents the triumph of the market, without stopping to think of how every nation, not least America, in practice views the market as a tool, not an ideology, which domestically is submitted to a moral and income distribution framework determined by society.

In the other corner are those who complain bitterly about all manner of evils that they attribute to globalization. These critics are divided between those in rich countries who fear its impact on them and those who attack it because it is, sometimes with good reason, passing them by. If they get beyond anger they often end up proposing solutions in line with the liberalization that contributes to globalization. (Bowring 2001, 8)

Try to construct an objective evaluation of these and other competing views of globalization. We ask you to contemplate two very different possible futures for world politics as a result of the globalization process that is so differently interpreted. That is, you will be forced to compare two forecasts for the global future. In one optimistic scenario, **neoliberal theory** sees sovereignty at bay as the globalization of markets and cultures transcends contemporary geopolitical boundaries and erodes the meaning of national identity, creating "global citizens" who assign loyalty to the common interests of all peoples. In the other, more pessimistic forecast, states will compete with one another to attain or retain the trappings of independence from and control over the homogenizing forces now sweeping the world. This competition will divide the world even as countries become more alike, making some wealthy and stable but others poorer and fragile.

Globalization stems from "the onrush of economic and ecological forces that demand integration and uniformity and that mesmerize the world with fast music, fast computers, and fast food—with MTV, Macintosh, and McDonald's pressing nations into one commercially homogenous global network: one McWorld tied together by technology, ecology, communications, and commerce" (Barber 1995). Such forces imply nothing less than a redistribution of global economic power "which will increasingly translate into a redistribution of political power" (Schwab and Smadja 1996).

In this and the next two chapters we will examine the diverse forces propelling the rapid globalization now sweeping the world. This chapter will look primarily at the economic influence of international trade, investment, finance, and production and their impact on markets, growth, and global governance. Chapter 9 broadens the coverage to encompass the implications of globalization for the new international political economy, and Chapter 10 examines the demographic (population) and ecopolitical (environmental) dimensions of a globalizing world. Together, all three chapters force consideration of how globalization is likely to affect the **human security** of people and their human rights (recall Chapter 7), as well as, at the **state level of analysis,** the well-being of countries in the Global North and the Global South. This evaluation will force consideration of the prospects for the continuation of states as sovereign and independent actors against the tide toward a cosmopolitan world culture

■ **neoliberal theory**
a philosophy that maintains that peaceful change with prosperity can be encouraged through cooperation in institutions that knit the states and peoples of the world together into a true global community (see p. 155).

■ **human security**
a concept that refers to the degree to which the welfare of individuals is protected and advanced, in contrast to national security which puts the interests of states first.

■ **state level of analysis**
an analytical approach to the study of world politics that emphasizes how the internal attributes of states explain their foreign policy behaviors.

Sally Wiener Grotta/The Stock Market

The World at One's Fingertips The revolution in telecommunications has contributed to "the death of distance," as virtually instantaneous communications are possible nearly everywhere. Here, in a remote and desolate region of northern Kenya, a Samburu warrior makes a call on his cellular telephone.

and an emerging global polity with institutions for global governance (see Controversy: Does Globalization Mean the End of the Age of States?). It will also force interpretation of the prospects for international cooperation and conflict. Before inspecting globalization's consequences—whether globalization is best seen as a plot by profit-hungry megacorporations to exploit workers and despoil the environment, a return to colonialism, a magic cure-all for economic problems, the last step in the creation of world government, or any number of potential possibilities—we must first inspect globalization's causes.

WHAT IS GLOBALIZATION?

Rapid and unrestrained communication is a hallmark of the **global village**—a metaphor used by many futurologists to portray a world in which borders will vanish and the world will become a single community. The major source of this global transformation is the growing speed and flow of communications, because "by drastically reducing the importance of proximity, the new technologies change people's perceptions of community" (Mathews 1997). Will cellular phones and other means of transnational communication portend consensus, and, perhaps, an integrated global village? Or is the vision of such a global village, in which shared information breeds understanding and peace, pure mythology? Worse, will the virus of interconnectiveness within globalization do away with private life, erasing what remains of identity, individualism, and independence?

■ **global village**
a popular image used to describe the growth of awareness that all people share a common fate, stemming from a macro perspective that the world is an integrated and interdependent whole.

CONTROVERSY

DOES GLOBALIZATION MEAN THE END OF THE AGE OF STATES?

What does globalization today mean for the survival of the state? To some thinkers "it's the end of sovereignty [which] has seen the rise of the European state as the epitome of political organization. The twenty-first century will see the end of state sovereignty as we have known it" (Howell 1998). Still others believe that globalization is simply a new manifestation of old patterns, one that will "in many ways be viewed as a resumption of a trend observed in the world economy a century ago. . . . The trends we have been observing in recent decades are in a sense taking us back to the future" (IMF 1997).

Consider this question as informed by the observations of journalist Neal R. Peirce, who attended the fiftieth Salzburg Seminar of global leaders in 1997 to contemplate the state's future in the face of transformative globalization. Peirce issued this provocative summary of the debate, which provides a good framework to consider rival ideas about globalization's causes, likely consequences, and probable impact on the survival of the nation-state.

> Is the nation-state at the end of its 500-year run? Is it about to succumb to rapid-fire economic globalization, resurgent regions or to ethnic and tribal rivalries?

Not entirely, say midcareer professionals from some 32 nations who came here in March [1997] to debate the nation-state's furture at the elegant 18th-century palace that has been the site of the Salzburg Seminar for 50 years.

Whether from advanced or undeveloped, Western or Eastern nations, most participants agreed we'll still need nation-states to give people identity, raise taxes, provide social safety nets, protect the environment and guarantee internal security.

But for a peek into the deep uncertainties of the 21st century and the astounding array of forces now undermining the nation-states, this conference was a remarkable tour de force.

Leading the parade of transformative change are globalization and its accomplices. The computer and telecommunications revolutions enable instant worldwide communications to create new relationships, new economics, whether central governments like them or not.

Multinational corporations now assemble goods from plants across the globe and have moved heavily into services, too—law, accounting, advertising, computer consultation—as if the world were borderless.

Financial markets are also globalized. Where nation-states once sought to set exchange rates, private traders now control currency flows—at a scarcely believable level of $1.5 trillion a day.

The Global Information Age

Cellular phones are becoming available worldwide, enabling many in the world, who have never before made a phone call, to communicate instantly with others. The "wireless world" of cellular phones which use radio waves rather than installed lines is growing almost 50 percent yearly, allowing communication between rural areas in developing Global South countries and "wired" Global North countries, where connected telephone lines are already abundant. The globe is linked directly by more than 1 billion telephone lines and nearly that many cellular phone subscribers, and the number of mobile subscribers worldwide doubled every twenty months in the 1990s (*Vital Signs 2002*, 84). As might be expected in a globalized world, the volume of international communications has increased proportionately. "The death of distance as a determinant of the cost of communications will probably be the single most important economic force shaping society in the first half of the [twenty-first] century," according to the *Economist* (September 30, 1995, 5–6). "It will alter, in ways that are only dimly imaginable, decisions about where people live and work; concepts of national borders; patterns of international trade. Its effects will be as pervasive as those of the discovery of electricity."

The nation-states fatefully shrank their own power by creating supernational institutions such as the United Nations, World Trade Organization and World Bank. Each creates its own cadres of civil servants unaccountable to any single state.

Now comes a rise of influential, globally active non-governmental organizations—the NGOs—ranging from Greenpeace to Amnesty International to animal rights groups. They got official UN recognition at the Rio Earth Summit in 1992; now they're negotiating to get a voice in official UN deliberations. Yet the NGOs, like multinationals, are mostly based in Europe and North America, feeding off cutting-edge technology, setting new global standards without much accountability to anyone.

Globalization is creating immense wealth. Yet countries unwilling or unequipped to become technologically connected—many in Africa today, for example—face "marginalization," another word for isolation and poverty.

At the Salzburg sessions there was real unease about globalization—a fear that the world order now emerging would be too cruel, too amoral, too exclusive in its power-wielding.

Anil Saldanha, a corporate executive from India, gave voice to these concerns.

"Man is not well," Mr. Saldanha said. "He is going through a process of insularity—insecurity, fright, fear. He doesn't know what's thrust on him, he must cope. So we need to look inward, to express our individuality, spirituality. If we do not put a human face on globalization, bring humanity to the forefront, we may not have far to go."

A global market does not create a global community, another speaker commented.

Yet the conference made it clear that the erosion of the nation-state is not only coming from above, it's creeping up from below.

One force is the rise of subnational regions impatient with the bureaucracy and unresponsiveness of large national governments. Nimble city-states—the "Asian tigers" of Hong Kong, Taiwan and Singapore, for example—have been recent models of success. In 1970, four U.S. states had trade offices abroad. Now virtually all do and all have official standing in the World Trade Organization.

Ethnic, racial and religious groups grasping for power are perhaps an even greater pressure from below. The end of the Cold War untapped myriad ethnic nationalistic tensions.

Indeed, we may end up with more nation-states. The United Nations had 166 member "states" in 1991. It now has 185 [now 190], and it could one day end up with 400 or more, just because of ethnic divisions. But how many will be viable nations? And what does the developed world do about the collapse of countries worlds removed from its sleek globalization?

New hybrid structures—African, Asian or Latin American emulations of the European Union, for example—may be needed.

Perhaps we'll see forms of community as unknown now as the nation-state was when it burst on the scene in the 16th century.

SOURCE: Peirce (1997), 9.

Computers are another significant symbol of globalization. They are also its most potent agents. No area of the world and no arena of politics, economics, society, or culture is immune from the pervasive influence of computer technology. Even victims of ethnopolitical conflict and natural disasters in the most remote corners of the world are connected to others by the laptop computers that relief workers from the International Federation of Red Cross and Red Crescent Societies bring with them.

More than 200 million computers are in use today; more than 95 percent are personal computers (PCs), which have replaced the mainframes of yester-year. Their number is growing by the millions annually, propelled by miniaturization. Microprocessors in today's PCs are incredibly small and growing more powerful at a phenomenal rate. "Computers owe their growth and impact to a phenomenon dubbed Moore's Law (after Gordon Moore, the founder of Intel), which says that computing power and capacity double every eighteen months. This exponential growth has led to the digital revolution.

The freedom people enjoy with personal computers without government intervention is most apparent on the Internet. Individuals routinely "surf the Net" without constraints, creating a global, electronic web of people, ideas, and

■ **cyberspace**
metaphorical term used to
describe the global
electronic web of people,
ideas, and interactions on
the Internet, which is
unencumbered by the
borders of the geopolitical
world.

interactions—a **cyberspace**—unencumbered by state borders. The Internet was developed in the late 1960s at the initiative of the U.S. Department of Defense. Its intent was to enable scientists and engineers working on military contracts to share computers, resources, and ideas—the latter through e-mail messages sent electronically. Designed to survive a nuclear war, information was transmitted in small "packages" through different routes, making it difficult to eavesdrop on the data and messages sent.

The popularity of the Internet spread slowly through the academic world, which by the mid-1980s was its principal user. By 1994, commercial companies surpassed universities as the leading users of the Internet. Today it is the functional equivalent of the "information superhighway" telecommunications specialists have long anticipated and promised.

Use of the Internet has grown—fueled by the growth of personal computers in homes and businesses—from less than 100,000 Internet hosts in 1988 to more than 172 million hosts connecting 689 million people in 2002 (*U.S. News & World Report,* April 22, 2002, 69). Most experts estimate that the Internet will grow by at least 50 percent each year. The number of Web pages is increasing nine times faster than world population and Internet users are growing by more than a million each week (Aronson 2001, 545, 547). "Today, one of every twelve people goes online to get news, send e-mail, buy goods, or be entertained" (*Vital Signs 2002,* 82).

The Internet is an engine for the conduct of business and the transfer of capital through e-commerce across borders. That said, even though

> the Internet is perceived as being everywhere, all at once . . . geography matters in the networked world, and now more than ever. . . . Taking a look at where the Internet actually is [and] the answer is . . . in cities [because of] the rise of "server farms," also known as data centers or web hotels—vast warehouses that provide floor space, power and network connectivity for large numbers of computers, and which are located predominantly in urban areas. A typical example can be found in Santa Clara, just off California's Highway 101. It is run by Exodus Communications, a web-hosting firm which has nine server farms in Silicon Valley and another 35 around the world. . . . Most of the world's biggest websites live in buildings like this; Exodus hosts 49 of the top 100. (*Economist,* August 11, 2001, 18)

In this sense, although the entire world is being wired and connected, it is at different rates: Only one in five Internet users lives in the Global South (*Vital Signs 2002,* 82). Thus, geography still matters. The Internet has not liberated most countries and people from their technological dependence on the places where management of Web sites is located. Therefore, even if the Internet has made for the worldwide hypermobility of ideas and information, the so-called digital arms race has resulted in the concentration and control of intellectual property in the Global North in such international Internet bandwidth giants as the most-wired country in the world, Finland, and the globe's economic powerhouse, the United States. This is made especially evident with respect to global e-commerce, which raises concerns. "Something like three-quarters of all e-commerce currently takes place in the United States. The country also accounts for 90 percent of commercial websites. Given that the Internet is, by its very nature, global in reach, theses two facts raise a vital question about e-commerce for the rest of the world: is America in general, and are American websites in particular, inevitably going to dominate it?" (*Economist* February 26, 2000, 49).

Communication technologies are driving much of the globalization process and are the underlying force in the global race for knowledge in the twenty-first century's information age:

> Communications technology set this era of globalization apart from any other. The Internet, mobile phones, and satellite networks have shrunk space and time. Bringing together computers and communications unleashed an unprecedented explosion of ways to communicate at the start of the 1990s. Since then tremendous productivity gains, ever-falling costs and rapidly growing networks of computers have transformed the computing and communications sector. If the automobile industry had the same productivity growth, a car today would cost $3. (UNDP 1999, 57–58)

To some enthusiasts, the advantages of the communications revolution are, through globalization, a blessing for humanity. Far-reaching changes "as the communications revolution turns digital promises . . . to connect everything to everything else, are creating . . . a tremendous force for human development for all those connected—by providing information, enabling empowerment, and raising productivity" (UNDP 1999). "Enthusiasts see a sort of digital Utopia, not because everything is admirable, but because [the communications revolution] defies centralized authority" (*Economist*, July 1, 1995). Envisioning the information age and globalization as liberating, advocates for the promotion of globalization as a policy regard it as a leveling factor that allows small businesses to successfully compete in the global marketplace, empowering the globe's 28,750 nongovernmental organizations (NGOs) "using the network to fire up debates and rally instant responses, bringing a new lobbying power to previously silent voices on the global stage, [and] at the same time [fostering] closer community formation [by allowing] a diversity of voices and cultures to be aired" (UNDP 1999). The Internet expands information and communication in ways that threaten dictatorial governments' rule, as China discovered when it sought to muzzle Web networking by the Falun Gong religious movement.

Critics, on the other hand, complain that the growing electronic network has created a new global condition known as **virtuality.** Claude Moisy (1997) defines this as "the ability to create a fictitious world using one's computers." In such a world one can conceal one's true identity, which threatens to make the activities of international organized crime and terrorist groups easier, as illustrated by the global terrorist network Al Qaeda's use of computers to coordinate the destruction of the World Trade Center towers in New York on September 11, 2001.

Critics also warn that even as Internet use and commerce grow, the communications revolution is widening the gap between the rich and the poor, leading to the globalization of poverty and the destruction of local culture. They point to the probability that although computer technology and communication are agents of rapid globalization, these forces accentuate the already wide differences in countries' abilities to shape (and be shaped by) a computer-driven world. As shown in Figure 8.1 for example, the spread of the Internet is heavily concentrated in the Global North to a handful of newly industrialized economies, primarily in Asia. Thus the communication revolution through computer technology suggests the peril that globalization will be increasingly uneven, benefiting a few privileged countries while putting the rest at a great

■ **virtuality**
imagery created by computer technology of objects and phenomena that produces a fictitious picture of actual things, people, and experiences.

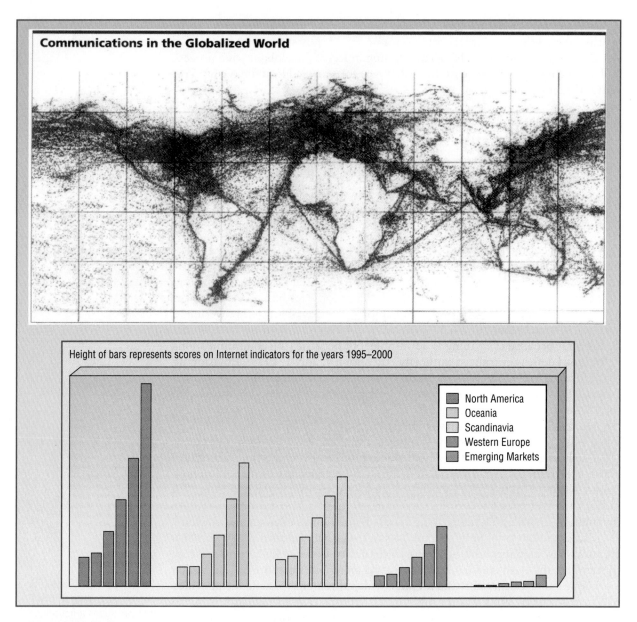

FIGURE 8.1
The Digital Divide

International communication is making a global village, but the rate at which information is transferring is uneven in different regions. The figure on the top taps the density with which communications occur in the world and captures what is meant by the so-called digital divide, the division of the technological "haves" in the Global North and the technological "have-nots" in the Global South. Note that the highest density of flows is shown in the darker shading across North America, Europe, and northeast Asia. Note also the figure on the bottom, which portrays the digital divide in an alternative manner, showing that with respect to Internet technology "the Web's reach within the developed world continues to dwarf its influence in developing countries. North America is 40 times more wired than the emerging markets [which] account for fewer that 20 percent of the world's Internet users and less than 5 percent of Internet hosts."

SOURCE: Flanagan, Frost, and Kugler, 2001, p. 24 (top); adapted from *Foreign Policy*, Jan./Feb. 2002, p. 50 (bottom). Used with permission.

disadvantage. For example, the doors to the communication revolution for small entrepreneurs in developing countries remain closed, creating a *digital divide* where one-third of the world's 6 billion people are denied access. The **digital divide** refers broadly to the access that people have to **information and communications technology (ICT).** The demographic, economic, and social patterns that explain the digital divide are not surprising. In the United States, for example, ICT access is greatest among young urban men in higher income groups. And because educational attainment is closely correlated with income and urban residence, level of education is the single most powerful determinant of ICT access and use.

At the Davos World Economic Forum in January 2001, the impact of communications technology was addressed, with the fears expressed that because the wealthy own more computers than the poor, the global village would divide itself into two classes, and these inequalities would grow. And there are good reasons for these fears. Consider the distribution and the number of Internet users, hosts, and secure servers. "Although emerging markets have seen Internet access grow at remarkable rates (on average twice the rate in the developed world in recent years), those same markets are still dwarfed by the industrialized countries. The Organization for Economic Cooperation and Development (OECD) estimates that 95.6 percent of the world's Internet hosts in 2000 were located in its member countries" (*Foreign Policy,* January/February 2002, 49). Hence, the so-called digital divide remains deep and wide. Yet the divide may close in the future because globalization has been more fierce in the spread of technology than originally thought, and "falling prices and skill requirements suggest that the digital divide would spontaneously shrink—and so it has [because] many computer skills aren't especially high-tech or demanding" as programming has made each generation of new software easier to use, and the pace of development has grown faster and faster (Samuelson 2002a). This helps to explain why increasingly the volume of digital communications evident in the United States is being matched not only elsewhere in the technologically sophisticated Global North but also in the Global South. But because education and income are in short supply in the Global South, it also is not surprising that the global digital divide closely tracks the inverse of the global demographic divide (see Figure 8.1). The International Labor Organization in its *World Employment Report 2001 (www.ilo.org)* estimates that "barely six percent of the world's people have ever logged onto the Internet and eighty-five to ninety percent of them are in the industrialized countries." Much the same holds for other ICT access devices, which include personal computers, wired and wireless telephones, and other consumer electronics, such as televisions. But the digital divide is also explained both by the capacity (or incapacity) of the public and private sectors to provide financial assess to ICT services and by the cognitive processes education encourages, including an ability to process and evaluate the information that information and communications technologies offer.

ICT technologies hold great promise for many of the poorer countries of the world, since these technologies may permit the Global South to "leapfrog" technologies in which the Global North invested heavily as they developed economically. Wireless phones, for example, enjoy both popularity and promise in many developing countries, where the cost of stringing line from pole to pole for traditional wired phones is often prohibitive. But because the individual,

■ **digital divide**
the division between the Internet technology-rich Global North and the Global South in the proportion of Internet users and hosts.

■ **information and communications technology (ICT)**
the technological means through which information and communications are transferred, such as through the worldwide Web.

The Internet and the Export of Mass Culture throughout the Globe As the Internet has expanded throughout the globe, in a wired world local customs and culture are becoming lost as the same language and messages are communicated around the world at the same time. "Mass culture is now exported from all over to all over [producing] a global hall of mirrors in which we do not always know what originated where" (Pells 2000). "Consider the word 'O.K.' How often do you use it? How often do you hear others use it? O.K. has found its way into the local vernacular of a vast number of languages—so much so that it may be the only word you will understand if you travel to foreign countries. This is globalization in process. . . . We are becoming a soup of

social, economic, and geographic factors that have created and perpetuated the digital divide are complex, narrowing it will prove difficult. The Global North remains at present the primary beneficiary of the communications revolution. In particular "the United States, where the Internet was developed, continues to dominate this electronic network. About a third of all people online are American" (*Vital Signs 2002*, 82). Consequently, many other countries fear that America's technological and information edge will enable it to dominate the world.

The Media: Markets or Monopoly?

Ours is often described as the information age, but a remarkably large portion of the information we receive is controlled by a remarkably small number of media sources. In the United States, despite more than 25,000 media outlets, only "twenty-three corporations control most of the business in daily newspapers, magazines, television, books, and motion pictures" (Bagdikian 1992, 4). And as corporate America merges its media sources into ever larger and fewer units—as witnessed in Disney Corporation's buyout of the ABC broadcasting network, as well as Viacom's acquisition of the CBS broadcasting network and

Francois Guillot/AFP

culture, politics, society, race and language sloshed into a large melting pot labeled 'humanity'" (Leow 2002). The Internet is the primary vehicle for the homogenization of the world through globalization that is erasing traditional identities. Above left is one example: new technology in Moorea. On the right is another example: the EasyEverything Internet Café in Paris, a crowded Web bar that is jammed around the clock with eager customers passing information and ideas through e-mail around the world. As a sign of the times, EasyEverything and other Web bars are making plans for global expansion.

the giant spread of Verizon Communications—fewer and fewer corporate executives will control what Americans hear and see about the world around them. The world's population may become a captive audience to what a few telecommunication corporate giants choose to present as information. Although thousands of potential sources of information about politics, society, and culture are available, the influence of such media midgets is negligible compared to that of the giants. This gives the rich Global North and, in particular the United States, extraordinary power over the way people throughout the world think, structuring what they believe and how they view the world.

The media's impact on the global diffusion of Western culture is widely seen as influential, as the handful of news and information agencies operate like a giant circulatory system, pumping ideas, information, and ideals from the wealthy center to the remote periphery in the Global South. This global reach is nowhere more striking than in the fact that the Internet reaches all over the world. The media's power is also attributed to CNN (Cable News Network), the twenty-four-hour news channel beamed around the world, and MTV which has been called "one of the first global television channels [to give] rise to a global teenage culture linked through music" (Etheredge 1999). Indeed, the recent merger of giant telecommunications companies concentrates further the control of information in the hands of conglomerates. The January 2000 merger of America Online and Time Warner, for example, gives it enormous clout with financial resources one-fourth larger than the annual budget of France (*Harper's,* March 2000, 19). What Global South opponents of globalization complain about is not so much modernization and trade; rather, they oppose "corporate globalization" dictated by MNCs which, they contend, ignores the values and needs of the vast majority in the developing world.

The type of power the media wields over international affairs is, in fact, a specific and limited type of power. Scholarship shows that the media influence what people *think about* more than what they *think*. In this way, the media primarily functions to *set the agenda* of public discussion about public affairs instead of determining public opinion. In the process of **agenda setting** the media demonstrably shape international public policy. For example, global broadcasts of violence and repression in Kosovo were often viewed as a cause of NATO's military intervention in 1999. This example of the positive contribution of information technology to international peacekeeping aside, some people caution that this kind of "virtual diplomacy," possible because of the development of a "global brain" circulating common information through 1,700 communication satellites weaving an information web around the globe (J. Peterson 1999), has real limitations. One critic has described the impact of CNN and the media this way:

> In foreign policy circles these days one often hears that the advent of instantaneous and global technology has given the news media far greater influence in international relations than ever before, robbing diplomacy of its rightful place at the helm in the process. Observers of international affairs call it the CNN curve. . . . It suggests that when CNN floods the airwaves with news of a foreign crisis, it evokes an emotional outcry from the public to "do something." Under the spell of the CNN curve, goes this refrain, policymakers have no choice but to redirect their attention to the crisis at hand or risk unpopularity, whether or not such revision is merited by policy considerations. (Neuman 1995–1996, 109)

Control of television and other media sources by the United States and a small number of European countries became the focus of hot dispute with the Global South during the 1980s. Dissatisfied with the media coverage it received from Global North news agencies and resentful of G-8 domination of other forms of communication, Global South leaders demanded a **New World Information and Communication Order (NWICO)** to create a new regime with fair rules to right the imbalance of the information flows from North to South. The image of the South painted by such sources, they believed, fostered Northern values, such as consumerism and conspicuous consumption, that perpetuated the South's dependence on the North. As the North-South conflict brewed, the United States angrily withdrew from the United Nations Educational, Scientific, and Cultural Organization (UNESCO), in part as a rejection of its role in promoting the new communications order. (In September 2002, in an effort to galvanize multilateral support for a preemptive war against Iraq, the U.S. announced that it would rejoin UNESCO.).

The NWICO has since receded on the global agenda, but the issues remain very much alive in NGOs concerned about the concentration of so much media power in so few hands. In 1995, Hollywood was able to beam the Academy

■ agenda setting
the thesis that by their ability to identify and publicize issues, the communications media determine the problems that receive attention by governments and international organizations.

■ New World Information and Communication Order (NWICO)
the controversial 1980 call by the less-developed Global South to combat what was termed "cultural imperialism" by circumscribing the news and information disseminated by the Western transnational news agencies.

Awards around the world to over a billion people, and American evangelist Billy Graham preached via electronic links to a similar number in over 185 countries. The new global information infrastructure is "especially disturbing because dominance in 'global' products implies not just the ability to ship products around the world, but dominance in cultural exports. This dominance provides the potential to displace indigenous culture with a tide of largely Western, largely consumerist, global conformity. Perhaps globalization is just a nice word that multinational corporations use to hide their efforts to infect the entire world with the cultural virus of commercialism" (Mowlana 1995).

Whatever its true character, the nearly $800 billion global telecommunications industry is without question the major vehicle for the rapid spread of ideas, information, and images worldwide. It also plays a role in the transfer of institutions and generation of income, as exhibited by the World Trade Organization's (WTO) World Telecom Pact. Issued by more than sixty countries, the accord to open the industry to the free market creates a new regime that ends government and private telecommunication monopolies in many states and has pumped new funds into the global economy by slashing phone costs to consumers and creating countless jobs. Estimating that liberalization could add $1 trillion, or 4 percent, to the value of world economic output over the next decade, WTO Director-General Renato Ruggiero in 1997 proclaimed that the accord "is good news for the international economy, it is good news for businesses and it is good news for the ordinary people around the world." That prediction proved to be on the mark. The WTO agreement on basic telecommunications services generated immediate results that exceeded expectations in four areas:

> Market access, the adoption of regulatory principles, liberalization of foreign investment rules, and satellite offers. Market access soared. Fifty-nine countries agreed to adopt transparent, pro-competitive regulatory principles, representing 99 percent of the WTO telecommunications market. Forty-four countries agreed to permit significant inward foreign investment. Fifty countries guaranteed market access for all domestic and international satellite services and facilities. (Aronson 2001, 543)

The success of the **regime** suggested the benefits perceived to result from international cooperation to conduct global transactions by rules. Advocates see global telecommunications as a vehicle for progress, liberating minds, expanding choices, penetrating societies closed to diplomatic communication, and creating a single, more united, homogenized global culture. Others disagree, however. They note that the airwaves can broadcast divisive messages as well as unifying ones, and that what is said is more important than how much is said.

One counterpoint to the "McWorld" of transnational media consumerism is "Jihad"—a world driven by "parochial hatreds," not "universalizing markets" (Barber 1995). In this context, it is sobering to note that the Ayatollah Khomeini, author of the revival of Islamic fundamentalism that swept the shah of Iran from power in 1979, "combined his access to networks of mosques and bazaars with that of electronic communication and cassette tapes" to carry on a successful long-distance bid to create an Iranian theocracy (Mowlana 1995).

Hence, because globalized communications and information may be used as tools for conflict and revolution as well as for community and peace, the creation of "a world without boundaries where everybody will know everything

■ **regime**
the rules agreed to by states to regulate their exchanges.

about everybody else" may not necessarily be a better world (Moisy 1997). We must ask, would the world be better or worse if it were to become an increasingly impersonal place, with "rootless, atomistic individuals floating free of any ties to society, . . . a world without ties of history, language, culture and kinship, in which it is costless for people and objects to move around?" (*Economist*, September 20, 1997, 29).

Global Health or Global Infection?

Humankind and the threat of disease have always coexisted uneasily. In the early 1990s, for example, in Kikwit, Zaire, the deadly Ebola virus—after lying dormant for twenty years—broke out and ravaged its victims with massive hemorrhaging and certain death. Globalization not only heightens awareness of health risks, but actually multiplies them. Truck drivers in India are primary agents for the AIDS (acquired immune deficiency syndrome) epidemic in that country and elsewhere in Asia. Rapid urbanization in much of the world also contributes to the rapid spread of diseases. Growing numbers of refugees forced into unsanitary camps are ravaged by cholera and other diseases that can prove as deadly as the violence and terrorism they flee. Excessive population growth forces people to move into habitats where unknown microorganisms and killer viruses await them. Millions of airline travelers share cabin-sealed environments filled with the carriers of potentially fatal diseases. A shrinking globe, in short, has made the spread of disease across borders rapid, frequent, and difficult to control:

> It is somewhat ironic that, in the face of an ongoing biomedical revolution, traditional diseases are making a comeback and new microbes are evolving to challenge human immune systems. The World Health Organization estimates that one-quarter of the world's population is subject to chronic intestinal parasitic infections. Of the nearly twenty million annual deaths due to communicable diseases, resurgent tuberculosis kills three million people annually, malaria two million, and hepatitis one million. (Pirages 1998, 393)

The AIDS virus has become a symbol for the global spread of disease in a shrinking world. It is an epidemic, global in scope, with the number of people infected with HIV—the virus that causes AIDS—climbing to more than an estimated 60 million people. The number is expected to continue to rise even though new public health measures have begun to slow the growth rate in the Global North. AIDS strikes most virulently in the impoverished Global South among youthful wage earners who are the foundation of the labor force, but it undermines economic growth everywhere on the planet. The human toll from AIDS-related disease has been most severe in Sub-Saharan Africa, where the devastating disease accounts for three-quarters of the globe's HIV infections and is the leading cause of death, cutting life expectancy almost in half. The virus is not confined to any quarter of the globe, however; it travels across borders and throughout the world (alongside the increase in travel throughout the world).

Adding to the challenge of preventing international infectious diseases beyond HIV/AIDS is another problem brought on by rising globalization: "As a result of underuse of antibiotics in the developing world and overuse in the developed world, viruses are developing stronger strains that are able to overcome standard antibiotics. A report by the World Health Organization indicates that 'almost all infection diseases are slowly but surely becoming resistant to existing medicines.' . . . Acute respiratory infections such as pneumonia kill a million more people each year than does AIDS. Diarrheal diseases, tuberculosis, malaria, and measles combined with AIDS and respiratory infections account for 90 percent of total infectious disease deaths worldwide" (Gilman and Gejdenson 2000, 6). And humans are not the only victims of so-called borderless diseases, as was made evident in 2001 when the contagious foot-and-mouth disease swept through Europe and Europeans desperately tried to seal their frontiers to a virus that spread with frightening speed, devastating livestock. As they pitched battle over how to respond, many noted that such epidemics in the European Union were increasingly difficult to contain because borders between countries had all but dissolved and it had been years since anybody needed a passport to travel between most European countries.

Another unfortunate product of globalization has been the spread of diseases throughout the globe that are causing massive ecological destruction to the environment. As the World Conservation Union (an NGO that includes more than 78 states and over 10,000 scientists) warns, alien animal, plant and insect invaders that cross national borders are doing irreparable damage to thousands of native species and, in the process, creating an enormous problem for the planet's environment and public health. In May 2001 the union used World Biodiversity Day to heighten awareness of the threat posed by this invasion, which it labeled "among the costliest and least understood aspects of globalization," proclaiming

> If this were an invasion from space, governments would be alarmed. But these are not extraterrestrials. They are ordinary animals, plants and insects that have escaped from their normal environment to wreak havoc someplace else.
>
> Consider these examples:
>
> - A poisonous brown tree snake from Australia and Indonesia has exterminated most of the native forest birds on Guam and is spreading across the Pacific, sometimes by hopping a ride in the wheel well of aircraft.
> - The Indian mongoose was introduced to the West Indies to control rats, but it has wiped out many native species of birds, reptiles and amphibians. It also carries rabies.
> - Crazy ants, proliferating in Asia, are indirectly destroying the rain forest on Christmas Island by exterminating land crabs that play an important role in the ecosystem. In one 18-month period, the ants were estimated to have killed three million crabs.
>
> Globalization is dramatically increasing the opportunities for plants and animals to get from where they form a normal part of the flora and fauna to other places where they can become destructive pests, weeds and parasites, either because people deliberately introduce new species such as exotic fish and plants, or because the invaders slip in aboard aircraft, ships and containers. (James 2001a, 1)

The globalization of health concerns is limited only by the extent to which contageous diseases, viruses, and infections respect state boundaries—which they don't. The world is too interconnected to isolate these threats to health in any location. Other kinds of communicative health problems cross national borders with increasing ease.

Consider the effect of narcotics. Many view narcotic use as a disease. The illicit use of drugs is widespread, hugely profitable, and difficult to control in a borderless world. Fueled by major production and distribution complexes in the Andes and southwest and southeast Asia, the narcotics industry generates profits estimated at $400 billion annually (Mathews 1997, 57). As profits have grown, traffickers' power has expanded, leading to other worrisome developments. Among them are "the [widening] impact of the illicit drug trade on illegal economic structures and processes in major producing or transit countries; the increasing political corruption in such countries; the growing intrusion of narcocriminal enterprises into the realm of the state and the law . . . ; the successes of narcotics businesses in innovation, avoiding detection, and increasing operating efficiency; and . . . the growing transnational cooperation among criminal empires that deal in drugs and other black-market items" (Lee 1995). **International organized crime (IOC)** syndicates have profited enormously by the opportunities created by globalization.

Global Migration

The movement of populations across frontiers has reached unprecedented proportions, producing a **global migration crisis.** Nearly 20 million people in each year from 1998 to 2002 qualified for and received refugee assistance. As floods of people leave their homeland for another country each year, the crossnational movement has become a norm—so common that leaving one's native country has become almost an expectation. "The ease of travel and communication, combined with looser borders, gives rise to endless crisscrossing streams of wanderers and guest workers, nomadic adventures, and international drifters" (Hoffman 2000). Global travel and emigration have become routine in the global age. But the mass movement of people living abroad has raised a host of moral issues, such as the ethnic balance inside host countries, the meaning of citizenship and sovereignty, the distribution of income, labor supply, xenophobia, the impact of multiculturalism, protection of basic human rights and prevention of exploitation, and the potential for large flows of migrants and refugees from **failed states** to undermine democratic governance and state stability (see Chapter 7). Particularly troubling is the moral inconsistency between liberal democracies that simultaneously defend the fundamental right of refugees to emigrate and the absolute right of sovereign states to control their borders.

As "national sovereignty is eroded from above by the mobility of capital, goods, and information across national boundaries" (Sandel 1996), whether existing institutions of global governance are able to cope with globalization's multiple challenges is a hotly contested issue. Meanwhile, the capacity of the state to cope with the forces of rapid change is also being tested. As we turn our attention to the globalization of finance, trade, and production, we will find further evidence that "globalization is uneven. It unites but it also divides, creating winners here and losers there." And in an anarchical international political system, "there is no global civil society that can be called on to support global governance" (Sørensen 1995). Like politics and markets, then, politics and the process of globalization are intimately intertwined, as "even the most powerful

■ **international organized crime (IOC)**
crime syndicates specializing in the use of technology to cooperatively network with each other throughout the world.

■ **global migration crisis**
a crisis stemming from the growing number of people moving from their home country to another country, straining the ability of the host countries to absorb the foreign migrants.

■ **failed states**
countries whose governments no longer enjoy support from their rebelling citizens and from displaced peoples who either flee the country or organize revolts to disintegrate the state into smaller independent units (see p. 242).

states cannot escape the imperatives of the global economy" (Sandel 1996). Meanwhile, realization of truly civic-spirited community in the global village remains elusive.

THE GLOBALIZATION OF FINANCE

Global finance encompasses "all types of cross-border portfolio-type transactions—borrowing and lending, trading of currencies or other monetary claims, and the provision of commercial banking or other financial services. It also includes capital flows associated with foreign direct investment—transactions involving significant control of producing enterprises" (Cohen 1996). The **globalization of finance** refers to the increasing transnationalization or centralization of financial markets through the worldwide integration of capital flows. The central characteristic of the emerging consolidated system of financial arrangements is that it is not centered on a single state. Thus globalization implies the growth of a single, unified world market. While telecommunications specialists talk about the "death of distance," financial specialists talk about the "end of geography," which "refers to a state of economic development where geographic location no longer matters in finance" (O'Brien 1992).

> ■ **globalization of finance**
> the increasing transnationalization of financial markets.

Evidence of financial globalization abounds. Although trade has grown dramatically. Since World War II, the volume of cross-border capital flows has increased even more. Financial flows now greatly exceed the volume of trade, and the gap continues to widen. Similarly, cross-border transactions in bonds and equities have increased at an astonishing rate over the past twenty years. In the mid-1990s, "$1,300 billion (roughly the equivalent of the French annual GNP) were being exchanged daily, compared to $18 billion at the beginning of the 1970s" (Pfetsch 1999, 3). "Each day well over a trillion dollars flows around the world, exceeding the volume of trade by 60 times" (Eizenstat 1999, 6).

Further evidence of financial globalization is the astonishing recent increases in the daily turnover on the foreign exchange market. On many days, private currency traders may exchange as much as $2 trillion to make profits through **arbitrage** on the basis of minute shifts in the value of states' currencies, and their activity continues to climb steadily. Consequently, interconnected markets require more than ever a reliable system of money to conduct business across borders while coping with an array of fluctuating national currencies. "It has become a well-known fact that the daily turnover on the currency markets now often exceeds the global stock of official foreign exchange reserves—so what chance have central banks in influencing exchange rates by buying and selling currency in the markets?" (*Economist*, September 10, 1997).

> ■ **arbitrage**
> the selling of one currency (or product) and purchase of another to make a profit on the changing exchange rates; traders ("arbitragers") help to keep states' currencies in balance through their speculative efforts to buy large quantities of devalued currencies and sell them in countries where they are valued more highly.

As the transnational economy becomes integrated, "most national central banks are now irrelevant [because] the world's money is essentially controlled by three key institutions: the U.S. Federal Reserve Board, the Bank of Japan, and the German Bundesbank, and global capital markets centered in London, Tokyo, and New York are facilitating increased internationalization in every area of finance. As the market value of stock transactions increased fourfold between 1980 and 2002, a major change occurred: a rise or fall in the security market of any one state began to immediately cause similar changes in other

■ **digital world economy**
a system based largely on globalized electronic debt and credit systems.

■ **commercial liberalism**
an economic theory advocating free markets and the removal of barriers to the flow of trade and capital as a locomotive for prosperity (see p. 306).

■ **capital mobility hypothesis**
the proposition that MNCs' movement of investment capital has led to the globalization of finance.

■ **realist theory**
the view that states are sovereign, unitary global actors in relentless competition with each other for position and prosperity in the international hierarchy, able to engineer policies to promote their own interests and to control conditions within their borders.

countries' stock indexes. In addition, "derivatives" emerged leading to new markets in which stocks are traded. Derivatives combine speculation in options and futures to hedge against volatility in financial markets, but they require no actual purchase of stocks or bonds. Derivatives now account for trillions of dollars in crossborder transactions and are now estimated to be the most globalized financial market. Automated online trading for equity sales on the Internet in the emerging **digital world economy** has lowered the costs and increased the volume of such crossborder exchanges.

The computerization of financial transactions and contracts occurred at the same time that, since the 1970s, **commercial liberalism** and its advocacy of state deregulation of global investments and capital movements gained acceptance. States reduced their authority by relaxing their legal control over their economies and by opening their markets to foreign capital.

The predictable result of financial liberalization has been great increases in capital mobility—an exploding expansion of international financial transactions. According to the **capital mobility hypothesis,** the free or unregulated flow of money across borders has produced the globalization of finance.

Because the accelerating mobility of capital means that financial markets are no longer centered within states, the globalized financial system is not subject to regulation by any one state in particular. Most states are losing their grip on their capacity to control the flow and level of finance in their national economies. The globalization of finance has expanded the power of private markets and corporations no longer tied to any one country "thereby increasingly undermining state power itself and institutionalizing that of the global marketplace. . . . Having set up the conditions in which more open international financial markets were established in the 1970s and 1980s, [states] are now having difficulty controlling their own creations" (Cerny 1994). As the globalization of finance has accelerated, the escalating mobility of capital has undermined the assumption of **realist theory** that states are autonomous, unitary actors capable of regulating their internal economic affairs. Globalization limits "the ability of governments to restrict—or even control—economic activity" (Thurow 1998).

The lightning speed of capital mobility has made national markets extremely volatile, and vulnerable to sudden reversals caused by their dependence on foreign capital and the rapid flight of capital at the first sign of economic trouble. Capital mobility is at historically high levels (inspect Map 8.1, which in the figure on the right provides a profile of this global trend). As Map 8.1 shows, capital mobility has some unintended consequences, affecting the developing countries of the Global South negatively, because the flow of capital has declined as the globalization of finance has risen. "Today's capital transactions seem to be 'mostly a rich-rich affair,' a process of 'diversification of finance' rather than 'development finance,' [note economists Maurice Obstfeld and Alan Taylor]. Compared with the previous peak of global capital, the amount of money flowing to poorer countries is already small [even though] the less developed countries' share of total debt is at an all-time low. . . . In 1913, the countries at the bottom fifth of income per person received around 25 percent of the world stock of foreign capital, much the same way as the countries in the richest fifth. By 1997, the poorest fifth's share was down to under 5 percent, compared with 36 percent for the richest fifth" (*Economist* May 18, 2002, 27).

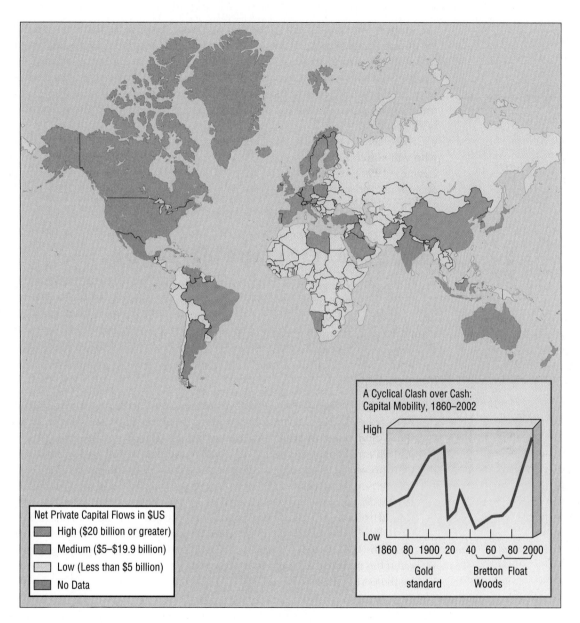

MAP 8.1
The International Flow of Finance Capital

Capital flows internationally through loans by commercial banks and private creditors and through foreign direct investments (FDI) in businesses located in countries different from those of the investors. The movement of capital across borders since the 1950s has expanded as shown in the figure (right) on transformations in capital mobility since 1860. In the globalized political economy the bulk of the money now lands in the rich Global North, and the forty-nine poorest Global South countries receive only 0.5 percent of the total even though their inflows have risen nearly ninefold since 1990 (*Economist*, May 19, 2001, 104). Note that, as we might expect, the wealthy Global North countries exert a disproportionate influence over the global flow of capital.

SOURCE: *Capital mobility figure—From *The Economist*, May 18, 2000, p. 27. Copyright © 2000 by The Economist Newspaper Ltd. All rights reserved. Reprinted with permission. Further reproduction prohibited. www.economist.com

Hence, the globalization of finance and "capital flight" has resulted in mounting inequalities. True, all countries are mutually vulnerable to rapid transfers of capital in an interdependent, globalized financial world. But the Global South is the most dependent and vulnerable. This circumstance suggests why bankers and economists have called for the creation of more reliable multilateral mechanisms for policy coordination to manage the massive cross-border capital.

"The near-instant flow of funds determines who, if anyone, will prosper and who will suffer, and this power holds poor nations at its mercy," warns Robert A. Levine (1999), who predicts that "The interaction between disintegrative economies and starving people and the self-interested rich states will be explosive."

THE GLOBALIZATION OF TRADE

Technological changes have led to the integration of states' economic markets. However, the extraordinary pace at which the countries of the world have linked their markets can be attributed to more than the increased speed of transport and communication. The organization of markets at a global level, and the convergence of commodity prices across countries, have been driven by the worldwide reduction of tariff rates that has made the expansion of international trade possible.

> After World War II, the General Agreement on Tariffs and Trade (GATT) was created by the international community, along with the IMF, the World Bank, and other international organizations. Based on the principles of multilateral cooperation, the GATT had a mandate to roll back tariffs from their prewar peaks and to continue reducing them in the future. The GATT was extremely successful in 1947 in the first Geneva Round in reducing tariffs by 35 percent. Successive rounds in the 1950s, 1960s (the Kennedy Round), and the 1970s (Tokyo Round) and the recent Uruguay Round have virtually eliminated tariffs on manufactured goods. The World Trade Organization (WTO), which succeeded GATT in 1994, is currently engaged in reducing nontariff barriers and protection, including in areas not covered by the GATT. (IMF 1997, 113)

The WTO has enlarged its membership, and the 145 countries that have agreed to adhere to its free-trade rules are spread across the globe, with other applicants eagerly seeking entry (see Map 8.2). If and when this expansion process is complete, the globalization of trade will escalate even further and faster.

In historical perspective, the globalization of trade serves as testimony to the wisdom of commercial liberalism, which held that trade liberalization to remove barriers to exports would permit the free trade crucial to growing prosperity. That theory has been supported by experience. The reduction of tariff rates since World War II (see Chapter 9) has permitted international trade and world output to grow hand in hand. "In the half-century since the founding of the **General Agreement on Tariffs and Trade (GATT),** the world economy has grown six-fold, in part because trade has expanded 16-fold" (Micklethwait and Wooldrige 2001, 22). The expansion of global trade, and with it global welfare, is expected to continue, especially if and when the U.S. economy recovers from

■ **General Agreement on Tariffs and Trade (GATT)**
an international organization affiliated with the United Nations that promotes international trade and tariff reductions.

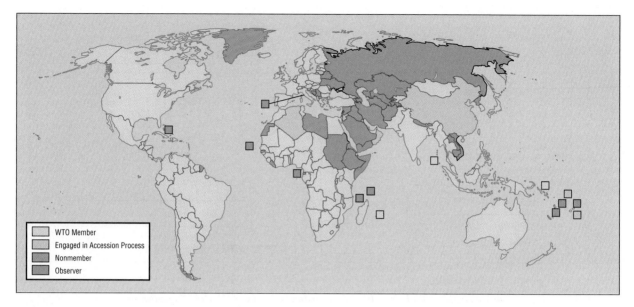

MAP 8.2
The World Trade Organization Goes Global

As of the end of 2002, almost every state has become a member of the World Trade Organization, whose purpose is to promote free trade throughout the globe. One hundred forty-five countries are now official members; 29 additional countries are "observers" who must begin accession negotiations within five years if they are to gain formal membership. If and when these states join, the volume of international trade will climb, contributing further to the integration of the world marketplace. Why states seek to join the WTO is a puzzle to those who see it as undermining states' sovereign independence. But they overlook the fact that by its rules the WTO is an intergovernmental rather than supranational IGO ruled by consensus. As the WTO is fond of saying, far from being antidemocratic it is "hyperdemocratic," because each and every one of the WTOs has a veto over the rules. The WTO acts as a mere referee when members face trade disputes. In addition, the WTO has few resources. With a staff of only 530 and a budget of $78 million (about one-half of what the World Bank spends on travel), the WTO is a midget in the world of nonstate actors. As WTO Director Mike Moore pointed out in 2001, the World Wildlife Fund has three times the financial budget of the WTO.
SOURCE: World Trade Organization.

the post-9/11 fears of recession fueled by rising U.S. debts to finance America's global war on terrorism and America resumes its role as the engine of global economic growth. In Chapter 9 we will examine the dynamics underlying transformations in the world economy. Here we focus attention on the primary product—the rising globalization of trade interdependence.

In 1950, exports accounted for 8 percent of worldwide GDP, and a half-century later they more than tripled. The impact of the rising volume of goods shipped from one country to another has been enormous, pushing economic growth to unprecedented levels. International trade has become increasingly important to all states, especially those which in the past were not very concerned about exports. Now every state has become increasingly dependent on

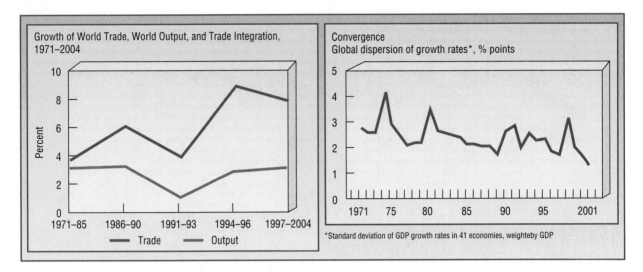

FIGURE 8.2
Trends in Global Trade Integration and the Mutual Interdependence of States' Economies

World economic transactions are more globalized than ever before, and the level of interdependence is growing at an accelerating rate. As the index of trends in world trade integration between 1971 and 2004 on the left shows, global trade has outpaced the rate of world output. The figure on the right measures the "convergence" of countries' economic fortunes, showing the growing extent to which growth rates across countries are tied to one another—"hit simultaneously by common global shocks. Different economies' business cycles are becoming more closely correlated over time [because] increased trade causes economies to move more closely in step [so that] increasing globalization could lead to bigger economic booms and busts" (*Economist* September 28, 2002).

SOURCE: Trade integration From *Global Trends 2005* by Michael J. Mazarr p. 160. Copyright © Michael J. Mazarr. Reprinted with permission of Palgrave Macmillan. Economic interdependence, from *The Economist*, Sept. 28, 2002. Copyright © 2002 by The Economist Newspaper Ltd. Reprinted with permission. Further reproduction prohibited. www.economist.com

---

exports for economic growth and aggressively compete with other countries for a share of the growing international trade market. This has made states interdependent—the key defining characteristic of globalization.

Trade integration is the measure of the extent to which the growth rate in world trade increases faster than does the growth rate of world gross domestic product. As trade integration grows, so does globalization, because states' interdependence grows when countries' exports account for an increasing percentage of their gross domestic product. As Michael Mazarr (1999) explains, "Measuring global trade as a percentage of GDP is perhaps the simplest and most straightforward measure of globalization. If trade in goods and merchandise is growing faster that the world economy as a whole, then it is becoming more integrated."

Figure 8.2 documents the remarkable speed at which trade integration has accelerated between 1971 and 2004. Countries have become increasingly interdependent, and the world increasingly globalized, because world trade has far outpaced growth in the world economy (and in world population as well). The increasing dependence of states' economies on exports knits a globalized world together in a tight web of interdependence. The globalization of trade means that states' prosperity depends increasingly on other states willingness to import their manufactured goods.

■ **trade integration**
economic globalization measured by the extent to which world trade volume grows faster than the globe's combined gross domestic product.

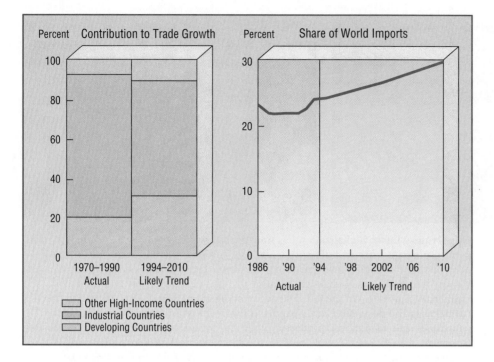

FIGURE 8.3
The Global South in World Trade
In recent years, international trade has grown more rapidly than the production of goods and services. The Global South's contribution to world trade growth and its rising share of world imports reveal its growing importance to the world political economy.
SOURCE: World Bank (1995a), 58; UNDP (1999), 26.

Countries differ in the degree to which their economies become integrated through trade in the global political economy. It is important to note that the pace of trade integration has been higher in the Global South than in the Global North, reflecting the less-developed Global South's increasing contribution to world trade—a trend expected to continue (see Figure 8.3). This also means that the Global South is becoming increasingly important to growing economic prosperity in the Global North. Some Global South countries' imports matter more than others, inasmuch as differences exist in the extent to which Global South countries are participants in the global marketplace.

"The global economy created in the 1990s by the spread of markets . . . and more open trade have yet to prove that it distributes its fruits more evenly: the rich still get richer and the poor get poorer—only faster" (Hoagland 1999b). The differences among these groups reflect their historical experiences and the different strategies of development each has chosen (see Chapter 6). They also reflect changes in technology and consumer demands in a global economy. High-technology electronic goods (i.e., data-processing equipment, telecommunications equipment, and semiconductors and microprocessors) make up an increasing proportion of trade in manufactured goods. Here, the twenty-eight advanced Global North economies have cornered the

Douglas Engle/AP/Wide World

Eraldo Peres/AP/Wide World

Opportunity Lost? Globalization has transformed world production and employment patterns, moving both manufacturing and jobs across borders in response to MNCs' perceptions of changing investment opportunities. These changes have provoked various responses, many negative, because change frightens people and threatens established interests. On the left, Fiat automobiles manufactured by the Italian-based carmaker in Rio de Janeiro await export to Europe. Fiat is one of many European companies that have moved production to Brazil, whose economy leads the Mercosur free-trade bloc. The rich countries in the Global North fear that manufacturing is passing into the hands of the poor Global South countries where production is inexpensive and some are lobbying against globalization. Globalization often wreaks havoc on local economies and leads to protests against the economic volatility it engenders, as shown at right in Brazil.

market as the major suppliers, accounting for nearly two-thirds of world exports in goods and services (World Bank 2002b, 238–239). The United States and Japan lead the pack, followed by the European Union (EU) countries. However, globalization has altered these patterns, creating new winners in the creation of new products and in their command of the market.

As noted, the Global South's share of global trade has grown (from 23 percent in 1985 to 28 percent in 2002) and is projected to expand in the future. The developing countries' share of global exports in manufactured products has also grown (increasing from 10 percent in 1980 to 27 percent in 2002. In this context the Global South's growth in the share of *new* products for exports is especially impressive; as a result of recent industrialization, the **newly industrialized economies (NIEs)** of the Global South have cornered about one-fifth of that portion of global trade (World Bank 2002b). Asia has taken the lead in developing new products; the three Asian tigers and the new "cubs"—Malaysia, Thailand, and India—account for almost two-thirds of this new export trade. Asian NIEs have been winners.

Trade in services also promises to make new winners. Because the United States enjoys comparative advantages in this area, it has been a strong advocate of brining services under the liberalizing rules of the WTO. Trade in services has already expanded more than threefold since 1980, with the Global North reaping most of the benefits, even though the Global South has increased its share of this growing trade even more rapidly. The spread of information technology and the comparatively lower wage costs in developing economies are among

■ **newly industrialized economies (NIEs)**
states such as Singapore and South Korea that have successfully grown into advanced industrialized societies. As wealthy countries, they are now members of the Global North and competitive players in global trade and investments, no longer in need of development assistance (see p. 206).

the reasons why the World Bank predicts that developing countries will capture an increasing share of world trade in the first two decades of the twenty-first century. In the case of services, then, it appears that—at least for the time being—Global North and Global South will both reap the growing profits from the globalization of trade.

It would be terribly inaccurate to picture trade globalization as a panacea for poverty, however. It is not proving to be a path to wealth for many developing countries. Globalization "has changed the distribution of these gains from trade. There are clear winners and losers, both between and within countries. More trade with developing countries hurts low-skilled workers while simultaneously increasing the incomes of more highly skilled workers" (Held et al., 1999). A backlash to these growing inequalities has grown as many groups see themselves as victims of an integrated trade world (Broad 2002; Aaronson 2002). The Global South's poorer countries are not participating in the advantages that globalization is providing the winners. The losers, "poor countries and poor people," often find their interests neglected. The Controversy Box: Is Globalization Producing Prosperity or Poverty? frames the issues surrounding the painful costs of trade globalization for the Global South's poor countries. While the shares of global exports of the Asian NIEs and the rapidly industrialized economies have increased since the late 1960s, the shares of most of the other Global South developing countries have not increased and in some cases have declined. If globalization is to continue, as appears highly likely, then perhaps in the long run globalization's success will depend on large "transfers of capital, tangible and intangible alike" from the Global North to the Global South (Reinicke 1997).

From a management point of view, traditionally MNCs' overseas operations were "appendages" of a centralized hub. The aim today, however, is to dismantle the hub by dispersing production facilities worldwide. MNCs are replacing national corporations, because the sales of large companies are now geared to the global market and a large proportion of their revenues are generated from sales outside the countries where they are headquartered. The growing globalization of production is transforming the international political economy:

> Global exports may be more important than ever, but transnational production is now worth even more. To sell to another country, increasingly you have to move there; this is the main way to sell goods and services abroad. The multinational corporation has taken economic interdependence to new levels. Today, 53,000 multinational corporations and 450,000 foreign subsidiaries sell $9.5 trillion of goods and services across the globe every year. Multinational corporations account for at least 20 percent of world production and 70 percent of world trade. A quarter to a third of world trade is intrafirm trade between branches of multinationals. (Held et al., 1999, 135)

MNCs are now the primary agents in the globalization of production. By increasingly forming **strategic corporate alliances** with companies in the same industry, and by merging with one another at a frenzied pace, MNCs have become massive NGOs rivaling states in financial resources (see Table 5.2, p. 175). These global actors have grown in influence also because many MNC parent companies are now linked with each other in **virtual corporations** and alliances of coownership and coproduction. These corporate networks of MNCs pursue truly global strategies for financial gain, often through long-term

■ **strategic corporate alliances**
cooperation between MNCs and foreign companies in the same industry, driven by the movement of MNC manufacturing overseas (see p. 177).

■ **virtual corporations**
agreements between otherwise competitive MNCs, often temporary, to join forces and skills to coproduce and export particular products in the borderless global marketplace.

CONTROVERSY   IS GLOBALIZATION PRODUCING PROSPERITY OR POVERTY?

Many people recommend globalization as a form of international public policy, because they believe that its consequences are basically good for humankind. However, critics argue that globalization's costs far outweigh its benefits. In particular, a major controversy revolves around the question of whether globalization punishes countries and people who are already poor by actually increasing their poverty. Despite the evidence that half a century of increasing globalization has been associated with unprecedented growth and general prosperity, others argue that this property has come at the great expense of some people and regions. According to "anti-globalists," writes Paul Krugman (2000), "again and again you see the less attractive features of the modern world contrasted with an imagined pre-globalization Arcadia of happy villagers living in harmony with nature."

Examine the evidence presented in Chapter 6 on the Global South, Chapter 7 on income inequality, and in this chapter. What do you think? Has globalization led to the "stark disparities between rich and poor, . . . with the fifth of the world's people living in the highest income countries [getting] 8.6 percent of world GDP [and] the bottom fifth just 1 percent?" (UNDP 1999, 2)? Or, is poverty in the world due to other causes besides globalization? In evaluating your assessment, consider how the UN Development Program describes the characteristics of contemporary globalization and the issues it creates:

A dominant economic theme of the 1990s, globalization encapsulates both a description and a prescription. The description is the widening and deepening of international flows of trade, finance and information in a single, integrated global market. The prescription is to liberalize national and global markets in the belief that free flows of trade, finance and information will produce the best outcome for growth and human welfare. All is presented with an air of inevitability and overwhelming conviction. Not since the heyday of free trade in the nineteenth century has economic theory elicited such widespread certainty.

The principles of free global markets are nevertheless applied selectively. If this were not so, the global market for unskilled labor would be as free as the market for industrial country exports or capital. Global negotiations are moving rapidly toward a free world market in foreign investments and services. But intervention in agriculture and textiles, an obstacle to developing countries, remains high. Lacking power, poor countries and poor people too often find their interests neglected and undermined.

Globalization has its winners and its losers. With the expansion of trade and foreign investment, developing coun-

Trade as Aid to Help the Poor In April 2002 the aid agency Oxfam International launched an international "Make Trade Fair" campaign with a report on trade, globalization, and the fight against poverty entitled "Rigged Rules and Double Standards." Arguing that the United States and the European Union have betrayed their own free-trade principles by tilting the rules of the global trading system overwhelmingly to their advantage, Oxfam mounted this display in Hong Kong to urge fair trade rules for rich and poor countries alike, which Oxfam says can fight poverty better than aid or debt relief.

tries have seen the gaps among themselves widen. Meanwhile, in many industrial countries unemployment has soared to levels not seen since the 1930s, and income inequality to levels not recorded since the [nineteenth] century.

A rising tide of wealth is supposed to lift all boats. But some are more seaworthy than others. The yachts and ocean liners are indeed rising in response to new opportunities, but the rafts and rowboats are taking on water—and some are sinking fast.

Inequality is not inherent in globalization. Because liberalization exposes domestic producers to volatile global markets and to capital flows that are large relative to the economy, it increases risks—but it also increases potential rewards. For poverty eradication the challenge is to identify policies that enable poor people to participate in markets on more equitable terms, nationally and globally.

SOURCE: UNDP (1997), 82–83.

Frank Fournier/Contact

Child Labor in a Global System Globalization is sped not only by the rapid expansion of technology but by the availability of cheap labor in some countries, which take advantage of their peoples' low wages to make products highly competitive in the globalized marketplace. Here a child labors at near slave wages in Bangladesh, producing goods that cost less than those made where labor unions protect workers. Such practices have mercantilist nationalists and free-trade critics up in arms, even though open global markets encourage them.

supplier agreements and licensing and franchising contracts, both using MNCs' international alliances and joint foreign direct investment strategies; today "about 70 percent of world trade is intra-industry or inter-firm" (Reinicke 1997, 128). The outward flow of **foreign direct investment (FDI)** stock attributable to their more than 45,000 foreign affiliates has increased rapidly. As they funnel large financial flows across national borders, these global corporate conglomerates are integrating national economies into a single global market.

The impact of FDI on creating an interconnected global capital market extends beyond money. With it comes technology, managerial expertise, and most importantly now, employment opportunities. Jobs are desperately needed, and there exists in the age of globalization (and because of it?) a huge surplus of available labor. The lack of jobs is a worldwide problem, even in the Global North where so-called **underemployment** is widespread; the conditions are worse in the Global South, where the UN estimates that about one in six workers and one-third of the world's work force was unemployed or underemployed in 2001, and predicts that at least 500 million new jobs will be needed in the next decade to accommodate new arrivals on the job market.

MNCs' investments are seen as an attractive potential cure to unprecedented levels of unemployment (although it is widely recognized that the growth of trade will not automatically create more employment and better wages). Not surprisingly, many Global South countries now actively seek MNC investment capital and the other advantages they perceive will result from it, such as new

■ **foreign direct investment (FDI)** purchase of stock, property, or assets in another country, with a goal of long-term involvement in the economy of that country (see p. 176).

■ **underemployment** a condition critics trace to trade globalization in which a large portion of the labor force only works part-time at low pay in occupations below their skill level.

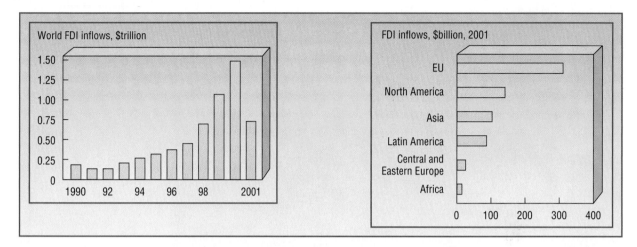

FIGURE 8.4

The Ebb and Flow of Foreign Investments, 1990–2001: Is Globalization a Global North Phenomenon?

Most foreign direct investment (FDI) is controlled by powerful multinational corporations, and their recent "urge to converge" to create monster transnational conglomerates has enhanced their economic clout. Through megamergers, the economic titans target their investments primarily toward the rich and large Global North markets in Europe and North America (figure on right). The figure on the left shows the annual average global level of FDI, in billions of dollars between 1990 and 2001, when it declined after reaching a record level in 2000. FDI is expected to resume its past brisk growth rate through the year 2006, as predicted by the International Monetary Fund.

SOURCE: *The Economist*, Sept. 21, 2002, p. 98. Copyright © 2002 by The Economist Newspaper Ltd. All rights reserved. Reprinted with permission. Further reproduction prohibited. www.economist. com

jobs (see Chapter 6). Global South countries pursue MNC investment as a way of emulating the economic success of the NIEs. Foreign capital is critical to this goal. In 1992, worldwide foreign direct investment was less than $175 billion; by 1998 it climbed to $643 billion, and in 2002 it exceeded $912 billion (Drezner 2002, 46; World Bank 2002b, 239). Most of this MNC investment in search of profit continues to flow into the Global North, and the MNCs headquartered there provide the primary source for the outward flow of FDI (see Figure 8.4).

The reason for the concentration of FDI in the Global North is self-interest: Profits are MNCs' primary motivation, and their investment returns are likely to be greatest in the Global North, where a combination of affluence and political stability reduces investment risks. Still, the Global South is the recipient of considerable and growing FDI. Although the amounts fluctuate yearly, at the start of the twenty-first century a growing number of developing countries were viewed as targets of investment opportunity, and inflows in 2002 totaled $185 billion (World Bank 2002b, 239).

Although MNCs are a key catalyst to trade integration and globalization, critics worry that MNGs have become too powerful for states to control:

Jeffrey Aaronson/Network Aspen

Trade Links Former Enemies The developing countries once shunned foreign investments, fearing their adverse economic and political consequences, but no longer. Even Vietnam, once a bitter communist enemy of the capitalistic United States, now welcomes American investment dollars.

The formidable power and mobility of global corporations are undermining the effectiveness of national governments to carry out essential policies on behalf of their people. Leaders of nation-states are losing much of the control over their own territory they once had. More and more, they must conform to the demands of the outside world because the outsiders are already inside the gates. Business enterprises that routinely operate across borders are linking far-flung pieces of territory into a new world economy that bypasses all sorts of established political arrangements and conventions. (Barnet and Cavanagh 1994, 19)

Nonetheless, some corporate visionaries extol the transnational virtues and the positive contribution they claim MNCs make by encouraging replacement of narrow nationalistic values with those of a truly global, cosmopolitarian culture. To the extent that this influence is operative, MNCs' globalization of production and investment will lead to the transfer of people's loyalties from individual countries to the world as a whole. By challenging "the operational sovereignty of a government, that is, its ability to exercise sovereignty in the daily affairs of politics" (Reinicke 1997), the globalization of production builds bridges across the **politics** that divides states—providing a common ground for people to cooperate. This would fulfill the humanist vision of international harmony resulting from acceptance of everyone's shared humanity and destiny. "There are no longer any national flag carriers," in the words of Kenichi Ohmae, a Japanese management consultant. "Corporations must serve their customers, not governments."

■ **politics**
the effort by actors to resolve controversial issues against the wishes of the other affected actors.

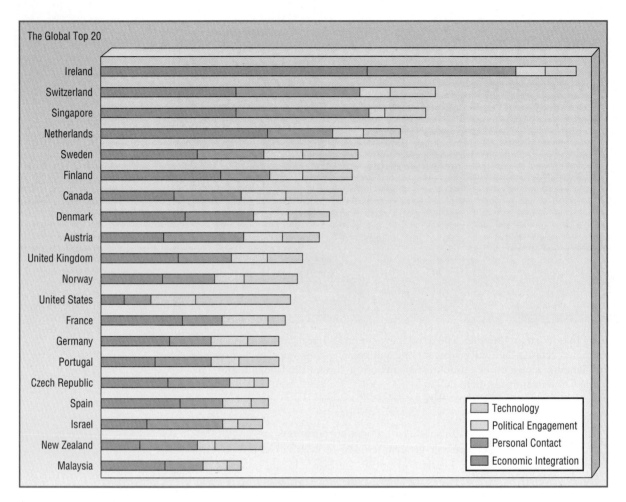

FIGURE 8.5
Levels of Globalization and the Degree of Satisfaction

There are various ways to measure the extent to which countries are integrated in the globalization of the world. These levels, of course, affect different countries differently, depending upon the degree to which each state is involved in the various dimensions of "globalization." The globalization index on the left calculates these levels yearly, in order to bring "globalization into sharper focus by assessing changes in its most important components, whether engagement in international relations and policymaking, trade and financial flows, or the movement of people, ideas, and information across borders" (*Foreign Policy* January/February 2002). This chart scales and ranks the global top 20 countries in 2002 on four measures. Globalization has slowed recently with the 9/11 terrorist attacks and economic recession, and "many of the countries that score high on the index are the ones most likely to bear the brunt of globalization's unwinding." At issue is whether globalization breeds happiness among the people living in countries that are the most globalized or integrated internationally. The survey (right) provides one estimate and shows that generally globalization tends to make people happy: "Countries that have a large portion of their population who describe themselves as 'happy' or 'very happy' and indicate a high degree of satisfaction with life also tend to be the most globally integrated countries" (*Foreign Policy*, January/February 2002).

SOURCE: A. T. Kearney/*Foreign Policy Magazine Globalization Index* (*Foreign Policy*, January/February 2002, 39, 29).

Globalization and Happiness

Globalization
Happiness

Peru Colombia Brazil Pakistan Turkey South Africa China Philippines Mexico India Bangladesh Argentina Ukraine Romania Russia Japan Chile Nigeria Taiwan South Korea Slovenia Poland Croatia Italy Hungary Slovakia Australia New Zealand Spain Czech Republic Portugal Germany* France United States Norway United Kingdom Austria Denmark Canada Finland Sweden Netherlands Switzerland Ireland

*World Values Survey data derived from former West Germany

GLOBALIZATION AND THE STATE: WHAT FUTURE?

Rapid globalization, fueled in large measure by technological revolutions, is likely to continue. Analysts differ on whether globalization is desirable or despicable, depending in part on the scenarios about the future world order that globalization will help create and the political perspectives that inform their worldviews. Some analysts focus on the benefits of globalization for economic well-being; others focus on its unevenness and the prospects for marginalizing large numbers of peoples and states. Some focus on the challenge globalization poses to an international system founded on the sovereign territorial state; others are more hopeful about the state's resilience and the prospects for global governance to cope with the challenge of steering globalization in rewarding directions. We can expect the controversies about globalization's alleged virtues and vices, benefits and costs, to heighten as finance, population, trade, labor, and culture continue to converge globally. While globalization has narrowed distance between the world's people, some have gained and others have lost ground. The global village is not proving to be an equally hospitable home for everyone. The losers resisting "corporate citizenship" or "stakeholder capitalism" are mounting a backlash, even though "no one can predict globalization's outcome" (Pfaff 1996). "Globalization rides mankind, but drives people to take refuge from its powerful forces" (Schlesinger 1997). Levels of satisfaction with cascading globalization vary widely, as do the levels to which countries are intertwined in the forces making for globalization (see Figure 8.5). Winners in the game of trade and investment play down the costs of global integration, while protectionist critics of free trade and open capitalist markets deny globalization's benefits, and the debate about globalization's problematic impact

In Defense of Jobs at Home Free trade and globalization are seen as threats to the job security of some workers, who seek protection to preserve their employment in vulnerable, relatively uncompetitive sectors of the global market. In 1993, American workers demonstrated against the North American Free Trade Agreement (NAFTA). If such protests succeed around the globe, free-trade agreements are likely to unravel, and the pace of globalization will slow.

has intensified without resolution as the debaters have hardened their positions without listening to the counterarguments.

The key question is really about fairness, ethics, and justice, not about the benefits of free trade, which both rich and poor countries recognize as they competitively seek to gain a larger share of the global export market. The evidence about the costs and payoffs is mixed, because globalization refers to different phenomena, the outcomes of which are open to interpretation. While many issues remain uncertain, it *is* clear that globalization is far from a win-win situation. Therefore, the debate will continue.

Is globalization eroding the ability of even the rich states to control their economic and political fortunes? To be sure, a world of vanishing borders challenges all territorial states, rich and poor alike. In an era of globalization, "one often hears that sovereignty is being undermined by the global market [and if] sovereignty is being steadily weakened, then we can eventually expect the state to no longer be the central form of political organization in the world" (Barkin 2001). However, states have proven themselves to be remarkably resilient since the time they were formally created in 1648, and states still rule and govern the institutions and laws that shape changes in the world economy. States remain the globe's major political unit, and some observers see the power of the state as being as strong as ever, even in the era of global interdependency that has forced states to reorganize themselves to more effectively manage international transactions (see Gelber 1998). Globalization may even strengthen the size and economic power of states. The age of big government is not dead.

At the beginning of the [twentieth] century government spending in today's industrial countries accounted for less than one-tenth of national income. [In 1997] in the same countries, the government's share of output was roughly half. Decade by decade, the change in the government's share of the economy moved in one direction only: up. During war it went up; during peace it went up. Between 1920 and the mid-1930s, years of greatly diminished trade and international economic contact, it went up. Between 1960 and 1980, as global trade and finance expanded, it went up. Between 1980 and 1990, as this breeze of globalization became a strong wind, it went up again. Between 1990 and 1996, as the wind became a gale, it went up some more. (*Economist,* September 20, 1997, 7)

The expansion of governmental control over states' spending notwithstanding, globalization has arguably reduced the sovereign control of states over activities within their borders and their relations with other states and nonstate actors.

Globalization reduces the capacity of states to exercise political power over the territory in which private-sector actors operate. This loss of control probably means that, "Probing further into the future, including the future of the nation-state itself, one must recognize that globalization has ended the nation-state's monopoly over internal sovereignty, which was formerly guaranteed by territory. This change deprives external sovereignty of its functional value. The nation-state as an externally sovereign actor in the international system will become a thing of the past" (Reinicke 1997).

International regimes such as those that evolved after World War II to promote global governance in monetary and trade affairs may also prove effective management strategies for coping with the challenge of globalization. Because "globalization implies that everyone and everything is more closely connected than ever before but on a foundation that is still shaky," a more effective architecture for global governance needs to be created (Garten 1999). As a former U.S. policymaker, Joseph S. Nye, Jr. (2001), urges, "We need to think harder about norms and procedures for the governance of globalization. Denial of the problem . . . will not do. We need changes in processes."

Expanding on this proposition, Klaus Schwab, president of the World Economic Forum, warned in 2002 that with a worldwide recession, rampant terrorist attacks, and other signs that fundamental transformations are occurring in the world, "fragility characterizes best the situation we are now in. With globalization we have much more synchronization—this is the first really synchronized world recession. A second factor is speed, time compression, mainly driven by technology advances." And to deal effectively with the challenges presented by globalization, cooperation and coordination may be an imperative. Thus it is no longer radical to call for changes and support multilateralism, because globalization's challenges compel all of us to become serious, for a change, about a concept that so far we have only touched upon: the sharing of sovereignty. To agree to share one's sovereignty is difficult," explains Peter Sutherland, former director-general of the WTO, in November 2001, but "in many ways the Europeans have shown the way forward. But I would submit that a genuine enhanced institutional sharing, or pooling of sovereignties is today the structural issue which has yet to be settled. Failing that, the globalization process, and the development of a rules-based international system, will fail and be derailed sooner or later."

A key issue is whether states can find a focal point, a norm, around which cooperation could coalesce. Liberal theorists, who focus on the mutual gains stemming from international cooperation, are optimistic about the possibilities. Realists and neomercantilists, who are concerned more with relative gains than absolute gains, are more pessimistic. But all accounts agree on one proposition:

"that the communications and technology revolution that facilitate the flow of capital, information, and jobs across old national boundaries will force a redefinition of the role of states [because] the process of globalization is remaking the economic world and inevitably will reshape the political world as well" (Broder 1999).

This chapter began by asking whether globalization is the route to a global village—one free of conflict and intent only on improving villagers' welfare—or whether this is mere mythology. *Global pillage* is an alternative description of the probable consequences that will flow from cascading globalization. There is no limit to the dangers attributed to globalization. If globalization means anything, it means that the sturdiness of the global economy is vulnerable to shocks that can overturn it, and faith in globalization as a motor of progress is destined to collapse whenever the international market begins to melt. In addition, September 11 shows that terrorism has become another unpleasant manifestation of globalization and that as terrorism becomes global it can wreck havoc everyplace. The cost of rapidly accelerating globalization promoted primarily by growing international trade must be balanced by the benefits. Will the continuing economic trade-offs that result from the globalization of world trade spell eventual doom, or will it spell growth and the consolidation of a cosmopolitan global culture? The next chapter investigates possible answers to this question.

KEY TERMS

globalization
neoliberal theory
human security
state level of analysis
global village
cyberspace
virtuality
digital divide
information and communications
   technology (ICT)
agenda setting
New World Information and
   Communication Order (NWICO)

regime
international organized crime
   (IOC)
global migration crisis
failed states
globalization of finance
arbitrage
digital world economy
commercial liberalism
capital mobility hypothesis
realist theory

General Agreement on Tariffs and
   Trade (GATT)
trade integration
newly industrialized economies
   (NIEs)
strategic corporate alliances
virtual corporations
foreign direct investment (FDI)
underemployment
politics

SUGGESTED READING

Aaronson, Susan Ariel. *Taking Trade to the Streets: The Lost History of Public Efforts to Shape Globalization.* Ann Arbor: University of Michigan Press, 2002.

Baylis, John, and Steve Smith, eds. *The Globalization of World Politics*, 2nd ed. New York: Oxford University Press, 2002.

Broad, Robin, ed. *Global Backlash: Citizen Initiative for a Just World Economy.* Lanham Md.: Rowman and Littlefield, 2002.

De Greiff, Pablo, and Ciaran P. Cronin, eds. *Global Justice and Transnational Politics: Essays on the Moral and Political Challenges of Globalization.* Cambridge, Mass.: MIT Press, 2002.

Friedman, Thomas L. *The Lexus and the Olive Tree: Understanding Globalization.* New York: Farrar, Straus, Giroux, 1999.

Held, David, Anthony McGrew, David Goldblatt, and Jonathan Perraton. *Global Transformations: Politics, Economics and Culture.* Stanford, Calif.: Stanford University Press, 1999.

Keohane, Robert O. "Governance in a Partially Globalized World," *American Political Science Review* 94 (March 2002): 1–13.

Mittelman, James H. *The Globalization Syndrome.* Princeton, N.J.: Princeton University Press, 2001.

Nye, Joseph S., Jr., and John D. Donahue, eds. *Governance in a Globalizing World.* Washington, D.C.: Brookings, 2000.

Rosenau, James N. *Along the Domestic-Foreign Frontier: Exploring Governance in a Turbulent World.* Cambridge, Eng.: Cambridge University Press, 1997.

Soros, George. *George Soros On Globalization.* New York: Public Affairs, 2002.

Stiglitz, Joseph E. *Globalization and Its Discontents.* New York: W. W. Norton, 2002.

WHERE ON THE WORLD WIDE WEB?

LaborNet
http://www.labornet.apc.org/

LaborNet provides labor news from around the world, Internet services, and Internet training to those interested in workers' causes. Want to be a sympathetic striker? Click on the Strike Page and find out the who, what, where, and why of current strikes anywhere in the world. This Web site also has extensive links to international labor unions. Want to form a student union organization? This is the place to look for support and more information. It also gives the reader a sense of how the Internet has contributed to the globalization of labor.

Migration Dialogue
http://www.migration.ucdavis.edu/

The University of California at Davis has created a Web site that "promotes an informed discussion of the issues associated with international migration, by providing unbiased and timely information on immigration and integration issues." Most useful to you at this site is "Migration News," which has up-to-date reports on migration issues in various states and regions of the world. Its archive allows you to search news by year and month, so you can track migration issues over time. Based on your exploration of the site's offerings, do you think there is a "global migration crisis"?

The Progress of Nations
http://www.unicef.org/pon99/

As described in the chapter, AIDS is a disease that has spread around the world through the process of globalization. The United Nations Children's Fund (UNICEF) has created a Web site that details the devastating impact of HIV/AIDS on children. Use this site to analyze the effects of AIDS on children in a variety of countries. Charts present a cross-country comparison of the number of children orphaned by AIDS and the impact it has had on their lives. What country's children are most affected by the AIDS epidemic?

Telecom Information Resources on the Internet
http://china.si.umich.edu/telecom/telecom-info.html

The University of Michigan has produced a Web site that references information sources related to technical, economic, public policy, and social aspects of telecommunications (voice, data, video, wired, wireless, cable television, and satellite). Map 8.1 displays the uneven distribution of Internet connections around the world, and offers evidence to support the concern that the globalization of telecommunications will be concentrated in the Global North. As you visit the Telecom site, see if you can find additional evidence that substantiates this concern. Click on Broadcasters to link to every television and radio broadcaster in the world. Count how many broadcasters are in each country; you will be amazed at the number in the United States.

INFOTRAC® COLLEGE EDITION

Taylor, Timothy. "The Truth about Globalization," *Public Interest* Spring 2002.

Hoffmann, Stanley. "Clash of Globalizations," *Foreign Affairs* July–August 2002.

James, Harold. "Globalization and Great Depressions," *ORBIS* Winter 2002.

Massing, Michael. "From Protest to Program," *The American Prospect* July 2, 2001.

For more articles, enter:

"globalization" in the Subject Guide, and then go to subdivision "analysis."

"globalization" in the Subject Guide, and then go to subdivision "evaluation."

"anti-globalization movement" in the Subject Guide.

MARKETS AND MONEY IN THE NEW GLOBAL POLITICAL ECONOMY

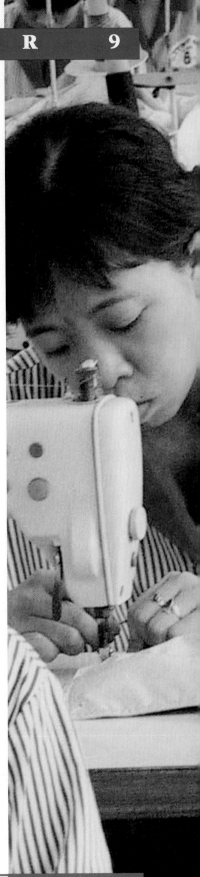

T O P I C S   A N D   T H E M E S

- The importance of trade and currency exchange in a globalized political economy

- The global context for interpreting contemporary world economic change
  Past commercial philosophy
  Liberal versus mercantile values
  Hegemony: A precondition for economic order and free trade?

- The changing free-trade regime

- Monetary matters: Can regimes promote trade and growth?

- The fate of free trade: Triumph or trouble?

- **CONTROVERSY** GLOBALIZATION'S GROWING PAINS: IS THE WORLD TRADE ORGANIZATION A FRIEND OR FOE?

Workers using sewing machines in Vietnam make sports clothes for European and U.S. markets.

I think trade is very important. . . . Trade not only helps spread prosperity but trade helps spread freedom.

—GEORGE W. BUSH, U.S. President, 2001

Efficiently functioning trade is an important prerequisite for a more stable and prosperous world. But such trade is not based on the rules of the poor. It is trade based on an agreed order that takes into account the weakest and systematically promotes their fuller integration. It facilitates access of less developed countries to foreign markets and thus to financial resources needed for development.

—VACLAV HAVEL, President of the Czech Republic, 2001

"Money makes the world go 'round," is an old saying. Today, more than ever, that adage is true at least in one sense: money is moving around the world at a quickening pace, as purchases at home are made increasingly of goods produced abroad. You are a participant in this process that is integrating a globalizing marketplace. When you buy a sandwich, a sweater, a car, or the gasoline to make it run, the chances are exceedingly high that what you purchased was produced at least in part in a foreign land. Your transaction contributed to the movement of money across borders, because the purchase you made will ultimately affect the balance of payments and the cash position of your country in international currency accounts. Congratulations! You have become an actor on the world stage, and your actions have registered an international impact. As a result of your decision, money has moved around the world and the distribution of income and wealth globally has shifted in a small way.

This chapter is about trading places and money markets in the global system. We will look at the processes governing international economics, concentrating on how international trade and currency exchanges operate and affect national and human security. We thus look at a phenomenon as old as recorded history and inspect how it influences life in the twenty-first century. The quest for wealth is an ageless pursuit. Because it provides the means by which many other prized values can be realized, the successful management of economics lies at the center of how governments define their national interests. What practices (and underlying philosophies justifying them) should they embrace to regulate commercial and monetary activities within their borders? And what foreign economic policies should each state adopt to influence trading and financial exchanges with other states?

These are the principal concerns of **international political economy.** This **paradigm,** or, that is, approach to study, is "concerned with the political determinants of international economic relations. International political economy tries to answer such questions as: How have changes in the international distribution of power among states affected the degree of openness in the international trading system? Do the domestic political economies of some states allow them to compete more effectively in international markets? Is the relative poverty of the [Global South] better explained by indigenous conditions in individual countries or by some attribute of the international economic system? When can international economic ties among states be used for political leverage?" (Krasner 2001).

To introduce these topics, this chapter will first examine the ways in which the global economic system has evolved. This will allow us to then investigate how trade and monetary activities today are creating new issues in the twenty-first century.

■ **international political economy**
the study of the intersection of politics and economics that illuminates the reasons why changes occur in the distribution of states' wealth and power.

■ **paradigm**
derived from the Greek *paradeigma*, meaning an example, a model, or an essential pattern; a paradigm structures thoughts about an area of inquiry.

THE GLOBAL CONTEXT FOR INTERPRETING CONTEMPORARY WORLD ECONOMIC CHANGE

Rapid changes in the world force people to think about and interpret world politics in fresh ways. Of all the many recent changes, perhaps none has been more profound and far-reaching than **globalization.** The growth of states' economic interdependence can be viewed as the recent culmination of a trend that began more than a century ago, but its current level is unprecedented. Accordingly, basic ideas about states, markets, trade, and currency exchange are at the center of debate, and issues in international political economy are at the vortex of global discussion. The contests between the rich Global North and the poor Global South, and between supplier and producer, have risen to prominence. While some might say (especially after 9/11) that the **high politics** governing national security remains a necessary preoccupation, most would also agree that **low politics,** where international economic issues such as inequalities are being negotiated, are of equal importance. The strong undercurrents in the latter are reshaping the former. International trade integration and the increasingly interlocked world economy compel attention to economic transactions. Today, high interest rates in one country lead to high interest rates in others, and a stock market freefall starting in New York will spread to Asia and London overnight. Depression abroad means recession at home. Inflation is shared everywhere, and it seems to be beyond the control of any single state. The balance of fiscal power is now as pertinent to national security and quality of

■ **globalization**
the increasingly close international integration of markets both for goods and services and for capital (see p. 45)

■ **high politics**
geostrategic issues of national and international security as related to war and peace (see p. 19).

■ **low politics**
the category of global issues related to the economic, social, demographic, and environmental aspects of relations between governments and people (see p. 19).

life as is the global balance of military power. These are some of the consequences of the growing international interdependence known as globalization (see Chapter 8).

Theories of political economy dating back to John Stuart Mill's *Principles of Political Economy* and Karl Marx's *A Contribution to the Critique of Political Economy* in the mid-nineteen century have been rediscovered. This reconsideration stems from the growing awareness that the conventional categories of politics and economics can no longer be separated, because now "much of politics is economics, and most of economics is politics" (Lindblom 1979).

In today's world, politics (states) and economics (markets) are merging. The relentless march in the volume of international commerce has made trade increasingly important to countries' economies and is expected to increase at an even faster rate through the year 2015 *(Global Trends 2015)*. Trade comprises a growing share of the global economy, now accounting for 40 percent of global domestic product, up from 20 percent in 1990 (World Bank 2002a). World trade is the most visible symbol of globalization and deserves our primary attention, but so do the dynamics of the floating **international monetary system** through which foreign currencies and credits are calculated when capital moves across borders through trade, investments, and loans.

We need to first step backward to understand leading ideas about states' trade and monetary policies, which are rooted in past thinking. In this chapter we will focus on the critical role of the United States as an economic superpower in shaping the contest between liberalism and mercantilism underlying the different trade and monetary strategies states are pursuing in the quest for power and wealth.

The Shadow of Past Commercial Policy Philosophy

In July 1944, forty-four states allied in war against the Axis powers met in the New Hampshire resort community of Bretton Woods. Their purpose was to devise new rules and institutions to govern international trade and monetary relations after World War II. As the world's preeminent economic and military power, the United States played the leading role. Its proposals were shaped by its perception of the causes of the 1930s' economic catastrophe and its beliefs about the role the U.S. dollar and economy should play in the postwar world. The United States sought free trade, open markets, and monetary stability—all central tenets of what would become the "Bretton Woods system"—based on the theoretical premises of **commercial liberalism,** which advocates free markets with few barriers to private trade and capital flows.

Britain also played an important role at the conference. Led by John Maynard Keynes—whose theories about the state's role in managing inflation, unemployment, and growth influenced a generation of economic thinking throughout the capitalist world—the British delegation won support for the principle of strong government action by states facing economic problems. That ideology conforms less closely with liberalism than with the principles of **mercantilism,** which assign states a greater role than markets in managing economic interactions and accepts protectionist trade policies to expand exports and limit imports as a strategy for acquiring national wealth.

■ **international monetary system**
the financial procedures governing the exchange and conversion of national currencies so that they can be bought and sold for one another to calculate the value of currencies and credits when capital is transferred across borders through trade, investment, and loans.

■ **commercial liberalism**
an economic theory advocating free markets and the removal of barriers to the flow of trade and capital as a locomotive for prosperity (see p. 284).

■ **mercantilism**
the seventeenth century theory preaching that trading states should increase their wealth and power by expanding exports and protecting their domestic economy from imports, which is still advocated by some today (see p. 195).

Despite these differences, the rules established at Bretton Woods reflected a remarkable level of agreement and governed international economic relations for the next twenty-five years, because they rested on three political bases (Spero and Hart 1997). First, power was concentrated in the rich Western European and North American countries, which reduced the number of states whose agreement was necessary for effective management by restricting the potential challenges by Japan, the Global South, and the then-communist states of Eastern Europe and the Soviet Union. Second, the system's operation was facilitated by the dominant states' shared preference for an open international economy with limited government intervention. The onset of the Cold War helped cement Western unity, because a common external enemy led the Western industrial countries to perceive economic cooperation as necessary for both prosperity and military security. That perception promoted a willingness to share economic burdens. Third, Bretton Woods worked because the United States assumed the burdens of leadership and others willingly accepted that leadership.

The political bases of the Bretton Woods system crumbled in 1972 when the United States suspended the convertibility of the dollar into gold and abandoned the system of fixed currency exchange rates at its core. Since then, as floating exchange rates and growing capital mobility have made monetary mechanisms unstable, more chaotic processes of international economic relations have materialized. Still, commercial liberalism's preference for market mechanisms over government intervention and the urge to privatize and otherwise reduce government regulation of markets has spread worldwide, since the Cold War collapsed, and multinational corporations (MNCs) are serving as a powerful pillar in support of the continuing strength of the liberal rules of the global trade regime. Thus it is still useful to characterize the contemporary international economic system as a **Liberal International Economic Order (LIEO)**—one based on such free market principles as openness and nondiscriminatory trade.

Not all states consistently support the liberal tenet that governments should not interfere by managing trade flows because they fear the potential costs of free trade. Commercial liberalism is under attack in many states, including some of liberalism's unenthusiastic proponents, which are pressured domestically to protect industries and employment at home. Globalization has not eliminated the urge to compete, because states fear that **interdependence** will compromise their sovereignty and security. Interdependence encourages states to maximize their gains through transborder transactions while minimizing their vulnerability. States' trade policies are naturally influenced by the selfish desire to increase the domestic benefits of international economic transactions and to lessen their adverse consequences, even if this will undermine the expansion of a global capitalist economy propelled by free trade.

The Clash between Liberal and Mercantile Values

How should states rationally cope in the globalized political economy to best manage economic change? The choices inspire different philosophies and policies. They force governments to attempt to reconcile the overriding need for states to cooperate with others in trade liberalization if they are to maximize their wealth with each state's natural competitive desire to put its own welfare first.

■ **Liberal International Economic Order (LIEO)** the set of regimes created after World War II, designed to promote monetary stability and reduce barriers to the free flow of trade and capital.

■ **interdependence** a situation in which the behavior of international actors greatly affects others with whom they have contact, making all parties mutually sensitive and vulnerable to the others' actions.

Most controversies in international political economy are ultimately reducible to the competing ideologies of liberalism and mercantilism, which represent "fundamentally different . . . conceptions of the relationships among society, state, and market" (Gilpin 2001). A comparison of the logic behind the two theoretical traditions can help us to appreciate why a reconciliation or balance is so hard to achieve, why particular protectionist domestic interests sacrifice collective prosperity in order to maximize their own parochial gains, and why others criticize mercantilism as self-defeating.

■ **theory**
a set of conclusions derived from assumptions (axioms) and/or evidence about some phenomenon, including its character, causes, and probable consequences and their ethical implications.

Commercial Liberalism. Commercial liberalism as a political **theory** explains economics by building on the presumption that humankind's natural inclination is to cooperate in order to increase prosperity and enlarge individual liberty under law. Consequently, it is closely related to liberal theory (described in Chapter 2), which is based on the assumption that individuals and groups usually make decisions on the basis of rational calculations through the application of intellect to analyze available facts. Commercial liberalism asserts that through mutually beneficial exchanges people can benefit and the problems of capitalism—boom-and-bust cycles, trade wars, and poverty—can be solved. Commercial liberal theory has many roots and variations, but all liberal thinkers agree that the promotion of free international trade to lift the poor from poverty and to expand political liberties is one of the globe's "great causes" (see Bhagwati 1999).

Adam Smith, the eighteenth-century political economist who helped define the precepts of classical liberalism as well as modern-day economics, used the metaphor of the unregulated market's "invisible hand" to show how the collective or public interest can be served by humans' natural tendency to "truck, barter, and exchange" in pursuit of private gain. Hence the importance of "free" markets, which produce collective as well as private gain. David Ricardo, a nineteenth-century British political economist, added an important corollary to liberal thought as applied to the international economy. Ricardo demonstrated conclusively that when all states specialize in the production of those goods in which they enjoy a **comparative advantage** and trade them for goods in which others enjoy an advantage, a net gain in welfare for both states, in the form of higher living standards, will result. The principle of comparative advantage underpins commercial liberalism's advocacy of free trade as a method for capital accumulation. Material progress is realized and mutual gains are achieved, according to this principle, providing countries specialize in the production of what they can produce least expensively, are willing to purchase, from other countries, goods that are costly for them to produce, and, in addition, do not restrict the flow of trade across borders.

■ **comparative advantage**
the concept in liberal economics that a state will benefit if it specializes in those goods it can produce comparatively cheaply and acquires through trade goods that it can only produce at a higher cost.

Liberalism maintains that open markets and free trade are both advantageous and the engines of economic progress. As Benjamin Franklin summarized commercial liberal theory more than two centuries ago, "No nation was ever ruined by trade." Another way of expressing this idea is to say that each country should specialize in producing those goods in which it has the greatest comparative cost advantage or least comparative cost disadvantage, and trade with others. The assumption is that trade competition is good for all. Competition stimulates technological innovation to improve production efficiency in order to meet the competition for trade by other producers, and in the long run the world's output and income will increase and everyone's standard of living

TABLE 9.1

Comparative Advantage and the Gains from Free Trade

Country	Worker Productivity per Hour		Before Specialization		Specialization, No Trade		Specialization with Trade	
	Camera	Computer	Camera	Computer	Camera	Computer	Camera	Computer
Japan	9	3	900	300	990	270	910	300
United States	4	2	400	200	320	240	400	210

will rise providing all abide by the rules of free trade and open markets. Commercial liberalism recognizes that in the short run free trade will result in unequal rewards for some and produce inequalities in countries' rate of growth, but argues that the long-term gains for all in a **laissez-faire economic** system of free markets are most important.

Why does free trade produce benefits for trade partners who specialize in the production of goods for which they each have comparative advantage? Consider a hypothetical illustration of Japan and the United States, each of which produces cameras and computers but with different worker productivity (output per hour) for each country, as shown in the first column of Table 9.1.

Clearly Japan has an absolute advantage in both products, as Japanese workers are more productive in turning out cameras and computers than the American workers are. Does this mean the two countries cannot benefit by trading with one another? If trade does occur, should each country continue to allocate its resources as in the past? The answer to both questions is no.

Each country should specialize in producing that item in which it has the greatest comparative cost advantage or least comparative cost disadvantage, and trade for others. Because Japan is three times more productive in cameras than computers, it should direct more of its resources into manufacturing that industry. One cost of doing so is lost computer output, but Japan can turn out three additional cameras for every computer given up. The United States, on the other hand, can obtain only two computers. Like their Japanese counterparts, American workers are also more productive in making cameras than computers. Still, U.S. resources should be directed to computers because the United States is at a smaller disadvantage compared with Japan in this area. If the United States specializes in computers and Japan in cameras and they trade with one another, each will benefit. The following scenario shows why.

Begin with one hundred workers in each industry without specialization or trade (second column). Next specialize production by shifting ten Japanese workers from computer to camera production and shifting twenty American workers from camera production to computers (third column). Then permit free trade so that eighty Japanese-manufactured cameras are exported to the United States and thirty U.S. computers are exported to Japan. With specialization *and* free trade the benefits to both countries improve.

By shifting Japanese resources into the production of cameras and U.S. resources into computers and allowing trade, the same total allocations will cause camera and computer output to rise ten units each (fourth column). Resources are now being used more efficiently. Both countries realize benefits

■ **laissez-faire economics**
from a French phrase (meaning literally "let do") that Adam Smith and other commercial liberals in the eighteenth century used to describe the advantages of free-wheeling capitalism without government interference in economic affairs.

when each trades some of its additional output for the other's. Japan ends up with more cameras than before specialization and trade and the same number of computers, while the United States finds itself with more computers and the same number of cameras. More output in both countries means higher living standards.

Liberals such as Smith, Ricardo, and Franklin believed that markets work best when free of government interference. They reasoned that economic processes governing the production, distribution, and consumption of goods and services operate according to certain natural laws. They saw **politics** as necessary if crass, and argued that while governments often performed their key tasks poorly, they had the capacity to overcome their historic proclivity to abuse power and could instead become engines for prosperity—providing they would not exercise a heavy hand in regulating the marketplace. Today people subscribing to these views are described as conservatives, not liberals. The tenets described here are those of "classical" liberalism. The hallmark of commercial liberal theory, then, is its commitment "to free markets and minimal state intervention. . . . Liberals believe economics is progressive and politics is regressive. Thus they conceive of progress as divorced from politics and based on the evolution of the market" (Gilpin 2001).

Transferred to the international level, these principles suggest that trade and other forms of economic relations "are a source of peaceful relations among nations because the mutual benefits of trade and expanding interdependence among national economies will tend to foster cooperative relations. . . . A liberal international economy will have a moderating influence on international politics as it creates bonds of mutual interests and a commitment to the status quo" (Gilpin 2001). Thus, trade liberalization is believed to produce many economic and political benefits: the removal of trade restrictions, currency devaluations, and other reforms generate rapid export and economic growth because they promote competition, improve resource allocations, reduce production costs, generate pressures for increased production efficiencies, attract foreign capital and expertise, provide foreign exchange needed for imports, and promote more equal access to scarce resources. These economic benefits are believed to have positive political consequences, leading to the growth of civil liberties and democratic governance (Todaro 2000).

There is a fly in this liberal ointment, however. Although commercial liberal theory promises that the "invisible hand" will maximize efficiency so that everyone will gain, it does not promise that everyone will gain equally. Instead, "everyone will gain in accordance with his or her contribution to the whole, but . . . not everyone will gain equally because individual productivities differ. Under free exchange, society as a whole will be more wealthy, but individuals will be rewarded in terms of their marginal productivity and relative contribution to the overall social product" (Gilpin 2001). This applies at the global level as well: The gains from international trade may be distributed quite unequally, even if the principle of comparative advantage governs. Commercial liberal theory ignores these differences, as it is concerned with **absolute gains** rather than **relative gains.** Other theorists, however, are more concerned with the distribution of economic rewards.

Mercantilism.   Mercantilism is an economic philosophy deeply entrenched in the long story of states' quest for power and wealth. Its theoretical underpinnings

---

■ **politics**
the use of power by those in authority to exercise influence against subordinates and other authorities, and their reciprocal use for the same purpose.

■ **absolute gains**
a measure of the degree to which all participants in an exchange become better off.

■ **relative gains**
a measure of how much some participants in an exchange benefit in comparison to others.

prompted Adam Smith to write his famous critique in *The Wealth of Nations,* and its practice prompted rebellious American colonists to dump British tea into the Boston harbor in 1773.

Mercantilism advocates government regulation of economic life to increase state power and security. It emerged in Europe as the leading political economy philosophy after the decline of feudalism and helped to stimulate the first wave of Europe's imperialist expansion, which began in the fifteenth century. Accumulating gold and silver was seen as the route to state power and wealth, and imperialistically acquiring overseas colonies was seen as a means to that end.

While states no longer try to stockpile precious metals, many continue to intervene in the marketplace. In the contemporary context, then, **neomercantilism** refers to "a trade policy whereby a state seeks to maintain a balance-of-trade surplus and to promote domestic production and employment by reducing imports, stimulating home production, and promoting exports" (Walters and Blake 1992). Its advocates are sometimes called "economic nationalists." In their view, states must compete for position and power, and economic resources are the source of state power. From this it follows that "economic activities are and should be subordinate to the goal of state building and the interests of the state. All nationalists ascribe to the primacy of the state, of national security, and of military power in the functioning of the international system" (Gilpin 2001).

As an ideology of political economy, mercantilism shares much in common with political realism: Realists and mercantilists both see the state as the principal world actor; both view the international system as anarchical; and both dwell on the aggressively competitive drive of people and states for advantage. "Economic nationalists . . . stress the role of power in the rise of a market and the conflictual nature of international economic relations; they argue that economic interdependence must have a political foundation and that it creates yet another arena of interstate conflict, increases national vulnerability, and constitutes a mechanism that one society can employ to dominate another" (Gilpin 2001).

While commercial liberals emphasize the mutual benefits of cooperative trade agreements, mercantilists are more concerned that the gains realized by one side of the bargain will come at the expense of the other. "The logical absurdity of all governments seeking a surplus at the same time was not perceived as a problem. Within a zero-sum world, there had to be winners and losers" (Mayall 2001). For mercantilists, relative gains are more important than both parties' absolute gains. An American economic nationalist, for instance, would complain about a trade agreement that promised the United States a 5 percent growth in income and the Chinese 6 percent. Although the bargain would ensure an eventual increase in U.S. living standards, its position compared with China's would erode. Indeed, projected over the long run, such seemingly small differences would eventually lead to China's replacement of the United States as the world's largest economy—an outcome declared in 2002 as highly unacceptable to American economic nationalists, as President Bush did when his new grand strategy proclaimed that preserving U.S. hegemonic supremacy was the highest priority. Calculations such as these explain why achieving mutual gains through multilateral international cooperation often encounters stiff resistance from domestic groups seeking to protect their profits from foreign competition. It also explains why specific, negatively affected domestic producers lobby for mercantilist measures, and why they sometimes succeed against the unorganized interests of consumers who benefit from free trade.

■ **neomercantilism**
a contemporary version of classical mercantilism which advocates promoting domestic production and a balance-of-payment surplus by subsidizing exports and using tariffs and nontarriff barriers to reduce imports.

Protectionism is the generic term used to describe a number of mercantilist policies designed to keep foreign goods out of a country and to subsidize the export of goods to encourage foreigners to buy domestically produced goods.

- **Beggar-thy-neighbor policies** seek to enhance domestic welfare by promoting trade surpluses that can be realized only at other countries' expense. They reflect a government's efforts to reduce unemployment through currency devaluations, tariffs, quotas, export subsidies, and other strategies that adversely affect its trade partners. These protective strategies encourage unequal exchanges between exporters and importers (see Chapter 5).

- **Import quotas** unilaterally specify the quantity of a particular product that can be imported from abroad. In the late 1950s, for example, the United States established import quotas on oil, arguing that they were necessary to protect U.S. national security. Hence the government, rather than the marketplace, determined the amount and source of imports.

- **Export quotas** result from negotiated agreements between producers and consumers and restrict the flow of products (e.g., shoes or sugar) from the former to the latter. An **orderly market arrangement (OMA)** is a formal agreement in which a country agrees to limit the export of products that might impair workers in the importing country, often under specific rules designed to monitor and manage trade flows. Exporting countries are willing to accept such restrictions in exchange for concessions on other fronts from the importing countries. The Multi-Fiber Arrangement (MFA) is an example of an elaborate OMA that restricts exports of textiles and apparel. It originated in the early 1960s, when the United States formalized earlier, informal **voluntary export restrictions (VERs)** negotiated with Japan and Hong Kong to protect domestic producers from cheap cotton imports. The quota system was later extended to other importing and exporting countries and then, in the 1970s, to other fibers, when it became the MFA.

- Import and export quotas are representative of a broader category of trade restrictions known as **nontariff barriers (NTBs)** that discriminate against imports without direct tax levies. They cover a wide range of creative government regulations designed to shelter particular domestic industries from foreign competition, including health and safety regulations, government purchasing procedures, subsidies, and antidumping regulations (to prevent foreign producers from selling their goods for less than they cost domestically).

- Among developing countries whose domestic industrialization goals may be hindered by the absence of protection from the Global North's more efficient firms, the **infant industry** argument is often used to justify mercantilist trade policies. According to this argument, tariffs or other forms of protection are necessary to nurture young industries until they eventually mature and lower production costs to compete effectively in the global marketplace. Import-substitution industrialization policies, once popular in Latin America and elsewhere, often depended on protection of infant industries (see Chapter 6).

- In the Global North, creating comparative advantages now motivates the use of what is known as **strategic trade policy** as a neomercantilist means of ensuring that a country's industries will remain competitive. Strategic trade is a form of government industrial policy that targets subsidies toward particular industries so they gain a competitive edge over foreign producers. Two protectionist strategies that are increasingly used are **countervailing duties,** the imposition of tariffs to offset alleged subsidies by foreign producers, and **antidumping duties** imposed to counter the alleged sale of products at below the cost of production.

Realist theory helps to account for states' impulse to practice mercantilist and neomercantilist protectionism. Recall that **realism** argues that states often shun cooperation, because international anarchy without global governance creates fear: Threatened states mistrust one another's motives. Moreover, in the self-help global system, states alone are responsible for their survival and well-being. As a result, uncertainty about others' expansionist aims encourages each state to spend "a portion of its effort, not forwarding its own good, but in providing the means of protecting itself against others" (Waltz 1979).

The insecurity that breeds competition rather than cooperation is often exhibited in international economic relations. Those who see states' power and wealth as inextricably linked conclude that "even if nation-states do not fear for their physical survival, they worry that a decrease in their power capabilities relative to those of other states will compromise their political autonomy, expose them to the influence attempts of others, or lessen their ability to prevail in political disputes with allies and adversaries" (Mastanduno 1991). Thus many states are "defensively positional actors" that seek not only to promote their domestic well-being but also to defend their rank (position) in comparison with others (see Grieco 1995).

The relative gains issue speaks to the difficulties of achieving international cooperation under anarchical conditions and explains why some domestic producers vigorously oppose liberal (open) international economies despite the evidence that free trade promotes economic growth. Different countries therefore practice dissimilar economic policies. Some endorse free trade, and others impose protectionist barriers; some see an unregulated market as the best method for protecting the greatest good for the greatest number, while others seek to tilt the playing field to their own advantage.

Hegemony: A Precondition for Economic Order and Free Trade?

Hegemonic stability theory, a blend of liberalism and mercantilism, holds that when a single state ascends to hold a preponderance of military and economic power such that a **hegemon** emerges, international economic stability based on liberal principles can materialize to alleviate the fears of nationalistic mercantilists. Unlike mercantilism, this realist worldview follows the logic of **long-cycle theory** (see Chapter 4) in viewing the balancing of power among competing actors in anarchy as the key to global economic order, but accepts the likelihood that order can best emerge at those phases in the long-term redistribution of global power when an all-powerful single hegemon uses its supremacy to enforce free-trade rules. Hegemonic stability theory thus "assumes that a liberal economic system cannot be self-sustaining but must be maintained over the long term through the actions of the dominant economy" (Gilpin 2001).

Hegemony is the ability to "dictate, or at least dominate, the rules and arrangements by which international relations, political and economic, are

infant industry
a newly established industry that is not yet strong enough to compete effectively in the global marketplace.

strategic trade policy
an industrial policy that targets government subsidies toward particular industries so as to gain competitive advantage over foreign producers.

countervailing duties
tariffs imposed by a government to offset suspected subsidies provided by foreign governments to their producers.

antidumping duties
duties imposed to offset another state's alleged selling of a product at below the cost to produce it.

realism
the theoretical tradition that operates from the assumption that competitive states seek self-advantage and are unlikely to cooperate (see p. 36).

hegemonic stability theory
the proposition that free trade and interstate peace depend on the existence of a predominant great power willing and able to use economic and military strength to promote global stability (see p. 101).

hegemon
a single, overwhelmingly powerful state that exercises predominant influence over other global actors (see p. 422).

Angel Franco/New York Times

Preparing the Pathways to Global Economic Recovery In the wake of the September 11, 2001, terrorist attacks in New York City, stock markets shut down as investor and consumer gloom spread quickly across the globe and the vulnerability of the United States undermined confidence in the capability of America to perform as an unchallenged hegemon in international economics to preserve the liberal system of free trade. After the world economy enjoyed spectacular growth of almost 5 percent in 2000, after 9/11 fears of a worldwide recession escalated. In order to avert a massive recession, prime ministers, bankers, and CEOs gathered in 2002 at the meeting of the World Economic Forum to talk about the most effective multilateral plans for propelling recovery, moving their annual conclave from Davos, Switzerland, to New York. Their goal: to signal their solidarity with the charred city, with terrorists still threatening to destroy the pillars of global capitalism. The terrorist attacks forced a major rethinking about how the global economy works and how to make the international economy resume its pace of growth since the early 1990s. Adding to the challenge is the continuing protest movement arrayed against globalization. Shown here are New York City police practicing to act as bodyguards to protect the participants at the 2002 World Economic Forum. "The success of the World Economic Forum, whose meetings began informally in 1982, attracted the criticism of those who objected to the economic and social values associated with Anglo-American-style capitalism [and in reaction in 2001] critics established an 'anti-Davos' to develop constructive alternatives to globalization" (Pfaff 2001). The critics held their first counter-meeting in Porto Alegre, Brazil, at the same time that the annual Davos forum was scheduled.

conducted" (Goldstein 1988). In the world economy it occurs when a single great power garners a sufficient preponderance of material resources so that it can dominate the international flow of raw materials, capital, and trade.

From its preponderant position, a hegemon is able to promote rules for the whole global system that protect the hegemon's own interests. Hegemons such as the United States (and Britain before it), whose domestic economies are based on capitalist principles, have championed liberal international economic systems, because their comparatively greater control of technology, capital, and raw materials has given them more opportunities to profit from a system free of mercantilist restraints. When they have enforced such free-trade rules, the hegemon's economies typically have served as "engines of growth" for others in the "liberal train."

However, historically hegemons have also had special responsibilities. They have had to coordinate states' **macroeconomic** policies, manage the international monetary system to enable one state's money to be exchanged for others', make sure that countries facing balance-of-payments deficits (imbalances in their financial inflows and outflows) could find the credits necessary to finance their deficits, and serve as lenders of last resort during financial crises. When the most powerful liberal states could not perform these tasks, they have often backtracked toward more closed (protected or regulated) domestic economies, and in doing so have undermined the open international system that was previously advantageous to them. This kind of departure historically has made tariffs, monetary regulations, and other mercantilist policies more widespread and thereby undermined the LIEO regime. In short, hegemonic states not only have had the greatest capacity to make a free-trade regime succeed but in the past they also have had the greatest responsibility for its effective operation and preservation. To interpret whether hegemonic stability theory is likely to hold in the future, a closer look at the theory's logic is useful.

The Hegemonic Pillars of Free Markets and Free Trade.   Nearly all economic theories accept particular principles about the preconditions for fostering the free movement of goods across national borders. A core concept that informs discussion is that of public or **collective goods**—benefits that everyone shares and from which no one can be excluded selectively. National security is one such collective good that governments try to provide for all of their citizens, regardless of the resources that individuals contribute through taxation. In the realm of economic analysis, an open international economy permitting the relatively free movement of goods, services, and capital is similarly seen as a desirable collective good, inasmuch as it permits economic benefits for all states that would not be available if the global economy were closed to free trade.

According to hegemonic stability theory, the collective good of an open global economy needs a single, dominant power—a hegemon—to remain open and liberal. If a hegemon does not exist or is unwilling to use its power to provide this collective good, states will be tempted to "free ride" rather than contribute to maintaining the liberal international economy. A major way in which the hegemon pays may be to open its own market to less-expensive imported goods even if other countries free ride by not opening their own markets. And if enough states take this easy route, the entire structure may collapse.

The analogy of a public park helps us to clarify this principle. If there were no central government to provide for the maintenance of the park, individuals themselves would have to cooperate to keep the park in order (the trees trimmed, the lawn mowed, and so on). But some may try to come and enjoy the benefits of the park without pitching in. If enough people realize that they can get away with this—that they can enjoy a beautiful park without helping with its upkeep—it will not be long before the once beautiful park looks shabby.

■ **long-cycle theory**
the proposition based on the evidence that great powers rise to positions of hegemonic global leadership but eventually decline when their leadership is challenged by ascendant rivals (see p. 422).

■ **hegemony**
the ability of one state to lead in world politics by promoting its worldview and ruling over arrangements governing international economics and politics.

■ **macroeconomics**
the study of aggregate economic indicators such as GDP, the money supply, and the balance of trade that governments monitor to measure changes in the national economy.

■ **collective goods**
goods such as safe drinking water from which everyone benefits (see p. 389).

■ free riders
those who enjoy the benefits of collective goods but pay little or nothing for them.

■ zero-sum
an exchange in which what one competitor gains is lost by the other party to the exchange (see p. 208).

Cooperation to provide a public good is thus difficult. This is also the case with the collective good of a liberal international economy, because many states that enjoy the collective good of an orderly, open, free market economy pay little or nothing for it. These are known as **free riders.** A hegemon typically tolerates free riders, partly because the benefits that the hegemon provides, such as a stable global currency, encourage other states to accept the leader's dictates. Thus both gain, much as liberalism sees the benefits of cooperation as a "positive-sum" outcome because both sides to a bargain stand to gain from their exchanges. If the costs of leadership begin to multiply, however, a hegemon will tend to become less tolerant of others' free riding. In such a situation cooperation will increasingly be seen as one-sided or **zero-sum** because most of the benefits come at the expense of the hegemon. Then the open global economy will crumble amidst a competitive race for individual gain at others' expense.

Charles Kindleberger (1973), an international economist, first theorized about the need for a preponderant liberal hegemon to maintain order and stability. In his explanation of the 1930s Great Depression, Kindleberger concluded that "the international economic and monetary system needs leadership, a country which is prepared, consciously or unconsciously, . . . to set standards of conduct for other countries; and to seek to get others to follow them, to take on an undue share of the burdens of the system, and in particular to take on its support in adversity." Britain played this role from 1815 until the outbreak of World War I in 1914, and the United States assumed the British mantle in the decades immediately following World War II. In the interwar years, however, Britain was unable to play its previous leadership role, and the United States, although capable of leadership, was unwilling to exercise it. The void, Kindleberger concluded, was a principal cause of the "width and depth" of the Great Depression throughout the world in the 1930s.

A Globe without Hegemonic Leadership? Although hegemonic powers benefit from the liberal economic systems that their power promotes, the very success of liberalism eventually erodes the pillars that support it.

> Economic competition and the price mechanism drive the market economy toward ever higher levels of productive efficiency, economic growth, and the integration of national markets. In time, the market produces profound shifts in the location of economic activities and affects the international redistribution of economic and industrial power. The unleashing of market forces transforms the political framework itself, undermines the hegemonic power, and creates a new political environment to which the world must eventually adjust. With the inevitable shift in the international distribution of economic and military power from the core to rising nations in the periphery and elsewhere, the capacity of the hegemon to maintain the system decreases. Capitalism and the market system thus tend to destroy the political foundations on which they must ultimately rest. (Gilpin 1987, 77–78)

The leading economic power's ability to adapt is critical to maintaining its dominant position. Britain was unable to adapt and fell from its top-ranked position. Many wonder if the United States is destined to suffer the same fate, not because of economic failure but because of the lack of political will to exercise leadership through concerted multilateral action (Nye 2002b). At the twenty-first century's dawn, the United States stood as an economic super-power, with few apparent ends in sight to economic dominance. However, the circumstances confronting the United States today are eroding its capacity to exercise hegemonic leadership.

The United States is a " 'dependent colossus' [because] although globalization today reinforces American power, over time it promises to have the opposite effects" (Nye 2002a). At present, the United States has the largest economy, but no one predicts that its position of dominance will increase. The trajectories are moving in the opposite direction. The U.S. share of world output has fallen steadily since World War II ended. In 1947, the United States accounted for nearly 50 percent of the combined gross world product. By 1960, its share had slipped to 28 percent, by 1970 to 25 percent, and "by the 1990s to 20 percent or less—less than of what it had been at its peak and less than it was at the time of the Spanish-American War, when the United States first emerged as a world power" (D. White 1998, 42). Another symptom of the U.S. erosion in the international pecking order is that the U.S. share of world financial reserves has declined. The United States went from being the globe's greatest creditor country in 1980 to the world's largest debtor by 1990 and remains "the biggest debtor in history" (D. White 1998). America's huge and growing current account deficit (what is owed to foreign creditors) has swelled and could reach almost 6 percent of GDP by the end of 2003—"the biggest deficit run by any G-7 economy in the past thirty years . . . that will require America to borrow from abroad almost $2 billion a day" (*Economist*, April 27, 2002, 12). A third symptom of U.S. vulnerability is the fact that the U.S. trade deficit at the start of 2003 reached the highest level ever. Finally, alongside these debt burdens and trade imbalances, U.S. investment in public infrastructure to stimulate future growth is lower than that of all the other G-7 industrialized powerhouses, a problem that will ultimately reduce the U.S.'s "ability to compete with other economies because of its low savings rate and insufficient investment in education" (Thurow 1998). These trends suggest that U.S. advantages in the global marketplace will not continue. "The U.S. clearly is the world's strongest economy, but weak spots are visible as we look to the decades ahead" (Widenbaum 1999). That prediction was made before 9/11, and the extraordinary costs of the U.S. war against terrorism worldwide and against Iraq could easily postpone recovery and cause a recession.

Because in many areas essential to lasting hegemony—control over capital, markets and robust production—U.S. preponderance may continue to be as secure as ever. This makes less convincing Paul Kennedy's popular thesis (1987) that **imperial overstretch** was likely to cause America's fall from its preeminent position at the pinnacle of global economic power. As Kennedy argued in the late 1980s, "The United States now runs the risk that the sum total of [its] global interests and obligations is nowadays for larger than the country's power to defend them all simultaneously." This prediction derived from a principle suggested by past hegemonic experiences, namely "that a power that wants to remain number one for generation after generation requires not just military capability . . . but also a flourishing and efficient economic base, strong finances and a healthy social fabric, for it is upon such foundations that the country's military strength rests in the long term."

An undisputed hegemonic power typically can afford to be less concerned about its relative power position than others. It is therefore less likely to

■ **imperial overstretch** Paul Kennedy's thesis that hegemons decline because they make costly global commitments in excess of their ability to fulfill them.

attempt to maximize its share of the global market than are aspiring hegemons or other economic powers threatened by an erosion in their relative power. As a hegemon's dominance erodes, however, its trade and other economic policies can be expected to become less benevolent (interested in general benefits for all) and more coercive (self-interested and exploitative). The United States today *is* less willing to assume the burdens of maintaining the liberal international economic order it once championed, emphasizing competitiveness more than the acceptance of the burdens of making sacrifices to maintain the stability of the global political economy.

The Uncertain Consequences of Waning Hegemonic Leadership.   What will happen if and when the U.S. hegemon's preponderant power persists, but its willingness to lead declines? Domestically we would expect the United States to abandon the torch of commercial liberalism as the forces of economic nationalism gain politically. Internationally, hegemonic stability theory predicts that disorder will result, because hegemonic leadership is "the cement that holds the system together" (Gilpin 1987).

Have the institutions and rules put into place to govern the liberal order in the post–World War II era of unilateral American hegemony now taken on a life of their own? This view is the most convincing one to commercial liberals, who believe that the rise of a liberal international regime and embedded network of complementary institutions to support its open rules explains the persistence of economic order and growth, even if American willingness to engage in hegemonic leadership fades.

The power of that conviction resides in the fact that the commercial liberalism institutionalized in the original Bretton Woods system persists. True, "America's defection could throw the process into reverse" (Bergsten 1997). However, even in the absence of a U.S. hegemon pushing for trade liberalization, and even in the face of the U.S. hegemon succumbing to the temptations of (free-riding) mercantilism (as the Bush administration did when it in 2002 imposed tariffs on steel imports to protect that fading sector), trade liberalization may now be too deeply entrenched for it to collapse. Does the free-trade regime have too many supporters, including powerful MNCs, for that regime to need a single hegemonic protector to preserve free trade as it did in the past two hundred years? To some optimists, institutionalized globalization has now progressed to a level that makes the continuation of a liberal trading system likely, because too many states and multilateral institutions have an enormous stake in its preservation. "Built-in restraints on imposing new trade barriers have never been greater" (Stokes 2000).

International regimes are created by states to devise rules for cooperation even under international anarchy. Most of the liberal international regimes (rules and institutions) that govern international trade today first developed after World War II when the United States was both dominant and willing to lead. "By providing more information, establishing mechanisms for monitoring and generating shared expectations, institutions can create an environment in which interstate cooperation is possible even without a single dominant leader" (Krasner 2001). The free-trade regime may no longer depend on the existence of an all-powerful hegemon.

To better probe that hypothesis and understand the likely future of global economics, let us now inspect how those international trade and monetary

■ **international regimes** the set of rules, norms, and decision-making procedures that coordinates state behavior in such areas as international trade.

rules have evolved from mere pledges to reduce trade barriers to entrenched customary policy practices.

THE CHANGING FREE-TRADE REGIME

In the period immediately following World War II, when the United States became the world's new political hegemon, it simultaneously became the pre-eminent voice in international trade affairs. The liberal trading system the United States chose to promote rejected the zero-sum, beggar-thy-neighbor competitive economic nationalism widely seen as a major cause of the economic depression of the 1930s. Removing barriers to trade became a priority and led to the recurrent rounds of trade negotiations that cumulatively produced remarkable reductions in tariff rates. As the large U.S. market was opened to foreign producers, other countries' economies grew, and rising trade contributed to a climate that encouraged others to open their markets also.

That movement toward free trade progressed in a series of steps. At the time of the Bretton Woods negotiations, the United States envisioned a new International Trade Organization (ITO) that would seek lower restrictions on trade and set rules of commerce. The organization was stillborn, however. The proposed trading scheme, popularly known as the Havana Charter, failed to win the approval of the U.S. Congress: "Protectionists opposed the arrangement for being too liberal, and liberals were against it for being too protectionist. . . . Without U.S. support the ITO was dead" (Isaak 2000).

Without the ITO, the United States needed to find another institutional base from which to create and enhance a liberalized trade regime. It turned to the **General Agreement on Tariffs and Trade (GATT)** that, after its birth in the late 1940s, became the principal international organization designed to promote and protect free trade in the postwar LIEO.

GATT was never intended to be a formal institution with enforcement powers. Instead, a premium was placed on negotiations and reaching consensus to settle disputes among parties to the agreement, which was first and foremost a commercial treaty. As the trading system changed and disputes multiplied, though, GATT—under pressure from the United States—increasingly became involved in dispute settlement following increasingly legalistic procedures. Those rules put into law an evolving regime whose primary mission has been increasing free trade.

The emergence of a global free trade regime is a history of starts and stops along the progressive path toward the reduction of barriers to the free flow of goods across national borders. Progress toward lower tariffs has encountered resistance along the way, but in 1994 the GATT sessions in the **Uruguay Round** of negotiations that had begun in 1986 culminated in the 1995 creation of the **World Trade Organization (WTO),** a new free-trade IGO with "teeth" (see Table 9.2 and Figure 9.1). That 22,000-page agreement was the most comprehensive trade deal in history, covering everything from paper clips to jet aircraft.

The WTO represents a breathtaking step in free-trade management, although it has also provoked much controversy (see Controversy: Globalization's Growing Pains). The WTO extended GATT's coverage to products, sectors, and conditions of trade not previously covered adequately. The WTO also enhanced previous dispute-settlement procedures by making the findings of its

■ **General Agreement on Tariffs and Trade (GATT)**
an international organization affiliated with the United Nations that promotes international trade and tariff reductions, now the World Trade Organization.

■ **Uruguay Round**
the multilateral trade negotiations of GATT that began in 1986 and concluded in 1994 with the creation of the WTO.

■ **World Trade Organization (WTO)**
a multilateral agency that monitors the implementation of trade agreements and settles disputes among trade partners.

TABLE 9.2 AND FIGURE 9.1

Round and Round: A GATT-WTO Chronology

Date	Summary
1947	Birth of the GATT, signed by twenty-three countries on October 30 at the Palais des Nations in Geneva.
1948	The GATT comes into force. First meeting of its members in Havana, Cuba.
1949	Second round of talks at Annecy, France. Some five thousand tariff cuts agreed to; ten new countries admitted.
1950–51	Third round at Torquay, England. Members exchange 8,700 trade concessions and welcome four new countries.
1956	Fourth round at Geneva. Tariff cuts worth $1.3 trillion at today's prices.
1960–62	The Dillon Round, named after U.S. Undersecretary of State Douglas Dillon, who proposed the talks. A further 4,400 tariff cuts.
1964–67	The Kennedy Round. Many industrial tariffs halved. Signed by fifty countries. Code on dumping agreed to separately.
1973–79	The Tokyo Round, involving ninety-nine countries. First serious discussion of nontariff trade barriers, such as subsidies and licensing requirements. Average tariff on manufactured goods in the nine biggest markets cut from 7 percent to 4.7 percent.
1986–93	The Uruguay Round. Further cuts in industrial tariffs, export subsidies, licensing, and customs valuation. First agreements on trade in services and intellectual property.
1995	Formation of WTO with power to settle disputes between members.
1997	Agreements concluded on telecommunications services, information technology, and financial services.
1999	The "Millennium Round" convenes at Seattle in November to organize for a new round of multilateral trade negotiations. Thousands demonstrate against globalization and trade liberalization, including numerous NGOs pressuring the WTO to advance their agendas.
2000	The WTO grows to 135 members, and more than 30 other states are applicants for membership. WTO opens new negotiations to revamp rules of trade on agricultural goods and services.
2001	WTO resumes discussions in Doha, Qatar, in hope that the remote setting will prevent protest disruptions from antiglobalization protestors. 142 states unsuccessfully chart a path for the world's biggest economies to deal cooperatively with regionalism between competitive trade blocs and to raise hopes for recovery.
2002	WTO convenes in New York. Later admits China and Taiwan to its membership, which grows to 145 members.

The liberalization of the international trading system is the product of cooperative efforts within the framework of the General Agreement on Tariffs and Trade, as shown in this summary of the major GATT multilateral negotiating rounds since its creation in 1947 (top) and the growth of trade among the WTO's members since 1985 (bottom). The free-trade regime has greatly aided the expansion of global trade, which more than doubled in the last fifteen years of the twentieth century. One indicator of the growing magnitude of trade interdependence is the fact that world trade now accounts for 25 percent of all countries' GDP— twice its share in 1970 (*Economist* September 28, 2002, 22).

SOURCE: Adapted from *The Economist*, May 16, 1998, p. 22 (top) and Aug. 28, 1998, p. 52 (bottom). Copyright © 1998 by The Economist Newspaper Ltd. All rights reserved. Reprinted with permission. Further reproduction prohibited. www.economist.com

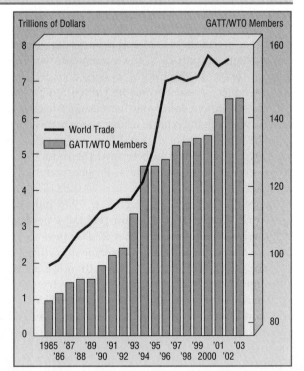

arbitration panels binding on the domestic laws of participating states (GATT's findings were not binding). Finally, the WTO deals with the problem of free riding by being available only to states that belong to GATT, subscribe to all of the Uruguay Round agreements, and make market access commitments (under the old GATT system, free riding was possible when some small states were permitted to benefit from trade liberalization without having to make contributions of their own).

The accord's acceptance was hailed as a big step toward keeping the liberal trade regime afloat in an increasingly competitive and globalized world economy. Today, three-fourths of the globe's countries derive at least 30 percent of their national income from exports (Allen 2002, 58). The WTO was reconfigured to guard against trade wars. The incentives for lowering barriers to free trade are powerful, since much evidence supports the liberal proposition that exports and imports contribute to higher standards of living (Mandelbaum 2002). The creation of the WTO signaled a victory for liberalism and a setback for neomercantilist free riding. At the same time, this transforming treaty advanced globalization and multilateralism, because it "reduced the powers of all governments to regulate behavior and set independent economic policies" (Thurow 1998). Trade squabbles will nonetheless continue despite overwhelming profits from trade liberalization. There are many tricks to free trade, and contentious issues will inevitably cast the spotlight on the continuing frictions caused by a shrinking globe of competitive states. Free trade generates new jobs and wealth, but laissez-faire international capitalism also brings unprecedented risks.

MONETARY MATTERS: CAN FINANCIAL REGIMES PROMOTE GROWTH?

States cannot always trade as they wish. The exports and imports depend on many factors, especially on changes in global demand and prices for the goods and services that countries' producers sell in the global marketplace. The mechanisms for setting the currency exchange rates by which the value of traded goods are priced heavily influence international trade. Indeed, the **monetary system** is crucial for international trade, for without a stable and predictable method of calculating the value of sales and foreign investments, those transactions become too risky, causing trade and investment activities to fall. As the World Bank argues, the success of international trade and "market reforms depends on the health of the financial system."

The Nuts and Bolts of Monetary Policy

Monetary and financial policies are woven into a complex set of relationships between states and the international system, and, because monetary and currency issues have their own specialized technical terminology, they are difficult to understand. However, the essentials are rather basic:

> **Monetary policy** works on two principal economic variables: the aggregate supply of money in circulation and the level of interest rates. The **money supply** (currency plus commercial bank demand deposits) is thought to be

■ **monetary system**
a stable and predictable method for calculating the value of sales and foreign investments across national currencies.

■ **monetary policy**
the decisions made by states' central banks to regulate the national economy and control inflation using policies such as changing the money supply and interest rates.

■ **money supply**
the total amount of currency in circulation in a state, calculated to include demand deposits, such as checking accounts, in commercial banks and time deposits, such as savings accounts and bonds, in savings banks.

CONTROVERSY

GLOBALIZATION'S GROWING PAINS
Is the World Trade Organization a Friend or Foe?

In late November 1999, the then 135-member countries of the World Trade Organization (WTO) and 30 additional observer states made final preparations to stage in Seattle what was billed as the Millennium Round on trade negotiations—the follow-up to the Uruguay Round of trade talks completed in 1993. At the time the mood was optimistic. The meeting promised to celebrate the free-trade regime for the global marketplace and the contributions that lower trade barriers arguably had made to the growth of international exports and, for many members (particularly the United States), their longest and largest peacetime economic expansion in the twentieth century. There appeared to be widespread recognition that

> Every country in history that has raised its living standards—including the United States—has done so by hitching its wagon to the world economy. . . . During the past [50] years, the world has seen a massive reduction in trade barriers—and consequently the biggest and longest economic boon in history. Between 1950 and [2000], world exports of manufactured goods multiplied [16-fold] and world economic output increased six-fold. All this has meant rising standards of living for people around the world, but most especially those in the West and the United States. (Zakaria 1998a, 40; Micklewhait and Wooldridge 2001)

A half-century of generally rising prosperity had generated a climate of enthusiasm for the power of free trade. Fears of imports tend to recede in good economic times, and, with the best decade ever, most leaders in the twilight of the twentieth century emphasized the sunnier side of free trade. Advocates share the liberal conviction that countries, companies, and consumers have much to gain by a globalized economy freed from restraints on the exchange of goods across borders. A world without walls promotes prosperity and welfare. Negotiators in 1999 expected added benefits from a new trade round that could slash tariffs and other trade barriers in agriculture, manufactured goods, and services.

That mood and the seeming consensus on which it was based was shattered when the Seattle trade talks opened. An estimated fifty thousand to one hundred thousand protesters and grassroots anti-WTO activists, who differed widely in their special interests (the poor, environment, labor, women, indigenous people), joined hands to shout their common opposition to the general idea of globalization and free trade. A plane trailed a banner proclaiming "People Over Profits: Stop WTO" as part of what became known as "The Battle in Seattle" or, alternatively, the "Carnival against Capitalism." A tirade against open trade ensued, fueled by citizen backlash (Broad 2002; Aaronson 2002).

The Seattle conference will be remembered as the moment when the debate over the benefits and costs of the globalized economy rose to the pinnacle of the global agenda. The immediate target of the demonstrations was the WTO; however, the organization itself was simply a convenient symbol of a much larger sea of discontent. The WTO protests—and the failure of the WTO conference attendees to compromise on tightly held positions and agree on even a minimal accord—exposed the deep divisions about the best ways to open global commerce and adopt new rules at a time of rapid change.

Controversies about globalization, free trade, and global governance are multiple. At the core is the question of whether a globalized economy is inevitable and, if so, is it an antidote to suffering or an enemy of human welfare. The debates are explosive, because everyone is affected, but in quite different ways. Many are enjoying the boom years under liberalized trade engineered by the WTO's trade agreements. But the celebration is confined largely to the top—the privileged,

directly related to the level of economic activity in the sense that a greater money supply induces expanded economic activity by enabling people to purchase more goods and services. This in essence is the *monetarist theory* of economic activity. Its advocates argue that by controlling the growth of the money supply, governments can regulate their nations' economic activity and control inflation. (Todaro 2000, 657)

Peter Dejong/AP/Wide World

powerful, and prosperous. Many others see themselves as clear victims of an open global economy, as when a factory closes and workers lose their jobs. Those discontented with globalized free trade include a diverse coalition of protestors, many of whom harbor very specific concerns about wages, the environment, and human rights issues. Labor leaders contend that the WTO is sacrificing worker rights; environmental groups complain that when green values collide with world commerce, environmental standards are left out of trade negotiations; and human rights activists accuse the WTO of serving the preferences of MNCs for erasing trade barriers in ways that fail to protect human rights. In addition, enraged trade ministers from the Global South's developing countries see a Global North conspiracy in the WTO's efforts to adopt core labor standards, because the less-developed Global South views such high-sounding rules as a method to impose

high tariffs on their products and take away the comparative advantages Global South developing nations enjoy with lower wage scales.

These, and other issues, are certain to continue as major controversies. What do you think? Is the WTO a valuable tool for improving global governance and human welfare or a threat? Is the WTO and the free trade practices it promotes too strong or too weak? Does the WTO put corporate greed and profits above human rights and environmental protection, as critics charge? Or do you agree with WTO Director General Mike Moore's defense of free trade, and his warning against what he called a "false debate" between people and the WTO, when he maintained "Trade is the ally of working people, not their enemy. As living standards improve, so does education, health, the environment and labor standards." What direction should global trade take?

To understand the importance of monetary policies as a determinant of states' trade, growth rates, and wealth consider both why **exchange rates** (see Table 9.3) fluctuate and the impact of these currency fluctuations. Money works in several ways and serves different purposes. First, money must be widely accepted, so that people earning it can use it to buy goods and services from others. Second, money must serve to store value, so that people will be willing to keep some of their wealth in the form of money. Third, money must act as a

■ **exchange rate**
the rate at which one state's currency is exchanged for another state's currency in the global marketplace.

TABLE 9.3

Currency Concerns: Concepts for Conversing about International Exchange Rates and Balance-of-Payments Issues

Term	Concept
Balance of Payments	A calculation summarizing a country's financial transactions with the external world, determined by the level of credits (export earnings, profits from foreign investment, receipts of foreign aid) minus the country's total international debts (imports, interest payments on international debts, foreign direct investments, and the like). A favorable balance of payments is achieved when a country's international credits exceed its national debits, as recorded in its current account (the market value of exports and imports with the rest of the world) and its capital account (the ratio of a country's private and foreign investments flowing into and outside the country).
Balance-of-Trade Deficit	A situation that results when a state buys more from abroad than it sells. The balance measures both the value of merchandise goods and services imported and exported. To correct a payments deficit, a country has available three basic but painful options: (1) its government can initiate deflationary policies at home by raising interest rates to tighten budgets; (2) it can restrict the outflow of money by imposing higher tariffs, import quotas, or other restrictions; or (3) it can borrow in capital markets or liquidate its foreign exchange reserves.
Central Bank	The major "financial institution [in a state] responsible for issuing currency, managing foreign reserves, implementing monetary policy, and providing banking services to the government and commercial banks" (Todaro 2000).
Devaluation	The lowering of the official exchange rate of one country's currency relative to the value of all other states' currencies, usually in the hope that the devaluation will encourage foreigners to purchase products through trade at the artificially reduced price.
Exchange Rate	The rate at which one state's currency is exchanged for another state's currency in the global marketplace. For 1 U.S. dollar, you might receive 1.5 Swiss francs or 9 Mexican pesos. Exchange rates are subject to rapid fluctuations, usually changing daily, though to small degrees. One day your 1 U.S. dollar might buy 1.51 Swiss francs and the next day 1.54 Swiss francs.
External Debt	"Debt owed by a country to non-residents repayable in foreign currency, goods and services" (UNDP 1999).
Fixed Exchange Rate	A system in which a government sets the value of its currency at a fixed rate for exchange in relation to another country's currency (usually the U.S. dollar) so that the exchange value is not free to fluctuate in the global money market.
Floating Exchange Rate	The system that replaced the Bretton Woods system of fixed exchange rates in the early 1970s, when the link between the dollar and gold was severed. Market forces, rather than government actions, are expected to adjust the relative value of states' currencies to reflect the underlying strengths and weaknesses of their economies. In principle, a floating exchange rate is based on the expectation that imbalances in states' payments to one another will more or less automatically adjust themselves, but in practice states have intervened frequently to ensure monetary stability and flexibility.
Managed Exchange Rate System	The kind of system constructed by the European Union (EU) when it created the single European currency, the euro. The European Monetary System (EMS) links the currencies of EU members whose governments pledge to stabilize currency values through government intervention if necessary.
Official Exchange Rate	The rate at which a state's central bank agrees to buy and sell its currency in exchange for a unit of another country's currency such as the U.S. dollar.

standard of deferred payment, so that people will be willing to lend money knowing that when the money is repaid in the future, it will still have purchasing power.

Governments attempt to manage their currencies to prevent inflation. Inflation occurs when the government creates too much money in relation to the goods and services produced in the economy. As money becomes more plentiful and thus less acceptable, it cannot serve effectively to store value or to satisfy debts or as a medium of exchange.

Movements in a state's exchange rate occur in part when changes develop in peoples' assessment of the national currency's underlying economic strength or the ability of its government to maintain the value of its money. A deficit in a country's balance of payments, for example, would likely cause a decline in the value of its currency relative to that of others. This happens when the supply of the currency is greater than the demand for it. Similarly, when those engaged in international economic transactions change their expectations about a currency's future value, they might reschedule their lending and borrowing. Fluctuations in the exchange rate could follow.

Speculators—those who buy and sell money in an effort to make it—may also affect the international stability of a country's currency. Speculators make money by guessing the future. If, for instance, they believe that the Japanese yen will be worth more in three months than it is now, they can buy yen today and sell them for a profit three months later. Conversely, if they believe that the yen will be worth less in three months, they can sell yen today for a certain number of dollars and then buy back the same yen in three months for fewer dollars, making a profit. The globalization of finance now also encourages managers of investment portfolios to move funds from one currency to another in order to realize gains from differences in states' interest rates.

In the same way that governments try to protect the value of their currencies at home, they try to protect them internationally by intervening in currency markets. Their willingness to do so is important to importers and exporters, who depend on orderliness and predictability in the value of the currencies they deal in to carry out transnational exchanges. Governments intervene when countries' central banks buy or sell currencies to change the value of their own currencies in relation to those of others. Unlike speculators, however, governments are pledged not to manipulate exchange rates so as to gain unfair advantages, for states' reputations as custodians of monetary stability are valuable. Whether governments can affect their currencies' values in the face of large transnational movements of capital is, however, increasingly questionable. So is the value of any country's currency in relation to any other's (see Figure 9.2).

The Bretton Woods Monetary System

When the leaders of the capitalist West met at Bretton Woods, they were acutely aware of the need to create a reliable mechanism for determining the value of countries' currencies in relation to one another, and agreed to a set of concepts to define monetary and currency policy for conducting international trade and finance. Recognizing that a shared system and vocabulary was a necessary precondition for trade, and from it post–World War II economic recovery and prosperity, the negotiating parties agreed that the postwar monetary regime should be based on **fixed exchange rates** and assigned governments primary responsibility

■ **fixed exchange rates**
a system under which states establish the parity of their currencies and commit to keeping fluctuations in their exchange rates within narrow limits.

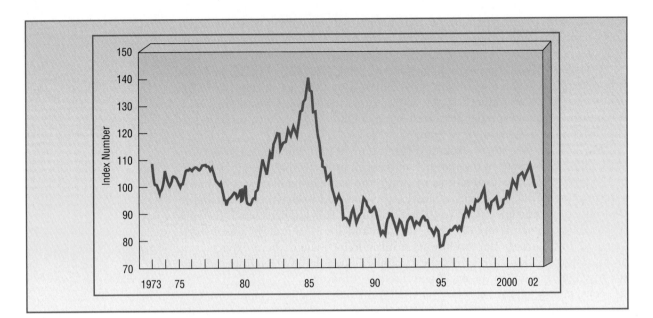

FIGURE 9.2

How to Tell a Real Bargain? Calculating the Cost of Goods in the Globe's Confusing Currency Exchange System

Countries must constantly estimate their current account trade balance with other countries, after trade transactions are made, because, in the U.S. case, the dollar has risen and fallen relative to the currencies of the other powers since 1980. The figure on the left shows the weighted average of the foreign exchange values of the U.S. dollar against a subset of the currencies of a large group of major U.S. trading partners. The value of the U.S. dollar declined since 1985 (making U.S. exports less expensive for people in many other countries to purchase), but rose seven straight years between April 1995 and 2001 as the world's (overvalued?) supercurrency before slipping in 2002 amidst fears of U.S. debt and a possible recession.

Anyone traveling abroad soon finds the costs of items difficult to calculate in terms of the home currency and difficult to compare to what it would cost at home. In each case, it is necessary to convert the foreign price to one's local price by calculating the currency exchange rate, which can change daily and even hourly. One way of calculating exchange rates is by the purchasing-power parity (PPP), which adjusts the price of goods to equalize their price across countries. The index on the right first formulated in the mid-1980s by the *Economist* displays the differentials according to one item, the price of a Big Mac sold by McDonald's in more than 120 countries. In the long run, countries' exchange rates should move towards rates that would equalize the prices of an identical basket of goods and services. . . . The Big Mac PPP is the exchange rate that would leave hamburgers costing the same in America as elsewhere. Comparing these with actual rates signals if a currency is under- or overvalued" (*Economist*, April 27, 2002, 76).

To compare the size of countries economies, the simplest method is to convert GDP into a common currency such as the U.S. dollar. But this method is misleading because it overlooks differences in *relative* prices, as the Big Mac Index suggests, because non-tradable goods are usually less expensive in poor countries than in wealthy ones. The center figure adjusts for differences in purchasing power, with the result that poor countries have relatively bigger GDPs when calculated by this method.

SOURCES: Major Currencies Index, U.S. Federal Reserve; *The Economist*, Dec. 22, 2001, p. 130 (Big Mac Index), and May 12, 2001, p. 110 (size of economies). Copyright © 2001 by The Economist Newspaper Ltd. All rights reserved. Reprinted with permission. Further reproduction prohibited. www.economist.com

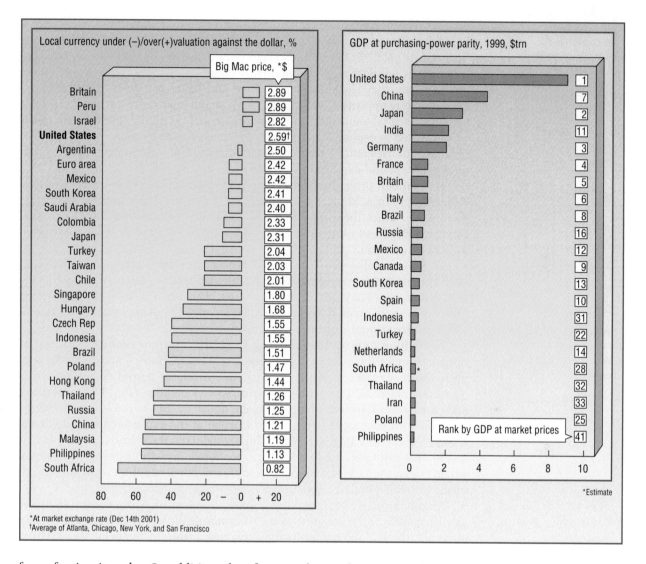

Local currency under (–)/over(+)valuation against the dollar, %

Big Mac price, *$

Britain	2.89
Peru	2.89
Israel	2.82
United States	2.59†
Argentina	2.50
Euro area	2.42
Mexico	2.42
South Korea	2.41
Saudi Arabia	2.40
Colombia	2.33
Japan	2.31
Turkey	2.04
Taiwan	2.03
Chile	2.01
Singapore	1.80
Hungary	1.68
Czech Rep	1.55
Indonesia	1.55
Brazil	1.51
Poland	1.47
Hong Kong	1.44
Thailand	1.26
Russia	1.25
China	1.21
Malaysia	1.19
Philippines	1.13
South Africa	0.82

80 60 40 20 – 0 + 20

*At market exchange rate (Dec 14th 2001)
†Average of Atlanta, Chicago, New York, and San Francisco

GDP at purchasing-power parity, 1999, $trn

United States	1
China	7
Japan	2
India	11
Germany	3
France	4
Britain	5
Italy	6
Brazil	8
Russia	16
Mexico	12
Canada	9
South Korea	13
Spain	10
Indonesia	31
Turkey	22
Netherlands	14
South Africa *	28
Thailand	32
Iran	33
Poland	25
Philippines	41

Rank by GDP at market prices

0   2   4   6   8   10

*Estimate

for enforcing its rules. In addition, they foresaw the need to create what later became the **International Monetary Fund (IMF),** to help states maintain equilibrium in their balance of payments and stability in their exchange rates with one another. The International Bank for Reconstruction and Development, known as the **World Bank,** was also created to aid recovery from the war.

Today the IMF and World Bank are important, if controversial, players in the global monetary and financial systems. Their primary mission is to serve as "lenders of last resort" when its member states face financial crises, providing those seeking assistance meet the often painful conditions requiring domestic adjustments to strengthen their economies'. In the period immediately after World War II, these institutions commanded too little authority and too few resources to cope with the enormous devastation of the war. The United States stepped into the breach.

The U.S. dollar became the key to the hegemonic role that the United States eagerly assumed as manager of the international monetary system. Backed by a vigorous and healthy economy, a fixed relationship between gold and the

■ **International Monetary Fund (IMF)** a financial agency with 185 members affiliated with the United Nations, formed in 1945, to promote international monetary cooperation, free trade, exchange rate stability, and democratic rule by providing financial assistance and loans to countries facing financial crises.

■ **World Bank**
also known as the International Bank of Reconstruction and Development (IBRD), the World Bank is the globe's major IGO for financing economic growth.

dollar (pegged at $35 per ounce of gold), and the U.S. commitment to exchange gold for dollars at any time (known as "dollar convertibility"), the dollar became "as good as gold." In fact, others preferred dollars to gold for use in managing their balance-of-payments and savings accounts. Dollars earned interest, which gold did not; they did not incur storage and insurance costs; and they were needed to buy imports necessary for survival and postwar reconstruction. Thus a dollar-based system, with the dollar a universally accepted "parallel currency," was accepted in exchange markets as the reserve used by monetary authorities in most countries and by private banks, corporations, and individuals for international trade and capital transactions.

To maintain the value of their currencies, central banks in other countries either bought or sold their own currencies, using the dollar to raise or depress their value. Thus the Bretton Woods monetary regime was based on fixed exchange rates and ultimately required a measure of government intervention for its preservation.

■ **international liquidity**
reserve assets used to settle international accounts.

To get U.S. dollars into the hands of those who needed them most, the Marshall Plan provided Western European states billions of dollars in aid to buy the U.S. goods necessary for rebuilding their war-torn economies. The United States also encouraged deficits in its own balance of payments as a way of providing **international liquidity** in the form of dollars.

In addition to providing liquidity, the United States assumed a disproportionate share of the burden of rejuvenating Western Europe and Japan. It supported European and Japanese trade competitiveness, permitted certain forms of protectionism (such as Japanese restrictions on importing U.S. products), and condoned discrimination against the dollar (as in the European Payments Union, which promoted trade within Europe at the expense of trade with the United States). The United States willingly incurred these leadership costs and others' free riding because subsidizing economic growth in Europe and Japan would widen the U.S. export markets and strengthen the West against communism's possible popular appeal.

Although this system worked well with the United States operating as the world's banker, the costs grew as the enormous number of dollars held by others made the U.S. economy increasingly vulnerable to financial shocks from abroad. As the British had discovered before, U.S. leadership made devaluing the dollar without hurting U.S. allies difficult; nor could inflationary or deflationary pressures at home be managed without hurting allies abroad. This reduced the United States' ability to use the normal methods available to other states for dealing with the disruption caused by deficits in a country's balance of trade, such as adjusting interest and currency exchange rates.

■ **commercial domino theory**
the notion that under conditions of globalization the depletion of one country's currency reserves panics investors worldwide and spreads like a contagious disease to other countries, which, in a chain reaction, witness the decline of their own currency reserves as the flight of capital also reduces the value of their currency.

The End of Bretton Woods

As early as 1960 it was clear that the dollar's top currency status could not be sustained by U.S. hegemony. A number of developments combined to destroy the monetary system, leading to a crisis in which the collapse of one country's economy and currency—in a modern version of the **commercial domino theory**—leads to "fiscal contagion" that spreads uncontrollably around the world, wreaking havoc on global capitalism. The fall of fiscal dominos rippling through the world economy has become a common experience in a tightly interconnected international monetary system, in which capital and currency

Dealing with Economic Integration New skyscrapers—a symbol of economic growth—dot the skyline of Shanghai, the venue of the ninth meeting of the Asia-Pacific Economic Co-operation (APEC) forum held in July 2001 to respond to growing economic and trade interdependence in the region.

move instantaneously outside borders at the slightest sign of fiscal troubles. In any imploding national market, when one country's currency reserves are depleted, it sets in motion panic abroad as investors reduce their holdings and the flight of capital brings down other countries in a chain reaction (Sanger 1998). For the first time in history a single, integrated global economic system had emerged, and the deficiencies of global financial institutions with unstable fixed and floating currencies have become apparent. Not much is being done to revise and reform the shaky existing global financial architecture. In a world of increasingly mobile capital, volatility in capital flows threatens, in the absence of international financial regulation, to end the continuation of world economic growth.

"Much of the international relations literature concerned with prospects for international monetary reform can be read as a search for an alternative to hegemony as a basis for international monetary stability" (Eichengreen 2000), and the need for a reformed system stems in large part from the failure of the United States to adjust its policies so it could continue to serve as a hegemonic stabilizing force in international finance or unilaterally regulate international monetary affairs.

Floating Exchange Rates

After 1971, U.S. President Nixon abruptly announced—without consulting with allies—that the United States would no longer exchange dollars for gold. With the price of gold no longer fixed and dollar convertibility no longer guaranteed, the Bretton Woods system gave way to a substitute system based on **floating exchange rates.** Market forces, rather than government intervention, were now expected to determine currency values. A country experiencing adverse economic conditions now saw the value of its currency fall in response to the choices of traders, bankers, and businesspeople. This was expected to make its exports cheaper and its imports more expensive, which in turn would pull its currency's value back toward equilibrium—all without the need for central bankers to support their currencies. In this way, it was hoped that the politically humiliating devaluations of the past could be avoided.

Those expectations were not met. Beginning in the late 1970s, escalating in the 1980s, and persisting through the 1990s, a rising wave of financial crises, both in currency and banking, has occurred (see World Bank 2002a, 85; 1999, 125). These have been compounded by massive defaults by countries unable to service their debts—a chronic problem that has pushed the international monetary regime to the brink of destruction. Thirty-seven countries currently have foreign debts in excess of $10 billion dollars—a staggering sum of indebtedness that leaves many countries exposed to external economic and political influence (*Economist* 2002, 38; see also Allen 2002, 56). Even the most powerful are vulnerable; the United States is in this danger zone, with a huge external deficit at over 4 percent of its GDP, a burden so large that the U.S. will have to pay on interest to foreigners nearly $2 billion everyday (*Economist*, April 27, 2002, 12).

Financial crises have become increasingly frequent around the world as a result of the inability of states to manage debt, inflation, interest, and income in a volatile monetary system fraught with wild currency exchange rate gyrations. In the past thirty-five years, more than one hundred major episodes of banking insolvency occurred in ninety developing and emerging countries. The financial cost of these crises, in terms of the percentage of GDP lost, has been huge. The disastrous debts generated by banking and currency disruptions forced governments to suffer, on average between 1970 and 1997, direct loses of nearly 15 percent of their GDP for each crisis and more than a 5 percent decline in output growth after each crisis (World Bank 1999a, 126).

In response to the growing awareness of the extent to which the health of others' economies depended on the value of the U.S. dollar internationally (which in turn depended on the underlying strength of the U.S. economy), since 1985 the Group of Five (or G-5 great powers, the United States, Britain, France, Japan, and Germany) has adhered to the landmark agreement reached secretly at the Plaza Hotel in New York City, in which they pledged to collectively coordinate their economic policies through management of exchange rates internationally and interest rates domestically.

The **Group of Seven** (the **G-7,** consisting of the G-5 plus Canada and Italy) and the **G-8** (with the inclusion of Russia in 1997) have sought to carry out the pledge to coordinate global monetary policy. However, at the G-8 summit in Genoa in July 2001, it was clear that the leading industrial powers were unable to reach consensus about the best way to manage exchange rates, monetary and fiscal policies, and trade relations in order to sustain global economic growth.

■ **floating exchange rates**
an unmanaged process where market forces rather than governments influence the relative rate of exchange for currencies between countries.

■ **Group of Seven (G-7)/Group of Eight (G-8)**
a group of advanced industrialized democracies composed of the United States, Britain, France, Japan, Germany, Canada, and Italy that meets in regular economic summit conferences; since 1997, known as the G-8 with the addition of Russia.

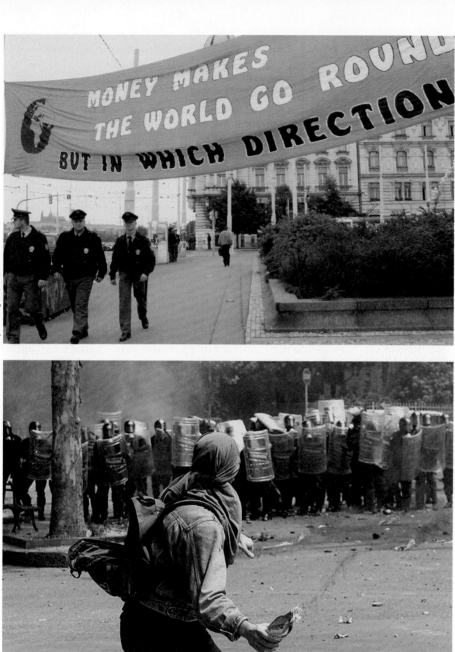

Financial Empires without Umpires? Currency moves rapidly throughout the world, and in principle in a free global marketplace it should gravitate to any location where investors believe they can make a profit. The game is played according to rules, but it remains true that the rules are created by the wealthy finance managers of powerful state governments which create the exchange-rate systems by which their currencies are adjusted to facilitate investments and trade. Monetary policies create currency dilemmas which sometimes unleash hostile feelings. For example, when finance ministers lower interest rates in ways that benefit a country with high unemployment, that shift breeds inflation in other countries with low unemployment. Some people opposed to the integration of international finance see monetary adjustments as a conspiracy designed to enrich the wealthy few at the expense of the many. Shown here are two examples. Top, Czech police pass under a protest banner reading, "Money makes the world go round—but in which direction?" at the September 2000 annual economic summit of the IMF and the World Bank in Prague. Bottom, a scene of a protestor preparing to throw a firebomb at the G-8 Genoa summit in July 2001, where 20,000 policeman pitched battles with demonstrators.

In the absence of true collective management of global monetary conditions, it appears likely that the volume of world trade and the activities of currency speculators (who use sophisticated global electronic technologies and rely on about two thousand "hedge funds" to make profits in currency trading) will increasingly determine national currency values. An average of over $1.5 trillion in currency trading occurs each day—a transfer of capital greater than one-fourth of the world's average *weekly* level of international trade. International sales of stocks and bonds have mushroomed as well and promise to rise through increased investor trading on the Internet. In the volatile world of increasingly mobile capital, wide fluctuations in national currencies' exchange rates have become common. The globalization of finance and the removal of barriers to capital flows across borders expose national economies to shocks, with little hope that such volatility will vanish.

Plans for Reforming the International Financial Architecture

"No institution has worldwide responsibility for the arrangement of capital flows at present [although there does exist] an entire set of principles, standards and rule of relatively universal scope" (Berthelot 2001). Hardly anyone is happy with the prevailing weak and somewhat haphazard global financial architecture, but it appears that only when severe financial crises occur which threaten a global recession that sufficient pressure mounts to engineer new reforms, beyond the cosmetic improvements in monitoring transactions and making money exchanges transparent in an attempt to control the money laundering practices of crime syndicates and terrorist groups.

Many proposals have been advanced for reforming the international monetary system to help cushion the aftershocks of the rapid movement of investment funds among countries that creates booms and busts, such as the 1980s Latin American debt crisis and the global crisis that followed on the heels of the 1997–1998 flight of capital from Asia. Some see reversion to the pre–World War I gold standard as preferable to the exchange rates with highly fluctuating currencies. Others recommend something like the Bretton Woods system of fixed but adjustable rates.

What these and other proposals seek is a mechanism for creating the currency stability and flexibility on which prosperity through trade depends and which the current system has failed to achieve. However, there is little agreement about how to bring reforms about. With global democratization, most governments face domestic pressures to sacrifice such goals as exchange rate stability for unemployment reduction, so it seems likely that floating exchange rates, with all their costs and uncertainties, are here to stay. As one observer notes,

> The world is a far different place than it was when currency rates were fixed during the first quarter century after World War II. At that time, governments maintained strict controls over the flow of capital across their borders. Today, money sloshes around the world . . . because of the widely accepted view that growth will be maximized if capital is free to seek the highest returns. And whatever action is taken to limit "hot" money flows, few if any experts believe the broad trend can or should be reversed. (Blustein 1999a, 6)

Frederick Brown/AFP

Eric Feferberg/AFP

The Domino Effect in Global Finance When a country's banks go bankrupt and its economy collapses, foreign capital flees in panic. No worldwide central bank exists to cushion such crashes. Money problems in one country lead to money problems in others, provoking currency depreciations and plunges in stock prices at home and abroad. Here stunned brokers react to the January 1998 plummet of Hong Kong stocks that caused the key indexes elsewhere in Asia, London, Frankfort, New York, and Paris to fall. Described as "the worst international financial crisis in fifty years [which] took global finance to the edge of collapse." (Altman and Cutter 1999), since then no serious reforms have been implemented.

The International Monetary Fund finds itself

> at the center of a host of proposals for reforming the "international financial architecture" [despite the fact that] there is a widely shared sense that the IMF had become overextended and overburdened, and hence, that it needs to return to its original mandate and concentrate on preventing and mitigating financial crises, especially liquidity and banking crises, leaving such tasks as reducing poverty to the World Bank. . . . The reality is that the leading powers in the world economy have too much of a stake in existing arrangements to show much appetite for reinventing the IMF or for charting a new Bretton Woods. For these actors, the IMF remains a preferred instrument for coping with financial crises. Hence, while the schemes for alternatives proliferate, the prospects are for incremental tinkering rather than wholesale restructuring. The prospects also tend to favor *ad hoc* case-by-case treatment of financial crises. (Babai 2001a, 418)

That said, it is discomforting that the global currency regime is unstable and erratic and that the lack of an effective exchange mechanism to orchestrate adjustments causes such disruptions in a globalize marketplace in which states' economies are so highly integrated. As long as the flow of trade across borders continues to expand, as is highly likely, the currency dilemmas facing the world are likely to intensify. Currency fluctuations and monetary instability are at the root of the difficulties, and the prevailing regime remains inadequate. No exchange rate system is perfect. Whether countries fix or float to manage their currencies, inevitably problems surface.

As Rubens Ricupero, secretary-general of UNCTAD, warned in 2001,

> The increased frequency and virulence of international currency and financial crises involving even countries with a record of good governance and macroeconomic discipline, suggest that instability is global and systemic. Although there is room to improve national policies and institutions, that alone would not be sufficient to deal with the problem. . . . A strengthening of institutions and arrangements at the international level is essential if the threat of such crises is to be reduced and if they are to be better managed whenever they occur. Yet, despite growing agreement on the global and systemic nature of financial instability, the international community has so far been unable to achieve significant progress.

Some small steps to address short-term financing problems have been taken, such as establishment of the Contingency Credit Line (CCL) through the International Monetary Fund to meet balance-of-payments problems arising from international financial contagion. However, these steps do not correct the major difficulties, and as Secretary-General Ricupero cautions, reform of the international financial architecture is needed: "Financial regulation is constantly struggling to keep up with financial innovation, and in this struggle, it is not always successful. . . . The key question is whether there exists a viable and appropriate exchange rate regime for developing economies when major reserve currencies are subject to frequent gyrations and misalignments, and when international capital exchanges are extremely unstable." In the meantime, the only option available for countries is the choice between "dollarization or regionalization" to weather currency and debt crises.

■ **regional currency union**
the pooling of sovereignty to create a common currency (such as the EU's euro) and single monetary system for members in a region, regulated by a regional central bank within the currency bloc to reduce the likelihood of large-scale liquidity crises.

That conclusion was highlighted by the "solution" to the currency problem adopted by the twelve European countries in 2002, which severed dependence on the U.S. dollar in preference for a **regional currency union** to try to stabilize today's erratic exchange rate fluctuations. To this end, the European Union created for its 305 million people the euro single currency in the hopes that the creation of a single currency will make the European Union a single market for business.

> The European Central Bank (ECB) minted 52 billion new coins (170 for each person in the "euro area") and printed 14.9 billion bank notes (49 per person). The total value is 649 billion euros, which, at present exchange rages (1 euro = 90 cents), is about $584 billion. . . . To its enthusiasts, the euro means economic vitality and political unity. Companies won't have to convert all those different moneys. Easier cross-border price comparisons will compel firms to become more efficient. As cross-border investment rises, money will increasingly go to the most deserving companies. Economics success will strengthen a European consciousness. (Samuelson 2002b, 38)

As innovative as the creation of the euro appears, it may not serve as a model for other countries and regions. The euro remains controversial even in Europe, especially among EU states (Britain, Denmark, and Sweden so far have rejected it). The new common currency is much more than an economic change; to critics it is an ambitious *political* change designed to create a European super-state and thereby erase the individuality and economic and political sovereignty of European states. This solution through currency integration in

Europe can only been seen as a response to the domination of the United States in the global economy, where the U.S. dollar reigns supreme as the global currency for settling international accounts. To many, globalization really means the "dollarization" of the international political economy. As long as U.S. economic and military supremacy continues, it is unlikely that the present free-floating exchange mechanism for currency exchanges valued in terms of the U.S. dollar will be overturned by creation of new global institutions accepting supranational management. And this means that the debate over currency and monetary policies will remain as intense as ever, particularly in the turbulent arena of international trade.

FROM CURRENCY CONCERNS TO TRADE TROUBLES IN THE TWENTY-FIRST CENTURY

Emerging Unilateral Trade Policies

To anticipate the future, we can look at the **unilateral** strategies of individual countries and at the regional strategies of groups of countries or blocs.

> ■ **unilateral**
> a state's policies to manage foreign policy problems independently through self-help measures (see p. 128).

In the past, the United States led the way to the decline of protectionist tariffs in the industrialized world (see Figure 9.3). However, the United States has not consistently advocated free trade; in reaction to its increasingly shaky global position in the 1980s, it began to practice "aggressive unilateralism" by retaliating against states perceived to be engaging in unfair trade practices. The Omnibus Trade Act incorporated a bellicose "Super 301" provision that required the president to identify countries believed to be engaging in unfair trade practices and to force them to either negotiate remedies or face U.S. retaliation. This is symptomatic of the fragility of commitments to free trade, because almost all countries viewed the Super 301 provision as a clear violation of GATT rules. Since then, however, the United States has acted under the milder, less accusatory "ordinary" 301 legislation (which does not carry automatic retaliatory penalties), but has still initiated hundreds of complaints. Hence, free trade remains under challenge. And of course, one of the reasons why the preservation of the free-trade regime is precarious is because the United States itself does not always live up to its own ideals and rhetoric. Many states complain bitterly that the United States imposes many elaborate restrictions on imports that undermine free competition through protectionist policies such as nontariff barriers. The United States has not supported free trade as enthusiastically as it claims and has not always led in the efforts to promote an open trading system. Like the other G-8 great powers, national interests are sometimes put above international ideals:

> The United States, Japan and the EU continue to maintain some of their highest tariffs on sugar, milk, meat, fruits and vegetables, as well as textiles and footwear—precisely the kinds of basic products in which developing countries enjoy a comparative advantage because of low labor costs.
>
> For example, the United States slaps a 244 percent tariff on sugar imports and 174 percent on peanuts, two products grown cheaply in poor countries such as Swaziland and Sudan. Meanwhile, the EU discourages

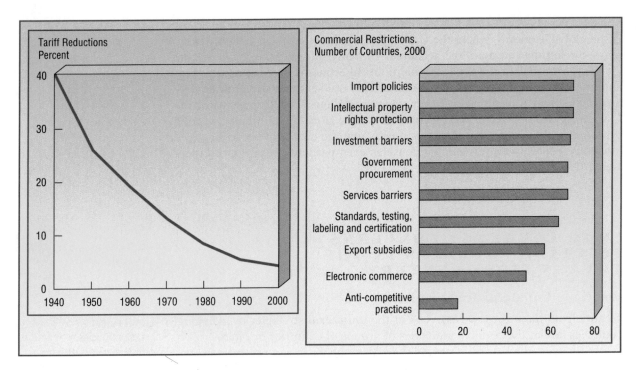

FIGURE 9.3
To Tariff or Not to Tariff—That Is the Question

■ **reciprocity**
the norm that accepts the ethical prescription that actors should treat others as they themselves would wish to be treated, so that the same standards of conduct apply.

All states want the same thing—for other countries to purchase their exports and to protect domestic producers from foreign imports. These goals are incompatible if **reciprocity** is to prevail so that all countries treat international trade according to the same rules that allow goods to be traded without interference. To promote trade, the industrialized countries have greatly reduced tariffs, from the peak period of economic nationalism through protectionism in the 1940s to less than 5 percent today, as shown in the figure on the left. The reduction of tariffs has fostered the growth of trade, thus serving the liberal goal of open trade. However, as the table on the right shows, the temptation to introduce barriers to free trade have been difficult to resist, and many countries have imposed various nontariff barriers to protect their domestic economies from external imports. According to the office of U.S. trade representative, in 2002 roughly sixty countries had established mechanisms for restricting trade with the rest of the world (not including America's own elaborate restrictions and anticompetitive policies and practices). Thus, the struggle between the liberal value of free trade and the mercantilist value of economic nationalism is far from over.

SOURCES: Office of the U.S. Trade Representative, with information on commercial restrictions on imports summarized by *The Economist*, April 7, 2001, p. 121. Copyright © 2001 by The Economist Newspaper Ltd. All rights reserved. Reprinted with permission. Further reproduction prohibited. www.economist.com

beef imports with a tariff of 213 percent, while Japan limits wheat with a 353 percent charge and Canada restricts butter with a 360 percent tax.

"This kind of protectionism as practiced by the wealthiest industrialized countries is simply indefensible," says Nicholas Stern, chief economist of the World Bank. "The cost to developing countries is much greater in lost export opportunities than the amount of official aid they receive each year."

The problem is compounded by "tariff escalation," in which the tariff rate increases when value is added through the processing of a product. For example, Morocco's attempts to sell packaged orange juice or Ghana's efforts to export chocolate candy instead of raw cocoa beans can encounter tariffs that run as much as 50 percent higher than those on the raw commodities. While this method may preserve Western manufacturing jobs, it prevents poor countries from taking the first steps to augment their wealth by moving into more advanced products. (Drozdiak 2001, 17)

U.S. trade policy reflects twin instincts: to push for trade liberalization in foreign markets and to cushion the impact of imports on the U.S. economy and employment rate. The stakes are high; in 1997, the Commerce Department estimated that one in five U.S. jobs was supported by trade. Awareness of this dependence was behind George W. Bush administration's 2002 successful reestablishment of the president's **fast-track negotiating authority** from Congress (suspended in 1994) to permit the president to negotiate trade pacts that U.S. Congress could approve or reject but not change.

■ **fast-track negotiating authority**
a concession by the U.S. Congress permitting the president to negotiate reciprocal tariff-reduction agreements with other countries which, when granted, enables the United States to reach bilateral trade treaties more easily.

How U.S. trade partners and rivals view the American commitment to free trade will shape their own trade policies and whether they will choose free trade over protectionism. Tough negotiations and countercharges plague U.S–China exports as well as the relationships between many other active international trade partners.

Domestic economic policies also tend to shape many countries' foreign trade policies. Observe in this context how countries differ in the extent to which they regulate their national economies within their borders and the degree to which the level of economic freedom within states predicts the level of growth they experience as well as their willingness to open their domestic markets to foreign imports in order to elevate their citizens' standard of living. Overwhelming evidence shows that economic freedom makes for prosperity; those countries which do not interfere with trade at home tend to have the highest average economic growth rates. Liberalism in domestic economic policy pays many financial, political and security dividends. Compare the rankings of countries according to their economic freedom, and we see much evidence supporting the view that open markets stimulate economic growth (Mandelbaum 2002).

Referring to Map 9.1, we see strong evidence suggesting that the most economically free states not only grow their wealth at the fastest rates, but also provide the best or safest environments for investments with the least risk. In addition, these open economies are the least corrupt and least prone to civil wars. This is because economically free countries are also politically free, that is, ruled democratically with civil and legal ways for resolving conflicts, as opposed to economically repressed countries which also politically repress civil liberties and violate citizens' **human rights.**

■ **human rights**
the political rights and civil liberties recognized by the international community as inalienable and valid for individuals in all countries by virtue of their humanity.

Given these seemingly clear-cut economic advantages to free markets and free trade, it is difficult to understand why many governments protectively resist open markets. The answer lies in the fact that trade is profoundly treacherous, and appears in the eye of the beholder to be inherently unfair. Trade unions in wealthy Global North states complain that the lower wages of the Global South countries give them "unfair" advantages and, for their part, the less-developed Global South states complain that they cannot "fairly" compete against their more productive, technologically advanced Global North counterparts. Hence, the age-old debate between free traders and mercantilists is likely to persist as a global issue in the brutally competitive globalized world economy.

Free
Score: 1.00 to 1.95
Mostly Free
Score: 2.00 to 2.95
Mostly Unfree
Score: 3.00 to 3.95
Repressed
Score: 4.00 to 5.00
Not Ranked

Political Risk Ranking (Safest to Riskiest)

USA	4	Singapore	3	China	1	Jordan	0
Canada	4	Finland	3	Malaysia	1	Colombia	0
Sweden	4	Italy	2	Israel	1	Venezuela	0
Switzerland	4	Japan	2	South Africa	1	Pakistan	0
Denmark	4	Taiwan	2	Thailand	1	Vietnam	0
Australia	4	Hong Kong	2	India	1	Turkey	0
Norway	4	Portugal	2	Hungary	1	Ecuador	0
New Zealand	4	Mexico	2	Czech Republic	1	Kenya	0
Netherlands	3	Greece	2	Kuwait	1	Peru	0
United Kingdom	3	South Korea	2	Poland	1	Indonesia	0
Germany	3	Chile	2	Panama	1	Slovakia	0
France	3	Brazil	2	Philippines	1	Bolivia	0
Ireland	3	Argentina	2	Cost Rica	1	Nigeria	0
Belgium	3	United Arab Emirates	2	Egypt	1		
Spain	3	Saudi Arabia	2	Romania	1		
Austria	3	Slovenia	2	Russia	0		

M A P   9 . 1
Ranking Countries by Their Economic Freedom and Political Risk
Much evidence points to the straightforward conclusion backed by the past ten years—that states with the most economic freedom have the highest rates of long-term economic growth. This validates a primary proposition of **neoliberalism,** that free markets promote prosperity. According to this index, economic liberty expanded for the eighth straight year when, at the start of 2003, of 155 countries 71 were either economically "free" or "mostly free" while 85 were "mostly unfree" or "repressed." The "political risk" ranking in the chart on the above suggests another finding in support of neoliberal theory—that the most economically free countries were also those that were the most stable and, as a consequence, the safest environments for corporations and private investors to make investments.
Note: Map based rankings through the year 2002, followed by political risk rankings (on above).
SOURCE: Map from Heritage Foundation website at www.heritage.org; political risk from *World Trade* 14, June 2001, p. 36.

Emerging Regional Trade Policies. A recent trend has been to construct trade partnerships within particular regions. The United States first experimented with this approach in 1984, with the Caribbean Basin Initiative to reduce tariffs and provide tax incentives to promote industrialization and trade. This was soon followed in 1987 with free-trade agreements with Israel and Canada and in 1989 with the **North American Free Trade Agreement (NAFTA)** (signed by Canada, Mexico, and the United States in 1993). NAFTA's purpose was the most ambitious—to integrate the North American region. In addition, at their April 2001 Quebec Summit, the United States and thirty-three Western Hemispheric democracies took a bolder step when they pledged to build the **Free Trade Area of the Americas (FTAA)** in that region by 2005. This would create the globe's largest barrier-free trade zone, from the Artic to Argentina, linking markets to 800 million people.

The successful Mercosur free-trade zone in South America is another example of a regional regime. Its six member countries—Argentina, Brazil, Paraguay, Uruguay, and later Chile and Bolivia—expanded trade sixfold in 1998 to $18.2 billion dollars (from only $3.6 billion dollars in 1991). However, Mercosur's progress stalled in 2002 when Argentina, facing a deep recession, raised tariffs in violation of the agreement, and the barriers posed by differences between Brazil's floating *real* and Argentina's *peso* pegged to the U.S. dollar exchange rate programs compounded the problem, as did nontariff barriers to the otherwise duty-free trade regime within Mercosur. The enlarged ten-member Association of Southeast Asian Nations (ASEAN) free-trade region is representative of yet another among the many multilateral regional trading blocs (see Map 9.2).

Many feel that NAFTA and other regional free-trade zones are consistent with GATT's rules and see regional regimes as vital pieces in the step toward a free-trade agreement for the entire global economy. Others see the division of the globe into competing trade blocs as an obstacle to the global integration of trade zones, fretting that existing regional free-trade zones actually violate the WTO's nondiscrimination principle by moving away from free trade toward inter-bloc competition. In particular, the critics fear that further development of regionalized markets centered on Asia, Europe, and North America has already split globalized trade into competing trade blocs (see Figure 9.4). Currently, almost three-quarters of exports in Asia go within the APEC region to other Asian countries, two-thirds of European exports go within the European Union, and more than half of exports by North American countries stay within the NAFTA bloc (World Bank 2002a, 345).

The ultimate impact of the trend toward regionalization of the world political economy, both nationally and globally, remains uncertain. Some analysts see the formation of trade blocs as likely to undermine the free-trade regime and thereby plague world economic growth in the years ahead. Others are concerned with the possibility that regional economic centers will undermine security relationships. If trade-bloc rivalry intensifies, others warn that result would be a cut-throat mercantile rivalry in which the fear of one another may be the only force binding the regional members together.

Those outside the globe's three major trading blocs have ample reason to be concerned about the prospect of a world divided into separate regional centers. It leaves them outside the system altogether, and even those it encompasses are left relatively weaker as their bargaining power is divided. Therefore, even

■ **North American Free Trade Agreement (NAFTA)**
an agreement that brings Mexico into the free-trade zone linking Canada and the United States.

■ **Free Trade Area of the Americas (FTAA)**
a set of rules to promote free trade among thirty-four democracies in North and South America.

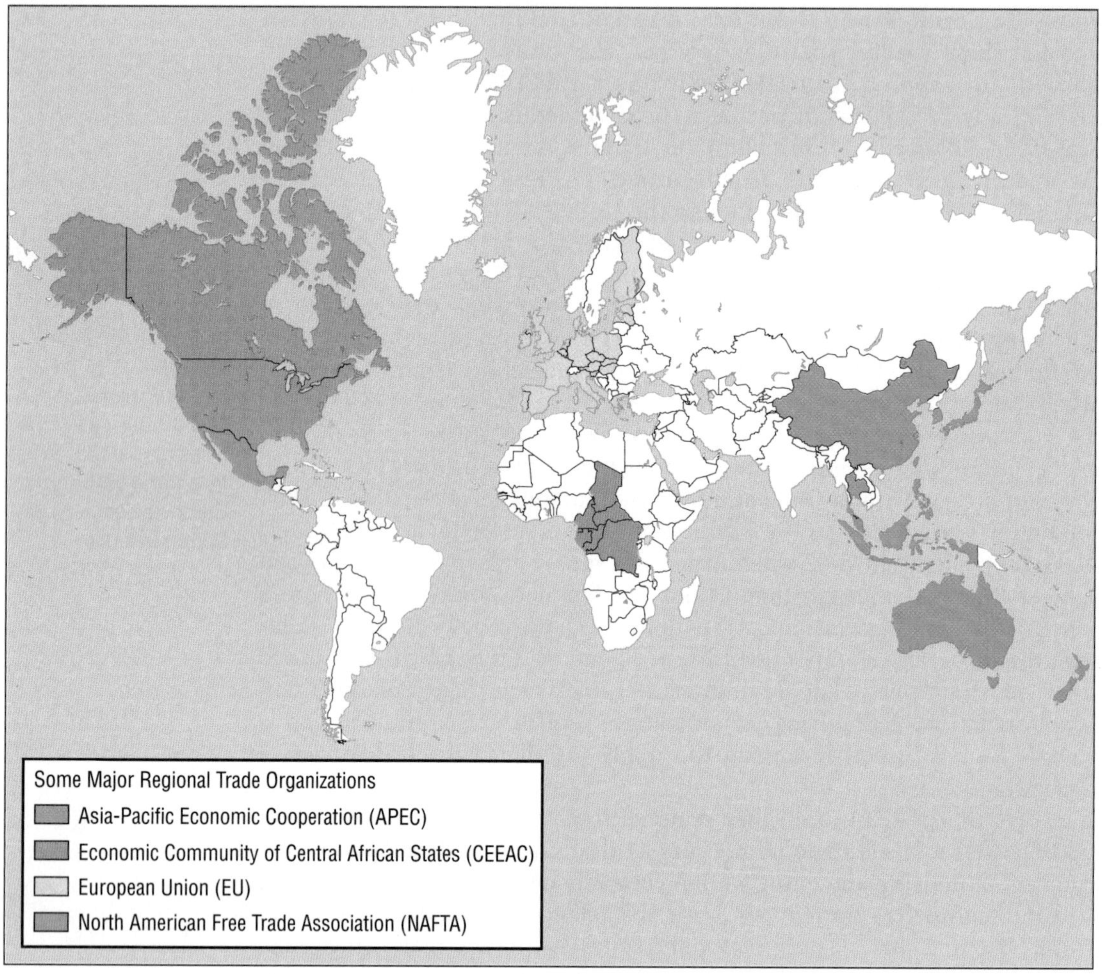

MAP 9.2

Putting Politics into the Management of Free Trade: The Global Network of Regional Trade Organizations

More than 150 regional trade agreements have been registered with the GATT/WTO since 1945, half of which were established after 1990 (*Economist*, October 3, 1998, 19). Shown here are examples of four of the major regional trade organizations whose regimes have been created to set rules for encouraging trade by reducing protectionist barriers. These agreements have tied states into an interlocking web of obligations to liberalize trade. Most states are members of more than one or two trade blocs—indeed many, as shown in the table. For example, Israel, France, the Netherlands, Spain, Belgium, Austria, Portugal, and Mexico have agreements with thirty-five or more separate trade blocs. Each of the regionally focused international trade organizations has been created to steer and secure growing prosperity through free trade under, and consistent with, the umbrella, the universal IGO designed to facilitate trade among countries without barriers, the World Trade Organization.

SOURCE: *World Trade* (2002, 14); Table data from Allen (2000).

The 20 Top-Ranking Countries for Trade Blocs/Agreements		
Country	**Trade Blocs/Agreements**	**Total Trade Block Points**
1 Israel	WIPO, WTO, US, Canada, Hungary, Poland, others	36
2 France	EU, EMU, WIPO, WTO, Sch, Israel, Mexico	35
2 Netherlands	EU, EMU, WIPO, WTO, Sch, Israel, Mexico	35
2 Spain	EU, EMU, WIPO, WTO, Sch, Israel, Mexico	35
2 Belgium	EU, EMU, WIPO, WTO, Sch, Israel, Mexico	35
2 Austria	EU, EMU, WIPO, WTO, Sch, Israel, Mexico	35
2 Portugal	EU, EMU, WIPO, WTO, Sch, Israel, Mexico	35
2 Mexico	NAFTA, WIPO, WTO, APEC, EU, Chile, others	35
9 Germany	EU, EMU, WIPO, WTO, Sch, Israel, Mexico	33
10 Ireland	EU, EMU, WIPO, WTO, Israel, Mexico	32
10 Finland	EU, EMU, WIPO, WTO, Sch, Israel, Mexico	32
10 Chile	Mercosur, WIPO, WTO, APEC, Can, Mex, others	32
13 Italy	EU, EMU, WIPO, Sch, Israel, Mexico	30
14 Canada	NAFTA, WIPO, WTO, APEC, Chile, Israel	28
14 Sweden	EU, WIPO, WTO, Sch, Israel, Mexico	28
14 Denmark	EU, WIPO, WTO, Sch, Israel, Mexico	28
17 USA	NAFTA, WIPO, WTO, APEC, Israel	26
18 United Kingdom	EU, WIPO, WTO, Israel, Mexico	25
18 Greece	EU, WIPO, WTO, Israel, Mexico	25
20 Bolivia	Mercosur, WIPO, WTO	19
20 Brazil	Mercosur, WIPO, WTO	19
20 Argentina	Mercosur, WIPO, WTO	19

though developing Global South countries in the past have regarded the GATT/WTO as a rich man's club, today they see it as a guardian for the clear and fair rules they need if they are to successfully enter the global arena. Beyond the now 145-member WTO, however, developing countries have also spawned a growing number of regional economic cooperation schemes of their own, as discussed in Chapter 6. However, their chances of superseding existing bilateral and multilateral agreements are poor.

THE FATE OF FREE TRADE: TRIUMPH OR TROUBLE IN A GLOBAL AGE?

Since 1950 world trade has grown sixteenfold, reaching in 2001 $7.4 trillion. In the same period, gross world product has grown sevenfold, reaching $45.9 trillion (*Vital Signs 2002,* 59–60). The exponential growth of trade has contributed measurably to the unprecedented rise in global economic prosperity. Reductions in barriers to free trade are expected to accelerate these trends if world trade continues, as in the past five decades, to expand three times faster than real world output (see Figure 9.5). The expected consequence is that **trade integration** will increasingly bind countries' economies ever more tightly in interdependent economic relationships, and thereby promote the further growth of globalization; one estimate predicts that by the year 2015 world trade will comprise 40 percent of world GDP (*Global Trends 2015*).

■ **trade integration**
the difference between growth rates in trade and gross domestic product.

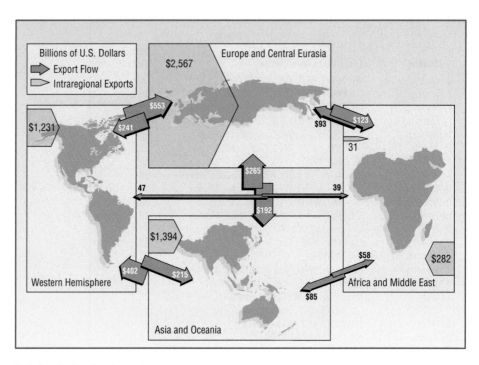

FIGURE 9.4

Trade Blocs and the Regionalization of Global Trade, 2002: A Growth Industry

A trend shaping the global political economy has been a tendency for trade flows to concentrate *within* regions instead of *between* them. The economist Paul Krugman terms this regional bias "the localization of the world economy" (in Mazarr 1999) to capture countries' increasing tendency to trade with regional neighbors rather than with distant regions. This trend has resulted in the formation of four major trade blocs all promoting the removal of state barriers to free trade but more so inside each bloc than among all countries. This map shows the shape of exports within and between the four major trade blocs. Note that trade flows are far from equal—the dollar value of exports varies in directional balance across the major trade regions, showing that the liberal goal of global economic integration—a single marketplace for all—remains just that, an ideal or aspiration yet to be realized. From the perspective of each individual state this presents a challenge, because all states seek imports from all others, irrespective of the regional location of the foreign trade partner.

SOURCE: World Trade Organization, 2002.

■ **most-favored-nation (MFN) principle**
unconditional nondiscriminatory treatment in trade between contracting parties guaranteed by GATT; in 1997, U.S. Sen. Daniel Patrick Moynihan introduced legislation to replace with the term "normal trade relations (NTR)" to better reflect its true meaning.

The projections assume that the process of liberalizing the global political economy will continue. Progress, however, remains problematic if the forces of neomercantilism also remain vibrant. Although hegemonic stability theory would predict that a U.S. leadership decline will inevitably be followed by the liberal trade regime's closure, a collapse of free trade is unlikely. The liberal trade regime may endure with the support of global institutions such as the WTO and liberal regional regimes such as FTAA.

Many states see advantages in rejecting mercantilism and accepting instead the **most-favored-nation (MFN) principle,** now known as normal trade relations (NTR) (which holds that the tariff preferences granted to one state must be granted to all others exporting the same product) as well as the reciprocity

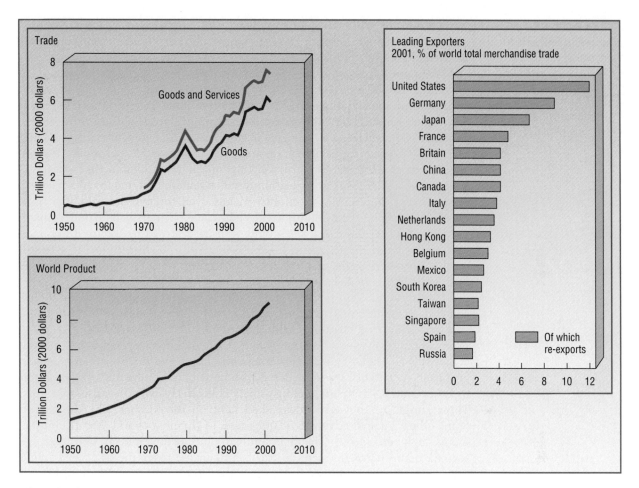

FIGURE 9.5

Global Economic Prospects: The Growth of Trade and Wealth

Since 1970, the volume of world trade has increased on average nearly 4 percent each year. When global trade has risen, almost always so has world wealth. Trade liberalization and liberal market reforms within many countries have spurred both these trends steadily upward. The top figure on the left captures the rising volume of world exports since 1950, and the bottom figure displays the increasing level of gross world product for the same 1950–2001 period. Although trade integration is deepening, the benefits of trade and of a booming global economy are not evenly distributed, as some countries are not participating at the same levels as others. The chart on the right rank orders the top exporting countries according to the percent of total world merchandize trade they control; these seventeen leaders in trade in 2002 captured most of the nearly $6 trillion in global merchandize exports.

Note: Annual growth rates beyond 2003 are projections.

SOURCES: Global trade and economic growth from *Vital Signs 2002*, p. 59, 61. Copyright © 2002 Worldwatch Institute. www.worldwatch.org; leading exporters from *The Economist*, May 18, 2002, p. 25. Copyright © by The Economist Newspaper Ltd. All rights reserved. Reprinted with permission. Further reproduction prohibited. www.economist.com

■ **nondiscrimination**
a principle for trade that proclaims that goods produced at home and abroad are to be treated the same for import and export agreements.

norm (countries will reduce their own tariffs in return for another's reductions) and the **nondiscrimination** rule (goods produced at home and abroad are to be treated the same).

"Free trade is about raising living standards; it is about looking after people better," Mike Moore, the WTO director argued in July 1999 in an attempt to better defend the benefits of free trade. However, free trade is attractive only if everyone, developed Global North and developing Global South countries alike, can benefit. Recall that the principle of comparative advantage is a central tenet of free trade, because specialization and trade are viewed as permitting trading states to enjoy a higher standard of living than they would otherwise (see Table 9.1, p. 309). Still, as we have seen, many states remain tempted to enhance their domestic well-being by protectionist means even though, according to commercial liberalism, their relations with their trade partners will be undermined, reducing the benefits free trade would otherwise provide to both. "Trade may be global," warn Ramesh Thakur and Steve Lee (2000), but "politics is still local." If neomercantilism spreads, the preservation of the free-trade regime is unlikely throughout the twenty-first century.

The simultaneous pursuit of liberalism and mercantilism today shows states' determination to reap the benefits of interdependence while minimizing its costs. It also reveals the tension between states and markets, between the promise that everyone will benefit and the fear that the benefits will not be equally distributed. As noted earlier, the absence of world government encourages each state to be more concerned with how it fares competitively in relation to other states—its relative gains—than collectively with its absolute gains. These simple yet powerful ideas shed light on the reasons why the United States, the principal advocate of free trade in the post–World War II era, has increasingly engaged in neomercantilism and protectionism and in 1999 seemed bent on waging a trade war with Europe (over the issue of banana imports!). Fearful of others' free riding, the United States looks more like an "ordinary country" than a hegemonic power, despite the fact that it remains the largest economic market and one of the world's leading exporting countries.

Premises for a Future Global Economy

Six premises dictate the boundaries within which the global economy is likely to vary in the future.

1. Free trade contributes to economic growth, and trade protection reduces prosperity in the long run.
2. The future will depend heavily on the rules the leading economic powers choose to support to govern trade and monetary policy. The choices are between the contrasting philosophies of commercial liberalism without burdensome regulation and mercantilist and neomercantilist approaches that seek protectionism.
3. The position of the globe's largest economy, the United States, will likely remain pivotal in the equation, for how this hegemon makes economic policy will influence the direction in which others' trade and monetary policies are likely to move.
4. The activities of powerful and wealthy mobile MNCs in foreign investment and trade will increasingly determine economic flows; these activities and

pressure for continuing trade liberalization are increasingly beyond the control of state governments, whose sovereign power is eroding.

5. Nonstate commercial and monetary actors (for example, transnational banks, many of which are negotiating mergers to consolidate their power) will provide much of the lubrication that can keep the global trade engine humming.

6. Globalization is likely to accelerate, and, as competition expands wealth and reduces the costs of both products and labor, the economic fate of the globe's 6 billion people will be tied together in increasingly interdependent ties, making the welfare of any one important to the welfare of all.

Global Economic Destiny?

The United States, Europe, and Japan have advocated quite different philosophies toward states and markets over the years, and their policies have evolved as their circumstances in the global economy have changed over time. At times, Japan has embraced mercantilism (even as it talked of liberalization), the United States has touted liberalism (even as it practiced mercantilism), and Europe historically has stood midway between the two (but looked more inward than outward). Increasingly, economic nationalism "could propel the preeminent economic powers—and the rest of the world with them—into an era of 'real-economik,' in which parochial economic interests drive governments to pursue marginal advantage in an international system marked by growing interdependencies" (Peterson 1998). Whether a collision of these competing capitalisms can be averted is questionable, especially if the relative position of American economic power declines in a country where a clear majority of Americans (56 percent) are protectionists and only 37 percent are free-trade supporters. Protectionist pressure is rising in the United States and elsewhere—as opinion surveys show, 48 percent worldwide now favor protectionism (*Economist*, January 25, 1999, 36). The erosion of U.S. hegemonical management, the rise of protectionist pressure, and other instabilities in the international political economy "do not augur well for the level of cooperation necessary to avoid the neomercantilist confrontation that could flow from competing national policies" (Peterson 1998). "Historically, recession is the midwife of protectionism. In good times, peoples and nations are happy to enjoy the benefits of open trade. Come bad times, they are tempted to minimize short-run pain through protection" (*Economist*, January 2, 1999). Unfortunately for the fate of the liberal international regime, the threats to global prosperity are multiplying at the same time that the dependency of countries on volatile foreign capital is creating an inherently unstable situation and the volume of world trade is fluctuating in periodic swings between expansion and contraction. If global trade experiences anemic growth or, worse, declines, this slump will cause the demand for exports to drop, and the world's consumers are likely to seek to cushion the impact of the slowdown by turning away from the free-trade regime that engineered their previous period of unprecedented growth.

Playing Games with Prosperity on a Global Scale: Tricks-of-the-Trade Debate

International trade and finance can be likened to a global game of dominoes. If, and when, the globe's biggest economy (the United States) falters, how, in an integrated global system fraught with competition alongside connection, can other countries' economies stay aloft? Does global growth require a resurgence by the economic hegemon? In a U.S. downdraft, can the rest find the resources and policies to cushion themselves from the dynamic repercussions? In a global recession, how does any country obtain a parachute when the economic fate of everyone depends on the economic growth of everyone else? Sinking under conditions of interdependence is synchronized; so is ascendance in times of economic expansion for the world's biggest economies. This principle was underscored in 2001 when the World Bank warned that the global economy could not fly forever on a single engine—the U.S. economy.

The architecture of the LIEO constructed at Bretton Woods a half-century ago appeared to depend not only on a consensus about the appropriate shape of the world political economy but also on U.S. leadership. The United States is still the dominant state in the world political economy and continues to perform many hegemonic functions: It tries to maintain a comparatively open market for others' goods, manage the international monetary system, provide capital to would-be borrowers facing financial stress, and coordinate economic policies among the world's leading economies. Today, however, U.S. willingness to absorb the costs of leadership has waned. More worrisome still, the United States under the administration of George W. Bush has shown a strong preference for taking a unilateral approach toward international problems, rather than accommodating itself to the interests and ideals of U.S. allies by addressing shared problems through a cooperative, multilateral action. This "go-it-alone" posture is especially evident with respect to free trade. True, in its early policy rhetoric, the Bush administration was an enthusiastic advocate of liberal free-trade principles, claiming its firm oppositions to trade protectionism and import tariffs.

However, in 2002, as economic circumstances deteriorated in America in the face of the threat of a deep recession alongside budget deficits, runaway military spending to wage the proclaimed war against international terrorism, and the continuing rise of its balance-of-trade deficit, professed U.S. ideals clashed with parochial U.S. interests. Instead of living up to its campaign pledges to promote free trade, the Bush administration began to practice protectionism. A strong signal was scent to the world when President Bush decided in March 2002 to place high tariffs on the import of steel. That is, as political journalist George Will (2002b) observed, "the Bush administration interrupted its proclamations in favor of free trade in order to protect the steel industry with tariffs of up to 30 percent [and the administration soon thereafter] imposed a tariff of 29 percent on Canadian softwood [and in the process began to acquire] a reputation for a certain plasticity of conviction." Elaborating, Will (2002a) chastised the Bush turnabout: "Proving himself less principled than Bill Clinton regarding the free-trade principles that are indispensable to world prosperity and comity, President Bush has done what Clinton refused to do. In the name of providing 'breathing space' for the U.S. steel industry, which has been on the respirator of protection for decades, Bush has cooked up an unpalatable confection of tariffs and import quotas that mock his free-trade rhetoric. Do not read his lips, read his actions, which will incite protectionist clamors from other industries (timber and textiles, for starters) and invite retaliation from penalized nations."

This prediction proved prophetic. In the international political economy, leaders lead and the others either follow the leader or resist it. In this case, the

U.S. rejection of free trade was met with prompt retaliation. Within days, a major trade battle ensued as European and Asian officials issued an immediate warning that it would challenge the U.S. violation of its commitment to free trade in the World Trade Organization. Shortly thereafter, the WTO cleared the way for the outraged European Union to seek up to $4 billion in retaliatory duties against the United States, and others among America's biggest trading partners joined in a coalition against the United States at the same time that the United States was loosing in its attempts to hold together the fragile antiterrorism coalition it painstakingly had built.

Put together, these events show how precarious the liberal trading agreements so slowly built up over five decades are, especially in the absence of support from the global hegemon, the United States. At risk is the entire edifice of prosperity that has materialized through the removal of barriers to trade. That liberal free-trade regime could collapse under further economic pressure. Merely contemplate the vulnerability of the liberal international economic order should international economic conditions worsen. The combination of a global slowdown, financial market volatility, a deepening of U.S. trade imbalances, and worldwide excess of manufacturing capacity could easily bring about a global upsurge in protectionism, because protectionism breeds protectionism.

However, traumatic and tragic world transforming events like the September 11 terrorist attacks do not necessarily spell the death knell of cascading globalization. It continues to unfold and unwind, and, with or without U.S. leadership, seems to proponents of open markets to instill faith in bringing the blessings of rising living standards, cheaper and better goods, and stable democracies. As the IMF's Stanley Fischer in 2002 pointed out, "Over the last few years almost every country that has had an economic crisis was advised by powerful domestic forces to stop free-market reforms. And yet after an initial period of doubt, almost all of them—Brazil, Russia, Turkey—came back to the same policy path. Often they have come back with greater resolve."

Thus, a new wave of mercantilism and trade wars is not preordained. A number of other important developments are also likely to influence the future direction of the world political economy, and these, in combination, are likely to sustain and strengthen the liberal free-trade regime that has contributed to global economic growth. World commerce has become globalized; global financial flows outstrip trade transactions within countries; and market forces almost everywhere are now being given a freer reign to determine economic outcomes. With trade growing rapidly in the absence of barriers, and with the expansion of free-trade areas, pressure to preserve the liberal trade regime has increased. Multinational corporations are playing a larger role in the continuing growth of commercial liberalism worldwide, and they are supported in this aspiration by the powerful WTO, the conversion of eastern Europe and China to acceptance of freer trade, and the opening up of restrictive markets to exports. All these developments suggest that the prospects for the momentum of commercial liberalism to gain strength are promising.

Some theorists believe that the spread of liberal market philosophies will eliminate the need for new institutions to cope with the changed and changing world political economy. Others caution that the unregulated market should not be considered the ideal and universal arrangement for economic activity, because coordinating institutions are needed to manage sustained growth. The task of reaching agreement about economic principles is made more daunting by the absence of a true consensus about what the world political economy should look like, as the continuing contest between liberalism and mercantilism (as well as the conflict between rich and poor countries) illustrates. Furthermore, the globalization of commerce and finance increasingly seems to shape, rather than be shaped by, states' policies—thus challenging the sovereign prerogatives of states themselves.

The face of the future thus remains uncertain. If liberals are correct, the process of rapid globalization already on the horizon will hasten the trend toward interdependence and integration and, with that, the prospects for economic prosperity and political harmony. If mercantilists are right, however, an emerging era of geo-economics will increase states' vulnerability and thus the likelihood of political conflict and states' efforts to dominate others. What the future holds is hard to foresee, because the various rules for trade and currency are likely to change in the twenty-first century, and these changes will undercut the usefulness of past economic philosophies. The world seems to be spinning out of control in a sea change of rapid globalization that hides the decisions that affect our daily lives. Globalization is entangling the functions of governments and markets and making it difficult to tell the difference between countries and corporations. In the next chapter we shall move from geo-economics to ecopolitics and examine how changes in world population and resources in a globalized planetary environment are also likely to transform world politics in the twenty-first century.

KEY TERMS

international political economy
paradigm
globalization
high politics
low politics
international monetary system
commercial liberalism
mercantilism
Liberal International Economic Order (LIEO)
interdependence
theory
comparative advantage
laissez-faire economics
politics
absolute gains
relative gains
neomercantilism
protectionism
beggar-thy-neighbor policies
import quotas
export quotas
orderly market arrangements (OMA)

voluntary export restrictions (VERs)
nontariff barriers (NTBs)
infant industry
strategic trade policy
countervailing duties
antidumping duties
realism
hegemonic stability theory
hegemon
long-cycle theory
hegemony
macroeconomics
collective goods
free riders
zero-sum
imperial overstretch
international regimes
General Agreement on Tariffs and Trade (GATT)
Uruguay Round
World Trade Organization (WTO)
monetary system
monetary policy

money supply
exchange rate
fixed exchange rates
International Monetary Fund (IMF)
World Bank
international liquidity
commercial domino theory
floating exchange rates
Group of Seven (G-7)/Group of Eight (G-8)
regional currency union
unilateral
reciprocity
fast-track negotiating authority
human rights
North American Free Trade Agreement (NAFTA)
Free Trade Area of the Americas (FTAA)
trade integration
most-favored-nation (MFN) principle
nondiscrimination

SUGGESTED READING

Bhagwati, Jagdish. *Free Trade Today*. Princeton, N.J.: Princeton University Press, 2002.

Caporaso, James A., and David P. Levine. *Theories of Political Economy*. New York: Cambridge University Press, 1992.

Eichengreen, Barry. *Globalizing Capital: A History of the International Monetary System*. Princeton, N.J.: Princeton University Press, 1996.

Ferguson, Niall. *The Cash Nexus: Money and Power in the Modern World, 1700–2000*. New York: Basic Books, 2001.

Gilpin, Robert, with Jean M. Gilpin. *Global Political Economy: Understanding the International Economic Order*. Princeton, N.J.: Princeton University Press, 2001.

Goddard, C. Roe, Patrick Cronin, and Kishore C. Dash, eds. *International Political Economy: State-Market Relations in a Changing Global Order*, 2nd ed. Boulder, Colo.: Lynne Rienner, 2003.

Gomory, Ralph E., and William J. Baumol. *Global Trade and Conflicting National Interests*. Cambridge, Mass.: MIT Press, 2001.

Grieco, Joseph M., and S. John Ikenberry. *State Power and World Markets: The International Political Economy*. New York: W.W. Norton, 2003.

Irwin, Douglas. *The Case for Free Trade*. Princeton, N.J.: Princeton University Press, 2002.

Isaak, Robert A. *Managing World Economic Change: International Political Economy*, 3rd ed. Upper Saddle River, N.J.: Prentice Hall, 2000.

Lindsey, Brink. *Against the Dead Hand: The Uncertain Struggle for Global Capitalism*. New York: Wiley, 2002.

Odell, John. *Negotiating the World Economy*. Ithaca, N.Y.: Cornell University Press, 2000.

Steger, Manfred B. *Globalism: The New Market Ideology*. Lanham, Md.: Rowman & Littlefield, 2002.

WWW WHERE ON THE WORLD WIDE WEB?

Exchange Rates
http://www.x-rates.com

There is no common international currency for carrying on financial transactions. Currency rates of exchange show the value of one country's currency in relation to another's. The Exchange Rates site allows you to compare currencies for thirty-five different countries. Using this site, see how the euro, the currency of the European Union, is doing in relation to the U.S. dollar, or use the Customs Table to compare the U.S. dollar with all other currencies. For fun, you can click on Photos to see what a Belgian franc looks like, or can even order foreign currencies before your trip abroad.

Organization for Economic Cooperation and Development
http://www.oecd.org/

The Organization for Economic Cooperation and Development (OECD) began with the purpose of rebuilding war-ravaged economies after World War II and administering the distribution of the Marshall Plan's aid to Europe. Today, the OECD promotes policies that contribute to the expansion of world trade on a nondiscriminatory basis. It provides a forum in which the governments of the twenty-nine member states can compare their experiences and further the principles of a market economy. From the OECD's home page, you can access the largest source of comparative statistical data on the industrialized countries. Look at the Frequently Requested Statistics to compare economies.

Trade Resources
http://www.usitc.gov/tr/tr.htm

The United States International Trade Commission (USITC) has created an information referral service for those seeking information related to international trade and investment. Interested in investing in a chemical company in Canada? Want to export tractors to Russia? This Web site provides Internet resources to help those interested in international trade and investment to obtain information on their client country, research various products, access trade assistance, understand patent law, or view international law.

U.S. Trade Representative
http://www.ustr.gov/

The Office of the U.S. Trade Representative (USTR) is responsible for "developing and coordinating U.S. international trade, commodity, and direct investment policy, and leading or directing negotiations with other countries on such matters." Learn about the history of the U.S. Trade Representative, read speeches by the current representative and by Charlene Barshefsky and other past trade representatives, and scan the trade agreements the United States has with many other countries of the world.

World Bank
http://www.worldbank.org/

The World Bank is the world's largest source of development assistance, providing nearly $30 billion in loans annually. The Bank was first created to aid European countries in their recovery from World War II. Today the Bank's mission is to help developing countries achieve stable, sustainable, and equitable growth. Its main focus is to help the poorest people and the poorest countries to grow economically. Explore this Web site to find out the eligibility requirements for borrowing money. What are some of the criteria?

World Trade Organization
http://www.wto.org/

The World Trade Organization (WTO) is a multilateral, global intergovernmental organization (IGO). The WTO's main purpose is to administer trade agreements between countries, monitor trade policies, and provide technical assistance and training for developing countries. Unlike many international organizations, the WTO has a mechanism for settling international disputes with limited enforcement abilities. Click on the Dispute Settlement link on the home page to review Overview of the State-of-Play of WTO Disputes. In how many disputes is the United States the defendant? In how many is the United States the complainant?

INFOTRAC® COLLEGE EDITION

Heginbotham, Eric, and Richard J. Samuels. "Mercantile Realism and Japanese Foreign Policy," *International Security* Spring 1998.

Sampson, Gary P. "The Environmentalist Paradox: The World Trade Organization's Challenges," *Harvard International Review* Winter 2002.

Taylor, Chantell. "NAFTA, GATT, and the Current Free Trade System: A Dangerous Double Standard for Workers' Rights," *Denver Journal of International Law and Policy* Fall 2000.

Litan, Robert E. "The "Globalization" Challenge," *Brookings Review* Spring 2000.

For more articles, enter:

"mercantilism" in the Subject Guide.

"World Trade Organization" in the Subject Guide, and then go to subdivision "powers and duties."

"International Monetary Fund" in the Subject Guide, and then go to subdivision "economic policy."

POPULATION PRESSURE, RESOURCE DEPLETION, AND THE PRESERVATION OF THE GLOBAL ENVIRONMENT

T O P I C S   A N D   T H E M E S

- The tragedy of the global commons
- Global demographic trends
  Factors affecting population growth rates
  The epidemic and impact of tuberculosis and HIV/AIDS
- How population policy colors world politics
- The international response to population issues
- Environmental security and sustainable development
  The ecopolitics of energy
  The ecopolitics of the atmosphere
  The ecopolitics of forests and biodiversity
- Trade, the environment, and sustainable development
- Toward sustainability

- CONTROVERSY HOW MANY PEOPLE CAN EARTH SUPPORT?

Sherwin Castro/AP/Wide World

The UN has estimated that India's population reached 1 billion in August 1999 and predicts that India will be the world's most populous country by 2050. Shown here is a railway station in Bombay, India, on the day world population reached 6 billion, October 12, 1999.

A host of contradictory demographic trends and measures will likely reshape the world during the next quarter century.

—NICHOLAS EBERSTADT, demographer, 2001

Today we abuse the Earth's resources. We feed on portions that belong to unborn generations. . . . Protection of the environment is a noble endeavor in itself. But the survival of the environment is also the strategic basis of human survival.

—THABO MBEKI, FERNANDO HENRIQUE CARDOSO, and GORAN PERSSON, presidents, respectively, of South Africa, Brazil, and Spain, 2002

■ **demography**
the study of population changes, their sources, and their impact.

■ **carrying capacity**
the maximum biomass that can be supported by a given territory.

"Chances are," notes an expert in **demography** Jeffrey Kluger (2002, 25), "that you will never meet any of the estimated 247 human beings who were born in the past minute. In a population of six billion, 247 is a demographic hiccup. In the minute before last, however, there were another 247. In the minutes to come, there will be another, then another, then another. By next year at this time, all those minutes will have produced nearly 130 million newcomers in the great human mosh pit. That kind of crowd is very hard to miss." What will that crowd do in the long run to the planet's **carrying capacity**—the earth's ability to support and sustain life? That concern has made population and environmental policy a central issue in world politics.

Increasing numbers of people are populating the planet, and globalization is bringing them closer together in an interdependent and crowded global village. Population growth is straining the planet's carrying capacity—its ability to support human and other life forms—evidence which strongly suggests that unrestrained population growth will result in environmental degradation and domestic strife. A world interdependent economically as well as ecopolitically is certain to be conditioned by population growth, and this problem has made population and environmental policy a key political issue on the global agenda of the twenty-first century.

The **tragedy of the commons** is a metaphor that highlights the potential impact of human behavior on the planet's resources and its delicately balanced ecological systems. First articulated in 1833 by English political economist William Foster Lloyd and later by contemporary human ecologist Garrett Hardin, the commons parable depicts a medieval English village, where the "green" was common property on which all villagers could graze their cattle. Freedom of access to the commons was a cherished village value. Sharing the common grazing area worked well as long as usage by individuals (and their cattle) didn't reduce the land's usefulness to everyone else. Assuming the villagers were driven by the profit motive and no laws existed to restrain their greed, herders had a maximum incentive to increase their stock as much as possible. In the short run, the addition of one more animal would produce a personal gain whose costs would be borne by everyone. But in the long run the overgrazed green was destroyed. The lesson? "Ruin is the destination toward which all men rush," Hardin (1968) concluded, "each pursuing his own best interest."

This chapter uses the tragedy of the commons metaphor to explore how changes in demography, resources, and the environment influence the global future by examining how changes in world population affect the prospects for preserving for future generations the planet's ecology on which life itself depends.

■ **tragedy of the commons**
a metaphor, widely used to explain the impact of human behavior on ecological systems, that explains how rational self-interested behavior by individuals may have a destructive collective impact.

POPULATION CHANGE AS A GLOBAL POLITICAL CHALLENGE

How many people can the earth support? What are the costs of population growth to human freedom and welfare and many environmental issues ranging from excessive fishing of the oceans to transboundary pollution caused when industries spew toxic wastes into the atmosphere? The right to produce children is a major unregulated freedom. "The most important aspect of necessity that we must now recognize," Hardin (1968) wrote in explaining the tragedy of the commons, "is the necessity of abandoning the commons in breeding. Freedom to breed will bring ruin to all. . . . The only way we can preserve and nurture other and more precious freedoms is by relinquishing the freedom to breed and . . . very soon. . . . Only so, can we put an end to this aspect of the tragedy of the commons."

Not everyone agrees with the **ethics** of Hardin's arguments. Some regard the freedom to parent as a human right. Others claim that controls on family size are unnecessary because the ultimate carrying capacity of the global ecosystem is unknown and the impact of unregulated population growth on social well-being and environmental quality remains uncertain. For this reason, **politics** governs debates about population policies. To understand why this issue has become so controversial, it is helpful to trace the global trends in population growth that have made the topic so problematic (see Figure 10.1).

■ **ethics**
the criteria by which right and wrong behavior and motives are distinguished.

■ **politics**
the exercise of influence in attempts to resolve controversial issues in one's favor.

Understanding Growth Rates: The Persian Chessboard

The rapid growth of world population is described by a simple mathematical principle articulated in 1798 by the Reverend Thomas Malthus: unchecked, population increases in a geometric or exponential ratio (e.g., 1 to 2, 2 to 4,

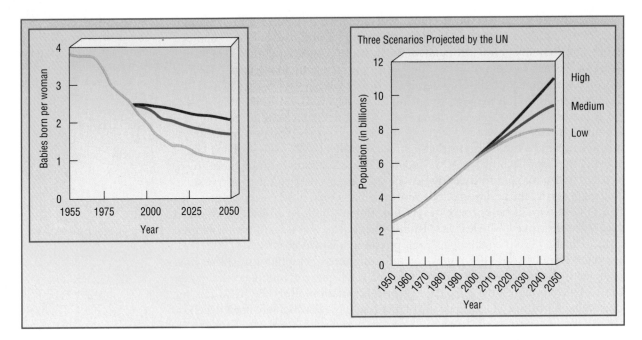

FIGURE 10.1
World Population Growth Projections to the Year 2050

In the twentieth century world population grew from less than 2 billion people to more than 6 billion, with each billion added in less time than the previous billion. World population is growing at 1.3 percent, each year. Between 1.2 and 2.2 billion additional people will be living on the earth by the middle of the twenty-first century, depending on how fast fertility rates (the number of babies born for each woman) fall (see figure on left) and life spans increase. The figure on the right sketches three potential scenarios for the future, showing that "by 2050 world population is expected to be between 7.9 billion (low variant) and 10.9 billion (high variant), with the medium variant producing 9.3 billion" (UNPD 2001).

SOURCE: United Nations Population Division (UNPD 2001).

4 to 8), whereas subsistence increases in only an arithmetic ratio (1 to 2, 2 to 3, 3 to 4). When population increases at such a geometric rate, the acceleration can be staggering. The astronomer Carl Sagan illustrated this principle governing growth rates with a parable he termed "The Secret of the Persian Chessboard":

> The way I first heard the story, it happened in ancient Persia. But it may have been India, or even China. Anyway, it happened a long time ago. The Grand Vizier, the principal adviser to the King, had invented a new game. It was played with moving pieces on a board of 64 squares. The most important piece was the King. The next most important piece was the Grand Vizier—just what we might expect of a game invented by a Grand Vizier. The object of the game was to capture the enemy King, and so the game was called, in Persian, shahmat—shah for king, mat for dead. Death to the King. In Russia it is still called shakhmaty, which perhaps conveys a lingering revolutionary ardor. Even in English there is an echo of the name—the final move is called "checkmate." The game, of course, is chess.

As time passed, the pieces, their moves and the rules evolved. There is, for example, no longer a piece called the Grand Vizier—it has become transmogrified into a Queen, with much more formidable powers.

Why a king should delight in the creation of a game called "Death to the King" is a mystery. But, the story goes, he was so pleased that he asked the Grand Vizier to name his own reward for such a splendid invention. The Grand Vizier had his answer ready: He was a humble man, he told the King. He wished only for a humble reward. Gesturing to the eight columns and eight rows of squares on the board he devised, he asked that he be given a single grain of wheat on the first square, twice that on the second square, twice that on the third, and so on, until each square had its complement of wheat.

No, the King remonstrated. This is too modest a prize for so important an invention. He offered jewels, dancing girls, palaces. But the Grand Vizier, his eyes becomingly lowered, refused them all. It was little piles of wheat he wanted. So, secretly marveling at the unselfishness of his counselor, the King graciously consented.

When the Master of the Royal Granary began to count out the grains, however, the King was in for a rude surprise. The number of grains starts small enough: 1, 2, 4, 8, 32, 64, 128, 256, 512, 1,024. . . . . But by the time the 64th square is approached, the number becomes colossal, staggering. In fact the number is nearly 18.5 quintillion grains of wheat. Maybe the Grand Vizier was on a high fiber diet.

How much does 18.5 quintillion grains of wheat weigh? If each grain were 2 millimeters in size, then all the grains together would weigh around 75 billion metric tons, which far exceeds what could have been stored in the King's granaries. In fact, this is the equivalent of about 150 years of the world's present wheat production. (Sagan 1989, 14)

To picture in another way how growth rates unfold, consider how money deposited in a savings account grows as it earns interest not only on the original investment but also on the interest payments. If one of our ancestors had put a mere 10 dollars in the bank for us two hundred years ago, and it accrued a steady 6 percent annual interest, today we would all be millionaires! Population grows in the same way: It is a function of increases in the original number of people plus those accruing from past population growth. Thus a population growing at a 1 percent rate will double in sixty-nine years, while a population growing at a 2 percent rate will double in only thirty-five years. (The impact of different growth rates on doubling times can be calculated by dividing 69 by the percentage of growth.)

The story of population growth is told in its statistics: The annual rate of population growth in the twentieth century increased from less than 1 percent in 1900 to a peak of 2.2 percent in 1964. It has since dropped to about 1.3 percent. Despite the recent drop in rate, however, the absolute number of people *added* each year has continued to grow, from 16 million in 1900 to a peak of 87 million in 1990, and thereafter has declined to an additional 77 million new people in 2001 when global population expanded by adding the equivalent of another Germany. Plainly, the planet is certain to have many more people by the mid-twenty-first century, well beyond the 6.2 billion already roaming the planet (*Vital Signs 2002*, 88). Yet the feared "population explosion" once believed

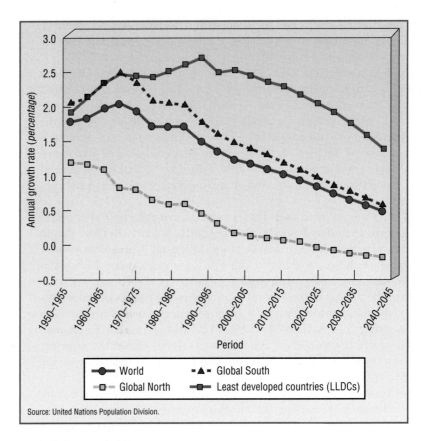

Source: United Nations Population Division.

FIGURE 10.2

The New Demographics: The Global North–Global South Population Divide

Overpopulation is much feared, but the UN estimates that we can expect a "slowing of population growth rates" followed by "slow reductions in the size of world population" (Wattenberg 2002). Population growth is not expected to occur everyplace at the same pace, however. Nearly all the population growth in the twenty-first century will occur in the Global South, whereas a "birth dearth" in the Global North is expected to reduce the absolute number of people living there, as shown in the figure. Assuming continuing declines in fertility, Global South population is expected to rise to 8.2 billion in 2050 (in the absence of such declining birth rates, the less-developed countries will reach 11.9 billion by 2050, and by 2050 the Global North's population is anticipated to change little, because fertility rates are expected to remain below replacement levels [UNPD 2001]. The map which accompanies this figure shows that life expectancy is increasing, as people everywhere are living longer, and this growth in the number of elderly people will affect the size of each country's expected population by the year 2050. When interpreting these projections, also take into account the number of people within each country as controlled by geographical size, known as "population density." Some countries are very crowded and others are not. For example, Singapore is the most congested country in the world, with 6,587 for each square kilometer, and people in Australia are the least likely to bump into each other, with only two people for each square kilometer.

SOURCES: Adapted from the United Nations Population Division (left); *The Economist*, Nov. 3, 2001, p. 3 (right). Copyright © 2001 by The Economist Newspaper Ltd. All rights reserved. Reprinted with permission. Further reproduction prohibited.

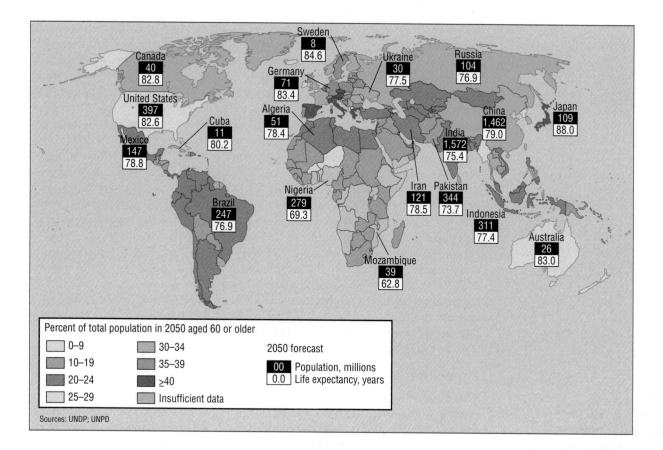

certain to overwhelm the earth's resources is now expected to be far less dramatic than previously predicted.

If a catastrophic population explosion is not necessarily assured and the probability of continuing population growth overwhelming a crowded planet is receding, why then does population remain such a political powder keg in world politics? The answers are numerous. Several salient features about population dynamics make demographic change the source of new global issues and problems.

The Demographic Divide between Global North and Global South

Population growth rates are not the same throughout the world. Population is growing much more rapidly in the developing Global South countries than in the wealthy countries in the Global North, and that trend is expected to continue. In fact, the population of the industrialized world is actually expected to decline. This "demographic divide," as projected in Figure 10.2, explains a large part of the problem making population such a hot political issue.

Because population growth is occurring in precisely those countries least able economically to support a growing number of people, global population cannot be expected to stabilize until it falls below replacement-level fertility in the developing countries. In 2002, the worldwide average number of children born to a woman during her lifetime—the total **fertility rate**—was around 2.8.

■ **fertility rate**
the average number of children born to a woman (or group of women) during her lifetime.

However, these projections for the entire globe overlook the different rates for the rich and the poor. Although the world's population grew by 77 million people in 2001, 95 percent of the continuing global population surge were added in the developing Global South (*Vital Signs 2002*, 88), already home to 5 billion people, or more than 80 percent of the world (UNPD 2001). Hence, global population growth is the result of new births in the developing Global South, where the average fertility rate averaged 3.1 children for each mother (5.8 for the least-developed countries). In contrast, the wealthy, developed Global North's fertility rate has actually declined to 1.6 children for each woman, which is below **replacement-level fertility** (each couple replacing itself with 2.1 children). Fertility rates around the world must fall to an average of 2.1 children for each woman in order to fall to replacement level. Yet, throughout much of the Global South, the preferred family size remains far in excess of the replacement level, especially in the poorest countries (UNDP 2001).

The developing countries' high fertility rates have important economic consequences. Almost all the problems in the North-South dispute can be traced to disparities in income and economic growth that are directly linked to the differentials in population growth rates. A brief look at these dynamics completes the picture of ongoing political conflict between the haves and the have-nots.

■ **replacement-level fertility**
one couple replacing themselves with two children, so that a country's population will remain stable if this rate prevails.

Population Momentum

The surge in the Global South's population in the twentieth century is easily explained as a combination of high birthrates and rapidly falling death rates. But to understand the population surge projected throughout the twenty-first century—when birthrates throughout the world will decline—we have to understand the force of population momentum, the continued growth of population for decades into the future because of the large number of women now entering their childbearing years. Like the inertia of a descending airliner when it first touches down on the runway, population growth simply cannot be halted even with an immediate, full application of the brakes. Instead, many years of high fertility mean that more women will be entering their reproductive years than in the past. Not until the size of the generation giving birth to children is no larger than the generation among which deaths are occurring will the population "airplane" come to a halt.

Western Europe and Sub-Saharan Africa illustrate the force of population momentum. Africa's demographic profile is one of rapid population growth, as each new age group (cohort) contains more people than the one before it. Thus, even if individual African couples choose to have fewer children than their parents, Africa's population will continue to grow because there are now more men and women of childbearing age than ever before. In contrast, Europe's population profile is one of slow growth, as recent cohorts have been smaller than preceding ones. In fact, Europe has moved beyond replacement-level fertility to become a "declining" population, described by low birthrates and a growing number of people who survive middle age. A product of an extended period of low birthrates, low death rates, and increased longevity, Europe is best described as an aging society, where the low birthrates and aging populations have caused alarms that the number of European newborns will not be sufficient to renew populations.

As the Global North generally ages, much of the Global South continues to mirror the Sub-Saharan African profile: because each cohort is typically larger than the one before it, the number of young men and women entering their reproductive years will also continue to grow. The resulting differences in these demographic momentums will produce quite different population profiles in the developed and the developing worlds. Two examples illuminate the contrast. Germany has at present a low birthrate of 1.3 per woman and between now and the year 2030, people over 65 in the world's third-largest economy will account for almost half the adult population (compared with one-fifth in 2001). The net result will be that Germany's total population of 82 million will shrink to about 70 million and the number of working-age people will fall about 25 percent (from 40 million to 30 million). Similarly, the population of Japan, the world's second-largest economy, will peak in the year 2005 at 125 million. Given the Japanese birthrate of 1.3 per woman, by the year 2030 the proportion of Japanese adults will have fallen in half, and twenty years thereafter in 2050, Japan's total population will shrink to around 95 million. "The figures are pretty much the same for most other developed countries—Italy, France, Spain, Portugal, the Netherlands, Sweden—and for a good many emerging ones, especially China. . . . The only developed country that has so far avoided this fate is America. But even there the birthrate is well below replacement level, and the proportion of older people in the adult population will rise steeply in the next 30 years" (Drucker 2001, 5). Thus, the population divide will grow; Japan, Europe, and the other Global North countries will become older and smaller while the United States is "getting older, to be sure, but also bigger. By 2050 the United States will be alone as the only developed country among the world's twenty most-populous countries" (Srodes 2001, 13).

From Population Explosion to Population Implosion—
A Demographic Transition?

High rates of population growth are, simply put, punitive and painful, condemning low economic growth. How can the poor Global South escape the population explosion that in many developing countries is blocking their economic development?

One path out of this economic prison is reducing population by following the path known as **demographic transition.** That term was coined to describe the change that Europe and, later, North America experienced between 1750 and 1930, when high birthrates combined with high death rates were replaced by low birthrates and low death rates. The transition started when death rates began to fall due to rising prosperity and living standards in addition to improved disease control. Although the potential for substantial population growth was high, birthrates soon began to decline as well. During this phase of the demographic transition, the population growth rate slowed to less than 1.5 percent each year.

Demographic transition is now under way virtually everywhere in the world, but at much different rates in different countries and regions. As noted above, with the exception of about twenty-five states now at near replacement levels, the experience of the Global South differs greatly from that of Europe and North America where death rates declined slowly. In most of the Global South, death rates have declined rapidly—the average life span of sixty-four is

■ **demographic transition**
an explanation of population changes over time that highlights the causes of declines in birth and death rates so that a country's population achieves a stable level.

now only fourteen years lower than the seventy-eight years people in the Global North can expect to live (UNDP 2002)—largely as a result of more effective public health "death control" programs introduced by the outside world. A population explosion inevitably followed.

There are two ways that changes in birth- and death rates enable demographic transitions to develop. First, a decline in death rates can itself stimulate a decline in birthrates. When people begin to expect to live longer lives, couples begin "to realize that more of their children will live to adulthood, and therefore, to feel secure that they can have fewer births and still achieve their desired number of surviving children" (Lutz 1994). Second, demographic transitions are a by-product of **modernization,** which leads to value changes about the preferred size of family. In traditional low-income societies children are economic bonuses because they provide labor that contributes to family income; as modernization proceeds, children can become economic burdens, inhibiting social mobility and capital accumulation of wealth. "In most every country where people have moved from traditional ways of life to modern ones, they are choosing to have too few children to replace themselves" (Singer 1999). Modernization changes family values and drives fertility rates toward the replacement level; a demographic transition then commences followed by low or no population growth.

If these trends continue, they are certain to make for a transformed world. Consider the impact of the "graying" of the world presently occurring as a revolution in longevity making for an increasingly aged world population. About 630 million people worldwide are now age sixty years or older (*Economist*, April 13, 2002, 104). What are the consequences? It was concern about this fact which propelled representatives from 160 countries to participate in Madrid at the April 2002 UN Second World Assembly on Aging to deal with the challenges. According to a 2001 U.S. Census Bureau report, the world's senior population over the age of sixty had tripled over the past fifty years, and global aging was occurring at rates never before seen. At issue are almost-cataclysmic predictions. If this present trend continues, in fifty years the number of people older than sixty will again triple, to comprise a third of humanity, and those 2 billion older people would outnumber the world's youths, with two older persons for every child. The "oldest old"—80 years or over—is expected to increase even faster, more than fivefold by 2050 (UNPD 2001).

This unprecedented aging of the world could create economic problems of crisis proportions. With the percentage of taxpaying workers shrinking, the budgets of state governments (especially in the developed Global North where the number of elderly is already the highest) could be overwhelmed by attempts to provide retirement and health benefits for the elderly. In addition, dwindling birthrates, lengthening life spans, and early retirements could spell trouble for a worker-hungry Global North in need of immigrants to supply labor. Without migration, the UN notes, the Global North population would start declining in 2003 rather than 2025, "and by 2050 would be 126 million less than the 1.18 billion under the assumption of continued migration" (UNPD 2001). For example, to maintain its present workforce through the year 2050, Japan will require 30 million new immigrants (*Harper's*, June 2000, 23). The graying of world population does not leave the developing countries immune from the challenge, because in the Global South the pace of aging is faster than in the developed countries, with the proportion of the population over sixty rising from 8 percent

■ **modernization**
a view of development popular in the Global North's liberal democracies which argues that wealth is created through efficient production, free enterprise, and free trade and that countries' relative ability to create wealth depends on technological innovation and education.

in 2002 to 20 percent in 2050, and this gives the poorest societies less time to cope as they continue to simultaneously try to confront the scourges of poverty and disease.

Against this scenario, consider as well alternative ways of visualizing the global future. All projections are dangerous, because natural or human-made events can overturn the conditions that make for today's prevailing trends. For example, current projections could be overturned overnight by a nuclear war or a terrorist act of mass destruction with biological weapons, rendering obsolete today's life expectancy of nearly eighty years in the Global North. Other threats, such as the outbreak of a widespread, deadly contagious disease, also could produce a **population implosion**—a severe reduction in world population. We take a brief look at two examples of life-ending diseases of epidemic proportions.

■ **population implosion** a rapid reduction of population that reverses a previous trend toward progressively larger populations.

New Plagues? The Global Impact of Tuberculosis and HIV/AIDS

Although infant and child mortality rates remain discouragingly high in much of the developing world, at least they are decreasing. On a global level, life expectancy at birth each year since 1950 has increased, climbing at the start of 2003 to sixty-six years. However, this trend in rising longevity could reverse if globally transmittable diseases cut into the extension of life spans made possible by improvements in health care, nutrition, water quality, and public sanitation. Throughout history the spread of bacteria, parasites, viruses, plagues, and diseases to various ecospheres, regardless of state borders, has suspended development or brought down once mighty states and empires. For example, drug-resistant strains of tuberculosis (TB) have developed recently, and whether at home or abroad TB knows no borders since in our age of globalization the disease can be passed on with a sneeze or cough on an international flight. It is not possible to control the disease within a country if it continues to spread in other parts of the world. This could certainly curtail population growth, because "about one-third of the world's population is infected with the bacteria that causes TB—over two billion people, and TB will kill nearly two million" each year (Clyburn 2001, A9).

The grim possibility that virulent disease will diminish the world's population, and that we all share a common fate, is made no more evident than in the spread of the **human immunodeficiency virus (HIV)** that causes **AIDS (acquired immune deficiency syndrome).** Since the 1970s onset of the AIDS pandemic, the UN estimates that, in the words of UN Secretary-General Kofi Annan in June 2001, "every day 14,500 more people become infected with HIV. Twenty-two million have died, with . . . the total of three million in 2000 the highest yet." Elaborating in November 2001 on the eve of World AIDS Day, Annan warned that the facts about AIDS are stark: "Every day more than 8,000 people die of AIDS. Every hour almost 600 people become infected. Every minute a child dies of the virus. Just as life and death go on after September 11, so must we continue our fight against the HIV/AIDS epidemic. Before the [9/11] terrorist attacks, . . . tremendous momentum had been achieved in that fight. To lose it now would be to compound one tragedy with another."

Most health experts agree with Annan's warning that "in the ruthless world of AIDS there is no us and them" and that international solidarity is required to fight the disease which in a globalized planet spreads across national borders.

■ **human immunodeficiency virus (HIV)** a virus that can lead to acquired immune deficiency syndrome (AIDS).

■ **AIDS (acquired immune deficiency syndrome)** an often fatal condition that can result from infection with the human immunodeficiency virus (HIV).

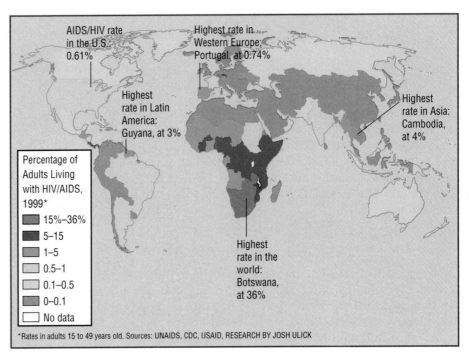

AIDS/HIV rate in the U.S.: 0.61%

Highest rate in Western Europe: Portugal, at 0.74%

Highest rate in Latin America: Guyana, at 3%

Highest rate in Asia: Cambodia, at 4%

Percentage of Adults Living with HIV/AIDS, 1999*

■ 15%–36%
■ 5–15
■ 1–5
□ 0.5–1
□ 0.1–0.5
■ 0–0.1
□ No data

Highest rate in the world: Botswana, at 36%

*Rates in adults 15 to 49 years old. Sources: UNAIDS, CDC, USAID, RESEARCH BY JOSH ULICK

MAP 10.1
The Spread of the Deadly HIV/AIDS Plague

Throughout the world, in 2001 more than 63 million people were believed to have HIV infections *(Vital Signs 2002,* 90*).* This is more than the population of France. The UN identifies forty-five countries as the "worst affected," where AIDS could kill 10 percent of the population, as shown on this map.

SOURCE: *Newsweek,* June 11, 2001, p. 36. Copyright © 2001 by Newsweek, Inc. All rights reserved. Reprinted by permission.

The circumstances are truly grim and likely to worsen: every day tens of thousands are newly infected, the number of those already HIV-infected has climbed to 63 million, and "the pace of the pandemic's spread is alarming. Some countries could lose 20 percent of their gross domestic product due to the effects of AIDS on their work force and productivity" (*Vital Signs 2002,* 90). The 2002 *UNAIDS* report warned that AIDS could kill nearly 30 million people worldwide over the next two decades unless the wealthy Global North countries paid for more prevention and treatment programs. The challenge is severe. As a U.S. CIA report warns, "The rate of infection from the AIDS virus in five of the world's most populous countries are rising so fast that they pose potential security threats to their regions and the United States. The countries—China, Ethiopia, India, Nigeria and Russia—comprise forty percent of the world's population and by 2010 the number of infected people will grow from an estimated 50 million to 75 million" (Altman 2002, 1). The virus is resistant to control because most HIV is contracted through heterosexual contact. It can also be spread through the use of injected drugs, unsanitary blood-selling practices, and the tragic infection of infants born to infected women during childbirth or through breast-feeding.

More than 90 percent of new infections occur in the Global South, but the contagion respects no borders and is a truly global epidemic, killing through-

Mike Hutchings/Reuters/Getty Images

Can AIDS Be Stopped? As the aids epidemic has spread throughout the world and become a transnational health problem, the demand has increased for assistance to those afflicted with the deadly disease. Shown here is a demonstration in November 2001 outside South Africa's parliament demanding that the government provide antiretroviral drugs to HIV-positive pregnant women to prevent the transfer of HIV from a mother to her child.

out the world (see Map 10.1). Are world death rates thus destined to rise in the future, reversing the upward trend in world population? The "age of AIDS" is a sobering reminder that population and power are heavily determined by natural phenomena in an era where what occurs anywhere often has consequences everywhere. The spread and control of infectious diseases such as AIDS, tuberculosis, malaria, Lassa fever, Ebola, mad cow disease—must be viewed as a global issue.

THE INTERNATIONAL RESPONSE TO POPULATION ISSUES

The world community convened its first World Population Conference to address the world's growing population in Bucharest in 1974. Many Global South delegates then concluded from Europe's and North America's demographic transitions that declining fertility rates flowed more or less automatically from economic growth and proposed policies that focused on economic development rather than population control. They called on the Global North for economic development assistance, reasoning that the population problem would then take care of itself. The slogan "development is the best contraceptive" reflected the prevailing view.

A decade later, a second World Population Conference was held in Mexico City. By then, a new consensus had converged around the critical importance of family planning. However, the United States, previously a major advocate of this viewpoint, resisted this emerging global consensus, and argued that free-markets and technological innovations to offset shortages created by population growth should take precedence over such government interventions in population programs as the use of mandatory sterilization and abortion as approaches to family planning.

The debate between optimists and pessimists has continued. In 1994 the UN-convened International Conference on Population and Development (ICPD) in Cairo concluded that population stabilization could be achieved only in conjunction with efforts to promote **human development** and sustainable economic growth, supported by increases in **multilateral aid.** This conclusion was reaffirmed at the August 2002 Johannesburg World Conference on Sustainable Development. Despite the contentious issue of abortion rights, the precedent-setting 1994 Cairo agreement and the 2002 Johannesburg resolutions set standards regarding other issues of environmental quality, resource conservation, demographic sources of political instability and ethnic conflict, urbanization, and inequalities between the Global North and Global South. Prominent among the key objectives, a global consensus has crystallized on

- stabilizing population growth levels consistent with sustainable development
- focusing assistance programs on the unmet need and demand for family planning and reproductive health services
- preventing HIV/AIDS infection
- addressing women's health needs and protecting children
- advancing the economic, political, and social rights of women
- increasing male responsibility in family planning and childbearing

Specific goals to be achieved were set at both global conferences, which included access to primary school education, family-planning services, and reproductive health and improved rates on infant and child mortality, maternal mortality, and life expectancy.

The proposals of these precedent-setting world conferences were only recommendations, not binding on governments. Indeed, few could be expected to act on all of them, particularly given the enormous resources their realization demands. By 2005, global family-planning expenditures alone are expected to balloon to $15 billion, nearly double the amount spent in the early 1990s. Even greater sums will be required to meet the goals of increased access to primary education and to health care. Global South countries cannot be expected to meet these demands by themselves. Others—meaning governments in the Global North—will also be asked to contribute more. Since domestic political support for foreign aid among donor countries has greatly declined, however, large subsidies are unlikely.

Mounting a sustained effort to stem the growth of world population thus remains a formidable challenge. However, the goal itself is no longer in serious

■ **human development**
the extent to which humans' ability to develop to their individual potential is protected, such that they are provided with sufficient schooling, income, and opportunity to live a full life.

■ **multilateral aid**
assistance provided through more than two states or other international actors for the purpose of collective action to combat perceived problems.

dispute, because most now agree with UN Secretary-General Kofi Annan's once controversial view, stated in 1999, the "We have to stabilize the population of this planet," inasmuch as the global community has agreed that the concurrent growth of human population and demands on the planet exceed some of the natural limits on the earth's carrying capacity. The world community now, in the age of globalization, has also begun to accept the once controversial view that the real problems are poverty and inequality. At the 1999 Hague conference, like the 2002 Johannesburg conference, more than one hundred countries convened to review the obstacles to carrying out the consensus commitment that first emerged at the 1994 Cairo conference, which emphasized the need to take a humane, noncoercive approach to population stabilization. In a comparatively short time, the "population problem" moved nearer to the top of the global agenda.

Food Fights: The Clash of Optimists and Pessimists

The impact of population growth centers on long-standing disputes in the so-called realm of **low politics.** In recent years, a new question has emerged: Is the planet running out of food? If world population grows to 9 billion and food supplies are depleted, many will be underfed and undernourished. Who will eat and who will starve? This kind of question makes for a continuing international controversy, with **neo-Malthusians,** alarmed about potential food shortages, debating **cornucopians** who claim these pessimists' concerns are unwarranted (see Controversy: How Many People Can Earth Support?). History does not provide a clear answer. Furthermore, the range of opinion and conviction separating them is less clear than the labels suggest. As noted in Chapter 6, for example, the absolute gap in income between Global North and Global South continues, but the gap in human development between people in rich and poor countries has narrowed, and many optimists are counting on such technological miracles as genetically engineered crops to revolutionize farming and feed future generations. **Genetic engineering** develops hybrid seeds for new plants, and genetically modified or genetically engineered **transgenetic crops** are altered by inserting genes to develop a desired trait, such as herbicide tolerance or increased oil content. Unlike crop varieties developed through traditional plant breeding, transgenetics often contain genes from unrelated species—of plant, animal, bacteria, or other origin—with which the crop could not reproduce naturally. Despite lingering consumer unease, genetically modified crops "are gaining ground. In 2001 53 million hectares were planted with transgenetic crops, a 19 percent rise over the previous year. Thirteen countries now grow genetically modified soybeans, maize, corn, cotton or canola. America accounts for two-thirds of global production but China, South Africa and Australia are rapidly increasing their share" (*Economist*, January 19, 2002, 90). As the risk of plant and animal extinction escalates, scientists have turned to the desperate strategy of seeking to replicate them in surrogate forms through cloning. Needless to say, this approach is controversial and has met with considerable opposition from groups who feel that tampering with nature and life is immoral.

Like the computer revolution, geneticists could revolutionize agriculture and transform the capability of the planet to feed the globe's growing population, increasing **food security.** However, the growing prevalence of commercially grown and globally marketed genetic agricultural production is a rising controversy on the global agenda. Should scientists manipulate nature for

■ **low politics**
the category of global issues related to the economic, social, demographic, and environmental aspects of relatins between governments and people.

■ **neo-Malthusians**
pessimists who warn of the global ecopolitical implications of uncontrolled population growth.

■ **cornucopians**
optimists who question limits-to-growth analyses and contend that markets effectively maintain a balance between population, resources, and the environment.

■ **genetic engineering**
research geared to discover seeds for new types of plant and human life for sale and use as substitutes for those produced naturally.

■ **transgenetic crops**
new crops with improved characteristics created artificially through genetic engineering which combines genes from species that would not naturally interbreed.

■ **food security**
access by all people at all times to enough food for an active, healthy life.

HOW MANY PEOPLE CAN EARTH SUPPORT?

Are there limits to the size of world population beyond which humanity will perish? Two thousand years ago, when the earth had about the same number of people as the United States does today, few would have pondered that question. They do now, however, because with 8 to 10 billion people expected to live on the earth and consume what can be grown on it in the twenty-first century, the possibility has arisen that there will not be enough food to feed the world. If so, food scarcities will lead to famine and mass starvation, and countries will engage in "food fights" over agriculture products.

It is unclear whether this grim outcome will materialize, however. Demographic and environmental scientists are divided in their evaluations about the planet's future carrying capacity—the limits on its ability to supply the resources to sustain life on a planet teeming with a growing human population. The two major broadly defined groups of analysts approach these issues quite differently. Taking their name and orientation from Thomas Malthus and his classic 1798 *Essay on the Principle of Population,* the first group, neo-Malthusians, believes that world population is pushing against the earth's resources, straining its ability to meet the needs of this generation and the next. Sometimes called "growth pessimists," many neo-Malthusian ecologists point to a host of disconcerting facts about the present global condition: "Since Malthus wrote, the human population has grown by a factor of six, and total human energy use by a factor of one hundred or so. . . . The forest cover of the earth has been cut by a third and the area of undisturbed wetlands by half. The composition of the atmosphere has been altered by human-generated pollution. Hundreds of millions of people have starved to death; thousands of species have gone extinct" (Meadows 1993).

In contrast with the pessimism of neo-Malthusians, the second group, the cornucopians (many of whom are economists and otherwise known as "growth optimists"), emphasizes quite different global trends.

Genetic Engineering in Agriculture A Chinese farmer harnesses a transgenetic cow to produce milk and power.

Observing that global life expectancy has more than doubled since 1950 to sixty-six years, they conclude that rapid population growth has occurred not because human beings suddenly started breeding like rabbits but because they finally stopped dropping like flies. Despite the growth of global population from 1.6 billion in 1900 to more than 6.3 billion in 2003, cornucopians argue that "global health and productivity have exploded. Today human beings eat better, produce more, and consume more than ever. . . . Overpopulation is a problem that has been misidentified and misdefined. The term has no scientific definition or clear meaning. The problems typically associated with over-

Isabelle Rouvillois/AFP

Freak Food or Unfair Foreign Trade? A Greenpeace activist in France protests the import of genetically modified corn, which the United States produces for export around the globe.

population (hungry families, squalid and overcrowded living conditions) are more properly understood as issues of poverty." Although some blame dwindling natural resources for the reversals and catastrophes that have recently befallen heavily populated low-income countries, such episodes are directly traceable to the policies or practices of presiding governments (Eberstadt 1995).

What do you think? How do you line up on the divisions of opinion which follow? Note that some governments understandably view too many people as a problem and will seek to control population growth. Other countries are facing the threat of shrinking populations and see additional people as critical to their future. These differences in national needs make population policies highly contentious, especially because divergent population policies affect everyone and will determine whether technological advances will be sufficient for the earth to provide enough resources for its people.

Some people have high hopes that genetically engineered agriculture will enable genetically modified or transgenetic livestock and crops to be developed to feed a growing world population. Shown here is one example on which these "cornucopian" enthusiasts pin their hopes: a farmer in Tienman, China, cultivates a field using a new breed of cow developed by researchers in Africa that is strong enough to work in the field without reducing its capacity to produce milk or to breed. Critics of genetically modified crops, like the Greenpeace activist shown in the photo on the right vandalizing a field of transgenic corn in 1998 in protest, complain that genetic engineering through biotechnology is dangerous because it is harmful to public health. "Far from being a solution to the world's hunger problem," complain some experts (Rosset 1999), "the rapid introduction of genetically engineered crops may actually threaten agriculture and food security."

human needs? Are gene-spliced plants and hormone-treated meat safe? Do transgenic foods created through genetic engineering contain allergens that cause serious allergic reactions that endanger health?

What makes population policy so difficult to forge is that some of the problems associated with demographic trends are declining, and others are growing worse. How is the globe responding?

Global environmental issues pose another controversy, one that engages the competing perspectives of optimistic cornucopians and pessimistic neo-Malthusians. Cornucopians adhere to the liberal belief that if free markets and free trade are practiced, ecological imbalances that threaten humankind eventually will be corrected. For them, prices are the key adjustment mechanism that in time produces the greatest good for the greatest number of people. Neo-Malthusians, on the other hand, share more in common with economic **mercantilism** which argues that free markets fail to prevent excessive exploitation of both renewable and nonrenewable resources, and that, accordingly, intervention by governing institutions is necessary (recall Chapter 9). More fundamentally, it requires rejecting the belief that the free market will always maximize social welfare, because neither an inexhaustible supply of natural resources nor "sinks" for disposing the wastes from consuming those resources are available.

■ **mercantilism**
a government trade strategy for accumulating state wealth and power by active government management of the state's economic, population, and environmental policies.

A Prescription for Optimism or Pessimism?

Neo-Malthusians and cornucopians paint quite different visions of our future. Might both be right? Rapidly expanding populations increase environmental degradation, poverty, and reproduction to hedge against the future. Economic development, on the other hand, encourages small families by stimulating reduced birthrates and hence declining rates of population growth. So, too, do government family-planning policies. Where each of us chooses to focus attention—dictated by our perceptual lens—will in turn frame our policy prescriptions.

The world community has made great strides in recent decades in recognizing the complex causes and consequences of rapid population growth. Whether it has the will and shared vision to cope with the problems and expand the possibilities remains to be seen. Meanwhile, an interdependent and rapidly globalizing world promises that none will be immune to world population trends, even as the effects of population growth play strain the natural environment on which we depend. Population politics are linked directly to the issue of protecting the planet's ecology, which we now examine.

■ **ecopolitics**
how political actors influence perceptions of, and policy responses to, changing environmental conditions, such as population density.

ENVIRONMENTAL SECURITY AND SUSTAINABLE DEVELOPMENT: AN OVERVIEW

To explore global environmental challenges and responses to them, broadly described by the concept **ecopolitics**—the intersection of ecology and politics—we need to examine the linkage between the two. Ecology deals with

NASA/AP File

The View From Afar People on the planet collectively face many threats to survival, one of which is the threat posed by heat-trapping greenhouse gases that contribute to climate change and destructive global warming. Taken from a NASA global satellite surveillance system, this photo shows how integrated the globalized, borderless planet appears from outer space. NASA monitors the geophysical and biological conditions that will affect the earth's climate and the prospects for sustaining human life.

the impact of human activity on the environment. Politics, as we have seen, is concerned with the exercise of power. Ecopolitics, then, centers on how political actors influence perceptions of, and policy responses to, managing the impact of human behavior on their environments. But not surprisingly, politics emerges as a powerful force that permeates all dimensions of environmental and resource issues, ranging from the evaluation of scientific evidence to policy prescriptions for dealing with that evidence.

What is almost self-evident is that the ecological preservation of the global environment is required if any other values are to be achieved, for without the means to a healthy life no other values can be realized. Awareness of the importance of environmental protection has expanded greatly in recent years. When U.S. astronauts first viewed the Earth from the Apollo spacecraft, they remarked to millions of listeners about the "big blue marble" planet they saw through their small windows and how the clouds and continents flowed into one another without regard to the political boundaries humans had imposed on

realist theory

the view that states are unitary global actors in relentless competition with each other for position and prosperity in the international hierarchy, dedicated to the promotion of their own interests at the expense of other states.

high politics

geostrategic issues of national and international security that pertain to matters of war and peace.

neoliberalism

a perspective that accounts for the way international institutions promote global change, cooperation, peace, and prosperity through collective reform approaches.

politics of scarcity

the view that the unavailability of resources required to sustain life, such as food, energy, or water, can undermine security in degrees similar to military aggression.

environmental security

a concept recognizing that environmental threats to global life systems are as important as the threat of armed conflicts.

liberalism

the school of thought that stresses the need for international cooperation through institutions to manage global problems and promote progress.

a pristine planet. Those images were often replayed. However, the improvement in space technology since the 1990s also enabled the world to see uncomfortable images—of atmospheric poisons that encircle the globe; of violent winter and summer storms pounding islands and continents with relentless fury; of massive holes in the ozone shield that protects humans from dangerous ultraviolet rays; of vanishing forests and widening deserts. Will the consumption habits and excessive toxic waste of industrialization cause irreparable environmental damage? There is no consensus on this question. Not surprisingly, then, there is no more consensus on how states ought to cope with ecological degradation than on how they should deal with the globalization of demographic changes and the economic and political transformations they cause.

Environmental issues are linked to other values that states prize, notably, security and economic and social well-being. "Security" means freedom from fear. It also means freedom from risk and danger. Because fear of a nuclear holocaust and other forms of violence such as terrorism have long haunted the world, security has been conventionally equated with "national security," the struggle for state power central to **realist theory** in the so-called realm of **high politics.** Today many analysts urge people to adopt a broader conception of what constitutes security at both the state and global levels. That rival view recommended by **neoliberalism** suggests that threats to national security should be defined as actions that reduce the quality of life for a country's inhabitants. This is the **politics of scarcity,** which predicts that future international conflict will likely be caused by resource scarcities—restricted access to food, oil, and water, for example—rather than by overt military challenges (see Klare 2001). Compelling as this unconventional viewpoint may be, scarcity continues to be studied primarily from a state-centric ecopolitical perspective.

Environmental security is a useful concept to broaden the definition of national security, pushing our vision beyond borders and their protection. Focusing on the transboundary character of challenges to preserving the global environment, it recognizes that threats by such phenomena as global warming, ozone depletion, and the loss of tropical forests and marine habitats can threaten the future of humankind just as much as can the threat of nuclear annihilation. Because environmental degradation undercuts states' economic well-being and the quality of life all governments seek for their citizens, **liberalism** informs thinking about how states can cooperate with intergovernmental organizations (IGOs) and nongovernmental organizations (NGOs) to preserve the global environment. The effort by the neoliberal **epistemic community** to redefine *security* seeks to move beyond realism's popular state-centric conception of international politics, although the attempt to broaden the definition is understandably controversial to realists.

The dominant cornucopian social **paradigm** stressing the right to conspicuous consumption is under serious attack by environmental activists. It is also under attack internationally. **Sustainable development** is now popularly perceived as an alternative to the quest for unrestrained growth. The movement began in earnest in 1972, when the United Nations (UN) General Assembly convened the first UN Conference of the Human Environment in Stockholm. Conferences have since been held on a wide range of environmental topics, with scores of treaties negotiated and new international agencies put into place to promote cooperation and monitor environmental developments. The concept of sustainable development enjoys widespread support among governments and a broad range of NGOs that are particularly active in shaping the global environmental agenda. Its heritage is even more directly traceable to *Our Common Future*, the 1987 report of the World Commission on Environment and Development, popularly known as the "Brundtland Commission" after the Norwegian prime minister who chaired it. The commission concluded that the world cannot sustain the growth required to meet the needs and aspirations of the world's growing population unless it adopts radically different approaches to basic issues of economic expansion, equity, resource management, energy efficiency, and the like. Rejecting the "limits to growth" maxim popular among neo-Malthusians, it emphasized instead "the growth of limits." The commission defined a "sustainable society" as one that "meets the needs of the present without compromising the ability of future generations to meet their own needs."

A second milestone in the challenge to the dominant cornucopian social paradigm was the Earth Summit, which took place in Rio de Janeiro, Brazil, in 1992—the twentieth anniversary of the Stockholm conference. Formally known as the UN Conference on Environment and Development (UNCED), the meeting brought together more than one hundred fifty states, one thousand four hundred nongovernmental organizations, and eight thousand journalists. Prior to the Earth Summit, environment and economic development had been treated separately—and often regarded as being in conflict with each other, as economic growth frequently imperils and degrades the environment. In Rio, the concept of sustainability galvanized a simultaneous treatment of environmental and development issues. That concept continued to be the key theme on environmental protection enthusiastically endorsed at the UN World Summit on Sustainable Development that concluded in early September 2002 in Johannesburg. These and other international conferences have punctuated the strong consensus behind the proposition that all politics—even global politics—are local, that what happens anyplace ultimately affects conditions everyplace, and accordingly that the protection of the earth's environment is a primary international security issue.

Sustainability cannot be realized without dramatic changes in the social, economic, and political practices throughout an increasingly interconnected world. Is that possible? Are individuals willing to sacrifice personal welfare for the common good? Will they sacrifice now to enrich their heirs? The tragedy of the commons provides little basis for optimism, whether applied to individuals or states, suggesting that greed and the striving for **relative gains** by some in the absence of strong international regulation leads to reductions in everyone's **absolute gains** and possibly to their destruction. Add to this that international anarchy without potent institutions for true global governance discourages states from cooperating with one another out of fear that some will gain more than others, and it becomes clear why environmental problems that cross national boundaries are seldom effectively managed.

To better understand the multiple tensions that global environmental problems pose in an anarchical world and how competition undercuts effective responses to them, consider next three interrelated clusters of problems on the global ecopolitical agenda: (1) oil and energy, (2) climate change and ozone

■ **epistemic community**
a group of experts from around the world who, based on their knowledge, develop a shared understanding of a problem on the global agenda and a set of preferences for responding to it.

■ **paradigm**
derived from the Greek *paradeigma*, meaning an example, a model, or an essential pattern; a paradigm structures thoughts about an area of inquiry.

■ **sustainable development**
economic growth that does not deplete the resources needed to maintain growth.

■ **relative gains**
a measure of how much some participants in an exchange benefit in comparison with others.

■ **absolute gains**
a condition in which all participants in exchanges become better off.

depletion, and (3) biodiversity and deforestation. The clusters illustrate the problems and pitfalls that states and nonstate actors (IGOs and NGOs) face as they seek sustainable development of common properties and renewable resources.

THE ECOPOLITICS OF ENERGY

In April 1990, the average price for a barrel of internationally traded crude oil was less than $15. Five months later—stimulated by Iraq's invasion of the tiny oil sheikdom of Kuwait—it rose to more than $40. For the third time in less than two decades, the world suffered an oil shock when the price paid for the most widely used commercial energy source skyrocketed.

The 1990 Persian Gulf War was precipitated by Iraq's Saddam Hussein's attempt to subjugate Kuwait and acquire its oil—an act of aggression—that culminated two decades of Middle Eastern turmoil during which oil disputes figured prominently. Concern about new oil wars, pitting buyers like the United States against major Middle East sellers, remains, because the prospects for global prosperity and peace depend heavily on the preservation of order in the volatile Middle East. Ensuring access to the region's oil is especially critical to the economic fortunes of the Global North, because "almost all the oil that is cheap to extract lies under the desert sands of a handful of countries around the Persian Gulf. . . . The world is increasingly dependent on Middle Eastern oil [and] after September 11 this could be a cause of increased alarm" inasmuch as the Middle East is the soil from which the new global terrorism is primarily growing (*Economist*, December 15, 2001).

Global Patterns of Oil Consumption

The importance of oil to the Global North generally and the United States in particular is evident from their disproportionate share of energy consumption. The average person living in Europe uses more than twice as much energy as people in the Global South, while Canada and the United States use more than six times as much. The differences parallel the gap between the globe's rich and poor countries apparent in so many other dimensions of a globalized world.

Throughout the twentieth century, demand for and consumption of oil spiraled upward. An abundant supply of oil at low prices facilitated the recovery of Western Europe and Japan from World War II and encouraged consumers to use energy-intensive technologies, such as the private automobile. An enormous growth in the worldwide demand for and consumption of energy followed. Oil consumption hit an all-time high of 3.5 billion tons per day in 2001, when oil supplied about 87 percent of the world's commercial energy (*Vital Signs 2002*, 38). The industrialization of many emerging Global South economies has contributed to the growing demand, and the global shift to oil has been propelled by the aggressive production and promotion of a small group of multinational corporations (MNCs). Their operations encompass every aspect of the business, from exploration to the retail sales of products at their gas stations. Their search for, production of, and marketing of low-cost oil was for decades largely unhindered. Concessions from countries in the oil-rich Middle East and elsewhere were easy to get. And incentives for developing technologies for alternative energy sources, such as coal, were virtually nonexistent. Eventually, to maximize profits, the Organization of Petroleum Exporting Countries (OPEC) emerged as an important IGO **cartel.** Because the resources OPEC controls cannot be easily replaced, it has monopoly power. In March 1999 OPEC began to flex its economic muscles by cutting production to limit supplies. Oil prices tripled within a year, showing that OPEC can still make oil a critical global political issue—as it again threatened to do in 2002 in an effort to use oil prices as an instrument of **coercive diplomacy** to influence the course of the unfolding war on terrorism, particularly between Palestine and Israel.

■ **cartel**
an organization of the producers of a commodity that seeks to regulate the pricing and production of that commodity to increase revenue.

■ **coercive diplomacy**
the use of threats or limited armed force to persuade an adversary to alter its foreign and/or domestic policies.

Running on Empty: Is Energy Security an Elusive Goal?

The question of oil supplies assumes great importance to world politics, because oil is not being discovered at the same rate it is being used: "For every two barrels pumped out of the ground, the [giant oil companies] find less than one barrel to add to reserves. Production in the United States peaked thirty years ago. Russia peaked in 1987. North Sea production appears to be peaking now. [About] 70 percent of the oil consumed today was found twenty-five years ago or longer. . . . Meanwhile, demand for oil keeps moving up [and] the era of cheap and abundant oil is drawing to a close" (Quinn 2002, 43).

To properly characterize the present problem, the world does not now face the immediate threat of running out of oil; it faces instead the problem that oil reserves are concentrated in a small number of countries. Because OPEC members, who control approximately half of the world's oil reserves, are drawing down their reserves at half the average global rate, it seems almost inevitable that OPEC's share of the world oil market will grow. This means that OPEC is critical to global oil supply, the Middle East is critical to OPEC, and countries that depend on oil imports from this volatile, unstable source are highly vulnerable to disruptions—such as the United States (the percentage of whose oil from foreign suppliers exceeds 60 percent [*Harper's*, November 2001, 92] and whose oil inventories hit a twenty-three-year low in 2002).

OPEC's future role could change significantly, however, as its finances and political clout depend heavily on factors largely outside its control: changes in international demand (consumption) and supply. And we now may be witnessing the advent of a potentially historic juncture that could overturn the place of oil in the twenty-first-century's global political economy. Why? Largely because "World energy needs are projected to double in the next several decades, but no credible geologist foresees a doubling of world oil production, which is expected to peak within the next few decades" (Brown and Flavin 1999, 6). The petroleum picture on the planet is undergoing a massive transformation. This presages enormous future transformations in the ways the global community will meet its growing energy needs throughout the twenty-first century. And it places oil-producing countries in a powerful bargaining position. Consider the estimated proven reserves of oil in billions of dollars. "Saudi Arabia remains the kingpin of oil. It has a quarter of the world's proven reserves, about 262 billion barrels of oil, under its vast desert expanses. Add in the reserves held by the country's allies in the OPEC cartel, and the total is a whopping 815 billion barrels—some three-quarters of world reserves. In contrast, OECD countries, which use much of the world's oil, have less than one-tenth of total reserves" (*Economist*, July 21, 2001, 88). This distribution of oil reserves means that "unless vast reserves are discovered outside the Middle East, global dependence on Persian Gulf oil will grow [and] this is a long-term problem [especially] for the United States in the wake of September 11 because for three decades Americans have only haphazardly tried to fortify themselves against a catastrophic cutoff of oil from the Middle East, which accounts for about a third or world production and two-thirds of known reserves" (Samuelson 2001a, A17).

The global energy system appears to be in the process of reinvention. Fossil fuel—coal, oil, and natural gas—provide 90 percent or more of industrialized countries' energy and 75 percent of energy worldwide. Petroleum, the most convenient and available energy source, now appears to be without an alternative. However, that seems destined to change in the wake of the events of September 11, 2001. Technological, economic, cultural, and environmental changes are unfolding which suggest that the early stages of a major global energy transition are underway.

"The broad outlines of a new energy system may now be emerging, thanks in part to a series of revolutionary new technologies and approaches. These developments suggest that our future energy economy may be highly efficient and decentralized, using a range of sophisticated electronics. The primary energy resources for this system may be the most abundant ones on Earth: the sun, the wind, and other renewable sources of energy [such as] hydrogen, the lightest and most abundant element in the universe." Humans only became dependent on nonrenewable finite stocks of fossilized fuel when Europeans began mining coal in the seventeenth century. For most of their existence, humans have relied on abundant renewable energy resources such as plants, sun, wind, and water to meet basic human needs for shelter, heat, cooking, lighting and transportation. "Fossilized fuels . . . remaining energy is now equivalent to less than 11 days of sunshine. From a millennial perspective, today's hydrocarbon-based civilization is but a brief interlude in human history" (Flavin and Dunn 1999, 23).

The impact of such a global transformation would be huge, overturning the past 125-year pattern in world energy development and consumption. Could the era of "big oil" really be ending? That could well be the case. A growing number of energy analysts and industry officials now argue that "two forces much more powerful than the fickle oil price are driving the [long-run shift from fossil fuels]: the rise of markets, and growing public alarm over global warming [and that] these twin forces . . . in time . . . may even make it yesterday's fuel" (Vaitheeswaron 2000, 89). This prophecy was captured in a remarkable speech in Houston in early 1999, when Mike Bowlin, chairman and CEO of the ARCO Oil Company, said, "We've embarked on the beginning of the Last Days of the Age of Oil." Bowlin went on to say that the world is moving "along the spectrum away from carbon and headed toward hydrogen and other forms of energy" (*Vital Signs 1999*, 48).

Long before we completely run out of fossil fuels, however, the environmental and health burdens of using them may force us toward a cleaner energy system. Fossil fuel burning is the main source of air pollution and a leading cause of water and land degradation. Combustion of coal and oil produces carbon monoxide and tiny particles that have been implicated in lung cancer and other respiratory problems; nitrogen and sulfur oxides create urban smog, and bring acid rain that has damaged forests extensively. Oil spills, refinery operations, and coal mining release toxic materials that impair water quality. Increasingly, oil exploration disrupts fragile ecosystems and coal mining removes entire mountains. Although modern pollution controls have improved air quality in most industrial countries in recent decades, the deadly experiences of London and Pittsburgh are now being repeated in Mexico City, São Paulo, New Delhi, Bangkok, and many other cities in the developing world. Each year, coal burning is estimated to kill 178,000 people prematurely in China alone. (Flavin and Dunn 1999, 25).

This transformation portends a probable global shift from oil to unconventional sources (such as tar sands and shale) and renewable forms of energy. In the latter category, solar, tidal, and wind power, as well as geothermal energy and bioconversion are among the alternatives to oil most likely to become technologically and economically viable. Their development would reduce dependence on oil from the volatile Middle East and reduce anxieties over possible scarcity. As Figure 10.3 shows, advocates of reliance on environmentally friendly, renewable energy supplies picture a radically different twenty-first century. They urge immediate planning for a new global "eco-economy, one that satisfies today's need without jeopardizing the prospects of future generations to meet theirs by altering how we light our homes, what we eat, where we live, how we use our leisure time, and how many children we have. It will give us a world where we are part of nature, instead of estranged from it" (Brown 2002).

Among known technologies, nuclear energy has often been championed as the leading alternative to fossil fuel dependence. But safety and financial problems have forced some countries to reduce their nuclear programs. Well-publicized nuclear accidents in the United States at the Three Mile Island nuclear power plant in Pennsylvania in 1979 and at Chernobyl in Ukraine in 1986 and no less than five major accidents between 1995 and 1999 at Japan's fifty-two nuclear power plants (which supply about a third of Japan's electricity) dramatized the potential dangers of nuclear power. Since then fears have not decreased, in part because 92 percent of U.S. nuclear power plants that were operating in 1996 had since broken U.S. federal safety regulations (*Harper's*, April 2001, 17). At Chernobyl, in 1986, catastrophe *did* strike. Thousands died; hundreds of thousands were forced to evacuate their homes; and the radioactive fallout—the equivalent of ten Hiroshima bombs—permanently poisoned agricultural land the size of the Netherlands. Radioactive fallout spread beyond Ukraine, multiplying the geographical scope and number of those ravaged by the catastrophe's long-term consequences and costs, with the environmental cleanup estimated to require billions of dollars and taking generations to complete. Political support for nuclear power in Japan has steadily fallen after the series of accidents since 1995, and Green Party environmental activists throughout Europe have led a crusade to shut down nuclear power plants and reactors. The Greens' arguments: Nuclear energy produces lethal wastes that endanger future generations for centuries because there is no way to render them harmless, and the meltdown of a nuclear reactor is a catastrophic possibility.

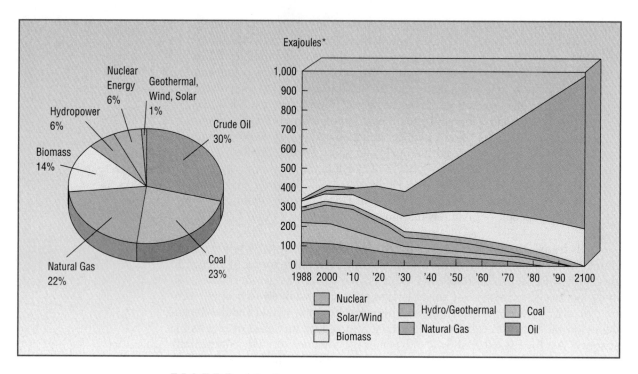

FIGURE 10.3

Phasing Out Fossil Fuels? The Potential for Renewable Energy to Supply the World's Energy Needs by the Year 2100

The global economy's need for energy continues to rise, requiring more energy than is ultimately available from nonrenewable resources. Thus rising demand is likely to change the current distribution of sources on which the world relies to meet its energy needs (left). As the Fossil Free Energy Scenario prediction (right) suggests, it would be possible to tap renewable sources to meet the world's entire energy needs by the end of the twenty-first century. For example, it is estimated that more than fifty Global South countries could produce as much energy from the biomass residues generated by sugar production as they presently obtain from oil; that less than 5 percent of the globe's small-scale hydropower has been exploited; and that land-based wind turbines could provide 20 million megawatt-hours of electricity each year—twice as much as the world consumed in 1987 (Crump 1998, 223). Renewable energy from replacable sources also has the advantage of doing relatively little damage to the environment. Whether these sources of energy will actually be harnessed remains to be seen, because the relatively low financial cost of using the planet's nonrenewable resources (like oil, which takes millions of years to form) makes them economically attractive.

*A joule is a unit of work or energy, equivalent to 0.239 calories (1 exajoule equals 10^{18} joules).

Note: Percentages do not equal 100 due to rounding errors.

SOURCE: Adapted from Crump (1998), 193 (left) and 223 (right).

Concerns about the risks of nuclear power extend beyond safety. How and where to dispose of highly radioactive nuclear wastes, for example, is an unresolved issue virtually everywhere. There are no safe procedures for handling toxic radioactive nuclear waste, some of which remains dangerous for hundreds of thousands of years. Ironically, after the Cold War ended, the problem compounded since dismantling both nuclear weapons and their production

Yanin Arthus Bertrand CORBIS

The Unforgiving Cost of Nuclear Power Failure Using nuclear power to generate energy appears inexpensive and cost-efficient, but involves risks, not only increasing the probability of nuclear weapons proliferation but also the potential of producing damage of toxic poisons to the environment. Show here is the town of Pripyat, Ukraine, that was abandoned after the Chernobyl accident. Rather than learning from this lesson, and despite strong opposition from the public, in 2001, Russia prepared to open its borders to become the largest international repository for radioactive nuclear wastes, in the hope of earning $21 billion over the next two decades (Tyler 2001).

facilities required unavailable means and places of disposal. "Not in my back yard" (NIMBY) is a divisive cry on the global ecopolitical agenda; the Global North prefers to dump wastes outside its own territory, and the Global South would prefer not to be the dump—but often is.

A related fear is that countries that do not now possess nuclear know-how might develop nuclear weapons. Most nuclear-energy generating facilities continue to produce weapons-grade material, specifically highly enriched uranium and plutonium, which is a national security concern because nonnuclear countries may use it to develop nuclear weapons. It was this concern that prompted the United States (with the help of South Korea and Japan) to give North

Korea—a longtime political-military adversary—nuclear reactors less suscepti-ble to nuclear weapons production than those it was admitted in late 2002 North Korea was attempting to develop secretly.

In a political world in which growing population means growing demand for energy, food, and other resources only the environment and technology can provide, the politics of scarcity becomes central. Common property resources and their preservation will be a core security concern in the twenty-first century. In an ecologically interdependent world without strong global governing institutions, where actions anywhere have external costs almost everywhere, the challenge of managing the global commons has reached unprecedented levels.

THE ECOPOLITICS OF THE ATMOSPHERE

The scores of government negotiators and nongovernmental representatives who converged on Rio de Janeiro in 1992 came in the wake of the hottest decade on record. For years scientists had warned that global warming—the gradual rise in world temperature—would cause destructive changes in world climatological patterns and that rising sea levels, melting glaciers, and freak storms would provoke widespread changes in the globe's political and eco-nomic systems and relationships. Perhaps because they had been burned by the chronic heat wave throughout the 1980s, negotiators agreed at Rio to a *Frame-work Convention on Climate Change* whose purpose was to address the human causes of climate change by reducing emissions of carbon dioxide and other greenhouse gases. Since then, fears have not subsided. The year 2001 was the warmest on record, and because of this, alongside hurricanes and tropical storms well above annual averages, the 2002 UN World Summit in Johannes-burg included in its sixty-five-page plan for action heavy emphasis on control-ling the sources of global warming.

In recent years, the world's top climate scientists have concluded that the extent of climate change is greater than once believed and furthermore, that evidence shows a discernible human influence. In response to many ecological alarm bells, the cry for greater attempts to curb the pollutants blamed for global warming has risen.

Climate Change

Major gaps in our knowledge of climate change remain, but few climate scien-tists think the world can afford to wait for answers. The changes are substan-tial and threatening. Most scientists believe that the gradual rise in the earth's temperature, especially evident since the late eighteenth century when the invention of power-driven machinery produced the Industrial Revolution, is caused by an increase in human-made gases that alter the atmosphere's insu-lating effects. The gas molecules, primarily carbon dioxide (CO_2) and chloro-fluorocarbons (CFCs), form the equivalent of a greenhouse roof by trapping heat remitted from Earth that would otherwise escape into outer space. As these gases are released into the atmosphere they have created a **greenhouse effect** that has caused the global temperature to rise. As shown in Figure 10.4, the temperature on the earth's surface has increased nearly a half degree since

■ **greenhouse effect**
the phenomenon producing planetary warming when gases released by burning fossil fuels act as a blanket in the atmosphere, thereby increasing temperatures.

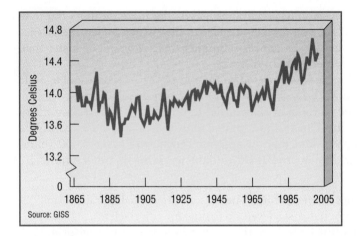

FIGURE 10.4

Rising Average Global Temperatures at the Earth's Surface since 1867

The World Meteorological Organization (WMO) monitors average global surface temperatures at thousands of sites around the world, and its records show that so-called global warming is not a myth. For nearly 140 years, the globe's temperature has seesawed up and down, usually by tiny fractions of degrees. But since the mid-1970s, the mercury has largely been on the rise, and the WMO predicts that the average global surface temperature could jump 3.6 degrees Celsius by the end of the twenty-first century—more than triple the rise of the past one hundred years.

Note: Five-year averages of global temperatures.

SOURCE: *Vital Signs 2002*, p. 51. Copyright © 2002 Worldwatch Institute. www.worldwatch.org

---

1950; thirteen of the hottest years since record-keeping began in 1866 have occurred since 1987, with 2001 exceeding new records in the 1990s—the hottest decade in the past 600 years (*Vital Signs 2002*, 51).

The globe's temperature is now between 0.3 and 0.6 degrees Celsius higher than it was in 1880 and is projected to further increase by 3.6 degrees Celsius by 2100 if preventive action is not taken (Soroos 2001). Although CO_2 is the principal greenhouse gas, concentrations of methane in the atmosphere are growing more rapidly. Methane gas emissions arise from livestock populations, rice cultivation, and the production and transportation of natural gas. To many scientists' alarm, the largest concentrations of methane are not in the atmosphere but locked in ice, permafrost, and coastal marine sediments. This raises the probability that warming will cause more methane to be released into the atmosphere, which would then accelerate the process because of methane's strong warming potential.

While some scientists believe that the rise in global temperature is part of the cyclical change the world has experienced for tens of thousands of years, that view has been steadily discredited. Since 1988, hundreds of atmospheric scientists from around the world organized several UN agencies to study global climate change. The team, known as the Intergovernmental Panel on Climate Change (IPCC), first conclusively stated in 1995 its belief that global climate trends are "unlikely to be entirely due to natural causes," that humans are to blame for at least part of the problem, and that the consequences are likely to be very harmful and costly. The implications were self-evident: Without significant efforts to reduce the emission of greenhouse gases, the increase in global temperatures by the year 2100 could be equivalent to that which ended the last ice age. Even at the lower end of the panel's estimates, the rise would be faster than any experienced in recorded human history.

Global climate change was elevated to the top of the international agenda (Luterbacker and Spinz 2001) as many countries expressed their appreciation of the need to respond to fresh evidence that temperatures were rising faster than previously thought—"faster and higher than most experts feared only a short time ago—faster, in fact than at anytime during the past 10,000 years" (James 2001b). According to the IPCC, global warming is not coming, it's here:

> Many strange things are happening. The seasons are changing, rainstorms are becoming more intense, sea levels are rising, mighty glaciers are receding, the permafrost (by definition, the permanently frozen subsoil in the polar regions) is thawing, trees are flowering earlier, insects are emerging sooner, and so on. . . . More people are projected to be harmed than benefited by climate change, even for global mean temperature increases of less than a few degrees centigrade. (Herbert 2001: A7)

Thus, the world has already entered a period of climatic instability likely to cause widespread economic, social, and environmental dislocation over the twenty-first century, because government leaders have not "responded to the problem with the sense of urgency that is called for [inasmuch as] carbon dioxide doesn't just float away in a day or two. It remains in the atmosphere for more than 100 years. The consequences of our failure to act will last for centuries" (Herbert 2001). The effects of continued temperature rises could be both dramatic and devastating:

- Sea levels could rise up to three feet, mostly because of melting glaciers and the expansion of water as it warms up. That will flood vast areas of low-lying coastal land, including major river deltas; most of the beaches on the U.S. Atlantic coast; part of China; and the Maldive Islands, the Seychelles, and the Cook and Marshall islands. More than 1 million people could be displaced, and 30 million would be put at risk of at least one flood per year.

- Winters would get warmer and warm-weather hot spells (such as the 1995 summer heat wave that killed five hundred people in Chicago) would become more frequent and more severe.

- Rainfall would increase globally, but only the areas already prone to flooding would flood more often and more severely, with freak storms such as the 1997 El Niño surge of storms in the Pacific and the flooding in the Dakotas becoming more common. Since water evaporates more easily in a warmer world, drought-prone regions would become even dryer. As oceans heat, hurricanes, which draw their energy from warm oceans, would become even stronger.

- Entire ecosystems would vanish from the planet, and a hotter earth would drive some plants to higher latitudes and altitudes and require farmers to irrigate and change their crops and agriculture practices.

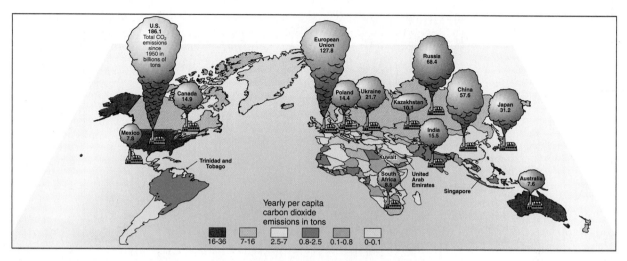

M A P   1 0 . 2
Global Warning about Global Warming: Who's to Blame?

This map shows the yearly carbon dioxide emissions in tons for each person in each country. The Kyoto Protocol of 2001 needed the support of countries accounting for 55 percent of greenhouse-gas emissions to come into force, and it received it even though the United States, which is responsible for most greenhouse gases, claimed it wanted nothing to do with the treaty: "Other countries have chosen their path," one senior U.S. negotiator belched, "and our answer is still 'No'" (*Economist*, November 17, 2001). The fight against global warming persists despite the 2002 rejection of the Kyoto Protocol by the United States. President George W. Bush's stance infuriated "other nations, since the U.S. is by far the biggest polluter on the planet. With only 4 percent of the world's population America produces 25 percent of its greenhouse gases" (Kluger 2001, 30).

SOURCE: From *TIME*, April 9, 2001, p. 30–31. Copyright © 2001 TIME, Inc. Reprinted by permission.

- The combination of flooding and droughts would cause tropical diseases such as malaria and dengue fever to flourish in previously temperate regions that were formerly too cold for their insect carriers.

Climate-Change Culprits

The politics of agreements to reduce the threat of global warming are divisive. The economics and financial stakes are enormous and every proposal generates stiff opposition. CO_2 emissions from the burning of fossil fuels have climbed steadily, rising fourfold since 1950. The industrial Global North states are the principal sources of global carbon emissions, accounting for three-fourths of global CO_2 emissions; the United States emits more CO_2 into the atmosphere that any other state. In large measure because of its big buildings, millions of cars, and relatively inefficient industries, the U.S. CO_2 emissions for each person are nearly those in all western Europe, and five times the world average. Elsewhere, China is a major and growing source of concern because coal emits more atmospheric pollutants than other fossil fuels, and three-fourths of China's energy for its fast-growing economy comes from coal. China now accounts for about 10 percent of all greenhouse gas emissions, making it the fastest-growing major contributor to global warming.

Daniel Beltra/Greenpeace

Cold Comfort for Global Warming Global emissions of carbon dioxide and other greenhouse gases are rising and contributing to global warming. If the earth continues to heat, oceans will rise and land will be submerged. Pictured here is the Bering Glacier at the edge of Vitus Lake in Alaska, which according to Greenpeace has shrunk about 40 feet in length during the past century due to global warming. An even more dramatic indicator of the effect of global warming began on January 31, 2002, when the Larsen B patch of floating ice shelf in Antarctica—30 to 40 miles across (the size of Rhode Island), weighing 500 billion tons and 700 feet thick—collapsed from warming temperatures in less than a month (Stott 2002). The U.S.-based National Snow and Ice Data Center described it as "the largest single event in a series of retreats by ice shelves in the peninsula over the last 30 years."

■ **acid rain**
precipitation that has been made acidic through contact with sulfur dioxide and nitrogen oxides.

Coal is a major source of atmospheric sulfur and nitrogen oxides. These pollutants return to Earth, typically after traveling long distances, in the form of **acid rain,** which adds to the acidification of lakes, the corrosion of materials and structures, and the impairment of ecosystems. Acid rain is a serious problem in much of China. Because the oxides that cause it are also transboundary pollutants, China's domestic energy policies have become a major irritant in its relations with its neighbors, particularly South Korea and Japan. Nonetheless, China plans to increase the amount of coal it burns by nearly 900 million tons a year by 2010. Other Asian states are following in its path, including populous India which, like China, has sizable coal deposits. Already China and India account for 15 percent of global greenhouse emissions, and their combined share of CO_2 emissions is expected to grow. "Human activity has now added more than 200 billion tons of carbon to the atmosphere since 1950. Among industrial nations, responsible for 45 percent of global carbon emissions, output increased 8.1 percent between 1990 and 1998. The United States, the world's leading emitter with 27 percent of the overall total, saw output rise 11.8 percent between 1990 and 1998. . . . Developing countries held a

41 percent share of global carbon emissions, and saw a 39.1 percent rise in output between 1990 and 1998" (*Visual Signs 1999*, 60). Hence, global warming will remain a hot topic on the global agenda.

To combat the danger of accelerating global warming, more than one hundred sixty states signed the 1992 *UN Framework Convention on Climate Change*, which sought to contain greenhouse gases at levels to avoid threatening climate change and aimed to return emissions to 1990 levels. But that agreement did not go far enough, and most industrial countries missed their targets for reductions. When yearly CO_2 emissions were predicted to reach "9 billion tons by 2010—49 percent above 1990 levels" (*Vital Signs 1997*, 58), the 1997 Kyoto Protocol was reached, requiring 28 industrial countries to reduce their current greenhouse gas emissions by between the years 2008 and 2012. If it had been followed, the United States would have cut emissions by 7 percent, the European Union by 8 percent, and Japan by 6 percent; and the protocol asked China, India, and other developing economies to voluntarily set sizable reduction targets.

In July 2001, 179 countries reached a new climate-control treaty that for the first time formally requires industrialized countries to cut emissions of gases linked to global warming. The agreement, reached after three days of marathon bargaining, rescued the 1997 Kyoto Protocol. However, to the shock of a stunned world, the United States refused to go along with the agreement and therefore stood in isolation as the only country in opposition to the treaty; *all* 190 other countries came aboard. President Bush labeled the treaty "fatally flawed," explaining "We will work together, but it's going to be what's in the interest of our country, first and foremost." Bush's hard line stunned environmentalists who were exasperated and enraged by the fact the U.S. carbon dioxide emissions had risen 13 percent in the 1990s (*U.S. News & World Report*, March 26, 2001, 7). The Bush administration's rejection of global opinion outraged U.S. allies, such as the European Union and Japan, which in March 2002 nonetheless went ahead and agreed to ratify the Kyoto Treaty in order to reduce the pollution blamed for global warming.

Ozone Protection

The story of climate change is similar to states' efforts to cope with depletion of the atmosphere's protective **ozone layer.** In this case, however, an international **regime** has emerged, progressively strengthened by mounting scientific evidence that environmental damage was directly caused by human activity.

Ozone is a pollutant in the lower atmosphere, but in the upper atmosphere it provides the earth with a critical layer of protection against the sun's harmful ultraviolet radiation. Scientists have discovered a marked depletion of the ozone layer—most notably an "ozone hole" over Antarctica that has grown larger than the continental United States, and they have conclusively linked the thinning of the layer to CFCs—a related family of compounds known as halons, hydrochlorofluorocarbons (HCFCs), methyl bromide, and other chemicals. Depletion of the ozone layer exposes humans to health hazards of various sorts, particularly skin cancer, and threatens other forms of marine and terrestrial life.

Scientists began to link halons and CFCs to ozone depletion in the early 1970s. Even before their hypotheses were conclusively confirmed, the **United Nations Environment Program (UNEP),** a UN agency created in the aftermath of the 1972 Stockholm conference, sought some form of regulatory

■ **ozone layer**
the protective layer of the upper atmosphere over the earth's surface that shields the planet from the sun's harmful impact on living organisms on the planet.

■ **regime**
norms, rules, and procedures for collective, cooperative action agreed to by a set of states.

■ **United Nations Environment Program (UNEP)**
a UN agency created in 1972 to study environmental deterioration and propose regulations to protect the global environment.

action. Despite scientific uncertainty and policy differences, the 1987 landmark Montreal Protocol on Substances That Deplete the Ozone Layer treaty was signed and "initiated dramatic declines in CFC output, which is many times below peak production years, the late 1980s." World CFC production between 1989 and 1999 declined 86 percent (*Vital Signs 2002,* 55). International cooperation for the construction of regimes sometimes works. However, in spite of reductions in CFCs over the past decade, the ozone hole over Antarctica continues to expand and under the current international regime depletion of the protective ozone shield is expected to accelerate before it begins to regenerate itself. Although production of CFCs in the Global North declined sharply in the 1990s as the largest producers (and consumers) prepared for their complete phase-out, production in the Global South surged, and increased demand for refrigerators, air conditioners, and other products using CFCs will offset the gains realized by stopping production in the Global North. Developed countries agreed to provide aid to help the developing countries adopt CFC alternatives, but have failed to provide all of the resources promised. Without this support, many in the Global South may not be able to keep their end of the global bargain. Meanwhile, a significant illegal trade in both virgin and recycled CFCs has emerged, threatening to further undermine the positive effects of the ozone regime.

Having scientific evidence, many believe, is what made the ozone initiative successful. Can it serve as a model for breakthroughs on other issues, notably climate change? Can environmental threats be given higher priority than vested interests? Again, consider the example of global warming. "There's a better scientific consensus on this than any other issue I know—except maybe Newton's second law of dynamics," observed D. James Baker of the U.S. National Oceanic Administration. "Man has reached the point where his impact on the climate can be as significant as nature's" (Warrick 1997). Global efforts to avert the tragedy of the commons on atmospheric issues are inadequate. Continued conflicts are predicated on efforts to negotiate new treaties to protect forests and the earth's biological heritage. The same is true with respect to pollution in the world's mountains. The UN designated 2002 the International Year of Mountains, highlighting the importance of mountains as the source of rich plant and animal life and more than half the world's fresh water. Mountains and highlands cover about a quarter of the globe and are home to 10 percent of the world's population, or 60 million people. According to the UN, mountains are the "water towers of the world," supplying more than half of the world's population; but that supply is endangered, because twenty-three of the globe's twenty-seven armed conflicts in 2002 were being fought in mountainous areas, destroying the environment.

THE ECOPOLITICS OF FORESTS AND BIODIVERSITY

Forests are critical in preserving the earth's biodiversity and to protecting the atmosphere and land resources. For these reasons they have been a rising ecological issue on the global agenda. Some rules have emerged to guide international behavior in the preservation of **biodiversity,** but issues concerning forests have proven much more difficult to address.

■ **biodiversity**
the variety of life on earth.

Wesley Bocxe/Photo Researchers

Deforestation Destruction of the world's forests contributes to climate change through global warming and threatens the earth's biodiversity and genetic heritage. Lumbering for commercial purposes exacts a toll on forests, but deforestation due to the expansion of agriculture to meet the needs of a growing population may be a more critical threat.

Shrinking Forests and Dust Bowls

Trends, since the 1980s, point toward considerable **deforestation** in the United States and throughout much of the Global South. Each minute, on average, fifty-two acres of the world's forests are lost (*Time*, April 13, 1998, 199). Destruction of tropical rain forests in such places as Brazil, Indonesia, and Malaysia is a matter of special concern, since much of the world's genetic heritage is found there.

The representatives sent to the 1992 Earth Summit hoped to secure an easy victory on a statement of principle for global forest conservation. But opposition quickly developed to the principle that the global interest makes all countries responsible for protecting national forests. The Global South—led by Malaysia, a principal exporter of tropical wood products—objected especially vigorously to the socially constructed view that the world's forest were a common property resource, the "common heritage of mankind." These developing countries feared that legally accepting this view would enable the Global North to interfere with the local management of their tropical forest resources. In the end, the Earth Summit backed away from the goal of establishing international guidelines for trade in "sustainably managed" forest products. The situation today remains largely unchanged, even though the International Tropical Timber Organization (ITTO), dominated largely by the timber interests centered in the Global North, continues to be the principal global forum for addressing the transnational issue (of trade) in timber products.

■ **deforestation**
the destruction of forests.

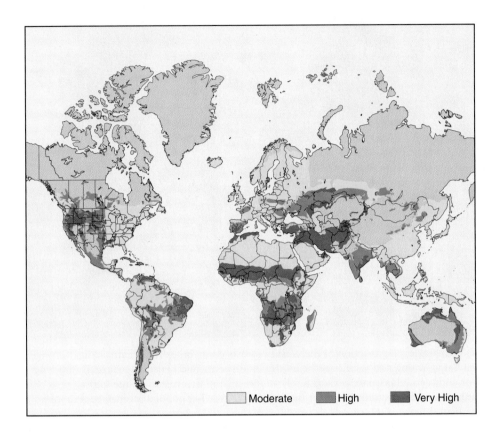

MAP 10.3
Loss of Forest and Ground to Deserts

Deforestation and desertification are global phenomena, destroying vast stretches of green forests and fields and turning them into brown deserts. "This map shows the degree to which certain regions of the world are at risk of desertification—formation or expansion of degraded dry lands as the result of climate change and human activity. Primary causes include adverse agricultural and industrial practices, deforestation and overgrazing" (James 2002). "Worldwide, more than 10 million acres of farmland are becoming unproductive deserts each year" (Seck 1999, 9), and tropical forests in Central and South America, Africa, and Southeast Asia are being cleared at an alarming rate. The 1999 UN Convention to Combat Desertification (CCD) seeks to stop the spread of deserts, which now cover 2 million square miles inhabited by one-third of the world's population" (Hottelet 1999, 8).

SOURCE: Originally developed from map located on U.S. Department of Agriculture website at www.nrcs.usda.gov.

■ **desertification**
the creation of deserts due to soil erosion, overfarming, and deforestation, which converts cropland to nonproductive, arid sand.

Meanwhile, high population growth rates, industrialization, and urbanization increase pressure on farm forests and marginal land poorly suited to cultivation. This has led to deforestation and **desertification,** which make an increasing portion of the earth's landmass deserts useless for agricultural productivity or wildlife habitats. "The world is running out of fresh water. There's water everywhere, of course, but less than three percent of it is fresh, and most of that is locked up in polar ice caps and glaciers, unrecoverable for practical purposes. Lakes, rivers, marshes, aquifers, and atmospheric vapor make up less than one percent of the earth's total water, and people are already using more

From Farmland to Dustbowl.
Desertiification has hit many areas
hard, such as this once productive soil.

Arko Datta/AFP

than half of the accessible runoff. Water demand, on the other hand, has been
growing rapidly—it tripled worldwide between 1950 and 1990—and water use
in many areas already exceeds nature's ability to recharge supplies. By 2025, the
demand for water around the world is expected to exceed supply by fifty-six
percent" (Finnegan 2002, 44).

Soil degradation has stripped billions of acres of the earth's surface from
productive farming; almost 4 billion acres of top soil are estimated to erode
worldwide each year (*Harper's,* June 2000, 23). Soil erosion and pollution are
problems both in densely populated developing countries and in the more
highly developed regions of mechanized industrial agriculture. "Since 1950,
11 percent of the planet's vegetation (approximately [2.9 billion acres]), has suffered land degradation" (Crump 1998, 78). Map 10.3 shows the regions of the
globe where desertification is occurring most rapidly. Based on previous trends,
it has been estimated that an area of one-fourth to one-half of an American football field is deforested each time another person is added to the world population (J. Cohen 1995, 338). This means that the addition of another billion people will require as much as 2.5 million square kilometers of additional land for
food production and other uses.

In the Global North, reforestation has alleviated some of the danger. This is
not the case in many cash-starved Global South countries, however, which
eagerly sell timber for income and to make room for their growing populations,

seemingly without concern for the long-term consequences of the destruction of their forests. The World Wide Fund for Nature (WWFN), a London-based environmental NGO, called 1997 "the year the world caught fire," complaining that more tropical forests were deliberately burned that year than in any other year in recorded history, 80 percent by multinational corporations (MNCs) clearing land for planting or development. Up to 12.4 million acres of forest were burned in Indonesia and Brazil alone in what the WWFN termed a "planetary disaster that is destroying our insurance for the future."

The clearing and burning of tropical rain forests to make room for farms and ranches is doubly destructive. From the viewpoint of climate change, green plants remove CO_2 from the atmosphere during photosynthesis. That is, the natural processes that remove greenhouse gases are destroyed when forests are cut down, and, as the forests decay or are burned, the amount of CO_2 discharged into the atmosphere increases.

Biodiversity

Biodiversity, or biological diversity, is an umbrella term that refers to the earth's variety of life. Technically it encompasses three basic levels of organization in living systems: genetic diversity, species diversity, and ecosystem diversity. Until recently public attention has been focused almost exclusively on preserving species diversity, including old growth forests, tall grass prairies, wetlands, coastal habitats, and coral reefs.

Forests, especially tropical forests, are important to preserving biodiversity because they are home to countless species of animals and plants, many of them still unknown. Scientists believe that the global habitat contains between 8 and 10 million species. Of these, only about 1.5 million have been named, and most of them are in the temperate regions of North America, Europe, Russia, and Australia (Edwards 1995, 215). Destruction of tropical forests, where two-thirds to three-fourths of all species are believed to live, thus threatens the destruction of much of the world's undiscovered biological diversity and genetic heritage. There exists overwhelming, alarming evidence that environmental deterioration is destroying a wide range of living organisms.

Many experts worry that the globe is relentlessly heading toward major species extinction. Of the 242,000 plant species surveyed by the World Conservation Union in 1997, some 33,000, or 14 percent, are threatened with extinction, mainly as a result of clearing land for housing, roads, and industries. Others doubt the imminence of a massive die-out, pointing out that only a small fraction of the earth's species have actually disappeared over the past several centuries. Indeed, optimistic cornucopians argue that species extinction may not be bad news, as new species may evolve that will prove even more beneficial to humanity (McKibben 1998).

Although threats to biodiversity have implications for all species, and thus the issue resembles threats to other common property resources, biodiversity's distributional characteristics also make it unique. In particular, because so much of the earth's biological heritage is concentrated in the tropics, the Global South has a special interest in this issue. It also has a growing concern about protecting its interest in the face of the recent surge of MNCs to reap profits from the sale of marketable products, based on the claim that the genetic character of the many species of plants and animals should be considered a part of the global commons and therefore available for commercial use by all, for their medical benefit.

The rapid growth of biotechnology has added incentives for preserving the earth's biological diversity so as to maintain a wide gene pool from which to develop new medical and agricultural products. MNCs in the Global North are major players in the so-called **enclosure movement** geared to privatize and merchandize the "products derived from plant and animal genes that are the building blocks of life. In India, for example, products from the neem tree have been used for medicine, contraception, toiletries, timber, fuel, and insecticide. In 1985 U.S. and Japanese firms began patenting a variety of neem compounds that Indians never patented. Now, local Indian populations must compete with MNCs for neem–derived products, often at sharply higher prices.

■ **enclosure movement** the claiming of common properties by states or private interests.

Pharmaceutical companies in particular have laid claim to Global South resources. They actively explore plants, microbes, and other living organisms in tropical forests for possible use in prescription drugs. In fact, approximately 25 percent of the prescription drugs used in the United States have active ingredients extracted or derived from plants (Miller 1995, 110).

Biogenetical engineering of harvests threatens to disrupt established trade and profits because most transgenetically altered foods and crops (primarily soybeans, beef, corn, and cotton) derived from the Global South are produced in North America and later exported for sale abroad in other countries' grocery stores. For example, food suppliers increasingly must acquire primitive germ plasma (the genetic material containing hereditary information) from the Global South to produce genetically altered seeds for the international market. Such seeds are patented and as private property can be sold back to Global South consumers. Most genetically altered seeds require expensive additives such as chemical fertilizers and pesticides that often are environmentally as well as financially costly. To compound the problem, when farmers in the Global South rely on hybrid varieties and genetically altered seeds, the risk increases that old varieties will disappear.

Biogenetic engineering threatens to escalate the loss of global diversity. Biological resources—animal and plant species—are distributed unevenly in the world. Map 10.4 shows the location of major "biodiversity bastions," where more than half the earth's species are found, primarily tropical wilderness territories laden with plant and animal species, covering only 2 percent of the land. It also shows the location of "biodiversity hot spots" where human activity threatens to disturb and potentially destroy many species that international law defines as **collective goods,** a resource for all humanity. According to the UN, about fifty thousand plant and animal species become extinct each year. This issue will intensify as the global community wrestles with the ethics of biodiversity preservation and management policies. The issue is also likely to influence and possibly poison relations between the Global North, where transgenetic crops are manufactured, and the Global South.

■ **collective goods** goods such as safe drinking water from which everyone benefits.

TOWARD PRESERVATION: THE INTERNATIONAL RESPONSE

The 1992 Earth Summit in Stockholm was precedent setting because, from it, a separate convention on biodiversity set forth a comprehensive framework for preservation of biodiversity. As finally ratified by 161 countries, the agreement established guidelines for sharing the profits of biotechnology between the

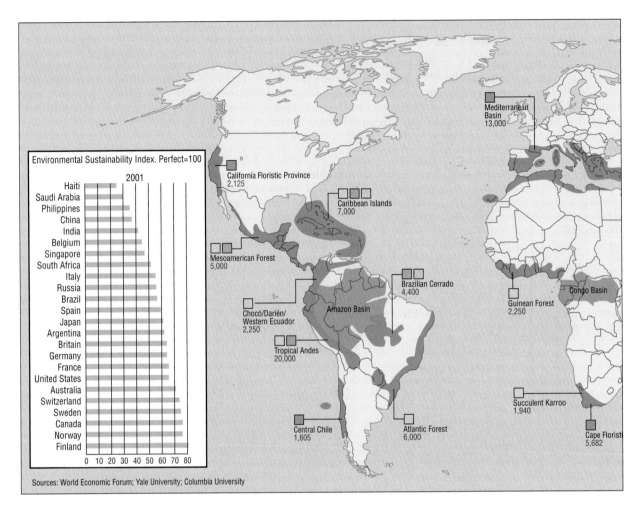

MAP 10.4

Measuring Environmental Sustainability and Locating Biodiversity Bastions and Endangered Biodiversity Hot Spots

To the left is a ranking of select countries based on an "environmental sustainability index" which measures "dozens of variables that influence the environmental health of economies. One of the strongest determinants, besides wealth, seems to be good governance including a broad commitment to the rule of law" (*Economist*, March 16, 2002, 110). The map provides another picture of the "danger zones" throughout the globe where the survival of a large number of plant and animal species is threatened. Biodiversity has become a hot global issue, and the magnitude of the danger has spread geographically, because of biologically rich areas that have been disturbed by human activity. "Scientists describe the current era as the greatest period of mass extinction since the disappearance of the dinosaurs. More than 800 species [of plants and animals] already have disappeared because of the degradation of their environments, and 11,000 more are threatened." (James 2002, 1).

SOURCE: Environmental sustainability, from *The Economist*, March 16, 2001, p. 110. Copyright © 2001 by The Economist Newspaper Ltd. All rights reserved. Reprinted with permission. Further reproduction prohibited. www.economist.com; map adapted from *TIME*, Dec. 14, 1998, p. 63–64, and *The Economist*, Jan. 29, 2000, p. 126. Copyright © 1998 TIME, Inc. Copyright © 2000 by The Economist Newspaper Ltd. All rights reserved. Reprinted with permission. Further reproduction prohibited. www.economist.com

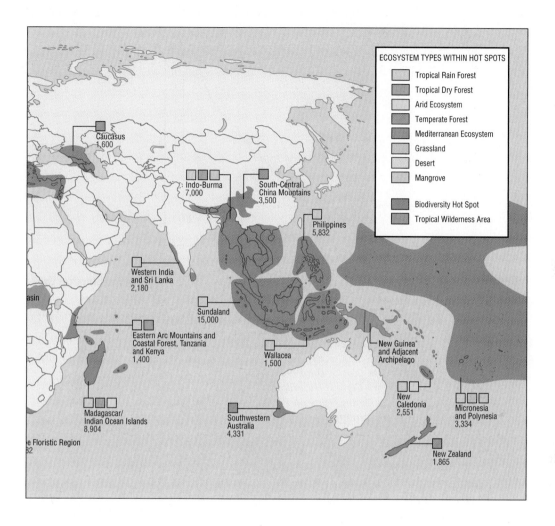

Global North and Global South and committed governments to devise national strategies for conserving species and habitats, protecting endangered species, expanding protected areas and repairing damaged ones, and promoting public awareness of the need to protect the earth's heritage. Since then, the world has attempted to cooperate through concerted efforts to reach agreements and back them with ratified treaties to protect and sustain the global commons.

Given the growing threats to environmental protection that are now recognized, this response is understandable. As documented above, there is ample evidence to mobilize for collective action, because there are strong reasons to believe that natural resources are running out, world population continues to grow at rates that threaten to leave less and less for humans to eat, forests are vanishing and fish stocks are disappearing, and the planet's air and water are becoming ever more polluted, as global warming exacerbates all of these alarming trends. The question facing the world is whether the response is adequate. International environmental treaties have grown exponentially in the last eighty years (see Figure 10.5). However, many skeptics fear that these efforts are too little, too late and that not enough is being done to save the global commons for future generations.

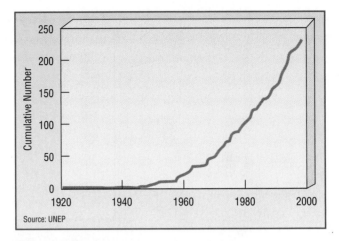

FIGURE 10.5
The Number of International Environmental Treaties since 1921: Protecting the Global Commons?

Recognizing the alarming trends toward environmental deterioration, the international community has taken a number of steps to address the major threats. Shown here is one inventory of existing environmental treaties. Recent examples include *UN Agreement Relating to the Conservation and Management of Straddling Fish Stocks* and *Highly Migratory Fish Stocks,* the 1998 *Rotterdam Convention on the Prior Informed Consent Procedure for Certain Hazardous Chemicals and Pesticides in International Trade,* the 2000 *Stockholm Treaty on Persistent Organic Pollutants,* and the 2001 *Kyoto Protocol on Global Warming.*

SOURCE: *State of the World 2000* p. 201. Copyright © 2000 Worldwatch Institute. www.worldwatch.org

To be seen in the long-term is whether the state of the global ecological environment is in peril. Many question the ability of today's existing treaties to manage the environmental dangers they are meant to address. Some are weak and introduce expressions of concern without commanding necessary policy changes to remedy the various problems they identify. Of particular concern is the reluctant backing of the globe's superpower, the United States. Of the UN's thirty-one major global environmental agreements, the United States has only ratified ten (*Harper's,* August 2001, 16). Environmental protection activists worry that if the United States refuses to lead, the prospects for strengthening the rules of the environmental preservation regime are dim. The decision by U.S. President George W. Bush in March 2001 that his administration would not regulate power plants' emissions of carbon dioxide which contributes to global warming (reversing his campaign promise) and his refusal to ratify the Kyoto Protocol on global warming that was signed by 179 other countries (leaving the United States the only state not to participate in that agreement), heightened fears throughout the world that meaningful controls of threats to the environment will not materialize.

Trade, the Environment, and Sustainable Development

A contrast may be drawn between free trade and sustainable development. Do these values complement one another, or are they in conflict? The question is

© Nik Wheeler/CORBIS

The Price of Progress?
Smog, produced by the emissions of modern society, covers the city of Los Angeles.

especially pertinent in a rapidly globalizing world in which trade increasingly links politics, economics, societies, and cultures in complex interdependencies (see Chapter 8).

Liberal economic theory argues that free trade produces benefits. If all states specialize in the production of goods in which they enjoy comparative advantages and trade them with others who enjoy advantages in other products, all will eventually prosper and new wealth will promote the means to address the environmental costs of the past.

Environmentalists question commercial liberal economists' logic, especially because they see economic growth and environmental protection as goals at cross-purposes. They argue that the focus on profits and production ignores hidden social and environmental costs that ultimately make us poorer, not richer.

Beyond the issue of the gains from and costs of trade, environmentalists and liberal economists differ in their assessments of the wisdom of using trade to promote environmental standards. Liberal economists see such efforts as market distortions, while environmentalists view them as useful instruments for correcting market failures, such as markets' inability to compensate for the "externalities" of environmental exploitation (for example, atmospheric pollution by chemical companies). Some countries, however, particularly in the Global South, view the use of trade mechanisms to protect the environment as yet another way in which the rich states block entry into lucrative Global North markets, thus keeping the Global South permanently disadvantaged.

Trade-offs must sometimes be made between goals that, in principle, all seem designed to increase human well-being. However, another interpretation maintains that trade encourages states to live beyond their means. According to some ecologists, trade magnifies the damaging ecological effects of production and consumption by expanding the market for commodities beyond state borders. Countries that have depleted their resource bases or passed strict laws to protect them can easily look overseas for desired products, in ways that shift the environmental stress of high consumption to someone else's backyard. These concern provoked Leon Brittan, the European Union commissioner for external trade, in 1999 to argue that "the economic case for pursuing the process of trade liberalization is an overwhelming one. But it is impossible to ignore the fact that . . . there are widespread fears of the social and environmental consequences of the combination of liberalization and globalization."

The issue to be faced is whether free trade and sustainable development are compatible or whether they work at cross-purposes. The path from the first Earth summits in Rio de Janeiro in 1992 and Johannesburg in 2002 has been paved with good intentions and high expectations about preserving the environment. However, pledges and promises about safeguarding the planet's ecology in the face of rising world population have *not* significantly improved conditions or expectations about the earth's capacity to expand economic growth while supporting life. When the Johannesburg World Summit on Sustainable Development concluded in September 2002, "Threats [were] higher than ever to natural resources such as forests, fish, and clean water and air. The richest one-fifth of mankind—including wealthy minorities in poor countries—[were consuming] energy and resources at such a high rate that providing a comparable lifestyle to the rest of the world's population would require the resources of four planets the size of the earth" (James 2002b, 1). "Conditions are worse," UN Secretary-General Kofi Annan bemoaned, "than they were ten years ago."

To reverse this global circumstance, 180 countries in Johannesburg signed agreements to protect global resources such as biodiversity. However, there emerged no firm commitments to sustainable development that might reconcile the conflicts between financial growth and environmental protection. Also left unresolved were the conflicting interests that separated the profits of MNCs from the value of environmental protection, at a time when "the area covered by tropical forests [was] disappearing at the rate of four Switzerlands every year [and] the global forestry industry [was picking] up $35 billion subsidies every year" (James 2002b, 8).

What happens when everyone does the same thing? The tragedy of the commons suggests a bleak future. Is ruin the destination toward which humankind rushes?

TOWARD SUSTAINABILITY?

"This is not a sprint, it's a marathon," is how U.S. Secretary of State Colin Powell in 2002 described sustainable development. Although the goal of sustainable development remains distant and frustrations about lost opportunities high, government and nonstate actors' acceptance of the concept continues to inspire creative, environmentally sensitive responses.

Differences between the rich Global North and the Global South will continue to spark controversy about such issues as the transfer of resources and technology needed to deal with climate change, ozone depletion, biodiversity, and a host of other specific problem areas. With growing populations and rising wealth, the Global South is beginning to face the same serious environmental challenges of the Global North, where consumption levels far exceed those of other states. However, one encouraging trend is that, as the industrialized countries move into the **information age** and their economies shift away from "dirty" manufacturing to much cleaner service-oriented activities, it is likely that the adverse environmental consequences of these advanced countries' economic activities will decline. Trade with other states, nevertheless, will ensure continuing pressures on global resources and the environmental burdens they pose.

■ **information age**
the era in which the rapid generation and transfer of information globally through mass communication and the Internet is contributing to the globalization of knowledge.

Is the world ready for the sacrifices required for balancing the desire for economic growth with the need to perverse the earth's regenerative capacity? Because, alongside expanding population growth pressures, "there are strong scientific indications of unsustainability, we must act on behalf of the future—even at the price of today's development. That may be expensive, so it is prudent to try to minimize those risks in the first place. Human ingenuity and a bit of luck have helped mankind stay a few steps ahead of the forces degrading the environment this past half century, the first full one in which the planet has been exposed to industrialization. In the [twenty-first century], the great race between development and degradation could well become a close call" (*Economist*, July 6, 2002, 18). "We need action at all levels—local, national, regional, and international—to promote sustainable development," warns Hans Christian Schmidt, the Danish environmental minister in 2002.

"The ability of states to regulate usage of the global common spaces in the twenty-first century has far-reaching consequences for the environment and for humankind" (Joyner 2001). In looking at the future, what is decided now will be crucial. Humankind is at a critical historical juncture. The path taken will determine the health of the planet for centuries. Because the stakes are so high, all the pieces in the puzzle—population, environmental, technology policy, and preferences in lifestyles—must be worked on simultaneously, through a global effort, if humanity is to survive and if human security is to be enhanced.

Perhaps the most immediate consequence of rapid population growth alongside the economic expansion driving excessive energy demands and shrinking supplies of natural resources, predicts Michael T. Klare (2001), will be a new era of "resource wars" in which future global conflicts will be increasingly fought over access to and supplies of vital natural resources and will occur less frequently over conflicts of interests and ideology in the struggle for power. That proposition serves as an introduction to the next arena in world politics on the global agenda which we shall consider in Part IV: the global character of armed conflict and its management.

KEY TERMS

demography

carrying capacity

tragedy of the commons

ethics

politics

fertility rate

replacement-level fertility

demographic transition

modernization

population implosion

human immunodeficiency
  virus (HIV)

AIDS (acquired immune
  deficiency syndrome)

human development

mulilateral aid

low politics

neo-Malthusians

cornucopians

genetic engineering

transgenetic crops

food security

mercantilism

ecopolitics

realist theory

high politics

neoliberalism

politics of scarcity

environmental security

liberalism

epistemic community

paradigm

sustainable development

relative gains

absolute gains

cartel

coercive diplomacy

greenhouse effect

acid rain

ozone layer

regime

United Nations Environment
  Program (UNEP)

biodiversity

deforestation

desertification

enclosure movement

collective goods

information age

SUGGESTED READING

Broadhead, Lee-Anne. *International Environmental Politics: The Limits of Green Diplomacy.* Boulder, Colo.: Lynne Rienner, 2003.

Brown, Lester R., Gary Gardner, and Brian Halweil. *Beyond Malthus: Nineteen Dimensions of the Populations Challenge.* New York: W. W. Norton, 1999.

Carter, Neil. *The Politics of the Environment.* Cambridge: Cambridge University Press, 2001.

Davis, Devr. *When Smoke Ran Like Water.* New York: Basic Books, 2002.

Diamond, Jared. *Guns, Germs, and Steel: The Fates of Human Societies.* New York: W. W. Norton, 1997.

Dobkowski, Michael N., and Isidor Wallimann, eds. *On the Edge of Scarcity: Environment, Resources, Populations, Sustainability, and Conflict.* Syracuse, N.Y.: Syracuse University Press, 2002.

Eberstadt, Nicholas. "The Population Implosion," *Foreign Policy* 123 (March–April 2001): 42–53.

Garrett, Laurie. *The Coming Plague: Newly Emerging Diseases in a World out of Balance,* rev. ed. London: Virago, 2000.

Hoerder, Dirk. *Cultures in Contact: World Migrations in the Second Millennium.* Durham, N.C.: Duke University Press, 2002.

Klare, Michael T. *Resource Wars: The New Landscape of Global Conflict.* New York: Holtzbrinck Academic, 2002.

Switzer, Jacqueline Vaughn. *Environmental Politics: Domestic and Global Dimensions,* 3rd ed. New York: Bedford/St. Martin's, 2001.

Worldwatch Institute, *State of the World 2003.* New York: W. W. Norton, 2003.

Young, Oran R., ed. *The Effectiveness of International Environmental Regimes.* Cambridge, Mass.: MIT Press, 1999.

WHERE ON THE WORLD WIDE WEB?

International Data Base
http://www.census.gov/ipc/www/idbnew.html

The U.S. Census Bureau offers you the chance to use their computerized bank of demographic data for all countries of the world. From their homepage you can look at the Summary Demographic Data to see totals in population and rates of growth for each country. Click on "Population Pyramids" to compare countries according to their population pyramids. First, choose the United States. What age groups had the largest concentration of people in 1997? Does this change in the year 2025? What about in the year 2050 (when you will probably be retired)? Is there a big difference between male and female populations? Now, choose a country in Africa. How is the pyramid for this country different from the one for the United States? How does it change across time? What conclusions can you draw about the problems each of the countries may face given the number of citizens in different age categories in different time periods?

UNAIDS
http://www.unaids.org/

UNAIDS is a joint program of the UN and a leading advocate for worldwide action against HIV/AIDS. Its mission is to support and strengthen an expanded response to the global AIDS epidemic. UNAIDS devises programs that will prevent the spread of HIV, provide care and support for those affected by the disease, and alleviate the socioeconomic and human impact of the epidemic. Explore the HIV/AIDS epidemic by country and find out about the World AIDS Campaign. What effect do you think AIDS will have on population growth rates?

World POPClock Projection
http://www.census.gov/cgi-bin/ipc/popclockw

The U.S. Census Bureau's World Population Clock projects the world population every second of every day. Look at the number of people in the world. Then, hit the Reload button on the top of your Web browser. How many more people were born in the time that it took you to *read* the number of people in the world? Click Reload again. How many more people were born?

Earth Times
http://www.earthtimes.org/

Earth Times is an independent international electronic newspaper devoted to reporting global and national issues relating to the environment, sustainable development, population, human rights, and current affairs. This award-winning site will give you up-to-date reports on and analyses of ecological issues. It is a very good resource on current events.

Greenpeace
http://www.greenpeace.org/

Greenpeace is an international nongovernmental organization (NGO) committed to global environmental advocacy. Its operation focuses on protecting the oceans and forests, phasing out use of fossil fuels, and promoting renewable energies in order to stop climate change. Visit this site to see how a nongovernmental actor affects global environmental issues. Find out how you can become a cyber-activist!

IISDnet
http://www.iisd.org/default.asp

The International Institute for Sustainable Development (IISD) has produced a Web site to help users learn about sustainable development, provide information on controversial topics, explore issues in environmental management, and show how businesses can turn sustainability into a competitive advantage. The site also includes a Sustainable Development Timeline, an especially interesting section. Find it by entering "sustainable development timeline" in the site's search engine. Here you can follow how your society has tried to integrate protection of the environment with the establishment of healthy societies and economies. Is there a specific event that you believe has crystallized global thinking on sustainable development? Which decade do you believe has seen the greatest advances? Follow some of the timeline links and read about the organizations that have been at the forefront of environmental protection.

Climate Change
http://www.nationalgeographic.com/

The National Geographic Society has an extensive Web site that covers many aspects of the interactions of humans with the environment. Enter the search terms "global warming" and "climate change" in the site's search engine. What are some sample articles that catch your interest? What are examples of climate change affecting a single animal or plant species? How is climate change affecting humans?

Rainforest Action Network
http://www.ran.org

The mission of the Rainforest Action Network is to protect the Earth's rain forests and support the rights of rain forest inhabitants through education, grassroots organizing, and nonviolent direct action. Visit the network's Web site and learn about the threats to rain forests and read about the campaigns that this group is waging. Learn what you can do to help protect the world's rain forests.

INFOTRAC® COLLEGE EDITION

Search for the following articles in the InfoTrac database:

Catley-Carlson, Margaret, and Judith A. M. Outlaw. "Poverty and Population Issues: Clarifying the Connections," *Journal of International Affairs* Fall 1998.

Lee, Kai N. "Searching for Sustainability in the New Century," *Ecology Law Quarterly* February 2001.

Rowland, F. Sherwood. "Climate Change and Its Consequences: Issues for the New U.S. Administration," *Environment* March 2001.

Postel, Sandra L., and Aaron T. Wolf. "Dehydrating Conflict," *Foreign Policy* September 2001.

For more articles, enter:

"population" in the Subject Guide, and then go to subdivision "economic aspects."

"population policy" in the Subject Guide.

"global warming" in the Subject Guide, and then go to subdivision "analysis."

MILITARY CONFLICT AND ITS CONTROL

T he threat of violence and warfare casts a dark cloud throughout the globe. Humanity lives in fear of aggression from terrorists, a neighboring state, or even their own government, bent on persecuting its citizens because of their nationality or religion. National and international security—freedom from fear of a military attack—remains precarious in the twenty-first century. Mil-

lions of people are the victims of aggression, and millions more have had to flee as refugees to seek sanctuary from the ravages of war.

Part IV explores the changing character of armed conflict and war (Chapter 11), looking closely at the growing number of prolonged civil wars in failing states and episodic terrorist attacks throughout the globe that undermine national secu-

rity and threaten human security. Chapter 12 addresses the national security strategies of states to provide for defense through military expenditures and to produce and import armaments. It discusses the new national security strategies of the great powers in light of anxieties about a new age of nuclear proliferation, global terrorism, and the rising danger posed by weapons of mass destruction, such as biological and chemical weapons. Chapter 13 examines how states seek to coerce other states to agree to their demands or to refrain from behaving in an undesired way by such means as economic sanctions or military interventions. Finally, we consider the alternative paths to peace prescribed by the realist (Chapter 14) and liberal (Chapter 15) theoretical traditions.

CHAPTER 11

THE NEW FACE OF TWENTY-FIRST-CENTURY ARMED CONFLICT

T O P I C S   A N D   T H E M E S

- The types of military conflict, past and present
- The causes of armed conflict: Rival theories
- Armed conflict within states: Civil wars, uncivil methods
- The new global terrorism

- **CONTROVERSY** DOES NATIONALISTIC LOVE OF COUNTRY CAUSE WAR WITH FOREIGN NATIONS?
- **CONTROVERSY** CAN THE WAR AGAINST GLOBAL TERRORISM BE WON?

The September 11, 2001, attacks marked the start of a new age of international terrorism.

Mankind must put an end to war or war will put an end to mankind.

—JOHN F. KENNEDY, U.S. president, 1961

The storms of violence cannot go on. Enough is enough.

—GEORGE. W. BUSH, U.S. president, 2002

In the calm summer of 2001, complacency had taken place in the zone of peace and prosperity in the Global North, where many thoughtful observers, noting the disappearance of interstate war among the economic giants, began to ask if interstate war was becoming obsolete. That mood and conclusion was shattered shortly thereafter on September 11 when international terrorists attacked and destroyed the symbol of global capitalism in the nerve center of the globe's most prosperous country, the Twin Towers of the World Trade Center in New York City. A shocked and stunned globe was given a grim reminder of the continuing danger of armed conflict. Peace seemed not to be on the horizon, but an illusion. Former U.S. President George Bush's lament in 1992—that "only the dead have seen the end of conflict"—appeared prophetic.

Since 1945, when the Second World War ended, not a single day has gone by without a war being fought. At the end of 2002, major armed conflicts were active in thirty-eight locations throughout the world, including Afghanistan, Iraq, the Ivory Coast, and the Philippines (*The Defense Monitor* 31 [January 2002], 1). The 9/11 terrorist attack reduced confidence in the capacity of the world to bring violence under control, despite the pledge by the United States and its allies to wage a victorious war against global terrorism and to strengthen their resolve to contain other forms of aggression. September 11 transformed the global landscape. Although no one knew quite how to define it, and there was little agreement about what to call it, clearly a strong consensus had emerged that the tragedy of the September 11 mass murders had ushered into existence a new chapter in human history in which prior hopes for national, international, and human security had vanished. Almost no one claimed they were safe. And in daily conversations, a new vocabulary had emerged to capture the threatening new realities. Students began to talk a new talk: bedrooms were "ground zero"—a total mess; a mean instructor—"He's a total terrorist;" a disciplined student—"*It* was total jihad." America's most frightening days had become slang and comic relief in an effort to alleviate the fear that violence would and could hurt anyone, anywhere, anytime—a new language to take horrific ideas and make them go away. Given the widespread occurrence of violence in today's world, it is little wonder that so many people think of international politics as the same thing as armed aggression.

In *On War,* Prussian strategist Karl von Clausewitz advanced his famous dictum that war is merely an extension of diplomacy by other means—"a form of communication between countries," albeit an extreme form. This insight underscores the realist belief that **war** is an instrument for states to use to resolve their conflicts. War, however, is the deadliest instrument of conflict resolution, and its onset usually means that persuasion and negotiations have failed.

In international relations, **conflict** regularly occurs when actors interact and disputes over incompatible interests arise. In and of itself, conflict (like **politics**—the exercise of influence) is not necessarily threatening, because war and conflict are different. Conflict may be seen as inevitable and occurs when two parties perceive differences between themselves and seek to resolve those differences to their own satisfaction. Some conflict results whenever people interact and may be generated by religious, ideological, ethnic, economic, political, or territorial issues; therefore we should not regard it as abnormal. Nor should we regard conflict as necessarily destructive, since it can promote social solidarity, creative thinking, learning, and communication—all factors critical to the resolution of disputes and the cultivation of cooperation (Coser 1956). However, the costs of conflict do become threatening when the partners turn to arms to settle their perceived irreconcilable differences. When that happens, violence occurs, and we enter the separate sphere of warfare.

This chapter explores the challenge that armed conflicts pose in world affairs, examining the character, causes, and magnitude of international violence, as well as changes in it over time. It investigates three primary ways that **armed conflict** most often occurs: *wars* between states, *civil wars* within states, and *terrorism*. The next chapters consider the ways in which states and other global actors are attempting to control this global problem.

■ **war**
a condition arising within states (civil war) or between states (interstate war) when actors use violent means to destroy their opponents or coerce them into submission.

■ **conflict**
discord, often arising in international relations over perceived incompatibilities of interest.

■ **politics**
activities aimed at getting another actor to do something it would not otherwise do (see p. 18).

■ **armed conflict**
combat between the military forces of two or more states or groups.

CONTINUITIES AND CHANGE IN ARMED CONFLICT

In a globe seemingly experiencing constant change, one grim continuity stands out: war and violence. Looking upon the tragic twentieth century, UN Secretary-General Boutros Boutros-Ghali described the global system as a "culture of death." The description is apt, because as many as 650 armed conflicts have occurred since 1900: "No other century on record equals the twentieth in uncivilized civil violence, in the number of conflicts waged, the hordes of refugees created, the millions of people killed in wars, and the vast expenditures for 'defense'" (Sivard 1996, 7).

■ **behavioralism**
the methodological research movement to incorporate rigorous scientific analysis into the study of world politics in order to base conclusions about patterns on measurement, data, and evidence rather than on speculation and subjective belief.

■ **constructivism**
a scholarly approach to inquiry emphasizing the importance of agents (people and groups) and the shared meanings they construct to define their identities, interests, and institutions— understandings that influence their international behavior.

Scientists who study war quantitatively from the perspective of **behavioralism** have attempted to estimate the frequency of armed conflicts and to ascertain if trends exist in the global system's level of violent conflicts. Different definitions and indicators produce somewhat different pictures of variations over time (as **constructivism** emphasizes they will). Various measures converge on the fundamental patterns since World War II ended in 1945, however. Consider the number of wars *underway* each year since then. This provides a good index of the globalization of international violence. Between 1945 and 2001, 225 armed conflicts have been underway, and the general trend has been a rising level of violence, with the number peaking in 1992 at 51—a level almost four times that of the 1950s (when the globe averaged thirteen each year) and nearly three times the average number of nineteen each year during the 1960s. More than thirty-one conflicts occurred each year in the 1970s and more than forty each year in the 1980s and 1990s (Gleditsch et al. 2002). "The overall conflict trends since 1990 are encouraging. Nevertheless, taken as a whole, the past century was extraordinarily violent. Milton Leitenberg of the University of Maryland estimates that from 1945 to 2000, some 50–51 million people were killed in wars and other violent conflicts. For the entire twentieth century, he estimates 130–142 million war-related deaths, and a chilling 214–226 million of government killings in non-war situations are included" (*Vital Signs 2002*, 95). The number of people killed from armed conflict since 1945 is twice that of the entire nineteenth century and seven times that of the eighteenth century (Kane 1995, 19).

Figure 11.1 charts the number of armed conflicts globally from two perspectives: the first long-term, looking at changes over the six hundred years from 1400 to 2000, and the second in the 1950–2001 more recent period. These inventories report in different ways what the mass media tell us: that violence and global insecurity are likely to remain core concerns in the twenty-first century.

The September 11, 2001, terrorist attacks and the war to counter global terrorism in Afghanistan and Iraq cast a dark shadow over public perceptions of the face of contemporary warfare. In the past, most armed conflicts were either between states or civil wars within an existing state. Indeed, between 1946 and 2001, of 225 armed conflicts there were 42 wars between two countries and an additional 178 internal conflicts, 32 of which had external participation by other states and 131 which did not (Gleditsch et al. 2002, 620), and until 9/11 most people expected this traditional form of organized violence to remain the norm. That expectation has now been shattered. Now military planners foresee the probability of many future small wars fought by irregular militia and private or semiprivate forces such as NGO terrorist movements against the armies of states. In short, the nature of contemporary warfare appears to be undergoing a major transformation, even though many of the traditional characteristics of armed conflict between states and within them continue. The general trends show that

- the proportion of countries throughout the globe engaged in wars has declined

- most wars now occur in the Global South, which is home to the highest number of states, with the largest populations, the least income, and the least stable governments

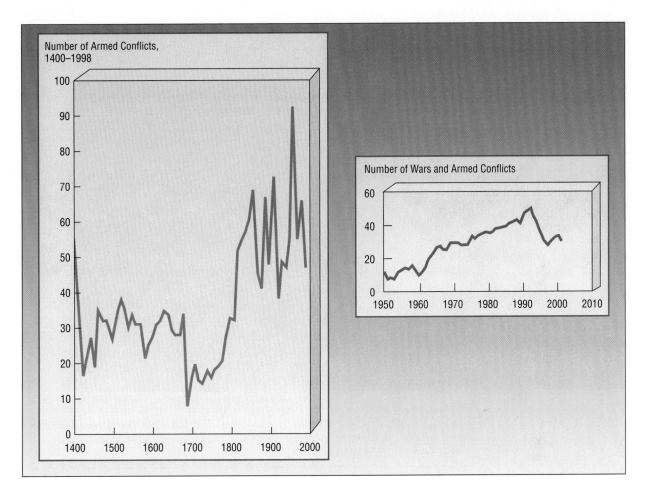

FIGURE 11.1
Two Pictures of the Changing Frequency of Armed Conflicts

Armed conflict between states has been around for as long as sovereign states have existed, as the trend on the left inventorying 2,566 individual wars for each decade since the year 1400 indicates. It shows that the number dropped considerably in the late 1600s in the aftermath of the Thirty Years' War, but has risen sharply in the three centuries since, peaking in the 1960s. The figure on the right captures the ebb and flow of active armed conflicts each year in the contemporary period since 1950. Most of these conflicts have occurred in the Global South; of the 38 underway in 2002, the vast majority began years and even decades earlier. The global landscape is dominated by armed conflicts arising from civil wars within states. "As has been the case in recent years, most extant conflicts are intrastate. In fact, aside from Angola, Congo, and Afghanistan, where countries overtly are supporting factions or governments, only three instances of interstate conflict (broadly defined) [existed] at the start of 2002: Iraq vs. the UN/U.S./Britain, Pakistan vs. India, and Palestine vs. Israel" (*Defense Monitor* 31 [January 2002], 13).

SOURCES: Left: Adapted from "The Characteristics of Violent Conflict since 1400 A.D." by Peter Brecke. Used with permission. Right: University of Hamburg, presented in *Vital Signs* 2002, p. 94–95.

Showing Force to Deter an Invasion. Iraqi soldiers march past a statue of dictator Saddam Hussein in a December 2000 parade staged in Baghdad. The alleged goal was **deterrence**—to discourage the United States from attacking Iraq in order to force a change in regime and disarmament.

■ **deterrence**
a military strategy in which the primary purpose is to prevent a foreign adversary's attack.

■ **long peace**
long-lasting periods of great-power peace.

- the goal of waging war to conquer foreign territory has ceased to be a motive
- wars between the great powers are becoming obsolete; since 1945 the globe has experienced a **long peace**—the most prolonged period in modern history in which no wars have occurred between the most powerful countries.

These changes raise questions about why wars occur. What ends motivate human beings to continue to resort to force, given the unspeakable casualties? The question provokes a more fundamental set of related questions about the causes of aggression generally. Accordingly, it is useful to review contending theories about the sources from which armed conflicts arise.

RIVAL THEORIES OF THE CAUSES OF AGGRESSION

Throughout history efforts have been made to explain why people resort to violence. Inventories of war's origins (see Cashman 2000; Midlarsky 2000) invariably conclude that they are incomplete, in part because most agree that war is rooted in multiple sources at various **levels of analysis.** For our purposes, the most plausible causes are divided here into three major levels or categories: individuals, states, and the global system.

The First Level of Analysis: Individuals' Human Nature

In a sense, all wars between states originate from the decisions of national leaders, whose choices ultimately determine whether armed conflict will occur (see Chapter 3). We must therefore consider the relationship of war to individuals and their choices, and for this, questions about human nature are central.

The repeated outbreak of war has led some, such as psychologist Sigmund Freud (1968), to conclude that aggression is an instinctive part of human nature that stems from humans' genetic programming and psychological makeup. Identifying Homo sapiens as the deadliest species, ethologists (those who study animal behavior in order to understand human behavior) such as Konrad Lorenz (1963) similarly argue that humankind is one of the few species practicing **intraspecific aggression** (routine killing of its own kind), in comparison with most other species, which practice **interspecific aggression** (killing only other species, except in the most unusual circumstances—cannibalism in certain tropical fishes being one exception). Ethologists are joined in their interpretation by those **realists** who assume that the drive for power is innate and cannot be eliminated. They therefore accept the conclusion suggested by Charles Darwin's theories of evolution and natural selection: Life entails a struggle for survival of the fittest, and natural selection eliminates the traits that interfere with successful competition, such as **pacifism,** which rejects the right of people to kill in order to obtain power.

Many question these theories on both empirical and logical grounds. If aggression is an inevitable impulse deriving from human nature, then should not all humans exhibit this genetically determined behavior? Most people, of course don't; they ethically reject killing as evil and neither murder nor accept others' killing on behalf of the state. In fact, at some fundamental, genetic level, argues Francis Fukuyama (1999a), human beings are built for consensus, not for conflict: "People feel intensely uncomfortable if they live in a society that doesn't have moral rules." In addition, liberal theory and social science research suggest that genetics fails to explain why individuals may be belligerent only at certain times. Social Darwinism's interpretation of the biological influences on human behavior can be countered by examining why people cooperate and act morally. As James Q. Wilson (1993) argues, Darwinian **survival of the fittest** realist theory overlooks the fact that "the moral sense must have adaptive value; if it did not, natural selection would have worked against people who had such useless traits as sympathy, self-control, or a desire for fairness in favor of those with the opposite tendencies."

Although the **nature versus nurture** controversy regarding the biological bases of aggression has not been resolved (see Nelson 1974; Ridley 1998), most social scientists now strongly disagree with this realist premise that humans are essentially selfish and aggressive and that people murder and kill because of their innate genetic drives to act out aggressively. Instead, war is interpreted as a learned cultural habit. Aggression is a propensity acquired early in life as a result of **socialization** and, therefore, is a learned rather than biologically determined behavior. The 1986 *Seville Statement,* endorsed by more than a

■ **levels of analysis**
the interpretation of the sources of international phenomena that looks separately at the influences of individuals, the characteristics of states, or the global system (see p. 17).

■ **intraspecific aggression**
killing members of one's own species.

■ **interspecific aggression**
killing members of species other than one's own.

■ **realism**
the theory that states are driven to compete for power through war and imperialism because of human nature, which is flawed by the urge to engage in aggression (see p. 36).

■ **pacifism**
the liberal idealist school of ethical thought that recognizes no conditions that justify the taking of another human's life, even when authorized by a head of state.

■ **survival of the fittest**
a realist concept derived from Charles Darwin's theory of evolution that advises that ruthless competition is ethnically acceptable to survive, even if the actions violate moral commands not to kill.

■ **nature versus nurture**
the controversy over whether human behavior is determined more by the biological basis of "human nature" than it is nurtured by the environmental conditions that humans experience.

■ **socialization**
the processes by which people learn the beliefs, values, and behaviors that are acceptable in a given society.

dozen professional scholarly associations, maintains that "it is scientifically incorrect" to say that "we have inherited a tendency to make war from our animal ancestors," "that war or any other violent behavior is genetically programmed into our human nature," "that humans have a 'violent brain,'" or "that war is caused by 'instinct' or any single motivation" (see Somit 1990). Ted Robert Gurr (1970) expresses the thesis, supported by behavioral research, that the "capacity, but not the need, for violence appears to be biologically entrenched in humans."

Individuals' willingness to sacrifice their lives in war out of a sense of duty to their leaders and country is one of history's puzzles. "The fog of war" is what the Russian author Leo Tolstoy and others have called the fact that people will give their lives in struggles, large and small, whose importance and purpose are sometimes not understood. Clearly, this self-sacrifice stems from learned beliefs that some convictions—such as loyalty to the state—are worth dying for. "It has been widely observed that soldiers fight—and noncombatants assent to war—not out of aggressiveness but obedience" (Caspary 1993). This, however, does not make human nature a cause of war, even if such learned habits of obedience are grounds for participation in the aggression authorized by others, and even if at times the mass public's jingoistic enthusiasm for aggression against foreign adversaries encourages leaders to start wars.

If human nature is not a direct cause of interstate conflict, how then do we explain the enduring rivalries and the repetitive recourse to genocide in some areas? It is the bloody history of territories such as the Balkans that inspires anthropologists to inquire if territoriality drives human aggression. Could it be that the genocide in Kosovo in 1999 stemmed from "an innate human aggression, inherited from our animal ancestors, to possess territory believed to be one's own"? Robert Ardrey (1966), the playwright turned anthropologist, proposed the notion of human territorial aggression in *The Territorial Imperative*. The controversial best-seller argued that "the territorial instincts of animals apply equally to man. . . . Simply put, Mr. Ardrey's theory proposes that humans, like animals, are compelled by instinct to possess and defend territory they believe belongs exclusively to them" (Levingston 1999). The **territorial imperative** has been resurrected as a theory to account for the kinds of ethnic wars that rage across the globe in so many regions today.

■ **territorial imperative**
the term coined by anthropologist Robert Ardrey to popularize the proposition that people and nations will defend to the death their territory, just like animals instinctively do.

■ **national character**
the collective characteristics ascribed to the people within a state

■ **rational choice**
the assumption that decision makers make choices through cool-headed calculations of cost and benefits and pick the options that have the best chance of realizing preferred goals (see p. 74).

Also to be questioned is that **national character** drives certain nationalities to aggression. Countries sharing cultural values and identity can express these in different ways and can change. For example, Sweden and Switzerland, once warlike, have managed conflicts without warfare since 1809 and 1815, respectively. In fact since 1500, one in five countries has never experienced war (Sivard 1991, 20). This suggests that other factors beyond the inborn collective traits of particular peoples better explain why certain countries engage in organized violence. As Ralph Bunche, a U.S. policymaker, argued before the UN, "There are no warlike people—just warlike leaders." "The common people do not go to war of their own accord, but are driven to it by the madness of kings," St. Thomas More advised in the sixteenth century. Thus, war most often occurs because of the choices leaders make, not the preferences of their entire societies. Some of those decisions by leaders are unwise and fail to conform to the **rational choice** model of decision making (see Chapter 3). In addition, even intelligent leaders and moral leaders are sometimes prone to take unnecessarily high-risk decisions to wage war because they are pressured through **groupthink** by advisers representing large-scale bureaucracies. This observation about the influences on leaders' choices about war and peace directs attention to the domestic factors that encourage some states to engage in foreign aggression.

The Second Level of Analysis: States' Internal Characteristics

Conventional wisdom holds that variations in states' governments, sizes, ideologies, geographical locations, population dynamics, ethnic homogeneity, wealth, economic performance, military capabilities, and level of educational attainment influence whether they will engage in war. Drawing on the possibility suggested by Russian political theorist Peter Kropotkin in 1884 that "the word *state* is identical with the word *war*" and the evidence that war has contributed to the rise of the state (Porter 1994), we need to examine some theories addressing the internal characteristics of states that influence leaders' choices regarding the use of force. Implicit in this approach to explaining armed conflict at the **state level of analysis** is the assumption that differences in the types or classes of states will determine whether they will engage in war. To argue that the prospects for war are influenced most heavily by national attributes and the types of leaders making policy decisions for states is to challenge the **neorealist** premise that international circumstances are the most powerful determinants of warfare, and that domestic factors have no influence.

Duration of Independence. New states, not long-lasting states, are the most likely to experience civil wars and engage in foreign wars. Newly independent countries typically go through a period of political unrest following their acquisition of **sovereignty,** as they struggle to resolve long-standing internal grievances and territorial disputes with their neighboring enemies—foreign disputes that frequently provoke great-power **intervention.** The high levels of civil wars and involvement in international conflicts in the Global South are linked to the fact that nearly all these less-developed countries have recently gained independence from colonialism, many through revolutions.

Cultural Determinants, Feminist Theory, and the Decay of Moral Constraints. Countries' behavior is strongly influenced by the cultural and ethical traditions of their peoples. In the state system governed by the rules championed by realism, moral constraints on the use of force do not command wide acceptance. Instead, most governments encourage their populations to glorify the state and to accept whatever decision their leaders claim are necessary for national security, including warfare against adversaries. Many scholars believe these kinds of cultural beliefs make violence more probable.

Advocates of the cultural origins of war argue that most people in most societies live an everyday experience of disengagement, or "numbness," which disinclines them to oppose their leaders' decisions to wage war. The modern state thus organizes its society to accept war and "builds a culture that affirms death" and accepts senseless carnage (Caspary 1993). In contrast, critics operating from the perspective of **feminist theories** of international relations argue that the foundation of war worldwide, alongside cultural numbing, is rooted in the masculine ethos of realism, which prepares people to accept war and to respect the warrior as a hero (see especially Enloe 2000 and Tickner 2002).

■ **groupthink**
the propensity for members of a decision-making group to accept and agree with the group's prevailing attitudes, rather than speaking out for what they believe would be the most rational choice.

■ **state level of analysis**
an analytical approach to the study of world politics that emphasizes how the internal attributes of states explain their foreign policy behaviours.

■ **neorealism**
the so-called structural version of realism that explains state conduct as a function of changes in the global system's structure, such as shifts in the distribution of states' military capabilities (see p. 39).

■ **sovereignty**
the legal doctrine that states have supreme authority to govern their internal affairs and manage their foreign relations with other states and IGOs.

■ **intervention**
external interference in a state's internal affairs.

■ **feminist theory**
a body of scholarship emerging from the social feminist movement to promote the political equality of women with men, critiquing sexual biases and challenging gender roles that encourage female subordination and warfare.

Gender roles, they assert, supported by realist values contribute to the prevalence of militarism and warfare:

> According to feminist critics, international relations theory as it has evolved incorporates "masculinist" prejudices at each of its three levels of analysis: man, the state, and war. Realists are "androcentric" in arguing that the propensity for conflict is universal in human nature ("man"); that the logic and the morality of sovereign states are not identical to those of individuals ("the state"); and that the world is an anarchy in which sovereign states must be prepared to rely on self-help, including organized violence ("war"). Feminist theorists would stress the nurturing and cooperative aspects—the conventionally feminine aspects—of human nature; they would expose the artificiality of notions of sovereignty, and their connection with patriarchy and militarism; and they would replace the narrow realist emphasis on security, especially military security, with a redefinition of security as universal social justice. (Lind 1993, 37)

To feminists and other constructivist theorists about the causes of war who embrace a cultural interpretation, the penchant for warfare does not evolve in a vacuum but is produced by the ways in which societies shape their populations' beliefs and norms. Many governments, through the educational programs they fund in schools and other institutions, indoctrinate values in their political culture that condone the practice of war. Ironically, in a world of diverse national cultures, the messages of obedience and of duty to make sacrifices to the state through such **cultural conditioning** are common. States disseminate the belief that their right to make war should not be questioned and that the ethical principles of religious and secular philosophies prohibiting violence should be disregarded. Consequently, critics stress the existence of powerful institutions that prepare individuals to subconsciously accept warfare as necessary and legitimate.

■ **cultural conditioning**
the impact of national traditions and moral principles on the behavior of states, under the assumption that culture affects national decision making about issues such as the acceptability of aggression.

Poverty. A country's level of economic development also affects the probability of its involvement in war. As U.S. Secretary of Defense Robert S. McNamara explained in 1966, "there is no question but that there is evidence of a relationship between violence and economic backwardness."

Before we conclude that poverty always breeds war, however, we must note that the *most* impoverished countries have been the least prone to start wars with their neighbors. The poorest countries cannot vent their frustrations aggressively because they lack the military or economic resources to do so. This does not mean that the poorest countries will always remain peaceful. If the past is a guide to the future, then the impoverished countries that develop economically will be those most likely to acquire arms and engage in future external wars. In particular, many studies suggest that states are likely to initiate foreign wars *after* sustained periods of economic growth—that is, during periods of rising prosperity, when they can most afford them (Cashman 2000). This signals danger if countries in the Global South develop rapidly and direct the new resources toward armament, as India and Pakistan chose to do by acquiring nuclear weapons in 1998, rather than by investing in sustained development.

The New Geography of Conflict. "Location, location, location"—the geographical roots of armed conflict are now being recognized as an important

War's Human Impact Innocent noncombatants, especially children and women, are often the primary victims of military conflict in the Global South. At the May 2002 World Summit for Children, the United Nations estimated that about 300,000 children under the age of eighteen were made soldiers and forced to fight in wars in more than thirty countries (*Newsweek*, May 13, 2002, 28). Shown here (left) is the 10-year-old son of an Afghani police commissioner carrying an assault rifle nearly as tall as him. The protection of children and women from warfare has usually required humanitarian military intervention by an outside power. Shown on the right are a starving Somalian mother and child in 1997 waiting for relief supplies delivered by U.S. military aircraft to a refugee camp in Kenya.

influence on the probability of instability and warfare. Geopolitical thinking has resurfaced as national security planners have assigned growing attention to the military consequences of a country's world position and topography. "Increased competition over access to major sources of oil and gas, growing friction over the allocation of shared water supplies, and internal warfare over valuable export commodities—have produced a new geography of conflict, a reconfigured cartography in which resource flows rather than political and ideological divisions constitute the major fault lines" (Klare 2001). The UN designated 2002 as the International Year of Mountains (partially because twenty-three of the twenty-seven armed conflicts that the UN identified as occurring in 2002 were being fought in mountainous areas), to address one dimension of the geographical impact on peace and war—how crippling poverty among mountain people and ecological destruction in the world's mountain ranges provide an environment conducive to the resource wars of the future.

Militarization. "If you want peace, prepare for war," realism counsels. It is questionable whether the acquisition of military power leads to peace or to war, but clearly most Global South developing countries agree with the realists' thesis that weapons contribute to their security. They have been by far the biggest customers in the robust global trade in arms and have built huge armies to guard against their neighboring states' potential aggression and to control their own citizens (see Chapter 12).

As Global South countries concentrate their budgets on equipping their militaries, many worry that war will become more frequent before it becomes less so. Militarization has *not* led to peace in the Global South. Will the curse of violence someday be broken there?

One clue comes from examination of the relationship between changes in military capabilities and war that occurred over centuries in Europe. During its transition to the peak of development, Europe was the location of the world's most frequent and deadly wars. The major European states armed themselves heavily and were engaged in warfare about 65 percent of the time in the sixteenth and seventeenth centuries (Wright 1942). Between 1816 and 1945, three-fifths of all interstate wars took place in Europe, with one erupting on average every other year (Singer 1991, 58). Not coincidentally, this happened when the developing states of Europe were most energetically arming in competition with one another. Perhaps as a consequence, the great powers—those with the largest armed forces—were the most involved in, and most often initiated, war (Cashman 2000). Since 1945, however, with the exception of war among the now-independent units of the former Yugoslavia, interstate war has not occurred in Europe. As the European countries moved up the ladder of development, they moved away from war with one another (internal conflict is another matter).

In contrast, the developing countries now resemble Europe prior to 1945. If the Global South follows the European pattern, the immediate future may well witness a peaceful, developed world surrounded by a violent, less-developed world.

Economic System.   Does the character of states' economic systems influence the frequency of warfare? The question has provoked controversy for centuries. Particularly since Marxism took root in Russia following the Bolshevik revolution in 1917, communist theoreticians claimed that capitalism was the primary cause of war—that capitalists practice imperialism and colonialism, and as they were fond of quoting Vladimir Lenin's 1916 explanation of World War I that war is caused by imperialistic capitalists' efforts "to divert the attention of the laboring masses from the domestic political crisis" of collapsing incomes under capitalism. According to the **communist theory of imperialism,** capitalism produces surplus capital. The need to export it stimulates wars to capture and protect foreign markets. Thus **laissez-faire economics**—based on the philosophical principle of free markets with little governmental regulation of the marketplace—rationalized militarism and imperialism for economic gain. Citing the demonstrable frequency with which wealthy capitalist societies engaged in aggression, Marxists believed that the only way to end international war was to end capitalism.

Contrary to Marxist theory is commercial liberalism's conviction that free market systems promote peace, not war. Defenders of capitalism have long believed that free market countries that practice free trade abroad are more pacific. The reasons are multiple, but they center on the premise that commercial enterprises are natural lobbyists for world peace because their profits

■ **communist theory of imperialism**
the Marxist-Leninist economic interpretation of imperialist wars of conquest as driven by capitalism's need for foreign markets to generate capital.

■ **laissez-faire economics**
free markets in which goods are exchanged within minimal management by the state (see p. 196).

depend on it. War interferes with trade, blocks profit, destroys property, causes inflation, consumes scarce resources, and encourages big government and counterproductive regulation of business activity. By extension, this reasoning continues, as government regulation of internal markets declines, prosperity will increase (see Chapter 9) and fewer wars will occur.

The evidence for these rival theories is, not surprisingly, mixed. Conclusions depend in part on perceptions regarding economic influences on international behavior, in part because alternative perspectives focus on different dimensions of the linkage. This controversy was at the heart of the ideological debate between East and West during the Cold War, when the relative virtues and vices of two radically different economic systems—socialism and capitalism—were uppermost in people's minds.

The end of the Cold War did not end the historic debate about the link between economics and war. This basic theoretical question commands increasing interest, especially given the "shift in the relevance and usefulness of different power resources, with military power declining and economic power increasing in importance" (Huntington 1991a).

Globalization, through which the growing economic interdependence of countries has tightly linked states' growth rates, has intensified the debate about the relationship between trade and international armed conflict. Although "most leaders still cling to the long-standing belief that expanding economic ties will cement the bonds of friendship between and within nations that make resort to arms unfathomable," observe Katherine Barbieri and Gerald Schneider (1999), "in contrast, realist and Marxist critics reject the liberal view" that the opening of free market economies within states and increased levels of trade between them will produce peace (see Chapters 8 and 9). Even though substantial evidence exists to support "the liberals' belief that economic interdependence [and economic and political freedom] have important pacific benefits" (Oneal and Russett 1999), that conclusion is unlikely to be widely accepted by the many poor Global South countries who maintain that under interdependent globalization the wealthy will profit disproportionally from trade, at their expense. This **relative gains** argument insists conflict is produced because the benefits of economic exchanges are distributed unequally (the rich get richer and the poor get poorer), and trade-war disputes and even wars are likely to undermine world peace. In addition, the relationship between types of states' political systems, such as democracy and cooperation in international trade, remains an issue of theoretical and policy debate (Mansfield, Milner, and Rosendorff 2002; Dai 2002). The future will tell if free markets and free trade will generate international conflict or cooperation in the globalized twenty-first century. In the meantime, the effects of economic changes such as the globalization of the sale of products worldwide on peace and war continue to provoke interest. For instance, in a tongue-in-cheek extension of this neoliberal logic, columnist Thomas Friedman (1999b) advanced the "Golden Arches Theory of Conflict Prevention"—that no two countries have fought a war once McDonald's was present in both countries. Friedman "attributes the phenomenon to the growth of a peaceable middle class. 'People in McDonald's countries didn't like to fight wars anymore. . . . They preferred to wait in line for burgers'" (Stross 2002).

Type of Government. Realist and especially neorealist theories discount the importance of government type as an influence on war and peace. Not so with

■ **globalization**
the integration of states, through increasing contact, communication, and trade, to create a holistic, single global system in which the process of change increasingly binds people together in a common fate.

■ **relative gains**
a situation in which some participants to an exchange benefit more than others (see p. 310).

■ **neoliberal theories**
the "new" liberal theories stressing the critical impact of free governments and free trade in promoting peace and prosperity through democratically managed institutions, following the liberal world politics philosophies of Immanuel Kant, Thomas Jefferson, James Madison, and Woodrow Wilson.

■ **human rights**
the political rights and civil liberties recognized by the international community as inalienable and valid for individuals in all countries by virtue of their humanity.

■ **democratic peace**
the liberal theory that lasting peace depends on the deepening of liberal democratic institutions within states and their diffusion throughout the globe, given the "iron law" that democracies do not wage wars against each other.

liberalism, especially **neoliberal theories.** As noted in Chapter 2, the liberal tradition assigns great weight to the kinds of political institutions that states create to make policy decisions and predicts that the spread of "free" democratically ruled governments will promote peaceful interstate relations. As Immanuel Kant in 1795 argued in *Perpetual Peace*, when citizens are given basic **human rights** such as choosing their leaders through ballots as well as civil liberties such as free speech and a free press, these democracies would be far less likely to initiate wars than would countries ruled by dictators and kings, because a government accountable to the people would be constrained by public opinion from waging war. Kant was joined by other liberal reformers, such as Thomas Jefferson, James Madison, and Woodrow Wilson in the United States—all of whom believed that an "empire of liberty" (as Madison pictured a growing community of liberal democracies) would be one freed of the curse of war, and that if democratic institutions spread throughout the world, the entire past pattern of belligerent international relations would be replaced by a new pacific pattern.

These liberal and neoliberal predictions have been fulfilled by the passage of time since they were first advanced. "We now have solid evidence that democracies do not make war on each other" (Russett 2001). Much research demonstrates that democracies resolve their differences with one another at the bargaining table rather than the battlefield (Mandelbaum 2002). This pattern provides the cornerstone for the **democratic peace** proposition (Ray 1995) holding that, as Bruce Russett summarizes,

> Democracies are unlikely to engage in any kind of militarized disputes *with each other* or to let any such disputes escalate into war. They rarely even skirmish. Pairs of democratic states have been only one-eighth as likely as other kinds of states to threaten to use force against each other, and only one-tenth as likely actually to do so. Established democracies fought *no wars* against one another during the entire twentieth century.
>
> The more democratic each state is, the more peaceful their relations are likely to be. Democracies are more likely to employ "democratic" means of peaceful conflict resolution. They are readier to reciprocate each other's behavior, to accept third-party mediation or good offices in settling disputes, and to accept binding third-party arbitration and adjudication. Careful statistical analyses of countries' behavior have shown that democracies' relatively peaceful relations toward each other are not spuriously caused by some other influence such as sharing high levels of wealth, or rapid growth, or ties of alliance. The phenomenon of peace between democracies is not limited just to the rich industrialized states of the Global North. It was not maintained simply by pressure from a common adversary in the Cold War, and it has outlasted that threat. (Russett 2001, 235)

The growing recognition that ballots serve as a barrier against the use of bullets and bombs by one democracy against another has been inspired by the growth of democratic governance over the past two centuries (see Figure 11.2). "The last two decades of the twentieth century have been dubbed the 'third wave' of democratization, as dictatorial regimes fell in scores of countries. . . . In the 1980s and 1990s . . . 81 countries took significant steps toward democracy, and today 140 of the world's 200 countries hold multiparty elections—more than ever before. But the euphoria of the Cold War's end has

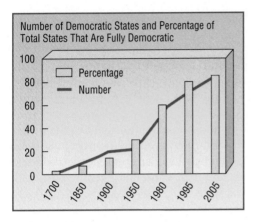

FIGURE 11.2

The Advance of Democracy, 1800–2005

Throughout the modern era, monarchs, despots, dictators, and autocrats have ruled states and made foreign policy choices about war. That has changed in a major global transformation, occurring in three "waves"; as shown in the figure, a "global shift from authoritarian to democratic regimes [is underway in the 'third wave']. According to Polity IV's [index of democratization data gathered by Ted Robert Gurr], the number of authoritarian countries fell from almost 70 in 1980 to fewer than 30 in 2000. Over the same period, the number of democratic regimes doubled, from 41 to 82" (UNDP 2002, 15). Whether this transition will foster peace is being tested.

SOURCES: Global Trends 2005, by Michael J. Mazarr, p. 107. Copyright © Michael J. Mazaar. Reprinted with permission of Palgrave Macmillan.

given way to the somber realities of twenty-first century politics" (UNDP 2002, 1, 14). There is no certainty that liberal democracy will become universal or that the continued growth of democracy will automatically produce a peaceful world order. The fact that leaders in elective democracies are accountable to public approval and electoral rejection does not guarantee that they will not use force to settle disputes with other democracies:

> It was, after all, the democratization of conflict in the nineteenth century that restored a ferocity to warfare unknown since the seventeenth century; the bloodiest war in American history remains the one fought between two (by today's standards flawed) democracies—the Civil War. Concentration camps appeared during another conflict between two limited democracies, the Boer War. World War I was launched by two regimes—Wilhelmine Germany and Austria-Hungary—that had greater representation and more equitable legal systems than those of many important states today. And even when modern liberal democracies go to war they do not necessarily moderate the scope of the violence they apply; indeed, sensitivity to their own casualties sometimes leads to profligate uses of firepower or violent efforts to end wars quickly. Shaky democracies fight each other all the time. . . . We must remind ourselves just how peculiar the wealthy and secure democracies of the West are, how painful their evolution to stability and the horror of war with each other has been. Perhaps other countries

will find short-cuts to those conditions, but it would be foolish to assume they will. (E. Cohen 1998, 39)

■ **nationalism**
sentimental devotion to the welfare of one's own nation without concern for the common interest of all nations and states in the global community (see p. 104).

Nationalism. **Nationalism**—love of and loyalty to a nation—is widely believed to be the cauldron from which wars often spring (Van Evera 1994; see also Chapters 4 and 5). "The tendency of the vast majority of people to center their supreme loyalties on the nation-state," Jack S. Levy explains, is a powerful catalyst to war. When people "acquire an intense commitment to the power and prosperity of the state [and] this commitment is strengthened by national myths emphasizing the moral, physical, and political strength of the state and by individuals' feelings of powerlessness and their consequent tendency to seek their identity and fulfillment through the state, . . . nationalism contributes to war" (Levy 1989a).

The connection between nationalism and war has a long history and provokes much debate (see Controversy: Does Nationalistic Love of Country Cause War with Foreign Nations?), but it has been especially pronounced in the twentieth century. The English essayist Aldous Huxley once termed nationalism "the religion of the twentieth century." Today, nationalism is particularly virulent and intense, and arguably, it and racism are "the most powerful movements in our world today, cutting across many social systems" (Gardels 1991).

Most armed conflicts today are fed by nationalist sentiments that promote "war fever . . . accompanied by overt hostility and contempt toward a caricatured image of the enemy," out of which sadistic violence and genocide have historically emanated (Caspary 1993). This entrenched linkage leads some to argue that "nationalism has often generated aggression abroad [and] has given us some three dozen costly wars in the Middle East since 1945" (Yoder 1991). And the danger could escalate. Nationalism's threat to world order led former Soviet President Mikhail Gorbachev to warn in May 1992 that "the demons of nationalism are coming alive again, and they are putting the stability of the international system to the test. Even the United States itself is not immune from the dangerous nationalism."

This discussion of the characteristics of states that influence their proclivity for war does not exhaust the subject. Many other potential causes internal to the state exist. But, however important domestic influences might be as a source of war, many believe that the nature of the international system is even more critical.

■ **global level of analysis**
an analytical approach to world politics that emphasizes the impact of global conditions on foreign policy behavior (see p. 17).

■ **self-help**
the principle that in anarchy states in the global system must rely on themselves (see p. 37).

The Third Level of Analysis: Cycles of War and Peace in the Global System

Realism emphasizes that the roots of armed conflict rest in human nature. In contrast, neorealism sees war springing from changes at the **global level of analysis,** that is, as a product of the decentralized character of the global system that requires sovereign states to rely on **self-help** for their security.

> Although different realist theories often generate conflicting predictions, they share a core of common assumptions: The key actors in world politics are sovereign states that act rationally to advance their security, power, and wealth in a conflictual international system that lacks a legitimate governmental authority to regulate conflicts or enforce agreements.

CONTROVERSY

DOES NATIONALISTIC LOVE OF COUNTRY CAUSE WAR WITH FOREIGN NATIONS?

What does *patriotism* mean? The most familiar definition is popularly expressed as "love for one's country." Often, it involves "love for the nation or nationality of the people living in a particular state," especially when the population of that state primarily comprises a single ethnonational racial or linguistic group. Because "love" for valued objects of affection, such as a person's homeland, is widely seen as a virtue, it is understandable why governments everywhere teach young citizens that love for country is a moral duty—it fosters a sense of political community. Nationalism encourages internal harmony and political stability, and thereby makes a positive contribution to civic solidarity and domestic peace. On these grounds, nationalism is not controversial. However, critics of nationalism find patriotism to be potentially dangerous in its extreme form. Superpatriots, these critics warn, are hypernationalists who measure their patriotism by the degree of hatred and opposition exhibited toward foreign nations and by the blind approval of every policy and practice of the "patriot's" own nation. In this sense, nationalistic patriotism can ignore transcendent moral principles such as the love for all humanity, even toward one's enemies, as preached by Jesus Christ in the Sermon on the Mount and other religious leaders such as Muhammad, the founder of Islam, and the legendary King Solomon in Judaism. If so, then is nationalistic superpatriotism sometimes a cause of war between nations? What do you think?

In contemplating your opinion about this controversial issue over values—about whether nationalism and internationalism are mutually exclusive, and whether nationalism makes for war by undermining justice under law for the world of nations—take into consideration the view of Karl Deutsch, a German-born immigrant and famous scholar who taught for many years at Harvard University. Deutsch, an authority on nationalism, described nationalism's linkage to armed conflict in these moving words:

Nationalism is an attitude of mind, a pattern of attention and desires. It arises in response to a condition of society and to a particular stage in its development. It is a predisposition to pay far more attention to messages about one's own people, or to messages from its members, than to messages from or about any other people. At the same time, it is a desire to have one's own people get any and all values that are available. The extreme nationalist wants his people to have all the power, all the wealth, and all the well-being for which there is any competition. He wants his people to command all the respect and deference from others; he tends to claim all rectitude and virtue for it, as well as all enlightenment and skill; and he gives it a monopoly of his affection. In short, he totally identifies himself with his nation. Though he may be willing to sacrifice himself for it, his nationalism is a form of egotism written large. . . .

Even if most people are not extreme nationalists, nationalism has altered the world in many ways. Nationalism has not only increased the number of countries on the face of the earth, it has helped to diminish the number of its inhabitants. All major wars in the twentieth century have been fought in its name. . . .

Nationalism is in potential conflict with all philosophies or religions—such as Christianity—which teach universal standards of truth and of right and wrong, regardless of nation, race, or tribe. Early in the nineteenth century a gallant American naval officer, Stephen Decatur, proposed the toast, "Our country! In her intercourse with foreign nations, may she be always in the right, but our country, right or wrong." Nearly 150 years later the United States Third Army, marching into Germany following the collapse of the Nazi regime, liberated the huge concentration camp at Buchenwald. Over the main entrance to that place of torture and death, the Nazi elite guard had thoughtfully written, "My Country, Right or Wrong." (Deutsch 1974, 124–125)

In confronting the impact of nationalism on armed conflict, we need to recognize its dual character: It is a force that (1) binds nations and nationalities together in common bonds, and (2) divides nation against nation, nationality against nationality, and is used to justify armed conflicts against other nations.

> For realists, wars can occur not only because some states prefer war to peace, but also because of unintended consequences of actions by those who prefer peace to war and are more interested in preserving their position than in enhancing it. Even defensively motivated efforts by states to provide for their own security through armaments, alliances, and deterrent threats are often perceived as threatening and lead to counteractions and conflict spirals that are difficult to reverse. This is the **"security dilemma"**—the possibility that a state's actions to provide for its security may result in a decrease in the security of all states, including itself. (Levy 1998b, 145)

■ **security dilemma**
the tendency of states to view the defensive arming of adversaries as threatening, and when they arm in response, everyone's security declines (see p. 114).

■ **anarchy**
at the global level, the absence of institutions for global governance with the power to enforce rules and regulate disputes between states to ensure that international relations are peaceful.

International **anarchy** may promote war's outbreak, but it fails to provide a complete explanation of changes in the levels of war and peace over time or why particular wars are fought. To capture war's many structural determinants, we must consider how and why systems change. This requires us to explore the impact of the distribution of military capabilities, balances (and imbalances) of power, the number of alliances and international organizations, and the rules of international law. At issue is how these factors—the system's characteristics and institutions—combine to influence changes in war's frequency. We will examine many of these factors in Chapters 14 and 15. Here we focus on cycles of war and peace at the international level and the structural determinants of armed conflict.

Does Violence Breed Violence? The adage "violence breeds violence" reflects the notion that the seeds of future wars are found in past wars. From this perspective World War II was an outgrowth of World War I, the U.S. bombing in 2002 of Iraq was an extension of the 1990 Persian Gulf War, and the successive waves of terrorism and war in the Middle East were seemingly little more than one war, with each battle stimulated by its predecessor. Because the frequency of past wars is correlated with the incidence of wars in later periods, war appears to be contagious and its future outbreak inevitable. If so, then something within the dynamics of world politics—its anarchical nature, its weak legal system, its uneven distribution of power, inevitable destabilizing changes in the principal actors' relative power, or some combination of structural attributes—makes the state system a war system.

Those believing in war's inevitability often cite the historical fact that war has been so repetitive. We cannot, however, safely infer that past wars have *caused* later wars. The fact that a war precedes a later one does not mean that it caused the one that followed.

Nor does war's recurrence throughout history necessarily mean we will always have it. War is not a universal institution; as we have seen, some societies have never known war, and others have been immune to it for prolonged periods. Moreover, since 1945 the outbreak of armed conflicts *between* states has greatly declined, despite the large increase in the number of independent countries. This indicates that armed conflict is not necessarily inevitable and that historical forces do not control people's freedom of choice or experiences.

Power Transitions. These trends notwithstanding, when changes have occurred in the major states' military capabilities, war has often resulted. Although not inevitable, war has been likely whenever competitive states' power

Nationalism's Dark and Deadly Past Under the fascist dictatorship of Adolf Hitler, shown on the left, the Nazi government glorified the state and claimed that the German people were a superior race. What followed from this extreme form of nationalism was war against Germany's neighbors and the campaign of genocide against the Jews and other ethnic minorities. U.S. troops under the command of General George Patton, shown on the right, are arriving to liberate the concentration camp at Buchenwald in May 1945, but not in time to save the lives of the prisoners the Nazi elite guard had put to death in the gas chambers. Experts estimate that more than 130 million victims perished in the twentieth century—the most genocidal period in history.

ratios (the differentials between their capabilities) have narrowed. Dubbed the **power transition theory,** this explanation rooted in **structural realism** holds that

> an even distribution of political, economic, and military capabilities between contending groups of states is likely to increase the probability of war; peace is preserved best when there is an imbalance of national capabilities between disadvantaged and advantaged nations; the aggressor will come from a small group of dissatisfied strong countries; and it is the weaker, rather than the stronger, power that is most likely to be the aggressor. (Organski and Kugler 1980, 19)

During the transition from developing to developed status, emergent challengers can achieve through force the recognition that their newly formed muscles allow them. Conversely, established powers ruled by risk-acceptant leaders are often willing to employ force to put the brakes on their relative decline. Thus when advancing and retreating states seek to cope with the changes in their relative power, war between the rising challenger(s) and the declining power(s) has become especially likely. For example, the rapid changes in the power and status that produced the division of Europe among seven great powers nearly equal in military strength are often (along with the alliances they nurtured) interpreted as the tinderbox from which World War I ignited.

■ **power transition theory**
the theory that war is likely when a dominant great power is threatened by the rapid growth of a rival's capabilities, which reduces the difference in their relative power.

■ **structural realism**
a neorealist theory that emphasizes the influence of the structure of world power on the behavior of the states within it.

As explained in Chapter 14, rapid shifts in the global distribution of military power have often preceded outbursts of aggression, especially when the new distribution nears approximate parity (equality) and thereby tempts the rivals to wage war against their hegemonic challengers. According to the power transition theory, periods in which rivals' military capabilities are nearly balanced create "the necessary conditions for global war, while gross inequality assures peace or, in the worst case, an asymmetric, limited war" (Kugler 1993). Moreover, transitions in states' relative capabilities can potentially lead the weaker party to start a war in order either to overtake its rival or to protect itself from domination. Presumably, the uncertainty created by a rough equilibrium prompts the challenger's (usually unsuccessful) effort to wage war against a stronger opponent. Equally persistent is the power transition theory's observation that advantages have shifted from the attacker to the defender: "In earlier centuries the aggressor seemed to have a 50-50 chance of winning the war, but this no longer holds. The chances of the starter being victorious are shrinking. In the 1980s only 18 percent of the starters were winners" (Sivard 1991, 20). As in the past (e.g., Japan's attack and subjugation of China in 1931 and 1937), there are notable exceptions: "Since 1945, six out of twenty wars have secured decisive advantage for the initiator (the Vietnam, Six Day, Bangladesh, Yom Kippur/Ramadan, Falklands, and Persian Gulf wars)" (Ziegler 1995).

Cyclical Theories. If war is recurrent but not necessarily inevitable, are there other international factors besides power transitions that might also explain changes over time in its outbreak? The absence of a clear trend in its frequency since the late fifteenth century, and its periodic outbreak after intermittent stretches of peace, suggest that world history seesaws between long cycles of war and peace. This provides a third structural explanation of war's onset.

The more recent formal analysis of such cycles is known as **long-cycle theory.** As noted in Chapter 4, its advocates argue that cycles of world leadership and global war have existed over the past five centuries, with a "general war" erupting approximately once every century, although at irregular intervals (Hopkins and Wallerstein 1996; Modelski 1987b; Modelski and Thompson 1996). Long-cycle theory seeks to explain how an all-powerful invisible hand built into the system's dynamics causes such peaks and valleys. Although this theory embraces many contending explanations (see Goldstein 1988), they converge on the proposition that some combination of systemic properties (economic, military, and political) produce the frequency with which major wars have erupted periodically throughout modern history.

The long-cycle perspective is based on the fact that a great power has risen to a hegemonic position about every one hundred years. Using as a measure of dominance the possession of disproportionate sea power, we observe the rise of a single **hegemon** regularly appearing after particular hegemonic periods (see Figure 11.3). Portugal and the Netherlands rose at the beginning of the sixteenth and seventeenth centuries, respectively; Britain climbed to dominance at the beginning of both the eighteenth and nineteenth centuries; and the United States became a world leader at the end of World War II. During their reigns, these hegemonic powers monopolized military power and trade and determined the system's rules. Yet no previous hegemonic power has retained its top-dog position for more than three or four decades. In each cycle, overcommit-

■ **long-cycle theory**
an interpretation of world history that focuses on repeating patterns of interstate behavior, such as the outbreak of systemwide general wars at different intervals, after long periods during which other patterns (global peace) were dominant.

■ **hegemon**
a single dominant military and economic state that uses its unrivaled power to create and enforce rules aimed at preserving the existing world order and its own position in that order.

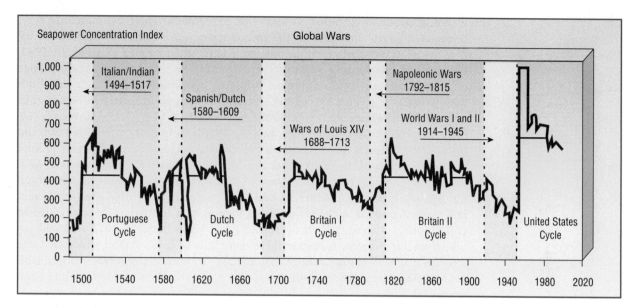

FIGURE 11.3

The Long Cycle of Global Leadership and Global War, 1494–2020

Over the past five hundred years, five great powers have risen to control the global system by dominating it. However, none of these hegemons (except Britain) has managed to reign for long. The past pattern shows that within a generation, the leader's grip on top-dog status has slipped, and in time new rivals have risen to challenge that leadership position by fighting a global war to settle the contest. The troubling question is whether this long cycle of war can be broken in the future or whether humankind will again experience a global war to determine which great power will lead.

SOURCE: Adapted from *Exploring Long Cycles* by George Modelski, ed., p. 6. Copyright © 1987 by Lynn Beinner Publishers. Reprinted by permission of the publisher.

ments, the costs of empire, and ultimately the appearance of rivals led to the delegitimation of the hegemon's authority and to the deconcentration of power globally. As challengers to the hegemon's rule grew in strength, a "global war" has erupted after a long period of peace in each century since 1400. At the conclusion of each previous general war, a new world leader emerged dominant (Modelski 1978, 1987b), and the cyclical process began anew.

Such deterministic theories have intuitive appeal. It seems plausible, for instance, that just as long-term downswings and recoveries in business cycles profoundly affect subsequent behaviors and conditions, wars will produce aftereffects that may last for generations. The idea that a country at war will become exhausted and lose its enthusiasm for another war, but only for a time, is known as the **war weariness hypothesis** (Blainey 1988). Italian historian Luigi da Porto expresses one version: "Peace brings riches; riches bring pride; pride brings anger; anger brings war; war brings poverty; poverty brings humanity; humanity brings peace; peace, as I have said, brings riches, and so the world's affairs go round." Because it takes time to move through these stages, alternating periods of enthusiasm for war and weariness of war appear to be influenced by learning, forgetting, and aging.

Cyclical theories of war's outbreak provoke much discussion. However, scholars attempting to construct a consensus about the existence of cycles of

■ **war weariness hypothesis**
the contention that a state at war will become exhausted and lose its enthusiasm for another war, but only for a time.

war and peace have failed to arrive at agreement. Their estimates diverge, because different measures of the frequency of war's outbreak construct rival pictures of the duration of periods of peace and war (compare Wright 1942, Richardson 1960a, and Sorokin 1937). What makes a true test for the presence of a cycle difficult is the increase in states' numbers over time, from about twenty-five during the 1816–1848 Concert of Europe to over two hundred in the post–Cold War period since 1989. The expansion of the global system's size increases the probability of war, but the numbers of wars between 1815 and today have actually been rather stable across time. The conclusion is suggested, therefore, that there is *not* a clear cycle operative in war's onset, and, given that, there is reason to doubt that the global system has properties which automatically produce recurrent cycles in wars (Singer 1981). The trends suggest, rather, that since the Congress of Vienna, war has been underway almost continuously. Although there were eighty-six years between 1816 and 2002 in which no interstate wars began, there were only twenty years in which no wars were in progress (Small and Singer 1982, 149; Singer 1991, 60–75; Gleditsch et al. 2002). Thus, throughout the modern era the level of warfare has been fairly stable.

The last decade of the twentieth century departed from this deadly pattern, however. The so-called outbreak of peace in the post–Cold War era is not mythical, as only eight large-scale wars were underway between states in the 1989–2001 period. Thus, the available evidence "suggests not so much that discrete wars come and go with some regularity, but that, with some level of such violence almost always present, there may be certain periodic fluctuations in the amount of that violence" (Small and Singer 1982). This characteristic draws attention to a puzzling trend. Since 1989, as the number of wars *between* states has plummeted, the number of civil wars *within* states has increased dramatically (recall Figure 1.1). War between states is ceasing to dominate world affairs, at least in frequency. "A tentative forecast: war in the twenty-first century is not likely to be as murderous as it was in the twentieth. But armed violence, creating disproportionate suffering and loss, will remain omnipresent and endemic—occasionally epidemic—in a large part of the world. The prospect of a century of peace is remote" (Hobsbawn 2002).

Although the disappearance of war *between* states may be possible over the long run, armed conflict and violence persists *inside* established states. We now turn from our exploration of the multiple causes of armed conflicts between states to examine armed conflicts within states.

ARMED CONFLICT WITHIN STATES

■ **civil war**
war between factions within the same country.

Civil wars—wars within states—have erupted far more frequently than have wars between states. It is these armed struggles that most often capture news headlines worldwide. The *New York Times* on May 7, 1995, for example, featured a story concluding that "for just about the first time since 1815, no great powers are at one another's throats [but] civil wars and snarling savageries continue on both sides of the Equator."

The Characteristics of Civil War

There is a basis in fact for the above assertion. Between 1989 and 2001, internal armed conflicts over government (civil wars) or over territory (state-formation conflicts) have been the most common by far. In this period, 118 civil wars erupted in comparison with only 8 between states. At the start of 2002, 35 civil wars were raging, and only 3 crossborder military conflicts were being fought worldwide (*Defense Monitor*, January 2002, 1).

Civil wars resulting in at least one thousand civilian and military deaths per year occurred 242 times between 1816 and 2001 (Small and Singer 1982; Singer 1991, 66–75; Wallensteen and Sollenberg 2001). Their outbreak has been somewhat irregular. Although at least one civil war was begun in eighty-four of these years, over time civil war has become increasingly frequent (see Table 11.1). Of the civil wars since 1816, three-fourths began after 1945, with a frequency steadily climbing each decade (almost half of the civil wars since the 1816 Congress of Vienna began since the Cold War ended in 1989). However, this accelerating trend is, in part, a product of the increase in the number of independent states in the global system, which makes the incidence of civil war statistically more probable. Nonetheless, civil wars stem from similar emerging conditions and center around several salient issues:

- Ethnic groups seeking greater autonomy or striving to create an independent state for themselves (such as the Kurds in Turkey and Chechens in Russia).

- Internal battles fought to gain control of an existing state. The confrontation between East and West during the Cold War provoked many of these conflicts and, even though sponsorship by a superpower for a particular internal faction has ended, active fighting in many civil wars has continued without interruption. Three-fourths of the major armed conflicts active in the year 2000 originated prior to 1989 (Wallensteen and Sollenberg 2001, 633). Many of these long-lasting civil wars—in Afghanistan, Colombia, Peru, Rwanda, Sri Lanka, and Sudan, for example—were fought over state control and fueled by ethnic, tribal, or religious disputes.

- "Failed states" where the authority of a national government has collapsed and armed struggle has broken out between the competing ethnic militias, warlords, or criminal organizations seeking to obtain power and establish control of the state.

The number of civil wars *underway* provides a different picture. Referring to the same inventories cited in Table 11.1, we see that between 1816 and 2001 civil wars were in progress somewhere in the world over 92 percent of the time. During the period from 1989–2000 a total of 111 armed conflicts were active in any one year around the world, and nine of these civil wars were "internationalized" through the military intervention of one or more foreign states (Wallensteen and Sollenberg 2001, 632). In the year 2001, five external powers intervened in the 35 civil wars that were underway (*Defense Monitor*, January 2002, 4–5). Thus, civil wars almost constantly cast their shadow over world politics, and between 1946 and 2001 one in five had the intervention of outside actors seeking to influence their outcome (Gleditsch et al. 2002, 620). Africa's so-called "First World War" in 2000 may be a symptom of the internal wars of the future—civil wars involving outside intervention by six states in the Congo where a dictatorship was waging a civil war against the rival rebel groups.

TABLE 11.1

The Frequency of 242 Civil Wars across Six Periods, 1816–2001

Period	Key System Characteristics	System Size (average number of states)	Number of Civil Wars Begun	Number (percent) of Civil Wars Internationalized through Large-Scale Military Intervention
1816–1848	Monarchies in Concert of Europe suppress democratic revolutions	28	12	3 (25%)
1849–1881	Rising nationalism and civil wars	39	20	1 (5%)
1882–1914	Imperialism and colonization	40	18	3 (17%)
1915–1945	World wars and economic collapse	59	14	4 (29%)
1946–1988	Decolonization and independence for emerging Global South countries during Cold War	117	60	14 (23%)
1989–2001	Age of failed states and civil wars	194	118	18 (15%)
Totals			242	41 (17%)

SOURCES: Data for 1816–1988, courtesy of the Correlates of War project under the direction of J. David Singer and Melvin Small; data for 1989–2001, based on Wallensteen and Sollenberg (2001), *Defense Monitor* (January 2002), 4–5, and Gleditsch et al. (2002).

Several characteristics of civil wars are especially noteworthy. The first, as noted, is the trend toward the globalization of external intervention into internal armed conflicts. One account of 111 armed conflicts between 1989 and 2000 recorded the involvement of more than eighty external state actors and a handful of regional IGOs—a proliferation that attests to the breakdown of borders as barriers through external interference which also "probably accounts for the difficulty in ending conflicts" (Wallensteen and Sollenberg 2001, 633).

A second notable characteristic of civil wars is their severity. The number of lives lost in civil violence has remained high since the Napoleonic Wars ended in 1815; one estimate places the battle deaths between 1815 and 1995 resulting directly from the fighting between combatants in excess of 12 million (Sivard 1996), and the collateral destruction of citizens is assuredly much greater. Casualty rates from civil wars show an alarming growth, especially since World War II. One symptom of the climbing lethality of civil rebellions is that ten of the fifteen most destructive civil wars between 1816 and 1980 occurred in the twentieth century; of those ten, seven have occurred since World War II (Small and Singer 1982, 241). The cliché that "the most savage conflicts occur in the home" captures the ugly reality, as genocide and mass slaughter aimed at depopulating entire regions have become commonplace in recent civil wars. That grim reality was illustrated in Rwanda, where "the Hutu government incited citizens to a genocidal slaughter, resulting in the murder of an estimated 500,000 people in a month's time" (Sivard 1996). Sudan provides another horrifying example of the mass slaughter of civilians that often occurs when governments seek to keep power by destroying minority opposition groups. "The Sudanese government, which displaced a democratically elected government in 1989, has engaged in a policy to divide and destroy the people of the predominately Christian and animist south. It uses terror against civilians as a weapon of choice and pits different ethnic groups against each other. . . . The scale of death and destruction has reached staggering proportions. Credible estimates from human rights organizations suggest the 2 million people have perished, 4 million have been internally displaced, and nearly 400,000 have been forced to live in neighboring countries as refugees" (Rice and Scheffer 1999, 6).

A third core characteristic of civil wars is their typically long duration.

> The dominant pattern is of rumbling conflicts that, from time to time across a decade, erupt viciously into action. . . . For the most part, modern [internal] war resembles a slow torture, [offering] few triumphs. . . . They simply continue. More than half the wars of the 1990s lasted more than five years, two-fifths lasted more than ten years and a quarter for more than twenty. The action is often fitful. (D. Smith 1997, 14)

A fourth characteristic of civil wars is their resistance to negotiated settlement. Making peace among rival factions that are struggling for power, driven by hatred, and poisoned by the inertia of prolonged killing that has become a way of life is very difficult. Civil wars rarely result in the decisive victory of one faction over another. The pattern of civil wars is that domestic enemies are rarely able to end the fighting through negotiated compromise at the bargaining table; over half end on the battlefield (Walter 1997, 335).

The growing frequency, severity, length, and indeterminate conclusion of the civil wars are accounted for by the multiple causes of these prolonged domestic disputes raging across the globe.

The Causes of Civil War

Civil wars stem from a wide range of ideological, demographic, religious, ethnic, economic, social-structural, and political conditions. Civil war and revolution have simultaneously been defended as instruments of justice and condemned as the immoral acceptance of violent change. They contain ingredients of both. Those who engineered the American, Russian, and Chinese revolutions claimed that violence was necessary to realize social change, political freedom, and independence; the powers from whom they sought liberation berated the immorality of their methods.

Internal Rebellion. Among the sources of civil war, internal violence is a reaction to frustration and **relative deprivation**—people's perception that they are unfairly deprived of the wealth and status that they deserve in comparison with advantaged others (Gurr 1970). When people's expectations of what they deserve rise more rapidly than their material rewards, the probability of conflict grows. That, of course, applies to most of the countries in the Global South today, where the distribution of wealth and opportunities is highly unequal (see Chapter 6).

Secessionist Revolts. The seeds of civil strife are often sown by national independence movements. "More than two thirds of all the armed combat in

■ **relative deprivation** inequality between the wealth and status of individuals and groups, and the outrage of those at the bottom about their perceived exploitation by those at the top.

John Stanmeyer

The Painful Birth of Democracy In the mid-1990s East Timor voted to secede from Indonesia. The Indonesian authorities sought to prevent by violence and repression the East Timorese bid for independence, prior to intervention by UN peacekeeping forces to halt the assault on human rights of hundreds of thousands of innocent East Timorese civilians. Here a rock-wielding protester is hunted down and killed by Jakarta-backed militia.

the world between 1945 and 1995 were manifestations of the state-creation enterprise" (K. Holsti 1995, 22). Violence often has been the means through which states have been given—or denied—birth.

Nationalism. Love of one's own country can provoke hatred of, and wars against, other countries, as noted above. Intense identification with one's own nationality or ethnic group can also easily provoke civil wars against a government, especially if it is repressive. There are as many as five thousand separate "nations" or separate indigenous peoples living in existing countries (see Chapter 5), and many of these nonstate nations have members seeking to use violence and terrorism against other nationalities or the governing majority. Between 1990 and 1995, half the countries that experienced civil wars were those in which ethnic minorities made up 10 to 15 percent of the population (D. Smith 1997, 30).

■ **ethnic warfare**
violence resulting from wars between two or more ethnic groups or from state-sponsored violence to terrorize or destroy an ethnic minority.

Ethnonational Conflict. Since World War II, civil wars provoked by ancient ethnic and racial hatreds have been commonplace in multiethnic states. Between 1945 and 1981, 258 cases of **ethnic warfare** were observed, 40 percent of which involved high levels of violence (Carment 1993, 141). More recently, this armed conflict has reached epidemic proportions. Ted Robert Gurr (1994, 351–352) estimated that 26,759,000 refugees fled the fifty major ethnonational

A. Yagsobzadeh/Sipa

Ethnic Warfare and Children Children have often been the major victims of civil strife. This photo, which received the World Press Award in 1985, depicts children caught in the ethnonational and religious civil war in Beirut, the capital of Lebanon—a country whose population is about two-thirds Muslim and one-fourth Christian, with each faction divided into further sects.

conflicts that were occurring in 1993–1994, each of which was responsible for an average of eighty thousand deaths. In today's civil wars, most of the victims are not soldiers; they are innocent noncombatant civilians such as women and children. Ninety percent of all killed are noncombatants (Sivard 1996, 17) and over half the **displaced people**—refugees within their own countries—are women and children (D. Smith 1997, 26).

As U.S. President Bill Clinton observed in his June 7, 1994, speech before the French National Assembly, militant ethnic nationalism was "on the rise, transforming the healthy pride of nations, tribes, religious and ethnic groups into cancerous prejudice, eating away at states and leaving their people addicted to the political painkillers of violence and demagoguery." Much of the internal revolt and ethnic warfare currently sweeping the world is inspired less by political motives and economic aims that it is by deeply rooted ethnic hatreds. Waged primarily by irregular militia and private gangs against their neighbors, extreme ethnonationalists are people are who are prepared to kill and die in large numbers. Ethnonational clashes differ greatly from the anti-colonial secessionist independence movement of the past.

Failed States. Many fledgling governments are fragile and fall apart as they fail to effectively manage the regulatory power sovereignty under international law gives them to govern affairs within their territorial borders. Mismanagement by government administration is causing an epidemic of **failing states** throughout the globe, as disarray, discontent, and disorder have mobilized

■ **displaced people**
people involuntarily uprooted from their homes but still living in their own countries (see p. 241).

■ **failing states**
those governments that are in danger of losing the loyalty of their citizens, who are rebelling against corruption and administrative failure, and, in the process, tearing the country into separate political parts.

desperate populations living in conditions of anarchy to rebel. The civil wars percolated by state failure have caused as many as one hundred and thirteen states to dissolve or fragment into separate units between 1955 and 1994 according to the U.S. Central Intelligence Agency's "State Failure Task Force" report. In 2002 no less than another eighteen states were "high-risk" countries vulnerable to destruction through civil rebellion against a feeble government.

The causes of state failure and civil disintegration are multiple, but failed states share some key characteristics. Among them, the CIA "State Failure Task Force" report finds that

- Democracy generally lowers the risk of state failure; autocracy increases it.
- Poor democracies, however, are more unstable than either rich democracies or poor nondemocracies, and poor democracies that do not improve living standards are exceptionally vulnerable.
- The best predictor of failure is high infant mortality.
- High levels of trade openness seem to inoculate any kind of regime against failure. States that have fair rules allowing a high degree of international trade gain stability.
- The existence of a "youth bulge"—a large proportion of young adults in the population—increases the risk of ethnic war because large pools of underemployed youths are easily mobilized into action.
- Mass killings are often associated with low levels of trade openness, in part, because countries with little foreign trade are usually of little concern to the international community. (Zimmerman 1996, 46)

Inasmuch as many of the 208 sovereign states in the world have one or more of these attributes, it is likely that failing states will grow as a problem in the globalized twenty-first century. As Map 11.1 shows, the globe is speckled with many dangerous civil war flashpoints where countries are highly vulnerable to dissolution as a result of state failure, mismanagement, and civil revolt.

The Economic Sources of Internal Rebellions. The destabilization caused by rapid growth also helps to account for the ubiquity of internal war. In contrast with what intuition might suggest, civil violence often erupts in countries in which conditions are improving, not deteriorating. "Economic modernization," former U.S. Secretary of State Henry Kissinger stated, "leads to political instability rather than political stability." When modernization generates rising expectations that governments are unable to satisfy, civil war often follows. This is the essence of relative deprivation as a cause of internal violence, as people who feel they have been denied the resources they deserve are often inclined to use force in acts of rebellion (Gurr 1970).

Having observed rapid growth as a source of civil war, we must not ignore the persistence of poverty as an ancient and continuing cause. Desperation has fomented domestic insurrection throughout all periods of history, and today, even in the period of democratization and economic growth through free trade and free markets, misery among those not sharing in the benefits is breeding revolt. "The chief causes of conflict remain—overwhelming poverty in cities and the dominance of a narrow elite in rural areas." This is made evident by the fact that 57 percent of the armed conflicts between 1990 and 1995 erupted in

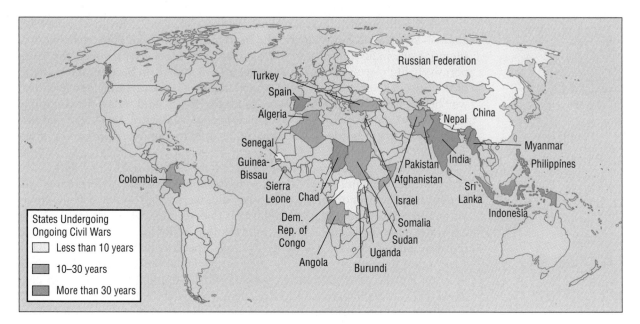

MAP 11.1

A World at War: States Threatening to Collapse in Civil Wars, 2002

Civil wars have broken out with steadily increasing frequency since the end of World War II, and most expect the contagion to continue. As failing states splinter and new states emerge, the United Nations predicts that by the year 2025 there could be as many as 500 sovereign states. This map underscores the magnitude of the epidemic, showing the location in 2002 of twenty-five long-term civil wars resulting in 1,000 or more deaths. Collectively, these ongoing civil wars across the globe are estimated to have taken the lives of at least 5 million people.

SOURCES: Copyright © 2002 by *Harper's Magazine*. All rights reserved. Reproduced from the March issue by special permission.

the poor countries ranking "low" on the UN **human development index (HDI;** see Chapter 7), and another 34 percent in the "medium-human-development" countries, in contrast to only 14 percent in the "high" countries providing relative prosperity, health and education for their citizens" (D. Smith 1997, 48, 50). It is therefore not surprising that "death rates from violence in poor countries are more than double the level in rich ones" (*Economist*, October 5, 2002, 98). As the UN High Commissioner for Refugees Sadaka Ogata concluded, "to establish a more peaceful, prosperous and secure world, poverty must be eliminated and income differentials reduced."

The International Dimensions of Internal War

It is tempting to think of civil war as stemming exclusively from conditions within countries. However, external factors often influence internal rebellions. "Every war has two faces. It is a conflict both between and within political systems; a conflict that is both external and internal. [It is undeniable that] internal wars affect the international system [and that] the international system affects internal wars" (Modelski 1964).

■ **human development index (HDI)**
an index that uses life expectancy, literacy, average number of years of schooling, and income to assess a country's performance in providing for its citizen's welfare and security.

We can distinguish several phases that have influenced the linkage between changes in the global system and the incidence of civil war. First, the effects of imperialism, industrialization, nationalism, and ideology provoked the comparatively high levels of civil war between 1848 and 1870. Second, the breakup of the European colonial empires contributed to the frequent incidence of civil war between the end of World War II and the 1960s. And today, the discipline imposed by Cold War bipolarity has disappeared, removing states' fear that turmoil within their borders will precipitate military intervention by the great powers.

Because the great powers have global interests, historically they have been prone to intervene militarily in civil wars to support friendly governments and to overthrow unfriendly ones. When they did, wars within states became internationalized. But today it is often difficult to determine where an internal war ends and another begins. As the information in Table 11.1 reveals, outside intervention in civil wars has been common, especially between 1945 and 2001, when more than two-thirds of all external participation in internal wars since 1816 took place. It is estimated that between 1946 and 2001, of the 178 civil wars, other states intervened in 32 of them (Gleditsch 2002, 620).

Many analysts believe that domestic conflicts become internationalized because leaders who experience internal opposition are inclined to provoke an international crisis in the hope that their citizens will become less rebellious if their attention is diverted to the threat of external aggression. This proposition has become known as the **diversionary theory of war.** This theory is based on the expectation that external war will result in increased domestic support for political leaders. It draws a direct connection between civil strife and foreign aggression, maintaining that when leaders suffer conflict at home, they are prone to attempt to contain that domestic strife by waging a war against foreigners in the hope that the international danger will take citizens' attention away from their dissatisfaction with their home leadership. "To put it cynically, one could say that nothing helps a leader like a good war. It gives him his only chance of being a tyrant and being loved for it at the same time. He can introduce the most ruthless forms of control and send thousands of his followers to their deaths and still be hailed as a great protector. Nothing ties tighter the ingroup bonds than an out-group threat" (Morris 1969).

There are powerful reasons for leaders to assume that national unity will rise when an external threat exists, and there are equally strong temptations for them to seek to manage domestic unrest by initiating foreign adventures. Indeed, many political advisers have counseled this strategy, as the realist theorist Niccoló Machiavelli did in 1513 when he advised leaders to undertake foreign wars whenever turmoil within their state became too great. He was echoed by Hermann Goering, Adolf Hitler's Nazi adviser, when he instructed, "Voice or no voice, the people can always be brought to do the bidding of the leaders. That is easy. All you have to do is tell them they are being attacked and denounce the pacifists for lack of patriotism." Similarly, in 1939 John Foster Dulles recommended before he became U.S. secretary of state that "The easiest and quickest cure of internal dissension is to portray danger from abroad."

Whether leaders actually start wars to offset domestic conflict remains a subject of debate. We cannot demonstrate that many leaders intentionally undertake diversionary actions to defend themselves against domestic opposition. Unpopular leaders may instead be highly motivated to exercise caution in

■ **diversionary theory of war**

the contention that leaders initiate conflict abroad as a way of increasing national cohesion at home (see p. 70).

foreign affairs and to avoid the use of force overseas in order to cultivate a reputation as a peacemaker; it is better to avoid further criticism that they are intentionally manipulative by addressing the domestic problems that cause civil unrest, rather than engaging in reckless wars overseas—especially unpopular wars that trigger protest demonstrations and reduce leaders' approval ratings from their constituents. Hence, there is reason to question the linkage between civil unrest and interstate war initiation. "The linkage depends," Jack Levy (1989b) observes, "on the kinds of internal conditions that commonly lead to hostile external actions for diversionary purposes." In general, the available evidence urges that we question the diversionary theory of war. Perhaps the most compelling reason for some doubt is that "when domestic conflict becomes extremely intense it would seem more reasonable to argue that there is a greater likelihood that a state will retreat from its foreign engagements in order to handle the situation at home" (Zinnes and Wilkenfeld 1971).

TERRORISM

Terrorism poses another alarming kind of violence in the contemporary world. The instruments of terror are varied and the motivations of terrorists diverse, but "experts agree that terrorism is the use or threat of violence, a method of combat or a strategy to achieve certain goals, that its aim is to induce a state of fear in the victim, that it is ruthless and does not conform to humanitarian norms, and that publicity is an essential factor in terrorist strategy" (Laqueur 2003).

Some terrorist activities, such as the 1995 bombing of the U.S. federal government building in Oklahoma City and the rampant terrorist bombings between 1999 and 2003 that inflicted Russia's desperate frontline fighters against random terror, begin and end in a single country. Many, however, cross national borders. At the start of the twenty-first century, most terrorists targeted citizens and property in external countries, and because terrorist acts are spread throughout the globe, the risks are also widespread.

Terrorism is a tactic of the powerless against the powerful. Thus it is not surprising that political or social minorities and ethnic movements sometimes turn to acts of terrorism on behalf of their political causes (see Chapter 5). Those seeking independence and sovereign statehood, such as the Basques in Spain, typify the aspirations that animate terrorist activity. Religion also sometimes rationalizes the terrorist activities of extremist movements, such as the efforts of the Sikh groups who wish to carve out an independent state called Khalistan ("Land of the Pure") from Indian territory, and of the Islamic extremist group HAMAS to destabilize Israel and sabotage a negotiated peace between Israel and its Arab neighbors. In November 1995, right-wing Jewish fanatics in the Kach religious terrorist group assassinated Israeli Prime Minister Yitzhak Rabin to derail the peace process in Palestine.

In the industrialized world, terrorism often occurs where discrepancies in income are severe and where minority groups feel deprived of the political freedoms and privileges enjoyed by the majority. In the urbanized areas of the industrialized world, guerrilla warfare—normally associated with rural uprisings—is not a viable route to self-assertion, but terrorist tactics are.

■ **terrorism**
premeditated politically motivated violence perpetrated against noncombatant targets by subnational groups or clandestine agents, usually intended to influence an audience (see p. 582).

Terrorism was well known in ancient times, as evident in the assassination of tyrants in ancient Greece and Rome, and killings by the *Zealots* in Palestine and the *Hashashin* of medieval Islam. In the nineteenth century, terrorism became associated with anarchist bombings and with murders and destruction of property by nationalist groups. The ethnic, political, or religious movements now practicing terrorism all seek to extract revenge against those states and populations that each terrorist group perceives as its oppressor. Often the terrorists are the "international homeless" whose main objective is to obtain for themselves a territory and state they can control. Whereas religious fanaticism is responsible for many terrorist incidents, the primary goals of most terrorist groups are independence and statehood.

Terrorist groups may be thought of as an unconventional type of nonstate actor (or global NGO) on the global stage, distinguished by the fact that they use violence as their primary method of exercising influence. However, terrorist groups are difficult to identify, and it would be a mistake to lump all terrorist movements together. Today terrorism is a strategy practiced by a very diverse group of movements, as seen by the fact that in 2002 the U.S. State Department identified thirty-three very different organizations as worldwide terrorist groups (see Table 11.2). Simply put, terrorist movements are more diverse than they are similar.

The difference between nationalistic "freedom fighters," whose major complaint is that they lack a country, and governments claiming to protect freedom, often lies in the eye of the beholder. This problem makes the definition of a terrorist group less obvious and more controversial, as what most distinguishes terrorist groups from liberation movements is the outcome—which faction succeeds or fails in a political struggle for power. We must keep in mind that those who are willing to use violence and terror outside the rules of warfare that have evolved over time tend to be condemned or praised, depending on whether those who condemn or praise accept or reject the terrorist's cause.

The popularity of the slogan that "one person's terrorist is another's freedom fighter" notwithstanding, there is a difference. Terrorists are defined by the *means* (terror) they use, and freedom fighters by the *end* (civil liberty) they pursue. Because freedom can be fought for by moral and legal methods that respect the immunity of noncombatant targets, freedom fighters can operate differently from terrorists, who are prepared to use violence against unarmed civilians and to promote good causes by evil methods.

Although many terrorist groups today are undeniably seeking sovereignty, a broader definition of terrorism would acknowledge that many governments undertake terrorist acts, sometimes against their own people and sometimes by supporting terrorism against other established sovereign states (see Crenshaw 2003). In fact, some states underwrite the activities of terrorist movements that advocate philosophies they embrace (or challenge the security of rival states). States have often financed, trained, equipped, and provided sanctuary for terrorists whose activities serve their foreign goals. The practice of such **state-sponsored terrorism** is among the charges that the United States leveled in 2002 against the so-called "axis of evil"—Iran, Iraq, and North Korea—as well as against Cuba, Libya, Sudan, and Syria. Similarly, others had previously accused the United States of sponsoring terrorist activities in Vietnam, Chile, El Salvador, Nicaragua, and elsewhere.

■ **state-sponsored terrorism**
formal assistance, training, and arming of foreign terrorists by a state in order to achieve foreign policy goals (see p. 514).

TABLE 11.2

Tribal Terrorists and Unholy Warriors: Some Active Terrorist Groups

Group	Description
Abu Nidal Organization (ANO)	Led by Sabri al-Banna, the ANO was headquartered in Iraq (1974–1983), Syria (1983–1987), and now Libya and operates internationally to coordinate the activities of various other Muslim terrorist groups.
Armed Islamic Group	An extremist group that seeks to overthrow the secular Algerian government and replace it with an Islamic state.
Basque Fatherland and Liberty (ETA)	Founded in 1959, and once committed to Marxism, the group seeks to create an independent homeland in Spain's Basque region.
HAMAS (Islamic Resistance Movement)	Emerging in 1987 from the Palestinian branch of the Muslim Brotherhood, HAMAS pursues—often by violent means—the goal of an Islamic Palestinian state in place of Israel.
Hizballah (Party of God)	Radical Shia religious group seeking to establish an Iranian-style Islamic Republic in Lebanon.
Kach and Kahane Chai	A right-wing Jewish extremist movement seeking to restore the biblical state of Israel and to halt the peace process in Palestine. A member of Eyal (an offshoot of the radical Kach movement) assassinated Israeli Prime Minister Yitzhak Rabin in November 1995.
Party of Democratic Kampuchea (Khmer Rouge)	Communist insurgents hoping to destabilize the Cambodian government. Under Pol Pot's leadership, a campaign of genocide killed more than 1 million people in the late 1970s.
Provisional Irish Republican Army (PIRA)	Radical group formed in 1969 as the secret armed wing of Sinn Féin, the legal political movement seeking to remove British forces from Northern Ireland and unify Ireland.
Sendero Luminoso (Shining Path)	Guerrilla insurgency formed in the late 1960s by a former university professor whose stated goals are ridding Peru of foreign influences, destroying existing Peruvian institutions, and replacing them with a peasant revolutionary regime.
Al Qaeda	Established by Osama bin Laden in the late 1980s to bring together Arabs who fought in Afghanistan against the Soviet invasion. Helped finance, recruit, transport, and train Sunni Islamic extremists for the Afghan resistance, which was covertly supplied with arms and money by the United States. Current goal is to establish a pan-Islamic Caliphate throughout the world by working with allied Islamic extremist groups to overthrow regimes it deems "non-Islamic" and expelling Westerners and non-Muslims from Muslim countries. Issued statement under banner of "the World Islamic Front for Jihad against the Jews and Crusaders" in February 1988, saying it was the duty of all Muslims to kill U.S. citizens—civilian or military—and their allies everywhere. On September 11, 2001, Al-Qaeda engineered the destruction of the World Trade Center in New York City.

Note: These descriptions of some terrorist movements active in the late 1990s are provided by the U.S. Department of State's counterterrorism office. Although not exhaustive, they convey the degree to which terrorist groups seek a combination of religious, ethnic, and political goals that generally aim to challenge the authority and cultural values of existing states.

The unspeakable horror that surrounded 9/11 and other equally unsettling incidents of terrorism, such as the bombing of Pan Am flight 103 over Scotland on December 21, 1988, which claimed 270 lives, provides conspicuous examples of the recurrent human tragedy and exemplifies the potency of terrorism and the frustration and failure of efforts to contain it. Past acts of ruthless terrorism have been committed on a regular basis, and their primary purpose usually has been to produce alarm. To instill paralyzing fear—to terrorize—has unfortunately become a common way of expressing grievances and attempting to realize political objectives.

The inherently sadistic nature of violent terrorism can obscure terrorist's identity, making states appear inherently blameless and dissimilar from revolutionary terrorists. However, an objective definition of terrorism as a strategy must acknowledge that *both* governments and countergovernment movements claim to seek liberty and both are labeled terrorists by their opponents.

> Those who are described as terrorists, and who reject that title for themselves, make the uncomfortable point that national armed forces, fully supported by democratic opinion, have in fact employed violence and terror on a far vaster scale than what liberation movements have as yet been able to attain. The "freedom fighters" see themselves as fighting a just war. Why should they not be entitled to kill, burn, and destroy as national armies, navies and air forces do, and why should the label "terrorist" be applied to them and not the national militaries? (O'Brien 1977, 56–57)

In addressing terrorism, we are dealing with a value-laden subject that resists precise definition and whose description is often motivated by the desire to condemn, not to offer detached evaluation. The task of objective analysis is complicated, because it requires comparing different ways in which transnational actors threaten violence and extracting valid generalizations about the characteristics terrorists share with other actors and those which set them apart. A definition must balance the need to identify commonalities against the need to recognize unique features of individual cases. Should suicide Al Qaeda and Taliban bombers, Palestinian skyjackers, Zionist hit squads, Basque separatists, Irish revolutionaries, and South American kidnappers be seen as similar? Are they properly classified with the insurgents who produced the American, French, and Russian revolutions? Do their actions resemble the tactics of the Red Brigade, the Ku Klux Klan, the Roman Catholic Church during the Inquisition, or big-time drug-trafficking street gangs and networks of international organized crime? Were the methods of the African National Congress and the racist South African government it opposed both cases of terrorist actors? Was the "state terrorism" of Pol Pot, Adolf Hitler, Joseph Stalin, and Mao Tse-Tung a part of the same terrorist syndrome? Is an attack on a principle such as freedom of the press different from a terrorist attack on human life? And what about the nuclear deterrence strategies pursued by the United States and the Soviet Union during the Cold War, which relied on terror to prevent attack (see Chapter 13)? Where does one draw the line?

How one addresses these questions shapes views about terrorism's purpose, challenge, and ultimate significance. Whether some forms of terrorism are found acceptable will similarly be shaped by the socially constructed images of it. As constructivist theorists remind us, what we see depends on what we look at, what we look for, what we expect to see, what we wish to see, and how we react to what we discern.

In this context, consider, for example, the seemingly simple question of whether global terrorism has increased in frequency since the 1960s. On the surface, this would appear to be an easy question to answer, yet estimates vary considerably. Indices select, screen, and filter what is perceived about the volume of international terrorism. For instance, the U.S. Department of State's Office of Counter-Terrorism, which employs the broad definition for international terrorism as any "premeditated, politically motivated violence perpetrated against noncombatant targets by subnational groups or clandestine agents, usually intended to influence an audience involving the citizens or territory of more than one country," began to inventory the frequency of terrorist acts after terrorism first emerged as a significant international problem in the 1960s and grew to epidemic proportions in the 1970s and 1980s. Figure 11.4 shows the changing frequency of terrorism and its level of destruction in today's world, as measured by this account, which reveals that global terrorist activity had increased nearly threefold between 1968 and 1987, after which the number of incidents has gradually but erratically declined. International terrorist attacks during 2002 fell to 199 from the prior year of 348 separate terrorist acts. However, in three fateful years—1995, 1989, and 2001—the number of people killed by terrorists' acts rose dramatically: nearly 3,000 people were killed as a result of the September 11 attack, the most lethal terrorist incident since World War II. This fourth wave of global terrorism continued to display its lethal face in 2002 when the latest manifestation of the Palestine-Israeli conflict intensified and more than 1,500 were killed in multiple suicide bombings by *Islamic Jihad* and *Hamas* that were met by Israeli attacks, reoccupation of Palestinian villages and land, and executions of suspected terrorists. As the so-called war on terrorism suggests, the threat of increasing global terrorism in the aftermath of September 11 is expected to persist and possibly grow, and with its growth global terrorism would likely become bloodier.

Regardless of the total volume global terrorist actions always exert a powerfully symbolic and dramatic impact, which heightens every time a major attack occurs. Until 9/11, terrorism was dismissed as a significant danger because even though international terrorism was increasingly lethal, global terrorism previously had seldom taken many lives; nevertheless, terrorism at all times has commanded high attention, because each spectacular terrorist act always has generated a powerful shock effect, elevated by its dramatic publicity in the news media. Consider the flash point of today's terrorism—the Middle East (see Map 11.2).

The New Global Terrorism.   The conventional view of terrorism as a rare and relatively remote threat to humans and security was challenged by the events of September 11, 2001, which forced people to rethink the meaning of terrorism and its previously marginal threat to global stability. The events of September 11, 2001, seem destined to remain permanently etched in the minds and memories of everyone. Few, if any, will ever forget where they were when they first heard the horrendous news. In a single flash the world was forced to confront grim new realities. Instantaneously, those absent towers in New York became the symbol for the shapelessness of an apparent new world disorder.

9/11 shattered the preexisting, prevailing sense of international safety and euphoria of a peaceful and prosperous post–Cold War era. "The prospect of another attack," warned U.S. Secretary of Defense Dick Cheney in 2002, "is not a matter of if, but when." A generation of fear was 9/11's primary product. That was precisely the terrorists' purpose behind this atrocious act. "America is full of fear," proclaimed a jubilant Osama bin Laden in the taped message he broadcast in anticipation of the U.S. response to his slaughter of thousands of innocent people. "They cry for their children," he gleefully asserted, while warning "Nobody in the United States will feel safe."

Provoking fear is the name of the terrorist's game. It's an old game, and traditional forms of the old terrorism are far from dead. However, terrorism after

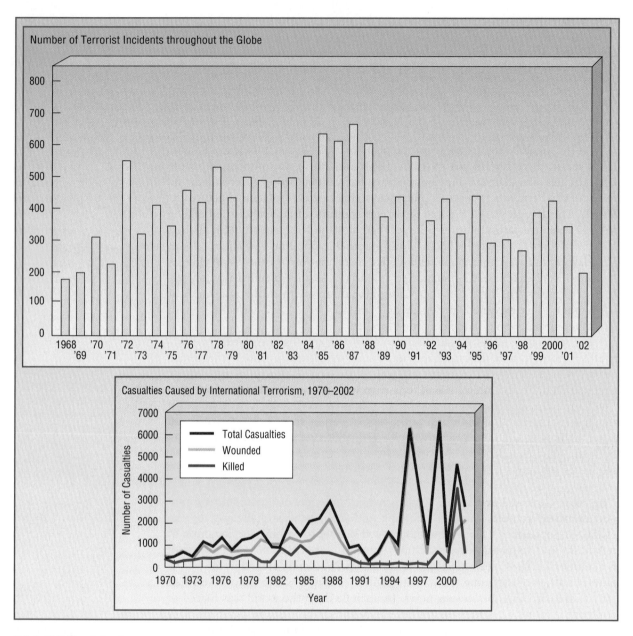

FIGURE 11.4

The Number of Terrorist Incidents throughout the Globe and the Changing Number of Casualties Caused by International Terrorism, since the Late 1960s

The frequency of international terrorist activity has changed over time since 1968, and the number of incidents each year has been between 174 (in 1968) and 666 (in 1987). These activities appear entrenched, but vary over time. Note also (bottom figure) the relatively modest toll of human life extracted by terrorism. No level is acceptable, but on average far fewer people die each year from terrorist acts than from the annual toll of U.S. homicides (25,000 Americans were murdered in 2002). Statistically, it is said that a person is more likely to be struck by lightning than by an act of terrorism. Note, however that casualty rates have begun to climb dramatically since 1995 and fears of mass destruction through terrorism have risen since 9/11.

SOURCE: Office of the Coordinator for Counter-Terrorism, U.S. Department of State.

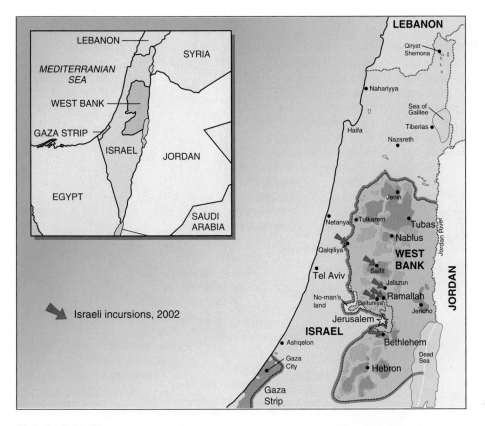

MAP 11.2
**The Dance of Death in the Middle East's Cauldron of Terror—the West Bank
Flash Point**

The state of Israel was carved in 1948 from the former British Protectorate of
Palestine—home of Muslim Arabs—and ever since a reign of tension and terror has
prevailed in the disputed West Bank area that was excluded from the original
settlement and taken from the Arab state of Jordan. Palestinian settlers remain the
region's majority population, but ever since the 1967 Six Day War Israel has established
a large number of settlements in this region, known as Judea in ancient times, and has
balked at ceding the disputed territory back to the Palestinian Arabs in order to end the
repeated and growing waves of Palestinian suicide terrorist attacks. In 2002 terrorist
fighting escalated when the United States removed itself from engagement in the so-
called peace process, and many innocent bystanders were killed. This map outlines the
troubled West Bank and identifies the major arenas of terrorist and counterterrorist
activities.

September 11 is now being practiced in what appears to be unprecedented
ways. Terrorism was no longer a marginal menace in other countries to be
watched on the evening news. 9/11 was a sadistic assault which exposed a previously complacent community's vulnerability to an enemy that recognized no
moral restraints, that was relentless in pursuit of violence, and that claimed to
be poised to strike anyone, anything, anywhere, anytime.

There *is* much that is new and therefore different about terrorism today
from the terrorism of the late twentieth century, prior to September 11. The two

AP/Wide World

Passions Aroused by Terrorism In reaction to Palestinian suicide bombings in 2002 Israeli Prime Minister Sharon ordered the construction of an "anti-terrorism" fence to keep militant Palesstinian terrorists from entering territory controlled by the state of Israel.

epochs can be distinguished, which is why many observers have asserted that *everything* has changed and that September 11 likely will be remembered as "the day the world changed."

What arguably has made September 11 a historic watershed ushering in a new age is that it marked the advent of new rules for a violent old game by the weak against the strong, but now conducted by ideological terrorists with grandiose revolutionary ambitions acting transnationally to transform the international *status quo*. Prior to 9/11, the primary purpose of terrorism was publicity, to elicit attention and sympathy for the terrorist's cause. Accordingly terror was previously regarded as mainly theater, and it was often observed that "terrorists want a lot of people watching, not a lot of people dead." No longer. Terrorists now began to engage in new practices for new purposes— intentionally seeking not simply to coerce changes in enemies' policies, but to

Terrorist Mastermind
The 9/11 terrorist attacks were coordinated by one man—Osama bin Laden, the wealthy Saudi expatriate, former CIA employee in the Afghan resistance against the Soviet Union, and zealous Islamic revolutionary shown here who financed and organized the Al Qaeda terrorist network responsible for the September 11 attack. The question is whether terrorism is primarily the product of individual fanatics motivated by religious, political, and ideological beliefs, or whether it arises from other sources such as poverty (Kaminski 2002), religion (Rubenstein 2003), or a clash between opposed civilizations (Howell 2003).

annihilate enemies; they now wanted a lot of people dead. In the past, when terrorists hit targets, they killed small numbers of people with modest weapons; 9/11 was a transformative step in a new direction, killing many more people than those who had perished in the December 7, 1941, Japanese attack on Pearl Harbor. The most deadly attack on U.S. territory in history, 9/11 signaled the specter of permanent terrorism throughout the globe—unless unchecked—with, as U.S. President George W. Bush pictured the scene in his January 2002 State of the Union address, thousands of "dangerous killers"—"ticking time bombs"—roaming the globe and eager to destroy, especially dangerous because these networks of global terrorists "threaten us with the world's most destructive weapons."

To Bush, "Night fell on a different world," marking not only, in his words, "the first war of the twenty-first century," but also inaugurating a defining moment. "We have found our mission and our moment." "The way I view this is that we're fighting evil, and I don't see any shades of gray." In April 2002, Bush's national security advisor, Condoleeza Rice, echoed his interpretation, declaring "an earthquake of the magnitude of 9/11 can shift the tectonic plates of international politics."

To be sure, there are many elements of truth in all these claims about the sea change that commenced. A new disease can be said to now stalk the face of the earth, a contagion that will severely test the targets' perseverance. And it raises unfamiliar issues. What is different today is that the new age of terrorism is

- Global, in the sense that with the death of distance borders no longer serve as barriers to terrorism
- Lethal, because now terrorists have shifted their tactics from theatrical violent acts seeking to alarm for publicity to purposeful destruction of a target populated entirely by civilian noncombatants, to kill as many as possible for the purpose of instilling fear in as many people as possible
- Novel, in the sheer size, destructiveness, and professionally coordinated planning of the September 11 attack
- Waged by civilians without state sanction in ways and by means that erase the classic boundaries between terrorism and a declared war between states
- Reliant on the most advanced technology of modern civilization to destroy through those sophisticated technological means the modern civilization seen as posing a threat to the terrorist's sacred traditions
- Orchestrated by transnational nonstate organizations through global conspiratorial networks of terrorist cells located in many countries, involving unprecedented levels of communication and coordination
- Pursued by fanatical extremists to annihilate through maximal bloodshed rather than to persuade, by carrying out crimes against humanity by suicidal methods requiring the terrorists to sacrifice their own lives in acts that cannot be deterred or prevented through negotiated compromise
- Driven by hatred of the target—by terrorists' desire to make the target suffer for what the target is, what it does, and the values for which the target stands

These changes will require a new compass to travel through the new global landscape, and new approaches to contain another wave of increasingly deadly global terrorism.

Counterterrorism. The nature of terrorism has been redefined to take account of terrorism's changing and multifarious characteristics. Terrorism is no longer seen as a conflict between enemies, but instead as a war of global dimensions that involves anyone and everyone. The globalization of the new terrorism was expressed by U.S. President George W. Bush, who declared that "our enemy is a radical network of terrorists and every government that supports them," and accordingly the war of terrorism "will not end until every terrorist group of global reach has been found, stopped, and defeated." The very definition of terrorism thus has been enlarged by his view that on September 11 "enemies of freedom committed an act of war" which would be fought to the end "to bring justice to our enemies" and that *all* would have to participate in this quest, one way or the other: "every nation in every region now has a decision to make," said President Bush, "either you are with us or you are with the terrorists."

Disagreement about the character and the cause of global terrorism past, present, and future remains pronounced, and, without agreement on these preliminaries, agreement on the best response to the new global terrorism is unlikely. Much like a disease which cannot be treated until it is first accurately diagnosed, so the plague of the new terrorism cannot be prevented until it is first defined, and successful strategies of control are contingent upon understanding its causes. Hence, "While the resolve to do whatever necessary to combat terrorism will remain undiminished, a great debate has already begun: What exactly is to be done? The answer will depend in large measure on the answer to a prior question, "What happened [on September 11] and why?" (Talbott and Chanda, 2002).

Those persuaded by one particular image of terrorism's character and primary causes are inevitably drawn to a particular set of policy recommendations, while those persuaded by a competing constructed image inevitably embrace an entirely different set of counterterrorist policy prescriptions and programs.

Consider the diametrically opposed views of whether repression or conciliation is the most effective remedy (see Controversy: Can the War against Global Terrorism Be Won?). Those advocating the former harsh approach see terrorism springing from the rational decisions of extremists to rely on political violence, and they advise prevention and even preemptive strikes that promise surgical attacks to kill terrorists, and failing that, swift and severe retaliation. In contrast are those who see terrorism rooted in frustrations with political oppression and deprivation; they recommend addressing these root causes in order to contain terrorism, taking as their point of departure the November 2, 1972, UN resolution that concluded: "measures to prevent international terrorism [require] study of the underlying causes of those forms of terrorism and acts of violence which lie in misery, frustration, grievance and despair." To those of this persuasion, long-term reforms and short-term conciliatory policies are proposed.

At issue therefore is how in fighting the new global terrorism should the line be drawn between the legitimate and illegitimate uses of military force. The debate about methods for waging a **just war** against the new global terrorism revolves around a series of interconnected issues: Are the policies effective? Ethical? Compatible with other values such as the preservation of civil liberties and democratic procedures? Require multilateral (international) cooperation (or can they be engineered through unilateral, go-it-alone independent national solutions?) Can technology provide a barrier? Can global terrorism be addressed through legal or institutional procedures? What are the relative benefits and costs of counterterrorist measures defined by the categories prevention, protection, and prosecution?

The dangers of stereotypes and the responses they rationalize show why the prospects are dim for eradicating terrorism through negotiated settlements and, conversely, also why combating terrorism through hard military operations tends to legitimize violence and thereby may inadvertently encourage further terrorist actions. The record of past efforts that have relied on these "solutions" reveals their deficiencies. Consider the impotence of promising punitive retaliation to acts of terrorism when those threats are not carried out: "although terrorists attacked U.S. interests more than 2,400 times between 1983 and 1998, the United States responded with overt military action only three times" (Reinares 2002, 92). Although most experts would agree that whereas "it is not possible to extirpate terrorism from the face of the globe," they share faith in the more modest goal—that "it should be possible to reduce the incidence and

■ **just war**
the theory originating in the Middle Ages that identifies the conditions under which it is morally permissible, or "just," for a state to go to war and the methods by which a just war might be fought.

CONTROVERSY

CAN THE WAR AGAINST GLOBAL TERRORISM BE WON?

In the wake of September 11, a new conventional wisdom has arisen—namely, in the words of U.S. Secretary of Defense Donald Rumsfeld, that "if the [United States] learned a single lesson from September 11, it should be that the only way to defeat terrorists is to attack them. There is no choice. You simply cannot defend in every place at every time against every technique. All the advantage is with the terrorist in that regard, and therefore you have no choice but to go after them where they are." This reflects the view that even if appeasement is tempting, the only way to respond is relentlessly and thoroughly.

A persistent and punitive approach to the eradication of global terrorism is the war on which the United States has embarked, as reflected in President George W. Bush's pledge: "You know, when I first started commenting about this new war, I reminded people that the farther we get away from September 11, the human mind is such that they'll want to forget the terror and the tragedy. . . ."

Exactly what *is* the right thing to do to control the new global terrorism is likely to remain controversial, as President Bush warned. Many experts question his characterization of the problem and the ambitious crusade he promised to undertake, including skeptical allies on whom the United States is dependent if the antiterror war is to be won. *Operation Enduring Freedom* to conduct a worldwide war requires an enduring commitment at very high costs. That is why proposals for an effective and just response to the new global terrorism differ, as do recommendations about how the world can most effectively reduce the probability that September 11 will never be repeated.

What makes counterterrorism so controversial is that strategists often fail to distinguish different types of terrorist movements and their diverse origins and therefore construct counter-terrorist strategies in the abstract—with a single formula—rather than tailoring approaches for dealing with terrorism's alternate modes. As one expert advises, "One lesson learned since September 11 is that the expanded war on terrorism has created a lens that tends to distort our vision of the complex political dynamics of countries" (Menkhaus 2002).

What do you think? If terrorism is the problem, and the goal is its complete eradication, how should those pursuing that quest proceed? In evaluating proposed controls in the fight against the latest wave of global terrorism, you will need to confront a series of incompatible clichés and conclusions: "concessions only encourage terrorists' appetite for further terrorism" as opposed to "concessions can redress the grievances that lead to terrorism," or "terrorism requires a long-term solution" as opposed to the claim that "terrorism cannot be cured but it can be prevented by preemption." Your search for solutions will necessarily spring from incompatible assumptions you make about terrorism's nature and sources, and these assumptions will strongly affect your conclusions about the wisdom or futility of contemplated remedies. Keep in mind that what may appear as a policy around which an effective counterterrorist program might be constructed could potentially only exacerbate the problem by provoking the very result your preferred plan was designed to solve: recourse to future terrorist actions. Counterterrorism is controversial because one person's solution is another person's problem, and the answers are often unclear. A counterterrorist program that may succeed in one location may backfire in another. Because promise and/or peril may result when the same countermeasure is deployed, what would you advise governments about the best methods of fighting terrorism?

effectiveness of terrorism." Maintaining a proper balance between respect for freedom and a capacity for decisive resolute action will prove to be a substantial challenge in the "war" against the new global terrorism.

It is unlikely that the danger of terrorism will decline. Indeed, terrorism has become more deadly and harder to curb in the borderless globalized system that makes the practice of terrorism so effortless. The previous reasons for terrorist activity remain as strong as ever, and the **information age** makes transnational networking among terrorist groups convenient. The new International Convention for the Suppression of the Financing of Terrorism adopted by the UN in 2000 failed to curb terrorist activity, despite the best of intentions, in an increasingly interdependent world which facilitates the free movement of people and goods across national borders. Adding to the persistent threat is that contemporary terrorism has become more radicalized and more violent. "Any survey of the world map of terrorism—the part of the world where the most casualties occur—reveals not only growing fanaticism but also the growth of indiscriminate murder, the desire to exercise power, and sheer bloodlust. In recent years, terrorists have become less hesitant to inflict heavy casualties and cause physical destruction" (Laqueur 2001). As former U.S. Secretary of Defense William Cohen warns, terrorism today is now the work of "cowards who rejoice in the agony of their victims" and are willing to use weapons of mass destruction (WMD, the initials preferred to ABC for atomic, biological, chemical weapons). Because terrorists now have available a variety of new tactics, such as the use of electronic threats so they can practice "cyber-terrorism" and engage in "Netwar" strategies, the dangers are climbing.

International terrorism is certain to persist for still other reasons. One of the most important and potent is the condition that Walter Laqueur terms **postmodern terrorism.** This phrase describes the globalized environment which today makes terrorism easy to practice. So-called postmodern terrorism is likely to expand because the globalized international environment without meaningful barriers allows terrorists to practice their ancient trade by new rules and methods, while at the same time encouraging state-sponsored terrorism as a substitute for warfare and making the most advanced countries the most vulnerable (Laqueur 2003). Another reason is the rapid spread of new weapons and technology, and their easy transport across borders, which provide unprecedented opportunities for terrorists to commit atrocities and to change their tactics in response to successes in countering them. A third reason is the growing difficulty in a globalized system of detecting and deterring the attacks of disciplined globalized terrorist networks that are generously funded by international organized crime (IOC) syndicates to facilitate their profit in the narcotics trade. And still another reason is the moral ambiguity that surrounds the activities of extremist militia, such as suicide bombers, who are glorified as religious martyrs. In addition, some of the mass media praise terrorists for their independent defiance of government authority.

Terrorists appear destined to be regarded either as hated villains or as honored heroes, depending on the view of the observer. This ensures that terrorism is likely to remain a fixture of twenty-first-century politics and that violence will continue to cast its shadow over international relations.

Could it be that a world so ingenious in perpetrating violence also will learn that war and violence are too costly, too destructive to continue? If so, can it discover effective paths to sustained peace? Can "the transformation of the warfare state into the welfare state" (Ferguson 2001) progress on its winding road? The chapters that follow examine some of the methods for controlling military conflict that policymakers and concerned global citizens have proposed.

■ **information age**
the era in which the rapid creation and global transfer of information through mass communication and the Internet is contributing to the globalization of knowledge.

■ **postmodern terrorism**
to Walter Laqueur, the terrorism practiced by an expanding set of diverse actors with new weapons "to sow panic in a society, to weaken or even overthrow the incumbents, and to bring about political change."

KEY TERMS

war
conflict
politics
armed conflict
behavioralism
constructivism
deterrence
long peace
levels of analysis
intraspecific aggression
interspecific aggression
realism
pacifism
survival of the fittest
nature versus nurture
socialization
territorial imperative
national character
rational choice

groupthink
state level of analysis
neorealism
sovereignty
intervention
feminist theory
cultural conditioning
communist theory of imperialism
laissez-faire economics
globalization
relative gains
neoliberal theories
human rights
democratic peace
nationalism
global level of analysis
self-help
security dilemma

anarchy
power transition theory
structural realism
long-cycle theory
hegemon
war weariness hypothesis
civil war
relative deprivation
ethnic warfare
displaced people
failing states
human development index (HDI)
diversionary theory of war
terrorism
state-sponsored terrorism
just war
information age
postmodern terrorism

SUGGESTED READING

Art, Robert J., and Kenneth N. Waltz, eds. *The Use of Force: Military Power and International Politics,* 6th ed. Lanham, Md.: Rowman & Littlefield, 2002.

Boot, Max. *The Savage Wars of Peace: Small Wars and the Rise of American Power.* New York: Basic Books, 2002.

Coker, Christopher. *Waging War without Warriors? The Changing Culture of Military Conflict.* Boulder, Colo.: Lynne Rienner, 2002.

van Creveld, Martin. *The Art of War: War and Military Thought.* London: Cassell, 2002.

Dershowitz, Alan M. *Why Terrorism Works: Understanding the Threat, Responding to the Challenge.* New Haven, Conn.: Yale University Press, 2002.

Gilpin, Robert. *War and Change in World Politics.* Cambridge, Eng.: Cambridge University Press, 1981.

Hedges, Chris. *War Is a Force That Gives Us Meaning.* New York: Public Affairs, 2002.

Henderson, Errol A. *Democracy and War: The End of an Illusion?* Boulder, Colo.: Lynne Rienner, 2002.

Holsti, Kalevi J. *War, the State, and the State of War.* New York: Cambridge University Press, 1996.

Kegley, Charles W., ed. *The New Global Terrorism: Characteristic, Causes, Controls.* Upper Saddle River, N.J.: Prentice Hall, 2003.

Lemke, Douglas. *Regions of War and Peace.* Cambridge, Eng.: Cambridge University Press, 2002.

Midlarsky, Manus I. ed. *Handbook of War Studies II.* Ann Arbor: University of Michigan Press, 2000.

WHERE ON THE WORLD WIDE WEB?

CAIN Web Service

http://cain.ulst.ac.uk/index.html

The Conflict Archive on the Internet (CAIN) is a joint project of three educational institutions in the United Kingdom (the University of Ulster, the Queen's University of Belfast, and the Linen Hall Library) that seeks to provide information on the ongoing conflict in Northern Ireland, historically known as "the Troubles." There are links to descriptions of the key events and issues of this long-term conflict and background on society in Northern Ireland. The site also includes full-length articles and lectures on the conflict that would be good sources for a research paper.

Dreams of Tibet

http://www.pbs.org/wgbh/pages/frontline/shows/tibet/

PBS Online offers this very educational Web site devoted to issues surrounding Tibet and its quest for independence. View the chronology of Tibet's history starting in the year 600. Then read background about Tibetan Buddhism and find out who the Dalai Lama is. Review over ten interviews, including those with Jamyang Norbu, a Tibetan author in exile; actor Richard Gere, who is a "free Tibet" activist; and Martin Scorsese, who directed the movie *Kundun,* based on the biography of the Dalai Lama. The site includes excerpts from media articles and reports on the tenuous relationship between Tibet and the Chinese government. You can share your own thoughts in a discussion forum.

INCORE

http://www.incore.ulst.ac.uk/cds/countries/index.html

The University of Ulster has developed an Internet Guide for the Initiative on Conflict Resolution and Ethnicity that allows you to examine the most recent international conflicts and nationalist movements in detail. Clearly arranged by geographic location, this site offers information about conflict from Kosovo to Ethiopia and Eritrea. Read about the Kurds' quest for their own state. There are links to research sources, news sources, maps, nongovernmental organizations, and email lists and newsgroups. You can also gather information according to theme. Want to know how war affects children? Visit the Children and Conflict link.

Institute for War and Peace Reporting

http://www.iwpr.net/

Students of international relations often have a hard time getting up-to-date information from conflict areas that is not heavily censored by government agencies. The main goal of the Institute for War and Peace Reporting (IWPR) is to bring unbiased information on international conflicts to Internet users. An independent media resource, IWPR informs readers on international conflicts and supports media development in war-torn areas. Special reports provide in-depth analysis of conflict, media, and human rights issues in regions across the globe. Read reports from Central Asia, the Balkans, and the Caucasus as events unfold. There is also an extensive list of Internet links for those who want more information on the conflicts.

International Crisis Group

http://www.intl-crisis-group.org/

The International Crisis Group (ICG) is a private, multinational organization dedicated to understanding and responding to international crises. The organization's analysts conduct field research and prepare reports about ongoing conflicts that are used to make recommendations to states' decision makers. Currently, ICG has projects in northern and central Africa, the Balkans, and Southeast Asia. Students who are interested in these regional conflicts will find useful overviews of specific countries, reports on developments, and maps.

War, Peace, Security Guide

http://www.cfcsc.dnd.ca/links/wars/index.html

The Canadian Forces College has created an information resource center on war and peace at this Web site. Graphical links to armed forces, peace and disarmament sites, and military information are available. Visit the clickable map of world conflicts. Choose two contemporary conflicts to explore. Who are the main combatants? What are the main issues? Can you identify any similarities between the two conflicts? Do you have any suggestions for resolution to the conflict? Are other international actors a help or a hindrance to the conflict?

INFOTRAC® COLLEGE EDITION

Search for the following articles in the InfoTrac database:

Serebriannikov, V. V. "On Cold and Hot Wars," *Military Thought* March–April 2002.

Kagan, Donald. "A Look at the Great Wars of the Twentieth Century," *Naval War College Review* Autumn 2000.

Bennett, D. Scott, and Allan C. Stam III. "The Duration of Interstate Wars, 1816–1985," *American Political Science Review* June 1996.

Van Evera, Stephen. "Hypotheses on Nationalism and War," *International Security* Spring 1994.

For more articles, enter:

"war" in the Subject Guide, and then go to subdivision "analysis."

"war" in the Subject Guide, and then go to subdivision "causes of."

"Persian Gulf War, 1991" in the Subject Guide.

MILITARY POWER AND NATIONAL SECURITY IN THE AGE OF GLOBALIZED TERRORISM

T O P I C S   A N D   T H E M E S

- **Power in international politics**
  What is "national security"?
  How states' military capabilities compare
  The changing nature of world power

- **The quest for military capabilities**
  Trends in military spending
  Changes in military capabilities
  Trends in weapons technology
  The proliferation problem

- **The great powers' national security strategies**
  The new U.S. grand strategy
  Russia's new strategy
  China's global clout and security posture
  Japan's search for a strategy
  Germany and the European Union search for a strategic vision
  Can an insecure world escape the security dilemma?

- **CONTROVERSY** DOES HIGH MILITARY SPENDING LOWER HUMAN SECURITY?

- **CONTROVERSY** A REVOLUTION IN WARFARE? THE NEXT GENERATION OF LETHAL AND NONLETHAL WEAPONS

CORBIS

The thriving
international trade in
the weapons of war
and terrorism.

It is an unfortunate fact that we can only secure peace by preparing for war.

—JOHN F. KENNEDY, U.S. presidential candidate, 1960

*I went into the British Army believing that if you want peace you must
prepare for war. I now believe that if you prepare thoroughly for war you
will get it.*

—SIR JOHN FREDERICK MAURICE, British military officer, 1883

Armed conflicts are frequent and destructive. Whenever and wherever they break out, they incite tension and terror. These features explain why states are preoccupied with security threats and why preparing for defense is a nearly universal preoccupation. Because the anarchical global system requires that states rely on **self-help** for protection, **national security**—a country's psychological freedom from fear of foreign aggression—is of paramount priority on policymakers foreign policy agendas.

This chapter examines why states often respond to perceived threats by arming. We begin by considering the place of power in the interdependent age of globalized world politics. We then evaluate states' efforts to reduce threats to their security, exploring trends in military spending (and their domestic socioeconomic consequences), the arms trade, and weapons technology. Later chapters will use this discussion to examine the dilemmas that armament acquisitions create, how weapons are used for coercive diplomacy, and which paths to peace realists and liberals advocate for escaping the danger of war.

■ **self-help**
the principle that because
in international anarchy all
global actors are
independent, they must rely
on themselves to provide
for their security and well-
being.

■ **national security**
a country's capacity to resist
external or internal threats
to its physical survival or
core values.

■ **power**
the factors that enable one
state to coerce another; to
realists, arms and military
capabilities are the most
important factor in
determining which state will
win a dispute (see p. 37).

POWER IN INTERNATIONAL POLITICS

What is this abstraction called **power,** which realists assume to be states' primary objective? Most leaders schooled in realpolitik conventionally operate from the traditional assumption that power is something which gives states the ability to promote national interests, to win in international bargaining, and to shape the rules governing the global system. Leaders thus view power primarily as a political phenomenon revolving around the capacity of one actor to persuade another to do what it otherwise would not. Thus, we will first evaluate this definition, which sees power as **politics**—the exercise of influence to control and dominate others. But we must keep in mind that power is an ambiguous concept (see Claude 1962; Rothgeb 1993) and therefore it is difficult to determine how states' power should be measured.

When we view power as the means to control, it is reasonable to ask, when **conflict** occurs, who is stronger and who is weaker to predict which party will get its way and which will be forced to make concessions. These considerations invite the more fundamental question: What enables states to achieve their goals?

THE ELEMENTS OF STATE POWER

To determine the comparative power of states, analysts usually rank them according to the capabilities or resources presumed necessary to achieve influence over others. For such purposes, multiple factors (most significantly, military and economic capability) measure countries' relative **power potential.** If we could compare each state's total capabilities, according to this logic, we could then rank them by their ability to draw on these resources to exercise influence. Such a ranking would reveal the global system's hierarchy of power, differentiating the strong from the weak, the great from the marginal.

Of all the components of state power, military capability is regarded by realists as the central element in states' power potential. "Throughout history, the decisive factor in the fates of nations has usually been the number, efficiency, and dispositions of fighting forces," they argue. "National influence bears a direct relationship to gross national strength; without that, the most exquisite statesmanship is likely to be of limited use" (German 1960). Because **realism** assumes that the ability to coerce is more important than the ability to reward or to purchase, realists reject the view of other neoliberal strategic thinkers that under conditions of twenty-first century **globalization,** economic resources will be increasingly more critical to national strength and human security than military capability.

Following traditional thinking, one way to estimate the power potential of states is to compare the extent to which they spend money on acquiring military capabilities. Figure 12.1 presents a ranking that taps what most people would likely regard as the world's most "powerful" states, according to their expenditures to wage war.

Money is not the measure of a man, or of a country. Yes, a state can spend without concern for cost in an effort to reach the elusive goal of obtaining national security. But there is never a guarantee that bucks will translate into bangs, or that, in the U.S. case, the $2.1 *trillion* that the Bush administration plans to spend on the military between 2003 and 2008 will automatically increase U.S. safety or reach the fighting men and women in the field. The size of the defense budget does not matter as much as how it is spent—whether it goes to the needs that really matter, such as protecting citizens in an effective homeland security system and protect a country from terrorist attacks, or

■ **politics**
the process by which important values are upheld or compromised when two or more actors become involved in a conflict in which a gain for one party will create a partial or total loss for the other party.

■ **conflict**
discord, often arising in international relations over perceived incompatibilities of interest.

■ **power potential**
the relative capabilities or resources held by a state that are considered necessary to its asserting influence over others.

■ **realism**
a paradigm based on the premise that world politics is essentially and unchangeably a struggle among self-interested states for power and position under anarchy, with each competing state single-mindedly pursuing its own national self-advantage without altruistic concern for others or sentimental attachment to moral values.

■ **globalization**
the processes by which the countries of the world are becoming linked to one another economically, politically, and militarily in interdependent bonds (see p. 21).

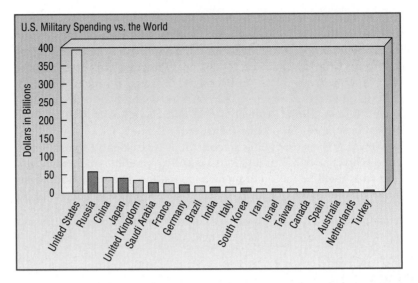

FIGURE 12.1

The Military Race for Hegemony: How the U.S. Military Spending Stacks Up against Its Competitors

All states seek safety from foreign attack, and many spend large sums of their national budgets for arsenals and armies for that defensive purpose. States vary widely, however, in their military expenditures. As this figure shows, the globe's "sole superpower" is the biggest spender on armaments, with U.S. President George W. Bush's proposed 2003 federal budget committing $396 billion for national security—more than the next twenty-six countries' military expenditures combined. The U.S. increase in 2002 of $48 billion was 13 percent above the past years' military budget (the single year's increase was larger than China's entire existing budget of $42 billion) (*Defense Monitor*, February 2002, 1). In terms of military spending as a measure, the United States stands at the apex of global power, predominate and without rival as a true hegemonic superpower. U.S. military spending overwhelms the $15 billion spent by "rouge" states.

SOURCE: Adapted with permission from *Defense Monitor*, Feb. 2002 p. 13.

whether the money is wisely spent. For the United States, the issue is critical. What are the returns for the investment? It now costs the average U.S. citizen $1,211 for defenses (as compared to $2.77 for international peacekeeping), and the anticipated U.S. increases now exceed the gross domestic product of over one-third of the globe's states (*Bulletin of the Atomic Scientists*, September/ October 2001, 35). The result has not paid large dividends, since the United States, the globe's greatest spender on defense, remains the primary target of and highly vulnerable to terrorist attacks (Crenshaw 2003).

Power potential also derives from factors other than military expenditures. Among the so-called elements of power, analysts take into account such capabilities as the relative size of a state's economy, its population and territorial size, geographic position, raw materials, degree of dependence on foreign sources of materials, technological capacity, national character, ideology, efficiency of governmental decision making, industrial productivity, volume of trade, savings and investment, educational level, national morale and internal solidarity, and especially "advances in technology and increases in social and economic transactions [which can] lead to a new world in which states, and their control of force, will no longer be important" (Koehane and Nye 2001b). For example, if power potential is measured by territorial size, Russia would be the globe's most powerful country, twice as large as its closest rivals (Canada, China, the United States, Brazil, and Australia, in that order). Likewise, if power is measured by the UN's projections for countries' populations by the year 2025, China, India, the United States, Indonesia, Pakistan, Nigeria and Brazil would, in that order, be the most powerful. In a similar comparison, the rankings of countries' expenditures on research and development to fund future economic growth and military might would rank Sweden, Finland, Japan, Switzerland, the United States, South Korea, and Germany as the countries with the brightest future to become world leaders in the pyramid of global power (*Economist*, October 27, 2001, 100). Clearly, strength is relative. The leading countries in some dimensions of power potential are not leaders in others, since power comes in many forms and the global spread of technology has made it increasingly difficult to distinguish between powerful and weak states.

There thus is little consensus on how best to weigh the various factors that contribute to military capability and national power; that is, there is no agreement as to what their relative importance should be in making comparisons, or what conditions affect the power potential of each factor. Although most analysts agree that states are not equal in their ability to influence others, few agree on how to rank their potential to exercise their power. Consider what divergent pictures of the global hierarchy emerge when the great powers relative capabilities are ranked in other categories that realists also define as especially important, such as the size of each state's economy and/or armed forces (see Maps 12.1 and 12.2).

Inferring Power from Capabilities

Part of the difficulty of defining the elements of power is that their potential impact depends (in a bargaining situation between conflicting actors, for example) on the circumstances and especially on how leaders perceive those circumstances. Such judgments are subjective, as power ratios are not strictly products of measured capabilities. Perceptions also matter.

In addition, power is not a tangible commodity that states can acquire. It has meaning only in relative terms. As Chapter 13 explains, power is relational: A state can have power over some other actor only when it can prevail over that actor. Both actual and perceived strength determine who wins in a political contest. To make a difference, an adversary must know its enemy's capabilities and willingness to mobilize those capabilities for coercive purposes. For example, it must regard the opponent's threat to use military capabilities as credible. Intentions—especially perceptions of them—are critically important when making threats. The mere possession of weapons does not increase a state's power if its adversaries do not believe it will use them.

Historically, those with the largest arsenals have not necessarily triumphed in political conflicts. Weaker states often successfully resist pressure from their military superiors. Although Vietnam was weak in the conventional military sense, it succeeded against a vastly stronger France and, later, United States. Similarly, U.S. superior military power did not prevent either North Korea's seizure of the USS *Pueblo* in 1968, Iran's taking of American diplomats as

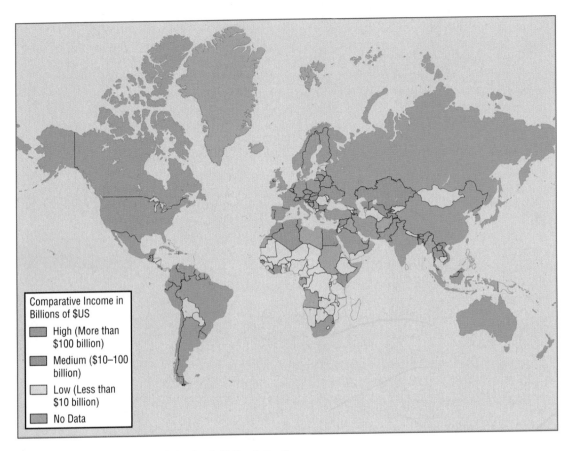

Comparative Income in
Billions of $US

High (More than
$100 billion)

Medium ($10–100
billion)

Low (Less than
$10 billion)

No Data

MAPS 12.1 AND 12.2
**Two Measures of Military Power Potential: National Wealth and the Size
of National Armies**

Many people look at economic indicators to measure national power, because a large
economy provides the means for acquiring the military capabilities necessary for
projecting political influence overseas. Indeed, wealth is a key measure of security and
political clout in the global marketplace, because rich countries possess the means of
exercising influence. The map on the left measures gross national income (GNI) across
countries to estimate national levels of economic well-being and shows the vast
differences in states' wealth that separate the rich from the poor (and the strong from
the weak?). Another measure of power projection is the number of the personnel in
uniform in states' armies, navies, and air forces. In the **information age** where high-
tech military equipment makes a huge difference, realists regard the size of a country's
armed forces as critically important in conducting modern warfare. This map on the
right shows the varying distribution of armed forces among the nations of the world.
SOURCE: National wealth, World Bank (2002c), 232–233; Armed forces personnel, World Bank
(2002b), 304–306.

■ **information age**
today's era in which mass
communication and the
Internet transfer information
instantaneously throughout
the globe.

hostages a decade later, or the Al Qaeda terrorist network's 9-11 attack on the
globe's reigning superpower. The Soviet Union's inability, prior to its disintegration, to control political events in Afghanistan, Eastern Europe, or even its
own constituent republics—despite an awesome weapons arsenal—shows that
the impotence of military power is not peculiar to the United States. History is
replete with examples of small countries that won wars or defended their inde-

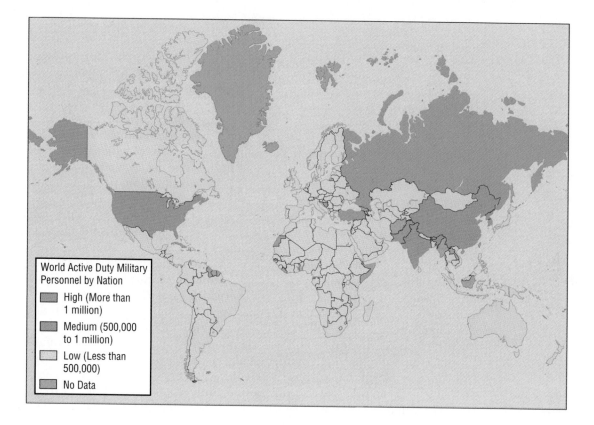

World Active Duty Military Personnel by Nation

- High (More than 1 million)
- Medium (500,000 to 1 million)
- Low (Less than 500,000)
- No Data

pendence against much more militarily powerful enemies. Think of Switzerland against the Hapsburg Empire, the Netherlands against Spain, and Greece against the Ottomans in the seventeenth century: In each case, intangible factors such as the will of the target population to resist against a more powerful army and their willingness to die to defend the homeland were a key element in the capacity of a weaker state to defend itself against a much stronger military force—as Great Britain reluctantly recognized in 1781 when it concluded that the price of conquering the American colonies was too great.

Nonetheless, the quest for security through arms and the realist belief in military force remain widespread. Most policymakers assume that "while it could be a mistake to assume that political influence is proportional to military strength, it would be an even bigger mistake to deny any connection between the two" (Majeed 1991). Many believe that this is because military capability is a prerequisite to the successful exercise of **coercive diplomacy** through the threat of limited force (see Chapter 13). Perhaps it was this conviction that inspired U.S. President George W. Bush to assert in 2000 that "a dangerous and uncertain world requires America to have a sharpened sword."

■ **coercive diplomacy**
the use of threats or limited armed force to persuade an adversary to alter its foreign and/or domestic policies.

The Changing Nature of World Power

Military power is central in leaders' conceptualizations of national security. As noted in previous chapters, however, many analysts now argue that "the sources of power are, in general, moving away from the emphasis on military force and conquest that marked earlier eras. In assessing international power today, factors such as technology, education, and economic growth are becoming more important, whereas geography, population, and raw materials are becoming less important" (Nye 1990). In part this is because military force has often proven ineffectual, notably against revisionist states and belligerent terrorist nonstate actors. Military superiority in raw numbers is especially questioned in the war against politically mobilized terrorist's movements, where intelligence and communications are arguably as important in counterterrorism as are military capabilities. Moreover, awareness of the importance of trade competitiveness to national standing has directed increasing attention to the nonmilitary dimensions of national security.

If we compare military, political, and trade strategies as alternative methods for realizing national security in the era of globalization, policies emphasizing economic and trade approaches to national power begin to appear increasingly effective as a strategy for acquiring political power and material advancement. Since 1945 only a handful of states have borne crushing military costs, while the others have gained a relative competitive edge by investing in research on the development of goods to export abroad and conserving resources by relying on allies and global institutions to provide defense against potential threats. While the United States (which in 2002 accounted for two-fifths of world military expenditures) has spent two-thirds of its research and development budget on military programs since the mid-1980s, European countries spent two-thirds on development of new technologies for consumers and civilians at home and abroad, and Japan's civilian product research exceeded 99 percent of all its research (SIPRI 2002).

■ **opportunity costs**
the concept in decision-making theories that when the opportunity arises to use resources, what is gained for one purpose is lost for other purposes, so that every choice entails the cost of some lost opportunity.

■ **peace dividend**
the global savings from arms expenditure reductions made possible by the end of highly hostile international rivalries such as the Cold War.

Military expenditures extract other **opportunity costs** as well that retard economic growth and create fiscal deficits. According to the International Monetary Fund (IMF), "military spending crowds out both private and public investment." Had U.S. military outlays remained at the 1990 levels established at the end of the Cold War, the **peace dividend** would have exceeded $400 billion in the next decade and potentially could have been made available for other purposes. The United States failed to do this, however, unlike many other countries. In addition to sacrificing other economic opportunities, this argument continues, military spending has direct costs, because expensive equipment quickly becomes outdated in the face of rapid technological innovations. This creates the need for even-more sophisticated new weapons, the costs of which are staggering.

Yet development of expensive new weapons, such as improved stealth aircraft and many others geared to fight the last century's threats, continue apace at the expense of lost revenue for other investments. At a time of uncontested U.S. military superiority, it was concern about reckless runaway spending on unneeded weapons that led U.S. Secretary of Defense Donald Rumsfeld in 2002 to cancel the contract on the army's expensive *Crusader* artillery program, even though Congress sought to fund its development.

Because "states can afford more 'butter' if they need fewer 'guns'" and eliminate plans to construct obsolete weapons, Richard Rosecrance (1997) notes, "the two objectives sometimes represent trade-offs: The achievement of one may diminish the realization of the other" and the substantial costs of defense can erode national welfare—what policymakers hope to defend with military might. Conversely, commercial clout and trade competitiveness for national exports may contribute more than military might to national power in a globalized marketplace without barriers to trade; in that setting, trade bloc competition replaces the military and diplomatic struggles of the past (see Controversy: Does High Military Spending Lower Human Security?).

Reuters/Corrine Dufka/Archive Photos

Who Pays for Defense? In many countries, military spending remains exceptionally high, and maintaining a large army comes at a high cost. Poor people often lose the most. One example is the United States. In October 1999, Stansfield Turner, a former director of the Central Intelligence Agency, complained that "Since the dawn of the nuclear age, the government has spent more than $5.5 trillion on nuclear forces, more than on education, the environment and transportation combined. . . . Cutting back our current force of more than 12,000 nuclear warheads . . . could save billions for schools, health insurance for the many children who lack it, Head Start and other needed initiatives." However, that proposal's acceptance is not likely, in part because of what President Dwight Eisenhower termed "the military-industrial complex," which continues to shape national budgets in the United States and elsewhere. Children often suffer unmet needs or are put in harm's way. In fact, outside the United States, children are frequently required to be soldiers. "Globally, an estimated 300,000 children are involved in 36 armed conflicts from the African jungles of Angola and Sudan to the Latin American mountains of Colombia and Peru; from Afghanistan to Indonesia; the Middle East and the Balkans. Fueled by civil wars, the numbers are climbing" (Schuler 1999). Here some of the newly trained child-soldiers ride through the streets of Monrovia in Liberia in April 1996, taking up arms to wage war on behalf of their government sponsors.

In addition to economic capability, other less-tangible sources of national power now figure more prominently in calculations regarding national defense, including the communications media empires' control of global information. "Political leaders and philosophers have long understood that power comes from setting the agenda and determining the framework of a debate. The ability to establish preferences tends to be associated with intangible power resources such as culture, ideology, and institutions." These intangible resources constitute *soft power*, in contrast with the *hard power* "usually associated with tangible resources like military and economic strength" (Nye 1990). Soft power is "the ability to achieve goals through attraction rather than coercion . . . by convincing others to follow or getting them to agree to norms and institutions that produce the desired behavior" (Keohane and Nye 2001b). If soft power grows in relative importance in today's so-called information age, military force ratios will no longer translate into power potential in the way they once did.

THE QUEST FOR MILITARY CAPABILITIES

How people spend their money reveals their values. Similarly, how governments allocate their revenues reveals their priorities. Examination of national budgets discloses an unmistakable pattern: Although the sources of global political power may be changing, many states continue to seek security by spending substantial portions of their national treasures on arms.

■ **national security**
a country's psychological freedom from fears that the state will be unable to resist threats to its survival and national values emanating from abroad or at home.

■ **human security**
a concept that refers to the degrees to which the welfare of individuals is protected and advanced, in contrast to national security, which puts the interests of states first.

■ **relative burden of military spending**
a measure of the economic burden of military activities calculated by the share of each state's gross domestic product allocated to military expenditures.

CONTROVERSY

DOES HIGH MILITARY SPENDING LOWER HUMAN SECURITY?

Politics requires making hard choices about priorities and about how public funds should be spent. One such difficult choice is between "guns versus butter"—how to allocate scarce finances for military preparedness as opposed to meeting the human needs of citizens and enabling them to live a secure and long life. The former category looks to arms for **national security**, and the latter stresses **human security.** Neither goal can be pursued without making some sacrifice for the realization of the other.

The "guns versus butter" trade-off is a serious controversy in every country, and different countries deal with it in different ways. That difference is captured by the range in states' willingness to pay a heavy burden for defense: by grouping states according to the share of gross national income (GNI) they devote to the military and then juxtaposing this relative burden with their GNI per citizen. The **relative burden of military spending,** the ratio of defense spending to GNI, is the customary way in which the sacrifices that

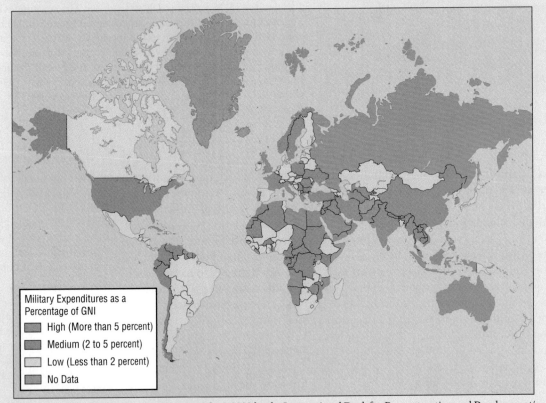

Military Expenditures as a Percentage of GNI

- High (More than 5 percent)
- Medium (2 to 5 percent)
- Low (Less than 2 percent)
- No Data

SOURCE: *World Bank Atlas 2002*, p. 50. Copyright © 2002 by the International Bank for Reconstruction and Development/ The World Bank. Reprinted by permission.

Trends in Military Spending

The weapons that governments believe they require for national security are costly. States' willingness to purchase military protection has kept world military spending high. "A decade after the end of the Cold War the decline in world military spending is changing into growth. It is a paradox that, in spite of an military spending requires is measured. As the map to the left shows, there exist wide variations, with many countries allocating high proportions of their total GNP to defense and other countries choosing to spend their wealth on enhancing human security. Indeed, note that some comparatively wealthy states (Kuwait, Israel, and Brunei) bear a heavy burden, whereas in contrast other states that provide a high average income for their citizens (Japan, Austria, and Luxembourg) have a low defense burden. Likewise, the citizens of some very poor countries (Sierra Leone, Mozambique, and Chad) are heavily burdened, whereas those of others (Bhutan and Zaire) are not. Thus, it is difficult to generalize about the precise relationship between a country's defense burden and its citizens' standard of living, human development, or stage of development.

"The problem in defense spending," as U.S. President Dwight D. Eisenhower observed in 1956, "is to figure how far you should go without destroying from within what you are trying to defend from without." How much should a country sacrifice for national security? To many realists, the price is never too high. However, others question this argument and maintain that the cost of high military spending reduces the states ability to provide for the human security of its citizens. This view was expressed by Eisenhower when he observed, "The world in arms is not spending money alone. It is spending the sweat of its children." This position was also argued by Oscar Arias, the 1987 Nobel Peace laureate and former president of Costa Rica who wrote in 1999 that "World leaders must stop viewing militaristic investment as a measure of national well-being. The sad fact is that half the world's governments invest more in defense than in health programs. If we channeled just $40 billion each year away from armies and into antipoverty programs in ten years all of the world's population would enjoy basic social services—education, health care and nutrition, potable water and sanitation. Another $40 billion each year over ten years would provide each person on this planet with an income level above the poverty line for his or her country."

The case of the United States, the globe's biggest spender on the military, speaks to Dr. Ariasa's proposition that high military spending reduces social welfare. Consider how the United States ranks on various nonmilitary indicators of human security:

U.S. Rank Compared to 160 Other States

Social Development

Percent population with safe water	1
Percent births attended by trained personnel	2
Female and male literacy rate	4
GNP for each person	5

Economic—Social Standing

Public health expenditures for each person	8
Public education expenditures for each person	9
Public education expenditures for each student	10
Maternal mortality rate	12
Infant mortality rate	13
Life expectancy	14
Percent school-age children in school	18
Under five mortality rate	18
Contraceptive prevalence	19
Percent infants with low birthweight	29
Number of physicians for each person	39
Number of teachers for each person	39

These rankings (UNDP 2000) suggest that when expenditures for arms go up, so do disease, illiteracy, and poverty, and the rate of economic growth goes down (Ward, Davis, and Lofdahl 1995). That said, every country is in need of a strong defense for national security. If you were a head of state, what budget priorities would you propose for your country's national security and your citizens' human security? How would you reconcile the need for defense with the need to provide for the common welfare? The choices you would make would be difficult, because they entail a necessary trade-off between competing values. For this reason military-spending decisions are highly controversial everywhere.

improved security environment in large parts of the world, since 1998 military expenditure has been rising in all regions [and] world military expenditure [in 2000] reached $798 billion (in current US dollars). . . . The amount of economic resources devoted to military activities is staggering when set in a global perspective. The overall level of world military spending in 2000 corresponds to . . . 2.5 percent of the world gross domestic product" (SIPRI, 2002).

Looking at the global military expenditures in 2000, the total of $798 billion exceeded more than $1.5 million each minute. However, world military spending could have been even higher had past levels continued. In fact, by 1998, it had declined by about a third since the peak year high of $1.35 trillion in 1987. Since 1998, however, expenditures have once again been rising, with the sharpest increases in Africa (37 percent between 1998–2000) and South Asia (23 percent), and the greatest absolute increases in Russia (44 percent) and the United States (2.3 percent) (SIPRI 2001).

Another impression results if the global outlay is measured in constant dollars adjusted for inflation. The 2000 level actually shows an increase over past levels, 2.7 times that spent in 1960, 1.9 times that of the 1970 total, and 1.2 times the 1980 level. These increases appeared especially noticeable in the 1980s, but on closer inspection they extend the growth rates of world military expenditures exhibited throughout the entire twentieth century. Military spending has increased fifteenfold since the mid-1930s. The growth-rate exceeded that of world population, the rate of expansion of global economic output, expenditures for public health to protect people from disease, and prices (U.S. ACDA 1997; Sivard 1991, 1993, 1996).

These aggregate figures require interpretation, because the global total spent for arms and armies conceals widely varying trends for particular groups of countries. Historically, the rich countries have spent the most money on arms acquisitions, a pattern that has continued. In 2000 the Global North spent $539 billion for defense, in contrast with the developing Global South's $259 billion. Thus the developed countries' share of the world total was 70 percent. However, when measured against other factors, the differences are not so great. Both groups spent exactly 2.6 percent of their GNPs, on average, on weapons, but the Global North's military spending as a portion of government revenues stood at 9 percent and the Global South's, at 13 percent. While these two groups' military spending levels were quite different, over time they are converging. The Global North's developed countries' expenditures declined 5.6 percent between 1985 and 1995, and the reduction of the Global South's developing countries fell only 1.7 percent. Since 1998, sharp rises in military spending in developing Asia and Africa, as noted above, support this trend of convergence. As Figure 12.2 reveals, the Global South's military expenditure in 1961 was about 7 percent of the world total, but by 2002 it had climbed threefold to approximately one-third. This trend indicates that poor states are copying the past, costly, military budgetary habits of the wealthiest states.

There are equally mixed regional and national variations in these levels and growth rates. The level of perceived threats in each region from potential or actual wars within (and, less frequently, between) states, and the spread of conventional and advanced weapons of mass destruction, exert a great impact on the rise or fall of states' levels of military spending. Similar variations are also exhibited in the rates of military expenditures across different regional organizations and military alliances.

Changes in Military Capabilities

The growing militarization of the Global South and of mobilized terrorist movements by nonstate actors manifests itself in other ways as well. Military capabilities are now more widespread than ever. Part of the reason is because weapons production capabilities are no longer concentrated in the industrial Global North.

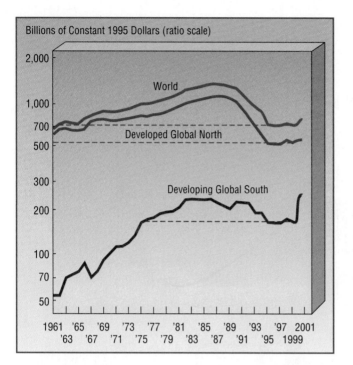

FIGURE 12.2

Changes in the Levels of Military Expenditures since 1960, Global North and Global South

Global military budgets have fluctuated since 1960, with total expenditures worldwide peaking in 1987, after which they fell about a third, but have been rising in the wake of the 9/11 war on terrorism (the United States spent more than $1 billion each month in the early phases of the intervention of Afghanistan, and budgets are expected to rise rapidly). As the trend lines show, the military budgets of the Global South's developing countries peaked in a 1982–1986 plateau, then declined before rising again since 1993 to more than $259 billion in 2000—about one-third of the world's total (U.S. ACDA 1997, 133; SIPRI 2001, 268). The Global North's defense spending began to decline after the threat of interstate wars receded in the wake of the Cold War, but has risen generally as the huge U.S. military budget increases pulled the developed countries' aggregate total higher, in excess of $539 billion in 2000. U.S. spending has widened considerably the gap between the United States and its great-power partners. "The gap in military capacity is so staggering that even professor Paul Kennedy, author of the highly influential *The Rise and Fall of the Great Powers* [in 1987], has now recanted the America-in-decline theory he fathered in the 1980s. Kennedy has been moved to express his awe at American resurgence: 'Nothing has ever existed like this disparity of power; nothing'" (in Krauthammer 2002).

SOURCES: 1961–1995, U.S. ACDA (1971). 1; 1996–2001 SIPRI (1999), 301, and www.SIPRI.

The Global South countries and terrorist organizations are now in the business of manufacturing modern aircraft, tanks, and missiles. A parallel change in the open and clandestine (secret) arms trade and in the destructiveness of modern weapons has accelerated the spread of military capabilities around the world.

Trends in the Weapons Trade.   During the Cold War's 40-year period of tension, many states sought to increase their security through the purchase of

Protecting National Security? Chinese missiles on display in Beijing

arms produced by suppliers eagerly seeking allies and profits. In 1961, world arms trade was valued at $4 billion. The traffic in arms imports thereafter climbed rapidly and peaked in 1987 at $82 billion (U.S. ACDA 1997, 10, 100). The end of the Cold War did not end the arms trade, however. Since 1991, the Global South developing countries have been the leading market for the traffic in arms (see Figure 12.3). Indeed, in the face of fierce competition among an expanding number of suppliers, the world's most advanced weapons were transferred to the Global South. The total value of all international arms deliveries between 1991 and 2001 exceeded $325 billion, of which 70 percent were exported to the developing countries (Grimmett 2002, 3).

Spurred by the developing countries' energetic search for armaments commensurate with those of the industrial countries, and their production of them for use at home and export abroad, the global arms trade has fueled the dispersion of military capability worldwide. Weapons delivered by major suppliers to developing countries between 1998 and 2001 included 3,252 tanks and self-propelled cannons, 2,158 artillery pieces, 821 supersonic combat aircraft, and a large number of warships, submarines, antishipping missiles, and other technologically advanced weapons systems (Grimmett 2002, 64).

The total value of international arms *deliveries* in 2001 was about $21 billion, a substantial decrease in the overall trend in the total value of all arms deliveries worldwide from the 1994–1997 period ($166 billion) and the $135 billion between 1998 and 2001 (Grimmett 2002, 3). In 2001, 69 percent of all global arms shipments were delivered to the developing countries. However, the recipients remain heavily concentrated in a subset of major Global South arms purchasers:

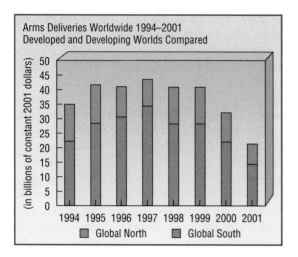

FIGURE 12.3
Arms Deliveries to the Global North and Global South, 1994–2001
The continuing global arms trade has led to the globalization of military capabilities throughout the Global North and especially the Global South. In 2001, arms deliveries were estimated to exceed $21 billion, and the estimated value of all global arms transfer agreements between 1998 and 2001 exceeded $131 billion (Grimmett 2002, 3). "During the years 1994–2001, arms deliveries to developing countries comprised 69 percent of all arms deliveries worldwide. Many Global South countries face the fear of collapsing in a civil war, or, as illustrated in the third war in 2002 between India and Pakistan, from an attack by a neighbor; in 2002, thirty-eight military conflicts were active and nearly all of them occurred within the poorer Global South developing countries (see Chapter 11). The least-stable states in recent years have spent among the largest percentages of their relatively small economies for the purchase of some of the most technologically advanced weapons of war available in the globalized arms market.
SOURCE: Grimmett (2002), 31.

between 1994 and 2001, weapon deliveries to the top ten recipients as a group accounted for half of all deliveries in the Global South. All of the top ten were in either Asia or the Middle East, with Saudi Arabia leading that group, spending $6.5 billion and accounting for almost half of the total deliveries. In rank order of the value of their purchases, the other leading recipients of imported arms after Saudi Arabia were Taiwan, South Korea, Egypt, China, United Arab Emirates, Kuwait, Israel, Malaysia, and Indonesia (Grimmett 2002, 59).

The regional distribution of arms deliveries seems to follow trends in the location of the world's flashpoints. The late 1990s, for example, saw the weapons trade gravitate toward the turbulent Asian region, which joined the feverish rush to purchase arms, spending $33 billion (32 percent) of the global total of imports between 1994 and 2001. The Middle East, with its numerous competitive states, is captive of an intense **arms race** as the main purchaser in the global arms market to seek to reduce its chronic national security problems. In the wake of the Persian Gulf War, rivalries endure between Israel and Palestine, Egypt and Libya, Iran and Iraq, Iran and Saudi Arabia, Iraq and Kuwait, Iraq and Syria, Iraq and Turkey, and Israel and Syria, and these states' high level of activity in the global arms market has continued. Middle Eastern countries accounted for 11 percent of world arms imports in 1967, and that share rose

■ **arms race**
the buildup of weapons and armed forces by two or more states that threaten each other, with the competition driven by the conviction that gaining a lead is necessary for security.

to 55 percent between 1998 and 2001. Recent brutal violence in the Israeli-Palestinian conflict has pushed arms sales in that region to an all-time high. In addition, the future is likely to see increased arms transfers to that theater for the global "war on terrorism" and increasing terrorist attacks from militant state and nonstate groups.

It is difficult to predict future trends in arms purchases. As mentioned above, regular shifts in procurement have occurred rapidly in response to emergent war and perceived threats. States' proportionate share of total weapons purchases is likely to change, depending on the location of the globe's next hot spots and each state's involvement in them. Similarly, aggregate levels of world arms imports are likely to be influenced by the performance of each state in the global economy, with activity fluctuating sharply from year to year and with weapons imported at high levels—not only in instable regions in countries where the risk of civil war and terrorism are high, in situations where pairs of enemy states are engaged in arms races, but also especially in countries when, in a period of growth in the business cycle, financial resources become available for arms purchases.

Alongside changing demands of arms importers, it is also important to observe changes in the activities of arms suppliers. During the Cold War the superpowers dominated the arms export market. Between 1975 and 1989 the U.S-Soviet share of global arms exports varied between one-half and three-fourths, and the United States alone had cornered 40 percent of the world arms export market when the Cold War ended (U.S. ACDA 1997, 19). In that period the two superpowers together "supplied an estimated $325 billion worth of arms and ammunition to the Third World" (Klare 1994, 139). But with the demise of the Soviet Union, the United States did not cease its supply of weapons worldwide: the U.S. reemerged as the unrivaled "arms merchant of the world" (a phrase used by then U.S. President Jimmy Carter to deplore what he sometimes regarded as an unsavory business). Between 1994 and 2001 the United States accounted for a higher proportion of worldwide contracts to sell arms than any other supplier, agreeing to weapons-export contracts exceeding $131 billion, or 44 percent of the $300 billion total worldwide. These contracts account for the suppliers' share of the arms that were *delivered* at the start of the twenty-first century.

> In 2001, the United States ranked first in the value of all international arms *deliveries*, making nearly $9.7 billion in such deliveries, or 45.6 percent [of $14.4 billion]. This was the eighth year in a row that the United States led in global arms deliveries, reflecting, in particular, implementation of arms transfer agreements made during and in the aftermath of the Persian Gulf War. The United Kingdom ranked second in worldwide arms deliveries in 2001, making $4 billion in such deliveries. Russia ranked third in 2001, making $3.6 billion in such deliveries. The top three suppliers of arms in 2001 collectively delivered nearly $17.3 billion, 81.2 percent of all arms delivered worldwide by all suppliers in that year. (Grimmett 2002, 3)

In this fierce race for income through arms sales, between 1994 and 2001 the United States, Russia, and France collectively made *agreements* for future sales of arms abroad that accounted for 70 percent of all the future arms transfer agreements by all suppliers (Grimmett 2002, 40). The U.S. monopoly on agreements rose to 34 percent of all arms deliveries, at $59.7 billion. The arms sale agreements already under contract assure that the arms trade will remain vigorous in the future, and that the United States will continue to be the largest exporter, followed by the other great powers.

Although the top ten major suppliers dominate the global arms market, the number of new suppliers has grown steadily, as many Global South developing countries also now produce arms for export. By 1990 more than sixty states had entered the business of "peddling arms" (Sivard 1991, 11). Still, most of these were small producers struggling for a share of the lucrative conventional armaments trade. In fact, for the countries in the Global South the struggle has not been very successful, considering their huge populations and combined economic clout; since 2001 they accounted for less than 8.7 percent of world arms exports (Grimmett 2002, 41).

A consequence of the increased competition for arms markets is the relaxation of export controls. The UN Register of Conventional Arms, begun in 1991 to monitor the weapons exports and imports of countries, has not curbed their sale. Supplier diversification, as well as joint ventures among arms manufacturers in different countries to produce and develop weaponry in a world where borders are no longer barriers, has ended many former solid supplier-consumer ties. Suppliers, it seems, are now eager to sell to any purchaser, and they continue the supply of weapons to both sides of a number of international disputes. To compound the danger, moreover, is the illegal export of nuclear, ballistic missile, and chemical weapons technology. As U.S. Secretary of Defense Donald Rumsfeld warned in May 2002, "terrorist networks have relations with terrorist states that have weapons of mass destruction and they [will get] their hands on them."

The threat of terrorists acquiring weapons of mass destruction on the black market through covert suppliers poses a real danger, although the extent of the threat is impossible to gauge, because this flow of the arms trade is invisible. Nonetheless, the absence of evidence is not evidence of absence. Terrorists are known to be actively searching for weapons of mass destruction, and as Rumsfeld warned it is likely they will succeed sooner or later. Consider this scenario: "It takes just a few kilograms of plutonium and less than 20 kilograms of highly enriched uranium to make a nuclear bomb [and] about 40 kilograms of weapons-usable uranium and plutonium have been stolen from poorly protected nuclear facilities in the former Soviet Union during the last decade. While most of that material has been retrieved, two kilos of highly enriched uranium taken from a research reactor in Georgia is still missing, and that's just for starters. The real amount of missing weapons-grade material [likely to be part of the illicit trafficking of nuclear material worldwide] could be 10 times higher than is officially known" (*USA Today* 130 [June 2002], 1).

Motives for the Arms Trade. Economic gain is an important rationale for foreign military sales, because producers sell arms abroad to subsidize their arms production at home. For example, the United States uses arms exports to offset its chronic balance-of-trade deficits and to ensure its lead in the lucrative arms business. In 1998, the United States assigned 6,493 full-time federal employees to handle U.S. arms deals and spent $477 million on promotional activities for U.S. arms dealers (*Harper's*, February 1998, 13). Following the disintegration of the Soviet Union, Russia sought to raise desperately needed hard currency by selling at bargain-basement prices its one product mix still in demand—weapons, weapons technology, and weapons expertise. Moreover, this aggressive sales campaign continues as "a cash-starved defense industry is selling Russian weapons to the world—latest models included" (Khripunov 1997). In February 2000, for example, Russia sold its most advanced destroyer armed with nuclear-capable missiles to China. In fact, Russia's $5.7 billion in arms sales agreements in 2001 was largely due to its deliveries of combat aircraft and ships to China. Cash is also the primary motive among other arms suppliers, for whom ideological considerations are virtually nonexistent.

Because the sale of weapons is big business, arms manufacturers constitute a powerful domestic lobby for the continuation of arms sales. A highly organized **military-industrial complex** is widely believed to exercise enormous power over defense budgets and arms sales agreements in both the United States and Russia. Arms manufacturers seek to increase their profits, and the best way of succeeding is by lobbying for military spending and the production and sale of new weapons in order to fill corporate coffers. The same pressures are operative in many other countries' civilian sectors for the same purposes (see Regan 1994).

The decline of interstate wars after the Cold War ended ironically increased states' incentives to sell arms merely for profit. Nonetheless, many states continue to sell arms (or make outright grants) for time-honored purposes: to support friendly governments, to honor allies' requests, and to cultivate cooperation. This was illustrated by U.S. arms export policy prior to and in the aftermath of the 1990 Persian Gulf War. The United States delivered 56 percent of the $101 billion in arms sold to the strife-torn Middle East between 1994 and 2001 (Grimmett 2002, 53, 5), allegedly for the purpose of anchoring allies and preserving the military balance of power in that explosive region. However, the profit motive, fueled in part by the desire of defense contractors to maintain income in an era in which many states are reducing their defense budgets, also continues to drive the for-profit sale of weapons across borders. As noted, an underground "black market" in weapons is flourishing and suggests that greed is behind many defense contractors' illegal participation in the global arms trade.

Recently, the United States had engaged in a program to encourage allies to co-fund weapons development initiatives such as the joint strike fighter program, introduced by the Bush administration in 2001. Facing increasing costs in arms production, the Pentagon thinks this would be the optimum way to continue production of what they see as necessary armaments. Some critics worry about the vulnerability of American security as allies involved in these programs are allowed access to sensitive weapons technology previously kept secret. In addition, antiproliferation advocates are concerned that involvement with other states in joint development efforts will make arms cuts nearly impossible, further fueling global weapons proliferation.

The Strategic Consequences of Arms Sales. Whether the arming of other countries has accomplished all of its intended goals is open to dispute. During the Cold War, for example, the United States and the Soviet Union thought they could maintain peace by spreading arms to politically pivotal recipients. Between 1983 and 1987 the United States provided arms to fifty-nine less-developed countries while the Soviet Union supplied forty-two (Klare 1990, 12). Yet many of the recipients engaged in war with their neighbors or experienced internal rebellion. Of the top twenty arms importers in 1988, more than half "had governments noted for the frequent use of violence" (Sivard 1991, 17). The toll in lives from the wars in the Global South since 1945 exceeds tens of mil-

■ **military-industrial complex**
the term coined by U.S. President Eisenhower to describe the coalition among arms manufacturers, military bureaucracies, and top government officials that promotes unnecessary defense expenditures for its own profit and power.

© Philip Wallick/Corbis

The Production of Weapons: Purchasing Protection or Protecting Profits? In the post–September 11 new age of global terrorism, U.S. military expenditures have climbed enormously to contain the threat. Many new weapons such as the SR-71 Blackbird, shown here, have been developed. Most are very expensive. Consider for example Boeing's 767-200 tanker designed to refuel an F-15, which the air force in 2002 renamed the A22 to reflect the fact that the new design with new weapons and enhanced air-to-ground capabilities was a new-generation fighter-attack jet. The manufacturer in 2002 sought a defense contract calling for $20 billion to be charged to the air force to lease one hundred of these refueling tankers, asking the Department of Defense to foot the bill for constructing the aircraft (at $150 million each), and pay $30 million to reconfigure each of the 767s for commercial use and ten years' later *give* the planes back to Boeing. It was this kind of cozy deal that reminded people of President Dwight Eisenhower's valedictory address in which he warned his fellow Americans "of the perils of ignoring the influence of what he christened the military-industrial complex. Ike's words have been repeated endlessly, and there have been countless editorials decrying 'beltway bandits' and their predilection for waste, fraud, and abuse" (*U.S. News & World Report*, May 13, 2002).

lions of people. Undoubtedly, the import of such huge arsenals of weapons from abroad aided this level of destruction. As the arms exporters "peddle death to the poor," they seldom acknowledge how this scouting for customers contradicts other proclaimed foreign policy goals. The U.S. arms export program, for example, undermines the current U.S. policy priority of promoting democracy, because no less than one-third (eighteen) of the recipients of U.S. arms exports were nondemocratic governments, which purchased $13.25 billion (41 percent) of the total U.S. arms sold ($32.43 billion) in 1993 (Blanton and Kegley 1997, 94–95).

Weapons for Sale The global arms trade is big business, and it remains brisk in many regions where perceptions of threats are intense. The Middle East, which accounts for more than two-thirds of global arms sales, is a prime example. Shown here are buyers examining a model of a warship at a defense exposition in Saudi Arabia in 1997. These "arms bazaars" are a regular feature of the global weapons market.

The inability of arms suppliers to control the uses to which their military hardware will be put is troubling. "The concern is that friends can become foes, and secrets can be stolen" (J. Brown 1999a). Loyalty is often a fragile commodity, and supplying weapons can backfire, as the United States discovered both when the weapons it sold to Iraq were used against U.S. forces by Saddam Hussein in the Persian Gulf War (Timmerman 1991) and when the Stinger missiles the United States supplied to Taliban forces resisting the Soviet Union's 1979 invasion in Afghanistan fell into the hands of terrorists later opposing the United States. Likewise, in 1982 Great Britain found itself shipping military equipment to Argentina just eight days before Argentina's attack on the British-controlled Falkland Islands (Sivard 1982), and in 1998 U.S. military technology sold to China was exported to Pakistan, making possible its nuclear weapons test.

Trends in Weapons Technology

The widespread quest for armaments has created a potentially explosive global environment. The description is especially apt when we consider not only trends in defense expenditures and the arms trade but also in the destructiveness of modern weapons.

Alain McLaughlin

Deadly Conventional Arms Sales The exact extent of global trade in so-called light conventional weapons is unknown, but growing. Of the armed conflicts fought worldwide since 1990, 90 percent were fought exclusively with small arms (*Harper's,* January 2000, 11), and small arms kill 300,000 people each year (*International Herald Tribune,* October 28, 2002, 8). In reaction, the UN Register of Conventional Arms in 1998 required that states' inventories and procurement of such weapons be reported. "Millions of the rifles now in the hands of the world's killers started out as legal weapons," Michael Renner (1999) warns. Shown here are M-16s from the El Salvadoran Battalion. This U.S.-trained unit massacred eight hundred civilians at El Mozote and murdered six Jesuit priests in San Salvador in 1989. During the Reagan-Bush years, the United States supplied El Salvador with 33,000 M-16s (Lumpe 1999).

Nuclear Weapons. Technological research and development has radically expanded the destructiveness of national arsenals. The largest "blockbuster" bombs of World War II delivered a power of ten tons of TNT. The atomic bomb that leveled Hiroshima had the power of over fifteen thousand tons of TNT. Less than twenty years later, the former Soviet Union built a nuclear bomb with the explosive force of fifty-seven megatons (million tons) of TNT. Since 1945 it is estimated that "more than 128,000 nuclear warheads had been built worldwide—all but 2 percent of them by the United States (55 percent) and the Soviet Union or Russia (43 percent)." Many have been dismantled, but in 2002 the global stockpile of intact nuclear warheads belonging to the world's eight nuclear states exceeded 30,000. Since its 1986 peak, the global nuclear arsenal has declined by 50 percent (*Bulletin of the Atomic Scientists,* (November/December 2002, 103). Even after these cuts, those nuclear warheads available for a strike collectively had the explosive force of over 1.3 million Hiroshima bombs.

The use of such weapons could destroy not only entire cities and countries but, conceivably, the world's entire population. Albert Einstein, the Nobel Prize–winning physicist whose ideas were the basis for the development of nuclear weapons, was well aware of the threat they posed. He professed uncertainty about the weapons that would be used in a third world war, but was confident that in a fourth they would be "sticks and stones." He warned that inasmuch as "the unleashed power of the atom has changed everything save our modes of thinking . . . we thus drift toward unparalleled catastrophe."

At the start of 2003, the number of operational nuclear stockpiles of the five major powers were estimated to total about 20,150 over strategic warheads. The U.S. arsenal then had 10,500 nuclear warheads, and Russia had about 8,600. In addition, France stockpiled an estimated 400 warheads; China had 400; Great Britain retained 200, and India and Pakistan were believed to have 100 nuclear warheads between them, and Israel as many as 200. Thus, in 2002 there were eight "official" members of the nuclear club—the United States, Russia, Great Britain, France, China, India, Pakistan and Israel. Moreover, Iraq and North Korea, in addition to as many as twenty states or nongovernmental terrorist organizations are generally believed the most likely to violate the spirit and law of the **Nuclear Nonproliferation Treaty (NPT)** by becoming members of the nuclear club (see Chapter 14). In short, the **proliferation** of arms is a serious global concern, because the so-called **Nth country problem** (the addition of new nuclear states) is expected to become an increasing likelihood. Both **horizontal nuclear proliferation** (the increase in the number of nuclear states) and **vertical nuclear proliferation** (increases in the capabilities of existing nuclear powers) are probable.

The obstacles to increased proliferation are fragile, as shown by the nuclear development programs of India and Pakistan in 1998 and the collapse of the nuclear test-ban's future following the U.S. rejection of the Comprehensive Test Ban Treaty (CTBT). The incentives to join the nuclear club and to acquire missiles and bombers for delivery are strong for several additional reasons.

First, the materials needed to make a nuclear weapon are widely available. This is partly due to the widespread use of nuclear technology for generating electricity. Today 428 nuclear power and research reactors are in operation in forty-four countries throughout the world (*Defense Monitor*, 1 [2000], 5). In addition to spreading nuclear know-how, states could choose to reprocess the uranium and plutonium, that power plants produce as waste, for clandestine nuclear weapons production. In the early 2000s, commercial reprocessing reactors were producing enough plutonium to make as many as forty thousand nuclear weapons.

Second, the scientific expertise necessary for weapons development has spread with the globalization of advanced scientific training. "In the near future it will be possible to duplicate almost all past technology in all but the most forlorn of Third World backwaters, and much of the present state-of-the-art will be both intellectually and practically accessible" (Clancy and Seitz 1991–1992).

Third, export controls designed to stop technology transfer for military purposes are weak. "A large and growing number of states can now export material, equipment, technology, and services needed to develop nuclear weapons" (Potter 1992). In addition, the leaks in nuclear export controls have weakened the antiproliferation regime (Krepon 2002). Conversion of peacetime nuclear energy programs to military purposes can occur either overtly or, as in the case of India and Pakistan, covertly. The safeguards built into the **nonproliferation regime** are simply inadequate to detect and prevent secret nuclear weapons development programs.

■ **Nuclear Nonproliferation Treaty (NPT)**
an international agreement that seeks to prevent horizontal proliferation by prohibiting nuclear weapons sales, acquistions, or production.

■ **proliferation**
the spread of weapon capabilities from a few to many states in a chain reaction, so that an increasing number of states gain the ability to launch an attack on other states with devastating (e.g., nuclear) weapons.

■ **Nth country problem**
the addition of new nuclear states.

■ **horizontal nuclear proliferation**
an increase in the number of states that possess nuclear weapons.

■ **vertical nuclear proliferation**
an increase in the capabilities of existing nuclear powers.

■ **nonproliferation regime**
rules to contain arms races so that weapons or technology do not spread to states that do not have them.

The ease with which Pakistan made a successful end-run around the technology-export controls illustrates the problem of control. In 1979, Pakistan quietly bought all the basic parts necessary for a uranium-enrichment plant, with funds supplied by Libya. Similarly, UN inspectors discovered after the Persian Gulf War that Iraq was much closer to building a nuclear weapon than previously suspected, despite UN restrictions and Iraq's continued pledge to adhere to the rules of the nonproliferation regime. Since 1997, until December 2002, Iraq successfully had resisted UN inspections to investigate possible production and storage sites for weapons of mass destruction within Iraq, as called for by the peace agreement. This illustrates the obstacles to preventing the illegal proliferation of weapons, as does the record elsewhere. No less than eight countries have constructed secret nuclear-production plants, underscoring the difficulties of managing effective inspections and monitoring nuclear developments (Albright 1993).

Fourth, nonnuclear weapons states have strong incentives to develop weapons similar to those of the existing nuclear club. They voice the complaint of former French President Charles de Gaulle, who argued that without an independent nuclear capability France could not "command its own destiny." Similarly, in 1960 Britain's Labour Party leader Aneurin Bevan asserted that without the bomb Britain would go "naked into the council chambers of the world." And in 1993 North Korea refused to allow monitoring of its five nuclear sites, and later, in 2002 admitted that it had secretly continued to operate a nuclear-weapon development program, despite pledges in exchange for technological assistance it would not.

Nuclear weapons serve as a symbol of status and power. Because of the widespread conviction rooted in realism that military might confers political stature, it is understandable why the nonnuclear powers regard the nuclear nonproliferation treaty as hypocrisy, which provides a seal of approval to the United States, Russia, China, Britain, and France for possessing nuclear weapons while denying it to all others. The underlying belief that it is acceptable to develop a nuclear capacity for deterrence, political influence, and prestige was expressed in 1999 by Brajesh Mishra, India's national security adviser to the Indian prime minister when he justified India's nuclear ambitions by asserting that "In the twenty-first century a new security order is likely to arise in the Asia-Pacific region, one in which India should be granted as much respect and deference by the United States and others as is China today."

It is unlikely that the nuclear threat will cease. "There's not a snowball's chance in hell we'll eliminate all nuclear weapons from the face of the earth," explains Matthew Bunn, editor of *Arms Control Today*. "That genie is long since out of the bottle and there's no chance of ever getting him back in." Moreover, a world nearing nuclear disarmament would not end the threat. "The problem is, if you eliminate them all, then any country that built just a few nuclear weapons would have enormous blackmail potential" (Davidson 1991).

That said, the most powerful nuclear states, the United States and Russia, took a bold step toward nuclear disarmament in May 2002 when they reached the Strategic Offensive Reduction Treaty (SORT) that pledged reducing their nuclear arsenals by two-thirds within the next ten years (see Figure 12.4). If enacted, that reduction will greatly reduce the number of nuclear warheads in the world. Whether that reduction will be followed by the other major powers remains to be seen. In the past, opportunities have been missed.

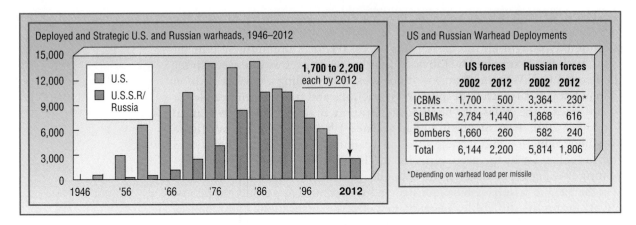

FIGURE 12.4

Caging the Nuclear Threat: The Rise and Fall of Deployed Strategic U.S. and Russian Warheads

The U.S.-Russian Moscow Treaty, or Strategic Offensive Reduction Treaty (SORT) of May 2002 promises to distance the former adversaries from the brink of nuclear destruction. Shown here is a comparison of their nuclear arsenals between 1946 and 2002, with the chart on the right breaking down both countries forces according to their warhead deployments.

SOURCES: Arms Control Association and the Carnegie Endowment for International Peace (left); *The Economist*, May 18, 2002, p. 30 (right). Copyright © 2002 by The Economist Newspaper Ltd. All rights reserved. Reprinted with permission. Further reproduction prohibited. www.economist.com

The opportunity for reducing deployments of strategic—that is, intercontinental—nuclear weapons was seized, when Presidents George Bush and Vladimir Putin signed the SORT accord in Moscow committing their countries to reducing their nuclear weapons from about six thousand on each side to between one thousand seven hundred and two thousand two hundred by the end of 2012. Neoliberal optimists cheered in the belief that the world would finally become a safer place as the danger of global annihilation showed promise of vanishing.

The continuing danger of annihilation was made evident at the same time, in 2002, when India and Pakistan squared off against each other poised for war in a standoff over Kashmir, the disputed province that has been the source of two of the three India-Pakistan wars since 1947. Over a million soldiers from each country massed on their common border, and preparations for fighting moved into high gear fueled by pledges on both sides that a "decisive battle" would be fought. A deadly game of nuclear brinkmanship unfolded. The India-Pakistan confrontation illustrates the **security dilemma.** Both sides sought to increase their national security by increasing their armaments and by developing nuclear weapons in 1998, and these preparations for war had the opposite effect—neither side was more secure than they had been prior to their build-up of war-making capabilities.

■ **security dilemma** the propensity of armaments undertaken by one state for ostensibly defensive purposes to threaten other states, which arm in reaction, with the result that their national security declines as their arms increase.

Technological Improvements and Weapons Delivery Capabilities. Advances in weapons technology have been rapid and extraordinary. Since the advent of the atomic age, with the "gravity bombs of 1945 . . . a whole warehouse of varied weapons, each with its own special purpose" has been created. These include:

clean bombs; dirty bombs; bombs that burrowed into the earth, seeking underground command posts; bombs that went off undersea, seeking submarines; bombs that went off high over earth, to fry the brains of electrical devices with a huge shower of electromagnetic pulses; bombs that killed tank crews with radiation but didn't flatten towns or cities; bombs delivered by guidance so precise that they could destroy anything with a known location on or near the surface of the earth. . . . The results of this tireless invention were weapons powerful enough to threaten human life on the planet. (Powers 1994, 123)

Particularly deadly have been the technological refinements that enable states to deliver weapons from as far away as 9,000 miles to within 100 feet of their targets in less than 30 minutes. The United States and Russia, for example, equipped their ballistic missiles with **multiple independently targetable reentry vehicles (MIRVs),** which enable a single missile to launch multiple warheads toward different targets simultaneously and accurately. One MIRV U.S. MX (Peacekeeper) missile could carry ten nuclear warheads—enough to wipe out a city and everything else within a 50-mile radius. As a result of MIRVing before the superpowers agreed to the START II treaty to ban MIRVed intercontinental ballistic missiles, the world's combined nuclear inventory grew nearly three times larger than the number of nuclear warheads previously in existence.

Other technological improvements have led to steady increases in the speed, accuracy, range, and effectiveness of weapons. Laser weapons, nuclear-armed tactical air-to-surface missiles (TASMs), Stealth air-launched cruise missiles (ACMs), and antisatellite (ASAT) weapons that can project force in and wage war from outer space, have become a part of the military landscape. In addition, a large number of innovative new weapons technologies are in use and under development—"wonder weapons" such as the so-called **nonlethal weapons** made possible by the **revolution in military technology (RMT),** so novel that they look like they belong in science fiction (see Controversy: A Revolution in Warfare?). These wonder weapons include an ever expanding inventory of new frontier weapons designed to fight the twenty-first century's likely wars. They include plans to develop information-warfare squadrons to protect military computer networks from electronic sneak attacks; energy pulses to knock out or take down enemies without necessarily killing them; biofeedback, beamed electromagnetic and sonic wavelengths that can modify the human behavior of targets (for example, putting people to sleep through electromagnetic heat and magnetic radiation); and underground **smart bombs** (at a speed of 1,000 feet per second, can penetrate a buried bunker and, at the proper millisecond, after calculating the level through which it crashes like a needle through flesh), can detonate 500 pounds of explosive to destroy an adversary's inventory of buried chemical and biological weapons. Many of these technological advances in warfare are already highly developed and are likely to make orthodox ways of classifying weapons systems as well as prior equations for measuring power ratios obsolete.

For decades, a **firebreak** has separated conventional from nuclear wars. The term comes from the barriers of cleared land that firefighters use to keep forest fires from racing out of control. In the context of modern weaponry, it is a psychological barrier whose purpose is to "prevent even the most intensive forms of conventional combat from escalating into nuclear war." As both

■ **multiple independently targetable reentry vehicles (MIRVs)**
a technological innovation permitting many weapons to be delivered from a single missile (see p. 554).

■ **nonlethal weapons**
the wide array of "soft-kill," low-intensity methods of incapacitating an enemy's people, vehicles, communications systems, or entire cities without killing either combatants or noncombatants.

■ **revolution in military technology (RMT)**
the sophisticated new weapons technologies that make fighting war without mass armies possible.

■ **smart bombs**
precision-guided military technology that enables a bomb to search for its target and detonate at the precise time it can do the most damage.

■ **firebreak**
the psychological barrier between conventional and nuclear war.

A Revolution in Warfare?
The Next Generation of Lethal and Nonlethal Weapons

It may seem strange, but the adage that defense planners are prone to prepare to fight and win the last war holds truth. There is a natural temptation to prepare for the "worst case" scenario, defined by the most recent war experience. That vigilant preparation seems reasonable, in principle, because military commanders are assigned the task of preparing their country for any contingency, and what better way than by perfecting the capabilities and strategies that would have ensured a quick victory over the last enemy in war, preferably at minimal loss of life?

More controversial are innovative preparations to wage the wars of the future when they have not yet been encountered. Yet, this challenge has been taken on boldly by defense planners in the United States who are designing new kinds of weapons to fight the wars they imagine will be fought in the twenty-first century. What makes these preparations so controversial is they require costly innovations in fighting technology that have very uncertain consequences for their country's national security. Will the new weapons work? Will they provide for better defense? Or will they backfire, taking warfare to a new level that unintentionally reduces human security? No one can know for sure; we can only ponder these questions with **counterfactual reasoning,** guessing what will happen if radically new weapons technology becomes part of many countries' arsenals. No wonder the issue is a topic for debate.

To proponents, revolutionary new weapons technology offer great promise. If warfare can be made less destructive, they argue, war can continue to serve as a political instrument for exercising power, in ways that make the use of military force civilized. In contrast, many critics question the effectiveness and ethics of remote and robotic killing with nonlethal arsenals. Many questions remain: Are smart bombs smart enough? Are precision weapons really effective? Or, given the high probability of technological and human error, is the front edge of high-tech warfare actually rather blunt?

What do you think? In contemplating your position on the promise or peril of the new weapons technology now being developed, take into consideration the kind of weapons now being planned by military engineers. Also factor into your assessment the fact that "miniaturization has made technology more accessible [and] globalization has been the engine driving its diffusion. . . . Today, almost every element of power can be acquired in the global marketplace" (Libicki 2000).

The stakes have been raised by the revolution in military affairs (RMA), the military-technical revolution (MTR), and by information age warfare. These concepts refer to the goal of seizing the opportunities created by microprocessors, instantaneous global communications, and precision-guided munitions technologies to confront and contain the armed conflicts of the future without relying on weapons of mass destruction. To advocates of the RMA, a kinder, gentler type of warfare promises to transform the ways wars will be fought.

Behind the technological revolution is the belief that nonlethal weapons are practical because they can obtain intelligence from computers and advanced technologies to enable precision strikes that can "blind, immobilize, and maintain the enemy at a distance while critical targets are identified, struck, and destroyed" (Tilford 1995). The value of these weapons was illustrated dramatically during the Persian Gulf War by the United States' use of smart bombs that could drop down chimneys, stealthy aircraft that could elude radar detection, and an airborne tracking system that could scout Iraqi military installations and movements. So-called smart bombs also were used with abandon during NATO's seventy-eight-day around-the-clock random bombing of Belgrade, which ended the war in Kosovo without a single U.S. soldier losing his or her life.

Talk of stealth, precision, information dominance, and missile defense anticipates a day when robots will replace soldiers in combat and unmanned aircraft will replace pilots, roaming the globe with laser weapons to destroy ground and air targets, and "cyberdefense" through the use of smart and brilliant weapons systems will be able to make sophisticated decisions about when and how to act. In this revolution, nonlethal weapons figure prominently. Among the devices already available are "guns that shoot rubber pellets, wooden batons and tiny beanbags to disperse a crowd; stinger grenades that fire rubber pellets; sticky foam that immobilizes people; and another foam system that creates a sudslike barrier 200 feet long, 20 feet wide, and four feet high, laced with tear gas" (Graham 1995). Today's arsenal includes lasers that can blind people from a distance and a variety of biological and chemical weapons. Some advocate using the latter, arguing that a day of fever, coughing, vomiting, and internal bleeding is preferable to incineration.

At issue, now and in the future, is an ageless question: Can technology make warfare safe, or will new technological innovation pave the way to humankind's destruction?

nuclear and conventional weapons technologies advance, there is danger that the firebreak is being crossed from both directions—by a new generation of near nuclear conventional weapons capable of levels of violence approximating those of a limited nuclear conflict and by a new generation of near conventional **strategic weapons** capable of causing destruction similar to that of the most powerful conventional weapons.

The precision and power of today's conventional weapons have expanded exponentially, at precisely the moment when the revolution in military technology is leading to "the end of infantry" because, in the computer age "the sky has eyes, bullets have brains, and victory will belong to the country whose military has the better data network" (Ross 1997) (see Controversy: A Revolution in Warfare?). Note also that even as the nuclear powers retain the capacity to turn cities into glass, they (and now, terrorist groups?) increasingly rely on a variety of new cyber-strategies to deter and demobilize enemies and are turning to **virtual nuclear arsenals** for **deterrence** of an adversary's attack. Examples include such futuristic weapons as the electromagnetic pulse (EMP) bomb, which can be hand delivered in a suitcase and can immobilize an entire city's computer and communications systems; computer viruses of electronic-seating microbates that can eliminate a country's telephone system; and logic bombs that can confuse and redirect traffic on the target country's air and rail system. Also planned are **information warfare (IW)** or **infowar tactics** that deploy information-age techniques "to disrupt the enemy's economy and military preparedness, perhaps without firing a shot." One example of these is the U.S. Air Force's Commando Solo psychological operations plane, which can disrupt signals and insert in their place a "morphed" TV program, in which the enemy leader makes unpopular announcements on the screen that alienate him from his population.

In addition, the production, trade, and use of so-called light weapons or small conventional arms is escalating. "Because of the global upsurge in ethnic and sectarian conflict, policymakers have become more attuned to the role played by [light] arms in sparking and sustaining low-level warfare and have begun to consider new constraints on trade in these munitions. . . . Although heavy weapons sometimes play a role, most of the day-to-day fighting is performed by irregular forces armed only with rifles, grenades, machine guns, light mortars, and other 'man-portable' munitions" (Klare 1999). Even space has become the subject of many militarization projections. U.S. Secretary of Defense Donald Rumsfeld has championed the need for weapons technology capable of protecting vital U.S. satellites and providing antiballistic missile defense.

Unconventional Weapons: Biological and Chemical. Biological and chemical weapons pose a special and growing threat, particularly in the hands of terrorists aiming at mass destruction rather than influencing public opinion. These unconventional weapons of mass destruction are sometimes regarded as a "poor man's atomic bomb," because they can be built at comparatively small cost and cause widespread injury and death. Despite the 1972 Biological Weapons Convention prohibiting the development, production, and stockpiling of biological weapons, according to U.S. Secretary of Defense Donald Rumsfeld in May 2002, Iran, Iraq, Libya, North Korea, and Syria were developing such weapons and, in addition, terrorists were certain to acquire biological weapons

■ **counterfactual reasoning**
thought experiments to consider the consequences that probably will result if something happens that has not yet occurred, such as speculating, "What if the United States once again becomes isolationistic as it did prior to World War II?" (see p. 102).

■ **strategic weapons**
weapons of mass destruction that are carried on intercontinental ballistic missiles (ICBMs), submarine-launched ballistic missiles (SLBM)s, or long-range bombers and are capable of annihilating an enemy state.

■ **virtual nuclear arsenals**
the next generation of "near-nuclear" military capabilities produced by the revolution in military technology that would put strategic nuclear weapons of mass destruction at the margins of national security strategies by removing dependence on them for deterrence.

■ **deterrence**
a preventive strategy designed to dissuade an adversary from doing what it would otherwise do (see p. 408).

■ **information warfare (IW) or infowar tactics**
attacks on an adversary's telecommunications and computer networks to penetrate and degrade an enemy whose defense capabilities depend heavily on these technological systems.

and "will not hesitate to use them." Similarly, chemical weapons proliferation is a worldwide concern. In addition to Iran, Iraq, Russia, and the United States (the only states confirmed to possess chemical weapons), twenty-one other countries—mostly in the Global South—are suspected to have produced chemical weapons (Stock and De Geer 1995, 340), and today's terrorists are widely perceived to be committed to acquiring and using these lethal weapons. Following the September 11, 2001, terrorist attacks on the United States, the spread of anthrax through the U.S. mail system was widely considered to be the work of Middle Eastern terror networks.

International law prohibits the use of chemical weapons: The 1925 Geneva Protocol banned the use of chemical weapons in warfare, and the Chemical Weapons Convention (CWC), signed by 184 countries by 2002, required the destruction of existing stocks. Nevertheless, legal restraints do not ensure that states will comply. Iran's and Iraq's use of gas in warfare demonstrated this; Iraq even used chemical weapons in 1989 against its own Kurdish people. In addition, many radical and extremist groups, often beyond the control of weak state governments, may find chemical and biological weapons to be a cheaper, effective means of promoting global terror. Thus, the firebreak against chemical warfare has already been breached. The proliferation of ballistic missiles among regional rivals in the Middle East, Asia and elsewhere particularly raises the danger of their use, because they enable chemical weapons to be readily delivered at great distances. The possibility that these weapons might be required and used by terrorists poses still another kind of threat.

In the early phases of the twenty-first century, a pervasive sense of the loss of security haunts much of the world. The danger of nuclear annihilation has not disappeared with the U.S.-Russian agreement to drastically cut their nuclear warheads, and in May 2002, at the exact moment when that historic SORT accord was signed, the famous "doomsday clock" of the *Bulletin of the Atomic Scientists* showed that the world was only 7 minutes from nuclear Armageddon—exactly the same number of minutes from the world's annihilation when the time was originally set on the clock in 1947. The world is *not* a safer place. And now, with terrorists roaming the globalized planet plotting mass destruction, and with Al Qaeda attempting in June 2002 to provoke a nuclear exchange between Pakistan and India over Kashmir, the human race is endangered by the constant threat worldwide of global terrorism. The twenty-first century is not a peaceful and prosperous period free of fear about survival as once hoped. International *in*security haunts the world.

In searching for national security, all states—big and small, strong and weak—face similar choices. How should they reconcile the need for a strong military with the need for economic growth? How should they reconcile their interest in acquiring power with their desire to promote principled and national ideals? The natural desire for freedom, flexibility, and independence in foreign affairs through unilateral "go it alone" strategies must be balanced against the need for multilateral action to confront many shared problems by working with allies and through global institutions. How should that balance to be obtained?

How to regain national and international security is the pressing issue of our time. How are the great powers responding to yesterday's old threats and to today's new threats? We conclude with a brief overview of the great powers' recent reformulations of their national security strategies and defense policies.

We look first at the United States—the globe's uncontested military superpower—its actions are influencing heavily how the other major powers are responding to both U.S. predominance and other security concerns as well.

THE GREAT POWERS' NATIONAL SECURITY STRATEGIES

In the wake of 9/11, the geostrategic landscape looks quite different from the terrain of the recent past. What is new, however, is not altogether different. The new age of global terrorism drives new strategic thinking, as defense planners in Washington, Moscow, Beijing, Tokyo, Berlin, and Brussels struggle to construct defense doctrines to manage the security threats on the horizon.

As noted in Chapter 4, the choices range between the extremes of isolationist withdrawal from participation in world affairs and active international engagement. The other choices need to be made between **unilateral** self-help actions on one end of the continuum, **multilateral** action with others on the other, and specialized **bilateral** alliances and ad hoc partnerships in between. And these choices force decisions to be made about honoring ideals without undermining self-interests: in short, to reconcile **liberalism** and realism.

What sort of national security response is most likely? We will look briefly at the emerging security policies of the five major great powers.

The U.S.'s New Security Policies

After September 11, U.S. global strategy shifted in new directions to confront the dangers posed by the new age of global terrorism. The United States immediately defined military security as its first priority, ahead of economic recovery and the promotion of such traditional U.S. ideals as free trade and free governments throughout the world (that also contribute, according to neoliberal thinking, to global prosperity and peace).

This preference about priorities is controversial, because three schools of thought about America's role in global affairs continue to divide U.S policymakers in the early years of the new millennium:

> Neoisolationists want the U.S. to deal only with threats to America's physical security, political independence, and domestic liberty. They . . . argue that the U.S. should let other powers, and regional balances of power, take care of all the world's woes. Realists such as Henry Kissinger want the U.S. to continue to be the holder of·the world balance of power, the arbiter of the main regional power groups, and the watchdog against all potential imperialistic troublemakers. Liberal internationalists want a greater role for multilateral institutions and more emphasis on human needs and rights, the environment and democracy. (Hoffmann 1992, 59)

The Bush administration's national security advisers have had to struggle to reconcile these divergent outlooks and to strike a balance among the need for self-help isolationism, the impulse to flex supreme U.S. military muscle in an activist push to run the world, and the desire to promote traditional U.S. liberal ideals such as human rights, democracy, and multilateral international cooperation. The

■ **unilateral**
a go-it-alone, self-reliant strategy for dealing with threats from another actor or global problem.

■ **multilateral**
a cooperative strategy of working with allies or with collective problem-solving institutions to face threats from another actor or global problem (see p. 541).

■ **bilateral**
an intermediary strategy of working with a specific ally or in a specially created ad hoc partnership to face threats from another actor or global problem.

■ **liberalism**
a paradigm predicated on the hope that the application of reason and universal ethics to inernational relations can lead to a more orderly, just, and cooperative world, and that international anarchy and war can be policed by institutional reforms that empower organizations and international law for global governance.

Paul J. Richards/AFP

Awakening to the New Age of Global Terrorism Shown here is U.S. President George W. Bush first learning on September 11, 2001, from an adviser, that terrorists had destroyed the World Trade Center and attacked the Pentagon. September 11 became known as "the day that changed the world, forever." Possible hyperbole aside, one thing without question *did* change overnight—U.S. national security policy, as the United States braced itself to wage a worldwide war to extricate terrorism from the face of the earth.

■ **zero-sum**
competitive situations in which there is little room for compromise, because the gains from one choice or one goal require a loss for another.

quest is challenging because they entail a **zero-sum** trade-off among choices, in which one goal can only be pursued by compromising pursuit of others. For example, the United States cannot play the role of hegemonic superpower leading the world and also isolationistically withdraw from the costs of paying for foreign aid, regional collective security alliances, or UN peacekeeping missions; nor can the United States avoid looking hypocritical if it undertakes a massive military buildup at the same time that it preaches the ideals of arms control, disarmament, and nonproliferation for others.

In 2003 the Bush administration sought to reconcile these partially incompatible goals, by pursuing the priorities its September 2002 report, "The National Security Strategy of the United States of America," identified:

- Wage, and win, the war against the worldwide network of terrorist organizations.
- Prevent any other great power from challenging the hegemonic position of the United States as the sole global superpower.
- Deter the use of nuclear, biological, or chemical weapons against the United States and its allies.

- Pursue regime change and disarmament in Iraq by all means necessary, including the preemptive use of military force, to overthrow Iraq dictator Saddam Huessin and to prevent Iraq from acquiring weapons of mass destruction.

- Attempt to recruit global support for U.S. military operations while, in those endeavors, preventing the United States from becoming isolated from those parts of the world opposed to U.S. operations overseas.

- Halt or at least slow the proliferation of such weapons, concentrating on the effort to keep these weapons of mass destruction out of the grasp of other alleged terrorists movements such as Al Qaeda.

- Pursue the search for technological solutions to military problems through the development of smaller smart bombs, nonlethal weapons, and an improved ballistic missile defense system in outer space.

- Remain capable of fighting (and winning) an armed conflict in at least two regions of strategic importance to the United States, in military interventions that in the best of circumstances minimize American casualties.

- Maintain U.S. technological superiority.

- Foster democratic values in other countries.

In the early stages of George W. Bush's administration, the **Bush Doctrine** was declared. It advocated "unabashed unilateralism [that aimed] to reshape norms, alter expectations and create new realities [by] unapologetic and implacable demonstrations of will" (Krauthammer 2001). This "go-it-alone" posture rejected accommodating American foreign policy to the wishes and interests of other countries in order for the U.S. to be seen as a good international citizen. Instead, the United States would venture forward as it chose and would break the straightjacket imposed by multilateral treaties—on arms control, antiballistic missiles, biological weapons, nuclear testing, the Kyoto treaty on greenhouses gases to control global warming, and the international criminal court. (It was said when the Bush administration first came to office that it never met a treaty that it liked.)

The trauma of the September 11 terrorist attacks forced the United States to retreat quickly from the bold unilateralism first asserted in the Bush Doctrine. After 9/11, the U.S. counterterrorism program required unrestrained global interventionism and needed the approval and assistance of allies and international organizations. Viewed in light of the **realpolitik** definition of its evolving defense doctrines, the United States is now especially committed to relying heavily on military might while also attempting to build liberal ideals into the definition of its goals (as seen in the way Bush defined the war on terrorism as a war to defend liberty). U.S. national security policy has reaffirmed the U.S. commitment to be prepared to wage two major wars simultaneously and to be able to intervene militarily around the world, while at the same time to deter an attack on the United States. For these objectives, the U.S. has increased its defense budget exponentially, planning to spend $2,100 billion on the military from 2003 to 2008. Power has been defined in terms of military might, not, as neoliberalism advocates, in terms of the promotion of high ideals such as free trade and free governments to secure a **democratic peace.**

As it faces an insecure future, the United States faces the awesome task of preserving U.S. predominance and its traditional reputation as a honorable peace-loving country abiding by moral principles. To some realists, American

■ **Bush Doctrine**
the declaration that the United States intended to behave globally in terms of its perceived national self-interests, without the necessary approval of others and, as a corollary, would consider taking unilateral preemptive military action against any security threat such as Iraq to defeat it before it could attack the United States.

■ **realpolitik**
the theoretical outlook prescribing that countries should prepare for war in order to preserve peace.

■ **democratic peace**
the theory that, because democratic states do not fight each other, the diffusion of democratic governance throughout the world will reduce the probability of war (see p. 71).

hegemonic leadership will require a warrior mentality and a pagan ethos. As the realist writer Robert D. Kaplan (2002) counsels, "the paramount question of world politics in the early twenty-first century will be the re-establishment of order," and for that crusade the United States will have to lead by using ruthless military methods as an imperial power that (like the Leviathan state envisioned by the realist Thomas Hobbes in the seventeenth century) crushes revisionist actors seeking to overturn the international status quo. The spirit underlying this advice was expressed in June 2002 when President Bush addressed the graduating class of the U.S. Military Academy at West Point.

> The war on terror will not be won on the defensive. We must take the battle to the enemy, disrupt its plans, and confront the worst threats before they emerge. The greatest danger to freedom lies at the perilous crossroads of radicalism and technology. When the spread of chemical and biological and nuclear weapons, along with ballistic missile technology occurs, even weak states and small groups could attain a catastrophic power to strike at great nations. [I ask Americans to] be ready for pre-emptive actions when necessary, to defend our liberty and to defend our lives. [The United States cannot afford to] put our faith in the word of tyrants who solemnly sign non-proliferation treaties and then systematically break them. All nations that decide for aggression and terror will pay a price. We will not leave the safety of America and the peace of the planet at the mercy of a few mad terrorists and tyrants.

Neoliberals question some of these assumptions, warning that suppressing freedom by force can undermine the very order that an imperial hegemon hopes to preserve. The fact is that in the present stage of world history the United States is stronger militarily than it (or any other great power) has ever been in history. However, the U.S. homeland in the age of global terrorism arguably has never been less secure or more vulnerable. So the United States faces a supreme test about the policies that should guide and preserve its power and reduce its vulnerability. As a neoliberal former U.S. policymaker, Joseph S. Nye, wrote in 2002, the "paradox of American power" is that at the height of its military capabilities the United States is more dependent on others than ever, because the United States is most affected by globalization. "The world's only superpower can't go it alone," and, as the threat of terrorism demonstrated, it is imperative that the United States seek constructive relations with others, for it cannot by itself ensure success and stability:

> In his election campaign, President George W. Bush said, "If we are an arrogant nation, they'll view us that way, but if we're a humble nation, they'll respect us." He was right, but unfortunately, many foreigners saw the United States as arrogantly concerned with narrow American interests at the expense of the rest of the world. They saw [the U.S.] focusing on the hard power of [U.S.] military might rather than soft power as [the U.S.] turned [its] back on many international treaties, norms, and negotiating forums. In their eyes, the United States used consultations for talking, not listening. Yet effective leadership requires dialogue with followers. American leadership will be more enduring if [the U.S.] can convince its partners that [the United States is] sensitive to their concerns. September 2001 was a start toward such sensitivity, by only a start. (Nye 2002a, xii)

Courtesy of Lockheed Martin Corporation

Remote-Control Warfare? In the twenty-first century, the United States plans to preserve its commanding edge in military capabilities by building a new generation of technologically sophisticated new weapons, instead of attempting to build up an overpowering inventory of big bombs that are risky to use, in order to combat the growing threat of insurgencies within the world's failing states. A wide variety of weapons are under construction, ranging from thousand-pound bombs (the concrete, nonexplosive bombs the U.S. bombarded Iraq with in late 1999) to landmines. Some of the nonnuclear strategic weapons systems on the drawing boards "may be able to engage 1,500 targets in the first hour, if not minutes, of a conflict." Shown here is one example: "An artist's conception of an advanced unmanned aircraft system—one possibility for strategic strike with conventional explosives" (Krepinevich and Kusiak 1998).

What is needed is a new U.S. strategic vision for a changed and changing world, Nye, concludes: one that relies less on the traditional measures of "hard power" defined in terms of military capabilities and more on the type of "soft power" that emanates from the appeal of America's humanitarian values and culture and its free institutions.

Standing at the pinacle of global power, the United States will have to struggle with the dilemmas of occupying—and holding—its lonely unipolar position as the supreme superpower at the top of the global pyramid of power. It will have to avoid the extremes of isolationism and imperialism if it is to lead in the world, but resist the temptation to dominate others and thereby drive them into hostile resistance. Globalization precludes the possibility of redesigning the world to advance U.S. prominence. The U.S. standing among the community of nations remains high, and that is a source of influence; but the U.S. capacity to use military force to compel other countries to act as the United States wishes is low, and the prospects of eliminating an entrenched phenomenon like terrorism worldwide are very low. The soft power that respect for U.S. ideals and ideas coupled with economic strength can provide can be the basis for the United States to fashion the globe into a prosperous and peaceful place, providing it leads by example rather than by force. Finding a global vision to chart its way in the complex twenty-first-century world that balances realist interests with liberal ideals will be America's continuing greatest challenge.

In the chaotic twenty-first century, American leaders can be expected to adapt U.S. strategy to the unknown dangers that lurk beneath the surface of turbulent global geostrategic waters. Limits on America's capacity to foresee the future—and limits on resources to take a unilateral approach to managing the new millennium's multiple security threats—suggest that a coherent strategy resting on a clear vision is likely to prove an elusive goal for the United States in the future.

Given the overwhelming military predominance of the United States, it is understandable that the other great powers have constructed their national security policies to a large extent around their uncertain relationship with the U.S. hegemon. (Ironically, so have the global terrorist movements that have made the U.S. superpower their major enemy and primary target.) We next briefly look at the policies the other great-power rivals to the United States have crafted, as they likewise attempt to deal with the prevailing reality of U.S. preponderance and with changes in both their national circumstances at home and in their region.

Russia Adjusts to Its New Geostrategic Circumstances

For Russia, perhaps the most important aspect of American foreign policy with which it has to wrestle is U.S. President George W. Bush's post–September 11 corollary to the Bush Doctrine. Bush declared, "I laid out a doctrine [that] if you harbor a terrorist, you're just as guilty as the terrorist; if you feed one or hide one, you're just as guilty as those who came and murdered thousands of innocent Americans." This message was a threat and a plea. It reaffirmed Bush's previous position that in the U.S. war against terrorism, other states were either with the United States or with the terrorists, and that each state would have to choose—ally with the United States or become its adversary. The United States needed allies because it recognized that "ultimately the fight against global terrorism [was] one the United States cannot win on its own" (Daalder and Lindsay 2002).

Confronting the United States as an adversary was similarly a fight Russia did not want and could not win. As a consequence, Russia has built its new security policies around the effort to cultivate a strategic partnership with the United States and, secondarily, the North Atlantic Treaty Organization (NATO) the U.S. dominates. That is why Russia in May 2002 rejoiced at NATO's decision to welcome Russia to participate fully in the alliance, a gesture dampened by the fact that NATO denied Russia the right to veto NATO security decisions. Russian military weakness has also forced Russia to forge ever closer political and economic relations with its neighbors in the European Union. Russia set its sights on integrating itself into the global institutions created by the United States and its allies in the West. This was seen in Russia's energetic effort to join the World Trade Organization—a goal that got a huge boost when in May 2002 the European Union announced that it formally recognized Russia as a free-market capitalist system. This step greatly spurred Russia's bid to join the World Trade Organization and the European Union—Russia's major trading partner with $73 billion in 2001.

Much of this shift reflected Russia's precarious geostrategic circumstances. Russia's army has lost its roar amidst its continuing financial shortfalls, which have required Russia to reduce its military spending to $60 billion—7 times smaller than the military budget of the United States. "Low salaries and ancient equipment plague a military that can't afford barracks for 93,000 officers" (Nichols 2002). Moreover, Russia has now dismantled much of the awesome strategic nuclear stockpile that formally was the backbone of its defense and the symbol of its military might. Simply put, Russia is undergoing **power transition** of unprecedented pace and magnitude and this has compromised Russia's capacity to deal with the many separatist movements active in the remaining

■ **power transition**
a situation resulting from the rapid increase or deterioration in one state's military capabilities relative to a rival's, often provoking fears that lead to warfare.

regions of Russia's shrunken empire (such as in the explosive war in the Chechnya breakaway republic and in Russia's southern rim, where Islamic terrorist bombings have become common). Russia simply does not have the resources to play the game of a global power: ten percent of the workforce is unemployed and "35 percent of the country's 145 million people are living in poverty, which is defined as a personal income of less than $40 a month" (Nichols 2002, 2A).

To deal with Russia's security predicament Russian President Vladimir Putin revised his original 1997 *The Concept of National Security* document. Putin's new doctrine set the following priorities:

- Cutting the meager Russian defense budget even further and undertaking fundamental restructuring to eliminate entire branches of the armed services, and putting the savings from this defense conversion toward stimulating economic recovery.

- Creating smaller, more mobile, and technologically adept fighting forces to manage civil rebellions within Russia as well as along Russia's troubled southern borders in the "near abroad."

- Following through with the SORT 2002 accord with the United States to cut Russia's nuclear arsenal by two-thirds by the year 2012, to no more than two thousand two hundred warheads.

- Repealing the **no first use** pledge previously made by Mikhail Gorbachev—that Russia would not be the first to use nuclear weapons in the event of a conventional or nuclear attack. For deterrence Russia relies on its remaining nuclear warheads to repel a foreign aggressor.

■ **no first use**
the doctrine that a nuclear state would not use its strategic weapons in the event of an attack by another state using nuclear or conventional weapons.

Aware of its vulnerability, Russia emphasizes a multilateral diplomatic approach to its many security problems and has isolationistically reduced the global scale of its international involvements. One example was the rejection of the previous strategy of building a countercoalition to balance what Russia had previously called a threat—U.S. hegemonial domination; Russia's doctrine now pursues the goal of **bandwagoning** by making Russia an alliance partner with the stronger United States and its European allies. In 2002, President Putin pushed hard toward closer relations with the West, and his efforts paid immediate dividends. President Bush announced, as a reward for Russian cooperation in the war against the terrorism, that to the United States Russia was no longer regarded as a threat in an oft-repeated statement that "Russia is not the enemy of the United States." Other payoffs occurred when Russia gained full participation in NATO, the European Union redefined Russia as a market economy to smooth its way into the World Trade Organization, and Russia's new partners offered to import oil from Russia's vast supplies as a means of cementing Russia's cooperation in the new war on international terrorism.

■ **bandwagoning**
the tendency for weak states to seek alliance with the strongest power, irrespective of that power's ideology or form of government, in order to increase security.

China's Global Clout and Security Posture

China figures prominently in U.S. and Russian conceptions of security.

> The rise of China, if it continues, may be the most important trend in the world for the [twenty-first] century. When historians one hundred years hence write about our time, they may well conclude that the most significant development was the emergence of a vigorous market economy—and army—in the most populous country of the world. This is particularly likely

if many of the globe's leading historians and pundits a century from now do not have names like Smith but rather ones like Wu.

China is the fastest growing economy in the world, with what may be the fastest growing military budget. It has nuclear weapons, border disputes with most of its neighbors, and a rapidly improving army that may—within a decade or so—be able to resolve old quarrels in its own favor. The United States has possessed the world's largest economy for more than a century, but at present trajectories China may displace it in the first half of the next century and become the number one economy in the world. (Kristof 1993, 59; see also Kaplan 1999)

China is now an economic giant, driven by the long-term goal of gaining respect and recognition as a great power. To that end, China has followed the realist script by attempting to harness its economic clout by modernizing its military. Since it abandoned Marxist-Leninist communism in the 1980s, China's economy has grown at a compound annual rate of about 10 percent; its GDP has quadrupled to over $5 trillion, making China the globe's fourth largest economy. These resources thus enable China, formerly regarded as sleeping giant, to awaken and convert finances into military power to symbolize and possibly act upon its new rising status.

However, China has far to go in order to become a military superpower. Its maritime and air capabilities remain antiquated, with only twenty DF-5 liquid-fueled ICMBs, no aircraft carriers, and only thirty-five hundred jet fighters. China's defense spending is growing, but at $42 billion in 2003 is only one-tenth that of the United States and inadequate for the major buildup required to rival the United States. Moreover, "the Chinese are not implementing these [military modernization] programs on a crash basis, and most of them will not bear fruit for years. Even then their military technology will lag far behind that of the United States" (Joffe 2001). Rather than building a modern military itself, China is allocating its military budget to purchase advanced arms from other suppliers, such as fighter aircraft and surface-to-air missiles from Russia and Israel.

China seeks to reduce other states' fears about its rising capabilities as the globe's most populous and fastest growing economy and repeatedly has asserted that China seeks peaceful relations with all. For example, China has ceased condemning the United States for pursuing the singular goal—"the hegemonic domination of the world." Taking a step further, in April 2002 Chinese Vice President Hu Jintao (regarded by the United States as the heir apparent to Chinese President Jiang Zemin) made a goodwill visit to the United States and expressed his hope—"May the friendship of the Chinese and American people last forever." That aspiration could become a reality, but the issue of China's pledge to recover Taiwan by force if necessary has renewed anxieties about potential Chinese militarism.

Like other great powers, China has struggled to find long-term solutions to its security problems. One direction is signaled by China's continuing arms buildup, its preservation of its modest strategic arsenal of nuclear weapons, and its feverish attempt to equip the globe's largest standing army of 2.9 million soldiers. The other direction is signaled by China's unrestrained efforts to increase further its diplomatic stature through continuing rapid economic growth. That path to security was made evident by the sacrifices China made in 2002 to

Chien-min Chung/AP/Wide World

A Hegemonic Challenger on the March? China is an ascendant superpower with the capacity to intimidate its Asian neighbors and strike fear into distant great-power rivals, who suspect that its rise to the top rankings of national economies will be followed by foreign aggressiveness. At the moment, China is not a serious challenger to U.S. supremacy. As this photo of Chinese soldiers suggests, China's military is more stylish pomp than it is a truly modern force able to credibly project power throughout the globe.

successfully gain membership in the World Trade Organization, which necessitated opening China to foreign imports and expanding civil liberties through political reforms. China has cast its fate in this neoliberal direction, hoping to win the benefits of active participation in the global marketplace, and so far this strategy is paying huge benefits: following membership in the World Trade Organization, foreign direct investment (FDI) in China rose 28 percent from the previous year and reached $10.1 billion in the first quarter of 2002 when the economic growth rate rose to 7.6 percent annually (Melloan 2002b, A17).

To find a safe place in the sun where it feels it belongs, China has defined its national security priorities through a strategy that seeks to

- Deter a large-scale conventional or nuclear attack on China by any other great power, such as the United States.
- To develop the military force required to successfully invade Taiwan should negotiations fail to integrate with the mainland what China sees as a renegade province.
- Lobby to see that the traditional international legal rule prohibiting external interference in sovereign states' domestic affairs is respected, to safeguard against foreign intervention to punish China for disregard of its citizens' human rights, while at the same time developing the military

capability to prevent U.S. intervention if Beijing decides to impose reunification with Taiwan by force.

China's national security policies emphasize the importance of "maintaining good and friendly relations with all countries" and above all avoiding becoming the next target of a U.S.-led coalition assembled to contain its rise. Establishing normalized diplomatic relations with the United States and the other great powers is crucial to Chinese security, because the last thing China needs is to be regarded as an enemy facing a new U.S. **containment** policy in a new Cold War. Mistrust prevails whenever great-power rivals clash, and to the other great powers these Chinese proclamations inspire divergent reactions.

China's strategic situation is at a crossroads. As China's vigorous rearmament and force-modernization program proceeds, China's growing arsenal will position China to play a dominant military role in Asia and eventually the entire world. Napoleon Bonaparte counseled in 1803 that the world should "let China sleep" because, he predicted, when China awakens, "the world will tremble." China has now awakened. What it will do with its power remains to be seen.

Japan's Search for a Strategy

An emerging economic superpower in the 1990s and proudly the second richest country behind the United States, Japan has recently struggled to keep pace economically and has been overshadowed by the "new star economy on the block," China (*Economist*, May 18, 2002). In addition to economic woes, Japan has an aging and shrinking population and now-staggering national debts that overshadow even America's enormous debts that have been compounded by the huge costs of waging the war on terrorism.

In the aftermath of World War II, Japan strictly adhered to the guidelines of the **Yoshida Doctrine,** in which Prime Minister Shigeru Yoshida argued that Japanese security policy should avoid international disputes, keep a low profile on divisive global issues, and concentrate on economic pursuits. That doctrine remains timely, given the 1990s' "lost decade" in which the Japanese economy actually declined, undermining Japan's ability to play a more active global role. Japan continues to stress words over deeds and to advocate a neoliberal foreign policy philosophy.

However, despite economic restraints, Japan has begun to expand its global involvement. Prime Minister Kiichi Miyazawa's policy departures in 1992 presaged the new direction that Japan's security policies are now following. Miyazawa won passage of the Peacekeeping Operations Bill, which enabled Japan to deploy a self-defense military force to participate in UN peacekeeping operations in Cambodia in 1992—the first use of Japanese armed forces abroad since World War II. Japan's acceptance of a large increase in its previous UN dues (over 20 percent in 2002), its push for inclusion as a permanent member of the UN Security Council, and its rise to the top of the world's foreign aid donors also suggest growing Japanese international activism. Such policies have continued in 2003.

As a sign of the Japanese effort to discard its traditional isolationism and be a player in world affairs, Japan increased defense expenditures to $40.4 billion in 2002. Japan in 2003 still adhered to the policy of spending no more than 1 percent of its gross national product on defense and remained committed to

■ containment
a term coined by U.S. policymaker George F. Kennan for deterring Soviet Russia's expansionist aims by counterpressures, which has since become a general term used by strategists to describe the methods used to prevent an expanding great power from using its military muscles for expansionist hegemonic purposes.

■ Yoshida Doctrine
Japan's traditional security policy of avoiding disputes with rivals, preventing foreign wars by low military spending, and promoting economic growth through foreign trade.

its postwar constitution, which forbids remilitarization. However, after a half-century of strict pacifism, alarmed that its neighbors' arms races are disrupting the Asian balance of power, and jittery over North Korea's launch of a three-stage long-range missile over Japan in August 1998, Japan is reconsidering how military might can contribute to national security and global standing. Japan's Self-Defense Force is impressive, with 235,000 soldiers in uniform and the Pacific's largest navy. Although it does not have advanced offensive weapons such as long-range bombers and aircraft carriers, Japan has seventeen of the most sophisticated submarines in the world. Japan's air force and navy may still be numerically less than China's, but they are more advanced and are likely to remain so for a long time. This shift in strategy worries its neighbors, who remember well Japan's history as a feared military power. Postwar Japanese pacifism could, with this military clout, give way to resurgent militarism aimed at its simmering territorial disputes with both Russia and China. From the Japanese perspective, Japan faces growing security concerns, which would intensify if the troubled situation in northeast Asia (especially North Korea) worsens or if the United States reduces its presence in Asia.

These fears have created pressures for Japan to participate in the growing Asian arms race. However, predictions about Japan's emergence as a global military power with global ambitions must be offset by the reality of other restraints. The Japanese government's official projections estimate that Japan's population of 124 million in 2002 will tumble rapidly, with the "birth dearth" reducing the population to 100 million in 2050 and 67 million in 2100. Add to that the problem of Japan's continuing reliance on its fifty-three accident-prone nuclear power processing plants for one-third of its energy, and the prospect of Japan playing a larger military role dims. In addition, new economic problems have placed financial constraints on military activities.

Given these structural weaknesses, Japan has sought to adapt the country's national security policies in several ways. First, Japan's security strategy seeks to further tie the country into the web of multilateral global institutions (the UN, the WTO, the G-8) on which it increasingly depends for preservation of the world order that has made Japan's prosperity since 1945 possible. Second, Japan has stepped up its efforts to lead in foreign assistance to developing Global South countries; it perceives advancing the poor a profitable investment in its own advancement. Third, Japan seeks to tie its security closer to America's: in 1997 it agreed to a new mutual defense treaty requiring Japanese troops to march with American troops in operations to keep the peace, and in 1999 it beefed up that military alliance treaty by giving Japanese forces new authority to provide logistic support to U.S. combat forces in the vaguely defined "area around Japan." Combinations of bilateralism and multilateralism have thus replaced Japan's traditional preference for unilateralism in foreign affairs.

More problematically, with its neighbors arming to the teeth, Japan has begun to have second thoughts about nuclear weapons. It balked at the Clinton administration's attempt to press for a Japanese commitment to support the indefinite and unconditional extension of the nuclear nonproliferation treaty, especially in light of the U.S. opening the path to nuclear weapons testing and ballistic missile defense, which gives Japan a green light to proceed with its plans to put its own spy satellite in orbit and begin research on a planned Star Wars ballistic missile defense system. Even more dramatically, "alarmed by the rising power of China and anxious about the effectiveness of security guarantees from the United States, some of Japan's most powerful politicians have begun to consider breaking with a half-century-old policy of pacifism by acquiring nuclear weapons" (French 2002). This potential reversal of traditional Japanese doctrine—the three nonnuclear principles never to own, produce, or allow nuclear weapons on Japanese territory—signals the possibility of a radical departure in Japan's posture toward its future military role in the world.

Germany and the European Union Search for a Strategic Vision

Now united with a rapidly growing economy, Germany has begun to show a new assertiveness now that most of the immense costs of reunifying and rebuilding the former German Democratic Republic in the east have been absorbed. Given its size, economic strength, and geographic location, the challenge for Europeans will be to find a way to absorb Germany within a broad European power-sharing arrangement. According to some analysts, however, Germany is too powerful to disappear into a wider European framework. It already accounts for almost one-half of the European Union's (EU) gross national product. In addition, its share of the EU budget is twice the amount of Great Britain and France combined. Moreover, most European states' economies are heavily linked to Germany's economy and trade, thereby giving Germany enormous leverage over the continent's economic growth. This extraordinary economic clout ensures Germany's continued dominance within any emergent amalgamated European political entity, whether it is built around the federalist idea of a supranational government or some other, and more modest, pan-European institutional structure. In either case, there is no set of states in the EU capable of balancing the power of a united Germany. "Too big for Europe, too small for the world" describes Germany's place in continental affairs.

If Germany's economic strength and diplomatic independence continue to grow, one consequence will be greater competition with the United States and other trade rivals. Yet this is not likely to result in a renewed push to flex German military muscle—even though Germany has one of the largest armies in Europe, and, at $21 billion in 2003, the eighth largest military budget in the world. Despite the parliamentary amendment to Germany's constitution, which permitted German troops to take part in international peacekeeping operations (for example, Germany's armed forces made up the second biggest contingent in NATO's 1999 peace force in Kosovo), an independent German military presence on the world stage is unlikely. Renewed militarism is even less so likely. Germany's armed forces are still deeply entrenched in and constrained by the joint command in NATO and the European Union's joint Eurocorps armed force. Because Germany remains a fervent advocate of the nuclear nonproliferation regime, economic rivalry is unlikely to culminate in an arms buildup in the foreseeable future. In fact, European states cashed in the so-called peace dividend after the Cold War ended and reduced their military budgets by large percentages. Total European military spending was once 60 percent of the U.S. allocation, but now it is a third of what the U.S. spends on defense, and the billions of dollars required for the EU to catch up with U.S. military technology stand as an enormous obstacle to the ability of a European force to act unilaterally without U.S. support through NATO.

That circumstance could change, however. After the September 11 crisis and the intervention into Afghanistan to root out the Taliban and Al Qaeda terrorist camps, Europe's leading military states in general, and Germany in particular, seized the opportunity provided by their engagement in the American-led coalition to strengthen their status in the global hierarchy of power. Great Britain, France, and especially Germany, but even Russia, perceived in the global battle against terrorism a chance to leverage their influence as regional leaders and global players, breaking out of their quasi-isolationistic roles as they moved in ways that expanded their international status. German Chancellor Gerhard Schroeder recast Germany's traditional sense of its place on the international stage—economically powerful but militarily timid—when he announced that his country's post–World War II role as a secondary player had "irrevocably passed." He announced "Germany needs to show a new international responsibility" as he called for a more muscular and independent German national security policy. Schroeder's advocacy of an expanded German global presence and his harsh criticism of the U.S. president's repeated threats to invade Iraq proved critical to Schroeder's September 2002 reelection.

Europe regards itself as "a second federal, democratic superpower [and] in the longer term, Euroland can—and probably will—look beyond its immediate borders. To be sure, it is not a military superpower like the United States and may not be one for some time. But that reality is less significant than is often thought. The deployment of Euroland's mammoth economic resources can have a strategic impact" (M. Elliott 1998). Thus, a strong German aversion to militarism persists and is likely to shape Germany's security policies well into the twenty-first century. In this regard, German defense strategy differs from the posture the other great powers have assumed.

What is more, Germany remains the most enthusiastic supporter of integration and institutional approaches to the preservation of peace. Its security strategy subscribes unflinchingly to the tenets of **neoliberal institutionalism:** Germany has cast its fate on the spread of international organizations, European unification, international law, disarmament, and the promotion of democracy, free markets, and free trade as the most effective strategy for ensuring that a twenty-first century peace will prevail. In that spirit, Germany is the leading proponent of the EU's quest to forge a common security policy, and Germany has been an enthusiastic supporter of the EU's decision to create an all-European expeditionary force of sixty thousand soldiers (over the U.S. protest that the European Rapid Reaction Force would reduce the need for NATO and would undermine the U.S.—European alliance). Despite U.S. objections, Europe is proceeding with its strategic vision, aiming no longer to be dependent on U.S. missiles for defense and willing to protest U.S. policies such as the U.S. preemptive strike against Iraq. As the realist analyst Fareed Zakaria characterizes the European mood,

> If it wants to be a global player in the Atlantic alliance, Europe needs a strike force that can fight with or without America. Europe has to get back into the business of making war. Since the end of the Cold War, every serious division between Europe and the United States has been over military action. Europeans simply do not believe in war anymore, largely because of their own experience. After an incredibly bloody past, Europe has moved beyond war—an amazing achievement. Within Western Europe, dialogue,

■ **neoliberal institutionalism**
the neoliberal theory in international relations that advocates creating global institutions to promote peace and security among states (see p. 570).

cooperation and trade have made conflict between the allies a distant memory. But the Europeans have now projected this mentally—born of highly unusual circumstances—onto a very difficult world. They spend lavishly on aid and send negotiation teams around the globe peddling their kinder, gentler power. . . . Even though many of them believe that Saddam Hussein is a dangerous aggressor, their solution is "anything but war." . . . With economies of roughly the same size ($8 trillion each), Europe spends only $140 billion on defense, compared with America's [$396] billion. Worse, Europe spends its money badly, maintaining large land armies (created to fight a Soviet invasion) rather than developing technology, logistics and strike forces, which are the needs of the present. The United States spends almost $30,000 per soldier on research and development, while Europe spends $4,000. Even after September 11, no European politician of note has urged a large increase in defense spending. (Zakaria 2002a, 35)

The core group of EU, NATO, and OSCE countries see nuclear weapons as legitimate and NATO's first use of nuclear weapons doctrine to deter an attack as necessary. The wisdom or folly of Germany's strategy—and the EU's bid to become a military power—will be tested by the consequences that flow from the "nuclearization" of the EU's approach to national security.

THE SEARCH FOR SECURITY IN AN INSECURE WORLD

Preparation for war continues to command support from defense planners as an approach to peace. Rationalized by realism, the quest is understandable in a world where states alone remain responsible for their own self-defense. As President Eisenhower once noted, "until war is eliminated from international relations, unpreparedness for it is well nigh as criminal as war itself."

The fears produced by visions of national vulnerability also explain why many defense planners base their plans on worst-case analyses of others' capabilities and intentions. The urge to arm is further stimulated by defense planners' influence in the policy-making process of most countries and the tendency of political leaders to adopt the vocabulary and concepts of their military advisers. A new arms race now appears to be underway as a consequence.

Asking whether military preparedness endangers, rather than ensures, national security raises an uncomfortable question that challenges the prevailing approach to national security throughout much of the world's history. Yet many experts believe such questioning is justified. To their way of thinking, now that fears of great-power war have receded, the economic and ecological dimensions of national security have assumed relatively greater prominence, and in the twenty-first century "security" should be defined more broadly so as to include both military and nonmilitary threats to human survival. Consider the argument made on behalf of a new definition of "national security":

The concept of "security" must include protection against all major threats to human survival and well-being, not just military threats. Until now, "security"—usually addressed as "national security"—has meant the maintenance of strong military defenses against enemy invasion and attack. This approach may have served us well in the past, when such attack was seen as the only real threat to national survival; today, however, when airborne poisons released by nuclear and chemical accidents can produce widespread death and sickness (as occurred with the Bhopal and Chernobyl disasters), and when global epidemiological and environmental hazards such as AIDS and the "greenhouse effect" can jeopardize the well-being of the entire planet, this perspective appears increasingly obsolete. As individual economies become ever more enmeshed in the world economy, moreover, every society becomes more vulnerable to a global economic crisis. And, as modern telecommunications bring us all closer together, we are made acutely aware of the pain and suffering of those living under oppression, tyranny, and injustice.

Given the fact that our individual security and well-being will depend to an ever-increasing extent on the world's success in mastering complex political, economic, environmental, and epidemiological problems, we must redefine "security" to embrace all of those efforts taken to enhance the long-term health and welfare of the human family. Defense against military aggression will obviously remain a vital component of security, but it must be joined by defenses against severe environmental degradation, worldwide economic crisis, and massive human suffering. Only by approaching the security dilemma from this multifaceted perspective can we develop the strategies and instruments that will be needed to promote global health and stability.

Given the multiplicity of pressing world hazards, the concept of "national security" must be integrated with that of "world security." Until now, most people have tended to rely on the nation-state to provide protection against external threats, and have viewed their own nation's security as being adversely affected by the acquisition of power and wealth of other nations. Thus, in the interests of "national security," nation-states have often engaged in a competitive struggle to enhance their own economic and military strength at the expense of other nations' capabilities. This us-versus-them, zero-sum competition for security is naturally biased toward unilateral solutions to critical problems, frequently entailing military and/or economic coercion. In today's interdependent world, however, the quest for security is rapidly becoming a positive-sum process, whereby national well-being is achieved jointly by all countries—or not at all. (Klare and Thomas 1991, 3)

Approaches to the study of national security now frequently advocate putting these nonmilitary dimensions of the problem into the picture (for example, Shultz, Godson, and Quester 1997). At issue is whether this new way of organizing perceptions of national security is an idea whose time has come.

It is an idea certain to be given close scrutiny, because a wide spectrum of problems has risen on political agendas, and the concerns of today's foreign policymakers are arguably different and more diverse than they were just a short time ago. Former U.S. Assistant Secretary of Defense Joseph Nye (2001) argues, "Power in the twenty-first century will depend on economic growth and mastering the information revolution, not on the brute nuclear force of the twentieth century. Nuclear weapons are not a power equalizer, and they cannot be used to blast one's way into an imagined great power club." Though the danger of nuclear weapons and inter- and intrastate warfare continues, it would be foolish to neglect the dangers posed by such emergent threats as trade-bloc competition, neomercantilism, trade protectionism, the continuing impoverishment of the least-developed countries, acid rain, deforestation, global warming, soaring population growth, the AIDS epidemic, international narcotic trafficking, the depletion of the earth's finite resources, and destruction of its protective ozone layer. These nonmilitary threats must command attention, as human survival may depend on addressing them.

However, the critical questions in an age of vulnerability to annihilation persist: How can states escape the prospect of destruction? How can they meet these emergent nonmilitary threats when the threat of warfare in a nationalistic age remains as pervasive as ever?

The security situation of the twenty-first century is unlikely to provide much room for maneuver. The world has yet to accept **common security** and nonoffensive defense, strategies that would eliminate offensive capabilities (Møller 1992). As demonstrated in the next chapter, many states still build weapons of attack for deterrence, even though conventional deterrence has failed frequently in the past. Moreover, contemporary deterrence theory remains based on the almost illogical premise that successful defense requires the continuing vulnerability of all states. Nonetheless, most believe that the threat system must be preserved to counter the threat and put more faith in the realist belief that for disputes to be resolved successfully it is safer to rely on the force of arms than on the force of arguments.

Thus, security may depend as much on the control of force as on its pursuit. The next chapter examines the ways in which national leaders put armaments and arsenals to use for purposes of coercive diplomacy. It then evaluates the effectiveness of the bargaining strategies of coercive diplomacy on which states rely to defend themselves and to exercise influence over others.

■ **common security**
a concept advocating replacing the notion of states competing with one another for their own national security with collective security to promote the security of all states.

KEY TERMS

self-help	relative burden of military	nonlethal weapons
national security	spending	revolution in military technology
power	arms race	(RMT)
politics	military-industrial complex	smart bombs
conflict	Nuclear Nonproliferation Treaty	firebreak
power potential	(NPT)	counterfactual reasoning
realism	proliferation	strategic weapons
globalization	Nth country problem	virtual nuclear arsenals
information age	horizontal nuclear proliferation	deterrence
coercive diplomacy	vertical nuclear proliferation	information warfare (IW) or
opportunity costs	nonproliferation regime	infowar tactics
peace dividend	security dilemma	unilateralism
national security	multiple independently targetable	multilateralism
human security	reentry vehicles (MIRVs)	bilateralism

liberalism   democratic peace   containment
zero-sum   power transition   Yoshida Doctrine
Bush Doctrine   no first use   neoliberal institutionalism
realpolitik   bandwagoning   common security

SUGGESTED READING

Buzan, Barry, Ole Waever, and Jaap de Wilde. *Security: A New Framework for Analysis.* Boulder, Colo.: Lynne Rienner, 1999.

Kaplan, Robert D. *Warrior Politics: Why Leadership Demands a Pagan Ethos.* New York: Random House, 2002.

Knox, MacGregor, and Williamson Murray. *The Dynamics of Military Revolution, 1300–2050.* Cambridge, Eng.: Cambridge University Press, 2001.

Mandel, Robert. *Armies without States: The Privatization of Security.* Boulder, Colo.: Lynne Rienner, 2002.

Nye, Joseph S., Jr. *The Paradox of American Power.* New York: Oxford University Press, 2002.

Plesch, Dan. *Sheriff and Outlaws in the Global Village.* London: Menard Press, 2002.

Powell, Robert. *In the Shadow of Power: States and Strategies in International Politics.* Princeton, N.J.: Princeton University Press, 2000.

Ralph, Jason G. *Beyond the Security Dilemma.* Brookfield, Vt.: Ashgate, 2001.

Rosecrance, Richard. *The Rise of the Virtual State: Wealth and Power in the Coming Century.* New York: Basic Books, 1999.

Sagan, Scott D., and Kenneth N. Waltz. *The Spread of Nuclear Weapons: A Debate Renewed,* 2nd ed. New York: W. W. Norton, 2002.

Schell, Jonathan. "The Unfinished Twentieth Century: What We Have Forgotten about Nuclear Weapons," *Harper's* 300 (January 2000): 41–56.

Wittkopf, Eugene R., Charles W. Kegley, Jr., and James Scott. *American Foreign Policy.* 6th ed. Belmont, Calif.: Wadsworth, 2003.

WHERE ON THE WORLD WIDE WEB?

Arms Sales Monitoring Project
http://www.fas.org/asmp/

Concerned with the global production and trade of weapons, the Federation of American Scientists is monitoring arms transfers and making data available to the public through this Web site. Click on the U.S. Arms Sales Table. Which country is the biggest recipient of U.S. arms sales? See what was sold to whom and for how much. Why do you think that certain countries got freebies?

The Henry L. Stimson Center
http://www.stimson.org/index.html

The Henry L. Stimson Center is a nonprofit, nonpartisan research center that concentrates on the intersection of national and international security policy and technology. It provides information on chemical and biological weapons, nuclear proliferation, and missile defense systems. It houses important international agreements and searches for ways to eliminate weapons of mass destruction. An excellent site for timely information.

International Code of Conduct on Arms Transfers
http://www.basicint.org/codeindx.htm

The British American Security Information Council (BASIC) is an independent research organization that analyzes government policies and promotes public awareness of defense, disarmament, military strategy, and nuclear policies. Since the United States and the Great Britain are the suppliers of 80 percent of the world light arms trade, BASIC's main goal is to petition the United States and Great Britain to create controls for weapons transfers. Visit this Web site to explore arms transfers and learn about initiatives such as Codes of Conduct, International Action Network on Small Arms, Illicit Weapons Trafficking, and Arms Brokering.

Military Spending Clock
http://www.cdi.org/sc/javaclock.html

The Center for Defense Information, a nonprofit organization, has created a military spending clock. See what the U.S. government has spent on the military to date this year. See how much is spent every second or per day and per week.

National Commission for Economic Conversion and Disarmament
http://www.webcom.com/ncecd/

The National Commission for Economic Conversion and Disarmament is a nonprofit public organization dedicated to public education on the need and ways to transfer military resources to civilian use. This Web site gives information on the costs associated with arms manufacturing and how monies can be better spent in other ways. Read the article comparing the exporting of arms to "green technologies" in the Fact Sheets or compare corporations and their conversion records. What is Washington's stance on this issue?

SIPRI Military Expenditure Country Graphs
http://sipri.se/projects/Milex/Introduction.html

The Stockholm International Peace Research Institute (SIPRI) monitors trends in military expenditures throughout the world. Its Web site lets you compare military expenditures and evaluate the economic burdens they pose. Choose a country from the Middle East, Far East, and Africa. How does their military spending compare to that of European countries? What conclusions can you draw?

INFOTRAC® COLLEGE EDITION

Search for the following articles in the InfoTrac database:

van Creveld, Martin. "Some Reflections on the Future of War," *Naval War College Review* Autumn 2000.

Mahnken, Thomas G., and Barry D. Watts. "What the Gulf War Can (and Cannot) Tell Us about the Future of Warfare," *International Security* Fall 1997.

Brooks, Stephen G., and William C. Wohlforth. "American Primacy in Perspective," *Foreign Affairs* July–August 2002.

Meilinger, Phillip S. "Force Divider: How Military Technology Makes the United States Even More Unilateral," *Foreign Policy* January–February 2002.

For more articles, enter:

"international relations" in the Subject Guide, and then go to subdivision "analysis."

"war" in the Subject Guide, and then go to subdivision "analysis."

"national security" in the Subject Guide, and then go to subdivision "analysis."

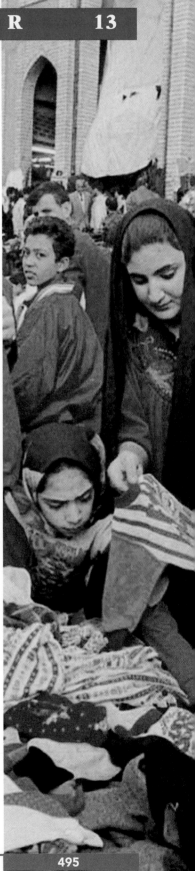

COERCIVE DIPLOMACY AND INTERVENTION IN THE AGE OF GLOBAL TERRORISM

TOPICS AND THEMES

- Coercive diplomacy as a necessary and widespread practice
- The security dilemma
- Nuclear deterrence and defense
- Deterring terrorism
  Conventional war and unconventional methods
  Prevention and preemption
- Intervention in international bargaining
- International crises
- Sanctions as instruments of coercion

- **CONTROVERSY** IS IT ETHICAL TO WAGE PREEMPTIVE WAR TO PRESERVE PEACE?

Iraq under trade
sanctions

All diplomacy is a continuation of war by other means.

—Chou En-Lai, premier, The People's Republic of China, 1954

*We all want to make the use of weapons of mass destruction less likely. The
way that you do that is to send a very strong signal to anyone who might try
to use weapons of mass destruction . . . that they'd be met with a
devastating response.*

—Condolezza Rice, U.S. national security adviser, 2002

In today's world, states often clash over conflicting national interests. Interstate discord colors visions of contemporary global realities as countries struggle to survive and to sort out the values that should guide their policies. Tensions often exist between principles and power, and unfortunately, the chaotic globe presents many dilemmas about how to pursue ideals and protect national interests. Because the world is so confusing many countries flounder in their struggle to deal with the multiple issues on the global agenda. We examine one category of bargaining behavior used by states to cope with others—coercive diplomacy.

THE PLACE OF COERCIVE DIPLOMACY IN WORLD POLITICS

Picking sides in interstate competition and responding to international crises has never been easy, which is why the German philosopher Hegel once wrote that "We learn from history that men learn nothing from history." "Hegel's wisdom aside," observed journalist Carl Rowan (1999), "there are not and never have been clear and easy lessons from history on matters that involve curbing the violent and ugly side of man's nature. That is why the United States faces what [President Bill Clinton] called 'a lot of bad alternatives.' In every generation or time, leaders and peoples are required to make hard new judgments as to how much risk they will take." Making a rational choice among unsatisfactory options is never easy, but, arguably, is now more challenging than it has been in any previous era of history.

The challenge of calculating the costs and benefits of alternative policy options was dramatized vividly in the winter of 2003. The Bush administration at that time had still not achieved its stated objective to "shut down terrorist camps, disrupt terrorist plans, and bring terrorists to justice." Osama bin Laden was still believed actively planning for Al Qaeda to stage another attack on the United States even more dreadful than the 9/11 destruction of the World Trade Center. Yet the administration chose to pursue another, equally ambitious goal: to "prevent regimes who seek chemical, biological, or nuclear weapons from threatening the United States and the world."

That policy decision extended the **Bush Doctrine** from targeting terrorist organizations to a state of war. The "doctrines of deterrence and containment," Bush announced, were no longer sufficient; hereafter "we must take the battle to the enemy, disrupt his plans, and confront the worst threats before they emerge"—in other words, wage war on other states preventively. But how? And why? Those were the questions.

Bush had to choose among options a strategy for **coercive diplomacy,** that is, for getting an enemy to do something it would otherwise not do. By what means should the danger be met? One option (for which the president sought and received congressional approval) was to use U.S. military intervention to attack Iraq, claimed to be the greatest threat. The benefit was to remove Iraqi leader Saddam Hussein from office, the Iraqi tyrant who was claimed to be acquiring weapons of mass destruction. The costs included the ethical and legal questions about a **preemptive** military strike to kill a head of state in order to force a change in regime and disarmament. Was this legal? Keep in mind that the UN Charter, following **just war theory,** permits a country to defend itself, but only in the event of an armed attack and only as a "last resort." Critics asked if by selecting preemptive actions the Bush administration, having made a commitment to the goal of intervening in a so-called rouge regime, might have been guilty of the very act that it accused Iraq of contemplating. In making its commitment to a specific goal by specific means, the Bush administration took upon itself responsibility for making many hard choices about alternative means to the declared objective.

States face many difficult choices about foreign policy ends and the means to achieve them. The complexities and contradictions in international politics increase the challenge of making a **rational choice.** The twenty-first century presents many issues about which fundamental tensions exist between conflicting values. How should states respond in the face of perceived evil or injustice? The choices in a world of borderless economies and stateless aggressors are never simple. How to reconcile power and principle, interests and ideals, puts all policymakers to the ultimate moral test, of biblical proportions, for the choices often mean the difference between life and death.

This chapter considers the dilemmas in the realm of high politics about strategic choices regarding war and peace. It looks at a perennial problem in conflict and conflict resolution: what actions should be taken against an actor

■ **Bush Doctrine**
the quest for unilateral, go-it-alone approaches to threats to U.S. security, advocating the military attack of aggressive enemies before they are able to attack the U.S., in order to prevent their own pre-emptive aggression.

■ **coercive diplomacy**
an approach to bargaining between states engaged in a crisis in which threats or the use of limited force are made to force an adversary to reach a compromise.

■ **preemptive war**
a quick first-strike attack that seeks to defeat an adversary before it can organize a retaliatory response.

■ **just war theory**
the theory originating early in the Middle Ages that identifies the criteria under which it is morally permissible, or "just," for a state to go to war and the methods by which a just war might be fought.

■ **rational choice**
the theory that decision makers choose on the basis of what they perceive to be in the best interests of themselves and their states, and select options according to their expectations about the relative usefulness of alternative means for the realization of their preferred goals. Sometimes called "expected-utility theory," this model derives from realist theories (see p. 74).

Resistance to Intervention Moral imperatives may need moral pioneers, but when a great power attempts to break down the barrier of sovereign borders by intervening for humanitarian purposes it can expect to encounter great resentment and resistance. Even the threat of military intervention by a great power in the internal affairs of another state will provoke stiff opposition in the target. Here, for example, following the Indonesian militia's rampage in East Timor after the territory voted for independence in 1999, protestors fearful of a U.S. intervention burned a U.S. flag in Jakarta. Elsewhere, wherever interventionist means of coercive diplomacy are used or threatened, opposition has produced protests.

■ **negotiation**
the process and art of discussing and debating issues when a conflict arises, in order for the disputing parties to reach a mutually satisfactory compromise agreement to resolve the issue.

■ **politics**
the exercise of influence (see p. 18).

attempting to do something illegal or immoral to others in order to get its way? The chapter thus inspects the ways states and nonstate global actors seek to influence those who do not always play by the rules and are not always interested in behaving ethically. Instead, their primary motive is to get what they want—seeking, often, to (1) protect themselves from attack by others; (2) to persuade others to act contrary to their self-serving interests; and (3) to convince others to agree to contracts that are not to their advantage. This domain of everyday international behavior, coercive diplomacy, not only involves diplomatic **negotiation** designed to settle disputes at the bargaining table, it also involves the most newsworthy category of activities for defense, deterrence, and bargaining—the ways most people think that **politics** unfolds globally as states make attempts to get other actors to change their behavior against their will. The occasions are unavoidably common because negotiators' efforts to peacefully resolve conflicts often fail, and the actors then turn to coercive methods. How coercive diplomacy *should* be managed, however, is hotly debated, because the ethics and practical payoffs of potential decisions are unclear. This chapter will concentrate on three arenas in world politics in which coercive diplomacy is especially prominent: strategic bargaining for nuclear deterrence, the place of conventional weapons in coercion and defense, and the use of economic sanctions as a policy instrument in bargaining. The prominence of these bargaining tactics is a product of the influential impact of weapons and economic resources in the equation that separates winners and losers in interstate competition. Their mismanagement is a primary reason for the frequency of war.

We look first at the changing role of armaments in interstate bargaining. This factor is pivotal to the survival capacity of coercively competing states, because, as documented in Chapter 11, one of the most disquieting long-term global trends is the exponential increase in the human toll of warfare. Preventing such human devastation is a primary security problem for all states—powerful and weak. As noted in Chapter 12, most state defense planners rely on **realism** and respond to the danger of foreign aggression by expanding their country's military capabilities. However, in and of themselves arms will not ensure peace, no matter how awesome the arsenal. To understand the predicaments that arming for war can create, the chapter first discusses the security dilemma that states face, and then examines the strategies states construct to prevent others from using arsenals against them, as well as how they use their military and economic resources in **bargaining** to exercise influence over other global actors.

THE SECURITY DILEMMA

What breeds the competition between states that leads to preparation for war? The eighteenth-century French political philosopher Jean-Jacques Rousseau argued that "the state . . . always feels itself weak if there is another that is stronger. Its security and preservation demand that it make itself more powerful than its neighbors. It can increase, nourish, and exercise its power only at their expense. . . . Because the grandeur of the state is purely relative, it is forced to compare itself to that of the others. . . . It becomes small or great, weak or strong, according to whether its neighbor expands or contracts, becomes stronger or declines."

Concern for relative power derives from states' desire for self-preservation, national identity, freedom from the control of others, status, and wealth. They seek these under anarchical conditions that provide little protection from rivals' hostile designs. Believing that their own strength will make them secure, many states attempt to build as much military might as their resources allow, often competing with one another in military capabilities.

Although states ostensibly arm for defensive purposes, their military might is often perceived as threatening. Alarmed, their neighbors arm in response. Thus, as Rousseau observed, security is relative. Such fear and its reciprocated behaviors create a predicament known as the **security dilemma**, defined as what results when "each party's power increments are matched by the others, and all wind up with no more security than when the vicious cycle began, along with the costs incurred in having acquired and having to maintain their power" (Snyder 1984).

Some scholars also describe the dynamics of this arms competition as the **spiral model** (Jervis 1976). The imagery captures the tendency of defense-

■ **realism**
an approach to world politics based on the assumption that all actors are naturally eager to compete and that they see the acquisition of weapons as a means of winning against their rivals (see p. 000).

■ **bargaining**
negotiation by states to try to settle their disputes without actually resorting to armed force.

■ **security dilemma**
the chronic distrust that actors living under anarchy feel because, without sanctions or regulatory rules, rivals will anything, including arming and using aggression, to get ahead, with the result that all lose their security in a climate of mistrust (see p. 000).

■ **spiral model**
a metaphor used to describe the tendency of efforts to enhance defense to result in escalating arms races.

enhancing efforts to result in escalating arms races that diminish the security of all. Sir Edward Grey, British foreign secretary before World War I, described this process well:

> The increase in armaments, that is intended in each nation to produce consciousness of strength and a sense of security, does not produce these effects. On the contrary, it produces a consciousness of the strength of other nations and a sense of fear. Fear begets suspicion and distrust and evil imaginings of all sorts, til each government feels it would be criminal and a betrayal of its own country not to take every precaution, while every government regards every precaution of every other government as evidence of hostile intent. (Grey 1925, 92)

Although the security dilemma affects all states, leaders still refuse to accept vulnerability. Searching for strength, they often proceed from the assumptions that (1) security is a function of power; (2) power is a function of military capability; and (3) military might is a measure of national greatness. Each of these suppositions is, of course, consistent with realpolitik.

Reformers in the liberal tradition question the logic by which states engage in competitive behavior that creates and sustains the security dilemma. To them, "the central theme of international relations is not evil but tragedy. States often share a common interest, but the structure of the situation prevents them from bringing about the mutually desired situation" (Jervis 1976). To escape this predicament, reformers adhering to **neoliberalism** call for changes in customary reliance on military approaches to national security. Many recommend disarmament, because armed countries are the most frequent target of attacks by fearful enemies. This reasoning was behind President John F. Kennedy's sober warning in 1963 that, in the event of another total war, regardless of how it might begin, those most heavily armed would automatically become primary targets and victims. Realists do not take this liberal thesis seriously. Even if leaders recognize the threats that arming for security provokes in others, they argue that global anarchy makes these threats inevitable. Because, by definition, there is no escaping a dilemma, the security dilemma explains why states sharing a common interest in security nonetheless engage in individual actions that prevent them from realizing it.

To understand how most states confront their lack of national security, consider the kinds of strategies they have created. As an object lesson we first examine the ways the two leading military powers, the United States and the former Soviet Union, sought during the Cold War to prevent nuclear attack through their evolving strategic doctrines regarding **nuclear deterrence.** We will then look at the strategies that other less militarily powerful states have used for purposes of **conventional deterrence**—prevention of an attack with conventional, nonnuclear weapons. In pursuing these topics, although nuclear and conventional deterrence are often seen as the same, most theories of the former are guided by historical investigation of cases in the latter category (Harknett 1994). It is important to keep the difference in mind.

■ **neoliberalism**
proponents of institutional reforms in governance, law, and economics as substitutes for warfare as an instrument of coercive diplomacy (see p. 43).

■ **nuclear deterrence**
dissuading an adversary from attacking by threatening retaliation with nuclear weapons.

■ **conventional deterrence**
dissuading an adversary from attacking by threatening retaliation with nonnuclear weapons.

NUCLEAR DETERRENCE AND DEFENSE

The dropping of the atomic bomb on Japan on August 6, 1945, is the most important event distinguishing pre– from post–World War II international politics. In the blinding flash of a single weapon and the shadow of its mushroom cloud, the globe was transformed from a balance-of-power to a balance-of-terror system.

In the following decades, policymakers in the nuclear states had to grapple with two central policy questions: (1) whether they should use nuclear weapons; and (2) how to prevent others from using them. The search for answers has been critical, for the immediate and delayed effects of a nuclear war are terrifying to contemplate. Even a short war using a tiny fraction of any country's nuclear warheads, life as we know it would cease. The planet would be uninhabitable, because a **nuclear winter** would result, with devastating consequences:

> As bad as the prompt and local effects of nuclear war would be, the delayed and global consequences might be much worse. . . . Forest fires ignited in such a war could generate enough smoke to obscure the sun and perturb the atmosphere over large areas. . . . That smoke from the burning of modern cities would provide a still more serious threat. . . . Provided cities were targeted, even a "small" nuclear war could have disastrous climatic consequences; a global war, . . . might lower average planetary temperatures by 15° to 20° C, darken the skies sufficiently to compromise green plant photosynthesis, produce a witches' brew of chemical and radioactive poisons, and significantly deplete the protective ozone layer. These effects, which had been almost wholly overlooked by the world's military establishments, [are] described as "nuclear winter." (Sagan and Turco 1993, 369)

It has been estimated that "the missiles on board a single [U.S.] SLBM submarine may be enough to initiate nuclear winter" (Quester 1992)—enough to end human existence. To defense planners, this prospect makes using nuclear weapons unthinkable. To the extent that nuclear states appreciate this fact, the purpose of nuclear weapons is reduced to one objective—deterring external aggression. However, many defense planners still advocate the threat of launching a nuclear strike as a declared policy option for coercive bargaining. The wisdom of a so-called first strike strategy is increasingly questionable, because if an enemy does not believe that a sane nuclear arms state would actually use its weapons in retaliation against aggression, that threat is useless as a deterrent—a bluff lacking credibility. Some experts believe that the recent voluntary reductions in the great powers' nuclear inventories have been due to the recognition that nuclear weapons are not useful as instruments in coercive bargaining. Nonetheless, those nuclear arsenals remain substantial, for whatever purpose.

The threat of nuclear war was, and remains, particularly pertinent to the United States and Russia, today's two most heavily armed nuclear powers. Their decisions during the Cold War—the formative period that still casts its

■ **nuclear winter**
the expected freeze that would occur in the Earth's climate from the fallout of smoke and dust in the event nuclear weapons were used, blocking out sunlight and destroying plant and animal life that survived the original blast.

Hiroshima In the first true test of the awful destructive capabilities of atomic weapons on cities, the United States dropped an atomic bomb on Hiroshima on August 6, 1945, in an attempt to bring World War II to a speedy close. In an instant, what later became known as "the nuclear age" was ushered in and the Japanese city lay in ruins.

■ **signaling**
in conflict situations, either explicit or implicit communication by states to reveal both their intentions and their capabilities.

shadow on defense planning—helps us to understand the larger subject of which it is a part: how states view deterrence as a method of coercive diplomacy for **signaling**—making threats in order to intimidate a potential enemy from using its weapons aggressively.

Superpower Deterrence and Defense Policies

Although weapons of mass destruction have existed since World War II, the superpowers' postures toward them have evolved as technologies, defense needs, capabilities, and global conditions have changed. For analytical convenience, we can treat those postures in terms of three periods. The first began at the end of World War II and lasted until the **Cuban Missile Crisis.** U.S. nuclear superiority was the dominant characteristic of this period. The second began in 1962 and lasted until the breakup of the Soviet Union in 1991. Growing Soviet military capability was the dominant characteristic of this period (which meant that the United States no longer stood alone in its ability to annihilate another country). The third phase began in 1992, as the former Cold War antagonists and other rising great powers revised their strategic doctrines.

■ **Cuban Missile Crisis**
the showdown in October 1962 between the United States and the Soviet Union over the deployment of Soviet missiles in Cuba.

■ **compellence**
a method of coercive diplomacy usually involving an act of war or threat to force an adversary to make concessions against its will.

Compellence, 1945–1962. Countries that enjoy military superiority often think of weapons as instruments for coercive bargaining—that is, as tools to be used for changing others' behavior. The United States, the world's first and, for many years, unchallenged nuclear power, adopted a **compellence** (Schelling 1966) strategic doctrine when it enjoyed a clear-cut superiority in the nuclear balance of power. Compellence made nuclear weapons instruments of political influence, used not for fighting but to convince others to do what they might not otherwise do. Thus it refers to nuclear weapons as instruments for "forceful persuasion" (George 1992), even if some question the ethics of a policy instrument that uses terror to pursue worthy ends such as peace (see Controversy: Is It Ethical to Wage War in Order to Make Peace?).

The United States sought to gain bargaining leverage by conveying the impression that it would actually use nuclear weapons. Its threatening posture regarding **commitments** in strategic negotiations was especially evident during the Eisenhower administration. In the 1950s, to win political victories Secretary of State John Foster Dulles practiced **brinkmanship,** deliberately threatening U.S. adversaries with nuclear destruction so that, at the brink of war, they would concede to U.S. demands. Others went even further, seeing the new weapons of mass destruction as instruments for bargaining. Brinkmanship became part of the overall U.S. strategic doctrine known as **massive retaliation.** It advocated the use of nuclear weapons to contain communism and Soviet expansionism. Massive retaliation was a **countervalue targeting strategy** because it targeted U.S. nuclear weapons at what the Soviets most valued—their population and industrial centers. The alternative is a **counterforce targeting strategy,** which targets an enemy's military forces and weapons, thus sparing civilians from immediate destruction.

Mutual Deterrence, 1962–1991. As U.S. strategic superiority eroded, American policymakers began to question the usefulness of weapons of mass destruction for political bargaining, or for **peace enforcement** to coerce an adversary to stop fighting. They were horrified by the destruction that could result if compellence should provoke a nuclear exchange. In contrast to so-called **limited war,** waged without recourse to all weapons in a state's arsenal, the nearly suicidal Cuban Missile Crisis of 1962 dealt coercive diplomacy a serious blow, and undermined faith in **total war,** waged against an enemy's civilian population and economy to destroy its fighting spirit and capacity to continue. With missiles and nuclear weapons, it was becoming recognized that there are no civilians. After the near-miss Cuban encounter, the objective of nuclear weapons shifted from compellence to deterrence to prevent an attack.

Ironically, the shift from compellence to deterrence stimulated rather than inhibited the U.S.-Soviet arms race. A deterrent strategy depends on the unquestionable ability to inflict unacceptable damage on an opponent. It requires a **second-strike capability** that enables a country to withstand an adversary's first strike and still retain the ability to retaliate with a devastating counterattack. To ensure a second-strike capability and an adversary's awareness of it, deterrence rationalized an unrestrained search for sophisticated retaliatory capabilities. Any system that could be built was built because, as President Kennedy explained in 1961, "only when arms are sufficient beyond doubt can we be certain without doubt that they will never be employed."

Policymakers coined the phrase **mutual assured destruction (MAD)** to describe the superpowers' essential military stalemate. Mutual deterrence, based on the principle of assured destruction, assumed the military potential for and psychological expectation of widespread death and destruction by both combatants in a nuclear exchange. Peace—or at least stability—was viewed as the product of mutual vulnerability, which was seen in turn as a precondition

■ commitment
a negotiator's promises during bargaining, designed to change the target's expectations about the negotiator's future behavior.

■ brinkmanship
the intentional, reckless taking of huge risks in bargaining with an enemy, such as threaning a nuclear attack, to compel submission.

■ massive retaliation
the Eisenhower administration's policy doctrine for containing Soviet communism by pledging to respond to any act of aggression with the most destructive capabilities available, including nuclear weapons.

■ countervalue targeting strategy
the bargaining doctrine that declares the intention to use weapons of mass destruction against an enemy's most valued nonmilitary resources, such as the civilians and industries located in its cities.

■ counterforce targeting strategy
targeting strategic nuclear weapons on particular military capabilities of an enemy's armed forces and arsenals.

■ peace enforcement
military actions undertaken to impose a peace settlement, truce, or agreement to surrender by a warring party, or to prevent the resumption of fighting by the participants in a past war.

CONTROVERSY

IS IT ETHICAL TO WAGE PREEMPTIVE WAR TO PRESERVE PEACE?

From the first recorded use of weapons by one society against another in human history, people have debated the ethical criteria by which a just war can be waged without violating the principle that it is morally wrong to kill. That debate has continued without a consensus emerging worldwide about the conditions under which it is morally acceptable to use armed force for political purposes. Experts in both defense and moral ethics remain divided as to the just means for containing aggression. International law also is divided (see Chapter 15).

Can war be stopped by waging it? Some realists believe so, arguing there are no moral limits: the ends justify the terrible means; might makes right; evil must be resisted; you can't negotiate with aggressors, so their aggression must be prevented. The savagery of war, of course, can never be justified to its victims. Critics argue that such strategies, which overlook the traditional right of innocent noncombatants to protection from genocide, violate international law and are crimes against humanity. Classic Christian and other pacifist theologians also condemn the extreme realist position that accepts evil methods, maintaining that a right intention does not automatically justify any means to achieve it.

The debate over the conditions justifying waging war to preserve peace heated up in 2002, when the Bush administration spelled out its grievances against Iraqi leader Saddam Hussein in attempting to justify why the United States planned a preemptive first strike to prevent Iraq from obtaining weapons of mass destruction for use against the United States. The United States prepared for an invasion, asserting that Saddam was too irrational for deterrence. "We do not have the luxury of doing nothing," National Security Advisor Condolezza Rice claimed. Critics questioned the logic and the morality. Germany's Chancellor Gerhard Schroeder barked that attacking an enemy simply because of what it might intend to do, to prevent its later aggression, was the same faulty argument Adolf Hitler had used in starting World War II. An attack also violates the established U.S. ban on assassination of foreign leaders, and the UN Charter's prohibition against waging war except in defense against an actual armed attack by an aggressor— not to remove another state's military capabilities. "Who can possibly argue that there is anything moral about killing other people's children?" the outraged British

Andrea Comas/Reuters/Getty Images

Protestors in Madrid, Spain, demonstrate against a possible U.S.-led preemptive strike against Iraq.

Minister Public Alice Mahon added. In planning a preemptive attack, critics claimed the Bush administration was ignoring the just war restraints against first strikes for either deterrence or revenge, and overturning 150 years of international law.

What do you think? Should the United States expect support for its radical new policy? If the U.S. actions are judged as justifiable, also ask what this means for others if they follow the same logic as that of the globe's reigning superpower. In the "categorical imperative," the German philosopher Immanuel Kant argued that, when evaluating the morality of a decision, the question to ask is what would happen if everyone else acted on the same basis. What will the world be like if preemptive strikes become a universal norm and *all* states base their peace strategies on the claimed right to make war for preemptive purposes?

Bernard Hermann/Liaison Agency

Nuclear Testing When informed of the possibility of designing a hydrogen bomb, U.S. President Truman asked, "What the hell are we waiting for?" Politicians hailed the nuclear weapon as a defensive force. However, scientists such as Robert Oppenheimer—who headed the Manhattan Project, which produced the atomic bomb—maintained that the hydrogen bomb was inherently immoral because it was a weapon of genocide that was so destructive that its use could not be restricted to military purposes. More than two thousand nuclear-weapons tests have occurred since 1945, and testing has continued. Pictured here is a 1995 French atomic test in the South Pacific of a nuclear bomb smaller than the hydrogen bomb that, in 1952, created a three-mile fireball one thousand times more powerful than the bombs used by the United States on Hiroshima and Nagasaki.

for successful deterrence. Each superpower sought to preserve the other's second-strike capability, trusting that neither would then dare to attack the other at the price of its own subsequent destruction.

As U.S.-Soviet relations evolved, debate in the United States concerning the best way to protect national security with strategic weapons broke into polar positions. Although MAD continued to dominate the thinking of some, others advocated **nuclear utilization theory (NUTs),** an approach whereby nuclear weapons would not simply play a deterrent role, but could also be used in war. Such a posture was necessary, some U.S. policy advisers argued, because the Soviet Union was preparing to fight—and win—a nuclear war (Pipes 1977). Furthermore, advocates of NUTs argued that use of nuclear weapons would not necessarily escalate to an unmanageable, all-out nuclear exchange. Instead, they reasoned that it was possible to fight a protracted "limited" nuclear war. By making nuclear weapons more usable, they argued, the United States could make nuclear threats more credible.

Proponents of MAD, on the other hand, held that deterrence remained the only sane purpose for nuclear weapons and contended that any use of nuclear weapons—however limited initially—would surely escalate to an unrestrained exchange.

■ **limited war**
the restrained use of armed force, short of full-scale warfare, to obtain limited objectives.

■ **total war**
wars, such as World Wars I and II, fought with all available weapons to threaten an enemy's survival, as opposed to limited wars waged with restricted capabilities for specific objectives.

■ **second-strike capability**
a state's capacity to retaliate after absorbing a first-strike attack with weapons of mass destruction.

■ **mutual assured destruction (MAD)**
a system of mutual deterrence in which both sides possess the ability to survive a first strike and launch a devastating retaliatory attack.

■ **nuclear utilization theory (NUTs)**
a body of strategic thought that claimed deterrent threats would be more credible if nuclear weapons were made more usable.

As the 1980s nuclear debate raged, U.S. and Soviet leaders both professed their commitment to avoiding nuclear war, viewing it as "unthinkable." This meant expanding the capabilities of both defensive and offensive systems. Thus each superpower continued developing and deploying the kinds of weapons that NUTs required—so-called discriminating low-yield nuclear weapons made possible by new technologies in guidance and precision. This weaponry prepared the contestants for warfare short of a massive, all-out nuclear attack and sought to provide them with effective deterrents against a conventional war.

A new shift in strategic thinking occurred in 1983, when U.S. President Reagan proposed building a space-based defensive shield against ballistic missiles. The **Strategic Defense Initiative (SDI),** as it was known, called for the development of a "Star Wars" ballistic missile defense (BMD) system using advanced space-based technologies to destroy offensive weapons launched in fear, anger, or by accident. The goal, as President Reagan defined it, was to make nuclear weapons "impotent and obsolete." Thus SDI sought to shift U.S. nuclear strategy away from reliance on offensive missiles to deterring attack—that is, away from dependence on MAD, which President Reagan deemed "morally unacceptable."

From the start, scientists questioned the feasibility of SDI's technological fix to the security dilemma posed by strategic weapons. There was simply no assurance that a reliable system was possible.

Deterrence and Defense after the Cold War.   Despite uncertainties about its effectiveness, even with technological advances, and its questionable legality as a repudiation of the 1972 Anti-Ballistic Missile (ABM) Treaty outlawing high-altitude theater missile defenses (TMD) systems, the United States has continued to proceed with the development of a ballistic missile defense system. In the first Bush administration, the primary purpose was to defend the United States from a nuclear attack by a great-power rival, such as the Soviet Union. The goal was protection as a substitute to reliance on the theory of deterrence. However, when the Cold War ended in 1991, that rationale faded, and with it the original U.S. incentive for constructing a missile defense system. The new geostrategic setting became especially clear after the United States and Russia negotiated a series of historic arms control and disarmament agreements, from the first START (Strategic Arms Reduction Treaty) in 1993 to the 2002 SORT accord that pledged by the year 2012 to shrink their nuclear warheads to between one thousand seven hundred and two thousand two hundred—a 92 percent decline for the 1986 peak (see Chapters 12 and 14).

Alongside what U.S. President George W. Bush termed the achievement—"the liquidation of the legacy of the Cold War"—other great powers also reduced the number of nuclear warheads in their arsenals deployed for strategic bargaining to threaten, wage, or deter nuclear war. Worldwide, the total number of nuclear warheads was cut in half in 2002 to less than 30,000. As a consequence, the strategic nuclear **balance of power** is radically different today than it was during most of the second half of the twentieth century.

To some, this sea change necessitates major rethinking of old assumptions. Strategic **doctrine,** defining when weapons of mass destruction should be used, is being reexamined. The superpowers' nuclear warheads have been slashed, and Russia has become a consultant in the North Atlantic Treaty Organization

---

■ **Strategic Defense Initiative (SDI)**
the so-called Star Wars plan conceived by the Reagan administration to deploy an antiballistic missile system using space-based lasers that would destroy enemy nuclear missiles before they could enter Earth's atmosphere.

■ **balance of power**
the theory that peace and stability are most likely to be maintained when military power is distributed so that no single power or bloc can dominate the others. (see p. 103).

■ **doctrine**
the guidelines a great power adopts defining the conditions under which it will use military power and armed force for political purposes abroad (see p. 209).

(NATO) (which was first created in 1949 to deter the then-Soviet Union from expansion and to contain communism's influence).

Was deterrence successful in bringing about this remarkable transformation? Some attribute the end of the Cold War without bloodshed to the effectiveness of the superpowers' deterrence strategies—the intimidating power of their weapons, which made aggression suicidal—and to the rationality of leaders, inspired by their awareness that survival was preferable to victory. This is called the **pax atomica.** Others believe that the superpowers averted apocalypse despite their awesome arsenals and deterrence doctrines rather than because of them. In fact, many of the critics of strategic nuclear deterrence (Johansen 1991; Vasquez 1991) complain that the doctrine's validity is suspect, because deterrence is the nonoccurrence of an event and by definition depends on **counterfactual reasoning** that cannot be proven because it is not testable. According to this line of reasoning, "Although it can be argued that nuclear deterrence worked during the Cold War, we do not know that for sure. (The USSR may never have wished to invade Europe or to attack the United States with nuclear weapons.) It is very difficult to prove deterrent successes because that would require showing why an event did not occur" (Haffa 1992).

Regardless of its causes, the suspension of the superpowers' Cold War rivalry has not loosened the grip of deterrence on strategic planning in the early twenty-first century. New threats are on the horizon, as the September 11, 2001, terrorist attacks on New York and Washington made evident. Against this threat a defense is needed. This is why the United States is presently pursuing a dual bargaining strategy to contain the terrorist and other threats it perceives to the U.S. homeland from such rogue states as Iraq, Iran, and North Korea—which President Bush termed in 2002 "the axis of evil" in the modern world. For defense, his administration has vigorously pushed forward with plans to develop the space-based antiballistic missile system, like that first purposed by Reagan's "Star Wars" design, to protect the United States against a nuclear attack by an enemy. To justify this costly program, the administration cites the proliferation of states with nuclear weapons (see Map 13.1). Many of the countries are U.S. adversaries that are expected to have the capacity to deliver nuclear weapons by missiles. To deter attacks involving weapons of mass destruction such as nuclear warheads, in March 2002 the Bush administration declared that the United States must be prepared to use its nuclear weapons. At that time Secretary of State Colin Powell stated the U.S. policy when he said that the United States has never ruled out using nuclear weapons against a nuclear-armed enemy, a policy he said should deter any would-be attacker, arguing "We think it is best for any potential adversary out there to have uncertainty in his calculus."

What 9/11 taught the world was that weapons of mass destruction can be delivered not only with short-range or intermediate-range ballistic missiles, but by other means—such as a hijacked airplane used as a missile to destroy a target like the World Trade Center, or a suitcase carried by a single suicide bomber. 9/11 demonstrated that terrorist groups have set their sites on using weapons of mass destruction, including not only nuclear but also, in all probability, biological and chemical weapons, and that they are now interested in inflicting heavy casualties instead of simply using, as in the past, terrorist acts as theater to draw attention to their cause (see Chapter 11). To wage a worldwide war against terrorism, the United States, its NATO allies, and other members of the antiterrorism coalition (such as China and Russia) have sought to deter terrorists' future

■ **pax atomica**
the notion that nuclear weapons have preserved peace.

■ **counterfactual reasoning**
thought experiments to consider the consequences that probably would have resulted had something happened that actually did not, such as speculating "what if Adolf Hitler had invaded Britain" or "what if John F. Kennedy had not been assassinated" (see p. 102).

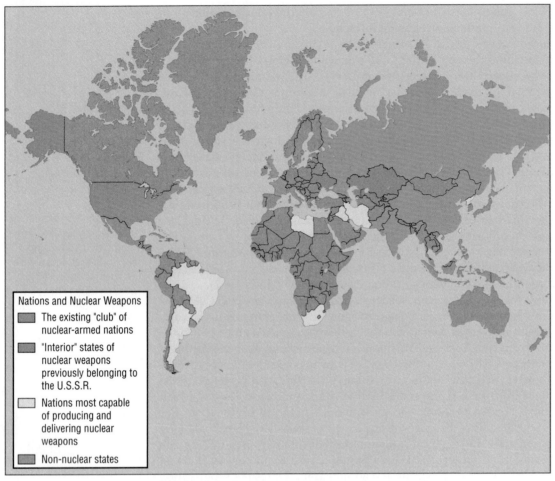

Nations and Nuclear Weapons

■ The existing "club" of nuclear-armed nations

■ "Interior" states of nuclear weapons previously belonging to the U.S.S.R.

□ Nations most capable of producing and delivering nuclear weapons

■ Non-nuclear states

MAP 13.1
Nuclear-Weapon Armed Countries, Today and Tomorrow

Despite the great decline in the number of wars between states since the end of the Cold War in 1989 (see Chapter 11), nuclear proliferation is a growing trend, as this map shows. Beyond the United States, Russia, Great Britain, France, China, India, Pakistan, and Israel, four new independent Soviet republics (Ukraine, Kazakhstan, Uzbekistan, and Georgia) still retain the nuclear weapons they acquired from the old Soviet Union. South Africa is believed to already possess the capacity to use nuclear warheads in wartime, and North Korea has pursued a secret uranium-enrichment program in violation of past agreements and in 2003 prepared to restart a nuclear reactor capable of producing weapons-grade plutonium. Six other countries have active nuclear-weapon development programs, which may include the capacity to manufacture and deliver these weapons of mass destruction—Argentina, Brazil, Iran, Iraq, Libya, North Korea, and Taiwan. Nuclear proliferation means that nuclear deterrence will remain a key component of national strategy and coercive diplomacy. SOURCE: Based on data from Bulletin of the Atomic Scientists (Nov–Dec 2002), 103.

capacity to attack through the various preemptive and proactive military strategies available (the mixed success of these approaches at various time throughout history notwithstanding). Deterrence as a method of coercive diplomacy continues as a popular bargaining tactic.

Few expect a war between the great powers in the foreseeable future, although most expect Global South wars to continue. The great powers have sought to restructure their armed forces in order to cope with the kinds of threats and weapons with which adversaries will fight such wars. This requires collective great-power efforts to keep nuclear weapons out of the hands of terrorists and other kinds of actors seeking to use aggression to get their way. The challenge is great, because illegal trafficking in the transborder transport of the nuclear materials necessary to produce a nuclear bomb is very active, with over four hundred confirmed incidents since 1993 (*Foreign Policy*, January/February 2002, 14).

The twenty-first-century security landscape also calls for increasing the capacity to wage conventional wars in emergent trouble spots. Military preparations have not ceased, but instead have been redirected toward short-term wars fought with increasingly sophisticated conventional weapons. The emerging strategies of the great powers now reflect their search for a new security architecture to contain regional conflicts, guard against the rising power of their rivals, and safeguard their homelands from the threat of terrorism.

DETERRING TERRORISM

The Global South is populated by many hypernationalist countries of growing military strength with an interest in controlling events in the areas where their primary security interests lie. This danger has increased the importance of conventional deterrence and reliance on unconventional methods of coercion against nonstate adversaries of terrorists.

> The most important challenge for deterrence strategists may not be in dealing with the increased frequency of military conflict, but rather in dealing with an increased *variety* of sources of conflict. . . . Nationalist aspirations, religious cleavages, and resurgent authoritarian coups may all cut against established international political alignments. Now, and in the foreseeable future, the sources of war will have to be viewed across a variety of dimensions. (Harknett 1994, 102–103)

Many states today are failing or in turmoil and perceive military force below the threshold of nuclear weapons as a viable means to achieve their political aims. Indeed, to the many states harboring historical grievances, armed coercion is a highly attractive option, as threats to initiate less-destructive and less-costly military actions with conventional weapons are far more likely to be believed than are threats to initiate a nuclear war. **Conventional war** is a more credible bargaining chip, because the risks are lower and the odds of retaliation by the target also are lower. The assumptions about the advantages of bargaining with the hard fist of conventional weapons and unconventional strategies are embedded, for example, in recent publications of the U.S. *Quadrennial Defense Review*. These strategic assessments assert that America's clear-cut lead

■ **conventional war**
armed conflicts waged with nonnuclear naval, air, and ground weapons.

in all conventional weapons would allow it to deter enemy states from the temptation of following Iraq's poor decision in the Persian Gulf War when Saddam Hussein concluded that Iraq could take on U.S. tanks, aircraft, and other conventional weapons.

After 9/11, these reviews have predicted that future U.S. wars were likely to be fought against nonstate challengers, such as elusive terrorist groups, which rely on conventional and nonconventional weapons such as jetliners used as missiles. "We are menaced less by fleets and armies than by catastrophic technologies in the hands of the embittered few," maintained *The National Security Strategy of the United States of America*, released by the Bush administration in 2002. "America is now threatened less by conquering states than by failing ones. . . . Traditional concepts of deterrence will not work against a terrorist enemy whose avowed tactics are wanton destruction and the targeting of innocents; whose so-called soldiers seek martyrdom in death and whose most potent protection is statelessness." This requires, it is argued, **preemption** over deterrence, relying on military power. To defeat faceless and stateless adversaries, conventional methods of coercive will not work because the enemy does not have things it values that can be used in bargaining. The logical conclusion: To confront enemies in wars without clear territorial objectives, the United States would require more of almost every conventional weapon—overseas bases, long-range aircraft, and technologically advanced surveillance and communication equipment—to protect the American homeland. For defense, huge investments are recommended for both high-tech and low-tech military instruments, such as information technology to project U.S. power in distant battlegrounds against adversaries armed with crude missiles, old-fashioned submarines, and the like.

Deterrence is a risky game, and the strategies on which most states today depend do not give them reliable protection. Conventional force can be used for coercive purposes and frequently is. The activity is not just practiced by weak states in the Global South; the use of conventional armed conflict short of war is a component of the great powers' bargaining strategies, as the **low-intensity conflict (LIC)** programs of the United States and others illustrate. In an interdependent world that is fraught with ethnic and religious rivalries, so-called **asymmetrical warfare,** or armed conflicts between enemies of unequal strength, short of full-scale war are likely to erupt often, and great powers are likely to influence the outcomes of the conflicts with low-intensity bargaining tactics using unconventional military methods. Low-intensity conflict is now a symbol of warfare between the haves and have-nots, referring primarily to methods for combating terrorism, insurgency, and guerrilla activities in the Global South and failed states. Such warfare below the level of overt military operations by a state's regular army includes proxy wars, wars fought with mercenaries, psychological operations to terrorize a populace, and death squads. "What is crucial to recognize," notes Michael T. Klare (1988), "is that low-intensity conflict is a form of warfare in which your side suffers very little death or destruction, while the other side suffers as much damage as possible without producing undue hardship for your own society."

The methods through which coercive diplomacy is pursued are varied, for both deterrence, compellence, and prevention. To bring about changes in other actors' behavior, states may rely on words and deeds, usually attempting to

■ **preemption**
a quick first-strike attack that seeks to defeat an adversary before it can organize a retaliatory response.

■ **low-intensity conflict (LIC)**
insurgency and counter-insurgency warfare fought with inexpensive conventional weapons that falls below the threshold of full-scale military combat between modern armies.

■ **asymmetrical warfare**
armed conflict between different types of enemies; one of which is much more militarily powerful than the other.

combine both. They talk tough by making threats and often act tough by using their military capabilities.

As the U.S.-led war on terrorism after 9/11 revealed, divisions regularly arise between diplomats and defense ministries over the best approaches to containing the multiple dangers posed by global terrorism—a form of armed conflict below the threshold of full-scale warfare. To what extent should a confrontational, militant, and preemptive counterterrorism strategy be pursued? Or should terrorism be addressed through negotiations, or perhaps even foreign assistance to alleviate the poverty and resentments of poor and marginalized societies which are the soil from which terrorism springs?

Terrorists are working hard at finding ways to inflict damage on enemy targets, usually in the most wealthy states. Terrorists' strategies include, among others, such tactics as infiltrating any one of the sixty-six U.S. nuclear power plants, hijacking by slipping potent conventional explosives past airport screening devices, using truck bombs loaded with explosives, causing panic by exploding uranium-packed devices that would spread toxic radiation over a wide area, or releasing cyanide into pipes that supply water for the target population. The issue: how to prevent such tactics, when complete deterrence and protection requires guarding everybody, everywhere, at every hour? In waging the antiterrorist wars of the future, unconventional methods are needed for this kind of unconventional combat waged by nonstate terrorist organizations. Defense against terrorist attacks requires tactics that go well outside the means for which most military establishments were originally created, because large armies and weapons systems were traditionally designed to fight and repel the armies of another state, not the subterranean underworld in which international terrorist networks operate in a global environment that facilitates their activities across state borders.

It is difficult to generalize about the effectiveness of various terrorist and counterterrorists strategies that work in some situations but not others. Bargaining strategies to deal with these security challenges, like those presented by traditional aggression waged by states, depend on the issue, the reputation of the actor pursuing a strategy of coercive diplomacy, and the actor's commitment to its goals. The use of alternative strategies also varies with the purpose of the action. **Preventive diplomacy**—managing emergent threats by swiftly demonstrating intentions and capabilities—is one thing. The actual use of force in retaliation for acts deemed immoral, illegal, or threatening to national interests is another. Although those who initiate war often see it as a necessary instrument to pursuing national interests, it takes the game to a higher level. The escalation can either work or backfire. Consequently, the relationship between promises of rewards and military threats of destruction is complex. It works at times when the goal is war prevention as opposed to **peacekeeping** (stabilizing a threatening dispute) and peace enforcement (operations to keep terminated military hostilities from reigniting), and it fails at other times.

Military Intervention

Making military threats to coerce others can be done in many forms at many levels. However, the most frequent practice is **military intervention**—sending troops onto others' territory in order to influence developments and policies there. Coercive diplomacy sometimes moves from talking to bombing, but more

■ **preventive diplomacy** diplomatic actions taken in advance of a predictable crisis to prevent or limit violence. (see p. 589).

■ **peacekeeping** external programs by intervening forces such as UN volunteers to stabilize war-torn regions, usually with only modest resources and in ways that avoid labeling an aggressor or provoking the hostility of a great power (see p. 589).

■ **military intervention** overt or covert use of force by one or more countries that cross the border of another country in order to affect the target country's government and policies.

frequently involves sending arms, armies, and aircraft to foreign territory. It can come in many forms, however; states can intervene physically through direct entry into another country or indirectly with propaganda through the penetration of another society's culture and spiritual life to alter its values. And intervention can be unilateral (by one state), or bilateral (two intervening states), or multilateral (with three or more intervening states acting together through an alliance or an international organization).

One way of conceptualizing foreign overt military intervention is as the type of international behavior "most closely associated with international war" (Tillema 1989). This conception includes as instances "battles involving regular foreign military forces, at least on one side" that seldom result in more than one thousand fatalities. Interventions thus involve "military operations undertaken openly by a state's regular military forces within a specific foreign land in such a manner as to risk immediate combat" (Tillema 1994). Conceived in this manner, intervention is a distinct category of militarized international behavior, which: (1) involves the use of force, (2) is intrinsically hostile in motive, (3) often results in the loss of soldiers' lives, and (4) is usually described by the target as an act of war. Based on this definition, evidence suggests that interventionary activities have been frequent, if erratically occurring, since World War II (see Figure 13.1)

Altogether, nearly 1,000 individual acts of military intervention have been initiated since 1945; if the 2.4 million fatalities resulting from an average of nearly fifteen military interventions each year between 1945 and 1991 (Tilleman 2001) are extrapolated, the human death toll will exceed 3 million deaths early in the twenty-first century. Excluded from this estimate of state military interventions worldwide is an unknown number of additional **covert operations.** If these were included in the total, military interventionism would appear to be an even greater part of the way the world pictures interventionism in world affairs. That role seems destined to grow, given the rise of the use of mercenaries as "private military companies . . . working hand in glove with various governments to fight their wars in a businesslike manner" (Isenberg 2001).

As a result of frequent overt and covert activity, military interventions have often heightened international tension and led to war. Between 1816 and 2001, forty-one cases of third-party military intervention into 242 civil wars occurred, with the result that 17 percent were "internationalized" as they were transformed into interstate wars (recall Table 11.1). The critical question about the use of military interventions for coercive diplomacy is their probable consequences. When states intervene, does this usually help peacekeeping, peacemaking, and preventive diplomacy by containing serious threats from escalating to full-scale war, or by providing a calming influence in a war-torn or famine-stricken failing state? Or does intervention more often result not in pacification but in war? Those questions have become perhaps the most hotly debated issue in world politics at the start of the twenty-first century. In the wake of humanitarian interventions in Kosovo and East Timor in 1999, the great powers struggled unsuccessfully in an effort to reach consensus about the need to intervene in sovereign states when innocent civilians are made the victims of acts of atrocity committed by dictators and tyrants. UN Secretary-General Kofi Annan's plea in September 1999 for the permanent members of the Security Council to make "a new commitment to intervention" stirred up an

■ **covert operations**
secret activities undertaken by a state outside its borders through clandestine means to achieve specific political or military goals with respect to another.

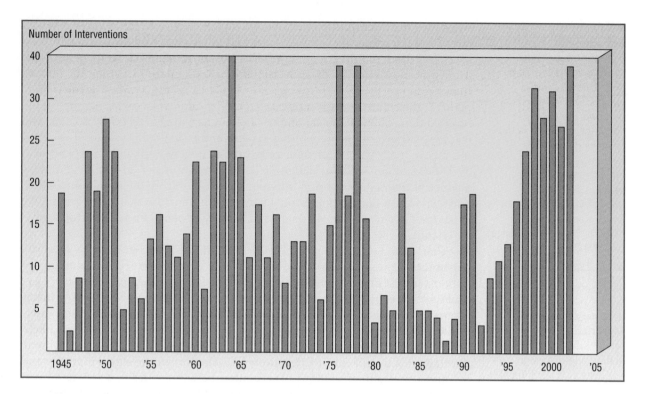

FIGURE 13.1

The Changing Incidence through Unilateral Military Intervention of Coercive Diplomacy, 1945–2002

States have frequently sent their troops into the sovereign territory of other states in order to influence the target, despite the fact that military intervention has traditionally been prohibited by international law. This figure shows fluctuations in the frequency of intervention since 1945.

SOURCE: Based on Pickering (1999), with estimates since 1999 based on data and projections in 2002 from *Facts on File*, as inventoried by Min Ye and Long Wang.

already intense debate about the limits to involvement and intervention, even in the name of morality, justice, and human rights.

Few question the necessity to stand up to genocide and intervene to protect the lives of persecuted peoples in theory. However, many great powers remain reluctant to pledge unconditionally to protect the **human rights** of innocent civilians. Even the United States has retreated from the blanket commitment of the Clinton Doctrine. "The real Clinton Doctrine [was] this: The U.S. will protect innocent civilians from bullies—but only bullies that don't count geopolitically. When China oppresses Tibet, Russia ravages Chechnya or Indonesia reduces East Timor to rubble, [the United States does] not intervene" (Krauthammer 1999).

Bcause the impulse to intervene for high moral and humanitarian purposes is tempting in a troubled world where evil terrorist acts and aggression are rampant, particularly in **failed states,** intervention in the name of global responsibility is likely to continue. At the same time, most great powers are likely to practice **selective engagement** by picking and choosing when and where they

■ **human rights**
the political rights and civil liberties recognized by the international community as freedoms to which all people are entitled, even though many such inalienable privileges are not universally protected by the laws of states.

■ **failed states**
countries whose governments have so mismanaged policy that they have lost the loyalty of their citizens who, in rebellion, threaten to divide the state into separate countries (see p. 209)

■ **selective engagement**
a great power grand strategy using economic and military power to influence only important particular situations, countries, or global issues by striking a balance between a highly interventionist "global policeman" and an uninvolved isolationist when crises erupt in a great-power's sphere of influence. (see p. 128)

■ **state-sponsored terrorism**
formal assistance, training, and arming of foreign terrorists by a state in order to achieve foreign policy goals.

■ **crisis decisions**
choices made in highly threatening and potentially grave situations, involving elements of surprise and restricted response time, by the highest level of authoritative decision makers.

■ **rational choice**
the theory that decision makers choose on the basis of what they perceive to be the best interests of themselves and their states, based on their expectations about the relative usefulness of alternative options for realizing goals. Sometimes called "expected utility theory," it was derived from realist theories.

will be willing to militarily intervene, because in low-scale interventions to root out global terrorism, the United States and other great powers face a new kind of enemy that requires a new kind of response—endless wars of attrition against faceless enemies. The decisions to avoid situations calling for outside intervention to pacify fighting are also likely to continue when great powers perceive their national self-interests served by noninvolvement—as the United States did in 2002 when it sat on the sidelines as waves of terrorist violence and counterattacks took the lives of both Israeli and Palestinian civilians. For years, the U.S. military was "sized and configured to deal with major wars," and with over 250 million soldiers deployed in foreign countries to honor America's alliance partners, intervention "fatigue" has set in. "From the standpoint of U.S. policy, a cautionary admonition by Abraham Lincoln is also relevant: 'We should not promise what we ought not, lest we be called upon to perform what we cannot.'"

That said, what appears likely is the impulse to fight the new, post–September 11 war on terrorism by balancing counterterrorism against active military intervention in efforts to root out the sanctuaries provided by rogue states believed by the great powers and the U.S. hegemon to be the primary supporters of **state-sponsored terrorism.** This will undoubtedly entail interventions fought in the shadows by covert and clandestine methods, in all likelihood through multilateral rather than unilateral operations in order to break the chain reaction of catastrophic destructive terrorism through deterrence and resistance by a united coalition. This contest between states and nonstate intergovernmental organizations' (IGOs) terrorist movements will likely also require, in the interest of coercive diplomacy through military intervention, the cooperation of some unlikely allies, as seen by the U.S. alignment with rulers it once opposed in Afghanistan to restore stability to a land freed by U.S. and British intervention from the rule by the Taliban and Al Qaeda terrorists.

In order to anticipate the extent to which interventionism will dominate world politics as a preferred method of coercive diplomacy in the future, it is helpful to examine one sure consequence that follows every act of military intervention: Each past war was begun by an act of military intervention; the byproduct of every military intervention is that it produces a crisis.

International Crises

Crisis is a commonly used word that describes a situation that has reached a critical stage. More precisely, a **crisis decision** in international affairs is a decision made in a situation that (1) "threatens the high-priority goals of the decision-making unit; (2) restricts the amount of time available for response before the decision is transformed; and (3) surprises the members of the decision-making unit by its occurrence" (Hermann 1972). Most of the conspicuous military crises of our age, such as the Cuban Missile Crisis, the Berlin blockade, the Sino-Soviet border clash, the Formosa Straits crisis in the 1950s, and the Taiwan Straits crises in 1997, 1999, and again in 2001 exhibited these attributes. Each contained the elements of surprise, threat, and time pressure, as well as the risk of war. None of these crises crossed the line into overt large-scale military hostilities, however; all were managed successfully without escalation to war, because, arguably, the feuding parties made decisions according to **rational choice** theory. In contrast, many crises in the Global South have not

AP/Wide World

Stand By Me in a Time of Need U.S. President George W. Bush introduces in April 2002 Zahir Shah, the 87-year-old former king of Afghanistan, as the new leader put into place after the U.S. military intervention drove out the Al Qaeda terrorists and Taliban religious extremists. The challenge for great powers which intervene in failed states is restoring order with justice and providing the means for economic recovery after civil and religious wars, ventures that have a sorry track record.

been managed successfully and have escalated to war. Even with respect to crises between the great powers, the unbroken record of successful crisis management since 1945 should not necessarily instill confidence about the future. For crises to be managed successfully without escalating to war, governments, as rational actors, must be able to keep their quarrels within controllable bounds, and not let name-calling incite them to violence. There is no assurance that rationality will calm passions: "There is scant evidence that along with more lethal weapons we have evolved leaders more capable of coping with stress" (Holsti 1989). Crises can easily escalate to war because of the time pressures, inadequate information, fear and anxiety, and impulsive risk-taking that normally accompany decision-making procedures during threatening situations.

Crises result when one actor attempts to force an adversary to alter its behavior. "The strategy of coercive diplomacy . . . employs threats or limited force to persuade an opponent to call off or undo an encroachment—for example, to halt an invasion or give up territory that has been occupied" (Craig and George 1990). "Military power does not have to be used for it to be useful"; a state may succeed simply by "coercing a country by demonstrating the quantity of force and highlighting the capability of, and intention to, use force" (Majeed 1991). "Coercive diplomacy offers the possibility of achieving one's objective economically, with little bloodshed, fewer political and psychological costs, and often with much less risk of escalation than does traditional military strategy" (Craig and George 1990).

The crises generated by coercive bargaining thus perform the function that war often traditionally played, namely, "to resolve without violence, or with only minimal violence, those conflicts that are too severe to be settled by ordinary diplomacy and that in earlier times would have been settled by war" (Snyder and Diesing 1977).

Figure 13.2 shows the annual frequency between 1918 and 2001 of 433 international crises. Each of these crises between two or more states threatened to escalate to military confrontations and destabilized the entire global system. Almost all were what is sometimes called **militarized disputes,** because the disputing parties confronted each other with reciprocated mobilizations that took the situation to the brink of war. The practice of **gunboat diplomacy**—sending ships and troops overseas to intimidate an enemy—is an example of the actions involved in crises.

Note the evidence from the crisis chronology. Since World War I, situations have reached crisis levels threatening to escalate to war every decade and in every region. However, the frequency varied yearly, with many peaks of international tension followed by short troughs of relative calm. We learn from this inventory (Brecher and Wilkenfeld 1997) also that most states—altogether, more than 850—have been involved in these crises; over 100 triggered at least one crisis and more than 125 were the principal target of the military action that provoked the crisis. In addition, most crises were initiated by the great powers, and two-thirds occurred in the Global South's developing countries.

The use of military threat for bargaining purposes between states and the crises that result are important, because crises often trigger war. Examples of violence that were preceded by a crisis include World War I (1914), Kashmir (1948 and 2002), Suez (1956), Tibet (1959), the Bay of Pigs (1961), Goa (1961), Kuwait (1990), Yugoslavia (Kosovo, 1999), Macedonia (2001), and Afghanistan (2001). About one of every three militarized disputes making for crises lead to full-scale war rather than deterrence, even if the latter was the threatener's original intention. Coercive diplomacy is clearly a dangerous game, and especially so when played by the great powers; 95 percent of the most serious crises involved the great powers (Brecher 1993, 333, 576).

The Future of Conventional Military Coercion

The sobering conclusion that international crises are likely to increase in the future raises concerns about the use of coercive bargaining by military means as a method of dispute management. Is this kind of bargaining a solution or part of the security dilemma problem?

Policymakers today disagree about the appropriate place of coercive military bargaining in their strategic doctrines. Enthusiasts argue that the successful use of such strategies in the second half of the twentieth century argues for applying the lessons of nuclear bargaining to situations requiring deterrence in

■ **militarized disputes** confrontations short of war characterized by the reciprocated threat, deployment, mobilization, or use of force.

■ **gunboat diplomacy** a show of military force; historically naval force.

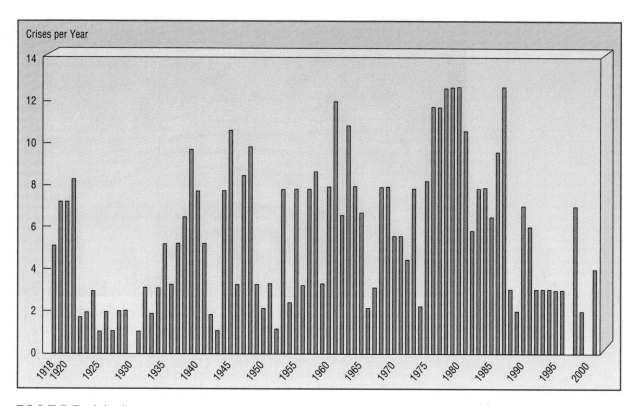

FIGURE 13.2

International Tension since World War I: The Annual Frequency of International Crises, 1918–2001

On occasions—433 occasions—states confronted each other militarily between 1918 and 2001, in the hopes of forcing concessions. The frequency has varied over time, but its recurrence attests to states' compulsion to threaten each other with military force to get their way. In February 2000, the world witnessed another crisis when two enemies, India and Pakistan, amassed troops on the mutual border and spoke openly of nuclear war; and, of course, on September 11, 2001, the entire world went on alert in reaction to the terrorist destruction of the World Trade Center in New York.

SOURCE: Based on International Crisis Behavior (ICB) data, provided courtesy of Jonathan Wilkenfeld at the University of Maryland, and Michael Brecher. Note that the 1995–2001 frequencies provided are preliminary, based on data not yet released when this book went to press.

the future. Skeptics disagree, maintaining that what may have worked in the realm of strategic deterrence is unlikely to work with respect to conventional deterrence, where in all probability most of the action will center. They feel that the kinds of armed conflicts and threats most in need of deterring will be most resistant to control through the strategies that help prevent nuclear attacks. Aggressors in the future—whether they are rough outlaw states, or criminal and terrorist organizations—very likely will employ advanced telecommunication networks to operate from dispersed locations, making the threat of massive retaliatory strikes against specific geographic regions ineffective.

It will clearly be much more difficult to deter the kinds of aggression that will employ conventional weapons than to deter aggression using nuclear weapons. The key elements of deterrence are: (1) *capabilities*—the possession

AP/Wide World

Tension in Taiwan In August 1997, the world held its breath as China and Taiwan squared off in a military showdown short of war. As democracy took root in Taiwan, the country signaled its desire to officially declare its independence from China, and China interpreted this as a provocative act, despite nearly fifty years of separation and the uninterrupted respect for the unwritten cease-fire between China and its "rebel province." As China threatened to invade, the threat of a military clash rose, with the danger compounded by the expectation that the United States would come to Taiwan's aid. Pictured here is an example of gunboat coercive diplomacy—new Taiwanese-made fighter jets poised for battle in August 1997 in the event of war. This crisis continued in February 2000 when China declared its intention to go to war, if necessary, to force Taiwan to proceed with unification negotiations and not to seek formal independence; painting Beijing as a military menace, Taiwan in response warned that "force won't work." Desperate for international support, Taiwan's president "established a secret $100 million fund to buy influence with foreign governments, institutions and individuals, including some in the United States" (Pomfret 2002).

of military resources that can make threats of military retaliation plausible; (2) *credibility*—the belief that the actor is willing to militarily defend its declared position; and (3) *communication*—the actor's ability to send a potential aggressor the clear message that it is willing to carry out its threat. In today's world, it is difficult to combine these elements to make conventional deterrence work. As Richard Harknett (1994) cautions, deterrence of conventional warfare "will succeed if threatened costs can be communicated to the challenger, assessed by the challenger, and believed by the challenger." These requirements are difficult to satisfy with the unconventional warfare employed by terrorists and irregular militia not answering to a particular state.

For the United States, the globe's so-called only superpower, reliance on military interventionism appears to comprise the major military method by which it seeks to exercise influence in the international arena: since 1990 the U.S. Army has been deployed abroad three times as often as the number of "major" deployments in the entire period between 1946 and 1989 (*Harper's*, July 1999, 17). But public opposition to and international criticism of the U.S. use

AL-JAZEERAAFDP AFP Photo

Bringing Terrorists to Justice? "We will defend the peace by fighting terrorists and tyrants," George W. Bush's September 2002 "National Security Strategy of the United States of America" pledged. Earlier, President Bush had vowed to capture Osama bin Laden (shown here), head of the Al Qaeda terrorist network, but he remained at large in 2003, plotting new acts of terrorism beyond 9/11. The U.S. preemptive strategy of "anticipatory self-defense" and "forward deterrence" signalled a bold doctrine, but, as U.S. National Security Advisor Condoleeza Rice warned in 2002, "Power is nothing unless you can turn it into influence."

of interventionary force overseas stands in the way of its practicing interventionism with abandon, however. "Intervention fatigue" and international complaints about the threat of intervention to the principle of sovereignty and the **nonintervention norm** in international law could result in the decline of this military instrument for exercising influence.

Bargaining by nonmilitary methods is also likely to be tried, and perhaps will be the method of choice, given the risks of military activities and the obstacles to their effective use. Economic sanctions will figure prominently among these alternative approaches.

■ **nonintervention norm** a fundamental international legal principle, now being challenged, that traditionally has defined interference by one state in the domestic affairs of another as illegal.

BOYCOTTS, NOT BULLETS, AS WEAPONS: SANCTIONS AS INSTRUMENTS OF COERCION

When the Arab members of OPEC placed an embargo on the shipment of oil to the United States and the Netherlands in 1973, their purpose was to alter these countries' policies toward the Arab-Israeli conflict. When the UN Security

Council decided in August 1990 that the world organization should cease trade with Iraq, its purpose was to accomplish the immediate and unconditional withdrawal of Iraqi forces from Kuwait. Both are examples of the use of **economic sanctions**—"deliberate government actions to inflict economic deprivation on a target state or society, through the limitation or cessation of customary economic relations" (Leyton-Brown 1987).

■ economic sanctions
the punitive use of trade or monetary measures, such as an embargo, to harm the economy of an enemy state in order to exercise influence over its policies.

We will look specifically at economic sanctions, keeping in mind that sanctions may be defined more broadly to include acts "intended to convince or compel another state to desist from engaging" in some unacceptable behavior by a wider range of methods than economic coercion. They may be military, involving the use of armed intervention; diplomatic or political (breaking formal relations); or cultural, aimed at undermining a deviant government's internal and international standing (Joyner 1995).

Economic sanctions are an increasingly popular choice from the broad array of instruments of statecraft available to governments.

> To the extent that there is a degree of optimism today about the potential effectiveness of sanctions, it is likely because of the perception shared by many that broad multilateral sanctions helped to end apartheid in South Africa, have forced Iraqi President Saddam Hussein to cooperate grudgingly (and sporadically) with the UN inspectors seeking to destroy his weapons of mass destruction, and induced Serbian leader Slobodan Milosevic to come to the negotiating table in Dayton, Ohio. Here the optimism is based on the fact that, with the end of the Cold War, it may now be possible for the United Nations to take action in defense of collective security and to protect international norms, as was originally intended. The hope is that multilateralism, combined with the relatively greater legitimacy accorded to UN enforcement actions, may restore to sanctions the leverage that they traditionally have had. (K. Elliott 1998, 50–51)

■ sanctions
punitive actions by one state against another to retaliate for its previous objectionable behavior.

■ boycotts
concerted efforts, often organized internationally, to prevent relations such as trade with a state, to express disapproval, or to coerce acceptance of certain conditions.

An alternative to applying military force, **sanctions** are enacted to express outrage and to change the target's behavior. Since World War I, there have been 120 observable episodes of foreign policy sanctions, 104 of which have been enacted since World War II (Hufbauer, Schott, and Elliott 1990). In the 1990s, the use of **boycotts** instead of bullets for exercising political influence became widespread. It was illustrated by the U.S. "dual containment" policy toward Iraq and Iran (alongside the continuation of sanctions against the North African "pariah state," Libya, which was accused of sponsoring terrorism), by the 1997 U.S. effort to sever economic ties with Burma for its human rights violations, and by the April 1997 Arab foreign ministers plan to launch a business boycott of Israel in response to its decision to place housing projects in East Jerusalem.

Sanctions are popular. They have been described as "the main tool of coercive diplomacy" (Hoagland 1996) and "the most favored tool of diplomats" (Pound and El-Tahri 1994). Sanctions are particularly relied upon by the United States, the ruling hegemon which, in that capacity, has the most responsibility for maintaining world order. Between 1945 and 1990, when more than sixty cases of sanctions were undertaken, "a rate averaging better than one new action per year, more than two-thirds were initiated and maintained by the United States" (Lopez and Cortright 1995, 5). By 1998, half the world's population lived in countries that had been placed under U.S. sanctions (*Harper's,* February 1998, 13).

The reason and rationale for using sanctions as instruments of influence stems largely from the fact that it avoids the dangers of using military force. Military approaches to coercion have many risks; they can easily backfire, take soldier's lives, drain government budgets, and provoke widespread public criticism at home and abroad, especially since it is difficult to mount a short-term military operation with few battle casualties. In comparison with military methods of coercion, sanctions appear less risky and far less costly. Hence, "policymakers continue to use sanctions with increasing frequency" (Baldwin 2000), because sanctions are an attractive substitute method.

Another primary reason for the rising use of economic sanctions is that today national economies are increasingly integrated through trade, and, because of the accelerating pace of **globalization,** people and states are bound together more closely than ever before in a single global capitalistic system which increases their dependence on others for their own prosperity. This circumstance makes sanctions that threaten targets with the loss of an export market more effective than in the past, when countries could better withstand a foreign embargo on the purchase of their products in the global marketplace. Likewise, countries dependent on foreign imports from abroad for their basic needs are highly vulnerable to sanctions, since disruptions for supplies could bring their economies to a standstill. As Maps 13.2 and 13.3 show, a large number of states are either trade dependent or energy dependent.

> ■ **globalization**
> the integrative tendencies that are linking the countries of the world into increasingly tight webs of economic, political, and cultural interdependence (see p. 21).

Through the globalization of trade, the dependence of many countries on exports for their growth and on foreign suppliers for their vital needs makes it difficult for them to withstand an embargo (a government order prohibiting commerce) or a boycott that interrupts the target's export-generated income or imports of critical resources such as oil. Economic sanctions are also gaining proponents because more than sixty states are highly vulnerable "single-commodity-dependent economies" which derive at least 40 percent of their export revenues from foreign purchase of a single product (*Handbook of International Economic Statistics* 2000, 72–73). This high level of vulnerability makes sanctions appear potent to exercise influence according to the classic reasoning of James Madison and Thomas Jefferson, who advocated "peaceable coercion" against those foreign governments that would have to yield to American pressure because U.S. goods were essential to their prosperity.

Five major policy goals are customarily pursued by states when they turn to economic sanctions in lieu of other options, such as military force, to punish a foreign target:

- *Compliance* ("to force the target to alter its behavior to conform with the initiator's preferences"), as in the case of the 1982 U.S. embargo of Libya, designed to force it to end its support of terrorism.

- *Subversion* ("to remove the target's leaders . . . or overthrow the regime"), as in the cases of the 1993–1994 U.S. trade embargo on Haiti and the 2002 U.S. efforts to topple Saddam Hussein in Iraq.

- *Deterrence* ("to dissuade the target from repeating the disputed action in the future"), as in the case of the Soviet grain embargo by the United States.

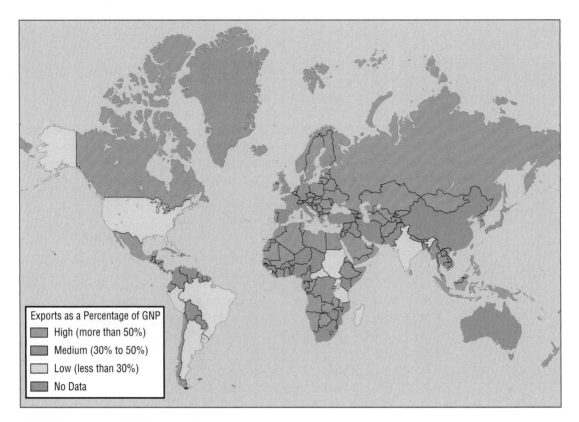

M A P S   1 3 . 2   A N D   1 3 . 3

Vulnerable to Sanctions—Countries Dependent on Trade and Energy Imports

Many states find themselves subject to external coercion and vulnerable to manipulations by states which impose sanctions on them, especially if they are highly dependent on exports for their economic prosperity and/or imports for their commercial energy use. Sanctions through boycotts or embargoes, undertaken to coerce change in a trade-dependent or energy-dependent country's policies, can be devastating. The map on the left shows the great extent to which many countries are today dependent on trade, and in the globalized marketplace the level of states' dependence on exports for economic prosperity is growing. The map on the right shows the varying levels on which countries are dependent on foreign suppliers for their energy needs; note that only a small number of states are net exporters, with the rest dependent on and therefore vulnerable to manipulation by the foreign sources from which they import their energy—such as the Organization of Petroleum Exporting Countries (OPEC).

SOURCES: Exports, World Bank (2002a) 332–334; Energy imports, World Bank (2002b) 158–160; Energy exports, Economist (2002), 52.

- *International symbolism* ("to send messages to other members of the world community"), as in the case of the British sanctions against Rhodesia after its unilateral declaration of independence in 1965.

- *Domestic symbolism* ("to increase its domestic support or thwart international criticism of its foreign policies by acting decisively"), as in the case of U.S. sanctions against Iran following its seizure of U.S. diplomats in 1979 (Lindsay 1986).

These multiple uses notwithstanding, it is rare for policymakers to advocate the use of economic sanctions as an instrument of bargaining without generating skepticism and criticism. Critics invariably argue that "the problem with economic sanctions is that they frequently contribute little to . . . foreign

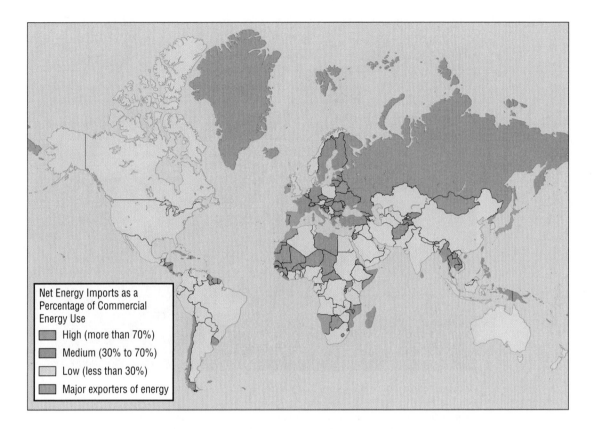

Net Energy Imports as a Percentage of Commercial Energy Use

■ High (more than 70%)
■ Medium (30% to 70%)
□ Low (less than 30%)
■ Major exporters of energy

policy goals while being costly and even counterproductive" (Haass 1997). Furthermore,

> policymakers often have inflated expectations of what sanctions can and cannot accomplish. . . . At most there is a weak correlation between economic deprivation and political willingness to change. The *economic* impact of sanctions may be pronounced; both on the sender and the target country, but other factors in the situational context almost always overshadow the impact of sanctions in determining the *political* outcome. (Hufbauer, Schott, and Elliott 1990, 94).

Stated differently, the most harsh criticism of sanctions is that they frequently do not work or fail to accomplish the objectives for which they were initiated. Indeed, sanctions have a very checkered history. At times they have succeeded, such as in South Africa, where two decades of economic pressure applied to the white minority regime finally brought an end to the segregationist **apartheid** system and opened the way for black majority rule in a democracy. Another example of success often cited is the case of Libya, where in 1999, after a decade of international pressure on Libyan dictator Muammar Qaddafi for his role in sponsoring terrorism, he finally turned over to Western powers for trial two Libyans alleged to have blown up the Pan Am flight 103 over Scotland in 1988 that killed all of its 280 passengers. However, these are exceptions to a deeply entrenched pattern of failed sanctions. Here the record casts great doubt on the capacity of unilateral sanctions to work, even when used by the globe's most powerful economic giant, the United States. That record is dismal. Between

■ **apartheid**
the former South African policy of racial separation.

AP/Wide World

Arming against Sanctions in Iraq In a war of words that punctuated the weakness of economic sanctions as a tool of coercive diplomacy, the Iraqi government in January 1998 called on 1 million men and women of all ages to take part in a weapons training program. Pictured here are armed Iraqi women who joined a paramilitary group in response to a call to arms by Iraqi President Saddam Hussein, who claimed his state must be ready for a U.S. attack over the issue of UN arms inspections and economic sanctions.

1970 and 1990, "just 5 of 39 unilateral U.S. sanctions [achieved] any success at all" (K. Elliott 1998, 58). Conspicuous in the many cases where U.S. economic coercion through sanctions failed is the U.S. experience with Cuba. The United States placed sanctions on the Castro regime shortly after it came to power in 1960 and created a communist government in alliance with the Soviet Union. In response, the United States banned all trade with Cuba and pressured other countries to do the same, hoping to overthrow the Castro regime. This goal was not realized. Castro has survived for over forty years.

Cuba is often cited as perhaps the best example of the inherent obstacles to successful sanctions. Other such U.S. failures include the inability of the United States to impose a partial embargo on the sale of grain to the Soviet Union after its 1979 intervention in Afghanistan as well as the inability of the Reagan administration in 1981 to use sanctions to stop Poland and the Soviet Union from building the trans-Siberian gas pipeline designed to bring Soviet energy into western European markets. These examples suggest that "Sanctions are seldom effective in impairing the military potential of an important power, or in bringing about major changes in the policies of the target country" (Hufbauer, Schott, and Elliott 1990), and "have been absolutely ineffective in bringing about a change of government leadership within a target country"

Charles Crowell/Black Star

Trade Interdependence and Sanctions In this photo a tanker carrying natural gas leaves Qatar for Japan. Qatar, with huge gas reserves, hopes exports will transform its economy; Japan badly needs natural gas to propel its consumer-rich economy. Japan's dependence on foreign suppliers for desperately needed energy sources reduces its willingness to use economic sanctions to influence the policies of suppliers. The use of economic sanctions is often influenced by the relationships between commodity-dependent importers and commodity-wealthy exporters. In April 2002, Crown Prince Abdullah visited U.S. President George W. Bush at his Crawford, Texas, ranch, and warned Bush that American support for Israel in Palestine undercut the war on terrorism, but promised that it would not use oil as a weapon.

(Cortright and Lopez 1995). This conclusion was also reached by U.S. Secretary of State Colin Powell when in 2001 he pleaded, "For gosh sake, please give [sanctions] a sunset clause, make them all go away at the end of the year. . . . [I ask Congress] to get rid of most of the sanctions already on the books."

The expected high payoff and usual high pitfalls of sanctions as a punitive form of diplomatic punishment were underscored by the prolonged case of the U.S.-led multilateral efforts to topple the Iraqi dictator Saddam Hussein after the Persian Gulf War and to prevent him from carrying out his crash program to build a nuclear weapon and to develop an arsenal of toxins for biological warfare. This long-lasting campaign demonstrated the limits of economic sanctions. In 2002, Saddam Hussein was still in power, being courted by major oil companies, making huge profits buying and selling oil futures after the United Nations in the Resolution 986 "oil for food" program partially lifted its oil embargo, and exporting oil on the black market through dummy companies to needy importers in order to buy illegal arms from foreign manufacturers to protect himself and his army from his own citizens. At the same time, U.S. firms were helping to rebuild Iraq's oil industry even while air raids continued. Sanctions failed to produce compliance or submission, as the Baghdad dictator prevented UN inspectors from determining whether Iraq had complied with Security Council's demands to scrap its long-range missiles and other chemical and biological weapons of mass destruction under the peace settlement that ended the 1991 Gulf War. The futility of the financially crippling UN embargo to drive Saddam Hussein out of office or to open his palaces to UN inspectors, and the repeated success of Saddam's stubborn brinkmanship bargaining, highlighted the impotence of sanctions; it was only after a tough new UN Security Council resolution threatening military enforcement that real inspections began in late November 2002.

The history of ineffectual sanctions against Iraq underscores the principles that "success importantly depends on the type of policy for government change sought [and that sanctions] are of little utility in achieving goals that depend on compelling the target country to take actions it stoutly resists" (K. Elliott 1998). This case explains why military force is still usually preferred as an alternative to sanctions in coercive diplomacy, and why in 2002, out of frustration, the Bush administration announced plans to unleash a preemptive strike to oust what it termed "the Butcher of Baghdad" before Hussein could build weapons of mass destruction and use them in terrorism against the United States and its allies.

The choice between the options of economic sanctions and military force is always a difficult one, and there is every reason to expect states to continue to pursue both strategies when they are confronted with situations that seem to demand coercive measures. In that context, note that in May 2002 the U.N. Security Council voted unanimously to impose new import controls on Iraq in an effort to overhaul the five-year-old set of sanctions that had been derided by critics as ineffectual and by citizens who felt, understandably, that the sanctions were punitive to ordinary Iraqi people who suffered the most from them. The sanctions have been a humanitarian disaster. More than 600,000 Iraqi children have died as a result of the UN sanctions—three times the number of Japanese killed in 1945 by the U.S. atomic bomb attacks (*Harper's*, November 2002, 13). The fatalities encouraged the UN to begin experimentation with so-called smart sanctions (Cortright and Lopez 2002), which would least harm those innocent people least responsible for the wrongdoing. To make sanctions effective, and smart, it will be necessary to rectify those features of sanctions that previously have made them a weak tool in statecraft. These include the following deficiencies:

- A typical response to economic coercion in the sanctioned society is a heightened sense of nationalism, a *laager* mentality (circle the wagons to face oncoming enemies), which stimulates resistance in the target state.

- Sanctions sometimes hurt the disempowered people they seek to help—the country's average citizens.

- Governments often act covertly to support the sanctioned state even as they publicly profess their support of sanctions.

- Sanctions are an invisible form of trade protectionism that interfere with liberal free trade and therefore profits.
- The credibility of the state(s) imposing sanctions is often low.
- Widespread and collective sustained cooperation from the international community and international organizations seldom materializes, and unilateral sanctions seldom succeed in a globalized market with many competitive suppliers of embargoed goods.

These limitations attributed to sanctions underscore why their use is often questioned whenever sanctions are proposed as an instrument for international bargaining. Nonetheless, the impulse to use this tool is likely to remain strong because sanctions enable a leader to show leadership without bearing the costs and dangers that other policy options, particularly military force, ential. Sanctions appear, therefore, destined to remain a part of states' strategies.

This chapter reviewed four basic approaches to controlling the behavior of others, concentrating especially on the use of force. Whether for deterrence or compellence, states will continue to rely on strategic weapons to prevent their own mass destruction. They will also continue to use conventional weapons and economic sanctions to defend themselves while bargaining to protect national interests. All three of these methods of coercive diplomacy place an emphasis on capabilities—both military and economic; all three are methods for bargaining that, when used, tell us that the fourth method, diplomatic negotiation, has failed or broken down. The next chapter evaluates how these approaches to the management of military conflict are often complemented by still other strategies advocated by realism.

KEY TERMS

Bush Doctrine	brinkmanship	asymmetrical warfare
coercive diplomacy	massive retaliation	preventive diplomacy
preemptive war	countervalue targeting strategy	peacekeeping
just war theory	counterforce targeting strategy	military intervention
rational choice	peace enforcement	covert operations
negotiation	limited war	human rights
politics	total war	failed states
realism	second-strike capability	selective engagement
bargaining	mutual assured destruction	state-sponsored terrorism
security dilemma	(MAD)	crisis decision
spiral model	nuclear utilization theory (NUTs)	rational choice
neoliberalism	Strategic Defense Initiative (SDI)	militarized disputes
nuclear deterrence	balance of power	gunboat diplomacy
conventional deterrence	doctrine	nonintervention norm
nuclear winter	pax atomica	economic sanctions
signaling	counterfactual reasoning	sanctions
Cuban Missile Crisis	conventional war	boycotts
compellence	preemption	globalization
commitment	low-intensity conflict (LIC)	apartheid

SUGGESTED READING

Brecher, Michael, and Jonathan Wilkenfeld. *A Study of Crisis*. Ann Arbor: University of Michigan Press, 1997.

Chan, Steve, and A. Cooper Drury, eds. *Sanctions as Economic Statecraft: Theory and Practice*. New York: St. Martin's, 2000.

Cortright, David, and George A. Lopez, eds. *Smart Sanctions: Targeting Economic Statecraft*. Lanham, Md.: Rowman and Littlefield, 2002.

Goldstein, Avery. *Deterrence and Security in the 21st Century*. Stanford, Calif.: Stanford University Press, 2000.

Harclerode, Peter. *Fighting Dirty: The Inside Story of Covert Operations from Ho Chi Minh to Osama bin Laden*. London: Cassell, 2001.

Holzgrefe, J. L., and Robert O. Keohane, eds. *Humanitarian Intervention: Ethical, Legal and Political Dilemmas*. New York: Cambridge University Press, 2003.

Lang, Anthony, Jr. *Agency and Ethics: The Politics of Military Intervention*. Albany: N.Y.: State University of New York Press, 2002.

Luttwak, Edward N. *Strategy: The Logic of War and Peace*. Cambridge, Mass.: The Belknap Press of Harvard University Press, 2001.

Manwaring, Magin, ed. *Deterrence in the 21st Century*. Portland, Ore.: Frank Cass, 2000.

Naylor, R. T. *Economic Warfare: Sanctions, Embargo Busting, and Their Human Cost*. Boston Northeastern University Press, 2001.

Regan, Patrick M. *Civil Wars and Foreign Powers: Outside Intervention in Interstate Conflict*. Ann Arbor: University of Michigan Press, 2000.

Starkey, Brigid, Mark Boyer, and Jonathan Wilkenfeld. *Negotiating a Complex World: An Introduction to International Negotiation*. Boulder, Colo.: Rowman & Littlefield, 2000.

WHERE ON THE WORLD WIDE WEB?

A-Bomb WWW Museum

http://www.csi.ad.jp/ABOMB/index.html

Visit this Japanese Web site for eyewitness accounts of the impact the first atomic bomb had on Hiroshima. The site includes pictures from the Peace Memorial Museum in Hiroshima that show the effect of the bombing and stories from survivors, many of them deeply disturbing. The A-Bomb WWW Museum was created as a perpetual reminder of the horrors of atomic bombing. It welcomes email responses from all around the world.

Atomic Bomb: Decision

http://www.dannen.com/decision/index.html

This Web site houses the available documents on the decision to use atomic bombs on the cities of Hiroshima and Nagasaki. Scan eyewitness accounts of the Trinity Test. Read what the individuals responsible for creating the bomb and for deciding to drop it had to say. See the official bombing order and hear an excerpt of President Truman's radio speech announcing the decision. Based on what you have read and heard, do you think the United States should have dropped the bomb?

Fourth Freedom Forum

http://www.fourthfreedom.org/

Are economic sanctions a useful tool in statecraft? Visit the Fourth Freedom Forum's Web site to get a prosanctions point of view. The Fourth Freedom Forum's works toward "a more civilized world based on the force of law rather than the law of force." It contends that the effective use of economic incentives and sanctions offers the greatest hope for creating a more secure and peaceful future. From the home page, click on Sanctions and Incentives. Here you will find an extensive collection of articles related to international sanctions and case studies. Do you think sanctions are effective? Under what circumstances should they be used?

Missile Threats & Responses

http://www.cdiss.org/tempor1.htm

Want to know the difference between ballistic, cruise, biological, chemical, or radiological missiles? How effective are missile defense systems? Do you want to join a forum to discuss issues relating to weapons of mass destruction (WMD)? Visit the site of the Center for Defence and International Security Studies at Cartmel College in Great Britain. It offers an overview of different WMD, raises awareness about the issues, and stimulates debate on a wide range of defence and security matters.

Remembering Nagasaki
http://www.exploratorium.edu/nagasaki/index.html

A stunning Web site, Remembering Nagasaki presents the photographs of Japanese army photographer Yosuke Yamhata, who took pictures the day after the bomb was dropped. A public forum on issues related to the atomic age includes memories from people all over the world of the moment when they heard about the explosion of the bomb and how they constructed the story in their minds, discussion of the decision to drop the bomb, the question of how to tell history, and the ethical responsibilities of scientists. This is a truly fascinating site that explores the issues from all sides.

Russian Roulette
http://www.pbs.org/wgbh/pages/frontline/shows/russia/

PBS's famous *Frontline* series is online with a look at the safety and security of Russia's nuclear arsenal and the potential for accidental launch or diversion of its nuclear weapons. Take a look at Russia's nuclear complex. Compare and contrast U.S. and Russian nuclear arsenals and become familiar with nuclear smuggling incidents. Read interviews with policy experts, smugglers, scientists, analysts, and law enforcement agents, and analyze Russian and U.S. articles for further perspective. On the other hand, you may not want to look at this Web site at all. As a Russian proverb states, "The less you know the better you sleep."

INFOTRAC® COLLEGE EDITION

Search for the following articles in the InfoTrac database:

Barnett, Roger W. "What Deters? Strength, Not Weakness," *Naval War College Review* Spring 2001.

Joseph, Robert G. "Nuclear Deterrence and Regional Proliferators," *The Washington Quarterly* Summer 1997.

Levine, Robert A. "Deterrence and the ABM: Retreading the Old Calculus," *World Policy Journal* Fall 2001.

Baldwin, David A. "The Sanctions Debate and the Logic of Choice," *International Security* Winter 1999.

For more articles, enter:

"nuclear arms control" in the Subject Guide, and then go to subdivision "international aspects."

"deterrence" in the Subject Guide.

"economic sanctions" in the Subject Guide, and then go to subdivision "analysis."

The Realist Road to Security through Alliances, the Balance of Power, and Arms Control

T O P I C S   A N D   T H E M E S

- Alliances and their impact on national and global security
- The balance of power
- Controlling military power through arms agreements
- Can the acquisition of allies and arms stabilize a twenty-first-century multipolar world?

- **CONTROVERSY** ARE ALLIES FRIENDS OR FOES? RECONSIDERING THE ADVANTAGES AND DISADVANTAGES OF ALLIES TO A STATE'S SECURITY
- **CONTROVERSY** IS A UNIPOLAR, BIPOLAR, OR MULTIPOLAR SYSTEM THE MOST STABLE? THREE SCHOOLS OF THOUGHT ON THE RELATIONSHIP OF POLARITY AND INTERNATIONAL PEACE

Leonid Brezhnev and Jimmy Carter sign the SALT II Treaty, 1979.

The September 11 attacks . . . were, in a sense, a consequence of the new unipolar world. . . . America were attacked because it is the master of the modern world, deploying its economic, political, and military powers across the globe. Because America is "No. 1," it is also target No. 1.

—FAREED ZAKARIA, realist analyst, 2002

The web of disarmament and anti-proliferation treaties, woven during the Cold War, has turned out to have gaping holes, large enough for suitcase bombs and even passenger jets to slip through. Only a multilateral approach can counter the new threats.

—ANNA LINDH and ERKKI TUOMIOJA, foreign ministers, respectively, of Sweden and Finland, 2002

■ **security dilemma**
the propensity of armaments amassed by one state for ostensibly defensive purposes to be perceived by others as threatening, which drive the alarmed competitors to undertake as a countermeasure a military buildup that heightens both states' insecurities (see p. 114).

Imagine yourself as the next secretary-general of the United Nations (UN). You face responsibility for fulfilling the UN's Charter to preserve world peace. Looking at the globe, you see that many countries have the capacity to annihilate their enemies with new weapons of mass destruction whenever they wish to unleash the military power in their states' arsenal. As a consequence, you see the **security dilemma** that has been created: Due to the escalating destructive power of modern weapons, most states' sense of national security has decreased, rather than increased, and the globe's more than 6 billion people live in fear that they will not see tomorrow. What course should you counsel the UN's 190 members to pursue?

Most states continue to reject the **liberal** and the neoliberal paths of peace, which recommend building institutions for world law, states' integration, and/or democratic governmental reforms (see Chapter 15). Rather, most states follow the realist road, seeing their viable choices as among three basic, time-honored options: States can (1) arm themselves; (2) form (or sever) alliances with other countries; or (3) negotiate arms control and disarmament agreements to reduce the threat of adversaries' weapons. Most leaders usually pursue various combinations of these military strategies.

Up to this point, our discussion of conflict and its management has followed a logical progression. Chapter 11 began by exploring why the frequency of war makes preparations for it so necessary. Chapter 12 examined the search for national security through the acquisition of military capabilities. Chapter 13 assessed states' use of coercive diplomacy, both to realize their national goals abroad and to deter their rivals from aggression. We now concentrate on the other two military approaches to national security—the use of alliances and arms control to maintain a favorable balance of power and thereby enhance security. These approaches draw their inspiration primarily from the assumptions that realist theory makes about the most prudent paths to peace (see Table 14.1).

■ **liberalism**
a paradigm predicated on the hope that the application of reason and universal ethics to international relations can lead to a more orderly, just, and cooperative world, and that international anarchy and war can be policed by institutional reforms that empower international organizations and law (see p. 33).

TABLE 14.1

The Realist Road to Security: Assumptions and Policy Recommendations

The Realist Picture of the International Environment

Primary global condition:	Anarchy; or the absence of authoritative governing institutions
Probability of system change/reform:	Low
Prime actors:	States, and especially great powers
Principal actor goals:	Power over others, self-preservation, and physical security
Predominant pattern of actor interaction:	Competition and conflict
Pervasive concern:	National security
Prevalent state priorities:	Acquiring military capabilities
Popular state practice:	Use of armed forces for coercive diplomacy

Realist Policy Prescription	*Premise*
Prepare for war:	If you want peace, prepare for war.
Remain vigilant:	No state is to be trusted further than its national interest.
Avoid moralism:	Standards of right and wrong apply to individuals but not states; in world affairs amoral actions are sometimes necessary and can produce positive results.
Remain involved and actively intervene:	Isolationism is not an alternative to active global involvement.
Protect with arms:	Strive to increase military capabilities, and fight rather than submit to subordination.
Preserve the balance of power:	Do not let any state or coalition of states become predominant.
Prevent arms races from resulting in military inferiority with rivals:	Negotiate agreements with competitors to maintain a favorable military balance.

ALLIANCES AND THEIR IMPACT ON NATIONAL AND GLOBAL SECURITY

■ **alliances**
coalitions that form when two or more states combine their military capabilities and promise to coordinate their policies to increase mutual security.

■ **deterrence**
a preventive strategy designed to dissuade an adversary from doing what it would otherwise prefer to do.

■ **self-help**
reliance only on one's state for defense since under anarchy no state can depend on others—even allies—to come to their defense if attacked.

■ **rational choice**
a decision made by careful definition of the situation, weighing of goals, consideration of all alternatives, and selection of the options most likely to achieve the highest goals (see p. 74).

Alliances usually form when two or more states face a common security threat. They are formal agreements among states to coordinate their behavior by heeding realism's first rule of statecraft: to increase military capabilities. By acquiring allies, states increase their mutual armaments, which provides them when facing a common threat with the means of reducing their probability of being attacked **(deterrence)**, obtaining greater strength in case of attack (defense) while preventing their allies from alliance with the enemy (preclusion; G. Snyder 1991).

These advantages notwithstanding, realists often see a downside and counsel against forming alliances, as Britain's Lord Palmerston did in 1848 when he advised that states "should have no eternal allies and no perpetual enemies." Their only duty is to follow their interests and whenever possible to rely on **self-help.** The greatest risk to forming alliances is that they bind a state to a commitment that may later become disadvantageous. This is why "wise and experienced statesmen usually shy away from commitments likely to constitute limitations on a government's behavior at unknown dates in the future in the face of unpredictable situations" (Kennan 1984a). Because conditions are certain to change sooner or later and the usefulness of all alliances is certain to change once the common threat that brought the allies together declines, the realist tradition advises states not to take a fixed position on temporary convergences of national interests and to forge alliances only to deal with immediate threats.

When considering whether a new alliance is a **rational choice** in which the benefits outweigh the costs, heads of state usually recognize that allies can easily do more harm than good (see Controversy: Are Allies Friends or Foes?). Many realists advise states against forming alliances for defense, basing their fears on five fundamental flaws:

- Alliances enable aggressive states to combine military capabilities for aggression.

- Alliances threaten enemies and provoke them to form counteralliances, which reduces the security for *both* coalitions.

- Alliance formation may draw otherwise neutral parties into opposed coalitions.

- Once states join forces, they must control the behavior of their own allies to discourage each member from reckless aggression against its enemies, which would undermine the security of the alliance's other members.

- The possibility always exists that today's ally might become tomorrow's enemy.

In a 1917 address to the U.S. Senate, President Woodrow Wilson proposed that "all nations avoid entangling alliances which would draw them into . . . a net of intrigue and selfish rivalry." In taking this position, which reflected his liberal belief that alliances and secret diplomacy transform limited conflicts into global wars with many participants, Wilson underscored the difficulties and the dangers of making alliance decisions. Despite their uncertain usefulness, many

ARE ALLIES FRIENDS OR FOES?
Reconsidering the Advantages and Disadvantages of Allies to a State's Security

When states make decisions about forging alliances, they must keep in mind the many risks of sharing their fate with other states. While realists generally see alliances as potentially beneficial, they caution that making a defense pact with an ally will also carry a heavy price. Creating alliances will:

- Foreclose options.
- Reduce the state's capacity to adapt to changing circumstances.
- Weaken a state's capability to influence others by decreasing the number of additional partners with which it can align.
- Eliminate the advantages in bargaining that can be derived from deliberately fostering ambiguity about one's intentions.
- Provoke the fears of adversaries.
- Entangle states in disputes with their allies' enemies.
- Interfere with the negotiation of disputes involving an ally's enemy by precluding certain issues from being placed on the agenda.
- Preserve existing rivalries.
- Stimulate envy and resentment on the part of friends who are outside the alliance and are therefore not eligible to receive its advantages.

These potential dangers explain why alliance decisions are so controversial, even when advocates enthusiastically propose that another state be sought as an ally for mutual defense. The posture of leaders about the advantage or disadvantage of alliances has depended on their personal philosophy and the country's circumstances. What do you think? What are the advantages of having alliance partners? In thinking about your options, look at the photo picturing, in

1796, George Washington, the first president of the United States, advising other leaders in American government that it should be the foreign policy of the United States to "steer clear of permanent alliances." He felt that whereas a state "may safely trust to temporary alliances for extraordinary emergencies" it is an "illusion . . . to expect or calculate real favors from nation to nation." Yet, almost every state is insecure in one way or another and is tempted to recruit allies to bolster its defense capabilities and protect its power as a united friend to adversaries that threaten it.

The Granger Collection, NY

states have chosen to ally throughout history because, the risks notwithstanding, the perceived benefits to security in a time of threat justified that decision.

To best picture how alliances affect global security, it is instructive to move from the state level of analysis, which views alliance decisions from the perspective of individual state's security, to the global **level of analysis** (recall Chapters 1 and 3) by looking at the impact of alliances on the frequency of interstate war. This view focuses attention on the possible contribution of alliance formation to maintaining the balance of power.

■ **levels of analysis**
variables at the global, state, and individual levels that explain why transnational actors behave as they do in international relations (see p. 17).

THE BALANCE OF POWER

International anarchy makes each state responsible for its own national security. The seventeenth-century English realist philosopher Thomas Hobbes observed that this condition encourages among states a perpetual "war of all against all." Realists, neorealists, and **neotraditional realists** argue that reforming this system is unrealistic because international anarchy is permanent, as is the selfish drive for power over rivals. Survival and world order rest on the proper functioning of a system of shifting military alignments commonly referred to as the "balance of power."

Assumptions of Balance-of-Power Theory

Balance of power is an ambiguous concept used nearly twenty different ways (see Claude 1962). At its core is the idea that peace will result when military power is distributed so that no one state is strong enough to dominate the others. If one state, or a combination of states, gains enough power to threaten others, compelling incentives will exist for those threatened to disregard their superficial differences and unite in a defensive alliance. The power resulting from such collaboration would, according to this conception, deter the would-be attacker from pursuing expansionism. Thus, from the laissez-faire competition of predatory and defensive rivals would emerge a balance of contending factions, which would maintain the status quo.

Balance-of-power theory is also founded on the realist premise that weakness invites attack and that countervailing power must be used to deter potential aggressors. Realists assume that the drive for expanded power guides every state's actions. It follows that all countries are potential adversaries, and each must strengthen its military capability to protect itself. Invariably, this reasoning rationalizes the quest for military superiority, because others pursue it as well.

On the surface, these realist assumptions appear dubious (especially to liberals). The arms races they justify can easily lead to the very outcome most feared—a destructive, global war. However, the realist policymakers in Europe who formulated classical balance-of-power theory after the Peace of Westphalia in 1648 were not irrational (Gulick 1955). They reasoned that a system founded on suspicion and competition, in which all states were independent and could make rational choices freely to advance their perceived national interests, would distribute power evenly through **alignments**—shifts by neutrals to one coalition or the other. A free-floating balance-of-power **security regime** without formal rules on how, where, and when to act for specified goals, they believed, could curtail the temptation of any actor to dominate others.

The Balance Process. In classic balance-of-power theory, fear of a third party would encourage alignments, because those threatened would need help to offset the power of the mutual adversary. An alliance would add the ally's power to the state's own and deny the addition of that power to the enemy. As alliances combine power, the offsetting coalitions would give neither a clear advantage. Therefore, aggression would appear unattractive and would be averted.

To deter an aggressor, counteralliances were expected to form easily, because states sitting on the sidelines could not risk **nonalignment.** If they

---

■ **neotraditional realists**
the "new" version of classical realist theorizing that emphasizes leaders, their perceptions of national interests, and changes in capabilities as the primary determinants of states' foreign policies, instead of the "structural" neorealist focus on the influence of the global system (see p. 000).

■ **balance of power**
the theory that peace and stability are most likely to be maintained when military power is distributed to prevent a single hegemon or bloc from controlling the world (see p. 103).

■ **alignments**
the acceptance by a neutral state threatened by foreign enemies of a special relationship short of formal alliance with a stronger power able to protect it from attack.

■ **security regime**
norms and rules for interaction agreed to by a set of states to cooperatively increase their mutual security.

■ **nonalignment**
a foreign policy posture in which states do not participate in military alliances with either of two rival blocs for fear that alliance will lead to involvement in an unnecessary war.

refused to ally, their own vulnerability would encourage the expansionist state to attack them at a later time. In theory, the result of these individual calculations would be the formation of coalitions approximately equal in power. This theory presumes that state actors (agents) are rational and that they make policies aimed at equalizing the power of competing coalitions because of their ability to recognize states' interest in stopping aggression. The so-called **size principle** accounts for the inclination of rational actors to form coalitions only sufficient in size to ensure victory and no larger, resulting in political coalitions that are roughly equal in size (see Riker 1962).

To maintain an even distribution of power, realists recommend certain *rules* be followed to promote fluid and rapidly shifting alliances. They recognize that a balance will develop only if states practice certain behaviors. One requirement is that a great power not immediately threatened by the rise of another power or coalition perform the role of a **balancer** by offsetting the new challenger's power. Since the seventeenth century, Great Britain often played this role by consistently supporting the weaker coalition to prevent an expansionist state and its allies from achieving dominance.

In addition to needing a balancer, all states have to obey the following "essential rules": "(1) increase capabilities but negotiate rather than fight; (2) fight rather than fail to increase capabilities; (3) stop fighting rather than eliminate an essential actor; (4) oppose any coalition or single actor that tends to assume a position of predominance within the system; (5) constrain actors who subscribe to supranational organizational principles; and (6) permit defeated or constrained essential national actors to reenter the system as acceptable role partners" (Kaplan 1957).

According to these rules, competition is proper because it leads to the equalization of capabilities among the major competitors. The balance-of-power approach deals with the problem of war in a way that preserves the problem. War is a way to measure states' relative power as well as a means for changing the distribution of global power in order to preserve the essential features of the balance-of-power system itself.

The successful operation of a global balance-of-power system also presupposes some important preconditions for its successful operation. To maintain a balance, for example, Kenneth Waltz (1979) advances the neorealist thesis that "balance-of-power politics prevail whenever two, and only two, requirements are met: that the order be anarchic and that it be populated by units wishing to survive." Most other theorists hold a more complex view and argue that the following conditions must exist:

- States must possess accurate information about others' capabilities and motives and react rationally to this information.
- There must be a sufficient number of independent states to make alliance formation and dissolution readily possible; stable balance-of-power systems usually require at least five great powers or blocs of states.
- There must be a limited geographic area.
- National leaders must have freedom of action.
- States' capabilities must be relatively equal.
- States must share a common political culture in which the rules of the security regime are recognized and respected.

■ **size principle**
the propensity for competitors to form coalitions only sufficient in size to ensure victory, even if by a narrow margin, with the result that over time opposed alliances tend to remain roughly equal to one another.

■ **balancer**
under a balance-of-power system, an influential global or regional great power that throws its support in decisive fashion to a defensive coalition. This role was often played by Great Britain in the eighteenth, nineteenth and twentieth centuries.

- States in the system must have similar types of government.
- No transnational ideology or religious cause (such as that believed to drive the Al Qaeda terrorist network) interferes with the creation of a balancing coalition.

■ **preemption**
a quick first-strike attack that seeks to defeat an adversary before it can attack or organize a retaliatory response.

- States must have a weapons technology that inhibits **preemption**—quick mobilizations for war by means of first-strike attacks that defeat the enemy before it can undertake military action—and wars of annihilation.
- No supranational institution is powerful enough to obstruct states' alignments and realignments.

These preconditions characterized the environment of international politics during most periods before World War II. But do they exist today? Are the assumptions underlying classic balance-of-power theory still warranted?

The Breakdown of Power Balances. Is international order truly a product of alliance formation and power balances, as most realists believe? Or, when arms races and alliance formation combine power into contending blocs, do the aligned states find that their security actually declines and that major wars then usually erupt?

If the assumptions of the balance-of-power theory are correct, historical periods in which the basic preconditions listed above were in evidence should also have been periods in which war was less frequent. What does the historical record show?

The Eurocentric system that existed from the mid-seventeenth century until World War I is generally regarded as the "golden age" of balance-of-power politics. But even then the balance of power was always precarious at best (Dehio 1962). Indeed, the regularity of wars in Europe between the mid–1600s and the early twentieth century (the period when the necessary conditions for the "invisible hand" of the balance of power most clearly existed) raises the question of whether this approach brings peace or, instead, is a cause of war.

Although the classical systems may at times have prolonged the intervals of peace between conflicts and possibly limited wars' duration and damage when they occurred, a balancing of power has never kept the peace. Research shows

■ **long peaces**
historical periods of long duration without a great-power war.

■ **hegemonic stability theory**
the argument that a dominant state is necessary to enforce international cooperation, maintain international rules and regimes, and keep the peace.

■ **hegemon**
a single dominant military and economic state (see p. 99).

that although during the nineteenth century alliance formation within the balance-of-power system was associated with the absence of war, throughout the first half of the twentieth century, this linkage no longer held; as many states became members of alliances, the frequency of war increased (Singer and Small 1968). However, this is not to argue that the pattern was entirely consistent in this time period. To be sure, several **long peaces**—long-lasting periods of great-power peace—occurred in Europe during the balance of power (between the Congress of Vienna in 1815 and the outbreak of war across Europe in 1848, and after the Franco-Prussian War in 1871 until 1914). An alternative explanation of the relative peace during these periods is offered by **hegemonic stability theory,** which postulates that the existence of a single, all-powerful military **hegemon** can safeguard system stability better than an equilibrium resulting from balance-of-power politics (Wohlforth 1999). At this time, it was the extraordinary dominance of power possessed and used by Great Britain, the world's hegemonic leader, that kept peace among its European rivals (Organski 1968). Whatever the causes of modern periods of peace followed by major wars, the most striking feature of the balance of power was the increasingly destructive general wars that erupted each time these balance-of-power systems collapsed. This led Inis L. Claude, perhaps the foremost realist theoretician on the balance of power, to soberly conclude:

> Balance-of-power theory is concerned mainly with the rivalries and clashes of great powers—above all—what we have come to describe as world wars, the massive military conflicts that engulf and threaten to destroy the entire multistate system. It is difficult to consider world wars as anything other than catastrophic failures, total collapses, of the balance-of-power system. They are hardly to be classed as stabilizing maneuvers or equilibrating processes, and one cannot take seriously any claim of maintaining international stability that does not entail the prevention of such disasters as the Napoleonic wars or World War I. Mention of those and similar disasters, however, frequently evokes the reminder that the would-be universal emperor—be it Louis XIV or Napoleon or Hitler—was defeated; in accordance with balance of power principles, a coalition arose to put down the challenger and maintain or restore the independence of the various states. In short, the system worked. Or did it? Is the criterion of the effectiveness of the balance of power that Germany lose its bid for conquest, or that it be deterred from precipitating World War I? It is not easy to justify the contention that a system for the management of international relations that failed to prevent the events of 1914–1918 deserves high marks as a guardian of stability or order, or peace. If the balance-of-power system does not aim at the prevention of world war, then it aims too low; if it offers no hope of maintaining the general peace, then the quest for a better system is fully warranted. (Claude 1989, 78).

In light of the repetitious breakdown of the balance of power, it is noteworthy that the pattern of recurrent general wars ended when the nuclear era began, after World War II. Since then, war among great powers has been virtually nonexistent. Another long peace (Gaddis 1991) has taken root. Could it be that the **balance of terror** created by atomic weapons has deterred great-power belligerence since 1945 more than the balance of power? Arguably, alliance formation and balance-of-power politics could not have caused this long peace. Rigid alliance blocs halted the rapid realignments necessary for the equilibrium that balance-of-power theory envisions. If that is so, then it seems likely that the annihilating destructiveness of atomic and nuclear weapons—a **pax atomica**—kept the peace since the 1950s—not the alliances and power balances that the great powers constructed.

Equally debatable is the realist assumption underlying balance-of-power theory that countries with dominant strength will be secure. Contrary evidence suggests that rapidly arming countries may actually invite attack. In five of the nine great-power wars that occurred in the 150 years following the 1815 Congress of Vienna, the countries attacked were stronger militarily than those initiating the war (Singer and Small 1974; see also Chapter 11). This belies the premise that seeking military advantages over others deters aggression. Instead, as liberals warn, the growth of a state's military power may so terrify its adversaries that they are motivated to initiate a preemptive strike in order to prevent their defeat.

■ **balance of terror**
situations of mutual nuclear deterrence.

■ **pax atomica**
the notion that nuclear weapons have preserved peace.

The Rise, Fall, and Revival of Collective Security as a Substitute for Power Balances

The outbreak of World War I, perhaps more than any other event, discredited balance-of-power politics and promoted the search for alternatives. The catastrophic proportions of that war led many to view the balance-of-power mechanism as a *cause* of war instead of an instrument for its prevention. These critics cited the arms races, secret treaties, and cross-cutting alliances driving balance-of-power politics before the outbreak of the war as its immediate causes.

U.S. President Woodrow Wilson voiced the most vehement opposition to balance-of-power politics. He and other liberal reformers hoped to replace the alliances and counteralliances within the balance of power with the principle of **collective security,** a system of world order in which aggression by any state would be met by a collective response.

The League of Nations embodied this belief, built on the assumption that peace-loving countries could collectively deter—and, if necessary, counteract—aggression. Instead of accepting war as a legitimate instrument of national policy, collective security advocates sought to inhibit war through the threat of collective action. The theory proposed: (1) to retaliate against *any* aggression or attempt to establish hegemony—not just those acts that threatened particular countries; (2) to involve the participation of *all* member states—not just a sufficient number to stop the aggressor; and (3) to create an international organization to identify threats to security and to organize a military response to them—not just to let individual states decide for themselves whether to undertake self-help measures. In essence, collective security may be defined as "collective self-regulation," occurring when "a group of states attempts to reduce security threats by agreeing to collectively punish any member state that violates the system's norms" (Downs 1994). As one realist authority impartially describes the concept,

> The rock bottom principle upon which collective security is founded provides that an attack on any one state will be regarded as an attack on all states. It finds its measure in the simple doctrine of one for all and all for one. War anywhere . . . is the concern of every state.
>
> Self-help and neutrality, it should be obvious, are the exact antithesis of such a theory. States under an order of neutrality are impartial when conflict breaks out, give their blessings to combatants to fight it out, and defer judgment regarding the justice or injustice of the cause involved. Self-help in the past was often "help yourself" so far as the great powers were concerned; they enforced their own rights and more besides. In the eighteenth and nineteenth centuries this system was fashionable, and wars, although not eliminated, were localized whenever possible. In a more integrated world environment, a conflict anywhere has some effect on conditions of peace everywhere. A disturbance at one point upsets the equilibrium at all other points, and the adjustment of a single conflict restores the foundations of harmony at other points throughout the world. (Thompson 1953, 755)

To the disappointment of its advocates, collective security was not endorsed by the very powers that after World War I had most championed it, such as the

■ **collective security**
a global or regional security regime agreed to by the great powers setting rules for keeping peace, guided by the principle that an act of aggression by any state automatically will be met by a combined military response from the rest.

United States. Japan's aggression against Manchuria in 1931 (and China in 1937) and Italy's invasion of Ethiopia in 1935 were widely condemned, but collective resistance was not forthcoming. Germany's so-called preemptive invasion of Czechoslovakia and other European countries in the late 1930s elicited no collective response. When World War II broke out, collective security was discredited, and balance-of-power politics regained favor, along with realism, as the most popular approach for preserving global peace. In the wake of that deadly global war, realists convinced many people that national self-help was the only trustworthy safeguard of security. They loudly preached that peace must come through states' unilateral preparations for war and use of acquired military might, to confront a potential aggressor with an abundance of power to successfully deter its aggression. Realists assume that the global system's **structure** encourages natural equilibrium among self-interested state actors. U.S. President Richard Nixon was one of many leaders who reaffirmed the balance-of-power approach and rejected **multilateral** collective peacekeeping; he argued "We must remember the only time in the history of the world that we have had any extended period of peace is when there has been a balance of power. . . . It will be a safer world . . . if we have a strong, healthy United States, Europe, Soviet Union, China, and Japan, each balancing the other."

That realpolitik philosophy fell on receptive ears throughout the tense Cold War and helped to propel the worldwide arms race that characterized it. It was only after the Cold War ended in 1991 that the global community began to once again consider collective security as the preferred method for letting the UN and regional defense organizations maintain world order (see Chapter 15). Changing times in the midst of cascading **globalization** seemed to justify a return to liberal approaches.

Models of the Balance of Power in the Twenty-First Century

Military power can be distributed in different ways—an idea scholars call **polarity.** Historically, these have ranged from highly concentrated power on one end of the continuum to highly dispersed distributions on the other. The former have included regional empires (e.g., the Roman Empire), while an example of the latter is the approximate equality of power held by the European powers at the conclusion of the Napoleonic Wars in 1815. Using the conventional ways historians separate turning points from one type of balance-of-power system to another, we identify four distinct periods of polarity. This evolution displays a **long cycle,** since the transformations went through four phases that conclude today the way the system began: (1) unipolarity, 1945–1949; (2) bipolarity, 1949–1991; (3) multipolarity 1991–2001; and (4) another unipolar system today with the United States again an unchallenged hegemon.

Unipolarity—the United States.   Most countries were devastated by World War II. The United States, however, was left in a clearly dominant position, its economy accounting for about half the world's combined gross national product (GNP). The United States was also the only country with the atomic bomb and had demonstrated its willingness to use the new weapon. This underscored to others that it was without rival and incapable of being counterbalanced. The United States was not just stronger than *anybody*—it was stronger than

■ structure
the defining characteristics of the global system—such as the distribution of military capabilities—that exists independently of all actors but powerfully shapes their actions.

■ multilateralism
agreements among many states to cooperate for the purpose of collective action (see p. 477).

■ globalization
the integration of states through increasing contact, communication, and trade to create a holistic, single global system, which increasingly binds people together in a common fate (see p. 21).

■ polarity
the degree to which the global system revolves around one or more extremely powerful states, or "poles," as power concentrates in a single (unipolar) center of power or is distributed between two (bipolar) main powers or among three or more (multipolar) great powers.

■ long cycle
an interpretation of world history that focuses on repeating patterns of interstate behavior, such as the outbreak of systemwide general wars at regular intervals, after long periods during which other patterns (global peace) were dominant.

everybody. In the period immediately following World War II, a unipolar distribution of power materialized, because power was concentrated in the hands of a single *hegemon* able to exercise overwhelming influence over all other states, either through leadership or through domination. So supremely powerful was the United States at that time that people spoke of a new "American Empire" ruling over an impoverished world ravaged by war. That hegemonic status was short lived, however, as ascendant challengers to U.S. preponderance, such as the Soviet Union, soon began to undermine America's supremacy and hegemonic status.

The U.S. capacity to act unilaterally by going it alone in pursuit of its interests and ideals in competition with others underwent a decline over the next four decades, as the U.S. grip on global developments and its ability to influence others eroded (see Kennedy 1987).

Bipolarity—the United States and Russia. The recovery of the Soviet economy, the growth of its military capabilities, its maintenance of a large army, and growing Soviet-U.S. rivalry less than five years after the end of World War II gave rise to a new distribution of world power. The Soviets broke the U.S. monopoly on atomic weapons in 1949 and exploded a thermonuclear device in 1953, less than a year after the United States. This achievement symbolized the creation of **bipolarity** in the global system. Military capabilities became concentrated in the hands of two competitive "superpowers," whose capacities to massively destroy anyone made comparisons with the other great powers meaningless.

■ **bipolarity**
the division of the balance of power into two coalitions headed by rival military powers, each seeking to contain the other's expansion.

■ **polarization**
the degree to which states cluster in alliances around the most powerful members of the state system.

Power combined to form two opposing blocs or coalitions through **polarization** when states joined counterbalanced alliances. In interpreting these dynamics, it is important not to use the concepts of polarity and polarization interchangeably. They refer to two distinct dimensions of the primary ways in which military power is aggregated (or dispersed) at any point in time in the international system. When states independently build arms at home, their differential production rates change the system's *polarity,* or number of power centers (poles). In contrast, when states combine their arms through alliance formation, the aggregation of power through *polarization* changes the system's balance of power. A system with multiple power centers can be said to be moving toward a greater degree of polarization if its members form separate blocs whose external interactions are characterized by increasing levels of conflict while their internal interactions become more cooperative (Rapkin and Thompson with Christopherson 1989). Conversely, polarization decreases when the number of cross-cutting alignments expands. The concept of polarization is especially apt in this context because a *pole* suggests the metaphor of a magnet—it both repels and attracts.

■ **North Atlantic Treaty Organization (NATO)**
a military alliance created in 1949 to deter a Soviet attack on Western Europe that now seeks to maintain peace and promote democracy.

The formation of the **North Atlantic Treaty Organization (NATO),** linking the United States to the defense of Western Europe, and the Warsaw Pact, linking the former Soviet Union in a formal alliance with its Eastern European clients, were produced by this polarization process. Through this process, states combined their military resources in two countercoalitions to reinforce a bipolar structure. The opposing blocs formed in part because the superpowers competed for allies and in part because the less-powerful states looked to one superpower or the other for protection. Correspondingly, each superpower's allies gave it forward bases from which to carry on the competition. In addition, the involvement of most other states in the superpowers' struggle globalized the East-West conflict. Few states remained outside the superpowers' rival alliance networks as neutral or nonaligned countries.

By grouping the system's states into two blocs, each led by a superpower, the Cold War's bipolar structure bred insecurity among all. The balance was constantly at stake. Each bloc leader, fearing that its adversary would attain hegemony, viewed every move, however defensive, as the first step toward world conquest. **Zero-sum** conflict prevailed as both sides viewed what one side gained as a loss for the other. Both superpowers attached great importance to recruiting new allies. Fear that an old ally might desert the fold was everpresent. Bipolarity left little room for compromise or maneuver and worked against the normalization of superpower relations (Waltz 1993).

The major Cold War coalitions associated with bipolarity began to disintegrate in the 1960s and early 1970s. As their internal cohesion eroded, new centers of power emerged. At the same time, weaker alliance partners were afforded more room for maneuvering. Diverse relationships among the states subordinate to the superpowers developed, such as the friendly relations between the United States and Romania and between France and the Soviet Union. The superpowers remained dominant militarily, but this less-rigid system allowed other states to perform more independent foreign policy roles.

Rapid technological innovation in the superpowers' major weapons systems was a principal catalyst to the crumbling of the blocs. Intercontinental ballistic missiles (ICBMs), capable of delivering nuclear weapons through space from one continent to another, eroded the necessity of forward bases on allies' territory for striking at the heart of the adversary.

In addition, the narrowed differences in the superpowers' arsenals loosened the ties that had previously bound allies to one another. The European members of NATO in particular began to question whether the United States would, as it had pledged, protect Paris or Bonn by sacrificing New York. Under what conditions might Washington or Moscow be willing to risk a nuclear holocaust? The uncertainty became pronounced while the pledge to protect allies through **extended deterrence** seemed increasingly insincere.

The acceptance of capitalism by many communist states since the late 1980s further eroded the adhesive bonds of ideology that had formerly helped these countries face their security problems from a common posture. Fissures in the military **doctrine** of both blocs widened. In addition, support for alliance commitments in general declined (Kegley and Raymond 1990) as fears of a new world war lessened.

The 1989 dismantling of the Berlin Wall tore apart the Cold War architecture of competing blocs. With the end of this division, and without a Soviet threat, the consistency of outlook and singularity of purpose that once bound NATO members together disappeared. Many perceived the need to replace NATO and the defunct Warsaw Pact with a new security arrangement. However, most leaders maintained that some configuration of an European defense architecture was still necessary to cement relationships and stabilize the rush of cascading events. That adaptation occurred eventually after the Cold War ended and a third multipolar phase began.

■ **zero-sum**
the perception in a rivalry that if one side gains, the other side loses (see p. 208).

■ **extended deterrence**
the protection received by a weak ally when a heavily militarized great power pledges to "extend" its capabilities to it in a defense treaty (see p. 117).

■ **doctrine**
the guidelines a great power embraces as a strategy to specify the conditions under which it will use military power and armed force for political purposes abroad (see p. 209).

The Vestiges of Communist Power In 1998, only five countries (China, Cuba Laos, North Korea, and Vietnam) then remained members of the "communist bloc." In 1988, before the Cold War ended, that coalition consisted of fifteen countries. Pictured here is Cuba's Fidel Castro being assisted by Vietnam's General Secretary Do Muoi and a Vietnamese soldier at farewell ceremonies of a 1995 summit in Hanoi. The Cuban leader visited both China and Vietnam to observe how they had adapted Marxism to market economies. The meeting raised the question of whether communist ideology can still unify what remains of the communist bloc in a common coalition. Perhaps national self-interests rather than ideology will cement future alignments, as suggested by the pledge of Russian President Vladimir Putin to strengthen ties with Cuba, its former communist ally.

Multipolarity

U.S. Secretary of State Lawrence Eagleburger proclaimed in 1989 that "we are now moving into a world in which power and influence [are] diffused among a multiplicity of states—[a] multipolar world." A multipolar system of relatively equal powers, similar to the classical European balance-of-power system, did indeed describe the distribution of power from 1991 until the start of the twenty-first century. A **power transition** occurred after the collapse of the Cold War, resulting in a new multipolar system consisting of the United States, China, Germany, Japan, and Russia (see Chapters 4 and 12), joined by the European Union. It appeared in 1991 that world politics would be dominated by great-power rivalry among these five or six centers of global power, which were growing closer in military and economic strength with one another.

■ **power transition**
a narrowing of the ratio of military capabilities between great power rivals that may either increase or decrease to increase the probability of war between them.

What unfolded was precisely the kinds of roles performed by great powers in previous multipolar systems. The search for the capacity to compete on an equal footing with the other centers of power is characteristically strong when power is spread across three or more poles. With the effort by the European Union to enter the playing field alongside the United States, China, Japan, Russia, and other regional players like Brazil and India, the game of rivalry and balancing was becoming much different from the strategies and alignments that materialize in unipolar and bipolar systems. As power became increasingly equally distributed, each player became assertive, independent, and competitive; diplomacy displayed a nonideological, chesslike character; and conflict intensified as each contender feared the power of its rivals. The enlarged global chessboard of multiple geostrategic relationships developed. A congested landscape led to confusion about the identity of friends and foes. To make this setting even more confusing, the interplay took place simultaneously on two playing fields—the first military and the second economic (recall Table 4.2 on p. 127). The major players aligned together against others on particular issues, as their interests dictated. Behind the diplomatic smiles and handshakes, one-time friends and allies began to grow apart, formally "specialized" relations began to dissolve, and former enemies forged friendly tips.

This competition under conditions of multipolarity was evident in the growing U.S.–Japan-EU trade-bloc rivalry on the economic battlefield (see Chapter 9). In addition, much counterbalancing and shifting in flexible and fluid alliances occurred, with the United States often casting itself in the role of balancer. For example, in December 2002 China and Russia signed a new friendship treaty, calling for a "multi-polar world" to express resentment of U.S. global dominance even though Russia at the same time was also energetically pursuing full membership in NATO.

The evolution of the North Atlantic Treaty Organization (NATO) in this period shows the dynamics of alliance politics in response to changes in the global balance of power. When the Cold War first began to collapse, many observers felt that NATO would also disintegrate. The purpose for which NATO was first created—containing Russian expansionism—no longer was relevant, because the threat no longer existed. However, NATO did not dissolve. It reinvented itself. Changing conditions motivated NATO to change its membership and its mission. In January 1994, NATO began to encourage **bandwagoning** by allowing four formerly communist bloc states (Poland, the Czech Republic, Slovakia, and Hungary) to join NATO by becoming peace partners under the **Partnership for Peace (PfP)** plan. The PfP did not then give them the same guarantee of aid in the event of an attack that the existing full members were promised. But it became a pivotal step in the process of enlargement aimed at creating a peaceful, united, and democratic Europe, as did the **Euro-Atlantic Partnership Council (EAPC)** whose forty-six-member countries at the time served to help coordinate NATO's efforts to manage crises and provide for greater security in Europe. As Map 14.1 shows, after admitting Poland, the Czech Republic and Poland in 1999, NATO took enlargement a big step forward in November 2002 when NATO undertook the biggest expansion in its fifty-three-year history. Bulgaria, Estonia, Latvia, Lithuania, Romania, Slovakia, and Slovenia were admitted as full members along with the nineteen existing countries under NATO's security umbrella. The expansion stretches NATO's territory from the Baltic Sea to Russia's west coast to the Black Sea on Europe's southeastern rim. In

■ **bandwagoning**
the tendency for weak states to seek alliance with the strongest power, irrespective of that power's ideology or form of government, in order to increase security.

■ **Partnership for Peace (PfP)**
a plan proposed in 1993 by the United States that established limited military partnerships between NATO and the former Warsaw Pact countries.

■ **Euro-Atlantic Partnership Council (EAPC)**
a coordinating institution within NATO created in 1998 to manage the common political, military, financial, and security issues confronting Europe.

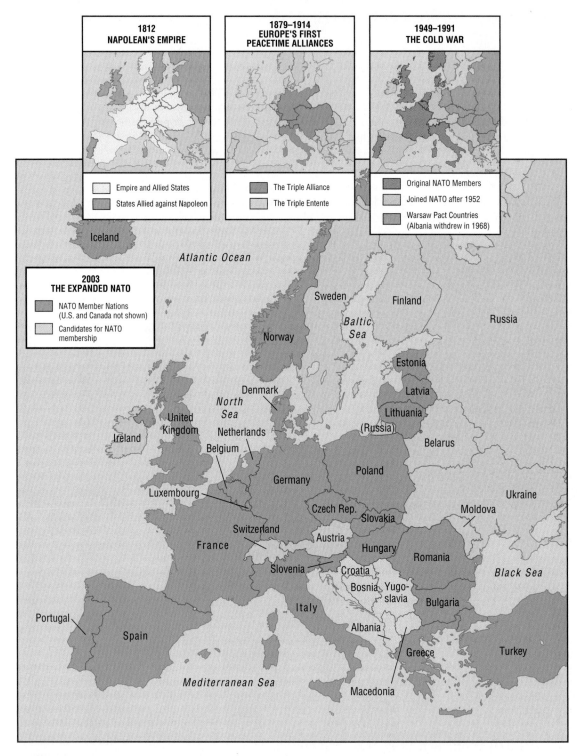

MAP 14.1

The Enlarged NATO in the New Geostrategic Balance of Power

The twenty-first-century geostrategic landscape has been transformed by NATO's expansion at the start of 2003 to twenty-seven full members. An additional thirty-eight countries work as Partners for Peace in the Euro-Atlantic Partnership Council (EAPC). As shown in this map, NATO now casts its security umbrella across and beyond Europe in its endeavor to create a collective security regime including states that once were its enemies. If NATO succeeds in redefining itself as a coalition of liberal democracies fighting tyranny, terrorism, and a range of other economic and environmental problems, the transformation will defy the tendency for Europe's alliances to collapse after the defeat of a common adversary.

SOURCE: From *U.S. New and World Report*, July 14, 1997. Copyright © 1997, U.S. News & World Report, L.P. Reprinted with permission.

addition, Russia has been invited to formally participate in full decision making on NATO security policies, in order to alleviate any lingering Russian fears that the alliance continues to perceive Russia as a potential enemy. Thus, NATO, a product of a bygone bipolar world, has become under multipolarity a new security IGO on the global stage, committed to defending its twenty-six members' borders as though they were their own. This membership includes the United States.

Enlargement of both NATO's membership and its mission opens a new chapter in NATO's history. Revitalized with a larger membership and territorial reach, NATO seeks to orchestrate a cooperative approach to security among liberal democracies. That goal was forcefully expressed by U.S. President George W. Bush in December 2001 at Warsaw University, when he declared that every European democracy—including former parts of the Soviet Union—must be permitted to join an expanded NATO. "The United States is no longer your enemy," Bush declared in urging Russia to be "a partner in peace, a partner in democracy." U.S. Secretary of State Colin Powell followed by noting that the Atlantic alliance after 9/11 remained more vital than ever despite NATO's exclusion from the U.S. war in Afghanistan. "The world has changed. Now more than ever, NATO matters," he stressed.

On September 13, 2001, for the first time NATO invoked the mutual defense principle when, following 9/11, the alliance declared that the terrorist attacks on New York and Washington were an attack on all of them and that they would act as a united coalition to punish those behind the atrocities. This further helped dispel doubts about NATO's usefulness in addressing twenty-first-century security challenges, and questions on whether NATO's cumbersome decision-making procedures will permit it to be used for fighting wars rather than peacekeeping missions. The advantages to enlargement are offset by the risk that expansion will reduce the alliance to a mere conference association for discussing security issues and end its role as a military alliance in the global balance of power.

Critics of NATO's enlargement complain that this monster alliance undermines the security of the other states it excludes. Not only at times Russia, but also China, Japan, and other powers have complained that the presence of a solidified military alliance in Europe without other strong military alliances to balance it poses a threat to global security. NATO asserts that these charges are unjustified because its new decision rules, giving every full member a veto over decisions regarding coercive military operations, remove the threat of a NATO preemptive strike. Other proponents of NATO and European Union enlargement claim that the maze of overlapping European security organizations (including the OSCE and the Council of Europe) are too cumbersome and slow to permit any of them to take decisive military actions outside their sphere of influence.

The innovative redesign of NATO and its expansion suggest the grip that realist thinking exerts on national security thinking as states and alliances seek to adjust to changes in the global distribution of military power. Coalitions form and dissolve in response to changes in security threats and national interests. One example was the division that developed between the United States and its NATO allies in late 2002 when Europeans did not accept the Bush administration's plan to launch a preemptive strike against Iraq. That episode of strained trans-Atlantic relationships shattered some of the enthusiasm for building a concert of great powers to wage a global war against global terrorism following

Andreas Striglos/AFP

Rivalry among Allies Seeking to disarm and defuse European allies' anxieties about his plan for the United States to build a missile defense system, Bush proclaimed his administration's "new receptivity" to the European allies at the June 2001 NATO summit. However, French, German, and other Europeans were not persuaded, and a climate of mistrust among allies prevailed. Shown here is a June 2001 protest demonstration in Europe against the United States.

the 9/11 attacks. Alignments shifted again after 9/11 when the friction grew between the United States and its closest allies over how to pursue the war on terrorism after President Bush condemned North Korea, Iran, and Iraq as an "axis of evil" and threatened to take military action against Iraq. As a measure of how sensitive particular issues can be among great powers, both the European Union's foreign affairs commissioner, Christopher Pattern, and the German foreign minister, Joschka Fischer, castigated President Bush for treating America's coalition partners as subordinate "satellites," and Russian President Vladimir Putin quickly joined their criticism of U.S. unilateralist disregard of the interests of America's would-be partners in the antiterrorist coalition. In multipolarity, alignments are inherently fragile.

Another indicator of continuing balance-of-power jockeying for global position and independence was the decision by the European Union to create its own rapid deployment force so it can undertake military actions on its own without the approval of the United States. The European reaction was a response to the growing recognition that U.S. power had grown so dramatically that it overshadowed everyone else combined. In short, history had cyclically "returned" to a previous condition: another era of unipolarity had arisen in the early twenty-first century.

Unipolarity Redux

Most analysts believe that a new era of unipolarity has arisen again like the one after World War II, with the United States once more reemerging as the globe's only superpower. Part of the basis for this constructed view of the new global realities stems from recent U.S. policy rhetoric and part from the tangible magnitude of the U.S. superpower's hegemonic dominance. Consider the U.S. policy proclamations first. Asserting a new and aggressive American unilateralism, the **Bush Doctrine** has embraced the motto "We will build to suit—ourselves" because it perceives the United States to be "the dominant power in the world, more dominant than any since Rome. Accordingly, America is in a position to reshape norms, alter expectations and create new realities . . . by unapologetic and implacable demonstrations of will" (Krauthammer 2001).

To enthusiasts, the United States has today regained sufficient supremacy in military might and economic clout to re-create a new unipolar period. "People are coming out of the closet on the word empire," noted columnist Charles Krauthammer, using it with approval as an acceptable "Pax Americana" to preserve peace as a hegemon, instead of condemning hegemony as **imperialism.** "The fact is," Krauthammer proclaimed in 2002, "no country has been as dominant culturally, economically, technologically, and militarily in the history of the world since the Roman Empire." The question is whether the assertive U.S. global ambition and active management of international affairs will prove beneficial or damaging. As German analyst Josef Joffe (in Friedman 2001) observes, American hegemonic supremacy is widely resented but no solid alliance has yet formed to counter it, and U.S. preeminence is perceived in incompatible ways—"America is both menace and seducer, both monster and model."

The effect of unipolarity under U.S. hegemony is regarded by some to be medicinal. Recall that to hegemonic stability theorists a unipolar concentration of power in a single hegemonic superpower would provide the global leader with the unrivaled power to police chaos and maintain international peace. Their faith in America as a well-intentioned peacekeeper is bolstered by President George W. Bush's pledge in 2001 that the U.S. role in the world would be "the story of a power that went into the world to protect but not possess, to defend but not to conquer."

Against this optimistic view currently runs a strong suspicion about the future stability of a unipolar world under U.S. management. Warns one critic, "It is virtually universal in history that when countries become hegemons—global superpowers—they tend to want everything their own way, and it never works. They decide that they no longer want to make realistic choices in keeping with their goals" (Mathews 2002). Others condemn the shortsightedness of U.S. hegemonic leadership, guided, as they see it, more by self-interests than by ideals and motivated primarily toward competition to preserve America's position as top dog and less toward cooperation to promote peace and prosperity:

> In reality, America's engineering of its dominance has at times been for the general good, when it used its clout to "think for the world." But often its

■ **Bush Doctrine**
the policy of assertive unilateral hegemonic leadership proclaimed by George W. Bush in 2001 as the policy principle that would guide American foreign policy, elaborated in the 2002 *National Security Strategy of the United States* pledges to maintain a unipolar world and to use preemptive warfare to prevent enemies' use of force.

■ **imperialism**
intentional imposition of one state's power over another, traditionally through territorial conquest but more recently through economic domination, denying the victim population's freedom to have a voice in the conquering regime's decisions.

clout has been used solely in the interests of its richest citizens and most powerful corporations. This latter tendency has been dominant lately. We see it in its new single-minded unilateralism in international relations, much exacerbated by the mixture of rage at September 11 and gung-ho jubilation at "success" in Afghanistan. And we see it in what the United States is now ramming through the international supervisory organizations. The United States and its allies can stamp out specific groups by force and bribery. But in the longer run, the structural arrangements that replicate a grossly unequal world have to be redesigned, as the Bretton Woods conference did after World War II, so that markets working within the new framework produce more equitable results. Historians looking back a century from now will say that the time to have begun was now. (Wade 2002, 7)

■ **unipolarity**
a condition in which an international system has a single dominant power center, or pole, able to exercise supreme authority by its superior economic resources and military capability.

Whatever the ultimate consequences of **unipolarity,** it is clear that most of the globe's other powers would agree with the skeptics about the instability of world politics if the overwhelming power of the United States persists. In the view of many Chinese, Germans, Japanese, and Russians, the growing accumulation of so much political, military, economic, and cultural clout by the United States is breeding an alarming arrogance and a dangerous impulse to bully the rest of the world. Some of America's closest allies fear that U.S. dominance will lead to a heavy-handed U.S. imperialism that threatens global stability.

As America's power became more apparent, foreign governments voiced their growing distaste for it. . . . Today, with no alternative ideology and no competitors, America stands alone in the world. Everyone else sits in its shadow. This doesn't mean that other countries will form military alliances against America; that would be pointless. But countries will obstruct American purposes whenever and in whatever way they can, and the pursuit of American interests will have to be undertaken through coercion rather than consensus. Anti-Americanism will become the global language of political protest—the default ideology of opposition—unifying the world's discontents and malcontents, some of whom, as we have discovered, can be very dangerous. (Zakaria 2002, 76, 81)

To put these concerns about unipolarity into historical context, consider another interpretation of the existing unipolar "moment," which predicts that the current phase of American hegemonic leadership will not persist in the long run and that another period of multipolarity will materialize:

Commentators were quick to recognize that a new "unipolar moment" of unprecedented U.S. power had arrived. In 1992, the Pentagon drafted a new grand strategy designed to preserve unipolarity by preventing the emergence of a global rival. But the draft plan soon ran into controversy, as commentators at home and abroad argued that any effort to preserve unipolarity was quixotic and dangerous. Officials quickly backed away from the idea and [eschewed] the language of primacy or predominance, speaking instead of the United States as a "leader" or the "indispensable nation."

The rise and sudden demise of an official strategy for preserving primacy lends credence to the widespread belief that unipolarity is dangerous and unstable. While scholars frequently discuss unipolarity, their focus is

Russia and China Seek to Balance U.S. Power When NATO approved formal enlargement in 1997, both Russia's and China's sense of security plummeted. In reaction, the old rivals, feeling excluded, repaired their broken alliance ties by agreeing to a new "strategic partnership" aimed at rearranging the global geostrategic chessboard. Russian Premier Vickor Cheknomyrdin (right) and Chinese President Jiang Zemin met in Moscow in April 1997 to negotiate the "new world order" joint statement, which called for creation of a new "multipolar" system cemented by a new Sino-Russian axis to counter the threat of global domination by the U.S. hegemonic superpower. This friendship treaty was renewed in 2002. The logic of balance-of-power politics rationalizes the formation of these kinds of strategic unions to check the growing influence of a rising great-power rival. The same thinking inspired the 1999 common defense treaty between Japan and the United States to offset the expanding military power of China.

always on its demise. For neorealists, unipolarity is the least stable of all structures because any great concentration of power threatens other states and causes them to take action to restore a balance. Other scholars grant that a large concentration of power works for peace, but they doubt that U.S. preponderance is fragile and easily negated by the actions of other states. As a result, most analysts argue that unipolarity is an "illusion," a "moment" that "will not last long," or is already "giving way to multipolarity." (Wohlforth 1999, 5–6)

Many agree with this assessment, believing that a new period of multipolarity will emerge, despite the commitment in the 2002 *National Security Strategy of the United States* to preserve unipolar American hegemony and predominance by assuring that U.S. power and position is not challenged by other great-power

IS A UNIPOLAR, BIPOLAR, OR MULTIPOLAR SYSTEM THE MOST STABLE?

Three Schools of Thought on the Relationship of Polarity and International Peace

In the early twenty-first century, a long-standing debate has intensified about which type of polarity distribution—unipolar, bipolar, or multipolar—is the most capable of preventing large-scale war. What do you think? Consider the divided opinions about this issue, as represented by the arguments in three contending schools of thought.

One interpretation holds that peace will occur when one hegemonic state acquires enough power to deter others' expansionist ambitions. This view maintains that the concentration of power reduces the chances of war because it allows a single superpower to maintain peace and manage the international system (Wohlforth 1999). The long peace under Britain's leadership in the 1800s (the Pax Britannica) and earlier, under the Roman Empire (the Pax Romana), offered support for the idea that unipolarity brings peace, and therefore inspires the hope that the twenty-first century under a Pax Americana will be stable as long as U.S. dominance prevails (Knickerbocker 1999).

In contrast, a second school of thought (e.g., Waltz 1964) maintains that bipolar systems are the most stable. According to this line of reasoning, stability, ironically, results from "the division of all nations into two camps [because it] raises the costs of war to such a high level that all but the most fundamental conflicts are resolved without resort to violence" (Bueno de Mesquita 1975). Under such stark simplicities and balanced symmetries, the two leading rivals have incentives to manage crises so that they do not escalate to war.

Those who believe that a bipolar world is inherently more stable than either its unipolar or multipolar counterparts draw support from the fact that in the bipolar environment of the 1950s, when the threat of war was endemic, major war did not occur. Extrapolating, these observers (e.g., Mearsheimer 1990) reason that because a new multipolar distribution of global power makes it impossible to run the world from one or two centers, disorder will result:

> It is rather basic. So long as there [are] only two great powers, like two big battleships clumsily and cautiously circling each other, confrontations—or accidents—[are] easier to avoid. [With] the global lake more crowded with ships of varying sizes, fueled by different ambitions and piloted with different degrees of navigational skill, the odds of collisions become far greater. (House 1989, A10)

A third school of thought argues that multipolar systems are the least war prone. While the reasons differ, advocates share the belief that polarized systems that either concentrate power, as in a unipolar system, or that divide the world into two antagonistic blocs, as in a bipolar system, promote struggles for dominance (see Thompson 1988; Morgenthau 1985). The peace-through-multipolarity school perceives multipolar systems as stable because they encompass a larger number of autonomous actors, giving rise to more potential alliance partners. This is seen as pacifying because it is essential to counterbalancing a would-be aggressor, as shifting alliances can occur only when there are multiple power centers (Deutsch and Singer 1964).

Abstract deductions and historical analogies can lead to contradictory conclusions, as the logic underlying these three inconsistent interpretations illustrates. The future will determine which of these rival theories is the most accurate.

---

rivals. Should a new multipolar world develop in the mid-twenty-first century, the probable consequences are here again not clear, as the three different schools of thought on the relationship between polarity and global stability suggest (see Controversy: Is a Unipolar, Bipolar, or Multipolar System the Most Stable?). Because there is no real consensus on whether systems with a certain number of poles are more war prone than others, it would be imprudent to conclude that a new multipolar system will necessarily produce another period of warfare or of peace.

Other scenarios are possible, with equally uncertain ultimate consequences. For example, some forecast the likely return of coalition politics, with a new bipolar but unstable configuration emerging from the formation of a new Sino-Russian bloc, European-Russian entente, or Sino-Japanese alliance to counter an alliance spearheaded by the United States (Brzezinski 1998). Here it is possible to visualize turmoil as various states join together to restrain the American behemoth or another great-power bloc from harming others with its power. It is, indeed, very difficult to predict what the twenty-first-century geostrategic chessboard will look like and whether it will be chaotic or stable. But if the past truly is a guide to the future, the distribution of global power will exert a strong influence on the kind of global system the world will experience.

The preservation of peace by states aggregating power in order to balance power has a rather checkered history. In the long run, the resulting alliances and distributions of power have failed to avert a breakdown of world order. The great powers have persistently been drawn into wars by the collapse of the balance of power in either Europe or East Asia or both. Yet history also suggests that the prospects for peace in unipolar, bipolar, and multipolar systems depend on other factors as well. Negotiated arms agreements designed to change the existing balance of power are a critical component that could alter the tendency of multipolar systems to culminate in widespread warfare.

CONTROLLING MILITARY POWER THROUGH ARMS AGREEMENTS

Liberal reformers have often attacked the theory that power can be balanced with power to preserve world order. They have advocated instead the biblical prescription that states should beat their swords into plowshares. The destructiveness and dispersion of today's weapons have inspired many people once again to take this tenet of liberal theory seriously. But this approach is not solely a liberal preserve. Most realists also see arms control as a way of influencing the global distribution of military power in ways that promote peace and individual states' national security. In fact, most policymakers who have negotiated arms control agreements have been realists who perceived these treaties as a prudent tool to promote their countries' security. At times, they have been the leading advocates of arms control to adjust their states' military power relative to the rivals' and to help maintain the balance of power.

Arms Control versus Disarmament

It will be useful to review the historical record of negotiators' efforts to preserve the global distribution of weapons and their uses. However, two concepts must first be distinguished. Many people incorrectly assume that the terms "arms control" and "disarmament" are synonymous. **Arms control** refers to agreements designed to regulate arms levels either by limiting their growth or by restricting how they may be used. This is a far less ambitious endeavor than **disarmament,** which is the reduction or elimination of weapons, and **demilitarization,** which occurs when a country's war-fighting capabilities are eliminated.

■ **arms control**
multilateral or bilateral agreements to contain arms races by setting limits on the number and types of weapons states are permitted.

■ **disarmament**
agreements to reduce or destroy weapons or other means of attack.

■ **demilitarization**
the forced complete elimination of the military power or potential of a state, usually imposed by victors on the vanquished after a war.

■ **bilateral agreements**
exchanges between two states, such as arms control agreements negotiated cooperatively to set ceilings on military force levels.

■ **multilateral agreements**
cooperative compacts among many states to ensure that a concerted policy is implemented toward alleviating a common problem, such as levels of future weapons' capabilities.

■ **Strategic Arms Limitation Talks (SALT)**
the negotiations begun in 1969 between the United States and the USSR to freeze offensive weapons at existing levels and promote balanced, verifiable limits on strategic nuclear weapons (see p. 118).

■ **START (Strategic Arms Reduction) Treaty**
the U.S.-Russian series of negotiations that began in 1993 and, with the 1997 START-III agreement ratified by Russia in April 2000, pledged to cut the nuclear arsenals of both sides by 80 percent of the Cold War peaks, in order to lower the risk of nuclear war by making a successful preemptive strike impossible.

■ **multiple independently targeted reentry vehicles (MIRVs)**
the technological innovation that permits many nuclear warheads to be delivered from a single ballistic missile.

We should also distinguish between **bilateral agreements** and **multilateral agreements.** Because the former are agreements between only two countries, they are often easier to negotiate and to enforce than are the latter, which are agreements among three or more countries. Negotiating a multilateral agreement, simultaneously binding on many states, poses many obstacles because states' security interests are very different, as are the domestic pressures which affect whether states can forge agreements. As a result, the record of bilateral arms control and disarmament agreements is stronger than those of multilateral agreements. By far the most revealing example of successful bilateral diplomacy is the superpower agreements to control nuclear arms. We first take a brief look at that record and the lessons it suggests.

The Superpowers Negotiate Arms Control

The Cold War never became hot. One of the reasons for that outcome was the series of more than twenty-five arms control agreements the United States and the Soviet Union (now Russia) negotiated since 1963, when the Hot Line Agreement established a direct radio and telegraph communication system between the governments to be used in times of crisis. Examples include the 1972 Antiballistic (ABM) missile treaty, the 1977 convention prohibiting military use of environmental modification techniques, the 1990 chemical weapons destruction agreement, and the 1992 open skies agreement. Each of these bilateral agreements reduced superpower tensions and contributed to confidence building between the former adversaries. The five strategic nuclear arms control agreements stand out in this history between superpowers as the most important achievements (**SALT** I, 1972; SALT II, 1979; **START** I, 1999; START II, 1993; START III, to be implemented December 2007; and the Strategic Offensive Reductions Treaty (SORT), 2002, to reduce warheads by 2012. The first two agreements stabilized the nuclear arms race, and the remaining agreements have reduced the arsenals in each side's inventories so as to cut significantly the number of nuclear warheads (see Figure 14.1). In 1991 when the Cold War ended the U.S. had more than 9,500 nuclear warheads and Russia had about 8,000. However, the January 1993 agreement pledged to cut their combined arsenals to about 6,500 by the year 2003. Even more dramatically, this amendment to the START agreement also altered drastically the kinds of weapons in each country's arsenal. Under the agreement, Russia and the United States gave up all the **multiple independently targeted reentry vehicles (MIRVs),** their land-based ICBM missiles. By banning all MIRVed ICBMs and reducing SLBM warheads to no more than 1,750 the most threatening preemptive capabilities were eliminated.

The next big step in the nuclear disarmament occurred in May 2002 when Presidents George W. Bush and Vladimir Putin signed the Strategic Offensive Reductions Treaty (SORT). This very brief document calls for the two countries to cut their combined number of strategic nuclear warheads by two-thirds over the next ten years to between one thousand seven hundred and two thousand two hundred by the year 2012. This jump was heralded by U.S. President George W. Bush as a milestone in ending the half-century of mutual suspicion that had terrorized Americans and Russians—an agreement "to liquidate the legacy of the Cold War."

To be sure, this accord sought to make both countries more secure by reducing the danger of nuclear war and sought to take another step to move

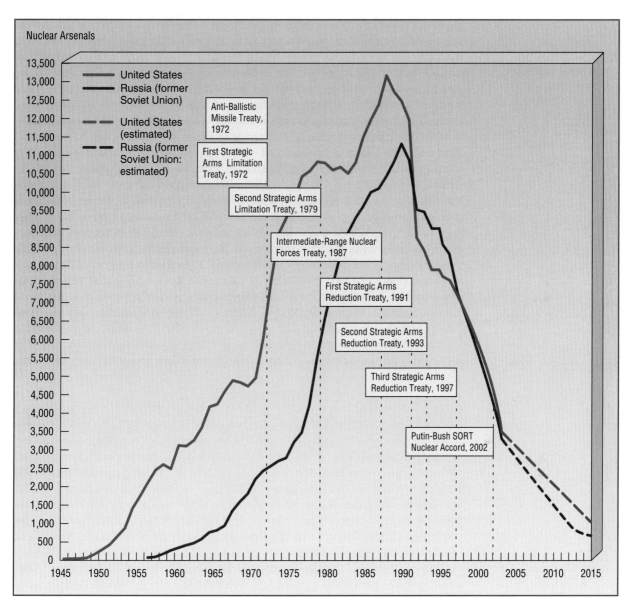

FIGURE 14.1

Countdown to Strategic Parity: The Negotiated End of the U.S.-Russian Arms Race

After decades of rapidly building the number of nuclear warheads in their arsenals, the United States and Russia have, through a series of disarmament agreements, pledged to cut dramatically the number of nuclear warheads in their stockpiles. This has inspired most of the other nuclear powers to also reduce the number of warheads they have deployed. Since its 1986 peak, the size of the global nuclear arsenal has declined by nearly 90 percent. However, fears that the 1990s disarmament process will be followed by a new arms race remain, as seen in the 2002 agreement that allows the United States to store rather than destroy its inventory of Cold War warheads and to preserve its missile defense program. The Putin-Bush Strategic Offensive Reductions Treaty (SORT) nonetheless took another sizable step in 2002 toward Russia's goal of eliminating nuclear warheads altogether.

SOURCES: Based on data from Worldwatch data diskette, U.S. Arms Control Association *Fact Files* and *SIPRI Yearbooks*. Worldwatch data Copyright © Worldwatch Institute and the Stockholm International Peace Research Institute.

■ **mutual assured destruction (MAD)**
a system of mutual deterrence in which both sides possess the ability to survive a first strike and launch a devastating retaliatory attack.

beyond the Cold War. However, diplomats recognized that much remained to be done and that the three-page treaty had serious limitations. Both parties were left with plenty of firepower to retain the threat of **mutual assured destruction (MAD)** that had guided deterrence throughout the Cold War (see Chapter 13), and untold thousands of smaller technical nuclear weapons (the kind far more likely than a large warhead to end up in a terrorist's suitcase) were unchecked by the accord. In addition, at the insistence of the Bush administration, the treaty contains no requirement to destroy warheads taken out of service; both sides were permitted and expected to store some rather than destroy them. Moreover, the pact (which Russian President Vladimir Putin wanted in writing while Bush suggested just a handshake would do) permitted either side to withdraw from the agreement with three months' notice by citing "a supreme national interest" and to return to any level it desires even prior to the treaty's expiration in 2012. Hence, while this treaty signaled a step toward disarmament, and was welcomed around the world, it was regarded as mostly symbolic in importance (Mendelsohn 2002). That said, the reduction of both armaments and threat between two former bitter enemies inspires hope that negotiations can improve relationships among other rivals threatening each other with nuclear warfare, such as India and Pakistan. If military rivalries between two parties can be pacified through arms control, then it might be possible to broaden those agreements to extend to the wider international community. The history of multilateral arms control and disarmament speaks to the prospects.

Multilateral Diplomacy: The Checkered Disarmament and Arms Control Record

It is hardly a novel idea that it is possible to control war by reducing the world's arsenals. Yet until very recently, one of the few constants in the changing international system has been the repetition with which states have advocated disarmament but failed to implement it. True, some countries in the past did reach agreements to reduce their armaments levels. For example, the Chinese states in 600 B.C.E. formed a disarmament league that produced a peaceful century for the league's members, and in the Rush-Bagot Agreement of 1818 Canada and the United States disarmed the Great Lakes. Disarmament proposals also figured prominently in the League of Nations' abortive World Disarmament Conference of 1932 and rather continuously in the UN since 1946 (especially in its many "special sessions" on disarmament). Nonetheless, these kinds of achievements have been relatively rare in history. Many more countries have raced to expand their arsenals than have tried to cut them. Most disarmament is involuntary, the product of reductions imposed by the victors in the immediate aftermath of a war, as when the Allied powers attempted (unsuccessfully) to permanently disarm a defeated and demilitarized Germany after World War I.

In contrast with disarmament, there are many historical examples of arms control efforts. As early as the eleventh century, the Second Lateran Council prohibited the use of crossbows in fighting. The 1868 St. Petersburg Declaration prohibited the use of explosive bullets. In 1899 and 1907, International Peace Conferences at the Hague restricted the use of some weapons and prohibited others. The leaders of the United States, Britain, Japan, France, and Italy signed treaties at the Washington Naval Conferences (1921–1922) agreeing to adjust the relative tonnage of their fleets.

The post–World War II period saw a variety of new arms control proposals. The Baruch Plan (1946) called for the creation of a United Nations Atomic Development Authority, which would have placed atomic energy under an international authority to ensure its use for only peaceful purposes. However, the great powers never approved the proposal. The Rapacki Plan (1957) to prevent the deployment of nuclear weapons in Central Europe also failed.

Nonetheless, leaders have made recurrent efforts to resolve differences so formal arms control agreements might be realized. Prominent among them were the arms control summit meetings of the great powers.

The great powers have devoted much energy negotiating treaties on particular issues, and these efforts have taken on the character of institutionalized processes used to reach arms control agreements. Table 14.2 identifies the nearly thirty major multilateral agreements with many parties that the ratifying states have signed since the Second World War. Of these, the historic 1968 Nuclear Nonproliferation Treaty (NPT) stands out as the most symbolic multilateral agreement, although the efforts of new states and terrorist groups to acquire nuclear weapons has greatly reduced confidence in the continuation of the **nonproliferation** regime. Other important multilateral agreements include the 1993 Chemical Weapons Convention (CWC). This convention lost some of its authority in 2001 when the Bush administration refused to accept the enforcement measures within the drafted amendment of the packet of chemical and biological germ warfare treaties that included the CWC. This erosion of support for arms control caused UN Secretary-General Kofi Annan to warn that "much of the established multilateral disarmament machinery has started to rust."

To these we might add an indeterminate number of tacit understandings about the level and use of weapons to which the great powers agreed. These understandings did not achieve the status of formal agreements but were observed by the major powers nonetheless. They included occasional pledges to refrain from the offensive use of nuclear arsenals, as indicated by President Carter's and Soviet Foreign Minister Andrei Gromyko's promises that their states would never be the first to use nuclear weapons in any conflict. Such commitments were not legally binding. Indeed, NATO based its "flexible response" strategy on the right to retaliate with nuclear weapons against an attack. More recently, in 2003, Russia's strategic doctrine reserved the right to use nuclear weapons in the event of an attack. Nonetheless, most understandings undeniably help enforce great-power respect for the no-first-use doctrine (as do China's vocal support for the same principle and the 1995 agreement between China and Russia to stop aiming nuclear weapons at each other). Such informal rules have paved the way to creating greater institutional controls over the use of strategic weapons.

■ **nonproliferation**
the commitment to no development of weapons or technology by countries that do not already possess them.

The Problematic Future of Arms Control

U.S. Secretary of State Madeleine Albright warned in March 2000, "The nuclear danger clearly has not ended. We have a long way to go on the road to disarmament." As promising as some of the great powers' recent arms control agreements might appear, the history of their past negotiations testifies to the many obstacles to arms control agreements that exist. It also attests to the extent to which they are dependent on prior improvement in adversaries' political

TABLE 14.2

Major Multilateral Arms Control Treaties since 1945

Date	Agreement	Number of Parties (2002)	Principal Objectives
1959	Antarctic Treaty	43	Prevents the military use of the Antarctic, including the testing of nuclear weapons
1963	Limited Test Ban Treaty	154	Prohibits nuclear weapons in the atmosphere, outer space, and under water
1967	Outer Space Treaty	127	Outlaws the use of outer space for testing or stationing any weapons, as well as for military maneuvers
1967	Treaty of Tlatelolco	33	Creates the Latin America Nuclear Free Zone by prohibiting the testing and possession of nuclear facilities for military purposes
1968	Nuclear Nonproliferation Treaty	187	Prevents the transfer of nuclear weapons and nuclear-weapons-production technologies to nonnuclear weapons states
1971	Seabed Treaty	117	Prohibits the deployment of weapons of mass destruction and nuclear weapons on the seabed beyond a 12-mile coastal limit
1972	Biological Weapons Convention	169	Prohibits the production and storage of biological toxins; calls for the destruction of biological weapons stockpiles
1977	Environmental Modifications Convention (Enmod Convention)	85	Bans the use of technologies that could alter the earth's weather patterns, ocean currents, ozone layer, or ecology
1980	Protection of Nuclear Material Convention	53	Obligates protection of peaceful nuclear material during transport on ships or aircraft
1981	Inhumane Weapons Convention	72	Prohibits the use of such weapons as fragmentation bombs, incendiary weapons, booby traps, and mines to which civilians could be exposed
1985	South Pacific Nuclear Free Zone (Roratonga) Treaty	18	Prohibits the testing, acquisition, or deployment of nuclear weapons in the South Pacific
1986	Confidence-Building and Security-Building Measures and Disarmament in Europe (CDE) Agreement (Stockholm Accord)	54	Requires prior notification and mandatory on-site inspection of conventional military exercises in Europe

SOURCE: Adapted from "Arms Control and Disarmament Agreements" by R. Ferm, published in *Stockholm International Peace Research Institute Yearbook 1995: Armaments, Disarmaments, and International Security.* Oxford University Press: Oxford 1995. Reprinted with the permission of SIPRI.

TABLE 14.2

(continued)

Date	Agreement	Number of Parties (2002)	Principal Objectives
1987	Missile Technology Control Regime (MTCR)	35	Restricts export of ballistic missiles and production facilities
1990 1992	Conventional Forces in Europe (CFE)	30	Places limits on five categories of weapons in Europe and lowers force levels
1990	Confidence- and Security-Building Measures (CSBM) Agreement	53	Improves measures for exchanging detailed information on weapons, forces, and military exercises
1991	UN Register of Conventional Arms	97	Calls on all states to submit information on seven categories of major weapons exported or imported during the previous year
1992	Open Skies Treaty	27	Permits flights by unarmed surveillance aircraft over the territory of the signatory states
1993	Chemical Weapons Convention (CWC)	169	Requires all stockpiles of chemical weapons to be destroyed within ten years
1995	Protocol to the Inhumane Weapons Convention	135	Bans some types of laser weapons that cause permanent loss of eyesight
1995	Wassenaar Export-Control Treaty	33	Regulates transfers of sensitive dual-use technologies to nonparticipating countries
1996	ASEAN Nuclear Free Zone Treaty	10	Prevents signatories in Southeast Asia from making, possessing, storing, or testing nuclear weapons
1996	Comprehensive Test Ban Treaty (CTBT)	156	Bans all testing of nuclear weapons
1996	Treaty of Pelindaba	48	Creates an African nuclear-weapon-free zone
1997	Treaty of Bangkok	10	Creates a nuclear-weapon-free zone in Southeast Asia
1998	Antipersonnel Landmines Treaty (APLT)	135	Bans the production and export of landmines and pledges plans to remove them
1999	Inter-American Convention on Transparency in Conventional Weapons Acquisitions	34	Requires all thirty-four members of the Organization of American States (OAS) to annually report all weapons acquisitions, exports, and imports
2000	Nuclear Non-Proliferation Treaty Review Conference		Attended by 155 of the 187 signatory states; consensus on the final communiqué was reached to continue support for the NPT treaty

SOURCE: Stockholm International Peace Research Institute, *SIPRI Yearbooks;* Arms Control Association *Fact Files.*

relations. That history raises questions as to whether arms control agreements can restrain the arms race in the long run. After all, these obstacles could resurface in a new multipolar system characterized by rivalry among five or more great powers and a potentially large number of new nuclear-weapon states.

Until recently, international agreements controlled only obsolete armaments or ones that the parties to the agreements had little incentive for developing in the first place. Do states purposely leave the most threatening problems outside negotiations and seek only to control the weapons they no longer deem necessary to their national security? Indeed, does the record demonstrate that states rarely take arms control seriously when they perceive their survival to be at stake? Many trends point to the tendency for more states to cling tenaciously to the realist belief that preparations for war are required than to accept the liberal belief that armament *reductions* can increase national and international security.

The limits to arms control are illustrated by several activities that undermine confidence in the ability of arms control to lower states' capacities for causing death in the twenty-first century. For example, the testing of nuclear weapons speaks to the tendency of states to make improving their weaponry a priority over controlling it (see Map 14.2). The eight known nuclear states conducted a total of 2,052 nuclear explosions in twenty-four different locations since 1945—an average of one test every ten days. Both China and the United States regularly conduct so-called zero-yield nuclear experiments and are suspected of conducting explosive tests so small that they can't be detected. Note that the pace of testing did not slow as a result of the partial test ban treaty of 1963, which prohibited atmospheric and underwater testing but not underground explosions. In fact, three-fourths of all nuclear tests took place after the ban went into effect in 1963.

Also note that while adherence to the Nuclear Nonproliferation Treaty (NPT) of 1968 that obligated the nonnuclear countries to refrain from manufacturing or acquiring nuclear weapons had been widespread, with 187 states as members of the arms control regime when the NPT was renewed in May 2000. However, India and Pakistan broke the barriers the NPT sought to create by becoming nuclear-weapon states; Israel is widely believed to have clandestinely produced nuclear weapons and openly refused to comply with NPT; and Iraq, Iran, Libya, and North Korea remain outside the treaty and are seeking to become nuclear-weapon states. In addition, even the existing nuclear states have sought to develop more imposing arsenals at the same time they were reducing the size of their arsenals.

If disarmament treaties are designed to eliminate the threat of mass annihilation, they have failed. For example, the SORT agreements would leave the United States and Russia defenseless against a handful of nuclear missiles launched in an accidental or unauthorized strike or by a radical rogue regime such as Iran, Iraq, North Korea, or Libya. Because the menace of nuclear proliferation is still very real and the capacity to use these weapons could easily be acquired by ruthless terrorist groups, states' efforts to guarantee their citizens' safety from such attacks persist.

Here policymakers read from the script of **realism,** which insists that national security is best protected by developing military capabilities and not by reducing armaments or military spending. Realists regard treaties to be dangerous in an anarchical world in which the promises of self-interested rivals

■ **realism**
a paradigm based on the premise that world politics is essentially and unchangeably a struggle among self-interested states for power and position under anarchy, with each competing state pursuing its own national interests by expanding military capabilities.

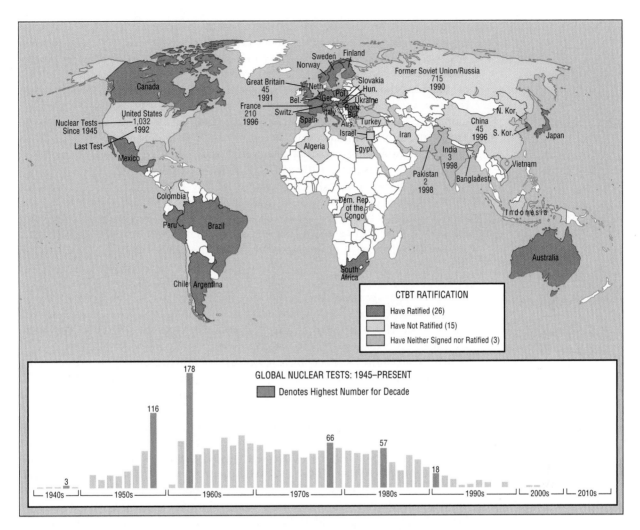

MAP 14.2

Trick on Treaty? Can Arms Control Treaties Arrest the Proliferation of Weapons?

Hope was rising in 1999 that the testing of nuclear weapons, which had been declining since 1945 (see chart at bottom of map of the number of nuclear tests yearly), would stop if the forty-four nuclear-capable states ratified the Comprehensive Test Ban Treaty (CTBT). Those hopes dissolved that October when the U.S. Senate rejected the test ban, and in so doing opened the way for ambitious regimes like India and Pakistan to resume testing. Headlines compared the U.S. repudiation of their arms-control treaty to the same kind of partisan **intermestic** politics for domestic payoffs that prompted the U.S. rejection of the 1919 Treaty of Versailles (an isolationistic fear of multilateral treaties that arguably paved the road to World War II). The CTBT would have banned all nuclear test explosions worldwide for all time, created a multilateral global monitoring network to detect explosions and verify compliance, and allowed for on-site inspections of areas of clandestine nuclear testing. This map shows that twenty-six of the forty-four nuclear-capable states had ratified the treaty, fifteen had not ratified, and three had neither signed nor ratified, and shows the number of nuclear tests conducted by each of the eight nuclear states through 2002. With the CTBT's colapse, termed by arms-control expert Brent Scowcroft as a "pathetic blow to global arms control," the prospect of continued testing of nuclear weapons is high.

SOURCE: Arms Control Association; Stockholm International Peace Research Institute.

■ **intermestic**
those issues confronting a state that are simultaneously international and domestic, encouraging policymakers to play two-level games when making decisions (see p. 64).

cannot be trusted, rather than putting faith in arms control treaties when threatened states turn to self-reliance and military preparedness. That propensity was exhibited in the first five months of the George W. Bush administration, when in January 2001 it announced that it would not send the treaty for establishing the International Criminal Court to the U.S. Senate for ratification, followed by the decision on March 28 to abandon the 1997 Kyoto Protocol on global warming, the May 1 decision to abrogate the 1972 Anti-Ballistic Missile Treaty, the July 21 threat to withdraw from a UN conference to impose limits on illegal trafficking of small arms, and the July 25 rejection of proposed enforcement measures for the 1972 Biological Weapons Convention.

Bush showed his realist colors by rejecting faith in treaties. He was not alone in this regard, of course. But as leader of the global hegemon, his disregard for arms control set a standard for other states to follow. Especially troublesome to America's allies was the U.S. repudiation of the 1972 Anti-Ballistic Missile (ABM) Treaty, regarded by many as the cornerstone of nuclear arms control. That announcement was the first time in modern history that the United States had renounced a major international accord, and it ignited fears that a global chain reaction of massive repudiations by other states of arms control agreements would follow. As Jack Mendelsohn, a U.S. delegate to the SALT I and SALT II treaty negotiations, complained in October 2002, "The Bush administration has been stunningly mute on the future of arms control [and] clearly believes that it has completed its arms control agenda. . . . By playing make-believe arms control . . . the Bush administration has sacrificed the security of structure and predictability for the putative virtues of flexibility and unilateralism."

Also reducing faith in the future meaningful arms control is the slow, weak, and ineffective ability of the international community to ban some of the most dangerous and counterproductive weapons. Consider the case of **antipersonnel landmines (APLs).** These are weapons that cannot discriminate between soldiers and civilians. Over 100 to 300 million landmines are believed to be scattered on the territory of more than seventy countries (with another 100 million in stockpiles). In the mid-1990s there was about one mine for every fifty humans on earth, and each year they killed or maimed more than twenty-six thousand people—almost all of them civilians. In 1994, not a single state would endorse a prohibition on these deadly weapons. It took a peace activist, Jody Williams, to organize the International Campaign to Ban Landmines that produced the Convention on the Prohibition of the Use, Stockpiling, Production and Transfer of Antipersonnel Mines and Their Destruction, which was opened for signature in December 1997. For her effort to remove those landmines and ban the production of new ones, Williams was awarded the Nobel Peace Prize. But the United States, Russia, and other great powers stubbornly resisted the APL convention until a coalition of NGO peace groups mounted sufficient pressure in world public opinion to coerce their consent to this epic convention. If adhered to, the challenge of enforcing the ban now signed by 158 states and the removal of APLs could prove staggering.

The globalization of weapons systems, making states' capabilities increasingly sophisticated and similar, has continued apace in the so-called new arms control era, because the globalized arms trade has few **arms control regimes** to control dispersion (see Held et al. 2001). The experience of the past fifty years thus does not generate confidence in the ability of arms control agreements to

■ antipersonnel landmines (APLs) weapons buried below the surface of the soil that explode on contact with any person—soldier or citizen—stepping on them.

■ arms control regimes rules accepted by the parties to treaties to prohibit the production, deployment, sale, or use of particular categories of weapons.

reduce the number of weapons or to contain their dispersion in the next fifty years. Technology has increased the problem. Its constant movement has led to the birth of an ever-widening range of novel new weapons—increasingly smaller, deadlier, easier to conceal, and capable of destroying by means unimaginable until recently. The next generation of lethal and **nonlethal weapons** on the drawing boards is claimed to make war safer and kinder. However, that hardly appears to be the case. The new robotic and laser weapons offer little protection to innocent noncombatants who can easily become the targets. In 1995, the United States had plans to develop an antipersonnel weapon known as the Laser Countermeasure, based on a secret technology that was "cruel and inhumane even by the standards of war. It is a 40–pound portable gun that fires a beam powerful enough to burn out human retinas from up to 3,000 feet away" (Arkin 1995). By blinding people—so the rationale for the construction of this and other equally awesome new weapons goes—war could be made safe for the attacker.

Why do states often make decisions to arm that apparently imprison them in the grip of perpetual insecurity? On the surface, the incentives for meaningful arms control seem numerous. Significant controls would save money, reduce tension and hence the dangers of war, symbolize leaders' desire for peace, lessen health hazards, reduce the environmental hazards of nuclear waste, diminish the potential destructiveness of war, dampen the incentive for one state to seek a power advantage over others, reduce the possibility of being the target of a preemptive attack, and achieve a propaganda advantage for those advocating peace. To these we can add moral satisfaction and the opportunity to live in a less threatening global environment.

However, states still do not significantly control the growth of arms. There are many reasons to rely on military preparedness as a path to peace; they stem from the fear that is endemic to international anarchy. Most countries are reluctant to engage in arms limitations in a self-help system that requires each state to protect itself. Thus states find themselves caught in a vicious cycle of fear. This creates the security dilemma—a condition that is in no actor's best interest but that permits no easy escape. Its influence on behavior is potent and helps explain why military establishments often subscribe to two basic principles: "(1) 'Don't negotiate when you are behind. Why accept a permanent position of number two?' and (2) 'Don't negotiate when you are ahead. Why accept a freeze in an area of military competition when the other side has not kept up with you?'" (Barnet 1977). Compounding the obstacles to arms reductions is the fact that many people benefit financially from arms races and lobby against arms agreements because they could lose their jobs if military spending is cut. **Military-industrial complexes**—defense contractors, journalists, labor unions, and government employees—exist in all societies whose influence is tied to high defense spending. "The business of defense is defending business" is the way one analyst summarized the problem (Mulhollin 1994).

Arms control still remains a murky policy area, and the past record suggests that we should not expect too much of arms control or exaggerate its potential.

> The history of the postwar era proves that arms control, if pursued wisely and properly, can reduce the threat; it can never eliminate the risk of war altogether. Arms control is not a substitute for weapons but a complement to them. Arms and arms control, one by creating the means to inflict

■ **nonlethal weapons**
the wide array of "soft-kill," low-intensity methods of incapacitating an enemy's people, vehicles, communications systems, or entire cities without killing either combatants or noncombatants (see p. 473).

■ **military-industrial complex**
the term coined by U.S. President Eisenhower to describe the coalition among arms manufacturers, military bureaucracies, and top government officials, that promotes unnecessary defense expenditures for their own profit and power (see p. 466).

unacceptable damage on a potential enemy and the other by protecting that capability from enemy attack, are both necessary for national security. A defense policy that fails to pursue the two together, that emphasizes one approach to the exclusion of the other, is dangerous and incomplete. . . .

True international security depends not as much on arms or arms control as on reducing as much as possible the sources of conflict in international relations and on finding effective nonviolent means of resolving the conflicts that remain. (Kruzel 1991, 268)

MILITARY POWER AND THE SEARCH FOR A TWENTY-FIRST-CENTURY PEACE

The obstacles to arms control are formidable. The idea that a disarmed world would be a more secure one does not have the force of history behind it, whereas the realist idea that military preparedness produces security does. As long as aggressive states exist, it would be imprudent to disarm. Arms control does not solve the basic problem of rivalry between states, because as long as states have and can use weapons, such agreements are little more than cooperative arrangements between adversaries. They define the competition and confine the potential destruction that war brings but do not remove the source of the conflict.

Alternatively, managing political conflicts without violence may be the key to arms control. Arms, after all, are less causes of war than symptoms of political tension: People "do not fight because they have arms. They have arms because [they are afraid and] they deem it necessary to fight" (Morgenthau 1985). From this perspective, controlling arms is contingent on removing the fears that underlie states' conflicts. The quest for national security in an anarchical world springs from states' fear of one another. Yet, because one country's security makes others insecure, nearly all states prepare for war to defend themselves. In this sense the realists' military paths to peace discussed in this chapter are intimately related to the widespread quest for armaments described in Chapter 12. As we have seen, the tragedy of world politics is captured by realists' pessimism, which harbors little hope for the optimistic liberal vision that the "end of history" (Fukuyama 1999b) is around the corner and that the world will move toward peace with minimal arms in a twenty-first century ruled by free-market democracies and international institutions that govern their relations. To realists, this happy vision is utopian. As the events after September 11 reveal, great-power politics still matters, and tragic struggle for security among rivals will continue (Mearsheimer 2001).

The validity of that realist interpretation is still at issue, however. So too is the question of whether global security is best served by states' military search for their own national security or whether the pursuit of peace and security through military means will sow the seeds of the world's destruction.

Chapter 15 examines some proposals—recommended especially by liberal theorists for preventing the damage caused by arms races, power transitions, and the wars they ignite—that were inspired by convictions such as those expressed by former U.S. Secretary of Defense Robert McNamara: "We have reached the present dangerous and absurd confrontation by a long series of steps, many of which seemed rational in their time. Step by step we can undo much of the damage."

KEY TERMS

security dilemma
liberalism
alliances
deterrence
self-help
rational choice
levels of analysis
neotraditional realists
balance of power
alignments
security regime
nonalignment
size principle
balancer
preemption
long peaces
hegemonic stability theory
hegemon
balance of terror
pax atomica
collective security

structure
multilateralism
globalization
polarity
long cycle
bipolarity
polarization
North Atlantic Treaty
    Organization (NATO)
zero-sum
extended deterrence
doctrine
power transition
bandwagoning
Partnership for Peace (PfP)
Euro-Atlantic Partnership Council
    (EAPC)
Bush Doctrine
imperialism
unipolarity

arms control
disarmament
demililtarization
bilateral agreements
multilateral agreements
Strategic Arms Limitation Talks
    (SALT)
START (Strategic Arms
    Reduction) Treaty
multiple independently targeted
    reentry vehicles (MIRVs)
mutual assured destruction
    (MAD)
nonproliferation
realism
intermestic
antipersonnel landmines (APLs)
arms control regimes
nonlethal weapons
military-industrial complex

SUGGESTED READING

Diehl, Paul F., and Gary Goertz. *War and Peace in International Rivalry.* Ann Arbor: University of Michigan Press, 2000.

Hybel, Alex Roberto. *Made in the USA: The International System.* London: Palgrave, 2002.

Ikenberry, G. John. "America's Imperial Ambition," *Foreign Affairs* 81 (September/October 2002): 44–60.

Kaplan, Robert D. *Warrior Politics: Why Leadership Demands a Pagan Ethos.* New York: Random House, 2002.

Kegley, Charles W., Jr., and Gregory A. Raymond. *A Multipolar Peace? Great-Power Politics in the*

Twenty-First Century. New York: St. Martin's Press, 1994.

Larsen, Jeffrey A., ed. *Arms Control: Cooperative Security in a Changing Environment.* Boulder, Colo.: Lynne Rienner, 2002.

Mead, Walter Russell. *Special Providence: American Foreign Policy and How It Changed the World.* New York: Knopf, 2001.

Mearsheimer, John J. *The Tragedy of Great Power Politics.* New York: W. W. Norton, 2001.

Redwood, John. *Stars and Strife: The Coming Conflict between the USA and the European Union.* London: Palgrave, 2002.

Rochester, J. Martin. *Between Two Epochs: What's Ahead for America, The World, and Global Politics in the Twenty-First Century?* Upper Saddle River, N.J.: Prentice Hall, 2002.

Rusi, Alpo M. *Dangerous Peace: New Rivalry in World Politics.* Boulder, Colo.: Westview Press, 1997.

Snyder, Glenn. *Alliance Politics.* Ithaca, N.Y.: Cornell University Press, 1997.

Vasquez, John A., and Colin Elman. *Realism and the Balancing of Power: A New Debate.* Upper Saddle River, N.J.: Prentice Hall, 2003.

W H E R E   O N   T H E   W O R L D   W I D E   W E B ?

Bulletin of the Atomic Scientists
http://www.bullatomsci.org/

After World War II, many of the scientists responsible for the production of the atomic bomb helped form a movement to control nuclear energy. In 1945, they founded the *Bulletin* to advocate international control of the means of nuclear production. Still published today, the *Bulletin* now appears online. Current and archived issues are available. While exploring this site, click on the Doomsday Clock to see how international tensions and nuclear developments have brought us alternatively closer to midnight or back from the brink. Read brief or detailed histories of technological and political developments. Scan the Nuclear Notebook to get up-to-date facts and figures on the world's nuclear arsenals.

Center for Nonproliferation Studies (CNS)
http://cns.miis.edu/index.htm

The Center for Nonproliferation Studies (CNS) at the Monterey Institute of International Relations is the largest nongovernmental organization in the United States devoted exclusively to research and training on nonproliferation issues. At this site you will find articles on featured topics as well as summaries on CNS projects. Its extensive electronic resources are organized according to region of the world, subject (nuclear, chemical, or biological weapons), and publication type. Which countries of the world are active in the production of weapons of mass destruction? Why do you think this is the case?

Federation of American Scientists
http://www.fas.org/

Students interested in examining international arms control treaties and related issues should visit the Federation of American Scientists' (FAS) Web site to find a comprehensive archive of nuclear, chemical, and biological arms control agreements. FAS is a privately funded nonprofit policy organization engaged in analysis and advocacy on science, technology, and public policy issues that concern global security. Topics such as arms sales monitoring, chemical and biological arms, space policy, and nuclear nonproliferation and disarmament are covered extensively.

NATO
http://www.nato.int/

The North Atlantic Treaty Organization's (NATO) Web site contains information on NATO's enlargement as well as the Partnership for Peace (PfP) initiative. Click on the Partnerships link to get a list of the countries participating in the PfP. What are some important current activities of NATO? What opinions of NATO and its role are expressed in the latest edition of *NATO Review?*

United Nations Conference on Disarmament
http://www.unog.ch/disarm/disarm.htm

The UN Conference on Disarmament Web page links to all the major international instruments on disarmament, from the 1949 Geneva Convention through the 1997 antipersonnel landmines convention. Read the texts of some of the most influential international agreements that seek to control or eliminate weapons of mass destruction.

United Nations Demining Database
http://disarmament.un.org/MineBan.nsf

Antipersonnel landmines (APLs) are internationally recognized as an inhumane and counterproductive weapon. In 1997, one hundred countries signed a treaty prohibiting the production of landmines and supporting the removal of those buried in the ground, but enforcing the treaty remains a challenge. This comprehensive site explores the issues involved with demining. Read about specific countries' problems demining their land and the origins of the mines found within their borders. See how many mines different countries have, the area contaminated, and the number of victims. Which countries have the greatest number of landmines? Why do you think this is so? Who are the biggest suppliers?

INFOTRAC® COLLEGE EDITION

Search for the following articles in the InfoTrac database:

Chace, James. "The Balance of Power," *World Policy Journal* Winter 1998.

Jervis, Robert. "Arms Control, Stability, and Causes of War," *Political Science Quarterly* Summer 1993.

Collina, Tom Z., and Jon B. Wolfsthal. "Nuclear Terrorism and Warhead Control in Russia," *Arms Control Today* April 2002.

Ross, Andrew L. "Thinking about the Unthinkable: Unreasonable Exuberance?" *Naval War College Review* Spring 2001.

For more articles, enter:

"balance of power" in the Subject Guide.

"war" in the Subject Guide, and then go to subdivision "causes of."

"nuclear arms control" in the Subject Guide, and then go to subdivision "international aspects."

THE LIBERAL INSTITUTIONAL PATHS TO PEACE

T O P I C S   A N D   T H E M E S

- Liberalism and conflict management
- International law as a means to world order
- International organizations and world order: The UN and regional organizations
- Political integration: The functional and neofunctional paths to peace
- Democracy as a means to peace
- Liberal institutions and world order

- **CONTROVERSY** LEGAL LIMITS ON SEX FOR SALE? INTERNATIONAL LAW VERSUS STATE'S RIGHTS ON PROSTITUTION

Liberal democracies give citizens the right of assembly and free speech and allow mass public participation in the policy-making process. Shown here are people exercising those rights in a protest demonstration in October 2002 against U.S. plans to attack Iraq.

My first axiom: The quest for international security involves the unconditional surrender by every nation, in a certain measure, of its liberty of action, its sovereignty that is to say, and it is clear beyond all doubt that no other road can lead to such security.

—ALBERT EINSTEIN, scientist, 1932

In this globalized world, fewer and fewer problems affect only individual countries, and they certainly cannot be solved by individual countries acting alone.

—WOLFGANG THIERSE, president of the German Bundestag, 2002

Since antiquity, the world has pursued two primary paths to peace. The realist road emphasizes *military* solutions; the liberal road emphasizes *political* solutions. This chapter examines four principal approaches to the control of armed conflict from the liberal theoretical tradition: international law, organization, integration, and democratization (see Table 15.1). Because all four stress institutions, the new advocates of these liberal paths are sometimes referred to collectively as **neoliberal institutionalists.** While they differ in their approach to security, they share a fear of states' historic tendency to make war.

■ **neoliberal institutionalism**
the recent theoretical effort to explain how peace and prosperity instead of war might be created through law, global governance, and liberal democracies' cooperation to engineer international change.

INTERNATIONAL LAW AND WORLD ORDER

In 1984, the United States announced that it would unilaterally withdraw from the World Court's jurisdiction. This move followed Nicaragua's accusation that the U.S. Central Intelligence Agency had illegally attempted to "overthrow and destabilize" the elected Sandinista government. Nicaragua charged that the

TABLE 15.1

Liberal Paths to International Security

Policy Prescription	Premise
Provide states rules of international law to regulate competition.	Interstate cooperation can be encouraged by creating rules for peaceful interaction.
Participate in the creation of international organizations.	If you want peace, prepare global institutions to keep it.
Practice collaboration to bind independent states together in integrated security communities.	Interdependence makes imperative the amalgamation of states, not their division.
Promote the spread of democratic governance.	Countries that protect their own citizens' civil liberties do not wage war against other governments that also protect their citizens' human rights.
Prepare rules to facilitate free trade.	Trade protectionism is counterproductive to prosperity and peace.
Produce agreements to reduce armaments to levels that discourage war.	States get what they plan for—beat swords into plowshares.
Provide humanitarian assistance to the impoverished.	Rich states can help themselves only by helping poor people also.
Principles are more important than power.	Principled moral behavior ultimately reaps higher rewards for all because it encourages reciprocity.

United States had illegally mined its ports and supplied money, military assistance, and training to the rebel *contra* forces. The United States denied the tribunal's authority. In so doing, however, it was not acting without precedent; others had done so previously. Nonetheless, by thumbing its nose at the court and the rule of law it represents, had the United States, as some claimed, become an "international outlaw?" Or, as others asserted, had it acted within its rights?

The World Court supported the former view. In 1984, the court ruled against the United States as follows:

> The right to sovereignty and to political independence possessed by the Republic of Nicaragua, like any other state of the region or of the world, should be fully respected and should not in any way be jeopardized by any military and paramilitary activities which are prohibited by the principles of international law, in particular the principle that states should refrain in their international relations from the threat or the use of force against the territorial integrity or the political independence of any state, and the principle concerning the duty not to intervene in matters within the domestic jurisdiction of a state. (*New York Times*, May 11, 1984, 8)

Yet this ruling had little effect, as neither the court nor Nicaragua had any means to enforce it.

Events such as this have led many critics to conclude that international law is "weak and defenseless" (Fried 1971). Indeed, many experts—whether they are realists or liberals—skeptically ask whether international law is really law. There are many reasons to answer this question affirmatively. Although international law is imperfect, actors regularly rely on it to redress grievances (see Joyner 2001b). Most of this activity falls within the realm of **private international law**—the regulation of routine transnational activities in such areas as commerce, communications, and travel. While largely invisible to the public, private international law is the locus for almost all international legal activities. It is where the majority of transnational disputes are regularly settled and where the record of compliance compares favorably with that achieved in domestic legal systems.

In contrast, **public international law** covers issues of relations between governments and the interactions of governments with intergovernmental organizations (IGOs) and nongovernmental organizations (NGOs) such as multinational corporations. Some believe that we should use the phrase *world law* to describe the mixture of public and private, domestic and international transactions that public international law seeks to regulate in an increasingly globalized world. However, it is the regulation of government-to-government relations that dominates the headlines in discussion of public international law. This area of activity also receives most of the criticism, for here, failures—when they occur—are quite conspicuous (see Controversy: Legal Limits on Sex for Sale?). This is especially true with respect to the breakdown of peace and security. When states engage in armed conflict, criticism of its shortcomings escalates. Israeli Ambassador Abba Eban lamented that "international law is that law which the wicked do not obey and the righteous do not enforce."

Because this chapter examines the capacity of public international law to control war, our discussion will address only the laws and institutional machinery created to manage armed conflict between states. That is, it will explore that segment of public international law popularly regarded as the most deficient.

Law at the International Level: Core Principles

Public international law is usually defined as the rules that govern the conduct of states in their relations with one another. The *corpus juris gentium* (the body of the law of nations) has grown considerably over the past four centuries, changing in response to transformations in international politics. An inventory of the basic legal principles relevant to the control of war reveals the character of the international system.

The Rules of International Law.   No principle of international law is more critical than state sovereignty. **Sovereignty** means that no authority is legally above the state, except that which the state voluntarily confers on the international organizations it joins. In fact, as conceived by theoreticians schooled in the tradition of **realism** since the seventeenth century, the rules of international law were written to protect states and permitted states "a complete freedom of action" (Parry 1968) to preserve their sovereign independence.

Nearly every legal doctrine supports and extends the cardinal principle that states are the primary subjects of international law. Although the Universal Declaration of Human Rights in 1948 expanded concern about states' treatment of

■ private international law
law pertaining to routinized transnational intercourse between or among states as well as nonstate actors.

■ public international law
law pertaining to government-to-government relations.

■ sovereignty
the legal doctrine that states have supreme authority to govern their internal affairs and manage their foreign relations with other states and IGOs.

■ realism
the theoretical tradition arguing that sovereign states are the most important global actors and should be unrestrained by law, principles of justice, or supranational organizations when making decisions regarding war and peace (see p. 36).

LEGAL LIMITS ON SEX FOR SALE?

International Law versus States' Rights on Prostitution

A revolution in human affairs is occurring. The international community is attempting the awesome challenge of revising international law. Even in a world where more and more of the global population lives in good health and prosperity and is increasingly secure from territorial aggression, many others live in marked poverty and despair. The twenty-first century is home to a global dichotomy between promise and peril, achievement and affliction.

What should the global community do to address the problems that still haunt humankind? At issue is whether international law can police the many problems in human affairs. Can modern perils and afflictions be brought under control by globally recognized legal doctrine? One argument holds that states should preserve their traditional sovereign right to manage human affairs within their borders as they see fit. To this way of thinking, international law should have no jurisdiction over a country's internal affairs and policies with respect to human rights. In contrast, a rival argument holds that human affairs are global affairs, and that international law should seek to protect human rights around the world, even when states resent such regulation as an unjust interference in their internal affairs.

What do you think? What are the limits of international law over the control of a state's conduct toward its citizens? What criteria should define the boundaries between global involvement and intervention that can assault national sovereignty and erode the traditions of local cultures? In contemplating your position, consider the example of the 2000 UN treaty, the Convention Prohibiting the Trafficking of Women and Children for

Prostitution. Sex trafficking is a serious human rights issue that has both international and national implications. Human rights groups estimate that hundreds of thousands, perhaps millions, of women and children are forced into lives of sexual exploitation. Many are transported across national borders by criminal organizations. The new treaty is designed to protect the victims of sex trafficking.

On the surface, few would question whether this treaty should be enforced, because it is designed to protect women's human rights. However, many countries have objected to the treaty because they see it as an infringement on their national sovereignty. These protestors are not alone. They are joined by a number of nongovernmental organizations (NGOs), including the National Organization for Women and the Planned Parenthood Federation of America, which complain that the wording of the treaty is too weak and in fact seeks to appease national governments. If the negotiators do not alter its wording, the treaty would make it difficult for human rights groups to prosecute prostitution rings, because the terms of the treaty would deal with only a limited range of sex trafficking practices. In effect, it would legally allow states to retain primary control over issues of prostitution.

Major human issues like prostitution highlight the tension between many ethical principles regarding national rights versus global responsibilities to protect human rights. A daunting question is whether states will agree on rules to control shared problems through international law or whether they will continue to resist letting international law control them.

---

individual people, states remain supreme. "Laws are made to protect the state from the individual and not the individual from the state" (Gottlieb 1982). Accordingly, the vast majority of rules address the rights and duties of states, not people. For instance, the principle of **sovereign equality** entitles each state to full respect by other states as well as equal protection by the system's legal rules. The right of independence also guarantees states' autonomy in their domestic affairs and external relations, under the logic that the independence of each presumes that of all. Similarly, the doctrine of **neutrality** permits states to avoid involvement in others' conflicts and coalitions.

■ **sovereign equality**
the principle that states are legally entitled to equal protection under international law.

■ **neutrality**
the legal doctrine that provides rights and duties for states who remain nonaligned with adversaries during wartime.

■ **nonintervention**
the principle prohibiting one state from interfering in another state's internal affairs (see p. 149).

■ **diplomatic immunity**
the legal doctrine that gives ambassadors immunity from the domestic laws of the countries where their embassies are located.

■ **extraterritoriality**
the legal doctrine that allows states to maintain jurisdiction over their embassies in other states.

■ **crimes against humanity**
a category of activities, made illegal at the Nuremberg war crime trials, condemning states that abuse human rights.

■ **divine right of kings**
the realist doctrine that because kings are sovereign they have the right to rule their subjects authoritatively and are not accountable to the public because their rule is ordained by God.

■ **statehood**
the legal criteria by which a country and its government become a state in the international community.

■ **diplomatic recognition**
the formal legal acceptance of a state's official status as an independent country.

Furthermore, the noninterference principle forms the basis for **nonintervention**—that is, states' duty to refrain from uninvited involvement in another's internal affairs. This sometimes-abused classic rule gives governments the right to exercise jurisdiction over practically all things on, under, or above their bounded territory. (There are exceptions, however, such as **diplomatic immunity** for states' ambassadors from the domestic laws of the country where their embassies are located and **extraterritoriality,** which allows control of embassies on other states' terrain.)

In practice, domestic jurisdiction permits a state to enact and enforce whatever laws it wishes for its own citizens. In fact, international law was so permissive toward the state's control of its domestic affairs that, prior to 1952, "there was no precedent in international law for a . . . state to assume responsibility for the crimes it committed against a minority within its jurisdiction" (Wise 1993). A citizen was not protected against the state's abuse of human rights or **crimes against humanity.** Note also that international law permits states to set their own rules for citizenship. Two basic principles govern the way nationality and citizenship are conferred: under *jus soli*, citizenship is determined by the state in whose territory the birth took place; under *jus sanguinis*, nationality is acquired by descent from a parent who is a national.

In addition, in earlier periods of modern international law, states were permitted to create whatever form of government they desired without regard to its acceptability to other states. This principle was expressed in the realpolitik language of the Treaty of Augsburg (1555) and the Westphalian Treaties (1648), which made states all-powerful by recognizing the **divine right of kings.** This doctrine was reaffirmed in the 1943 Atlantic Charter's pledge of "the right of all people to choose the form of government under which they will live." However, the right of people to live under the liberties of democracy is increasingly being defined as an "entitlement" or a basic human right. At Geneva in 1999, states proclaimed that all individuals have a right to democracy," thereby revising international law through a United Nations resolution and by the same vote dealing "a severe blow to those countries which continue to deny their citizens not only democracy but other fundamental human rights" (Rubin 1999; see also Sellers 1998). International law still gives states the complete freedom to regulate economic transactions within their boundaries and empowers the state to draft those living on its soil into its armed forces to fight—and die, if necessary—to defend the state.

The Montevideo Convention of 1933 on the Rights and Duties of States summarizes the major components of **statehood.** A state must possess a permanent population, a well-defined territory, and a government capable of ruling its citizens and of managing formal diplomatic relations with other states. Essentially, the acquisition of statehood depends on a political entity's recognition as such by other states. Whether a state exists thus rests in the hands of other states; that is, preexisting states are entitled to extend **diplomatic recognition** to another entity. **De facto recognition** is provisional and capable of being withdrawn in the event that the recognized government is superseded by another. It does not carry with it the exchange of diplomatic representatives or other legal benefits and responsibilities. **De jure recognition,** on the other hand, extends full legal and diplomatic privileges from the granting state. This distinction emphasizes that recognition is a political tool of international law, through which approval or disapproval of a government can be expressed.

Other rules specify how treaties are to be activated, interpreted, and abrogated. International law holds that treaties voluntarily entered into are binding *(pacta sunt servanda)*. However, it also reserves for states the right to unilaterally terminate treaties previously agreed to, by reference to the escape clause known as *rebus sic stantibus*. This is the principle that a treaty is binding only as long as no fundamental change occurs in the circumstances that existed when it was concluded.

Procedures for Dispute Settlement. In addition to these general principles, international law provides a wide variety of legal methods for states to resolve their conflicts. The laws of negotiation do not obligate states to reach agreement or to settle their disputes peacefully. They do, however, provide rules for several conflict resolution procedures, including:

- **Mediation:** when a third party proposes a nonbinding solution to a controversy between two other states.
- **Good offices:** when a third party offers a location for discussions among disputants but does not participate in the actual negotiations.
- **Conciliation:** when a third party assists both sides but does not offer any solution.
- **Arbitration:** when a third party gives a binding decision through an ad hoc forum.
- **Adjudication:** when a third party offers a binding decision through an institutionalized tribunal, such as a court.

The Limitations of the International Legal System

Sovereignty and the legal principles derived from it shape and reinforce international anarchy. World politics is legally dependent on what governments choose to do with one another and the kinds of rules they voluntarily support. Throughout most of modern history, international law as constructed by realists was designed by states to protect the state and so made sovereignty the core principle to ensure states' freedom to act in terms of their perceived national interests.

To liberal theoreticians, putting the state ahead of the global community was a serious flaw that undermined international law's potential effectiveness. Many theorists consider the international legal system institutionally defective due to its dependence on states' willingness to participate. Because formal legal institutions (like those within states) are weak at the global level, critics make the following points. First, in world politics no legislative body capable of making binding laws exists. Rules are made only when states willingly observe or embrace them in the treaties to which they voluntarily subscribe. There is no systematic method of amending or revoking treaties. Article 38 of the Statute of the International Court of Justice (or World Court) affirms this. Generally accepted as the authoritative definition of the "sources of international law," it states that international law derives from (1) custom; (2) international treaties and agreements; (3) national and international court decisions; (4) the writings of legal authorities and specialists; and (5) the "general principles" of law recognized since the Roman Empire as part of "natural law" and "right reason."

■ **de facto recognition**
a government's acknowledgment of the factual existence of another state or government short of full recognition.

■ **de jure recognition**
a government's formal, legal recognition of another sovereign government or state.

■ **mediation**
a conflict-resolution procedure in which a third party offers a nonbinding solution to the disputants.

■ **good offices**
the offering by a third party of a location for discussion among disputants.

■ **conciliation**
a conflict-resolution procedure in which a third party assists both parties to a dispute but proposes no solution.

■ **arbitration**
a conflict-resolution procedure in which a third party makes a binding decision between disputants through a temporary ruling board created for that ruling.

■ **adjudication**
a conflict-resolution procedure in which a third party makes a binding decision about a dispute in an institutional tribunal.

Second, in world politics no judicial body exists to authoritatively identify the rules accepted by states, record the substantive precepts reached, interpret when and how the rules apply, and identify violations. Instead, states are responsible for performing these tasks themselves. The World Court does not have the power to perform these functions without states' consent, and the UN cannot speak on judicial matters for the whole global community (even though it has recently defined a new scope for Chapter VII of the UN Charter that claims the right to make quasi-judicial authoritative interpretations of global laws).

Finally, in world politics there is no executive body capable of enforcing the rules. Rule enforcement usually occurs through the self-help actions of the victims of a transgression or with the assistance of their allies or other interested parties. No centralized enforcement procedures exist, and compliance is voluntary. The whole system rests, therefore, on states' willingness to abide by the rules to which they consent and on the ability of each to enforce through retaliatory measures the norms of behavior they value.

Consequently, states themselves—not a higher authority—determine what the rules are, when they apply, and how they should be enforced. This raises the question of greatest concern to liberal advocates of a world law: When everyone is above the law, is anyone ruled by it? It was precisely this problem that prompted UN Secretary-General Kofi Annan in 1999 to push for abandonment of traditional "state sovereignty" and acceptance of a new conceptualization of sovereignty. He argued:

> [I]t is clear that traditional notions of sovereignty alone are not the only obstacle to effective action in humanitarian crises. No less significant are the ways in which states define their national interests. The world has changed in profound ways since the end of the Cold War, but I fear our conceptions of national interest have failed to follow suit. A new, broader definition of national interest is needed in the 21st century, which would induce states to find greater unity in the pursuit of common goals and values. In the context of many of the challenges facing humanity today, the collective interest is the national interest.

Beyond the barriers to legal institutions that sovereignty poses, still other weaknesses reduce confidence in international law. Critics and reformers usually cite these additional alleged deficiencies:

- *International law lacks universality.* An effective legal system must represent the norms shared by those it governs. According to the precept of Roman law, *ubi societas, ibi jus* (where there is society, there is law), shared community values are a minimal precondition for forming a legal system. Yet the contemporary international order is culturally and ideologically pluralistic and lacks consensus on common values, as evidenced by the peculating "clash of civilizations" (Berger and Huntington 2002) and the rejection by terrorists and others of the Western-based international legal order. The simultaneous operation of often incompatible legal traditions throughout the world undermines the creation of a universal, cosmopolitan culture and legal system (Bozeman 1994).

- *International law justifies the competitive pursuit of national advantage without regard to morality or justice.* As in any legal system, in international politics what is legal is not necessarily moral. In fact, international law legitimizes the drive for hegemony and contributes to conflict (Lissitzyn 1963). The principle of **self-help** fails to check states' pursuit of power at others' expense; it is a concession to power. By accepting the unbridled autonomy of sovereign independence, international law follows the realists' "iron law of politics"—that legal obligations must yield to the national interest (Morgenthau 1985).

- *International law is an instrument of the powerful to oppress the weak.* In a voluntary consent system, the rules to which the powerful willingly agree are those that serve their interests. These rules therefore preserve the existing hierarchy (Friedheim 1965). For this reason, some liberal theorists claim that international law has bred the so-called **structural violence** resulting from the hierarchical organization of world politics in which the strong benefit at the expense of the weak (Galtung 1969). Enforcement is left "to the vicissitudes of the distribution of power between the violator of the law and the victim of the violation." Therefore, Hans J. Morgenthau (1985) concedes, "it makes it easy for the strong both to violate the law and to enforce it, and consequently puts the rights of the weak in jeopardy."

- *International law is little more than a justification of existing practices.* When a particular behavior pattern becomes widespread, it becomes legally obligatory; rules *of* behavior become rules *for* behavior (Hoffmann 1971). Eminent legal scholar Hans Kelsen's contention that states ought to behave as they have customarily behaved (see Onuf 1982) and E. Adamson Hoebel's dictum (1961) that "what the most do, others should do" reflect the **positivist legal theory** that when a type of behavior occurs frequently, it becomes legal. In fact, the highly regarded positivist legal theorists stress states' customary practices as the most important source from which laws derive. In the absence of formal machinery for creating international rules, for evidence of what the law is, positivists observe leaders' foreign policy pronouncements, repeated usage in conventions voluntarily accepted by states, general practices (by an overwhelmingly large number of states), the judicial decisions of national and international tribunals, and legal principles stated in the resolutions of multinational assemblies such as the UN General Assembly. When the sources of international law are interpreted in this way, the actions of states shape law, not vice versa.

- *International law's ambiguity reduces law to a policy tool for propaganda purposes.* The vague, elastic wording of international law makes it easy for states to define and interpret almost any action as legitimate. "The problem here," observes Samuel S. Kim (1991), "is the lack of clarity and coherence [that enables] international law [to be] easily stretched, . . . to be a flexible fig leaf or a propaganda instrument." This ambivalence makes it possible for states to exploit international law to get what they can and to justify what they have obtained (Wright 1953).

■ **self-help**
the principle that in anarchy actors must rely on themselves (see p. 37).

■ **structural violence**
the condition defined by Norwegian peace researcher Johan Galtung as the harm and injury caused by the global system's unregulated structure, which effectively allows strong states to victimize weak states that cannot protect themselves.

■ **positivist legal theory**
a theory that stresses states' customs as the most important source of law.

The Relevance of International Law

Although international law has deficiencies, that should not lead to the conclusion that it is irrelevant or useless. States themselves find it useful and expend much effort attempting to shape its evolution. "The reality as demonstrated through their behavior," legal scholar Christopher Joyner (2001) observes, "is that states do accept international law as law and, even more significant, in the vast majority of instances they . . . obey it."

The major reason even the most powerful states adhere to international legal rules is because they recognize that adherence pays benefits that outweigh the costs of expedient rule violation. International reputations are important. Those who play the game of international politics by recognized rules receive rewards, whereas states that ignore international law or opportunistically break customary norms pay costs for doing as they please. Other countries will be reluctant to cooperate with them. They must also fear retaliation by those victimized, as well as the loss of prestige. For this reason, only the most ambitious or reckless state is apt to flagrantly disregard accepted standards of conduct.

A primary reason why states value international law and affirm their commitment to it is that they need a common understanding of the "rules of the game." International law is an "institutional device for communicating to the policymakers of various states a consensus on the nature of the international system" (Coplin 1965). Law helps shape expectations, and rules reduce uncertainty and enhance predictability in international affairs. These communication functions serve every member of the international system.

Formal institutions for rule enforcement do not guarantee compliance. No legal system can deter all of its members from breaking existing laws. Consequently it is a mistake to expect a legal system to prevent all criminal behavior or to assert that any violation of the law proves the inadequacy of the legal structure. Law is designed to deter crime, but it is unreasonable to expect it to prevent it.

Similarly, we should not view every breakdown of international law as confirming general lawlessness. Conditions of crisis strain all legal systems, and few, when tested severely, can contain all violence. Since 1500, more people have died from civil wars than from wars between sovereign states (Sivard 1991). Today, with street crime in cities worldwide at epidemic proportions and ethnopolitical warfare within countries exacting a deadly toll against hundreds of minority groups, states' domestic legal systems are patently failing to prevent killing. Thus, the allegedly "deficient" international legal system performs its primary job—inhibiting interstate violence—more effectively than the supposedly more sophisticated domestic systems. Perhaps, then, the usual criteria by which critics assess legal systems are dubious. Should they be less concerned with structures and institutions and more concerned with performance?

The Legal Control of Warfare

Liberal reformers often complain that law clearly fails in the realm of behavior most resistant to legal control—conflict management. If under international law, as fashioned by realist leaders, states are "legally bound to respect each other's independence and other rights, and yet free to attack each other at will" (Brierly 1944), international law may actually encourage war. The ethical and

War and the Birth of Modern International Law Enraged by the inhumane international conditions he witnessed during his lifetime, Dutch reformer Hugo Grotius (1583–1645) wrote *De Jure Belli et Pacis (On the Law of War and Peace)* in 1625 in the midst of the Thirty Years' War. His treatise called on the great powers to resolve their conflicts by judicial procedures rather than on the battlefield and specified the legal principles he felt could encourage cooperation, peace, and more humane treatment of people. Grotius consequently became known as the "founder of international law."

jurisprudential **just war doctrine** from which the laws of war stem shapes discussions of contemporary public international law. Because throughout history changes in international law have followed changes in the moral consensus about the ethics of using armed force in interstate relations, it is important to understand the origins of just war theory and the way it is evolving today, before reviewing contemporary changes in the legal rules of warfare, which have led to the formation of **security regimes**—sets of rules to contain armed conflict.

Just War Doctrine: The Changing Ethics Regarding the Use of Armed Force. Many people are confused by international law because it both prohibits and justifies the use of force. The confusion derives from the just war tradition in "Christian realism," in which the rules of war are philosophically based on **morals** (principles of behavior) and **ethics** (explanations of why these principles are proper). In the fourth century, St. Augustine questioned the strict view that those who take another's life to defend the state necessarily violate the commandment "Thou shalt not kill." He counseled that "it is the wrong-doing of the opposing party which compels the wise man to wage just wars." The Christian was obligated, he felt, to fight against evil and wickedness. To St. Augustine, the City of Man was inherently sinful, in contrast to the City of God; thus in the secular world it was sometimes permissible to kill—to punish a sin by an enemy (while still loving the sinner) to achieve a "just peace." This realist logic was extended by Pope Nicholas I, who in 866 proclaimed that any defensive war was just.

From this perspective evolved the modern just war doctrine as developed by such medieval secularists as Hugo Grotius, who challenged the warring Catholic and Protestant Christian powers in the Thirty Years' War (1618–1648) to abide by humane standards of conduct and sought to replace the two "cities," or ethical realms, of Augustine with a single global society under law. For Grotius, a just war was one of self-defense or punishment for inflicted damages: "No other just cause for undertaking war can there be excepting injury

■ **just war doctrine**
a doctrine regarding moral considerations under which war may be undertaken and how it should be fought once it begins.

■ **security regimes**
the norms and rules for interaction agreed to by a set of states to increase their security.

■ **morals**
principles clarifying the difference between good and evil and the situations in which they are opposed.

■ **ethics**
the branch of philosophy that deals with the sources, status, and justification of moral rules and why right and wrong behavior and motives should be distinguished.

received." For war to be moral it must be fought by just means without harm to innocent noncombatants. From this distinction evolved the modern version of just war doctrine, consisting of two categories of argument, *jus ad bellum* (the justice of a war) and *jus in bello* (justice in a war). The former sets the criteria by which a political leader may determine whether a war should be waged. The latter specifies restraints on the range of permissible tactics to be used in fighting a just war.

These distinctions have been hotly debated since their inception. Drawing the line between murder and just war is a controversial task. Yet just war theory seeks to define these boundaries. According to this legal tradition, some circumstances in which lethal force may be justifiable are recognized under international law, which also provides guidelines for sanctioned methods.

At the core of the just war tradition is the conviction that the taking of human life may be a "lesser evil" when necessary to prevent further life-threatening aggression. St. Thomas More contended that the assassination of an evil leader responsible for starting a war was justified if it would prevent the taking of innocent lives. From this premise, a number of other principles follow. The criteria today include ten key ideas:

1. All other means to a morally just solution of conflict must be exhausted before a resort to arms can be justified.

2. War can be just only if employed to defend a stable political order or a morally preferable cause against a real threat or to restore justice after a real injury has been sustained.

3. A just war must have a reasonable chance of succeeding in these limited goals.

4. A just war must be proclaimed by a legitimate government authority.

5. War must be waged for the purpose of correcting a wrong rather than for malicious revenge.

6. Negotiations to end the war must be in continuous process as long as fighting continues.

7. Particular members of the population, especially noncombatants, must be immune from intentional attack.

8. Only legal and moral means may be employed in prosecuting the war.

9. The damage likely to be incurred from a war may not be disproportionate to the injury suffered.

10. The final goal of the war must be to reestablish peace and justice.

These ethical criteria continue to color thinking about the rules of warfare and the circumstances under which the use of armed force is legally permissible. However, the advent of nuclear and chemical or biological weapons of mass destruction that would violate many of these principles has created a crisis of relevance in just war doctrine. Fuzzy circumstances have materialized with the innovations of the **revolution in military affairs (RMA).** Because containment and prevention of violence have become the the chief purposes of arms and armies today, leaders and scholars are struggling to revise just war doctrine to deal with the new strategic realities of contemporary weapons and warfare, especially in light of post-9/11 global terrorism.

As Figure 15.1 shows, since World War I the international community has increasingly rejected the traditional legal right of states to use military force to

■ **revolution in military affairs (RMA)**
the goal of seeking to increase military capabilities and effectiveness with new technology that does not rely on weapons of mass destruction.

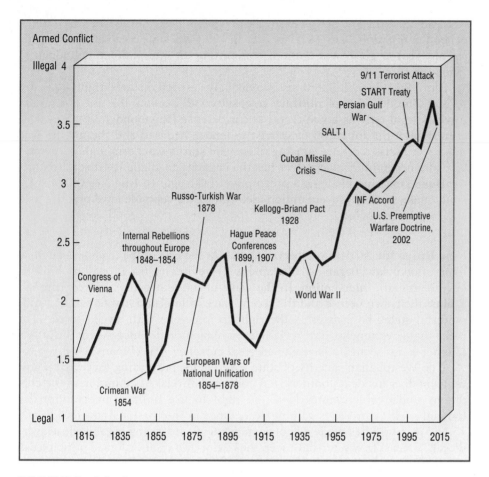

FIGURE 15.1

The Legal Prohibition against Initiating Wars, 1875–2005

Legal restraints on the historic right of states to start a war *(jus ad bellum)* have fluctuated over time, but have grown steadily since World War I when the carnage prompted the global community to make wars of conquest illegal. Since 9/11 these legal prohibitions of the traditional right of states to initiate war have been questioned in the aftermath of the U.S. efforts to promote **preemption** as a legal right to repel potential aggression by another state or by a nonstate terrorist movement.

SOURCE: Adapted from Transnational Rules Indicators Project, as described in *When Trust Breaks Down: Alliance Norms and World Politics* by Charles W. Kegley, Jr. and Gregory A. Raymond. Copyright © 1990 Charles W. Kegley, Jr. and Gregory A. Raymond. Reprinted with the permission of the University of South Carolina Press.

■ **preemption**
a quick first-strike attack that seeks in self-defense to defeat an adversary before it can undertake military action or can organize a retaliatory response.

achieve their foreign policy objectives. Just war theory reflects this continuing quest to place legal constraints on the use of armed force, in order to create a moral consensus about the conditions under which ends justify means, even though "today there is a sharp difference of opinion about the criteria that should be accepted" (von Glahn 1996). These differences became especially evident in debate after 9/11 about the just means of waging a war against global terrorism (see Falk 2003; Johnson 2003).

The Hague conferences of 1899 and 1907 were early developments in shaping new attitudes toward the start of armed conflict. World War I, however, revealed more than any other event the dangers inherent in the fact that "under general international law, as it stood up to 1914, any state could at any time and for any reason go to war without committing an international delinquency" (Kunz 1960).

Until 9/11, legal injunctions increasingly restricted states' rights to resort to war. The doctrine of **military necessity** still accepts the use of military force as legal only as a last recourse for defense (Raymond 1999). However, even though the initiation of war is no longer licensed and the intention to make war is still a crime (labeling those who start a war "criminals"), the posture of a hegemonic superpower has the capacity to challenge this norm, and the **Bush Doctrine** pledging a preemptive strike against Iraq (see Chapter 13) could make wars to prevent anticipated wars an acceptable legal practice as it was in past centuries.

New Rules for Military Intervention. At the end of the twentieth century, international law began to fundamentally revise its traditional prohibition against military intervention. In the wake of mass atrocities by governments against their own people and the recent wave of international terrorism, some powerful states have asserted the right to intervene with armed force. "The belief that governments have a right, even obligation, to intervene in the affairs of other states seems to have gained great currency" (Blechman 1995).

The Westphalian sanctity of state sovereignty, purporting that what a government does inside it's borders, has collapsed. A relaxed definition of the conditions under which states have the right to use military intervention for humanitarian purposes is gaining acceptance in international law (see Figure 15.2). The world has made a choice on genocide, declaring organized savagery illegal: "the last fifty years have seen the rise of universal endorsed principles of conduct" defining humanitarian intervention as a legal right to protect **human rights** by punishing acts of genocide and by interpreting intervention as "a spectrum of possible actions ranging from mild diplomatic protest to military invasion, even occupation" (Smith 2000).

International law, it appears, develops most rapidly when global problems arise which require collective solutions and legal remedies. The acceptance of intervention arose in response to the atrocities that grew alongside genocide and the need to rewrite the rules to permit interventions in an attempt to contain a problem in which international law was traditionally weakest—the control of civil wars and **terrorism,** for which a global response was needed to contain their spread:

> Attention to terrorism has led to increased cooperation and spawned new branches of international law. . . . Terrorism, far from disrupting the legal and organizational structures of the world community, has prompted states to step up their mutual cooperation on criminal matters and devise mechanisms based on common interest, designed both to prevent terrorist groups from attacking innocent civilians or state officials, and, in case such attacks are carried out, to arrest the culprits and bring them to justice. Treaties which demand that states either extradite or prosecute those accused of terrorism committed outside their territory have multiplied and are now copied in fields such as money laundering, corruption, and drug trafficking. (Cassese and Clapham 2001, 411)

■ **military necessity**
the legal doctrine asserting that violation of the rules of warfare may be excused during periods of extreme emergency.

■ **Bush Doctrine**
the declaration underscored in the 2002 National Security Strategy of the United States that the Bush administration would act unilaterally to preserve American unipolar predominance and, if necessary, undertake preemptive warfare to prevent adversary's military action, without the approval of allies.

■ **human rights**
the political rights and civil liberties recognized by the international community as inalienable and valid for individuals in all countries by virtue of their humanness. (see p. 23).

■ **terrorism**
criminal acts and threats against a targeted actor for the purpose of arousing fear in order to get the target to accept the terrorists' demands.

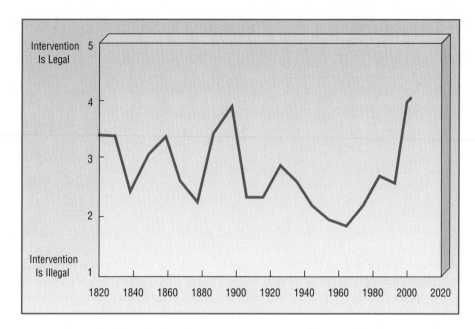

FIGURE 15.2

The Changing Status of the Nonintervention Rule in International Law since 1820

Over time, the illegality of intervening in sovereign states has changed, as measured by changes in authoritative international law texts about the prevailing consensus regarding rules for international conduct in each period. Since 1960, international law has adopted an increasingly permissive posture toward this form of coercive diplomacy for a variety of purposes including humanitarian aid, preventing genocide, protecting civil liberties, promoting democracy through "reform interventions," and combating global terrorism.

SOURCE: From Transnational Rules Indicators Project, as measured in "The Rise and Fall of the Nonintervention Norm: Some Correlates and Potential Consequences" by Charles W. Kegley, Jr., Gregory A. Raymond, and Margaret G. Hermann from the Fletcher Forum of International Affairs (Winter 1998).

The Rules for War's Conduct and the Expansion of Human Rights Legislation.   Laws regulating the methods that states may use in war *(jus in bello)* have also grown. These restraints include the principles of discrimination and **noncombatant immunity,** which attempt to protect innocent civilians by restricting military targets to soldiers and supplies. The laws of retaliation specify conditions under which certain practices are legitimate. One category, **reprisals** (hostile and illegal acts permitted only if made in proportionate response to a prior hostile and illegal act), stipulates procedures for military occupations, blockades, shows of force, and bombardments. Another category, **retorsion** (hostile but legal retaliatory acts made in response to similar legal acts initiated by other states), provides rules for embargoes, boycotts, import quotas, tariffs, and travel restrictions to redress grievances.

The advent of a new set of legal justifications for military intervention to protect civilians is explained by the fact that noncombatants have become the primary victims in warfare. "World War I was mass-conscription, democratic war with a vengeance, but it still was limited in its direct effect on civilians. The ratio of soldiers to civilians killed between 1914 and 1918 is about 90-to-10. In

■ **noncombatant immunity**
the legal principle that military force should not be used against innocent civilians.

■ **reprisals**
hostile but legal retaliatory acts to punish prior illegal military actions.

■ **retorsion**
hostile but legal retaliatory acts.

World War II, the ratio was 50-to-50. In recent years, it has been 90 civilian casualties to every 10 military losses—a reversal of the World War I ratio" (Pfaff 1999, 8).

To prevent the horror of civilian casualties and contain the mass slaughter that increasingly has taken place, the global community has radically revised the rules of international law. For the first time international law holds leaders of countries accountable for war crimes as war criminals. Traditionally, international law prohibited leaders from allowing their militaries to undertake actions in violation of certain principles accepted by the international community, including the protection of innocent noncombatants. However, when violations occurred, there was little that could be done except to condemn such actions. Another weakness was that traditional international law did not hold government leaders to the same standards to which it held soldiers and military officers who committed atrocities against enemy civilians and captured soldiers. Although international law set standards for both individuals and states, leaders were free from jurisdiction under the doctrine of "sovereign immunity," even when their commands flouted the laws of war. Though they might behave as criminals, leaders were treated with respect because they were the people with whom the global community had to negotiate to settle conflicts.

While many people and states still commit war crimes without facing punishment, the resumption of war crime tribunals in 1993 signaled to would-be perpetrators the global community's intolerance for these atrocities. In 1999, the prosecutor's office of the UN's **International Criminal Court (ICC)** indicted seventy-seven people and arrested seven for crimes in Bosnia. Building on this step, a **permanent world criminal court** was created in The Hague to try leaders for the most terrible of mass crimes—especially acts of genocide such as those perpetrated by terrorists. A goal the UN had pursued for half a century became a reality: the world community now has an international court with teeth, through a treaty ratified by more than fourteen states (and all major states except China, Iran, and Iraq, and the United States, which in May 2002 "unsigned" the ICC agreement by informing the UN that the United States was pulling out, to the dismay of U.S. allies). Moreover, heads of state are now held accountable for war crimes against humanity, removing the protection they had received under traditional international law. Ever since The Hague tribunal's 1997 founding statute, a head of state can be charged with war crimes committed at any time the leader was in office; even a sitting head of state can now be indicted for past war crimes. In fact, Slobodan Milosevic of Yugoslavia and President General Augusto Pinochet of Chile were indicted in 1999. The criminalization of rulers' **state-sponsored terrorism** raises the legal restraints on the initiation and conduct of war to an all-time high, widening the scope of acts now classified as **war crimes.**

Law's Contribution to Peace.   Cynics who contented that international law is irrelevant to the control of war overlook several dimensions of law's character.

- International law is not intended to prevent all warfare. Aggressive war is illegal, but defensive war is not. It is a mistake, therefore, to claim that international law has broken down whenever war breaks out.
- Instead of doing away with war, international law preserves it as a sanction against breaking rules. Thus war is a device of last resort to punish aggressors and thereby maintain the system's legal framework.

■ **International Criminal Court (ICC)**
a court established by the United Nations for indicting and administering justice to people committing war crimes.

■ **permanent world criminal court**
a standing international court to judge mass crimes such as genocide.

■ **state-sponsored terrorism**
formal assistance, training, and arming of foreign terrorists by a state in order to achieve foreign policy and/or domestic goals.

■ **war crimes**
acts performed during war that the international community defines as illegal crimes against humanity, including atrocities committed against an enemy's prisoners of war, civilians, or the state's own minority population.

Reuters/Rubin Sprich/Archive Photos, William Campbell/Time Magazine, Vienna Report/
Sygma, Kathy Willens/AP/Wide World, P.F. Gero/Sygma, Matthieu Polak, Sygma, Sygma

UGANDA
Idi Amin

IRAQ
Saddam Hussein

HAITI
Jean-Claude
Duvallier

UNITED STATES
George Bush
(Persian Gulf War)

BRITAIN
Margaret Thatcher
(Falklands/Malvinas
War)

YUGOSLAVIA
Slobodan Milosevic
(Convicted)

Identifying War Criminals In 1994, the UN Security Council got serious about prosecuting war criminals and created two special crimes tribunals in The Hague. Swiss criminal lawyer Carla del Ponte (left) was appointed in September 1999 as chief prosecutor for the UN's war crimes tribunals for Yugoslavia and Rwanda, in which eighty prisoners were tried. The principle that national leaders cannot get away with mass murder and torture was established after World War II at the Nuremberg and Tokyo war crimes trials, but the norm was not reinforced until the UN responded in 1999 to the genocide and state terrorism in Bosnia, Rwanda, and Tanzania by setting up special-purpose war crimes tribunals. The performance of these tribunals is believed critical to the credibility of the newly created International Criminal Court.

The question about precisely what behavior is proscribed for a head of state is creating a new controversy. International law still is unclear about the limits. At right are some past heads of state who potentially, according to *Time* (December 14, 1998, 42) could be called before courts to defend their use of arms, either against their own people or its wars. In February 2002, Slobodan Milosevic, the president of the former Yugoslavia, was convicted of criminal charges for starting three wars of ethnic cleansing.

- International law is an institutional substitute for war. Legal procedures exist to resolve conflicts before they erupt into open hostilities. Although they cannot prevent war, they sometimes make recourse to violence unnecessary by resolving disputes that might otherwise escalate to war.

The demonstrable capacity of pacific methods to reduce the frequency of war does not mean that international adjudicative machinery is well developed or functionally effective. Nowhere is this more evident than with the International Court of Justice (ICJ), known as the World Court, which was created after World War II as the highest judicial body on earth. The World Court was an inactive judicial institution until very recently. Between 1946 and 1991 it heard only sixty-four contentious cases between states, rendered judgments on less than half of these, and handed down only nineteen advisory opinions, and over the last century has averaged only about three cases per year. Since 1991, however, the ICJ has expanded its workload and considered cases dealing with many new issues. Even though only governments of states may apply for an appearance before the court (and are hesitant to do so because ICJ decisions are final, without a possibility of appeal), an increasing number have done so: between 1992 and 1995, the ICJ heard twenty-four cases, and the judicial activity jumped to an average of sixteen cases each year between 1996 and 2002. The court also became increasingly active in responding to requests for advisory opinions; for example, in 1996 the ICJ rendered an advisory opinion on the highly controversial question of whether the use or threat of nuclear weapons could be declared illegal (answering that for the most part it should be).

World order in the twenty-first century will depend to a considerable extent on the uses to which states put international law. Alleged shortcomings of international law lie not with the laws but with their creators—states and their addiction to sovereignty as a legal right. The intentions of states acting individually or in concert, and not the slow processes by which legal development grows, will be decisive.

Crucial in determining the role that international law will play will be which trend shall prevail—whether states choose to strengthen international law or insist on continuing to resist the compulsory jurisdiction to the World Court and other international tribunals. One path is displayed by the United States, which the Bush administration in 2002 pledged would continue to act in accordance to its so-called Connally amendment that reserves the U.S. right to determine which cases it will permit the World Court to hear. The U.S. preference is to try cases in U.S. courts and to let others use U.S. courts as global arbiters of global rights and wrongs (as happened in 2001 when five Chinese civilians sued former Chinese Prime Minister Li Peng in an American court for his role in the crackdown in Beijing's Tiananmen Square that killed hundreds of civilians). The trend toward use of U.S. courts to conduct criminal prosecutions of foreign terrorists captured abroad is accelerating as the United States is transforming itself from "global policeman" to "global attorney" (Glaberson 2001). A quite different path follows the tenet of liberal theory advanced by U.S. President Eisenhower, who counseled that it "is better to lose a point now and then in an international tribunal and gain a world in which everyone lives at peace under the rule of law." That approach has been accepted at the regional level in the European Union, where the European Court of Justice (ECJ) has authority over state members and acts as a legal engine for the integration of the European Union (EU); and in the European Court of Human Rights, under the Council of Europe, which exercises authoritative jurisdiction—in South America, the Inter-American Court on Human Rights has also considered cases.

The global community could, in principle, follow Europe's lead and strengthen international law's capacity. Still, many barriers remain to creating, as John F. Kennedy expressed liberal theory's hope, "a new world of law, where the strong are just and the weak secure and the peace preserved." We next consider the role of international organizations in maintaining such a world peace.

INTERNATIONAL ORGANIZATIONS AND WORLD ORDER

Liberal theorists recommend the creation of international organizations as a second political path to peace. To understand this approach, we must also understand its theoretical underpinnings. The expectations about and performance of the UN exemplify those theoretical premises.

The United Nations and the Preservation of Peace

The UN's purposes are multiple; but, as Article I of the UN Charter signals, peace is primary among the UN's objectives as follows:

- Maintain international peace and security.
- Develop friendly relations among nations based on respect for the principle of equal rights and self-determination of peoples.
- Achieve international cooperation in solving international problems of an economic, social, cultural, or humanitarian character and in promoting and encouraging respect for human rights and for fundamental freedoms for all.
- Function as a center for harmonizing the actions of nations in the attainment of these common ends.

The UN Charter states that all members are required to "settle their international disputes by peaceful means." That said, on many occasions UN members have *not* honored that promise—taking up arms to resolve their differences on the battlefield. In addition, many members have militarily intervened in nonmembers' internal wars, and especially in the past two decades the UN has faced the difficult choice of what to do with the rampant outbreak of civil wars, ethnic or religious warfare and terrorism in **failed states.** "Everywhere we work," lamented Secretary-General Boutros-Ghali in 1995, "we are struggling against the culture of death."

> ■ **failed states** countries whose governments have so mismanaged policy that they have lost the loyalty of their citizens and face anarchy and revolution.

To evaluate the prospects for meeting the cursed challenge of controlling militarized conflict, it is important to understand how states have organized the UN to carry out the missions it has asked it to perform. Recall from Chapter 5 that the UN Charter divided authority and decision power into three separate organs: The Security Council of fifteen members, the General Assembly of representatives of all 190 member states, and the Secretariat administrative staff under the secretary-general. This unwieldy structure enshrined the great powers on the Security Council with with final authority over peacekeeping decisions, although the General Assembly attempted to expand its jurisdiction in matters of security when the Security Council was paralyzed by the great powers' use of vetoes during the Cold War. The end of the Cold War in 1989 allowed the UN to step up to the plate and begin to assume a greater role in attempting to police the cascade of civil wars that erupted (see Chapter 11). However, budgetary constraints have reduced the capacity to play a more active security role. That said, at the heart of the barriers to more active UN security activities is the continuing inefficiency of the UN's administrative bureaucracy, although recent reforms have reduced that problem (see Chapter 5).

There remains a huge gap between the UN's mandate to keep the peace and the resources that member states have provided as means to fulfill those objectives. Two basic approaches continue to be pursued. The first seeks to address the underlying social and economic roots of armed conflict (recall Chapter 11) by attempting to alleviate the human suffering which often causes aggression and terrorism. These efforts are carried out through the UN's "specialized agencies," such as the World Health Organization (WHO), the Food and Agriculture Organization (FAO), the International Labor Organization (ILO), the UN Educational Scientific and Cultural Organization (UNESCO), and many others. In addition, various UN programs operate to assist these efforts in the realm of

■ **low politics**
the category of global issues related to the economic, social, demographic, and environmental aspects of relations between governments and people.

low politics, such as the UN Development Programme (UNDP), the UN Children's Emergency Fund (UNICEF), the UN Conference on Trade and Development (UNCTAD), the World Food Programme (WFP), and many others. The second approach is more ambitious: taking on the task of directly bringing fighting under control, resolving armed conflicts when they arise, and maintaining the peace when the fighting stops. Let us look more closely at that central goal as pursued by the United Nations.

■ **collective security**
a security regime agreed to by the great powers setting rules for keeping peace, guided by the principle that an act of aggression by any state will be met by a collective response from the rest (see p. 34).

Collective Security. **Collective security** is often viewed as a liberal alternative to the competitive balanced alliances that realists recommend. In a balance-of-power system, it is assumed that each state, acting in its own self-interest through self-help for its individual protection, will form coalitions offsetting others and that the resulting equilibrium will prevent war. In contrast, collective security asks each state to share responsibility for all other states' security. It "assumes that every nation perceives every challenge to the international order in the same way, and is prepared to run the same risks to preserve it" (Kissinger 1992). All states are to take joint action against any transgressor, and all are to act in concert. This presumes that the superior power of the entire community will deter those contemplating aggression or, failing this, that collective action will defeat any violator of the peace.

Faced with the League of Nations' inability to put collective security into practice, realist critics attacked what they regarded as the illusory expectations on which liberal proponents had built the model. The league's failures stemmed from the U.S. refusal to join the organization; the other great powers' fear that the league's collective strength might be used against them; disagreement over objectively defining an instance of aggression in which all concurred; states' pervasive dread of inequities in sharing the risks and costs of mounting an organized response to aggression; and their tendency to voice approval of the value of general peace but unwillingness to organize resistance except when their own security was threatened. In the final analysis, the theory's central fallacy was that it expected a state to be as anxious to see others protected as it was to protect itself. That assumption did not prove true in the period between World War I and World War II. As a result, the League of Nations never became a valid collective security system.

The architects of the UN were painfully aware of the league's disappointing experience. While they voiced support for collective security, their design restored the **balance of power** to maintain peace. The 1945 UN Charter permitted any of the Security Council's five permanent members (the United States, the Soviet Union, Great Britain, France, and China) to veto and thereby block any proposed enforcement action that any of them disapproved. Because the Security Council could act in concert only when the permanent members fully agreed, the UN Charter was a concession to states' sovereign freedom:

■ **balance of power**
the theory that peace and stability are most likely to be maintained when threatened states form a military coalition and thereby redistribute power to prevent any single great power hegemon or bloc from dominating the global system.

> In the final analysis, the San Francisco Conference must be described as having repudiated the doctrine of collective security as the foundation for a general, universally applicable system for the management of power in international relations. The doctrine was given ideological lip service, and a scheme was contrived for making it effective in cases of relatively minor importance. But the new organization reflected the conviction that the concept of collective security had no realistic relevance to the problems posed by conflict among the major powers. (Claude 1962, 164–165)

To further enhance the great powers' authority relative to the UN, the charter severely restricted the capacity of the General Assembly to mount collective action. The charter authorized it only to initiate studies of conflict situations, bring perceived hostilities to the attention of the Security Council, and make recommendations for initiatives to keep the peace. Moreover, it restricted the role of the secretary-general to that of chief administrative officer. Article 99 confined the secretary-general, and the working staff of the Secretariat created to aid that person, to alerting the Security Council to peace-threatening situations and to providing administrative support for the operations that the Security Council authorized.

Although the UN's structure compromises the organization's security mission, it is still much more than a mere debating society. It is also more than an arena for power politics. During the Cold War the UN fell short of many of the ideals its more ambitious founders envisioned, principally because its two most powerful members in the Security Council, the United States and the Soviet Union, did not cooperate. Over 230 Security Council vetoes were cast, stopping action of any type on about one-third of the UN's resolutions. In this period, UN action was only taken when a conflict was outside the East-West rivalry and did not involve either superpower, with decolonization disputes involving relatively small and weak countries receiving most of the UN's attention. Between 1945 and 1984 the UN only attempted to mediate 40 percent of the 319 interstate conflicts that erupted (Holsti 1988, 423). To put it mildly, the UN's peace-making achievements during the Cold War were at best modest.

Like any adaptive institution, the UN found other ways besides peacekeeping to overcome the compromising legal restrictions and lack of great-power cooperation that inhibited its capacity to preserve world order. For example, in contrast to peace enforcement as in the Korean War, the UN undertook a new approach, termed **peacekeeping,** that aimed at separating enemies. The UN Emergency Force (UNEF) in 1956 authorized by the Uniting for Peace Resolution in the General Assembly in response to the Suez crisis was the first of many other peacekeeping operations that followed. In addition, in 1960 Secretary-General Dag Hammarskjold sought to manage peace and security through what he termed **preventive diplomacy** by attempting to resolve conflicts before they reached the crisis stage, in contrast to ending wars once they erupted. Likewise, in 1989 then-Secretary-General Javier Perez de Cuellar, frustrated with the superpowers' prevention of the UN to "play as effective and decisive a role as the charter certainly envisaged for it," pursued what was called **peace-making** initiatives designed to obtain a truce to end the fighting so that the UN Security Council could then establish operations to keep the peace. UN Secretary-General Kofi Annan has since taking office in 1997 in his first term concentrated the UN's efforts on **peace building** by creating the conditions that make renewed war unlikely, while at the same time working on peace making (ending fighting already underway) and managing the UN's **peace operations** to police those conflicts where the threat of renewed fighting between enemies is high. These endeavors have emphasized **peace enforcement** operations, relying on UN forces trained and equipped to use military force if necessary without the prior consent of the disputants.

For more than four decades, the UN was a victim of superpower rivalry. However, the end of the Cold War removed many of the impediments to the

■ **peacekeeping**
the efforts by third parties such as the UN to intervene in civil wars and/or interstate wars or to prevent hostilities between potential belligerents from escalating, so that by acting as a buffer a negotiated settlement of the dispute can be reached.

■ **preventive diplomacy**
diplomatic actions taken in advance of a predictable crisis to prevent or limit violence. (see p. 511).

■ **peace making**
the process of diplomacy, medition, negotiation, or other forms of peaceful settlement that arranges an end to a dispute and resolves the issues that led to conflict.

■ **peace building**
postconflict actions, predominantly diplomatic and economic, that strengthen and rebuild governmental infrastructure and institutions in order to avoid recourse to armed conflict.

■ **peace operations**
a general category encompassing both peacekeeping and peace enforcement operations undertaken to establish and maintain peace between disputants.

■ **peace enforcement**
application of military force, or the threat of its use, normally pursuant to international authorization, to compel compliance with resolutions or sanctions designed to maintain or restore peace and order (see p. 503).

Maya Vidon/AFP.

International Peacekeepers on the March In response to desperate please for help, the UN has selectively authorized peacekeeping forces to intervene. In September 1999, Australian soldiers marched off to lead the UN-authorized peacekeeping force in East Timor, where after voting four to one for independence from Indonesia, the people in East Timor were killed and raped in an act of state-sponsored terrorism. This mission restored order, and democracy was born.

UN's ability to return to its primary mission of preserving international security by means that the founders of the UN originally envisioned. The potential to play an active security role was demonstrated in 1990 when Iraq invaded Kuwait. The Security Council promptly passed Resolution 678, authorizing member states "to use all necessary means" to coerce Iraq's withdrawal from Kuwait. Under the authority of this resolution, on January 16, 1991, U.S. President Bush ordered an air war against Iraq's military machine, the fourth largest in the world. Forty-three days later, Iraq agreed to a cease-fire and withdrawal from Kuwait.

Bolstered by this success at collective security, optimism about the UN's capacity to take the lead in peace making started to grow. This optimism was facilitated by the shift of power from the General Assembly back to the Security Council. Acting in concert, it authorized the UN to launch twice as many peacekeeping missions between 1988 and 2002 as it had in the previous four decades of its existence. The level of activity has remained high, with the UN managing an average of fifteen peacekeeping operations each year since the end of the Cold War (see Map 15.1), and between 1996 at 2001 only six vetoes were cast.

Supporters of the UN as a peacekeeping organization still encounter resistance. The UN seems to have many critics because many countries make demands on the organization which cannot be met with existing resources and which other countries oppose. Countries call on the UN in times of need, but

Reuters/Peter Morgan/Archive Photo

Superclerk to the World Running the United Nations as secretary-general is perhaps the most challenging job in the world. In 1997, that position changed hands, as Kofi Annan of Ghana (at right) replaced Boutros Boutros-Ghali. Annan undertook massive reforms while seeking, with reduced finances, "to maintain the organization's capacity to manage existing operations and, if necessary, to launch new operations." As a key element in his organizational reform package, Annan won approval for the appointment of Louise Frechette (at left) as the UN's first deputy secretary-general. The popular Annan was elected to a second five-year term in 2002.

attack it when it fails to comply with the request made. For example, in October 2002 U.S. President George W. Bush warned the UN to act quickly on Iraq or "face irrelevance." However, at the time Russian, Chinese, and French opposition to the U.S. and British determination to use force against Iraq stiffened, and did not ease for another seven weeks until, after much diplomatic squabbling and rising U.S. criticism of the entire UN, the Security Council unanimously backed a new but weakened resolution requiring Iraq to show that it had abandoned its weapons of mass destruction or face "serious consequences."

In order to deflect criticism, the UN, through the offices of Secretary-General Kofi Annan, has undertaken organizational reforms to make it more efficient and cost-conscious. These reforms require a **selective engagement** peacekeeping policy, resulting in the streamlining and downsizing of existing missions and a reluctance of the part of the Security Council to launch new missions. Financial restraints have reduced total peacekeeping personnel from 78,000 at the start of 1994 to 46,500 at the start of 2003, with peacekeeping expenditures reduced from $3.4 billion in 1994 to $2.9 billion in 2002. But the UN remains active, with seventeen peacekeeping operations underway in seventeen locations at the start of 2003, and Secretary-General Annan continued to pursue plans to establish a Rapidly Deployable Mission Headquarters (RDMH) and to energize the UN's Counterterrorism Committee (CTC) created in response to 9/11.

UN peacekeeping operations remain understaffed, underfunded, and overwhelmed, and the prospects for Blue Helmet participation in future hot spots remain inadequate. To respond to the challenge, the UN has increasingly sought

■ **selective engagement**
a state's or an IGO's choosing to intervene militarily in some situations but declining to do so in others (see p. 128).

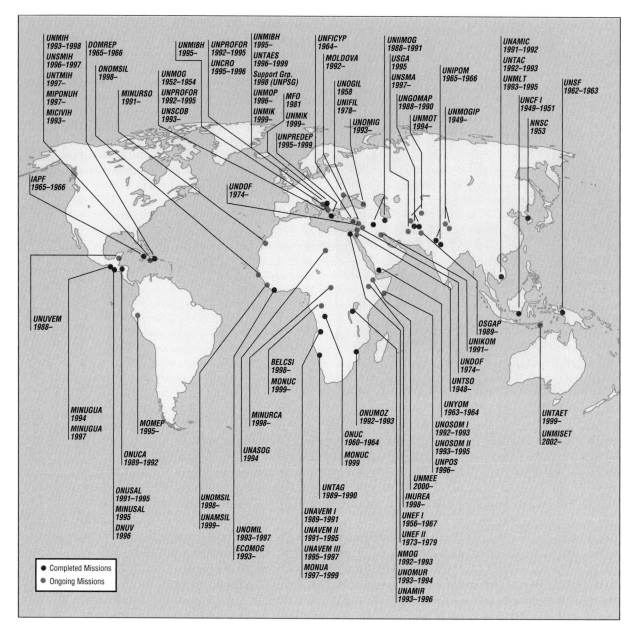

MAP 15.1

UN Peace Missions since 1948

In its first forty years, only thirteen UN peacekeeping missions were undertaken. But between 1986 and 2002 thirty-eight major new missions were launched, and as this map shows, UN peacekeepers were sent to flash points in nearly every region of the globe. Since 1989, in each year, on average, more than fifteen peacekeeping operations have been active, with seventeen underway at the start of 2003 (see figure at top right). As the figure below it on the right shows, since 1993 the number of military and civilian police participating in UN peacekeeping operations each month has averaged over forty-five thousand personnel from nearly all the UN's 190 members. The cost of keeping UN Blue Helmets in the world's trouble spots has climbed, but so have the budget deficits of members' arrears, compromising the capacity of the UN to carry out the missions the UN members have authorized. Sadly, the need is greatest now when the resources and commitments to global peacekeeping may be declining.

SOURCE: Based on data from the United Nations Department of Public Information.

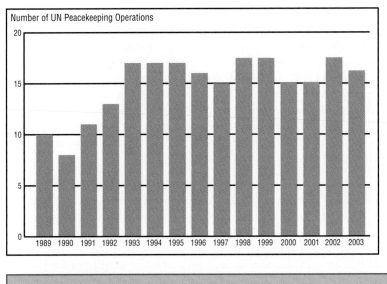

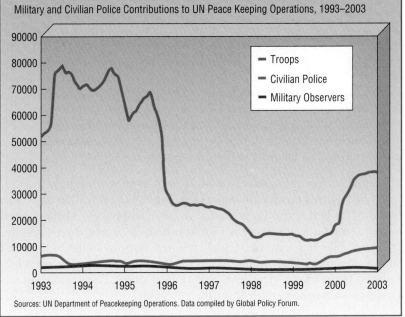

Sources: UN Department of Peacekeeping Operations. Data compiled by Global Policy Forum.

to deploy UN peacekeeping missions alongside non–UN forces and at other times has requested regional organizations or multiparty state alliances to step in the breach as a substitute for the UN. This has raised questions about in whose interest these forces are acting and whether they can be held accountable. Altogether, in 2002 at least twelve non–UN observer, peacekeeping, and peace enforcement missions were active in situations that UN forces were unavailable to assist.

The UN's problems raise concerns about its future ability to police the many ethnic conflicts and potential civil (and interstate) wars on the horizon. The UN is not yet a true collective security organization. Its blueprint for global involvement is just that—a blueprint. It is a design without a realistic structure,

■ **public goods**
shared values from which
everyone who has access to
them benefits, such as safe
drinking water, even if not
everyone contributes to
their preservation or
creation.

and the UN is not yet empowered for the high purposes it has been asked to perform. Currently, its advocates' expectations exceed its capabilities.

The global **public goods** of peace, prosperity, sustainable developments, and good governance cannot be achieved by any single country acting on its own. For the UN to succeed, the world community must match the demands made on it with the means given to it. The organization has to strike a balance between realism and idealism. The United Nations will be incapacitated if it alienates its most important members, in particular the United States. As John Bolton, the U.S. Secretary of State for Arms Control and International Security in the second Bush administration, wrote in 2001,

> Only the United States can lead the United Nations effectively. . . . The UN neither has, nor should have, the capability for independent action. It follows that when [the U.S. hegemon entrusts] it with responsibility for an independent undertaking, the United States must understand that it alone can lead the effort to a successful conclusion. . . .
>
> In fact, this observation should lead logically to the question; what exactly is the United Nations? In practical terms, it is simply an agglomeration of member states, served (at least in theory) by a staff that has no power or autonomy—and no independent democratic or other political legitimacy—to act except as directed by the member governments. Thus understood, there really is no "United Nations;" there is no "there" there, only the shifting reflections of the several views of the members. The UN has no more legitimacy or permanence than those members, and especially the largest, most important members, choose to give it. In particular, the secretary-general according to Article 97 of the Charter . . . has no independent political mandate or authority. Needless to say, the subordinate Secretariat staff has no independent legitimacy either.

The UN must reflect the current realities of U.S. economic military predominance. However this poses a dilemma, because the organization also risks losing all credibility if it compromises core values. "Opponents of the United Nations, who have long argued that it should not act as a world government, will object. But, while less than perfect, the United Nations is the only global mechanism for effective collaboration in circumstances where states are reluctant or ill-placed to act alone" (DeVecchi and Helton 1999). The reasons underlying this assessment are summarized by the view that,

> In the great uncertainties and disorders that lie ahead, the United Nations, for all its shortcomings, will be called on again and again, because there is no other global institution, because there is a severe limit to what even the strongest powers wish to take on themselves. . . . Either the UN is vital to a more stable and equitable world and should be given the means to do its job, or peoples and governments should be encouraged to look elsewhere. But is there really an alternative? (Urquhart 1994, 33)

Actually, there is a conspicuous alternative. The great powers' reluctance to equip the UN to contain civil wars lends credence to the 1995 prophecy of Karel Kovanda (the Czech Republic's UN ambassador), that the "important issues are going to be taken care of by regional organizations . . . with the United Nations giving its blessings."

Regional Security Organizations and Conflict Management

If the UN reflects the lack of shared values and common purpose characteristic of a global community, perhaps regional organizations, whose members already share some interests and cultural traditions, offer better prospects. The kinds of wars raging today do not lend themselves to control by a worldwide body, because these conflicts are now almost entirely civil wars. The UN was designed to manage only interstate wars; it was not organized or legally authorized to intervene in battles within sovereign borders. This, however, is not the case for regional institutions; regional IGOs see their security interests vitally affected by armed conflicts within countries in their area or adjacent to it, and historically have shown the determination and discipline to police bitter civil conflicts "in their backyards." Hence, regional security organizations can be expected to play an increasingly larger role in the future security affairs of their regions.

The North Atlantic Treaty Organization (NATO) is the best-known regional security organization. Others include the Organization for Security and Cooperation in Europe (OSCE), the ANZUS pact (Australia, New Zealand, and the United States), and the Southeast Asia Treaty Organization (SEATO). Regional organizations with somewhat broader political mandates beyond defense include the Organization of American States (OAS), the League of Arab States, the Organization of African Unity (OAU), the Nordic Council, the Association of Southeast Asian Nations (ASEAN), and the Gulf Cooperation Council.

Although Article 51 of the UN Charter encourages the creation of regional organizations for collective self-defense, it would be misleading to describe NATO and the other regional organizations as a substitute collective security instrument for the UN. They are not. More accurately, **regional collective defense** systems are designed to deter a potential common threat to the region's peace, one typically identified in advance.

> ■ **regional collective defense**
> organizations and military alliances within a specific region created to preserve peace and security for their members collectively.

Many of today's regional security organizations face the challenge of preserving consensus and solidarity without a clearly identifiable external enemy or common threat. Cohesion is hard to maintain in the absence of a clear sense of the alliance's mission. Consider NATO. The ambiguous European security setting is now marked by numerous ethnopolitical conflicts for which NATO was not originally designed to deal. Its original charter envisioned only one purpose—mutual self-protection from external attack; it never defined policing civil wars as a goal. Consequently, until 1995, when NATO took charge of all military operations in Bosnia-Herzegovina from the UN, it was uncertain whether the alliance could adapt to a broadened purpose to give it a new lease on life. Since that intervention, NATO *has* redefined itself, and in March 1999 it performed the same interventionary peace-making assignment in Kosovo. Today, NATO is an enlarged alliance, with seven new members joining in 2002 (see Map 14.1), and has transformed itself to become both a *military* alliance for security between states, within them, and for containing the spread of global terrorism, as well as a *political* alliance for encouraging the spread of democracy. That said, the primary purpose remains putting NATO's 26 members under a security umbrella, with the promise that an attack on one would be considered an attack on all. This **collective security** clause was invoked for the first time after 9/11 when the Al Qaeda terrorist network attacked the United States. This reaffirmed NATO's security-protecting capacity.

> ■ **collective security**
> a security regime created by a group of allied states that sets rules for keeping peace, guided by the principle that an act of aggression against any member will be met by a collective response from the rest.

Likewise, in other regional mutual security systems, controversies among the coalition partners about the identity of "the enemy" and the conditions warranting intervention raise doubts about their capacity to engineer collective defense projects. These doubts are fueled by the history of regional organizations in peacemaking efforts. Between 1945 and 1984, of 291 high-intensity armed conflicts involving military units, less than one-fourth, or only sixty-eight, were handled by regional organizations (Holsti 1992, 353). This record suggests that although regional collective defense institutions were, to some extent, created to overcome the deficiencies of global institutions, they may not be able to perform that task any better than global institutions.

The overlapping memberships in Europe's major international organizations illustrate the obstacles to the maintenance of peace through regional organizations, because in that region their institutional development has been most rapid. Since World War II, Europe has built, in a series of steps, an increasing number of political, military and economic organizations encompassing more and more countries throughout an enlarged geographic network of institutions. The overlapping architecture includes OSCE, NATO, EAPC, the Council of Europe, and the EU defense organizations. As Anne-Else Holjberg in NATO's Political Affairs Division complained in 1997, "there is still a certain degree of rivalry between [these] different organizations," and the multilayered structure has made collective decision making difficult. The crisis in Kosovo again exemplifies these barriers to collective security that regional organizations face. This case and others suggest that regional organizations have the capacity to bring conflict under control only when their members are in agreement. However, it also indicates that they often lack the consensus and political will to control controversial conflicts and require pressure from world public opinion mobilized in global organizations such as the UN to take action.

In the twenty-first century, regional collective defense institutions, assisted by unilateral peacekeeping forces from particular interested states, and now supported by mercenaries that regional organizations and states hire or "outsource" from private multinational corporations (Isenberg 2000), may help to build a global security community in which the expectation of peace exceeds the expectation of war. The processes through which such metamorphoses might occur are addressed by the functional and neofunctional approaches to peace within the liberal paradigm.

POLITICAL INTEGRATION: THE FUNCTIONAL AND NEOFUNCTIONAL PATHS TO PEACE

■ **political integration**
the processes and activities by which the populations of two or more states transfer their loyalties to a merged political and economic unit.

■ **world federalism**
a reform movement proposing as a path to peace combining two or more previously independent countries be combined to form a single unified federal state.

Political integration refers to either the process or the product of efforts to build new political communities and supranational institutions that transcend the state. Their purposes are to remove states' incentives for war and to engineer reform programs to transform international institutions from instruments *of* states to structures *over* them.

World Federalism: A Single Global Government

Integration in its various forms does not necessarily make a frontal attack on the state by proposing to replace it with some central authority. That radical remedy is represented by **world federalism,** a school of thought advocating the merger of

Boris Grdanski/AP/Wide World

The Interventionist Road to Peace? The chaos and killing in failed states provoke widespread concern, but until recently many states and IGOs have been reluctant to intervene militarily to keep the peace in civil wars outside their spheres of influence. NATO's 1999 humanitarian intervention in Kosovo is an exception—the first time that alliance used force "out of area" to prevent a campaign of state-sponsored terror against an ethnic minority. Here a British tank heading to the Kosovo border in June 1999 is greeted by jubilant Albanian Kosovars thankful that NATO's KFOR (Kosovo Force) peacekeepers appeared on the scene to rescue them. The mission was supported by three hundred Eurocorps soldiers provided by the EU, made up largely of French and German officers, in what became the first mission of the EU's newly created Rapid Reaction Force of 60,000 soldiers. At its November 2002 Summit in Prague, NATO created its own rapid-reaction force "to fight anywhere in the world." Humanitarian military interventions could become frequent now that international law has relaxed traditional prohibitions against external interference in the internal affairs of an established state.

previously sovereign states into a single integrated federal union. Federalists follow the liberal conviction of Albert Einstein "that there is no salvation for civilization, or even the human race, other than the creation of a world government."

Federalists reason that if people value an **absolute gain** such as humanity's survival more highly than a **relative gain** such as an individual state's national advantage over its rivals, they will willingly transfer their loyalty to a supranational authority to dismantle the anarchical system of competitive territorial states that produces war. "World government," they believe, "is not only possible, it is inevitable," because it appeals to the patriotism of people who "love their national heritages so deeply that they wish to preserve them in safety for the common good" (Ferencz and Keyes 1991).

■ **absolute gains** conditions in which all participants in exchanges become better off (see p. 310).

■ **relative gains** conditions in which some participants benefit more than others (see p. 310).

■ nationalism
the feeling of loyalty to a particular state and/or nationality or ethnic group, to the exclusion of attachment to other states, universal religious values, or the collective welfare of all people.

■ nongovernmental organizations (NGOs)
transnational organizations of private citizens maintaining consultative status with the UN; they include professional associations, foundations, multinational corporations, and internationally active groups in different states joined together to work toward common interests.

■ functionalism
the theory advanced by David Mitrany and others explaining how people can come to value transnational institutions (IGOs, integrated or merged states) and the steps to giving those institutions authority to provide the public goods (for example, security) previously supplied by their state.

It is not surprising that ardent adherents to **nationalism** have vehemently attacked the revolutionary federalist "top-down" peace plan. Because it seeks to subvert the system of sovereign states, the plan threatens many entrenched interests. More abstractly, other critics reject the world federalists' proposition that governments are bad but people are good, wise, and enlightened (see Claude 1971). Likewise, they question the assumption that the need for changes will automatically lead to global institutional innovation.

Many of the globe's nearly thirty-thousand **nongovernmental organizations (NGOs)** are sympathetic to peace plans that seek to reduce the capability of states to make wars. Some accept the bold view of NGOs like United World Federalists that still actively promote creation of a world government. Nevertheless, aversion to war and raised consciousness of its dangers have not mobilized widespread grassroots enthusiasm for this radical step. Other approaches to reforming the world political system have attracted more adherents.

Functionalism

Classical functionalism is a rival but complementary reform movement associated with liberalism. In contrast to federalism, **functionalism** is not directed toward creating a world federal structure with all its constitutional paraphernalia. Rather, it seeks to build "peace by pieces" through transnational organizations that emphasize the "sharing of sovereignty" instead of its surrender. Functionalism advocates a "bottom-up," evolutionary strategy for building cooperative ties and unity among states.

According to functionalists, technical experts, rather than professional diplomats, are the best agents for building collaborative links across national borders. They see diplomats as being overly protective of their country's national interests at the expense of collective human interests. Rather than addressing the immediate sources of national insecurity, the functionalists' peace plan calls for transnational cooperation in technical (primarily social and economic) areas as a first step. Habits of cooperation learned in one technical area (such as telecommunications or medicine), they assume, will "spill over" into others—especially if the experience is mutually beneficial and demonstrates the potential advantages of cooperation in other areas (such as transportation and communication).

To enhance the probability that cooperative endeavors will prove rewarding, the functionalist plan recommends that less-difficult tasks be tackled first. It assumes that successful mastering of one problem will encourage attacking other problems collaboratively. If the process continues unabated, the bonds among countries will multiply, because no government would oppose a web of functional organizations that provide such clear-cut benefits to its citizens. Thus, "the mission of functionalism is to make peace possible by organizing particular layers of human social life in accordance with their particular requirements, breaking down the artificialities of the zoning arrangements associated with the principle of sovereignty" (Claude 1971). Its intellectual parent, David Mitrany (1966), argued in *A Working Peace System* (first published in 1943) that functionalism is based on self-interest.

Functionalism proposes not to squelch but to utilize national selfishness; it asks governments not to give up sovereignty which belongs to their peoples but to acquire benefits for their peoples which were hitherto unavailable, not to reduce their power to defend their citizens but to expand their competence to serve them. It intimates that the basic requirement for peace is that states have the wit to cooperate in pursuit of national interests that coincide with those of other states rather than the will to compromise national interests that conflict with those of others. (Claude 1971, 386)

Persuaded by the logic of this argument, farsighted liberals such as Jean Monnet applied functionalist theory to begin the process by which war-prone Europe began to form an integrated "security community" after World War II.

The permanent problem-solving organizations created in the 1800s, such as the Rhine River Commission (1804), the Danube River Commission (1857), the International Telegraphic Union (1865), and the Universal Post Union (1874), suggested a process by which states might cooperate to enjoy mutual benefits and hence to launch the more ambitious experiments that functionalists anticipated. Their lessons informed the early organizational ideology that also inspired the missions assigned to the UN's specialized agencies (such as the World Health Organization) and the growth of **intergovernmental organizations (IGOs)** and NGOs generally.

Functionalism, as originally formulated, did not pertain to **multinational corporations (MNCs),** the institutions some now consider the "dominant governance institutions on the planet" (Korten 1995). However, many now believe that MNCs' roles in the integration of states' economies and the globalization of world politics are consistent with functionalist logic. Individuals who manage global corporations often think and speak of themselves as a "revolutionary class," possessing a holistic, cosmopolitan, or supranational vision of the earth that challenges traditional nationalism (Barnet and Müller 1974). This **ideology** and the corresponding slogan "Down with borders" are based on the assumption that the world can be managed as a single, integrated market. From it comes a view of the world that sees global corporations as the primary catalysts to a borderless world opposed to governments that interfere unnecessarily with the free flow of capital and technology. According to this perspective, MNCs' investments and trade promote the growing level of cooperation and compromise exhibited between otherwise competitive states that is creating the emerging global culture—a culture that is eroding state sovereignty as states' economies become interdependent and states' foreign policies become increasingly **intermestic** (simultaneously international and domestic).

Critics charge that as a theory of peace and world order, functionalism does not take into account some important political realities. First, they question its assumption about the causes of war. Functionalism argues that poverty and the lack of public goods cause war. Critics question this assumption. They counter that war may instead cause poverty and the lack of public goods. Addressing issues of poverty may not alleviate war, they also argue, especially if the rapid acquisition of wealth enables dissatisfied states to build armies for war.

Second, functionalism assumes that political differences among countries will be dissolved by the habits of cooperation learned by experts organized transnationally to cope with technical problems such as global warming, environmental deterioration, or contagious disease. The reality, say critics, is that technical cooperation is often more strongly influenced by politics than the other way around. The U.S. withdrawal in the 1980s from the International Labor Organization (ILO) and the UN Educational, Scientific, and Cultural Organization (UNESCO) because that hegemon then felt that those IGOs were too politicized illustrated the primary of politics (the U.S. re-entry in UNESCO in 2002 to seek UN support for anti-terrorism punctuates the proposition, too).

■ **intergovernmental organizations (IGOs)** international organizations whose members are states, such as the World Trade Organization (see p. 000).

■ **multinational corporations (MNCs)** business enterprises headquartered in one state that invest and operate extensively in other states.

■ **ideology** a set of core philosophical principles collectively held about the ways people and governments ought to behave ethically and politically (see p. 13).

■ **intermestic policies** those issues confronting a state that are both local (domestic) and global (international).

As skeptics conclude, functionalists are naive to argue that technical (functional) undertakings and political affairs can be separated. If technical cooperation becomes as important to state welfare as the functionalists argue that it will, states will assume an active role in technical developments. Welfare and power cannot be separated, because the solution of economic and social problems cannot be divorced from political considerations. The expansion of transnational institutions' authority and competency at the expense of national governments and state sovereignty is, therefore, unlikely. Functionalism, in short, is an idea whose time has passed.

Neofunctionalism

A new, albeit derivative, theory arose in the 1950s to question the assumption that ever-expanding functional needs for joint action to address property rights, health, technological change, and other shared problems would force the resolution of political disputes. Termed **neofunctionalism,** the reconstructed liberal theory sought to directly address the political factors that dominate the process of merging formerly independent states.

> *Neofunctionalism* holds that political institutions and policies should be crafted so that they lead to further integration through the process of . . . "the expansive logic of sector integration." For example, [the first] president of the ECSC [European Coal and Steel Community], [Jean] Monnet, sought to use the integration of the coal and steel markets of the six member countries as a lever to promote the integration of their social security and transport policies, arguing that such action was essential to eliminate distortions in coal and steel prices. [The] neofunctionalism of Monnet and others [had] as its ultimate goal . . . the creation of a federal state. (Jacobson 1984, 66)

Neofunctionalism thus proposes to accelerate the processes leading to new supranational communities by purposely pushing for cooperation in politically controversial areas, rather than by avoiding them. It advocates bringing political pressure to bear at crucial decision points to persuade opponents of the greater benefits of forming a larger community among formerly independent national members.

The European Integration Example. Europe has shown the world how neofunctionalism can work to create an integrated political community. In 2002, the **European Union (EU)** put its official stamp on adding by 2004 ten European countries to the fifteen-country regional bloc (see Map 15.2). This enlargement created the globe's biggest free-trade area, swelling the EU to bring together under a single administrative umbrella over 450 million people. The single "euro" currency is the most potent symbol of European integration, so if and when all twenty-five EU members begin using it for economic transactions, nearly all the continent will be united for the first time in history.

In order to speak with one voice and act collectively not only in economics but also in defense and foreign policy, the EU took a big step when it endorsed its **Common Foreign and Security Policy (CFSP),** which defined as the EU's objectives safeguarding "the common values, fundamental interests, and independence of the Union," strengthening the EU's security, preserving "world peace and international security [as well as promoting] international cooperation to develop and consolidate democracy and the rule of law, and respect for

■ **neofunctionalism**
the revised functional theory explaining that the IGOs that states create to manage common problems provide benefits that exert new pressures for further political integration, the creation of additional IGOs, and the globalization of international relations in an expanding network of interdependence that reduces states' incentives to wage war.

■ **European Union (EU)**
a regional organization created by the merger of the European Coal and Steel Community, the European Atomic Energy Community, and the European Economic Community, called the Europe Community until 1993.

■ **Common Foreign and Security Policy (CFSP)**
the agreement reached by the European Union defining the goals in foreign and defense policy the EU pledges to jointly pursue.

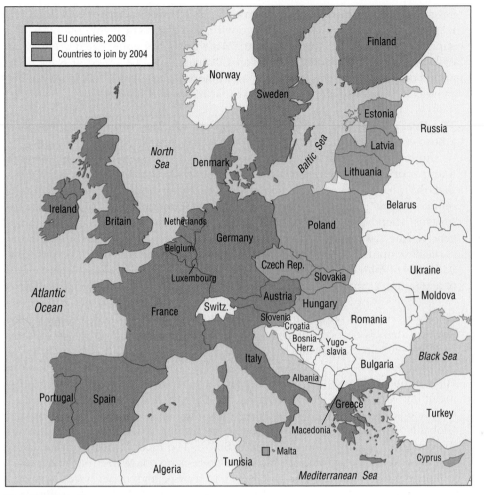

MAP 15.2
The European Union Expands

The European Union is a premier example of a supranational regional organization. In December 2002, the current fifteen EU members agreed to admit ten new members by 2004. The scheduled fast-track entry of Cyprus, the Czech Republic, Slovakia, Estonia, Hungary, Latvia, Lithuania, Malta, Poland, and Slovenia gives weight to EU aspirations to play a greater role in international peacekeeping.

SOURCE: European Union.

human rights and fundamental freedoms." To fulfill these goals, at the 2001 Nice Summit, the EU established the European Rapid Reaction Force, taking the next step toward becoming a military presence on the world stage capable of *unilateral* action. This sixty thousand strong military force enables the EU to reduce both its dependence on the United States and U.S. domination of NATO.

The political unification of Europe represents an enormous achievement, overturning a past of chronic suspicion and warfare—the dark side of European history. Instead of competing, the EU has created a **security community** (Deutsch et al. 1957) in which the expectation of war between states has vanished from one of the historically most violence-prone regions of the world. The

■ **security community**
a group of states whose high level of noninstitutionalized collaboration results in the settlement of disputes by compromise rather than by force (see p. 155).

sovereign state in Europe has lost ground, as "a serious sense of European citizenship, along with the rights that go with it, seems to be laying the basis of a supranational identity" (Cohen 2000). With unity has come greater efforts at collective security through a common European posture aimed at preventing armed conflicts. Those aspirations inspire hopes that Europe will leave behind the tragic cycle of rivalry and mistrust that haunted it for centuries.

The Preconditions for Regional Integration. The record of previous integrative experiments demonstrates that the factors promoting (or inhibiting) successful integration efforts are many and their mixture complex. It is not enough that two or more countries choose to interact cooperatively. Research indicates that the probability of such cooperative behavior resulting in integration is remote without geographical proximity, steady economic growth, similar political systems, supportive public opinion led by enthusiastic leaders, cultural homogeneity, internal political stability, similar experiences in historical and internal social development, compatible forms of government and economic systems, similar levels of military preparedness and economic resources, a shared perception of a common external threat, bureaucratic compatibilities, and previous collaborative efforts (Cobb and Elder 1970; Deutsch et al. 1957). While not all of these conditions must be present for integration to occur, the absence of more than a few considerably reduces the chances of success. The integration of two or more societies—let alone entire world regions—is, in short, not easily accomplished.

European institution building nonetheless has served as a model for the application of the neofunctionalist approach to integration in other regions, including Africa, Asia, the Caribbean, and South America. However, current evidence suggests that political integration may be peculiarly relevant to the Global North's advanced industrial democracies but of doubtful applicability to the developing countries of the Global South. The record, moreover, indicates that even where conditions are favorable there is no guarantee that integration will proceed automatically. As noted, even in Europe high hopes have alternated with periods of disillusionment. When momentum has occurred, **spillover**—involving either the deepening of ties in one functional area or their expansion to another to ensure the members' satisfaction with the integrative process—has led to further integration. But there is no inherent expansive momentum in integration schemes. Thus, **spillback** (when a regional integration scheme fails, as in the case of the East African Community) and **spillaround** (when a regional integration scheme stagnates, or its activities in one area work against integration in another, as occurred in June 2001 when an Irish referendum rejected the Treaty of Nice's reforms for decision making) are also possible.

Political Disintegration

The substantial difficulty that most regions have experienced in achieving a level of institution building similar to that of the EU suggests the magnitude of existing barriers to creating new political communities out of previously divided ones. Furthermore, the paradox that the planet is dividing precipitately and coming together reluctantly at the very same moment confounds predictions. We are witnessing a convulsive splintering of states, as hundreds of ethnic nationalities are currently seeking autonomy. Consider Europe, where in 1991 hypernationalism led to the creation of fifteen newly independent countries. Since then five addi-

■ **spillover**
the propensity for successful integration across one area of cooperation between states to propel further integration in other areas.

■ **spillback**
the reversal of previous steps toward integration, reducing the number of sectors in which integrating states are engaged in cooperative exchanges.

■ **spillaround**
the stagnation or encapsulation of regional integration activities.

tional European states have been created from the former Yugoslavia. Between 1990 and 1998, the global rate of new-country creation as a consequence of civil wars within states was 3.1 new countries each year (Enriquez 1999, 30). Ironically, this fragmentation occurred in precisely the same period when elsewhere political units were reintegrating, as Hong Kong in 1997 and Macao in 2000 did when, after centuries of colonialism, they once again became a part of China.

The surge of ethnic and religious secessionist movements tearing countries apart is not confined to eastern and southern Europe. Disintegration of many of the globe's 208 currently separate states could multiply the number of independent countries to as many as 500 by the year 2025, according to UN estimates. With fewer than twenty-five countries ethnically homogeneous and with three thousand to five thousand **indigenous peoples** interested in securing a sovereign homeland, the prospects are high that **political disintegration** will continue, especially if the number of failed states where central governing institutions have imploded in a sea of chaos continues to rise (see Chapters 5 and 11). This division of the globe into more and more smaller states could be slowed if existing states accepted **devolution** (the granting of greater political power to quasi-autonomous regions), as many central governments have done for the purpose of containing separatist revolts. However, in many countries where governmental institutions are fragile, the leadership has refused to accept devolution and repressed by force the minority peoples seeking to share power. In these the hypernationalist quest for independence under the banner of the **self-determination** principle threatens to dismember some formerly integrated sovereign states, including such widely dissimilar states as Canada, Russia, Spain, South Africa, and the United Kingdom, where minorities (the proportion of a state's population made up by different ethnic, nationality, or racial groups) are often a repressed subclass ripe for revolution. About a third of the globe's countries contain restless, politically repressed minorities struggling at various levels for human rights and independence (see Allen 2002, 33; Gurr 2000, 2001). Such struggles and revolutions are not new, of course. The U.S. Civil War between 1861 and 1865 and the thirty-year civil war in Ethiopia that enabled Eritrea to gain independence in 1991 remind us that states may either integrate into larger unions or disintegrate into smaller states. Hence, there is little reason to expect integrative processes, once underway, to automatically continue by the force of their own momentum. Globalization, uneven growth rates, and income inequalities could easily pull history in the opposite direction, toward the disintegration of states to create many new national flags.

A DEMOCRATIC PEACE: CAN VOTES STOP VIOLENCE?

Historically liberal theory has emphasized the need for global institutional reforms to promote peace. For this reason, liberalism is most closely identified with international law, organization, and integration. However, liberalism embraces a fourth institutional approach: that democratization is critical, because if states are ruled democratically the world will become more peaceful. (This liberal thesis runs directly counter to realism's assumption that state's forms of government do not influence their foreign policy very much, because all governments, realists maintain, will respond similarly to similar security threats.)

■ **indigeneous peoples** the native ethnic and cultural inhabitant populations within countries ruled by a government controlled by others, known as the "Fourth World."

■ **political disintegration** the separation of a failed state into fragments to create two or more newly independent countries.

■ **devolution** states' granting of political power to ethnopolitical national groups and indigenous people under the expectation that greater autonomy for them in particular regions will curtail their quest for independence as a new state.

■ **self-determination** the standard advocated strenuously in U.S. President Woodrow Wilson's "14 Points" address that national and ethnic groups have a right to statehood so they can govern themselves as independent countries.

■ **democratic peace**
the theory that, because democratic states do not fight each other, the diffusion of democratic governance throughout world will reduce the probability of war (see p. 71).

■ **behavioralism**
an approach to the study of international relations that emphasizes the application of scientific methods (see p. 41).

■ **doctrine**
the guidelines a state specifies to identify the conditions under which it will use power for political purposes abroad.

■ **Group of Eight (G-8)**
the major industrialized countries including Russia, whose leaders participate in annual summit conferences to set economic, political, and military goals for the global future.

James Madison in 1792 voiced the liberal ideas underlying expectations about a **democratic peace** when he argued that "in the advent of republican governments [would be found] not only the prospect of a radical decline in the role played by war but the prospect as well of a virtual revolution in the conduct of diplomacy" (Tucker and Hendrickson 1990). Evidence generated by a quantitative **behavioral** research has convincingly demonstrated that there are sound reasons for accepting this liberal proposition. Studies have repeatedly shown that "well-established democracies have never made war on one another [and] republics and only republics have tended to form durable, peaceful leagues" (Weart 1994; see also Mandelbaum 2002).

This lesson has not been lost on leaders in democratic states seeking to find a principle on which to ground their twenty-first-century national security policies. "Ultimately the best strategy to insure our security and to build a durable peace is to support the advance of democracy elsewhere," the 1994 *U.S. National Strategy* concluded. That **doctrine** was officially endorsed by the other major EU and NATO liberal democracies who members insist on states being democratically ruled as a condition for membership. In addition, the major international organizations have also endorsed the promotion of democracy as a policy priority, including the **Group of Eight (G-8),** the World Bank, the International Monetary Fund (IMF), the Organization for Economic Cooperation and Development (OECD), and the Organization of American States.

The active promotion of democratic reforms in the past three decades has produced significant results. The reform-minded rhetoric to "export democracy" has been met with a great amount of action to back it up (Schraeder 2002). Since the mid-1970s freedom and civil liberties have grown, in a series of transitions, and today the enlarged community of liberal democracies make up three-quarters of the globe's governments, ruled by free or partially free institutions (see Figure 15.3).

Skeptics grounded in realism question whether democracies can be counted on to put their liberal ideals for promoting liberties worldwide ahead of their narrow national interests by risking their soldiers' lives in humanitarian crusades in countries of low geopolitical importance. Needless to say, confidence in the liberal path to peace through democratization will remain shaky in a precarious globalized world where the institutional foundations of lasting peace are still fragile. Some have been provoked to predict that global politics will constrain democracy, rather than democratization taming world politics (Gilbert 2000). Others fret that global terrorism will undermine the democratic project, observing that the war on terrorists like Osama bin Laden (who believe they can change U.S. policy through terror) will force democratic states to suspend their civil liberties.

These doubts notwithstanding, past trends provide strong evidence to support the liberal tenet that democracy has the capacity to deter wars within and between members of the democratic community of states. Therefore, providing that democratic states continue to abide by their past record of dealing with conflicts by compromise through negotiation, mediation, arbitration, and adjudication, the existing liberal democracies efforts to enlarge their community could potentially usher in a major transformation of twenty-first-century world politics and the 1995 hopes that Pope John Paul II expressed could make an ancient dream a reality: "No more war, war never again."

However, promise dictates neither performance nor destiny. As Prime Minister Ingvar Caarlsson of Sweden warned, "If we fail to nurture democracy—the

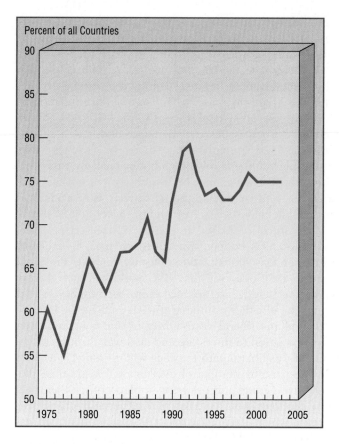

FIGURE 15.3
The Global Growth of Democratic Governance since 1974

The number of free and partly free countries that are members of the community of democracies has increased as a percent of the world's state governments since 1974 in fits and starts. As this figure shows, as the year 2003 began three-fourths of the countries in the world were either fully or partially democratic, according to Freedom House. Eighty-five "free" countries had governments that provided their citizens with a high degree of political and economic freedom and civil liberties, and another fifty-nine "partly free" countries had electoral governments.

SOURCE: Freedom House annual surveys.

most fundamental political project of this century—we will never be able to realize our goals and the responsibilities which the future will call for."

LIBERAL INSTITUTIONS AND WORLD ORDER: FROM SECURITY TO STABILITY?

Liberal and neoliberal theories that focus on international law, organization, integration, and democratization see armed conflict as deriving from prevailing and deeply rooted institutional deficiencies. Neoliberal reformers believe that the current anarchical system is the problem, not the solution, because weak institutions make security dear and global welfare subservient to national welfare. To change this, they advocate legal and institutional methods to pool sovereignty and reform the character of nondemocratic governments. Seeing the international system as underdeveloped and unstructured, advocates of these reforms believe that a rebuilt state system can best eliminate the roots of war. As one liberal scholar argues, global change requires innovation, because "During the coming decades global challenges will continue and may increase. . . . There is more and more of an overlap between national interests and global responsibilities. The task of multilateral diplomacy is to cope with new issues, new demands and new situations [through] 'shared responsibilities' and 'strengthened partnership' " (Kinnas 1997).

To liberal advocates, the big problems on the global agenda are ones that simultaneously affect many states. They cannot be meaningfully managed unilaterally; they are transnational and cannot be met effectively with a national response. With respect to such global issues as free trade, environmental degradation, global warming, the control of AIDS, the global refugee crisis, failed states, and civil wars, a multilateral cooperative approach may be required under conditions of interdependent globalization. In this context, President Martti Ahtisaari of Finland in 1999 observed that "the world has turned from mere coexistence to cooperation [and it has] succeeded in reaching beyond the boundaries of state sovereignty." Whether multilateral IGOs such as the UN, the democratically driven EU, and the liberal community of states at large can orchestrate their collective opposition to interstate and civil war through multilateral action will determine if this liberal path to peace will ultimately succeed.

The contributions of the expanding number of international institutions created in the twentieth century to this grand purpose were, until recently, rather modest. Despite some promising developments, armed conflict has been frequent. This is not surprising in a system in which, during the mid-1990s, states allocated less than $2 for every man, woman, and child to the UN for humanitarian and security emergencies, while at the same time their combined annual defense expenditures exceeded $960 billion (Evans 1995, 8). However, the impact of multilateral management of strife-torn areas should not be minimized. As Inis L. Claude maintains,

> Particular *organizations* may be nothing more than playthings of power politics and handmaidens of national ambitions. But international *organization*, considered as an historical process, represents a secular trend toward the systematic development of an enterprising quest for political means of making the world safe for human habitation. It may fail, and peter out ignominiously. But if it maintains the momentum that it has built up in the twentieth century, it may yet effect a transformation of human relationships on this planet which will at some indeterminate point justify the assertion that the world has come to be governed—that mankind has become a community capable of sustaining order, promoting justice, and establishing the conditions of that good life which Aristotle took to be the supreme aim of politics. (Claude 1971, 447–448, emphasis added)

At the advent of the twenty-first century, liberal institutionalists have appropriately raised various concerns about the capacity of independent and competing sovereign states to engineer a hopeful future for humanity. On balance, sovereign states have not used their foreign policies to create a safe and secure global environment in which their youth can survive and prosper. Instead, states have historically been instruments for making war with others, and recently national governments have proven inefficient at either preventing civil wars or commanding widespread loyalty and respect from their constituents. The global "crisis of confidence" in governments has resulted in the disintegration of failing states at the same time that these fragile states have become tied together in an interdependent globalized community. "Liberal internationalists see a need for international rules to solve states' problems, proclaim the end of the nation-state, [and see] transgovernmentalism rapidly becoming the most widespread and effective mode of international governance," said Anne-Marie Slaughter (1997) in defining the contemporary currents of public opinion. States are, to be sure, uniting by creating global institutions and a common culture to jointly protect themselves against the many shared problems they face. They appear to increasingly accept the once radical liberal view that, as Kofi Annan argued in 1999, "a new, broader definition of national interest is needed in the [twenty-first] century," which would unify states to work on common goals that transcend national interests. Borders and oceans cannot isolate or insulate states from these threats to security; they can only be controlled in the global commons by a collective effort. It is for this reason that many intergovernmental organizations (IGOs) originally came into being, and it is the persistence of collective threats produced by an increasingly globalized world that makes IGOs durable. As the globe shrinks and borders become even more porous, we can predict that liberal paths to peace and prosperity will continue to find favor and policymakers will take seriously the call to help create what Swedish Foreign Minister Anna Lindh describes as "a global culture of conflict prevention." If pursued, will the liberal approaches to the control of armed conflict create a different pattern? The world awaits an answer.

KEY TERMS

neoliberal institutionalism
private international law
public international law
sovereignty
realism
sovereign equality
neutrality
nonintervention
norm
diplomatic immunity
extraterritoriality
crimes against humanity
divine right of kings
statehood
diplomatic recognition
de facto recognition
de jure recognition
mediation
good offices
conciliation
arbitration
adjudication
self-help
structural violence
positivist legal theory

just war doctrine
security regimes
morals
ethics
revolution in military affairs (RMA)
preemption
military necessity
Bush Doctrine
human rights
terrorism
noncombatant immunity
reprisals
retorsion
International Criminal Court (ICC)
permanent world criminal court
state-sponsored terrorism
war crimes
failed states
low politics
collective security
balance of power
peacekeeping
preventive diplomacy
peace making
peace building

peace operations
peace enforcement
selective engagement
public goods
regional collective defense
collective security
political integration
world federalism
absolute gains
relative gains
nationalism
nongovernmental organizations (NGOs)
functionalism
intergovernmental organizations (IGOs)
multinational corporations (MNCs)
ideology
intermestic policies
neofunctionalism
European Union (EU)
Common Foreign and Security Policy (CFSP)
security community
spillover

spillback

devolution

behavioralism

spillaround

self-determination

doctrine

indigenous peoples

democratic peace

Group of Eight (G-8)

political disintegration

SUGGESTED READING

Aksu, Esref, and Joseph A. Camilleri, eds. *Democratizing Global Governance*. London: Palgrave, 2003.

Calleo, David P. *Rethinking Europe's Future*. Princeton, N.J.: Princeton University Press, 2001.

Franceschet, Antonio. *Kant and Liberal Internationalism: Sovereignty, Justice, and Global Reform*. London: Palgrave, 2002.

Goldstein, Judith L., Miles Kahler, Robert O. Keohane, and Anne-Marie Slaughter. *Legalization and World Politics*. Cambridge, Mass.: MIT Press, 2001.

Hampson, Fen Osler, and David M. Malone, eds. *From Reaction to Conflict Prevention: Opportunities for the UN System*. Boulder, Colo.: Lynne Rienner, 2002.

Joyner, Christopher C. *International Law in the Twenty-First Century*. Lanham, Md.: Rowman & Littlefield, 2000.

Kegley, Charles W., Jr., and Gregory A. Raymond. *Exorcising the Ghost of Westphalia: Building World Order in the New Millennium*. Upper Saddle River, N.J.: Prentice Hall, 2002.

Mandelbaum, Michael. *The Ideas That Conquered the World: Peace, Democracy, and Free Markets in the Twenty-First Century*. New York: Public Affairs Press, 2002.

Rittberger, Volker, ed. *Global Governance and the United Nations*. Tokyo: United Nations University Press, 2002.

Russett, Bruce, and John Oneal. *Triangulating Peace: Democracy, Interdependence, and International Organization*. New York: W. W. Norton, 2000.

Schrader Peter J., ed. *Exporting Democracy: Rhetoric vs. Reality*. Boulder, Colo.: Lynne Rienner, 2002.

Wapner, Paul, and Lester Edwin J. Ruiz, eds. *Principled World Politics: The Challenge of Normative International Relation*. Lanham, Md.: Rowman & Littlefield, 2000.

WWW WHERE ON THE WORLD WIDE WEB?

Carnegie Council on Ethics and International Affairs
http://www.cceia.org/

The best inventory of global issues, with Point of View commentary links to other Web sites dealing with each issue.

Human Rights Watch
http://www.hrw.org/

Human Rights Watch (HRW) is an independent, nongovernmental organization dedicated to protecting the human rights of people around the world. To this end, the organization investigates and exposes human rights violations and holds abusers accountable. As chapter 15 notes, the international community has impressively expanded the human rights protection granted under international law. HRW challenges governments to respect these laws. Its Web site houses stories on breaking news concerning human rights around the globe. The site delivers HRW reports on specific countries' human rights abuses. Which countries have the best and worst human rights records?

The International Court of Justice
http://www.icj-cij.org/

The International Court of Justice (ICJ) is the principal judicial organ of the United Nations. Examine the court's statute to find out who can bring cases before the court. Then, read the biographies of the court's fifteen members. Finally, access the Decisions link to examine some of the ICJ's contentious cases. Which countries have brought the United States to court? What were the ICJ's rulings in these cases?

International Court of Justice Considers Genocide
http://oz.uc.edu/thro/genocide/index.html

Professor Howard Tolley of the University of Cincinnati has created an interactive Web site on which you can role-play the judge at the International Court of

Justice when Bosnia brought charges against Yugoslavia in 1993. You can explore the facts, research the law, and consider opposing arguments, and then make your judgement. How does it compare to the court's actual decision?

International Criminal Tribunal for the Former Yugoslavia (ICTY)
http://www.un.org/icty/

Established by the United Nations Security Council in 1993, the ICTY is mandated to prosecute persons responsible for serious violations of international humanitarian law committed on the territory of the former Yugoslavia since 1991. Visit this Web site to see who was indicted for war crimes and what judgment was rendered. What has happened with the case against Slobodan Milosevic, the former Yugoslavian leader? Do you believe that the international community's ability to punish individuals for war crimes will be a deterrent against future acts of genocide and inhumanity?

Multilaterals Project
http://www.tufts.edu/fletcher/multilaterals.html

The Fletcher School of Law and Diplomacy makes available the texts of international multilateral conventions and other instruments. It has a searchable

database as well as a list of conventions organized by subject, such as the rules of warfare, the environment, cultural protection, or biodiversity. You can also view the Treaty of Westphalia and the League of Nations covenant. For thorough historical background on a subject, read the documents chronologically.

United Nations Peacekeeping Operations
http://www.un.org/Depts/dpko/dpko/home.shtml

The United Nations has deployed numerous international military and civilian personnel to conflict areas to stop or contain hostilities and supervise the carrying out of peace agreements. Click on an ongoing mission and read about the profile, background, and facts and figures concerning the mission. Do the same thing for an older mission. Are there any similarities or differences?

Universal Declaration of Human Rights
http://www.un.org/Overview/rights.html

This chapter discusses the development of international human rights protections. Read the document that started it all—the Universal Declaration of Human Rights. Did you know that Eleanor Roosevelt, serving as a delegate to the United Nations, chaired the committee that produced this document?

INFOTRAC® COLLEGE EDITION

Search for the following articles in the InfoTrac database:

Johnson, James Turner. "The Broken Tradition (Just-War Doctrine)," *The National Interest* Fall 1996.

Schwebel, Stephen M., and Dietmar Prager. "The International Court of Justice: As a Partner in Preventive Diplomacy," *UN Chronicle* Summer 1999.

Chomsky, Noam. "In a League of Its Own," *Harvard International Review* Summer 2000.

Tucker, Robert W. "The International Criminal Court Controversy," *World Policy Journal* Summer 2001.

For more articles, enter:

"just war doctrine" in the Subject Guide.

"International Court of Justice" in the Subject Guide.

"international law" in the Subject Guide, and then go to subdivision "evaluation."

THE PROBLEMATIC TWENTY-FIRST CENTURY

How are the trends that are emerging in world politics today likely to influence the global future? Will the twenty-first century find past approaches to world order useful, or will it reject past approaches as new questions that demand new answers arise?

Part V presents ten thought-provoking questions that ask how current trends in world politics are likely to impact the early part of the twenty-first century. These questions, which expand on those originally introduced in Chapter 1, draw on ideas you have encountered as you have read this book. Thinking about possible answers will require you to analyze these ideas, looking ahead to the global future informed by your knowledge of the contemporary character of international relations and recently constructed images about how world politics work.

CHAPTER 16

TEN QUESTIONS ABOUT TWENTY-FIRST-CENTURY GLOBAL PROSPECTS

T H E M E S   A N D   T O P I C S

- Should global interests be placed ahead of national interests?
- If war between states is obsolete, what is the purpose of military power?
- Can the new global terrorism be contained?
- Will separatist conflict within states lead to hundreds of new states?
- Will the great powers intervene to protect human rights?
- Will globalization tie the world together or tear it apart?
- Is realism still realistic and is liberalism still too idealistic?
- Is the world preparing for the wrong war?
- Is this the "end of history"?
- Is there a reordered global agenda?

Global inequalities have widened the gap between rich and poor. The World Urban Forum in 2002 sought to instill awareness of the destitute in many cities worldwide, as shown here, to conceive of more sensible public policies, arguing that, ethically, the advantages of modern civilization ought to be within the grasp of all.

AFP/Corbis

Trend is not destiny.

—RENÉ DUBOS, French author, 1975

The historical significance of September 11, like the fall of the Berlin Wall, will be debated for years to come. Was it the end of history? Was it our entry into the 21st century through a "gate of fire," as my secretary-general [Kofi Annan] has put it? That it brought the issue of terrorism into the forefront of the global agenda—far from being a purely national or regional concern— is indisputable. And yet, the rest of the global agenda before September 11 remains with us.

—JAYANTHA DHANAPALA, United Nations undersecretary-general for disarmament affairs, 2002

The opposing trends toward integration and fragmentation point toward a new global system—one whose character has yet to develop definition. Uncertainty and unpredictability define the contemporary mood. But one thing is certain: The seismic shifts underway will challenge the wisdom of old beliefs and orthodox visions. Because turmoil and turbulence govern contemporary international affairs, they require that we ask unconventional questions about conventional ideas. They push us to try to think four-dimensionally in order to perceive how political, military, market, and environmental pressures—intensified through globalization—are increasingly being brought to bear on the countries of the world, the people who reside in them, and their interactions.

Chapter 1 suggested that the investigative challenge to interpreting the future of world affairs would require the consideration of five controversial questions:

1. Are states obsolete?

2. Is globalization a cure or a curse?

3. Is technological innovation a blessing or a burden?

4. Will geo-economics supersede geopolitics?

5. What constitutes human well-being on an ecologically fragile planet?

Answers to these questions are elusive. The conclusions boldly asserted by would-be prophets are not likely to prove definitive, because, as former UN Secretary-General Boutros Boutros-Ghali warned in 1996, "those caught up in revolutionary change rarely understand its ultimate significance." It is hard to recognize, and to describe, the bewildering array of problems that we carry into the new millennium. As President Bill Clinton lamented in his 1997 National Security Strategy of the United States,

> The dangers we face are unprecedented in their complexity. Ethnic conflict and outlaw states threaten regional stability; terrorism, drugs, organized crime and proliferation of weapons of mass destruction are global concerns that transcend national borders; and environmental damage and rapid population growth undermine economic prosperity and political stability in many countries.

Given this complex and dangerous environment, it is important to weigh plausible answers to these same five key questions as we attempt to prepare ourselves intellectually for understanding the problematic future of twenty-first-century world politics.

This final chapter addresses ten additional questions about the future, based on the preceding discussion of the major trends currently unfolding in world politics.

TOWARD THE FUTURE: CRITICAL QUESTIONS AT THE START OF THE NEW MILLENNIUM

Leaders and policy analysts worldwide are debating a number of controversial issues that require policy choices. How these and other questions are answered will significantly shape world politics in the twenty-first century.

1. Should Global Interests Be Placed Ahead of National Interests?

What goals should states pursue? In earlier times, the answer was easy: The state should promote the internal welfare of its citizens, provide for defense against external aggression, and preserve the state's values and way of life. States followed a largely realist script, putting their national interests ahead of global interests. This meant competing with other states for power, position, and prestige, and above all else protecting the state from external attack by acquiring arms for defense. Working with other states on common problems or with many other countries in building institutions for global governance was secondary—to be considered only after national security was enhanced by acquiring political clout and military might.

Leaders pursue the same goals today, but their domestic and foreign policy options are increasingly limited. Many problems can be resolved only at the risk of worsening others. Under such conditions, the national quest for narrow self-advantage and global position often carries prohibitively high costs. The historic tendency toward chauvinism (my country, right or wrong) in defining national interests can be counterproductive domestically as well as internationally. No country can long afford to pursue its own welfare in ways that reduce its competitors' security and welfare.

In the past, those who questioned the primacy of the national interest seldom found support. Few accepted the notion that the global community's "moral meaning is better expressed in the notion of a 'human community,' which exists prior to the sovereign state" (Hehir 2002). That is changing. As Margaret Mead (1968) noted, people are beginning to endorse the view that "Substantially we all share the same atmosphere today, and we can only save ourselves by saving other people also. There is no longer a contradiction between patriotism and concern for the world." Former U.S. Secretary of State Cyrus Vance voiced a similar idea when he observed that "more than ever cooperative endeavors among nations are a matter not only of idealism but of direct self-interest."

■ **realism**
the orthodox theory of world politics based on the assumption that because humans are born to seek self-advantage, international politics is doomed to be a struggle for power involving war (see p. 36).

E. H. Carr (1939), a British pioneer of **realism,** was convinced of the realism of idealism, maintaining that opposing the general interests of humankind does not serve a country's self-interest. Failing to recognize the plight of others can ultimately threaten one's own well-being—a view underscored by Martin Luther King, Jr., who urged that "injustice anywhere is a threat to justice everywhere." Indeed, it was largely enlightened awareness of the limitations of traditional notions of state sovereignty and the conventional ways in which states have defined their national interests that prompted UN Secretary-General Kofi Annan in September 1999 to warn: "The world has changed in profound ways . . . but I fear our conceptions of national interest have failed to follow suit. A new, broader definition of national interst is needed . . . which would induce states to find greater unity in the pursuit of common goods and values." These proposals put human interests and global security ahead of national interests and national security. If such conceptions, largely rooted in the legacy of **liberalism,** gain a wider following in world public opinion, will the collective concerns of all humanity begin to better compete with states' continuing competitive preoccupation with their own narrow national interests?

■ **liberalism**
the optimistic view that because humans are capable of compassion, cooperation, and self-sacrifice for collective gain, it is possible for world politics to progress beyond narrow competition and war (see p. 33).

2. If War between States Is Obsolete, What Is the Purpose of Military Power?

Prevalent practices tend to wither away when they cease to serve their intended purpose, as the examples of slavery, dueling, and colonialism illustrate. Is war between states subject to these same forces? Since World War II, legal prohibitions against military aggression have expanded, and war has occurred almost exclusively in the Global South. And since the end of the Cold War in 1989, military conflicts between states have neared the vanishing point. Even more impressively, the period since 1945 has been the longest span of great power peace since the seventeenth century, raising expectations that large scale wars between states will continue to decline and perhaps cease altogether. (This hope exists even as internal or civil wars and terrorism are on the rise and humanitarian concerns about genocide and war crimes increasingly require interventionary peacekeeping.) "For modern states the anticipated costs [of waging war], political and economic as well as human, generally exceed the benefits" (Mack 1996).

It is, of course, debatable whether the disincentives and dangers of using today's destructive weapons are truly making war between states obsolete. Instead, this kind of war may eventually disappear in another, far more frightening way—because resorting to weapons of mass destruction will obliterate humankind. The puzzle, then, is when and by what means war will become obsolete. As Martin Luther King, Jr., put it, "The choice is either nonviolence or nonexistence."

In the past, military might enabled states to project power, exercise influence, and dominate others. Today nuclear, biological, and chemical weapons of mass destruction make the use of military might by states against other states risky. Continuing arms proliferation raises new questions. Does the acquisition of more weapons increase **national security**—a psychological phenomenon? Or are preparations for war and defense responsible for the **security dilemma** that all countries face?

Most leaders agree with the ancient Greek philosopher Aristotle, who argued that "a people without walls is a people without choice." Thus most accept the realist premise that preparing for war is necessary for peace, especially against terrorist groups. Yet the capacity to destroy does not always make for a convincing threat, especially against countries and transnational terrorists with the capacity to retaliate, whose citizens, not soldiers, would die in the largest numbers. Today, the threat of force often lacks credibility especially against terrorist groups willing to die for their cause. Military power has become impotent by its very strength. And when military might no longer compels others' compliance, then weapons will have lost their primary role as a basis, or substitute, for diplomacy.

No level of military might can guarantee a state's invulnerability. And states' primary security problem today is the rise of internal, not external, aggression, or an attack by a transnational terrorist. Therefore, preparations for war can be assessed only in terms of other consequences. Thresholds may exist, beyond which the addition of greater destructive power or the discovery of technologically revolutionary new kinds of lethal and nonlethal weapons are meaningless. Furthermore, excessive and financially costly preparations for war may leave a country heavily fortified with little left to defend, as U.S. President Eisenhower warned in 1961. To avoid debt and inflation, some states have adjusted to the diminishing usefulness of weapons by slashing their military budgets, inspired by their recognition that in the long run high military spending can reduce their industrial growth, weaken global economic competitiveness, and ultimately undermine the ability to satisfy citizens' cravings for a reasonable standard of living and a promising financial future.

Although immediate fears of another great power conflict causing a world war have declined and further eroded justifications for acquiring military power, states' traditional quest for military advantage has not disappeared. Military spending by the United States, China, the European Union (EU), and other aspiring global powers is scheduled to climb, fueled by enormous expenditures for homeland defense against terrorist attacks. Another sign of the persistent belief that military power increases political influence and national security is found in the fact that the global trade in weapons is the world's largest industry. In addition, the proliferation of weapons of mass destruction continues, as India's and Pakistan's nuclear weapons suggests, as does the pursuit of weapons of mass destruction by Iraq and untold numbers of nonstate terrorist movements. The

■ **national security**
a country's psychological freedom from fears that the state will be unable to resist threats to its survival and national values emanating from abroad or at home (see p. 450).

■ **security dilemma**
the propensity of armaments undertaken by one state for ostensibly defensive purposes to threaten other states, which arm in reaction, with the result that all arming states' national security declines as their arms increase (see p. 114).

Noresen/Greenpeace

People Power? States continue to seek sovereignty and supremacy, but increasingly world politics is being transformed at the grassroots level by networks of nongovernmental organizations (NGOs)—people dissatisfied with states' definitions of national interests. Individuals have formed nearly thirty thousand NGOs that advocate global changes and reforms. One such well-known NGO is Greenpeace, whose goal is to protect humanity from environmental degradation of the global commons. Shown here are Greenpeace members in action. NGOs have emerged as a major force to overcome global problems such as war, famine, human rights abuse, gender inequality, and poverty, that many people feel are not being tackled effectively by states' governments; these organizations wish to see human interests reinterpreted as states' primary national interests.

one predicament that nearly every state finds unacceptable is being vulnerable to foreign aggression or subject to other states' dictates. Consequently, the pursuit of military power is likely to continue at the same time that concerns about the social and financial costs of preparations to use military force in war are likely to rise.

Concurrently, in the information age states are increasingly likely to invest in nonmilitary methods of acquiring **soft power,** reasoning that "if a state can make its power legitimate in the eyes of others and establish international institutions that encourage others to define their interests in compatible ways, it may not need to expend as many costly traditional economic or military resources" (Keohane and Nye 2001b). That outcome could diminish substantially states' traditional faith in the proposition that overwhelming military might is required to play the game of international **politics** because it gets others to accommodate themselves to the demands of a more militarily powerful state. If the power to destroy does not provide the power to control, then states' willingness to spend for destructive weapons will decline.

■ **soft power**
the ability to exercise influence in world politics due to intangible resources such as culture and ideas as opposed to methods that rely on military might.

■ **politics**
the pursuit and exercise of power to promote self-interests and goals (see p. 18).

3. Can the New Global Terrorism Be Contained?

September 11, 2001, has been called by many people the day that changed the world—forever. The destruction of the World Trade Center and damage to the Pentagon by terrorists using hijacked airplanes as missiles shattered the prevailing illusion that terrorism was merely "theater" aimed primarily at shocking to gain attention; it was now aimed at killing large numbers. The goal of the Al Qaeda terrorist network that is spread across seventy countries and orchestrated by the former U.S. CIA client and Islamic extremist Osama bin Laden was to hit the enemy, and hard—to provoke widespread terror at the alarming thought that even more deadly acts were likely.

This transforming event gave birth to the new age of global terrorism, pitting terrorist movements against the states to rectify perceived injustices. In the bull's eye on their target was the globe's sole superpower, the United States, seen as a demonic global evil. Also on the screen were America's allies which also symbolized all that had gone wrong in the world, such as the loss of cultural traditions and religions by alien forces—globalization, consumerism, atheism, and modernization generally. In response, the United States under George W. Bush launched a global war to eliminate all terrorists and their sponsors from the face of the earth.

Extricating terrorism from the world is, of course, an extremely ambitious goal. Terrorism has been practiced for over 3,000 years, and ending a practice that has been around since antiquity will require vast resources and unswerving perseverance. To fight a war against terrorism is to fight a phenomenon, not an adversary actor. It is like fighting the war on poverty and on drugs—a noble undertaking against a perpetual phenomenon resistant to control.

How does a fragile worldwide coalition committed to counterterrorism win this kind of war? Can it? Opinions diverge on the answers to both questions.

One one extreme are experts who maintain that terrorism cannot be eliminated unless the conditions that cause it are first corrected. To them, circumstances of misery, poverty, persecution, and marginalization are the preconditions that pave the way to the outbreak of terrorist acts, and alleviating the suffering and despair by desperate people and reducing their grievances is the only long-term solution. To root out terrorism is to repair the soil from which terrorism grows—the kinds of terrain that breed people willing to take high risks and even to die as martyrs in suicide missions. At another extreme are counterterrorist strategists who see the new terrorism perpetrated by maniacs and fanatics and who conclude that because these terrorist leaders are responsible for today's terrorism, the answer lies in militarily striking and destroying the people who organize terrorist movements. This is the posture advocated by many in the Bush administration counseling the necessity of attacking Iraq and destroying its dictator, Saddam Hussein, who is believed to be bent on acquiring and using weapons of mass destruction. **Preemption**—militarily attacking the enemy before it obtains the capacity to strike first—is recommended by these advocates (although they have been less bold in pledging proactive attacks against Iran and North Korea, the other state sponsors of terrorism who Bush included along with Iraq, calling them an "axis of evil" in the world). In addition, this policy forces all countries to take a position. In April 2002 Bush stated "I laid out a doctrine [that] said if you harbor a terrorist, you're just as guilty as the terrorist; if you feed one or hide one, you're just as guilty as those who came and murdered thousands of innocent Americans."

■ **preemption**
a quick fast-strike military attack that seeks to defeat an adversary before it can organize a retaliatory response.

Courtesy of INA/Getty Images

The United States Takes on a Terrorist In 2003 the United States used its military might to oust Saddam Hussein from power in Iraq in order to prevent him from developing what was believed to be a secret stockpile of weapons of mass destruction and using them against the United States and its allies. Shown here is Saddam Hussein firing a rocket-propelled grenade.

■ **military necessity**
the legal doctrine asserting that the violation of the rules of warfare may be executed during periods of extreme emergency.

Military approaches may be required in the short run, rationalized by the principle of **military necessity.** But even if the primary targets such as Osama bin Laden and Saddam Hussein are killed, is there any certainty that a new generation of terrorists will not arise eager to avenge their deaths? And to successfully wage a war against worldwide terrorism, everyone recognizes that a broad-based international coalition of allies will be required. Global terrorism is a global problem that requires a global, multilateral approach. This reality was stressed by President Bush in May 2002 when, facing protests in Berlin over the direction of the U.S. war on terror, he warned German lawmakers that they had no choice but to fight because they, too, are targets.

Dividing the world into two camps—the just and the unjust, the good and the evil—is risky in the turbulent international world where friends and foes are hard to distinguish and where alignments on one global issue dissolve in the face of other issues and allegiances (see photo, p. 621). National interests are bound to conflict at times, even among allies united against a common enemy as threatening as global terrorism. This was illustrated when President Bush warned Russian President Vladimir Putin in May 2002 that the U.S.-Russian strategic partnership depended on Russian willingness to end arms sales to Iran, a terrorist state. "If Iran gets a weapon of mass destruction, deliverable by a missile, that's going to be a problem for all of us, including Russia," Bush said.

Xinhua/Fan Rujun/AP/Wide World

Friends or Foes in the Fraying Alliance against Global Terrorism? September 11 was said to have enabled China and the United States to put aside their differences and ally as friends in the war against terrorism, and in fact their relationship warmed as they began to cooperate for that purpose. However, all great powers have multiple interests, which sometimes conflict and than weaken the ties that bind them. In April 2002, Hu Jintao, China's vice president, made an official visit to the United States to coordinate their partnership in the war on terror. En route, he interrupted his journey to visit Malaysia, where he announced that China "opposes the strong lording it over the weak and the big bullying the small," implying a contrast between U.S. policy and that of China which, he claimed "has long pledged not to seek hegemony." He next visited Iran, which was labeled by the United States as a state sponsor of terrorism, and later (shown here) met with Muammar Qaddafi, the Libyan leader long described by the United States as a sponsor of terror. Politics does make strange bedfellows.

Putting an immediate end to global terrorism is not regarded likely in the near future, by whatever means. Not even U.S. policymakers are optimistic that the war on terrorism can be won quickly and without high risk and causalities. The threat will not vanish soon. As Bush warned, all countries are vulnerable to terrorist groups wielding missiles with chemical, biological, or even nuclear weapons, and this meant that "There can be no lasting security in a world at the mercy of terrorists—for my nation, or for any nation." U.S. Vice President Dick Cheney underlined the danger in May 2002 when he declared that terrorists would strike again in the United States and that "It's not a matter of if, but when." "There will be another terrorist attack. We will not be able to stop it. It's something we all will have to live with," U.S. FBI Director Robert Mueller added. So it remains to be seen if the war on terrorism can ultimately be contained, but at present it is unlikely that the danger of global terrorism will recede.

■ ethnocentrism
a propensity to see one's nationality or state as the center of the world and therefore special, with the result that the values and perspectives of other groups are misunderstood and ridiculed.

■ clash of civilizations
political scientist Samuel Huntington's controversial thesis that in the twenty-first century the globe's major civilizations will conflict with one another, leading to anarchy and warfare similar to that resulting from conflicts between states over the past five hundred years (see p. 165).

■ Fourth World
indigenous people or native ethnic and tribal groups who often live in poverty and deprivation within a state that occupies the land from which they originate (see p. 245).

■ state terrorism
formal assistance, training, and arming of terrorists by a state in order to achieve foreign and domestic policy goals.

■ ethnic cleansing
the extermination of an ethnic minority group by a state, in violation of international law (see p. 242).

■ self-determination
the doctrine that asserts nationalities have the right to determine what political authority will represent and rule them (see p. 35).

4. Will Separatist Conflict within States Lead to Hundreds of New States?

Throughout world history, when distinct cultures have come into contact, either the collisions have sparked communication and a healthy respect for diversity or familiarity has bred contempt. When followers have embraced **ethnocentrism,** the view that their own group's values are inherently superior, animosity and disrespect for differences have been especially characteristic, and persecution and killing have often followed.

Civilizations such as those of both the Western and the Islamic traditions tend to think of themselves ethnocentrically, which is why Samuel Huntington (1996) predicts that a **clash of civilizations** will dominate world politics. Another possibility is the rise of ethnic clashes *within* states between tribes and religions. An epidemic of violent conflicts has erupted already between nationalities whose identity is defined by a shared language, religion, or race that makes their members feel different from others. Most of these have involved the indigenous peoples of the **Fourth World** threatened with **state terrorism** and **ethnic cleansing.** The predictable result is that many civil wars have erupted which threaten to break existing states into many new separate states. East Timor's formal entry in the international community in 2002 as an independent sovereign state following four hundred years of Portuguese colonial rule and another twenty years of brutal occupation by Indonesia is another recent example of the state-formation trend underway. Between 1980 and 1998, more than thirteen new states on average were created *each year* (Enriquez 1999, 40).

Many of the globe's 208 independent countries are made up of many different nationality and ethnic groups, and it is not surprising that a large number of the globe's three- to five-thousand indigenous peoples and ethnic minorities are seeking **self-determination.** Rebellion is especially prevalent in **failing states** where governments have lost the support of the population, can no longer maintain law and order, and have massacred rebelling peoples instead of protecting their human rights. If every major "political and ethnic and religious group" won independence, President Bill Clinton warned in October 1999, "we might have eight hundred countries in the world, [perhaps even] eight thousand."

The dilemma created by the striving for independence around the globe is that it pits important values against one another. Sovereign independence and human rights are treasured, but so are prosperity and peace. How will these values be reconciled, if at all? Would the breakup of states into smaller units be a blessing or a burden to the long-term collective interests of humanity?

5. Will the Great Powers Intervene to Protect Human Rights?

Conflicts within countries are raging throughout the world. Many civilians are the targets of overt oppression and violence by the governments presumably created to preserve law and order in courts and through ballots. Of great concern is whether the moral outrage of the globe's major powers will be sufficient for them to make concerted peacekeeping and peace-making interventions to end **human rights** abuses in those countries where standards of conduct accepted in international law have been blatantly disregarded. Atrocities in many failed states are forcing a mass exodus of more than 20 million refugees each year, and another 80 million **displaced people** have left their homes to seek safety elsewhere within their countries. The global community is being put to a test of its true ideals and its capacity to defend them, at potentially high costs. Will a humanitarian concern for the victims targeted for extermination crystallize into a response? Or will the victims perish in a sea of indifference?

Human rights law now provides unprecedented protection in principle for people everywhere to live in freedom without fear. The traditional legal rule of state sovereignty and its corollary—the **nonintervention norm** prohibiting external interference in the internal affairs of states—has been revised. In September 1999 UN Secretary-General Kofi Annan described well the redefinition when he noted that "States are now widely understood to be instruments at the service of their people, and not vice versa. At the same time . . . the fundamental freedom of each individual, enshrined in the charter of the UN and subsequent international treaties—[has] been enhanced by a renewed and spreading consciousness of individual [human] rights. When we read the charter today, we are more than ever conscious that its aim is to protect individual human beings, not to protect those who abuse them."

Principle is one thing; the reality of human suffering another. Will the great powers in the globalized community back their expressed convictions with action to free humanity from the oppression of mass murder? Can the great powers agree on a **doctrine** for **humanitarian intervention** that defines when it is legitimate to militarily respond to gross violations of "human rights, wherever they take place, and also on ways of deciding what action is necessary, and when, and by whom"? The challenge, Kofi Annan elaborated, is to transcend traditional notions of sovereignty. Those old ideas remain an "obstacle to effective action in humanitarian crises" that still encourages states "to stand idly by while the horror unfolds," instead of taking military action to enforce international human rights law. If the global community truly recognizes that all people have rights that transcend national borders, and defines those human rights as the core of the community's "common global interests," then it will have to answer and act on the essential unresolved questions: "What is the common interest? Who shall define it? Who shall defend it? Under whose authority? And by what means of intervention?" (Annan 1999). True global governance will begin if a consensus can be reached on such monumental questions and the world's commitment to humanitarian action worldwide is then backed by collective action irrespective of region or state.

6. Will Globalization Tie the World Together or Tear It Apart?

Former Soviet President Mikhail Gorbachev observed in 1999, "Politics is being conducted in a terribly clumsy way everywhere." Why does it suddenly appear that the world and the states within it are spinning out of control? One answer is ascribed to **globalization,** a widely accepted socially constructed code word understood as a transforming force that is creating sweeping governance crises in a new age of increasing interdependent complexity. Globalization captures the idea that everyone and everything on the planet is now more closely connected than ever before, but on an institutional foundation that is shaky and unprepared for managing the massive adjustments brought on by accelerating worldwide changes. Most affected and at a loss are the so-called sovereign states, no longer able to exercise control over the economic, political, and

■ **failing states** those governments that are in danger of losing the loyalty of their citizens, who are rebelling against corruption and administrative failure and in the process tearing the country into separate political parts (see p. 429).

■ **human rights** the political rights and civil liberties recognized by the international community as inalienable and valid for individuals in all countries by virtue of their humanity.

■ **displaced people** people involuntarily uprooted from their homes and forced either to flee outside their state or to seek sanctuary within their own countries (see p. 241).

■ **nonintervention norm** a fundamental international legal principle, now being challenged, that traditionally has defined interference by one state in the domestic affairs of another as illegal.

■ **doctrine** a great power's statement of the principles its leaders will follow when making decisions about solutions to anticipated national security problems, such as the conditions under which it will use military power and armed force for political purposes abroad (see p. 209).

■ **humanitarian intervention**
the use of peacekeeping troops by foreign states or international organizations to protect endangered people from gross violations of their human rights and from mass murder and starvation.

■ **globalization**
the integration of states through increasing contact, communication, and trade to create a holistic, single global system in which the process of change increasingly binds people together in a common fate (see p. 21).

■ **sovereignty**
the legal doctrine that states have supreme authority to govern their internal affairs and manage their foreign relations with other states and IGOs.

■ **nationalism**
a mindset glorifying the nationalities of a people living in a state that holds loyalty to the state's national interests as a supreme value (see p. 104).

■ **self-help**
the principle that because in international anarchy all global actors are independent, they must rely on themselves to provide for their security and well-being.

■ **public goods**
shared values from which everyone who has access to them benefits, such as safe drinking water, even if not everyone contributes to their preservation or creation.

environmental problems within their territories. States everywhere are experiencing a sense of lost **sovereignty** as they attempt to cope with the pressures originating outside their borders. Simply put, the communications and technology revolution has sped the flow of information, capital, people, and jobs across state boundaries, and the integration of the globe is forcing a redefinition—of historic proportions—of the role of states within this transformed, interconnected world.

The shrinking of distances and sharing of knowledge and ideas characteristic of a borderless world and common cosmopolitan culture have reduced old feelings of independence, identity, and autonomy and driven many states to surrender some of their sovereignty in order to benefit from collaborative participation in a competitive global marketplace. The message has been heard everywhere: borders and barriers cannot be revived in a nationalistic effort to close off a country in solitary isolation. "Join the world or become irrelevant" is the way Edward Ballador, a former French prime minister, described "the end of **nationalism.**"

Many people feel that UN Secretary-General Boutros Boutros-Ghali was correct when in 1996 he wrote, "Globalization is the world's problem." To be sure, it is not just a threat, but an opportunity as well. When everyone depends on everyone else, they *must* work together. "People are recognizing that if there is a serious problem with the Brazilian economy," British Prime Minister Tony Blair counseled in 1999, "it develops into a serious problem for the British economy or the European economy or the American economy. It is similar with security problems." The challenge of globalization resides primarily in the fact that it reduces states' control over their national future and their capacity to govern, in conjunction with the pressing need to create stronger institutions of international governance to regulate the global system's integrated free market economy. The crisis of complexity makes it imperative that states work together and undertake bold departures from the **self-help** approaches of the past. "The only practical prospect for universal peace [and prosperity] must be more civilization" through globalization, and so to attain this goal "we should strive to create the largest social, economic, and political units possible, ideally one encompassing the whole world" (Keeley 1996). These observers see globalization optimistically as an unstoppable engine for unity and progress. They reason that people who trade have shared interests and fewer incentives to fight; by integrating countries' investments and consumers in the global economy, the capacity for troublemaking and warmaking among countries will be reduced. At the extreme is the Thomas Friedman's (1999b) celebratory view in his best-selling book *The Lexus and the Olive Tree: Understanding Globalization* that globalization is a **public good** to be promoted as a cause for human development because it will ultimately increase the wealth of everyone everywhere. Adds Francis Fukuyama (2002), "The September 11 terrorist attacks on the United States represent a serious detour, but in the end modernization and globalization will remain the central structuring principles of world politics."

There are in actuality serious questions about how future domestic and international problems will be addressed in such a globalized world without organized global governance. There are "many globalizations" operating in a culturally diverse world that affect different peoples differently (Berger and Huntington 2002). How will this complexity be managed? Can it be managed when so many people are not participating in the benefits of globalization and

A Worldwide Integrated Market Today, products made anywhere are available for sale everywhere. Internet access is common worldwide, even in countries such as China that fear the growth of electronic underground journals that circulate information critical of state policies. Here a billboard advertises for a computer company in Shenzen, China. The information age is rapidly making every place more like everyplace else, in part because "Computing power has doubled every eighteen months for the last thirty years. . . . Similarly, growth of the Internet and the World Wide Web has been exponential. Internet traffic doubles every 100 days" (Keohane and Nye 2001b, 28).

are threatened by it and anxious to reverse it? These questions were allegedly uppermost in the 9/11 suicide terrorists' minds, those who sought to overturn their hated symbol of globalization's commercial culture, the United States (Howell 2003). These complaints are symptomatic, too, of the challenge of the minority groups' quest for autonomy from within and of the challenge of NGOs (such as Doctors without Borders and multinational corporations) from outside. Many observers blame globalization for leaders' confusion about how to react to the crisis of globalization's economic and social impact on those not benefiting. "We need to be concerned," Kofi Annan advised in October 2002, "about the gulf between insiders and outsiders in a globalized world . . . where the privileges of the few are painfully apparent to those multitudes who still yearn for liberty and opportunity."

To make globalization a green, clean, and compassionate process for engineering sustainable development for all humanity, a global civil society will require greater global governance to manage a world knit closer together. Globalization may have emasculated the sovereign power of states, but in various respects this same force has strengthened many governments (Pfaff 2000). The question for the future is whether humanity can count on relatively powerless NGOs at the grassroots level seeking through global public policy networks to assume responsibility for engineering human progress. If states do not respond to the challenge, can the world's people expect a new global architecture with accepted supranational global governance and global norms to crystallize? This may be the most important issue facing twenty-first-century world politics.

7. Is Realism Still Realistic and Is Liberalism Still Too Idealistic?

Since the eve of World War II, leaders and scholars alike have constructed their thoughts and images almost exclusively from the perspective of realism. Their reliance on realism to explain and predict international developments was understandable. Finding a fertile ground in which to flourish during the conflict-ridden fifty-year period between 1939 and 1989, realism accounted for, better than any other theoretical perspective, the great powers' prevailing lust for power, the appetite for imperial expansion and struggle for hegemony, the all-consuming arms race, and the obsession with military security.

At least until the shattering events of 9/11, and still after it, however, a window opened to expose quite different dimensions of world politics that were previously neglected. The global agenda has shifted as new issues and problems have risen to prominence. "The problem . . . today is not new challengers for hegemony; it is the new challenge of transnational interdependence" (Nye 2001). Welfare, not warfare, is the primary global threat; global warming and trade balances now seem higher on the global agenda than does preventing the use of force by one state against another. As a consequence of these changing issues commanding the world's concern, the realist image of states as unitary rational actors has looked increasingly archaic. In the borderless global village, nongovernmental organizations (NGOs) composed of private citizen groups have flexed their muscles and raised their voices, and they are being heard and are orchestrating changes in people's values. "More and more," observed Espen Barth Eide of the Norwegian Foreign Policy Institute in 1997, "the global agenda is being set by others . . . rather than [by] superpowers and governments."

To a number of theorists, the broadened and transformed global agenda goes beyond what realism can be expected to address accurately. To their minds, realist preoccupations threaten to mask the deeper political, economic, and social challenges in international affairs. Many critics are disturbed by realism's failure to anticipate the democratic revolutions that accompanied the Cold War's end, the voluntary retreat of the Soviet Union, and global change and cooperation generally. "The wisdom [that] calls itself 'realism,'" scolded Harvard University's Stanley Hoffmann (in Friedman 1993), "is utter nonsense today." Perhaps it was this sentiment that prompted Jeffrey Legro and Andrew Moravcsik (1999) to ask, "Is anybody still a realist?" If these critics of realism's receding accuracy and relevance are correct, then pressure will mount for a new theoretical approach that places less emphasis than realism, neorealism, and **neotraditional realism** on conflict in world politics and on military power and self-help to maintain international stability.

What a new theory will or should look like is not presently obvious, as challengers to realism differ in their prescriptions. Yet many agree with the general view that "it is time for a new, more rigorous idealist alternative to realism" (Kober 1990) and that "there are good reasons for examining aspects of the liberal international legacy once again" (Fukuyama 1992a) by giving Woodrow Wilson's liberal vision "the fair test it has never received" (Gaddis 1990; see also McNamara and Blight 2001). A number of scholars and policymakers have advocated a **neoliberal** approach for interpreting world politics and the transformed conditions of globalization. Such a new liberal approach emphasizes the transnational interdependence that drives cooperation in international

■ **neotraditional realism**
a body of recent realist theorizing that departs from neorealism by stressing foreign policy more than international structure and that focuses on the internal influences on states' external behavior instead of the global determinants of states' foreign behavior (see p. 39).

■ **neoliberalism**
a perspective that accounts for the way international institutions promote global change, cooperation, peace, and prosperity through collective reform approaches (see p. 43).

affairs; it attaches importance to global governance, international law, and high ideals such as the promotion and protection of human rights and democracy as methods for reforming international anarchy and weapons proliferation and for creating a world order guided by a shared global consensus about international morality.

This liberal perspective places a greater value on principles than on power, on ideals rather than national self-interest. To the extent that global tensions recede and global harmony and cooperation prevail over warfare, neoliberalism is likely to grow increasingly popular as a way to describe and explain international relations. However, if the world experiences a new arms race and even another war between highly armed adversaries, then liberalism will once again be perceived as too idealistic and optimistic, as it was when World War II began. Should a major war break out between old enemies, such as between India and Pakistan, or if the United States unilaterally follows through with its 2002 plans to attack Iraq, this climate of heightened tension will propel the resurgent popularity of realism and neorealism as theories of international security. That resurgence of realism was already highly evident in the wake of 9/11 and the war against international terrorism, and the interpretation that realism constructs of world affairs is certain to regain many adherents if terrorists use weapons of mass destruction to carry out their deadly goals. Realism accounts for violence and the absence of security better than any rival theoretical perspective focusing on humanity's cooperation in such areas as trade.

In all probability, twenty-first-century world politics will continue to display combinations of both conflict and cooperation, unity and disunity, order and disorder. Should those dual properties simultaneously characterize the future of world politics, a synthesis of the rich insights of both realism and liberalism will be needed to capture the divergent trajectories. A reconstructed theory of world politics that fuses the most useful and reasonable assumptions of neorealist and neotraditional realist theories of international politics with those of neoliberalism may provide the intellectual framework needed to understand and guide policy making in twenty-first-century world politics.

8. Is the World Preparing for the Wrong War?

To preserve peace, one must prepare for war. That remains the classical realist formula for national security. But would states not be wiser to prepare to conquer the conditions that undermine prosperity, freedom, and welfare? "War for survival is the destiny of all species," observes philosopher Martin J. Siegel (1983). "In our case, we are courting suicide [by waging war against one another]. The world powers should declare war against their common enemy—the catastrophic and survival-of-the-fittest forces that destroyed most of the species of life that came before us."

Increasingly, fewer world leaders are succumbing to the single-mindedness of preparing to compete with other states. President François Mitterrand of France warned in 1983 that "together we must urgently find the solutions to the real problems at hand—especially unemployment and underdevelopment. This is the battlefield where the outlines of the year 2000 will be drawn." India's Prime Minister Indira Gandhi predicted that "either nuclear war will annihilate the human race and destroy the earth, thus disposing of any future, or men and women all over must raise their voices for peace and for an urgent attempt to combine the insights of different civilizations with contemporary knowledge. We can survive in peace and goodwill only by viewing the human race as one, and by looking at global problems in their totality." These prescriptions adhere to a fundamental premise, as expressed in 1995 by Martti Ahtisaari, president of Finland: "To deal with the great security challenges of our time, including population growth, the spread of weapons of mass destruction, crime, environmental degradation and ethnic conflicts, we must resolutely adopt new methods of managing change and building global security."

These rhetorical positions doubtless reflect the problems and self-interests the leaders faced at home and abroad. Nonetheless, they reveal a minority view. The war of people against people goes on. Human security remains precarious, as a large percentage of humanity faces famine, poverty, and a denial of their basic human rights; millions are threatened by genocide and terrorism sponsored by their own governments. Humankind may consequently self-destruct, not because it lacks opportunities, but because of its collective inability to see and to seize them. "Perhaps we will destroy ourselves. Perhaps the common enemy within us will be too strong for us to recognize and overcome," the eminent astronomer Carl Sagan (1988) lamented. "But," he continued, "I have hope. . . . Is it possible that we humans are at last coming to our senses and beginning to work together on behalf of the species and the planet?"

9. Is This the "End of History"?

To many observers, the history of world affairs is the struggle between tyranny and liberty. The contest has taken various forms since antiquity: between kings and mass publics; despotism and democracy; ideological principle and pragmatic politics. Labels are misleading and sometimes dangerous. However, they form the vocabulary of diplomacy and inform theoretical discussion of governance and statecraft. History, in this image, is a battle for hearts and minds. It is an ideological contest for the allegiance of humankind to a particular form of political, social, and economic organization.

With the defeat of fascism in World War II and the collapse of the international communist movement a generation later, it has become fashionable to argue that we have witnessed the end of a historic contest of epic proportions— and thus the triumph of liberalism and what Francis Fukuyama called the **end of history**:

> The twentieth century saw the developed world descend into a paroxysm of ideological violence, as liberalism contended first with the remnants of absolutism, then bolshevism and fascism, and finally an updated Marxism that threatened to lead to the ultimate apocalypse of nuclear war. But the [twentieth] century that began full of self-confidence in the ultimate triumph of Western liberal democracy seems at its close to be returning full circle to where it started: . . . to the unabashed victory of economic and political liberalism. (Fukuyama 1989, 3; see also Fukuyama 1999b)

The abrupt repudiation of communism has raised expectations that history has indeed "ended," in the sense that liberal democratic capitalism has triumphed throughout most of the world. Liberals, inspired by the belief that "lib-

■ **end of history**
the thesis that the philosophy of economic and political liberalism has triumphed throughout the world, ending the contest between market democracies and centrally planned governance (see p. 71).

eral democracy and a market-oriented economic order are the only viable options for modern societies" (Fukuyama 1999b), are heartened by the doubling since the mid–1980s of the number of countries practicing multiparty elections and capitalism at home and in foreign trade. World order, they believe, can best be created by free governments practicing free trade. As Woodrow Wilson argued, making the world "safe for democracy" would make the world itself safe. From this liberal perspective, the diffusion of democratic capitalism bodes well for the future of world politics.

A less-reassuring possibility is that history has not "ended" and that the battle between totalitarian and democratic governance is not truly over. There remain many democracies ruled by one-party despots who, although elected, disregard constitutional limits on their power and deny their citizens basic political freedoms and religious and economic human rights. Many governments continue to abuse fundamental civil liberties and freedoms. This persistence of leaders not accountable to the electorate suggests that we may not be witnessing history's end. Like previous turning points in history, tomorrow may signal history's resumption: the return to the ageless search for barriers against the resurgence of tyranny, nationalism, and terrorism and war. Especially to followers of realpolitik, the most salient feature of world politics—the relentless competitive struggle for power under international anarchy—is permanent, and they take as evidence the continuing efforts of terrorist movements to use violence against such despised targets as the United States and the republic for which it stands. There is not assurance that the global community has moved beyond tyranny or interstate competition and militarized conflict. As former Soviet President Mikhail Gorbachev warned in 1992, "A major international effort will be needed to render irreversible the shift in favor of a democratic world—and democratic for the whole of humanity, not just half of it."

10. Is There a Reordered Global Agenda?

The paradox of contemporary world politics is that a world liberated from the paralyzing grip of the Cold War must now face a series of challenges every bit as threatening and as potentially unmanageable. Globalization has simultaneously enlarged the responsibilities and expanded the issues to be confronted. In a prosperous and stable period of history, when confidence in peace and economic growth was high, and his administration was still in office, U.S. President Bill Clinton found it necessary to warn that "Profound and powerful forces are shaking and remaking our world. And the urgent question of our time is whether we can make change our friend and not our enemy."

The changes in recent years have spawned transnational threats to world order, other than the resurgence of nationalism, ethnic conflict, failed states, and separatist revolts. These include acid rain, **AIDS** and other contagious diseases, drug trafficking, international organized crime, ozone depletion, climate change, obstacles to gender equality, energy and food insecurity, desertification and deforestation, financial crises and collapsing economies, and neomercantile trade protectionism.

The potential impact of these additional threats is formidable, as emerging trends suggest that nonmilitary dangers will multiply alongside the continuing threat of arms and armed conflicts in civil wars, as well as interstate wars in particular regions and terrorism almost any place and at any time in the world. As distance and borders cease to be barriers in the global village, low politics is becoming high politics; conversely, as weapons cut across state boundaries and reduce human security, whenever bombs and bullets are fired, killing people and degrading the environment, high politics has become low politics. Accordingly, the distinction between **high politics** (war and peace) and **low politics** (economic and other issues of human welfare) may disappear. How will humanity set priorities for action in a system crowded with so many interrelated issues and problems, all of which require attention if peace and prosperity with justice is to prevail?

■ **high politics**
geostrategic issues of national and international security that pertain to matters of war and peace (see p. 19).

■ **low politics**
the category of global issues related to the economic, social, demographic, and environmental aspects of relations between governments and people (see p. 19).

A NEW WORLD ORDER OR NEW WORLD DISORDER?

Previously established patterns and relationships have been obliterated. Something revolutionary, not simply new, appears to be unfolding. This book has focused on global change. It has identified the most important changes under way that are potentially leading to transformations in world politics. Change, as we have seen, can be abrupt or slow. It moves constantly, but at its own pace, and history reminds us that the evolutionary direction of global change is uncertain. Many trends are unfolding at the same time, and their impact in combination can move the world along an unexpected trajectory. In addition, trends can reverse themselves, and each trend that moves forward advances at its own rate. Some trends move incredibly slowly in an evolutionary process that can only result in dramatic transformations over many centuries, where others exhibit short bursts of rapid change, interrupted by long periods of stasis or continuity. Many examples of reversible, interrupted, and constant trends exist, as you have learned in this book's survey. It is in their mix that the future will be shaped.

From the early part of the twenty-first century, it now appears that the collective impact of the divergent trends under way is signaling a major transformation in world politics. Yet, juxtaposed against the revolutionary is the persistent—the durability of accepted rituals, existing rules, established institutions, and entrenched customs that resist the pull of the momentous recent changes in world politics. Persistence and change coexist uneasily, and it is this mixture that makes the future so uncertain. The twin forces of integration and disintegration, continuity and change, create a mood of both confidence and disorientation. As Australia's Prime Minister John Howard put it in 1997, "In one sense, you are a remarkably lucky generation, but in another sense you have been born into a period of social and technological change . . . and economic evolution."

The outcomes of two races will determine the difference between the world that is and the world that will be. The first is the race between knowledge and oblivion. Ignorance stands in the way of global progress and justice. Advances in science and technology far outpace resolution of the social and political problems they generate. Building the knowledge to confront these problems may therefore present the ultimate challenge. "The splitting of the atom," Albert

NASA

Picturing Global Destiny Globalization "implies a holistic worldview and a rejection of the traditional realist paradigm. A globalist perspective embraces a much wider range of important internation actors than realism does and addresses a much broader range of issues, as well as expanding the definition of existing concepts such as security" (Sheehan 1996). This view of a globe without borders is captured by this photo taken of the eastern Mediterranean from the Earth-orbiting space shuttle *Columbia*. It pictures an integrated world community, in which humanity shares a common destiny. It also captures the kinds of threats confronting humanity in a globalized world, where problems do not stop at borders. According to scientists studying this photo, the difference in visibility in this panorama suggests that a pollution event near the Black Sea contaminated the atmosphere.

Einstein warned, "has changed everything save our modes of thinking, and thus we drift toward unparalleled catastrophe. Unless there is a fundamental change in [our] attitudes toward one another as well as [our] concept of the future, the world will face unprecedented disaster."

"Knowledge is our destiny," philosopher Jacob Bronowski declared. If the world is to forge a promising future, it must develop more sophisticated knowledge. Sophistication demands that we see the world as a whole, as well as in terms of its individual parts. We must overcome the temptation to picture others according to our images of ourselves and to project onto others our own aims and values. We must discard belief in a simple formula for a better tomorrow and resist single-issue approaches to reform. Toleration of ambiguity, even the pursuit of it, is essential.

The future of world politics also rests on the outcome of a race between states' ability to cooperatively act in concert and their historic tendency to compete and fight. Paraphrasing a line from William Shakespeare's *Julius Caesar*, U.S. National Security Advisor Samuel Berger, noting in 1997 that it was time for the international community to get beyond settling conflicts by force, said, "I come not only to praise the post–Cold War era, but to bury it." Only concerted international cooperation can avert slipping back into military conflicts guided by the belief that "might alone makes right." Because "policymakers have a deep-seated penchant for putting off hard choices as long as possible" (George 2000), the world's political will to implement the reforms necessary to meet global challenges is uncertain.

The future is cloudy, but it is ours to shape. The moving words of President John F. Kennedy thus describe a posture we might well assume: "However close we sometimes seem to that dark and final abyss, let no man of peace and freedom despair. For he does not stand alone. . . . Together we shall save our planet or together we shall perish in its flames. Save it we can, and save it we must, and then shall we earn the eternal thanks of mankind."

KEY TERMS

realism
liberalism
national security
security dilemma
soft power
politics
preemptive war
military necessity
ethnocentrism
clash of civilizations

Fourth World
state terrorism
ethnic cleansing
self-determination
failing states
human rights
displaced people
nonintervention norm
doctrine
humanitarian intervention

globalization
sovereignty
nationalism
self-help
public goods
neotraditional realism
neoliberalism
end of history
high politics
low politics

SUGGESTED READING

Balkin, Jack M. *The Laws of Change*. New York: Pantheon, 2003.

Berger, Peter L., and Samuel P. Huntington, eds. *Many Globalizations: Cultural Diversity in the Contemporary World*. Oxford, Eng.: Oxford University Press, 2002.

Booth, Ken, and Tim Dunne, eds. *Worlds in Collision: Terror at the Future of Global Order*. London: Palgrave, 2002.

Friedman, Thomas L. *Longitudes and Attitudes: Exploring the World after September 11*. New York: Farrar, Straus & Giroux, 2002.

Harrison, Lawrence E., and Samuel P. Huntington, eds. *Culture Matters: How Values Shape Human Progress*. New York: Basic Books, 2000.

Hopkins, Terence K., and Immanuel Wallerstein. *The Age of Transition: Trajectory of the World-System, 1945–2025*. London: Zed Books, 1996.

Kegley, Charles W., Jr., ed. *The New Global Terrorism: Characteristics, Causes, Controls*. Upper Saddle River, N.J.: Prentice Hall, 2003.

Keylor, William. *A World of Nations: The International Order since 1945*. New York: Oxford University Press, 2002

Lewis, Bernard. *What Went Wrong? Western Impact and Middle Eastern Response*. New York: Oxford University Press, 2002.

Mazarr, Michael J. *Global Trends 2005*. London: Palgrave, 1999.

Mills, Nicolas, and Kira Brunner, eds. *The New Killing Fields: Massacre and the Politics of Intervention.* New York: Basic Books, 2003.

Rosecrance, Richard, ed. *The New Great Power Coalition: Toward a World Concert of Nations.* Lanham, Md.: Rowman & Littlefield, 2002.

Sylvester, Christine. *Feminist International Relations: An Unfinished Journey.* New York: Cambridge University Press, 2002.

Volgy, Thomas J., and Alison Bailin. *International Politics and State Strength.* Boulder, Colo.: Lynne Rienner, 2003.

WWW WHERE ON THE WORLD WIDE WEB?

International Futures Programme
http://www1.oecd.org/sge/au/index.htm

The Organization for Economic Cooperation and Development (OECD) has designed a program to help decision makers in government and industry deal with the formidable challenge of assessing the long-term trends that shape our global future. Scan the Web site and read about conferences and projects now under way. Do you think this is a good model for other organizations that strive to understand the changes occurring in the international system? What suggestions can you give?

World Citizen Foundation
http://www.worldcitizen.org/

As a student of international relations, you may ask yourself if there is a better way to organize international relations than the state system. The World Citizen Web site allows you to think about your world citizenship, asking how we, as sovereign world citizens, can collectively govern our world. The World Citizen Foundation believes that the Internet can help serve as a communication tool whereby the citizens of the world can vote on common global issues. Do you believe that one day soon we may be able to vote on world issues like we do national issues? Is it possible to form a world government?

World Future Society
http://www.wfs.org/

The last chapter of *World Politics* asks you to think about future global trends. To help with this task, visit the World Future Society Web site. The World Future Society is a nonprofit educational and scientific organization whose main interest is how social and technological developments are shaping the future. Its Web site is a neutral clearinghouse for ideas about the future. Participate in one or more of the several discussion forums. You can also read quotes offering wisdom on the new millennium. Feel creative? Submit your own quotes to be posted.

INFOTRAC® COLLEGE EDITION

Search for the following articles in the InfoTrac database:

Huntington, Samuel P. "The Clash of Civilizations," *Foreign Affairs* Summer 1993.

Maiti, Prasenjit. "Clash of Civilizations?" *The Humanist* November–December 2001.

Friedman, Thomas. "States of Discord," *Foreign Policy* March 2002.

Strong, Maurice. "Reforming the United Nations," *The Futurist* September 2001.

For more articles, enter:

"war" in the Subject Guide, and then go to subdivision "analysis."

"globalization" in the Subject Guide, and then go to subdivision "evaluation."

"United Nations" in the Subject Guide, and then go to subdivision "forecasts."

REFERENCES

Aaronson, Susan Ariel. (2002) *Taking Trade to the Streets: The Lost History of Public Efforts to Shape Globalization.* Ann Arbor: University of Michigan Press.

Abramowitz, Morton. (2002) "The Bush Team Isn't Coping," *International Herald Tribune* (August 20): 6.

Adelman, Kenneth L., and Norman R. Augustine. (1992) "Defense Conversion," *Foreign Affairs* 71 (Spring): 26–47.

Albright, David. (1993) "A Proliferation Primer," *Bulletin of the Atomic Scientists* 49 (June): 14–23.

Albright, Madeleine. (2000) "Time to Renew Faith in the Nonproliferation Treaty," *International Herald Tribune* (March 7): 8.

Allen, John L. (2002) *Student Atlas of World Politics,* 5th ed. New York: Dushkin/McGraw-Hill.

———. (2001) *Student Atlas World Geography,* 2nd ed. New York: McGraw-Hill.

———. (2000) *Student Atlas of World Politics,* 4th ed. New York: Dushkin/McGraw Hill.

———. (1998) *Student Atlas of World Politics,* 3rd ed. Guilford, Conn.: Dushkin/McGraw-Hill.

Allison, Graham, and Philip Zelikow. (1999) *Essence of Decision: Explaining the Cuban Missile Crisis,* 2nd ed. New York: Longman.

Allison, Graham T. (1971) *Essence of Decision: Explaining the Cuban Missile Crisis.* Boston: Little, Brown.

Al-Sammarrai, Bashir. (1995) "Economic Sanctions against Iraq," pp. 133–139 in David Cortright and George A. Lopez (eds.), *Economic Sanctions.* Boulder, Colo.: Westview Press.

Altman, Lawrence K. (2002) "AIDS Is Called a Security Threat," *International Herald Tribune* (October 2): 1, 10.

Altman, Roger C., and C. Bowman Cutter. (1999) "Global Economy Needs Better Shock Absorbers," *International Herald Tribune* (June 16): 7.

Ambrose, Stephen E. (1995) "The Bomb: It Was More Than Death," *New York Times* (August 5): A15.

Amoore, Louise, et al. (1997) "Overturning 'Globalisation,'" *New Political Economy* 2 (No. 1): 179–195.

Angell, Norman. (1910) *The Great Illusion: A Study of the Relationship of Military Power in Nations to Their Economic and Social Advantage.* London: Weidenfeld & Nicholson.

Annan, Kofi. (1999) "Two Concepts of Sovereignty," *Economist* (September 18): 49–50.

Appleby, R. Scott. (2000) *The Ambivalence of the Sacred: Religion, Violence, and Reconciliation.* Boulder, Colo.: Rowman & Littlefield.

Apter, David E., and Louis W. Goodman (eds.). (1976) *The Multinational Corporation and Social Change.* New York: Praeger.

Ardrey, Robert. (1966) *The Territorial Imperative: A Personal Inquiry into the Animal Origins of Property and Nations.* New York: Atheneum.

Arkin, William M. (1995) "The Pentagon's Blind Ambition," *New York Times* (May 10): A19.

Aronson, Jonathan D. (2001) "The Communications and Internet Revolution," pp. 540–551 in John Baylis and Steve Smith (eds.), *The Globalization of World Politics,* 2nd ed. Oxford: Oxford University Press.

Art, Robert J. (1999) "Geopolitics Updated: The Strategy of Selective Engagement," *International Security* 23 (Winter): 79–113.

Atwood, Brian. (1999) "Trade, Not Aid," *Christian Science Monitor* (July 6): 9.

Auguste, Byron G. (1999) "What's So New about Globalization?," pp. 45–47 in Helen E. Purkitt (ed.), *World Politics 99/00,* 20th ed. Guilford, Conn.: Dushkin/McGraw-Hill.

Avery, Dennis. (1995) "Saving the Planet with Pesticides," pp. 49–82 in Ronald Bailey (ed.), *The True State of the Planet.* New York: Free Press.

Ayoob, Mohammed. (1995) *The Third World Security Predicament.* Boulder, Colo.: Lynne Rienner.

Babai, Don. (2001a) "International Monetary Fund," pp. 412–418 in Joel Krieger (ed.), *The Oxford Companion to Politics of the World,* 2nd ed. New York: Oxford University Press.

Babai, Don. (2001b) "International Political Economy," pp. 420–422 in Joel Krieger, (ed.), *The Oxford Companion to Politics of the World,* 2nd ed. New York: Oxford University Press.

Bagdikian, Ben H. (1992) *The Media Monopoly.* Boston: Beacon Press.

Baker, Raymond W., and Jennifer Nordin. (1999) "A 150-to-1 Ratio Is Far Too Lopsided for Comfort," *International Herald Tribune* (February 5): 6.

Balaam, David N., and Michael Veseth. (1996) *Introduction to International Political Economy.* Upper Saddle River, N.J.: Prentice Hall.

Baldwin, David A. (2000) "The Sanctions Debate and the Logic of Choice," *International Security* 24 (Winter): 80–107.

———. (ed.). (1993) *Neorealism and Neoliberalism: The Contemporary Debate.* New York: Columbia University Press.

———. (1989) *Paradoxes of Power.* New York: Basil Blackwell.

Ball, Nicole. (1991) *Briefing Book on Conventional Arms Transfers.* Boston: Council for a Livable World Education Fund.

Barber, Benjamin R. (1998) "Fantasy of Fear: Huntington and the West versus the Rest," *Harvard International Review* 20 (Winter): 66–71.

———. (1995) *Jihad vs. McWorld.* New York: Random House.

Barbieri, Katherine, and Gerald Schneider. (1999) Globalization and Peace: Assessing New Directions in the Study of Trade and Conflict," *Journal of Peace Research* 36 (July): 387–404.

Barkin, Samuel. (2001) "Resilience of the State," *Harvard International Review* 22 (Winter): 40–46.

Barkun, Michael. (1968) *Law without Sanctions: Order in Primitive Societies and the World Community.* New Haven, Conn.: Yale University Press.

Barnet, Richard J. (1980) *The Lean Years.* New York: Simon & Schuster.

———. (1977) *The Giants: Russia and America.* New York: Simon & Schuster.

Barnet, Richard J., and John Cavanagh. (1994) *Global Dreams: Imperial Corporations and the New World Order.* New York: Simon & Schuster.

Barnet, Richard J., and Ronald E. Müller. (1974) *Global Reach: The Power of the Multinational Corporations.* New York: Simon & Schuster.

Baron, Samuel H., and Carl Pletsch (eds.). (1985) *Introspection in Biography: The Biographer's Quest for Self-Awareness.* Hillsdale, N.J.: Analytic Press.

Bayard, Thomas O., and Kimberly Ann Elliott. (1994) *Reciprocity and Retaliation in U.S. Trade Policy.* Washington, D.C.: Institute for International Economics.

Baylis, John, and Steve Smith (eds.). (2002) *The Globalization of World Politics,* 2nd ed. New York: Oxford University Press.

Beckman, Peter R., and Francine D'Amico (eds.). (1994) *Women, Gender, and World Politics.* Westport, Conn.: Bergin & Garvey.

Beckman, Peter R., et al. (2000) *The Nuclear Predicament: Nuclear Weapons in the Twenty-First Century.* Upper Saddle River, N.J.: Prentice Hall.

Beer, Francis A. (1981) *Peace against War: The Ecology of International Violence.* San Francisco: Freeman.

Beitz, Charles R. (2001) "Human Rights as a Common Concern," *American Political Science Review* 95 (June): 269–282.

Bell, Coral. (1995) "The Future of Power in World Affairs," *Quadrant* 39 (September): 49–56.

Belsie, Laurent. (1999) "Signs of the Food Fight to Come," *Christian Science Monitor* (March 10): 1, 4.

Benedick, Richard Elliot. (1991) "Protecting the Ozone Layer: New Directions in Diplomacy," pp. 112–153 in Jessica Tuchman Mathews (ed.), *Preserving the Global Environment.* New York: Norton.

Bennett, A. Leroy. (1988) *International Organizations,* 4th ed. Englewood Cliffs, N.J.: Prentice Hall.

Berger, Peter L., and Samuel P. Huntington (eds.). (2002) *Many Globalizations: Cultural Diversity in the Contemporary World.* Oxford: Oxford University Press.

———. (2002) *Many Globalizations: Cultural Diversity in the Contemporary World.* Oxford: Oxford University Press.

Bergesen, Albert, and Ronald Schoenberg. (1980) "Long Waves of Colonial Expansion and Contraction, 1415–1969," pp. 231–277 in Albert Bergesen (ed.), *Studies of the Modern World-System.* New York: Academic Press.

Berghahn, Volker R. (1995) *Imperial Germany, 1871–1914.* Providence, R.I.: Berghahn Books.

Bergsten, C. Fred. (2000) "Free Trade Is a Real Boon for the Developing World," *International Herald Tribune* (February 9): 9.

———. (1997) "American Politics, Global Trade," *Economist* 344 (September 27): 23–26.

Bertelsen, Judy S. (ed.). (1977) *Nonstate Nations in International Politics.* New York: Praeger.

Berthelot, Yves. (2001) "The International Financial Architecture—Plans for Reform," *International Social Science Journal* 170 (December): 586–596.

Bhagwati, Jagdish. (1999) *A Stream of Windows: Trade, Immigration, and Democracy.* Cambridge, Mass.: MIT Press.

———. (1993) "The Case for Free Trade," *Scientific American* 269 (November): 41–49.

Bienefeld, Manfred. (1994) "The New World Order: Echoes of a New Imperialism," *Third World Quarterly* 15 (March): 31–48.

Birdsall, Nancy. (2001) "Life Is Unfair: Inequality in the World," pp. 361–374 in Charles W. Kegley, Jr. and Eugene R. Wittkopf (eds.), *The Global Agenda,* 6th ed. Boston: McGraw-Hill.

Blainey, Geoffrey. (1988) *The Causes of War,* 3rd ed. New York: Free Press.

Blanton, Shannon Lindsey. (1999) "Examining the Impact of Arms Transfers on Human Development," *Journal of Third World Studies* 16 (Fall): 75–93.

Blanton, Shannon Lindsey, and Charles W. Kegley, Jr. (1997) "Reconciling U.S. Arms Sales with America's Interests and Ideals," *Futures Research Quarterly* 13 (Spring): 85–101.

Blechman, Barry M. (1995) "The Intervention Dilemma," *Washington Quarterly* 18 (Summer): 63–73.

Blechman, Barry M., and Stephen S. Kaplan, et al. (1978) *Force without War.* Washington, D.C.: Brookings Institution.

Block, Fred L. (1977) *The Origins of International Economic Disorder.* Berkeley: University of California Press.

Blumenthal, W. Michael. (1988) "The World Economy and Technological Change," *Foreign Affairs* 66 (No. 3): 529–550.

Blustein, Paul (1999a) "Currencies in Crisis," *Washington Post National Weekly Edition* (March 1): 6–7.

———. (1999b) "The Downside of an Upside: Last Year's Record Trade Deficit Signals Concern about the Impact of Faltering Economies," *Washington Post National Weekly Edition* (March 17): 19.

Bolton, John R. (2001) "United Nations," pp. 871–873 in Joel Krieger (ed.), *The Oxford Companion to Politics of the World,* 2nd ed. New York: Oxford University Press.

Bonnart, Frederick. (2000) "Europe Has Set Itself a Tough Military Challenge," *International Herald Tribune* (January 13): 8.

Boot, Max. (2000) "Paving the Road to Hell: The Failure of UN Peacekeeping," *Foreign Affairs* 79 (March/April): 143–148.

Borrus, Michael, Steve Weber, John Zysman, and Joseph Willihnganz. (1992) "Mercantilism and Global Security," *National Interest* 29 (Fall): 21–29.

Bostdorff, Denise M. (1993) *The Presidency and the Rhetoric of Foreign Crisis.* Columbia: University of South Carolina Press.

Boswell, Terry. (1989) "Colonial Empires and the Capitalist World-Economy: A Time Series Analysis of Colonization, 1640–1960," *American Sociological Review* 54 (April): 180–196.

Bowring, Philip. (2001) "Thinking at Cross-Purposes about Globalization," *International Herald Tribune* (February 1): 8.

Bozeman, Adda B. (1994) *Politics and Culture in International History.* New Brunswick, N.J.: Transaction.

Bracken, Paul. (1999) *Fire in the East: The Rise of Asian Military Power in the Second Nuclear Age.* New York: HarperCollins, 1999.

Braudel, Fernand. (1973) *The Mediterranean and the Mediterranean World at the Age of Philip II.* New York: Harper.

Brecher, Michael. (1993) *Crises in World Politics: Theory and Reality.* Oxford, Eng.: Pergamon.

Brecher, Michael, and Jonathan Wilkenfeld. (1997) *A Study of Crisis.* Ann Arbor: University of Michigan Press.

Brecke, Peter. (1999) "The Characteristics of Violent Conflict since 1400 A.D.," paper presented at the annual meeting of the International Studies Association, Washington, D.C., February 17–20.

Brierly, James L. (1944) *The Outlook for International Law.* Oxford, Eng.: Clarendon Press.

Broad, Robin, ed. (2002) *Global Backlash: Citizen Initiatives for a Just World Economy.* Lanham Md.: Rowman and Littlefield.

Broder, David. (2002) "Senator Brings Vietnam Experiences to Bear on Iraq," (Columbia, S.C.) *The State* (September 18): A15.

———. (1999) "Global Forces May Change Balance between States and Federal Government," (Columbia, S.C.) *The State* (August 11): A9.

Bronfenbrenner, Urie. (1971) "The Mirror Image in Soviet–American Relations," *Journal of Social Issues* 27 (No. 1): 46–51.

Brooks, Stephen G. (1997) "Dueling Realisms," *International Organization* 51 (Summer): 445–477.

Brown, Justin. (1999a) "Arms Sales: Exporting U.S. Military Edge?" *Christian Science Monitor* (December 2): 2.

———. (1999b) "Fight over Raptor Trims Military's Talons," *Christian Science Monitor* (October 18): 1, 3.

Brown, Lester R. (2002) "Planning for the Eco-economy," *USA Today* (March): 31–35.

———. (1999) "Feeding Nine Billion," pp. 115–132 in Lester R. Brown, et al., *State of the World 1999.* New York: Norton.

———. (1995) *Who Will Feed China? Wake-Up Call for a Small Planet.* New York: Norton.

Brown, Lester R., et al. (2000) *State of the World 2000.* New York: Norton.

———. (1999) *State of the World 1999.* New York: Norton.

———. (1998) *State of the World 1998.* New York: Norton.

Brown, Lester R., and Brian Halweil. (1999) "How Can the World Create Enough Jobs for Everyone?" *International Herald Journal* (September 9): 9.

Brown, Lester R., and Christopher Flavin. (1999) "A New Economy for a New Century," pp. 3–21 in Lester R. Brown, et al., *State of the World 1999.* New York: Norton.

Brown, Lester R., Gary Gardner, and Brian Halweil. (1999) *Beyond Malthus: Nineteen Dimensions of the Population Challenge.* New York: Norton.

Brzezinski, Zbigniew. (1998) "The Grand Chessboard," *Harvard International Review* 20 (Winter): 48–53.

Bueno de Mesquita, Bruce, (1975) "Measuring Systemic Polarity," *Journal of Conflict Resolution* 22 (June): 187–216.

Bueno de Mesquita, Bruce, and David Lalman. (1992) *War and Reason: Domestic and International Imperatives.* New Haven, Conn.: Yale University Press.

Bull, Hedley. (1977) *The Anarchical Society: A Study of Order in World Politics.* New York: Columbia University Press.

Bundy, McGeorge. (1990) "From Cold War to Trusting Peace," Foreign Affairs 69 (No. 1): 197–212.

Burkhart, Ross E., and Michael S. Lewis-Beck. (1994) "Comparative Democracy: The Economic Development Thesis," *American Political Science Review* 88 (December): 903–910.

Butterfield, Herbert. (1944) *The Englishman and His History.* Cambridge University Press.

Buzan, Barry, and Gerald Segal. (1998) *Anticipating the Future.* London: Simon & Schuster.

Cahn, Anne H. (1995) "Does the Defense Industry Really Need Welfare?" *Christian Science Monitor* (May 15): 19.

Caldwell, Dan. (1977) "Bureaucratic Foreign Policy Making," *American Behavioral Scientist* 21 (September–October): 87–110.

Calvocoressi, Peter, Guy Wint, and John Pritchard. (1989) *Total War: The Causes and Courses of the Second World War,* 2nd ed. New York: Pantheon.

Caporaso, James A., and David P. Levine. (1992). *Theories of Political Economy.* New York: Cambridge University Press.

Carment, David. (1993) "The International Dimensions of Ethnic Conflict," *Journal of Peace Research* 30 (May): 137–150.

Carothers, Thomas. (1997) "Democracy without Illusions," *Foreign Affairs* 76 (January/February): 85–99.

Carpenter, Ted Galen. (1991) "The New World Disorder," *Foreign Policy* 84 (Fall): 24–39.

Carr, Barry. "Globalization from Below: Labor Internationalism under NAFTA," *International Social Science Journal* 159 (March 1999): 49–59.

Carr, E. H. (1939) *The Twenty-Years' Crisis, 1919–1939.* London: Macmillan.

Carter, Ashton B. (1990–1991) "Chairman's Note," *International Security* 15 (Winter): 3–4.

Carter, Jimmy. (2000) "Lapsed Disarmament Brings on a Nuclear Crisis," *International Herald Tribune* (February 24): 6.

Cashman, Greg. (2000) *What Causes War?* Boston: Lexington Books.

———. (1993) *What Causes War? An Introduction to Theories of International Conflict.* New York: Lexington Books.

Cassel, Douglass. (2001) "A Framework of Norms," *Harvard International Review* 22 (Winter): 60–75.

Caspary, William R. (1993) "New Psychoanalytic Perspectives on the Causes of War," *Political Psychology* 14 (September): 417–446.

Cassese, Antonio, and Andrew Clapham. (2001) "International Law," pp. 408–411 in Joel Krieger (ed.), *The Oxford Companion to Politics of the World,* 2nd ed. Oxford: Oxford University Press.

Cerny, Philip G. (1994) "The Dynamics of Financial Globalization: Technology, Market Structure, and Policy Response," *Policy Sciences* 287 (No. 4): 319–342.

Chaliand, Gérald, and Jean-Pierre Rageau. (1993) *Strategic Atlas,* 3rd ed. New York: Harper Perennial.

Chan, Steve. (1997) "In Search of Democratic Peace: Problems and Promise," *Mershon International Studies Review* 41 (May): 59–91.

———. (1987) "Military Expenditures and Economic Performance," pp. 29–37 in U.S. Arms Control and Disarmament Agency, *World Military Expenditures and Arms Transfers 1986.* Washington, D.C.: U.S. Government Printing Office.

———. (1984) "Mirror, Mirror on the Wall . . . : Are the Free Countries More Pacific?" *Journal of Conflict Resolution* 28 (December): 617–648.

Checkel, Jeffrey T. (1998) "The Constructivist Turn in International Relations Theory," *World Politics* 50 (January 1998): 324–348.

Chossudovsky, Michel. (1997) *The Globalisation of Poverty: Impacts of IMF and World Bank Reforms.* London: Zed Books.

Chubin, Shahram. (1998) "Southern Perspectives on World Order," pp. 208–220 in Charles W. Kegley, Jr. and Eugene R. Wittkopf (eds.), *The Global Agenda,* 5th ed. New York: McGraw-Hill.

Cirincione, Joseph. (2000a) "The Asian Nuclear Reaction Chain," *Foreign Policy* 118 (Spring): 120–136.

———. (2000b) "The Assault on Arms Control," *Bulletin of the Atomic Scientists* 56 (January/February): 32–37.

Clad, James C. (1994) "Slowing the Wave," *Foreign Policy* 95 (Summer): 139–150.

Clancy, Tom, and Russell Seitz. (1991–1992) "Five Minutes Past Midnight—and Welcome to the New Age of Proliferation," *National Interest* 26 (Winter): 3–17.

Clapham, Andrew. (2001) "Human Rights," pp. 368–370 in Joel Krieger (ed.), *The Oxford Companion to Politics of the World,* 2nd ed. New York: Oxford University Press.

Claude, Inis L., Jr. (1989) "The Balance of Power Revisited," *Review of International Studies* 15 (January): 77–85.

———. (1988) *States and the Global System: Politics, Law, and Organization.* New York: St. Martin's Press.

———. (1971) *Swords into Plowshares,* 4th ed. New York: Random House.

———. (1967) *The Changing United Nations.* New York: Random House.

———. (1962) *Power and International Relations.* New York: Random House.

Clausewitz, Karl von. (1976 [1832]) *On War.* Princeton, N.J.: Princeton University Press.

Clegg, Liz. (1999) "NGOs Take Aim," *Bulletin of the Atomic Scientists* 52 (January/February): 49–52.

Clyburn, James E. (2001) "Global Action on TB Needed," *The State* (Columbia, S.C.) (March 24): A9.

Cobb, Roger, and Charles Elder. (1970) *International Community.* New York: Harcourt, Brace & World.

Cockburn, Andrew. (1995) "A U.S. Military Porkfest Fattens Contractors," *International Herald Tribune* (October 5): 9.

Cohen, Benjamin J. (2002) *The Geography of Money.* Ithaca, N.Y.: Cornell University Press.

———. (2000) *The Geography of Money.* Ithaca, N.Y.: Cornell University Press.

———. (1996) "Phoenix Risen: The Resurrection of Global Finance," *World Politics* 48 (January): 268–296.

———. (1973) *The Question of Imperialism.* New York: Basic Books.

Cohen, Eliot A. (1998) "A Revolution in Warfare: The Changing Face of Force," pp. 34–46 in Charles W. Kegley, Jr. and Eugene R. Wittkopf (eds.), *The Global Agenda,* 4th ed. New York: McGraw-Hill.

———. (1995) "The Future of Military Power: The Continuing Utility of Force," pp. 35–43 in Charles W. Kegley, Jr. and Eugene R. Wittkopf (eds.), *The Global Agenda,* 4th ed. New York: McGraw-Hill.

Cohen, Joel E. (1998) "How Many People Can the Earth Support?" *New York Review of Books* 45 (October 8): 29–31.

———. (1995) *How Many People Can the Earth Support?* New York: Norton.

Cohen, Roger. (2000) "A European Identity: Nation-State Losing Ground," *New York Times* (January 14): A3.

———. (1999) "Europe Seeks a New Parity: Dependence on U.S. Grows Uncomfortable," *New York Times* (June 15): A1, A14.

Commager, Henry Steele. (1983) "Misconceptions Governing American Foreign Policy," pp. 510–517 in Charles W. Kegley, Jr. and Eugene R. Wittkopf (eds.), *Perspectives on American Foreign Policy.* New York: St. Martin's Press.

Commission on Transnational Corporations. (1991) "Recent Developments Related to Transnational Corporations and International Economic Relations," UN Doc. E/E.10/1991/2, United Nations Economic and Social Council.

Conger, Lucy. (1999) "A Fourth Way? The Latin American Alternative to Neoliberalism," pp. 197–201 in Robert M. Jackson (ed.), *Global Issues 1999/00.* Guilford, Conn.: Dushkin/McGraw-Hill.

Connelly, Matthew, and Paul Kennedy. (1994) "Must It Be the Rest against the West?" *Atlantic Monthly* (December): 61–84.

Constable, Pamela. (1999). "India's Clock Just Keeps on Ticking," *Washington Post Weekly Edition* (August 30): 16.

Copeland, Dale C. (2000) "The Constructivist Challenge to Structural Realism," *International Security* 25 (Fall): 187–212.

Coplin, William D. (1971) *Introduction to International Politics.* Chicago: Markham.

———. (1966) *The Functions of International Law.* Chicago: Rand McNally.

———. (1965) "International Law and Assumptions about the State System," *World Politics* 17 (July): 615–634.

Cortright, David, and George A. Lopez, eds. (2002) *Smart Sanctions: Targeting Economic Statecraft.* Lanham, Md.: Rowman and LittleField.

Cortright, David, and George A. Lopez. (1995) "The Sanctions Era: An Alternative to Military Intervention," *Fletcher Forum of World Affairs* 19 (May): 65–85.

Coser, Lewis. (1956) *The Functions of Social Conflict.* London: Routledge & Kegan Paul.

CQ Press. (2001) *Global Issues.* Washington, D.C.: CQ Press.

Craig, Gordon A., and Alexander L. George. (1990) *Force and Statecraft,* 2nd ed. New York: Oxford University Press.

Crenshaw, Martha. (2003) "The Causes of Terrorism," pp. 92–105 in Charles W. Kegley, Jr. (ed.), *The New Global Terrorism.* Upper Saddle River, N.J.: Prentice Hall.

Crook, Clive. (1997) "The Future of the State," *Economist* 344 (September 20): 5–20.

Crossette, Barbara. (2000) "The UN's Unhappy Lot: Perilous Police Duties Multiplying," *New York Times* (February 23): A3.

———. (1999) "The Internet Changes Dictatorship's Rules," *New York Times* (August 1): Section 4, 1.

———. (1995) "The Second Sex in the Third World," *New York Times* (September 10): E1, E3.

Crump, Andy. (1998) *The A to Z of World Development.* Oxford, Eng.: New Internationalist Publications.

Curtis, Bronwyn. (1998) "What Asia Could Learn from Europe," *New York Times* (January 25): A12.

Daalder, Ivo H., and James M. Lindsay. (2002) "Nasty, Brutish and Long: America's War on Terrorism," pp. 74–79 in Helen Purkitt (ed.), *World Politics 02/03.* Guiford, Colo.: McGraw-Hill Dushkin.

Dahrendorf, Ralf. (1999) "The Third Way and Liberty," *Foreign Affairs* 78 (September/October): 13–17.

Dai, Xinyuan. (2002) "Political Regimes and International Trade," *American Political Science Review* 96 (March): 159–169.

D'Amato, Anthony. (1982) "What 'Counts' as Law?" pp. 83–107 in Nicholas Greenwood Onuf (ed.), *Law-Making in the Global Community.* Durham, N.C.: Carolina Academic Press.

Daly, Herman E. (1993) "The Perils of Free Trade," *Scientific American* 269 (November): 50–57.

Daly, Herman E., and John B. Cobb, Jr. (1989) *For the Common Good.* Boston: Beacon Press.

Daniels, Ted (ed.). (1999) *A Doomsday Reader.* New York: New York University Press.

Davidson, Keay. (1991) "Slashing U.S. Nuclear Arsenal Now Thinkable," *Baton Rouge Sunday Advocate* (November 10): E1.

Davis, Bob. (1994) "Global Paradox: Growth of Trade Binds Nations but It Can Also Spur Separatism," *Wall Street Journal* (June 20): A1, A10.

Davis, Wade. (1999) "Vanishing Cultures," *National Geographic* (August): 62–89.

Deger, Saadet, and Ron Smith. (1983) "Military Expansion and Growth in Less Developed Countries," *Journal of Conflict Resolution* 27 (June): 335–353.

Dehio, Ludwig. (1962) *The Precarious Balance*. New York: Knopf.

Demko, George J., and William B. Wood. (1994) *Reordering the World: Geopolitical Perspectives on the Twenty-First Century*. Boulder, Colo.: Westview Press.

Dentzer, Susan. (1993) "Meet the New Economic Bogeymen," *U.S. News and World Report* (October 18): 67.

DeRivera, Joseph H. (1968) *The Psychological Dimension of Foreign Policy*. Columbus, Ohio: Merrill.

Desch, Michael C. (1998) "Culture Clash," *International Security 23* (Summer): 141–170.

de Tocqueville, Alexis. (1969 [1835]) *Democracy in America*. New York: Doubleday.

Deutsch, Karl W. (1974) *Politics and Government*. Boston: Houghton Mifflin.

———. (1953) "The Growth of Nations: Some Recurrent Patterns in Political and Social Integration," *World Politics 5* (October): 168–195.

Deutsch, Karl W., et al. (2004) *Backgrounds to Community*. Columbia: University of South Carolina Press.

Deutsch, Karl W., et al. (2001) *Backgrounds to Community*. Columbia: University of South Carolina Press.

———. (1957) *Political Community and the North Atlantic Area*. Princeton, N.J.: Princeton University Press.

Deutsch, Karl W., and J. David Singer. (1964) "Multipolar Power Systems and International Stability," *World Politics 16* (April): 390–406.

DeVecchi, Robert, and Arthur C. Helton. (1999) "The United Nations Requires an Upgrade," *International Herald Tribune* (September 20): 16.

Diehl, Paul F., and Gary Goertz. (2000). *War and Peace in International Rivalry*. Ann Arbor: University of Michigan Press.

Dillin, John. (2000) "Which Freedom First: Political or Economic?" *Christian Science Monitor* (February 7): 12–13.

Diouf, Jacques. (2000) "Global Trade Alone Will Not End World Hunger," *International Herald Tribune* (February 18): 8.

DiRenzo, Gordon J. (ed.). (1974) *Personality and Politics*. Garden City, N.Y.: Doubleday-Anchor.

Diwan, Isaac, and Ana Revenga. (1995) "Wages, Inequality, and International Integration," *Finance & Development 32* (September): 7–9.

Dixon, William J. (1994) "Democracy and the Peaceful Settlement of International Conflict," *American Political Science Review 88* (March): 14–32.

Doremus, Paul N., William W. Keller, Louis W. Pauly, and Simon Reich. (1998) *The Myth of the Global Corporation*. Princeton, N.J.: Princeton University Press.

Dorraj, Manochehr. (1995) "Introduction: The Changing Context of Third World Political Economy," pp. 1–13 in Manochehr Dorraj (ed.), *The Changing Political Economy of the Third World*. Boulder, Colo.: Lynne Rienner.

Dos Santos, Theotonio. (1970) "The Structure of Dependence," *American Economic Review 60* (May): 231–236.

Dougherty, James E., and Robert L. Pfaltzgraff, Jr. (2001) *Contending Theories of International Relations*, 5th ed. New York: Longman.

Dower, John W. (1999) *Embracing Defeat: Japan in the Wake of World War II*. New York: Norton.

Downs, George W. (ed.). (1994) *Collective Security beyond the Cold War*. Ann Arbor: University of Michigan Press.

Doyle, Michael W. (1997) *Ways of War and Peace*. New York: Norton.

———. (1995) "Liberalism and World Politics Revisited," pp. 83–106 in Charles W. Kegley, Jr. (ed.), *Controversies in International Relations Theory: Realism and the Neoliberal Challenge*. New York: St. Martin's Press.

Doyle, Michael W., and G. John Ikenberry (eds.). (1997) *New Thinking in International Relations Theory*. Boulder, Colo.: Westview Press.

Drezner, Daniel W. (2002) "Bottom Feeders," pp. 44–49 in Robert J. Griffiths (ed.), *Developing World 02/02*. Guilford, Conn.: Dushkin/McGraw-Hill.

Drozdiak, William. (2001) "Protectionism in the Global Age," *Washington Post National Weekly* (May 21–27): 17.

———. (1999) "Germany Shifts Its Focus Eastward," *International Herald Tribune* (September 11–12): 1, 4.

Drucker, Peter. (2001) "A Survey of the Near Future," *Economist* (November 3): 3–19.

———. (1997) "The Global Economy and the Nation-State," *Foreign Affairs 76* (October): 159–171.

Dulles, John Foster. (1939) *War, Peace, and Change*. New York: Harper.

Dunn, Seth. (1999) "Cut Back on the Global Use of Coal," *International Herald Tribune* (August 30): 8.

Dupont, Alan. (2002) "Sept. 11 Aftermath: The World Does Seem to Have Changed," *International Herald Tribune* (August 6): 6.

Durbin, Andrea C. (1995) "Trade and the Environment," *Environment 37* (September): 16–20, 37–41.

Durning, Alan Thein. (1993) "Supporting Indigenous Peoples," pp. 80–100 in Lester R. Brown, et al., *State of the World 1993*. New York: Norton.

Dworkin, Ronald. (2001) *Sovereign Virtue*. Cambridge, Mass.: Harvard University Press.

Dyson, Freeman. (1997) *Imagined Worlds*. Cambridge, Mass.: Harvard University Press.

Eakin, Emily. (2002) "Pax Americana: The Case for American Empire," (Columbia, S.C.) *The State* (April 7): D1, D5.

Easterbrook, Gregg. (2002) "Safe Deposit: The Case for Foreign Aid," *New Republic*. (July 29): 16–20.

Easton, David. (1969) "The New Revolution in Political Science," *American Political Science Review 63* (December): 1051–1061.

Easton, Stewart C. (1964) *The Rise and Fall of Western Colonialism*. New York: Praeger.

Eberstadt, Nicholas. (2001) "The Population Implosion," *Foreign Policy 123* (March–April): 42–53.

———. (1995) "Population, Food, and Income: Global Trends in the Twentieth Century," pp. 7–47 in Ronald Bailey (ed.), *The True State of the Planet*. New York: Free Press.

Economist. (2002) *Pocket World in Figures*. London: Profile Books.

———. (1999a) *Pocket World in Figures, 2000*. London: Profile Books.

———. (1999b) *The World in 2000*. London: *Economist*.

Edwards, Stephen R. (1995) "Conserving Biodiversity: Resources for Our Future," pp. 212–265 in Ronald Bailey (ed.), *The True State of the Planet*. New York: Free Press.

Eichengreen, Barry. (2000) "Hegemonic Stability Theories of the International Monetary System," pp. 220–244 in Jeffrey A. Frieden and David A. Lake (eds.), *International Political Economy*. Boston: Bedford/St. Martin's.

Eisendrath, Craig, Melvin A. Goodman, and Gerald E. Marsh. (2001) *The Phantom Defense: America's Pursuit of the Star Wars Illusion*. Westport, Conn.: Greenwood.

Eizenstat, Stuart. (1999) "Learning to Steer the Forces of Globalization," *International Herald Tribune* (January 22): 6.

Elliott, Kimberly Ann. (1998) "The Sanctions Glass: Half Full or Completely Empty?" *International Security 23* (Summer): 50–65.

———. (1993) "Sanctions: A Look at the Record," *Bulletin of the Atomic Scientists* 49 (November): 32–35.

Elliott, Michael. (1998) "A Second Federal Democratic Superpower Soon," *International Herald Tribune* (November 24): 8.

Emerson, Sarah A. (1997) "Resource Plenty: Why Fears of an Oil Crisis Are Misinformed," *Harvard International Review* 19 (Summer): 12–15, 64.

Emmanuel, Arghiri. (1972) *Unequal Exchange: An Essay on the Imperialism of Trade.* New York: Monthly Review Press.

Emmott, Bill. (2002) "Present at the Creation: A Survey of America's World Role," *Economist* (June 29): 1–34.

Enloe, Cynthia H. (2001) "Gender and Politics," pp. 311–315 in Joel Krieger (ed.), *The Oxford Companion to Politics of the World,* 2nd ed. New York: Oxford University Press.

———.(2000) *Maneuvers: The International Politics of Militarizing Women's Lives.* Berkeley: University of California Press.

———. (1993) *The Morning After: Sexual Politics at the End of the Cold War.* Berkeley: University of California Press.

Enriquez, Juan. (1999) "Too Many Flags?" *Foreign Policy* 116 (Fall): 30–50.

Esbobar, Arturo. (2000) "The Invention of Development," pp. 93–96 in Robert M. Jackson (ed.), *Global Issues 00/01,* 16th ed. Guilford, Conn.: Dushkin/McGraw-Hill.

Etheredge, Lloyd S. (1999) "The Internet and World Politics," paper presented to the Columbia University Seminar on Human Rights, New York, May 10.

Etzioni, Amital. (1968) "Toward a Sociological Theory of Peace," pp. 403–428 in Leon Bramson and George W. Goethals (eds.), *War.* New York: Basic Books.

Evans, Gareth. (1995) "A Struggling UN Must Now Appreciate the Art of the Possible," *International Herald Tribune* (October 7–8): 8.

Evans, Gareth (ed.). (1998) *Human Rights Fifty Years On.* New York: Manchester University Press.

Evans, Tony. (1997) *What a Way to Live!* Dallas, Tex.: Word Publishing.

Falk, Richard A. (2003) "The Aftermath of 9/11 and the Search for Limits: In Defense of Just War Thinking," pp. 216–222 in Charles W. Kegley, Jr. (ed.), *The New Global Terrorism.* Upper Saddle River, N.J.: Prentice Hall.

———. (2001a) "The New Interventionism and the Third World," pp. 189–198 in Charles W. Kegley, Jr. and Eugene R. Wittkopf (eds.), *The Global Agenda,* 6th ed. Boston: McGraw-Hill.

———. (2001a) "The New Interventionism and the Third World," pp. 189–202 in Charles W. Kegley, Jr. and Eugene R. Wittkopf (eds.), *The Global Agenda.* Boston: McGraw-Hill.

———. (2001b) "Sovereignty," pp. 788–791 in Joel Krieger, ed., *The Oxford Companion to Politics of the World.* 2nd ed. New York: Oxford University Press.

———. (1993) "Sovereignty," pp. 851–854 in Joel Krieger (ed.), *The Oxford Companion to Politics of the World.* New York: Oxford University Press.

———. (1970) *The Status of Law in International Society.* Princeton, N.J.: Princeton University Press.

———. (1965) "World Law and Human Conflict," pp. 227–249 in Elton B. McNeil (ed.), *The Nature of Human Conflict.* Englewood Cliffs, N.J.: Prentice Hall.

———. (1964) *The Role of Domestic Courts in the International Legal Order.* Syracuse, N.Y.: Syracuse University Press.

Falk, Richard, and Andrew Strauss. (2001) "Toward Global Parliament," *Foreign Affairs* 80 (January/February): 212–218.

———. (1999) "Globalization Needs a Dose of Democracy," *International Herald Tribune* (October 5): 8.

Falkenheim, Peggy L. (1987) "Post-Afghanistan Sanctions," pp. 105–130 in David Leyton-Brown (ed.), *The Utility of International Economic Sanctions.* New York: St. Martin's Press.

Fedarko, Kevin. (1995) "Louder Than Words," *Time* (September 11): 49–59.

Ferencz, Benjamin B., and Ken Keyes, Jr. (1991) *Planet-Hood.* Coos Bay, Ore.: Love Line Books.

Ferguson, Niall. (2001) *The Cash Nexus.* New York: Basic Books.

———. (1999) *The Pity of War.* New York: Basic Books.

Festinger, Leon. (1957) *A Theory of Cognitive Dissonance.* Evanston, Ill.: Row, Peterson.

Fetter, Steve. (1991) "Ballistic Missiles and Weapons of Mass Destruction: What Is the Threat? What Should Be Done?" *International Security* 16 (Summer): 5–42.

Fieldhouse, D. K. (1973) *Economics and Empire, 1830–1914.* Ithaca, N.Y.: Cornell University Press.

Fields, Gary S. (2001) *Distribution and Development: A New Look at the Developing World.* Cambridge, Mass.: MIT Press.

Finnegan, William. (2002) "Leasing the Rain," *The New Yorker* (April 18): 43–53.

Fitzgerald, Frances. (2000) *Way Out There in the Blue: Reagan, Star Wars, and the End of the Cold War.* New York: Simon & Schuster.

Flanagan, Stephen J., Ellen L. Frost, and Richard Kugler. (2001) *Challenges of the Global Century.* Washington, D.C.: Institute for National Strategic Studies, National Defense University.

Flavin, Christopher, and Seth Dunn. (1999) "Reinventing the Energy System," pp. 23–40 in Lester R. Brown, et al., *State of the World 1999.* New York: Norton.

Førland, Tor Egil. (1993) "The History of Economic Warfare: International Law, Effectiveness, Strategies," *Journal of Peace Research* 30 (May): 151–162.

Forsythe, David. (1997) "The International Court of Justice at Fifty," pp. 385–405 in A. S. Miller et al. (eds.), *The International Court of Justice.* Amsterdam: Klumer Law International.

Francis, David R. (1999) "A Richer World—But Poorer Too," *Christian Science Monitor* (May 4): 1, 8.

———. (1997) "Welcome Mat Now Offered Foreign Firms," *Christian Science Monitor* (May 28): 1, 8–9.

Francis, Emerich K. (1976) *Interethnic Relations.* New York: Elsevier.

Franck, Thomas M. (2001) "Are Human Rights Universal?" *Foreign Affairs* 80 (January/February): 191–204.

Frank, Andre Gunder. (1969) *Latin America: Underdevelopment or Revolution.* New York: Monthly Review Press.

Freeman, Orville L. (1990) "Meeting the Needs of the Coming Decade: Agriculture vs. the Environment," *Futurist* 24 (November–December): 15–20.

French, Hillary. (2000) *Vanishing Borders: Protecting the Planet in the Age of Globalization.* Washington, D.C.: Worldwatch Institute.

French, Hilary F. (1994) "Can the Environment Survive Industrial Demands?" *USA Today* 122 (January): 66–69.

French, Howard W. (2002) "Japan Considering Nuclear Weapons," *New York Times* (June 9): A12.

Freud, Sigmund. (1968) "Why War," pp. 71–80 in Leon Bramson and George W. Goethals (eds.), *War.* New York: Basic Books.

Fried, John H. E. (1971) "International Law—Neither Orphan nor Harlot, Neither Jailer nor Never-Never Land," pp. 124–176 in Karl W. Deutsch and Stanley Hoffmann (eds.), *The Relevance of International Law.* Garden City, N.Y.: Doubleday-Anchor.

Frieden, Jeffrey A. (2001) "International Debt," pp. 404–406 in Joel Krieger (ed.), *The Oxford Companion to Politics of the World,* 2nd ed. New York: Oxford University Press.

Friedheim, Robert L. (1965) "The 'Satisfied' and 'Dissatisfied' States Negotiate International Law," *World Politics* 18 (October): 20–41.

Friedman, Thomas L. (2001) "Love It or Hate It, but the World Needs America," *International Herald Tribune* (June 16–17): 6.

———. (2000) "Corporations on Steroids," (Columbia, S.C.) *The State* (February 8): A9.

———. (1999a) "America's Technological Revolution," *International Herald Journal* (August 24): 11.

———. (1999b) *The Lexus and the Olive Tree: Understanding Globalization.* New York: Farrar, Straus, Giroux.

———. (1996) "Answers Needed to Globalization Dissent," *Houston Chronicle* (February 8): 30.

———. (1993) "Friends like Russia Make Diplomacy a Mess," *New York Times* (March 28): E5.

Fukuyama, Francis. (2002) "The West May Be Cracking," *International Herald Tribune* (August 9): 4.

———. (1999a) *The Great Disruption: Human Nature and the Reconstitution of Social Order.* New York: Free Press.

———. (1999b) "Second Thoughts: The Last Man in a Bottle," *National Interest* 56 (Summer): 16–33.

———. (1992a) "The Beginning of Foreign Policy," *New Republic* (August 17 and 24): 24–32.

———. (1992b) *The End of History and the Last Man.* New York: Free Press.

———. (1989) "The End of History?" *National Interest* 16 (Summer): 3–16.

Fuller, Graham E. (1995) "The Next Ideology," *Foreign Policy* 98 (Spring): 145–158.

———. (1991–1992) "The Breaking of Nations—and the Threat to Ours," *National Interest* 26 (Winter): 14–21.

Gaddis, John Lewis. (1997) *We Now Know: Rethinking Cold War History.* New York: Oxford University Press.

———. (1991) "Great Illusions, the Long Peace, and the Future of the International System," pp. 25–55 in Charles W. Kegley, Jr. (ed.), *The Long Postwar Peace.* New York: HarperCollins.

———. (1990) "Coping with Victory," *Atlantic Monthly* (May): 49–60.

———. (1983) "Containment: Its Past and Future," pp. 16–31 in Charles W. Kegley, Jr. and Eugene R. Wittkopf (eds.), *Perspectives on American Foreign Policy.* New York: St. Martin's Press.

Galtung, Johan. (1969) "Violence, Peace, and Peace Research," *Journal of Peace Research* 6 (No. 3): 167–191.

Gardels, Nathan. (1991) "Two Concepts of Nationalism," *New York Review of Books* 38 (November 21): 19–23.

Garrett, Laurie. (2000) *The Coming Plague: Newly Emerging Diseases in a World Out of Balance,* rev. ed. London: Virago.

Garrett, Laurie. (1998) "Runaway Diseases," *Foreign Affairs* 77 (January/February): 139–142.

Garten, Jeffrey A. (1999). "Beware the Weak Links in Our Globalization Chain," *International Herald Tribune* (August 19): 8.

Garwin, Richard L. (2000) "The Wrong Plan," *Bulletin of the Atomic Scientists* 50 (March/April): 36–41.

Gedman, Jeffrey. (1999) "Continental Drift," *New Republic* (June 28): 23–24.

Gelb, Leslie H. (1993) "Tailoring a U.S. Role at the UN," *International Herald Tribune* (January 2–3): 4.

———. (1979) "The Future of Arms Control: A Glass Half Full," *Foreign Policy* 36 (Fall): 21–32.

Gelb, Leslie H., and Morton H. Halperin. (1973) "The Ten Commandments of the Foreign Affairs Bureaucracy," pp. 250–259 in Steven L. Spiegel (ed.), *At Issue.* New York: St. Martin's Press.

Gelber, Harry. (1998) *Sovereignty through Interdependence.* Cambridge, Mass.: Kluwer Law International.

George, Alexander L. (2000) "Strategies for Preventive Diplomacy and Conflict Resolution," *PS: Political Science and Politics* 33 (March): 15–19.

———. (1992) *Forceful Persuasion: Coercive Diplomacy as an Alternative to War.* Washington, D.C.: United States Institute of Peace.

———. (1986) "U.S.–Soviet Global Rivalry: Norms of Competition," *Journal of Peace Research* 23 (September): 247–262.

———. (1972) "The Case for Multiple Advocacy in Making Foreign Policy," *American Political Science Review* 66 (September): 751–785.

German, F. Clifford. (1960) "A Tentative Evaluation of World Power," *Journal of Conflict Resolution* 4 (March): 138–144.

Gibney, Frank, Jr. (1999) "Birth of a Superpower," *Time* (June 7): 40–42.

Gilbert, Alan. (2000) *Must Global Politics Constrain Democracy?* Princeton, N.J.: Princeton University Press.

Gill, Stephen. (1993a) "Group of 7," pp. 369–370 in Joel Krieger (ed.), *The Oxford Companion to Politics of the World.* New York: Oxford University Press.

———. (1993b) "Hegemony," pp. 384–386 in Joel Krieger (ed.), *The Oxford Companion to Politics of the World.* New York: Oxford University Press.

Gilman, Benjamin A., and Sam Gejdenson. (2000) "Preventing Disease: We're All in This Together," *International Herald Tribune* (July 4): 6.

Gilpin, Robert. (2001) "Three Ideologies of Political Economy," pp. 269–286 in Charles W. Kegley, Jr. and Eugene R. Wittkopf (eds.), *The Global Agenda,* 6th ed. Boston: McGraw-Hill.

———. (2000) *The Challenge of Global Capitalism: The World Economy in the Twenty-First Century.* Princeton, N.J.: Princeton University Press.

———. (1987) *The Political Economy of International Relations.* Princeton, N.J: Princeton University Press.

———. (1985) "The Politics of Transnational Economic Relations," pp. 171–194 in Ray Maghroori and Bennett Ramberg (eds.), *Globalism versus Realism: International Relations' Third Debate.* Boulder, Colo.: Westview Press.

———. (1981) *War and Change in World Politics.* Cambridge, Eng.: Cambridge University Press.

———. (1975) *U.S. Power and the Multinational Corporation.* New York: Basic Books.

Glaberson, William. (2001) "U.S. Courts Become Arbiters of Global Rights and Wrongs," *New York Times* (June 21): A1; A20.

Glahn, Gerhard von. (1996) *Law among Nations,* 7th ed. Boston: Allyn & Bacon.

Gleditsch, Kristian S., and Michael D. Ward. (1999) "A Revised List of Independent States since the Congress of Vienna," *International Interactions* 25 (No. 4): 393–413.

Gleditsch, Nils Petter. (1995) "35 Major Wars?" *Journal of Conflict Resolution* 39 (September): 584–587.

Gleditsch, Nils Petter, et al. (2002) "Armed Conflict 1946–2001: A New Dataset," *Journal of Peach Research* 39 (September): 615–637.

Global Trends 2015. (2002) Washington, D.C.: Central Intelligence Agency

Gochman, Charles S., and Zeev Maoz. (1984) "Militarized Interstate Disputes, 1816–1976: Procedures, Patterns, and Insights," *Journal of Conflict Resolution* 28 (December): 585–616.

Goldgeier, James M., and Michael McFaul. (1992) "A Tale of Two Worlds: Core and Periphery in the Post–Cold War Era," *International Organization* 46 (Spring): 467–491.

Goldstein, Joshua. (2002) *War and Gender.* Cambridge: Cambridge University Press.

Goldstein, Joshua S. ed. (1999) *Longman Atlas of War and Peace.* New York: Longman.

———. (1988) *Long Cycles: Prosperity and War in the Modern Age.* New Haven, Conn.: Yale University Press.

Goldstein, Morris. (1995) *The Exchange Rate System and the IMF: A Modest Agenda.* Washington, D.C.: Institute for International Economics.

Gordon, Michael R. (1999) "Russians Firmly Reject U.S. Plan to Reopen ABM Treaty," *New York Times* (October 21): A3.

Gottlieb, Gidon. (1982) "Global Bargaining: The Legal and Diplomatic Framework," pp. 109–130 in Nicholas Greenwood Onuf (ed.), *Law-Making in the Global Community.* Durham, N.C.: Carolina Academic Press.

Gowa, Joanne. (1999) *Ballots and Bullets: The Elusive Democratic Peace.* Princeton, N.J.: Princeton University Press.

Graham, Bradley. (1995) "Revolutionary Warfare: New Technologies Are Transforming the U.S. Military," *Washington Post National Weekly Edition* (March 6–12): 6–7.

Graham, Edward M., and Paul R. Krugman. (1995) *Foreign Direct Investment in the United States.* Washington, D.C.: Institute for International Economics.

Grant, Rebecca, and Kathleen Newland (eds.). (1991) *Gender and International Relations.* Bloomington: Indiana University Press.

Green, Faktuurdatum. (1999) *The Contemporary Law of Armed Conflict.* Manchester, Eng.: Manchester University Press.

Greenberg, David. (2000) "The Empire Strikes Out: Why Star Wars Did Not End the Cold War," *Foreign Affairs* 79 (March/April): 136–142.

Greene, David. (1997) "Economic Scarcity: Forget Geology, Beware Monopoly," *Harvard International Review* 19 (Summer) 16–19, 65.

Greenfield, Meg. (1997) "Back to the Future," *Newsweek* (January 27): 96.

———. (1995) "When the Budget Is Colonized: Cutting a Program Is Like Bombing a Settlement," *Newsweek* (May 22): 78.

Greenstein, Fred I. (1987) *Personality and Politics.* Princeton, N.J.: Princeton University Press.

Grey, Edward. (1925) *Twenty-Five Years, 1892–1916.* New York: Frederick Stokes.

Grieco, Joseph M. (1995) "Anarchy and the Limits of Cooperation: A Realist Critique of the Newest Liberal Institutionalism," pp. 151–171 in Charles W. Kegley, Jr. (ed.), *Controversies in International Relations Theory: Realism and the Neoliberal Challenge.* New York: St. Martin's Press.

Grimmett, Richard F. (2002) *Conventional Arms Transfers to Developing Nations, 1994–2001.* Washington, D.C.: Congressional Research Service.

Grimmett, Richard F. (2001) *Conventional Arms Transfers to Developing Nations, 1993–2000.* Washington, D.C.: Congressional Research Service.

———. (1999) *Conventional Arms Transfers to Developing Nations, 1991–1998.* Washington, D.C.: Congressional Research Service.

Gruber, Lloyd. (2000) *Ruling the World: Power Politics and the Rise of Supranational Institutions.* Princeton, N.J.: Princeton University Press.

Gulick, Edward V. (1999) *The Time Is Now: Strategy and Structure for World Governance.* Lanham, Md.: Lexington Books.

———. (1955) *Europe's Classical Balance of Power.* Ithaca, N.Y.: Cornell University Press.

Gurney, Kevin Robert. (1996) "Saving the Ozone Layer Faster," *Technology Review* 99 (January): 58–59.

Gurr, Ted Robert. (2001) "Managing Conflict in Ethnically Divided Societies: A New Regime Emerges in the 1990s," pp. 173–186 in Charles W. Kegley, Jr. and Eugene R. Wittkopf (eds.), *The Global Agenda,* 6th ed. Boston: McGraw-Hill.

———. (2000) *Peoples versus States: Minorities at Risk in the New Century.* Washington, D.C.: United States Institute of Peace Press.

———. (1998) "Communal Conflicts and Global Security," pp. 197–207 in Charles W. Kegley, Jr. and Eugene R. Wittkopf (eds.), *The Global Agenda,* 5th ed. New York: McGraw-Hill.

———. (1994) "Peoples against States: Ethnopolitical Conflict and the Changing World System," *International Studies Quarterly* 38 (September): 347–377.

———. (1993) *Minorities at Risk: A Global View of Ethnopolitical Conflicts.* Washington, D.C.: United States Institute of Peace Press.

———. (1970) *Why Men Rebel.* Princeton, N.J.: Princeton University Press.

Gurr, Ted Robert, et al. (2002) *Peace and Conflict 2002.* College Park, Md.: Integrated Network for Societal Conflict Research, University of Maryland.

Haas, Ernst B. (1986) *Why We Still Need the United Nations: The Collective Management of International Conflict, 1945–1984.* Berkeley: Institute of International Studies, University of California.

Haas, Ernst B., and Allen S. Whiting. (1956) *Dynamics of International Relations.* New York: McGraw-Hill.

Haas, Peter M., Robert O. Keohane, and Marc A. Levy (eds.). (1993) *Institutions for the Earth: Sources of Effective International Environmental Protection.* Cambridge, Mass.: MIT Press.

Haass, Richard N. (1997) "Sanctioning Madness," *Foreign Affairs* 76 (December): 74–85.

Haffa, Robert P., Jr. (1992) "The Future of Conventional Deterrence," pp. 5–30 in Gary L. Guertner, Robert Haffa, Jr., and George Quester (eds.), *Conventional Forces and the Future of Deterrence.* Carlisle Barracks, Pa.: U.S. Army War College.

Hagan, Joe D. (1993) *Political Opposition and Foreign Policy in Comparative Perspective.* Boulder, Colo.: Lynne Rienner.

Haggard, Stephan, and Beth A. Simmons. (1987) "Theories of International Regimes," *International Organization* 41 (Summer): 491–517.

Hajnal, Peter I. (2000) *The G7/G8 System: Evolution, Role, and Documentation.* Brookfield, Vt.: Ashgate.

Hall, John A. (1993) "Liberalism," pp. 538–542 in Joel Krieger (ed.), *The Oxford Companion to Politics of the World.* Oxford, Eng.: Oxford University Press.

Hallenbeck, Ralph A., and David E. Shaver (eds.). (1991) *On Disarmament.* New York: Praeger.

Halliday, Denis J. (1999) "Iraq and the UN's Weapon of Mass Destruction," *Current History* 98 (February): 65–68.

Halliday, Fred. (2001) *The World at 2000.* New York: Palgrave.

Hammond, Grant T. (1996) "The Difficult Pursuit of Peace," *USA Today* 125 (November): 13.

Handbook of International Economic Statistics 2000. (2001) Langley, Va.: U.S. Central Intelligence Agency.

Handbook of International Economic Statistics 1998 (1999) Langley, Va.: U.S. Central Intelligence Agency.

Hardin, Garrett. (1993) *Living within Limits.* New York: Oxford University Press.

———. (1968) "The Tragedy of the Commons," *Science* 162 (December): 1243–1248.

Hardt, Michael, and Antonio Negri. (2001) "The New Faces in Genoa Want a Different Future," *International Herald Tribune* (July 25): 6.

Harknett, Richard J. (1994) "The Logic of Conventional Deterrence and the End of the Cold War," *Security Studies* 4 (Autumn): 86–114.

Harries, Owen. (1995) "Realism in a New Era," *Quadrant* 39 (April): 11–18.

Hausmann, Richardo. (2002) "Prisoners of Geography," pp. 9–15 in Robert D. Griffiths, (ed.), *Developing World 02/03,* 12th ed. Guilford, Conn.: McGraw-Hill/Dushkin.

Hedges, Chris. (2002) *War Is a Force That Gives Us Meaning.* New York: Public Affairs.

Hehir, J. Bryan. (2002) "The Limits of Loyalty," *Foreign Policy* (September/October): 38–39.

Heilbroner, Robert L. (1991) *An Inquiry into the Human Prospect.* New York: Norton.

Held, David, and Anthony McGrew. (2001) "Globalization," pp. 324–327 in Joel Krieger (ed.), *The Oxford Companion to Politics of the World,* 2nd ed. New York: Oxford University Press.

Held, David, and Anthony McGrew, with David Goldblatt, and Jonathan Perraton. (2001) "Managing the Challenge of Globalization and Institutionalizing Cooperation through Global Governance," pp. 136–148 in Charles W. Kegley, Jr. and Eugene R. Wittkopf (eds.), *The Global Agenda,* 6th ed. Boston: McGraw-Hill.

———. (1999) *Global Transformations: Politics, Economics and Culture.* Stanford, Calif.: Stanford University Press.

Helman, Udi. (1995) "Sustainable Development: Strategies for Reconciling Environment and Economy in the Developing World," *Washington Quarterly* 18 (Autumn): 189–207.

Helms, Jesse. (1999) "An Epidemic of Sanctions? It's Sheer Nonsense," *International Herald Tribune* (December 16): 9.

Helprin, Mark. (1995) "What to Do about Terrorism, Really," *Wall Street Journal* (May 10): A14.

Henderson, Errol A., and Richard Tucker. (1999) "Clear and Present Strangers: The Clash of Civilizations and International Conflict," paper presented at the annual meeting of the American Political Science Association, Atlanta, September 2–5.

Herbert, Bob. (2001) "Global Warming Is Already upon Us," (Columbia, S.C.) *The State* (February 26): A 7.

Heredia, Blanca. (1999) "Prosper or Perish? Development in the Age of Global Capital," pp. 93–97 in Robert M. Jackson (ed.), *Global Issues 1999/00,* 15th ed. Guilford, Conn.: Dushkin/McGraw-Hill.

———. (1997) "Prosper or Perish: Development in the Age of Global Capital," *Current History* 96 (November): 383–388.

Hermann, Charles F. (1988) "New Foreign Policy Problems and Old Bureaucratic Organizations," pp. 248–265 in Charles W. Kegley, Jr. and Eugene R. Wittkopf (eds.), *The Domestic Sources of American Foreign Policy.* New York: St. Martin's Press.

———. (1972) "Some Issues in the Study of International Crisis," pp. 3–17 in Charles F. Hermann (ed.), *International Crises.* New York: Free Press.

Hermann, Charles F., Charles W. Kegley, Jr., and James N. Rosenau (eds.). (1987) *New Directions in the Study of Foreign Policy.* Boston: Allen & Unwin.

Hermann, Margaret G. (1988) "The Role of Leaders and Leadership in the Making of American Foreign Policy," pp. 266–284 in Charles W. Kegley, Jr. and Eugene R. Wittkopf (eds.), *The Domestic Sources of American Foreign Policy.* New York: St. Martin's Press.

———. (1976) "When Leader Personality Will Affect Foreign Policy: Some Propositions," pp. 326–333 in James N. Rosenau (ed.), *In Search of Global Patterns.* New York: Free Press.

Hermann, Margaret G., and Charles W. Kegley, Jr. (2001) "Democracies and Intervention," *Journal of Peace Research* 38 (March): 237–245.

Hermann, Margaret G., and Bengt Sundelius (eds.). (2004) *Comparative Foreign Policy Analysis: Theories and Methods.* Upper Saddle River, N.J.: Prentice Hall.

Herz, John H. (1951) *Political Realism and Political Idealism.* Chicago: University of Chicago Press.

Hiatt, Fred. (1997) "Globalization: Real Benefits, but Also Real Costs for Many," *International Herald Tribune* (June 12): 8.

Higgins, Benjamin, and Jean Downing Higgins. (1979) *Economic Development of a Small Planet.* New York: Norton.

Higgins, Rosalyn. (1994) *Problems and Process: International Law and How We Use It.* Oxford, Eng.: Oxford University Press.

Hilsman, Roger. (1967) *To Move a Nation.* New York: Doubleday.

Hirsh Michael. (1999) "At War with Ourselves," *Harper's* (July): 59–69.

Hoagland, Jim. (1999a) "At Present the Brutal Colonialists Aren't Westerns," *International Herald Tribune* (September 20): 12.

———. (1999b) "Is the Global Economy Widening the Income Gap?" *International Herald Tribune* (April 27): 6.

———. (1996) "Yes, Sanctions Can Be Effective, but You Have to Work at It," *International Herald Tribune* (February 8): 8.

———. (1993a) "A Breakthrough for Clinton Too," *Washington Post National Weekly Edition* (September 20–26): 29.

———. (1993b) "Economic Sanctions Sometimes Do More Harm Than Good," (Columbia, S.C.) *The State* (November 11): A12.

Hobsbawm, Eric. (2002) "War and Peace in the 20th Century," *London Review of Books* 21 (February): 16–18.

Hodges, Michael R., John H. Kirton, and Joseph P. Daniels. (2000) *The G-8's Role in the New Millennium.* Brookfield, Vt.: Ashgate.

Hoebel, E. Adamson. (1961) *The Law of Primitive Man.* Cambridge, Mass.: Harvard University Press.

Hoffman, Eva. (2000) "Wanderers by Choice," *Utne Reader* (July/August): 46–48.

Hoffmann, Stanley. (1998) *World Disorders: Troubled Peace in the Post–Cold War Era.* Lanham, Md.: Rowman & Littlefield.

——. (1992) "To the Editors," *New York Review of Books* (June 24): 59.

——. (1971) "International Law and the Control of Force," pp. 34–66 in Karl W. Deutsch and Stanley Hoffmann (eds.), *The Relevance of International Law.* Garden City, N.Y.: Doubleday-Anchor.

——. (1961) "International Systems and International Law," pp. 205–237 in Klaus Knorr and Sidney Verba (eds.), *The International System.* Princeton, N.J.: Princeton University Press.

Hollingsworth, J. Rogers, and Robert Boyer (eds.). (1997) *Contemporary Capitalism: The Embeddedness of Institutions.* New York: Cambridge University Press.

Holsti, Kalevi J. (2001) "Power, Capability, and Influence in International Politics," pp. 13–25 in Charles W. Kegley, Jr. and Eugene R. Wittkopf (eds.), *The Global Agenda,* 6th ed. Boston: McGraw-Hill.

——. (1996) *The State, War, and the State of War.* New York: Cambridge University Press.

——. (1995) "War, Peace, and the State of the State," *International Political Science Review* 16 (October): 319–339.

——. (1992) *International Politics: A Framework for Analysis,* 6th ed. Englewood Cliffs, N.J.: Prentice Hall.

——. (1991) *Peace and War: Armed Conflicts and International Order, 1648–1989.* Cambridge, Eng.: Cambridge University Press.

——. (1988) *International Politics: A Framework for Analysis,* 5th ed. Englewood Cliffs, N.J.: Prentice Hall.

Holsti, Ole R. (2001) "Models of International Relations: Realist and Neoliberal Perspectives on Conflict and Cooperation," pp. 121–135 in Charles W. Kegley, Jr. and Eugene R. Wittkopf (eds.), *The Global Agenda,* 6th ed. Boston: McGraw-Hill.

——. (1989) "Crisis Decision Making," pp. 8–84 in Philip E. Tetlock, et al. (eds.), *Behavior, Society, and Nuclear War.* New York: Oxford University Press.

Homer-Dixon, Thomas F. (1998) "Environmental Scarcities and Violent Conflict—Global Implications," pp. 465–472 in Charles W. Kegley, Jr. and Eugene R. Wittkopf (eds.), *The Global Agenda,* 5th ed. New York: McGraw-Hill.

Hopf, Ted. (1998) "The Promise of Constructivism in International Relations Theory," *International Security* 23 (Summer): 171–200.

Hopkins, Terence K., and Immanuel Wallerstein, eds. (1996) *The Age of Transitions: Trajectory of World Systems 1945–2025.* London: Zed Books.

Hottelet, Richard C. (1999) "Desertification: Forgotten Threat," *Christian Science Monitor* (December 15): 8.

House, Karen Elliot. (1989) "As Power Is Dispersed among Nations, Need for Leadership Grows," *Wall Street Journal* (February 21): A1, A10.

Howard, Michael E. (1983) *The Causes of War.* Cambridge, Mass.: Harvard University Press.

——. (1978) *War and the Liberal Conscience.* New York: Oxford University Press.

Howell, Llewellyn D. (2003) "Is the New Global Terrorism a Clash of Civilizations?" pp. 173–184 in Charles W. Kegley, Jr. (ed.), *The New Global Terrorism.* Upper Saddle River, N.J.: Prentice Hall.

——. (2000) "Global Warming, Global Warning," *USA Today* 129 (March): 35.

——. (1998) "The Age of Sovereignty Has Come to an End," *USA Today* 127 (September): 23.

——. (1995) "Economic Sanctions as Weapons," *USA Today* 124 (July): 37.

Hufbauer, Gary. (1998) "Foreign Policy on the Cheap," *The Washington Post National Weekly Edition* (July 20–27): 22–23.

——. (1994) "The Futility of Sanctions," *Wall Street Journal* (June 1): A14.

Hufbauer, Gary Clyde, Jeffrey J. Schott, and Kimberly Ann Elliott. (1990) *Economic Sanctions Reconsidered: History and Current Policy,* 2nd ed. Washington, D.C.: Institute for International Economics.

Hughes, Barry B. (2000) *Continuity and Change in World Politics,* 4th ed. Upper Saddle River, N.J.: Prentice Hall.

——. (1999) *International Futures: Choices in the Face of Uncertainty,* 3rd ed. Boulder, Colo.: Westview Press.

Hughes, Emmet John. (1972) *The Living Presidency.* New York: Coward, McGann, & Geoghegan.

Huntington, Samuel P. (2001a) "The Coming Clash of Civilizations or, The West against the Rest," pp. 199–202 in Charles W. Kegley, Jr. and Eugene R. Wittkopf (eds.), *The Global Agenda,* 6th ed. Boston: McGraw-Hill.

——. (2001b) "Migration Flows Are the Central Issue of Our Time," *International Herald Tribune* (February 2): 6.

——. (1999a) "Big Powers Have Little Sway When Rival Civilizations Clash," *International Herald Tribune* (December 17): 10.

——. (1999b) "The Many Faces of the Future," pp. 15–18 in Robert M. Jackson (ed.), *Global Issues 1999/00,* 15th ed. Guilford, Conn.: Dushkin/McGraw-Hill.

——. (1996) *The Clash of Civilizations and the Remaking of World Order.* New York: Simon & Schuster.

——. (1991a) "America's Changing Strategic Interests," *Survival* 33 (January/February): 3–17.

——. (1991b) *The Third Wave: Democratization in the Late Twentieth Century.* Norman: University of Oklahoma Press.

Hurwitz, Jon, and Mark Peffley. (1987) "How Are Foreign Policy Attitudes Structured? A Hierarchical Model," *American Political Science Review* 81 (December): 1099–1120.

Hutcheson, Ron. (2002) "Bush Vows 'To Deal with' Iraqi President," (Columbia, S.C.) *The State* (March 14): A4.

Hutzler, Charles. (2000) "China Increases Military Spending," (Columbia, S.C.) *The State* (March 7): A4.

Hyndman, Jennifer. (2000) *Managing Displacement: Refugees and the Politics of Humanitarianism.* Minneapolis: University of Minnesota Press.

Ignatieff, Michael. (2001a) "The Danger of a World without Enemies," *The New Republic* 234 (February 26): 25–28.

——. (2001b) *Human Rights as Politics and Ideology.* Princeton, N.J.: Princeton University Press.

Ignatieff, Michael. (1999) "Human Rights: The Midlife Crises," *New York Review of Books* 46 (May 20): 58–72.

Ignatius, David. (2001) "The Global Economy Is Tailor Made for Money Laundering," *International Herald Journal* (June 1): 8.

——. (1999) "A Dangerous Indifference to Global Warming," *International Herald Tribune* (June 2): 9.

———. "Webbing the World's Rich and Poor Together," *International Herald Tribune* (August 2): 8

Ikenberry, G. John. (1993) "Salvaging the G-7," *Foreign Affairs* 72 (Spring): 132–139.

Iklé, Fred Charles. (1991–1992) "Comrades in Arms," *National Interest* 26 (Winter): 22–32.

International Monetary Fund (IMF). (1999) *World Economic Outlook September 1999.* Washington, D.C.: International Monetary Fund.

———. (1997) *World Economic Outlook May 1997.* Washington, D.C.: International Monetary Fund.

Isaak, Robert A. (2000a) *Managing World Economic Change: International Political Economy,* 3rd ed. Englewood Cliffs, N.J.: Prentice Hall.

———. (2000b) *International Political Economy,* 3rd ed. Upper Saddle River, N.J.: Prentice Hall.

———. (1995) *International Political Economy,* 2nd ed. Englewood Cliffs, N.J.: Prentice Hall.

———. (1975) *Individuals and World Politics.* North Scituate, Mass.: Duxbury.

Isenberg, David. (2001) "Combat for Sale: The New Post–Cold War Mercenaries," *USA Today* 129 (March): 12, 16.

Jackson, John H. (1994) "Managing the Trading System: The World Trade Organization and the Post–Uruguay Round GATT Agenda," pp. 131–151 in Peter B. Kenen (ed.), *Managing the World Economy: Fifty Years after Bretton Woods.* Washington, D.C.: Institute for International Economics.

Jacobson, Harold K. (1984) *Networks of Interdependence: International Organizations and the Global Political System.* New York: Knopf.

Jaggers, Keith, and Ted Robert Gurr. (1995) "Transitions to Democracy: Tracking Democracy's Third Wave," *Journal of Peace Research* 32 (November): 469–482.

Jain, Subhash, and Piotz, Chelminski. (1999) "Beyond Buzzwords—Defining 'Globalization,' " *International Herald Tribune* (April 25): 9.

Jakobson, Max. (1991) "Filling the World's Most Impossible Job," *World Monitor* 4 (August): 25–33.

James, Barry. (2002a) "Summit Aims, Again, for a Better World," *International Herald Tribune* (August 8): 1, 8.

———. (2002b). "Talks to Tackle Threat to Biodiversity," *International Herald Tribune* (August 23): 1, 9.

———. (2002c) "World Loses Ground to Deserts," *International Herald Tribune* (April 4): 1, 10.

———. (2001a) "Mischievous Species Capitalize on Globalization," *International Herald Tribune* (May 21): 1, 9.

———. (2001b) "Warming on Earth Raises New Alarm," *International Herald Tribune* (January 23): 5.

———. (1995) "Religious Fanaticism Fuels Terrorism," *International Herald Tribune* (October 31): 6.

James, Patrick. (1993) "Neorealism as a Research Enterprise: Toward Elaborated Structural Realism," *International Political Science Review* 14 (No. 2): 123–148.

Janis, Irving. (1982) *Groupthink: Psychological Studies of Policy Decisions and Fiascoes,* 2nd ed. Boston: Houghton Mifflin.

Janning, Josef. (1999) "European Integration Needs to Expand Its Horizons," *International Herald Tribune* (July 24–25): 6.

Jenkins, Simon. (1995) "Dresden: Time to Say We're Sorry," *Wall Street Journal* (February 14): A22.

Jensen, Lloyd. (1982) *Explaining Foreign Policy.* Englewood Cliffs, N.J.: Prentice Hall.

Jervis, Robert. (2002) "Theories of War in an Era of Leading-Power Peace," *American Political Science Review* 96 (March): 1–14.

———. (1999) "Realism, Neoliberalism, and Cooperation: Understanding the Debate," *International Security* 24 (Summer): 42–63.

———. (1992) "A Usable Past for the Future," pp. 257–268 in Michael J. Hogan (ed.), *The End of the Cold War.* New York: Cambridge University Press.

———. (1991–1992) "The Future of World Politics: Will It Resemble the Past?" *International Security* 16 (Winter): 39–73.

———. (1991) "Will the New World Be Better?" pp. 7–19 in Robert Jervis and Seweryn Bialer (eds.), *Soviet-American Relations after the Cold War.* Durham, N.C.: Duke University Press.

———. (1982) "Security Regimes," *International Organization* 16 (Spring): 357–378.

———. (1976) *Perception and Misperception in World Politics.* Princeton, N.J.: Princeton University Press.

Joffe, Ellis. (2001) "Don't Exaggerate the Military Threat from China," *International Herald Tribune* (July 28–29): 4.

Joffe, Josef. (1990) "Entangled Forever," *National Interest* 21 (Fall): 35–40.

———. (1985) "The Foreign Policy of the Federal Republic of Germany," pp. 72–113 in Roy C. Macridis (ed.), *Foreign Policy in World Politics,* 6th ed. Englewood Cliffs, N.J.: Prentice Hall.

Johansen, Robert C. (1995) "Swords into Plowshares: Can Fewer Arms Yield More Security?" pp. 253–279 in Charles W. Kegley, Jr. (ed.), *Controversies in International Relations Theory: Realism and the Neoliberal Challenge.* New York: St. Martin's.

———. (1991) "Do Preparations for War Increase or Decrease International Security?" pp. 224–244 in Charles W. Kegley, Jr. (ed.), *The Long Postwar Peace.* New York: HarperCollins.

Johnson, James Turner. (2003) "Just War Theory: Responding Morally to Global Terrorism," pp. 223–238 in Charles W. Kegley, Jr. (ed.), *The New Global Terrorism.* Upper Saddle River, N.J.: Prentice Hall.

Johnson, Kevin. (1999) "Law Enforcement Plays Catch-Up with Reorganized Crime," *USA Today* (September 2): 15A.

Jones, Dorothy V. (1991) *Code of Peace: Ethics and Security in the World of the Warlord States.* Chicago: University of Chicago Press.

Joyner, Christopher C. (2002) "The United Nations: Strengthening an International Norm," pp. 147–172 in Peter J. Schraeder (ed.), *Exporting Democracy.* Boulder, Colo.: Lynne Rienner.

———. (2001a) "Global Commons: The Oceans, Antarctica, the Atmosphere, and Outer Space," pp. 354–389 in P. J. Simmons and Chantal de Jonge Oudraat (eds.), *Managing Global Issues: Lessons Learned.* Washington, D.C.: Carnegie Endowment for International Peace.

———. (2001b) "The Reality and Relevance of International Law in the Twenty-First Century," pp. 243–256 in Charles W. Kegley, Jr. and Eugene Wittkopf (eds.), *The Global Agenda,* 6th edition. Boston: McGraw-Hill.

———. (2000) *International Law in the Twenty-First Century.* Boulder, Colo.: Rowman & Littlefield.

———. (1995) "Collective Sanctions as Peaceful Coercion," pp. 241–270 in *The Australian Yearbook of International Law 1995.* Canberra: Australian National University.

Juergensmeyer, Mark. (2003) "The Religious Roots of Contemporary Terrorism," pp. 185–193 in Charles W. Kegley, Jr. (ed.), *The New Global Terrorism.* Upper Saddle River, N.J.: Prentice Hall.

Juergensmeyer, Mark. (1993) *The New Cold War? Religious Nationalism Confronts the Secular State.* Berkeley: University of California Press.

Kagan, Donald. (1995) *On the Origins of War and the Preservation of Peace.* New York: Doubleday.

Kaiser, David. (1990) *Politics and War: European Conflict from Philip II to Hitler.* Cambridge, Mass.: Harvard University Press.

Kaminski, Matthew. (2002) "Anti-Terrorism Requires Nation Building," *Wall Street Journal* (March 15): A10.

Kane, Hal. (1995) *The Hour of Departure: Forces That Create Refugees and Migrants.* Washington, D.C.: Worldwatch Institute.

Kaplan, Morton A. (1957) *System and Process in International Politics.* New York: Wiley.

Kaplan, Morton A., and Nicholas DeB. Katzenbach. (1961) *The Political Foundations of International Law.* New York: Wiley.

Kaplan, Robert D. (2002) *Warrior Politics: Why Leadership Demands A Pagan Ethos.* New York: Random House.

———. (1999) "China: A World Power Again," *Atlantic* 284 (August): 16–18.

Kaplan, Robert. (1994) "The Coming Anarchy," *Atlantic* 279 (February): 44–76.

Kaplan, Stephen S. (1981) *Diplomacy of Power.* Washington, D.C.: Brookings Institution.

Kapstein, Ethan Barnaby. (1991–1992) "We Are Us: The Myth of the Multinational," *National Interest* 26 (Winter): 55–62.

Kapstein, Ethan B., and Michael Mastanduno. (1999) *Unipolar Politics: Realism and State Strategies after the Cold War.* New York: Columbia University Press.

Kapuz, Devesh. (2001) "The IMF: A Cure or a Curse?" pp. 60–67 in Robert J. Griffiths, (ed.), *Developing World 01/02.* Guilford, Conn.: Dushkin/McGraw-Hill.

Katzenstein, Lawrence C., and Stefanie Lenway. (2001) "Multinational Corporations," pp. 564–566 in Joel Krieger (ed.), *The Oxford Companion to Politics of the World,* 2nd ed. New York: Oxford University Press.

Kearney, A. T./Foreign Policy Magazine. (2002) "Globalization's Last Hurrah?" *Foreign Policy* (January/February): 38–71.

Keegan, John. (1999) *The First World War.* New York: Knopf.

Keeley, Lawrence. (1996) *War before Civilization.* New York: Oxford University Press.

Keeny, Spurgeon M., Jr. (1993) "Arms Control during the Transition to the Post-Soviet World," pp. 175–197 in Joseph Kruzel (ed.), *American Defense Annual,* 8th ed. New York: Lexington Books.

Keeny, Spurgeon M., Jr. and Wolfgang K. H. Panofsky. (1981) "MAD vs. NUTS: Can Doctrine or Weaponry Remedy the Mutual Hostage Relationship of the Superpowers?" *Foreign Affairs* 60 (Winter): 287–304.

Kegley, Charles W., Jr. (ed.). (1995) *Controversies in International Relations Theory: Realism and the Neoliberal Challenge.* New York: St. Martin's Press.

———. (1993) "The Neoidealist Moment in International Studies? Realist Myths and the New International Realities," *International Studies Quarterly* 37 (June): 131–146.

Kegley, Charles W., Jr., and Margaret G. Hermann. (2002) "In Pursuit of a Peaceful International System," pp. 15–29 in Peter J. Schraeder (ed.), *Exporting Democracy.* Boulder, Colo.: Lynne Rienner.

———. (2001) "Democracy and Peace," forthcoming in Peter Schraeder, ed., *Exporting Democracy? Rhetoric versus Reality in the International Pursuit of Democratization.* Boulder, Colo.: Lynne Rienner.

———. (1997) "Putting Military Intervention into the Democratic Peace: A Research Note," *Comparative Political Studies* 30 (February): 78–107.

Kegley, Charles W., Jr., and Gregory A Raymond. (2002a) *Exorcising the Ghost of Westphalia: Building World Order in the New Millennium.* Upper Saddle River, N.J.: Prentice Hall.

———. (2002b) *From War to Peace: Fateful Decisions in World Politics.* Belmont, Calif.: Wadsworth.

Kegley, Charles W., Jr. and Gregory A. Raymond. (1999) *How Nations Make Peace.* Boston: Bedford/St. Martin's.

———. (1994) *A Multipolar Peace? Great-Power Politics in the Twenty-First Century.* New York: St. Martin's Press.

———. (1990) *When Trust Breaks Down: Alliance Norms and World Politics.* Columbia: University of South Carolina Press.

Kegley, Charles W., Jr., Gregory A. Raymond, and Margaret G. Hermann. (1998) "The Rise and Fall of the Nonintervention Norm: Some Correlates and Potential Consequences," *Fletcher Forum of World Affairs* 22 (Winter/Spring): 81–101.

Kelman, Herbert C. (1965) *International Behavior: A Social-Psychological Analysis.* New York: Holt, Rinehart & Winston.

Kelsen, Hans. (1945) *General Theory of Law and State.* Cambridge, Mass.: Harvard University Press.

Kennan, George F. (1984a) *The Fateful Alliance: France, Russia, and the Coming of the First World War.* New York: Pantheon.

———. (1984b) "Soviet-American Relations: The Politics of Discord and Collaboration," pp. 107–120 in Charles W. Kegley, Jr. and Eugene R. Wittkopf (eds.), *The Global Agenda.* New York: Random House.

———. (1982) *The Nuclear Delusion.* New York: Pantheon.

———. (1976) "The United States and the Soviet Union, 1917–1976," *Foreign Affairs* 54 (July): 670–690.

———. (1967) *Memoirs.* Boston: Little, Brown.

———. (1954) *Realities of American Foreign Policy.* Princeton, N.J.: Princeton University Press.

———. (1951) *American Diplomacy, 1900–1950.* New York: New American Library.

——— ["X"]. (1947) "The Sources of Soviet Conduct," *Foreign Affairs* 25 (July): 566–582.

Kennedy, Paul. (1999) "In the Shadow of the Great War," *New York Review of Books* 45 (August 12): 36–39.

———. (1994) "Overpopulation Tilts the Planet," *New Perspectives Quarterly* 11 (Fall): 4–6.

———. (1993) *Preparing for the Twenty-First Century.* New York: Random House.

———. (1992) "A Declining Empire Goes to War," pp. 344–346 in Charles W. Kegley Jr. and Eugene R. Wittkopf (eds.), *The Future of American Foreign Policy.* New York: St. Martin's Press.

———. (1987) *The Rise and Fall of the Great Powers.* New York: Random House.

Keohane, Robert O. (2002) "Governance in a Partially Globalized World," *American Political Science Review* 94 (March): 1–13.

———. (1989) "International Relations Theory: Contributions from a Feminist Standpoint," *Millennium* 18 (Summer): 245–253.

——— (ed.). (1986a) *Neorealism and Its Critics.* New York: Columbia University Press.

———. (1986b) "Realism, Neorealism and the Study of World Politics," pp. 1–26 in Robert O. Keohane (ed.), *Neorealism and Its Critics.* New York: Columbia University Press.

———. (1984) *After Hegemony: Cooperation and Discord in the World Political Economy*. Princeton, N.J.: Princeton University Press.

———. (1983) "Theory of World Politics: Structural Realism and Beyond," pp. 503–540 in Ada Finifter (ed.), *Political Science: The State of the Discipline*. Washington, D.C.: American Political Science Association.

Keohane, Robert O., and Stanley Hoffmann. (1991) "Institutional Change in Europe in the 1980s," pp. 1–39 in Robert O. Keohane and Stanley Hoffmann (eds.), *The New European Community: Decisionmaking and Institutional Change*. Boulder, Colo.: Westview Press.

Keohane, Robert O., and Joseph S. Nye. (2001a) *Power and Interdependence*, 3rd ed. New York: Addison Wesley-Longman.

———. (2001b) "Power and Interdependence in the Information Age," pp. 26–36 in Charles W. Kegley, Jr. and Eugene R. Wittkopf (eds.), *The Global Agenda*, 6th ed. Boston: McGraw-Hill.

Keohane, Robert O., and Joseph S. Nye, Jr. (2001) "Power and Interdependence in the Information Age," pp. 26–36 in Charles W. Kegley, Jr. and Eugene R. Wittkopf (eds.), *The Global Agenda*, 6th ed. Boston: McGraw-Hill.

———. (2000) "Globalization: What's New? What's Not? (And So What?)," *Foreign Policy* 118 (Spring): 104–119.

———. (1989) *Power and Interdependence*, 2nd ed. Glenview, Ill.: Scott, Foresman/Little, Brown.

———. (1988) "Complex Interdependence, Transnational Relations, and Realism: Alternative Perspectives on World Politics," pp. 257–271 in Charles W. Kegley, Jr. and Eugene R. Wittkopf (eds.), *The Global Agenda*, 2nd ed. New York: Random House.

———. (1977) *Power and Interdependence*. Boston: Little, Brown.

Khripunov, Igor. (1997) "Have Guns Will Travel," *Bulletin of the Atomic Scientists* 53 (May/June): 47–51.

Kidder, Rushworth, M. (1990) "Why Modern Terrorism?" pp. 135–138 in Charles W. Kegley, Jr. (ed.), *International Terrorism: Characteristics, Causes, Controls*. New York: St. Martin's Press.

Kidron, Michael, and Ronald Segal. (1995) *The State of the World Atlas*, 5th ed. London: Penguin Reference.

Kim, Dae Jung, and James D. Wolfensohn. (1999) "Economic Growth Requires Good Governance," *International Herald Tribune* (February 26): 6.

Kim, Samuel S. (1991) "The United Nations, Lawmaking and World Order," pp. 109–124 in Richard A. Falk, Samuel S. Kim, and Saul H. Mendlovitz (eds.), *The United Nations and a Just World Order*. Boulder, Colo.: Westview Press.

Kindleberger, Charles P. (1973) *The World in Depression, 1929–1939*. Berkeley: University of California Press.

Kinnas, J. N. (1997) "Global Challenges and Multilateral Diplomacy," pp. 23–48 in Ludwik Dembinski (ed.), *International Geneva Yearbook*. Berne, Switzerland: Peter Lang.

Kissinger, Henry A. (2001) *Does America Need a Foreign Policy?* New York: Simon and Schuster.

Kissinger, Henry. (1999) *Years of Renewal*. New York: Simon & Schuster.

———. (1997) "A World We Have Not Known," *Newsweek* (January 27): 74–81.

———. (1994) *Diplomacy*. New York: Simon & Schuster.

———. (1992) "Balance of Power Sustained," pp. 238–248 in Graham Allison and Gregory F. Treverton (eds.), *Rethinking America's Security*. New York: Norton.

———. (1979) *White House Years*. Boston: Little, Brown.

———. (1969) "Domestic Structure and Foreign Policy," pp. 261–275 in James N. Rosenau (ed.), *International Politics and Foreign Policy*. New York: Free Press.

Klare, Michael T. (2001) "The New Geography of Conflict," *Foreign Affairs* 80 (May/June): 49–61.

———. (1999) "The New Arms Race," pp. 139–143 in Robert M. Jackson (ed.), *Global Issues 1999/00*, 15th ed. New Guilford, Conn.: Dushkin/McGraw-Hill.

———. (1994) "Adding Fuel to the Fires: The Conventional Arms Trade in the 1990s," pp. 134–154 in Michael T. Klare and Daniel C. Thomas (eds.), *World Security*. New York: St. Martin's Press.

———. (1990) "Wars in the 1990s: Growing Firepower in the Third World," *Bulletin of the Atomic Scientists* 46 (May): 9–13.

———. (1988) "Low-Intensity Conflict," *Christianity and Crisis* 48 (February 1): 11–14.

———. (1987) "The Arms Trade: Changing Patterns in the 1980s," *Third World Quarterly* 9 (October): 1257–1281.

———. (1985) "Leaping the Firebreak," pp. 168–173 in Charles W. Kegley, Jr. and Eugene R. Wittkopf (eds.), *The Nuclear Reader: Strategy, Weapons, War*. New York: St. Martin's Press.

Klare, Michael T., and Daniel C. Thomas (eds.). (1991) *World Security: Trends and Challenges at Century's End*. New York: St. Martin's Press.

Kluckhohn, Clyde. (1944) "Anthropological Research and World Peace," pp. 143–152 in L. Bryson, Laurence Finkelstein, and Robert MacIver (eds.), *Approaches to World Peace*. New York: Conference on Science, Philosophy, and Religion.

Kluger, Jeffrey. (2002) "The Big Crunch," pp. 25–27 in Robert M. Jackson (ed.), *Global Issues 02/03*. Guilford, Conn.: McGraw-Hill/Dushkin.

———. (2001) "A Climate of Despair," *Time* (April 9): 30–35.

Knickerbocker, Brad. (1999) "Who Rules Next? Where America Stands among World Empires," *Christian Science Monitor* (December 29): 1, 4.

Knight, W. Andy. (2000) *A Changing United Nations*. London: Palgrave.

Knorr, Klaus. (1977) "International Economic Leverage and Its Uses," pp. 99–126 in Klaus Knorr and Frank N. Trager (eds.), *Economic Issues and National Security*. Lawrence: Regents Press of Kansas.

Knorr, Klaus, and James N. Rosenau (eds.). (1969) *Contending Approaches to International Politics*. Princeton, N.J.: Princeton University Press.

Knorr, Klaus, and Sidney Verba (eds.). (1961) *The International System*. Princeton, N.J.: Princeton University Press.

Knox, MacGregor, and Williamson Murray. (2001) *The Dynamics of Military Revolution: 1300–2050*. Cambridge: Cambridge University Press.

Kober, Stanley. (1990) "Idealpolitik," *Foreign Policy* 79 (Summer): 3–24.

Kobrin, Stephen J. (1997) "Electronic Cash and the End of National Markets," *Foreign Policy* 107 (Summer): 65–77.

Kokoski, Richard. (1994) "Non-Lethal Weapons: A Case Study of New Technology Developments," pp. 367–388 in the Stockholm International Peace Research Institute, *SIPRI Yearbook 1994*. New York: Oxford University Press.

Korany, Bahgat. (1986) *How Foreign Policy Decisions Are Made in the Third World*. Boulder, Colo.: Westview Press.

Korb, Lawrence J. (1995a) "The Indefensible Defense Budget," *Washington Post National Weekly Edition* (July 17–23): 19.

———. (1995b) "Our Overstuffed Armed Forces," *Foreign Affairs* 74 (November/December): 23–34.

Koretz, Gene. (1996) "Fewer Guns, More Butter," *Business Week* (July 1): 22.

Korten, David. (1995) *When Corporations Rule the World.* West Hartford, Conn.: Berrett-Koehler.

Krasner, Stephen P. (2001) "International Political Economy, pp. 420–422 in Joel Krieger (ed.), *The Oxford Companion to Politics of the World*, 2nd ed. New York: Oxford University Press.

Krasner, Stephen D. (1993) "International Political Economy," pp. 453–455 in Joel Krieger (ed.), *The Oxford Companion to Politics of the World*. New York: Oxford University Press.

Krauthammer, Charles. (2002) "NATO Is Dead; We Should Not Work to Revive It," (Columbia, S.C.) *The State* (May 26): D3.

———. (2001) "The Bush Doctrine," *Time* (March 5): 42.

———. (1999) "The Limits of Humanitarianism," *Time* (September 27): 118.

———. (1991) "The Unipolar Moment," *Foreign Affairs* 70 (No. 1): 23–33.

Krepinevich, Andrew F., and Steven M. Kusiak. (1998) "Smarter Bombs, Fewer Nukes," *Bulletin of the Atomic Scientists* 54 (November/December): 26–32.

Krepon, Michael. (2002) "Weakening the Anti-Proliferation Regime," *International Herald Tribune* (October 20): 8.

Kristof, Nicholas D. (1993) "The Rise of China," *Foreign Affairs* 72 (November/December): 59–74.

Krugman, Paul. (2000) "Some Don't Want to Be Saved from Globalization," *International Herald Tribune* (February 17): 7.

Kruzel, Joseph. (1993) "American Security Policy in a New World Order," pp. 1–23 in Joseph Kruzel (ed.), *American Defense Annual*, 8th ed. New York: Lexington Books.

———. (1991) "Arms Control, Disarmament, and the Stability of the Postwar Era," pp. 247–269 in Charles W. Kegley, Jr. (ed.), *The Long Postwar Peace*. New York: HarperCollins.

Kugler, Jacek. (1993) "War," pp. 962–966 in Joel Krieger (ed.), *The Oxford Companion to Politics of the World*. New York: Oxford University Press.

Kunz, Josef L. (1960) "Sanctions in International Law," *American Journal of International Law* 54 (April): 324–347.

Landes, David S. (1998) *The Wealth and Poverty of Nations: Why Are Some So Rich and Some So Poor?* New York: Norton.

Laqueur, Walter. (2003) "Postmodern Terrorism," pp. 151–159 in Charles W. Kegley, Jr. (ed.), *The New Global Terrorism*. Upper Saddle River, N.J.: Prentice Hall.

———. (2001) "Terror's New Face," pp. 82–89 in Charles W. Kegley, Jr. and Eugene R. Wittkopf (eds.), *The Global Agenda*, 6th ed. Boston: McGraw-Hill.

———. (1998) "Postmodern Terrorism," pp. 89–98 in Charles W. Kegley, Jr. and Eugene R. Wittkopf (eds.), *The Global Agenda*, 5th ed. New York: McGraw-Hill.

———. (1986) "Reflections on Terrorism," *Foreign Affairs* 65 (Fall): 86–100.

Lauren, Paul Gordon. (1999) *The Evolution of Human Rights*. Philadelphia: University of Pennsylvania Press.

Lavin, Douglas. (2002) "Globalization Goes Upscale," *Wall Street Journal* (February 1): A18.

Lebow, Richard Ned. (1981) *Between Peace and War: The Nature of International Crisis*. Baltimore: Johns Hopkins University Press.

Lebow, Richard Ned, and Janice Gross Stein. (1994) *We All Lost the Cold War*. Princeton, N.J.: Princeton University Press.

Lee, Rensselaer W., III. (1995) "Global Reach: The Threat of International Drug Trafficking," *Current History* 94 (May): 207–211.

Legro, Jeffrey W., and Andrew Moravcsik. (1999) "Is Anybody Still a Realist?" *International Security* 24 (Fall): 5–55.

Lemke, Douglas. (2002) *Regions of War and Peace*. Cambridge: Cambridge University Press.

Leow, Rachel. (2002) "How Can Globalization Become 'O.K.' for All?" *International Herald Tribune* (February 15): 9.

Leventhal, Paul L. (1992) "Plugging the Leaks in Nuclear Export Controls: Why Bother?" *Orbis* 36 (Spring): 167–180.

Levi, Isaac. (1990) *Hard Choices: Decision Making under Unresolved Conflict*. New York: Cambridge University Press.

Levine, Robert A. (1999) "The Global Market Holds Poor Nations at its Mercy," *International Herald Tribune* (October 17–18): 8.

Levingston, Steven. (1999) "Does Territoriality Drive Human Aggression?" *International Herald Tribune* (April 14): 9.

Levy, Jack S. (2001) "War and Its Causes," pp. 47–56 in Charles W. Kegley, Jr. and Eugene Wittkopf (eds.), *The Global Agenda*, 6th edition. Boston: McGraw-Hill.

———. (1998a) "The Causes of War and the Conditions of Peace," *American Review of Political Science* 1: 139–165.

———. (1998b) "Towards a New Millennium: Structural Perspectives on the Causes of War," pp. 47–57 in Charles W. Kegley, Jr. and Eugene R. Wittkopf (eds.), *The Global Agenda*, 5th ed. New York: McGraw-Hill.

———. (1997) "Prospect Theory, Rational Choice, and International Relations," *International Studies Quarterly* 41 (March): 87–112.

———. (1992) "An Introduction to Prospect Theory," *Political Psychology* 13 (June): 171–186.

———. (1991) "Long Cycles, Hegemonic Transitions, and the Long Peace," pp. 147–176 in Charles W. Kegley, Jr. (ed.), *The Long Postwar Peace*. New York: HarperCollins.

———. (1990–1991) "Preferences, Constraints, and Choices in July 1914," *International Security* 15 (Winter): 151–186.

———. (1989a) "The Causes of War: A Review of Theories and Evidence," pp. 209–333 in Philip E. Tetlock, Jo L. Husbands, Robert Jervis, Paul C. Stern, and Charles Tilly (eds.), *Behavior, Society, and Nuclear War*. New York: Oxford University Press.

———. (1989b) "The Diversionary Theory of War: A Critique," pp. 259–288 in Manus I. Midlarsky (ed.), *Handbook of War Studies*. Boston: Unwin Hyman.

Lewis, Flora. (2001) "Needy Migrants Will Keep Coming." *International Herald Tribune* (February 23): 8.

Lewis, George, and Theodore Postol. (1997) "Portrait of a Bad Idea," *Bulletin of the Atomic Scientists* 53 (July/August): 18–24.

Lewis, Paul. (1999) "Corporate Conduct Code Is Proposed for Third World Nations," *New York Times* (April 29): A7.

Leyton-Brown, David. (1987) "Introduction," pp. 1–4 in David Leyton-Brown (ed.), *The Utility of International Economic Sanctions*. New York: St. Martin's Press.

Libicki, Martin. (2000) "Rethinking War: The Mouse's New Roar?" *Foreign Policy* 117 (Winter): 30–42.

Lifton, Robert Jay, and Richard Falk. (1982) *Indefensible Weapons: The Political and Psychological Case against Nuclearism*. New York: Basic Books.

Lilly, James, and Carl Ford. (1999) "China's Military: A Second Opinion," *National Interest* 57 (Fall): 71–77.

Lind, Michael. (1993) "Of Arms and the Woman," *New Republic* (November 15): 36–38.

Lindblom, Charles E. (1979) "Still Muddling, Not Yet Through," *Public Administration Review* 39 (November/December): 517–526.

Lindsay, James M. (1986) "Trade Sanctions as Policy Instruments: A Re-examination," *International Studies Quarterly* 30 (June): 153–173.

Lipman, Masha. (2000) "In Russia's Future, Hard Work Instead of Tempests," *International Herald Tribune* (February 21): 8.

Liska, George. (1968) *Alliances and the Third World*. Baltimore: Johns Hopkins University Press.

———. (1962) *Nations in Alliance: The Limits of Interdependence*. Baltimore: Johns Hopkins University Press.

Lissitzyn, Oliver J. (1963) "International Law in a Divided World," *International Conciliation* 542 (March): 3–69.

Little, David. (1993) "The Recovery of Liberalism," *Ethics and International Affairs* 7: 171–201.

Livingston, Donald. (2002) "Dismantling Leviathan," *Harper's* (May): 13–17.

Lomborg, Bjorn. (2001) "The Truth about the Environment," *Economist* (August 4): 63–65.

Lopez, George A., and David Cortright. (1995) "Economic Sanctions in Contemporary Global Relations," pp. 3–16 in David Cortright and George A. Lopez (eds.), *Economic Sanctions*. Boulder, Colo.: Westview Press.

Lopez, George A., Jackie G. Smith, and Ron Pagnucco. (1995) "The Global Tide," *Bulletin of the Atomic Scientists* 51 (July/August): 33–39.

Lorenz, Konrad. (1963) *On Aggression*. New York: Harcourt, Brace & World.

Lumpe, Lora, (1999) "The Lender of the Pack," *Bulletin of the Atomic Scientists* 58 (January–February): 27–33.

Lundestad, Geir. (1994) *The Fall of the Great Powers*. Oslo: Scandinavian University Press.

Luterbacher, Urs, and Detlef F. Sprinz (eds.). (2001) *International Relations and Global Climate Change*. Cambridge, Mass.: MIT Press.

Lutz, Wolfgang. (1994) "The Future of World Population," *Population Bulletin* 49 (June): 1–47.

Lynch, Colum. (2000) "Split U.S. Policy on Iraq: Bombing while Trading," *International Herald Tribune* (February 21): 1, 14.

Maalouf, Amin. (2002) *In the Name of Identity: Violence and the Need to Belong*. New York: Arcade.

Mack, Andrew. (1996) "Allow the Idea of Nuclear Disarmament a Hearing," *International Herald Tribune* (January 26): 8.

Mackinder, Sir Halford. (1919) *Democratic Ideals and Reality*. New York: Holt.

Mahan, Alfred Thayer. (1890) *The Influence of Sea Power in History*. Boston: Little, Brown.

Majeed, Akhtar. (1991) "Has the War System Really Become Obsolete?" *Bulletin of Peace Proposals* 22 (December): 419–425.

Malaquias, Assis V. (2001) "Humanitarian Intervention," pp. 370–374 in Joel Krieger (ed.), *The Oxford Companion to Politics of the World*, 2nd ed. New York: Oxford University Press.

Mandelbaum, Michael. (2002) *The Ideas That Conquered the World: Peace, Democracy, and Free Markets in the Twenty-First Century*. New York: Public Affairs/Perseus.

Mandle, Jary R. (2001) "Trading Up: Why Globalization Aids the Poor," pp. 56–59 in Robert J. Griffiths (ed.), *Developing World 01/02*. Guilford, Conn.: Dushkin/McGraw-Hill.

Mansfield, Edward D., and Jack Snyder. (1995) "Democratization and the Danger of War," *International Security* 20 (Summer): 5–38.

Mansfield, Edward D., Helen V. Milner, B. Peter Rosendorff. (2002) "Replication, Realism, and Robustness: Analyzing Political Regimes and International Trade," *American Political Science Review* 96 (March): 167–169.

Marantz, Paul. (1987) "Economic Sanctions in the Polish Crisis," pp. 131–146 in David Leyton-Brown (ed.), *The Utility of International Economic Sanctions*. New York: St. Martin's Press.

Markusen, Ann, Peter Hall, Scott Campbell, and Sabina Dietrick. (1991) *The Rise of the Gunbelt: The Military Remapping of America*. New York: Oxford University Press.

Marshall, Tyler. (1999) "Anti-NATO Axis Could Pose Threat, U.S. Analysts Say," *Los Angeles Times World Report* (October 11): 1, 4.

Mastanduno, Michael. (1991) "Do Relative Gains Matter? America's Response to Japanese Industrial Policy," *International Security* 16 (Summer): 73–113.

Masters, Roger D. (1969) "World Politics as a Primitive Political System," pp. 104–118 in James N. Rosenau (ed.), *International Politics and Foreign Policy*. New York: Free Press.

Mathews, Jessica T. (2000) "National Security for the 21st Century," pp. 9–11 in Gary Bertsch and Scott James (eds.), *Russell Symposium Proceedings*. Athens: University of Georgia.

Mathews, Jessica T. (1997) "Power Shift: The Rise of Global Civil Society," *Foreign Affairs* 76 (January/February): 50–66.

———. (1996) "Global Warming: No Longer in Doubt," *Washington Post National Weekly Edition* (January 1–7): 29.

May, Ernest R. (2000) *Strange Victory: Hitler's Conquest of France*. New York: Hill and Wang.

Mayall, James. (2001) "Mercantilism," pp. 535 and 540 in Joel Krieger (ed.), *The Oxford Companion to Politics of the World*, 2nd ed. New York: Oxford University Press.

Mazarr, Michael J. (1999) *Global Trends 2005*. London: Palgrave.

McGowan, Patrick J. (1981) "Imperialism in World-System Perspective," *International Studies Quarterly* 25 (March): 43–68.

McGranahan, Donald. (1995) "Measurement of Development," *International Social Science Journal* 143 (March): 39–59.

McGurn, William. (2002) "Pulpit Economics," *First Things* 122 (April): 21–25.

McKibben, Bill. (1998) "The Fortune of Population," *Atlantic Monthly* (May): 55–78.

McNamara, Robert S., and James G. Blight. (2001) *Wilson's Ghost*. New York: Public Affairs.

Mead, Margaret. (1968) "Warfare Is Only an Invention—Not a Biological Necessity," pp. 270–274 in Leon Bramson and George W. Goethals (eds.), *War*. New York: Basic Books.

Mead, Walter Russell. (2001) *Special Providence: American Foreign Policy and How It Changed the World*. New York: Knopf.

———. (1995) "Forward to the Past," *New York Times Magazine* (June 4): 48–49.

Meadows, Donella H. (1993) "Seeing the Population Issue Whole," *The World & I* 8 (June): 396–409.

Meadows, Donella H., Dennis L. Meadows, Jøngen Randers, and William W. Behrens III. (1974) *The Limits to Growth*. New York: New American Library.

Mearsheimer, John J. (2001) *The Tragedy of Great Power Politics*. New York: Norton.

———. (1990) "Back to the Future: Instability in Europe after the Cold War," *International Security* 15 (Summer): 5–56.

Medley, Richard. (1999) "Europe's Next Big Idea: Strategy and Economics Point to a European Military," *Foreign Affairs* 78 (September/October): 18–22.

Melanson, Richard A. (1983) *Writing History and Making Policy: The Cold War, Vietnam, and Revisionism*. Lanham, Md.: University Press of America.

Melko, Matthew. (1999). "Cycles of General War in World History," *International Interactions* 25 (No. 3): 287–299.

Mendelsohn, Jack. (2002) "America and Russia: Make-Believe Arms Control," *Current History* 101 (October): 325–329.

Menkhaus, Ken. (2002) "Somalia: In the Crosshairs of the War on Terrorism," *Current History* (May): 210–218.

Melloan, George. (2002a) "Bush's Toughest Struggle Is with His Own Bureaucracy," *Wall Street Journal* (June 25): A19.

———. (2002b) "Meet Mr. Hu—Or Should It Be Mr. Who?" *Wall Street Journal* (April 30): A17.

Menand, Louis. (2002) "Faith, Hope, and Clarity," *New Yorker* (September 16): 98–104.

———. (2002) "September 11th and the American Soul," *New Yorker* (September 16): 98–104.

Metz, Steven, and James Kievit. (1995) *Strategy and the Revolution in Military Affairs*. Carlisle Barracks, Pa.: U.S. Army War College.

Michael, Marie (2001) "Food or Debt," pp. 78–79 in Robert J. Griffiths (ed.), *Developing World 01/02*. Guilford, Conn.: Dushkin/McGraw-Hill.

Micklethwait, John, and Adrian Wooldridge. (2001) "The Globalization Backlash," *Foreign Policy* (September/October): 16–26.

Midlarsky, Manus I. (1988) *The Onset of World War*. Boston: Unwin Hyman.

Midlarsky, Manus I. (ed.). (2000) *Handbook of War Studies II*. Ann Arbor: University of Michigan Press.

Miller, Judith. (1999) "Globalization Widens Rich-Poor Gap, UN Report," *New York Times* (July 13): A8.

Miller, Marian A. L. (1995) *The Third World in Global Environmental Politics*. Boulder, Colo.: Lynne Rienner.

Mills, C. Wright. (1956) *The Power Elite*. New York: Oxford University Press.

Mitrany, David. (1966) *A Working Peace System*. Chicago: Quadrangle.

Mittelman, James H. (2000) *The Globalization Syndrome: Transformation and Resistance*. Princeton, N.J.: Princeton University Press.

Modelski, George (ed.). (1987a) *Exploring Long Cycles*. Boulder, Colo.: Lynne Rienner.

———. (1987b) "The Study of Long Cycles," pp. 1–15 in George Modelski (ed.), *Exploring Long Cycles*. Boulder, Colo.: Lynne Rienner.

———. (1978) "The Long Cycle of Global Politics and the Nation-State," *Comparative Studies in Society and History* 20 (April): 214–235.

———. (1964) "The International Relations of Internal War," pp. 14–44 in James N. Rosenau (ed.), *International Aspects of Civil Strife*. Princeton, N.J.: Princeton University Press.

Modelski, George, and William R. Thompson. (1999) "The Long and the Short of Global Politics in the Twenty-First Century: An Evolutionary Approach," *International Studies Review*, special issue, ed. by Davis B. Bobrow: 109–140.

———. (1996) *Leading Sectors and World Powers*. Columbia: University of South Carolina Press.

———. (1989) "Long Cycles and Global War," pp. 23–54 in Manus I. Midlarsky (ed.), *Handbook of War Studies*. Boston: Unwin Hyman.

Moffett, George D. (1994) *Critical Masses: The Global Population Challenge*. New York: Viking.

Moisy, Claude. (1997) "Myths of the Global Information Village," *Foreign Policy* 107 (Summer): 78–87.

Møller, Bjørn. (1992) *Common Security and Nonoffensive Defense: A Neorealist Perspective*. Boulder, Colo.: Lynne Rienner.

Moon, Bruce E., and William J. Dixon. (1992) "Basic Needs and Growth—Welfare Trade-offs," *International Studies Quarterly* 36 (June): 191–212.

———. (1985) "Politics, the State, and Basic Human Needs: A Cross-National Study," *American Journal of Political Science* 29 (November): 661–694.

Moore, Mike. (1995) "Midnight Never Came," *Bulletin of the Atomic Scientists* 51 (November/December): 16–27.

Moran, Theodore H. (1999) *Foreign Direct Investment Development: the New Policy Agenda for Developing Countries*. Washington, D.C.: Institute for International Economics.

Moravcsik, Andrew. (1997) "Taking Preferences Seriously: A Liberal Theory of International Politics," *International Organization* 51 (Autumn): 513–553.

Morgan, T. Clifton, and Kenneth N. Bickers. (1992) "Domestic Discontent and the External Use of Force," *Journal of Conflict Resolution* 36 (March): 25–52.

Morgan, T. Clifton, and Sally Howard Campbell. (1991) "Domestic Structure, Decisional Constraints and War," *Journal of Conflict Resolution* 35 (June): 187–211.

Morgan, T. Clifton, and Valerie L. Schwebach. (1992) "Take Two Democracies and Call Me in the Morning: A Prescription for Peace?" *International Interactions* 17 (No. 4): 305–320.

Morgenthau, Hans J. (1985) *Politics among Nations*, 6th ed. Revised by Kenneth W. Thompson. New York: Knopf.

———. (1983) "Defining the National Interest—Again," pp. 32–39 in Charles W. Kegley, Jr. and Eugene R. Wittkopf (eds.), *Perspectives on American Foreign Policy*. New York: St. Martin's Press.

———. (1959) "Alliances in Theory and Practice," pp. 184–212 in Arnold Wolfers (ed.), *Alliance Policy in the Cold War*. Baltimore: Johns Hopkins University Press.

———. (1948) *Politics among Nations*. New York: Knopf.

Morris, Desmond. (1969) *The Human Zoo*. New York: Dell.

Morse, Edward L., and James Richard. (2002) "The Battle for Energy Dominance," *Foreign Affairs* 81 (March/April): 16–31.

Mowlana, Hamid. (1995) "The Communications Paradox," *Bulletin of the Atomic Scientists* 51 (July): 40.

Mulhollin, Gary. (1994) "The Business of Defense Is Defending Business," *Washington Post National Weekly Edition* (February 14–20): 23.

Muravchik, Joshua. (2002) "Democracy Is Quietly Winning," *International Herald Tribune* (August 21): 6.

Murray, Williamson, and Allan R. Millett. (2000) *A War to Be Won: Fighting the Second World War.* Cambridge, Mass.: Harvard University Press.

Myers, Steven Lee. (1999) "Without Public Debate, Pounding of Iraq Goes On," (Columbia, S.C.) *The State* (August 20): A8.

Nardin, Terry. (1983) *Law, Morality, and the Relations of States.* Princeton, N.J.: Princeton University Press.

Nardin, Terry, and David R. Mapel (eds.). (1992) *Traditions of International Ethics.* New York: Cambridge University Press.

Nathan, James A. (1997) "Can Economic Sanctions Succeed as Foreign Policy?" *USA Today* 126 (September): 37.

Neild, Robert. (2000) "Expose the Unsavory Business behind Cruel Wars," *International Herald Tribune* (February 17): 6.

Nelson, Stephan D. (1974) "Nature/Nurture Revisited: A Review of the Biological Bases of Conflict," *Journal of Conflict Resolution* 18 (June): 285–335.

Neuman, Johanna. (1995–1996) "The Media's Impact on International Affairs, Then and Now," *National Interest* 16 (Winter): 109–123.

Newland, Kathleen. (1994) "Refugees: The Rising Flood," *World Watch* 7 (May/June): 10–20.

Nichols, Bill. (2002) "After Two Years at the Top Russia's Putin Still an Enigma," *USA Today* (March 27): 1A–2A.

Nicholson, Michael. (1992) *Rationality and the Analysis of International Conflict.* Cambridge, Eng.: Cambridge University Press.

Niebuhr, Reinhold. (1947) *Moral Man and Immoral Society.* New York: Scribner's.

Nietschmann, Bernard. (1991) "Third World War: The Global Conflict over the Rights of Indigenous Nations," pp. 172–176 in Robert M. Jackson (ed.), *Global Issues 91/92.* Guilford, Conn.: Dushkin.

Nikovich, Frank. (1999) *The Wilsonian Century.* Chicago: University of Chicago Press.

Nincic, Miroslav. (1982) *The Arms Race.* New York: Praeger.

Nnoli, Okwudiba. (1993) "Ethnicity," pp. 280–284 in Joel Krieger (ed.), *The Oxford Companion to Politics of the World.* New York: Oxford University Press.

Nye, Joseph S., Jr. (2002a) "The Dependent Colossus," *Foreign Policy* (March/April): 74–76.

———. (2002b) *The Paradox of American Power.* New York: Oxford University Press.

———. (2001) "The Changing Nature of World Power," pp. 95–107 in Charles W. Kegley, Jr. and Eugene R. Wittkopf (eds.), *The Global Agenda,* 6th ed. Boston: McGraw-Hill.

———. (1990) *Bound to Lead: The Changing Nature of American Power.* New York: Basic Books.

———. (1987) "Nuclear Learning and U.S.-Soviet Security Regimes," *International Organization* 41 (Summer): 371–402.

Oberdorfer, Don. (1991) *The Turn: From the Cold War to a New Era.* New York: Poseidon.

O'Brien, Conor Cruise. (1993) "The Wrath of Ages," *Foreign Affairs* 72 (November–December): 142–149.

———. (1977) "Liberty and Terrorism," *International Security* 2 (Fall): 56–67.

O'Brien, Richard. (1992) *Global Financial Integration: The End of Geography.* New York: Council on Foreign Relations Press.

Odell, John S. (2000) *Negotiating the World Economy.* Ithaca, N.Y.: Cornell University Press.

Olson, Elizabeth. (2001) "UN Rights Panel Faces Hard Issues," *International Herald Tribune* (March 19): 6.

Olson, Mancur. (1971) "Rapid Growth as a Destabilizing Force," pp. 215–227 in James C. Davies (ed.), *When Men Revolt and Why.* New York: Free Press.

Oldstone, Michael B. A. (1998) *Viruses, Plagues, and History.* New York: Oxford University Press.

Oneal, John R., and Bruce Russett. (1999) "Assessing the Liberal Peace with Alternative Specifications: Trade Still Reduces Conflict," *Journal of Peace Research* 36 (July): 423–442.

Onuf, Nicholas. (2002) "Worlds of Our Making: The Strange Career of Constructivism in International Relations," pp. 199–241 in Donald J. Puchala (ed.), *Visions of International Relations: Assessing an Academic Field.* Columbia: University of South Carolina Press.

———. (1989) *World of Our Making: Rules and Rule in Social Theory and International Relations.* Columbia: University of South Carolina Press.

———. (1982) "Global Law-Making and Legal Thought," pp. 1–82 in Nicholas Greenwood Onuf (ed.), *Law-Making in the Global Community.* Durham, N.C.: Carolina Academic Press.

Opello, Walter C., Jr., and Stephen J. Rosow. (1999) *The Nation-State and Global Order: A Historical Introduction to Contemporary Politics.* Boulder, Colo.: Lynne Rienner.

Organski, A. F. K. (1968) *World Politics.* New York: Knopf.

Organski, A. F. K., and Jacek Kugler. (1980) *The War Ledger.* Chicago: University of Chicago Press.

Osgood, Robert E. (1968) *Alliances and American Foreign Policy.* Baltimore: Johns Hopkins University Press.

Ostrom, Charles W., and Brian L. Job. (1986) "The President and the Use of Force," *American Political Science Review* 80 (June): 554–566.

Ostry, Sylvia. (2001) Review of *The Challenge of Global Capitalism* by Robert Gilpin, *American Political Science Review* 95 (March): 257–258.

Owen, John M., IV. (1997) *Liberal Peace, Liberal War.* Ithaca, N.Y.: Cornell University Press.

Packenham, Robert. (1992) *The Dependency Movement: Scholarship and Politics in Dependency Studies.* Cambridge, Mass.: Harvard University Press.

Parry, Clive. (1968) "The Function of Law in the International Community," pp. 1–54 in Max Sørensen (ed.), *Manual of Public International Law.* New York: St. Martin's Press.

Passel, Jeffrey S., and Michael Fix. (1994) "Myths about Immigrants," *Foreign Policy* 95 (Summer): 151–160.

Pastor, Robert A. (ed.). (1999) "The Great Powers in the Twentieth Century," pp. 1–31 in *A Century's Journey: How the Great Powers Shape the World.* New York: Basic Books.

Payne, James E., and Anandi P. Sahu (eds.). (1993) *Defense Spending and Economic Growth.* Boulder, Colo.: Westview Press.

Pear, Robert. (1997) "AIDS' Numbers Make a Giant Leap," *International Herald Journal* (November 27): 1, 6.

Peceny, Mark. (2000) *Democracy at the Points of Bayonets.* College Station: Penn State Press.

Peceny, Mark, Caroline C. Beer, and Shannon Sanchez-Terry. (2002) "Dictatorial Peace?" *American Political Science Review* 96 (March): 15–26.

Peirce, Neal R. (2000) "Keep an Eye on 'Citistates' Where Economic Action Is," *International Herald Tribune* (January 11): 8.

———. (1997) "Does the Nation-State Have a Future?" *International Herald Tribune* (April 4): 9.

Pells, Richard. (2002) "Mass Culture Is Now Exported from All Over to All Over," *International Herald Tribune* (July 12): 9.

Penttila, Risto E. J. (2001) "The Concert Is Back, and It Seems to Be Working," *International Herald Tribune* (December 28): 8.

Peterson, Erik. (1998) "Looming Collision of Capitalisms?" pp. 296–307 in Charles W. Kegley, Jr. and Eugene R. Wittkopf (eds.), *The Global Agenda*, 5th ed. New York: McGraw-Hill.

Peterson, John L. (1999) "Getting Ready for the Twenty-First Century," *USA Today* 128 (May): 56–58.

Peterson, Niels Helveg. (1999) "Place Priority on Human Rights in Applying International Law," *International Herald Tribune* (July 27): 7.

Peterson, V. Spike, and Anne Sisson Runyan. (1993) *Global Gender Issues*. Boulder, Colo.: Westview Press.

Petit, Pascal, and Luc Soete. (1999) "Globalization in Search of a Future," *International Social Science Journal* 160 (June): 163–181.

Pettis, Michael. (2001) "Will Globalization Go Bankrupt?" *Foreign Policy* (September/ October): 52–59.

Pfaff, William. (2001a) "Anti-Davos Forum Is Another Sign of a Sea Change," *International Herald Tribune* (July 25): 6.

———. (2001b) "The Question of Hegemony," *Foreign Affairs* 80 (January/February): 50–64.

———. (2000) "Look Again: The Nation-State Isn't Going Away," *International Herald Tribune* (January 11): 8.

———. (1999) "Getting the Facts on a Bumper Century for War Crimes," *International Herald Tribune* (September 4–5): 8.

———. (1996) "Seeking a Broader Vision of Economic Society," *International Herald Tribune* (February 3–4): 6.

Pfetsch, Frank L. (1999) "Globalization: A Threat and a Challenge for the State," paper presented at the European Standing Conference on International Studies, Vienna, September 11–13.

Philips, Rosemarie, and Stuart K. Tucker. (1991) *U.S. Foreign Policy and Developing Countries: Discourse and Data 1991*. Washington, D.C.: Overseas Development Council.

Pickering, Jeffrey. (1999) "The Structural Shape of Force: Interstate Interaction in the Zones of Peace and Turmoil," *International Interactions* 25 (No. 4): 363–391.

Pierre, Andrew J. (1984) "The Politics of International Terrorism," pp. 84–92 in Charles W. Kegley, Jr. and Eugene R. Wittkopf (eds.), *The Global Agenda*. New York: Random House.

Pincus, Walter. (1999) "Their Soldiers Aren't Ready to Fight," *Washington Post National Weekly Edition* (March 1): 18.

Pipes, Richard. (1977) "Why the Soviet Union Thinks It Could Fight and Win a Nuclear War," *Commentary* 26 (July): 21–34.

Pirages, Dennis. (1998) "An Ecological Approach to International Relations," pp. 387–394 in Charles W. Kegley, Jr. and Eugene R. Wittkopf (eds.), *The Global Agenda*, 5th ed. New York: McGraw-Hill.

Pollack, Andrew. (1999) "Growing Pains: Why Hopes for a Global Biotech Treaty Withered," *International Herald Tribune* (February 25): 1, 4.

Pollack, Kenneth M. (2002) "Next Stop Baghdad?" *Foreign Affairs* 81 (March/April): 32–47.

Pomfret, John. (2002) "Taiwan Set Up Fund to Buy Global Influence," *International Herald Tribune* (April 6–7): 1, 7.

———. (1999) "China Maps Changes in Defense Strategy," *International Herald Tribune* (June 12–13): 1, 4.

Population Reference Bureau. (2000) *2000 World Population Data Sheet*. Washington, D.C.: Population Reference Bureau.

———. (1981) *World Population: Toward the Next Century*. Washington, D.C.: Population Reference Bureau.

Porter, Bruce D. (1994) *War and the Rise of the State*. New York: Free Press.

Porter, Gareth. (1995) "Environmental Security as a National Security Issue," *Current History* 94 (May): 218–222.

Porter, Gareth, and Janet Welsh Brown. (1996) *Global Environmental Politics*, 2nd ed. Boulder, Colo.: Westview Press.

Potter, William C. (1992) "The New Nuclear Suppliers," *Orbis* 46 (Spring): 199–210.

Pound, Edward T., and Jihan El-Tahri. (1994) "Sanctions: The Pluses and Minuses," *U.S. News & World Report* (October 31): 58–71.

Powell, Robert. *In the Shadow of Power: States and Strategies in International Politics*. Princeton, N.J.: Princeton University Press.

Powers, Thomas. (1994) "Downwinders: Some Casualties of the Nuclear Age," *Atlantic Monthly* (March): 119–124.

Puchala, Donald J. (2001) "Building Peace in Pieces: The Promise of European Unity," pp. 160–174 in Charles W. Kegley, Jr. and Eugene R. Wittkopf (eds.), *The Global Agenda*, 6th ed. Boston: McGraw-Hill.

———. (1994) "Some World Order Options for Our Time," *Peace Forum* 11 (November): 17–30.

Putnam, Robert D. (1988) "Diplomacy and Domestic Politics: The Logic of Two-Level Games," *International Organization* 42 (Summer): 427–460.

Quester, George, ed. (1992) "Conventional Deterrence: The Past as Prologue," pp. 31–51 in Gary L. Guertner, Robert Haffa, Jr., and George Quester, *Conventional Forces and the Future of Deterrence*. Carlisle Barracks, Pa.: U.S. Army War College.

Quinn, Dennis. (1997) "The Correlates of Change in International Financial Regulation," *American Political Science Review* 91 (September): 531–551.

Quinn, Jane Bryant. (2002) "Iraq: It's the Oil, Stupid," *Newsweek* (September 30): 43.

Ralph, Jason G. (2001) *Beyond the Security Dilemma: Ending America's Cold War*. Brookfield, Vt.: Ashgate.

Rapkin, David, and William Thompson, with Jon A. Christopherson. (1989) "Bipolarity and Bipolarization in the Cold War Era," *Journal of Conflict Resolution* 23 (June): 261–295.

Ratner, Stephen A. (1997) *The New UN Peacekeeping: Building Peace in Lands of Conflict after the Cold War*. New York: St. Martin's Press.

Rauch, Jonathan. (2001) "The New, Old Economy: Oil, Computers, and the Reinvention of the Earth," *Atlantic Monthly* 287 (January): 35–47

Ray, James Lee. (1995) *Democracy and International Conflict: An Evaluation of the Democratic Peace Proposition*. Columbia: University of South Carolina Press.

Raymond, Gregory A. (2003) "The Evolving Strategies of Political Terrorism," pp. 71–105 in Charles W. Kegley, Jr. (ed.), *The New Global Terrorism*. Upper Saddle River, N.J.: Prentice Hall.

———. (1999) "Necessity in Foreign Policy," *Political Science Quarterly* 113 (Winter): 673–688.

———. (1994) "Democracies, Disputes, and Third-Party Intermediaries," *Journal of Conflict Resolution* 38 (March): 24–42.

Reardon, Betty. (1985) *Sexism and the War System.* New York: Teachers College Press.

Redfield, Robert. (1962) *Human Nature and the Study of Society,* vol. 1. Chicago: University of Illinois Press.

Regan, Patrick M. (2000) *Civil Wars and Foreign Powers: Outside Intervention in Interstate Conflict.* Ann Arbor: University of Michigan Press.

———. (1994) *Organizing Societies for War: The Process and Consequences of Societal Militarization.* Westport, Conn.: Praeger.

Reich, Robert. (1990) "Who Is Us?" *Harvard Business Review* 68 (January–February): 53–64.

Reinares, Fernando. (2002) "The Empire Rarely Strikes Back," *Foreign Policy* (January/February): 92–94.

Reinicke, Wolfgang H. (1997) "Global Public Policy," *Foreign Affairs* 76 (November/December): 127–38.

Renner, Michael. (1999) "Arms Control Orphans," *Bulletin of the Atomic Scientists* 58 (January/February): 22–27.

Repetto, Robert, and Jonathan Lash. (1997) "Planetary Roulette: Gambling with the Climate," *Foreign Policy* 108 (Fall): 84–98.

Rice, Susan, and David Scheffer. (1999) "Sudan Must End Its Brutal War against Civilians," *International Herald Tribune* (September 1): 6.

Richardson, Lewis F. (1960a) *Arms and Insecurity.* Pittsburgh: Boxwood Press.

———. (1960b) *Statistics of Deadly Quarrels.* Chicago: Quadrangle.

Richardson, Michael. (1995) "Fears of a Militarily Resurgent Japan," *International Herald Tribune* (August 15): 1, 7.

Richardson, Neil R. (1995) "International Trade as a Force for Peace," pp. 281–293 in Charles W. Kegley, Jr. (ed.), *Controversies in International Relations Theory.* New York: St. Martin's Press.

Riddell-Dixon, Elizabeth. (1995) "Social Movements and the United Nations," *International Social Science Journal* 144 (June): 289–303.

Ridley, Matt. (1998) *The Origins of Virtue: Human Instincts and the Evolution of Cooperation.* New York: Viking.

Rieff, David. (1999) "The Precarious Triumph of Human Rights," *New York Times Magazine* (August 8): 36–41.

Riggs, Robert E., and Jack C. Plano. (1994) *The United Nations: International Organization and World Politics,* 2nd ed. Belmont, Calif.: Wadsworth.

Riker, William H. (1962) *The Theory of Political Coalitions.* New Haven, Conn.: Yale University Press.

Roca, Sergio. (1987) "Economic Sanctions against Cuba," pp. 87–104 in David Leyton-Brown (ed.), *The Utility of International Economic Sanctions.* New York: St. Martin's Press.

Rodrik, Dani. (2002) "Trading in Illusions," pp. 38–44 in Robert J. Griffiths (ed.), *Developing World 02/02.* Guilford, Conn.: Dushkin/McGraw-Hill.

———. (1997a) *Has Globalization Gone Too Far?* Washington, D.C.: Institute for International Economics.

———. (1997b) "Sense and Nonsense in the Globalization Debate," *Foreign Policy* 107 (Summer): 19–37.

Rosa, Jean-Jacques. (2000) *Euro Error.* New York: Algrera.

Rosecrance, Richard. (1997) "Economics and National Security: The Evolutionary Process," pp. 209–238 in Richard Shultz, Roy Godson, and George Quester (eds.), *Security Studies for the Twenty-First Century.* New York: Brassey's.

Rosenau, James N. (1998) "Disorder and Order in a Turbulent World: The Evolution of Globalized Space," pp. 145–169 in Charles W. Kegley, Jr. and Eugene R. Wittkopf (eds.), *The Global Agenda,* 5th ed. New York: McGraw-Hill.

———. (1997) *Along the Domestic-Foreign Frontier: Exploring Governance in a Turbulent World.* Cambridge, Eng.: Cambridge University Press.

———. (1995) "Security in a Turbulent World," *Current History* 94 (May): 193–200.

———. (1990) *Turbulence in World Politics: A Theory of Change and Continuity.* Princeton, N.J.: Princeton University Press.

———. (1980) *The Scientific Study of Foreign Policy.* New York: Nichols.

Rosenberg, Shawn W. (1988) *Reason, Ideology and Politics.* Princeton, N.J.: Princeton University Press.

Rosenburg, Tina. (1999) "International Law Is Dissolving the World's Borders," *International Herald Tribune* (July 3–4): 6.

Rosenthal, Joel H. (1991) *Righteous Realists.* Baton Rouge: Louisiana State University Press.

Ross, Philip E. (1997) "The End of Infantry?" *Forbes* (July 7): 182–185.

Rosset, Peter. (1999) "Biotechnology Won't Feed the World," *International Herald Tribune* (September 2): 8.

Rostow, W. W. (1960) *The Stages of Economic Growth.* Cambridge, Eng.: Cambridge University Press.

Rothgeb, John M., Jr. (1993) *Defining Power: Influence and Force in the Contemporary International System.* New York: St. Martin's Press.

Rothstein, Linda. (2001) "After September 11," *Bulletin of the Atomic Scientists* (November/December): 44–48.

Rowan, Carl. (1999) "U.S. Is on Right Side of History in Kosovo Campaign," (Columbia, S.C.) *The State* (March 30): A9.

Rubenstein, Richard E. (2003) "The Psycho-Political Sources of Terrorism," pp. 139–150 in Charles W. Kegley, Jr. (ed.), *The New Global Terrorism.* Upper Saddle River, N.J.: Prentice Hall.

Rubin, Nancy. (1999) "It's Official: All of the World Is Entitled to Democracy," *International Herald Tribune* (May 18): 8.

Ruggie, John Gerald. (1993) "Wandering in the Void: Charting the UN's New Strategic Role," *Foreign Affairs* 72 (November/December): 27–31.

———. (1983) "Continuity and Transformation in the World Polity: Toward a Neorealist Synthesis," *World Politics* 35 (January): 261–285.

Rummel, Rudolph J. (1994) *Death by Government.* New Brunswick, N.J.: Transaction Books.

———. (1983) "Libertarianism and International Violence," *Journal of Conflict Resolution* 27 (March): 27–71.

Runyan, Curtis. (1999) "NGOs Proliferate World Wide," pp. 144–145 in Lester R. Brown, et al., *Vital Signs 1999.* New York: Norton.

Rupert, James. (1995) "The Cloud over Chernobyl," *Washington Post National Weekly Edition* (June 26–July 2): 6–7.

Rusi, Alpo. (1997) *Dangerous Peace.* Boulder, Colo.: Westview Press.

———. (1997) *Dangerous Peace: New Rivalry in World Politics.* Boulder, Colo.: Westview Press.

Russett, Bruce. (2001) "How Democracy, Interdependence, and International Organizations Create a System for Peace," pp. 232–242 in Charles W. Kegley, Jr. and Eugene Wittkopf (eds.), *The Global Agenda,* 6th ed. Boston: McGraw-Hill.

———. (1993) *Grasping the Democratic Peace: Principles for a Post–Cold War World.* Princeton, N.J.: Princeton University Press.

———. (1982) "Defense Expenditures and National Well-Being," *American Political Science Review* 76 (December): 767–777.

Russett, Bruce, and John Oneal. (2001) *Triangulations Peace: Democracy, Interdependence, and International Organizations.* New York: Norton.

———. (2000) *Triangulating Peace: Democracy, Interdependence, and International Organization.* New York: Norton.

———. (1982) "Defense Expenditures and National Well Being," *American Political Science Review* 76 (December): 767–777.

Russett, Bruce, and Harvey Starr. (1996) *World Politics: The Menu for Choice,* 5th ed. New York: Freeman.

Russett, Bruce, Harvey Starr, and David Kinsella. (2000) *World Politics: The Menu for Choice,* 6th ed. Boston: Bedford/St. Martin's.

Russett, Bruce, and James S. Sutterlin. (1991) "The UN in a New World Order," *Foreign Affairs* 70 (Spring): 69–83.

Sachs, Jeffrey. (1997) "The Limits of Convergence," *Economist* (June 14): 19–22.

Sadowaski. Yahya, (1998) "Ethnic Conflict" *Foreign Policy* 112 (Summer): 12–23.

Sagan, Carl. (1989) "Understanding Growth Rates: The Secret of the Persian Chessboard," *Parade* (February 14): 14.

———. (1988) "The Common Enemy," *Parade* (February 7): 4–7.

Sagan, Carl, and Richard Turco. (1993) "Nuclear Winter in the Post–Cold War Era," *Journal of Peace Research* 30 (November): 369–373.

Samuelson, Robert J. (2002a) " 'Digital Divide' Facing Poor Looks Like Fiction." (Columbia, S.C.) *The State* (April 3): A13.

———. (2002b) "The New Coin of the Realm," *Newsweek* (January 7): 38.

———. (2001a) "Better Energy Policy a Critical Need for U.S.," (Columbia, S.C.) *The State* (October 11): A17.

———. (2001b) "The Spirit of Capitalism," *Foreign Affairs* 80 (January/February): 205–211.

Sandel, Michael J. (1996) "America's Search for a New Public Philosophy," *Atlantic Monthly* (March): 57–74.

Sandler, Todd, and Keith Hartley. (1995) *The Economics of Defense.* New York: Cambridge University Press.

Sanger, David E. (1998) "Contagion Effect: A Guide to Modern Domino Theory," *New York Times* (August 2): Section 4, 1, 5.

Saurin, Julian. (2000) "Globalization, Poverty, and the Promises of Modernity," pp. 204–229 in Sarah Owen Vanderslvis and Paris Yeros (eds.), *Poverty in World Politics.* New York: St. Martin's.

Scarborough, Grace E. Iusi, and Bruce Bueno de Mesquita. (1988) "Threat and Alignment," *International Interactions* 14 (No. 1): 85–93.

Schelling, Thomas C. (1978) *Micromotives and Macrobehavior.* New York: Norton.

———. (1966) *Arms and Influence.* New Haven, Conn.: Yale University Press.

Schlagheck, Donna M. (1990) "Superpowers, Foreign Policy, and Terrorism," pp. 170–197 in Charles W. Kegley, Jr. (ed.), *International Terrorism.* New York: St. Martin's Press.

Schlesinger, Arthur, Jr. (1997) "Has Democracy a Future?" *Foreign Affairs* 76 (September/October): 2–12.

———. (1986) *The Cycles of American History.* Boston: Houghton Mifflin.

———. (1983) "Pretension in the Presidential Pulpit," *Wall Street Journal* (March 17): 26.

Schmemann, Serge. (1999) "What Makes Nations Turn Corrupt?" *New York Times* (August 28): A15, A17.

Schneider, Barry R., and Lawrence E. Grinter (eds.). (1995) *Battlefield of the Future: Twenty-First Century Warfare Issues.* Maxwell Air Force Base, Ala.: Air War College.

Schraeder, Peter J. (ed.). (2002) *Exporting Democracy.* Boulder, Colo.: Lynne Rienner.

Schuler, Corinna. (1999) "Helping Children Warriors Regain Their Humanity," *Christian Science Monitor* (October 20): 1, 12–13.

Schulz, William F. (2001) *In Our Own Best Interest: How Defending Human Rights Benefits Us All.* Boston: Beacon Press.

Schulz, William F. (2000) *In Our Own Best Interest: How Defending Human Rights Benefits Us All.* Boston: Beacon.

Schwab, Klaus, and Claude Smadja. (1999) "Globalization Needs a Human Face," *International Herald Tribune* (January 28): 8.

———. (1996) "Start Taking the Backlash against Globalization Seriously," *International Herald Tribune* (February 1): 1, 8.

Schwartz, Regina M. (1997) *The Curse of Cain: The Violent Legacy of Monotheism.* Chicago, Ill.: University of Chicago Press.

Schwartz, Stephen I. (2000) "Outmaneuvered, Outgunned, and Out of Sight," *Bulletin of the Atomic Scientists* 56 (January/February): 24–31.

Schweller, Randall L. (1999) Review of *From Wealth to Power,* by Fareed Zakaria, *American Political Science Review* 93 (June 1999): 497–499.

———. (1992) "Domestic Structure and Preventive War," *World Politics* 44 (January): 235–269.

Scott, Bruce R. (2001) "The Great Divide in the Global Village," *Foreign Affairs* 80 (January/February): 160–177.

Seabright, Paul. (2001) "The Road Upward," *The New York Review of Books* 48 (March 29): 41–48.

Seck, Manadon Manosour. (1999) "Shrinking Forests," *Christian Science Monitor* (May 3): 9.

Seib, Gerald F. (1999) "Another Great Threat Looms: China as New Demon," *Wall Street Journal* (May 26): A21.

Sellers, M. N. S. (1998) "Separatism and the Democratic Entitlement in International Law," in *The Challenge of Non-State Actors.* Washington, D.C.: American Society of International Law.

Sen, Amartya. (1994) "Population: Delusion and Reality," *New York Review of Books* 41 (September 22): 62–71.

Shambaugh, David. (2001) "Facing Reality in China Policy," *Foreign Affairs* 80 (January–February): 50–64.

Shannon, Thomas Richard. (1989) *An Introduction to the World-System Perspective.* Boulder, Colo.: Westview Press.

Shannon, Victoria. (1999) "What's Lurking behind Those Slow Downloads," *International Herald Tribune* (May 27): 6.

Shawcross, William. (2000) *Deliver Us from Evil: Peacekeepers, Warlords, and a World of Endless Conflict.* New York: Simon & Schuster.

Sheehan, Michael. (1996) "A Regional Perspective on the Globalization Process," *Korean Journal of Defense Analysis* 8 (Winter): 53–74.

Shiva, Vandana. (2001) "Is 'Development' Good for the Third World?" pp. 154–155 in Robert J. Griffiths (ed.), *Developing World 01/02.* Guilford, Conn.: Dushkin/McGraw-Hill.

Shultz, Richard, Roy Godson, and George Quester (eds.). (1997) *Security Studies for the Twenty-First Century.* New York: Brassey's.

Shultz, Richard H., Jr., and William J. Olson. (1994) *Ethnic and Religious Conflict: Emerging Threat to U.S. Security.* Washington, D.C.: National Strategy Information Center.

Siegel, Martin J. (1983) "Survival," *USA Today* 112 (August): 1–2.

Simmel, Georg. (1956) *Conflict.* Glencoe, Ill.: Free Press.

Simon, Herbert A. (1997) *Models of Bonded Rationality.* Cambridge, Mass.: MIT Press.

———. (1982) *Models of Bounded Rationality.* Cambridge, Mass.: MIT Press.

———. (1957) *Models of Man.* New York: Wiley.

Sinding, Steven W. (1999) "Now We Can Be Serious about Population Politics," *International Herald Tribune* (February 8): 8.

Singer, Hans W., and Javed A. Ansari. (1988) *Rich and Poor Countries,* 4th ed. London: Unwin Hyman.

Singer, J. David. (1991) "Peace in the Global System: Displacement, Interregnum, or Transformation?" pp. 56–84 in Charles W. Kegley, Jr. (ed.), *The Long Postwar Peace.* New York: HarperCollins.

———. (1981) "Accounting for International War: The State of the Discipline," *Journal of Peace Research* 18 (No. 1): 1–18.

———. (ed.). (1968) *Quantitative International Politics.* New York: Free Press.

———. (1961) "The Level-of-Analysis Problem in International Relations," pp. 77–92 in Klaus Knorr and Sidney Verba (eds.), *The International System.* Princeton, N.J.: Princeton University Press.

Singer, J. David, and Melvin Small. (1974) "Foreign Policy Indicators," *Policy Sciences* 5 (September): 271–296.

———. (1968) "Alliance Aggregation and the Onset of War, 1815–1945," pp. 247–285 in J. David Singer (ed.), *Quantitative International Politics.* New York: Free Press.

Singer, Max (1999) "The Population Surprise," *Atlantic* (August): 22–25.

Singer, Max, and Aaron Wildavsky. (1993) *The Real World Order: Zones of Peace/Zones of Turmoil.* Chatham, N.J.: Chatham House.

Sivard, Ruth Leger. (1996) *World Military and Social Expenditures 1996.* Washington, D.C.: World Priorities.

———. (1993) *World Military and Social Expenditures 1993.* Washington, D.C.: World Priorities.

———. (1991) *World Military and Social Expenditures 1991.* Washington, D.C.: World Priorities.

———. (1982) *World Military and Social Expenditures 1982.* Leesburg, Va.: World Priorities.

———. (1979) *World Military and Social Expenditures 1979.* Leesburg, Va.: World Priorities.

Siverson, Randolph M., and Julian Emmons. (1991) "Democratic Political Systems and Alliance Choices," *Journal of Conflict Resolution* 35 (June): 285–306.

Sivy, Michael. (1999) "The Buzz of Money in Motion," *Time* (July 26): 71.

Skjelsbaek, Kjell. (1991) "The UN Secretary-General and the Mediation of International Disputes," *Journal of Peace Research* 28 (February): 99–115.

Sklair, Leslie. (1991) *Sociology of the Global System.* Baltimore: Johns Hopkins University Press.

Slaughter, Anne-Marie. (1997) "The Real New World Order," *Foreign Affairs* 76 (September–October): 183–197.

Small, Melvin, and J. David Singer. (1982) *Resort to Arms: International and Civil Wars, 1816–1980.* Beverly Hills, Calif.: Sage.

———. (1976) "The War-Proneness of Democratic Regimes, 1816–1965," *Jerusalem Journal of International Relations* 1 (March): 50–69.

———. (1972) "Patterns in International Warfare, 1816–1965," pp. 121–131 in James F. Short, Jr. and Marvin E. Wolfgang (eds.), *Collective Violence.* Chicago: Aldine-Atherton.

Smith, Dan. (1999) "The Norm of Sovereignty in the Age of Intervention," paper presented at the International Peace Conference, "Will World Peace Be Achievable in the Twenty-First Century," Kyung Hee University, Seoul, October 11–13.

———. (1997) *The State of War and Peace Atlas,* 3rd ed. New York: Penguin.

Smith, Jackie, and Timothy Patrick Moran. (2001) "WTO 101: Myths about the World Trade Organization," pp. 68–71 in Robert J. Griffiths (ed.), *Developing World 01/02,* Guilford, Conn.: Dushkin/McGraw-Hill.

Smith, Michael J. (2000) "Humanitarian Intervention Revisited," *Harvard International Review* 22 (April): 72–75.

Smith, Ron P., and George Georgiou. (1983) "Assessing the Effect of Military Expenditures on OECD Economies: A Survey," *Arms Control* 4 (May): 3–15.

Smith, Steve. (1997) "Bridging the Gap: Social Constructivism," pp. 183–187 in John Baylis and Steve Smith (eds.), *The Globalization of World Politics.* New York: Oxford University Press.

Smith, Steve, and Michael Clarke. (1985) *Foreign Policy Implementation.* London: Allen & Unwin.

Snidal, Duncan. (1993) "Relative Gains and the Pattern of International Cooperation," pp. 181–207 in David A. Baldwin (ed.), *Neorealism and Neoliberalism: The Contemporary Debate.* New York: Columbia University Press.

Snider, Lewis W. (1991) "Guns, Debt, and Politics: New Variations on an Old Theme," *Armed Forces and Society* 17 (Winter): 167–190.

Snyder, Glenn H. (1991) "Alliance Threats: A Neorealist First Cut," pp. 83–103 in Robert L. Rothstein (ed.), *The Evolution of Theory in International Relations.* Columbia: University of South Carolina Press.

———. (1984) "The Security Dilemma in Alliance Politics," *World Politics* 36 (July): 461–495.

Snyder, Glenn H., and Paul Diesing. (1977) *Conflict among Nations: Bargaining, Decision-Making, and System Structure in International Crisis.* Princeton, N.J.: Princeton University Press.

Snyder, Jack. (1993) "The New Nationalism: Realist Interpretations and Beyond," pp. 179–200 in Richard Rosecrance, and Anthony A. Stein (eds.), *The Domestic Bases of Grand Strategy.* Ithaca, N.Y.: Cornell University Press.

Sobel, Andrew C. (1994) *Domestic Choices, International Markets: Dismantling National Barriers and Liberalizing Securities Markets.* Ann Arbor: University of Michigan Press.

Sodaro, Michael J. (2001) *Comparative Politics: A Global Introduction.* Boston: McGraw-Hill.

Somit, Albert. (1990) "Humans, Chimps, and Bonobos: The Biological Bases of Aggression, War, and Peacemaking," *Journal of Conflict Resolution* 34 (September): 553–582.

Sommaruga, Cornelio. (1999) "Renew the Ambition to Impose Rules on Warfare," *International Herald Tribune* (August 12): 8.

Sørensen, Georg. (1995) "Four Futures," *Bulletin of the Atomic Scientists* 51 (July/August): 69–72.

Sorensen, Theodore C. (1963) *Decision Making in the White House.* New York: Columbia University Press.

Sorokin, Pitirim A. (1937) *Social and Cultural Dynamics.* New York: American Book.

Soroos, Marvin S. (2001) "The Tragedy of the Commons in Global Perspective," pp. 485–499 in Charles W. Kegley, Jr.

and Eugene R. Wittkopf (eds.), *The Global Agenda,* 6th ed. Boston: McGraw-Hill.

Spector, Michael. (1998) "Low Birth Rates Cause Alarm," *New York Times International Edition* (July 11–12): 1, 10.

Spero, Joan E., and Jeffrey A. Hart. (1997) *The Politics of International Economic Relations,* 5th ed. New York: St. Martin's Press.

Speth, James Gustave. (1999a) "Debt Relief, Yes, but Development Aid as Well," *International Herald Tribune* (May 7): 6.

———. (1999b) "The Neglect of Growing Poverty Poses a Global Threat," *International Herald Tribune* (July 17–18): 6.

———. (1999c) "The Plight of the Poor," *Foreign Affairs* 78 (May–June): 13–17.

Spykman, Nicholas. (1944) *Geography of Peace.* New York: Harcourt Brace.

Srodes, James. (2001) "Importing Economic Muscle," *World Trade* 14 (June): 13–15.

Stanley Foundation. (1999) *The United Nations and Civil Society.* Muscatine, Iowa: Stanley Foundation.

———. (1993) *The UN Role in Intervention.* Muscatine, Iowa: Stanley Foundation.

The State of Indigenous People. (2002) Olympia, Wash.: Center for World Indigenous Studies. www.soroptimisi.org

State of the World 2002. (2002) Worldwatch Institute. New York: Norton.

Starkey, Brigid, Mark Boyer, and Jonathan Wilkenfeld. (2000) *Negotiating a Complex World: An Introduction to International Negotiation.* Boulder, Colo.: Rowman & Littlefield.

Steger, Manfred B. (2002) *Globalism: The New Market Ideology.* Lanham, Md.: Rowman & Littlefield.

Stein, Janice Gross. (1993) "Reassurance in International Conflict Management," pp. 77–97 in Demetrios Caraly and Cerentha Harris (eds.), *New World Politics.* New York: Academy of Political Science.

Stein, Janice Gross, and Louis W. Pauly. (1993) *Choosing to Cooperate: How States Avoid Loss.* Baltimore: Johns Hopkins University Press.

Stephenson, Carolyn M. (2000) "NGOs and the Principal Organs of the United Nations," pp. 270–294 in Paul Taylor and R. J. Groom (eds.), *The United Nations at the Millennium.* London: Continuum.

Sterling, Claire. (1994) *Thieves' World: The Threat of the New Global Network of Organized Crime.* New York: Simon & Schuster.

Stevens, William K. (1997) "Five Years after Rio Summit, Old Ways Still Dominate," *International Herald Tribune* (June 18): 4.

Stevenson, Richard W. (1997) "The Cost of 'Fast-Track' Setback," *International Herald Tribune* (November 11): 3.

Stock, Thomas, and Anna De Geer. (1995) "Chemical and Biological Weapons, pp. 337–57 in the Stockholm International Peace Research Institute. *SIPRI Yearbook 1995.* New York Oxford University Press.

Stockholm International Peace Research Institute (SIPRI). (2002) *SIPRI Yearbook 2002.* New York: Oxford University Press.

———. (2001) *SIPRI Yearbook 2001.* New York: Oxford University Press.

———. (1999) *SIPRI Yearbook 1999.* New York: Oxford University Press.

Stokes, Bruce. (2000) "The Protectionist Myth," *Foreign Policy* 117 (Winter): 88–102.

Stopford, John. (2001) "Multinational Corporations," pp. 72–77 in Robert J. Griffiths (ed.), *Developing World 01/02.* Guilford, Conn.: Dushkin/McGraw-Hill.

Stott, Philip. (2002) "Cold Comfort for 'Global Warming,' " *Wall Street Journal* (March 25): A18.

———. (2000) "Multinational Corporations," *Foreign Policy* 117 (Winter): 12–20.

Strang, David. (1991) "Global Patterns of Decolonization, 1500–1987," *International Studies Quarterly* 35 (December): 429–545.

———. (1990) "From Dependence to Sovereignty: An Event History Analysis of Decolonization 1870–1987," *American Sociological Review* 55 (December): 846–860.

Strange, Susan. (1996) *The Retreat of the State.* Cambridge, Eng.: Cambridge University Press.

———. (1982) "Cave! Hic Dragones: A Critique of Regime Analysis," *International Organization* 36 (Spring): 479–96.

Strasser, Steven, and Mazumdar, Sudip. (1999) "A New Tiger," p. 119 in Robert Jackson, ed., *Global Issue 99/00,* 15th ed., Guilford, Conn.: Dushkin/McGraw-Hill.

Streeten, Paul. (2001) "Human Development Index," pp. 367–368 in Joel Krieger (ed.), *The Oxford Companion to Politics of the World,* 2nd ed. New York: Oxford University Press.

Strom, Stephanie. (2000) "Group of G-8 Nations Seek Their Own Path to a Common Goal," *International Herald Tribune* (January 23): 4.

Stross, Randall E. (2002) "The McPeace Dividend," *U.S. News and World Report* (April 1): 36.

Sumner, William Graham. (1968) "War," pp. 205–228 in Leon Bramson and George W. Goethals (eds.), *War.* New York: Basic Books.

Switzer, Jacqueline Vaughn. (2001) *Environmental Politics: Domestic and Global Dimensions.* Boston: Bedford/St. Martin's.

Talbott, Strobe. (1990) "Rethinking the Red Menace," *Time* (January 1): 66–72.

Talbott, Strobe, and Nayan Chanda (eds.). (2002) *The Age of Terror.* New York: Basic Books.

Tammen, Ronald J., et al. (2000) *Power Transitions: Strategies for the Twenty-First Century.* New York: Chatham House.

Taylor, Paul. (2000) "The Institutions of the United Nations and the Principle of Consonance," pp. 295–326 in Paul Taylor and R. J. Groom (eds.), *The United Nations at the Millennium.* London: Continuum.

Taylor, Peter J. (ed.). (1990) *World Government.* New York: Oxford University Press.

Thakur, Ramesh. (1998) "Teaming Up to Make Human Rights a Universal Fact," *International Herald Tribune* (December 10): 10.

Thakur, Ramesh, and Steve Lee. (2000) "Defining New Goals for Diplomacy in the Twenty-First Century," *International Herald Tribune* (January 19): 8.

Thompson, Kenneth W. (1960) *Political Realism and the Crisis of World Politics.* Princeton, N.J.: Princeton University Press.

———. (1953) "Collective Security Reexamined," *American Political Science Review* 47 (September): 753–72.

Thompson, William R. (ed.). (1999a) *Great Power Rivalries.* Columbia: University of South Carolina.

———. (1999b) "Why Rivalries Matter and What Great Power Rivalries Can Tell Us about World Politics," pp. 3–28 in William P. Thompson (ed.), *Great Power Rivalries.* Columbia: University of South Carolina Press.

———. (1988) *On Global War: Historical-Structural Approaches to World Politics.* Columbia: University of South Carolina Press.

Thurow, Lester C. (1999) *Building Wealth: The New Rules for Individuals, Companies, and Nations in a Knowledge-Based Economy.* New York: HarperCollins.

———. (1998) "The American Economy in the Next Century," *Harvard International Review* 20 (Winter): 54–59.

———. (1992) *Head to Head: Coming Economic Battles among Japan, Europe, and America.* New York: Morrow.

Tickner, J. Ann. (2002) *Gendering World Politics: Issues and Approaches in the Post–Cold War Era.* New York: Columbia University Press.

———. (1999) "Searching for the Princess? Feminist Perspectives in International Relations," *Harvard International Review* 121 (Fall): 41–48.

———. (1997) "You Just Don't Understand: Troubled Engagements between Feminists and IR Theorists," *International Studies Quarterly* 41 (December): 611–632.

———. (1992) *Gender in International Relations: Feminist Perspectives on Achieving Global Security.* New York: Columbia University Press.

Tilford, Earl H., Jr. (1995) *The Revolution in Military Affairs: Prospects and Cautions.* Carlisle Barracks, Pa.: U.S. Army War College.

Tillema, Herbert K. (2004) *Overt Military Intervention in the Cold War Era.* Columbia: University of South Carolina Press.

———. (1994) "Cold War Alliance and Overt Military Intervention, 1945–1991," *International Interactions* 20 (No. 3): 249–278.

———. (1989) "Foreign Overt Military Intervention in the Nuclear Age," *Journal of Peace Research* 26 (May): 179–195.

Tillema, Herbert K., and John R. Van Wingen. (1982) "Law and Power in Military Intervention: Major States after World War II," *International Studies Quarterly* 26 (June): 220–250.

Timmerman, Kenneth. (1991) *The Death Lobby: How the West Armed Iraq.* Boston: Houghton Mifflin.

Todaro, Michael P. (2000) *Economic Development,* 7th ed. Reading, Mass.: Addison-Wesley.

———. (1994) *Economic Development in the Third World,* 5th ed. New York: Longman.

Toffler, Alvin, and Heidi Toffler. (1993) *War and Anti-War: Survival at the Dawn of the Twenty-First Century.* New York: Little, Brown.

Toner, Robin. (2002) "FBI Agent Gives Her Blunt Assessment," *The State* (Columbia, S.C.) (June 7): A5.

Toynbee, Arnold J. (1954) *A Study of History.* London: Oxford University Press.

Trachtenberg, Marc. (1990–1991) "The Meaning of Mobilization in 1914," *International Security* 15 (Winter): 120–150.

Triffin, Robert. (1978–1979) "The International Role and Fate of the Dollar," *Foreign Affairs* 57 (Winter): 269–286.

Tuchman, Barbara W. (1984). *The March of Folly.* New York: Ballentine.

———. (1962) *The Guns of August.* New York: Dell.

Tucker, Neely. (1999) "AIDS Slashes Life Expectancy across Africa by 25 Years or More," (Columbia, S.C.) *The State* (March 19): A11.

Tucker, Robert C., and David C. Hendrickson. (1990) *Empire of Liberty.* New York: Oxford University Press.

Turk, Danilo. (2001) "Genocide," p. 316 in Joel Krieger (ed.), *The Oxford Companion to Politics of the World,* 2nd ed. New York: Oxford University Press.

Tyler, Patrik E. (2001) "Seeing Profits, Russia Prepared to Become World's Nuclear Waste Dump," *International Herald Tribune* (May 28): 5.

Ullman, Richard. (1983) "Refining Security," *International Security* 8 (Summer): 129–153.

United Nations. (1999) *World Economic and Social Survey 1999.* New York: United Nations.

———. (1998) *World Investment Report 1998.* New York: United Nations.

———. (1995a) *World Economic and Social Survey 1995.* New York: United Nations.

———. (1995b) *World Population Prospects: The 1994 Revision.* New York: United Nations.

United Nations Development Program (UNDP). (2002) *Human Development Report 2002.* New York: Oxford University Press.

United Nations Development Program (UNDP). (2002) *Human Development Report 2002.* New York: Oxford University Press.

———. (2001) *Human Development Report 2001.* New York: Oxford University Press.

———. (2000) *Human Development Report 2000.* New York: Oxford University Press.

———. (1999) *Human Development Report 1999.* New York: Oxford University Press.

———. (1998) *Human Development Report 1998.* New York: Oxford University Press.

———. (1997) *Human Development Report 1997.* New York: Oxford University Press.

———. (1995) *Human Development Report 1995.* New York: Oxford University Press.

———. (1994) *Human Development Report 1994.* New York: Oxford University Press.

———. (1993) *Human Development Report 1993.* New York: Oxford University Press.

———. (1991) *Human Development Report 1991.* New York: Oxford University Press.

United Nations Environment Programme. (2002) *Global Environment Outlook.* New York: Oxford University Press.

United Nations Population Division (UNPD). (2001) *World Population Projects.* New York: United Nations.

United Nations Population Division (UNPD). (2001) *World Population Prospects.* New York: United Nations.

U.S. Arms Control and Disarmament Agency (ACDA). (1997) *World Military Expenditures and Arms Transfers 1995.* Washington, D.C.: U.S. Government Printing Office.

U.S. Census Bureau. (2000) *Statistical Abstract of the United States.* Washington, D.C.: U.S. Government Printing Office.

U.S. Commission on Integrated Long-Term Strategy. (1988) *Discriminate Deterrence.* Washington, D.C.: U.S. Government Printing Office.

U.S. Department of State. (2000) *Patterns of Global Terrorism: 1999.* Washington, D.C.: U.S. Department of State.

———. (1994) *Dispatch 5,* Supplement No. 8. (September): 9.

———. (1993) *State 2000: A New Model for Managing Foreign Affairs.* Washington, D.C.: Office of Management Task Force.

———. (1983) *Security and Arms Control: The Search for a More Stable Peace.* Washington, D.C.: U.S. Government Printing Office.

Urquhart, Brian. (2001) "Shameful Neglect," *International Herald Tribune* (April 25): 12–14.

———. (2001) "Mrs. Roosevelt's Revolution," *New York Review of Books* 49 (April 26): 32–34.

———. (1994) "Who Can Police the World?" *New York Review of Books* 41 (May 12): 29–33.

Vaitheeswaron, Vijay. (2000) "Big Oil in Big Trouble," in *The World in 2000.* (London) *Economist* 89–90.

Van Evera, Stephen. (1999) *Causes of War: Power and the Roots of Conflict.* Ithaca, N.Y.: Cornell University Press.

———. (1990–1991) "Primed for Peace: Europe after the Cold War," *International Security* 15 (Winter): 7–57.

Vandersluis, Sarah Owen, and Paris Yeros (eds.). (2000a) "Ethics and Poverty in a Global Era," pp. 1–31 in Sarah Owen Vandersluis and Paris Yeros (eds.), *Poverty in World Politics.* New York: St. Martin's.

———. (2000b) *Poverty in World Politics.* New York: St. Martin's.

Vanhanen, Tatu. (2002) "Democratization in 2000," paper presented at the annual meeting of the International Studies Association, New Orleans, March 24–27.

———. (2000) "A New Dataset for the Measurement of Democracy 1810–1998," paper presented at the forty-first annual meeting of the International Studies Association, Los Angeles, March 14–18.

Vasquez, John A. (1998) *The Power of Power Politics: From Classical Realism to Neotraditionalism.* Cambridge, Eng.: Cambridge University Press.

———. (1997) "The Realist Paradigm and Degenerative versus Progressive Research Programs," *American Political Science Review* 91 (December): 899–912.

———. (1993) *The War Puzzle.* Cambridge, Eng.: Cambridge University Press.

———. (1991) "The Deterrence Myth: Nuclear Weapons and the Prevention of Nuclear War," pp. 205–223 in Charles W. Kegley, Jr. (ed.), *The Long Postwar Peace.* New York: HarperCollins.

Vasquez, John A., and Colin Elman (eds.). (2003) *Realism and the Balancing of Power: A New Debate.* Upper Saddle River, N.J.: Prentice Hall.

Väyrynen, Raimo. (1992) *Military Industrialization and Economic Development.* Aldershot, Eng.: Dartmouth.

Verba, Sidney. (1969) "Assumptions of Rationality and Non-Rationality in Models of the International System," pp. 217–231 in James N. Rosenau (ed.), *International Politics and Foreign Policy.* New York: Free Press.

Vernon, Raymond. (1971) *Sovereignty at Bay.* New York: Basic Books.

Vital Signs 2002. (2002) *Vital Signs 2002: The Trends That Are Shaping Our Future.* New York: W. W. Norton, for the Worldwatch Institute.

Vital Signs 2000. (2000) Lester Brown and colleagues of the Worldwatch Institute, et al., New York: Norton.

Vital Signs 1999. (1999) Lester R. Brown, Michael Renner, and Brian Halweil (et al.), eds. New York: Norton.

Vital Signs 1997. (1997) Lester R. Brown, Michael Renner, and Christopher Flavin (et al.), eds. New York: Norton.

Volgy, Thomas J., and Alison Bailin. (2002) *State Strength and the New World Order: An Analysis of Post-Cold War Architecture and its Consequences.* Boulder, Colo.: Lynne Rienner.

Wade, Robert Hunter. (2002) "America's Empire Rules an Unbalanced World," *International Herald Tribune* (January 3): 7.

Walker, William O. (1991) "Decision-Making Theory and Narcotic Foreign Policy: Implications for Historical Analysis," *Diplomatic History* 15 (Winter): 31–45.

Wallace, Brian. (1978) "True Grit South of the Border," *Osceola* (January 13): 15–16.

Wallensteen, Peter, and Margareta Sollenberg. (2001) "Armed Conflict 1989–2000." *Journal of Peace Research* 38 (September): 629–644.

———. (1999) "Armed Conflict, 1989–98," *Journal of Peace Research* 36 (September): 593–606.

———. (1998) "Armed Conflict and Regional Conflict Complexes, 1989–97," *Journal of Peace Research* 35 (September): 621–634.

Waller, Douglas. (1995) "Onward Cyber Soldiers," *Time* (August 21): 40–46.

Wallerstein, Immanuel. (2002) "The Eagle Has Crash Landed," *Foreign Policy* (July/August): 60–68.

———. (1988) *The Modern World-System III: The Second Era of Great Expansion of the Capitalist World-System, 1730–1840.* San Diego: Academic Press.

———. (1980) *The Modern World-System II.* New York: Academic Press.

———. (1974a) *The Modern World-System: Capitalist Agriculture and the Origins of the European World-Economy in the Sixteenth Century.* New York: Academic Press.

———. (1974b) "The Rise and Future Demise of the World Capitalist System: Concepts for Comparative Analysis," *Comparative Studies in Society and History* 16 (September): 387–415.

Walter, Barbara F. (1997) "The Critical Barrier to Civil War Settlement," *International Organization* 51 (Summer): 335–364.

Walters, Robert S., and David H. Blake. (1992) *The Politics of Global Economic Relations,* 4th ed. Englewood Cliffs, N.J.: Prentice Hall.

Waltz, Kenneth N. (2000) "Structural Realism after the Cold War," *Internatinal Security* 25 (Summer): 5–41.

———. (1999) "Globalization and Governance," *PS: Political Science and Politics* 32 (December) 693–700.

———. (1995) "Realist Thought and Neorealist Theory," pp. 67–83 in Charles W. Kegley, Jr. (ed.), *Controversies in International Relations Theory: Realism and the Neoliberal Challenge.* New York: St. Martin's Press.

———. (1993) "The Emerging Structure of International Politics," *International Security* 18 (Fall): 44–79.

———. (1979) *Theory of International Politics.* Reading, Mass.: Addison-Wesley.

———. (1964) "The Stability of a Bipolar World," *Daedalus* 93 (Summer): 881–909.

———. (1954) *Man, the State, and War.* New York: Columbia University Press.

Ward, Michael D., David R. Davis, and Corey L. Lofdahl. (1995) "A Century of Tradeoffs: Defense and Growth in Japan and the United States," *International Studies Quarterly* 39 (March): 27–50.

Warrick, Joby. (1998) "Turning Cool toward the Kyoto Accords," *Washington Post National Weekly Edition* (February 23): 31.

———. (1997) "How Warm Will It Get?" *Washington Post National Weekly Edition* (December 1): 6–7.

Watson, Douglas. (1997) "Indigenous Peoples and the Global Economy," *Current History* 96 (November): 389–391.

Wattenberg, Ben J. (2002) "Over-population Turns Out to Be Overhyped," *Wall Street Journal* (March 4): 10.

Watts, Sheldon. (1998) *Epidemics and History: Disease, Power, and Imperialism.* New Haven, Conn.: Yale University Press.

Weart, Spencer R. (1998) *Never at War: Why Democracies Will Not Fight One Another,* New Haven, Conn.: Yale University Press.

———. (1994) "Peace among Democratic and Oligarchic Republics," *Journal of Peace Research* 31 (August): 299–316.

Weidenbaum, Murray. (1999) "Weighing U.S. Advantages in Global Marketplace," *International Herald Tribune* (March 18): 11.

Weinberg, Gerhard L. (1994) *A World at Arms: A Global History of World War II*. Cambridge, Eng.: Cambridge University Press.

Weiner, Myron. (1995) *The Global Migration Crisis: Challenges to States and Human Rights*. New York: HarperCollins.

Weiss, Stanley A. (1999) "Food Sanctions Are Bad Policy, So Just Lift Them," *International Herald Tribune* (March 18): 6.

Weldes, Jutta, Mark Laffe, Hugh Gusterson, and Raymond Duvall (eds.) (2000) *Cultures of Insecurity: States, Communities, and the Production of Danger*. Minneapolis: University of Minnesota Press.

Wendt, Alexander. (2000) *Social Theory of Internatinal Politics*. Cambridge: Cambridge University Press.

———. (1992) "Anarchy Is What States Make of It: The Social Construction of Power Politics." *International Organization* 46 (Spring): 395–424.

Wendzel, Robert L. (1980) *International Relations: A Policymaker Focus*. New York: Wiley.

White, Donald W. (1998) "Mutable Destiny: The End of the American Century?" *Harvard International Review* 20 (Winter): 42–47.

White, Ralph K. (1990) "Why Aggressors Lose," *Political Psychology* 11 (June): 227–242.

Whiting, Allen S. (1985) "Foreign Policy of China," pp. 246–290 in Roy C. Macridis (ed.), *Foreign Policy in World Politics*, 6th ed. Englewood Cliffs, N.J.: Prentice Hall.

Whitney, Craig R. (1999) "European Union Vows to Become Military Power," *New York Times* (June 4): A1, A16

Will, George. (2002a) "Bush Move on Steel Shows Soft Principles," (Columbia, S.C.) *The State* (March 8): A11.

———. (2002b) "Tough-Taking Administration Getting Soft on Trade," (Columbia, S.C.) *The State* (April 14): D3.

Wilmer, Franke. (1993) *The Indigenous Voice in World Politics: Since Time Immemorial*. Newbury Park, Calif.: Sage.

Wilson, James Q. (1993) *The Moral Sense*. New York: Free Press.

Wise, Michael Z. (1993) "Reparations," *Atlantic Monthly* 272 (October): 32–35.

Wittkopf, Eugene R., Charles W. Kegley, Jr., and James M. Scott. (2003) *American Foreign Policy*, 6th ed. Belmont, Calif.: Wadsworth.

Wohlforth, William C. (1999) "The Stability of a Unipolar World," *International Security* 24 (Summer): 5–41.

Wolf, Charles, Jr. (2002) "To Intervene or Not to Intervene? America Ought to Decide," *International Herald Tribune* (November 8): 8.

Wolf, Martin. (2001) "Will the Nation-State Survive Globalization?" *Foreign Affairs* 80 (January/February): 178–190.

Wolfers, Arnold. (1962) *Discord and Collaboration*. Baltimore: Johns Hopkins University Press.

Woodward, Bob. (1991) *The Commanders*. New York: Simon & Schuster.

Woodward, Bob, and Rick Atkinson. (1990) "Launching Operation Desert Shield," *Washington Post National Weekly Edition* (September 3–9): 8–9.

World Bank. (2003) *World Development Report 2003*. New York: Oxford University Press.

———. (2002a) *World Bank Atlas*. Washington, D.C.: World Bank.

———. (2002b) *World Development Indicators 2002*. Washington, D.C.: World Bank.

———. *World Development Report 2002*. New York: Oxford University Press.

———. *World Development Report 2000—2001*. New York: Oxford University Press.

———. *Entering the 21st Century: World Development Report 1999/2000*. New York: Oxford University Press.

———. (1999a) *Global Economic Prospects and the Developing Countries, 1998/99*. Washington, D.C.: World Bank.

———. (1999b) *World Development Report, 1998/99*. New York: Oxford University Press.

———. (1998) *World Bank Atlas*. Washington D.C.: World Bank.

———. (1997) *World Development Report 1997*. New York: Oxford University Press.

———. (1996) *World Debt Tables 1996*, vol. 1. Washington, D.C.: World Bank.

———. (1995a) *Global Economic Prospects and the Developing Countries 1995*. Washington, D.C.: World Bank.

———. (1995b) *World Development Report 1995*. New York: Oxford University Press.

———. (1992) *World Development Report 1992*. New York: Oxford University Press.

The World in 2000. (2000) Worldwatch Institute. New York: Norton.

World Population Prospects: The 2000 Revisions. (2001) New York: United Nations Development Programme.

World Trade (2002) *World Trade* 14 (June 2002): 13–15.

Wren, Christopher S. (1999) "UN Reporting Cuts in Global Drug Crops' " *New York Times* (July 11): 11.

Wright, Quincy. (1953) "The Outlawry of War and the Law of War," *American Journal of International Law* 47 (July): 365–376.

———. (1942) *A Study of War*. Chicago: University of Chicago Press.

Wright, Robert. (2000a) "Continental Drift," *New Republic* (January 17): 18–23.

———. (2000b) *Nonzero: The Logic of Human Destiny*. New York: Pantheon.

Yearbook of International Organizations, 2001/2002, vol. 3. Munich: K. G. Sauer.

Yoder, Edwin M., Jr. (1991) "Isolationists Would Put America on a Dangerous Course," (Columbia, S.C.) *The State* (December 14): A10.

Young, Oran R. (1995) "System and Society in World Affairs: Implications for International Organizations," *International Social Science Journal* 144 (June): 197–212.

Zacher, Mark W. (1987) "Trade Gaps, Analytical Gaps: Regime Analysis and International Commodity Regulation," *International Organization* 41 (Spring): 173–202.

Zacher, Mark W., and Richard A. Matthew. (1995) "Liberal International Theory: Common Threads, Divergent Strands," pp. 107–149 in Charles W. Kegley, Jr. (ed.), *Controversies in International Relations Theory: Realism and the Neoliberal Challenge*. New York: St. Martin's Press.

Zagare, Frank C. (1990) "Rationality and Deterrence," *World Politics* 42 (January): 238–260.

Zakaria, Fareed. (2002a) "Europe: Make Peace with War," *Newsweek* (June 3): 35.

———. (2002b) "Stop the Babel over Babylon," *Newsweek* (October 16): 34.

———. (2002c) "The Trouble with Being the World's Only Superpower," *New Yorker* (October 14 and 21): 72–81.

———. (2001) "New Dangers amid the Ruins," *Newsweek* (March 5): 29.

———. (1999) "The Empire Strikes Out: The Unholy Emergence of the Nation-State," *New York Times Magazine* (April 18): 99.

———. (1998a) *From Wealth to Power: The Unusual Origins of America's World Role.* Princeton, N.J.: Princeton University Press.

———. (1998b) "The Future of Statecraft," p. 42 in *The World in 1999.* London: *Economist.*

———. (1992–1993) "Is Realism Finished?" *National Interest* 30 (Winter): 21–32.

Zelikow, Philip. (1987) "The United States and the Use of Force: A Historical Summary," pp. 31–81 in George K. Osburn, et al. (eds.), *Democracy, Strategy, and Vietnam.* Lexington, Mass.: Lexington Books.

Ziegler, David. (1995) Review of *World Politics and the Evolution of War,* by John Weltman, *American Political Science Review* 89 (September): 813–814.

Zimmerman, Tim. (1996) "CIA Study: Why Do Countries Fall Apart?" *U.S. News & World Report* (February 12): 46.

———. (1994) "Arms Merchant to the World," *U.S. News & World Report* (April 4): 37.

Zinnes, Dina A., and Jonathan Wilkenfeld. (1971) "An Analysis of Foreign Conflict Behavior of Nations," pp. 167–213 in Wolfram F. Handieder (ed.), *Comparative Foreign Policy.* New York: McKay.

INDEX

Note: Glossary terms appear in **bold faced** type. Page numbers followed by italicized letters *f, m,* and *t,* indicate figures, maps, and tables, respectively.

ABC broadcasting network, 276
A-Bomb WWW Museum, 528
Abramowitz, Morton, 85
absolute gains, 44, 310, 371, 597
Academic Council on the UN System, 139
Academic Info Religion (Web site), 184
acid rain, 382
ACMs. *See* air-launched cruise missiles
acquired immune deficiency syndrome (AIDS), 280, 361–63, 491
actor(s), 62
  nonstate, 19, 45, 59, 62, 136–40, 207
  unitary, 73, 73–80, 163
adjudication, 575
Afghanistan, 119, 228, 242, 254, 413, 468
  armed conflict and, 404, 406
  civil war and, 425
  end of Cold War and, 120
  Soviet invasion of, 118
Africa, 159–61, 196
  decolonization of, 199
  disease and, 280
  IGOs and, 160*m*
  population and, 358, 359
  refugees and, 242
  Third World countries in, 193
African Charter of Human and Peoples Rights (1981), 255
African Studies WWW, 221
Africa's First World War, 425
The Age of Imperialism (Web site), 221
agenda setting, 278
aging population, 360–61
Ahtisaari, Martti, 606, 628
AIDS. *See* acquired immune deficiency syndrome
air-launched cruise missiles (ACMs), 473
Al Qaeda, 62, 85, 165, 171, 242, 272, 441, 497, 519, 619
Albright, Madeleine, 557
Algeria, 199
alignments, 536
All India Women's Conference, 139
Allende, Salvador, 176
alliances, 534–35
Allied powers, 106–7, 108*m,* 112
Allison, Graham, 81–82
America Online, 278
American Journalism Review News Link, 25–26

Amin, Idi, 585
Amnesty International, 59, 162, 258, 271
  Web site, 262
anarchy, 11, 44, 48, 142, 209, 420
Andean Group, 212
Andropov, Yuri, 119
Angell, Norman, 33
Angola, 119
Annan, Kofi, 7, 143, 146, 147, 228, 253, 361, 365, 394, 512, 557, 576, 589, 591, 607, 616, 623, 625
Anti-Ballistic Missile (ABM) Treaty (1972), 506, 562
anticommunism, 114
antidumping duties, 313
antipersonnel landmines (APLs), 562
antisatellite (ASAT) weapons, 473
ANZUS (Australia, New Zealand, United States) pact, 595
apartheid, 523
APEC. *See* Asia Pacific Economic Cooperation
appeasement, 108
Arab Maghreb Union (AMU), 160
Arafat, Yasser, 77
arbitrage, 283
arbitration, 575
Arbotov, Georgi, 120
ARCO Oil Company, 374
Ardrey, Robert, 410
Argentina, 212, 339, 468
Arias, Oscar, 459
Aristotle, 188, 617
armed conflict, 404. *See also* wars
  between states, 408–24
  causes of, 408–24
  contemporary transformation of, 406, 408
  continuities and changes in, 405–8
  frequency of, 407*f*
  geography and, 412–13
  globalization and, 406, 415
  terrorism, 133–45
  within states, 424–33
Armey, Dick, 84
arms control, 553
  future of, 557–64
  multilateral diplomacy, 556–57
  negotiation of, 554–56
  treaties, 555*f,* 558–59*t,* 561*m*
  versus disarmament, 553–54
arms control regimes, 562
Arms Control Today, 471

arms race, 117–18, 209–10, 463
Arms Sales Monitoring Project (Web site), 493
arms trade, 617
  future trends in, 464
  motives for, 465–66
  strategic consequences of, 466–68
  to Global North, 463*f*
  to Global South, 463*f*
ASEAN. *See* Association of Southeast Asian Nations
Asia Pacific Economic Cooperation (APEC), 158, 212, 329
Asia, 242, 290
Asian Studies WWW Virtual Library, 221
Asian Tigers, 206, 271, 290
Asociación Latinoamericana de Integración (ALADI). *See* Latin American Integration Association
Association of Southeast Asian Nations (ASEAN), 159, 212, 339, 595
asylum, 245
asymmetrical warfare, 510
Atlantic Charter (1943), 574
atmosphere, ecopolitics of, 378
atomic bomb, 541
Atomic Bomb: Decision (Web site), 528
atrocities, 245
Atwood, Brian J., 215
Augustine, Saint, 579
Australia, 590, 595
Austria, 107, 155, 198, 340*m*
Austrian-Hungarian Empire, 101, 104, 105, 198, 417
authoritarian government, 69, 70
autocratic rule, 69
autonomy, 65
The Avalon Project—World War II (Web site), 132
axis of evil, 434, 507, 548, 619
Axis powers, 106–7, 108*m*

Baker, James A., 7, 84
Baker, James D., 384
balance of power, 103, 124, 506, 588
  assumptions of, 536–39
  collective security as substitute for, 540–41
  globalization and, 540–41
  models of, 541–43
  multipolarity, 544–49
  new geostrategic and, 546*m*

balance of power—(continued)
as peacekeeping strategy, 538–39
process of, 536–38
unipolarity, 549–53
balance of terror, 539
balancer, 537
Balkans, 109
Ballador, Edward, 624
ballistic missile defense
(BMD) system, 506
ballistic missile weapons, 465
Ban the Bomb, 92
bandwagoning, 483, 545
Bangladesh, 293
Bank of Japan, 283
Barbieri, Katherine, 415
bargaining, 499
Barnet, Richard J., 177
Baruch Plan (1946), 557
Basques, 63
beggar-thy-neighbor policies, 312
behavioral scientists, 39
behavioralism, 40, 41, 406, 604
Beijing '95: Women, Power, and
Change (Web site), 263
Belgium, 109, 155, 340m
Berger, Samuel R., 84, 632
Berlin Wall, 10, 120
Bevan, Aneurin, 471
Bietz, Charles R., 255
Big Mac Index, 326–27f
Big Three, 98, 112
bilateral, 148, 477
bilateral agreements, 554
bin Laden, Osama, 85, 437, 441, 497,
519, 619, 620
biodiversity, 384, 388–89, 390–91m
biological weapons, 475–77
Biological Weapons Convention
(1972), 475, 562
bipolarity, 104, 117, 542–43, 552
Blair, Tony, 189, 624
Boeing, 467
Boer War, 417
Bolivia, 212, 339
Bolshevik Revolution, 32, 114
Bolton, John, 594
Bonaparte, Napoleon, 91, 486
Bosnia, 259, 584
bounded rationality, 77
Boutros-Ghali, Boutros, 405, 587, 591,
614, 624
Bowlin, Mike, 374
boycotts, 520
brain drain, 243
Braudel, Fernand, 229
Brazil, 212, 339
Bretton Woods Monetary System, 306,
307, 319, 325, 327–29
Brezhnev, Leonid, 119, 532
brinkmanship, 503
Britain. See Great Britain
Brittan, Leon, 394
Bronowski, Jacob, 631
Brundtland Commission, 371
Brunei, 212

Brzezinski, Zbigniew, 83
Bulgaria, 545
Bulletin of the Atomic Scientists, 476
Web site, 566
Bunche, Ralph, 410
Bundesbank, 283
Bunn, Matthew, 471
bureaucracies, 80, 81
attributes of, 85–87
consequences of, 87–88
efficiency and rationality, 81
limits of, 81–85
sabotage, 87
bureaucratic politics model, 81–82
Burger, Julian, 166m
Bush Doctrine, 88, 128, 479, 497,
549, 582
Bush, George, 122, 404, 585
Bush, George W., 7, 9, 62, 67, 69,
75–76, 83–84, 86, 128, 136, 304,
311, 337, 346, 381m, 383, 392,
404, 441, 442, 444, 455, 472,
477–82, 497, 504, 506, 515, 519,
546, 549, 554, 556, 562, 590, 591,
619–21
Butterfield, Herbert, 229

Caarlsson, Ingvar, 604–5
CAIN Web Service, 447
Canada, 147, 212, 330, 339, 603
Canadian Chemical Producers
Association, 139
capabilities, 44
capital investments, in the Global
South, 218f
capital mobility hypothesis, 284, 285m
capitalism, 197
capitalistic imperialism, 114
Cardoso, Fernando Henrique, 352
CARE International, 139
Caribbean Basin Initiative
(1984), 339
Caribbean Community and Common
Market (CARICOM), 159
Carnegie Council of Ethics and
International Affairs (Web
site), 608
Carpenter, Ted Galen, 121
Carr, E. H., 36, 616
carrying capacity, 352
cartel, 373
Carter Doctrine, 118
Carter, Jimmy, 16, 30, 82, 118, 464,
532, 557
cartographers, 14
Castor, Fidel, 75, 544
caucuses, 82
CBS broadcasting network, 276
CFCs. See chlorofluorocarbons
CFSP. See Common Foreign and
Security Policy
Center for Middle Eastern Studies
(Web site), 222
Center for Nonproliferation Studies
(CNS) (Web site), 566
Central America, 119

Central Intelligence Agency, 86, 457
Central Intelligence Agency State
Failure Task Force, 430
Central Powers, 105
Chamberlain, Neville, 109
chaos theory, 52
Cheknomyrdin, Vickor, 551
Chemical Weapons Convention
(CWC), 557, 476
chemical weapons, 465, 475–77
Cheney, Dick, 84, 437, 621
Chernenko, Konstantin, 119
Chernobyl nuclear power plant, 375
child labor, 293
children
as soldiers, 457
as victims, 254
Chile, 259, 339, 434, 584
Chiltelco, 176
China, 18p, 66, 106, 117, 122, 125,
129, 147, 192–93, 196, 468, 518,
544, 551, 584, 621, 625
AIDs and, 362
ethnic cleansing and, 248
genetic engineering and, 368
imported arms and, 463
multipolar politics and, 126
national security strategies of,
483–86
nuclear club, 470
nuclear weapons and, 210
population and, 359
UN and, 141
UN Security Council and, 588
World Bank and, 150
China Investigation Report (2002), 248
chlorofluorocarbons (CFCs), 383–84
Churchill, Winston, 8, 91, 98, 112
citistates, 20
citizenship, 254
civil society, 230
Civil War, American, 417, 603
civil war(s), 424. See also war(s)
causes of, 427–31
characteristics of, 425–27
economic sources of, 430–31
ethnic groups and, 425
ethnonational conflict and, 428–29
failed states and, 429–30
frequency of, 426
internal rebellion and, 427
international dimensions of, 431–33
issues of, 425
nationalism and, 428
secessionist revolts and, 427–28
states threatening to collapse in, 431m
civilizations, 168m
Clarke, Jonathan, 98
clash of civilizations, 165, 200,
248, 622
classical economic development
theory, 203
classical liberal economic theory, 196
Claude, Inis L., 199, 539, 606
climate change, 378–83
Web site, 398

Clinton, Bill, 8, 43, 73, 75, 77, 89, 429, 622, 629, 614
Clinton Doctrine, 88, 513
closed systems, 69
CNN (Cable News Network), 277, 278
  Web Site, 26
CNS. *See* Center for Nonproliferation Studies
coal, 382–83
Cobden, Richard, 33*f*
coercive diplomacy, 373, 455
  changing incidence of military intervention in, 513*f*
  deterring terrorism, 509–19
  military approach to, 516–19
  nuclear deterrence and defense, 501–9
  place in world politics, 496–99
  sanctions as instruments of, 519–27
  security dilemma, 499–500
coexistence, 118
cognitive dissonance, 13, 77–78
Cohen, William, 445
cold peace, 122
Cold War, 9, 31, 99, 113, 142
  causes of, 113–21
  characteristics of, 114–16
  coexistence to détente, 1963–1978, 118
  confrontation, 1945–1962, 116–118
  consequences of, 121–22
  end of, 120
  key events in evolution of U.S.-Soviet relationship, 116*f*
  nuclear deterrence and defense after, 506–9
  peaceful ending of, 120
  renewed confrontation to rapprochement, 1979–1991, 118–20
  Web site, 132
collective goods, 315, 389
collective security, 34, 130, 142, 540, 588–94, 595
Cologne European Union (EU) Summit (1999), 128
Colombia, 212, 425
colonialism, 109, 191, 198–200, 204
colonization, 198
commercial domino theory, 328–29
commercial liberalism, 284, 306, 308–10, 414
commitments, 503
Common Foreign and Security Policy (CFSP), 600
Common Market for Eastern and Southern Africa (COMESA), 160
common security, 492
communication technologies, 273–76
communism, 114, 115, 196
communist bloc, 544
communist theory of imperialism, 414
comparative advantage, 308, 309*t*, 344
compellence, 502–3

competition, versus transnational collaboration, 21–22
complex interdependence, 45
compliance, 521
Comprehensive Test Ban Treaty (CTBT), 470, 561*m*
computers, 271–72, 475
Comte, August, 21
The Concept of National Security (Putin), 483
concert, 129–30
Concert of Europe (1815), 125, 130, 424
conciliation, 575
conflict, 405, 451
Congress of Vienna, 424
constitutional democracy, 69
constructivism, 19, 31, 49–55, 80, 163, 164, 178, 406
containment, 117, 486
Contemporary Philosophy, Critical Theory, and Postmodern Thought (Web site), 56
Contingency Credit Line (CCL), 334
A Contribution to the Critique of Political Economy (Marx), 306
Convention on the Prohibition of the Use, Stockpiling, Production and Transfer of Antipersonnel Mines and Their Destruction, 562
Convention Prohibiting the Trafficking of Women and Children for Prostitution (2000), 573
Convention to Combat Desertification (CCD) (1999), 386*m*
conventional deterrence, 500
Conventional Forces in Europe (CFE) Treaty, 120
conventional war, 509
conventions, for human rights protection, 260*t*
core states, 205
cornucopians, 365–68
Corporate Conduct Code for Third World Nations, 219
corpus juris gentium, 572
cost of goods, 326–27*f*
Council of Arab Economic Unity (CAEU), 159
Council of Europe, 596
Council of Ministers (EU), 156
counterfactual reasoning, 102, 474, 475, 507
counterforce targeting strategy, 503
counterterrorism, 86, 128, 442–45
Counterterrorism Committee (CTC), 591
countervailing duties, 313
countervailing powers, 179
countervalue targeting strategy, 503
countries. *See* states *or specific countries*
covert operations, 512
credit tranche, 154
crimes against humanity, 574

crises decisions, 514
crises, international, 514–16, 517*f*
Crusades, 167
CTBT. *See* Comprehensive Test Ban Treaty
Cuba, 75, 117, 120, 434, 544
Cuban Missile Crisis, 75, 81–82, 87, 117–18, 502
  Web site, 94
cultural conditioning, 412
cultural diversity, 249
cultural domains, 165
culture, war and, 41
current history approach, 32
cyberspace, 272
cyber-terrorism, 445
cycles, 11
Cyprus, 156
Czech Republic, 156, 248, 545
Czechoslovakia, 104, 107, 109, 112, 117, 198, 248

Danube River Commission (1857), 599
Darwin, Charles, 409
Data on the net, 56
Davos World Economics Forum (2001), 275
debt relief, 218–19
Declaration on the Granting of Independence to Colonial Countries and Peoples (1960), 199
decolonization, 193, 198–200
deconstruction, 52
deconstructivism, 40, 41
de Cuellar, Javier Perez, 589
de facto recognition, 574
deforestation, 385
de Gaulle, Charles, 471
de jure recognition, 574
del Ponte, Carla, 585
Delay, Tom, 84
demilitarization, 553
democracies, 35, 72*m*, 120
  advance of, 417*f*
  human development and, 235–37
  war and, 416
democratic capitalism, 11, 106
democratic peace, 71, 416, 479, 603–5
democratic systems, 69–73
demographic divide, 356*f*, 357–58
demographic transition, 359–61
demography, 352. *See also* population growth
Denmark, 109, 155
Department of Defense, 467
Department of Homeland Security, 86
dependency, 204
dependency theory, 203–4, 234
dependent development, 205
dependentistas, 204
derivatives, 284
Desai, Nitin, 209
desertification, 386–87
détente, 118, 119

deterrence, 475, 521, 534
  elements of, 517–18
  terrorism and, 509–19
Deutsch, Karl, 419
developed countries, 200. *See also* Global North
developing countries, 200. *See also* Global South
development, 202
  classical economic development theory, 203
  human, 234–39, 364
  neoclassical theory, 205–7
devolution, 162, 247, 603
Dhanapala, Jayantha, 209, 614
digital divide, 274*f*, 275
digital world economy, 284
diplomatic immunity, 574
diplomatic recognition, 574
disarmament, 35, 120, 471–72, 553–54, 556–57
Disney Corporation, 276
displaced people, 241, 429, 623
diversionary theory of war, 70, 432
divine right of kings, 574
Doctors Without Borders, 162, 625
doctrine, 209, 506, 543, 604, 623
dollar convertibility, 328
domestic jurisdiction, 572–74
domestic symbolism, 522
domino theory, 115
Dos Santos, Theotonio, 204
Dreams of Tibet (Web site), 447
dualism, 203, 204–5
Dubos, René, 614
Dulles, John Foster, 432, 503
Duvallier, Jean-Claude, 585
Dworkin, Ronald, 229

Eagleburger, Lawrence, 7, 84, 127, 544
EAPC. *See* Euro-Atlantic Partnership Council
Earth Summit (1992), 371, 389
Earth Times (Web site), 397
Earthjustice Legal Defense Fund, 139
East Germany, 66, 108*m*
East Timor, 428, 498, 512, 590
Eban, Abba, 572
Eberstadt, Nicholas, 352
Ebola virus, 280
Economic and Social Council (UN), 143
Economic Community of Central African States (CEEAC), 160
Economic Community of West African States (ECOWAS), 159, 160
economic conditions, states, 68–69
economic development, foreign policy and, 65
economic freedom, political risk and, 338*m*
economic hierarchy, 11
economic rivalries, 127*t*
economic sanctions, 520
  countries vulnerable to, 522–53*m*
  globalization and, 521

policy goals related to, 521
  reasons for, 521
  unsuccessful, 523–26
economics, 22–23, 37
  globalization and, 288*f*, 305–6
  human development and, 237–39
  multipolarity and, 126
  new imperialism and, 196–98
  war and, 414–15
ecopolitics, 368
  of atmosphere, 378–82
  of biodiversity, 384, 388–89, 390–91*m*
  of energy, 372–78
  of forests, 384–88
Ecuador, 212
Egypt, 77, 117, 213, 463
Eide, Espen Barth, 626
Einstein, Albert, 469–70, 570, 597, 630–31
Eisenhower, Dwight D., 89, 457, 459, 467, 490, 586, 617
El Salvador, 434, 469
electromagnetic pulse (EMP) bombs, 475
Emerson, Ralph Waldo, 88
enclosure movement, 389
end of history, 71, 120, 628–29
enduring rivalries, 101
energy
  ecopolitics of, 372–78
  global transformation of, 374–75
  nuclear, 375–78
  security, 373–78
En-Lai, Chou, 496
England. *See* Great Britain
entente, 129
Entente Cordiale, 102
environment, 392–94. *See also* ecopolitics
environmental protection, 391–92
environmental security, 246, 368–72
environmental sustainability index, 390–91*m*
epistemic community, 370, 371
epistemology, 52
Essay on the Principle of Population (Malthus), 366
Essence of Decision (Allison), 81–82
Estonia, 104, 112, 156, 545
ethics, 229, 353, 504, 579
Ethiopia, 247, 362
ethnic cleansing, 242, 244, 248, 622
ethnic groups, 63, 164, 425
ethnic nationalism, 164
ethnic warfare, 428
ethnicity, 163, 164
ethnocentrism, 248, 622
ethnonational conflict, war and, 428–29
ethnonationalism, 249
ethnopolitical groups, 59, 163, 164
ethnopolitical movements, 164–65
EU. *See* European Union
Euro-Atlantic Partnership Council (EAPC), 545, 546*m*, 596
Euroland. *See* European Union

Europe, 10, 65, 414
  population and, 358, 359
  post–World War I boundaries, 105*m*
  post–World War II boundaries, 108*m*, 112
European Atomic Energy Committee (Euratom), 155
European Central Bank (ECB), 334
European Coal and Steel Community (ECSC), 155, 600
European Commission, 156
European Court of Human Rights, 586
European Court of Justice (ECJ), 157, 586
European imperialism, 194–98
European Parliament, 156–57
European Rapid Reaction Force, 489, 601
European Union (EU), 7, 11, 59, 66, 136, 155–58, 290, 334, 544, 596, 600–602
  free trade and, 335–37
  governmental structure, 157*f*
  national security strategies of, 488–90
  Russia and, 483
  Web site, 183
Evans, Gareth, 136
exchange rates, 323–25
  Web site, 349
exclusionism, 172
export quotas, 312
export-led industrialization, 210–11
extended deterrence, 117, 543
extraterritoriality, 574
extreme militant religious movements, 172

failed states, 209, 242, 282, 587
  civil war and, 425, 429–30
  intervention and, 513
failing states, 429, 622
Falkland Islands, 468
fascism, 32, 107, 111
fast-track negotiating authority, 337
FDI. *See* foreign direct investment
Federal Bureau of Investigations (FBI), 86
Federal Republic of Germany, 66, 108*m*
federalism, 596–98
Federation of American Scientists (Web site), 566
feminist theory, 45, 46, 47*f*, 231, 253, 411–12
  Web site, 56
Feminist Theory and Gender Studies (Web site), 56
Ferdinand, Archduke, 101
fertility rate, 357
Fides et Ratio, 54*f*
Fifth Committee, 144
finance, globalization of, 283–86
Finland, 66, 104, 112, 155
firebreak, 473
First World, 191
Fischer, Joschka, 548

Fischer, Stanley, 347
Five Power Treaty (1922), 106
fixed exchange rates, 325, 327
floating exchange rates, 330, 332
Food and Agriculture Organization
 (FAO), 587
food security, 365
Ford, Gerald, 82
Foreign Affairs, 84, 117
Foreign Affairs Online, 26
foreign aid, 213–19
foreign debts, 330
foreign direct investment (FDI), 173,
 204, 215, 217, 285m, 293, 294f
foreign policy, 16, 59, 62
 bureaucratic politics of, 80–88
 domestic determinants of, 63–73
 geography and, 65m
 global determinants of, 63–73
 Global South, 207–19
 modern state system, 63
 problems and prospects of, 91–93
 role of leaders in, 88–91
 unitary actors and rational
  decisions, 73–80
forests, ecopolitics of, 384–88
Fossil Free Energy Scenario, 376f
fossil fuels, 374–75, 376f
Four Power Treaty, 106
Fourth Freedom Forum (Web site), 528
Fourth Way, 219
Fourth World, 164, 165, 622
 indigenous cultures of, 166m, 167m
 indigenous peoples in, 245–49
 Documentation Project (Web
  Site), 262
*Framework Convention on Climate
 Change* (1992), 378, 383
France, 101–9, 147
 as arms supplier, 464–65
 disarmament and, 556
 European Commission, 156
 European Union and, 155
 immigration and, 241
 monetary policy and, 330
 nuclear club, 470
 nuclear weapons and, 471
 population and, 359
 trade blocs and, 340m
 UN Security Council and, 588
 World Bank and, 150
Franco, Francisco, 109
Frank, Andre Gunder, 204
Franklin, Benjamin, 16, 308, 310
Frechette, Louise, 591
free riders, 316
free trade, 213, 319–21. *See also* trade
 globalization and, 322–23
 hegemony and, 313–19
 sustainable development and, 392–94
**Free Trade Area of the Americas
 (FTAA),** 339
freedom fighters, 434
Freedom House (Web site), 94
Freedom, Democracy, Peace; Power,
 Democide, and War, (Web site), 94

Freud, Sigmund, 409
Friedman, Thomas, 21, 266, 415, 624
Frost, Robert, 55
FTAA. *See* Free Trade Area of the
 Americas
Fukuyama, Francis, 43, 71, 120, 409,
 624, 628
functionalism, 598–600
future, of great-power politics, 122–30

G-5, 330
G-7. *See* Group of 7
G-8. *See* Group of Eight
G-77. *See* Group of 77
Gandhi, Indira, 627
GATT. *See* General Agreement on
 Tariffs and Trade
GDP. *See* gross domestic product
gender empowerment, 252
gender empowerment index, 250
gender inequalities, 46, 249–53
gender myopia, 252
**General Agreement on Tariffs and
 Trade (GATT)** (1947), 48,
 148–49, 286, 319–21
General Assembly (UN), 143–44, 587
General Motors, 62
genetic engineering, 365
Geneva Convention (1949), 253
Geneva Protocol, 476
genocide, 247, 248–49, 259, 421, 582,
 584
Genocide Convention (1948), 247
geo-economics, 23
geography, armed conflict and,
 412–13
geopolitics, 23, 32, 66
German Democratic Republic, 66,
 108m
Germany, 32, 66, 101–11, 142, 147,
 417, 544
 ethnic cleansing and, 244
 European Commission, 156
 European Union and, 155
 monetary policy and, 330
 national security strategies of,
  488–90
 population and, 359
 World Bank and, 150
 WWII and, 106–9
global agenda, 18, 147, 629–30
*Global Dreams: Imperial Corporations
 and the New World Order,* 177
global economics, 124f
global governance, 178
global hierarchy, 123m
global imperialism, 194m
global interests, versus national
 interests, 615–16
global level of analysis, 17, 41,
 73–74, 102, 137, 138, 190, 418
global migration crisis, 282
Global North, 17, 144, 191
 GNP and, 23
 military spending and, 460, 461m
 versus Global South, 189m, 191–94

global patterns, 19
Global Reach (Barnet), 177
Global South, 17, 182, 188–91
 AIDS and, 280
 as arms supplier, 465
 capital investments in, 218f
 colonial plight origins, 191–200
 democracy and, 200
 foreign policy, 207–19
 future role of, 219–20
 gender gap and, 251–52
 GNP and, 23
 living conditions of, 232–34
 migration and, 243
 military spending and, 460, 461m
 UN and, 144
 underdevelopment, 202–7
 versus Global North, 189m, 191–94,
  200–202
 war and, 406, 407f
 world trade and, 289–94
global system, 11, 190–91
global terrorism, 69, 75, 126, 437, 604,
 619–21
global village, 269
global warming, 6, 378–83
Global Youth Connect, 162
globalization, 9, 18p, 21–22, 45, 64, 65,
 130, 153, 176, 200, 234, 451, 631
 armed conflict and, 406
 balance of power and, 541
 communication technologies and,
  273–76
 consequences of, 267–68
 defining, 269–83
 disease and, 280–82
 economic sanctions and, 521
 economics and, 266–67, 305–6
 of finance, 283–86
 free trade and, 322–23
 human development and, 239–41
 impact of, 623–25
 information age and, 270–73
 media and, 276–80
 states and, 270–71, 297–300
 of terrorism, 436–42
 of trade, 286–96
 of war, 415
globalization of finance, 283–86
GNP. *See* gross national product
Goering, Hermann, 431
good offices, 575
Gorbachev, Mikhail, 23, 91, 120, 418,
 483, 623, 629
government type
 foreign policy and, 65
 states, 69–73
 war and, 415–18
governmental politics, 82–83
Graham, Billy, 279
Grand Coalition, 108
Great Britain, 65, 101–9, 142, 147,
 422, 468, 585, 603
 as arms supplier, 464–65
 Bretton Woods and, 306
 disarmament and, 556

Great Britain—*(continued)*
economic leadership and, 316
European Commission, 156
European Union and, 155
expansion of, 196
immigration and, 241
monetary policy and, 330
nuclear club, 470
nuclear weapons and, 471
UN Security Council and, 588
World Bank and, 150
Great Depression, 110, 316
great powers, 19, 59, 98
Cold War, 113–22
evolution of rivalry for world
leadership, 100*t*
future politics, 122–30
national security strategies of,
477–90
quest for hegemony, 99–101
World War I, 101–6
World War II, 106–13
Greece, 70, 117
greenhouse effect, 378–79, 491
greenhouse gases, 381*m*
Greenpeace, 59, 271, 368
Web site, 397
Grey, Edward, 500
Gromyko, Andrei, 557
gross domestic product, 237*f*
gross national income (GNI), 200,
454*m*, 458
gross national product (GNP), 23,
68, 541
Grotius, Hugo, 579–80
Group of Eight (G-8), 188, 219,
330, 604
Group of 5, 330
Group of 7 (G-7), 148, 330
Group of 77 (G-77), 144, 211
groupthink, 87, 411
Gulf Cooperation Council, 595
gunboat diplomacy, 516, 518
guns versus butter, 458
Gurr, Ted Robert, 410, 417*f*, 428–29

Hagel, Chuck, 76
Hague peace conferences, 32
Hague Tribunal (1997), 259
Haiti, 585
Hammarskjold, Dag, 589
Haq, Mahbud ul, 235
hard power, 457, 481
Hardin, Garrett, 353
Harknett, Richard, 518
Havana Charter, 319
Havel, Václav, 180, 304
HDI. *See* Human Development Index
**Heavily Indebted Poor Countries
(HIPCs),** 219
Hegel, Georg Wilhelm Freidrich,
496–97
hegemonic stability theory, 101,
313, 518
hegemon(s), 99, 125, 313–15,
422, 538

hegemony, 99–101, 113, 122, 126,
129, 313–19
Henry L. Stimson Center (Web
site), 493
Hermann, Margaret G., 90
hierarchies, 11
high politics, 19, 179, 305, 370, 630
HIPCs. *See* Heavily Indebted Poor
Countries
Hiroshima, 10*p*, 111, 469, 502
**history-making individuals
model,** 88
Hitler, Adolf, 32, 66, 88, 101, 108, 110,
111, 247, 421, 504
HIV. *See* human immunodeficiency
virus
Hobbes, Thomas, 36, 37, 234, 253, 536
Hobson, J. A., 198
Hoebel, E. Adamson, 577
Hoffmann, Stanley, 6, 10, 626
Holiberg, Anne-Else, 596
Hong Kong, 206, 271
**horizontal nuclear
proliferation,** 470
Howard, John, 630
Hughes, Emmet John, 89
human development, 234–35, 364
democracy and, 235–37
economics and, 237–39
Human Development Index (HDI),
235, 236*t*, 237*f*, 238*m*, 239, 431
Human Development Reports, 233,
235, 236–37, 238–39
**human immunodeficiency virus
(HIV),** 280, 361–63
human impact of war, 413
human nature, war and, 409–11
human needs, 235
human rights, 23, 228, 231, 337, 416,
513, 582
abuses, 256–61
conventions for protection, 260*t*
gender inequalities, 249–53
groups, 47
indigenous peoples, 245–49
intervention and, 622–23
legislation, 583–84
protection of people, 253–56
refugees, 241–45
Human Rights Watch (Web site), 608
human security, 234–35, 241, 246,
268, 457, 458
humanitarian intervention, 256–59,
623, 624
humanity, state and, 254–55
Hume, David, 33
Hungary, 117, 156, 198, 545
Huntington, Samuel P., 136, 165,
168*m*, 248, 622
Hussein, Saddam, 7, 62, 67–68, 69,
75–76, 83–84, 247, 372, 408, 467,
479, 504, 510, 520, 525–26, 585,
619, 620
Huxley, Aldous, 418
hyperdemocratic, 287*m*
hypernationalism, 110, 419

ibi jus, 576
IBRD. *See* World Bank
ICBMs. *See* intercontinental ballistic
missiles
ICT. *See* information and
communications technology
idealists, 33–34
ideology, 13, 114, 115, 116, 142,
253, 599
IGOs. *See* intergovernmental
organizations
IISDnet, 397
ILO. *See* International Labor
Organization
images, 12–13, 16
IMF. *See* International Monetary Fund
immigrants, 241
imperial overstretch, 317
imperial reach, 68
imperialism, 66, 110, 197, 549
European, 194–97
global, 194*m*
Imperialism (Hobson), 198
*Imperialism, The Highest Stage of
Capitalism* (Lenin), 197
import quotas, 312
**import-substitution
industrialization,** 210
income inequalities, 232
INCORE (Web site), 447
independence, war and, 411
India, 63, 193, 199, 280, 560
AIDS and, 362
devolution and, 247
export trade and, 290
multipolar politics and, 126
nuclear club, 470
nuclear weapons and, 210
population of, 352
war and, 412
indigenous nationalities, 62
indigenous peoples, 164–65, 166*m*,
167*m*, 191, 245–49, 603
individual level of analysis, 17, 103, 190
Indochine, 199
Indonesia, 212, 248–49, 428, 463,
498, 590
Industrial Revolution, 196, 198
industrialization, 32
infant industries, 312, 313
inflation, 325
The Influence of Sea Power in History
(Mahan), 66–67
information age, 395, 454*m*, 625
globalization and, 270–73
terrorism and, 445
**information and communications
technology (ICT),** 275
information warfare (IW), 475
informed choices, 78
infowar tactics, 475
inhumanity, morality and, 261
INS, 86
Institute for War and Peace Reporting
(Web site), 447
instrumental rationality, 88–89

intelligence agencies, 85–86
intentions, 44
Inter-American Court on Human Rights, 586
intercommunal warfare, 244
intercontinental ballistic missiles (ICBMs), 543
interdependence, 21, 130, 181, 307
interest groups, 178
interests, global versus national, 615–16
intergovernmental organizations (IGOs), 19, 59, 137–40, 514, 599
  classification of, 138*t*
  European Union, 155–58
  International Monetary Fund, 152–54
  others, 158–61
  United Nations, 140–47
  World Bank, 150–52
  World Trade Organization, 148–50
  Africa and, 160*m*
  versus NGOS and states, 137*f*
Intergovernmental Panel on Climate Change (IPCC), 7, 379
intermestic policies, 64, 561*m*, 599
International Bank for Reconstruction and Development (IBRD). *See* World Bank
International Bill of Rights, 255
International Campaign to Ban Landmines, 562
International Chamber of Commerce, 162
International Civil Aviation Organization (1944), 161
International Code of Conduct on Arms Transfers (Web site), 493–94
international commerce, 306
International Commission on Intervention and States Sovereignty (2001), 256
International Conference on Population and Development (ICPD), 364
international cooperation, 44
International Court of Justice (ICJ) (UN), 143, 585–86. *See also* World Court Web site, 608
International Criminal Court (ICC) (UN), 562, 584, 585
International Criminal Tribunal for the Former Yugoslavia (ICTY) (Web site), 609
International Crisis Group (Web site), 447
International Data Base (Web site), 397
International Development Association (IDA), 150
International Federation of Red Cross, 271
International Futures Programme (Web site), 633
international inequalities, terrorism and, 200

International Labor Organization (ILO), 161, 275, 587, 599
international law
  core principles of, 572–75
  dispute settlement procedures, 575
  foreign policy and, 64
  human rights and, 583–84
  limitations of, 575–76
  military intervention rules, 582
  nonintervention rule in, 583*f*
  peace contribution, 584–86
  private, 572
  public, 572
  relevance of, 578
  rules of, 572–75
  sources of, 575
  versus states' rights on prostitution, 573
  war conduct and, 583–84
  war crimes and, 259
  warfare control and, 578
  world order and, 570–86
international liquidity, 328
International Monetary Fund (IMF), 48, 147–48, 152–54, 181, 202, 327, 334, 604
  Enhanced Structural Adjustment Facility, 219
  foreign aid and, 215
  military spending and, 456
  monetary reform and, 333
  underdevelopment and, 206
  Web site, 183
international monetary system, 306
international organizations, 11, 62
international organized crime (IOC), 282, 445
International Peace Conference, 556
international political economy, 305
international political system, 8
international politics, 37
international regimes, 45, 48, 253, 318
international relations, 32
  behavioral science and, 40
  perceptions of, 13
international security, 127–30, 179
international symbolism, 522
international system, 10
International Telecommunication Union (1865), 161
International Telegraphic Union (1865), 599
International Telephone and Telegraph (ITT), 176
international terrorism, 172, 248, 436–37
international trade, foreign policy and, 64
International Trade Organization (ITO), 148, 319
International Tropical Timber Organization (ITTO), 385
International Year of Mountains (2002), 384, 413
Internet, 271–73, 275–77, 625

interspecific aggression, 409
intersubjective consensus, 31
intervention, 256–59, 411
intervention fatigue, 519
interventionism, 16, 68, 597
intraspecific aggression, 409
IPCC. *See* Intergovernmental Panel on Climate Change
Iran, 62, 83, 279, 434, 475–76, 507, 520, 548, 560, 584, 620, 621
Iran-Contra Affair, 86
Iraq, 7, 62, 67–68, 75–76, 83–84, 247, 372, 408, 434, 468, 471, 479, 497, 504, 507, 510, 520, 548, 560, 584, 585, 590
  armed conflict and, 404, 406
  biological weapons and, 475–76
  chemical weapons and, 475
  ethnic cleansing and, 249
  nuclear weapons and, 210
  sanctions bomb, 525–26
Ireland, 155, 244
irredentism, 107, 172, 249
Islamic fundamentalism, 11
isolationism, 107, 128
Israel, 7, 77, 560
  devolution and, 248
  foreign aid and, 213
  free-trade agreements, 339
  immigration and, 241
  imported arms and, 463
  nuclear club, 470
  trade blocs and, 340*m*
Italy, 105–11, 142, 147
  disarmament and, 556
  European Commission, 156
  European Union and, 155
  monetary policy and, 330
  population and, 359
  xenophobia and, 244
ITO. *See* International Trade Organization
ITTO. *See* International Tropical Timber Organization
Ivory Coast, armed conflict and, 404

James, Patrick, 43
Japan, 62, 101, 106, 108, 109, 112, 126, 129, 142, 148, 196, 290, 544
  atomic bomb and, 501
  disarmament and, 556
  ethnic cleansing and, 244
  free trade and, 335–37
  monetary policy and, 330
  national security strategies of, 486–88
  nuclear power plants and, 375
  nuclear weapons and, 377–78
  population and, 359
  World Bank and, 150
Jefferson, Thomas, 33, 71, 416
Jerusalem, 7
Jihad, 279
Jintao, Hu, 484, 621
Joffe, Josef, 549
John Paul II (Pope), 171, 54*f*, 604

Joint Declaration on the Multipolar World and a New World Order (1997), 129
Jordan, 77
Joyner, Christopher, 578
jus ad bellum, 580, 581*f*
jus in bello, 580, 583
jus sanguinis, 574
jus soli, 574
just war, 443
just war doctrine, 579–82
just war theory, 497

Kant, Immanuel, 33, 71–72, 231, 416, 504
Kaplan, Robert D., 266, 480
Kashmir, 199
Kautilya, 36
Kegley, Charles, 30
Kellogg-Briand Pact (1928), 34, 106
Kelsen, Hans, 577
Kennan, George F., 36, 71, 117, 121, 258
Kennedy, John F., 75, 87, 92, 118, 404, 450, 500, 503, 505, 586, 632
Kennedy, Paul, 317, 461*f*
Kennedy, Robert, 82
Kennedy Round, 286
Kenya, 413
Keohane, Robert O., 47–48, 178
Keynes, John Maynard, 306
Khmer Rouge, 247
Khomeini, Ayatollah, 279
Khrushchev, Nikita, 117
Kim, Samuel S., 577
Kindleberger, Charles, 316
King Hussein, 77
King, Martin Luther, Jr., 616, 617
Kissinger, Henry A., 30, 62, 68, 74–75, 78, 82, 87, 89, 118, 119, 127, 430, 477
Klare, Michael T., 395, 510
Kluger, Jeffrey, 352
Korea, 112
Korean War, 117, 589
Kosovo, 75, 247, 248, 278, 512, 597
Kovanda, Karel, 594
Krauthammer, Charles, 549
Kropotkin, Peter, 411
Krstic, Radislav, 247
Krugman, Paul, 292
Kurds, 62
Kurile Islands, 112
Kuwait, 67, 206, 372, 463, 590
Kyoto Protocol, 381*m*, 383, 562

labor, 293
LaborNet, 301
LAIA. *See* Latin American Integration Association
laissez-faire economics, 196, 309, 414
Laos, 544
Laser Countermeasure, 562
Latin America, 66
Latin American Integration Association (LAIA), 159
Latvia, 104, 112, 156, 545

leaders
foreign policy and, 88–91
war and, 410
League of Arab States, 595
League of Nations (1919), 16, 34, 35, 106, 125, 142, 540
collective security and, 130
mandate system, 199
World War II, 110
least developed of the less-developed countries (LLDCs), 193, 202
Lebanon, 429
Lebow, Richard Ned, 12
Lee, Steve, 344
Legro, Jeffrey, 43, 626
Leitenberg, Milton, 406
Lemkin, Raphael, 247
Lenin, Vladimir, 104, 115, 196, 197, 414
levels of analysis, 17, 64, 231, 409, 535
Levine, Robert A., 286
Levy, Jack S., 418, 433
The Lexus and the Olive Tree: Understanding Globalization (Friedman), 624
liberal institutions, world order and, 605–7
Liberal International Economic Order (LIEO), 48, 211, 307
liberal internationalists, national security and, 477
liberal theory, 106
liberalism, 32–35, 50–51*t*, 115, 120, 153, 370, 477, 532, 533, 616, 626–27
human rights and, 231
international security and, 571*t*
post–World War I, 106
liberals, 121
Libya, 89, 434, 471, 475–76, 520, 523, 560, 621
LIEO. *See* Liberal International Economic Order
limited war, 503, 505
limits-to-growth proposition, 23
Lincoln, Abraham, 89, 514
Lindh, Anna, 532, 607
linkage strategy, 119
Lithuania, 104, 112, 156, 545
LLDCs. *See* least developed of the less-developed countries
Lloyd, William Foster, 353
Locke, John, 33
logic bombs, 475
long cycle, 541
long-cycle theory, 99–101, 123*f*, 313, 315, 422, 423*f*
long peace, 408, 538
Lorenz, Konrad, 409
low politics, 19, 48, 179, 305, 365, 588, 630
low-intensity conflict (LIC), 510
Luftwaffe, 109
Luxembourg, 109, 155

Machiavelli, Niccoló, 36, 56, 432
machtpolitik, 107
Mackinder, Halford, 32, 67
macroeconomics, 315
MAD. *See* mutual assured destruction
Madison, James, 33, 416, 604
Maginot Line, 109
Mahan, Alfred Thayer, 32, 66–67
Mahon, Alice, 504
Malaysia, 212, 290, 463, 621
Malta, 156
Malthus, Thomas, 353, 366
Manhattan Project, 505
Marx, Karl, 196, 197, 306
Marxism, 414
Marxism-Leninism, 11, 115, 196
massive retaliation, 503
Maurice, John Frederick, 450
Mazarr, Michael, 288
Mazzini, Giuseppe, 6
Mbeki, Thabo, 188, 352
McCarthy, Joseph, 115
McNamara, Robert S., 82, 412
Mead, Margaret, 616
media, globalization and, 276–80
mediation, 575
megadiversity countries, 249
Melloan, George, 86
Mendelsohn, Jack, 562
mental maps, 12
mercantilism, 195, 306, 310–13, 368
Mercator projection, 15*f*
Mercosur agreement, 212, 339
Mexico, 212, 339, 340*m*
MFA. *See* Multi-Fiber Arrangement
Middle East, 126, 463–64
migration, 241, 243, 244, 282–83
Migration Dialogue (Web site), 301
militant religious movements, 172–73
militarism, 109
militarization, 210, 413–14
militarized disputes, 516
military alliances, foreign policy and, 64
military capabilities
changes in, 460–68
foreign policy and, 65
quest for, 457–77
states, 67–68
military force, 22
military hierarchy, 11
military intervention, 209, 511–14, 582
military necessity, 582, 620
military power, 454–55*m*, 564–65, 616–18
military rivalries, 127*t*
military spending, 617
nuclear weapons and, 210
trends in, 458–60
U.S. versus world, 452*f*
Military Spending Clock (Web site), 494
military-industrial complex(es), 457, 466, 563
military-technical revolution (MTR), 474

Mill, John Stuart, 33, 306
Millennium Round, 322–23
Milosevic, Slobodan, 75, 259, 520, 584, 585
The Minorities at Risk Project (Gurr), 249
mirror images, 16, 114
MIRVs. *See* multiple independently targetable reentry vehicles
Mishra, Brajesh, 471
Missile Threats and Responses (Web site), 528–29
Mitrany, David, 598–99
Mitterand, François, 627
Miyazawa, Kiichi, 486
MNCs. *See* multinational corporations
Modelski, George, 62
modernization, 203, 360
Mohammed, Akhtar, 254
Moisy, Claude, 273
Moldova, devolution and, 247
monetarist theory, 322
Monetary and Financial Conference (UN) (1944), 150
monetary policy, 321–25, 330, 331
monetary system, 321
money supply, 321–22
Monnet, Jean, 599, 600
Montevideo Convention (1933), 574
Montreal Protocol on Substances That Deplete the Ozone Layer (1987), 384
Moore, Mike, 287*m*, 344
morality, 229
inhumanity and, 261
war and, 411–12
morals, 579
Moravcsik, Andrew, 626
More, St. Thomas, 410, 580
Morgenthau, Hans J., 36, 38, 98, 577
most-favored-nation (MFN) principle, 342–44
Mubarak, Hosni, 77
muddling through, 79
Mueller, Robert, 621
mulitpolarity, 544–49
Multi-Fiber Arrangement (MFA), 312
multilateral, 477, 541
multilateral agreements, 554
multilateral aid, 213, 364
multilateral diplomacy, 556–57
Multilaterals Project (Web site), 609
multinational corporations (MNCs), 59, 62, 173–77, 200, 215, 599
dualism and, 204–5
in the Global South, 216
importance of, 175*t*
world trade and, 291
multiple advocacy, 81
multiple independently targetable reentry vehicles (MIRVs), 473, 554
multipolar, 124, 552
multipolarity, 110, 122–30
Munich Conference (1938), 109
Muoi, Do, 544

Mussolini, Benito, 107
mutual assured destruction (MAD), 503, 505, 556
mutual deterrence, 503, 505–6
My American Journey (Powell), 84

NAFTA. *See* North American Free Trade Agreement
Nagasaki, 111
Napoleonic Wars (1815), 541
narcotics, globalization and, 282
Nasser, Gamal Abdel, 66
Nathanson Center for the Study of Organized Crime and Corruption (Web site), 184
national character, 410
National Commission for Economic Conversion and Disarmament (Web site), 494
The National Geographic Society (Web site), 26
national interest, 37, 615–16
National Organization for Women, 573
National Public Radio Online, 26
national security, 86, 245, 246, 450, 457, 458, 490–92, 617, 627–28
China's strategies, 483–86
European Union's strategies, 488–90
Germany's strategies, 488–90
Japan's strategies, 486–88
realism and, 39
Russia's strategies, 482–83
U.S. strategies, 477–82, 510, 551
National Security Strategy of the United States (2002), 510, 551
National Snow and Ice Data Center, 382
nationalism, 104, 111, 163, 164, 419, 624
civil war and, 428
federalism and, 598
war and, 418
nationality groups, 209
nations, 35, 63
nation-state, 63
Native Americans, 63
NativeWeb, 263
NATO. *See* North Atlantic Treaty Organization
natural barriers, of countries, 64*m*
nature versus nurture, 409
Nauru, 195
Nazism, 32, 107, 421
negotiation, 498
neoclassical theory, 205–7
neocolonial penetration, 204
neocolonialism, 194, 215
neofunctionalism, 600–602
neoidealism, 43
neoimperialism, 194, 215
neoisolationists, national security and, 477
neoliberal institutionalism, 43, 489, 570
neoliberal theory, 155, 268, 416
neoliberalism, 43–49, 50–51*t*, 73, 370, 500, 626

environmental security and, 370
free trade and, 338*m*
versus neorealism, 44
neoliberals, 71, 121, 206
neo-Malthusians, population and, 365–68
neomercantilism, 311
neorealism, 39, 41–42, 50–51*t*, 92
structuralism, 102
versus neoliberalism, 44
war and, 418, 420
neorealists, 121, 411
neotraditional realism, 39, 42, 536, 626
neotraditional realists, 536
NetAid, 263
the Netherlands, 109, 422
European Union and, 155
population and, 359
trade blocs and, 340*m*
Netwar, 445
neutrality, 573, 574
new imperialism, 196–98
New International Economic Order (NIEO) (1974), 211
New World Information and Communication Order (NWICO), 278
New York Times, 424
Web site, 26
New Zealand, 595
Newly Industrialized Countries (NICs), 205
newly industrialized economies (NIEs), 206–7, 290
NGOs. *See* nongovernmental organizations
Nicaragua, 119, 247, 434
Niebuhr, Reinhold, 36
Nicholas I (Pope), 579
NICs. *See* Newly Industrialized Countries
NIEO. *See* New International Economic Order
NIEs. *See* newly industrialized economies
NIMBY. *See* not in my backyard
Nigeria, 362
9/11. *See* September 11, 2001
Nine Power Treaty, 106
Nixon Doctrine, 88
Nixon, Richard, 82, 92, 118, 119, 330, 541
no first use, 483
Nonaligned Movement (NAM), 208
nonaligned states, 208
nonalignment, 208, 536
noncombatant immunity, 253, 583
noncombatants, 259
nondiscrimination, 344
nonethical weapons, 473
nongovernmental organizations (NGOs), 19, 47, 59, 62, 137, 161, 271, 598
multinational corporations and transnational banks, 173–77

nongovernmental organizations (NGOs)—*(continued)*
nonstate nations, 163–66
religious movements, 167–73
transforming world politics, 177–80
versus states and IGOs, 137*f*
nonintervention, 149, 574
nonintervention norm, 519, 623
nonlethal weapons, 563
nonmilitary containment, 121
nonprofit organizations, as NGOs, 140
nonproliferation, 557
nonproliferation regime, 470
nonstate actors, 19, 45, 59, 62, 136–40, 207
advantages and disadvantages, 180–82
IGOs, 137–61
NGOs, 137–40, 161–80
nonstate nations, 63, 163–66, 193, 209, 247
nontariff barriers (NTBs) , 312
Nordic Council, 62, 595
normalization, of Soviet-American relations, 120
North Africa, 109
North America, 10
North American Free Trade Agreement (NAFTA) (1993), 212, 298, 339
North Atlantic Treaty Organization (NATO), 75, 138, 158–59, 542, 595, 596
evolution of, 545–48
Russia and, 482, 483, 506–7
Web site, 183–84, 566
North Korea, 434, 507, 544, 548, 560
biological weapons and, 475–76
nuclear weapons and, 210, 377–78, 471
North, Oliver, 86
Northern Territories, 112
Norway, 109, 237*f*
not in my backyard (NIMBY), 377
NPT. *See* Nuclear Nonproliferation Treaty
Nth country problem, 470
nuclear arms race, 115
nuclear club, 470
nuclear deterrence, 500
compellence and, 502–3
mutual, 503, 505–6
post–Cold War, 506–9
nuclear energy, 375–78
nuclear nonproliferation regimes, 48
Nuclear Nonproliferation Treaty (NPT) (1968), 470, 557, 560
nuclear utilization theory (NUTs), 505
nuclear weapons, 38, 68, 92, 121, 377–78, 465, 469–72
expansion and reduction of, 472*f*
impact of war with, 501
nonproliferation of, 470–71
proliferation of, 470, 508*f*
testing of, 505, 560, 561*m*

nuclear winter, 501
NWICO. *See* New World Information and Communication Order
Nye, Joseph S., 47–48, 98, 178, 299, 480–81, 491–92

Obasanjo, Olusegun, 188
ODA. *See* official development assistance
OECD. *See* Organization for Economic Cooperation and Development
Office of the High Commissioner for Human Rights (UN), 166*m*
official development assistance (ODA), 213, 214*f*
Ogata, Sadaka, 431
Ohmae, Kenichi, 295
oil, 372–74
Omnibus Trade Act, 335
On the Law of War and Peace (Grotius), 579
On War (von Clausewitz), 405
OPEC. *See* Organization of Petroleum Exporting Countries
open systems, 69
Operation Enduring Freedom, 444
Oppenheimer, Robert, 505
opportunity costs, 456
orderly market arrangements (OMA) , 312
Organization for Economic Cooperation and Development (OECD), 275, 604
Web site, 349
Organization for Security and Cooperation in Europe (OSCE), 155, 595, 596
Organization of African Unity (OAU), 595
Organization of American States (OAS), 138, 595, 604
Web site, 184
Organization of Petroleum Exporting Countries (OPEC), 205–6, 373
Organization of the Islamic Conference (OIC), 159
organizational process, 82
orthographic projection, 15*f*
OSCE. *See* Organization for Security and Cooperation in Europe
Ottoman Empire, 101, 104
Our Common Future (1987), 371
overpopulation, 366–67
ozone layer, 383

Pacific Rim, 10
pacifism, 409
pacta sunt servanda, 575
Pakistan, 199, 468, 471, 560
nuclear club, 470
nuclear weapons and, 210
war and, 412
Palestine, 7, 141, 248
Palestine Liberation Organization, 77, 159

Palmerston, Lord, 534
Panama Canal Zone, 196
paradigm, 31, 231, 305, 370, 371
Paraguay, 212, 339
parallel currency, 328
Partnership for Peace (PfP), 545, 546*m*
patriotism, 419
Pattern, Christopher, 548
Patterns of Global Terrorism (Web site), 185
Patton, George, 421
Pax Americana, 549, 552
pax atomica, 507, 539
Pax Britannica, 552
Pax Romana, 552
peace building, 589
peace dividend, 456
peace enforcement, 503, 589
peace making, 589
Peace of Paris, 107
Peace of Westphalia (1648), 63, 125, 136, 149, 180, 190, 536
peace operations, 589
cycles of, 418, 420–24
democratic, 603–5
law's contribution to, 584–86
military power and search for, 564–65
political integration and, 596–603
UN and, 587–94
peaceful coexistence, 117
peacekeeping, 511, 589
Peacekeeping Operations Bill, 486
Pearl Harbor, 109
Peirce, Neal R., 270–71
Peng, Li, 586
perceptions, versus reality, 12–16
perceptual psychologists, 14
periphery states, 205
Perle, Richard, 84, 121
Permanent Court of International Justice, 34
permanent world criminal court, 584
Perpetual Peace (Kant), 71, 416
Persian Chessboard, 353–55
Persian Gulf, 118, 126
Persian Gulf War, 67, 70, 122, 242, 372, 468, 471, 510
Persson, Goran, 352
Peru, 212, 425
Peter's projection, 15*f*
PfP. *See* Partnership for Peace
Philippines, 212, 404
Pinochet, Augusto, 259, 584
Pipes, Richard, 119
Planned Parenthood Federation of America, 573
Poland, 104, 107, 109, 112, 156, 198, 545
polarity, 541, 542
polarization, 542
policy agendas, 78
policy making, as rational choice, 74–76

policy networks, 82
political asylum, 244
Political Database of the Americas (Web site), 222
political disintegration, 602–3
political economy, 110
political efficacy, 90
political freedom, human development and, 235–37
political hierarchy, 11
political integration
  functionalist approach, 598–600
  neofunctionalist approach, 600–602
  political disintegration, 602–3
  world federalist approach, 596–98
political risk, economic freedom and, 338m
politics of scarcity, 370
politics, 18, 33, 141–42, 196–98, 295, 310, 353, 405, 451, 498, 618
pooled sovereignty, 158
poor states, 68
population density, 356
population growth, 23, 352. *See also* demography
  demographic transition and, 356f, 357m, 359–61
  diseases and, 361–63
  division between Global North and Global South, 357–59
  as global political problem, 353
  impact of, 361–63
  international response to, 363–68
  mathematical principle of, 353–55
  projections, 354f
  understanding rates of, 353–57
population implosion, 361
Porto, Luigi da, 423
Portugal, 155, 340m, 359, 422
positivist legal theory, 577
postbehavioral movement, 40, 41
postmodern terrorism, 445
poverty, 209, 232–34, 240, 292
  Global South and, 202
  war and, 412
Powell, Colin, 84, 395, 507, 546
power, 37, 41
  changing nature of, 455–57
  hard, 457, 481
  in international politics, 450–51
  inferring from capabilities, 453–55
  soft, 457, 481, 618
  state elements, 451–57
power balances, breakdown of, 538–39
Power and Interdependence (Keohane and Nye), 47
power politics, 107
power potential, 451
power transition, 113, 482, 544
power transition theory, 421
PPP. *See* purchasing power parities
preemption, 510, 538, 581, 619
preemptive war, 497
The Presidents: PBS's *The American Experience* (Web site), 94

preventive diplomacy, 511, 589
primus inter pares, 154
Principles of Political Economy (Mill), 306
private international law, 572
procedural rationality, 88
productivity, 668
The Progress of Nations (Web site), 301
proliferation, 470
prospect theory, 78–79
prosperity, 68
protectionism, 110, 312–13, 346
protesters, 92
public goods, 594, 624
public international law, 572
purchasing power parities (PPP), 123f, 239, 326–27f
Putin, Vladimir, 472, 483, 544, 548, 554, 556, 620
Putnam, Robert, 79

Qaddafi, Muammar, 67, 89, 523, 621
Qatar, 206
Quadrennial Defense Review, 509–10

Rabin, Yitzhak, 77, 433
Race for the Superbomb (Web site), 132
Rainforest Action Network (Web site), 398
Rapacki Plan (1957), 557
Rapid Reaction Force, 597
Rapidly Deployable Mission Headquarters (RDMH), 591
rapprochement, 120
rational choice, 103–4, 149, 410, 497, 514, 534
  impediments to, 76–80
  policy making as, 74–76
Reagan Doctrine, 88, 119
Reagan, Ronald, 83, 86, 89, 119, 121, 506
realism, 35–39, 41–42, 50–51t, 73, 98–99, 111, 115, 122, 155, 178, 313, 409, 451, 477, 499, 572, 616, 626–67
  Cold War and, 113
  human rights and, 229
  leaders and, 88
  mercantilism and, 311
  national security and, 560, 562
  security approach, 533t
  war and, 418, 420
  WWI and, 106
realist theory, 120, 285, 370
reality, versus perceptions, 12–16
realpolitik, 36, 106, 141, 479
rebus sic stantibus, 575
recession, 7
reciprocity, 336
Red Crescent Societies, 271
Red Cross, 162
Redfield, Robert, 229–30
refugees, 241–45
regime, 147–48, 162, 178, 257, 279, 383

regional collective defense, 595
regional currency union, 334
regional integration, 43, 602
regional security organizations, 595–96
regionalization, 339–41, 342f
Register of Conventional Arms (UN), 465, 469
relative burden of military spending, 457, 458
relative deprivation, 239, 427
relative gains, 44, 310, 371, 415, 597
religions, 169m
religious movements, 59, 167–73
religious roots of terror, 171
Remembering Nagasaki (Web site), 529
Renner, Michael, 469
replacement-level fertility, 358
representative government, 69
reprisals, 583
Resolution 678, 590
resource hierarchy, 11
The Responsibility to Protect (2001), 256
retorsion, 583
revolution in military affairs (RMA), 474, 580
revolution in military technology (RMT), 473
Rhine River Commission (1804), 599
Ricardo, David, 308, 310
Rice, Condoleezza, 441, 496, 504, 519
rich states, 68
Ricupero, Rubens, 334
right to intervene, 256
Rights and Duties of States, 574
The Rise and Fall of the Great Powers (Kennedy), 461f
Robinson, Mary, 234
Romania, 112, 198, 545
Roosevelt, Eleanor, 261
Roosevelt, Franklin D., 91, 98, 109, 112
Rosecrance, Richard, 456
Rostow, Walt W., 203, 204
Rousseau, Jean Jacques, 33, 231, 499
Rowan, Carl, 496–97
Rowley, Coleen, 86
Ruggiero, Renato, 279
rule of law, 120
Rumsfeld, Donald, 83, 444, 456, 465, 475
Rush-Bagot Agreement (1818), 556
Rusk, Dean, 98
Russett, Bruce, 416
Russia, 13, 32, 101–10, 105m, 129, 142, 414, 468, 544, 551, 603
  AIDS and, 362
  as arms supplier, 464–65
  bipolarity and, 542–43
  chemical weapons and, 475
  Cold War and, 113–22
  disarmament and, 471–72
  multipolar politics and, 126
  national security strategies of, 482–83
  nuclear bombs and, 469

Russia—*(continued)*
  nuclear club, 470
  UN Security Council and, 588
  World Bank and, 150
Russian Roulette (Web site), 529
Rwanda, 242, 247
  civil war and, 425, 426–27
  ethnic cleansing and, 244

SAARC. *See* South Asian Association
  for Regional Cooperation
SADC. *See* Southern African
  Development Community
Sagan, Carl, 354, 628
Saldanha, Anil, 271
SALT. *See* Strategic Arms Limitation
  Talks
Salzburg Seminar, 270–71
Samuelson, Robert J., 9
sanctions, 231, 520. *See also*
  economic sanctions
sanctuary, 245
Santayana, George, 8
satisficing, 78
Saudi Arabia, 70, 150, 192, 257, 463
Save the Children, 162
Scalfaro, Oscar Luigi, 248
scapegoat phenomenon, 70
schematic reasoning, 12
Schlesinger, James, 82–83
Schmidt, Hans Christian, 395
Schneider, Gerald, 415
Schroeder, Gerhard, 489, 504
Schwab, Klaus, 299
Scowcroft, Brent, 7, 84, 561*m*
secession, 172
Second World, 191
second-strike capability, 503
Secretariat (UN), 143, 587
security, 246. *See also* national
  security
  alliances and, 534–35
  collective, 34, 130, 142, 540,
    588–94, 595
  common, 492
  environmental, 246, 370–72
  food, 365
  issues, 19
  realist approach to, 533*t*
  search for, 490-92
security committee, 155
security community, 601
Security Council (UN), 62, 113, 141,
  143, 587–91
security dilemma, 114, 420, 472,
  499–500, 532, 617
security regimes, 48, 115, 117,
  536, 579
seeing is believing, 14
selective engagement, 128, 513,
  514, 591
self-determination, 35, 198–200, 248,
  603, 622
self-fulfilling prophecies, 114
self-help, 37, 418, 450, 534, 577, 624
self-image, 90

self-righteousness, 16
semiperiphery, 206
semiperiphery states, 205
SEATO. *See* Southeast Asia Treaty
  Organization
Senator Joe McCarthy: A Multimedia
  Celebration (Web site), 132
separative revolts, 172
September 11, 2001, 6, 9–11, 69, 165,
  241, 404–6
  alignments and, 548
  bureaucratic politics and, 85–86
  collective security and, 595
  global terrorism and, 437–42, 444,
    619–21
  new U.S. security policies, 477–82
  rational choice and, 75
  religious movements and, 171
  weapons of mass destruction
    and, 507
Serbia, 103
services, trade in, 290–91
Sevill Statement (1986), 409–10
Shah, Zahir, 515
Shotwell, James T., 33
Shultz, George, 83
Siegel, Martin J., 627
Sierra Leone, 237*f*
signaling, 502
Sikhs, 63
Simon, Herbert, 78
ingapore, 193, 206, 212, 271
SIPRI Military Expenditure Country
  Graphs (Web site), 494
size principle, 537
Slaughter, Anne-Marie, 607
Slovakia, 156, 248, 545
Slovenia, 156, 545
smart bombs, 473, 474
smart sanctions, 526
Smith, Adam, 33, 196, 308, 310, 311
social constructivism, 13, 52
Social Contract (Rousseau), 231
socialism, 32, 111
socialization, 409, 410
soft power, 457, 481, 618
Somalia, 47*f*
Sony, 62
Sorenson, Theodore, 76, 82
SORT. *See* Strategic Offensive
  Reduction Treaty
South Africa, 603
South America, 10
South Asian Association for Regional
  Cooperation (SAARC), 159
South Korea, 206, 251
  imported arms and, 463
  multipolar politics and, 126
  nuclear weapons and, 377–78
Southeast Asia Treaty Organization
  (SEATO), 595
Southern African Development
  Community (SADC), 159, 160, 212
sovereign equality, 573
sovereignty, 247, 411, 572, 624
Soviet Exhibit (Web site), 132

Soviet Union, 11, 66, 91. *See also*
  Russia
  ethnic cleansing and, 248
  and U.S. relationship, key events in
    evolution of, 116*f*
Spain, 63, 603
  European Commission, 156
  European Union and, 155
  population, 359
  trade blocs and, 340*m*
Spanish-American War (1898), 196
speculators, 325
spheres of influence, 113, 196
spillaround, 602
spillback, 602
spillover, 602
spiral model, 499–500
Spykman, Nicholas, 67
Sri Lanka, civil war and, 425
St. Petersburg Declaration (1868), 556
The Stages of Economic Growth
  (Rostow), 203
Stalin, Joseph, 98, 109, 112
**standard operating procedures
  (SOPs),** 82
START. *See* Strategic Arms Reduction
  Treaty
state goals, 44
state level of analysis, 17, 104, 110,
  190, 268, 411
state sovereignty, 20, 37, 63
state terrorism, 436, 622
statehood, 574
state(s), 11, 20, 35, 62, 622
  elements of power, 451–57
  emergence of, 63
  foreign policy behavior, 63–73
  globalization and, 270–71, 297–300
  humanity and, 254–55
  internal characteristics of, and
    armed conflict, 411–18
  international law and, 572–78
  versus IGOs and NGOs, 137*f*
  war between, 616–18
states' attributes, foreign policy
  and, 65
state-sponsored terrorism, 434,
  514, 584
Statute of the International Court of
  Justice, 575. *See also* World Court
Stern, Nicholas, 336
stock indexes, 284
**Strategic Arms Limitation Talks
  (SALT),** 118, 554
**Strategic Arms Reduction Treaty
  (START)** (1993), 120, 506
strategic corporate alliances, 177,
  291, 293–95
**Strategic Defense Initiative
  (SDI),** 506
Strategic Offensive Reduction Treaty
  (SORT), 471–72, 506, 554, 555*f*
strategic trade policy, 312–13
strategic weapons, 475
structural realism, 39, 190, 421
structural violence, 577

structuralism, 102–3, 203–5
structure, 541
subsistence economy, 202
subversion, 521
Sudan, 434, 425, 426–27
suicide-bombings, 7
superpatriots, 419
superpowers, 68, 113
supranatural organization, 158
supremacy, 98
survival of the fittest, 409
sustainable development, 23, 370,
    371, 392–94, 395
Sutherland, Peter, 299
Sweden, 155, 237f, 359, 410
Switzerland, 20, 65, 70, 150, 410
Syria, 434, 475–76

tactical air-to-surface missiles
    (TASMs), 473
Taiwan Straits, 117
Taiwan, 141, 206, 271, 463, 518
tariffs, 7, 286, 335–37
technology, 24p
   advantages and disadvantages of, 22
   Global North versus Global South, 200
   weapons, 472–73, 475
Telecom Information Resources on
    the Internet, 301
territorial imperative, 410
The Territorial Imperative (Ardrey), 410
territorial states. *See* states
terrorism, 6, 11, 62, 69, 404–5,
    433–45, 465, 582, 619–21. *See*
    also international terrorism;
    global terrorism
   active groups, 435t
   counterterrorism, 442–45
   cyber, 445
   defining, 434, 436
   deterring, 509–19
   fighting, 444
   globalization of, 436–42
   incidents of, 438f
   information age and, 445
   international inequalities and, 200
   international organized crime
     and, 445
   Netwar, 445
   new age of, 442
   postmodern, 445
   post–September 11 changes in,
     440–41
   state, 436
   state-sponsored, 434
   versus freedom fighters, 434
   weapons of mass destruction and,
     507, 509
   worldwide recession and, 314
Terrorism Research Center (Web
    site), 185
Thailand, 212, 290
Thakur, Ramesh, 344
Thatcher, Margaret, 585
theater missile defenses (TMD), 506
theoretical interpretation, 30

Theory of International Politics
    (Waltz), 41
theory, 32, 308
Thierse, Wolfgang, 570
Third Way, 155, 239
Third World, 191
Third World's Third World, 193
Thirty Years' War, 63, 136, 167, 579
Thompson, Kenneth W., 36
Thousand-Year Reich, 110–11, 112
Three Mile Island nuclear power
    plant, 375
Thucydides, 36, 70
Thurow, Lester, 126
Tibet, 117
Time Warner, 278
Tocqueville, Alexis de, 24, 70, 113
Tokyo Round, 286
Tolstoy, Leo, 410
total war, 503, 505
totalitarianism government, 69
Toynbee, Arnold J., 99
trade. *See also* free trade
   blocs, 10, 212, 339, 342f
   globalization of, 286–96
   policies, 335–41
trade integration, 288, 341
Trade Resources (Web site), 349
tragedy of the commons, 353
transformation, 9, 54
transgenetic crops, 365
transnational actors, 59
transnational banks (TNBs), 173–77
transnational collaboration, versus
    competition, 21–22
transnational interdependence, 45–48
transnational players, 62
transnational religious movements, 11
Treaty of Augsburg (1555), 574
Treaty of Brest-Litovsk (1918), 112
Treaty of Nice (2000), 128
Treaty of Utrecht (1713), 125
Treaty of Versailles, 107
trickle-down hypothesis, 239
Tripartite Pact (1940), 109
Triple Alliance, 102
Triple Entente, 104
Truman Doctrine, 117
Truman, Harry S, 112, 117, 505
Trusteeship Council (UN), 143
tuberculosis (TB), 361
Tuomioja, Erkki, 532
Turkey, 62, 105, 117
Turkish Empire, 104
Turner, Stansfield, 457
two-level games, 79, 214

ubi societas, 576
Uganda, 585
underdevelopment, 202–7
underemployment, 293
unilateral approach, 128, 335–37, 477
Union of Arab Banks, 139
Union of Concerned Scientists, 162
Union of International
    Associations, 139

Union of International
    Organizations, 137
Union of Soviet Socialist Republics.
    See Russia; Soviet Union
unipolarity, 116, 117, 122, 541–42,
    552, 549–53
unitary actors, 73, 73–80, 163
United Arab Emirates, 206, 463
United Kingdom. *See* Great Britain
United Nations (1945), 7, 20, 44, 47,
    54–55, 59, 62, 75, 113, 125, 136,
    140, 150, 271
   changing membership of, 141f
   decolonization and, 199
   global network, 145m
   human development and, 240
   ideology of, 142
   peace and, 587–94
   peace missions, 592–93m
   purpose and agenda, 141–43
   system and structure, 143–47
   Web site, 184
United Nations AIDS report, 362
   Web site, 397
United Nations and the Status of
    Women: Setting the Global
    Gender Agenda (Web site), 263
United Nations Atomic Development
    Authority, 557
United Nations Charter, 249, 587
United Nations Children's Fund
    (UNICEF), 144, 254, 588
United Nations Conference of the
    Human Environment (1972), 371
United Nations Conference on
    Disarmament (Web site), 566
United Nations Conference on
    Environment and Development
    (UNCED), 371
United Nations Conference on Trade
    and Development (UNCTAD),
    211, 588
   Web site, 222
United Nations Demining Database
    (Web site), 566–67
United Nations Development Program
    (UNDP) (Web site), 222, 235,
    292, 588
United Nations Educational
    Scientific and Cultural
    Organization (UNESCO), 278,
    587, 599
United Nations Emergency Force
    (UNEF), 589
**United Nations Environment
    Program (UNEP),** 383–84
United Nations General Assembly, 255
United Nations High Commission for
    Refugees (UNHCR), 241
   Web site, 263
United Nations Human Rights
    Commission, 257
United Nations International Crime
    Court (ICC), 259
United Nations Millennium Summit
    (2000), 142

United Nations Peacekeeping
  Operations (Web site), 609
United Nations Second World
  Assembly on Aging (2002), 360
United Nations University, 144
United Nations World Summit on
  Sustainable Development, 371
United States, 62, 63, 67–68, 75, 77,
  101, 105, 106, 108, 126, 142, 422,
  468, 504, 544, 584, 585, 595
  AIDS and, 362
  as arms supplier, 464–65
  bipolarity, 542–43
  chemical weapons and, 475
  Cold War and, 113–22
  defense budget of, 451–52
  disarmament and, 471–72
  disarmament and, 556
  economic leadership and, 316
  ethnic cleansing and, 244
  expansion of, 196
  free trade and, 335–37
  GATT and, 319–21
  global warming and, 381m
  international trade and, 306
  military expenditures and, 467
  monetary policy and, 330
  NAFTA and, 212, 339
  national security and, 477–82
  nuclear bombs and, 469
  nuclear club, 470
  nuclear weapons and, 377–78
  refugees and, 241
  service trade and, 290
  and Soviet relationship, key events
    in evolution of, 116f
  terrorism and, 404
  trade deficit and, 317
  trade representative (Web site), 350
  UN Security Council and, 588
  unipolarity and, 541–42
  World Bank and, 150
United States Agency for International
  Development (USAID) (Web
  site), 222
United States Federal Reserve
  Board, 283
United States National Oceanic
  Administration, 384
United States National Security
  Council, 86
United States National Strategy
  (1994), 604
United States Secretary of State for
  Arms Control and International
  Security, 594
Uniting for Peace Resolution, 589
*Universal Declaration of Human
  Rights* (1948), 228, 230, 255, 261,
  572–73
  Web site, 609
Universal Postal Union (1874),
  161, 599
universalism, 172
universalistic civilizations, 165
universality, 255

University of Texas Library Online
  Map Collection, 26
unsustainable debt, 218
Urban II (Pope), 167
Uruguay, 212, 339
Uruguay Round, 148, 286, 319, 321,
  322–23
USSR. *See* Russia; Soviet Union

Vance, Cyrus, 83, 616
Venezuela, Mercosur agreement
  and, 212
Verizon Communications, 277
Versailles treaty, 107
vertical nuclear proliferation, 470
Viacom, 276
Vienna Declaration (1993), 249
Vienna World Conference on Human
  Rights (1993), 255
Vietnam War, 16, 82
Vietnam, 92, 212, 434, 544
virtual corporations, 291
Virtual Library on International
  Development, 222
virtual nuclear arsenals, 475
virtuality, 273
**voluntary export restrictions
  (VERs)** , 312
von Clausewitz, Karl, 405

Wallerstein, Immanuel, 128
Waltz, Kenneth N., 41–43, 537
war(s), 253. *See also* armed conflict;
  civil war(s)
  commercial liberalism and, 414
  communism and, 414
  cultural determinants of, 411
  cycles of, 418, 420–24
  cyclical theories of, 422–24
  democracy and, 416
  economics and, 414–15
  ethics and, 504
  feminist theories, 411–12
  Global South and, 406, 407f
  government type and, 415–18
  human impact of, 413
  human nature and, 409–11
  human rights protection and, 259
  independence and, 411
  intervention and, 411
  just, 443
  leaders and, 410
  legal control of, 578–86
  legal restraints on, 581f
  levels of analysis, 409–24
  morality and, 411–12
  nationalism and, 418
  neoliberal theories and, 416
  neorealism and, 418, 420
  neorealists and, 411
  poverty and, 412
  realism and, 418, 420
  refugees and, 242
  religious movements and, 171
  rules for conduct, 583–84
  sovereignty and, 411

  state level of analysis and, 411
  versus conflict, 405
war crimes, 259
war criminals, 585
War, Peace, Security Guide (Web
  site), 447
war weariness hypothesis, 423
Warsaw Pact, 120
Washington, George, 535
Washington Naval Conferences
  (1921–1922), 106, 556
Washington Naval Disarmament
  Treaties, 35
The Wealth of Nations (Smith), 196, 311
weapon technology, 11
weapons. *See also* nuclear weapons
  technology, 468–77
  trade, 461–65
  unconventional, 475–77
weapons of mass destruction (WMD),
  445, 465, 507, 617–18, 619, 620
Weber, Max, 81
Weimar Republic, 66
Weinberger, Caspar, 83
welfare issues, 19
Wendt, Alexander, 52
West Germany, 66, 108m
Westphalian system, 63
Westphalian Treaties, 574. *See also*
  Peace of Westphalia
Wilhelm, Kaiser II, 66, 90, 103
Will, George, 346
Williams, Jody, 562
Wilson, James Q., 409
Wilson, Woodrow, 33, 35, 56, 71, 106,
  198, 416, 534, 540, 626, 629
Winter War (Finnish War), 110
WMD. *See* weapons of mass
  destruction
Wolfensohn, James D., 151, 188,
  215, 218
Wolfowitz, Paul, 84
Women's International League for
  Peace and Freedom, 139
women's rights, 249–53
A Working Peace System (Mitrany),
  598–99
World AIDS Day, 361
World Bank, 147–48, 150–52, 181,
  271, 327, 328, 336, 604
  class divisions, 200–201
  Enhanced HIPC initiative, 219
  poverty and, 232–33
  underdevelopment and, 206
  Web site, 350
World Biodiversity Day, 281
World Citizen Foundation (Web
  site), 633
World Commission on Environment
  and Development, 371
World Conference of Indigenous
  Peoples (1992), 166m
World Conference on Sustainable
  Development (2002), 364
World Conference on Women (1995),
  252–53

World Conservation Union (1997), 281, 388
World Court, 570, 575, 585. *See also* International Court of Justice
World Disarmament Conference (1932), 556
World Economic Forum, 299, 314
world federalism, 596–98
World Federation of Trade Unions, 139–40
World Food Programme (WFP), 588
World Future Society (Web site), 633
world geography, 14, 15*f*
World Health Organization (WHO), 280–81, 587
  Web site, 184
world law, 572
World Meteorological Organization (WMO), 161, 379
world order
  international law and, 570–86
  international organizations and, 586–94
  liberal institutions and, 605–7
world politics, 30
  coercive diplomacy and, 496–99
  liberalism, 32–35
  realism, 35–39, 41–42
  understanding, 31–32
World POPClock Projection (Web site), 397
World Population Conference, 363–64

World Summit for Children (2002), 413
World Summit for Social Development (1995), 235
World Summit on Sustainable Development (2002), 7, 252, 378, 394
world trade, 289–91, 343*f*
World Trade Organization, 7, 11, 18*p*, 44, 48, 147–50, 181, 271, 286, 287*m*, 319, 322–23, 347
  China and, 485
  GATT and, chronology, 320*t*
  Russia and, 483
  trade blocs and, 340*m*
  Web site, 184, 350
  World Telecom Pact, 279
World Urban Forum (2002), 614
World Veterans Association, 140
world view, 12
World War I, 9, 16, 31, 32, 90, 99, 101, 142, 417, 540, 580
  casualties of, 583
  causes of, 101–4
  consequences of, 104–6
  economic leadership and, 316
  European boundaries following, 105*m*
The World War I Document Archive (Web site), 132
World War II, 9, 13, 16, 31, 38, 48, 99, 106, 142, 173
  casualties of, 584

  causes of, 107–12
  consequences of, 112–13
  economic leadership and, 316
  European boundaries following, 108*m*, 112
World Wide Fund for Nature (WWFN) (Malaysia), 139, 388
World Wide Web, 625
World Wildlife Federation, 62, 162
World Young Women's Christian Association, 139
world-system theorists, 205
world-system theory, 197–98
WTO. *See* World Trade Organization

xenophobia, 244–45

Yalta Conference (1945), 112
Yoshida Doctrine, 486
Yoshida, Shigeru, 486
Yugoslavia, 75, 104, 198, 414, 584, 585
  ethnic cleansing and, 242, 248
  war crimes and, 259

Zaire, 280
Zakaria, Fareed, 43, 84, 489–90, 532
zeitgeist, 91, 92
Zemin, Jiang, 484, 551
zero-sum, 208, 316, 478, 543
zero-yield nuclear experiments, 560
Zimmerman, Alfred, 33

PHOTO CREDITS